GLOBAL SCIENCE

EARTH/ENVIRONMENTAL SYSTEMS SCIENCE

SEVENTH EDITION

John W. Christensen
Teri L. Christensen

KENDALL/HUNT PUBLISHING COMPANY
4050 Westmark Drive   Dubuque, Iowa 52002

Cover image by R. B. Husar, Washington University; the land layer from the Sea WiFS Project; fire maps from the European Space Agency; the sea surface temperature from the Naval Oceanographic Officer's Visualization Laboratory; and cloud layer from SSEC, University of Wisconsin.

This globe shows data collected from multiple sensors and integrated into one image. Notice the three-dimensional cloud measurements. An El Niño temperature anomaly is visible as red in the Pacific Ocean, while the red dots on land show the locations of forest fires. This type of information helps us understand Earth as a whole integrated system.

All Shutterstock images used under license from Shutterstock, Inc.

Scilinks® is owned and provided by the National Science Teachers Association. All rights reserved.

Copyright © 1981, 1984, 1991, 1996, 2000, 2006, 2009 by Kendall/Hunt Publishing Company
ISBN 978-0-7575-4979-3

Printed in the United States of America

3 4 5 6 7 8 9 10   16 15 14 13

Contents

CHAPTER 1

The Nature of Science — 2

CHAPTER 2

A Grand Oasis in Space (The Ecosystem Concept) — 28

CHAPTER 3

Energy Flow and Matter Cycles 68

CHAPTER 4

Mineral Resources 124

CHAPTER 5

Growth and Population 186

CHAPTER 6

Seeds of Life (The Continuity of Life) 220

CHAPTER 7

Agriculture and Nutrition 254

CHAPTER 8

Energy Today 298

CHAPTER 9

Nonrenewable Resource Depletion

CHAPTER 10

Nuclear Energy

CHAPTER 11
Energy Alternatives   408

CHAPTER 12
Strategies for Using Energy   450

CHAPTER 13
Water Quantity 484

CHAPTER 14
Water Quality 526

Contents ix

CHAPTER 17

Options for the Future   **658**

Acknowledgments

Global Science has been developed over a lifetime. Scores of friends, students, professional acquaintances, and fellow educators have made suggestions. No person is an island; hence, each of my ideas, no matter how novel, has been enhanced by comments of friends and associates. To the extent that I am aware of my intellectual debts, I have tried to acknowledge them and give proper credit. If I have left anyone out, I apologize.

A special thank you to the following organizations:

- The Colorado Section of the American Institute of Mining, Metallurgical & Petroleum Engineers (AIME) for financial help, encouragement, and the duplication of the preliminary draft of this course.

- The Mineral Information Institute for encouragement in the development of all seven editions, and continuing efforts to promote the use of this course.

- The Mining and Metallurgical Society of America (MMSA), and the Seeley W. Mudd Memorial Fund of AIME for financial assistance that provided for numerous pilot schools and field tests.

- The National Science Teachers Association (NSTA) for choosing me as a writer for its *Project for an Energy-Enriched Curriculum* (PEEC), and for allowing me to use several of their activities in the text.

- Colorado's Cherry Creek School District for providing the atmosphere where such a course could be pioneered.

- To (Harvard) *Project Physics, Inc.*, for encouragement and for financial help in the production of the initial phases of the course.

- To the many individuals and organizations that allowed the use of figures and illustrations, I am most grateful.

The pilot testing of this program was a most ambitious undertaking. Generous financial assistance was provided by the Colorado Endowment for the Humanities; the National Endowment for the Humanities; the Kettering Family Foundation; Walter S. Rosenberry, III; the Richard King Mellon Foundation; The Frost Foundation, Ltd.; Joy R. Hilliard; Richard Ballantine; St. Mary Parish Land Company; MGA Inc.; and others.

The pilot teachers were most helpful with their suggestions, criticisms, and compliments when the project seemed overwhelming. They reinforced the fundamental belief that science is of value to all students and has an important message for all of us.

To improve and expand the curriculum, generous in-kind support was provided by Public Service Company of Colorado; Pacific Gas & Electric; City of Colorado Springs Energy Department; University of Northern Colorado; Colorado College; Cherry Creek School District; and many others.

The development of the third edition enabled *Global Science* to become a national (global) curriculum that started as a dream.

The Mineral Information Institute (MII) has provided important support for all the editions of this text, but most extensively during the development of the third through seventh editions. Jackie Dorr coordinated the tracking of all the permissions. Her commitment to the *Global Science* curriculum is strong and enthusiastic. I am most grateful.

MII coordinated the work of several editors, each providing specific expertise to ensure accuracy and clarity in this latest edition. I am truly indebted for the hours they spent reviewing the manuscript and researching and preparing the comments that led to this finished text. Thought, discussion, suggestions, debate, and research culminate in this seventh edition.

I am delighted to have my daughter on board as my coauthor. Her training in the biological sciences complements my formal training, which is mostly physical science. Most important, she is in the classroom—where the action is.

Many individuals, organizations, and industries have assisted in the preparation of the seventh edition. Of special note are the following:

- Chris Young of the biology department at Alverno College for assistance in developing Activity 1.11 on the history of environmental science.

- Charles Bottinelli for the revision of the information on the structure of science that appears in the Teacher Edition (Chapter 1).

- Robert L. Sanford, Jr., of the biology department at the University of Denver, for advice on the expanded material on ecological succession.

- Demographers at the Population Reference Bureau for updated data used in Chapter 5.

- Elizabeth (Betty) Wolonyk, director of agricultural education for the American Farm Bureau Foundation for Agriculture, for reviews of Chapters 6 and 7, along with providing documented data and suggestions.

- The M. King Hubbert Center for Petroleum Supply Studies at the Colorado School of Mines for the information necessary to keep Chapter 9 up-to-date.

- Kevin Kamps, nuclear waste specialist at the Nuclear Information and Resource Service, for documented information on how France, Great Britain, Germany, and Japan are dealing with their nuclear wastes. This information is in the Teacher Edition (Chapter 10).

- Byron Stafford at the National Renewable Energy Laboratory for analyzing the solar cell used in Activity 11.7.

- Gregg Marland at the Carbon Dioxide Information Analysis Center at the Oak Ridge National Laboratory for assistance with the update of Figure 15.36.

- Mineral Information Institute (www.mii.org) for assistance in expanding and documenting information on land use in Chapter 16.

A special thank you to Kendall Hunt Publishing Company for its strong commitment to the *Global Science* curriculum.

A very special thanks to my family who suffered through months and then years of research and writing. Thank you for your love, help, and understanding.

And finally, to all my students and those around the globe to whom this whole endeavor is dedicated, may the content help each of you prepare and plan for a better world.

—John W. Christensen

About the Authors

About the Authors

John W. Christensen taught science in the Cherry Creek School District in Englewood, Colorado, for 27 years. He pioneered in the development of global science materials as early as 1968. Broadening and improving these materials has involved years of study and travel to conferences, workshops, conventions, and resource-related facilities from coast to coast.

Mr. Christensen received a B.A. from Augsburg College* in Minneapolis, Minnesota, and an M.S. in Natural Science from New Mexico Highlands University, majoring in physics, chemistry, and mathematics. He has both attended and taught at numerous summer institutes across the nation supported by the National Science Foundation (NSF). He was on the writing team that produced Harvard *Project Physics* and spent two summers working on the National Science Teachers Association's (NSTA) *Project for an Energy-Enriched Curriculum.*

Mr. Christensen spent four summers on an NSF team focusing on the production of relevant classroom materials for uncommitted students. Mr. Christensen recently retired from the high school classroom. He works full time on the *Global Science* Curriculum Project.

Teri L. Christensen teaches high school biology, global science, and AP environmental science in the Cherry Creek School District located in the Denver metropolitan area. She works on expanding global science materials during the summer months.

Ms. Christensen received a B.S. degree from California Lutheran University where she majored in biology with an emphasis on marine biology. She interned with the National Resource Conservation Service (formerly the U.S. Soil Conservation Service). She earned a M.S. in biology from the University of Northern Colorado with an emphasis on botany. Her graduate thesis was a seed viability study done through the Center for Genetic Resource Preservation (formerly the National Seed Storage Laboratory) in Fort Collins, Colorado. She earned her Colorado teaching license through the University of Denver.

*Dr. Peter Agree, Class of 1970: 2003 Nobel Prize in Chemistry

About the Mineral Information Institute and This Course

This course is about natural resources and how we develop and use them. We truly hope it will help you make wise decisions in the future about how we develop and use our natural resources. Meeting our basic needs for food, clothing, and shelter are possible because of human's ingenuity in using the resources that are available from our planet.

While the lifestyle the civilized world enjoys today is based on the science and technology of the last two centuries, nearly 25 percent of the world's population still lives without electricity. That is changing as many countries in the world are rapidly expanding the consumption of the world's natural resources to help raise the standard of living for their citizens. This has created a concern about Earth's ability (and our ingenuity) to provide a sustainable supply of those resources to meet the new demands for those resources and still protect the environment.

During the last two generations, governments and industry have made substantial improvements in their quest to simultaneously develop our resources and protect our environment. Yet there are some people who feel hostile toward those who are responsible for maintaining and improving our standard of living. Many have focused on the costs of scientific technology and ignored the benefits—perhaps because the benefits are so familiar that they are taken for granted.

Science is a process of learning about things that happen and then, hopefully, being able to apply our knowledge to help things happen better. Our hope is that this program will help you face (with understanding) the complicated scientific, technological, and societal issues that will confront you in the 21st century.

In aiding with this course, the Mineral Information Institute has accepted the challenge of explaining that many of our natural resources can be extracted in an environmentally sound manner, while providing social and economic benefits. We hope the information in this program helps you develop the knowledge and perspective that will be necessary to make those wise decisions in the future. We need to develop and use our natural resources wisely.

Teachers and students are invited to inquire about other activities of the Mineral Information Institute and to participate in them.

Mineral Information Institute
505 Violet Street
Golden, Colorado 80401
www.mii.org

An Open Letter to Students

" *My interest is in the future because I am going to spend the rest of my life there.* "

—*Charles F. Kettering*

Dear Student:

You are living at an exciting time. During your lifetime, important decisions will be made, and you have a role in making them. These decisions will affect the position of your country in the world of nations; your feeling of who you are and how you relate to others and the environment that surrounds you; the quality of life you will have; and the amount of personal freedom you will enjoy. Many decisions will relate to how you use energy, resources, and our environment.

Wise decisions will depend on how well you understand the issues. It is the purpose of this course to build a basic background for understanding energy, resources, and environmental benefits and problems. *Global Science* is not just another science course. The questions we will discuss relate to today as well as tomorrow. You will find that the road you travel as you work through these pages can be an exciting journey.

Science is a powerful tool at our disposal. Science plays an important role for every living creature on Earth. Some of the questions this science course will discuss are

- What is exponential growth?

- Does Earth have a carrying capacity?

- Is there an energy, resource, and environmental concern?

- Can we live better with less? Do we have to?

- What are our alternatives?

It is true that people cause some of the concerns we will study. It is also true that people are keys to the solutions. *Global Science* helps provide the vision of tomorrow. It describes alternatives and suggests possible solutions.

To be part of the solution, you need to

- understand how the scientific issues relate to you and your needs;

- have a vision of what a sustainable world might be like; and

- act on what you know. That is something you do for yourself.

African environmentalist Baba Dioum said:

" *In the end, we will conserve only what we love. We will love only what we understand. We will understand only what we are taught.* "

Global Science teaches the wonders of our planet. Studying this text will not provide all the answers, but you will be much better prepared to face the challenges of tomorrow because of your experiences in this course.

—*John W. Christensen and Teri L. Christensen*

Using This Textbook

Using a textbook to its fullest potential should be a goal you want to pursue. To help you use it fully, we want to point out the main features of this book.

Quickly page through a portion of your book and note that most pages have a white background. Some pages, however, have a green or brown background. Normal text is on the white background, and special sections have the colored backgrounds. Special sections contain such items as special focus topics, biographical sketches, career opportunities, and the acknowledgment of sources where necessary. Some pages have a beige edge. This colored edge indicates an activity. The beginning and end of an activity are also indicated by a blue bar running across the page.

Now turn to Chapter 1. Note the following features:

- **Marginal notes** provide a clue into the content of the passages they match. Use them to help you understand the passage, focus on the content, or identify the most important material in the chapter.

- **Vocabulary** you need to know is placed in **boldface type** the first time a new key word appears in a chapter. This is done to draw your attention to that word. All key words are defined in the **glossary**, which is located near the end of this textbook. Emphasized words are in italics.

- **Chapter questions/tasks** give you an opportunity to practice and apply what you have learned. In this textbook, the important questions/tasks appear in the relevant sections or in marginal notes. Most are part of an activity. Do these carefully and completely.

- **Key ideas/questions** are provided to give you an idea of what is important in the chapter. They appear as marginal notes with a key symbol next to them. This will enable you to focus your attention on key ideas as they are being presented.

- **Tables, graphs, illustrations, and photos** help you visualize the concept being discussed. Important tables and illustrations have a colored background to help emphasize their importance. Note that the source of the information is given in the figure legend when it is not the author's. Knowing where data come from is as important as the actual data.

- **Readings, activities, and figures are numbered** by chapter. The first number is the number of the chapter. This is followed by the number of the reading, activity, or figure within the chapter. This system should help you locate material anywhere within the textbook.

- **Chapter summaries** are provided at the end of each chapter. Read them before you read the entire chapter. They will help you find the important ideas. Read them again at the end to help you put together all the different concepts of the chapter.

- **References** for further reading and research follow the chapter summary. It is often useful to find and examine the information sources an author has used.

- **Websites** that give additional information related to the topics you are studying can be found at the end of most chapters. Websites are also included within specific activities for further reference and with SciLinks.

In addition to these features, the book contains **appendixes**, a **glossary**, and an **index**. The appendixes contain useful information on making graphs, doing scientific notation, using units of measure, understanding conversion factors, and having other useful data and information on careers handy. The index should help you locate topics anywhere in the text.

Key to the Symbols

Throughout the *Global Science* textbook, you will find symbols that alert you to the features of this course.

A key indicates key ideas and questions. This symbol is placed with the relevant marginal note.

Be safe! This symbol alerts you to safety concerns in the lab and in the field.

A special warning or caution when working in the lab or field. These warnings/cautions are there for your safety. Read and follow them carefully!

This symbol indicates an activity, simulation, research project, or laboratory investigation.

This question mark draws attention to questions or tasks you need to consider.

The book symbol indicates key reference material.

This symbol indicates websites that relate to a topic of interest.

This symbol is your gateway to more information on key topics. Go to www.scilinks.org and enter the topic code. A host of information on that topic is just a click away!

This symbol directs you to Appendix 1, which is a collection of career vignettes.

Laboratory Safety

This program contains a variety of activities. Many involve the use of laboratory equipment and chemicals. Some of the equipment and chemicals can cause problems if used incorrectly. None of the activities, however, are dangerous if you have a good attitude, think clearly, and follow the directions.

The following guidelines should help make all your laboratory experiences safe and positive.

1. Work in the lab only when your teacher is present.

2. Think about safety each time you do a lab. Read through the directions and plan what you will do before you begin. Pay close attention to safety alerts and warnings in the activities.

3. Know the location and how to use all safety equipment in the laboratory. This includes the safety shower, eye wash, sink, faucets, first-aid kit, fire extinguisher, and blanket.

4. Wear a lab coat or apron and protective glasses or goggles in all labs that involve heating and/or the use of chemicals. Tie back loose hair—especially when heat and flames are involved.

5. Clear your lab station of all unnecessary materials before you begin.

6. Carefully read the labels on all containers. Make sure you are using the correct chemical before you start measuring.

7. Do not return any excess materials to their original container unless your teacher instructs you to do so.

8. Stay on task. When in the lab, emphasize the *labor* and deemphasize the *oratory*.

9. Never taste laboratory materials. In addition, no food of any kind should be brought into the lab.

10. Never place the opening of a container near your nose. If you are instructed to smell something, do so by fanning some of the vapor toward your nose with your hand. Your teacher can show you the proper technique.

11. Never look directly down into a test tube. Always view the contents from the side. Never point the open end of a test tube toward yourself or your neighbor.

12. Any laboratory accident, however small, should be reported immediately to your teacher.

13. If you *spill* a chemical on your skin or clothing, quickly rinse the affected area with plenty of water. If the eyes are affected, cleanse with water immediately and continue for 10 to 15 minutes or until professional assistance is obtained.

14. Place minor skin burns under cold, running water.

15. Do not discard chemicals unless instructed to do so. In those cases, carefully follow the instructions provided.

16. Return all equipment, chemicals, and protective glasses to their designated locations.

17. Before leaving the laboratory, make sure that gas lines and water faucets are turned off.

18. Finally, if in doubt, ask!

Biological Sciences Curriculum Study

CHAPTER 1

The Nature of Science

GOAL

- To build an understanding of the purpose, methods, and effectiveness of science.

The meaning of it all: the meaning of the pattern of nature, and of our place in nature ... it is the quest of everyone, whether scientist, or artist, or person in the street.

—*J. Bronowski, science philosopher*

Science as a Way of Thinking

1.1 What Is Science?

Science is more than a body of knowledge. It is a way of thinking.

—Carl Sagan, astronomer and science writer

Think of *Global Science* as a survival manual for life on Spaceship Earth.

You are about to embark on an exciting exploration into the world of global science. But first let's begin by looking at the nature of science itself. The activities in this chapter help you examine the purpose, methods, and effectiveness of science. Learning about what science is and what science isn't will help you gain a better understanding of the rest of the topics you will study in this course.

ACTIVITY 1.1

What Do You Think Science Is?

In this activity, you will think about what science is and what scientists do. This will help you come up with your own definition of science.

Procedure

1. Based on your own experiences, write down 4 ideas or statements about what science is.

2. List 4 things that you think scientists do. See Figures 1.1 and 1.2 for ideas.

3. Share your ideas from steps 1 and 2 with a partner. Revise your lists by adding, deleting, and clarifying items.

4. Compare the Sagan quote above to your list. How are they similar? How are they different? Be ready to discuss your thinking with the class.

Helpful Hint!

Record your thinking in your science notebook. Using a science notebook is a good way to keep all your observations in one place.

5. Write a definition of science based on your experiences, the Sagan quote, and the ideas you obtained in class.

▲ FIGURE 1.1 Kristy Richie, a research chemist, examines a fluorescent gel used in a DNA "fingerprinting" technique.
(National Institute of Standards and Technology [NIST])

▲ FIGURE 1.2 An artist's sketch of an 18th-century chemical laboratory.
(Fisher Scientific Company)

1.2 What Scientists Do

Scientists start their work by asking questions about the natural world. Most of us do this all the time. We simply don't make an effort to answer these questions. Scientists do.

Science begins with observations and questions about those observations.

ACTIVITY 1.2

Asking Scientific Questions

In this activity, you will have a chance to ask questions in a scientific manner.

Materials (for each lab station—individual, pair, or team)

- sealed test tube filled with colored water (use cork or rubber stopper)
- strip of paper with the words URANIUM DIOXIDE written in capital letters
- metric ruler

Procedure

1. Place the paper strip on a flat, level surface with the words showing. Hold the test tube at least 2 centimeters (cm) above the paper strip.

2. Look at the words through the test tube. (Do not read through any air bubbles that may be present.)

3. Record your observations in your science notebook. What questions do you have right now? Why do the letters do this?

4. Based on your question(s), try to explain your observations. This is your hypothesis. A **hypothesis** is a first explanation of what is happening. It is an explanation "on trial."

5. Work with your partner to develop a way to test your hypothesis. The possibility must exist that you could be wrong.

6. Test your ideas and record your results.

7. After you are satisfied that you have tested your ideas thoroughly, answer these questions:

   a. What is your explanation of what happened?

   b. How do you know that your explanation is correct?

8. Make a representation (for example, a chart, diagram, or outline) that shows the process you used to answer your original question(s).

9. How do you think this process might be useful in answering other questions?

10. For what kinds of questions would this process *not* be useful?

[Adapted with the permission of Donald Uhland, Westlake Middle School, Broomfield, Colorado.]

1.3 Scientific Problem Solving

Think about This!

A hypothesis must be testable and falsifiable. If there is no test for its "wrongness," it is not a hypothesis. In that case, it is simply opinion.

There is no one way to do science; however, scientists often use the following pattern:

1. Make *observations*.

2. Form a *question* based on those observations.

3. Form a *hypothesis* that attempts to explain the observations.

4. *Test* the hypothesis. (This may require making more observations, taking measurements, or reworking the original question.)

5. Develop an *explanation* based on the results of the tests.

Apply Your Understanding

How similar was the process you developed in Activity 1.2 to this process?

Lists of steps to answer scientific questions can be useful tools, but we must not be bound by them. Percy Bridgman, an American Nobel Prize winner in physics, says:

> It seems to me that there is a good deal of ballyhoo about scientific method. I venture to think that the people who talk the most about it are the people who do least about it. Scientific method is what working scientists do . . . and there are as many scientific methods as there are individual scientists.

There is no single scientific method.

Science philosopher and writer Gerald Holton states:

> The well planned experiment is by far the most frequent one and has generally the best chance of success; yet successful scientists have often not even mapped out a tentative plan of attack but have instead let their enthusiasm, their hunches, and their sheer joy of discovery suggest the line of work.

Topic: scientific investigations
Go to: www.scilinks.org
Code: GloSci7e6

One might conclude, then, that it is a myth that there is a single best method for doing an experiment. As a rule-of-thumb in this course, the best way to write up an experiment is the way your teacher wants it. We will not confine you to a single way of doing lab reports. What we do emphasize is this: In science, we start with observations and related questions. We don't start with answers.

Think about This!

Science does not start with answers.

ACTIVITY 1.3

Modeling the Weathering Process

Introduction

In this activity, you will design an experiment that models the weathering process.

Observation

People, including scientists, have observed that rocks seem to weather (or break down) faster in some climates than in others. You will use methods from both Activity 1.2 and the text to answer this question:

The question. What is the effect of temperature on the process of chemical weathering?

Background

Sometimes, natural events and processes are too large, too small, too fast, or too slow to study directly. So scientists develop models of these events. In this experiment, you will model the process by which rocks are broken down in nature. The natural process of breaking down rocks into smaller pieces is called **weathering**.

> **Helpful Hint!**
> A model is something that imitates the behavior of something else.

Wind, flowing water, moving ice, and the pull of gravity all result in the slow breakdown of rock. Also, naturally occurring chemicals in water often react with soil and rock, slowly breaking them apart. This process is called *chemical weathering*. We will use antacid tablets to represent (model) limestone rocks, and water to model the action of natural water.

Materials (per lab group)

- stopwatch or wall clock
- room-temperature water
- 3 beakers (250 mL)
- Celsius thermometer (°C)
- cold water
- waste container
- hot water (45°C−50°C)
- 4 antacid tablets (limestone rocks)
- safety goggles

Procedure

1. Review the observation, the question, and the list of materials.

2. Think of a way you might answer the question based on the background information, what you know about the methods of science, and the materials available. This is your testable hypothesis.

3. Write your proposed experimental design in your science notebook. Include safety procedures and your hypothesis.

WARNING
Use care when handling hot water.

4. Have your teacher review and approve your design.

5. Gather your materials and conduct your experiment.

6. Record your data and observations in a table in your science notebook.

7. Clean up your lab station.

QUESTIONS & TASKS

1. Graph your data. It is up to you to decide how to do the graph.

2. What does your graph show? Was your hypothesis correct?

3. What explanation about weathering can you give based on your data?

4. What information would strengthen your explanation?

[Adapted from an activity developed by the Graduate School of Education at the University at Buffalo (SUNY).]

The Nature of Scientific Explanation

In this activity, you will use what you did in Activities 1.2 and 1.3 to identify the characteristics of a scientific exploration.

Procedure

1. Think about Activity 1.2. Write an explanation about what happened.

2. Identify the characteristics of your scientific explanation. Use these questions as a guide:

   a. Was your explanation based on something observable?

   b. Does your explanation tie together many observations? Explain.

   c. What natural phenomenon does your explanation explain?

3. Repeat steps 1 and 2 for Activity 1.3.

1.4 Scientific Explanations

Think about This!

To scientists, what is the purpose of science?

In science, an explanation for a natural event is accepted when that explanation consistently predicts what will happen.

Think about This!

To most people, what is the purpose of science?

Scientific explanations tie together many observations in an attempt to explain the natural world. These explanations help us understand what happens around us and inside our bodies. These explanations are based on questions such as those in Activities 1.2 and 1.3.

For scientists, scientific explanations define the *purpose* of science. This purpose is to develop concepts, laws, and theories that function as enduring explanations. That is, scientists assume that the concept, law, or theory will be true for all similar situations, now and in the future. For example, when Sir Isaac Newton (Figure 1.3) stated the law of gravity, he said *all* objects attract one another. This means that any object raised above Earth's surface will fall to the ground when released. The law has endured, helping scientists develop explanations about the movement of Earth around the sun, satellites around Earth, and other similar happenings in space.

For most people, scientific explanations may have a different purpose. In many instances, the explanations are useful in our daily life (Figure 1.4a). For example, an understanding of the laws of motion can help you drive more safely.

▶FIGURE 1.3 Sir Isaac Newton is one of the greatest scientists of all time. He helped popularize the experimental method. He also developed many of the concepts and laws that are fundamental to the development of the physical sciences, mathematics, and applications such as modern transportation systems and space exploration. *(Yerkes Observatory)*

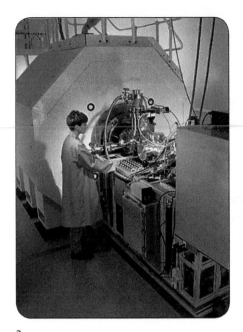

a
b
c

▲ FIGURE 1.4 Ways of searching for meaning and explanation.
(a) Mass spectrometer in the Environmental Molecular Sciences Laboratory at Pacific Northwest National Laboratory *(U.S. Department of Energy Genomics: GTL Program, http://doegenomestolife.org)*; (b) Religious quest. *John W. Christensen;* (c) *The Thinker (Rodin, Auguste, 1880. The Rodin Museum: Philadelphia: Gift of Jules E. Mastbaum).*

Most people find the methods of science useful in dealing with questions about the natural world. Why did my lawn turn brown? What foods are best for me to eat?

But sometimes, people have questions that cannot be answered by scientific explanations or by using the methods of science. We have developed other ways of addressing these questions. These ways include religion and philosophy. *Religion* is a system of beliefs often centered on a divine or supernatural power or powers to be obeyed and worshiped as God and/or ruler(s) of the universe. Religion often involves a code of conduct and a theology tied to the meaning and purpose of life (Figure 1.4b).

Philosophy is the study of the processes that govern thought and conduct. Philosophy includes the study of beauty, ethics, logic, and metaphysics. Philosophy is based on the belief that clear, logical reasoning reveals some truths to humans (Figure 1.4c).

To some, our ways of searching for meaning and explanation are in conflict. They need not be. Religion deals with the purpose and meaning of life. Philosophy deals with patterns of reasonable thought. Science deals with the patterns of the natural world—that which we can see, touch, feel, and measure.

Helpful Hint!

Ethics is the study of standards of conduct and correct behavior.

Logic is the study of correct reasoning and valid thought.

Metaphysics is the study of ideas in an effort to explain the nature of reality and the origin and structure of the world.

Religion and philosophy tie to our quest for purpose.

❓ QUESTIONS & TASKS

1. What is the purpose of science?

2. Give an example of how a scientific explanation has been useful to you or to someone you know.

ACTIVITY 1.5

Sorting Out the Questions

In this activity, you will think about and identify different ways of knowing.

> **Think about This!**
> Science ties to our desire to know how things happen.

Procedure

1. Quickly write down 10 questions that are important to you.

2. Sort your questions into 3 categories: scientific, religious, and philosophical.

3. Exchange lists and discuss these ideas with your partner(s).

   a. Do you agree with the sorting?

   b. Defend your sorting to your partner(s).

4. Revise your list based on your discussion.

 The Scientific Attitude

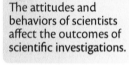

The attitudes and behaviors of scientists affect the outcomes of scientific investigations.

1.5 Thinking in a Scientific Manner

Being a scientific thinker involves more than asking questions and developing explanations. Certain habits of mind or attitudes and behaviors determine how scientists approach their work. Anyone can develop these behaviors and attitudes.

ACTIVITY 1.6

Scientific Habits of Mind

In this activity, you will learn about the attitudes and behaviors that will make you a scientific thinker.

The Habit of Skepticism

While browsing the Internet for information, (then) junior high student Nathan Zohner (Figure 1.5) came across some disturbing information about a dangerous chemical in our environment. This chemical is dihydrogen monoxide, or DHMO. Nathan researched the scientific properties of DHMO. He then designed an informational bulletin to acquaint his classmates with the dangers of this compound. Nathan's bulletin, *Dihydrogen Monoxide—The Unrecognized Killer!*, is reproduced here. Read it carefully and then answer the questions that follow.

Dihydrogen Monoxide—The Unrecognized Killer!

Dihydrogen monoxide (DHMO) is a colorless, odorless, tasteless chemical that kills uncounted thousands of people each year. Most of these deaths are caused by the accidental inhalation of DHMO, but the dangers of this chemical do not end there. Prolonged exposure to its solid form causes severe tissue damage. Symptoms of DHMO ingestion can include excessive sweating and urination, and possibly a bloated feeling, nausea, vomiting, and body electrolyte imbalance. For those who have developed a dependency on DHMO, complete withdrawal means certain death.

Consider the KNOWN facts. Dihydrogen monoxide:

- is also known as hydroxyl acid, and is the major component of acid rain.

- contributes to the "greenhouse effect."

- may cause severe burns, especially in gaseous form.

- contributes to the erosion of our natural landscape.

- accelerates the corrosion and rusting of many metals.

- may cause electrical failures and decrease effectiveness of automobile brakes.

- has been found in excised tumors of terminal cancer patients.

- is allowed to be present in many food products.

- is sold in pure form (without warning labels!) by many profit motivated grocery store chains.

Contamination of our natural environment is reaching epidemic proportions!!! The presence of DHMO has been confirmed in every river, stream, lake, and reservoir in America. During recent months, DHMO has caused millions of dollars of damage in northern Idaho and on the coast of California.

Despite the known dangers, dihydrogen monoxide continues to be used:

- as an industrial solvent and coolant.

- by contractors like Lockheed Martin (aerospace) and Newport News (ships and submarine builders) who are conducting experiments with DHMO, and are designing multi-billion (that's billion with a "b"!!) dollar devices to utilize this chemical for applications in warfare. Hundreds of military research facilities receive tons of it through a highly sophisticated underground distribution network. The Idaho National Engineering and Environmental Laboratory (INEEL) has admitted that it has received the chemical through its own underground network and has released tons of it into the environment. It is an open fact that employees at the INEEL contact this chemical in the workplace daily, yet neither the government nor its contractors make any effort whatsoever to monitor employees for DHMO contamination when they go home at night.

It's not too late!!!

Act NOW to prevent further contamination. Find out more about this dangerous chemical that kills thousands each year. What you don't know can hurt you, those you love, and others throughout the world. Coalition to Ban DHMO.

[Courtesy of Nathan Zohner, Idaho Falls, Idaho. Adapted from *Factsheet* by Coalition to Ban DHMO.]

QUESTIONS & TASKS

1. Think about the scientific information provided in Nathan Zohner's fact sheet. Do you think that action should be taken to ban the release of DHMO into the environment? Why?

2. Should the banning of DHMO be done at the local, state, federal, or international level? How should such a ban be enforced?

3. After reading the information on DHMO, most people think it should be banned. That is, of course, until they learn that DHMO is water. Knowing this, can you explain the facts about DHMO in the bulletin?

4. Nathan intended to use the fact sheet to show how easily people can be manipulated. How does this activity illustrate the habit of skepticism? Can this habit be useful to most of us as we read the newspaper and follow political campaigns? Explain.

The Habit of Intellectual Honesty

In its purest form, science is the pursuit of truth about the natural world. Scientists start with questions; gather data in an honest, unbiased manner; and then look for patterns and relationships in those data. If meaningful patterns are discovered, they are announced to other scientists in the form of published papers and presentations. This allows the relationships to be verified independently by others. That is how it is supposed to happen. Scientists, however, are human and are subject to temptation like everyone else. Sometimes, the process breaks down.

In 1973, Dr. William T. Summerlin (Figure 1.6), a researcher at the Sloan-Kettering Institute for Cancer Research, announced that he had successfully cultured skin tissue from a white mouse and grafted it onto a black mouse. He also claimed to have done the reverse. This announcement generated a lot of interest. At that time, living organisms usually rejected transplants from dissimilar hosts. This could have been the breakthrough that would pave the way for wide-scale skin grafting and organ transplants.

Almost immediately, other scientists attempted to duplicate Dr. Summerlin's work. They were unsuccessful. This led to a debate about whether or not the original claims were true, or if those who were unsuccessful were culturing the skin tissue correctly.

As a result of this debate, Dr. Summerlin was asked to show his boss the best evidence to support his claims. As he rode up an elevator with 18 mice as evidence, he noticed the new skin had a dull, grayish look. So he whipped out his felt-tip pen and painted the skin grafts of two of the mice to make the results look better. After the meeting, the mice and their cages were returned to the animal room.

Unfortunately for Dr. Summerlin, one of the laboratory assistants noticed that two of the black grafts looked "unfamiliar." He applied alcohol to the skin and discovered that the color washed away. He informed a senior research technician, who then informed others. A few hours later, Dr. Summerlin was back in the boss's office. He admitted to the paint job and was immediately suspended.

More recently, South Korean research scientist Hwang Woo-Suk claimed to be the first person to clone a human embryo and to extract human stem cells. His claims were published in the journal *Science* in 2004. Soon after, the results of his claims were challenged by other scientists. An investigation by Seoul National University found that he had fabricated his data. Steps were taken to hold him accountable for his deception.

▶ FIGURE 1.6

Dr. Summerlin with one of his lab mice.
*(Newsweek-Tony Rollo.
© 1974, Newsweek, Inc.
All rights reserved.
Reprinted by permission.)*

QUESTIONS & TASKS

1. Why do you think some scientists were skeptical after they became aware of Dr. Summerlin's claims?

2. Why do you think Dr. Summerlin painted the skin-grafted regions on the mice he was showing to his boss?

3. Scientists are often under pressure to produce results in their research because results bring in the money necessary to continue their work. Results also enable them to get published and receive recognition and promotions. How can

these conditions put pressure on a scientist to be dishonest? Explain. Is this any different than the pressure on some high school students to get good grades? Explain.

4. When Dr. Summerlin painted the mouse to make the skin graft look better than it actually was, he compromised

Helpful Hint!

Integrity is the quality of being honest, sincere, and morally strong.

his own integrity. Your integrity protects you from feelings of guilt, shame, and pity. How can emphasizing honesty and good judgment help you to not repeat Dr. Summerlin's mistake? Explain.

The Habit of Tolerating Uncertainty

The results of science depend upon measurements and data analysis. However, neither measurements nor scientists who interpret data are perfect. For this reason, science must allow for elements of uncertainty. To a scientist, this is a *strength*, not a weakness. Richard D. Feynman, a Nobel Laureate in physics, states:

> *The scientist has a lot of experience with ignorance and doubt and uncertainty, and this experience is of very great importance. When a scientist doesn't know the answer to a problem, he is ignorant. When he has a hunch as to what the result is, he is uncertain. And when he is pretty darn sure of what the result is going to be, he is in some doubt. We have found it of paramount importance that in order to progress, we must recognize the ignorance and leave room for doubt. Scientific knowledge is a body of statements of varying degrees of certainty—some most unsure, some nearly sure, none absolutely certain . . . . It is our responsibility as scientists, knowing the great progress and great value of a satisfactory philosophy of ignorance, the*

> *great progress that is the fruit of freedom of thought, to proclaim the value of this freedom, to teach how doubt is not to be feared but welcomed and discussed, and to demand this freedom as our duty to all coming generations.*

QUESTIONS & TASKS

1. How can admitting your uncertainty lead to a better discussion of ideas?

2. List two or three ideas scientists are unsure of that are being discussed and researched.

3. Absolute knowledge is not penetrable by facts and evidence. This can be dangerous. Explain.

The Habit of Openness to New Ideas

The scientific process begins with curiosity—asking questions, paying attention, and wanting to find out more. Sometimes, that curiosity leads to discovery. Discovery occurs when someone looks at one thing and sees something different. Stated another way, discovery consists of seeing what everyone else has seen, but thinking what no one else has thought. Try it!

Think about This!

When do discoveries happen?

Procedure

1. Below are 9 dots placed in a square pattern. Recopy these 9 dots near the center of a blank $8\frac{1}{2} \times 11$-inch sheet of paper.

2. Can you connect all of these dots with 4 straight lines, all of which connect? Can you do it with fewer than 4 straight lines? Use your imagination. Be creative.

```
•   •   •

•   •   •

•   •   •
```

Make Your Own Contribution to the Global Pool of Scientific Data

GLOBE is an ongoing international education and science program that unites students, teachers, and scientists in the study of Earth as a system. Students participating in GLOBE engage in inquiry-based scientific research of their local environment (Figure 1.7). GLOBE students collect, analyze, share, and report their data and findings with other students and with scientists around the world via the GLOBE website and database (www.globe.gov).

Students benefit from GLOBE through a better understanding and appreciation of Earth system science and through improved achievement and interest in science. Teachers benefit from GLOBE through professional development workshops and educational materials that support the integration of inquiry-based scientific investigations into their curricula. Scientists benefit from GLOBE through access to quality ground truth data from around the world that is unavailable by other means and through their interactions with teachers and students. Communities and countries benefit from GLOBE through enhanced awareness of and attention to local and regional environmental problems and through the building of cross-cultural relationships.

The GLOBE data are available at no cost to students and scientists worldwide. In the United States, GLOBE is primarily sponsored by the National Aeronautics and Space Administration (NASA), the National Science Foundation (NSF), the University Corporation for Atmospheric Research (UCAR), Colorado State University (CSU), and the U.S. Department of State.

To begin making your contribution to the global pool of scientific data, go to www.globe.gov. Work with your teacher to establish your school's involvement.

▲ FIGURE 1.7 Students in Thailand prepare to work on GLOBE water quality protocols. (*Courtesy: The GLOBE Program*)

The Tools and Skills of Science

1.6 Scientific Tools and Skills

Everyone can be a scientist at some level; each of us can learn about the world from a scientific point of view. We learn science by reading and listening, by watching videos, and by making observations of the world around us. We do science by performing experiments. Sometimes, we repeat experiments that others have done; at other times, we design experiments on our own. All of these methods will be available to you in this course.

ACTIVITY 1.7

Quality and Quantity of Data

In this activity, you will collect data about students in your class and then interpret the significance of your measurements.

Procedure

1. Choose 1 person to represent your entire class.

2. Record the following data about your representative in your science notebook:

   a. age

   b. gender

   c. height in centimeters

   d. eye color

   e. hair color

   f. number of fingers

3. Do these data give an accurate picture of your class? Explain.

4. Randomly select 5 people from your class by drawing names from a container.

5. Collect the same data as you did in step 2, and display the measurements in a chart on the board. Compute the average values for items a, c, and f.

QUESTIONS & TASKS

1. How well do these data represent the class?

2. How much data would it take to accurately represent the class?

3. Even with data from everyone in class, would someone be able to read the data chart and really *know* your class? Why or why not?

1.7 Challenges to Taking Measurements

Scientists want to make accurate and precise measurements because these measurements can lead to a better understanding of what the scientists are studying. But there are two things that make the measuring process imperfect. The first is that the act of making a measurement disturbs what is being measured. Consider this problem: You want to use a thermometer to accurately measure the temperature of some cold water in a beaker. What temperature must the thermometer be before it is placed in the water? Answer: The same temperature as the water. Since this hardly ever happens, most temperatures taken using this method are a little off.

The second problem is that once measurements are taken, the scientist must interpret them. Since scientists aren't perfect, their interpretations aren't either.

Think about This!

Why can't science provide a perfect view of the natural world?

Think about This!

This is called the effect of the knower on the known.

The Blind Men and the Elephant

In this activity, you will read a poem that illustrates some of the problems related to obtaining information. Read the poem carefully and then examine Figure 1.8.

The Blind Men and the Elephant

A Hindu Fable by John Godfrey Saxe, 1816–1887

It was six men of Indostan
To learning much inclined,
Who went to see the Elephant
(Though all of them were blind),
That each by observation
Might satisfy his mind.

The FIRST approached the Elephant,
And happening to fall
Against his broad and sturdy side,
At once began to bawl:
"God bless me; but the Elephant
Is very like a wall!"

The SECOND, feeling of the tusk,
Cried, "Ho! What have we here.
So very round and firm and sharp?
To me 'tis mighty clear
This wonder of an Elephant
Is very like a spear!"

The THIRD approached the animal
And happening to take
The squirming trunk within his hands,
Thus boldly up and spake
"I see," quoth he, "The Elephant
Is very like a snake!"

The FOURTH reached out an eager hand,
And felt about the knee.
"What most this wondrous beast is like
Is mighty plain," quoth he:

"Tis clear enough the Elephant
Is very like a tree!"

▲FIGURE 1.8 **The fable of the blind men and the elephant.**
(Caricatures adapted by permission of Smith Kline Beecham Consumer Healthcare.)

The FIFTH, who chanced to touch the ear,
Said: "E'en the blindest man
Can tell what this resembles most;
Deny the fact who can,
This marvel of an Elephant
Is very like a fan!"

The SIXTH no sooner had begun
About the beast to grope,
Then, seizing on the swinging tail
That fell within his scope,
"I see," quoth he, "The Elephant
Is very like a rope."

And so these men of Indostan
Disputed loud and long,
Each in his own opinion
Exceeding stiff and strong,
Though each was partly in the right
And all were in the wrong!

QUESTIONS & TASKS

1. Who or what might the blind men represent?

2. Who or what might the elephant represent?

3. Why was each "partly in the right" but "all were in the wrong"?

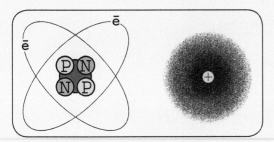

◄FIGURE 1.9 Drawings that represent atoms as illustrated in many science textbooks. On the left is an earlier model of the atom. In this model, electrons travel in definite paths like planets around the sun. The more recent model on the right shows an electron cloud. This model came about because scientists realized they did not know the precise path of each electron but only the likelihood of where it might be.

4. Compare the blind men and the elephant fable to attempts by scientists to draw pictures of what the atom looks like (see Figure 1.9).

5. If scientists can't give a perfect picture of the natural world, why have science?

1.8 Data Collection and Interpretation

Data are pieces of information that are collected in an attempt to answer a question. The last two activities illustrate this process. Data provide the raw material, or evidence, used by scientists to develop an explanation. For data to be useful, scientists must carefully consider what forms of data to collect and how much to collect. In the next activity, you will have the opportunity to collect a variety of data. You will then determine how to analyze and interpret the data. By making meaningful choices about the analysis and interpretation of data, you can develop more powerful explanations.

Data provide the raw material from which science is built.

Sometimes, the outline of a plan for an investigation can help you focus on the collection and interpretation of data. This is the approach we will use in Activity 1.9.

ACTIVITY 1.9

Measuring Aluminum

In this activity, you will practice some measuring techniques and improve your ability to analyze and interpret data.

Materials

- 5 different aluminum samples
- set of graduated cylinders
- metric ruler
- *Handbook of Chemistry and Physics*
- balance (to mass in grams)
- water
- beakers
- medicine dropper
- graph paper

Procedure

1. Reproduce the table in Figure 1.10 in your science notebook.

DO NOT WRITE IN THIS BOOK.

2. Number the 5 aluminum samples (1–5).

3. Measure and record in your table the length (in centimeters) of each sample. Figure 1.11a shows how to determine length.

4. Use the balance to determine the mass of each sample in grams (g).

5. Determine the volume of each sample in milliliters (mL). Use the water displacement method to do this. Figure 1.11b shows how to read a graduated cylinder. To determine the volume, use the smallest graduated cylinder that will hold the sample. *Do not try to force the sample into*

Sample (No.)	Length (cm)	Mass (g)	Original Water Level	New Water Level	Volume (NWL − OWL)	m/V (g/mL)
1						
2						
3						
4						
5						

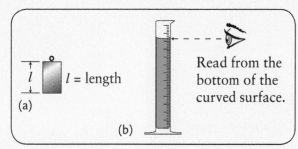

l = length

Read from the bottom of the curved surface.

(a)

(b)

▲ FIGURE 1.11 (a) How to measure the length of your samples. (b) How to read a graduated cylinder.

the graduated cylinder. If it doesn't fit, use the next larger size. For each sample, record in your table the original water level (OWL) and the new water level (NWL). Determine the volume of each sample by subtracting the original water level from the new water level (NWL−OWL).

6. Determine the ratio mass/volume for each sample. Record this measurement in the last column of your table.

QUESTIONS & TASKS

1. Plot a graph of length vs. mass for your 5 samples. See Appendix 2 for information on graphing data.

2. Plot a graph of length vs. volume for the 5 samples.

3. Plot a graph of mass vs. volume for the 5 samples.

Answer the following questions (in your lab notebook):

4. Which graph shows the most meaningful relationship? Why?

5. Look up the density of aluminum in the *Handbook of Chemistry and Physics*. Record your finding in your science notebook.

6. Based on what you have done in this lab, what is the equation for determining density?

7. Knowing that 1 mL = 1 cm^3 = 1 g of water at 4°C, what is the density of water?

8. From what you have determined, why does aluminum sink into water?

9. What would the numerical value of the density of a substance (in g/cm^3) have to be for it to float?

10. What kind of graph did you get when you plotted mass vs. volume for the aluminum samples?

11. Determine the slope of the mass vs. volume graph. See Appendix 2 for information on determining the slope of a graph.

12. What physical quantity does the slope represent?

13. The equation $y = mx$ is the general form for any straight-line graph that passes through the origin. The symbol for slope is m. Substitute for y, m, and x using your straight-line graph. Did this provide a meaningful equation? Explain. (This is how many of the equations in science books were found.)

14. Did all lab groups obtain the same value for the slope? Why or why not?

15. **Interpolate** means to obtain information *between* known data points. **Extrapolate** means to obtain information *beyond* known data points. In this case, it means to extend the line of the graph in both directions into regions where you have no data. Are you justified when you interpolate and extrapolate your mass vs. volume graph? Explain.

16. How does this activity demonstrate that scientists search for patterns? Sometimes they find them, often they don't.

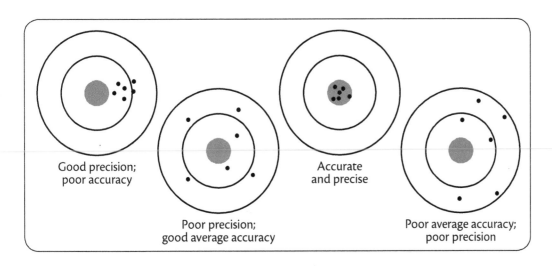

Good precision; poor accuracy

Poor precision; good average accuracy

Accurate and precise

Poor average accuracy; poor precision

1.9 Accurate Data, Precise Data

In Activity 1.8, none of the blind men had enough data to develop an accurate picture of an elephant. To develop strong, accurate, and reasonable explanations, one must have a sufficient *quantity* of data.

You may have noticed in Activity 1.9 that the graphs varied based on how carefully people made their measurements. This happened because of the quality of the data. *Quality* data are data that are accurately and precisely measured (see Figure 1.12).

Accurate measurements are something we rely on so often, we take them for granted. We give little thought to the fact that modern societies are built on our ability to measure hundreds of different quantities accurately and precisely over and over again. For example, accurate and uniform measurements maximize efficiency and promote customer confidence in the sale of goods. These range from oranges at the grocery store, to crude oil flowing through a transnational pipeline, to ultrapure gases purchased by semiconductor manufacturers.

QUESTIONS & TASKS

1. Explain the difference between accurate and precise.

2. Were accurate and precise measurements involved in building the phone you use? Explain.

ACTIVITY 1.10

Measurement, Modern Life, and Your Home

In this activity, you will think about accurate measurements in connection with a familiar structure. Your home is a good example of the use of accurate measurements. The materials and objects in your home exist as they do because of a variety of accurate measurements.

Procedure

1. Look at the drawing in Figure 1.13.

2. In each of the 5 categories below, list 2 measurements that may have been made in the production of this house or that are used as people live in this house.

   a. length

   b. time

The Nature of Science 19

c. temperature

d. mass

e. electrical energy

3. Make a drawing of your home.

4. Identify 10 locations where accurate measurements were used or are being used.

5. How do you think your life would change if it were not possible to make these accurate measurements?

 To learn more about the standards of measurement, call up http://www.nist.gov on your computer. Click on "A-Z subject index" and then "NIST in Your House."

► FIGURE 1.13 Measurement, modern life, and your home. *(Adapted from original art by National Institute of Standards and Technology.)*

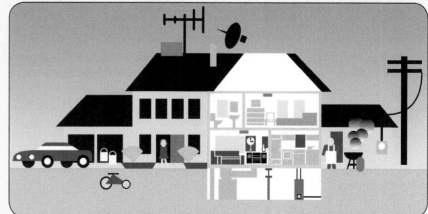

Measurement Systems

In science, it is important that we measure quantities using an agreed-upon method (Figure 1.14). That way, we can compare results. Over a long period of time, two measurement systems have survived. We will use both in this course.

U.S. Customary System

The **U.S. Customary System**, formerly the English System, is the measurement system that is used daily in the United States. The most common units are inches (in), feet (ft), miles (mi), quarts (qt), gallons (gal), ounces (oz), pounds (lb), degrees Fahrenheit (°F), and British Thermal Units (Btu).

Metric System

Most of the world uses the **metric system** of measurement. This is the measurement system

▲ FIGURE 1.14 Electronics engineer Katherine MacReynolds readies an antenna for near-field measurements. *(© Geoffrey Wheeler)*

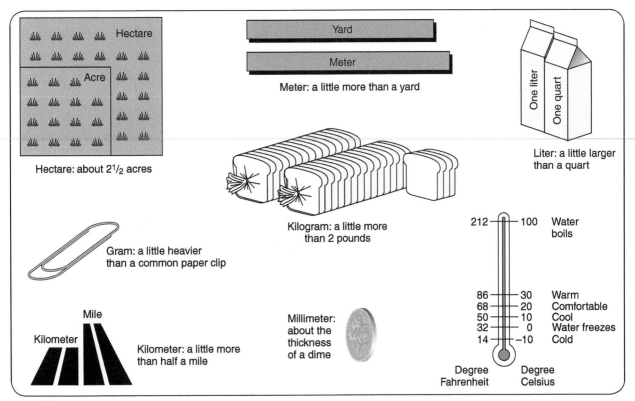

▲ **FIGURE 1.15** Comparison between U.S. Customary units and metric units. (*Adapted from original art by National Institute of Standards and Technology.*)

used by scientists around the world. The United States is the only industrialized nation that does not mainly use the metric system. Common metric units are the meter (m), kilogram (kg), second (s), degrees Celsius (°C), calorie (cal), volt (V), and watt (W).

The sizes of the various units in the U.S. Customary System are not related in any simple way. There are 12 inches in a foot, 5,280 feet in a mile, 4 quarts in a gallon, and 16 ounces in a pound. This makes it difficult to change from one unit to another. The metric system is more convenient because all units are related by multiples of 10. There are 10 millimeters in a centimeter, and 100 centimeters in a meter. Also, 1,000 grams = 1 kilogram, and 1,000 calories = 1 kilocalorie.

The metric system is easy to learn. As you examine the names of metric units in Figure 1.15 and Figure 1.17, notice that these names sometimes include prefixes such as *milli, centi,* and *kilo,* as in milliliter, centimeter, and kilogram. These prefixes indicate multiples or divisions of the unit. The meanings of the prefixes are shown in Figure 1.16 and in Appendix 4.

Figure 1.16 also introduces scientific notation. Scientific notation is the method used in science to deal with very large and very small numbers. See Appendix 3 for more information on scientific notation.

Because scientists use the metric system, and because the United States is converting to the metric system, you will want to learn it. You will then be better prepared to work with, visit, or exchange ideas with people from other countries. Many American industries already use the system; others are converting to make it easier to sell products in a global market.

Examine the drawings in Figure 1.15 to become familiar with comparisons between U.S. Customary and metric units. Then do the following problems. Record your work in your science notebook. The conversion factors in Appendix 6 will also be helpful.

Focus Conversion Problems

1. Convert 690 millimeters to centimeters.

2. How many liters is 7,950 milliliters?

3. Convert 38.2 kilograms to grams.

4. How many kilometers is 465 miles?

5. What is the mass of a 175-pound person in kilograms?

6. If the thermometer in a room reads 21°C, what is the temperature in Fahrenheit?

7. How many degrees Celsius is 180°F?

8. If you buy 25 liters of gasoline in Canada, how many quarts of fuel did you buy? How many gallons?

9. How many liters is 14 gallons of gasoline?

10. A 120-hectare farm is how many acres?

11. Is a person healthy if his or her body temperature averages 37°C?

12. Is a room comfortable if the thermostat is set at 27°C?

13. Will water boil at 100°C at sea level?

► FIGURE 1.16 Metric prefixes, symbols, and what they mean. (SI is the abbreviation for Système International, or International System. This is another name for the metric system. (*National Institute of Standards and Technology*)

Topic: measurement and data
Go to: www.scilinks.org
Code: GloSci7e22

Multiples and Prefixes
These Prefixes May Be Applied to All SI Units*

Multiples and Submultiples	Prefixes	Symbols
1 000 000 000 000 000 000 000 000 =	10^{24} yotta	Y
1 000 000 000 000 000 000 000 =	10^{21} zetta	Z
1 000 000 000 000 000 000 =	10^{18} exa	E
1 000 000 000 000 000 =	10^{15} peta	P
1 000 000 000 000 =	10^{12} tera	T
1 000 000 000 =	10^{9} giga	G
1 000 000 =	10^{6} mega	M
1 000 =	10^{3} kilo	k
100 =	10^{2} hecto	h
10 =	10^{1} deka	da
1 =	10^{0}	
0.1 =	10^{-1} deci	d
0.01 =	10^{-2} centi	c
0.001 =	10^{-3} milli	m
0.000 001 =	10^{-6} micro	μ
0.000 000 001 =	10^{-9} nano	n
0.000 000 000 001 =	10^{-12} pico	p
0.000 000 000 000 001 =	10^{-15} femto	f
0.000 000 000 000 000 001 =	10^{-18} atto	a
0.000 000 000 000 000 000 001 =	10^{-21} zepto	z
0.000 000 000 000 000 000 000 001 =	10^{-24} yocto	y

*Apply to gram in case of mass.

(continued)

Measurement Systems *(continued)*

Common Conversions
(Approximate Conversions)

◄ FIGURE 1.17
Common conversion factors between the U.S. Customary System and the metric system. You will notice that most symbols are written with lowercase letters. Exceptions are L for liter and units named after people, in which case the symbols are capitalized. Periods are not used with any symbols.

Symbol	When You Know	Multiply by	To Find	Symbol
Length				
in	inches	2.5	centimeters	cm
ft	feet	30	centimeters	cm
yd	yards	0.9	meters	m
mi	miles	1.6	kilometers	km
mm	millimeters	0.04	inches	in
cm	centimeters	0.4	inches	in
m	meters	3.3	feet	ft
m	meters	1.1	yards	yd
km	kilometers	0.6	miles	mi
Mass (Weight)				
oz	ounces	28	grams	g
lb	pounds	0.45	kilograms	kg
g	grams	0.035	ounces	oz
kg	kilograms	2.2	pounds	lb
Volume				
fl oz	fluid ounces	30	milliliters	mL
qt	quarts	0.95	liters	L
gal	gallons	3.8	liters	L
mL	milliliters	0.03	fluid ounces	fl oz
L	liters	1.06	quarts	qt
L	liters	0.26	gallons	gal
Temperature				
°F	degrees Fahrenheit	{ subtract 32, then multiply by 5/9 }	degrees Celsius	°C
°C	degrees Celsius	{ multiply by 9/5 and add 32 }	degrees Fahrenheit	°F

14. If two cities are 90 miles apart, what is the distance between them in kilometers?

15. About how many fluid ounces of refreshment are 2 liters?

16. If a girl jumps 24 inches off the ground, how high did she jump in meters? in centimeters?

Another way to learn to use measuring tools is to do experiments. We will wait to talk more about measuring systems until you do some experiments and take more measurements.

Science in Everyday Life

1.10 Using the Results of Science

To educate a man in mind, and not in morals, is to educate a menace to society.

—Teddy Roosevelt, 26th President of the United States

Topic: bioethics
Go to: www.scilinks.org
Code: GloSci7e24

The ethical neutrality dilemma.

Science and technology make many things possible. It is possible to travel all over the globe by airplane, car, or ship. We can talk to others by phone almost anywhere on our planet or send them e-mail. Doctors can use a knowledge of diseases (what causes them, how to cure them) to increase the overall health of large numbers of people. Unfortunately, a terrorist can use that same knowledge to kill thousands of people.

One of the problems in science is that the results of science come with no directions for use. Science is ethically neutral, but scientists are not.

Helpful Hint!

A *clone* is an organism genetically identical to the donor of the cell from which it was produced.

Should we try to restrict what scientists do or how certain ideas from science are applied? Informed societies debate scientific issues and sometimes decide to hold back. An example is the use of nuclear power. We must also keep in mind that, in the past, those societies that have placed the strongest limits on what people could or could not do have been the cruelest societies. Is there any hope for an enlightened future in a censored society?

? QUESTIONS & TASKS

Think about This!

Should scientists "do things" just because they can be done? Because we can clone sheep (Figure 1.18), for example, should we try to clone humans?

1. Genetic manipulation has the potential to do an enormous amount of good. Give an example.

2. Genetic manipulation has the potential to do a lot of harm. Give an example.

3. Should we regulate genetic engineering? Why or why not? If so, how?

4. If science cannot provide answers to how we should use genetic engineering, where can we find such answers?

1.11 Evaluating "Scientific" Information

In its purest form, science is an unbiased search for truth about the natural world. But because scientific issues are also tied to political and monetary gain, the true nature of

►Figure 1.18 In 1997, scientists in Scotland cloned a sheep, Dolly. *(Johnston/SIPA)*

scientific debate is often lost. The methods of politics and advertising are not an accepted part of science. In the real world, however, scientific information is often misused and presented with distorted logic and selective use of data. This helps promote the agenda of the user. It also makes it difficult for the average person to find out the "truth."

With this in mind, read the following guidelines carefully and think about our use and misuse of scientific information.

Beware of lists of experts (sometimes even Nobel Prize winners) on various sides of issues. Scientific debates are not settled by popular vote or by pointcounterpoint arguments. The appearance or "smoothness" of the scientist makes little difference. Scientific issues are settled by debates over experimental design, accuracy of data, and the reliability of predictions. This process is usually slow. As such, it does not fit well into the drama of the evening news.

Look for the source of the information (Figure 1.19). The source is as important as the information itself. In this textbook, the source is listed with the data. Sources are also listed as part of the caption for figures. Many of the books you use do not list their sources of information up front. Credits are listed in very small print near the back of the book—if they are listed at all. As a textbook user, you should always demand to know the source of information.

Beware of fancy titles of organizations and agencies. Try to find out who the source is and what that source represents. Special interest groups often give themselves attractive titles to help promote their agenda.

Simple experiments and simulations can help you understand some scientific concepts, but they cannot be extended too far. Placing a shoe box containing dark soil and a plastic cover in the sun and taking data may help you understand the greenhouse effect, but it doesn't help you settle the greenhouse debate. The debate is over the accuracy of a computer model that is best understood by climatologists. The best an average person can do is to analyze the issues as reported in scientific journals—not as presented in political debates.

Extrapolation of scientific data can sometimes lead to discovery. However, extrapolation of uncertain data far into the future can also lead to wrong conclusions. Beware of extrapolated information.

Science does not speak with absolute authority. Much of modern living, however, is tied to what science can offer. Safe travel and food, disease prevention, and computers all have their origin in the scientific process.

Use these guidelines to help you separate the "wheat from the chaff" as you analyze what is said on the news, in advertising, and in political debates.

Environmental Science: Its History and Those Who Built It

In this activity, you will construct a time line for the history of environmental science by highlighting a number of individuals who made significant contributions to the discipline.

Background

For most of our history, humans have had a local and fairly limited impact on the environment. In the last 10,000 years, agricultural practices have increased that level of impact. In the most recent two centuries, human impact on the environment has grown to global proportions. The most significant response to this global impact has been the development of scientific studies. These studies are designed to determine the causes of changes to the air, water, and soil at the local level, and to changes in the atmosphere, oceans, and landmasses on a global scale.

Generally referred to as environmental science, these studies are mostly quite recent. However, they arise out of the older studies of natural history and natural philosophy. These studies became specialized as botany, zoology, geology, chemistry, and physics in the 19th century. Environmental science is unique not so much for being recent as for the fact that it includes all of the scientific specialties. As sciences continued to grow more specialized in the 20th century, a few new disciplines developed at the fringes of the main areas of study. These new sciences include ecology, meteorology, and biochemistry. Environmental science includes elements of the older specialties and the more recent hybrids, along with even broader viewpoints. Researchers from fields usually regarded to be outside the natural sciences —anthropology and economics—also joined the ranks of environmental scientists.

Procedure

1. Construct a time line for the history of environmental science based on the accomplishments of the 11 contributors whose names are listed. This list includes naturalists, scientists, and environmentalists who have contributed to environmental science. Use library reference materials (for example, *American Men and Women of Science*; encyclopedias such as *Environmental Encyclopedia* [Detroit: Gale Research, 1994]; and *The Environmentalists: A Biographical Dictionary from the 17th Century to the Present,* Facts on File, 1993); web-based information; and history textbooks.

Rachel Carson	James Lovelock	Eugene and Howard Odum
Paul and Anne Ehrlich	Amory Lovins	
	George Perkins Marsh	Theodore Roosevelt
Lois Gibbs		
Aldo Leopold	John Muir	Edward O. Wilson

2. Place the names of the individuals near the date or time span of their major contribution. In a few words, state their contribution.

3. After constructing your time line, divide the time line into 2 or more meaningful periods of time.

QUESTIONS & TASKS

1. In the history of environmental science, what specialized fields of scientific study have been most important?

2. What concerns contributed to the development of sciences related to the environment?

3. What were (and are) some of the most recent developments in environmental science?

[Developed in cooperation with the author by Chris Young, Alverno College.]

Summary

As humans, we seek to find purpose, meaning, and explanation. Science is one of the methods humans use in this quest. Science is based on the idea that there is some order or regularity in the natural world. We can discover some of that order or regularity by doing experiments. There is a general pattern for doing experiments; the process is best learned by doing science over a period of time. It is important to note, however, that science begins with observations and related questions. If you know the answer before doing an experiment, you are not doing science. You are simply confirming your biases. Science is the search for information using well-established procedures, behaviors, and methods. Scientists measure everything that can be measured. They use agreed-upon measuring devices and a common set of units called the metric system. This allows them to compare measurements with one another. They hypothesize about the patterns they discover in their measurement data. Each hypothesis is then tested and either confirmed, revised, or thrown out.

Certain attitudes and behaviors are common to the way scientists approach their work. Good scientists are skeptical of new scientific claims, but they are open to new ideas. They know all scientific information is uncertain to some degree. They work hard to gather and interpret data in an honest, unbiased matter. Finally, they trust that the information they provide is of value.

REFERENCES

1. Adler, Mortimer J. *The Conditions of Philosophy: Its Checkered Past, Its Present Disorder, and Its Future Promise* (New York: Dell Publishing Co.), 1965.

2. Barbour, Ian G. *Issues in Science and Religion* (Englewood Cliffs, NJ: Prentice-Hall), 1966.

3. Feynman, Richard P. The Value of Science. In *Frontiers in Science* (New York: Basic Books), 1958.

4. Christensen John W. and Teri L. Christensen. *Global Science,* 7th Ed., Teacher Edition. "Questions Science Cannot Answer." [Chapter 1 extension] (Dubuque, IA: Kendall/Hunt Publishing Co.), 2009.

5. Christensen, John W. and Teri L. Christensen. *Global Science,* 7th Ed., Teacher Edition. "Understanding the Nature of Science: The Relationships among Facts, Hypotheses, Laws, and Theories." [Chapter 1 extension] [Dubuque, IA: Kendall/Hunt Publishing Co.), 2009.

6. Meine, Curt. *Aldo Leopold: His Life and Work* (Madison, WI: University of Wisconsin Press), 1988.

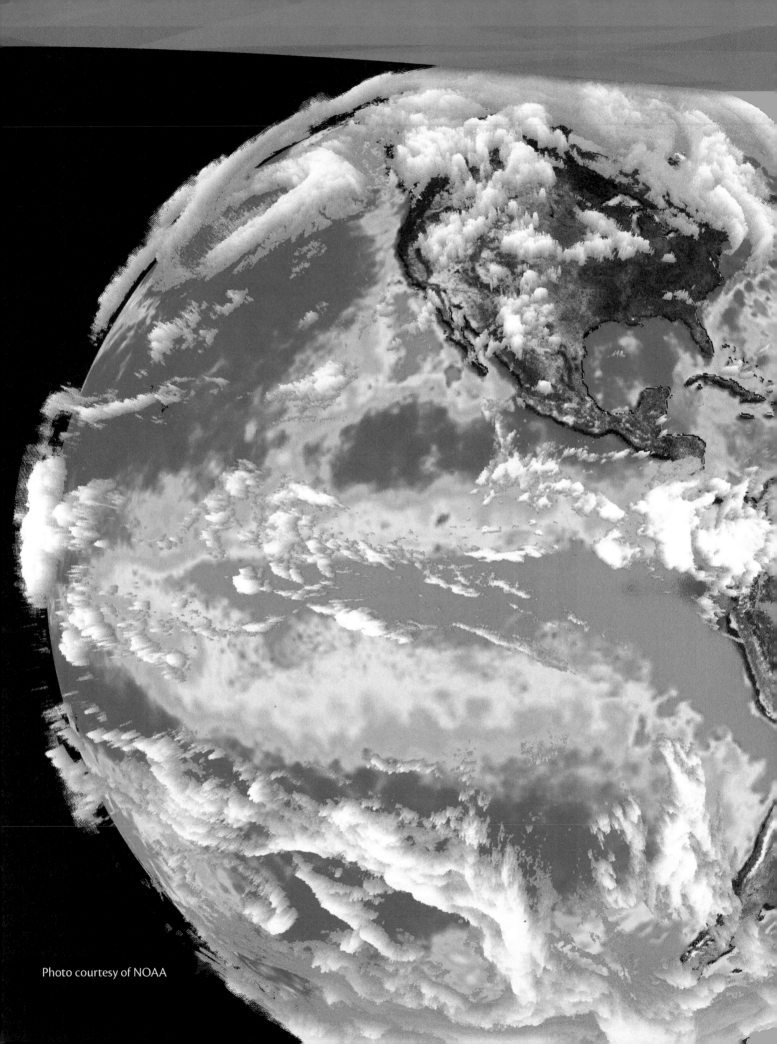

Photo courtesy of NOAA

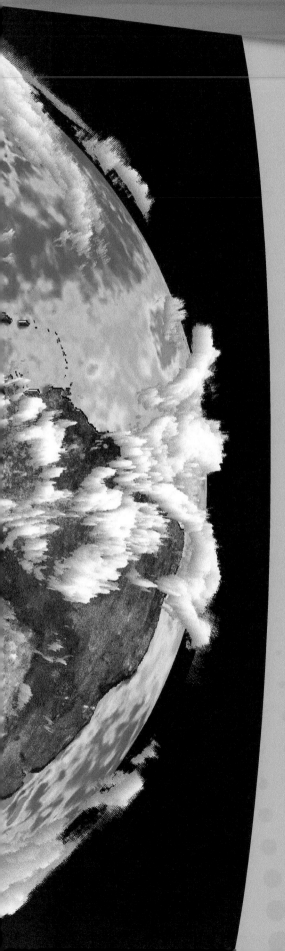

CHAPTER 2

A Grand Oasis in Space

(The Ecosystem Concept)

GOAL

- To understand Earth as a system of which humans are a part.

The vast loneliness up here is awe-inspiring, and it makes you realize just what you have back there on Earth. The Earth from up here is a grand oasis in the big vastness of space.

—James A. Lovell, Jr., astronaut; aboard the *Apollo* 8 spacecraft, 1968

Our Unique Planet

Why is Earth called a global spaceship?

We live on what has been called a global spaceship. Because it travels through space alone, Earth is like a spaceship, with no outside resources except sunlight. With the exception of a few astronauts, all humans are bound to Earth for life. Even those astronauts who leave Earth do so only temporarily and under very special conditions. They must return to the unique and delicate life-support system of Spaceship Earth before their supplies are gone.

Most of us take Earth's life-support system for granted. We think about it rarely and observe it only casually. Since most of us will spend every moment of our lives on Earth, it makes sense to examine and understand how our "spaceship" operates. Equally important, we need to see how our daily actions interact with this life-support system.

Global science is the study of how individuals and societies use Earth's resources and affect the environment to satisfy human needs and wants. Through your study, you should gain a greater appreciation of the human struggle and a better understanding of how our planetary home sustains us.

ACTIVITY 2.1

This Place Called Earth

In this activity, you will learn more about Earth by discussing your ideas and completing a series of lab activities. You will examine some of the properties that make water a distinctive and amazing substance.

Procedure

Part A: What characteristics distinguish Earth from other planets?

1. Work with a partner to complete this think-pair-share activity. First, think about these 3 questions:

   a. What are 3 characteristics that make Earth different from other planets?

   b. What are 3 characteristics that make Earth similar to other planets?

   c. Of these 6 characteristics, which do you think are essential for life as we know it?

2. When both you and your partner have finished thinking about your answers to these questions, share your ideas with each other.

3. After you finish your discussion, record your thinking in your science notebook so you can refer to your ideas later.

Part B: How do Earth's features make it such a unique planet?

1. Visit each of 6 lab stations according to your teacher's instructions. The directions and questions for each station are listed below. Answer the questions for each station in your science notebook.

2. After you have visited all 6 stations, write your responses to the following questions in your science notebook:

   a. What features of Earth do you now consider essential for the existence of life?

   b. How does your response to question 2a compare to your earlier ideas from Part A of this activity?

   c. If you were looking for evidence that life could or did exist on other planets, what types of evidence would be of most interest to you?

   d. Explain why Earth is the only planet in our solar system that currently supports life as we know it.

Task

Determine the part of Earth where life can exist.

Background

Earthquake waves imply that Earth is made of three main layers: the **core**, the **mantle**, and the very thin **crust** (see Figure 2.1). The core forms only 15 percent of Earth's volume. The mantle is the largest layer, occuping 84 percent of Earth's volume. The crust makes up the remaining 1 percent.

Each layer has different features. The core is actually made of two layers. The inner layer, which is called the solid core, is thought to be made of a combination of solid iron and nickel. The same source of information (earthquake waves) implies that the outer core is a liquid made of iron and nickel.

> **Content Clue**
>
> Earthquake waves give clues about Earth's interior.

Earthquake waves indicate that the mantle is also made of two layers. The lower mantle is solid and made of silicate materials. The upper mantle is hot enough to melt rocks. This is the zone of rock that is pushed around when volcanoes erupt or mountains form. (In Chapter 4, you will study the tectonic plates that ride on this layer of Earth.)

The crust is directly accessible to us. Scientists have been able to collect more data on this layer than on any of the other layers. Some of the ways scientists collect data about Earth include analyzing earthquake waves; conducting experiments on rocks with high pressure; analyzing Earth's motion in the solar system; and studying Earth's heat flow, gravity, and magnetic fields.

The crust is less dense than the other layers. It also varies in thickness, ranging from 0 to 44 miles (mi) or 0 to 70 kilometers (km). It is thickest under the continents and thinnest under the oceans. All known life on Earth interacts with this thin zone of solid material that is sometimes called the **lithosphere**. Life

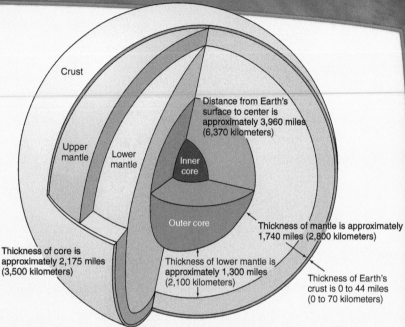

▲ **FIGURE 2.1** Current depiction of Earth's layers.
(Based on art by the U.S. Geological Survey.)

is possible in this zone because of two other features of the outer layer of Earth. Earth is surrounded by a layer of gases or air called the **atmosphere**. In addition, much of Earth has water on top of the solid materials. This layer is called the **hydrosphere**.

The area that includes the air, water, and rock is known as the **ecosphere** or **biosphere**. It is this zone that is our focus in this course because of the importance of air, water, and solid materials to all life. Figure 2.2 illustrates how air, water, and rock intermingle to support living systems.

Materials

- cutaway model of Earth (optional)

Procedure

1. Share with your partner 3 things you noticed in Figures 2.1 and 2.2. Tell your partner 2 things you understood from reading the background information.

2. After you and your partner have shared your observations and understandings, answer the questions for this station and record your thinking in your science notebook.

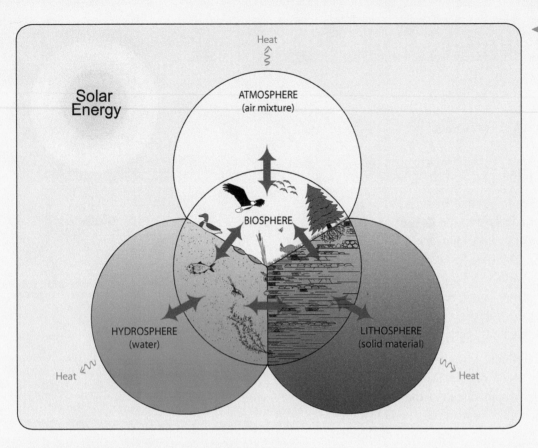

QUESTIONS & TASKS

1. How does the top layer of Earth differ from the other layers?

2. Why are air, water, and solid materials essential to life?

3. What role do air, water, and solid materials play in your body?

Topic: biosphere
Go to: www.scilinks.org
Code: GloSci7e32

STATION 2: HOW MUCH WATER IS THERE?

Task

Determine the percentage of Earth that is covered with water.

Background

From space, Earth is seen as the "blue planet." The color blue is caused by the vast amount of water. Oceans cover much of the globe (see Figure 2.3). Water is also found in lakes, rivers, streams, in soils, and in underground reservoirs. About half the water is found in the atmosphere as water vapor, and some water remains frozen as ice caps and glaciers. Water is the most abundant compound in all living organisms. Without water, there would be no life.

Materials

- scissors
- graph paper
- colored pencils (at least 2 colors)
- transparent tape
- globe (optional)
- Handout: *World Map*

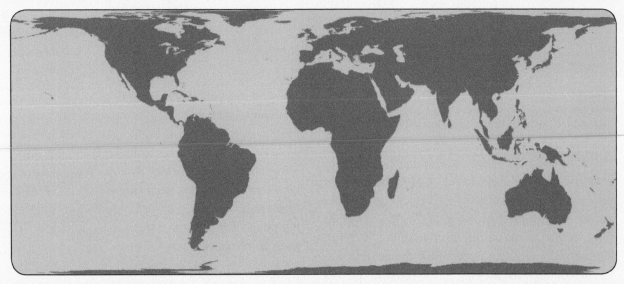

▲ **FIGURE 2.3** This map shows Earth's land areas and large areas of water. The map is an equal area projection, which means it correctly represents the true size of the areas shown on the map. *(Peter H. Dana, Department of Geography, University of Texas at Austin)*

Procedure

1. Looking at Figure 2.3 or at a globe, estimate the percentage of Earth that is covered by water. Record your estimate in your science notebook.

   > **Think about This!**
   >
   > Why do some call Earth the "blue marble"?

2. Using Figure 2.3 or a globe as a reference, color the land on your map in one color and the water with a second color.

3. Cut out the land pieces. Fit them close together, and tape them on the graph paper.

4. Count the number of squares of graph paper that the land covers. Record this number.

5. Cut out the water pieces. Fit them close together, and tape them on the graph paper.

6. Count the number of squares of graph paper that the water covers. Record this number.

7. Add the number of land squares and the number of water squares together. This number is your total number of covered graph squares. Record this number.

8. To find the percentage of Earth that is covered by water, you will need to divide the number of water squares by the total number of covered graph squares. (This means you will be dividing a bigger number into a smaller number.) Record this number.

9. The number you obtained in step 8 can be converted to a percentage by multiplying that number by 100 or by moving the decimal point 2 places to the right.

10. Check your work by calculating the percentage of land on Earth in the same manner you used to determine the percentage of water. When you add the percentage of water to the percentage of land, it should total 100%. If your answer does not equal 100, you have made a mistake somewhere. Repeat the process, or talk to another team to determine where you made your mistake.

QUESTIONS & TASKS

1. How close was your estimation of the percentage of Earth that is covered by water to your calculation?

2. Did your calculation surprise you? Why or why not?

3. How do you think the percentage of Earth that is covered by water compares to the amount of water on other planets?

4. What does the percentage of water on Earth mean for your life?

A Grand Oasis in Space   33

Task

Identify several unique characteristics of water.

Background

Picture a pond on a winter day. Air temperatures are slightly above freezing. Snow is on the ground. As snow, water is frozen *solid* in the form of ice crystals. Ice also forms a solid layer on top of the pond. *Liquid* water is in the pond below the ice and percolates through the melting snow. Water also exists as a *gas* in the form of water vapor, both within the snow and in the air above the snow. Thus, at normal climatic temperatures, water exists in three different physical states: a solid, a liquid, and a gas. All three forms of water can be present at the same time (Figure 2.4).

The form or physical state of water depends on the speed of motion of its molecules. Molecular speed is tied to temperature. In the solid state, water molecules are relatively quiet with little energy.

These ice crystals have geometric, six-sided shapes, like snowflakes. When molecules are activated by heat, water becomes a liquid. The molecules are close together, yet slip around freely, giving liquid water its flowing motion. At high temperatures, molecules move about violently, spreading out to form water vapor, an invisible gas (Figure 2.5).

> **Helpful Hint!**
>
> The physical state is determined by molecular motion.

Water requires heat to change its physical state. Heat is necessary to melt ice. Even more heat is needed to change water from a liquid to water vapor. To help you understand, think about what happens in a ice chest. A block of ice in a closed chest cools food because heat from the food is absorbed by the ice. The absorbed heat energy breaks bonds holding the ice crystals together. As a result, the ice melts.

This same principle works in climate control. When hot, dry air passes over water, the water absorbs heat from the air. This cools the air and warms the water.

◀ FIGURE 2.4 The three phases of water can be present at the same time. Locate each phase in this picture of icebergs in the Arctic. *(Konrad Steffen)*

► FIGURE 2.5 The rate of motion of water molecules increases as temperatures increase. This motion breaks the bonds between the molecules, and the water changes from a solid to a liquid to a gas. (*Adapted from Marine Biology by H.V. Thurman and H.H. Webber; copyright © 1984 by Bell and Howell Company. Reprinted by permission of Addison-Wesley Educational Publishers.*)

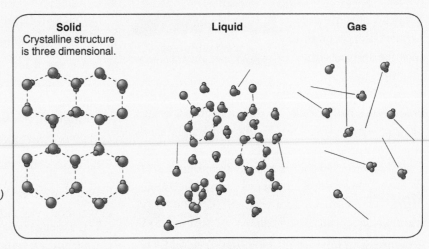

Solid
Crystalline structure is three dimensional.

Liquid

Gas

When water is warmed enough to evaporate, it is converted to vapor. A great deal of heat energy is required to break bonds between water molecules before gaseous vapor can move rapidly and expand.

Materials

- liquid water in a large beaker or bowl
- ice cubes
- small paper or plastic cups (2–3 ounces)
- access to a freezer

Procedure

1. Make a prediction for each of the following questions:
   a. Does a given amount of liquid water take up more, less, or the same amount of space when it is frozen?
   b. If you mix cold liquid water and frozen water, which one floats on top of the other?

2. Using the materials available, develop short experiments to answer each of the questions in step 1.

3. Show your written plans to your teacher for approval.

4. Conduct each experiment and record your results in your science notebook. (You may need to move to another station while you are waiting for some results.)

QUESTIONS & TASKS

1. How accurate were your predictions?

2. If your predictions were different from your results, explain what led to your predictions. If your predictions were the same as your results, explain what experience or knowledge you had that helped you make the prediction.

3. What do the results of your experiments tell you about the characteristics of water?

4. Why are these characteristics important to life on Earth?

STATION 4: WHAT IS THE HEAT CAPACITY OF WATER?

Task

Determine how well water holds heat in comparison to other materials.

Background

Heat capacity refers to the ability of a substance to absorb and

Think about This!

What is heat?

retain heat without becoming very hot itself. Water has a high heat capacity. This can be demonstrated by comparing an empty pan to one filled with water. If an empty pan is heated on a stove, it quickly becomes red hot. If that same pan is filled with water before it is heated, the pan becomes hot but not red hot, and the temperature of the water does not rise past 100° Celsius (C).

Water absorbs five times as much heat per gram as rock for a given change in temperature. Because of water's high heat capacity, oceans act as huge reservoirs of solar warmth. Oceans moderate climates of nearby landmasses, first by absorbing and then by slowly giving off heat. Lands farther away from large bodies of water have more extreme temperatures.

Think about This!

How does water's heat capacity influence climate?

Materials

WARNING

Isopropyl alcohol is flammable; its vapors may explode. Keep away from heat and sparks. Extinguish any flames in the area. Locate the fire blanket and fire extinguisher. Be sure you are wearing your safety goggles.

- 3 paper or plastic cups with lids
- 3 thermometers
- sand
- isopropyl alcohol
- water
- access to refrigerator, freezer, and/or incubator
- safety goggles

Procedure

1. To test the idea that water has a relatively high heat capacity, set up an experiment. Look at the materials that are available. How can you compare water's ability to hold heat with that of other substances?

2. Discuss your ideas from step 1. Then record 2 ideas for experiments in your science notebook that will help you show the difference in heat capacity among 3 or more substances.

3. Choose 1 idea and design the steps for your experiment. Be sure to identify how you will **control** your experiment.

4. Show your written plan to your teacher for approval.

5. Conduct your experiment *only after* your plan is approved. Be sure to record your results.

Helpful Hint!

A *control* is a part of an experiment that you keep the same so you can compare your results fairly. For example, say you are growing radish seeds and bean seeds to see which grow the fastest. You would need to keep the kind of soil, amount of soil, amount of light, amount of water, type of container, and other parts of the experiment exactly the same.

QUESTIONS & TASKS

1. Based on the results of your experiment, explain what you know about the heat capacity of water.

2. Use what you know about the heat capacity of water to explain the difference in climate in this example. Florida and the Sahara Desert are at the same latitude and receive a comparable amount of sunlight. Florida is surrounded by water and has a moist, balmy climate. The Sahara Desert is blistering hot during the day and cold at night.

STATION 5: WHAT IS SPECIAL ABOUT SURFACE TENSION?

Task

Place as many drops of water on a penny as possible.

Background

If you watch a drop of water fall from a spout, you notice it clings to the tap, stretches very thinly, then finally lets go. Immediately, it forms a sphere-shaped drop (Figure 2.6). Likewise, raindrops form droplets of water rather than a small stream of water. This ability of water molecules to stick together is called **surface tension**.

▶FIGURE 2.6 Sphere-shaped drops of water cling to a blade of grass. (*Dick Thomas/Visuals Unlimited*)

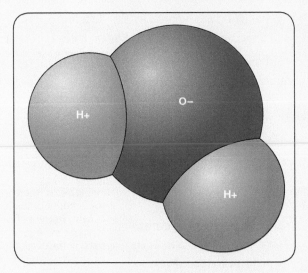

▲ FIGURE 2.7 A model of a water (H_2O) molecule.

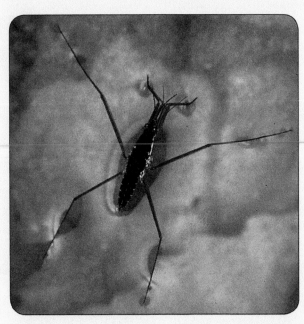

▲ FIGURE 2.8 A water strider can stay on top of the water because of its minimal mass and the surface tension of water. (*P. Starborn/Visuals Unlimited*)

Surface tension is caused by the attraction between positive and negative sides of water molecules (see Figure 2.7). The attraction also causes water to adhere to other surfaces, wetting them. The wetting ability of water is important in the movement of water upward through small cracks in soil and through small tubes in plant roots and stems.

Because it has a high surface tension, water forms a "skin" upon which materials that are actually more dense than water can float. Surface tension makes it possible for some insects to run around on the surface of water (Figure 2.8).

Materials

- eye dropper
- penny
- container of water

Procedure

1. Using the eye dropper, place as many drops of water on a penny as you can.

2. In your science notebook, record the maximum number of drops you were able to place on the penny before water ran over the side.

3. Compare your maximum number to the maximum number obtained by other groups in class. An easy way to do that is to design a class record sheet.

Think about This!

Why do paper towels soak up water?

QUESTIONS & TASKS

1. How does this activity demonstrate the concept of surface tension?

2. How does surface tension aid some natural processes?

STATION 6: WHERE IS EARTH IN THE "BIG PICTURE"?

Task

Make a scale diagram of the solar system. Use 1 AU = the mean distance between Earth and the sun.

Background

Theories that attempt to explain the origin of our own solar system (Figure 2.9) are uncertain. The currently

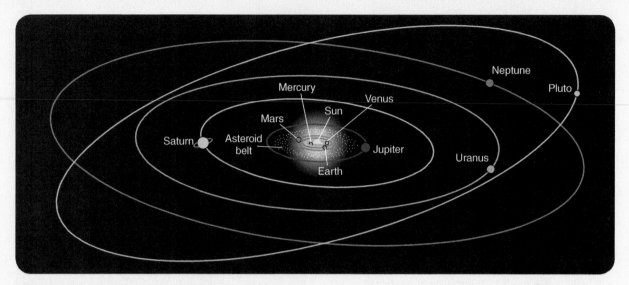

▲ FIGURE 2.9 The solar system.

accepted explanation is that our solar system originated as a cloud of slowly rotating gas and dust particles. Under the influence of its own gravity, the cloud began to collapse and spin faster. As the collapse proceeded, the cloud flattened into a disk of whirling particles. Most of the material slowly condensed into the disk's center and became our sun. The contraction heated the sun enough for atomic fusion to begin. The energy source for almost all life processes began to operate.

In regions far from the center of the disk, smaller condensations of particles became our solar system's planets. Gravity pulled these particles of matter together during the planet-forming process. The planets formed in different ways, partly because of their distances from the sun.

The distance from the sun to the planets is measured in astronomical units (AU). The chart in Figure 2.10 lists the AUs for each planet in our solar system.

Think about This!

Why is an astronomical unit a useful form of measurement?

 To learn more about the planets and the solar system, you may want to do an Internet search or visit the library.

Materials

- poster board
- markers or colored pencils
- metric ruler
- drawing compass

Planet	Average Distance from the Sun (AU)
Mercury	0.39
Venus	0.72
Earth	1.0
Mars	1.5
Jupiter	5.2
Saturn	9.5
Uranus	19.2
Neptune	30.0
Pluto	39.3

▲ FIGURE 2.10 This chart lists the average distance of each planet from the sun. Average distance is helpful because there are times when each planet is much closer and much farther away from the sun. (Remember, Pluto is now classified as a dwarf planet.)

Procedure

1. Use the background information to make a model of the solar system. How can you use the AUs to help you make your drawing of the solar system to scale?

   Helpful Hint!

   In this activity, you assume the orbits of the planets are circles. They are actually elliptical.

2. Compare your model (drawing) to Figure 2.9. As you may know, Pluto is no longer a planet. In 2006, the International Astronomical Union reclassified Pluto as a dwarf planet.

1. Where is Earth in comparison to the sun?

2. Where is Earth in comparison to other planets?

3. How completely have you answered the question, "Where is Earth?"

4. Using what you know about other planets, explain why Earth's placement is unique for supporting life.

5. How does reclassifying Pluto as a dwarf planet indicate the tentative nature of science?

SPECIAL FOCUS

Scientific Explanations Change over Time

One of the characteristics of science is that ideas are always changing. Scientists gather information about the world and the universe. They use this information to develop explanations about Earth and the rest of the universe. Not all scientists collect information about the same part of the universe. Some scientists focus on understanding plants. These scientists are called *botanists*. Some scientists try to understand more about water. These scientists are called *hydrologists*.

Scientists who study the composition and structure of Earth are *geologists*. It is very difficult to study the inside of Earth because of its thickness and density. The distance from where you are sitting right now to the center of Earth is about 3,960 mi (6,370 km). That's like driving east from Seattle, Washington, to Halifax, Nova Scotia. To get to the center of Earth, however, you would have to go straight down.

People have probably always been curious about the inside of Earth. Scientists' explanations about the inside of Earth change as new tools and ways of collecting information are developed. Some of the first information about the center of Earth was based on the water, gases, and chemicals found inside paint pots, volcanoes, and geysers (see Figure 2.11).

◀FIGURE 2.11 Material from inside Old Faithful, a geyser at Yellowstone National Park, provides evidence about the inside of Earth. *(Photo by National Park Service, courtesy of www.parkphotos.com.)*

► FIGURE 2.12 Layers of rock in the Grand Canyon tell part of the story about what is inside Earth. *(Photo by National Park Service, courtesy of www.parkphotos.com.)*

Scientists also gathered evidence about Earth by looking at eroded canyons and mountainsides. The layers of rock show the order in which different minerals and other materials formed as part of Earth's crust (see Figure 2.12).

Centuries ago, two men hypothesized about the composition of Earth. René Descartes and Sir Isaac Newton proposed very different models of the inside of Earth.

René Descartes (1596–1650) was a philosopher, mathematician, and scientist who lived in France. He believed in a Divine Creation that was based on physical and mathematical principles that humans could discover. His ideas about Earth are illustrated in Figure 2.13 (top). This part of the drawing shows that Descartes thought Earth had a particular layered structure before the mountains and oceans were formed. He coded his drawing so that 'E' stands for Earth's crust. This layer is surrounded by a layer of air. Under the crust is another

layer of air, labeled 'F,' then a layer of water, labeled 'D.' The interior crust ('C') is composed of metals. At numbers 2, 3, 4, 5, and 6, cracks have developed in the dry outer crust.

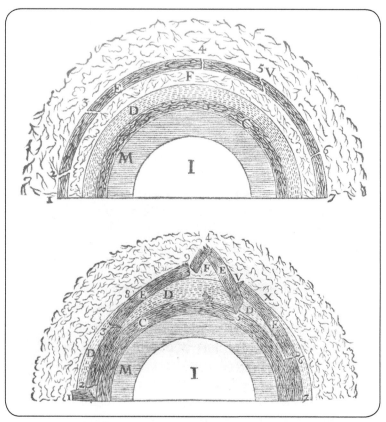

▲ FIGURE 2.13 Descartes drew these pictures to illustrate his ideas about the inside of Earth. *(From Renati Descartes Philosophia. Department of Special Collections, Charles E. Young Research Library, UCLA.)*

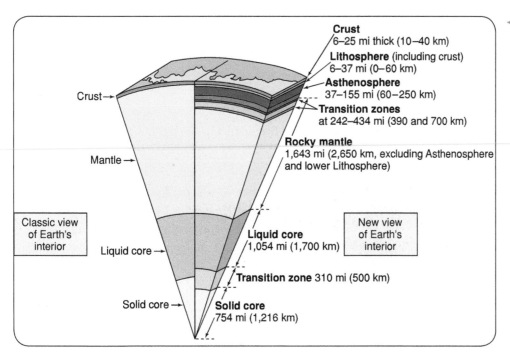

◄ FIGURE 2.14 Changing models of Earth's layers. You will revisit this model of Earth when you study mineral resources in Chapter 4. (*Adapted from* Continents in Motion *by Walter Sullivan, New York: McGraw-Hill, 1974. Reprinted by permission.*)

Descartes could not access the interior regions (labeled 'I' and 'M') and did not discuss them in his writings.

Descartes hypothesized that when the cracks weakened the upper crust, mountains were created. This change in the crust allowed water to escape from underneath the crust and form the oceans. This idea is illustrated in Figure 2.13 (bottom).

Sir Isaac Newton (1642–1727) was a scientist and mathematician who lived in England. He made careful observations of Earth. From these observations, he calculated that the density of Earth was twice that of rocks on the surface. This meant that the inside of Earth must be made of much denser material than the surface was.

Two hundred years later, scientists had more direct evidence with which to check Newton's calculations. In 1906, R.D. Oldham studied earthquake records. He saw how the waves changed as they traveled through the layers of Earth. This study confirmed Newton's calculations. It led scientists to propose a three-layer model for Earth. This classical model is illustrated on the left side of Figure 2.14. Additional evidence gathered during the next 50 years helped scientists refine this model of Earth. The currently accepted model is illustrated on the right side of Figure 2.14.

Focus Questions

You can see the progression of scientific ideas about Earth by looking at Figures 2.13 and 2.14. As you study the illustrations, think about these questions:

1. What are the major changes between each illustration?

2. What information or tool was available that resulted in the changes you identified?

3. How are these illustrations different from the one you used in Station 1 in Activity 2.1?

4. What scientific evidence gathered by Newton and later scientists caused them to modify Descartes' model?

Focus Extension

The August 2002 issue of *Discover* describes a new hypothesis about the structure of Earth's interior. Are you open to this new idea?

ACTIVITY 2.2

A Voyage to Mars

In this activity, you will think about and begin making plans to colonize Mars. Colonizing a planet is different from traveling to a planet. Think about the early colonists who came to North America before it became the United States. The colonists did not come to North America just to visit. They came to escape such things as unfair taxes and religious oppression. They also came hoping to live in a manner that they considered better than their previous lifestyle.

Materials

- Handout: *Confidential, Classified Government Document* (optional)

- Handout: *Earth–Mars Data*

Procedure

1. Read the classified government document in Figure 2.15 or from the handout your teacher supplies.

TOP SECRET FOR TRAINING ONLY
SOURCE: **INTSCOM**, INCLUSIONS: **NOFOR**

Confidential Classified Government Document
Under no conditions are you to divulge any of the information reported in this document. Failure to comply will be dealt with in the severest possible manner.

On October 25 last year, astronomers at Kitt Peak Observatory in Arizonaun expectedly sighted a huge comet that had never been seen before. Confirmation of their sighting made at several other observatories in the United States. During a period of more than two months, the comet's position was observed and carefully plotted. Initial calculations indicated that the comet would pass very close to Earth. In fact, within estimated margin of experimental error, a collision with Earth was deemed possible. Because of this possibility and because of the apparent size of the comet, U.S. government officials and astronomers decided not to announce the discovery until a later date.

The gravity of the situation prompted the U.S. government to fund a first-rate study of the comet. The goal was to gather all possible information on the comet and its predicted path. The nation's top astronomers gathered at Kitt Peak National Observatory near Tucson, Arizona, to conduct this study. Their initial work was completed a month ago. Their report states:

"We have firmly established that comet a-X is on a collision course with Earth. We have also firmly established that the mass and velocity of the comet are great enough to cause the collision to be fatal. The collision will change Earth's axis of rotation by more than two degrees. This change will result in massive tidal waves, extremely high velocity winds, and abrupt and severe weather changes. Collision will occur 327 days from today's date."

The decision has been made not to inform the peoples of the world of these facts until a well thought-out program has been established. Psychologists, psychiatrists, members of the clergy, scientists, sociologists, and government officials will draw up this plan. In the meantime, the U.S. government will undertake a project to colonize Mars with ten people.

Mars was selected because it is the closest object now known that can, with some ingenuity, support life as we know it. Because of the many factors involved in such a project, a team of people with a combination of a science background and other diverse strengths will work on the project.

This is an extremely important project; thus, you have a very large budget to work with. Your main limitations are the technologies available to you at this time. Present technology will limit you to sending five rockets; each will carry two passengers and a payload of 100,000 pounds. Five additional unoccupied rockets carrying 100,000 pound payloads each may also be sent.

It has tentatively been determined that the first launchings will begin in approximately eight months. All ten rockets are to be launched during a period of time not to exceed one month. Public announcement of Earth's situation and the exact nature of this project will be made no less than two weeks after the last rocket is launched and no more than two months before the collision occurs. False information will be given, as necessary, until the appropriate time arrives.

▲ FIGURE 2.15 Confidential, classified government document.

Place in the solar system:	Fourth from the sun
Distance from the sun:	227,940,000 km or 1.52 AU (astronomical units)
Diameter:	6,794 km
Mass:	6.4219×102^3 kg
Polar caps:	made of frozen carbon dioxide with frozen water underneath
Moons:	two, Phobos and Deimos (Greek for "fear" and "panic")
Name:	Mars is the Roman god of war; the month of March is named after Mars.

[Sources: http://www.astro.indiana.edu/,strom/a100_s96/Class/6_04/no_mo_h2o_7.html and http://web.eecs.nwu.edu/,pred/TNP/nineplanets/mars.html on 23 August 1998]

2. Based on your experience in Activity 2.1 and your background knowledge, respond to this question: What are the 10 most important items you will need to bring from Earth to Mars? Record your thinking in your science notebook.

Helpful Hint!

The information on the *Earth–Mars Data* sheet and in Figure 2.16 may be helpful in answering this question.

3. Share your responses with your assigned group. Develop a list of 10 items that you can all agree on. (This may take some patience and negotiation.) Record this list in your science notebook.

4. Because of size and weight limitations, you need to narrow your list to 5 items. Do this as a group. Record this list in your notebook.

 To learn more about Mars, visit the FAS website (Federation of American Scientists). FAS maintains a website with hot links to many other sites about Mars, including current NASA plans about a mission to Mars. You can visit this site at http://www.fas.org/mars/.

5. As a class, decide on and make a list of the 5 or 6 most important items and the reasons those items must be brought to Mars.

6. Your teacher will provide an "expert list" of essential items and the reasons those items are essential. Compare your class list to this expert list.

Think about This!

Even if you bring all the essential items in the correct amounts, you will not survive if you cannot get along. That is why the skills and knowledge of those who go are so important.

7. Select 10 people who will go on the trip. You can select the people by occupation, nationality, skills, or training, or by any other method that makes sense to your group.

Think about This!

The items you bring to Mars are those items that are essential to life as we know it. Make sure you understand why each item is important.

8. Create a chart that describes each person and gives 2 reasons why that person belongs on the trip. Submit your recommendations in the form of a group report.

The Needs of Living Things

2.1 The Basic Needs of Living Organisms

As you probably discussed in the activity A Voyage to Mars, certain conditions are necessary for life to continue. The basic needs for most living things include these six items: water, air, shelter, food, minerals, and decomposers. This list is based on the perspective of humans.

Water

Water is needed to transport nutrients to cells and to carry waste products away. Evaporating water helps to moderate body temperature in humans. Water is also essential for key processes in plants.

Air

A mixture of gases (nitrogen, oxygen, carbon dioxide, and other gases) makes up air. Nitrogen is required for building structural protein, enzymes, and other organic molecules. Nitrogen also dilutes the oxygen in our atmosphere. That is, it slows down combustion, which allows materials to burn at a controllable rate. Nitrogen also prevents certain respiratory problems. Oxygen is required for the breakdown of food. Carbon dioxide is essential for the process of photosynthesis. It also serves as nature's thermostat, keeping Earth's average temperature at a level suitable for life as we know it.

Think about This!

Can you explain what each of these gases has to do with humans?

Shelter

On Earth, gravity holds our atmosphere in place and makes our global home, the biosphere, possible. Most humans live in structures that moderate climate changes and make life more pleasant. Anyone who ventures out of the biosphere must take shelter along. During space walks, astronauts' suits provide conditions necessary for human life.

Food

Humans need a variety of food. Plants and animals provide carbohydrates and fats for energy, proteins for energy and tissue building, vitamins for specific biological functions, and minerals and chemical elements that are indispensable for life.

Minerals (Soil Nutrients)

Helpful Hint!

Minerals (soil nutrients) are often called fertilizers.

Food cannot be grown without minerals. Nitrogen, phosphorus, potassium, iron, zinc, sulfur manganese, and molybdenum are contained in some of the minerals and natural solutions that provide the necessary nutrients for plant life. Through the food chain, plants also provide the minerals and elements essential for a healthy human body.

Decomposers

Apply Your Understanding

Which decomposers have helped you today?

The organisms of decay (mainly bacteria and fungi) recycle sewage and dead plants and animals. This keeps the soil fertile. Without decomposers, Earth would quickly be covered in dead organisms.

? QUESTIONS & TASKS

1. Make a chart with two columns. In the left column, list each item necessary for life. In the right column, explain why each item is important.

2. Why is the information in your chart important to know?

2.2 Ecosystems Are Dynamic Systems

The items you just read about in section 2.1 are related and interact within ecosystems. **Ecosystems** consist of groups of organisms that interact in a variety of ways with one another and with the nonliving environment. The interactions within each ecosystem are unique to that ecosystem. Many of these interactions are driven by each organism's basic need for food.

Ecosystems consist of many communities living together in the same area. The place where an animal lives is its **habitat**. What an organism does, or how it affects and is affected by its habitat, is called its **niche**. The idea of a niche is not easy to understand. It's helpful to think of it as the animal's job. For example, the grassland community is a habitat suitable for antelope. This habitat includes nutritional grasses and open spaces that allow the antelope to escape its predators. If you were to study all the activities of the antelope, you would be studying the niche of the antelope.

The environment determines the *boundaries* of an ecosystem. That is, as the environment (moisture, soil type, temperature, and wind) changes, so does the ecosystem. The boundaries may be the result of change in moisture, such as that found between a marsh and the adjacent dry land, or between grassland and an adjacent forest. The separation of ecosystems is not often as distinct as that between a pond ecosystem and the adjacent forest ecosystem.

Ecosystems are dynamic (changing) systems in which there is a constant movement of energy and materials. Within this flow of energy, however, environmental resources and organisms tend to be in balance. If the primary consumers eat too much grass (or too many producers) and deplete their food reserve, then many of the consumers will die until a balance is reached between the number of consumers and the amount of food available. Figure 2.17 summarizes the major components and processes in an ecosystem. Refer to it often as you read more about ecosystems.

Ecosystems must be powered by an energy source. The sun is the source of the radiant energy that supports the ecosphere. Figure 2.18 summarizes what happens to the solar energy that strikes Earth. Note that 31 percent is directly reflected back into space. Forty-seven percent is converted into heat after being absorbed by such things as the ground, the oceans, and roofs. Twenty-two percent evaporates water, which causes precipitation. About

An ecosystem is an area of nature that includes living organisms and nonliving substances. These organisms and substances interact to produce an exchange of materials between the biotic and abiotic parts.

Helpful Hint!

Biotic means living; **abiotic** means nonliving.

Apply Your Understanding

How does a niche differ from a habitat?

Ecosystems are powered by the sun.

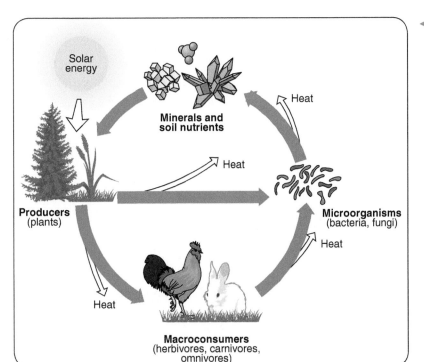

◀ **FIGURE 2.17** A summary of energy flow and matter recycling in ecosystems. The red arrows indicate movement of matter; the white arrows show energy flow.

➤ FIGURE 2.18 Earth's solar budget. *(Adapted from NASA. The figure 0.08 percent for photosynthesis is based on a literature search by John W. Christensen.)*

Think about This!

What happens to the solar energy that strikes Earth?

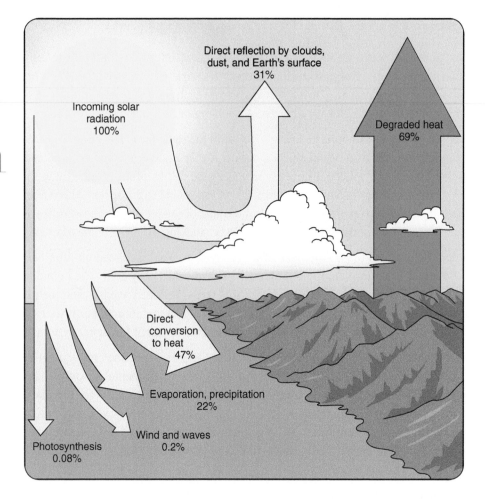

Direct reflection by clouds, dust, and Earth's surface
31%

Incoming solar radiation
100%

Degraded heat
69%

Direct conversion to heat
47%

Evaporation, precipitation
22%

Photosynthesis
0.08%

Wind and waves
0.2%

➤ FIGURE 2.19 The interaction between photosynthesis and respiration. Minerals are in the soil, the plants (food), and the waste products.

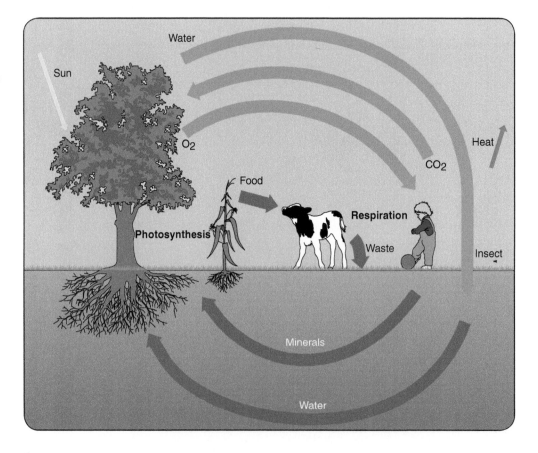

Water

Sun

O_2

Food

Photosynthesis

Respiration

CO_2

Heat

Waste

Insect

Minerals

Water

0.2 percent drives all the winds, waves, and the ocean's convection currents. Less than 0.1 percent is used in the process of photosynthesis.

Topic: photosynthesis
Go to: www.scilinks.org
Code: GloSci7e47a
Topic: respiration
Go to: www.scilinks.org
Code: GloSci7e47b

Photosynthesis is the process by which plants use light energy to convert carbon dioxide, water, and various minerals into the sugars and starches that make up plant cells. Through photosynthesis, plants produce the food and oxygen that sustain all life, including their own. For that reason, plants are called producers. Photosynthesis is summarized by this general equation:

$$\text{carbon dioxide} + \text{water} + \text{minerals} + \text{energy} \rightarrow$$
$$\text{food (plant cells)} + \text{oxygen}$$

or

$$6CO_2 + 6H_2O + \text{solar energy} \rightarrow C_6H_{12}O_6 \text{ (glucose)} + 6O_2$$

Respiration is the process organisms use to break down food to obtain energy. Respiration provides the energy both plant and animal organisms need to live. It is the reverse of the photosynthesis equation. Respiration may be represented by this general equation:

$$\text{food} + \text{oxygen} \rightarrow \text{carbon dioxide} + \text{water} + \text{minerals} + \text{energy}$$

or

$$C_6H_2O_6 \text{ (glucose)} + 6O_2 \rightarrow 6CO_2 + 6H_2O + \text{energy}$$

As organisms process food, they give off carbon dioxide, water, and a variety of minerals. Figure 2.19 shows how photosynthesis and respiration interact.

Helpful Hint!

Glucose is a form of sugar.

Content Clue

Photosynthesis is a process that stores energy. Respiration is a process that releases energy.

Helpful Hint!

Note: Minerals are not shown in these equations.

? QUESTIONS & TASKS

1. Think about your plan for the activity A Voyage to Mars. How did you take care of the need for oxygen?

2. How did you plan for the release of CO_2 by the people and other living organisms in the space colony?

3. The items you brought to Mars are the components of an ecosystem. What is an ecosystem?

SPECIAL FOCUS

Levels of Organization of Matter

Scientists classify matter according to size and function. The classification scheme is referred to as levels of organization. This system of classification will be useful to us as we develop the concept of ecosystem. Figure 2.20 summarizes the relationships between the various levels. The levels of concern to us are defined as follows:

- **atom:** the smallest particle of an element that can exist as that element. (There are more than 100 fundamental substances called elements. They make up all matter.)

Atoms are made up of still smaller parts called protons, neutrons, and electrons.

- **molecule:** the smallest particle of a substance that can exist as that substance. Molecules are combinations of like or differing atoms.

- **protoplasm:** the substance that makes up living parts of a cell.

- **cell:** a group of atoms and molecules that interact in an organized way to exhibit life.

A Grand Oasis in Space   47

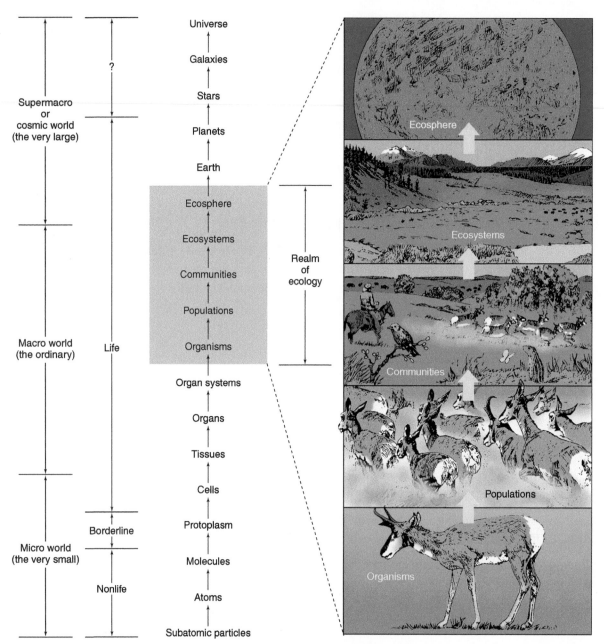

▲ FIGURE 2.20 Levels of organization of matter. (*Adapted From* Living In The Environment 2nd Edition *by G. Tyler Miller, Jr., Wadsworth Publishing Co., Belmont, California 94002.*)

- **tissue:** a group of similar cells that perform a similar function; for example, muscle tissue or blood tissue.

- **organ:** a group of tissues that perform a specific function; for example, the heart, the lungs, or the kidneys.

- **organ system:** a group of organs that perform a similar function; for example, the digestive system.

- **organism:** any living thing.

- **species:** a group of closely related organisms that can interbreed.

- **population:** a group of the same type of organisms living in a certain area.

- **community:** a group of populations living in a given area.

- **ecosystem:** any area of nature that includes living organisms and nonliving substances. These organisms and substances interact by transforming energy to produce an exchange of materials between the living (biotic) and nonliving (abiotic) parts. The boundaries of an ecosystem are not distinct. Major ecosystems are often called biomes.

- **ecosphere** or **biosphere:** the global ecosystem; the sum total of all the various ecosystems on Earth.

- **Earth:** a grand oasis in space.

Topic: ecology
Go to: www.scilinks.org
Code: GloSci7e49

ACTIVITY 2.3

Investigating Ecosystems

To complete the Mars voyage successfully, the team of scientists working on the project must plan for the production of oxygen. From your reading, you know something about the relationship among plants, animals, and oxygen. In this activity, you will design a **controlled experiment** to test your understanding of that relationship.

Background

To complete this activity, you must understand what a controlled experiment is, what an indicator is, and how the BTB indicator works. A controlled experiment is one in which you change only one factor to test the effect of that factor on your setup. Indicators are substances that show the presence of a particular substance by changing color. The color change indicates that a chemical is present. Bromthymol blue (BTB) is an indicator that changes from blue to green or yellow if an acid is present. When carbon dioxide is released into water, it reacts to form a weak acid called carbonic acid.

Materials

- 8–10 test tubes, 20 × 150 mm
- tops to seal the test tubes
- parafilm (optional, but improves the seal)
- marker or tape (to label test tubes)
- 2 test-tube racks
- 4 pieces of elodea (*Anacharis*)
- BTB solution in a dropper bottle
- tap water
- 4 small water snails
- small metric ruler
- pond water
- light source
- dark place (a box will work)
- Handout: *The Indicator*
- Handout: *Experimental Design*

Procedure

1. Watch the demonstration your teacher will do. Record your observations on Handout: *The Indicator*.

2. Consider your understanding of the relationship among plants, animals, photosynthesis, and respiration, and the results of the demonstration. Then make a list of at least 3 questions you think you could test with the equipment available. You do not need to use all of the equipment, but you must use the BTB indicator.

3. Discuss your questions with your teacher; choose 1 question for your experiment.

4. Record in your science notebook the materials you will need and the procedure you will follow for your experiment. Use Figure 2.21 to help you organize your plan.

5. Before you do your experiment, write down in your notebook what you think will happen and why. This is your hypothesis.

6. Review your procedure. Make sure you have a controlled experiment. What is your control? What are you testing? How are you using the BTB?

7. Show your procedure to your teacher for approval. Make any necessary changes.

8. Set up your experiment. You will need to leave it for at least 24 hours to see a reaction with the indicator.

9. Record your results in your science notebook.

1. Was your hypothesis correct? Why or why not?

2. Based on your results, describe what you know now about the relationship among plants, animals, and photosynthesis.

3. Share your results with the class.

4. Summarize your understanding of the role of photosynthesis and respiration within ecosystems in your notebook. Write a paragraph with at least 4 sentences.

Investigating Ecosystems: Experimental Design

Major Components	Lab Materials	Experimental Plan

Major Components

Pond water

Tap water

Aquatic plant

Snail

Lab Materials

BTB indicator

Test tube, cork, and parafilm

Light source

Box or other dark place

Test-tube rack

Experimental Plan

1. My hypothesis about how ecosystems work:

2. Drawing of my experiment to test my hypothesis:

3. Control setup:

4. Data (24–hour test):

5. Conclusion:

▲ FIGURE 2.21 Outline of the experimental options for planning your ecosystem investigation.

ACTIVITY 2.4

Ecosystem Experts

In this activity, you will become an expert on one ecosystem. You will then create a poster to interest someone else in visiting that ecosystem.

Materials

- resources about ecosystems, including this book
- poster board
- markers or colored pencils

Procedure

1. Choose an ecosystem from this list

- tundra (arctic, alpine)
- wetlands
- deserts
- deciduous forests
- open ocean
- grasslands
- coniferous forests
- estuaries
- rain forests

2. Make a poster that displays and summarizes important information about your ecosystem (see Figure 2.22). Be sure to include the following specific information on your poster:

a. name of ecosystem
b. description of ecosystem
c. physical features
d. life-forms
e. location map (world)
f. climate information (temperature, precipitation, etc.)
g. endangered species
h. human impact
i. food web
j. bibliography (use proper format)

3. You may want to begin your search for information by reading sections 2.3 and 2.4, Terrestrial Ecosystems (Biomes) and Aquatic Ecosystems, in this book. The library, SciLinks, and Figures 2.23 and 2.24 will also be sources of good information. Your teacher will provide ideas for constructing your food web.

4. Prepare and give an oral presentation on your poster ecosystem. Your presentation should not exceed 3 minutes.

▼ FIGURE 2.22 Outline of the ecosystem poster.

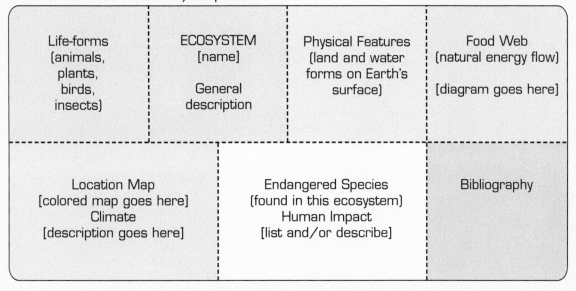

| Life-forms (animals, plants, birds, insects) | ECOSYSTEM [name] General description | Physical Features (land and water forms on Earth's surface) | Food Web (natural energy flow) [diagram goes here] |
| Location Map [colored map goes here] Climate [description goes here] | Endangered Species (found in this ecosystem) Human Impact [list and/or describe] | | Bibliography |

▼ FIGURE 2.23 The vegetative biomes (ecosystems) of the world. (The Vegetative Biomes of the World [1999] map was produced by reclassification of the Fedorova, et al., World Vegetation Cover map [*Fedorova, I. T., Y. A. Volkova, and D. L. Varlyguin. 1994. World Vegetation Cover. Digital Raster Data on a 10-minute Geodetic (lat/long) 1080 × 2160 grid. In: Global Ecosystems Database Version 2.0. Boulder, CO: NOAA National Geophysical Data Center*]. Reproduced by permission from Patricia and John Kineman, GAIA Institute of Geographical Ecology, 1101 Bison Drive, Boulder, Colorado 80302 USA.)

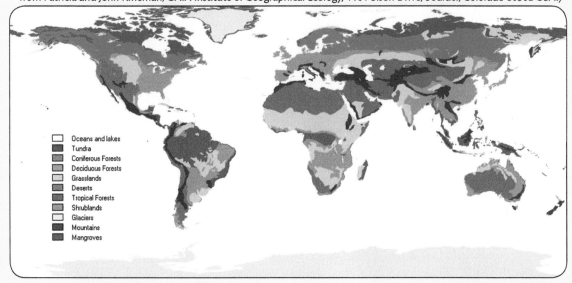

Oceans and lakes
Tundra
Coniferous Forests
Deciduous Forests
Grasslands
Deserts
Tropical Forests
Shrublands
Glaciers
Mountains
Mangroves

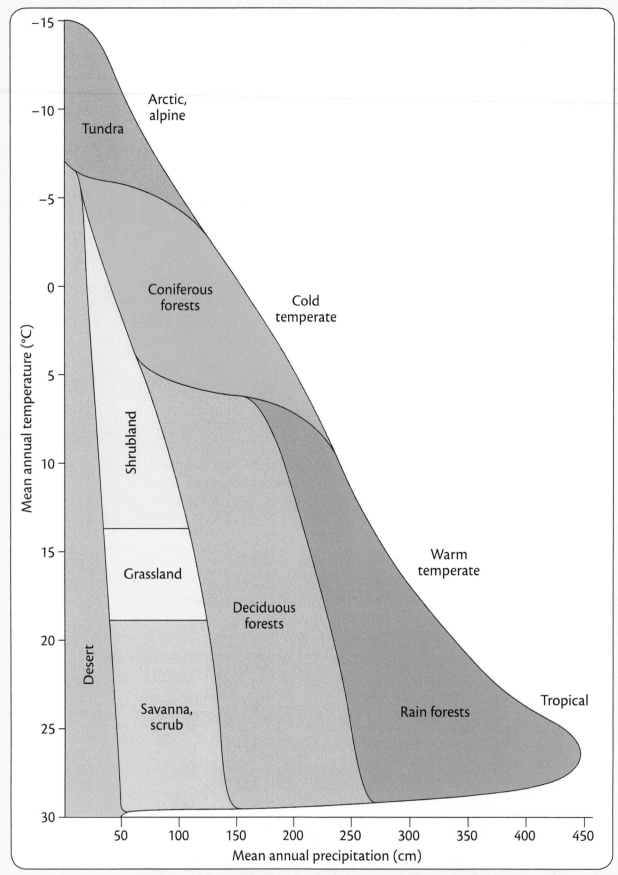

▲**FIGURE 2.24** A simple classification of vegetative biomes (ecosystems) of the world based on annual precipitation and mean annual temperature. In reality, the division boundaries are fuzzy. (*Adapted from Whittaker, R. H.* Communities and Ecosystems, *New York: MacMillan, 1975).*

2.3 Terrestrial Ecosystems (Biomes)

All land-based ecosystems are grouped together as terrestrial ecosystems (biomes). Each biome has its own set of organisms. The type of organisms present depends on the average temperature and annual rainfall of that biome. Descriptions of the major biomes follow.

Tundra

The region north of the tree line and near the Arctic Circle is known as the *arctic* **tundra**. This area is unique because the angle of the sun is low for much of the year. This results in long nights during the winter and nearly 24 hours of daylight each day during a short summer. Its few plant species must survive a cold, severe climate. The growing season in the arctic tundra is often less than 60 days. This does not allow trees the time required to store food until the next growing season. Thus, only dwarfed trees are seen here.

Precipitation rarely exceeds 10 inches (in) or 25 centimeters (cm) a year. Low temperatures freeze the soil permanently as deeply as 100 to 1,500 feet (ft) or 30 to 450 meters (m). Only a top layer 2–14 ft (about one-half to 4 m) thick thaws during the summer. The frozen soil beneath, called permafrost, does not allow root or water penetration. Consequently, water collects on the surface and forms many lakes (see Figure 2.25). This further reduces the chance for tree growth.

The tundra is the least complex of all the ecosystems. It does not have the structured vegetation of other ecosystems. Most of the plants are dwarfed and grow in marshy plains. Mosses and willows are common. Many of the animals are large, such as caribou. Having a small surface area to body mass ratio helps them conserve body heat.

At lower latitudes, *alpine tundra* occurs on mountaintops and in high mountain valleys above the timberline. Alpine tundra is common throughout the high mountains of the North American continent. At higher altitude, the colder air produces conditions much like those at a higher latitude (see Figure 2.26).

Northern Coniferous Forests

South of the tundra (or at levels lower than alpine tundra) lies the northern coniferous forest. This type of forest is found in Canada, the northern United States, and parts of Europe and Asia. The climate of this region is less severe than the tundra. It remains cool to

Topic: biomes
Go to: www.scilinks.org
Code: GloSci7e53

Apply Your Understanding

Why are lakes abundant in the tundra during the summer months?

SCIENCE at work

◀ FIGURE 2.25 Arctic tundra. *(Steve McCutcheon/ Visuals Unlimited)*

➤ FIGURE 2.26 Alpine tundra. *(Ivo Lindauer)*

cold with more precipitation and a longer growing season. The coniferous, needle-leafed trees that conserve moisture, such as spruce, pine, and fir, dominate this biome. Aspen and birch (deciduous trees) also are common, especially where disturbances such as forest fires have occurred.

Because much of the northern United States was covered by sheet glaciers during the ice age, this region contains many bogs and lakes. The area is dominated by black spruce, white spruce, hemlock, several pine species, tamarack, and alder thickets (Figure 2.27). Most of these are evergreens. Soils of this region tend to have deep litter layers, are acidic, and are usually mineral deficient. The dense forests that grow on these soils allow little light to pass through. Little vegetation, other than moss and fern, grows on the shady forest floor.

This biome is a haven for large mammals including deer, elk, moose, bear, wolverine, marten, lynx, fox, and wolf. Smaller mammals, such as weasels, snowshoe hares, moles, chipmunks, shrews, and bats and a variety of birds including juncos, jays, warblers, and nuthatches, thrive in this biome. Much of the original forest was harvested by logging in the late 1800s and early 1900s. The trees were converted to houses, wagons, and ships, or

Apply Your Understanding

What is the main economic value of northern coniferous forests?

➤ FIGURE 2.27 Northern coniferous forest.

were used for fuel. Today, the use and management of forests is an important issue because of the current and future demand for forest products.

Deciduous Forests

Much of the eastern half of the United States is dominated by the temperate deciduous forest biome (Figure 2.28). As the name suggests, the temperature of this biome is moderate. Its climate is characterized by humid, warm summers and cold winters. Abundant moisture is evenly distributed throughout the year. Annual rainfall averages from about 30 to 60 in (75–150 cm). These forests are dominated by broadleaf deciduous trees, which lose their leaves each year. The soil is rich, with much accumulation of litter (such as fallen leaves).

There is little fluctuation among the stable populations of this forest. The dry uplands are dominated by oak and hickory. Maple, basswood, and beech take over habitats that are moist. Cottonwood, willow, elm, and sycamore thrive in stream and river habitats.

The deciduous forest provides a lush habitat for many different organisms. White-tailed deer, red deer, squirrels, and skunks are common. Although present, black bears are rarely seen. Many bird species, such as woodpeckers, vireos, flycatchers, and ravens, also live there. Insects, which are very diverse and common, provide an extensive food source for the birds.

Grasslands

Grassland regions (often called prairies) are usually found in the interiors of continents such as the great plains of North America, the pampas of South America, the steppes of Russia and Asia, and in isolated spots of Europe. They occur in both temperate and tropical climates where precipitation is insufficient to support tree growth, but is not less than 10 in (25 cm) per year (Figure 2.29). In the United States, precipitation ranges from 20 in (50 cm) per year on the eastern edge to 10 in (25 cm) per year on the western and southern edges.

Most grasslands today are now farmlands and are frequently referred to as the "bread-baskets of the world." The fertile soils of these lands produce the wheat and corn we use for flour, breads, and breakfast cereals. The North American grassland once supported great herds of bison which, for the most part, have been replaced by cattle and sheep. Other regional animals include antelope, coyote, fox, badgers, prairie dogs, ground squirrels, rattlesnakes, and spade foot toads. Meadowlarks and prairie chickens are common. However, they have little impact on the large populations of insects that occupy this ecosystem.

Apply Your Understanding

Why aren't trees common on grasslands?

Apply Your Understanding

How are grasslands used in much of the world today?

The major natural herbivores and consumers of the grasslands are insects, which consume thousands of tons of plant material each year. These insects include grasshoppers, locusts, and aphids. Interestingly, the herds of wild grazing animals and today's grazing livestock seem to have little effect on the grasses. This is because the grasses developed over several million years of grazing pressure.

Deserts

Generally, regions that receive less than 10 in (25 cm) of precipitation annually are identified as **deserts**. Even more important than the amount of precipitation, however, is the rate of water loss through evaporation. Desert vegetation varies considerably. Much of it, however, consists of shrubs that have a variety of special adaptations for conserving water (see Figure 2.30). Many annual plants are found in the desert. Annuals can complete most of their life cycle when there is moisture; they survive the drought conditions in seed form.

► FIGURE 2.30 Organ Pipe Cactus National Monument. *(Jack Dykinga Photography)*

Their seeds are resistant to moisture loss. The great varieties of desert plants are the result of a great variety of desert conditions. Death Valley, in California's Mojave Desert, has a precipitation level often below 2 in (5 cm) per year. The lush woodlands of the Sonoran Desert in Arizona receive nearly 20 in (50 cm) of precipitation each year during the two rainy seasons. They dry out greatly during the dry seasons.

Deserts occupy about one-seventh of Earth's land surface. The largest desert is the Sahara Desert in Africa. It covers more than 3,000,000 square miles. (This is about the size of the 48 contiguous states.) Drought, overgrazing by livestock, and woodcutting for fuel are increasing the size of the Sahara. The next largest desert is the Gobi Desert in Mongolia and China, which covers 500,000 square miles.

In the past, humans have had less impact on the deserts of the world than on any other ecosystem. But desert ecosystems are easily damaged. The expansion of irrigation projects and the increase in human population, along with city growth, wind farms, livestock grazing, off-road vehicles, backpacking, hiking, camping, and other recreational activities, are now having a severe effect on these regions.

Apply Your Understanding

Describe at least three adaptations of desert plants.

Tropical Forests

In areas of the world where there is no freezing and moisture is plentiful, you will find lush tropical growth (see Figure 2.31). These **tropical forest** regions are located near the equator. They contain the greatest plant and animal diversity of any ecosystem on Earth. Thousands of different tree species grow here (compared with less than 100 in other types of forests).

Soils of these forests are typically thin and poor. The few nutrients that result from decomposition are quickly taken up by plants. Where the trees are burned or otherwise eliminated, the nutrients are washed away with the heavy rain runoff.

Think about This!

Tropical forests cover only 7 percent of Earth's surface, but they house over half of all plant and animal species in the world.

◄ FIGURE 2.31 Lowland tropical rain forest in Costa Rica. *(Robert L. Sanford, Jr.)*

Apply Your Understanding

What are some of the benefits we gain from rain forests?

The largest rain forests occur in the Amazon Basin of South America, where the average tree height exceeds 100 ft (30 m). These forests serve as major reservoirs for the production of atmospheric oxygen and the consumption of carbon dioxide. Today, they are seriously threatened by the expansion of human populations into the forest. Large expanses are being cleared for farming and grazing. Some are being cut for lumber.

Shrublands

Apply Your Understanding

Why are shrublands subject to fire?

Much of the arid and semiarid lands of the world are covered by shrubby vegetation. The climate of these **shrublands** is typically that of hot, dry summers and cool to cold, wet winters. These major land ecosystems are found in both temperate and semitropical regions. The *chaparral* ecosystem along the coast of California is an example of a well-developed shrubland (see Figure 2.32). The dense stands of shrubs growing there have hard, thick, waxy leaves that are drought resistant. These stands are frequently subject to fire; fire aids in the maintenance of the ecosystem.

2.4 Aquatic Ecosystems

Freshwater

Topic: aquatic ecosystems
Go to: www.scilinks.org
Code: GloSci7e58

Freshwaters are those inland waters that have very little or no soluble salts. They may be described as either flowing or standing waters. Standing waters may be puddles, ponds, or lakes. Flowing waters are divided into springs, brooks, streams, and rivers.

Helpful Hint!

Plankton are microscopic floating plants and animals that live in lakes, rivers, and oceans.

Small flowing springs are usually cool and contain much dissolved oxygen. They give rise to brooks. Brooks often contain leaves and other decaying material, but little plankton. Many insects live in this habitat during their reproduction and early development stages. Thus, predators such as small fish and trout do well in these small flowing waters.

Apply Your Understanding

How do rivers contribute to agriculture?

Brooks come together to form streams that are larger and slower. Streams provide a better habitat for plankton. Food chains originating from small plants support a much larger and more diverse population of organisms. These populations increase and become more complex as streams form small rivers (creeks). Creeks, in turn, become larger rivers, which provide the ultimate habitat in flowing water. Rivers are erosional and carry a great deal of sediment, which consists of nondecomposed organic matter, clay, silt, sand, and gravel.

The sediments are deposited along the banks and at the mouth of the river. These deposits become the very fertile soils that make up some of the best agricultural land in the world.

Standing waters (puddles, ponds, bogs, and lakes) all have one thing in common. Their water is contained. The water's salt content may vary from a little amount, such as in the Great Lakes (see Figure 2.33), to a large concentration, such as that of the Great Salt Lake in Utah. All standing waters are temporary. Someday, they will become filled with sediments and provide the basis for a forest or grassland.

Swamps and bogs are shallow, wet land areas; trees and shrubs grow in their midst. These wet land areas tend to contain a great amount of organic matter in various states of decomposition. Since bogs and swamps are shallow, photosynthesis is common, which allows healthy producer populations to become established. These areas provide the food for many organisms. Swamps (see Figure 2.34) and marshes are frequently the breeding and rearing habitats for many insects, birds, amphibians, reptiles, shrimp, and other crustaceans.

Think about This!

Why is photosynthetic production so great in swamps, bogs, and marshes?

◀ FIGURE 2.33 The north shore of Lake Superior. *(Minnesota Department of Natural Resources)*

◀ FIGURE 2.34 Swampy areas where water lilies grow tend to be much shallower than lakes. *(Minnesota Department of Natural Resources)*

▲ FIGURE 2.35 Ocean surf breaks on a rocky shoreline. *(Courtesy of National Parks and Conservation Association.)*

Marine Waters

Apply Your Understanding

How do oceans affect climate?

All of Earth's oceans are connected and are described as one large ecosystem. The oceans absorb a great deal of solar energy during warm seasons, and release this energy slowly during the cold seasons. This provides a stabilizing effect on Earth's climate.

The dissolved salts and minerals of the ocean increase with depth and nearness to the equator. Next to the shoreline and near the mouths of rivers, ocean salinity is less. Here, tides and wave action circulate the nutrients from the shallow water and provide a more fertile habitat (see Figure 2.35).

Oceans have zones similar to those of lakes. These zones are more complex since the oceans are so deep. Most productivity occurs along the continental shelf, the shorelines, and in the estuaries where nutrients are plentiful.

Think about This!

Where are oceans not productive? Why?

The open ocean is often described as a desert. However, a considerable amount of photosynthesis occurs near the surface. Because the oceans are so vast, they are the major photosynthetic ecosystem of the world. Small phytoplankton called diatoms are responsible for much of this production.

Estuaries

Think about This!

What are estuaries and why are they important?

Estuaries are transitional zones between freshwater and the open ocean. They often occur in bays or coves, sheltered from direct wind and oceans waves. They contain seawater that is diluted by the freshwater inflow and mixed by the tides, which serves to remove waste and nutrients. These regions are extremely productive compared to other natural ecosystems, and they provide a nursery for many sea animals. Figure 2.36 shows a typical estuary.

2.5 Ecosystems Change over Time

Ecosystems are not static. They continuously change over time because both natural forces and human activity disturb them. Some disturbances are gradual such as those that occur during slow climate change. Others are quick and dramatic—volcanoes, high winds, floods, and fires. The process by which an ecosystem restores itself after a disturbance is called **ecological succession**. This happens in a series of somewhat predictable stages.

Ecologists study two kinds of succession. **Primary succession** occurs when life is established on lifeless ground. This is what happens after lava flows over an area or a glacier retreats up a valley. The first steps involve the attachment of species such as lichens and moss to rock surfaces and the related weathering (breakdown) of rock-to-rock fragments. **Secondary succession** occurs when the remnants of a previous ecosystem remain after the disturbance. The most important remnants are organic material and seeds. This is almost always the case after a flood, tornado, or forest fire moves through an area. Figure 2.37 illustrates the process of secondary succession in an abandoned farm field located in a temperate deciduous forest biome.

As succession begins, the first set of species to establish itself is called pioneer, or early successional species. Pioneer plants grow rapidly, are short-lived, and do well in bright sunlight where nutrients are abundant. Their seeds tend to be widely and rapidly disbursed. Late successional plants are generally slow growing and long-lived. They do well in the shade. They have seeds that are not easily scattered, and the plants persist a rather long time.

As succession progresses, the total mass of organic matter present in a region increases rapidly at first, builds to a maximum, and then drops a little. This is shown in the graph in Figure 2.38.

Succession involves changes not only in vegetation. Everything changes—from the insects and birds to the animals and other organisms present. The changes brought about by the vegetation, however, are the most significant. In a given area, there is a predictable sequence of species that occurs as succession progresses. Figure 2.39 shows secondary succession on an abandoned farm field in Michigan.

SC/ LINKS
NSTA
Topic: succession
Go to: www.scilinks.org
Code: GloSci7e61

Apply Your Understanding

Distinguish between primary and secondary succession.

Apply Your Understanding

Distinguish between the characteristics of early and late successional plants.

► **FIGURE 2.37** Secondary succession happening on an abandoned farm field in a temperate deciduous biome. The time from beginning to end may be a century or more.

► **FIGURE 2.38** The change in biomass with succession. In the early stages, photosynthesis mainly goes into growth of new biomass. In the late stages, less solar energy is available for new growth because more energy is required to maintain existing biomass. The waviness at the end of the graph is the result of short-term climatic changes.

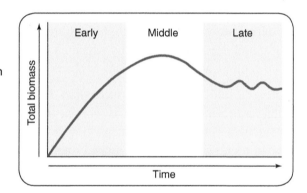

► **FIGURE 2.39** Secondary succession happening on abandoned farmland in Michigan. Young red cedar trees are taking hold on the hillside. *(John Sohlden/Visuals Unlimited)*

62 Chapter 2

Ecologists believe that succession occurs because each stage modifies its environment and prepares the way for the next stage. A knowledge of succession is useful when analyzing the strategy of agriculture and when planning for the restoration of land damaged by mining or other human activity. We will look at these closely in Chapters 7 and 15.

QUESTIONS & TASKS

1. Explain how life on a plot of land where you live will change after a fire, flood, or high winds destroy an existing biological community.

2. Explain how a disturbance such as a forest fire or flood may be beneficial to the ecological health of a community.

3. Find one or two areas in your community where ecological succession is in progress. Describe the changes and estimate the approximate stage of the succession.

The Needs of Humans

2.6 Do Humans Have Special Needs?

Even if all our basic needs were met, most humans could not survive as individuals alone. Most of us require companionship—an exchange of ideas and feelings. Interaction is necessary, but sometimes it leads to conflict. Conflict can lead to destruction. As a result, humans have developed techniques for trying to resolve conflicts and punish destructive behavior. This Special Focus shows how one group of people endured both physical danger and isolation from the outside world. As you read, note what strategies they used to cooperate and to deal with a stressful situation.

Think about This!

What are some special needs of humans?

SPECIAL FOCUS

Surviving an Antarctic Winter

By Robert Reinhold
The New York Times

SOUTH POLE STATION, Antarctica—The events of Aug. 17, 1979, will not get into the official history books, but they were something of a psychological milestone in the history of the South Pole. Outside, temperatures dipped to 71 degrees below zero in a blinding blizzard, but inside, emotional temperatures among the crew of 16 men and one woman, after nearly half a year of total darkness, were reaching the flash point.

Foaming at the mouth and roaring drunk, a member of the crew who has recently learned of his father's death, piles into the galley in rage. He yells and begins to smash cups wildly. Blood and glass are everywhere. Soon he spies his rival for the affections of the station's lone woman and charges with a two-by-four, then runs out into the blizzard. It is hours before the mayhem ends, with gashes, bruises, and frostbite.

In the three days of eerie calm that followed, Andrew Cameron, the 22-year-old supply man who witnessed all this, reflects in his diary: "Most people would never winter over if they knew what it really is like. Well the truth of it is that it can be fun at times but the deep dark winter with hopeless isolation for eight months is a sheer mental hell." He wonders how the crew, afflicted by deep jealousies and divisions, can survive another three months.

Though an extreme example, that night of violence underscores the powerful mental effects of protracted isolation. And many psychologists believe the unusual nature of Antarctic isolation may hold lessons for an approaching age of prolonged space travel and space colonization. In both instances, a small group of scientists and support personnel is confined to a tiny life-sustaining cocoon surrounded by an impenetrable hostile environment that permits no quick escape.

Though the Navy does the screening, the entire winter crew belongs to the United States Antarctic Research Program, an arm of the National Science Foundation. Seven of the 17 are scientific personnel making observations of the weather, upper atmosphere, and geophysical phenomena. The rest are support workers—a cook, engineers, mechanics, a doctor— employed by a private contractor, ITT Antarctic Services Inc., of Paramus, New Jersey.

Psychologists say the best candidates for isolation are hard-working personalities, somewhat diffident, with higher than average intelligence and education, and without close family ties. Above all, they say, isolated personnel should be competent in their work, since criticism can be devastating in such confines. They must be flexible and tolerant of other people's habits and beliefs.

Probably the best bets are "professional isolates," the kind of men who work on offshore oil rigs and Alaskan pipelines. Such men do not relate well to women and seem to thrive on isolation.

According to Cameron,

Some of the people who are most gung-ho for this experience are not well adapted," said Cameron. "They tend to be misfits, seeking something they'll not find. And when the bubble bursts, their depressive experience is very difficult for others to handle. This is the big league of isolation.

As for Andrew Cameron, now living in Gaithersburg, Maryland, he says it took him nearly a year to calm down from the winter. Toward the end, he wrote in his diary: "I am sick of this chunk of ice. I want to get out of this cesspool. Let me get the hell out of here. I want to go home." Today, he calls it "the greatest year of my life."

Human Behavior and Conflict Resolution

Scientific knowledge and skills are only part of what it takes to survive in a situation like the one just described. Independence and absorption in work are helpful. As this account illustrates, social skills in human relations and conflict resolution are also important. The same type of skills will be needed when attempting to resolve problems related to population, food supply, pollution, resource distribution, and land use at local, regional, and global levels. Keep this in mind as you study these problems in upcoming chapters.

Focus Questions

1. How might survival in this Antarctic episode be related to the voyage to Mars examined in Activity 2.2?

2. Does it take more scientific knowledge to survive in a Mars or Antarctic–type situation or in your everyday setting? Explain.

3. According to the article, what does stress bring out in people? Give examples.

4. What are the best personal traits to have if cooperation among individuals is a major goal?

5. Based on the information in this article and your responses to these questions, how would you change your list of who should go on the Mars voyage?

6. What lessons do these accounts (Mars and Antarctica) teach us that might be applicable to the resolution of conflicts related to regional and global pollution, food supply, and land use?

ACTIVITY 2.5

Our Quest for the "Good Life"

In this activity, you will examine what the "good life" means to you.

Background

Most people want more out of life than mere existence. In addition to their basic needs, most humans desire

To love and be loved

To do meaningful work and feel useful in society

To learn new things and teach them to others

To benefit from a variety of healthful foods

To enjoy clean air and water

To have modern-day conveniences

To seek the beauty and meaning of life

To help rid our planet of disease

To promote world peace and rid our planet of war

To relax and enjoy life on occasion

Achieving some of these desires requires the ability to interact and resolve conflicts. The wise use of our natural resources is also essential. In this course, we will examine the challenge of obtaining and using these resources. We also will speculate about how related issues might be resolved. We need to understand resources and their uses, design and use new technology, learn from mistakes of the past, and improve our ability to communicate. By making those things a priority, we are more likely to assure the good life for ourselves and for our children.

> **Apply Your Understanding**
>
> What kinds of knowledge are necessary or helpful for achieving the good life?

Procedure

1. Make a chart with 2 columns.

2. Label the left column "Basic Needs." Label the right column "Wants for My Lifestyle."

3. Begin filling in the left column by listing the 5 items you decided to take on the Mars journey.

4. Finish the list with other items you consider basic needs.

5. In the right column, list the things you use and want to maintain your lifestyle.

6. Next to each item in the right column, write down some of the resources or products necessary to produce these things.

QUESTIONS & TASKS

Discuss these questions with your classmates:

1. Does a growing human population create competition for natural resources?

2. Describe at least 2 possible ways to resolve conflicts that may result from competition for natural resources.

3. Is there more to living the good life than having material things?

4. What are some of your nonmaterial desires?

5. How well can one live the good life without consuming large quantities of energy and mineral resources?

6. What is the good life?

7. How do you achieve it?

8. What percentage of the world's population lives a good life (according to your definition)?

9. How can this percentage be increased?

Summary

We live on a global spaceship. It seems permanent and firm beneath our feet. But this is only an illusion. Processes within Earth cause the lithospheric plates to move. As the plates move, new minerals are brought to Earth's surface, and volcanoes add gases to our atmosphere. The atmosphere (air zone), hydrosphere (water zone), and lithosphere (rock zone) make up the ecosphere (life zone). The ecosphere is the global ecosystem that supports all life.

In an ecosystem, living organisms and nonliving substances interact to produce an exchange of materials between the biotic and the abiotic. The sun provides the energy necessary for this exchange to occur. Plants store energy and minerals. Animals (including humans) directly or indirectly take these things from plants for their needs. Finally, decomposers break down dead organic material and return minerals (nutrients) to the soil. Thus, the cycle is complete. It is repeated over and over again. As humans, we are totally dependent on this process. Figure 2.40 provides a visual summary.

Most humans want more out of life than mere existence. We desire various comforts (home, cars, appliances). We also desire peace, beauty, and love. Our ability to interact reasonably with our fellow human beings will determine the degree to which these desires are realized.

▼FIGURE 2.40 Basic components of an ecosystem. The green arrows show the cyclic movement of matter through the system. The orange arrows show the one-way flow of energy through the system.

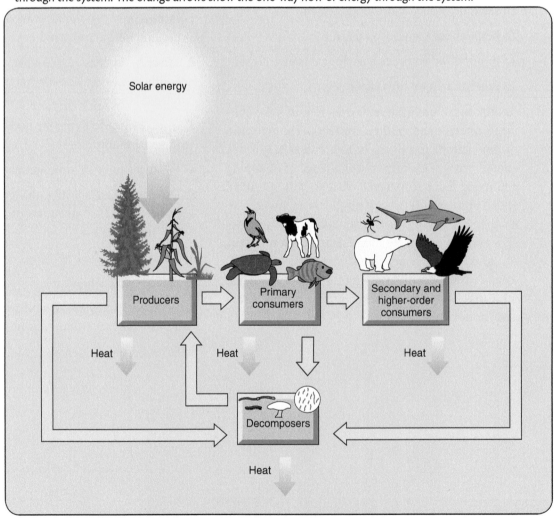

REFERENCES

Aber, John D. and Jerry M. Melillo. *Terrestrial Ecosystems* (Philadelphia: Saunders), 1991.

Akin, Wallace E. *Global Patterns: Climate, Vegetation and Soils* (Norman: University of Oklahoma Press), 1991.

Cunningham, William P. and Barbara W. Saigo. *Environmental Science*, 6th ed. (New York: McGraw-Hill), 2001.

Goldsmith, Edward, et al. *Imperiled Planet: Restoring Our Endangered Ecosystems* (Cambridge, MA: MIT Press), 1990.

Leopold, Aldo. *A Sand County Almanac* (New York: Oxford University Press), 1949.

Lieth, Helmut and Robert H. Whittaker, eds. *Primary Productivity of the Biosphere* (New York: Springer-Verlag), 1975.

Northington, David K. and J. R. Goodin. *The Botanical World* (St. Louis: Times Mirror/Mosby College Publishing), 1984.

Raven, Peter H. and Linda R. Berg. *Environment*, 3rd ed. (Philadelphia: Harcourt College Publishers). 2001.

Whittaker, R. H. *Communities and Ecosystems* (New York: MacMillan), 1975.

WEBSITES

Indiana University Astronomy Department: http://www.astro.indiana.edu

The Federation of American Scientists: http://www.fas.org/mars/

Satellite composite view of Earth by Tom Van Sant and the Geosphere™ Project, Santa Monica, California. With assistance from NOAA, NASA. Eyes on Earth. Technical direction Lloyd Van Warren. Source data derived from NOAA/TIROS-N Series Satellites. Completed April 15, 1990. © Tom Van Sant/Corbis.

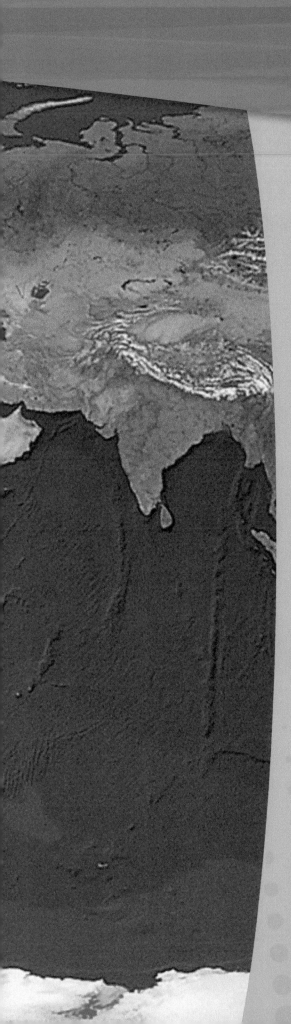

CHAPTER 3

Energy Flow and Matter Cycles

GOAL

- To build an understanding of the relationships among energy flow, the cycling of matter, and human use of energy and mineral resources.

Before I flew, I was already aware of how small and vulnerable our planet is, but only when I saw it from space, in all its ineffable beauty and fragility, did I realize that humankind's most urgent task is to cherish and preserve it for future generations.

—Sigmund Jahn, *Soyuz 31*

The Geosphere Image

The spectacular image of Earth shown on the preceding page marks a milestone in history. Unobstructed by clouds, we see Earth revealed. Meteorologists used NOAA weather satellites to obtain hundreds of individual satellite images from space. They then combined these to produce this image of the world. Like a jigsaw puzzle, this composite was assembled over a 10-month period; it was completed on April 15, 1990.

 Energy and Matter—The Big Picture

Although Earth is isolated in space, it is continuously renewed from the outside. Energy is carried to Earth in the rays that come from the sun. This energy is all around us and inside us. It is locked for a time inside all living things. It is released from these living organisms in countless ways as life on Earth continues.

Because of our sun, energy is readily available. That energy flows through our ecosystem (see Figure 3.1). It makes life possible. Humans, other animals, plants, fungi, bacteria and other single-cell organisms—all life depends on the sun.

▲ FIGURE 3.1 The sun is the most important of all our energy sources. Without it, there would be no life on Earth. (*Dick Thomas/Visuals Unlimited*)

 ACTIVITY 3.1

What Eats What?

One of the ways that energy flows through ecosystems is through food. When an animal eats another animal or plant, it is processing the energy stored in that organism. In this activity, you will model the feeding interactions in two different aquatic ecosystems to learn more about the flow of energy.

Materials (for each student)

- 1 role card
- ball of string or yarn

Procedure

1. Work with a partner to brainstorm a list of at least 8 specific interactions in an ecosystem.

2. Discuss your list of interactions with the class. Then group the interactions into large categories.

Helpful Hint!

You can use an ecosystem you studied in Chapter 2 or the ecosystem you featured in your poster in Activity 2.4. You can also use an ecosystem that you have direct experience with, such as the ecosystem where you live.

3. Read the role card your teacher gives you. This card tells you what plant or animal you represent. It also describes the animals that eat your organism and the animals, if any, that your organism eats.

4. Hold your ball of string or yarn in your hand. Find another student who can eat your organism or who represents one your organism can eat.

5. If your organism can eat the other organism, take the loose end of that student's string. If that organism can eat yours, give your loose end of the string to that student.

6. Keep moving and talking to other students about their organism. If your organism can eat their organism, take hold of their string. If theirs can eat your organism, give them some of your string.

7. Stop when your teacher calls time and look around the room. Think about and remember what you observe.

QUESTIONS & TASKS

Record your responses in your science notebook.

1. Use your observations to answer these questions:
   a. What happened during the activity?
   b. Why did the results require such a short period of time?
   c. What does the string or yarn represent?
   d. Did all students get string? Explain what happened.
   e. Did all students give away string? Explain what happened.
   f. Think of a dramatic change that could occur in the ecosystem. Which organisms would be most affected? Why?

2. Watch a demonstration by four volunteer students. Then answer these questions:
   a. How is the pattern of what happened similar to the large-class activity?
   b. How is the pattern of what happened different from the large-class activity?

3. Think back to the ecosystem you used in step 1. Draw a set of interactions between plants and animals that shows which organism eats another.

4. This activity is a model of the flow of energy in an ecosystem. But no model is perfect. In what ways is this model accurate? In what ways is this model inaccurate?

3.1 Energy Flow in Nature and Human-Built Systems

The energy flow in natural ecosystems is governed by the same laws that operate in human-built systems. One of these laws is that energy can be changed from one form to another. Energy must be transformed (changed) to drive either living or human-built systems. The **chemical energy** stored in carbon compounds must be changed to the **mechanical energy** of movement. This is true whether we are talking about the food that moves a person or the gasoline that powers a car. A second law is that the total amount of energy never changes. With living things, energy is lost to the environment as heat. This is much like burning fuel to run an engine, or using electricity to light a bulb.

In addition, **efficiency** is just as important in natural systems as it is in the energy systems people have created. The same principles apply. No conversion is ever 100 percent efficient. Some energy is always lost (as heat). The final efficiency of a series of energy

Content Clue

You can't see chemical energy because it is stored in the chemical bonds between atoms. This energy is released when the bonds are broken.

Content Clue

You can see evidence of mechanical energy when something moves.

► FIGURE 3.2 Diagram of
an electric power plant
showing how energy flows
from coal to alternating
current. (Diagram is not
drawn to scale, and not
all systems are shown.)
(*National Coal Association*)

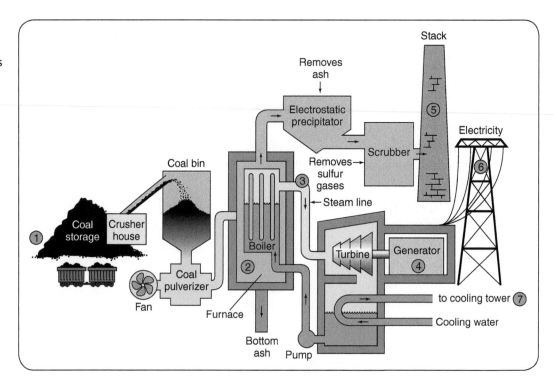

Helpful Hint!

Efficiency refers to how
much of the energy that
is used goes toward doing
something useful. If a
lot of energy does useful
tasks, it is an efficient
system. If a lot of energy
is just lost as heat, the
system is not efficient.

changes is the product of all the intermediate efficiencies. Figures 3.2 and 3.3 have more in common than may seem apparent at first. Can you see how they show the same idea?

Figure 3.3 starts with a certain amount of the energy that arrives on the surface of a green leaf. It is captured in the sugar molecules that plants produce through the process of photosynthesis. Through photosynthesis, a plant converts solar energy to chemical energy. The chemical energy is stored in the plant's cells. Plants (and animals) can use this energy to perform their daily functions. Special enzymes break down the energy compounds, which releases the energy for the body's needs.

▼ FIGURE 3.3 Simple food chain showing how energy flows though various levels.

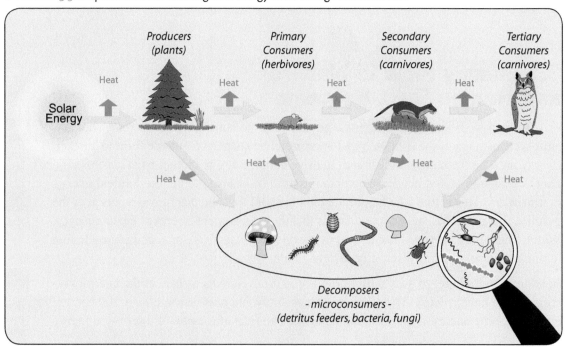

But photosynthesis is nowhere near 100 percent efficient. Whatever energy is trapped in this way is all the energy that the ecosystem has. It is the living equivalent of a full tank of gas. If the tank were not constantly refilled by the sun and the action of green plants, the ecosystem would "run out of gas" very quickly.

When a **primary consumer** eats a plant, energy is transferred and transformed. The chemical energy stored in the plant food materials is changed to kinetic energy. This energy helps move the organism, and heat energy is released into the environment. Some of the plant's energy is stored in the bones and tissues of the animal.

If that animal is eaten, its energy becomes available to the **secondary consumer** (or **carnivore**) that ate it. But energy is lost at each transfer. As a result, the total amount of energy available to secondary consumers is always less than what was available to primary consumers. Likewise, the total amount of energy available to primary consumers is always less than what came from the sun, or even what the plants trapped through photosynthesis.

A **food chain** is the transfer of energy from one organism to another. Green plants, the **producers**, transfer a certain portion of their energy to the **herbivores** or primary consumers such as rabbits or cows. However, a major portion of the energy (often as much as 90 percent) is lost in the transfer, usually in the form of heat energy. At each of the steps that follow in the food chain, more energy is lost. This is one of the reasons there are not very many animals at the top of the food chain. It takes a lot of energy to support them. This also explains why animals spend much of their time eating and behaving in ways that conserve energy.

These relationships are sometimes drawn as an **energy pyramid**. An energy pyramid shows producers on the bottom and secondary or **tertiary consumers** on the top (see Figure 3.4).

Food chains usually become diverse and weblike instead of linear as in Figure 3.3. Secondary consumers may have many choices and sometimes become primary consumers as well. When that happens, we have a food web. Figure 3.5 illustrates a food web. As the animals die, their remains are converted to nutrients, gases, and heat by **decomposers** that break them down. Much of the decomposition energy is lost to adjacent material or to the atmosphere. The heat created in a compost pile is one example of this energy release.

Helpful Hints!

Primary consumers eat plants. They are called primary consumers because they are the first organisms to use the energy stored in the plant.

A *carnivore* is an animal that eats other animals. It is a secondary consumer because it gets its energy from an animal that ate a plant.

If you can describe the relationship between a plant, the animal that eats the plant, and an animal that eats the first animal, then you can describe a *food chain*.

Plants are called *producers* because they take solar energy and lock it into plant molecules. In this way, plants produce the energy that powers the ecosystem. Producers are organisms that make, or produce, food from sunlight.

Topic: ecosystem factors
Go to: www.scilinks.org
Code: GloSci7e73

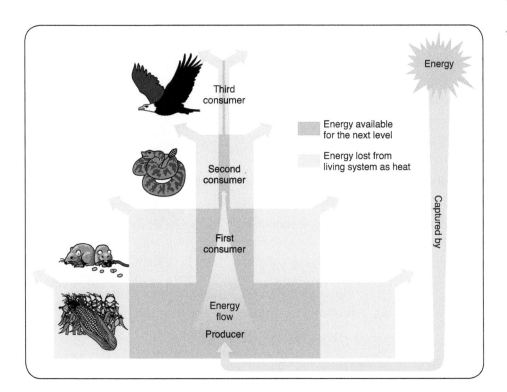

◀ FIGURE 3.4 Every living organism carries on activities that result in the release of energy. As a result, each consumer level that follows obtains a smaller percentage of the energy that was trapped by the producer. *(From BSCS, Biological Science: An Ecological Approach, Green Version, 3rd ed., 1973.)*

Energy Flow and Matter Cycles 73

▶FIGURE 3.5 Food web. The many food chains in a given area form a complex food web. *(From Wildlife Management Institute.)*

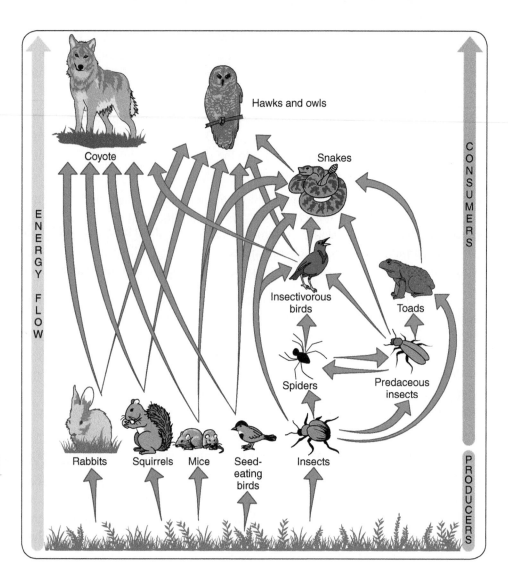

Hawks and owls

Coyote

Snakes

Insectivorous birds

Toads

Spiders

Predaceous insects

Rabbits   Squirrels   Mice   Seed-eating birds   Insects

ENERGY FLOW

CONSUMERS

PRODUCERS

What is the system efficiency of an ecosystem? The answer varies depending on the type, variety, and number of plants and animals in the system and how they interact with non-living factors. In general, the more plant life present, the greater the energy flow through an ecosystem. Warmer climates typically support more plant life than cooler climates. Lower elevations are usually more productive than higher elevations.

? QUESTIONS & TASKS

Think about these questions and be ready to contribute to a discussion. Record your responses in your science notebook.

1. Explain why vegetarians use food energy more efficiently than people who are not vegetarians.

2. Why don't lions hunt mice?

3. Elephants and blue whales are the largest animals on Earth. Both are vegetarians. Why don't meat-eaters get as large as elephants and blue whales?

4. Why are there more rabbits than coyotes?

Designing Your Ecodome

In Chapter 2, you identified the major parts or components of an ecosystem. You analyzed how they interact with one another. In this activity, you will use additional information about cycles to understand energy flow and matter cycling on Earth. You will use this information to design an ecodome. An ecodome is a small, enclosed biosphere such as Biosphere 2 (Figure 3.6) in Arizona or the International Space Station.

Materials (for each team)

- large sheet of paper
- markers (6 different colors)
- assorted art supplies

Procedure

1. Meet in your team of 4. Decide who will become the expert for each of these cycles: mineral/nutrient cycle, nitrogen cycle, carbon cycle, and water cycle.

2. Begin researching your cycle. You can use the information that follows in section 3.2 to help with your study. You may also want to access other available resources. Each expert should be able to answer these questions about his or her cycle:

   a. What is the material that cycles?

   b. What form does the material take as it cycles?

   c. What source of energy fuels your cycle?

3. Communicate your understanding of your cycle to the rest of your team.

4. As a team, plan an ecodome to be located on Mars, on the moon, or in the middle of a large desert. Your ecodome plan should meet the following criteria:

   a. Ten people will live there for more than 3 years without outside supplies.

   b. The dome will be sealed after the people are inside.

   c. Sunlight can enter the structure.

   d. All the components of an ecosystem you identified in the activity A Voyage to Mars must be present.

   e. Your plan must account for all 4 cycles.

   f. Your plan needs an illustration to show the following: 2 of the people, different-colored arrows to represent the 4 cycles, how the sunlight gets in, and where the ecodome is located. You also may show some of the high-tech equipment you will need to monitor the conditions inside. Only the short carbon cycle and mineral cycle need to be shown.

5. Make a short presentation to the class about your ecodome. Describe how the matter cycles inside your dome and how the sun provides the energy to power the cycles.

 Biosphere 2 is a project in which a team of scientists and others tried to create an ecodome in the desert in Arizona. To learn more about this project, visit these websites: http://www.bio2.com; http://www.paragonsdc.com/; and http://www.bioquest.org/simbio2.html.

◄FIGURE 3.6 Biosphere 2 in Oracle, Arizona.

(Photo by David Mayhew. © Biosphere 2 Center, Inc.)

3.2 Resource Recycling in Nature: The Biogeochemical Cycles

There are many chemical cycles in nature. The four major cycles are the water, mineral, carbon, and nitrogen cycles (see Figure 3.7). Each cycle is described below. Because there are many mineral cycles, the information provided here describes a generic mineral cycle.

▼ FIGURE 3.7 All life on Earth depends on the recycling of chemical nutrients and the one-way flow of energy through the biosphere. The sun provides the energy for both of these processes.

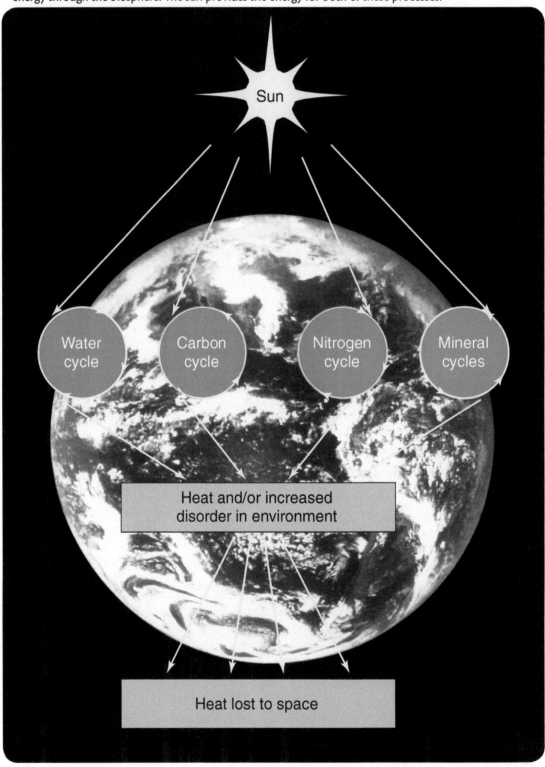

The Water (Hydrologic) Cycle

The water used by plants, animals, and people is never destroyed. It is used and reused by living and nonliving forms. This process of use and reuse is called the **water cycle** (see Figure 3.8). Refer to this figure often as you read the next paragraphs.

During a rainstorm, water is absorbed by the soil in a process called **infiltration**. Some water percolates farther down into porous rock. How far water sinks into the ground depends on the surface vegetation, the soil texture, and the types of rock beneath the soil.

Water in the underground part of the water cycle is known as **groundwater**. Groundwater is water in cracks and rocks, and in spaces between rock fragments, gravel, and sand grains. Water moves through pores, holes, and cracks in the soil and rock. These spaces become fewer and fewer the deeper you go. Finally, the movement of water becomes impossible.

Not all water from a rainstorm infiltrates the soil. Some runs off the ground surface into streams, lakes, and reservoirs. This water is called **runoff**. The flowing water in streams and rivers and the water stored in natural lakes, wetlands, and reservoirs is called surface water. Precipitation on land slowly works its way to the ocean.

Surface water absorbs heat from the sun and surrounding materials and changes from liquid water to water vapor. This change from a liquid to a gas is called **evaporation**. In liquid form, water contains dissolved impurities. As water evaporates, these impurities are left behind. As a result, water vapor contains only pure water. Because vaporization purifies water, water can be used over and over. Water is a naturally recyclable resource.

Huge amounts of water also evaporate from plants. Water rises from the soil into roots, stems, and finally into leaves. Water evaporates from the leaves by moving through small

Think about This!

Why is the water cycle so important?

Apply Your Understanding

Why is water not used up?

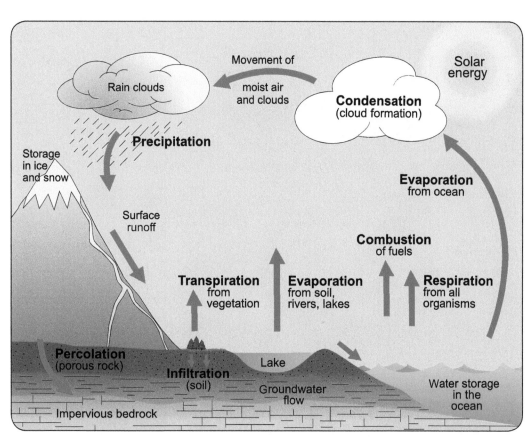

◄ FIGURE 3.8 The water cycle.

Apply Your Understanding

Use a drawing to explain the water cycle to someone who is unfamiliar with the concept.

Think about This!

Why are the mineral/nutrient cycles so important?

Apply Your Understanding

Name two ways humans use minerals.

Think about This!

The long mineral cycle involves the formation and weathering of rock.

The short mineral cycle involves the cycling of minerals by organisms.

openings in the leaf into the surrounding air. This process is called **transpiration**. An acre of corn transpires the equivalent of 15 inches (in) or 38 centimeters (cm) of rainfall during its growing season. Smaller amounts of water vapor are added to the air when fuels are burned (combustion) and as organisms respire.

As water vapor rises and cools, it condenses into a liquid and forms clouds. The clouds move as air circulates.

To use water wisely, we must know about renewal time. Renewal time is the time it takes water to renew or clean itself. The freshwater available to use comes from groundwater and runoff from streams and rivers. Rivers renew themselves quite rapidly, but the renewal of groundwater is much slower. As a result, the pollution of groundwater can affect the quality of human life for centuries.

Mineral/Nutrient Cycles

In addition to water, oxygen, carbon, and nitrogen, living organisms require a variety of nutrients in the form of metal ions. Metal ions are used by enzymes and some have special functions. Iron in our blood, for example, carries oxygen from the lungs. The variety of nutrients organisms need are provided in nature by a number of *mineral/nutrient cycles*.

Minerals originate in rocks. As rocks weather, the minerals required for life are slowly released and moved by wind, water, and gravity. Eventually, they end up in the soil and bodies of water. Because there is such a variety of these minerals, we will lump them all together in a generic mineral cycle (see Figure 3.9)

Soluble minerals are removed from the soil and taken in by plants as the plants photosynthesize. Plants build essential minerals into large molecules that are useful to themselves and to the organisms that eat them. Plants build these minerals into their structures. These minerals are then transferred to animals and other organisms that eat and digest plant material. The minerals are used in a variety of ways and then discarded with the organism's waste. Decomposers break down organic wastes and dead organisms, which releases CO_2,

▶FIGURE 3.9 A generic mineral/nutrient cycle. This figure does not show the industrial gathering of minerals to produce fertilizers and vitamin/mineral pills and supplements. Dark red arrows show the long mineral cycle; bright red arrows show the short mineral cycle.

Topic: phosphorus cycle
Go to: www.scilinks.org
Code: GloSci7e78

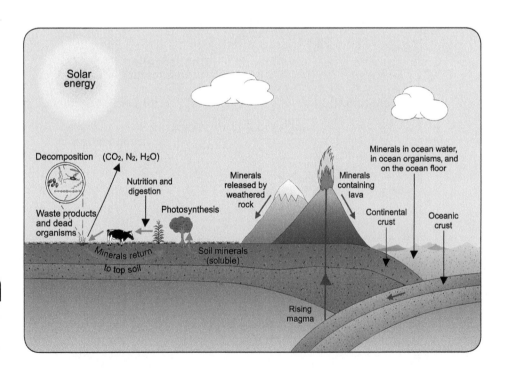

N$_2$, and water to the atmosphere. Minerals return to the soil for plants to use again. The process then repeats.

Some minerals are lost as water moves down through soil in a process called leaching. The lost minerals are replaced over time as rock at the Earth's surface weathers.

The Carbon Cycle

The **carbon cycle** is a special mineral cycle because carbon is the key element in organic molecules—the molecules of life. This cycle is summarized in Figure 3.10. Follow the arrows as you read about this cycle.

The carbon cycle can be broken into two parts, a short cycle and a long cycle. The short cycle involves the interplay between photosynthesis and respiration. It takes a carbon atom about 1 to 5 years to journey around the short cycle.

During photosynthesis, plants combine carbon dioxide, water, and minerals into **carbohydrates**. Oxygen gas is released. As food, carbohydrates represent a rich store of energy and carbon. The stored energy is released in cell respiration by plants, animals, and decomposers as carbohydrates are broken apart to yield carbon dioxide and water. Minerals, which are built into an organism's structure, are also released. The released energy enables organisms to perform their life functions. The carbon dioxide is returned to the air. When organisms die, decomposers break them down. In the process, carbon dioxide is released into the atmosphere.

The long cycle involves the storage of carbon compounds for long periods of time. The carbon begins its journey as part of a carbon dioxide molecule. It is taken in by a plant and becomes part of a carbohydrate. The carbon can become part of a plant and remain there

Apply Your Understanding

Use a diagram to explain the mineral/nutrient cycle to someone who is unfamiliar with the concept.

Think about This!

Why is the carbon cycle so important?

Topic: carbon cycle
Go to: www.scilinks.org
Code: GloSci7e79

Content Clue

Carbohydrates are large chemical molecules made mostly of carbon atoms. Food material like the starch in potatoes is an example of a carbohydrate.

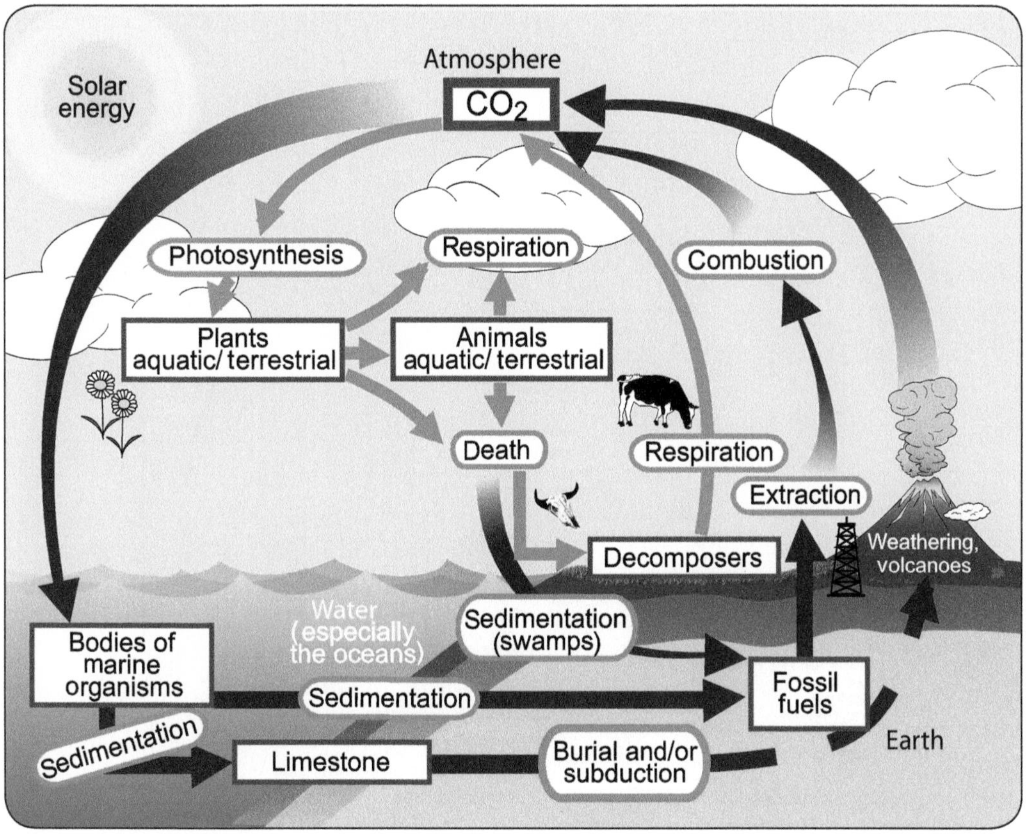

◀ Figure 3.10 The carbon cycle. The arrows show the movement of carbon atoms. Rectangles show places where carbon is stored; ovals indicate processes. Light-green arrows show flow in the short cycle; dark-green arrows show flow in the long cycle.

Content Clue

Most mineral cycles have no gaseous storage in the atmosphere. The carbon and nitrogen cycles are exceptions.

for a long time, such as in the wood of a very old tree. It can be stored in the remains of dead plants that become buried and changed into fossil fuel deposits. Or it could be locked up as calcium carbonate ($CaCO_3$) in the bodies of shells and the skeletons of other marine organisms such as corals. Most of these remains accumulate at the bottom of the oceans. Through geologic processes and time, they become limestone deposits that work their way into molten layers deep inside Earth. This carbon can eventually be released into the atmosphere by volcanic activity. Limestone can also be uplifted to the surface (not shown in Figure 3.10) as mountains form. Eventually, it is broken down as rocks weather and CO_2 is released to the atmosphere.

Another part of the long cycle involves the use of fossil fuels. Fossil fuels (coal, oil, natural gas, oil shale, and tar sands) are extracted (removed) from the ground in a variety of ways. We burn fossil fuels to use the energy stored in their molecules. In the process, carbon dioxide is released into the air. A carbon atom can take hundreds to millions of years to complete its journey around the long cycle.

The Nitrogen Cycle

Another special mineral cycle is the **nitrogen cycle**. Nitrogen plays a special role in the atmosphere, in our bodies, and as a soil nutrient. Nitrogen is part of amino acids, which are the building blocks of proteins, and the genetic molecules RNA and DNA. The nitrogen cycle is diagrammed in Figure 3.11. Follow the arrows as you read about this cycle.

Nitrogen in the air (N_2) is useless to plants. It does not react or combine readily with other molecules. Therefore, nitrogen must be supplied in "fixed" or combined form, as in ammonium ions (NH_4^+) or nitrite ions (NO_3^-). Some nitrogen is fixed by lightning and other processes in the atmosphere. Much more is fixed by bacteria that live in the soil and aquatic environments. Other important nitrogen-fixing bacteria live in the root nodules of legumes (see Figure 3.12).

Content Clue

Fossil fuels store carbon atoms for a long period of time.

Think about This!

Why is the nitrogen cycle so important?

Topic: nitrogen cycle
Go to: www.scilinks.org
Code: GloSci7e80

FIGURE 3.11 The nitrogen cycle. The boxes indicate places where nitrogen is stored. Arrows show the movement of nitrogen from one storage reservoir to the next.

Think about This!

Some farmers use commercial fertilizer. Others use the natural process of alternating legumes (such as soybeans) with nonlegume crops (such as corn). Farmers also use plant and animal waste.

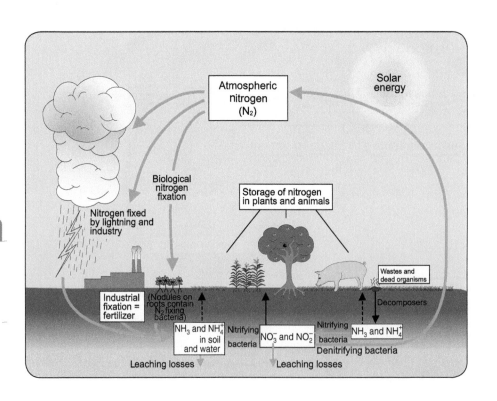

Helpful Hint!

Legumes are a group of pod-bearing land plants that have the ability to fix nitrogen. Legumes include such plants as beans, peas, alfalfa, and locust trees. They are found throughout natural ecosystems, plus they play a special role in agriculture.

Helpful Hint!

Leaching is the process by which minerals in the soil dissolve in water and are removed from the soil as the water drains into the rock below.

Nitrogen-fixing bacteria convert atmospheric nitrogen (N_2) into ammonia (NH_3). Ammonia and ammonium ions (formed when ammonia dissolves in water) are converted first to nitrate (NO_2^-) and then to nitrate (NO_3^-) by nitrifying bacteria in the soil. Plants take in nitrate, ammonia, and ammonium and use them to produce proteins and nucleic acids. Animals eat plant protein and produce animal protein. When plants, animals, and other organisms die, decomposers break down their nitrogen compounds, which releases ammonia that can be reused. This ammonia is converted to nitrate (NO_3^-) that can be taken in by plants. It can also be broken down by denitrifying bacteria that release nitrogen back into the air as N_2.

The pool of available nitrogen in most soils is small. Nitrogen is removed from the soil by leaching and by the bacteria that return it to the atmosphere. It is also lost through the harvesting of crops. To make up for these losses, animal manure and fertilizer are applied to the soil. Fertilizers contain nitrogen that was fixed through industrial processes. Industrial fixation is now a major part of the nitrogen cycle.

Apply Your Understanding

Use a diagram to explain the nitrogen cycle to someone who is unfamiliar with the concept.

⟹ Matter and Energy—A Closer Look

To understand how natural and human-built systems work, we must clearly define the terms matter and energy. We must also be aware of some of the natural laws that describe their behavior. The next section of readings and activities will enable you to build useful definitions of matter and energy.

3.3 So What Are Matter and Energy?

Energy is what moves our world. Our lifestyle and our standard of living are based on energy and resource use. Without an adequate and varied supply of minerals, we would have no automobiles or airplanes. Without sufficient energy in the proper form, those machines wouldn't run. We use coal to fire our power plants, natural gas to heat our homes, and electricity to power our refrigerators, computers, televisions, and radios. And the list goes on and on. Our appetite for energy and minerals seems to have no end. And the needs and wants of the rest of the world for such resources are growing as well.

Topic: matter and energy
Go to: www.scilinks.org
Code: GloSci7e81

Mass is the amount of "stuff" in an object

Matter occupies space and has mass.

Energy is the ability to move matter around.

This chapter provides a foundation for understanding energy and resource use. Certain laws govern our behavior when it comes to obtaining and using resources. We must be conscious of these laws because they help us understand the basic ideas about energy, resources, and the environment. With this knowledge, we can make intelligent plans for the future. But before we examine the laws that govern the use of energy and mineral resources, we need to define the terms *mass, matter,* and *energy.*

Mass is a measure of the amount of "stuff" in an object. More precisely, mass is a measure of an object's resistance to change. Try throwing a golf ball. Then throw the metal shot used by the track team. Which one goes farther? The answer is obvious. The metal shot is composed of a lot more stuff. It has a much larger mass than the golf ball. Therefore, it resists change in its state of motion. It is much harder to throw. But once going, it is also much harder to stop. Would a drag race between a sports car and a heavily loaded semi be very interesting? Why not?

Matter is anything that occupies space and has mass. All the objects that we see, touch, and feel are composed of matter.

Energy is the capacity to take action. It is the ability to move matter around. Energy is necessary to maintain life and a vibrant society. When our energy supplies are low, gasoline is harder to get, people lose their jobs, and homes are cooler in the winter. All life would cease without energy.

 QUESTIONS & TASKS

Record your responses in your science notebook.

1. Why do you buy gasoline? Relate your answer to the definition of energy. Use the word *matter* in your explanation.

2. How can you judge the mass of an object?

 ACTIVITY 3.3

Exploring Mass

In this activity, you will test some ideas to help you understand the relationship between energy and mass.

Materials

- string
- objects of different mass
- balance

Procedure

1. Watch your teacher's demonstration (see Figure 3.13) and then answer these questions:

   a. What happened when your teacher jerked the bottom string?

   > **Helpful Hint!**
   > A *force* is a push or a pull.

   b. What happened when your teacher pulled slowly on the bottom string?

   c. Discuss the 2 events, and then explain what happened. See the hint boxes in this activity for ideas. Record your thinking in your science notebook.

   > **Helpful Hint!**
   > On a diagram, indicate where forces are applied.

▶ FIGURE 3.13 The setup used in the demonstration in step 1.

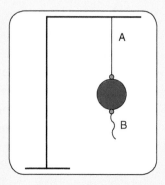

2. Use the materials available to test your explanation. You will have successfully completed your experimenting when you can answer these questions with confidence:

Helpful Hint!
Show where forces do not balance. When forces do not balance, what happens?

a. Describe the characteristics of the objects and string you used in terms of their size, mass, and strength.

b. What is the relationship between the force used to move the object and the mass of the object?

3. Present your results to the class.

QUESTIONS & TASKS

Based on your experiments and your class discussion, try these two challenges. Record your responses in your science notebook.

1. Describe what mass is.

2. Make a statement about the relationships among mass, force, and energy.

3.4 Kinetic and Potential Energy

When you experimented with the masses and string in Activity 3.3, you applied a force to the string. Unbalanced forces cause objects to move. A moving car, for example, has energy that we see in the form of the car's motion. A tank of gasoline has energy as well, but you do not get to "see" that energy until it is burned in the engine. In this example, there are two distinctly different forms of energy present. The energy you can observe in a moving car (see Figure 3.14) is called kinetic energy. The energy that is stored in the gasoline is potential energy.

Potential energy is stored energy. It is energy that has the ability, or potential, to produce motion. A tank of gas, a bowl of cereal, a stick of dynamite, and a compressed spring are all examples of potential energy. Can you think of another example of stored energy?

When potential energy is released, that energy is called kinetic energy. **Kinetic energy** usually is seen as motion. The moving car, a person running, a falling rock, and an avalanche are all examples of kinetic energy. You can also observe kinetic energy where the motion is less obvious, such as a burning candle, a person singing, or a tree growing.

Moving objects have kinetic energy. Potential energy is stored for future use.

◀ FIGURE 3.14 The kinetic energy possessed by this race car is made possible by the energy stored in the fuel that powers it. (*Roger Penske, Detroit Diesel Corporation*)

The kinetic energy (KE) of a mass (m) moving at a velocity (v) is given by this equation:

$$KE = \frac{1}{2} mv^2$$

How do objects obtain kinetic energy? The answer is, we must do work on them. **Work** is defined as the product of a force times the distance through which it acts. Thus,

$$work = force \times distance \text{ or}$$
$$W = F \times d$$

Helpful Hint!

The mathematical symbol Δ means "change in."

If a mass is at rest and we apply an unbalanced force (F) over a distance (d), our work will cause the mass to gain an amount of kinetic energy that is given by this equation:

$$F \times d = \Delta (KE) = \frac{1}{2} mv^2$$

 QUESTIONS & TASKS

Record your responses in your science notebook.

1. Picture two large rocks sitting on top of a hill. Do they have potential energy? How do you know? Describe a way to convert the potential energy in the rocks to kinetic energy.

2. Assign each of the following to one of these categories: potential energy, kinetic energy, or both. For each item, explain briefly why you chose that category.

   a. gallon of gasoline

   b. flying arrow

   c. rock balanced on a cliff

   d. charged battery

   e. stick of dynamite

   f. pitched baseball

3.5 Closed and Open Systems

Helpful Hint!

Global science is the study of Earth and environmental systems.

All the cycling of matter and the flow of energy on Earth occurs in a system. A system is a defined area, space, or region that is under study. For the purpose of the study, the system is limited by a boundary. The boundary may be imaginary.

You learned in Chapter 2 that in terms of matter, Earth is essentially a closed system. In terms of energy, however, Earth is an open system. The following definitions and examples will help us examine these two important statements.

closed system—a system where nothing enters or leaves; a system where everything is used and reused.

open system—a system where things both enter and leave.

steady state—a system in which properties are constant because substances are entering and leaving at the same rate.

Figure 3.15 shows a series of bathtubs that illustrates the relationship among the concepts of open systems, closed systems, and steady state systems. The questions that follow will help you discover more about these relationships.

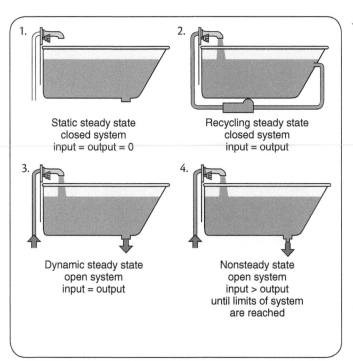

◄ Figure 3.15 **Four states of a bathtub.** (*Adapted from* Living in the Environment. *1st edition, by G. Tyler Miller, Jr.*)

Helpful Hint!

The mathematical symbol > means "is greater than."

QUESTIONS & TASKS

Record your responses in your science notebook.

1. Which tub is more like
   a. the world's present population situation?
   b. the quantity of water in the world's oceans?
   c. a lake with an inlet and an outlet?
   d. the average temperature of Earth?
   e. zero (no) population growth?
   f. your average weight?
   g. a recycling program?

2. Think about the ecodome you designed. What characteristics of your design make the ecodome a closed system? What characteristics make it an open system?

3. Explain why Earth is an open system in terms of energy.

3.6 Conservation Laws

There are several conservation laws in nature. A **conservation law** states that in a closed system, some quantity (such as total mass or energy) remains conserved (unchanged) forever. One such law is the **conservation of matter-energy**. This law states that the total amount of matter plus energy in the universe is constant.

On Earth, we break this conservation law into two parts. Both are important to us because they relate to our use of energy and mineral resources.

►FIGURE 3.16 Matter cannot be destroyed, but it can be rearranged and reused. We must design for recycling whenever possible. *(Institute of Scrap Recycling Industries, Inc.)*

Law of conservation of matter: Matter can neither be created nor destroyed. It can be rearranged.

Law of conservation of energy: Energy can neither be created nor destroyed. It can be changed from one form to another.

The **law of conservation of matter** states that the total mass of Earth is constant. This is because Earth is neither gaining mass nor losing mass. Stated another way, matter can neither be created nor destroyed, but it can be rearranged (see Figure 3.16).

The **law of conservation of energy** states that energy can neither be created nor destroyed. It can, however, be transformed (changed) from one form to another. This statement is also known as the first law of thermodynamics.

? QUESTIONS & TASKS

1. The conservation of matter is often stated as, "There is no 'away.'" What does that mean? How does this relate to you? How does this relate to current waste disposal problems?

2. In the activity A Voyage to Mars, many students suggested bringing an oxygen-making machine along. "Just plug it in and it makes oxygen." What are the drawbacks to that idea?

3. What do you think about a pollution-control device that can be attached to the tailpipe of a car to "eat up" pollutants?

4. If there is no "away," why doesn't trash build up in nature?

5. If the conservation of matter is such a simple concept, why do we have problems with solid waste and hazardous waste?

6. Many communities have aluminum can recycling centers. How does this change the amount of aluminum on Earth?

7. Give two examples of changing energy from one form to another.

8. If heat given off by a burning candle is not destroyed, where does it go?

The Conservation of Mass

In this activity, you will record the individual mass of two solutions. You will then predict what will happen to the combined mass after the two solutions are mixed. This experiment will allow you to experience the conservation of mass.

Materials (for each team)

- 2 100-mL beakers
- 2 50-mL graduated cylinders
- 20 mL 0.1M $Ca(CH_3COO)_2$
- 20 mL 0.1M Na_2CO_3
- balance

Procedure

1. Before you begin, make a prediction about the mass of the combination of the 2 solutions: solution A and solution B. Will the new mass be equal to or less than the 2 separate masses?

BE SAFE

Wear safety goggles when working with chemicals.

2. Create a data collection chart like the one in Figure 3.17 in your science notebook. Make sure you have a place to record the following:

   a. the mass of the 2 beakers
   b. the beakers with the solutions
   c. the 2 solutions
   d. the beaker with the combined solution
   e. the combined solution alone

3. Label one beaker "A" and the other "B." Record the mass of the 2 empty beakers.

4. Pour 20 mL of solution A (0.1M $Ca(CH_3COO)_2$) into beaker A.

5. Pour 20 mL of solution B (0.1M Na_2CO_3) into beaker B.

6. Measure and record the mass of each beaker containing the solutions.

7. Calculate the mass of each solution alone. Do this by subtracting the mass of the beaker from the mass of the beaker with the solution.

Helpful Hint!

If they are not premeasured, use a graduated cylinder to measure each solution.

▼ FIGURE 3.17 Sample chart for data collection. Solution A is the 0.1M $Ca(CH_3COO)_2$ solution; solution B is the 0.1M Na_2CO_3 solution.

Initial Mass		
Beaker A	**Beaker A with Solution A**	**Solution A**
_____ g	_____ g	_____ g
Beaker B	**Beaker B with Solution B**	**Solution B**
_____ g	_____ g	_____ g
Combined Mass of Original Materials		
Solution A + Solution B = _____ g		
Mass after Mixing Solutions		
Beaker B	**Beaker B with Solution A + B**	**Solution A + B**
_____ g	_____ g	_____ g

8. Pour the contents of beaker A into beaker B.

9. Observe the new combined solution. What is your prediction now about the mass of this solution? Will the mass be the same as, higher than, or lower than the sum of the numbers you calculated in step 7?

10. Determine the mass of the combined solutions.

11. How does the mass you measured compare to your 2 predictions in steps 1 and 9?

12. Calculate the percentage difference between the mass of the new materials and the mass of the original materials. Use this formula:

$$\left(\frac{\text{mass of original} - \text{mass of new}}{\text{mass of original}} \right) \times 100\%$$

13. How does the mass of the new materials compare with the sum of the masses of the original materials?

14. Return your materials to the location designated by your teacher.

QUESTIONS & TASKS

Consider these questions in light of this experiment. Record your responses in your science notebook.

1. Matter can neither be created nor destroyed. What can happen to it?

2. What kind of system did you work with? How do you know?

3. The balanced chemical equation for the addition of hydrochloric acid (HCl) to calcite ($CaCO_3$) is $2HCl + CaCO_3 \rightarrow CaCl_2 + H_2O + CO_2$. Use this equation to explain how matter is conserved in the reaction but the particles are rearranged.

ACTIVITY 3.5

Forms of Energy Experts

The first law of thermodynamics (the conservation of energy) may make more sense after you know more about the forms of energy that power the universe. In this activity, you will become an expert on one form of energy. You will then teach others what you have learned.

Materials

- resources about energy, including this book
- assorted markers and art supplies
- poster board

Procedure

1. Meet with your team of 6, as directed by your teacher. Each team member will choose one of these forms of energy: mechanical, thermal (heat), radiant (light), chemical, electrical, or nuclear.

2. You may want to begin your search for information by reading sections 3.7 and 3.8, The Six Forms of Energy and Energy Sources, in this book. The library and SciLinks will also help you become an expert on your energy form.

3. As an expert, you should be able to provide clear answers to the following:

   a. Give 3 examples of your form of energy.

   b. What are common sources of your form of energy?

   c. Describe 2 interesting facts or ideas about your form of energy.

4. Meet with other experts from the other teams who are studying the same form of energy. Share your findings and compare your responses to steps 3a–c. You may revise your responses if you choose.

5. Meet with your original team. Teach one another about the forms and sources of energy by explaining what you learned to your team members.

6. Create a poster that illustrates the 6 forms of energy, and hang your poster in a place where others can learn from your work.

Helpful Hint!

The 6 forms of energy are summarized in Figure 3.18.

Energy Form	Definition	Examples	Common Units of Measure
Mechanical	Kinetic: the energy of a moving object	A ball moving through the air; energy stored in a wound-up spring	joule (J); foot-pound (ft · lb)
Thermal (heat)	Potential: stored energy The energy of the random motion of the particles of a substance	The warmth of a campfire; a hot bath	British thermal unit (Btu); calorie (cal)
Radiant (light)	Energy carried as a wave motion; produced when charges are accelerated	Solar energy, used for photosynthesis by plants or causing a sunburn in humans	watt-hour (Wh); kilowatt-hour (kWh)
Electrical	The energy associated with magnets, electric circuits, and in combinations of the two	Energy for running a television, lamp, refrigerator, toaster, or radio	kilowatt-hour (kWh)
Chemical	The energy stored in chemical bonds (the energy of foods and fuels)	Energy in gasoline that runs your car; food that gives you energy	*Energy content: calories/mole (cal/mol); calories/gram (cal/g); Btu/pound (Btu/lb)
Nuclear	The energy locked in the nucleus of an atom; caused by the movement of nuclear particles	Reactions used in atomic weapons, nuclear medicine, and nuclear reactors	tons of TNT *Energy content is examined in Chapter 8.

▲ FIGURE 3.18 Six forms of energy. The common units of measure are defined in section 3.9, Energy Units and Conversion Factors.

3.7 The Six Forms of Energy

Mechanical Energy

Mechanical energy is the energy of an object as shown by the object's movement, its position, or both. Mechanical energy is the most familiar form of energy (see Figure 3.19). The moving pistons in an engine have mechanical energy and do work by making the wheels of a car go around. A hammer moving toward a nail has mechanical energy; it has the ability

Know the 6 forms of energy.

►FIGURE 3.19 "Big Muskie," a Bucyrus-Erie® 4250-W, is the world's largest walking dragline. This machine weighs 27 million pounds—more than 150 Boeing 727 jetliners. It is as wide as a football field. Why? So it can do a huge amount of work. Each filling of its 220 cubic yard bucket moves enough material to more than fill two average-size railroad coal hoppers. (*Courtesy of Bucyrus-Erie Company, South Milwaukee, Wisconsin.*)

to force a nail into a board. A boulder on the edge of a cliff has mechanical energy because of its position. It has the potential of moving something, if only a little soil, through a distance before it comes to rest.

Heat (Thermal) Energy

When you rub your hands together rapidly, your hands get warm. The mechanical energy of rubbing is transformed (changed) into heat.

Scientific evidence of the equivalence between mechanical work and heat was provided by the experiments of Scottish physicist James Prescott Joule. Joule's most famous experiment used an apparatus in which slowly falling weights turned a paddle wheel in an insulated container of water (see Figure 3.20). Friction between the paddle wheel and the water warmed the water. Joule measured the temperature increase.

From this and similar experiments, Joule concluded that heat was a form of energy. This understanding proved to be an important idea that changed how scientists and inventors thought about energy. Joule realized that the mechanical work did not disappear. Instead, it reappeared as heat energy! As the idea grew that energy never disappears, scientists were able to understand the law of conservation of energy.

►FIGURE 3.20 This is what the apparatus for Joule's famous experiment looked like. In the experiment, Joule observed the conversion of mechanical energy to internal (thermal) energy. (*From Physical Science Study Committee, PSSC Physics, Boston: D. C. Heath & Company.*)

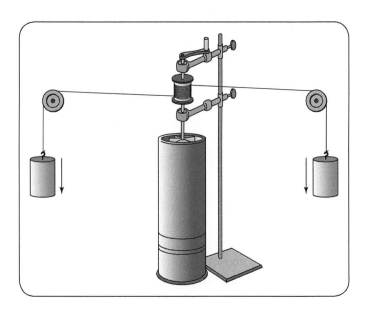

Another idea followed Joule's experiments. **Heat energy** actually is the *kinetic energy* of moving molecules. Temperature is a measure of this motion. For gases at low pressure, it was found that,

$$\tfrac{1}{2} mv^2 = kT$$

where k is a constant that relates the kinetic energy of the molecules to the Absolute (or Kelvin) temperature scale. This equation shows that as the temperature increases, the molecules of a substance move faster. As the substance cools down, its molecules move more slowly.

Radiant Energy (Including Light)

Radiant energy is the energy of electromagnetic waves. Light, radio waves, infrared radiation, microwaves, X-rays, and gamma rays are all examples. Waves of this type are sent out by accelerating electric charges. If electric charges (in a wire) move back and forth fast enough, radio waves will leave the wire. Electrons, accelerated by the high temperatures that exist in the hot filament of a lightbulb, send out visible (light) radiation.

Electromagnetic radiation is characterized by two properties: the frequency (f) and the wavelength (λ). These waves move with constant velocity (c), the velocity of light. These three quantities are connected by the relationship $c = f \times \lambda$. Wavelength and frequency (λ and f) are inversely related. This means a "long wavelength" radiation (large λ) must have "low frequency" (small f). Figure 3.21a shows familiar examples of electromagnetic radiation. Within a certain range of frequency and wavelength, electromagnetic radiation is visible as light.

Our most important form of radiation is solar (from the sun). Solar radiation includes not only visible light, but also the rest of the electromagnetic spectrum.

The fact that radiation is a form of energy can be shown in a variety of ways. For instance, we know that with a magnifying glass we can concentrate the sun's rays and start a fire. Another example is how a solar cell changes the sun's energy into electrical energy.

Content Clue

The connection between molecular motion and kinetic energy is explored further in a Special Focus in section 3.10. The Kelvin temperature scale is studied in chemistry classes.

Apply Your Understanding

What is the electromagnetic spectrum?

▼ FIGURE 3.21 (a) The electromagnetic spectrum. (b) This chart shows the relationship between frequency and wavelength for waves of constant velocity. As frequency increases, wavelength decreases. The wavelength of wave 1 (λ_1) is twice that of wave 2. Note, however, that the second set of waves has twice the frequency.

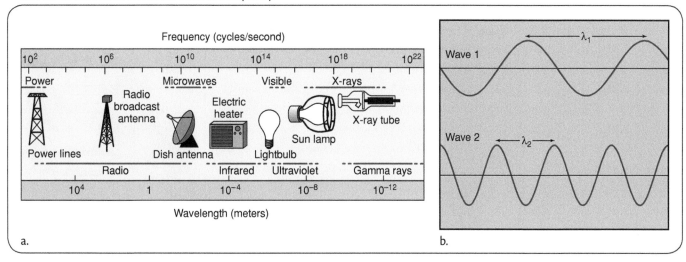

a. b.

Electrical Energy

Think about This!

Why is electrical energy so useful?

The three forms of energy we have discussed so far—mechanical, heat, and radiant energy—are familiar because they are used in those forms. We can see their end uses. Moving trucks, cars, or buses; heated buildings; lighted rooms; and foods cooked in microwaves are examples of such end uses. One of the most common forms of energy, however, is never an end use. Electrical energy is always an intermediate, or middle form. We only see its effects, such as the light from a lightbulb, the heat in a toaster, or the work done by an electric motor.

Electrical energy is useful because it is easily converted to other forms of energy. Usually, it is converted and used as it is produced. (This is because it is difficult and expensive to store electricity.)

Electrical energy is a special kind of kinetic energy. It is the energy of electric charges, usually electrons, in motion. Passed through a wire, this current can cause heating. If the wire gets hot enough, it will glow and produce light. An electric current produces a magnetic field. This field can cause a motor to turn if it is properly arranged.

Electricity is most commonly produced when the magnetic field that passes through a closed electric circuit (usually a coil) is caused to change. The basic principles involved are illustrated in Figure 3.22.

Chemical Energy

Chemical energy is the energy that is stored in the bonds that hold molecules together. Common examples of chemical energy include the energy that is stored in food, dried plant material, crude oil, natural gas, and coal. Figure 3.23 illustrates one need for chemical energy.

The products of photosynthesis are examples of chemical energy. Through photosynthesis, plants capture the sun's energy. This energy is used to combine carbon dioxide, water, and minerals into more complex molecules. These more complex molecules lock up solar energy in their chemical bonds. When the molecules are broken up as we digest food and burn fuel, the energy is released. With that energy, muscles can move and a body can do work.

▶FIGURE 3.22 This AC generator produces electrical energy. The wire coil is forced to rotate between the poles (N and S) of the magnet. This rotation causes an alternating current in a closed circuit. *(Used with permission of 3M Company, © 1966. Adapted by the author.)*

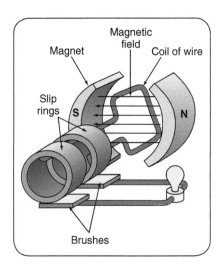

◄ Figure 3.23 Chemical energy for your tank. As we move into the future, the gasoline we buy may contain increasing percentages of alcohol. (*National Renewable Energy Laboratory [NREL]*)

Nuclear Energy

Nuclear energy is locked in the nuclei of atoms and is caused by the movement of the nuclear particles. When these particles are rearranged, nuclear energy is released.

Nuclear energy is the most difficult form of energy to release. It can only be released in two ways. One way nuclear energy is released is by combining small nuclei to make a bigger nucleus. This combination is called **fusion**. The second way is through the breakdown of a larger nucleus into smaller nuclei. This breakdown is called **fission**. Nuclear reactions are of interest because they can release large amounts of energy. However, it is a difficult form of energy to work with. The radiation that is released can be harmful to living things if uncontrolled.

Content Clue

We will examine the structure of atoms in more detail in Chapter 10.

3.8 Energy Sources

A close analysis reveals that the energy we use comes from only five primary sources. Those sources are described below and summarized in Figure 3.24 that follows.

The Sun

The sun is basically a hugh fusion reactor that radiates energy in all directions. Most solar radiation is used as it arrives on Earth. A much smaller amount is stored in chemical bonds and used later.

Only a small fraction of the sun's energy arrives at Earth, but that is still a huge amount of energy. Measurements outside the atmosphere indicate that Earth intercepts 1.353 kilowatts (kW) of power per square meter perpendicular to the sun's rays. That means that the total solar radiation intercepted by Earth's cross-sectional area of 1.275×10^{14} square meters is 1.73×10^{17} watts!

But how much power is that? It is enough to warm Earth, evaporate water, and drive the water cycle. It drives all the winds, waves, and Earth's climate systems. It also provides the energy for all photosynthesis. Simply put, it fuels all life processes. It is especially interesting to note that all these processes occur even though 30 percent of the sun's energy never reaches Earth. This 30 percent is reflected back into space by materials such as clouds and ice.

At Earth's surface, the solar input is approximately 1.0 kW per square meter. Although very spread out, this power density can accomplish many useful tasks. Solar radiation makes

Know the 5 primary energy sources.

Apply Your Understanding

How can the sun's energy be used to produce electricity?

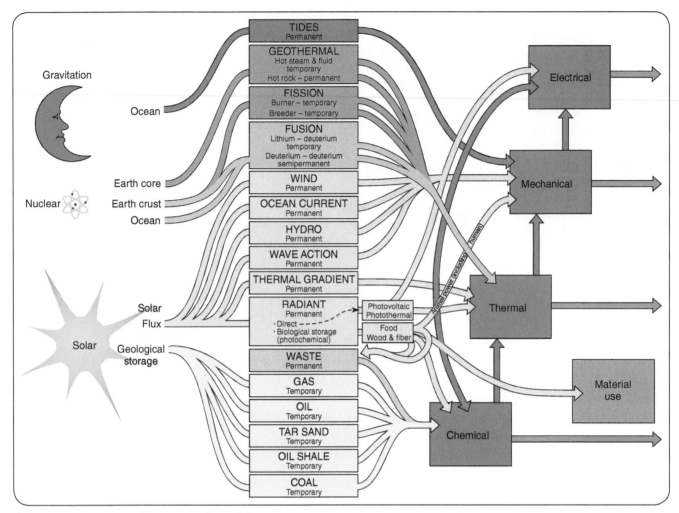

▲ FIGURE 3.24 Integrated energy supply model. *(From the Office of Energy Research and Planning, State of Oregon.)*

solar heating and cooling of homes possible (see Figure 3.25). It also makes possible the options of solar-powered electricity-generating plants and wind power. In addition, solar radiation causes temperature differences in the ocean that can be used to generate electricity. Each of these will be discussed in more detail in Chapter 11.

Solar energy is stored in living plants (when they photosynthesize food) and in animals (when they eat plants). Significant quantities of energy are available to us from these sources. For example, decomposing plant and animal waste can be converted into methane gas and alcohol; methane can be directly substituted for natural gas. Solar energy is also stored in plants that have died recently (dead wood and hay) and in trash (wood and plastic). Solar energy is stored in plants that died many millions of years ago, forming fossil fuels (oil, gas, coal, oil shale, and tar sands). Modern societies run primarily on oil, gas, and coal.

▶ FIGURE 3.25 This solar home uses flat-plate collectors to capture the sun's energy.

Tides

Tides orginate in the gravitational pull between Earth, our moon, and the sun. Tides offer a fascinating energy option. This option, however, is only useful in tidal areas that have a way to trap large quantities of water. Few such places exist on Earth.

Earth's Heat

Heat stored just below Earth's surface is caused by tremendous subsurface pressures and by the energetic decay of radioactive substances. This source of **geothermal energy** is used to provide steam to turn generators to supply electricity.

Think about This!

Why do we call this Earth's heat?

Fission Fuels

The energy stored in unstable uranium and thorium nuclei can be released and used to produce electricity. Uranium and thorium compounds can be extracted from Earth's crust like other minerals.

Fusion Fuels

Fusion involves combining very small nuclei to make larger nuclei. Since stability is gained in the process of combining, energy is released. Deuterium and tritium have been found to be the easiest light nuclei to fuse. The supply of deuterium in the world's oceans is huge. Tritium is made from lithium, which, although rare, can be mined from Earth's crust.

? QUESTIONS & TASKS

1. Name the five sources from which all our energy comes.

2. Nuclear fusion does not generally occur on Earth under natural conditions, yet no ecosystem could function without fusion energy. How can this be so?

3. Name the ways in which solar energy has been stored for later use.

4. Which type of stored solar energy have we been using the most during the past several decades?

ACTIVITY 3.6

Energy Transformations

Each form of energy can be converted, or transformed, to the others. Some transformations, however, are more difficult to accomplish than others. In this activity, you will look at both familiar and unusual forms of energy transformation.

Materials (for each student)

- Handout: *Forms of Energy—Transformation Chart*
- Handout: *Devices/Processes Grid*

Procedure

1. Examine the stations your teacher has set up around the room. Identify the energy transformations taking place at each station.

2. Chemical energy is changed to heat as wood burns. Heat is changed to mechanical energy in a car's engine. List 3 other transformations that you experience each day.

3. Figure 3.26 summarizes some energy transformations. What forms of energy or transformations are not shown?

Energy Flow and Matter Cycles 95

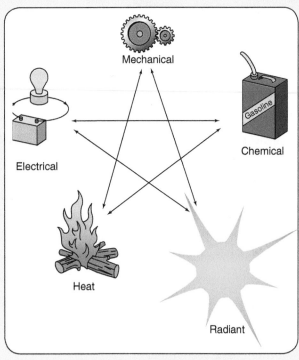

Mechanical

Gasoline

Chemical

Electrical

Heat

Radiant

▲ FIGURE 3.26 **Various energy transformations.**

4. Working in a team of 6, complete the *Forms of Energy* chart using the *Devices/Processes Grid* supplied by your teacher.

QUESTIONS & TASKS

Record your responses in your science notebook.

1. Choose one task that a human performs, such as lighting a match, and diagram the energy transformations. Begin with the food the human ate that was stored as chemical energy and end with the task you chose.

2. Give an example of the following:

- A household appliance that changes electrical energy into heat.

- A process that involves at least three energy transformations.

ACTIVITY 3.7

Plants as Energy Transformers

You know from reading about energy sources that the sun is the major source of energy for Earth. You may also know that the sun's energy is transformed by plants in the process of photosynthesis. In this activity, you will design an experiment to show your understanding of this type of energy transformation.

Materials

- plants or seeds
- access to sunlight or other light source
- potting soil
- peat pots
- water

Procedure

1. Organize your thoughts about plants and energy by creating a web, concept map, or other diagram that connects the following in a meaningful way: plants, sun, water, energy, sugar (glucose), food, photosynthesis. Record your diagram in your science notebook.

2. Based on the connections in your diagram, what questions do you have about plants and energy? Write down one of your questions.

3. Use your question to design an experiment that demonstrates that plants transform energy.

4. Show your teacher your experimental design.

5. Set up your experiment.

6. Collect your data (this may take some time).

7. Organize your data into a table.

QUESTIONS & TASKS

Record your responses in your science notebook.

1. Based on your experiment, write a conclusion that demonstrates what you learned about plants and energy transformation.

2. What would life on Earth be like if there were no plants? Discuss this question with your class.

Using Energy to See in a New Way

Remote sensing is the science and art of obtaining information about an object, area, or event through measurements made from a distance. For example, a person can determine whether or not a metal object is hot by placing a hand near the object. If the object is hot, the heat can be felt without touching the object. In a similar way, remote sensing devices measure electromagnetic radiation reflected or emitted from features of interest. Photography, for instance, uses an optical lens to record visible light on film. Any remote sensing system consists of parts that collect, record, store, and finally process and analyze information (see Figure 3.27).

Humans have eyes and ears to serve as sensors (collectors), and brains to record, store, analyze, and interpret information. Yet, as "remote sensors" we are very limited; our senses can detect only a fraction of the electromagnetic spectrum. We do not see or hear X-ray, ultraviolet (UV) and infrared (IR) radiation, microwaves, or radio waves. To make up for our human limitations, scientists have developed technologies for detecting and analyzing electromagnetic radiation. These remote sensing technologies can gather detailed information by processing wavelengths we cannot perceive. If these detecting devices are placed on satellites and aimed properly, we can gather a great deal of information about our Earth (see Figure 3.28).

Digital remote sensing systems convert records of electromagnetic energy to numeric values. This information is stored on a magnetic tape. Remote sensing satellites beam the data back to Earth where the data are picked up by a receiver. To display digital data, a computer program translates each number on the magnetic tape into a pixel or small shaded box. Rows of pixels

▼ FIGURE 3.27 **The major components of a remote sensing system.** *(Adapted from Denver Museum of Natural History.)*

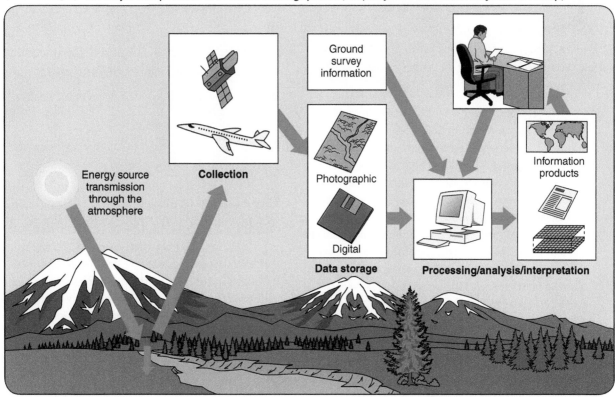

Energy source transmission through the atmosphere

Collection

Ground survey information

Photographic

Digital

Data storage

Information products

Processing/analysis/interpretation

▶ FIGURE 3.28 The Landsat remote sensing satellite. (*From Earth Observation Satellite Company, Lanham, Maryland.*)

form scan lines; a series of scan lines builds up an image or picture.

An ever-expanding number of fields of study make use of remote sensing technologies. These include agriculture, climate studies, demographic studies, forestry, geologic mapping, land use classification and monitoring, mineral resource exploration, oceanography (see Figure 3.29), resource management, and tectonics. These are all areas of study in this course.

Remote sensing provides valuable information about biomes and the impact humans have on them. Parts of the African continent are the subject of constant research, as drought cycles and desertification cause worldwide concern. Desert ecosystems are extremely delicate and do not recover readily from stress. Increasing demand for livestock grazing land, firewood, and cropland, coupled with changing climate, virtually assures that desert areas will continue to expand. Remote sensing plays a part in monitoring desertification by providing periodic data. These data help form a basis for planning corrective measures. Figure 3.30 shows the kind of display that can be made available to planners.

Technology has enabled us to escape the bonds of gravity and atmosphere. Views of Earth's sphere suspended in space reinforce the idea that despite political, philosophical, and geographic boundaries, the planet on which we live is a single entity. Remote sensing is a tool that can help us better manage and enjoy that entity.

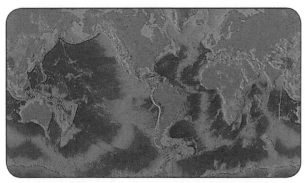

▲ FIGURE 3.29 Topography of Earth generated from synthesized digital databases. Color-coded topographic contours have been overlaid on a black-and-white–shaded relief map to give an indication of both relative and absolute relief. The continental data illustrated in the image were acquired by several methods, including field measurements and satellite altimetry. The oceanic data were acquired using down- and side-looking sonars. The resulting image depicts the topographic relief that could be observed from space if the oceans were transparent. The color scale illustrates altitudes from 7 miles (11 kilometers) below sea level to 6 miles (9 kilometers) above sea level. (*Source: Margo H. Edwards, Raymond E. Arvidson, Washington University in St. Louis, and James R. Heirtzler, Woods Hole Oceanographic Institute.*)

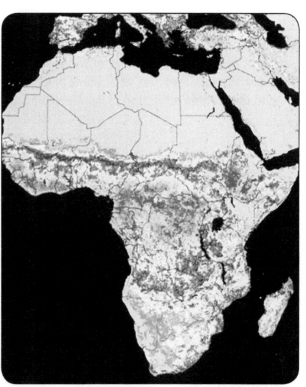

▲ FIGURE 3.30 This map shows vegetation density in Africa. It was made using data from eight 21-day composites. The Sahara Desert of northern Africa is seen to be nearly devoid of vegetation. The rain forests in central Africa show very high densities. The short transition between these two regions is also clearly visible. (*NASA/GSFC*)

3.9 Energy Units and Conversion Factors

Energy is found in six different forms. These forms are all directly related. The bad news is we have several different units for measuring energy in the English and metric systems. The good news is conversion factors allow us to change from one unit to another. The more common energy-related units are as follows:

Apply Your Understanding

What is a conversion factor?

- **calorie (cal)** The amount of heat necessary to raise the temperature of one gram of water one Celsius degree at standard atmospheric pressure.

- **British thermal unit (Btu)** The amount of heat required to raise the temperature of one pound of water one Fahrenheit degree at standard atmospheric pressure.

- **foot-pound (ft · lb)** The amount of work done or energy used when a force of one pound acts through a distance of one foot.

- **joule (J)** An internationally accepted unit equal to 0.738 foot-pound.

- **barrel of oil (bbl)** The amount of energy that can be obtained through the burning of one barrel (42 U.S. gallons) of oil.

- **ton of TNT** The amount of energy stored in or released by one ton of trinitrotoluene (TNT).

- **watt-hour (Wh)** The amount of electrical energy that will light a 10-watt bulb for 6 minutes. One kilowatt-hour (kWh) of electrical energy will light a 100-watt bulb for 10 hours.

Since energy is conserved during transformations, the various energy units are directly related. This means that they can be readily converted to each other by simple mathematical calculation. This is done using conversion factors. The conversion factors used in this course are shown below.

Conversion factors enable us to change from one energy unit to another. Practice making energy unit conversions by doing some of the problems in Activity 3.8. If you need to refresh your mathematical memory (or learn something new), see Appendix 6.

Energy Conversion Factors

$1 \text{ cal} = 3.968 \times 10^{-3} \text{ Btu} = 4.184 \text{ J}$

$1 \text{ kcal} = 1{,}000 \text{ cal} = 1 \text{ dietetic Cal} = 3.97 \text{ Btu}$

$1 \text{ Btu} = 252.0 \text{ cal} = 772 \text{ ft} \cdot \text{lb}$

$1 \text{ ft} \cdot \text{lb} = 1.285 \times 10^{-3} \text{ Btu} = 0.3239 \text{ cal}$

$1 \text{ J} = 0.2389 \text{ cal} = 0.7376 \text{ ft} \cdot \text{lb}$

$1 \text{ ton of TNT} = 1.04 \times 10^{9} \text{ cal} = 4.14 \times 10^{6} \text{ Btu}$

$1 \text{ bbl} = 5.8 \times 10^{6} \text{ Btu}$

$1 \text{ kWh} = 3{,}413 \text{ Btu} = 1{,}000 \text{ Wh}$

ACTIVITY 3.8

Conversion Factors

In this activity, you will try some problems to find out how well you understand energy conversion factors. Record your answers in your science notebook.

DO NOT WRITE IN THIS BOOK.

1. Measure and record the length of the line shown below in centimeters first, then in inches. Divide the length in centimeters by the length in inches and record the answer. (The answer is the conversion factor for changing inches to centimeters.) Answer: _____cm/in.

$$\longleftarrow \text{\_\_\_\_ cm} \longrightarrow$$

$$\longleftarrow \text{\_\_\_\_ in} \longrightarrow$$

2. Use the conversion factor you determined in question 1 to find your height in centimeters.

   My height = _____ ft + _____ in = _____ in (total) × _____ cm/in = _____ cm.

   Other conversion factors:

   1 foot = 12 inches   1 kilogram = 2.2 pounds
   1 yard = 3 feet   1 year = 365 days

3. How many centimeters are there in 10 yards?

   10 yd × 3 ft/1 yd = _____ ft × 12 in/1 ft = _____ in × 2.5 cm/1 in = _____ cm

4. How many inches are there in 30 centimeters?

   30 cm × 1 in/2.5 cm = _____ in

5. How many pounds are there in 25 kilograms?

6. How many calories are required to raise 8 grams of water 7 degrees Celsius?

   Number of calories = (temperature change in degrees Celsius) × (number of grams of water) = _____ × _____ = _____ calories.

7. How many calories are given off when 150 grams of coffee cools from 95°C to 88°C?

8. How many calories of heat will be given off when 200 grams of water cools from 80°C to 20°C?

9. A small solar panel raised the temperature of 4.4 pounds of water 20 degrees Fahrenheit. How many Btu of heat were absorbed by the water?

   Number of Btu = (temp. change in degrees Fahrenheit) × (number of pounds of water) = _____ × _____ = _____ Btu.

10. If 50 pounds of water cools from 85°F to 62°F, how many Btu of heat are given off by the water?

11. How many calories of heat are needed to raise 4,300 grams of water from 20°C to 80°C?

12. If the heating in question 11 is done electrically, how many watt-hours of energy should you be billed for if 1 watt-hour = 860 calories?

13. If 1,000 watt-hours = 1 kilowatt-hour (kWh), how many kWh did you use in question 12?

14. If electricity costs 7¢ per kWh, how much will the kWh in question 13 cost?

15. How many years are there in 1,022 days?

16. A car consumed 210 gallons of gasoline in 2 months. How many barrels of gasoline is this?

17. A large tank holds 750 pounds of water. The temperature of the water was originally 75°F. Because of cool weather, the temperature of the water dropped to 68°F. How many Btu of heat did the water lose?

18. How much energy (in Btu) is released when six barrels of oil are burned?

19. A mover slides a refrigerator across a smooth floor. She exerts a 75-pound force while pushing it 4 feet. How much work has she done in moving the refrigerator?

20. Assume that all of the work done by the mover in problem 19 went to overcome friction between the refrigerator and the floor. How much heat was generated by the time the mover had done 193 foot-pound of work? (Hint: Give your answer in Btu.)

The Second Law of Thermodynamics

3.10 Three Forms of the Second Law of Thermodynamics

The first law of thermodynamics states that energy can neither be created nor destroyed. Thus, we are neither gaining nor losing energy. If this is the case, why should we worry about running out of energy? There's just as much energy now as there has always been!

We know that when we fill our car's tank with gasoline and drive around, we lose something. If we didn't lose energy, what did we lose? The answer to that question is given by the second law of thermodynamics. We will state this law three ways. Each statement will add to your understanding of what the law says. (Mathematics can be used to show that all three statements are the same. However, this is beyond the scope of this course.)

Form 1: *In any transformation of energy from one form to another, there is always a decrease in the amount of useful energy.*

Useful energy is energy that can *easily* be used to move objects or to generate electricity. Modern societies prefer to do both of these things with the major portion of the energy they use.

The least useful form of energy is low-temperature heat. This is heat that is near the temperature of the surroundings. That's why we throw so much of it away. The purpose of the cooling towers at electric power-generating plants is to release low-temperature heat into the atmosphere. Likewise, the fins on gasoline engines are there to help dissipate (dump) heat. The radiator in your car is another example.

Form 2: *Heat cannot, by itself, flow from cold to hot. It spontaneously flows from hot to cold.*

Work (the moving of objects) can only be done when there is a difference in the energy content of objects. When the universe reaches a uniform temperature, there will be *no* difference in energy content. Life anywhere in the universe will cease. This is referred to as the "heat death of the universe." Why must it occur? If people manage their affairs well, how long can humans survive on planet Earth? (The answer is, as long as the sun lasts. The heat death of our sun is expected in about 5 billion years or so.)

Form 3: *In any closed system, disorder has a natural tendency to increase.*

Some synonyms for disorder are chaos, randomness, and entropy. We will use these words interchangeably. The concepts of disorder and of form 3 of the second law will become especially meaningful to you as you do Activity 3.10.

Second law of thermodynamics, Form 1: As energy is used, it becomes less useful.

Apply Your Understanding

Can you think of other examples of ways we throw away heat?

Second law of thermodynamics, Form 2: Heat spontaneously flows from hot to cold.

Second law of thermodynamics, Form 3: In a closed system, disorder tends to increase.

SPECIAL FOCUS

The Kinetic Theory of Matter

The kinetic theory of matter is used to explain how matter behaves. The theory is based on three assumptions.

1. All matter is made of small particles called atoms, molecules, or ions. Molecules are

made of atoms that are bound together in specific arrangements. For example, a water molecule consists of two hydrogen atoms bound to an oxygen atom (H_2O). A drop of water contains billions of water molecules. An **ion** is an atom or molecule that has an electric charge (+ or −).

A molecule is the smallest particle into which a substance can be divided and still have the chemical properties of that substance. If a molecule is divided further, you obtain the atoms from which the molecule is made. There are about 90 different kinds of atoms that exist in nature.

2. Atoms, molecules, and ions are not at rest; they are in constant thermal motion. The warmer an object, the greater the thermal motion of its particles.

3. Moving particles do not lose energy when they collide with one another or with a rigid container.

According to the kinetic theory of matter, a **gas** is made of small molecules that are in constant, rapid, and random motion. The molecules are relatively far apart, so a gas is mostly empty space. That is why gases weigh so little. When a gas is heated in a container, the pressure inside the container increases. This is because heating causes the molecules to move faster, so they hit the sides of the container harder and more often. Pressure is due to particle collisions. At the same temperature, lighter particles move faster than heavier ones do. In a **solid**, particles are bound in place in a fixed structure; the particles vibrate about fixed positions. In **liquids**, these bonds are broken, and groups of particles are thought to slide over one another. Hence, a liquid can be poured (see Figure 3.31).

▼ FIGURE 3.31 The three states of matter. In a solid, each particle vibrates about a central position. In a liquid, particles can slide to new positions. In a gas, particles travel in straight lines between collisions.

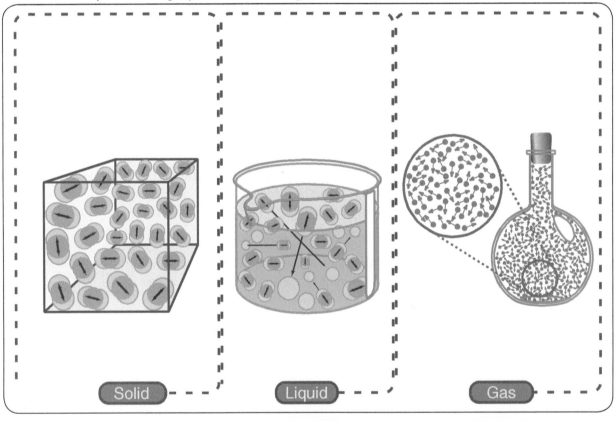

Solid   Liquid   Gas

ACTIVITY 3.9

Examining the Second Law

Understanding the second law of thermodynamics is sometimes easier if you consider a specific situation. In this activity, you will solve three tasks that illustrate the second law of thermodynamics.

Procedure

Task 1 Think about the agony of the heat by examining spontaneous heat flow.

1. Look at Figure 3.32. This engine is enclosed in a perfectly insulated box. Heat cannot enter or leave the box; it is a closed system. The chamber on the left contains a very hot gas, and the chamber on the right contains a cold gas. The axle of the paddlewheel is mounted on bearings that turn with almost no friction. A very small amount of energy is required to turn the generator and light the bulb. To start the heat engine, the valve between the two chambers is opened.

2. Answer the following challenges. Use ideas from the Special Focus The Kinetic Theory of Matter, and from studying Figure 3.32 and reading step 1. Record your responses in your science notebook.

    a. Why does the lightbulb light when the valve is first opened?

b. What do you think happens to the brightness of the bulb as time passes? Explain why.

c. List the 3 things that occur as time passes.

d. What is the direction of heat flow in this experiment? Is this spontaneous (occurs by itself)?

e. List the useful tasks that the energy performed when the valve was first opened.

f. Based on this experimental model, write a definition of useful energy.

g. Was energy lost in this experiment? Did usefulness change?

Task 2 Investigate perpetual motion.

1. Perpetual motion is the theoretical possibility that a machine could be built that could stay in motion forever, once it was started. Figures 3.33 and 3.34 are illustrations and descriptions of theoretical perpetual motion machines. Examine the machines.

2. Use the law of conservation of energy to explain why these machines could not work.

Reference: "Perpetual Commotion" by John Tierney. *Science 83*, May, 1983, pp. 30–39, © 1983 by AAAS.

▼ FIGURE 3.33 A magnet is mounted atop a ramp. An iron ball is pulled up the ramp to a hole near the top of the ramp. The ball then drops through the hole, rolls back to the start, and is then pulled back up again.

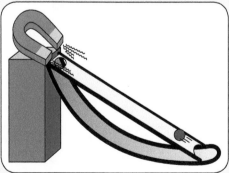

▼ FIGURE 3.32 An imaginary heat engine.

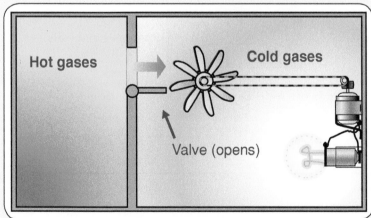

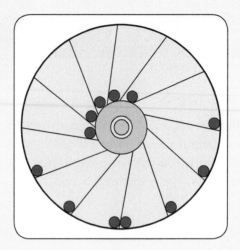

►FIGURE 3.34 This wheel was built with a series of identical chambers. Each chamber contains a steel ball that is free to roll within the chamber. Each ball is pulled by gravity to the lowest level. In the process, the balls on the right cause a downward torque (turning force) that is larger than the counter force produced by the balls on the left, which are nearer the hub. The unbalanced force causes the wheel to perpetually spin clockwise.

Task 3 Examine the natural tendency toward disorder.

1. To relate the second law of thermodynamics to real-world happenings and to understand the concept of energy quality, one must first have a good grasp of what is meant by disorder. Look at the 5 pairs of pictures in steps 1a–e below. Choose the picture in each pair that represents the most disordered state. Record your choice (either #1 or #2) in your science notebook.

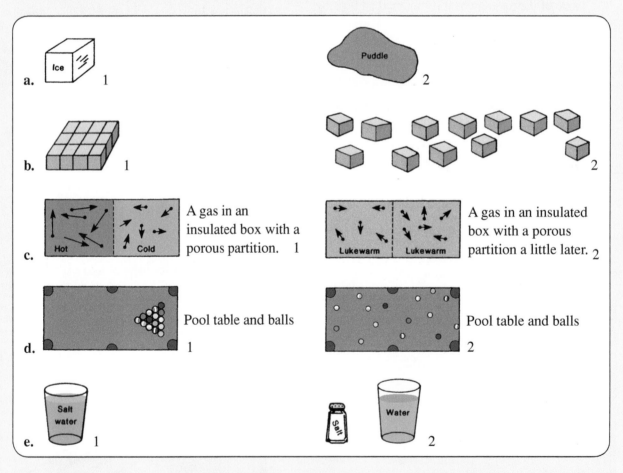

2. Answer this true/false question in your science notebook:

The most disorderly arrangement is the arrangement in which the particles of matter are all "doing their own thing." Hence, the most disordered state is the one most likely to be found.

[Adapted from PEEC Packet: *There Is Enough Energy, So What's the Problem?* National Science Teachers Association, Washington, D.C.]

ACTIVITY 3.10

It's a One-Way Street

In this activity, you will look for order in the world by dumping pennies on the table. If most of the pennies land with the same side up, then that is an indication of order. If they do not, then you have disorder, chaos, randomness, or entropy.

Materials

- 100 pennies
- large plastic can or tray
- access to a tabletop or floor

Procedure

1. Place all the pennies on the tray or in the can with the heads side up.

2. Predict how many of the pennies will land "heads up."

3. Shake the pennies and then dump them onto a tabletop or floor.

4. Record the results of your experiment by writing down in your science notebook how many pennies landed heads up and how many landed tails up.

5. Repeat steps 1–4 four more times.

QUESTIONS & TASKS

Respond to these questions based on your experience and the data you collected. Record your responses in your science notebook.

1. Describe the system the pennies are part of.

2. As the pennies fall to the floor, are they becoming more or less ordered? (See the hint box to the right.) Why do you think so?

3. To restore the pennies to their original state, what do you need to add to the system?

> **Helpful Hint!**
>
> Classification:
>
> 90–100 heads or tails = highly ordered
>
> 70–89 heads or tails = somewhat ordered
>
> 50–69 heads or tails = disordered

Respond to these questions and statements by generalizing from this activity and from your understanding of the second law of thermodynamics.

4. As plants grow, they create order by making CO_2 and H_2O into structured plant material (see Figure 3.35). Are plants violating the second law of thermodynamics? Why or why not?

5. If there is as much silver in the world today as there always has been, why are we "running out" of silver?

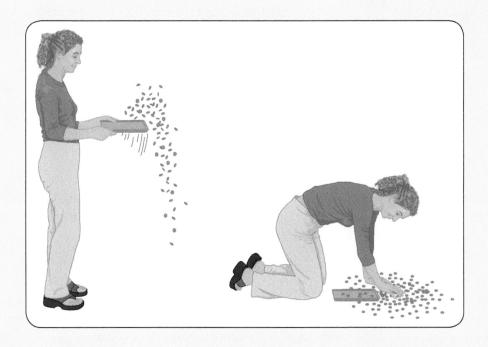

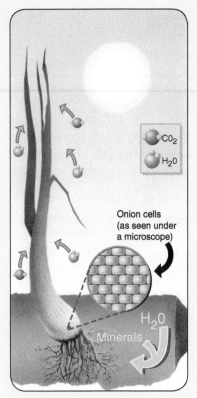

▲ FIGURE 3.35 Photosynthesis implies order. Consider what is happening with this onion.

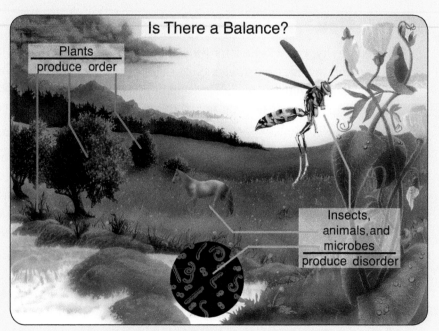

▲ FIGURE 3.36 The balance of nature.

6. Why can't automobile exhaust be easily recycled and changed back into gasoline again?

7. How would you explain this statement: "Little children are truly entropy's little helpers."

8. Iron is extracted from concentrated iron ore and made into thousands of different products, all of which will eventually end up in hundreds of dumps. Which form of the second law of thermodynamics does this illustrate? Explain your answer.

9. Things tend to go from an orderly condition to one of disorder. To reverse this process, what must be provided?

10. Relate the balance implied in Figure 3.36 to form 3 of the second law. Is there a balance in our biosphere today? If a balance is achieved, theoretically, how long can human life last on Earth?

[Adapted from PEEC Packet: *There Is Enough Energy, So What's the Problem?* National Science Teachers Association, Washington, D.C.]

3.11 Energy and Efficiency

An efficient person gets a lot done with little effort. The definition of an efficient machine is the same. The efficiency of a machine is the ratio of the desired output (work or energy) to the input. As an equation, this becomes

efficiency = (useful energy or work out/energy or work in) × 100%

The first law of thermodynamics (the conservation of energy) places a limit on how high efficiency can go. Since you can't create energy, no efficiency can be greater than 100 percent. You can't get more useful work out of any process than the energy you put into it. In other

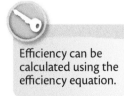

Efficiency can be calculated using the efficiency equation.

words, you can't get something for nothing. In most real-world situations, efficiencies are much less than 100 percent. In industry, for example, much energy is lost as heat caused by friction. For that reason, industrial engineers try to reduce friction. Their efforts have included machining smooth surfaces, developing new lubricants, inventing better electrical conductors, and so on. Though the losses may be small, they are still there.

Any device that converts heat energy into mechanical energy is called a heat engine. Heat engines are important. Some examples of heat engines are the internal combustion engine in our cars, jet engines, and the coal-fired steam turbines at electric power plants. Unfortunately, heat engines are very inefficient.

Figure 3.37 lists the efficiencies of various energy converters. Devices that are inefficient are at the bottom of the illustration; those with high efficiency are at the top. Note that

Think about This!

French physicist Sadi Carnot showed that heat engines can never be very efficient.

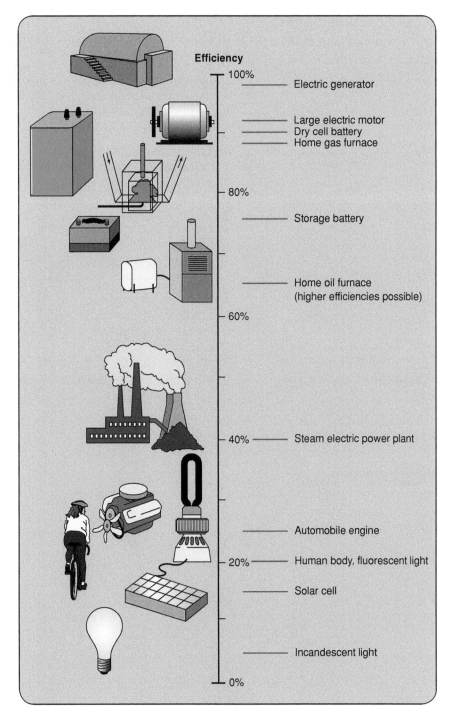

◀ FIGURE 3.37 The energy efficiency of some common energy-conversion devices used by modern society. (*Sources: Xcel Energy, NREL, EPA*)

Energy Flow and Matter Cycles 107

electric motors, generators, and batteries are highly efficient, whereas heat engines are inefficient. Heat engines made of metal must be cooled quickly, which adds to their inefficiency. Devices used for lighting are also very inefficient.

ACTIVITY 3.11

Let's Have Tea!

In countries around the world, people enjoy the late afternoon custom of having tea. This ritual includes boiling water and putting tea in the water. The tea is left to steep until it reaches the desired strength. From a scientific perspective, we can look at this tradition of having tea in a new way. In this activity, you will examine how efficiently energy is used in brewing tea.

Materials

- thermometer
- foam cup
- watch or clock with a second hand, or stopwatch
- tea bag (if allowed in your science laboratory)
- 100-mL graduated cylinder
- water
- immersion heater

Procedure

1. Your challenge in this activity is to determine the efficiency of making a cup of tea. Remember, efficiency = (useful energy output/ energy input) × 100%. Based on this equation, make a list of variables you think you will have to monitor or measure during the experiment. Record your thinking in your science notebook.

2. Read the following protocol for measuring efficiency:

   a. Use the graduated cylinder to determine the volume of water necessary to make a cup of tea.

   Helpful Hint!

   A *protocol* is a standard method for doing something.

   b. Convert the volume of water to a mass based on the fact that 1 milliliter (mL) of water equals 1 gram (g).

   c. Pour the water into the foam cup.

   d. Note the wattage of the immersion heater. (It is stamped on the heater.) Record the rating.

    WARNING

   Do not plug in the heater when it is not immersed in water. It will burn out in about 2 seconds!

   e. Place the *unplugged* immersion heater in the cup of water and take an initial temperature reading of the water (see Figure 3.38). Record the temperature.

▼ FIGURE 3.38 Experimental setup to take initial temperature reading of water.

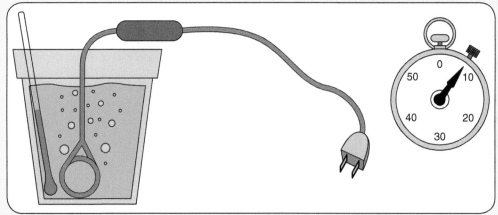

f. Plug in the immersion heater and begin timing.

g. Time how long it takes the water to reach 80°C. Unplug the heater. Record the time and final temperature.

h. After the unplugged heater has cooled down (to about 60°C) remove it from the water and place it on a paper towel.

3. Compare the variables you listed in step 1 to the protocol in step 2. Does this protocol allow you to collect the data you need? If so, you can use it as stated. If not, adjust the protocol to fit your needs. Ask your teacher to check your revised protocol.

4. Use the protocol in step 2 or your revised protocol to collect the data you need to measure efficiency.

5. Use the data you collect to determine the efficiency of heating water for tea. These ideas and equations may be helpful:

- Efficiency = (useful energy output/energy input) × 100%.

- Energy input can be determined by knowing that electrical energy is converted into heat according to this equation: 1Wh = 860 cal.

- Useful energy output can be determined by knowing that 1 cal is the amount of heat required to raise the temperature of 1 g water 1°C.

QUESTIONS & TASKS

After you have calculated the efficiency of making tea, answer these questions. Record your responses in your science notebook.

1. A completely efficient system has no loss of energy. If your system was not completely efficient, where do you think the lost energy went?

2. How could you increase the efficiency of your tea-making system?

3. What would it take to have a completely efficient system?

4. Would you rate this system of making tea as efficient or inefficient?

5. Based on your rating of this system of making tea, explain why tea is commonly made this way.

QUESTIONS & TASKS

Record your responses in your science notebook.

1. Why can't the efficiency of a device be over 100 percent?

2. Why are the items at the top of Figure 3.37 more efficient than those placed at the bottom?

3. Why are steam (electric) power plants, automobile engines, and incandescent lightbulbs so inefficient?

4. Why do energy systems become more inefficient as more steps are added?

5. If the energy input of a system is 50 cal and the output is 25 cal, what is the system efficiency?

6. If the average adult eats 3,000 kilocalories (kcal) of food per day and is capable of doing 150,000 ft · lb of work in a day, how efficient is the average adult?

Efficiency can't be more than 100 percent.

Energy Systems and Strategies

In modern societies, energy is usually not used in one or two simple steps. Gone are the days when large numbers of people would go out and chop wood, carry it to the house, and then burn it in a metal stove or fireplace. Today, we pay a power company to drill for natural gas, purify it, and then pump it through a vast pipeline network to the furnace in our home. Even making something as simple as toast requires many steps. Farmers must first plant, fertilize, and harvest grain. The grain must then be shipped, stored, and ground, and the resulting flour hauled to a bakery. At the bakery, the flour is made into dough that is baked into a loaf, packaged, and then shipped to a supermarket. Consumers buy the loaves and take them to make toast. The energy to power the farm equipment, trucks, and cars, and the electricity to power the toaster are also produced in systems composed of many steps.

A **system**, in this case, is a series of steps designed to produce a useful product or service. This way of doing things has both advantages and problems.

3.12 System Efficiency

Let's examine the system for lighting an incandescent lightbulb using energy that originally comes from coal. Refer to Figure 3.39 often as you read the next four paragraphs. The numbers in parentheses refer to the related sections of the figure.

Coal that is mined contains a certain amount of energy, but energy was used to mine the coal. This energy must be counted as part of the input. After washing and sorting, the coal must be transported to the power plant. It takes energy to transport coal. This must be added to the input side of the record. Coal (1) is burned in the furnace (2) at the electric power plant. The heat produced is used to create steam. The steam (3) turns a turbine, which turns the generator (4). Each of these conversion steps has its own efficiency. In the end, only about one-third of the energy of the coal at the plant appears as electrical energy (6). The other two-thirds is wasted as heat. The heat goes up the stack (5) with the hot exhaust gases or into the cooling tower (7).

Turbines won't work unless the pressure is high where the steam goes in, and low where it leaves. Without this pressure difference, the steam could not act on the turbine blades.

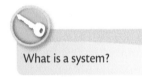

What is a system?

Content Clue

See Chapter 12, section 12.4, Energy Conversion Technologies, for information on another option called cogeneration, which helps boost overall efficiency.

►FIGURE 3.39 A coal-fired electric power-generating plant. (Diagram is not drawn to scale, and not all systems are shown.) *(National Coal Association)*

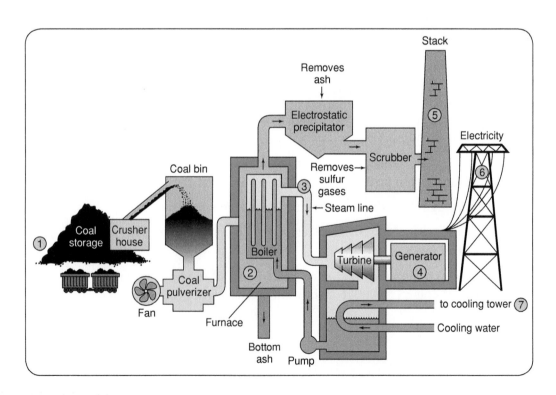

To create this difference, the steam-escape side of the turbine must be cooled. The cooling water both condenses steam and carries heat away. It is this heat that utilities (electric power plants) release into the environment (air, lakes, or rivers). Some energy is used internally for running the plant and the pollution control devices, or for other functions.

Next, the electrical energy must be transported over high-voltage transmission lines (6) and a lower-voltage distribution system. It must flow through transformers to step the voltage up or down. Energy is lost in transmission as it heats up the conductors and disappears into the surroundings.

At long last, the remaining energy arrives at the lamp. Figure 3.40 illustrates the whole process from generating plant to your home. At the lamp, most of the energy is lost in the process of heating the lamp filament to give off light. Only 5 percent of the energy that enters the lightbulb is actually converted to visible light. This means only 5 percent of the energy that goes into the bulb lights up the room. This light energy is finally absorbed by objects and converted into heat.

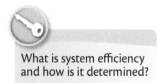

We described this process to make a point. The efficiency of the process of using energy to obtain light does not depend just on the efficiency of the final conversion. Instead, it depends on the efficiency of each step of the flow. The cumulative efficiency of the whole process is called the **system efficiency**. System efficiency is the real measure of how efficiently we are using our energy sources. In the case of lighting the incandescent bulb, it is only 1.3 percent.

What is system efficiency and how is it determined?

The concept of system efficiency is very important in understanding the energy problem. Many of our energy conversion processes require several steps. To produce electricity, for example, we usually mine, crush, and transport coal. We then burn it to turn a turbine, which turns a generator. Finally, the electricity must be brought to our homes by wires. There it is transformed to some end use, such as lighting a bulb.

At each conversion of energy along the energy's path, some energy is "lost" in the form of waste heat. This waste heat is discharged into the atmosphere or into our rivers and lakes by the electric utility plants. Waste heat is given off by the wires that carry electricity, lost through our poorly insulated houses and commercial buildings, lost by inefficient furnaces, and lost to the atmosphere by the inefficient engines of our automobiles. In each conversion

▼ FIGURE 3.40 The generation, transmission, and distribution of electricity. (*Adapted from* Coal in Your World, *National Coal Association.*)

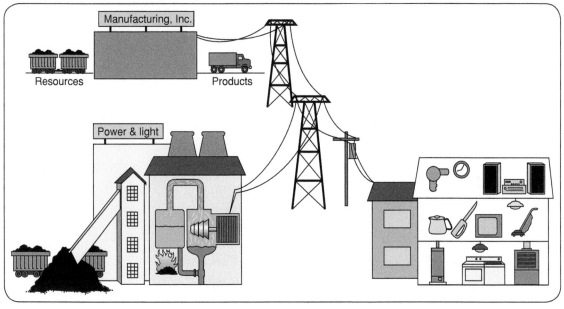

of energy in a multistep process, a "heat tax" must be paid because some of the energy is lost to future use. As a result, the overall system efficiency is equal to the *product* of the efficiencies of the various steps in the process (see Figures 3.41 and 3.42 for examples).

▼ **FIGURE 3.41** Energy system efficiency of the automobile. *(Mineral Information Institute; Colorado School of Mines)*

Step	Efficiency of Step (in percent)	Cumulative Efficiency (in percent)
Production of crude oil	96	96
Refining of gasoline	87	84
Transportation of gasoline	97	81
Thermal to mechanical engine	25–30	20–24
Mechanical efficiency transmission (includes auxiliary systems)	50–60	10–14
Rolling efficiency	60	6–8

▼ **FIGURE 3.42** Energy system efficiency of electric lighting (from coal-fired generation). *(Mineral Information Institute; Colorado School of Mines)*

Step	Efficiency of Step (in percent)	Cumulative Efficiency (in percent)
Production of coal	96	96
Transportation of coal	97	93
Generation of electricity	35	31
Transmission of electricity	85	26
Lighting incandescent (fluorescent)	5 (20)	1.3 (5.2)

? QUESTIONS & TASKS

Record your responses in your science notebook.

Calculating system efficiency.

1. Calculate the system efficiency of operating an electric car from the original energy stored in coal. Write the steps and their percentage of efficiency; then calculate the cumulative efficiency percentage.

Step	Efficiency of Step (in percent)	Cumulative Efficiency (in percent)
a. Produce coal	96%	96%
b. Transport coal	97%	___
c. Generate electricity	35%	___
d. Transmit electricity	85%	___
e. Charge storage battery	93%	___
f. Operate large electric motor	93%	___

2. Calculate the system efficiency for space heating with electric heaters, fuel oil, and natural gas. Fill in the blanks in your science notebook as you did in question 1. From a total energy use perspective, which system uses energy most wisely?

Step	Efficiency of Step (in percent)	Cumulative Efficiency (in percent)
Electric (coal fired)		
a. Coal production	96%	96%
b. Coal transportation	97%	____
c. Electricity generation	35%	____
d. Electricity transmission	85%	____
e. Heater efficiency	95%	____
Fuel Oil		
a. Crude oil production	96%	____
b. Fuel oil refining	90%	____
c. Fuel oil transportation	97%	____
d. Furnace efficiency	75%	____
Natural Gas		
a. Natural gas production	96%	____
b. Natural gas transportation	97%	____
c. Furnace efficiency	90%	____

3.13 Net Energy

Energy system analysis encourages us to look at each step of the process of energy transfer from source to end use. We need to determine if we are getting our "energy's worth." In this examination, we usually confine our bookkeeping to direct energy input and loss. We take into account the gasoline and diesel fuel used to run mining equipment and transport vehicles. However, we do not take into account the energy used to build the trucks and tractors, or to build the buildings, transmission lines, transformers, and so on.

When coal was mined with a pickax and carried by wagon to a home and stove, the indirect energy input could be neglected. The wagonload of coal had much more energy in it than was used in any of the equipment. This is no longer the case. In the case of coal, a significant amount of energy is used to build the huge shovels and drag lines, trucks, train cars, and power plants.

When we move beyond coal to uranium, we have an even more energy-intensive process to consider. It takes enormous amounts of energy to enrich the uranium in the fuel rods and build the thick stainless steel vessels that surround a nuclear reactor.

Figure 3.43 traces the flow of energy from a coal mine to a home. The size of the circles represents the amount of useful energy available. In terms of usefulness, we pay a significant price for the luxury of having electricity available at the flick of a switch.

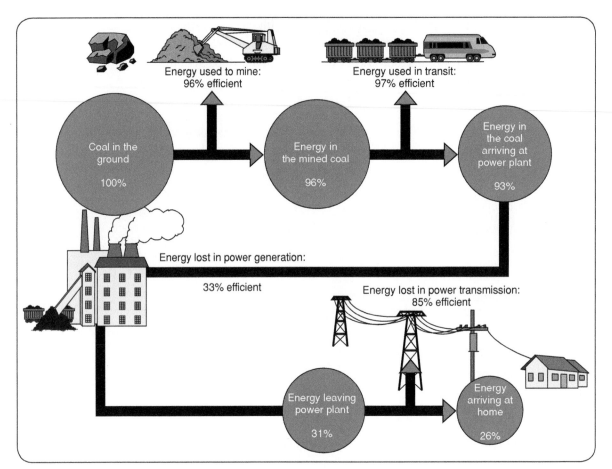

▲ FIGURE 3.43 The efficiency of electric power delivery systems.

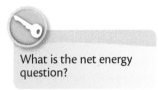

What is the net energy question?

The fact that energy production now requires massive and complex equipment makes it useful to add the concept of net energy to our efficiency measures. The **net energy** of an energy production system is the ratio of the total energy produced over the lifetime of the system to the total energy, direct and indirect, used to produce that energy.

Net energy is clearly a useful tool for analysis. It is of no benefit to us to use a system for which the ratio is less than one. We should also look skeptically at ratios near one, because they indicate we are running in place.

Unfortunately, net energy studies are hard to do because indirect energy measurements are hard to obtain. In the past, we have not computed the energy needed to manufacture a truck, build a power plant, or drill an oil well in the ocean. Such studies are now in progress.

Something to Ponder

Relate the concept of net energy to Figure 3.44.

3.14 The Concept of Energy Quality

What do we mean by energy quality?

Energy quality is an idea that is useful in modern societies. Much of what these societies consider to be the good life involves moving things around (mechanical energy) and using electrical appliances. (Have you ever tried washing clothes on a scrub board?) We consider

◀ FIGURE 3.44 Net energy analysis. *(Mike Keefe, The Denver Post)*

mechanical and electrical energy to be high in quality. Hence, high-quality energy is energy that can easily be used to move things or to generate electricity.

Organized energy is high-quality energy. "Organized" means that the molecules and atoms of the system under study are behaving in an orderly way. Thus, mechanical energy has the highest quality. When a car is in motion, all the molecules and atoms are moving forward— at least in part. Electrical energy is also high-quality energy because the electrons in the wires move in a predictable (nonrandom) way.

Energy quality is also high when energy is concentrated. Gasoline and sugar are ranked high on the quality scale because energy is concentrated in their highly structured chemical bonds. Because you can make steam and cook with it, focused sunlight is also high-quality energy.

Ambient temperature heat has the lowest quality. You can't move things with it. You can't cook with it. You can't even heat with it. Cars and electric power plants are designed to release ambient temperature heat into space. That is why we lose so much usefulness as these devices operate.

The quality of an energy source is a measure of its ability to be used to produce mechanical or electrical energy. It is difficult to rank all sources of energy on a quality scale. A crude ranking would look something like the information in Figure 3.45.

People use energy to accomplish certain tasks. We want to move the car, watch TV, heat the house, and cook dinner. The task accomplished is called the end use. It is useful to rank in terms of quality the tasks (or end uses) we use energy for. That ranking is also shown in Figure 3.45.

It makes sense to match energy sources to end-use tasks. High-quality sources should be saved for high-quality tasks. Using high-quality energy to do low-quality tasks is wasteful, both from an energy and an economic point of view. One can kill flies with a sledgehammer, but much effort has been wasted.

Helpful Hint!

Ambient temperature heat is heat at a temperature near that of the surroundings.

Matching source to end use should be a goal in all energy planning.

Record your responses in your science notebook.

1. Is energy more useful when it is concentrated or when it is spread out? Why?

▶ FIGURE 3.45 Sources of energy and tasks to be accomplished ranked by quality.

Source of Energy	Quality of Source or Task	End Use (task)
Mechanical	HIGH	Mechanical motion (move vehicles, move products, run industry)
Electrical Focused sunlight		Electrical devices (lighting, electronics, communications, motors, appliances)
Gasoline Coal		Heat: T > 100°C (cooking, steam production)
Wood and crop wastes Normal sunlight Ambient temperature heat	LOW	Heat: T < 100°C (home heating)

Helpful Hint!

The mathematical symbol > means "is greater than." The symbol < means "is less than."

ACTIVITY 3.12

Matching Source to End Use

In this activity, you will evaluate two different pairs of source-to-end-use strategies. For each pair, you will select the strategy that you think is the best choice from the standpoint of energy quality. This activity is designed to help you understand energy quality, not economics or technology. Whether the technology exists or is affordable is not the issue and should not be used in your discussion.

Procedure
Pair I

Decide which of these two heating systems is the best choice based on your understanding of energy

quality. Defend your decision. Record your thinking in your science notebook.

1. A home is heated electrically with resistance strip heaters. The electricity is produced at a nuclear generating plant.

2. A home is heated by burning natural gas in a furnace. Natural gas is supplied by a local utility.

Pair II

Decide which of these two systems for use of electricity is the best choice based on your understanding of energy quality. Defend your decision. Is this option available where you live? If not, why not?

1. Electricity is restricted to uses such as powering electronic devices, electrochemical processes, and running electric motors in home appliances. Larger tasks such as heating homes and transporting goods and people must be accomplished by various solar options.

2. Electrical consumption is expanded to include the heating of homes because of the increased scarcity of natural gas. Electricity is produced in coal-fired and nuclear power plants.

3.15 Another Energy Unit

Figure 3.46 shows the flow of energy through the U.S. economy. Since modern nations use such huge quantities of energy, we use a very large unit to describe this process. This unit is the quad. One **quad** equals 1 quadrillion (10^{15}) Btu. Put another way, a quad of energy can power the United States for 3.7 days.

In Figure 3.46, we see that energy enters the economy mainly as coal, crude oil, gas, nuclear fuels, and renewable resources. Some of these sources are obtained within the United States; others are imported. The energy is used in homes and buildings, industry, and transportation. This figure does not show the solar energy that may go into heating a home. We have no easy way to measure such a quantity. Also, this figure does not show how much energy is wasted. This number is hard to estimate. Some experts estimate the efficiency of the economy to be about 40 percent. A thermodynamic analysis of the American economy indicates we could, with real commitment, achieve an efficiency of more than 60 percent. You may wish to learn more about this technical and economic problem.

The quad is a very large energy unit used when comparing the energy use of nations.

Helpful Hint!

The metric equivalent of the quad is the exajoule (10^{18} joules). The conversion factor is 1 quad = 1.06 EJ.

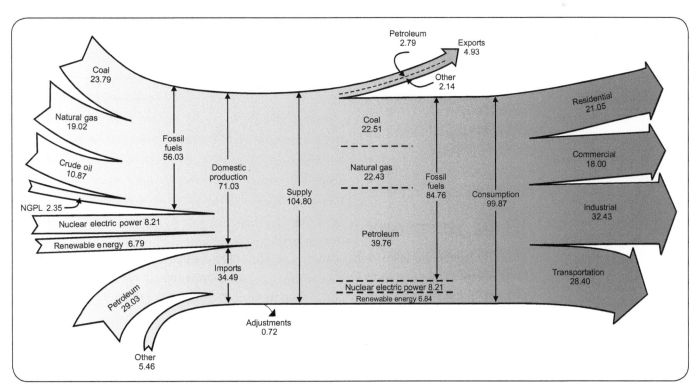

▲ FIGURE 3.46 Energy flow in the United States in 2006. (The abbreviation NGPL stands for natural gas plant liquids.)

(*Energy Information Administration/Annual Energy Review 2006*)

ACTIVITY 3.13

People and Energy Use

Energy use varies greatly around the world. In this activity, you will learn about the use of energy in other countries. You will produce a skit or poster about the way people in that country use energy.

Materials

- resources about energy use
- props for skit or poster board

Procedure

1. Choose a country, other than the United States, that you would like to learn more about and how it uses energy.

2. Research your country so that you can answer these questions:

   a. What are the primary energy sources for your country?

   b. What are the most common forms of energy used in your country?

   c. How does the personal use and the industrial use of energy differ in your country?

   d. How efficient is the energy use in your country?

   e. What are 3 typical energy transformations you would expect to see in your country?

   f. Compare the quality of life in your country to the quality of life in the United States.

3. Think about your answers to the questions in step 2. What would it be like in your country to prepare a meal, travel to school, have a garden or farm, buy food, heat a house or other dwelling, and clean yourself and your clothing?

4. Use the ideas from step 3 to create a short (3 minute) skit about daily life in your country. Your skit should illustrate how energy is used by people in your country, and should illustrate the forms, sources, and uses of energy that are most common.

5. As you watch the skits, use a chart to keep track of key differences among the various countries. Record your observations in your science notebook.

6. Review the information in your chart and write a short paragraph that summarizes how energy forms, sources, and uses vary around the world.

 To learn more about the primary energy consumption per person for various nations of the world, call up http://www.eia.doe.gov/emeu/international/contents.html. Click on Total Energy—Consumption & Intensity. Also see Figure 12.35 in Chapter 12.

3.16 Strategies for Resource Users

In this chapter, we learned that energy can be neither created nor destroyed. It is merely transformed from one form to another. In these transformations, however, energy quality (or usefulness) is lost as matter proceeds to its most probable (most disordered) state. Thus, we don't have an energy crisis—we have a quality crisis.

In an energy-dependent society, it makes sense to try to manage that quality. We also need to stretch out our losses. Instead of losing energy's usefulness over decades and centuries, we need to extend its usefulness to last the lifetime of our sun (or other stars). We need to develop a resource use policy. This can be done in a variety of ways (see Figure 3.47).

1. Change our lifestyles by consuming fewer resources and recycling waste.
2. Redesign our technology so that cars, homes, and buildings are more efficient.
3. Develop new energy sources.
4. Match the quality and quantity of the energy source to the task being performed.

◀ FIGURE 3.47 Techniques for managing energy use.

These are not easy changes to make; they are simply easy to list. The beginning of change starts with awareness. As we become more aware of our actions and their consequences, we fuel the desire to change.

There is no one best route into the future. The path we follow is not clearly marked and understood. Perhaps some of your new insights into the nature of energy and the laws that govern its flow will help you make a more successful journey. We will revisit this topic in Chapter 12.

QUESTIONS & TASKS

1. The U.S. economy is about 41 percent efficient. Where does the other 59 percent of the energy that is fed into the economy go?

2. What can be done to improve our use of energy?

3. List ways that we (as individuals and as members of society) can increase the amount of time high-quality energy will be available for our use.

Understanding energy use and efficiency are key to a clean environment and a stable economy.

Summary

A small number of scientific laws govern our use of energy and mineral resources. We can neither create nor destroy matter; we can only rearrange it. We can neither create nor destroy energy (first law of thermodynamics). We can, however, transform energy from one form to another. There are six forms of energy: thermal (heat), radiant (light), mechanical, electrical, chemical, and nuclear (see Figure 3.48).

As we go through life, we continuously rearrange matter and transform energy. The second law of thermodynamics summarizes what happens in the process. Most human activity results in matter becoming more disordered or scattered. It requires our deliberate and constant action to slow down this process. As we use (transform) energy, it goes to less useful forms. This means our energy supply is continuously losing its ability to move objects and/or generate electricity. Energy ultimately ends up as low-temperature heat and is radiated into space. We cannot stop these natural tendencies, but we can slow them down (see Figure 3.49). In the process, we increase the benefits to be gained from the use of our energy and mineral supplies. Wise use can improve our quality of life (see Figure 3.50).

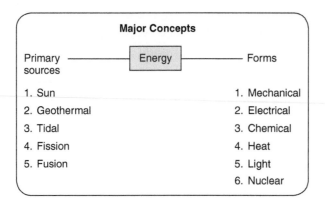

Major Concepts

Primary sources —— Energy —— Forms

Primary sources
1. Sun
2. Geothermal
3. Tidal
4. Fission
5. Fusion

Forms
1. Mechanical
2. Electrical
3. Chemical
4. Heat
5. Light
6. Nuclear

► FIGURE 3.49 The second law of thermodynamics.

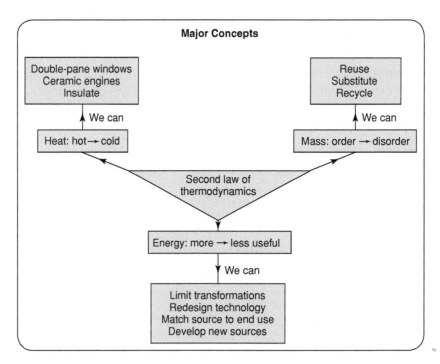

Major Concepts

Double-pane windows
Ceramic engines
Insulate

We can

Heat: hot → cold

Reuse
Substitute
Recycle

We can

Mass: order → disorder

Second law of thermodynamics

Energy: more → less useful

We can

Limit transformations
Redesign technology
Match source to end use
Develop new sources

► FIGURE 3.50 Energy systems.

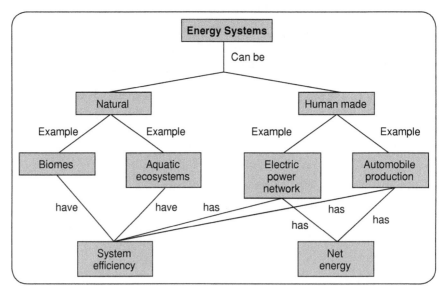

Energy Systems

Can be

Natural

Human made

Example — Biomes

Example — Aquatic ecosystems

Example — Electric power network

Example — Automobile production

have — System efficiency

have — System efficiency

has — System efficiency

has — Net energy

has — Net energy

has — Net energy

120   Chapter 3

Anderson, Victor. *Energy Efficiency Policies* (New York: Routledge), 1993.

Bolin, Bert and R. Cook. *The Major Biogeochemical Cycles and Their Interactions* (New York: John Wiley), 1983.

Hubbard, Harold M. The Real Cost of Energy. *Scientific American* (April 1991): 36–42.

Miller, G. Tyler, Jr. *Living in the Environment;* 14th ed. (Belmont, CA: Wadsworth/Thomson Learning), 2007.

Office of Technology Assessment. *Building Energy Efficiency* (Washington, D.C.: USGPO), 1992.

Office of Technology Assessment. *Fueling Development: Energy Technologies for Developing Countries* (Washington, D.C.: USGPO), 1992.

Post, Wilfred M. et. al. The Global Carbon Cycle. *American Scientist* 78 (1990): 310–326.

Smil, Vaclav. *General Energetics: Energy in the Biosphere and Civilization* (New York: John Wiley), 1991.

U.S. Department of Energy. *Annual Energy Review* (Washington, D.C.: USGOP), annual.

World Resources Institute. *World Resources*. (Annual Compendium.)

SPECIAL FOCUS

A Summary of Principles and Values for Using Resources

As humans seek to achieve a desired quality of life, we use Earth's natural resources. In many cases, this use has caused environmental damage. Sometimes, we have lacked knowledge of how Earth functions; at other times, we have failed to value the wise use of resources.

To lessen the impact on our environment in the future, and to correct mistakes of the past, it helps to understand the scientific principles that govern the behavior of matter and energy in living and nonliving systems. Scientific principles are based on logic and supported by evidence.

We need to make decisions from an Earth-sensitive point of view. That includes knowing and using scientific principles; it also includes making value judgments. Values may change from one generation to the next, or from one country to another. Scientific principles come from the ongoing work of scientists. The values of human ecology, however, are contributed by many people. The value statements below come from a variety of sources—scientists, philosophers, spiritual leaders, and the authors of this course. All reflect concern for Earth and its future.

Energy Flow and Matter Cycles 121

Some of the scientific laws and principles and value statements relating to human ecology are listed below. We will emphasize these ideas throughout this course.

Scientific Statements

- **Law of conservation of matter:** Matter can be neither created nor destroyed, but it can be rearranged. This law implies that everything must go somewhere (there is no "away") and that Earth itself is finite.

- **First law of thermodynamics:** Energy can be neither created nor destroyed. However, it can be transformed from one form to another.

- **Second law of thermodynamics:** Once energy and other resources are used, there is an overall decrease in their future usefulness. Here "useful" means objects can be moved or electricity can be generated.

- **Principle of diversity:** The greater the diversity of a natural system, the greater its stability.

- **Principle of continuous change:** Everything is becoming something else.

- **Optimum-size principle (Brontosaurus principle):** Up to a point, the bigger the better. Beyond that point, benefits may be reduced.

- **Interrelatedness:** Everything is connected to everything else, so you can't do one thing without affecting other things. Humans, too, interact with one another and everything around them.

Value Statements

- **Matter/energy quality:** Matter and energy are more useful when they are highly concentrated, such as in mineral deposits, petroleum, or bright sunlight.

- **Wise resource use:** High-quality resources should not be used on low-quality tasks.

- **Rights of future generations:** Our environment does not belong to one generation alone. It was used by our ancestors, it is used by us, and it will be used by future generations. We must not ignore how our use may affect future generations.

- **Responsibility for pollution:** Every person must be responsible for his or her contribution to pollution.

- **Nature knows best:** In many cases, but not always, nature provides the best solutions to problems of human ecology. (Nature doesn't really "know" anything, of course; it just is.)

- **Minimal change:** In using a natural resource, we should choose the least-harmful method. Damage should be repaired.

- **True cost:** The market price of any product should include the cost of remedying societal and environmental damage resulting from its production and use.

- **Your environment is you:** In the words of Winston Churchill, "We shape our buildings (environment) and afterwards our buildings (environment) shape us."

- **Ideas unlimited:** The creativity of the collective human mind is nearly limitless. If humans understand the laws that govern our ecosphere and live within their limits, human creativity should enable us to live comfortably on our planet for an indefinite period.

- **Equity:** All humans should have equal rights to live in dignity and peace and to have a meaningful existence. Everyone should be responsible for his or her impacts on the environment and resources.

- **Technology—Part of the problem, part of the solution:** Our use of technology, not the technology itself, aids or harms the environment. We should proceed into the unknown with caution.

- **Goal of society:** A major goal should be to live in comfort with minimal impact on the environment.

- **Give Earth a chance:** No national goal, however urgent, no political or economic necessity, however pressing, can possibly justify the risk of bringing all human history to an end. The end of humans would not be the end of the world.

Our technological dependence is strong and widespread. Technology has helped us achieve the highest standard of living in the history of humankind. Technology has also contributed to many of our environmental problems. You, as a student, citizen, future voter, and potential leader, or perhaps as a future decision maker, parent, or engineer, are challenged to use your creativity as we attempt to fashion a better future for the generations to come.

Phelps Dodge Corporation

CHAPTER 4

Mineral Resources

GOALS

- To learn about the nature of Earth's crust and its mineral resources, and how mineral deposits are formed, located, and mined.

- To understand why minerals are important and how to manage mineral resources wisely.

We mine the Earth seeking those minerals that are the foundation of our material well being. We change minerals into those things that are an important part of our world. Used wisely and well, they will take us into a promising future.

—*National Mining Association*

Minerals and Rocks

4.1 Where Does It All Come From?

Natural resources are both nonliving and living raw materials essential for our survival.

It all comes from minerals! Because global science is the study of our planet's **natural resources**, it makes sense to understand what these resources are and where they come from. In this chapter, we will investigate resources that come from the mostly nonliving parts of our Earth. We will examine the minerals that make up the soil and rock beneath our feet.

ACTIVITY 4.1

What Is Your MAQ?

In this activity, you will figure out your mineral awareness quotient (MAQ).

Procedure

Part A: What objects in your classroom have never been alive?

1. Look around the classroom and pick out objects that have never been alive. List on a sheet of paper as many of these objects as you can in 60 seconds (s).

> **Helpful Hint!**
> Good science begins with careful observation. Remember, wood was once part of a living tree.

2. Create a table like the one in Figure 4.1 in your science notebook.

3. Select 5 objects from your list in step 1 and record them in the first column of your table. In the next column, try to list the "ingredients" that object is made of. See Figure 4.2 for ideas.

4. In the last column, try to guess the source of the object's ingredients. Where do we get this material? Give it a try!

Part B: What is your MAQ?

1. Why was it difficult to say where many of these objects came from?

2. How might this activity be different if you had to identify the name and source of all the ingredients of your last meal?

3. How many different kinds of ingredients in the second column could you identify? Give yourself 1 point for each different ingredient listed. Record your score in your science notebook.

4. How many different places in the third column could you list? Score 2 points for each different place listed.

5. Total your score from questions 3 and 4. This is your MAQ.

6. Since many things are also derived from living or once-living plants or animals, they too are considered natural resources. Write a thorough definition of a natural resource in your science notebook.

▼ FIGURE 4.1 Objects in the classroom that have never been alive.

Name of Object	Ingredient(s)	Where Ingredient(s) Came From
1. Window	Glass	A sand or silica mine

Almost everything you use, every day, is made from minerals.

The cedar wood in a pencil is from the forests in California and Oregon. The graphite (not lead) might come from Montana or Mexico, and is reinforced with clays from Kentucky and Georgia. The eraser is made from soybean oil, latex from trees in South America, reinforced with pumice from California or New Mexico, and sulfur, calcium, and barium. The metal band is aluminum or brass, made from copper and zinc, mined in no less than 13 states and nine Canadian territories and provinces. The paint to color the wood and the lacquer to make it shine are made from a variety of different minerals and metals, as is the glue that holds the wood together.

Apply Your Understanding

What parts of a pencil are grown? What parts are mined?

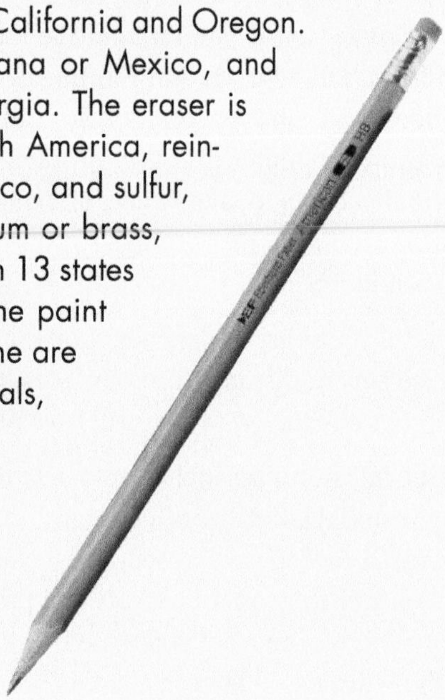

▶Figure 4.2 Something as simple as a wood pencil takes minerals from half a dozen different mines and resources from at least two different continents to produce. *(Mineral Information Institute)*

How Many Minerals and Metals Does It Take to Make a Lightbulb?

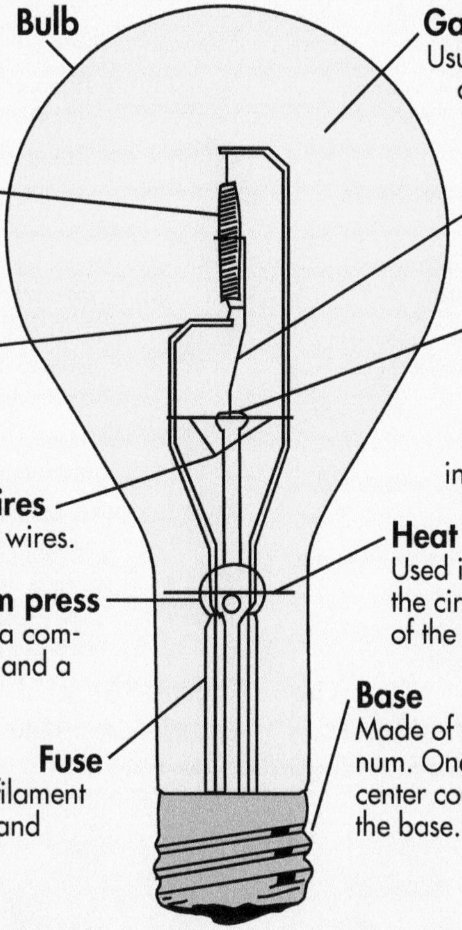

Bulb
Soft glass is generally used, made from silica, trona (soda ash), lime, coal, and salt.

Filament
Usually is made of tungsten. The filament may be a straight wire, a coil, or a coiled coil.

Lead-in wires
Made of copper and nickel to carry the current to and from the filament.

Tie wires
Molybdenum wires support lead-in wires.

Stem press
The wires in the glass are made of a combination of a nickel-iron alloy core and a copper sleeve.

Fuse
Protects the lamp and circuit if the filament arcs. Made of nickel, manganese, and copper and/or silicon alloys.

Gas
Usually a mixture of nitrogen and argon to retard evaporation of the filament.

Support wires
Molybdenum wires support the filament.

Button and button rod
Glass, made from the same materials listed for the bulb (plus lead), is used to support and to hold the tie wires placed in it.

Heat deflector
Used in higher wattage bulbs to reduce the circulation of hot gases into the neck of the bulb. Made of aluminum.

Base
Made of brass (copper and zinc) or aluminum. One lead-in wire is soldered to the center contact and the other is soldered to the base.

4.2 The Importance of Minerals

In Activity 4.1, if you thought the ingredients came "from a mine," you were right. Minerals are mined from holes in Earth; that is where they begin. They end up in our homes, offices, and schools. Televisions, computers, roller blades, and even ingredients in toothpaste are examples of useful products that wouldn't be possible without minerals. In fact, virtually every convenience of our everyday lives depends on mineral resources. The truth is we want these things for ourselves, but often have little understanding of how we obtain them.

Our lifestyles are so dependent on minerals that a lack or even a shortage of minerals would cause severe disruption to our lives. Can you imagine factories without iron tools, homes without electricity, or construction sites without sand and gravel to make concrete?

Mineral resources include a variety of earth materials such as metals and nonmetals, building materials, fertilizers, ceramics, and chemicals such as salt or gypsum. We also depend on fossil fuel mineral resources such as coal, oil, and gas. These natural resources provide the energy to extract minerals and process them into the various finished products we use. For now, we are most concerned with nonfuels (see Figures 4.3 and 4.4). Energy resources will be discussed later in Chapter 8.

4.3 What Is a Mineral?

The best way to learn about mineral resources is to observe them firsthand. After growing your own mineral sample, you will be able to define what a mineral is.

Mineral resources provide materials we need for the "good life."

▼ FIGURE 4.3 Every year, an average 48,000 pounds (21,818 kilograms) of new mineral, metal, and energy resources are produced for every person* in the United States to maintain our standard of living. *(Mineral Information Institute)*

 11,779 lbs. **Stone** used to make roads; buildings; bridges; landscaping; numerous chemical and construction uses

 8,857 lbs. **Sand & Gravel** used to make concrete; asphalt; roads; blocks & bricks

 841 lbs. **Cement** used to make roads; sidewalks; bridges; buildings; schools; houses

380 lbs. **Iron Ore** used to make steel— buildings; cars, trucks, planes, & trains; other construction; containers

 365 lbs. **Salt** used in various chemicals; highway deicing; food & agriculture

 254 lbs. **Phosphate Rock** used to make fertilizers to grow food; animal feed supplements

 247 lbs. **Clays** used to make floor & wall tile; dinnerware; kitty litter; bricks & cement; paper

  73 lbs. **Aluminum (Bauxite)** used to make buildings; beverage containers; autos; airplanes

17 lbs. **Copper** used in buildings; electrical & electronic parts; plumbing; transportation

 12 lbs. **Lead** 75% used for transportation— batteries; electrical; communications; TV screens

 9 lbs. **Zinc** used to make metals rust resistant; various metals & alloys; paint; rubber; skin creams; health care; and nutrition

 45 lbs. **Soda Ash** used to make all kinds of glass, in powdered detergents, medicines, as a food additive, photography, water treatment.

 7 lbs. **Manganese** used to make almost all steels for: construction; machinery; transportation

 704 lbs. **Other Nonmetals** numerous uses glass; chemicals; soaps; paper; computers; cell phones; etc.

 28 lbs. **Other Metals** numerous uses same as nonmetals, but also electronics; TV & video equipment; recreation equipment; etc.

Plus These Energy Fuels

• 1,055 gallons of **Petroleum**   • 7,539 lbs. of **Coal**   • 72,979 cu. ft. of **Natural Gas**   • 1/3 lb. of **Uranium**

To generate the energy each person uses in one year— equivalent to 300 people working around the clock for each of us.

Every American Born Will Need . . .

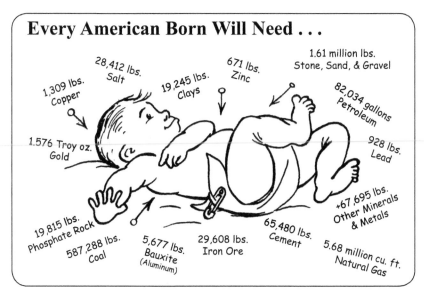

1,309 lbs. Copper

28,412 lbs. Salt

1.576 Troy oz. Gold

19,245 lbs. Clays

671 lbs. Zinc

1.61 million lbs. Stone, Sand, & Gravel

82,034 gallons Petroleum

928 lbs. Lead

+67,695 lbs. Other Minerals & Metals

19,815 lbs. Phosphate Rock

587,288 lbs. Coal

5,677 lbs. Bauxite (Aluminum)

29,608 lbs. Iron Ore

65,480 lbs. Cement

5.68 million cu. ft. Natural Gas

◄ **FIGURE 4.4** Add it up: 3.7 million pounds (lbs) of minerals in a lifetime. How is that possible? Half is for the energy we use to heat and cool our homes and buildings, to travel by car or by air, and to generate electricity to power the numerous things you use every day. The other half is minerals and metals; for example, a quarter million pounds in an average house, 3,000 lbs in a car, and 60 lbs in a desktop computer. Fertilizers to grow your food, recreational equipment, all electronics, paints, plastics, and more . . . think about all the things you use every day. (*Mineral Information Institute*)

ACTIVITY 4.2

Grow Your Own

Although we usually think of growth in terms of living things, minerals can grow in their own way. In this activity, you will grow minerals in a dish and then describe some physical properties that all minerals share. This experiment works best when you can allow enough time for the minerals to crystallize. Remember, close observation is the cornerstone of good science.

> **Content Clue**
>
> Minerals are chemicals.

Materials

- petri dish or shallow pan
- measuring spoon (tablespoon)
- 15 mL table salt
- glass rod or stirrer
- magnifying glass or hand lens
- clamp lamp apparatus
- water supply

Procedure

1. Fill a clean petri dish about halfway with tap water.

2. Add 15 mL table salt and stir gently.

3. Set aside for a long weekend or vacation break, or place under a clamp lamp with reflector.

4. After the break, carefully examine the bottom and sides of the dish. What do you see? To answer the following questions, you will need a magnifying glass or hand lens to help you see the tiny details of what you have "grown."

> **BE SAFE**
>
> Do not taste laboratory specimens.

a. What are you looking at? Explain with sketches or descriptions in your science notebook.

b. Name 3 physical properties (for example, size, shape, and color) of this mineral.

c. The word *crystallize* describes how minerals grow. Can plants crystallize? Why or why not?

QUESTIONS & TASKS

Record your responses in your science notebook.

1. Based on what you have observed here, try to come up with a working definition for all minerals. This is your hypothesis of what a mineral is.

2. Now check your definition with the one listed in the glossary in this book. Write the complete definition in your notebook.

3. Using the following materials, test what you know about minerals. For each one, ask, "Is it a mineral?"

- charcoal briquette
- salt

- fool's gold
- diamond
- snowflake
- ice cube
- sugar cube

What distinguishes minerals from living things?

Topic: minerals
Go to: www.scilinks.org
Code: GloSci7e130

4.4 Mineral Properties: Clues from Chemicals

In Activity 4.2, you probably concluded that a **mineral** is defined as a solid, nonliving substance that has a crystal form. What you can't see, however, is the internal structure of a mineral—that is, its chemicals and how they are arranged. Some minerals, such as gold, are composed entirely of only one kind of chemical or element. Most minerals, such as halite and quartz, consist of two or more elements that are combined in constant proportions—much like the repetitive arrangement of bricks in a wall. Figure 4.5 shows the crystal shapes of three different minerals. The structure determines a mineral's properties such

▼FIGURE 4.5 Minerals with differing internal structure and, therefore, differing crystal form. How does the inner chemical structure of these minerals affect their outward properties? *(Photographs by Mineral Information Institute/Gary Raham, Biostration.)*

Gold   Halite   Quartz

as its color, crystal form, cleavage, fracture, and hardness. How do we know this? Salt, or the mineral halite, gives us some clues.

Halite's cubic crystal structure reflects the orderly nature of its smallest chemical parts—its atoms and molecules. This structure is not random; rather, it is highly ordered. The structure controls the shape of its crystals. These molecules are made of the elements sodium (Na^+) and chlorine (Cl^-) bonded together in a regular, repeating pattern that forms a simple cube. Halite's cubic structure is always the same no matter where we find it. The tiniest grain of salt from your salt shaker has the same cubic crystal shape as a 2-ton boulder excavated from a mine. That's because the "recipe" for any mineral is the same no matter where the mineral formed or how long it has existed. Salt, like all minerals, contains an orderly arrangement of atoms. This accounts for its distinct physical and chemical properties. Examine Figure 4.6 for descriptions of common mineral properties.

Helpful Hint!

A *crystal* is a solid form of a substance whose atoms are arranged in a definite pattern. In this pattern, the outer surfaces are plane faces in a symmetrical arrangement.

Minerals with such beautiful forms, as shown in Figure 4.5, are difficult to find. Why? One reason is that both **physical weathering** (such as caused by gravity and running water) and **chemical weathering** (such as through dissolving or oxidation) wear down the sharp edges of mineral crystals when they are exposed at the surface. Even when we do find unweathered minerals, it is rare to find perfectly formed crystal faces. This is because growing minerals often crowd one another as they crystallize.

▼ FIGURE 4.6 Physical and chemical properties of minerals. *(Photographs by Mineral Information Institute/Gary Raham, Biostration.)*

Mineral Properties

Mineral Property	Reason	Example	Photo
Color (physical)	Reflects chemical composition of mineral	Quartz's many colored varieties reflect the presence of trace impurities.	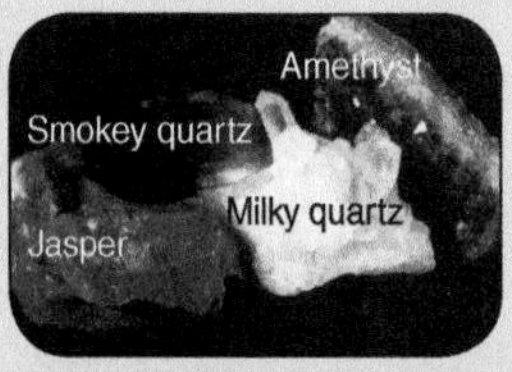 Varieties of quartz
Crystal form (physical)	Reflects internal arrangement of atoms	Pyrite and halite are cubic because their molecules form cubic lattices. Calcite is rhombohedral because its molecules form unit rhombs.	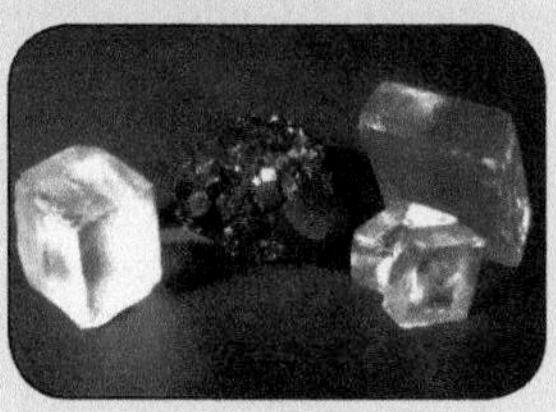 Different crystals
Hardness (physical)	Reflects internal structure and strength of bonds between atoms	Quartz (hardness = 7), which is harder than glass (hardness = 6), can scratch gypsum (hardness = 2.5).	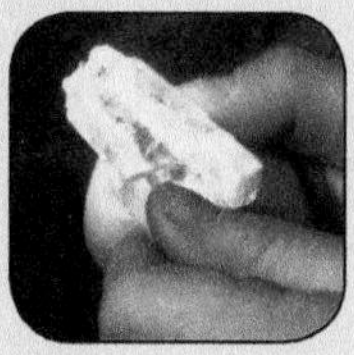 Gypsum

(continued)

Mineral Properties (continued)

Mineral Property	Reason	Example	Photo
Cleavage (physical)	Tendency of a mineral to break in a preferred direction because of its internal arrangement of atoms; not the same as crystal face	Muscovite (mica) peels apart along a well-defined cleavage plane. Potassium feldspar has three good cleavage directions. Fluorite has four cleavage directions. Quartz has no cleavage, and breaks along irregular surfaces called fractures. Be careful not to confuse cleavage with crystal faces.	Mica — Quartz with fracture/crystal — Feldspar — Fluorite
Streak (physical)	Reflects chemical composition of mineral	Hematite's streak always powders red because of the presence of Fe_2O_3 iron oxide (natural rust).	Red streak with hematite
Luster (physical)	Quality of reflected light from a mineral's surface; depends on composition of mineral	Pyrite and lead (galena) have metallic lusters; feldspar and quartz have nonmetallic lusters; and hematite has a rusty luster.	Pyrite and galena
Density or heft (physical)	Reflects density or "heaviness" of mineral	Gold's density is 19.3 g/cm³; quartz is only 2.6 g/cm³.	Gold — Quartz
Solubility (chemical)	Ability of a mineral to dissolve in natural solvents such as water in lakes, rivers, oceans, or groundwater	Salt or halite dissolves in pure water; calcite dissolves in the presence of weak acids such as hydrochloric or carbonic acid.	Fizzing calcite

What Mineral Is It?

In this activity, you will identify common rock-forming minerals by using their distinct physical and chemical properties.

Background

With about 3,000 different kinds of minerals, which ones are worth learning about? Fortunately, almost any rock you find will contain one or more of the minerals you will investigate in this activity. These are the **rock-forming minerals** because every rock contains at least one or more of these minerals. In fact, of the thousands of minerals that are known to exist in nature, only 20 common minerals make up 95 percent of Earth's crust. The remaining minerals are referred to as rare minerals.

> **Content Clue**
>
> Minerals are the ingredients of rocks.

Once you've been introduced to the most common minerals, you will find it easy to recognize them wherever you go. Valuable minerals, gems, and metals can also be identified using the techniques you learn in this activity.

Materials (for each lab station)

- basic mineral collection containing some or all minerals listed in Figure 4.8
- streak plate
- dilute HCl (about 10%–15% solution)

> **WARNING**
>
> Dilute hydrochloric acid can be dangerous. If you spill any on yourself, wash immediately and thoroughly with water. Tell your teacher. Be sure you are wearing your safety goggles.

- dull knife (or nail)
- hand lens or magnifying glass
- copper coin
- safety goggles
- glass plate

Procedure

Located at each lab table is a collection of numbered minerals. Your task is to identify each of the minerals and record its number on a chart in your science notebook. Your teacher will specify how many specimens you will identify and how you should record your answers. The table in Figure 4.7 is a sample of how you can record your information. Make sure you study the reference specimens and photos your teacher makes available during this lab. Refer to Figure 4.6 to review the various mineral properties and what they tell you about the specimen you are identifying. To begin, use the identification key "What Mineral Is It?" in Figure 4.8 to complete the following steps:

1. Examine 1 mineral at a time. Follow the flowchart in the What Mineral Is It? key (Figure 4.8). Begin by noting the color of the mineral and then continue.

2. If the mineral is light colored, proceed by testing the specimen's hardness.

3. If the specimen is dark colored, determine its luster before moving on. You may have some difficulty making choices. That's okay. Science works best

> **Helpful Hint!**
>
> Remember, the symbol < means "is less than," and the symbol > means "is greater than."

▼ FIGURE 4.7 Sample table for mineral identification.

Sample No.	Mineral Name	Color	Hardness	Cleavage	Luster	Interesting Facts
	Gypsum	White to clear	< Fingernail	One direction	Pearly	Fine, fibrous to bladed crystals

when your new observations help you reevaluate your initial decisions.

4. Continue testing for other properties such as presence of cleavage, crystal form, streak, or reaction with dilute HCl acid. Ask your teacher for help if you get stuck.

5. After each mineral is identified and your table is complete, check the accuracy of your work and turn it in.

Helpful Hint!

Color is helpful, but can be misleading. Be sure to rely on other physical properties as well.

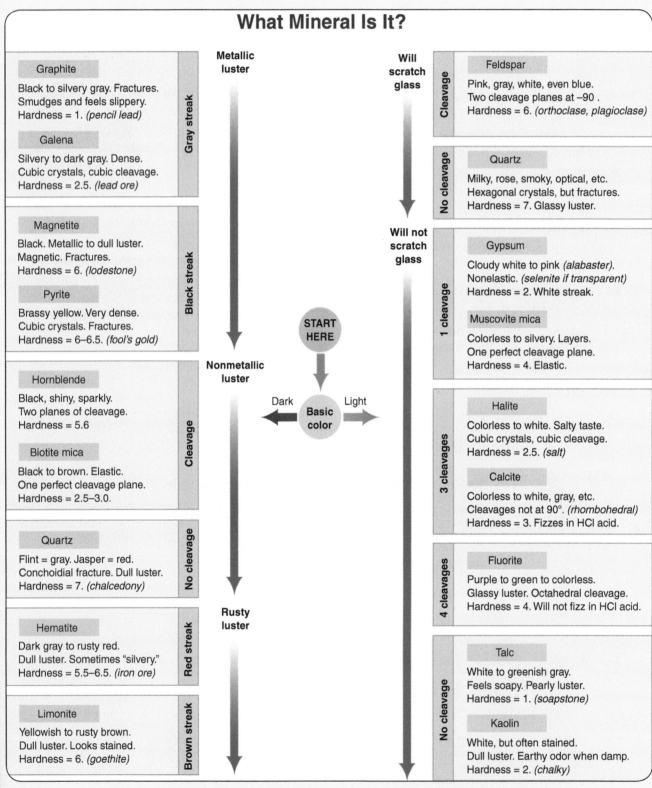

What Mineral Is It?

Metallic luster

Gray streak

Graphite
Black to silvery gray. Fractures. Smudges and feels slippery. Hardness = 1. *(pencil lead)*

Galena
Silvery to dark gray. Dense. Cubic crystals, cubic cleavage. Hardness = 2.5. *(lead ore)*

Black streak

Magnetite
Black. Metallic to dull luster. Magnetic. Fractures. Hardness = 6. *(lodestone)*

Pyrite
Brassy yellow. Very dense. Cubic crystals. Fractures. Hardness = 6–6.5. *(fool's gold)*

Nonmetallic luster

Cleavage

Hornblende
Black, shiny, sparkly. Two planes of cleavage. Hardness = 5.6

Biotite mica
Black to brown. Elastic. One perfect cleavage plane. Hardness = 2.5–3.0.

No cleavage

Quartz
Flint = gray. Jasper = red. Conchoidial fracture. Dull luster. Hardness = 7. *(chalcedony)*

Red streak

Hematite
Dark gray to rusty red. Dull luster. Sometimes "silvery." Hardness = 5.5–6.5. *(iron ore)*

Brown streak

Limonite
Yellowish to rusty brown. Dull luster. Looks stained. Hardness = 6. *(goethite)*

START HERE

Basic color

Dark ← → Light

Rusty luster

Will scratch glass

Cleavage

Feldspar
Pink, gray, white, even blue. Two cleavage planes at –90 . Hardness = 6. *(orthoclase, plagioclase)*

No cleavage

Quartz
Milky, rose, smoky, optical, etc. Hexagonal crystals, but fractures. Hardness = 7. Glassy luster.

Will not scratch glass

1 cleavage

Gypsum
Cloudy white to pink *(alabaster)*. Nonelastic. *(selenite if transparent)* Hardness = 2. White streak.

Muscovite mica
Colorless to silvery. Layers. One perfect cleavage plane. Hardness = 4. Elastic.

3 cleavages

Halite
Colorless to white. Salty taste. Cubic crystals, cubic cleavage. Hardness = 2.5. *(salt)*

Calcite
Colorless to white, gray, etc. Cleavages not at 90°. *(rhombohedral)* Hardness = 3. Fizzes in HCl acid.

4 cleavages

Fluorite
Purple to green to colorless. Glassy luster. Octahedral cleavage. Hardness = 4. Will not fizz in HCl acid.

No cleavage

Talc
White to greenish gray. Feels soapy. Pearly luster. Hardness = 1. *(soapstone)*

Kaolin
White, but often stained. Dull luster. Earthy odor when damp. Hardness = 2. *(chalky)*

▲ **FIGURE 4.8** Mineral identification key, including 18 common rock-forming minerals. *(Adapted from Scott Resources, Inc.)*

4.5 Rocks: The Solid Materials of Earth's Crust

In section 4.4, we learned that relatively few kinds of minerals make up most of the rocks on Earth. Since **rocks** are made of minerals, identifying rocks involves deciding what mineral or group of minerals the rocks contain (see Figure 4.9). To determine the uses of a rock, we must be able to identify the minerals that make up that rock.

Let's look at an example. The mineral gold (Au) sometimes occurs naturally in a form called "native gold." The mineral gold is in its most basic form as a single uncombined **element**. More commonly though, gold is found as a trace ingredient in one of several kinds of rocks.

To find gold or any other economic mineral, geologists must be able to accurately describe the rocks that contain the mineral they are looking for. All rocks can be classified into one of three types. The three types are *igneous, sedimentary*, and *metamorphic*.

Deciding if a rock is igneous, metamorphic, or sedimentary requires scientific detective work—much like the process you undertook in identifying minerals. We name rocks according to the process in which they formed.

Igneous Rock

Igneous rocks result from the cooling and solidification of hot fluid materials. **Magma** refers to the molten material that exists beneath Earth's surface. Molten material that escapes onto the surface is called **lava**.

Igneous rocks are divided into two main classifications: extrusive and intrusive. The cooling and hardening of lava poured out onto Earth's surface form **extrusive** igneous rock. If the lava cooled rapidly, the resulting rock may be glassy with few crystals (obsidian) or filled with bubbles of gas that didn't have time to escape (pumice). If the lava cooled less rapidly, the igneous rocks will display a fine-grained crystalline texture. The crystals in these rocks are hard to see without a hand lens or microscope.

Much slower cooling and solidification of magma beneath Earth's surface form **intrusive** igneous rock (see Figure 4.10). The longer time spans allow crystals to grow to much larger

Distinguish between rocks and minerals.

Quartzite   Granite

◄ FIGURE 4.9 A rock is made of minerals. You can see the minerals that make up granite. Granite is one of the most common rock types on Earth. Quartzite is made of only one kind of mineral. What mineral is that? (*Photograph by Mineral Information Institute/ Gary Raham, Biostration.*)

►FIGURE 4.10 Devil's Tower, Wyoming, is the remnant of molten material that cooled just below the surface of an ancient volcano. The distinctive columns are characteristic of rapidly cooling igneous rock. *(Courtesy of National Park Service.)*

sizes, which can be studied easily. These rocks are referred to as coarse-grained crystalline rocks. Figure 4.11 shows how the mineral gold has crystallized together with quartz.

Metamorphic Rock

Think about This!

Why do flat minerals become rearranged during metamorphism?

Metamorphic rock is usually formed deep within Earth's crust. All types of pre-existing rock can be recrystallized as the result of high temperature and/or high pressure. The minerals are changed chemically and rearranged in a more compact way. This modifies the texture of the pre-existing rock by producing distinct patterns called **foliation**. Foliation is caused by a parallel or nearly parallel arrangement of platy minerals such as mica. If platy minerals are not present, the rock is said to be nonfoliated.

It is easiest to begin studying metamorphic rocks by looking at samples and reading the related descriptions. Carefully examine Figure 4.12, which shows two types of common metamorphic rocks.

Sedimentary Rock

Apply Your Understanding

How do sedimentary rocks form?

The erosion of any of the three major rock types forms **sedimentary rocks**. The eroded products accumulate in low spots or basins, floodplains, lakes, and oceans. Under certain conditions, the sediment becomes buried by additional sediment, which piles on top of the older layers (see Figure 4.13). This deep burial increases temperature (as much as 572°F or 300°C) and pressure, compacting, and squeezing in the soft sediment. Many sedimentary rocks have angular to rounded grains and may contain fossils.

▼FIGURE 4.11 The mineral gold in combination with other minerals. In the right-hand photo, the mineral gold has crystallized with the mineral quartz. *(Samples courtesy of Fred Hart; photographs by Mineral Information Institute/Gary Raham, Biostration.)*

Think about This!

What causes the distorted layering in this sample of gneiss?

▲ FIGURE 4.12 Gneiss (pronounced "nice") has a similar composition to granite (at the left), but its texture is layered. Pre-existing rock, granite, and some sedimentary and metamorphic rocks can metamorphose into gneiss. The close-up view (right) shows schist (pronounced "shist"). Schist is made of mostly mica or other platy minerals. Although the crystals are small, their uniform arrangement results in a shiny surface. Schist originates from the metamorphism of clay-rich rocks such as mudstone, shale, or slate. *(Photographs by Mineral Information Institute/Gary Raham, Biostration.)*

There are two major categories of sedimentary rocks, depending on their origin. **Clastic** sedimentary rocks result from the accumulation of particles of broken rock and the skeletal remains of dead organisms. Over time, these materials become compacted and cemented together. Sandstone and conglomerate are examples. **Chemical** sedimentary rock is formed by chemical precipitation from solution. Halite and limestone are common examples.

Under certain conditions, the spaces or pores between adjacent sediment grains become filled with fluids or gases. In some places, fossil fuels such as petroleum (oil) or natural gas fill these pores. (We will learn about these natural resources in Chapter 8.) In most places, however, water is the most common fluid. Where pore waters contain dissolved chemicals such as calcium carbonate, silica, or even iron oxide, the dissolved chemicals often precipitate out as solid minerals. This forms a kind of "mineral glue" that binds loose grains of sediment into hard, sedimentary rock.

The three major rock types all tie together in the rock cycle (see Figure 4.14).

Apply Your Understanding

Can you hypothesize how the layers in the Grand Canyon formed?

▼ FIGURE 4.13 Grand Canyon, Arizona. Alternating bands of sedimentary rock line the canyon walls of the Colorado River. The majority of minerals contained in these rocks are grains of quartz, calcite, hematite, and a variety of clay minerals. *(National Park Service)*

Helpful Hint!

Groundwater is water that occupies the tiny spaces or cracks in any type of rock. In some places, groundwater is a source of freshwater. Over thousands or even millions of years, groundwater forms mineral deposits.

Think about This!

Why is the rock cycle more like a web than a simple, circular cycle?

SCiLINKS®
NSTA

Topic: rock cycle
Go to: www.scilinks.org
Code: GloSci7e137

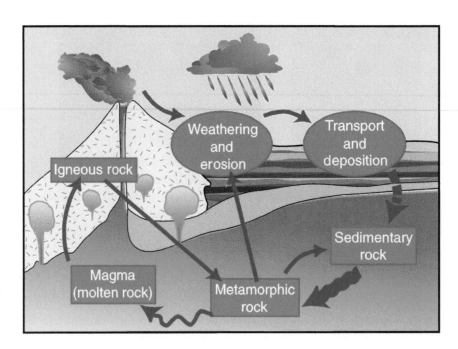

► FIGURE 4.14 The rock cycle represents how the three rock types are linked in time and space. Weathering and gravitational processes wear down the surface of pre-existing igneous, metamorphic, and sedimentary rock, breaking it down into particles of sediment. This sediment accumulates in basins or oceans. The sediment may then be cemented into sedimentary rock, or it may become squeezed, broken, or melted to form igneous and metamorphic rock.

ACTIVITY 4.4

What Rock Is It?

In this activity, you will identify common rocks types by observing textural characteristics and mineral content.

Materials (for each lab station)

- basic rock collection containing some or all of the three rock types shown in Figure 4.16

- dilute HCl (about 10%–15% solution)

- hand lens or magnifying glass

- safety goggles

WARNING

Dilute hydrochloric acid can be dangerous. If you spill any on yourself, wash immediately and thoroughly with water. Tell your teacher. Be sure you are wearing your safety goggles.

Procedure

Located at each lab table is a collection of numbered rock specimens. As with the mineral activity, your task is to identify each of the rock samples and record its number on a chart in your science notebook. Your teacher will specify how many specimens you will identify and how you should record your answers. The table in Figure 4.15 is a sample of how you can record your information. Refer to Figure 4.17 to review the names and descriptions of various rock textures. To begin, use the identification key "What Rock Is It?" in Figure 4.16 to complete the following steps:

1. Examine 1 rock at a time. Follow the flowchart in the What Rock Is It? key (Figure 4.17). Begin by deciding whether or not your specimen has crystals or sediment. You will need to use your hand lens or magnifying glass if one is available. If this proves difficult, start with another specimen that contains larger grains.

2. If the specimen is layered, proceed to the right side of the key.

3. If the specimen has no obvious layers, proceed to the left side of the key.

4. From here, try to determine the rock's overall mineral content (color), its chemical composition (using dilute HCl), or other unique features that aid in identification. Remember to ask your teacher for help if you get stuck.

5. After each mineral is identified and your table is complete, check the accuracy of your work and turn it in.

Sample No.	Rock Name	Rock Type	Color	Crystals (yes/no)	Crystal Size (small/ medium/ large)	Foliated (yes/no)	Sediment Grains (yes/no)	Interesting Facts	Composition
	Slate	Metamorphic	Blue gray to red to black	No	None visible	? Some streaks seen	No	Used for building stones	Clay minerals

▼ FIGURE 4.16 Rock identification key, including 15 common rocks. *(Adapted from Scott Resources, Inc.)*

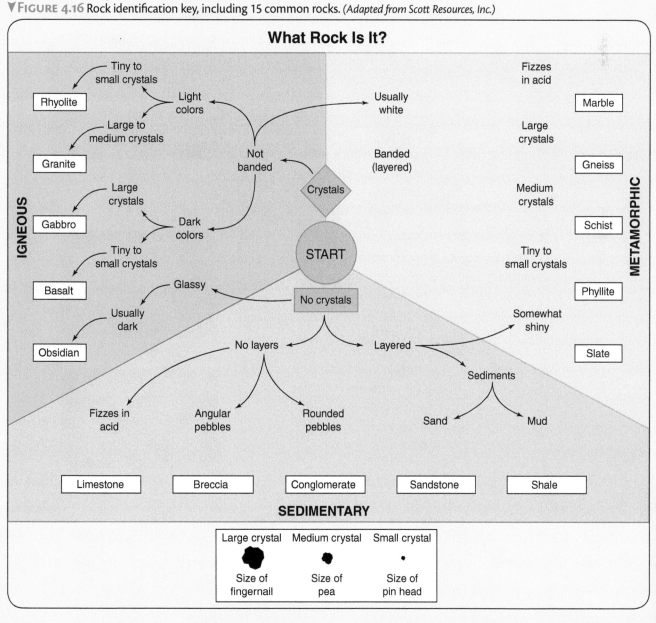

Textural Characteristics of Rocks

Texture	Reason	Example (with photos)
Sediment or fossils	Almost always indicates sedimentary rock. May be impossible to see if the grains are too small.	Large grains are apparent in conglomerate breccias, some sandstones, and in some fossil limestones. Small to microscopic grains such as shale or mudstone may be difficult to distinguish from fine-grained crystalline rocks. Conglomerate Fossil Limestone Shale Sandstone Conglomerate
Mineral or grain orientation	Indicates conditions under which rock formed.	Crystal grains that are strongly aligned or foliated texture as in gneiss indicate minerals grew under conditions of extreme pressure. Random texture, such as granite, indicates conditions lacking directional stress. Gneiss Granite
Crystallinity	The presence of crystals indicates minerals grew by cooling from a melt, from intense heat and pressure, or from precipitation.	Gneiss (metamorphic) and granite (igneous) are crystalline rocks because crystals grew in response to cooling or to added heat and pressure. Calcite crystals in limestone (chemical sedimentary) precipitate as the result of changes in water chemistry. Gneiss Granite Limestone

Textural Characteristics of Rocks (continued)

Texture	Reason	Example (with photos)	
Crystal size	In igneous rocks, large crystals indicate a slowly cooling magma; tiny, microscopic crystals indicate rapid cooling such as in cooling lava.	Gabbro is coarsely crystalline because it crystalizes slowly, deep below Earth's surface. Obsidian is fine-grained because it cools almost instantly as lava pours onto Earth's surface.	Gabbro Obsidian
Color	Indicates general mineral composition for all rock types.	The richer in quartz or calcite, the lighter color the rock. Rhyolite is a quartz-rich volcanic rock. The richer in iron and magnesium minerals (such as biotite, hornblende, or magnetite), the darker color the rock. Basalt is rich in iron and magnesium minerals.	Rhyolite Basalt

Earth's Structure

4.6 A Layered Look at Earth

Now that we have an idea of what minerals and rocks are, where can we find them? The answer is "just about everywhere we look."

On and just below Earth's surface, minerals are extracted from a layer of the earth. This layer is called the crust or lithosphere. On land, the crust may be exposed along valley walls of mountain ranges (Figure 4.18) and road cuts (see Figure 4.19). More commonly, the crust is covered with soil and vegetation, layers of sediment, or thick sheets of ice. Hence, our patchwork view of the crust is incomplete. Finding mineral resources requires a more complete picture of Earth's crust. Scientists piece this picture together by studying rocks and mineral samples from underground mines, drill holes, or caves.

What about the crust beneath Earth's oceans? The oceans cover nearly two-thirds of all Earth's crust. Thanks to advances in technology, scientists are now getting a more complete picture of this once hidden terrain of oceanic crust that lies beneath the ocean waves (see Figure 4.20).

The lithosphere and the minerals it contains represent just the top layer of the entire Earth. Below the crust, other layers lie completely hidden from our direct view. These layers form the hot interior of Earth. They drive the dynamic processes we experience as earthquakes and volcanoes.

► **FIGURE 4.18** Teton Range, Wyoming. Like most mountains, the Tetons are part of a mass of uplifted crust, now exposed at Earth's surface. *(Photograph by Herb Saperstone.)*

► **FIGURE 4.19** A view of Earth's crust exposed along a highway road cut near Palmdale, California. Hypothesize the origin of the rock's contorted layers. *(Photograph by Gerald N. Craig.)*

► **FIGURE 4.20** Computer-generated topographic map of a portion of the Scotia Plate. The southern tip of South America juts down from the top. The Antarctic Peninsula juts up from the bottom. The deep South Sandwich Trench is at the right. *(National Oceanic and Atmospheric Administration)*

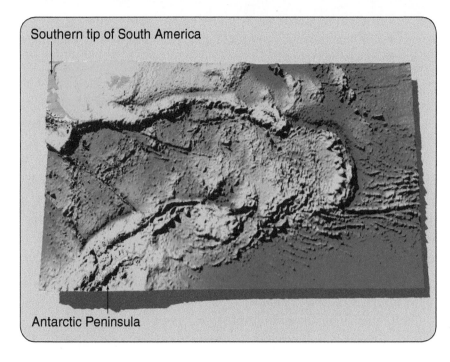

Southern tip of South America

Antarctic Peninsula

To put this all in perspective, consider the fact that currently the deepest hole ever drilled is more than 7.6 miles (mi) or 12.2 kilometers (km) deep. How far into Earth is 7.6 mi? The next activity will give you a more complete picture of Earth's crust and our planet's vast interior.

ACTIVITY 4.5

What's Inside Earth?

In this activity, you will construct a scale model of Earth's interior.

Materials (for each pair)

- 2 sheets of unlined $8\frac{1}{2} \times 11$-inch paper
- metric ruler
- calculator
- drawing compass
- set of colored pencils

Topic: Earth's layers
Go to: www.scilinks.org
Code: GloSci7e143

Think about This!

A model is a representation of a real object or process. Why are models of Earth useful?

- reference materials such as earth science textbooks, encyclopedias, CD-ROMs, or on-line resources (for class use)

Procedure

1. Examine Figure 4.21 and identify the 5 major layers of Earth.

2. Reproduce the table in Figure 4.22 in your science notebook.

Content Clue

The crust is the outermost layer of Earth. It is made up of a rocky, rigid layer between 0 and 70 km thick.

Content Clue

Earth's layers are located by studying seismic (earthquake) waves.

▼ FIGURE 4.21 Cross section of Earth revealing its five main layers.

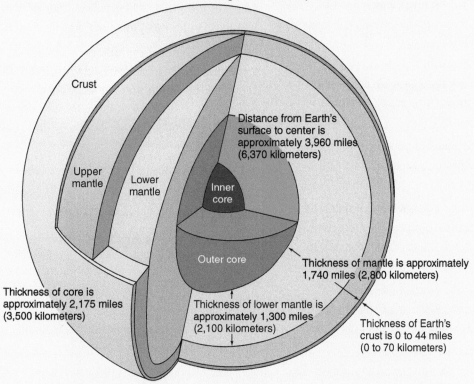

Layer Name	Actual Thickness	Model Thickness	Compass at
Inner core	1,250 km	2.0 cm	2.0 cm

▲ FIGURE 4.22 Sample table for Earth's five layers.

3. List the 5 major layers of Earth (in order) in the first column of your Earth's layers table. Start with the inner core.

4. Fill in the blanks in the column titled "ActualThickness." Use data from Figure 4.21 and a calculator to obtain your answers. (Because the thickness of the inner core is measured from its center to its edge, the sum of all the thicknesses should be 6,370 km. If it is not, recheck your work.)

> **Content Clue**
>
> The mantle forms the thickest layer of Earth, averaging above 2,800 km thick. Hot temperatures and high pressure keep minerals within the outer mantle soft and "plastic" like putty. The inner mantle is believed to be more rigid. Both layers of the mantle contain heavier, more dense minerals than the overlying crust.

5. Solve for the model thickness of each layer. The scale for the model you are to construct is 1 centimeter (cm) = 625 km.

6. Carefully locate the center of your 8.5 × 11-inch sheet of paper. (Each of you should complete your own drawing.)

7. From the center, use a drawing compass to draw successive circles to represent each layer. Complete the column titled "Compass at" to help with the process. Note that the radius of the inner circle will be 2.0 cm.

8. Label the layers on your scale drawing of Earth's interior. Record the scale below the drawing, and write a title at the top of the page.

9. Use outside references to obtain additional data on each of the 5 layers. This might include density (specific gravity), average temperature, nature of material (solid/liquid/gas), and elements or minerals present. Make a chart that summarizes this new information.

> **Content Clue**
>
> The core forms the central portion of Earth and has a radius of about 3,5000 km. The inner core is solid; the outer core is liquid. Both contain dense, iron-rich minerals.

10. Using colored pencils, color-code your average temperature information from step 9. Record your color code in a key below your drawing. Use these colors on your drawing.

11. At present, the deepest hole ever drilled was to a depth of 12.2 km below Earth's surface. Plot and label this depth on your scale drawing.

QUESTIONS & TASKS

Record your responses in your science notebook.

1. What mineral resources could possibly be obtained from layers other than the crust?

2. List some problems engineers encounter when drilling extremely deep wells.

3. Is it practical to attempt to dig these deep wells? Why or why not?

Plate Tectonics

4.7 Upper Crust on the Move

You have shaken the foundations of geology!

—Dr. Harry H. Hess to Dr. Bruce Heezen, on hearing for the first time a lecture about newly discovered submarine rifts in Earth's crust

Topic: plate tectonics
Go to: www.scilinks.org
Code: GloSci7e145

A simple model of Earth resembles a hard-boiled egg. It has a brittle and extremely thin outer layer (the lithosphere) that covers a much softer and warmer layer below (the asthenosphere). But this tells only part of the story. Earth's lithosphere and underlying asthenosphere (see Figure 2.14) more closely resemble the model of a *cracked* egg. Across the egg's broken surface, the shell fragments represent (on Earth) a series of thin, interlocking plates. These crustal plates actually float on and are moved by the underlying flexible asthenosphere.

Why do scientists think this? Because evidence gathered over the past 70 years has opened new doors to our understanding of the Earth—especially its outermost layer, the lithosphere. Let's look at some of the clues scientists have uncovered in piecing together the theory of **plate tectonics**.

ACTIVITY 4.6

Matching Continents

In this activity, you will study the movement of Earth's continents.

Background

Ever since the 1600s when accurate maps of the Atlantic Ocean were drawn, people have speculated about the apparent fit between South America and Africa. The fact that continents were once joined together but have since "drifted" apart is known as the *continental drift hypothesis*. Until the 1960s, no one could explain how continental drift worked. After completing the following activities, see if you can offer hypotheses of your own.

Continental drift was an incomplete, yet popular scientific theory. After World War II, new evidence supported a more complete explanation of "drifting continents"—the theory of plate tectonics.

Think about This!

Why does new evidence give rise to more complete scientific explanations?

Materials

- physical globe or map of the world
- scissors and tape

- unlined $8\frac{1}{2} \times 11$-inch paper (optional)
- Handout: *Partial World Map*

Procedure

1. On the world map or globe, note the orientation of the 5 large land masses bordering the Atlantic Ocean. Then look at the orientation of the 5 large land masses as shown on the partial world map in Figure 4.23. Note that the partial world map shows both the sea level continental boundaries and the outer edges of the continental shelf.

2. Label—Africa, Europe, Greenland, North America, and South America—on Handout: *Partial World Map*.

3. Cut out the 5 land masses. Separate North America from South America by cutting through the Panama Canal and the narrow part of Mexico. This small chunk, which includes most Central American countries, can be thrown away. Separate Africa from Europe by cutting through the Mediterranean Sea and the Red Sea. Arrange the 5 land masses in various ways to form a supercontinent. Cut along either

Helpful Hint!

No continent is to be placed upside down!

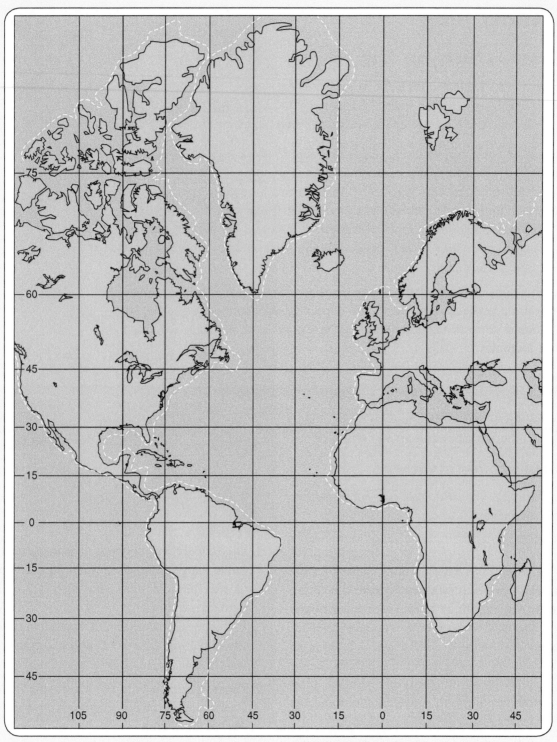

▲ **FIGURE 4.23** Partial world map (Mercator projection) showing present distribution of continents adjacent to the Atlantic Ocean. Dashed lines mark the approximate outer edge of the continental shelf.

the sea level boundaries or the continental shelf edge.

4. After you determine the "best fit," tape the land masses together. Then tape your supercontinent on a blank page in your science notebook or on a separate sheet of paper.

5. Examine your newly constructed supercontinent and answer the following questions.

QUESTIONS & TASKS

Record your responses in your science notebook.

1. Which gives a better fit—matching sea level boundaries or matching continental shelf boundaries? Why might this be the case?

2. How can areas of overlap of land masses (when they are joined) be explained?

3. If land masses were once joined together into a supercontinent, how are Europe and Africa moving relative to North and South America?

4. If the size of Earth doesn't change with time, and if the continents are moving as you indicated in question 3, what must be happening somewhere else on the globe?

5. What modern technology could help you test your hypothesis?

6. Since Earth is not changing in size, only one of three things can occur at plate boundaries. What are those three things?

[Adapted from *Activities and Demonstrations for Earth Science* by Robert E. Boyer and Jon L. Higgins. Copyright © 1970 by Parker Publishing Co., Inc., Englewood Cliffs, NJ 07632.]

ACTIVITY 4.7

Map Evidence for Plate Tectonics

In this activity, you will examine some of the map evidence supporting the theory of plate tectonics.

Background

The study of Earth's moving crustal plates, or plate tectonics, is a relatively new scientific field. Post-World War II technology such as sonar, deep-diving submarines (Figure 4.24), satellite imagery, and deep seismic detection enabled scientists to piece together many previously unsolved parts of the plate tectonic puzzle.

> **Think about This!**
> Technology advances scientific thinking.

Materials

- colored plate tectonic maps (see Appendix 9)

- reference materials such as a physical world map or globe, earth science textbooks, encyclopedias, CD-ROMs, or online resources (optional)

Procedure

Examine the 5 plate tectonic maps in Appendix 9 found in the back of your textbook. Then respond to the following in your science notebook:

1. In 1 or 2 sentences, briefly summarize the theory of plate tectonics.

◀ FIGURE 4.24 Although satellites and ship-board instruments remotely "sense" the details of the ocean bottom, scientists must continue to observe firsthand the nature of the crust and to retrieve samples for study. Here, U.S. Geological Survey scientist Jan Morton enters a research submarine before its launch to begin a research dive. (*Photograph by Randolph A. Koski, U.S. Geological Survey.*)

2. What does map A show?

3. Where do most of the world's earthquakes occur?

4. Where are most of the world's volcanoes located?

5. Note that Hawaii is not on a plate boundary. How might you explain the volcanoes of the Hawaiian Islands?

6. According to the plate tectonic theory, why is the seafloor much younger in the mid-Atlantic, in the Southern Ocean south of Australia, and in the Pacific Ocean about 30° of longitude west of South America?

7. Are earthquakes more common where plates separate or where they come together? Why might this be the case? As shown in Figure 4.25, plates can also slide past each other.

8. The geodesy map (map D) shows differences in the pull of gravity at the surface of the ocean at various locations. Make a statement that summarizes what this map shows.

9. What might cause the earthquake pattern shown in map B?

10. What might cause the volcanic activity shown in map C?

Content Clue

Geologic forces are most active along plate boundaries. Which plate boundaries border California's San Andreas Fault?

Helpful Hint!

More-dense minerals pull harder than less-dense minerals.

Check out these websites for helpful information.
- Rice University: http://www.geophysics.rice.edu
- U.S. Geological Survey National Earthquake Information Center: http://wwwneic.cr.usgs.gov
- Volcano World: http://volcano.und.nodak.edu/vw.html
- Photos of earthquakes and volcanoes: http://www.earthscienceworld.org/imagebank

▶ FIGURE 4.25 Aerial view of the San Andreas fault. Sometimes, plate boundaries are neither colliding nor separating. These transform plate boundaries are marked by faults that separate sliding crustal blocks. (*Courtesy U.S. Geological Survey.*)

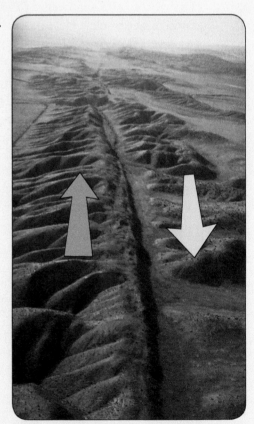

Earthquakes and Seismology

Plate tectonic theory is based on observations and measurements that indicate Earth's crust is fractured into a series of "plates" that have been moving very slowly over Earth's surface for millions of years (see Appendix 9, map A). Since Earth's size is not changing, one of three things can occur at plate boundaries: separation, collision, or sliding. All three movements can result in earthquakes (see Appendix 9, map B). This is especially true when plates collide or slide past each other.

An **earthquake** is the sudden release of energy caused by the movement of Earth's crust. During an earthquake, Earth shakes and cracks, there are landslides, and sandy areas with a lot of water may turn to liquid for seconds or minutes. Damage can be severe (see Figure 4.26).

Earthquakes under the ocean cause tsunamis, which we will examine in Chapter 13.

An examination of Appendix 9, map B will reveal that earthquakes also occur at locations not on plate boundaries. This is because there are cracks and faults all over Earth's crust. Movement of material below the surface can cause stress to build over time. When the resulting stress exceeds the strength of the frictional forces that lock blocks of rock together, the stress is quickly released and the earth "snaps" to a new position. In the process of snapping, vibrations are set up that are the earthquake. The vibrations, called *seismic waves*, are of two types: compression waves and transverse (sideways) or shear waves. Because the compression waves travel faster through Earth, they arrive first at a distant point. These waves are known as primary or "P" waves. The transverse waves that arrive later are referred to as shear or "S" waves. In an earthquake, people may note a sharp thud or blastlike shock first. That marks the

◄FIGURE 4.26 Apartment building after an earthquake. (© *Robert Paul Van Beets 2008, Shutterstock.*)

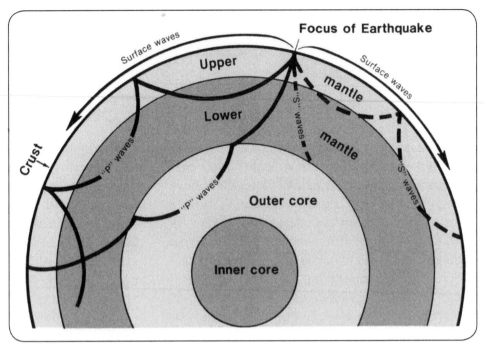

► FIGURE 4.27 Cross section of Earth showing the paths of some compression (P or primary) waves and transverse (S or shear) waves generated by earthquakes. (U.S.G.S.)

arrival of the P wave. A few seconds later, they may feel a swaying or rolling motion that marks the arrival of the S wave (see Figure 4.27). The study of earthquakes has revealed much about the makeup of Earth's interior.

Seismology is the study of earthquakes, seismic waves, and their propagation (movement) through Earth. Seismologists study earthquakes and seismic waves as a career. Their main tool is the **seismograph**, an instrument that measures and records seismic waves. By comparing data from the global network of seismographs, seismologists can locate the focus or starting point of an earthquake. The **epicenter** is the point on Earth's surface just above the focus. Seismologists also determine how much energy Earth releases during a quake. In the past, scientists used the Richter scale, but it is not as accurate as the Energy Magnitude (or moment magnitude) scale. This scale uses a mathematical formula to calculate magnitude. In brief, the scale measures as follows:

1.0–2.0	Usually detected by instruments only
3.0–4.0	Can hardly be felt
4.0–5.0	Generally felt, slight damage
6.0	Moderately destructive
7.0	Major earthquake
8.0	Great earthquake

Seismologists face many challenges. They are continuously developing and perfecting methods to predict earthquakes. At present, seismologists can determine with some accuracy when earthquakes might happen. However, they don't know exactly when one will occur. Seismologists aid the public with earthquake safety: If you are outside during an earthquake, stay outside and away from power lines. If inside, move to supporting archways and inside walls, or get under heavy furniture. Seismologists also work with engineers to design earthquake-resistant structures for quake-prone areas.

Many seismologists work for companies that explore for energy and mineral resources. Their task is to conduct seismic reflection surveys that reveal the structure of the rocks below the surface. A survey consists of generating seismic waves at a source and recording the arrival of the waves at a series of detectors (called geophones) usually arranged along a straight line from the source (see Figure 4.28). The waves travel downward from the source, and are reflected back to the surface from the boundaries between the rock layers. They are then recorded by the geophones, and the

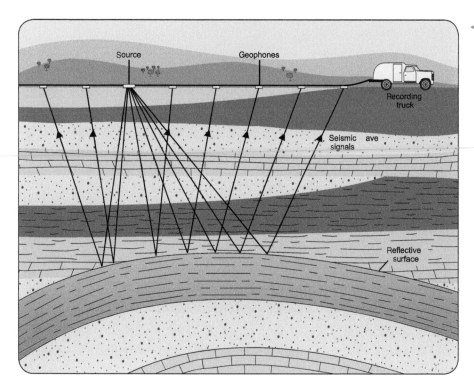

◄FIGURE 4.28 The overall setup for conducting a seismic reflection survey on land. The arrows indicate the collection of data from just one of many reflective surfaces.

information is fed into a software program that creates a seismic reflection profile of the rock structure below. These profiles often reveal oil and gas traps or other types of mineral concentrations.

On land, chemical explosives are the most widely used seismic energy source. A gas-propelled piston that thumps the surface is also used. Most marine (lake and ocean) surveys use an air gun as a sound source. When the gun is fired under water, high-pressure compressed air is released, which creates seismic pulses.

Focus Questions & Tasks

Record your responses in your science notebook.

1. What is an earthquake and why do earthquakes occur?

2. How are earthquakes measured?

3. Summarize the Energy Magnitude scale for earthquakes.

4. List four things a seismologist might work on.

5. If you are in an earthquake, what should you do?

Mineral Ores

4.8 Origin of Ore Minerals

In the last activity, you probably arrived at a number of conclusions about the nature of Earth's dozen or so tectonic plates. Your answers and those offered by your teacher provide the basis for understanding the global processes of plate tectonics. Why is this important?

The theory of plate tectonics explains the dynamic nature of the Earth's crust—especially the distribution and occurrence of life-threatening geologic events such as earthquakes and volcanoes (Figure 4.29). This is the most important reason to understand plate tectonics. But there is another reason. Plate boundaries and the interactions between them provide the basis for our understanding about Earth's vast mineral resources. This is because plate

Plate tectonics helps explain many earth science events such as the distribution of earthquakes, volcanoes, and certain mineral deposits.

► FIGURE 4.29 Mt. St. Helens lies above the boundary between the Pacific Plate and the North America Plate. The eruption on May 18, 1980, blasted away 1,300 feet (400 meters) of the volcano's summit and blew down forests as far as 12 mi (20 km) away. *(From U.S.G.S., David A. Johnston Volcano Observatory, Vancouver, Washington. Photo by Lyn Topinka.)*

Many of the world's most significant mineral deposits formed as a result of the interaction between crustal plates.

boundaries are active sites of heating, melting, cooling, and crystallization—a major source of minerals in Earth's crust.

What Is an Ore?

Everything on and in Earth is made up of about 90 natural elements. Various combinations of these elements make up all the earth materials we encounter. Figure 4.30 shows the percentages of the elements in Earth's crust. Recall that only 20 rock-forming minerals constitute most of the rocks we find.

An examination of Figure 4.30 reveals some startling facts. Almost three-fourths of the crust is composed of the elements oxygen and silicon. Aluminum and iron make up 13 percent of the total. Calcium, sodium, potassium, and magnesium total another 12 percent. Everything that remains is contained in the remaining 2 percent of the total. This includes the elements gold, silver, copper, lead, zinc, nitrogen, phosphorus, sulfur, and chlorine. These elements must occur in very small or trace quantities, yet many of them seem to be in ample supply. How is that possible?

The answer lies in the concentration of those elements in scattered places. A question equivalent to "Who is buried in Grant's tomb?" is "Where do they mine copper?" The obvious answer is, of course, a copper mine! Why? Because a copper mine is a place

► FIGURE 4.30 Pie graph showing the percentage, by weight, of the most abundant eight elements in Earth's crust. Most minerals are made of combinations of these eight elements.

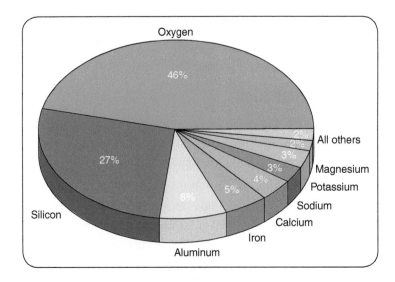

where the amount of copper is far above normal. By weight, the average crustal abundance of copper is only 0.007 percent. This means that 7 tons of crustal rocks contain about 1 lb or about .5 kilograms (kg) of copper. Obviously, no one can economically recover such a small amount of copper from such a large amount of rock.

A copper deposit that is mined is called an ore body. An **ore** is a mineral occurrence that can be mined for a profit. **Ore bodies** are deposits or local accumulations of ore in a mass of rock.

To be potentially profitable, copper must be concentrated at least 50 times its crustal average. Gold must be concentrated at least 1,000 times and mercury more than 100,000 times its crustal average. Any occurrence of a mineral we find in nature might be called a "mineral deposit." However, only one that can be removed at a profit is called an ore. Some mineral deposits that are classified as ores today weren't considered ores a few years ago. Likewise, some considered ores a few years ago are not classified as ores today. This is because the pricing of minerals and mining technologies have changed.

How did copper become more concentrated at some locations than at others? Why was gold concentrated in California, Nevada, Colorado, Alaska, and North Carolina, but not in Nebraska or Alabama? Obviously, mineral deposits are not distributed evenly around the country or the world. They are concentrated in specific places by specific processes. You will learn more about this in Activity 4.8.

ACTIVITY 4.8

Concentrate on Your Minerals

In this activity, you will examine five processes by which minerals become concentrated in Earth's crust.

Materials

- Bunsen burner or electric heater
- Erlenmeyer flask, 250-mL
- graduated cylinder, 10-mL
- graduated cylinder, 100-mL
- ring stand and utility clamp
- 2 test tubes with stoppers
- 25 mL 0.3M copper sulfate solution
- 2 nails
- 100 mL cooking oil
- potassium permanganate
- table salt
- Epsom salts
- distilled water
- 2 beakers, 50-mL
- 3 beakers, 100-mL

- test-tube rack
- petri dish
- gloves
- safety goggles

Procedure

1. Reproduce the table in Figure 4.31 in your science notebook. You will use this table to record your observations of these 5 concentrating processes:
   a. replacement
   b. immiscible liquids
   c. selective crystallization
   d. evaporation from lake and seawater
   e. secondary enrichment

2. Follow the directions in each of the Procedure sections that follow. If you did Activity 4.2, record the data from that activity in part D of this expanded chart.

Mineral Resources 153

Concentrating Process	Observations	Short Description of Process
Replacement	Day 1: Day 2:	Some minerals are more chemically active than other minerals. When minerals come in contact, they may react. In the replacement process, copper becomes more concentrated as a solid on the nail than it is as blue particles in solution.

▲ FIGURE 4.31 Sample table for recording observations of five mineral concentration processes.

Part A: Replacement

By nature, some minerals are chemically more reactive than others. When minerals of differing reactivity come in contact with each other, replacement can occur. Replacement deposits result when one mineral takes for itself the space once occupied by another. For example, as mineral-rich solutions move in carbonate sedimentary rocks, calcite might be replaced by zinc and/or lead sulphides. Petrified wood is an example of replacement (see Figure 4.32).

Procedure for Part A: Replacement

1. Pour 25 mL of 0.3M copper sulfate solution into a 50-mL beaker.

2. Place an iron nail into the beaker. Let the nail interact with the copper sulfate solution for 1 full day. Observe the nail right after it is

placed in the solution. Record your observations. Then note and record any changes on the second day.

3. Place an iron nail in 25 mL of distilled water and repeat the procedure.

Part B: Immiscible Liquids

When shaken together, oil and water won't mix. They are said to be immiscible. Instead of mixing, they separate into two layers. Magma can separate and cause minerals to concentrate in layers.

Procedure for Part B: Immiscible Liquids

1. Place 10 mL of water in a test tube. Add 10 mL of cooking oil to the same test tube. Also add 1 potassium permanganate crystal.

▶ FIGURE 4.32 Petrified Forest, Arizona. Under certain conditions, trees become "petrified" as a result of the replacement of the original woody material with dense, rock-hard silica. Silica, carried in solution by groundwater, precipitates within the pores of once-living wood or bones. Is petrified wood a real mineral? (Photograph by Herb Saperstone.)

2. Cork the test tube and shake the contents vigorously for about 1 minute.

3. Mount the tube upright and observe it for a couple of minutes. Record your observations. Then observe the tube on the second day. You may assume the purple material is a valuable material.

Part C: Selective Crystallization

As magmatic and other hot solutions cool, minerals with higher crystallization temperatures come out of solution first. Often, the minerals that crystallize first, such as chromite, are denser than the solution itself. In such instances, the denser material sinks to the bottom. If these segregated mineral layers are useful to us, a valuable ore deposit has been created.

BE SAFE

Be very careful working around hot plates and when pouring hot solutions. Be sure you are wearing your safety goggles. Report any spills or problems to your teacher immediately.

Procedure for Part C: Selective Crystallization

1. Place about 50 mL of distilled water into a 100-mL beaker and heat until boiling. (Your teacher may choose to provide the solution already made up.

2. Dissolve as much alum (*hypo*, or Epsom salts) as possible into the boiling water.

3. Fill a test tube about half full with the hot solution. Mount the test tube vertically.

4. Record your initial observations. Let the solution stand for 24 hours. Observe this solution the next day and record your observations.

Part D: Evaporation from Lake or Seawater

As you observed in Activity 4.2, some minerals form when chemically rich solutions evaporate. In nature, these dissolved elements come from the weathering of rocks. Streams transport these elements into lakes and seas. During dry periods, water in the lakes and seas may evaporate, concentrating the elements in a shrinking volume of water. Eventually, evaporation leaves behind only the solid material, which includes mineral crystals (see Figure 4.33). Halite (table salt) and salts of potassium and boron are concentrated this way.

The sediments formed in shallow seas are an especially rich source of metals and salts. Two kinds of calcium sulfates, gypsum and anhydrite, are formed in this way. We use gypsum and anhydrite in making plaster. The largest iron concentrations in the world, called iron formations, were also once dissolved in shallow seas and then precipitated as sedimentary iron.

Manganese, copper, iron, cobalt, and other elements are concentrated in mineral form on the deep ocean floor. They originate in hot solutions that shoot out of cracks in the seafloor. The solutions are quickly cooled by ocean water, and mineral precipitates that contain these elements form ore deposits (see Figure 4.34).

Content Clue

Groundwater carries high concentrations of dissolved elements, which can often precipitate out as solid minerals.

Procedure for Part D: Evaporation

- Repeat Activity 4.2, or use your data from that experiment to record your observation notes.

◄FIGURE 4.33 Solar evaporating ponds and mechanical harvesting of salt in the Great Salt Lake, Utah. Water evaporates, leaving behind extensive layers of salt. (*Morton Salt/Jim Huizingh*)

➤ **FIGURE 4.34** Plume of hot, mineral-rich water spouts from a mineralized chimney on the East Pacific Rise. The chimney and adjacent formations build up from dissolved minerals that precipitate around the hot jet as it mixes with the near-freezing waters at the ocean bottom. *(Photographed from the deep-diving submarine* Alvin, *by D. B. Foster, Woods Hole Oceanographic Institution.)*

Part E: Secondary Enrichment Caused by Groundwater

A common form of mineral concentration occurs when groundwater changes a pre-existing mineral deposit. **Secondary enrichment** makes the original deposit "richer" because it concentrates the ore minerals in a way that allows the minerals to be mined at a profit.

This process happens in two different ways. Secondary enrichment occurs when a valuable substance is dissolved, carried downward or laterally, and redeposited in a concentrated form a short distance away from its original location. Selective crystallization concentrated much of the copper at Utah's Bingham Canyon copper mine. Secondary enrichment, however, created the richest portion of the ore. At one time, this mine was the largest producer of copper in the United States (Figure 4.35).

Sometimes, a residue of valuable substance is left behind when other material is dissolved and carried away. This is called **residual enrichment**. An example is bauxite, a mixture of various aluminum oxide minerals. Bauxite is the main source of the metal aluminum.

Procedure for Part E: Secondary Enrichment

1. Your teacher will demonstrate this process for you.

2. Note the appearance of the column each time water passes through the mineral deposit. Also note the appearance of the liquid in the beaker. Record your observations in your table.

Many of these processes are not random. Instead, they take place where Earth's crust is active. Where do we look? What we know about plate tectonics can help.

▼**FIGURE 4.35** The Bingham Canyon Mine, known as "The Richest Hole on Earth," has produced more copper than any mine in the world. Since 1906, more than 7 billion tons of material has been mined, making Bingham Canyon the largest humanmade excavation on Earth. The dimensions of the mine are 2.5 mi (4 km) wide and .75 mi (1.2 km) deep. *(Kennecott Utah Copper Corporation)*

4.9 Ore Minerals and Plate Tectonics

Why do ore minerals tend to concentrate in some places? To understand why, we must take a larger view. We must go beyond individual events such as the cooling of a magma body or the dissolution of minerals by groundwater. In a cycle that spans tens of millions of years, tectonic plates shift, grind, and recycle earth material in many ways. These processes create patterns of change that are detectable by earth scientists. This is a long and complex process. It may help to think of this process as a never-ending cycle highlighted by three kinds of events. (See the websites listed at the end of this chapter for help with some of these terms.)

The formation of many ores is not a random process. How can plate tectonics explain this?

1. Mid-ocean **rifting** and **seafloor spreading** results in an overall "thinning" of Earth's lithosphere (crust). During this event, some of the asthenosphere melts because of the reduced pressure. This molten material then rises up into gaps or fractures created when plates move away from each other. Figure 4.36a shows how this process brings new minerals to Earth's crust, creating new plate material. Geologists refer to these long submarine canyons as **rift zones**. The pre-existing crust "rifts" apart to make way for the upward movement of the newer molten material through vents and submarine volcanoes. As the lava cools along these narrow rifts, many mineral deposits are created. These are among the few places on Earth where we can actually observe mineral formation.

2. Subduction results in mountain building and an overall thickening of the lithosphere. It occurs at continental margins, along island arcs, and at points of continental collisions (see Figures 4.36b, c, and d). This plate boundary zone of mountain building is an important region of ore body formation. Unique geological conditions cause subduction and melting, creating a new crust. The creation of new crust results in mountain building and, ultimately, the concentration of minerals. In one kind of plate collision, two distinct plates, each made of oceanic crust, collide with each other (Figure 4.36b). One of the plates is always somewhat denser than the other. The denser plate slides under the less dense plate. This is called **subduction**. As the subducted (pulled under) plate sinks, it produces a region of melting. Where magma forces its way to the surface, a distinct chain of volcanoes forms. This chain ultimately forms a **magmatic arc**.

   Figure 4.36c illustrates another form of subduction where dense oceanic crust meets less dense continental crust. This also creates melting and the generation of large volumes of magma associated with chains of volcanoes and frequent earthquakes. The result of all these events is the creation of thick, granitic continental crust and the storehouse of minerals contained within it. Many well-known mountain chains originated in this way. These include parts of the Rocky Mountains, California's Sierra Nevada Range, and the Andes Mountains, which stretch the entire length of South America.

3. Once minerals are uplifted by plate movements, weathering and erosion processes concentrate them through deposition, evaporation, and groundwater movement (see Figure 4.36d). Boundary interactions between shifting plates eventually fade. Smaller amounts of magma intrude into cracks and other openings that have developed in Earth's crust. Where newly formed igneous rocks are exposed at Earth's surface, particles will erode from mountains and hills. These will be carried in rivers and streams. As Figure 4.36d (right) implies, the eroded particles will ultimately end up as deposits of sediment accumulating in low spots such as valleys and at the bottoms of lakes and seas. In some places, water in lakes and seas will evaporate, leaving behind mineral deposits. In other places, such as near springs and wetlands, shallow groundwater will alter the chemistry of minerals and soils just below Earth's surface.

Content Clue

Changes in the earth are dramatic. Eighty million years ago, an inland sea covered large portions of the southern and western United States. The Rocky Mountains, as they are today, did not exist.

Content Clue

Figure 4.36d shows continental crust meeting continental crust. When this occurs, the rock must go somewhere. Most of it goes up to form our highest mountains, such as the Himalayas.

Apply Your Understanding

Plate boundaries recycle Earth's crust through subduction and seafloor spreading. How might Figure 4.37 help you begin a scientific search for a specific mineral ore?

Content Clue

Surface processes include running water, wind, ice, and gravity.

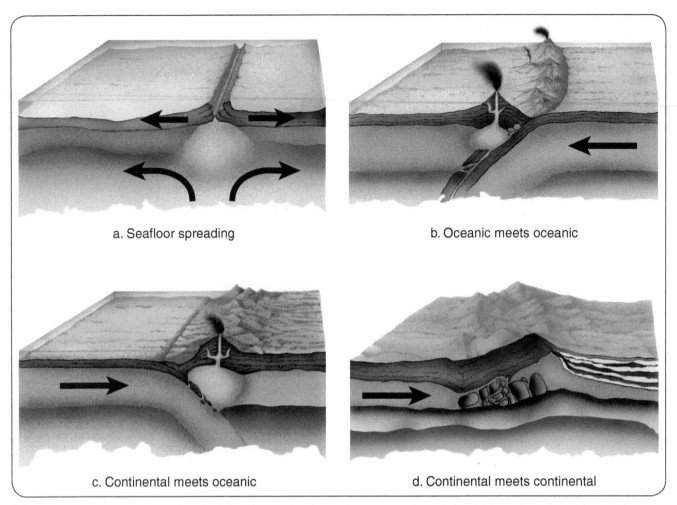

a. Seafloor spreading

b. Oceanic meets oceanic

c. Continental meets oceanic

d. Continental meets continental

▲ FIGURE 4.36 Block diagrams of Earth's lithosphere and asthenosphere at plate boundaries. (a) Spreading plates (rift zones); (b) and (c) colliding plates (**subduction zones**); (d) uplift, followed by weathering and erosion. Uplift results from subduction as shown in (b) or (c), or from the collision of two plates, each made of continental crust.

▶ FIGURE 4.37 Metals are concentrated where geologic processes separate, deposit, or crystallize various earth materials. Keep in mind, minerals originally deposited at the bottom of ancient seas may now be exposed as mineral-rich rock weathering on the slopes of high mountains.

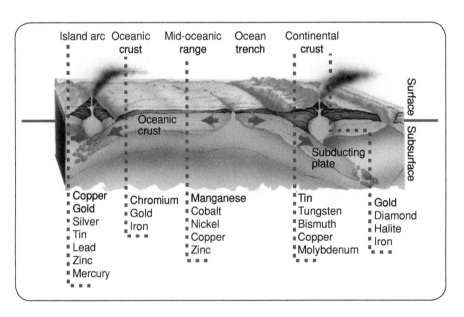

What do all these processes have in common? They represent processes at or near Earth's surface where temperatures and pressures are lower than those deep below the crust. They are processes that also concentrate important mineral deposits. It is the creation of mineral resources that interests us here.

Good as Gold

In the last activity, you read about the different ways minerals become concentrated. You then observed for yourself how these processes work. In this activity, you will have a chance to describe in your own words how a very different mineral-concentrating process works.

Materials

- empty 5-gallon bucket
- 25 pounds of sand seeded with "nuggets" (copper shot)
- large bucket or plastic tub
- gold pan or shallow pie pan
- hose or source of running water
- dictionary
- forceps (tweezers)
- vial
- reference materials such as American history textbooks, encyclopedias, CD-ROMs, or online resources

Procedure

1. Place 15–20 lbs (7–9 kg) of sand or fine gravel in a large plastic bucket. Your teacher will seed the sand or gravel with simulated gold nuggets. Add water to the "gold-bearing ore," and mix all the contents to make a slurry of river sediment.

2. Use a small, shallow pan to scoop up some of the slurry. Swirl the slurry over a large bucket or tub. Do not tip the pan too far or the contents will all spill out. Try to let the lower density solids spill over the edges of the pan into the bucket or tub.

3. Continue adding water while swirling until only a mixture of heavy minerals, including the nuggets, remains.

4. Using tweezers, remove any visible pieces of "gold" from your pan and put them in the vial.

5. When you are finished panning, answer the following questions.

QUESTIONS & TASKS

Record your responses in your science notebook.

1. In nature, where would you find the slurry mixture? (Hint: See the diagram on the next page.)

   Helpful Hint!
   See Figure 4.38 for clues.

2. What is the key physical characteristic that allows this process to work?

3. Would this process be effective in separating turquoise from ordinary quartz sand? Why or why not?

4. What natural process could concentrate gold in this manner?

5. Name another kind of metal ore you think this process would be appropriate for. Explain your thinking.

Mineral Name	Specific Gravity (density)
Feldspar	2.5
Quartz	2.65
Turquoise	2.7
Mica	3
Topaz	3.5
Diamond	3.5
Garnet	3.5
Pyrite	5
Magnetite	5.2
Galena	7.5
Copper	9
Silver	10.7
Gold	19.3
Platinum	21.5

▲ FIGURE 4.38 Selected minerals in order of increasing specific gravity.

6. What type of equipment would you need to mine this kind of deposit on a large scale?

7. Look up the word **placer** and write down its definition. Sketch a picture to illustrate this concept.

8. Write a story about a real or imaginary adventure during the American West's great Gold Rush that began in 1849. Use library or electronic resources to gather historical information. Be sure to use any scientific terms and concepts you have learned about in this chapter.

Here are some ideas for your project:

- a scientific journal that reports your discovery of gold

- a report or claim to the U.S. government that describes a location you would like to mine

- an advertisement for Easterners, luring them to seek their fortunes in the West

[Adapted from "The History of Gold Is the History of the World," Mineral Information Institute.]

4.10 Exploring for Minerals Today

At the start of the Gold Rush in 1849, mineral prospectors had little more than a pick, a shovel, and a gold pan. Maps were of little help as thousands of fortune seekers scoured unnamed hillsides and creek bottoms for traces of gold, silver, and copper (Figure 4.39).

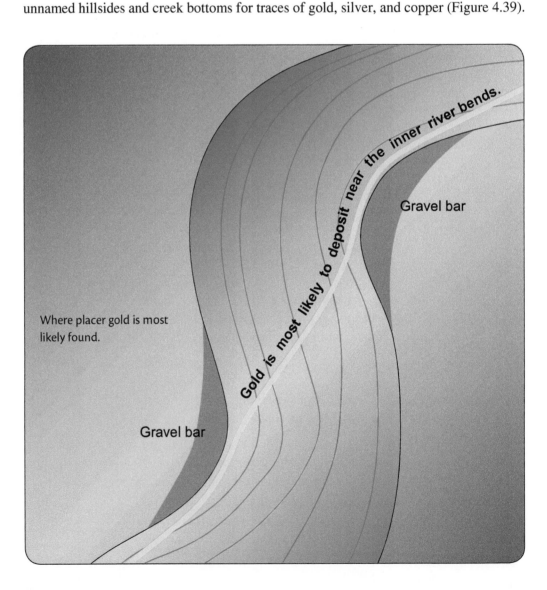

Gold is most likely to deposit near the inner river bends.

Gravel bar

Where placer gold is most likely found.

Gravel bar

Today, more than a century and a half later, most of the "easy" mineral ores have been located. These have been discovered near the surface or close to rail lines, highways, or navigable waterways. As the search for new mineral deposits expands, modern explorers are looking in places early prospectors could only have dreamed of. Today's geologists rely on a combination of applied earth science, high-tech tools, and a little bit of old-fashioned prospecting to locate new mineral deposits.

Geophysical Tools

Techniques used by geophysicists to explore for minerals rely on one basic fact. All earth materials exhibit different physical properties such as varying density, magnetism, radioactivity, or electrical properties. For example, geologists and geophysicists use a technique called **seismic reflection** to learn about the arrangement of underground rock strata. Seismic reflection sends miniature shock waves down into the earth. These waves strike the various rock layers and then bounce back to the surface. The reflected waves are studied to identify contrasts in the densities of the rocks. Results of these surveys reveal how deep the formations are, what they might be made of, and how far each layer extends. Maps and cross sections made from seismic data help scientists either promote or discourage future mineral exploration in certain areas.

Another useful tool relies on Earth's gravity. When measured in fine detail, gravity varies from place to place, again depending partially on the density of the rocks underneath the surface. Usually, sedimentary rocks are less dense than igneous or metamorphic rocks. Rocks containing metal ores are the most dense. The pull of gravity at the surface is measured using a **gravimeter**. The readings are plotted on a map.

A third test is based on the fact that some rocks contain more magnetite than others. The more magnetite a rock contains, the more magnetic it is. A **magnetometer** is used to measure the force of magnetism at the surface of Earth. Since magnetite is a form of iron, magnetic surveys are useful for locating iron-rich mineral deposits (see Figure 4.40). Combined with the results of other geophysical techniques, magnetic surveys can be plotted on maps to reveal patterns of dense rock or concentrations of ore minerals.

Think about This!

Fieldwork requires a love of the outdoors, long hours, and a commitment to careful scientific observation and record-keeping.

Helpful Hint!

Gravity is the force of attraction between all things that have mass. When one of the objects is massive (like Earth), it is easy to notice the effects of gravity.

Apply Your Understanding

Which of these geophysical techniques were used to produce the maps in Appendix 9?

➤ **FIGURE 4.40** An aerial electromagnetic survey in progress. Note the large transmitting "loop" and the receiving "bird" in the lower right corner. (*Geoterrex Limited, Ottawa, Canada*)

Geochemical Tools

As discussed earlier, rock-forming minerals are combinations of elements that exhibit distinct properties such as solubility in an acid or reactivity with oxygen in Earth's atmosphere. For example, soils overlying a copper deposit may have unusually high levels of copper. If plants grow there, they too may concentrate higher-than-normal levels of copper in their roots, stems, and leaves. That's why exploration geochemists analyze plants and soils to detect occurrences of *anomalous* (unusual) amounts of metals.

Remote Sensing Tools

Remote sensing is simply a means of detecting earth resources from a distance. Techniques can be as straightforward as taking photographs from an airplane or as complex as beaming radar waves from an Earth-orbiting satellite to obtain images of the ocean floor. One of the most widely used remote sensing tools for mineral exploration has been the **Landsat** family of Earth-orbiting satellites. Landsat takes pictures of Earth's land areas in different wavelengths. This allows scientists to see features not visible to the eye such as the presence of moisture in leaves or the existence of minerals or trace elements hidden in soils. Landsat and other remote sensing tools have created a revolution in mineral exploration. They offer scientists an opportunity to probe the most distant places on Earth.

Think about This!

Landsat-type satellites also provide the photos of your house from space.

Mapping, Collecting, and Drilling

Of all the techniques discussed, nothing can replace the need to verify what is actually "out there" (Figure 4.41). Data collected from geophysical, geochemical, and remote sensing surveys, combined with previous knowledge about crustal composition and movements, send the geologists to the field (the area they have investigated using the above techniques). In the field, they take pictures, collect samples, and plot geologic features on maps. They also see firsthand the outcrops and soils derived from the underlying rocks, the waters that flow through the area, and the vegetation that covers the area.

Collectively, the geological and geophysical data are used to determine the most likely places to drill for ore. Drilling is very expensive, but it is the only way to prove an ore body is present and to determine the character, grade (percentage or content of minerals/ metals sought), and size of the deposit.

▲ FIGURE 4.41 Although the modern geologist relies on many different tools, there is no substitute for on-site fieldwork, which allows for close observation and sampling. (*U.S. Geological Survey*)

▲ FIGURE 4.42 Today's drilling rigs can have minimal impact in sensitive areas. (*Courtesy Resolution Copper Company.*)

4.11 Mine It, Mill It, Concentrate It

Once a mineral deposit has been discovered, it is a matter of years before the ore can be placed into production. Most often, this is done by digging the ore out by means of a **mine**. To begin this process, geologists and engineers have to first determine which type of mining method to use. Many things have to be considered. These include the deposit's overall shape and thickness; its grade, quality, or content of valuable metals and minerals; its depth below the surface; the distance to transportation routes; and any environmental restrictions that may disrupt fragile ecosystems or populated areas (Figure 4.42). As a result, some deposits may be producing within 3 years, but others may take as long as 20 years. Figure 4.43 shows the steps and period of time needed for developing a typical mine.

Milling is a way of concentrating minerals so they can be used in manufacturing.

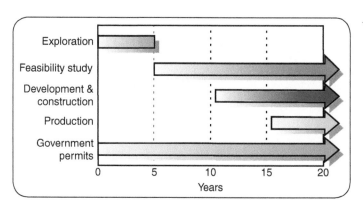

◀ FIGURE 4.43 The time required to find, plan, and build a working mine can take decades. Sometimes, no deposit is even found. (*Mineral Information Institute*)

►FIGURE 4.44 Most underground mines are larger than most people think. The front-end loader and dump truck in this limestone operation in Tennessee help demonstrate the size of some underground work areas in today's mines. *(Mineral Information Institute photo from Franklin Industries.)*

Mining Methods

Topic: mining methods
Go to: www.scilinks.org
Code: GloSci7e164

Ore deposits are extracted from the earth in the most economical way. If the ore deposits are deep, a decision may be made to remove the minerals by **underground mining**. This method requires the use of explosives and specialized machinery to drill and blast solid rock under Earth's surface. Small haulage trucks, trains, conveyors, or hoists are needed to remove the ore from the earth (see Figure 4.44).

In contrast, **open pit mining** uses huge equipment to remove ores such as copper or iron. The Bingham Canyon copper mine was the world's largest open pit copper mine (see Figure 4.35). Surface mining is the most common form of mining for shallow deposits of coal and phosphate minerals. Gravel pits and rock quarries (see Figure 4.45) are mined to remove other earth resources such as building stone and crushed rock.

►FIGURE 4.45 Sand, gravel, and rock are called *aggregate* minerals. By volume, they represent the largest fraction of all mined earth materials. These resources are important ingredients in concrete, roads, and other construction and landscaping materials. *(Photo by Rhonda S. Myers.)*

Superheated steam or other solvent

Surface

Dissolved mineral to process

Ore zone

Solution

For salt and other soluble minerals such as potash or sulfur, **solution mining** is the preferred method. Hot water is pumped down a drill hole into the zone where the minerals are easily dissolved. These mineral-rich fluids, or brines, are pumped out of another drill hole. The brines carry the minerals, which are then concentrated by evaporation (see Figure 4.46.) Oil and natural gas are also "mined" from Earth and are removed using methods you will read about in Chapter 8.

ACTIVITY 4.10

Milling Lab

In this activity, you will devise a plan for milling a crushed ore.

Background

Finding an ore body doesn't immediately produce a usable mineral. Nature has concentrated the desired mineral within Earth; however, it is up to human ingenuity to concentrate it further. The challenge is to separate the desired minerals from the unwanted materials they are combined with. The unwanted material is called **gangue**. Most mined ores contain a large quantity of gangue.

Milling is the process of separating the desired, valuable ore minerals from the unwanted gangue. Not all ores undergo the same process at the mill. Variations depend on the type of ore. The ore is usually crushed and ground until the particles of the mineral are broken apart from the gangue. If possible, the particles are separated further by physical means such as washing, flotation (Figure 4.47), or magnetic separation. The residue that remains after the valuable mineral has been separated from the gangue is called the **tailing**.

Whatever the process, the end result is a mineral concentrate that is shipped off to the smelter and the refinery for further processing and purification. **Smelting** is the fusing or melting of a concentrate to separate the metal or metals it contains from other elements such as oxygen, iron, or sulfur. **Refining** is the general term for the process by which a metal is further processed to a finished or more pure form (Figure 4.48).

Topic: milling
Go to: www.scilinks.org
Code: GloSci7e165

Apply Your Understanding

What is the difference between milling, smelting, and refining?

► **FIGURE 4.47** Flotation machines in the milling process. *(AMAX Inc.)*

► **FIGURE 4.48** Steps in metal production. *(Adapted from Mineral Information Institute.)*

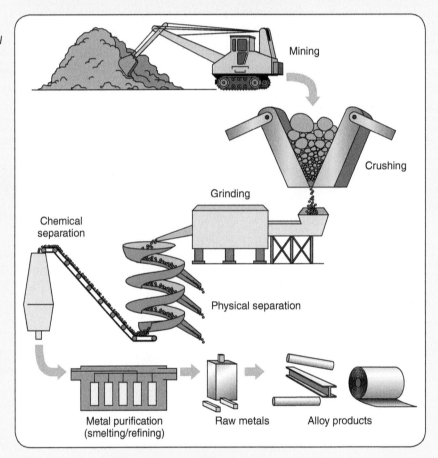

Materials (for each team)

- ore sample
- dilute HCl (hydrochloric acid)
- safety goggles
- other materials as necessary (based on your plan for separation)

Procedure

1. Your teacher will give you a sample of ground-up ore. Your task is to separate it into as many parts as you can.

2. To do this, you must develop a plan that takes advantage of the different properties of

the materials that are present. Here are some potential properties:

a. different solubilities in different solvents

b. different melting points

c. magnetic properties

d. color differences

e. variations in hardness

f. different densities or specific gravities

g. solubility or reactivity with an acid

h. solubility or reactivity with a base

3. The lab consists of 2 parts. On day 1, examine your ore and develop a plan for separation. Give your teacher a copy of your plan with a request for the materials you need to mill the ore. Your teacher will suggest a method for illustrating your milling procedure.

4. On day 2, carry out your milling

WARNING

Dilute hydrochloric acid can be dangerous. If you spill any on yourself, wash immediately and thoroughly with water. Tell your teacher. Be sure you are wearing your safety goggles.

operation. Turn in your separated substances, and report your results. Reproduce the table in Figure 4.49 in your science notebook.

5. Keep detailed notes in your science notebook and plan carefully. You will be limited to 2 class periods and a small sample of ore. Your grade will depend primarily on the separation you make. Thus, the milling operation has a definite payoff. Write a group report of your procedure and results.

BE SAFE

Use tongs or heat-resistant gloves to lift hot objects.

Identity of Substance	Characteristics

▲ FIGURE 4.49 Sample table for your milling operation.

4.12 Alloys

Once the ore has been processed at the mill (separated by smelting and made pure by refining), it is ready for use. Metals are seldom used in their pure state. The properties of metal *mixtures* may be preferable to those of the pure metals. These metal mixtures are known as **alloys**.

Alloys have different characteristics than their individual ingredients.

Although there are only 75 metallic elements, there are thousands of different combinations. Each alloy has its own special properties. For example, the melting point of an alloy may be higher or lower than the melting point of any of one of its individual elements. Also, alloys are usually harder and stronger than the parent metals. Pure iron is quite soft and ductile (easily formed). But when carbon is added, the resulting steel alloy is stronger and harder. Stainless steel is an alloy of steel with the elements chromium and nickel. Alloys also usually resist corrosion better than pure metals.

Apply Your Understanding

What elements can be alloyed?

You can find examples of alloys in your dentist's office. Alloys of gold, silver, platinum, and other metals are used for fillings and crowns. These alloys can be melted more easily, can retard heat conduction, and can bond to porcelain. None of the pure metals have all those properties.

Other alloys are used in the manufacture of sporting equipment such as tennis rackets, bicycle frames (Figure 4.50), and baseball bats. Figure 4.51 lists some examples of alloys and their composition.

▲ FIGURE 4.50 Modern bicycles, aluminum bats, and tennis rackets are among the many products we rely on for lightness and strength. Here, Elke Brutsaert—member of the Schwinn-Toyota RAV4 Mountain Bike Race Team—fights to get the maximum from both herself and her bike. *(Courtesy: Schwinn Cycling & Fitness Inc.)*

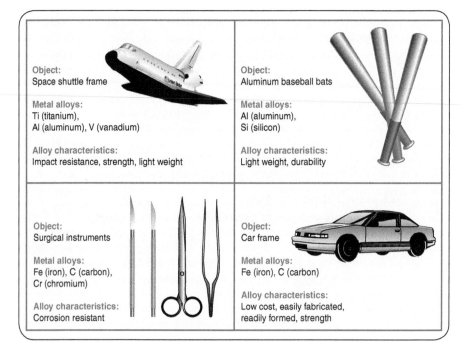

Object:
Space shuttle frame

Metal alloys:
Ti (titanium),
Al (aluminum), V (vanadium)

Alloy characteristics:
Impact resistance, strength, light weight

Object:
Aluminum baseball bats

Metal alloys:
Al (aluminum),
Si (silicon)

Alloy characteristics:
Light weight, durability

Object:
Surgical instruments

Metal alloys:
Fe (iron), C (carbon),
Cr (chromium)

Alloy characteristics:
Corrosion resistant

Object:
Car frame

Metal alloys:
Fe (iron), C (carbon)

Alloy characteristics:
Low cost, easily fabricated,
readily formed, strength

▲ FIGURE 4.51 Some familiar objects, their physical properties, and their metal alloy composition.

Minerals and Society

ACTIVITY 4.11

Importance of Minerals Revisited

In this activity, you will learn about the nature of 12 essential minerals or mineral resources vital to our experience of the good life in our present society. You will associate each of these natural resources with common objects, tools, machines, or parts of manufactured items. You will also identify where these mineral and mineral resources come from.

Apply Your Understanding

List some of the ways minerals help us lead the good life.

Helpful Hint!

Luster is the physical property that will help you distinguish between metals and nonmetals.

Materials

- reference materials about minerals, including this book, encyclopedias, CD-ROMs, and online resources

Procedure

1. In your science notebook, or on a separate sheet of paper, reproduce the table in Figure 4.52. You will complete the data requested in the table for these 12 mineral resources:

   a. Gypsum
   b. Lead
   c. Salt
   d. Sand
   e. Potash
   f. Copper

g. Hematite   k. Zinc

h. Granite   l. Aluminum
(from bauxite ore)

i. Sulfur

j. Cement (about 65% limestone rock)

2. Fill in your table by referring to information from this chapter. To help you get started, the first row (gypsum) has been completed. Figures 4.53 and 4.57 list information on mineral uses and imports that you will need.

▼**FIGURE 4.52** Activity table for importance of minerals. The first row has been filled in for you.

Minerals or Mineral Resources Obtained from Minerals	Metal (M), Nonmetal (N), or Source (S)	Description or Special Properties	Principal Uses	Leading Suppliers
Gypsum	N	A white, chalky mineral; soft	A filler in candy and paint; plasterboard; plaster of Paris	25% imported from Canada, Mexico

Column 1: List the identity of the sample here.

Column 2: Record M if the sample is a metal, N if the sample is a nonmetal, or S if the sample is the source of a metal or nonmetal.

Column 3: Describe the properties of the sample that can be used to identify it or give it its value.

Column 4: The mineral-related samples you are examining are valuable to our society. They all have a variety of uses.

Column 5: If a mineral is not listed in Figure 4.57, you may assume we don't import it (so the U.S. is the main supplier). List the percentage imported and the 2 leading suppliers.

4.13 Minerals and Society

So far, we have examined the nature of minerals and the rocks they form. We have also looked at the ways minerals become concentrated through both geologic and human-engineered processes. Now we will see how these raw materials become the essential ingredients for nearly every convenience we can think of. Figure 4.53 lists many of the mineral resources our society depends on and some of the sources of those materials. Study the information carefully because it demonstrates our heavy reliance on mineral resources.

We don't have to travel far to grasp the importance of minerals in our everyday lives. In fact, one of the best places to begin looking is right in our own home. Figure 4.54 illustrates a home and some of its more familiar contents. Refer to the labeled topics that follow for more detail.

A base metal is of less comparative value relative to a precious metal such as gold or silver.

Think about This!

Look around... everything is made from mineral resources.

Basic Resources	Primary Uses	Mineral Sources
Fuels	Fossil fuel	Coal, natural gas, oil
	Nuclear fuel	Uranium ore, thorium ore
Nonmetals	Construction materials	Sand and gravel, limestone, cement materials, gypsum, granite
	Chemicals	Coal, oil, natural gas, sulfur, salt, trona, sodium sulfate, compounds of boron
	Fertilizers	Phosphorite, potash, nitrates, air, natural gas
	Refractories/fluxes	Clay, magnesite
	Abrasives	Garnet, sandstone, industrial diamonds
	Insulators	Fiberglass (molten sand), rock wool (basaltic rock), polystyrene and urethane (petroleum), vermiculite (mica), perlite (volcanic ash), poly-isocyanurate (petroleum)
	Plastics	Petroleum
	Pigments/fillers	Clay, limestone, talc
	Precious stones/gems	Diamonds, amethyst, jade
Metals	Iron	Iron ore
	Alloying	Manganese, chromite, nickel, molybdenum, cobalt, vanadium
	Base metals*	Copper, lead, zinc, tin
	Light weight	Aluminum, magnesium, titanium
	Precious	Gold, silver, platinum
	Rare earth minerals	Bastnasite, monazite

*Base metals is a classification and not a use. It refers to certain metals (such as copper, lead, or zinc) of less monetary value per unit weight than the precious metals.

A. Insulation, Roofing, and Hardware

All homes and buildings rely on building materials that contain mineral resources. Consider the following products that help make up an average home:

- 779 pounds of insulation, usually made of glass wool (silica, feldspar, and trona) or vermiculite (mica containing magnesium, aluminum, iron, silica, manganese, phosphorus, and sulfur);

- 2,841 square feet of roofing shingles, usually made of wood or asphalt (composed of silica sands, limestone, and petroleum);

- 302 pounds of nails and screws (iron and zinc) used to fasten lumber together; and

- 12 interior doors, six closet doors, and three exterior doors, each with doorknobs, locks, and hinges made of steel or brass (alloy of copper and zinc).

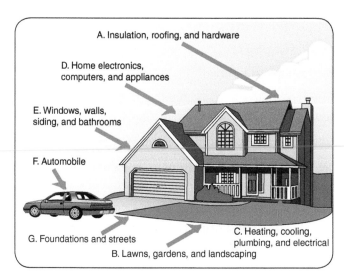

A. Insulation, roofing, and hardware

D. Home electronics, computers, and appliances

E. Windows, walls, siding, and bathrooms

F. Automobile

G. Foundations and streets

C. Heating, cooling, plumbing, and electrical

B. Lawns, gardens, and landscaping

B. Lawns, Gardens, and Landscaping

Growing plants draw the many chemical nutrients they need from the soil. Nature has its own way of recycling these necessary nutrients. When the soil lacks the right kind or the right amount of nutrients, we must add them to ensure the growth of healthy plants. These nutrients are added to the soil in the form of soluble **fertilizers**.

The three elements most needed in common fertilizer are nitrogen, phosphorus, and potassium. An analysis of a fertilizer is often stated in terms of these elements and is given in alphabetical order. For example, an 8-6-8 fertilizer contains, by weight, 8 percent nitrogen, 6 percent phosphorus pentoxide (P_2O_5), and 8 percent potassium oxide (K_2O) (see Figure 4.55). (The phosphorus and potassium are usually not present as oxides, but are reported as oxides in accordance with the universal practice of the fertilizer industry.)

These three elements are gathered from different sources. Nitrogen is recovered by chemical means from the atmosphere. Potassium is recovered from marine evaporite deposits as the soluble salt potassium chloride. Phosphorus is recovered as calcium phosphate from a special class of marine chemical sediments known as phosphorites or phosphate rock.

◀FIGURE 4.55 How much phosphorus does this fertilizer contain? How much potassium? How much nitrogen?

C. Heating, Cooling, Plumbing, and Electrical

In our homes and behind our walls lies a network of pipes, wires, and cable made of dozens of different kinds of minerals. Some examples include

Apply Your Understanding

How many of these items can you identify in your own home?

- 226 feet of galvanized (zinc-coated) heating or air-conditioning ducts to carry the heated or cooled air throughout the house;

- 100 plumbing fittings to connect the pipe (copper or iron and different steel alloys);

- 170 feet of plastic or metal pipe to carry wastewater away to the sewer, plus the connecting fittings; and

- 501 pounds of copper, used for 280 feet of plumbing pipes and 750 feet of electrical wiring. Pipes can also be made of steel, plastics, and clay. Newer, optical fiber cables are spun from silica.

D. Home Electronics, Computers, and Appliances

In our society, high technology adds new products to our homes each year. This growing list of products and materials uses almost all of the naturally occurring elements in the periodic table. Many of these products were first developed in the fields of industrial electronics and aerospace, but they have now found their way into our homes as consumer items.

Apply Your Understanding

How many of these can you locate on a periodic table of elements? How many are minerals?

Most electronics equipment such as televisions, microwave ovens, telephones and cell phones, computers, VCRs, CD and DVD players, radios, and electronic games contain no fewer than 30 different metals and minerals. These include aluminum, antimony, barite, beryllium, cobalt, columbium, copper, gallium, germanium, gold, indium, iron, lanthanides, lithium, manganese, mercury, mica, molybdenum, nickel, platinum, quartz, rhenium, selenium, silicon, silver, strontium, tantalum, tellurium, tin, tungsten, vanadium, yttrium, zinc, and zirconium.

E. Windows, Walls, Siding, and Bathrooms

In our homes, ceramic materials are used extensively. Some ceramics have properties that make them desirable substitutes for certain metals. The following items may be found in a typical home:

- 210 pounds of ceramic (clay, feldspar, and limestone) sinks, toilets, bathtubs and/or shower stalls, and tile used to cover walls and floors;

- 268 pounds of glass for 18 windows and one sliding glass door (glass is made of silica sand with lesser amounts of trona, limestone, and feldspar);

- 14,218 pounds of gypsum to make interior wallboard; and

- 3,011 square feet (400–1,500 pounds) of exterior siding material.

Content Clue

Gasoline, motor oil, and plastics are derived from fossil fuels, not inorganic minerals.

F. Automobile

For most of us, cars are necessary for our lifestyles. They are also among the most desired possessions for people all over the world. This high demand causes increased pressure for a steady, affordable supply of certain mineral resources (see Figure 4.56).

G. Foundations and Streets

Finally, parts of our homes and their surroundings may be built from many nonmetallic minerals such as limestone, cut and crushed stone, sand, and gravel. This includes the materials that are part of our streets and roads. For example,

► FIGURE 4.56 There are more than 212 million motor vehicles (of all types) in the U.S. The average weight of an automobile is 2,600 to 3,000 pounds. It is made by combining at least 39 different minerals and metals, each performing a special function when used in combination with the other. (Source: The Smithsonian Institution)

Plastics	250 lbs	Graphite	trace	Niobium	<.5 lb
Rubber	140 lbs	Halite	trace	Nitrogen	trace
Aluminum	240 lbs	Iron and Steel	2,124 lbs	Palladium	trace
Antimony	trace	(cast iron	435 lbs)	Platinum	.05–.1 troy oz.
Asbestos	.66–1.2 lbs	(steel*	1,382 lbs)	Phosphorus	< 1 lb
Barium	trace	(HSLA**	263 lbs)	Potash	trace
Cadmium	trace	(Stainless steel	45 lbs)	Sand	89 lbs
Carbon	50 lbs	Lead	24 lbs	Silicon	41 lbs
Cobalt	trace	Limestone	trace	Strontium	trace
Copper	42 lbs	Magnesium	4.5 lbs	Sulfur	2 lbs
Chromium	15 lbs	Manganese	17 lbs	Tin	trace
Fluorspar	trace	Molybdenum	1 lb	Titanium	trace
Gallium	trace	Mica	trace	Tungsten	trace
Gold	trace	Nickel	9 lbs	Vanadium	< 1 lb
				Zinc	22 lbs
				Zirconium	trace

* Conventional steel
** High strength low alloy

- 120,538 pounds of concrete made by mixing water with sand, gravel, and cement. Cement is made of limestone, bauxite, clay, shale, and gypsum. Concrete is reinforced with steel rods (rebar) to provide extra strength.

- 15,300 pounds of concrete block

- 21,440 pounds of brick made from mixing various kinds of sand with different types of clay

- 54,000 pounds of gravel and stone for decoration, landscaping, and drainage

- 5-inch-thick paving, made from 94 percent aggregate and 6 percent oil or asphalt concentrate, used to cover the surface of driveways, streets, and highways

- 8 inches of 3/4-inch aggregate and smaller-sized sediment used as a base underneath the paving

Apply Your Understanding

Why are aggregate minerals such as crushed rock and building stone more abundant and easier to extract than ore minerals?

Think about This!

There are nearly 4 million miles of roads in the U.S.; 2.6 million miles are hard-surfaced (asphalt or concrete).

4.14 Economic and Political Issues

Many social and economic issues become interwined with our dependence on minerals and agriculture. As people around the world strive to improve their standard of living, they compete for the available supply of resources. In addition, the extraction and use of resources leads to environmental problems, which you will read more about in section 4.15 Mining and the Environment.

Mineral Imports and Exports

As we have seen, mineral deposits are not evenly distributed around the globe because of the way geologic processes work. Some regions have a great variety of useful minerals; others have little or none at all. No country has all the minerals it needs. As a result, it must depend at least partially on imports. Japan, for example, has never been a major mineral or energy producer, so it imports most of its needs.

Most of the world's largest consumers of minerals are now in decline as producers. One reason for this decline is that some countries, such as the European nations, have depleted their higher-grade mineral reserves; they now must rely mostly on imports. Another reason for the decline is that some resources are cheaper when obtained from developing countries.

The United States is a major producer and supplier of certain minerals (such as coal, gold, soda ash, and fertilizers) for other countries. And, although the United States could produce some of those minerals it now imports, many of them are still imported, as you saw in Figure 4.57. Why must so much be bought from other countries? The major reasons are that some foreign ore deposits are of a higher grade and are less expensive to mine. Experts agree that the United States will continue to depend on minerals from other countries for many decades to come.

ACTIVITY 4.12

Mineral Imports

In this activity, you will see that minerals are not evenly distributed around the globe. This fact leads to patterns of international trade and, in some cases, international conflict.

Materials

- colored pencils or markers
- world atlas, globe, or geography book
- Handout: *World Map*

> **Think about This!**
>
> Why does the United States import so many mineral resources?

Procedure

Examine Figure 4.57 and answer the following questions. Mark your answers on the *World Map* handout, which you can label "U.S. Mineral Imports."

1. In your science notebook, list the names of all the minerals the United States must import completely.

> **Helpful Hint!**
>
> These minerals are not produced in the United States, so 100% of them are imported.

2. On your map, record the name(s) of the mineral on the country where we obtain it. To save space, use abbreviations for those mineral commodities listed on the periodic table shown in Chapter 10, section 10.1 The Atomic Model.

3. Next, list the names of the rest of the mineral resources the United States must import. Which countries supply the bulk of these mineral resources?

4. Plot the minerals from step 3 onto your world map.

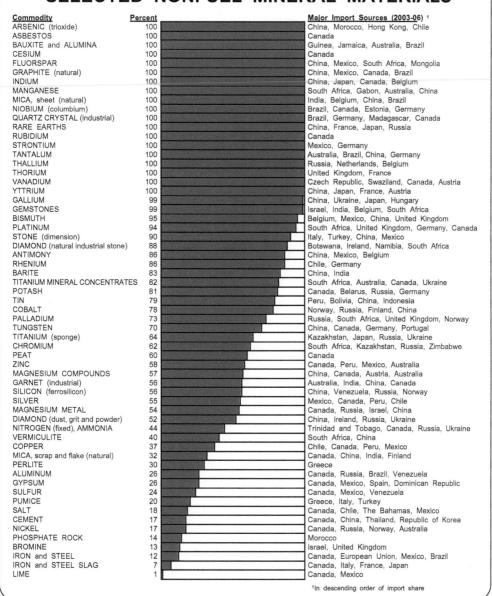

2007 U.S. NET IMPORT RELIANCE FOR SELECTED NONFUEL MINERAL MATERIALS

Commodity	Percent	Major Import Sources (2003-06) [1]
ARSENIC (trioxide)	100	China, Morocco, Hong Kong, Chile
ASBESTOS	100	Canada
BAUXITE and ALUMINA	100	Guinea, Jamaica, Australia, Brazil
CESIUM	100	Canada
FLUORSPAR	100	China, Mexico, South Africa, Mongolia
GRAPHITE (natural)	100	China, Mexico, Canada, Brazil
INDIUM	100	China, Japan, Canada, Belgium
MANGANESE	100	South Africa, Gabon, Australia, China
MICA, sheet (natural)	100	India, Belgium, China, Brazil
NIOBIUM (columbium)	100	Brazil, Canada, Estonia, Germany
QUARTZ CRYSTAL (industrial)	100	Brazil, Germany, Madagascar, Canada
RARE EARTHS	100	China, France, Japan, Russia
RUBIDIUM	100	Canada
STRONTIUM	100	Mexico, Germany
TANTALUM	100	Australia, Brazil, China, Germany
THALLIUM	100	Russia, Netherlands, Belgium
THORIUM	100	United Kingdom, France
VANADIUM	100	Czech Republic, Swaziland, Canada, Austria
YTTRIUM	100	China, Japan, France, Austria
GALLIUM	99	China, Ukraine, Japan, Hungary
GEMSTONES	99	Israel, India, Belgium, South Africa
BISMUTH	95	Belgium, Mexico, China, United Kingdom
PLATINUM	94	South Africa, United Kingdom, Germany, Canada
STONE (dimension)	90	Italy, Turkey, China, Mexico
DIAMOND (natural industrial stone)	88	Botswana, Ireland, Namibia, South Africa
ANTIMONY	86	China, Mexico, Belgium
RHENIUM	86	Chile, Germany
BARITE	83	China, India
TITANIUM MINERAL CONCENTRATES	82	South Africa, Australia, Canada, Ukraine
POTASH	81	Canada, Belarus, Russia, Germany
TIN	79	Peru, Bolivia, China, Indonesia
COBALT	78	Norway, Russia, Finland, China
PALLADIUM	73	Russia, South Africa, United Kingdom, Norway
TUNGSTEN	70	China, Canada, Germany, Portugal
TITANIUM (sponge)	64	Kazakhstan, Japan, Russia, Ukraine
CHROMIUM	62	South Africa, Kazakhstan, Russia, Zimbabwe
PEAT	60	Canada
ZINC	58	Canada, Peru, Mexico, Australia
MAGNESIUM COMPOUNDS	57	China, Canada, Austria, Australia
GARNET (industrial)	56	Australia, India, China, Canada
SILICON (ferrosilicon)	56	China, Venezuela, Russia, Norway
SILVER	55	Mexico, Canada, Peru, Chile
MAGNESIUM METAL	54	Canada, Russia, Israel, China
DIAMOND (dust, grit and powder)	52	China, Ireland, Russia, Ukraine
NITROGEN (fixed), AMMONIA	44	Trinidad and Tobago, Canada, Russia, Ukraine
VERMICULITE	40	South Africa, China
COPPER	37	Chile, Canada, Peru, Mexico
MICA, scrap and flake (natural)	32	Canada, China, India, Finland
PERLITE	30	Greece
ALUMINUM	26	Canada, Russia, Brazil, Venezuela
GYPSUM	26	Canada, Mexico, Spain, Dominican Republic
SULFUR	24	Canada, Mexico, Venezuela
PUMICE	20	Greece, Italy, Turkey
SALT	18	Canada, Chile, The Bahamas, Mexico
CEMENT	17	Canada, China, Thailand, Republic of Korea
NICKEL	17	Canada, Russia, Norway, Australia
PHOSPHATE ROCK	14	Morocco
BROMINE	13	Israel, United Kingdom
IRON and STEEL	12	Canada, European Union, Mexico, Brazil
IRON and STEEL SLAG	7	Canada, Italy, France, Japan
LIME	1	Canada, Mexico

[1] In descending order of import share

◀ FIGURE 4.57 The dependence of the United States on imports of selected minerals and metals. (*Mineral Information Institute*)

5. Which countries supply only 1 kind of mineral to the United States? Which countries supply more than 1 kind? Next to each country listed, indicate whether it is a developing (d) or developed (D) country. If unsure, leave blank. For more information on developing and developed countries, see Chapter 5, section 5.3 The Growth of Human Population.

Helpful Hint!

Developed and *developing countries* are names we use to distinguish between richer and poorer countries. Richer countries enjoy a higher standard of living than poorer countries. The terms industrialized and nonindustrialized carry similar meanings.

6. Write an essay that describes the nature of U.S. mineral imports. Include in your essay concepts discussed in your reading such as the distribution of minerals, geologic factors that concentrate minerals, cost of mining, mineral dependence, developing vs. developed countries, and self-sufficiency. Also include a statement about what, if anything, the United States should do to maintain its future supply of minerals.

Content Clue

"Strategic" minerals are minerals considered essential for a country's economic and defense needs. Examples include metals for defense weapons (Figure 4.58), satellite communications, automobile parts, and medical instruments.

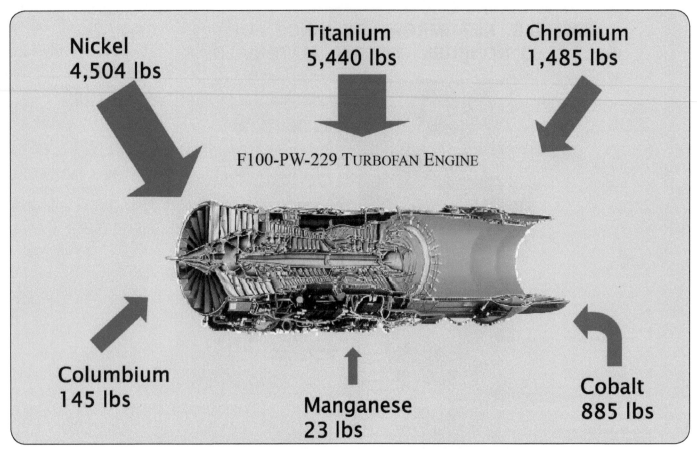

Nickel
4,504 lbs

Titanium
5,440 lbs

Chromium
1,485 lbs

F100-PW-229 TURBOFAN ENGINE

Columbium
145 lbs

Manganese
23 lbs

Cobalt
885 lbs

▲FIGURE 4.58 What does it take to build a jet engine? There are two F100 engines on an F-15 fighter and one on an F-16 fighter. The dependence of the United States on imports of minerals for these engines ranges between 54 and 100 percent (2005). Metals and other minerals are essential to the functioning of our economy and military capabilities. *(Pratt & Whitney)*

4.15 Mining and the Environment

Think about This!

How are environmental concerns about mining being addressed?

Mining has an environmental impact because minerals must be removed from the ground to be used. The amount and type of impact depends on many factors, including the geology of the mining site, the quantity of material moved, the depth of the ore deposit, the chemical makeup of the ore and its surrounding rocks, groundwater and soils, the mining method used, and the nature of the milling process. In most mineral-producing countries, environmental protection and land restoration are required in a company's original plans before mining operations begin. In the United States, such provisions are required by federal and state laws and most local city and county ordinances and regulations.

Land, Water, and Air

Many people regard mining as ugly because extraction can leave behind large holes and piles of unwanted rock and soil. The United States, along with a growing number of other countries, now has strict environmental controls that require mines to undergo careful reclamation. **Reclamation** involves (a) contouring the disturbed area, (b) spreading topsoil stockpiled during mine production over the area, and (c) replanting vegetation (Figure 4.59). Although underground mines rarely produce surface damage, occasional subsidence causes overlying land to collapse.

In addition to disturbing the land, mining can cause water pollution, especially where tailings and other accumulations of waste materials are exposed to water either from

◄**FIGURE 4.59** In the 1930s, a predecessor of Cyprus Amax developed and operated a lead, zinc, silver, and gold mine called the Terro Mine in northern New Mexico along the Pecos River. Reclamation of this site was initiated in the early 1990s and the land has now been returned to nature. *(Phelps Dodge Corporation)*

rainfall, stream flow, or from shallow groundwater movement. As the grade of mined ore decreases, the quantity of tailing increases. In places where water quality is tightly regulated, impacts of mine and mill-related water pollution have been greatly reduced or eliminated.

The impacts of mining can also affect our atmosphere. If not controlled, mine dust contaminates the air. Also, smelting can produce large quantities of air pollutants. Aside from the impact on the environment, air pollution can pose health hazards to mine workers and others who live or work near mines and smelters. Some countries, especially those with weak environmental restrictions, have few controls over this kind of pollution. In the last 20 years, laws restricting the release of these pollutants have dramatically improved air quality in many parts of the world.

Environmental Costs

Modern practices demonstrate that mining can be carried out in environmentally acceptable ways. Laws, rules, and regulations mandate that (a) tailings be disposed of properly; (b) the water used in mining, milling, and refining must be cleaned before it is released into streams; and (c) mined land be reclaimed and made suitable for other uses. The immediate costs may be high, but they may be less in the long run than those of restoring a badly damaged area.

Apply Your Understanding

How does mining impact the environment?

Apply Your Understanding

How can the impact of mining be minimized?

Think about This!

Ideally, the real cost of a mineral resource should include the cost to keep our environment clean.

Mineral Resources 177

For corporations to be able to pay the costs and make a profit, the sale price of the mineral produced must include all the costs of production (mining, milling, smelting, refining). In addition, there are safety and environmental costs to keep the air, water, and land as clean as possible. Consumers must be willing to pay that price. Otherwise, mines would close and their resources would no longer be available.

We must remember, though, that laws and regulations mean little if enforcement is lax. In addition, the global environment is not improved when cleanup laws are passed in a nation that then turns around and imports cheaper minerals from other nations that have lower environmental standards. This practice creates problems in both nations. Unemployment goes up in the first; the environment suffers in the other.

4.16 Wise Use of Minerals

Question This!

Should we be concerned
about future supplies of
mineral resources? Why or
why not?

Think about the length of time it takes for an ounce of gold to be deposited, erode, and then accumulate in sediment along a flowing stream. The process may begin with subducting tectonic plates. Magma melts, rocks solidify, and fluids infiltrate the hardened mass. Eventually, tiny crystals of gold form. Uplift takes place. Then a stream erodes the hillside; gold flakes tumble into a river and come to rest on a gravel bank. Now gleaming in the sunlight, the gold in your pan took 10 million years to arrive.

Such is the rate at which minerals form—some slower, some faster. But all form at a rate that is thousands of times slower than crops raised for food or trees grown for lumber. That is why we refer to most mineral resources as nonrenewable or limited in supply. Once we have used them, they usually take a great deal of time to regenerate.

Assuming that mineral resources are nonrenewable in their supply for present and future generations, we must use them with care. This is essential if the mineral requirements of modern society are to be met. It is also essential because of the impact of mining on our environment. What can we do? Fortunately, there are many options to help us extend the fixed supply we already have. We call this mineral **conservation**.

Conservation Strategies

A. Substitution

If you are having school lunch and the cook tells you "we're running low on potatoes," a side dish of corn might substitute just fine. Minerals can also be substituted to help conserve a mineral or a group of minerals in short supply. For example, aluminum can sometimes be substituted for steel and copper. Have you ever seen steel pennies? During World War II, copper was needed for military purposes, so steel was used to make pennies. In some cases, plastic pipe can take the place of metal pipe. The use of optical fibers made of silica in place of copper communications wire is yet another example of substitution. When it is economical and the supply is adequate, substitutes should be considered.

B. Recycling

Think about This!

How does recycling
promote the wise use of
resources?

What happens to materials when we are finished with them? The iron in a junked car, the aluminum in your soda can, and the lead from an old battery are too often tossed into the trash. This trash, in turn, is probably trucked to your community's solid waste landfill. The materials still exist, but they are "scattered." There is no less gold, copper, or mercury today than before humans appeared on Earth. But in the process of using these and all other minerals, they become more scattered. Recycling is a conscious

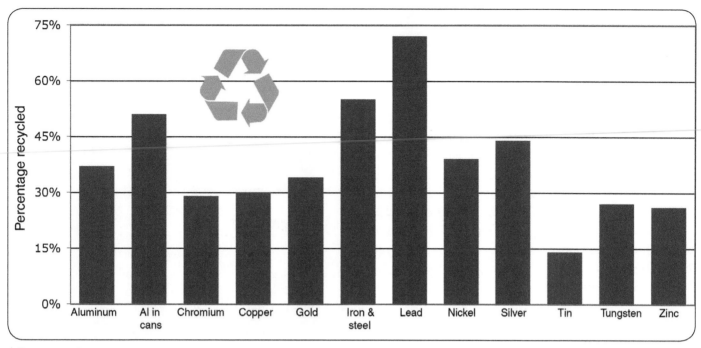

▲FIGURE 4.60 Some important metals used and recycled in the United States (*Mineral Information Institute*)

effort to conserve resources by slowing down this scattering of resources in the form of waste and scrap. Figure 4.60 illustrates a number of important metals that are recycled in the United States. We can use our technologies and economics to slow down this wasteful process. People can be made aware of and economically responsible for their own pollution. When the reward for recycling an aluminum can rose above a penny a can, the amount of aluminum recycled increased. It became worth the effort to save that can. In the economy of the future, it will be worth the effort to save almost everything from careless disposal. It will also be important to design for recycling. This means that we must design out the potentially hazardous materials from manufacturing processes and the products created. A worn-out car should be returned for maximum economic recycling, not thrown away.

C. Taxation

Concerns for a clean environment and our desire to ensure an uninterrupted supply of mineral resources for future generations is often not enough. Appropriate economic incentives also encourage conservation while providing additional revenues. Many states in the United States, for example, impose a *severance tax* on some of the minerals that are mined in that state. The tax is paid on the mineral resources removed from the earth. The rationalization for the severance tax is that since the minerals are located within the state, they in part belong to the state. Therefore, the people of the state should be compensated for that loss. The monies paid by mining companies are distributed to the state, local counties, or communities for roads, schools, hospitals, and other public services.

Some people argue that severance and other taxes unfairly discriminate against them. Too high a severance tax can be a severe handicap to a mine's operation; worse, it can prevent a mine from operating at all. When mining companies are successful, they increase employment and provide minerals to other industries at a competitive cost. These minerals can later be turned into products of higher value, thus increasing real wealth.

Think about This!

The recycling rate of automobile scrap steel in the United States is more than 100 percent. What does that mean?

Think about This!

How can economic factors affect our conservation efforts?

Question This!

Do you think states should collect a severance tax?

Car Battery Recycling

Reduce. Reuse. Recycle. These three words are paramount to the future of natural resources and the planet. In the 1940s and 1950s, recycling rubber from tires was important to the war effort. Today, recycling efforts have expanded to include everything from TVs and computers to cell phones and personal electronics. And yet, the single most recycled consumer product is the lead-acid car battery.

This standard battery starts more than 600 million passenger vehicles globally. It also powers golf carts, forklifts, and other modes of transportation. With a recycle rate of 97 percent, the lead-acid battery is recycled more often than aluminum cans and newspaper (see comparison in the box on the next page).

The world's largest, single-site lead recycling facility is located in the rural community of Boss, Missouri. Owned and operated by the Doe Run Company, North America's top lead producer, the Buick Resource Recycling facility processes more than 13 million spent lead-acid batteries annually. If you placed that many batteries end to end, they'd reach from Los Angeles to Indianapolis.

Each lead-acid car battery contains a set of metal grids, lead posts, lead oxide paste, sulfuric acid, and a plastic case (see quantities in the box on the next page). After the batteries are dismantled mechanically, the plastic case material is collected, washed, and sent to a designated plastics recycler. The plastic recycler will use this plastic to manufacture new battery cases.

New techniques for recycling existing lead products are extending the life of Earth's lead deposits. This, in turn, helps future generations by conserving this valuable natural resource. By recovering and recycling the lead in common products like batteries, computer monitors, and ammunition, recycling facilities are also helping the environment and saving space in landfills (Figure 4.61).

▲ FIGURE 4.61 In just 4 days, these batteries were collected for recycling at one small auto parts store.

Many communities now actively encourage recycling of all kinds. Common programs include collection points for electronics, curbside recycling containers, drop-off recycling zones, community recycling centers, and composting programs.

Most states now have battery recycling laws that offer consumers a $5 or $10 cash incentive for returning spent car batteries to stores where they were bought (see Figure 4.62). The batteries are then sent to companies like Doe Run for breakdown and recycling, eventually

▼ FIGURE 4.62 Most states provide a cash incentive to encourage recycling of used car batteries.

reappearing in new car batteries. This cyclical process, which brings together the efforts of consumers, manufacturers, retailers, government, and metals producers, makes car battery recycling one of the most impressive environmental success stories in recent years.

Recycling Rate for Common Products		Battery Contents
		On average, each car battery contains
Lead-acid batteries	97 percent	20 pounds of lead: recycled for use in future batteries
Newspaper	89 percent	1 gallon of sulfuric acid: used to make sodium sulfate used in paper, glass, and laundry detergents
Aluminum cans	52 percent	
Plastic soft drink bottles	34 percent	2 pounds of plastic: sent to a plastics recycler

4.17 Where Do We Mine Next?

As we have seen, mining has been and will continue to be a necessary function of our modern society. The world's demand for minerals is growing and so is the concern for the environment. An important question for the future is, "Where do we mine next?"

The majority of people live within a 30-minute drive of an active mine and never know it exists. In fact, many inner-city parks and golf courses are built on land that was once mined for the sand and gravel that helped build that city (Figure 4.63). Even when minerals are discovered in remote and unpopulated areas, mining still faces challenges.

Less than 0.5 percent (6 million acres) of the land in the United States has been used by mining in the last 100 years, but mining has an image problem. Some people believe that the best place to mine is always somewhere (anywhere) else. The problem is, we can mine minerals only where those minerals have been deposited, not where we would wish they

Think about This!

NIMBY ("not in my backyard") is a common complaint that mines, landfills, factories, and jails belong "somewhere else." Where should these places be located?

◀ FIGURE 4.63 Many parks and recreation sites in cities are built in areas that were once aggregate mines, like this golf course in Maryland. (*Courtesy Chaney Enterprises.*)

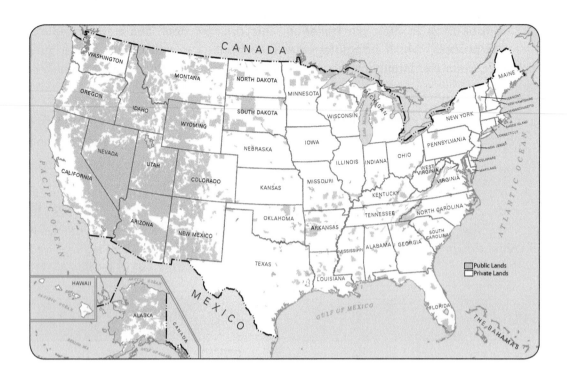

► **FIGURE 4.64** Federal public lands in the United States. (*www.NationalAtlas.gov*)

were. That means land use controversies will occur. You will learn more about land use processes and controversies in Chapter 16.

In the United States, most of the metal and energy resources are located in the West, which is where the majority of the public lands are located. About one-fourth of the land in the United States (643 million acres of 2.3 billion acres) is owned and managed by the federal government. Just the national park system comprises nearly 400 parks, which cover more than 84 million acres. Figure 4.64 shows the location of the federal public lands, and Figure 4.65 shows the geologically favorable locations for the occurrence of minerals. By comparing these two figures, we can assume that any new deposits of minerals that will be found will occur on public lands.

The two largest federal land management agencies are the Bureau of Land Management (264 million acres) and the Forest Service (193 million acres). The mission of both agencies is "the management of the public lands and their various resource values so that they are utilized in the combination that will best meet the present and future needs of the American people." This is called "multiple use" management because it does not emphasize one type of land use over another.

▼ **FIGURE 4.65** Known mineral occurrences in the United States. Alaska is shown to scale with U.S. map. (*www.mii.org*)

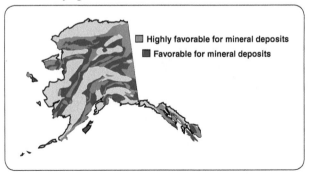

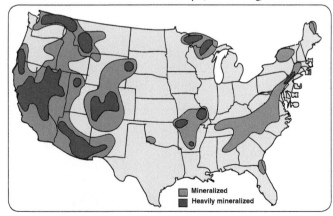

Public lands are increasingly viewed for their recreational opportunities, their cultural resources, and (in an increasingly urban world) their vast open spaces. However, the more traditional land uses (grazing, timber production, and energy and mineral extraction) also remain important, especially to the economic and social well-being of many rural Western communities.

These lands contain an unknown wealth of minerals and other resources that may be vital to the future of our economy. In some cases, denying ourselves access to these resources forces us to purchase them from foreign countries.

Some argue that public land preserves both valuable ecosystems and untapped ore deposits for future generations, assuming mining is allowed again. Others argue that the minerals can be removed without destruction of the environment and that reclamation can restore much of the mined land to a natural state or even (from the human point of view) an improved condition.

The natural forces that created the scenic beauty of our mountains and deserts also created mineral deposits. Thus, geologic placement of mineral and energy resources is scattered wherever earth processes have concentrated them—again, not necessarily where we want them to be located. The last activity in this chapter will help focus your thinking about this and other debates that arise from the process of locating, extracting, and processing mineral resources.

ACTIVITY 4.13

Mineral Issues

In this activity, you will identify key ideas about mineral issues and the challenges they pose. You will also present choices for dealing with these issues from multiple points of view.

Materials

- poster board, butcher paper, or other media for presentation
- markers or colored pencils

Procedure

1. Read the material on one of the following mineral issues your teacher assigns. Write down 2 or 3 sentences in your science notebook that summarize your reading.
    a. Mineral Imports (and exports) (Activity 4.12)
    b. Minerals and the Environment (section 4.15)
    c. Substitution (section 4.16)
    d. Recycling (section 4.16)
    e. Taxation (section 4.16)
    f. Where Do We Mine Next? (section 4.17)

2. On a sheet of paper or poster board, create a catchy headline that describes your topic. Be original.

3. Write 2 or 3 summary statements that focus your topic and clearly answer the following questions:
    a. Why is this topic an issue to begin with?
    b. Are there any choices or options available?
    c. What should be done to ensure the economic well-being of future generations?

4. If you work with a partner, make an illustration that shows some aspect of your topic.

5. Describe your topic to the class in a brief presentation (2 minutes or less).

To help you get organized, try using the following format:

> **Headline**
> - Bullet Statement #1
> - Bullet Statement #2
> |— — — — — — —|
> |— — — — — — —|

Summary

Mineral resources play a vital role in modern society. They provide the raw materials for virtually every manufactured item we can think of. They also serve as essential nutrients that all living things need to survive. Mineral resources are nonliving, chemical substances that are usually solid in form and are found in nature as part of Earth's crust or lithosphere. There are more than 3,000 naturally occurring minerals whose definite composition, crystalline structure, and distinct properties serve a wide variety of uses.

Most minerals arise from the hot, molten substance called magma. As magma rises from the asthenosphere and solidifies, it forms a host of minerals at or below Earth's surface. Other minerals form at lower temperatures on or just below Earth's surface.

Rocks, which are made up of minerals, are of three types. Igneous rock is formed by the solidification of magma. When any kind of rock erodes, settles, and becomes cemented in layers, the resulting new rock is called sedimentary rock. Metamorphic rock is rock that has been changed by high temperature and/or pressure. Both rocks and minerals have distinguishing chemical and physical properties that allow us to identify them by name and, in many cases, their origin.

Any mineral substance that can be mined at a profit is called an ore. Ores arise from the concentration of minerals through a number of natural processes. Techniques have been developed for locating, mining, and milling these minerals. In recent decades, advances in our understanding of Earth's crust and its dynamic processes (such as the theory of plate tectonics) have led to numerous successes in mineral exploration. Advances in technology have also helped scientists recover lower-grade minerals from deposits once considered unprofitable.

Obtaining these minerals involves a variety of issues such as mineral imports, taxation, environmental concerns, and policies for future mining. All these issues are colored by our world's rapidly evolving global economy and our ever-increasing demand for mineral resources.

Experts believe that the future of mineral supplies will be similar to the future of energy supplies. We will manage to get by, but present patterns will change. Some minerals will become more important; other minerals will become less significant. And some substances not used today will assume major importance. We can make one prediction safely: Mining operations will get bigger and more materials will be used. How we choose to deal with the challenges of our need for and use of mineral resources should involve all of us.

 REFERENCES

Canby, Thomas Y. Reshaping our Lives: Advanced Materials. *National Geographic* 176 (December 1989): 746.

Davidson, K. and A. R. Williams. Under Our Skin: Hot Theories on the Center of the Earth. *National Geographic* 106 (January, 1996).

Dickey Jr., John S. *On the Rocks: Earth Science for Everyone* (New York: John Wiley & Sons), 1988.

Dorr, Ann and Alma Paty. *Minerals—Foundations of Society*, 3rd ed. (Alexandria, Virginia: American Geological Institute), 2002.

French, Hilary F. Assessing Private Capital Flows to Developing Countries. In *State of the World 1998* (New York: W. W. Norton & Co.), 1998.

Hutchinson, Richard W. Some Broad Processes and Affects of Evolutionary Metallogeny. *Resource Geology Special Issue*, no. 15 (1993): 45–54.

Kious, W. J. and Robert I. Tilling. *This Dynamic Earth: The Story of Plate Tectonics* (U.S. Geological Survey), 1994.

Kusnick, Judi. Mining for Educational Resources on Mineral Resources. *Journal of Geoscience Education* (September, 1998): 395–397.

Skinner, Brian J. and Stephen C. Porter. *The Dynamic Earth* (New York: John Wiley & Sons), 1989.

Tapp, B. A. and J. R. Watkins. *Energy and Mineral Resource Systems: An Introduction* (New York: Cambridge University Press), 1990.

U.S.G.S. *Mineral Commodity Summaries* (Washington, D.C.: GPO), annual.

VanCleave, Janice. *Earth Science for Every Kid* (New York: John Wiley & Sons), 1991.

WEBSITES

Mineral Information Institute: http://www.mii.org

Rice University: http://www.earthscience.rice.edu

U.S. Geological Survey Earthquake Hazards Program: http://www.earthquake.usgs.gov

U.S. Geological Survey Volcano Hazards Program: http://www.volcanoes.usgs.gov

CHAPTER (5)

Growth and Population

GOALS

- To understand the basic properties of exponential growth.

- To relate that knowledge to world population issues.

In order to understand the impact of population growth on your own life and on the future of the world, you must first know how populations are studied.

—*John R. Weeks (demographer)*

Human Population Growth

Every living organism lives in a group called its *population*. When the population is small, the organism sometimes has difficulty finding other members of the same species to mate with. If a species' population is large, however, there are many choices for potential mates. But there also are new problems. In this chapter, you will focus on the human species and the issues that arise as the result of the size of our population and the rate that population is growing.

The Mathematics of Growth

Once two kings in Babylon enjoyed the game of chess and played with gusto. After one of their matches, the winner asked for an unusual prize. He handed the chessboard to the loser and asked that it be returned to him with one grain of wheat on the first square, two grains on the second, four on the third, and so on. The grains were to double on each square until all 64 squares were filled.

The losing king was delighted at the seemingly modest request and quickly agreed to it. He was soon sorry he had. The situation he found himself in is illustrated in the chart in Figure 5.1.

Square 64 represents 2^{63} grains of wheat. The total grains on the board would be one grain less than 2^{64}. How much wheat is 2^{64} grains? It is about 1,000 times the annual harvest of wheat for the entire world in 2005. This amount is probably larger than all the wheat harvested by humans in the history of Earth! How did we get to this enormous number when we started with just one grain of wheat and doubled it a mere 63 times? To grasp how this happened, we must first understand the properties of this kind of growth.

▶ FIGURE 5.1 Grains of wheat on a chessboard.

Square Number (number of the square)	Grains on Square (quantity required to double)	Number of Grains on the Board So Far (total amount of resource used)
1	1 (2^0)	1
2	2 (2^1)	3
3	4 (2^2)	7
4	8 (2^3)	15
5	16 (2^4)	31
6	32 (2^5)	63
7	64 (2^6)	127
64	2^{63}	$2^{64} - 1$

Modeling Exponential Growth

One of the best ways to learn how populations grow is to model that behavior. In this activity, you will use dice or colored wooden cubes to model growth. You will then change the variables in an attempt to slow down and stop the growth. Finally, you will compare this model to actual human population growth to see if the model is a good one.

> **Helpful Hint!**
>
> The type of growth you are modeling is called *exponential growth*. You will learn about this pattern of growth as you proceed through the activity.

Materials (for each team of 6–8 students)

- plastic container with about 250 dice or colored wooden cubes

Procedure

The directions that follow assume that you are using dice. If you use wooden cubes, make the substitution shown in the chart following step 5.

1. Each die or cube represents 1 person.

2. Each throw represents 1 year.

3. The numbers or colors in this chart determine the birth or death of an individual.

4. A "3" or "6" represents the birth of a child. Each time one of these numbers comes up, add a die to the population.

5. If a "1" comes up, an individual has died. Remove the die from the population.

Event	Dice	Cube
Birth	3 or 6	White, red
Death	1	Blue

Part A: What is unrestricted exponential growth (UEG)?

1. Create a chart like the one in Figure 5.2 in your science notebook. Make the chart long enough to allow up to 30 throws of the dice.

2. Take your covered plastic container of dice and carefully dump the dice onto a table. Push the dice to the side.

3. Put 10 dice into the container. These dice represent the population in year "0" (see Figure 5.2).

4. Carefully shake the covered container and dump the 10 dice onto the center of the table.

5. Count all the 1s that were thrown. Record that number in the column titled "Number of Deaths (N_d)" for year 1.

6. Total all the 3s and 6s that were thrown. Record this number in the column titled "Number of Births (N_b)" for year 1.

7. Now subtract N_d from N_b. If the number is negative, remove that many dice from your

▼ FIGURE 5.2 **Data for unrestricted exponential growth (UEG).**

Throw Number (year)	Number of Births (N_b)	Number of Deaths (N_d)	Number of Dice (population)	Growth Rate* (change/year = $N_b - N_d$)
0	—	—	10	—
1				
2				
3				
30				

*This column is the population change per throw.

Throw Number (year)	Number of Births (N_b)	Number of Deaths (N_d)	Number of Dice (population)	Population Growth Rate (change/year = $N_b - N_d$)

▲ FIGURE 5.3 Data for the effect of a limited birth control program (LBC).

population. Then record the new population in the fourth column titled "Number of Dice" for year 1. If the number is positive, add that many dice to the population. Then record the new population in the same column. If the number is zero, there is no change. Record a 10 in the fourth column.

Helpful Hint!

You are modeling a situation in which the birthrate is twice the death rate. In this case, the population growth rate is 1/6, or about 17%.

8. Repeat steps 4–7 until the total population exceeds 400 people. If you were given fewer than 400 dice, figure out a way to get a full set of data using the dice you were given.

Part B: What is the effect of a limited birth control program (LBC)?

1. Make a chart like the one in Figure 5.3 in your science notebook. Label the chart "Data for the Effect of a Limited Birth Control Program (LBC)."

2. Look at your data from Part A. In what year was your population closest to, but not larger than, 100? Record that year in the first row of the column titled "Throw Number." Also, record the population of that year in the first row of the column titled "Number of Dice."

3. Count out the number of dice you just recorded in the Number of Dice column, and place the dice in the covered plastic container.

4. You will now start modeling a limited birth control program. This will be done by having a "3" represent a birth, as before, as well as *every other* "6." The remaining half of the 6s will represent people using effective family planning, so no births will occur. (If you roll an odd

Helpful Hint!

You have essentially cut the population growth rate from 17% to about 8%.

number of 6s, round off in favor of a birth half the time and in favor of a prevented birth in the other half of cases.) Model this situation for a total of 12 throws.

Part C: What is the effect of a zero population growth program (ZPG)?

1. Make another chart in your science notebook like the one in Figure 5.3. This time label the chart "Data for a Zero Population Growth Program (ZPG)."

2. Start with the same year and population you began with in Part B. Record these 2 numbers in the first row of your chart.

3. Again, count out the number of dice you recorded in the Number of Dice column, and place the dice in the covered plastic container.

4. You will now model a ZPG program. This will be done by having 6s represent births and 1s represent deaths. All the 3s are now using effective family planning, so no births occur. Model this situation for a total of 12 throws.

QUESTIONS & TASKS

Record your responses in your science notebook.

1. Plot the data for Part A on a full sheet of graph paper. Label your graph "Population vs. Time."

2. Plot the data for Parts B and C onto the graph you made in step 1. Use two new colors to show the new lines, or use a dotted line and a dashed line. Clearly label the three lines you plotted.

3. Write a conclusion for this graph. Your conclusion should describe the growth in each case, hence, it will consist of three statements.

4. Plot the data for Parts A–C on two-cycle semilog paper. You do not need to know how semilog

paper works to use it. Make the little "1" in the bottom-left corner a "10." This was your beginning population. The little 1 in the middle of the page and to the left is now a "100."

The 1 at the top and to the left is 1,000. Label your graph "Population vs. Time" (semilog). Now, plot

Helpful Hint!

Semi means half, so the scale going up is logarithmic. The scale going across is ordinary. Thus, your time scale will be the same as on your ordinary graph.

the same numbers you plotted on your first graph on the semilog paper. Label each of the lines and make a statement about how exponential growth plots on semilog paper (on the average).

5. On a new sheet of ordinary graph paper, plot world population vs. time from 1650 to the present. Use the population estimates in Figure 5.4 and label your graph. Based on what your learned in Part A, how has world population been changing?

▼ FIGURE 5.4 World population estimates for selected years during the period 1650–2008. Statistics such as these are determined by scientists called **demographers**. The statistics are gathered by organizations and published in most almanacs.

Year	Population	Year	Population	Year	Population
1650	.47 billion	1930	2.1 billion	1970	3.7 billion
1750	.69 billion	1940	2.3 billion	1980	4.5 billion
1850	1.1 billion	1950	2.5 billion	1990	5.3 billion
1900	1.6 billion	1960	3.0 billion	2008	6.7 billion

[Sources: W.F. Wilcox (1650–1900) and United Nations (1930–2008).]

5.1 The Nature of Exponential Growth

The greatest shortcoming of the human race is man's failure to understand the exponential function.

—Albert A. Bartlett, Professor of Physics, University of Colorado

What are the main characteristics of exponential growth?

Topic: exponential growth
Go to: www.scilinks.org
Code: GloSci7e191

Exponential growth, like that on the chessboard and in Activity 5.1, is occurring around us in many situations. Because this pattern of growth is a major factor of our energy/resource/environment concerns, we must make every effort to understand it. The chessboard problem illustrates the following properties of exponential growth:

1. Exponential growth is marked by doubling. A few doublings can lead quickly to enormous numbers.

2. Exponential growth is deceptive because it starts out slowly, but gets out of hand rapidly (see Figure 5.5).

3. The total growth in any one doubling is more than the total of all preceding growth. Check this out by analyzing the chessboard data.

An analysis of your data and graphs from the activity on modeling exponential growth will show additional characteristics of exponential growth.

4. Exponential growth occurs whenever the rate of growth (r), $\Delta N/\Delta t$, is directly proportional to ($\propto$) the number (N) present:

$$\Delta N/\Delta t \propto N$$

Two quantities are directly proportional if their ratio is constant. As one increases, the other increases. Thus, when a population is doubled, if nothing else changes, the population will also grow twice as fast.

Helpful Hint!

Exponential growth plots as a "J" on ordinary graph paper.

N = number
t = time
Δ = change
ΔN = change in N
Δt = change in t
$\propto$ = is directly proportional to

▶FIGURE 5.5 Plot of grains of wheat added vs. square number for the first 14 squares on a chessboard. Note that exponential growth plots as a "J" on ordinary graph paper.

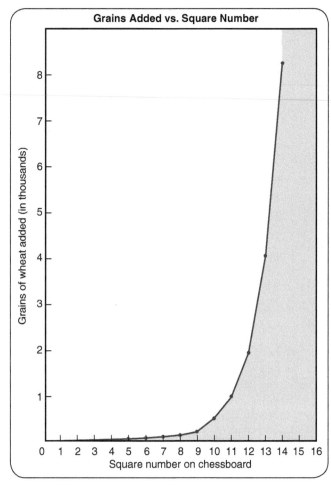

Grains Added vs. Square Number

Grains of wheat added (in thousands)

Square number on chessboard

5. A *quantity* exhibits exponential growth when it increases by a constant percentage of the whole in a constant time period (like a savings account bearing compound interest):

$$\Delta N/N \propto \Delta t$$

6. Plotted on semilog paper, exponential growth is seen as a straight line (see Figure 5.6).

7. It is useful to think of exponential growth in terms of **doubling time**. The doubling time equation is

doubling time (in years) $\simeq$ 70/percent annual growth rate, r

Helpful Hint!

The symbol "$\simeq$" means "is about equal to."

If the annual growth rate is 10 per 1,000 persons (1 percent per year), then the population will double in 70 years. If r = 2 percent, for example, the doubling time is $\frac{70}{2}$ = 35 years.

? QUESTIONS & TASKS

Record your responses in your science notebook.

1. Solve the doubling time (T_d) equation for r (the percentage annual growth rate). You now have a growth rate equation.

2. If the annual population growth rate is 5 percent, what is the doubling time? (Hint: Doubling time = 70/growth rate.)

3. If the doubling time is 7 years, what is the percentage annual growth rate?

4. Say you invest $5,000 in a business venture that guarantees 11 percent annual interest. How long will it take your investment to grow to $10,000?

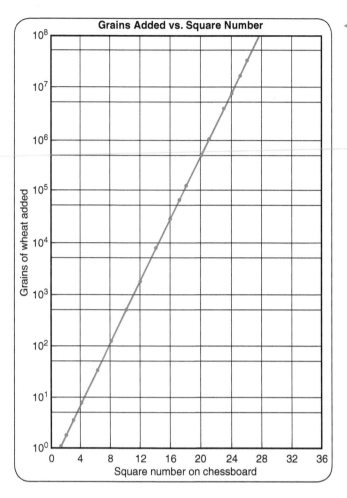

Grains Added vs. Square Number

Grains of wheat added (y-axis): 10^0, 10^1, 10^2, 10^3, 10^4, 10^5, 10^6, 10^7, 10^8

Square number on chessboard (x-axis): 0, 4, 8, 12, 16, 20, 24, 28, 32, 36

◀ FIGURE 5.6 Graph of grains of wheat added vs. square number for first 28 squares on a chessboard. Note that exponential growth plots as a straight line on semilog paper.

5. A bank advertises doubling your investment money in 12.3 years. What percentage simple interest will the bank be paying?

6. A city growing at a 15 percent rate will double its population in how many years?

7. At the present time, estimates are that it will take 117 years for the human population of the North American continent to double. What is the percentage annual growth rate?

8. The population of Latin America is growing at 1.5 percent per year. At this rate, how long will it take for the population of Latin America to double?

9. The population of Africa is growing at 2.3 percent each year. At this rate, how long will it take the population of Africa to double?

10. If the doubling time for the population of Western Europe is 700 years, how fast is the Western European population growing?

11. A parent invests $500 for a newborn infant in a savings account with a 10 percent interest rate. How long will it take to double? How old will the child be when the account has grown to $2,000? What will the value of the account be when the child is 28? If the child never touches the account until retiring at age 70, how much money will be in the account?

12. Make a bar graph of doubling time in years for the list of countries and regions that follows. Obtain data from the World Population Data Sheet

Think about This!

Israel has a population growth rate of 1.5 percent. The Palestinian Territory has a population growth rate of 3.3 percent. What are the political implications of these figures?

▲ FIGURE 5.7 "Stand up and be counted." *(Reprinted with special permission of King Features Syndicate.)* How many people do you know who can count exponentially?

Helpful Hint!

If the rate of natural increase is negative, the doubling time is infinite and can only be indicated by an arrow.

posted in class or found at www.prb.org. Click on World Population Data Sheet and download the data sheet. What does this bar graph indicate?

a. world

f. Nigeria

b. more developed regions

g. Palestinian Territory

c. less developed regions

h. India

d. United States

i. China

e. United Kingdom

j. Russia

Many situations in our lives can be explained by scientific principles such as exponential growth. The application of principles from science and mathematics to the real world, however, does not guarantee peace or happiness. It never has and it never will. Instead, the application of principles from science and mathematics can help us understand some of the problems we face with regard to population, food, pollution, and resource use. As the cartoon in Figure 5.7 indicates, we must know how to count.

Apply Your Understanding

Why is it important to understand exponential growth?

In this chapter, we examine the mathematics of exponential growth. Unlike you, most people have never learned to count exponentially. However, many things around us are changing at exponential rates. Knowledge of exponential growth will help us understand those events. We will first focus our mathematical knowledge on current population issues. This will offer new understanding as we examine food, energy supply, pollution, and re-source management issues in later chapters.

5.2 The Limits of Exponential Growth

Why is exponential growth abnormal in finite systems?

Bacteria multiply by division (see Figure 5.8). (Sounds odd, doesn't it?) One bacterium divides and becomes two, the two become four, the four become eight, and so on. Assume that for a certain strain of bacteria the time for this division is 1 minute. This process is recognized as exponential growth with a doubling time of 1 minute. Suppose one bacterium is put into a bottle at 11:00 AM. Then suppose the bottle is full at noon. This is a simple example of exponential growth in a finite environment. It is mathematically similar to the exponentially growing consumption of our nonrenewable resources. Keep this in mind as you consider these questions and answers about bacteria.

1. At what time was the bottle half full? Answer: 11:59 AM.

2. If you were an average bacterium in the bottle, at what time would you first realize that you were running out of space? There is no one answer to this question, so consider this: At 11:55 AM, when the bottle is only about 3 percent filled and 97 percent empty, would you be likely to perceive a problem?

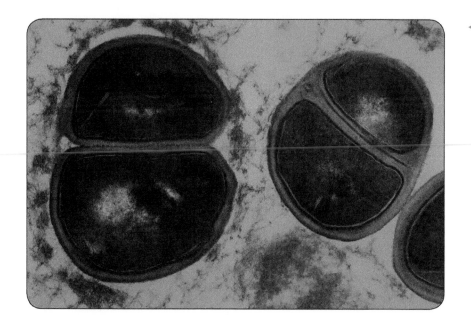

◀FIGURE 5.8 Cell division. The bacterium at the left has nearly finished dividing. (*George Musil/ Visuals Unlimited*)

Suppose that at 11:58 AM, some farsighted bacteria realize they are running out of space in the bottle. Consequently, with a great expenditure of effort and funds, they launch a search for new bottles. They look offshore and in the Arctic, and at 11:59 AM, they discover three empty bottles. Great sighs of relief come from all the worried bacteria. This magnificent discovery is three times the number of bottles that had previously been known!

The discovery quadruples the total space resource known to the bacteria. Surely this will solve the problem so that the bacteria can be self-sufficient in space. The bacterial "Project Independence" must have achieved its goal.

3. How long can the bacterial growth continue in the quadrupled space resources? Answer: Two more doubling times (minutes)! The following table documents the last minutes in the bottles.

The Effect of the Discovery of New Bottles

11:58 AM	Bottle 1 is one-quarter full.
11:59 AM	Bottle 1 is half full.
12:00 noon	Bottle 1 is full.
12:01 PM	Bottles 1 and 2 are both full.
12:02 PM	Bottles 1, 2, 3, and 4 are all full.

Quadrupling the resource extends the life of the resource by only two doubling times. When consumption grows exponentially, enormous increases in resources are consumed in very short times.

Like the bacteria, we are growing and using resources at an exponential rate. Figure 5.9 summarizes the energy history and possible energy future of the United States. The area of each rectangle represents the quantity of resources consumed or required during the 35-year period it represents. Although the percentage annual growth rate has varied, the average for the last hundred years or so has been around 2 percent. Many of our political leaders would like to "stabilize" the annual growth rate at about 2 percent. Figure 5.9 makes use of the fact

Helpful Hint!

Chapters 8–12 focus on energy supply, demand, and sources. At the end of Chapter 12, you will have a chance to propose an energy strategy for the United States.

▶FIGURE 5.9 The energy history and possible energy future of the United States.

Energy used before 1880 (wood)	Energy used 1880 to 1915 (coal)		
Energy used 1915 to 1950 (coal and oil)		Energy used 1950 to 1985 (oil and natural gas)	
Energy required for the years 1985 to 2020 (oil, gas, coal, and ????)			Energy required for the years 2020 to 2055 (Where will the energy come from?)
Energy required for the years 2055 to 2090 (This chart assumes a 2% annual growth rate or a 35-year doubling time.)			

that the total growth in any doubling is slightly more than the total of all preceding growth. If × equals all the energy used in the United States up until the year 2020, how much energy will be used in the 35 years between 2020 and 2055? in the 35 years after that?

Where will our future energy supplies come from? How do we plan for such growth? How long can this growth continue? The human population cannot continue to grow at exponential rates forever. Why? These are serious questions that we will address as you work your way through this course.

ACTIVITY 5.2

Now What's a Billion?

In this activity, you will use simple dots to help you comprehend just how much a billion is.

Procedure

1. Look at Figure 5.10. How many dots do you count on this page?

2. Apply this number to the questions that follow.

QUESTIONS & TASKS

Record your responses in your science notebook.

1. How many pages would it take to make 1 million (1,000,000) dots?

2. How many pages would it take to make 1 billion (1,000,000,000) dots?

▲ FIGURE 5.10 Dot matrix.

3. Imagine that you had a stack of pages with dots like in Figure 5.10. If in each inch thickness of the stack of paper there are 250 pages, how many inches of paper would it take to make a total of 1 million dots?

Helpful Hint!

There are 500 sheets in a ream of paper. A ream of paper is about 2 inches thick.

4. How many inches would it take to make a total of 1 billion dots? How many feet?

5. There are approximately 6.7 billion people in the world. If each dot represented one person, how many pages would be necessary to show the population of the world?

6. How many inches of dot-filled paper would represent the population of the world? How many feet? If there are 12 feet per story of an office building, how tall is the building represented by this stack of paper?

The Growth of Living Populations

Although we share Earth with millions of different species of plants and animals, it is helpful to focus our study of populations on humans. This is because humans have a major impact on all other populations, as well as their own. However, much of what you will learn about human population applies to all populations.

5.3 The Growth of Human Population

Apply Your Understanding

Note the impact of the "black death" as indicated in Figure 5.11. How might the current AIDS epidemic affect this graph? Provide evidence to back up your prediction.

One of the numbers increasing exponentially on Earth today is the number of people. Because population size is related to food availability, energy and resource consumption, industrial output, and pollution, it deserves our careful consideration.

World population size grew very slowly through most of human history (see Figure 5.11). This is because births and deaths were almost in balance. In the 1600s, however, things began to change. The standard of living increased significantly in Europe. Diseases and

▶FIGURE 5.11 Human population growth through time, 8000 BCE to AD 2020. (*Population Reference Bureau, 1875 Connecticut Avenue, NW, Suite 520, Washington, DC 20009-5728.*)

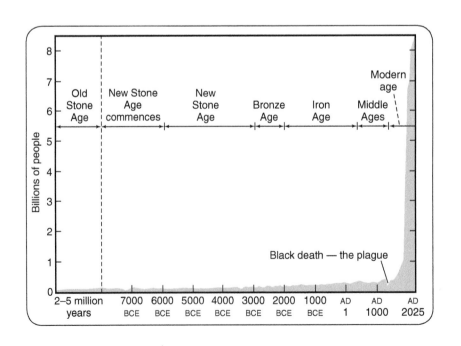

their causes were better understood. Medical practices improved. For various religious, social, humane, and political reasons, people made major efforts to eliminate disease and premature deaths, but only minimal effort to understand and control births. Births consistently began to outnumber deaths. And since the birthrate was higher than the death rate, population began to increase. At first, the natural increase was small. By about 1850, however, the situation had changed greatly.

Changes in the population size have been recorded by demographers. Demographers use a numerical equation to express the rate at which all populations grow. Considering the world as a whole, the fundamental demographic equation is

population growth rate = birthrate − death rate

In Figures 5.12 and 5.13, the population growth rate is shown as "natural increase"—the distance between birthrate and death rate in any one year. When we study the population in small regions, this equation must be modified to

population growth rate = rate of increase − rate of decrease

This takes **immigration** (moving into a region) and **emigration** (moving out of a region) into account. The rate of increase equals the birthrate plus the immigration rate; the rate of decrease equals the death rate plus the emigration rate.

We can choose to ignore the effects of immigration and emigration and write the equation as

rate of natural increase = birthrate − death rate

This is often done when immigration or emigration rates are small compared to birth and death rates. This is the case in both Figures 5.12 and 5.13.

In studying population growth, demographers find it useful to divide the world into "developed" regions and "developing" regions. More **developed regions** are those that are technologically advanced and have a high standard of living. These include countries in North America, Europe, Japan, and Australia. Less **developed regions** are those that have lower standards of living. Most are agricultural nations. In this category are India, the countries of East and Central Africa, and the People's Republic of China. China and India are now changing.

The reason for this division is shown in Figures 5.12 and 5.13. In both regions, the death rate has fallen as medical practices, sanitation, and education have improved. In the more developed regions, however, the birthrate also has declined, resulting in very slow population growth. In the less developed regions, the death rate has fallen much faster than the birthrate. This has resulted in rapidly growing populations, poverty, and starvation.

At present, the world population is growing at 1.2 percent per year, giving it a doubling time of approximately 58 years. The addition of more and more people has significant implications. Since Earth is a finite system, exponential growth cannot continue forever.

The maximum population Earth can sustain at a reasonable average living standard for its inhabitants is called the **carrying capacity**. The world human population today is approaching 7 billion. Some experts feel Earth's carrying capacity for humans is about 10–12 billion. Some argue it is less than that. Can we adequately provide for the minimal needs of 10 billion people?

Raising the standard of living in developing regions to anything approaching that in developed regions will be difficult. Thus, the population problem is one that must receive serious

Topic: human population growth
Go to: www.scilinks.org
Code: GloSci7e199

Helpful Hint!

Demography is the study of human populations.

What factors determine the growth rate of a population?

Think about This!

India is slated to become the world's most populous country by 2030.

Apply Your Understanding

Distinguish between developed and developing regions.

Apply Your Understanding

The present population growth rates for some developing regions are Africa—2.3 percent; western Asia—2.0 percent; Southeast Asia— 1.4 percent; and Central America—1.9 percent.

Apply Your Understanding

The present population growth rates for some of the developed regions are East Asia—0.5 percent; Australia—0.6 percent; North America— 0.6 percent; and Europe— −0.1 percent.

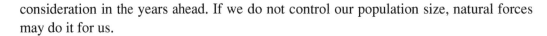

consideration in the years ahead. If we do not control our population size, natural forces may do it for us.

Whatever God's will for man may be, surely it is not that population is best controlled by starvation, disease and nuclear holocaust.

—Clare Booth Luce

► FIGURE 5.12 World birth and death rates in less developed regions (1775–2010). *(Population Reference Bureau, updated using U.N. Population Database.)*

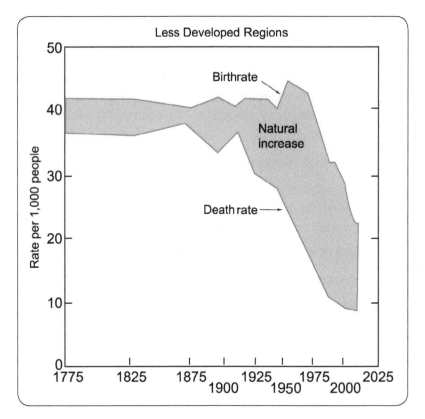

► FIGURE 5.13 World birth and death rates in more developed regions (1775–2010). *(Population Reference Bureau, updated using U.N. Population Database.)*

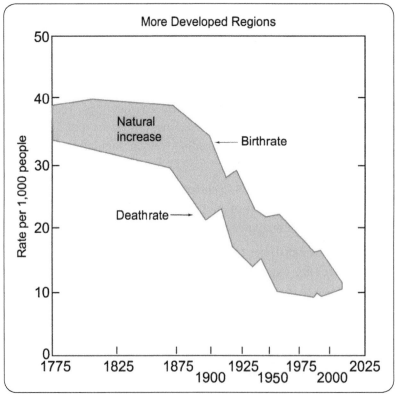

Picturing Population Growth

In this activity, you will look at population data based on specific countries and gender.

Background

Population statistics are often shown as histograms (see Figure 5.14). Because of their shape, population histograms are sometimes referred to as population pyramids. A **population histogram** is a bar graph that divides a population by age and gender. Each horizontal bar represents the percentage of the population that falls into a particular age/gender group. A relatively stable population would be represented by approximately equal percentages of the population in all age groups except for the very old.

> **Apply Your Understanding**
>
> What is a population histogram and what information does it give?

Materials

- Handout: *Population in Thousands—Student Worksheet 1*
- Handout: *Population in Thousands—Student Worksheet 2*
- graph paper (male and female)
- colored pencils
- tape

Procedure

1. Obtain a copy of Student Worksheet 1 or 2. Record the country and gender you were assigned in your science notebook.

2. The figures on the worksheet represent the population (in thousands) of each age group

> **Helpful Hint!**
>
> Example: The total population of the United States in 2004 was 293,027,000. The population of females age 0–4 in the U.S. was 9,887,000. Thus: 9,887,000/293,027,000 = 0.034, or 3.4%.

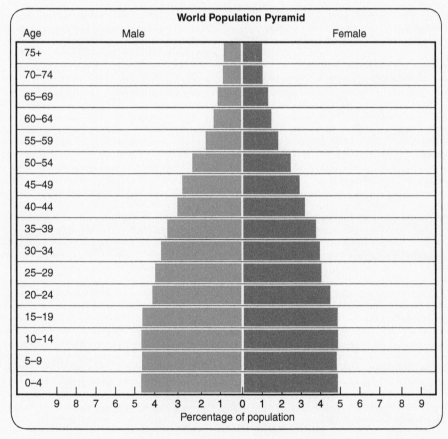

◄ **FIGURE 5.14** World population pyramid (2004) showing age/gender distribution. (*Adapted from Multiplying People, Dividing Resources: Global Math Activities, Population Connection, 2004.*)

within each gender for each country indicated. Calculate the percentage of the population in each subgroup for the country and gender you were assigned.

3. Obtain a copy of the graph paper for the activity. You are now ready to construct a population histogram for your country.

Topic: population histograms
Go to: www.scilinks.org
Code: GloSci7e202

The figures on the *x*-axis (the horizontal axis) of your graph represent the percentages of the population. The scale on the *y*-axis (the vertical axis) represents the age groups in the population. Draw in the percentages (vertical lines) for the age groups on the graph for the country and gender you were assigned. Connect these vertical lines with horizontal connectives to form a stair-step pattern. Use a colored pencil to color in the area under your graph.

4. Match the male histogram with the female histogram for your country. Tape the 2 graphs together and display them on the board at the front of the classroom.

5. Examine the 6 population histograms and answer the questions that follow.

QUESTIONS & TASKS

Record your responses in your science notebook.

1. Which gender has the higher population in the youngest age groups on every pyramid? Why is that the case?

2. Which gender has the higher population in the oldest age groups? Why might that be so?

3. Of the six graphs, which look most like pyramids? What does that indicate about their population growth rates? If birth and death rates remain the same, what will this pyramid look like in 25 years? What factors would change the shape of the pyramid?

4. Looking at the histograms, which country appears to have the slowest rate of population growth? How can you tell? If current trends continue, how might this histogram look in 25 years?

5. Which are the largest age groups in the United States? Why is there concern that smaller age groups are located under these groups?

> **Think about This!**
>
> In the year 2000, for the first time in history, people over age 60 outnumbered children aged 14 or younger in the developed countries.

6. What is different about the shape of China's pyramid? What unique factors have given the pyramid this shape?

7. Which country has the highest rate of growth? Why is this the case?

8. How would you expect the Mexican histogram to look if you graphed it 40 years from now?

[Adapted from *Multiplying People, Dividing Resources: Global Math Activities.* Population Connection, 2004.]

ACTIVITY 5.4

A Demographic Survey: Questions About Marriage and Children

In this activity, you will each complete a demographic survey about marriage and having children. The results of this survey will provide a statistical profile of your class. You and your classmates will then interpret the meaning of that profile.

Background

Demography is the study of human populations. Scientists who study populations are called demographers. Much of demography centers around obtaining, organizing, and interpreting statistical data.

You will take part in a demographic survey of your class to obtain statistical data on questions about marriage and children. You will receive credit for filling out this survey. Much of the survey is based on opinion. People have their own reasons for getting married or not getting married. Some of these reasons are "good"; others are not. The same can be said about having children. Couples have their own reasons for having or not having children. Rarely do they have children because of what a scientific study implies or what a professor said.

Materials (for each student)

- Handout: *Demographic Survey about Marriage and Children*

Procedure

1. Eight items make up a survey that will be passed out in class. Answer the questions as honestly as you can as you view your situation right now. Your opinion may change later; that's okay.

2. When you are finished, turn in the survey.

SURVEY QUESTIONS

1. What is your gender?

2. After high school, do you plan to go to college or to some type of trade school?

3. Do you plan to get married?

4. If you foresee marriage in your future, at what age do you think you will marry? (For most of you, this is only a guess; however, your opinion is important.)

5. If you plan to marry, would you like to have children?

6. If your answer to question 5 is yes, how many children would you like to have?

7. What advantages, if any, do you see in having children? In other words, what benefits and pleasures do you think you would derive from having children? Which of these benefits and advantages are most important to you personally? Rank your advantages by putting a "1" next to the advantage that is most important to you. Put a "2" next to the second most important advantage, and so on.

8. What disadvantages do you see in having children? That is, what prices do you think you would have to pay? What would you have to give up? List some of the disadvantages and, as before, rank your disadvantages in order of importance.

5.4 Understanding Population Growth

Topic: demography
Go to: www.scilinks.org
Code: GloSci7e203

Demographers look at many factors when they analyze population growth. You discussed some of these factors in Activity 5.4. Three factors of particular interest are examined next.

Family Size

Human population growth is not an automatic process. Many individual decisions contribute to both the birthrate and the death rate. Among these are decisions about when or whether to marry and how large a family to have. Family size is one of the critical factors in the determination of population growth. If the "average" couple has three or more children, a population will grow rapidly. When the average drops to two or less children, the population begins to level off (Figure 5.15). If two-child families are the average, the children replace the parents; over the long term, population tends to stabilize.

What must be the average number of births per woman for population to stabilize?

Apply Your Understanding

What are some of the reasons that the population size continues to increase in the United States?

At present, population in the United States and the world will continue to grow for a number of years even if the overall preference is for the two-child family. The continued increase

is because the birthrate is not the only factor involved in population growth. The death rate is also important. Other contributing factors include the age at marriage, the proportion of women who are of child-bearing age, and the rate of immigration. The percentage of women of child-bearing age in the United States is relatively large.

 QUESTIONS & TASKS

Helpful Hint!

The *gross national income,* or GNI, per person of a country is a measure of that country's wealth, economic strength, and standard of living.

Make a bar graph of the total fertility rate (TFR) per woman for the list of countries and regions that follows. Obtain data from the World Population Data Sheet posted in class or found at www.prb.org. Click on World Population Data Sheet and download the data sheet. How does the TFR relate to the gross national income (GNI)?

  a. world

  b. United States

  c. Mexico

  d. Africa

  e. Palestinian Territory

  f. India

  g. China

  h. Europe

Age at the Time of Marriage

Think about This!

Why is the replacement fertility rate 2.1 children per woman (in developed regions) instead of simply 2 children per woman?

Women are generally capable of having babies between their early teens and late 40s. The older a woman is when she first marries, the slower the population grows. This is because most couples do not wish to have children until they are married and can adequately provide for their family. Thus, if a woman stays single until she is 25, she has, on average, 19 years during which she may have children. If she marries at age 15, this span increases to 29 years. In addition, a woman who postpones having her first child is less likely to have a large family. She may become infertile, be divorced, or even die before having a second or third child. Postponement of marriage is a very effective way of lowering population growth.

The world population histogram in Figure 5.14 illustrates why world population will continue growing for several decades. It will continue even if the average preference around the world is suddenly for the two-child family. Replacement-level reproduction (two-child families) must be maintained for about 50 to 70 years before a population will stop growing. This is because several generations are alive at one time, and because growing populations have large proportions of young people.

Immigration

Immigration into the United States, both legal and illegal, contributes to our population growth. The United States is one of only a few countries that does not have severe restrictions on immigration. In 2005, 1,122,373 immigrants were granted permanent residence in the United States. The U.S. population also grew by 1,704,036—the number by which births exceeded deaths that year. In addition, the Pew Hispanic Center estimates illegal/undocumented immigration to be about 525,000 annually.

5.5 Problems Related to Growth Reduction

Although the major problems related to population change are associated with population growth, problems also result when populations stop growing. For a population to stabilize, it must go through a transition period. As the stabilization of a population begins, the base of the histogram shrinks. However, a bulge exists above the narrowed base.

This bulge represents a large age group followed by a smaller age group. Several things happen as the bulge moves upward. When the large group gets to high school, the demand for resources such as larger or more high school buildings and more teachers goes up. The group behind this large group is smaller. As a result, elementary schools must close and teachers are laid off. High schools are affected eventually when the larger group goes to college and the smaller group enters high school.

The biggest problem results when the larger, older group retires. Much of their retirement income will come from pensions and from social security deductions from the paychecks of the younger group. As you can see, the situation is difficult. If more money is withheld, less money remains for starting families and buying homes. Since the early years of marriage can be expensive, it is difficult for young people to put money away for retirement. A better solution may be to have the older group retire at a later age. In this way, retirement funds are used for a shorter period of time.

Retirement is not the only problem. The smaller group also represents a smaller demand for the items industry makes—homes, cars, radios. This means a smaller domestic market and production of consumer goods.

Another kind of problem appears when some countries stabilize their populations more than others. Since it is the developed world that is stabilizing its populations first, the percentage of the world's people who first reaped the benefits of industrialization is shrinking. What are the implications of this on the course of human history? What happens when the present developed nations represent less than 10 percent of the world's people (see Figure 5.16)?

Apply Your Understanding

Why does early marriage generally result in larger families?

What problems are encountered when human population growth is reduced?

Think about This!

The Japanese have the highest life expectancy—86 years for women and 79 years for men. On average, Japanese women are now giving birth to 1.3 children. Currently, one pensioner is supported by less than four people of working age. Shortly after the year 2010, there will be only two workers for every pensioner in Japan.

Think about This!

By 2030, almost 20 percent of the U.S. population will be 65+ years old.

► FIGURE 5.16 The shrinking West. You may know that East and West Germany are now Germany, and that the Soviet bloc is now a group of independent countries. *(Copyright © June 22, 1987, U.S. News & World Report. Adapted by the author.)*

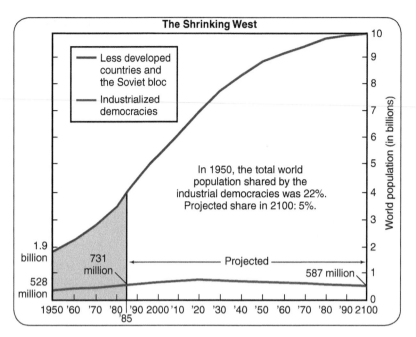

The Shrinking West

Legend:
— Less developed countries and the Soviet bloc
— Industrialized democracies

In 1950, the total world population shared by the industrial democracies was 22%. Projected share in 2100: 5%.

1.9 billion
528 million
731 million
587 million
Projected

(vertical axis: World population (in billions), 0 to 10)
(horizontal axis: 1950 '60 '70 '80 '85 '90 2000 '10 '20 '30 '40 '50 '60 '70 '80 '90 2100)

Note: Industrial democracies include Canada, United States, Australia, New Zealand, Japan, Austria, Belgium, Denmark, Finland, France, West Germany, Iceland, Italy, Luxembourg, Netherlands, Norway, Spain, Sweden, Switzerland, United Kingdom. Soviet bloc includes former U.S.S.R., Albania, Bulgaria, Czechoslovakia, East Germany, Hungary, Poland, Romania. Less developed countries include those in standard United Nations definitions.

The Birth Dearth—Basic data: *World Population Prospects*, United Nations, 1985; projections for industrial democracies from special World Bank projection; for rest of world from *World Population Projections*, 1984, World Bank.

5.6 The Demographic Transition

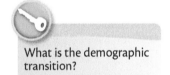

What is the demographic transition?

Apply Your Understanding

Use Figure 5.17 to explain what the demographic transition is and why it should occur.

As you have seen, human populations grew very slowly before the 1600s. Because the difference between birthrates and death rates was small, there was little or no growth. As medical care, sanitation, industrialization, food production, and knowledge about disease improved, however, the death rate among children dropped. But birthrates remained relatively constant. This combination led to rapidly growing populations.

After a time, people realized that fewer of their children would die young. They didn't need to have six or more children to guarantee that one or two would survive to care for them in old age. Slowly, birthrates dropped. In many countries, the result was population stabilization brought about by low birth and death rates. For example, in 1988 the birthrate in Denmark was 11.5 (per 1,000 population). The death rate was also 11.5. In Germany, the figures were similar. This series of changes is known as the **demographic transition**. It is summarized in Figure 5.17.

The exact cause of the demographic transition is not fully understood or agreed upon. Some scholars think that the decline in birthrates is brought about by improved economic conditions associated with industrialization. Others argue that industrialization is not necessary. They think any combination of events that can bring about an improved standard of living will eventually result in population stabilization.

As a society makes the transition, the drop in birthrates is brought about by a shift in attitudes toward children. Before the transition, children are viewed as valuable labor and as insurance

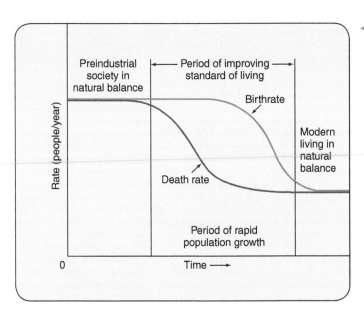

for care in old age. After the transition, children become an economic liability. Children are desired for other reasons: companionship; the family experience of parenting—raising another to be a good person; and the desire to have something of one's life continue. Some couples, however, desire only small families or no children at all. Reasons for these decisions include financial costs; emotional demands; time requirements related to child rearing coupled with career goals; and the desire for independence and privacy.

This attitude shift can be caused by social, political, or economic forces—separately or in combination. Often, for example, women will be better educated as economic conditions improve. They will also have more access to family planning. When men and women can control the number of children they have, they can affect the population's birthrate.

If a country can be helped to become modern, its birthrate is likely to fall. Prior to World War II, developed nations partially built their industrial base by using large quantities of cheap natural resources obtained from the poorer nations they dominated. Can China, India, Egypt, or Mexico accomplish now what Great Britain and Germany did in the 19th and early 20th centuries without access to large reserves of energy and mineral wealth? Do they have the necessary financial resources and knowledge base? It appears their best hope is for the development of technologies that provide modern conveniences at lower cost and use fewer resources. (More about that later.)

Topic: demographic transition
Go to: www.scilinks.org
Code: GloSci7e207

The drop in death rates and the rise in the standard of living occurred during the same short time period for many of today's economic giants (United States, Great Britain, France). Thus, their period of rapid population growth was relatively short. The situation in many developing countries is much different. After World War II, modern disease control and sanitation practices were introduced to these countries. This resulted in a dramatic drop in infant mortality. Unfortunately, economic conditions did not always improve. The result has been a population explosion and stagnation in the middle of the demographic transition.

Think about This!

Wealth, rather than poverty, paves the road to a cleaner environment.

If world population becomes too large, it may be desirable to go through a post-transition phase in which birthrates drop even lower than death rates. This way, the population could be reduced to some desired, optimum level.

Growth and Population 207

ACTIVITY 5.5

Analyzing the Demographic Transition

In this activity, you will extend your knowledge of the demographic transition by answering a series of questions.

Procedure

1. Carefully analyze the idealized demographic transition in Figure 5.17.

2. Apply your understanding to the questions that follow.

QUESTIONS & TASKS

Record your responses in your science notebook.

1. Why do preindustrial societies have high birth and death rates?

2. Why do we say preindustrialized (primitive) societies existed in natural balance?

3. Why does the death rate drop as the standard of living improves? Give at least two reasons.

4. Why does the birth-rate eventually drop as the standard of living in a region improves? Give at least two reasons.

> **Helpful Hint!**
>
> For ideas for question 4, think about changes that have taken place in the United States over the past 100 years. Think about your own goals and desires as you move through life. Recall the results of Activity 5.4, the demographic survey of your class.

5. Use the World Population Data Sheet posted in your classroom, select five nations with high GNI per capita. Also select five nations with lower GNI per capita. Then reproduce the table in Figure 5.18 in your science notebook. List the five developed nations at the top half of the chart. List the five developing nations below them. Then use the World Population Data Sheet posted in your classroom to fill in the data columns.

> **Helpful Hint!**
>
> Recall that the gross national income (GNI) per person of a country is a measure of its wealth, economic strength, and standard of living. Developed nations have a high GNI/person. Developing countries have a lower GNI/person.

6. Where on the idealized demographic transition graph (Figure 5.17) are the developed countries you located? Explain.

7. Where on the idealized demographic transition graph are the developing countries you located? Defend your answer.

8. The right side of the idealized demographic transition graph is labeled "Modern living in natural balance." What does that mean? (Be sure to mention both population growth and environment issues in your answer.)

9. The demographic transition suggests a humane solution to the world's population problems. What is it? (Ideally, how can we solve the population problem?)

10. Make a bar graph of total life expectancy (years) for the following countries: United States, Liberia, Sudan, Sweden, and Italy. Tie your graph to the demographic transition. Which countries have the best health care? Defend your answer. Obtain data from the World Population Data Sheet posted in class or found at www.prb.org. Click on World Population Data Sheet and download the data sheet.

▼ FIGURE 5.18 Sample table for collecting current data about some developed and developing countries.

Nation	GNI per Capita	Percentage Annual Growth	Doubling Time (years)	Percentage of Population < 15	Total Life Expectancy

5.7 World Population Trends

The world population passed the 6 billion mark in 2000. The present average growth rate is 1.2 percent, with a doubling time of about 58 years. About 98 percent of that growth is in the less developed world. Figure 5.19 shows the implications of that growth. Figure 5.20 shows the population histograms for these two very different regions.

It does appear that the demographic transition is beginning to occur for the world as a whole. This is indicated by a slow decline in the world population growth rate that began around 1965. This pattern is show in Figure 5.21. If this trend continues and as more and more nations modernize, the world population should begin to stabilize.

Apply Your Understanding

Why is population growing faster in developing regions than in developed regions?

Apply Your Understanding

When do you think the world population might stabilize?

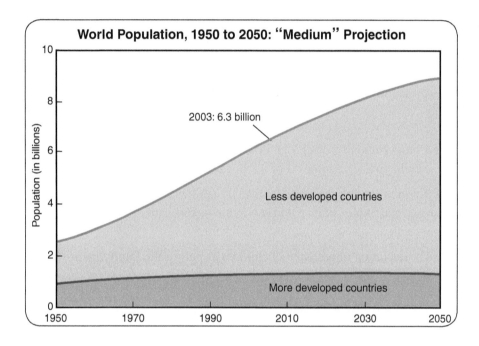

◀ FIGURE 5.19 World population growth and projection for less developed and more developed countries. *(Source: UN Population Division, World Population Prospects: The 2002 Revision.)*

▼ FIGURE 5.20 Population by age and gender: The world's more and less developed countries. *(Population Reference Bureau)*

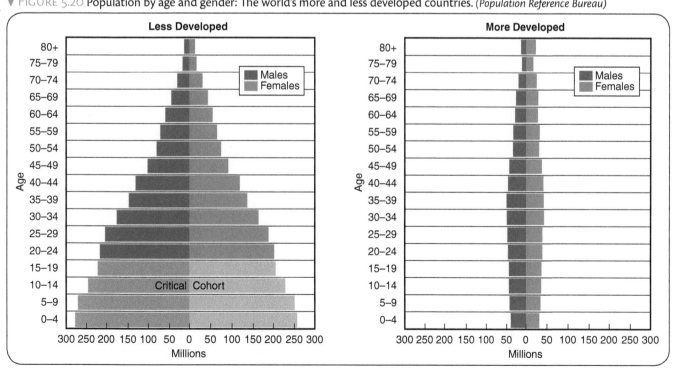

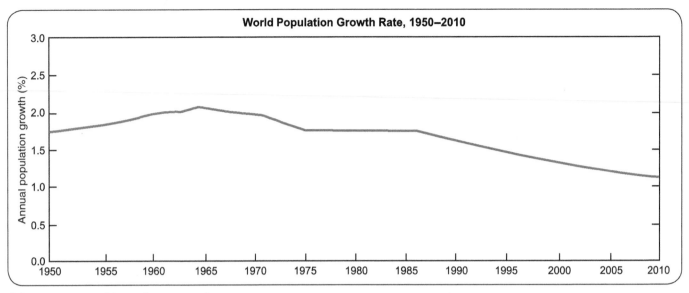

World Population Growth Rate, 1950–2010

Annual population growth (%) — y-axis: 0.0, 0.5, 1.0, 1.5, 2.0, 2.5, 3.0

x-axis: 1950, 1955, 1960, 1965, 1970, 1975, 1980, 1985, 1990, 1995, 2000, 2005, 2010

▲ FIGURE 5.21 World population growth rate, 1950–2010. *(Source: U.N. Population Database.)*

What factors may contribute to the stabilization of world population?

Apply Your Understanding

How does a National Aeronautics and Space Administration (NASA) photo of Earth from space help us understand the problems brought about by exponential growth?

▶ FIGURE 5.22 More women than men are enrolling in American colleges and universities. *(James Shaffer Photography)*

The United Nations projects stabilization of the world population at 10.2 billion by 2100 if the average replacement level of 2.1 births per woman is reached by 2035.

The reasons for the projected eventual stabilization of world population are many. An interplay of complex human and economic factors cause the demographic transition. These factors appear to center around the following:

1. The declining importance of children as part of the family labor force

2. The increased cost of raising and educating children

3. The improved social status of women

4. Rising educational attainment and improved employment patterns for women (Figure 5.22)

5. Increased urbanization

6. Concern about natural resources and pollution

Present trends seem to indicate that worldwide human and economic interactions will complete the demographic transition on a worldwide scale.

Controlling Growth

There are two accepted approaches to controlling human population: *economic development* and *family planning*. As you have just seen, economic development raises the standard of living and alters the economic importance of children and the social status of women. Family planning helps people have the number of children they want when they want them. Family planning strategies are the topic of the next section.

5.8 Family Planning

Family planning is the process by which couples discuss and determine the number and spacing of their children. It is based on

1. the desire of couples to control the number and spacing of their children;

2. a basic understanding of the reproductive process;

3. the availability of reliable birth control methods for married couples who choose to use them (Figure 5.23); and

4. The expected economic evolution of the family.

Birth control consists of all the methods humans can use to interrupt the production, movement, or joining of egg and sperm cells. In doing so, they prevent conception, the forming of a fertilized egg.

Birth control consists of a variety of strategies. Because these strategies are tied to questions of birth, life, and intimacy, people have strong feelings about them. What is acceptable and reasonable to one person or group of people may not be acceptable and reasonable to others.

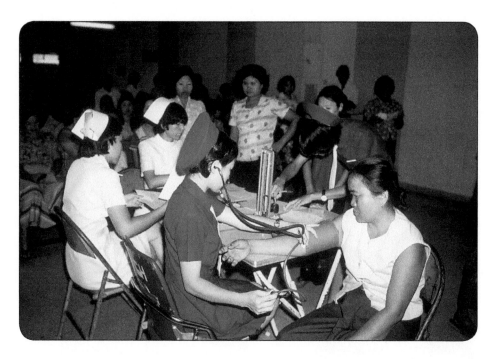

◀FIGURE 5.23 A family planning clinic in Asia. *(E.F. Anderson/Visuals Unlimited)*

Why do societies believe that total abstinence should be practiced by young people?

Think about This!

Abstinence protects one from pregnancy.

Think about This!

Abstinence is the accepted standard for school-age children.

Think about This!

Don't have children until you can assume the financial and time commitments.

Think about This!

What does the phrase "Every child a wanted child" mean to you?

Think about This!

Name some advantages of being young and not being a parent.

5.9 The Case for Total Abstinence for Young People

Because having children is such a tremendous responsibility, society as a whole believes that sexual relations should be practiced within the bonds of marriage. This belief is not always clear to young people because of what they see on television and in the movies, hear in some music, or read in magazines. However, the case for total abstinence is based on several strong arguments.

1. Abstinence from sexual activity is the only certain way to avoid out-of-wedlock pregnancy, sexually transmitted diseases, and other associated health problems.

2. Stable societies are built on a foundation of responsible citizens. Responsible behavior is the glue that binds together a free and stable society. Abstinence from sexual activity is the responsible standard for school-age children. Deviation from this standard adds unneeded strain on the surrounding community.

3. Couples should not have children until they can assume the full responsibility for raising children. This includes both the financial responsibility and the time commitment (Figure 5.24). Raising children is too expensive to do with simply a part-time job or by relying on the help of others. Many taxpayers do not look kindly on, and feel they should not be made responsible for, footing the bill for raising the children of irresponsible youth. Activities 5.6 and 5.7 will help you determine what some of these costs of raising children might be.

4. People desire to be good parents. The likelihood of being a good parent is greatly diminished if one cannot provide the love, time, money, and resources that enable a child to experience the richness of a quality life. The family experience can help provide the love and support necessary for children to become happy, healthy, and productive adults (Figure 5.25). Young people should want no less for their children.

5. Becoming a parent before one is ready robs young people of the full experience of youth. How often we hear adults say, "You're only young once!" or "Oh, to be young again!" Being young is not problem-free. Far from it. However, for many, it is the only time they have to try out a variety of subjects, clubs, theater roles, sports, and other experiences (Figure 5.26). Don't waste the chance.

▶ FIGURE 5.24 Raising children is an expensive undertaking. (*Adobe EyeWire*)

◀ FIGURE 5.25 The family experience is an important part of helping children become responsible adults. *(Adobe EyeWire)*

◀ FIGURE 5.26 School may not be perfect, but dropping out can pose a whole new set of problems.

ACTIVITY 5.6

Estimated Cost of Raising a Child to 18 Years

In this activity, you will estimate the cost of raising a child, in today's dollars, from birth to age 18. Note especially that the costs are for today. They should not be what was paid 15 years ago, nor should they be projected using some assumed inflation factor.

Procedure

1. Reproduce the table in Figure 5.27 in your science notebook.

2. Add your cost estimates in the column titled Total ($). Complete this activity by coming up with an adjusted grand total spent in raising a child from birth to age 18.
DO NOT WRITE IN THIS BOOK.

Growth and Population   213

▼ FIGURE 5.27 Sample table for estimating costs of raising a child from birth to age 18.

Item	Comments	Total ($)
1. Food	Average cost/month for infants, grade school years, and current costs. Average it all out.	
2. Clothing	Average cost/month for infants, grade school years, and current costs. Average it all out.	
3. Medical (include drugs)	Base on an average/year.	
4. School	Cost of preschool, if any, plus 12 years of regular school.	
5. Housing	Add in so much/year if you will buy a larger home because of the child. You may need an extra bedroom.	
6. Transportation	Cost of the additional use of a car to drive the child to the doctor, dentist, friends, clubs, etc., plus any help given to buy a car when the child can drive.	
7. Entertainment	Are children in your family provided $/month for entertainment? Include camp, team fees, etc.	
8. Utilities	Extra money that is spent for 18 years because children use extra lighting, TV, washer and dryer, etc.	
9. Dental/eyes	Add in the number of $/year for X number of years spent on dental and/or eye care.	
10. Vacations	Dollars/year spent on children for X number of any vacations. Include weekend outings.	
11. Recreation room, toys, bikes, presents, video games, sporting goods, musical instruments	How much will you spend to provide all this for 18 years?	
12. Insurance	Add up premiums on life insurance, and increased cost of medical/dental insurance, and increased cost of auto insurance for 3 years.	

Grand total _____

What additional costs might you incur during 4 to 5 years of college or post-high school training? _____

Adjusted grand total _____

ACTIVITY 5.7

Am I Ready for This Responsibility?

In this activity, you will answer a series of questions about the responsibilities of being a parent. Your teacher will provide a handout of this questionnaire. DO NOT WRITE IN THIS BOOK.

Am I ready to raise a child?	Yes	I Think So	I'm Not Sure	I Think Not	No
1. Do I communicate easily with others? Do I enjoy teaching others?	_____	_____	_____	_____	_____
2. Do I have enough love to give to a child?	_____	_____	_____	_____	_____
3. Would I have the patience to raise a child? Can I tolerate noise and confusion? Can I deal with disrupted schedules?	_____	_____	_____	_____	_____
4. How do I handle anger? Would I hurt my child if I lost my temper?	_____	_____	_____	_____	_____
5. Do I know my own values and goals? Could I help my child develop constructive values?	_____	_____	_____	_____	_____

What do I expect to gain from the parenting experience?

	Yes	I Think So	I'm Not Sure	I Think Not	No
6. Would I feel comfortable if my child had ideas different from mine? How different?	_____	_____	_____	_____	_____
7. Would I expect my child to make contributions I wish I had made in the world?	_____	_____	_____	_____	_____
8. Would I expect my child to keep me from being lonely in my old age? to take care of me? What if my child neglected me?	_____	_____	_____	_____	_____
9. Would I be prepared to let my child leave when she or he grows up?	_____	_____	_____	_____	_____
10. Do I need parenting to fulfill my role as a man or woman—to make my life more meaningful?	_____	_____	_____	_____	_____

Is my lifestyle conducive to parenting?

	Yes	I Think So	I'm Not Sure	I Think Not	No
11. Am I financially able to support a child? (Am I prepared to spend $100 a week, or a total of over $100,000 to raise a child to age 18? Can I afford this without the second income of my spouse if she or he chooses to remain at home?)	_____	_____	_____	_____	_____
12. Would I be willing to give up the freedom to do what I want, when I want?	_____	_____	_____	_____	_____
13. Would my partner and I be prepared to spend more time at home? Would we have enough time to spend with a child?	_____	_____	_____	_____	_____
14. Would I be willing to devote a great part of my life, at least 18 years, to being responsible for a child and spend my entire life being concerned about my child's welfare?	_____	_____	_____	_____	_____
15. Would I be prepared to be a single parent if my partner left or died?	_____	_____	_____	_____	_____

5.10 Reducing Problems Related to Population Growth

Problems related to population growth can be reduced. We can act individually or collectively.

Individually

1. Abstain from sexual relations until marriage. Only have as many children as you can financially afford and take care of properly.

2. Plan early for retirement so that family/society is not left with the problem of costly elder care.

Collectively (Nations/Society)

1. Make birth control information and devices available to those married couples who desire this service.

2. Expand educational and employment opportunities for women. This increases interest in family planning.

3. Where religious preferences discourage the use of artificial birth control, provide education in natural birth control methods.

4. Increase funding for research and development of new methods of birth control that are easier to use, more reliable, and more acceptable in some cultures than some current methods.

5. Raise the standard of living (in a sound environmental way) in poorer nations. Speed up the demographic transition.

SPECIAL FOCUS

To Have or Have Not? The Question of Children

All across the U.S., married couples who have put off having children to get head starts on careers or to gain good financial footings are reaching decision time. Now in their 30s, many can't afford to wait much longer to start families.

Typical are Michael and Deirdre Searles, both in their early 30s. He is vice president of an oil-drilling and exploration firm; she is communications director for a large computer company. How is this San Antonio couple dealing with the important question of parenthood? Deirdre provides a glimpse.

—San Antonio

For professional couples in their 30s, such as Michael and myself, the decision on whether to have children is a pressing and difficult one. In many ways, it is the first irrevocable life decision that we've had to make.

The passage of time, rather than clarifying our feelings, has tended to make the issues more complex. As the biological clock winds down, we are being forced to confront our feelings toward parenthood and come to grips with how having children will affect our careers, lifestyle and marriage.

Why is this decision more difficult for us in our 30s than it would have been in our 20s? First,

I feel we wouldn't have been making a rational choice if we had decided in our 20s whether or not to have children. At that time, having gone to college and found jobs, we might have borne children as our "next logical step" rather than making a well-reasoned choice.

In our 20s, we had a far more idealistic view of the world. We would not have really thought about the cost of college in 2025 or the physical drain of going three months without a good night's sleep when an infant comes home from the hospital. By our early 30s, we had ample opportunity to observe in other families the less enchanting aspects of parenthood.

Over the years, our careers have also made the decision more difficult. In our 20s, our major goal was gaining the financial security we felt was necessary before having children. As time passed, our careers gained importance to the point where the jobs that were to be the financial vehicle to enable us to afford parenthood actually became obstacles.

Both of us have challenging jobs that require travel, overtime and a lot of emotional involvement.

If we have children, we question whether we will be able to maintain the delicate balancing act necessary to provide time with the children, keep a healthy marriage and not neglect our careers. Even if we can manage to handle all of these things, will we enjoy our lives? As we see in many families, will we just exist on a never-ending treadmill of demands with no time to enjoy ourselves?

Many, including some of our friends, would say that we are selfish. To an extent that is true. On the other hand, we have known people who have had children for extremely selfish reasons. At least if we have children, we know it will not be for such reasons as insurance against our old age, a hedge against regretting it if we didn't have them, to prove that we are responsible, functioning adults or to find extensions of our own egos.

Yet, we know that you really can't analyze what it feels like to have pudgy little arms grab you and give you a hug or project the joy in watching a 3-year-old rip open Christmas packages. There are the twinges you feel when the young child of a friend, all scrubbed and ready for bed, comes to you for a good-night kiss. The fleeting feelings of envy on seeing parents and their laughing children at a beach or an amusement park. We can't hope to comprehend the emotions involved in watching the baby you raise go off to college, get married, or go to war. Can we deprive ourselves of these experiences and really be complete people?

We sit, firmly ambivalent at the moment. In the typical American way, we want it all— challenging jobs, well-adjusted children, and a good marriage. We are mature enough to realize that wanting something doesn't always result in having it. Maybe we're not wise enough to determine what's truly worth having.

If we don't decide, time will make the decision for us, and that is something neither of us wants. Therefore, we'll decide. Maybe not today or next month, but soon. We only hope it will be a decision without remorse.

—From: *U.S. News & World Report*, March 22, 1982, page 81. Copyright 1982, U.S. News & World Report, L.P. Reprinted with permission.

Summary

Earth's carrying capacity is finite. Exponential growth in a finite system is abnormal and cannot continue unchecked. Failure to understand this fact can lead to human tragedy because both population size and quality of life are linked. Exponential growth is hard to deal with because it creeps up on you. It starts slowly, but it can generate huge numbers very quickly. It can produce large human populations and demands for resources.

We must understand how populations grow, what good nutrition involves, and the demands populations place on natural resources including the natural environment. We must understand that the growth rate is equal to the birthrate *minus* the death rate. Lowering the death rate was a desirable accomplishment. However, doing nothing about the birthrate can cause huge population growth.

Population histograms, growth rate versus time graphs for developed and developing countries, analysis of family size, and the concept of age at marriage all help us understand population issues.

The demographic transition explains why many modern populations stabilize. There are indications that human population may stabilize around the 10–12 billion figure.

Family planning is the process by which married couples discuss and determine the number and spacing of their children. Many couples desire to maintain some control over when they bring babies into the world and size of their family.

Questions of birth, life, and intimacy are serious questions we all face. The ways we answer them have a significant impact on how successful most of us will be in life. These questions play an important role in what happiness we experience. We must choose wisely.

 REFERENCES

Bartlett, Albert A. The Exponential Function. *The Physics Teacher* (October, November, and December issues, 1976).

Bloom, David E., et al. *The Demographic Dividend* (Santa Monica, CA: RAND), 2003.

Brown, Lester R., and Jodi Jacobson. *Our Demographically Divided World* (Washington, DC: Worldwatch Institute), 1986.

Carlson, Allan. Depopulation Bomb: The Withering of the Western World. *Washington Post* (April 13, 1986): C1, C2.

Friedman, Thomas L. *The World Is Flat* (New York: Farrar, Straus and Giroux), 2005.

Haupt, Arthur and Thomas Kane. *Population Handbook*, 4th ed. (Washington, DC: Population Reference Bureau), 1998.

National Geographic. *Population* (October, 1998).

Population Reference Bureau. *World Population Data Sheet* (Washington DC: Population Reference Bureau), annual.

United Nations. *Demographic Yearbook* (New York: United Nations), annual.

Wattenberg, Ben J. *The Birth Dearth* (New York: Pharos Books), 1987.

Weeks, John R. *Population: An Introduction to Concepts and Issues*, 9th ed. (Belmont, CA: Wadsworth), 2005.

WEBSITES

Population Connection: http://www.populationeducation.org

Population Reference Bureau: http://www.prb.org

U.N. Population Information Network: http://www.un.org/popin/

U.S. Census Bureau: http://www.census.gov/

Photo by Stephen Ausmus, ARS/USDA

CHAPTER 6

Seeds of Life

The Continuity of Life

GOAL

- To examine properties of seeds, their importance, seed diversity, crop protection, and the role diversity plays in the continuity of life.

For 15,000 years of agriculture, nature and human nature have worked in partnership creating the seeds of survival. They're the stuff of life. Human continuity has always depended on the continuity of seed—its hidden power to adapt, survive, and multiply. Seed is our past and our future.

—From *Seeds* (video produced by Kensington Communications, Toronto; distributed by Bullfrog Films)

The Nature of Life

6.1 What Is Life?

One goal of a civilized society should be to preserve the continuity of life on our planet.

Content Clue

Six properties of life help distinguish living things from nonliving things.

An ecosystem is a region in nature that functions for the purpose of maintaining life on Earth. Just exactly what do we mean by "life"? A scientific answer to this question is that all life has these six properties.

1. **Growth and repair.** All living things grow by taking in nutrients. Plants make their food by using energy from the sun; animals get their food by eating plants or other animals. Living things use nutrients to grow larger from the inside; nonliving things grow from the outside. Living things also use energy from food to repair themselves; nonliving things cannot repair themselves.

2. **Reproduction.** All living things can make copies of themselves through a series of complex steps. The process of reproduction allows a species to continue for many generations.

3. **Change and adapt.** Living things have the ability to change and adapt as their surroundings change. This ability allows species to survive over millions of years. Change is tied to the great variety of different organisms that live on our planet.

4. **Movement.** Life is active. Movement can be subtle, such as a plant positioning a leaf to capture more sunlight, or drastic, like a rabbit running for cover from a predator. Movement of living things is more purposeful than movement of nonliving things.

5. **Response.** Living things have the ability to respond to their surroundings. They can control their responses unlike nonliving things. For example, when you are hungry you eat; when you are tired, you sleep.

6. **Death.** A single organism cannot live forever and ultimately dies. Death is necessary for life to continue. When an organism dies, decomposers break it down into nutrients and minerals. These then become available for use by other living things. In order for life to continue, there must be death and decomposition. Nutrients recycle and life begins again.

 ACTIVITY 6.1

Is It Alive?

All living things have six properties that separate them from nonliving things (see Figure 6.1). In this activity, you will examine several different objects and determine if they are living or nonliving.

Procedure

1. Reproduce the table in Figure 6.2 in your science notebook. You should have 1 line for each object you examine. DO NOT WRITE IN THIS BOOK.

2. Visit each station and write down the name of each object in the appropriate column. Spend a minute or two at each station.

c. Reproduction

d. Movement

a. Growth and repair   b. Death

▲ FIGURE 6.1 Various characteristics of living things. (a) *Giant star regeneration—KenLucas/Visuals Unlimited*; (b) *mushrooms on a fallen tree—Theo Allofs/Visuals Unlimited*; (c) *onion cell division—Robert Calentine/Visuals Unlimited*; (d) *Pacific dolphins—Brandon Cole/Visuals Unlimited*.

Sample Number	Name of Object	Growth & Repair	Reproduce	Change/ Adapt	Movement	Response	Death	Living? (yes/no)
1								
2								
3								
•								
•								
•	Earth							

▲ FIGURE 6.2 Sample table for recording observations of living and nonliving things.

3. Carefully examine each object at each station. Touch it, pick it up, smell it, and turn it over.

4. Then decide if the object has any of the properties of living things by placing a checkmark in the appropriate column.

5. In the last column, indicate whether the object is living or not.

6. The last station is a photo of Earth taken from space. The Gaia hypothesis argues that Earth, itself, is like a living organism. Rank Earth in terms of the 6 properties of living things.

QUESTIONS & TASKS

Record your responses in your science notebook.

1. Which samples did you find to be living? Why?

2. Which samples did you find to be nonliving? Why?

3. Were there nonliving object(s) that had some of the properties of living things? Explain your answer.

4. Do you think Earth is a living organism? Defend your answer.

Levels of Organization of Life

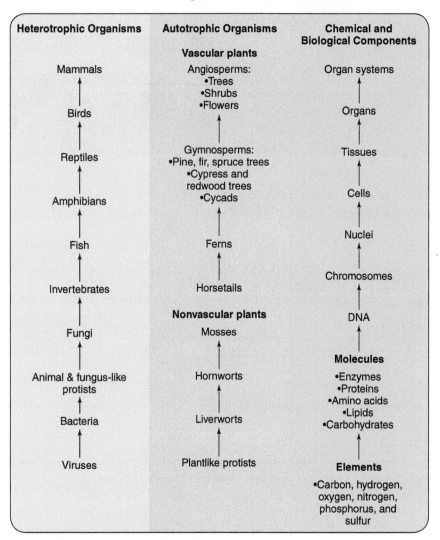

▲ FIGURE 6.3 Organisms and the materials that they are composed of can be grouped in a variety of ways. Three of those ways are shown above. Heterotrophic organisms must find ways to get food. Autotrophic organisms make their own food. The third column lists the elements, molecules, and other groupings of the components that make up various organisms, starting with the simplest and working up.

Note: *Global Science* is not a biology textbook. However, much of what is studied in environmental science (global science) focuses on the life sciences. It is useful to place and order many of the life science–related topics and terms. This illustration can help. It is not our purpose to define and understand all these terms. Greater understanding can come from reading life science textbooks, using the SciLinks features, and researching reference materials in a library.

6.2 Cells

The basic unit of life is the cell. All cells are microscopic. In other words, they cannot be seen without the aid of a microscope. Cells come in all shapes and sizes (see Figure 6.4). Usually the shape of the cell will determine the function of that cell. For example, muscle cells are long so they can contract and extend. Blood cells are small and round so they can flow through veins and arteries more easily. Most plant cells are brick-shaped so they can provide structure.

Topic: cells
Go to: www.scilinks.org
Code: GloSci7e225

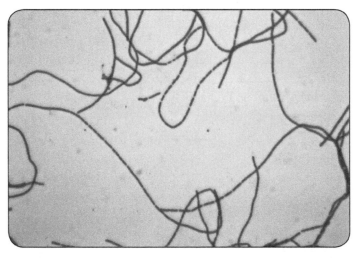

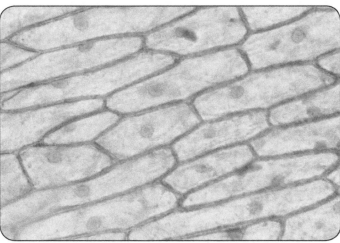

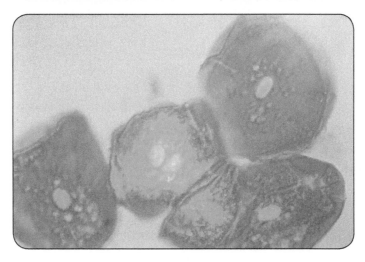

◀ FIGURE 6.4 Different types of cells show their diversity and complexity. *(Bacillus anthracis [top]— George Wilder/Visuals Unlimited; onion cells [middle]—Kevin & Betty Collins/Visuals Unlimited; cheek cells [bottom]—SIU/ Visuals Unlimited.)*

There are several different kinds of cells, but generally they can be grouped into two main categories. The first group is the most simple type of cells. These cells are called *prokaryotes*. Prokaryotes do not have a nucleus, and they have very few cell organelles (parts that help the cell function). Examples of this type of cell are bacteria and viruses. The second group of cells is more complex than the prokaryotes. This group of cells is called *eukaryotes*. All eukaryotes have a true nucleus and many cell organelles to carry out the cell's functions.

All organisms are composed of cells. Some organisms, such as an amoeba and a bacterium, have only one cell. Most organisms, however, are made up of many cells. A group of cells working together is called a tissue. Different tissues working together to perform a task are called organs. Ultimately, several organs working together are called organ systems. As an organism becomes more complex, it has more tissues, organs, and organ systems.

Content Clue

A cell is like a small factory.

As mentioned earlier, a cell has different parts, or organelles, that help it function. These parts work together so that a cell can perform the task it needs in order to stay alive. One can think of a cell as a microscopic factory and the cell organelles as the machines that keep the factory running. Probably the most important cell organelle is the nucleus. It acts as the control center for the cell.

Essentially, every action performed by all living things is a result of the function of cells. Without cells, life could not exist.

ACTIVITY 6.2

Cells: A Quick Look

As you have learned, the cell is the basic unit of life. Cells come in a wide variety of shapes and sizes. In this activity, you will look at different types of cells and become familiar with their differences.

For this activity, you can look at prepared slides or you can make your own. Find out from your teacher which method you will use.

Materials

- slides
- crystal violet
- onion pieces
- prepared slides of various organisms
- razor blades
- forceps
- water
- iodine
- microscope
- *Elodea* leaves

- toothpicks
- coverslips
- cheek cells
- medicine dropper
- safety goggles

BE SAFE

Wear safety goggles when working with chemicals. Report any spills to your teacher. Wash areas thoroughly with water if skin contact occurs. Use razor blades with care. See Material Safety Data Sheets for the chemicals you use.

Procedure

1. With a partner, obtain a microscope and 3 slides with coverslips.

2. If you are using prepared slides, make sure you and your partner observe each type that your teacher provides.

3. Look at each slide under the microscope. Start with low power and work up to high.

4. Draw a typical cell for each organism that you observe in your science notebook.

Cheek

1. On the first slide, add 1 drop of water with the medicine dropper.

2. Next, take a toothpick and very gently scrape the inside of your cheek. Be careful not to scrape too hard or to poke yourself.

3. Take the toothpick with the cheek cells and swirl it in the drop of water on the slide.

4. Add 1 drop of crystal blue to the drop of water. Then carefully place a coverslip over the cells by holding it at an angle and slowly lowering it down to the slide.

Onion

1. Take a piece of onion and break it in half.

2. Carefully pull the 2 halves apart. There should be a thin "skin" hanging off of one half.

3. Take forceps and peel off this skin. Place the skin on a slide.

4. Add 1 drop of iodine. Then carefully place a coverslip using the method described for cheek cells.

Elodea

1. Take a leaf off a fresh *Elodea* plant.

2. Place the leaf on a slide and add a drop of water to the leaf.

3. Carefully place a coverslip using the method described for cheek cells.

4. Use high power to observe whether any chloroplasts are moving. If so, use arrows to show the direction in which the chloroplasts are moving.

QUESTIONS & TASKS

Record your responses in your science notebook.

1. What were some similarities among all the cells that you observed?

2. What were some differences that you observed?

3. What are some big differences between plant and animal cells?

4. Explain why you used a stain on some of the cells. How did it help in your observations?

SPECIAL FOCUS

A Primer on Cells, DNA, Chromosomes, and Genes

Cells are the fundamental working units of every living system. All the instructions needed to direct their activities are contained within the chemical DNA (deoxyribonucleic acid).

DNA from all organisms is made up of the same chemical and physical components. The DNA *sequence* is the particular side-by-side arrangement of bases along the DNA strand (for example, ATTCCGGA). This order spells out the exact instructions required to create a particular organism with its own unique traits.

The *genome* is an organism's complete set of DNA. Genomes vary widely in size. The smallest known genome for a free-living organism (a bacterium) contains about 600,000 DNA base pairs, while human and mouse genomes have some 3 billion. Except for mature red blood cells, all human cells contain a complete genome.

DNA in each human cell is packaged into 46 *chromosomes* arranged into 23 pairs. Each chromosome is a physically separate molecule of DNA that ranges in length from about 50 million to 250 million base pairs. A few types of major chromosomal abnormalities, including missing or extra copies or gross breaks and rejoinings (translocations), can be detected by microscopic examination. Most changes in DNA, however, are more subtle and require a closer analysis of the DNA molecule to find perhaps single-base differences.

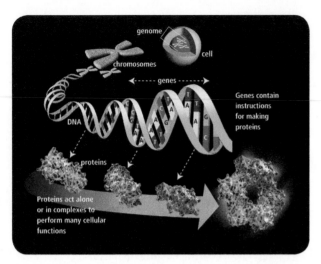

▲ **Figure 6.5** From genes to proteins. *(U.S. Department of Energy Human Genome Program, http://www.ornl.gov/hgmis)*

Each chromosome contains many *genes*, the basic physical and functional units of heredity. Genes are specific sequences of bases that encode instructions on how to make proteins. Genes comprise only about 2 percent of the human genome. The remainder consists of noncoding regions, whose functions may include providing chromosomal structural integrity and regulating where, when, and in what quantity proteins are made. The human genome is estimated to contain some 25,000 genes.

Although genes get a lot of attention, the *proteins* perform most life functions and even make up the majority of cellular structures. Proteins are large, complex molecules made up of chains of small chemical compounds called amino acids. Chemical properties that distinguish the 20 different amino acids cause the protein chains to fold up into specific three-dimensional structures that define their particular functions in the cell.

The constellation of all proteins in a cell is called its *proteome*. Unlike the relatively unchanging genome, the dynamic proteome changes from minute to minute in response to tens of thousands of intra- and extracellular environmental signals. A protein's chemistry and behavior are specified by the gene sequence and by the number and identities of other proteins made in the same cell at the same time and with which it associates and reacts. Studies to explore protein structure and activities, known as proteomics, will be the focus of much research for decades to come and will help elucidate the molecular basis of health and disease.

[*Source*: U.S. Department of Energy Genomics Program: DOEgenomes.org.]

 Seeds for Thought

Topic: seeds
Go to: www.scilinks.org
Code: GloSci7e228

Seeds are often the connection between soil and the food we eat. Good soil is necessary for seeds to grow quickly and produce strong plants. And plants are either a food we eat directly or the food for animals we will eat. Because seeds are the connection between the soil and the food on your plate at lunch, the next few activities will focus on the characteristics of seeds.

ACTIVITY 6.3

Characteristics of Seeds

In this activity, you will identify the characteristics of seeds that make them unique. You will use these ideas to consider the role of seeds in agriculture.

Materials

- 4–5 packets of seeds
- hand lens (optional)
- clear metric rulers (optional)

Procedure

1. With a partner, list 5 or 6 things you know about seeds in your science notebook.

2. Share your list with another group. Add ideas that you did not think of to your list.

3. Prepare a class list of 15–20 facts about seeds.

4. If you found a seed on the floor, how would you know what kind of seed it is? How might you find out?

5. Examine the clear plastic packets of seeds (4–5 unidentified species).

6. Develop a way to compare and record information about the seeds. Consider such characteristics as color, size, and shape.

7. Although you don't know what kind of seed each sample is, what information is stored inside each seed?

ACTIVITY 6.4

Seed Adaptation

In this activity, you will design and conduct an inquiry into seed adaptation.

Background

The fossil record indicates that plants have been on Earth for 650 million years. During that time, Earth has changed quite a bit. Yet plants have adapted and survived these changes. Sometimes, the changes in the genetic makeup of a plant occur naturally. Sometimes, these changes are induced (caused) by humans.

In searching for a new variation of a plant that might be able to respond to and survive certain environments, scientists will try to change a seed. This can be done by crossbreeding, genetic engineering, applying chemicals to seeds, or by radiating them. For example, scientists may radiate some seeds. They would then compare those seeds to nonradiated seeds to see how the seeds germinate and grow in polluted air. Some plants from the changed seeds may do better than the plants from regular seeds. That means the genetic makeup of these plants was changed by the radiation in a way that is favorable. Scientists would then study the plants in more detail.

Materials

- various seeds
- planting soil
- small containers
- water
- microwave oven (optional)
- UV light (optional)
- chemicals such as bleach, vinegar, baking soda (use your imagination)
- safety goggles

⚠ WARNING

Wear safety goggles when working with chemicals or UV light. Heed the warnings on the containers of chemicals you choose to work with. Report any spills to your teacher. Do not look directly at UV light.

Procedure

1. Think about the background information you just read and your class discussion. Develop a testable question for an experiment you can conduct in class with the available time and equipment.

2. Choose a type of stress to expose your seeds to.

3. Based on your work in steps 1 and 2, design an experiment to see the effect of the stress you exposed your plants to. Remember, you will need to control all the variables in your experiment except the one you are testing.

4. Have your teacher review your experimental design before proceeding.

5. Conduct your experiment.

Helpful Hint!

Examples of stresses to seeds are exposure to microwaves, UV light, chemicals, sound, heat, or gases.

Helpful Hint!

Be sure to use your science notebook to record your testable question, your experimental design, and the results of your experiment.

6. Record the results of your experiment. Based on your data, draw a conclusion about the idea you were testing.

7. Share your results and conclusion with the class.

QUESTIONS & TASKS

Record your responses in your science notebook.

1. What stresses seem to cause changes in plant seeds? What is your evidence for your response?

2. What changes would you consider positive changes? Why?

3. What changes would you consider negative changes? Why?

4. What is the importance of induced, or human-caused, changes to seeds when considering their use in agriculture?

6.3 The Importance of Seeds

Think about This!

Why are seeds the basic food of life?

Just as cells are the basic units of life, seeds are the basic food of life. Most animal species depend on seeds or the plants that grow from seed as a food source. On land without seeds, very few animals and plants would exist.

Apply Your Understanding

What are the two main parts of a seed?

Seeds are reproductive structures that contain a plant embryo (beginning plant) and its stored food. As many as 250,000 species of plants produce seeds. The seeds of these plants grow into the offspring of many plant species. Seed-producing plants are grouped into two main categories: enclosed seed plants (*angiosperms*) and naked seed plants (*gymnosperms*).

Seeds are a major source of food for humans.

Seeds are a very important part of our daily lives (see Figure 6.6). Many different types of seeds provide food for millions of people. Some of the more important seeds are those of the cereal grains. These include plants like corn, oats, rice, and wheat. Other major crops include seeds from the legume family, which include beans, peas, and peanuts.

Seed products are used in cooking. Vegetable oil comes from a large group of seeds. Some of the more common seeds are corn, peanut, soybean, canola, safflower, and sunflower. These seeds are also used to make other products such as margarine, salad oil, and shortening. Certain spices used to flavor food come from seeds like dill, mustard, and pepper. In addition, seeds are used to make other products such as beer, coffee, and cocoa.

Think about This!

Seeds are used by animals and industry.

Seeds are not only important in producing food. They are also important ingredients in products like detergent, soap, paints, varnishes, and stains. One particularly important seed, corn, is used to make cornstarch. This substance is used to make a variety of products such as adhesives and explosives. The biofuel alcohol can be made from corn and sugarcane. Biodiesel can be made from corn and soybeans. Seeds are also used to make food for other animals. The most common seeds used in livestock feed are corn, soybeans, oats, and other grains. Seeds such as belladonna and castor oil are important in making medicines. Finally, seeds are used in the flower industry as well as in reforesting land that has been logged. Seeds are essential in conservation and timber production. Ultimately, many seeds are responsible for the maintenance of the food supply for wildlife.

Apply Your Understanding

Name some industrial, medical, and fuel products that come from seeds.

◀ FIGURE 6.6 Seeds are the foundation of many of the products we use.

The Diversity of Life

The diversity of the organisms around us ties to our own survival.

ACTIVITY 6.5

If You've Seen One Tomato Seed, You Haven't Seen 'Em All!

If you go to the grocery store, you might see a variety of tomatoes. There are cherry tomatoes, yellow tomatoes, plum tomatoes, and beefsteak tomatoes (see Figure 6.7). Tomatoes come in many shapes, sizes, and colors. In this activity, you will examine tomato seeds that grow different kinds of tomatoes to see if you can tell the difference.

Materials

- tomato seed bank, displaying 9 photos and names and 9 clear plastic packages of seeds

◀ FIGURE 6.7 Tomatoes come in many shapes, colors, and sizes. (Agricultural Research Service)

Procedure

1. Make a 2-column chart in your science notebook. Label the left column "Tomato Variety." Label the right column "Seed Package Number."

2. The top half of the tomato seed bank displays photos of 9 varieties of tomatoes (numbered 1–9). Record these numbers and names in the left column of your chart.

3. The bottom half of the tomato seed bank displays clear plastic packages. These packages contain samples of the seeds for each variety of tomato. They are labeled A–I, but have been placed in random order. Try to match the seed with its picture. Correctly write the letters in the right column of the chart.

QUESTIONS & TASKS

Record your responses in your science notebook.

1. Why was this matching hard to do?

2. Do the seeds "know" which variety they are? Explain.

3. How do you think the tomato varieties differ?

4. What are the advantages of these differences? What are the disadvantages?

6.4 Nonhuman Organisms and Agriculture

Think about This!

How is food lost to nonhuman organisms?

Up to this point, we have implied that humans are the main organisms that eat products of agriculture. Clearly, that is not the case. Other organisms compete for the food available in the ecosphere. Quite often, they are so successful that they greatly reduce the amount of food available to people.

We have all seen some loss of food to other organisms. For instance, food left too long in the refrigerator spoils and must be thrown away. The spoilage is the result of the food's breakdown by fungi, bacteria, and other decomposers. These cannot be seen at first, but they often grow to visible size. The mold on bread is a kind of fungus. Have you learned never to open and consume the contents of a can when the ends bulge? The bulging is evidence of the production of gas inside the can. The gas is made by bacteria living and growing within the can. Toxins produced by these bacterial strains can be fatal to human beings. Another "decomposer" of foods can be found in flour and cereals left on the shelf for a long time. These products can support large populations of weevils and mealworms.

Spoilage is less of a problem in the United States than in many other parts of the world because of our technology. The energy required for food processing and refining techniques is normally available. Refrigeration, freezing, vacuum packing, curing, drying, culturing, sterilizing, and pasteurizing all retard bacterial growth. And the use of preservatives extends the shelf life of products ranging from soda crackers to instant pudding.

Bacteria, fungi, and other microorganisms are not our only competitors for food. Among the most widespread and serious threats to the human food supply are insects. A scientist at the Smithsonian Museum of Natural History estimates there are 30 million species of insects in the world. Furthermore, it is estimated that "in poundage, insects collectively outweigh the human race by a ratio of 12 to 1" (*U.S. News and World Report,* June 14, 1982, page 44).

Many people assume that ridding crops of *insect pests* is a simple matter of using "bug killers" in the fields. However, there are some downsides to using *insecticides*. For instance, various insecticides may pose hazards to human health. In addition, using chemicals to control agricultural pests sometimes has limited effectiveness. A look at some fundamental principles of biology, modeled in the next activity, will help you to understand why.

Competing to Survive, Surviving to Compete

In Activity 6.4, you learned about the adaptations plants can exhibit. As agricultural plants evolve through natural or artificial selections, so do the organisms that feed on those plants. We consider these organisms pests because they destroy our crops (see Figure 6.8). It is possible to find organisms that will destroy the pests before the pests have a chance to destroy the crop. In this activity, you will model the process of natural selection.

Materials (for each team of 4 students)

- 1 cup of assorted food units
- 4 plastic cups
- plastic knife, fork, and spoon (1 each)
- calculator
- watch (or clock) that indicates seconds
- Handout: *Data Tables*

Procedure

1. Form a group of 4 and collect the materials listed above for your group.

▲ FIGURE 6.8 These aphids will quickly suck the water out of the plant and kill it. (*Photo by Dr. Harold Hungerford.*)

2. Each group member assumes a trait: knife, fork, spoon, or pincher (use your hand). Each group member can assume only 1 of these traits and all traits must be assumed.

3. Empty the cup of food units onto the table. Spread them out so they cover much of the available space.

4. Use only 1 hand to model the use of your trait. Use the utensil you were given or your thumb and forefinger if you are the "pincher."

5. On a given signal, begin collecting food units for 1 minute. Collect as many food units as you can during this minute. *Collect only 1 food unit at a time.* Place food units into your plastic cup. Stop when the minute is over.

6. Count the food units that you collected and record the number in the first row on the *Data Tables* handout labeled "Food Units Acquired." In addition, record the number of units collected by the individuals with the other traits.

7. Next, make calculations for the data your team has recorded. (See the box titled Calculations.) Then go on to step 8.

8. Repeat steps 5 and 6 for generation 1. Record all data. Calculate the total food units acquired, the reproduction potential, and the number of individuals for each trait. Then repeat steps 5 and 6 for generation 2. After the calculations are completed, repeat steps 5 and 6 for generation 3. Finalize your calculations.

QUESTIONS & TASKS

Record your responses in your science notebook.

1. Based on your understanding of *natural selection*, would you say that natural selection occurred in this activity? Explain. (You will need to read section 6.5 Natural Selection, Pests, and the Food Supply to answer this question.)

2. Which trait was the most advantageous? Why?

3. How long did it take (or would it take) for one of the traits to disappear (become **extinct**)? Estimate if necessary.

4. Would you expect your data tables to be exactly like the data tables of other teams? Why or why not?

5. Would you expect your data tables to be similar to the tables of other teams? Why or why not?

6. Did the type of food unit make a difference in the number of units picked up? Explain your answer.

Calculations

1. Examine the section of the Data Tables handout labeled "Individuals." Note that this activity begins with 4 groups ("utensils") of 25 individuals each. Each group exhibits 1 of the 4 traits. Thus, we begin with 100 individuals. That means each group member represents 25 individuals in round 1.

2. Total the number of food units acquired by all individuals. Place the total in the first box of the last column of the Food Units Acquired table.

3. Determine the survival potential for each trait as follows: Multiply the number of individuals for a trait by the number of food units collected using that trait. Example: 25 individuals (knife) × 23 food units collected with knife = 575. Turn to the table labeled "Survival Potential." Enter the number (575) in the box for Knife/generation 1.

4. Determine the survival potential for each of the other traits. Record your answers in the table.

5. Convert the survival potential for each trait to a percentage by dividing the potential for that trait by the total potential for that generation. Multiply by 100 to change to a percent.

> **Helpful Hint!**
> The total number of individuals in each generation should be 100 (or very close to 100 due to rounding off). Use this fact to help check your accuracy.

Potential #/total potential × 100 = _____ percent having that trait for that generation.

Round all percentages to the nearest whole number. This whole number represents the individuals to be recorded in the Individuals table. Record this number in that table for generation 1.

[Adapted from an activity by Kevin Fisher, Region XI Education Service Center, Fort Worth, Texas.]

6.5 Natural Selection, Pests, and the Food Supply

What is natural selection?

Topic: natural selection
Go to: www.scilinks.org
Code: GloSci7e234

Biologists speak of genetic changes in organisms in terms of **natural selection**. During this process, organisms that survive have genetic characteristics that are advantageous for survival in their particular environments. That is, the genetic characteristics are naturally selected for the environment. Organisms possessing a characteristic that increases their chances of survival and reproduction are said to have a **selective advantage**. When conditions in the environment change, that advantage may no longer be advantageous. Another genetic variation in the population may become more likely to survive and reproduce. The survival of one form over another leads to changes in the proportions of certain genes in the population. This process results in changes in species.

When considering agriculture production, we have to think about ways to control losses of food crops to other organisms, especially to insect pests. What are the advantages and disadvantages of using pesticides to control insect pests?

Insects are widespread, diverse, and numerous. They reproduce rapidly. Tremendous genetic variability exists within a single species. There is even greater variability across species. Variability is the raw material of natural selection. When one genetic form is at a disadvantage, another is at an advantage.

Why do insects adapt so readily?

Beginning in 1981, California farmers were plagued by hordes of gnat-sized flies that carried a virus. As the virus infected plants, millions of dollars worth of melons, lettuce, and squash were lost. How can such losses be prevented?

Suppose a farmer sprays a field of squash with an insecticide known to be effective in killing flies. At first, the spraying works. Most of the flies are susceptible to the spray and are killed by it. A few flies have a genetic resistance to the chemical. They survive and reproduce, passing their genetic advantage on to most of their offspring. At first, the population is small. In fact, it may go unnoticed for years. The farmer may decide the problem is solved. Eventually, however, a large, new population of flies appears. This time, most flies are resistant to the pesticide that was so effective only a few years earlier. Now a new spray must be found. The selective process starts all over again.

Apply Your Understanding

Why did flies survive the spray?

Farmers cannot win the battle against natural selection. However, there are strategies that reduce the loss of valuable crops to insects. One strategy is to employ the principles of diversity that protect natural ecosystems. For example, in a monoculture like the field of squash, only one plant species is present. One insect population can destroy the entire crop, and all is lost. If, instead, a farmer plants some squash, beans, and spinach, only the squash would be lost. Part of the crop could be saved.

Integrated pest management (IPM) is another strategy used. The approach of this system to pest management combines the use of chemicals with cultural, mechanical, and biological control methods to minimize pest damage. The goal of IPM is not to completely eradicate pests or pesticide use. It is, rather, to control pest populations in order to prevent both the pests and the pest management activities from having an adverse effect on both crops and the environment. The methods of doing this vary among crops and among regions of the country.

How does integrated pest management work?

IPM is not an antipesticide program. It involves selective use of pesticides designed specifically for an intended pest. These pesticides are used only in necessary amounts, since overuse can cause insects to build up resistance to pesticides. Some of the control techniques used in IPM include crop rotation, mechanical removal, development and use of pest-resistant and disease-resistant strains, and use of natural enemies and parasites. In an IPM program, both the pest populations and the beneficial populations are monitored. Naturally occurring beneficial organisms—such as ladybugs, preying mantises, and green lacewing larvae—frequently prevent pest damage by reducing pest numbers (see Figures 6.9 and 6.10).

Topic: integrated pest management
Go to: www.scilinks.org
Code: GloSci7e235

A successful IPM program relies on farming practices such as uniform planting and plow-up dates to prevent pests from moving from field to field. Planting crops before insects become active and using varieties that are pest-resistant or faster-maturing enable farmers to harvest before pests become too abundant. The use of intermixed plantings can help control pests by attracting beneficial insects or by attracting pests away from one crop into other plantings.

Entomologists are now breeding sterile males of some insect species. They also are using insect pheromones to confuse the breeding habits of others as additional weapons in the insect control arsenal. Will there ever come a time when no food is lost to other organisms? Probably not. Perhaps the most we can hope for is to reduce our losses to manageable levels. As competitors survive, pests evolve and new methods must be developed to keep those pests under control.

▲ FIGURE 6.9 This stingless wasp attacks a cereal leaf beetle larva by inserting wasp eggs into its body. After the wasp larvae hatch, they kill the beetle, a potentially costly pest of small grains. *(USDA, Animal and Plant Health Inspection Service)*

▲ FIGURE 6.10 A stingless wasp attacks a Mexican bean beetle larva by inserting wasp eggs. The developing wasp larvae feed on the beetle until all that is left is an empty shell. Some farmers use natural predators like this wasp as a **biological control** for pests. This cuts down on the use of various pesticides. *(USDA, Animal and Plant Health Inspection Service)*

ACTIVITY 6.7

Pesticide Application Simulation

When is the last time you used a pesticide? Were there dandelions in your lawn, a wasp nest under the eaves, caterpillars eating your tomato plants, a mouse invading your pantry, or a line of ants marching across the kitchen floor to recently dropped food? Ridding ourselves of pests can make our lives healthier and happier *if* use and application are done properly. In this activity, you will learn more about the challenge of proper pesticide use.

Background

A **pesticide** is a generic term that refers to anything used to kill or control pests. An *herbicide* is a pesticide that kills plants, an *insecticide* kills insects, *fungicides* kill fungi, *rodenticides* kill rodents, *nematocides* kill nematodes, and *arachnicides* kill spiders.

Anyone who applies a pesticide commercially must be trained and licensed or certified. Annual retraining to maintain licensing and certification is required. Private homeowners are exempt from these controls. Except for a very few "restricted use" pesticides, anyone can buy and use pesticides. For the most part, the main difference between the pesticides the general public uses and those that farmers and other commercial applicators use is the quantity that can be purchased. The average homeowner uses *eight times* the amount of pesticides per acre than the average farmer. The proper use of pesticides enables us to grow more food, at a higher quality and at a reasonable cost, on less land.

The use of herbicides to control weeds in no-till and conservation tillage farming has drastically reduced soil erosion in the United States. Because of IPM, new technology, cost, and newer, more effective pesticides, pesticide use in the United States continues to decrease annually. Newer, safer pesticides that break down quickly in the environment and are effective in much smaller doses are continually replacing older, less effective and less safe ones. Plant varieties that are resistant to certain pests enable farmers to use less pesticide.

Instruments are available that allow routine detection of chemical concentrations as small as one part per billion—that is .000000001. One part per billion is similar to a six-person hockey team playing against the entire human population. It is the *dose* that makes the poison. Detection of a pesticide in drinking water does not automatically mean the water is unsafe to drink.

Biomagnification is a concern when pesticides are used. **Biomagnification** is the increased concentration of toxic chemicals, heavy metals, and certain pesticides in the tissues of organisms as these materials move up the food chain. Organisms that feed high on the food chain can suffer serious health effects. The goal is to eliminate this danger during the research and development of new and better pesticides.

Materials

- white vinegar
- distilled water
- small spray bottle
- 1000-mL beaker
- 250- or 500-mL graduated cylinder
- 10-mL graduated cylinder
- 3-mL dropping pipette
- pH test strips
- newspaper
- safety goggles

BE SAFE

Wear safety goggles throughout this activity.

Procedure

1. Reproduce Tables I and II (Figures 6.11 and 6.12) in your science notebook.
   DO NOT WRITE IN THIS BOOK.

2. Determine the pH of white vinegar. Record the value in Table I in your science notebook.

3. Determine the pH of distilled water. Record the value in Table I in your science notebook.

4. Carefully pour 249.5 milliliters (mL) of distilled water into a graduated cylinder.

Table I: pH Determinations

Liquid	pH
White vinegar	
Distilled water	
Vinicide	

▲ FIGURE 6.11 Sample table for recording pH levels.

5. Draw 0.5 mL of vinegar into a dropping pipette and then add it to the 249.5 mL of distilled water in the graduated cylinder. Let the mixture stand for 2–3 minutes as you fill out Table II in your science notebook. The vinegar/distilled water solution you prepared represents a simulated pesticide we will call vinicide.

6. Pour the diluted vinegar solution, vinicide, into a 1000-mL beaker and swirl to mix. Test the pH of the vinicide. Record the value in Table I in your notebook.

7. Calibrate your sprayer as instructed by your teacher.

8. Carefully pour vinicide into a small graduated cylinder to the 10 mL level.

9. Carefully pour the 10 mL of vinicide into the small spray bottle.

10. Cover your lab table with newspaper. Measure and record the length and width of your lab table in centimeters (cm).

11. Determine the area of your lab table surface in square centimeters (cm^2) as follows:

    area = _____ cm × _____ cm = _____ cm^2

12. In this activity, the covered area represents a potato field. The potato crop is being attacked by a fungus that vinicide can kill. Assume 1 cm^2 = 1 acre of farmland. How many acres of cropland does your lab table represent?

    acres of potato cropland = _____

13. Carefully spray the 10 mL of vinicide solution over your covered area (simulated potato field). Use the optimum spray distance

Helpful Hint!

Be sure to make your calculations in your science notebook.

Table II: ppm and Dose Determinations

Determination	Show Your Calculations Here
1. Concentration of the vinicide spray solution (2 mL in 1,000 mL means 2 parts in 1,000 mL solution)	0.5 parts vinicide in 250 mL of solution is the same as _____ parts in 1,000 mL of solution or _____ parts in 1,000,000 mL of solution or _____ ppm (parts per million) Note: The "parts" are the *dose* delivered.
2. Dose of vinicide in 10 mL of solution	2,000 ppm means 2,000 parts vinicide in 1,000,000 mL of solution, or _____ parts in 10 mL of solution
3. Vinicide/acre	_____ parts of vinicide were sprayed on _____ acres Thus, there were _____ parts ÷ _____ acres = _____ parts/acre
4. Parts (dose)/plant	_____ parts/acre ÷ 16,000 plants/acre = _____ parts/plant
5. Parts (dose)/potato	_____ parts/plant ÷ 7 potatoes/plant = _____ parts/potato

▲ FIGURE 6.12 Sample table for recording calculations.

and pattern to cover the newspaper with a fine mist. The spray areas covered in each pass should touch but not overlap. Mist the area only once. (Producers only make a single pass. They do not go back and spray the area again.)

Content Clue

If you do not apply the vinicide, the fungus will devastate your crop.

14. Measure the remaining vinicide. Then calculate the actual amount of vinicide sprayed on your field.

15. Use Table II to help you determine the following:

  a. What is the concentration of vinicide spray in parts per million (ppm)?

  b. How many parts (the dose) are in 10 mL of spray?

  c. How many parts of vinicide did each acre of land receive (on average)?

Helpful Hint!

You are determining a maximum dose because some vinicide may not have landed on the plant or soil in the spraying operation. Also, the chemicals used on today's crops break down in the environment.

16. How many parts of vinicide ended up on each plant? in each potato? Assume there are about 16,000 potato plants/acre and about 7 potatoes/plant.

QUESTIONS & TASKS

Record your responses in your science notebook.

1. How is trying to spray 10 mL of vinicide evenly across the simulated potato field similar to how a farmer spreads pesticide on a field? How is it different?

2. Most accidents with pesticides happen during the mixing and transfer stage. Why do you think this happens? What could be done to prevent this from happening?

3. How can research and development help reduce pesticide use? (Think back on your reading of section 6.5 Natural Selection, Pests, and the Food Supply.)

4. Why does the detection of a pesticide in drinking water not automatically mean the water is unsafe to drink?

[Adapted from *Pesticides, Agriculture, and the Environment*, Texas Farm Bureau, P.O. Box 2689, Waco, TX 76702.]

6.6 Why So Much Diversity?

Charles Darwin came up with the concept that in nature, only the fittest survive. This concept became known as the law of natural selection. If the fittest survive, however, why are there so many survivors and so much diversity? Several reasons answer this question.

One reason is that over time, organisms develop niches in an ecosystem. A niche can be thought of as a job or role in a particular ecosystem. There can be thousands of niches in a small area. Therefore, thousands of organisms can coexist in that small area. (See Special Focus: The Galápagos Finches at the end of this section.)

Another reason deals with geologic separation of populations over long periods of time. Populations of the same organism can be separated by many factors. Some of these include the movement of land caused by plate tectonics and/or the migration of a portion of the population. These separations can result in new species that cannot reproduce with the old population (see Figure 6.13).

Topic: biodiversity
Go to: www.scilinks.org
Code: GloSci7e239

There are many reasons for the diversity we see around us.

◀ FIGURE 6.13 Scientists propose that the ostrich (Africa), rhea (S. America), and emu (Australia) originate from a common ancestor. Years of geographic separation resulted in the formation of three distinct species. *(Ostrich [left]—Gerald and Buff Corsi/Visuals Unlimited; rhea [right]—Ken Lucas/ Visuals Unlimited; emu [below]—David Fleetham/ Visuals Unlimited.)*

A third reason deals with environmental factors that can influence diversity. For example, warm, wet climates can support more diverse ecosystems than can cold, dry climates. This is because warmer, wetter climates are more stable with fewer temperature fluctuations than colder, dryer climates. The more stable a climate is, the less severe environmental changes are. In addition, the more types of climates there are, the more niches there can be for organisms to occupy. Since Earth contains a variety of climatic regions, or biomes, there are many niches for organisms to occupy. This includes the aquatic environments as well, such as oceans, lakes, rivers, and estuaries.

Finally, as organisms go through their life processes, they can receive benefits from each other. This process is called **symbiosis**. For example, bacteria that help us digest food live in our intestines. In return for that help, we provide the habitat that supplies all of their food and the conditions necessary for them to stay alive.

It is important to note that all of these factors require long spans of time. These are not processes or events that simply happen overnight. Some of them take thousands of years.

SPECIAL FOCUS

The Galápagos Finches

The process of ecological succession described in Chapter 2 (section 2.5 Ecosystems Change over Time) is somewhat different on islands far from the mainland. An island may undergo a catastrophic event such as formation from a volcanic eruption or devastation by a powerful hurricane or tsunami. The first new life-forms to arrive on the island are carried there by wind, water, or other organisms. This is because islands are isolated by the water that surrounds them. As a result, many islands have large bird populations because birds reach islands more easily than land animals.

Organisms that arrive on a remote island, and can find a mate, have many ecological opportunities. Many unfilled niches are available to them that would not be available on the mainland. Charles Darwin found exactly this situation when he arrived on the Galápagos Islands (600 miles west of Ecuador) in 1835.

He found several species of finches, each with unique feeding habits (see Figure 6.14). Darwin hypothesized that all the finches evolved from a common ancestor to fill the many available niches.

Without competition, the finches easily adapted to the many niches. Several species of finches evolved, some of which could occupy more than one niche. This process continues as new predators arrive on the islands and climate conditions change.

Focus Questions

1. Why are so many niches available on recently devastated islands?

2. If a pair of mice is released on an island, what might happen to the population of finches living there?

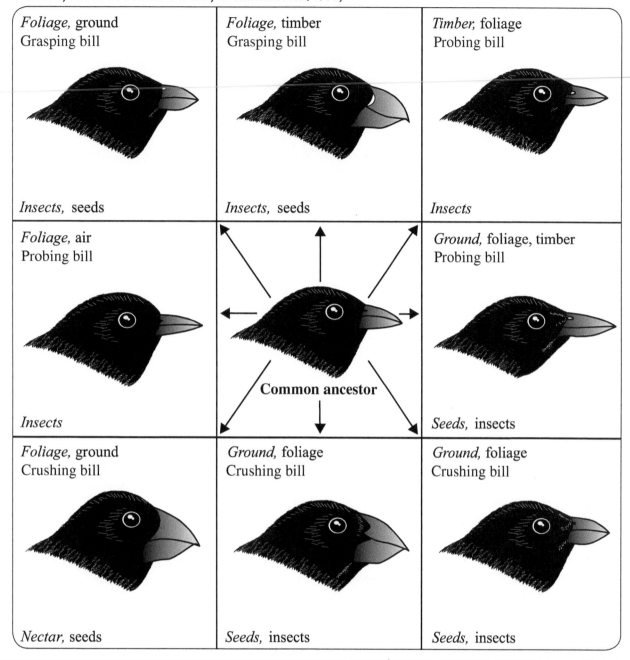

▼ FIGURE 6.14 The relationships between bill structure and feeding habits in eight species of finches from Indefatigable (Santa Cruz) Island in the Galápagos Islands. (Adapted from *Morphological Differentiation and Adaptation in the Galapagos Finches* by Robert I. Bowman. University of California Press, 1961.)

Foliage, ground
Grasping bill

Insects, seeds

Foliage, timber
Grasping bill

Insects, seeds

Timber, foliage
Probing bill

Insects

Foliage, air
Probing bill

Insects

Common ancestor

Ground, foliage, timber
Probing bill

Seeds, insects

Foliage, ground
Crushing bill

Nectar, seeds

Ground, foliage
Crushing bill

Seeds, insects

Ground, foliage
Crushing bill

Seeds, insects

6.7 The Importance of Diversity

Experience has taught us the importance of biodiversity and how critical it is to human survival. We can see an example of this in the potato famine in Ireland in the 1840s. Only a few varieties of potatoes were planted. When a fungus began to spread among the plants, there was nothing to stop it. As a result, 2 million Irish people died of hunger and disease. Two million more emigrated. Another example is the Southern corn leaf blight epidemic of 1970 in the United States. Most of the corn crop was of one variety and was wiped out by a

Past experience teaches us the need to preserve diversity.

Why we should save biological diversity.

fungus (Figure 6.15). A similar incident occurred in 1980 when the peanut crop, consisting of only two varieties, was almost entirely destroyed by drought and disease.

All of these examples contained crops that consisted of only one or two varieties. After disasters like these, we realized the importance of diversity. But of even more value, we are realizing the importance of *preserving* this diversity.

A variety of reasons exists for saving biological diversity, including the following:

1. **All life has a right to exist.** Most societies teach that it is immoral to kill other humans, and general acceptance of this belief is fundamental to our survival on Earth. However, the creatures with which we share the planet also have a right to exist. They are genetic wonders that took millions of years to adapt and fill their current niches. Who are we to eliminate them?

2. **The variety in nature adds enjoyment and meaning to life.** Most of us enjoy a trip to the forest, the mountains, or the lake. Part of that enjoyment comes from seeing a wild animal, an intricate flower, or strange insects. We delight at the crazy antics of penguins at the zoo, or the beauty of a butterfly. We owe it to future generations to pass on the variety that was given to us.

3. **Variety adds to the diversity of ecosystems, and diversity means stability of our life-support system.** Ecosystems provide tremendous economic services to us. They moderate climate, cleanse air and water, recycle waste, protect crops from pests, replenish soils, cycle nutrients, pollinate plants, supply our food, and maintain a genetic library. Diversity ensures their survival. The stability of our biosphere is life insurance for us and for our children.

4. **Every different organism is a genetic marvel that may someday be valuable to us or to other species.** Many plants and animals have proven to be useful in agriculture, science, and the production of medicines. For example, about 1,400 plants in tropical forests are believed to offer cures for cancer. In fact, a drug made from the periwinkle plant found in tropical forests is now used to treat childhood leukemia and Hodgkin's disease. One out of four pharmaceuticals used by Western chemists comes from a tropical plant. We should retain as many species as possible for future generations because we cannot predict which species will later prove to be valuable.

The future of civilization depends on high-yield agriculture. We have learned from past events that this entire enterprise rests on having adequate supplies of varying genetic combinations to be used in artificial selection. Commercial grains must be constantly modified to resist attack by disease or insects. It is diversity that makes that modification possible.

Think about This!

Modern agriculture is tied to biodiversity.

SPECIAL FOCUS

Invasive Species: An Example of Biological Pollution

Purple loosestrife (Figure 6.16), a perennial plant of wetlands, is a beautiful but aggressive invader that arrived in eastern North America from Europe in the early 1800s. Plants were brought by settlers for their flower gardens. Seeds were present in the ballast holds of ships that used soil to weigh down the vessels for stability on the ocean. Since its introduction, purple loosestrife has spread rapidly across much of the United States and Canada.

Purple loosestrife is very hardy and can rapidly degrade wetlands, the most biologically diverse and productive ecosystems. Once established, the plant can quickly choke the habitat of native plants, fish, birds, insects, and other wildlife in the area. This happens because Earth's ecosystems developed over long periods of time and isolation (see section 6.6 Why So Much Diversity?). The introduction of long-separated species from one part of the world into another usually leads to problems. Without the natural enemies of their native habitats, invasive species can spread rapidly and threaten the biodiversity of their new habitats.

Aggressive efforts are being made across North America to control purple loosestrife. The battle is difficult because its roots are very resistant

SCLINKS NSTA

Topic: invasive species
Go to: www.scilinks.org
Code: GloSci7e243

Helpful Hint!

Invasive species are introduced organisms that become widespread and threaten other organisms and ecosystems.

▲ FIGURE 6.16 Purple loosestrife, an invasive plant introduced into North America from Europe. (*Copyright State of Minnesota Department of Natural Resources*)

to cutting, burning, and spraying. It must be completely removed both above and below ground. Biological control relies on reuniting a pest with its natural enemies. However, extreme caution must be taken when introducing one organism

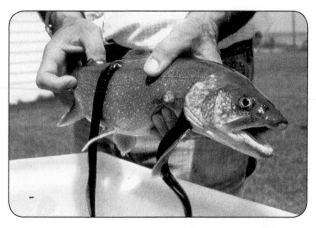

▲ FIGURE 6.17 Sea lamprey attached to a whitefish. (USGS)

to control another. Otherwise, the problem could be compounded. After rigorous testing, five species of beetles that attack purple loosestrife have been approved for release in North America.

The purple loosestrife is just one of a long list of invasive species. International commerce and travel greatly accelerated the problem with both accidental and intentional introductions. The sea lamprey (Figure 6.17) is a predaceous, eel-like fish native to the coastal regions of both sides of the Atlantic Ocean. Sea lamprey entered the Great Lakes through the Welland Canal about 1921. They contributed greatly to the decline of whitefish and lake trout in the Great Lakes.

Zebra mussels (Figure 6.18) are small, fingernail-sized mussels native to the Caspian Sea region of Asia. They were discovered in Lake St. Clair near Detroit in 1988. Tolerant of a wide range of environmental conditions, zebra mussels have now spread to parts of all the Great Lakes and the Mississippi River and are showing up in inland lakes. They clog the water systems of power plants, water treatment plants, and irrigation systems. They have severely reduced or eliminated native mussel species.

The introduction of new species is not always a bad thing. We must remember that almost all the fruits, vegetables, and meats we eat in North America came from somewhere else. The kudzu plant was introduced for erosion control in the southeastern United States and has provided that benefit. Tamarisk, a salt cedar tree, was introduced in the early 1800s because of

▲ FIGURE 6.18 Zebra mussel cluster attached to a freshwater clam. (Copyright State of Minnesota Department of Natural Resources)

its ability to grow rapidly (up to 12 feet a year) in heavily saline soils where little else will grow. Salt cedar invasions have aided the populations of the endangered willow flycatcher, which prefers salt cedars for nesting. The European honey bee aids farmers and gardeners across North America. It is true that over geologic time, all species were introduced at one time. The real question is, how should we manage change?

Use the SciLinks feature to learn more about invasive species.

Focus Questions

1. Why do invasive species often spread so fast?

2. Do all introduced species cause harm? Explain.

3. Obtain information on two or three additional invasive species. Write a short report.

4. What can be done to slow the spread of invasive species? What is effective action? Is there more than one approach?

6.8 How to Preserve Diversity

The need to preserve biodiversity is increasingly more important for both plants and animals. As humans expand their presence over all portions of the globe, we are eliminating complex ecosystems and the genetic material that helped to keep those ecosystems stable. We can preserve the genetic material, and biological diversity, in these five ways.

How we should preserve biological diversity.

1. Preserve large expanses of various ecosystems in the form of **wilderness**, parks, and monuments. These serve as living banks from which we can withdraw genetic materials when the need arises. This is becoming increasingly more difficult to do, however, because of the growing human population. Fortunately, humans have developed other ways to preserve diversity.

2. Collect, preserve, and maintain the **germplasm** (plant hereditary material) of naturally growing native plants and strains of food crops in genetic **seed banks** in different areas. These seed banks can be high-tech in regions that can afford them. Storage methods can include drying out germplasm and storing it in cold storage at temperatures of $-4°F$ $(-20°C)$; freeze-drying genetic materials in liquid nitrogen called *cryopreservation* (Figure 6.19); and using in vitro preservation, which allows germplasm to be stored as clones. In regions that are less affluent, seed banks can be run more economically using methods such as storage in a partial vacuum (T. L. Christensen, 2000).

3. Use **genetic engineering** to create diversity. Genetic engineering is any technique used to identify or change genes at the molecular level. This process allows humans to manipulate genes of an organism and change the organism's characteristics for our benefit. Genetic engineering is a relatively new process and could provide many new benefits for humans and the biosphere.

Topic: seed bank
Go to: www.scilinks.org
Code: GloSci7e245

◄ FIGURE 6.19 Cryogenic preservation of seeds at the National Center for Genetic Resources Preservation in Fort Collins, Colorado. (*Photo by Stephen Ausmus, ARS/USDA.*)

4. Maintain the diversity of animal species by preserving large expanses of natural habitats. This can be done through rare breeding trusts, through the establishment of zoological parks and managed wildlife refuges, and by preserving animal germplasm in animal gene banks.

5. Provide species with legal protection through laws and treaties. Species needing legal protection must first be identified. Criteria for protection can be that the species is endangered; it has the best chance for survival; it has the most ecological value to an ecosystem; and it is potentially valuable for agriculture, medicine, or industry. Laws and treaties must then be agreed upon to provide that protection. One example is the 1973 Convention on International Trade in Endangered Species (CITES). This treaty, signed by more than 150 countries, lists several hundred species that cannot be commercially traded as live specimens or wildlife products.

SPECIAL FOCUS

Endangered Species Act

In the United States, the Endangered Species Act of 1973 (ESA), amended in 1982, 1988, and 2003, requires the federal government to protect all animal and plant life threatened with extinction. The purpose of the ESA is to conserve the ecosystem upon which endangered and threatened species depend. It also prohibits the import, export, interstate, and foreign commerce of the listed species. The ESA provides programs for the recovery of these species. It also prohibits the government or any person from beginning a project that may harm an endangered species or destroy its habitat. This law puts intense pressure on landowners who want to develop their land, whether it is for residential, agricultural, recreational, or mining purposes. Projects that encompass an endangered or threatened species have to develop a mitigation plan prior to the project's approval by the authorities. In some

Helpful Hint!

An **endangered species** is one that is in danger of becoming extinct worldwide or in significant portions of its range.

A **threatened species** is one that is likely to become endangered within the foreseeable future.

instances, projects are not given approval, even after extensive studies of and accommodations for the species in question.

In late 2006, the U.S. Fish and Wildlife Service listed 412 animals and 598 plants as endangered in the United States. Another 155 animals and 146 plants were categorized as threatened. This list is a constant source of debate. As a species recovers, it can be downlisted from endangered to threatened or delisted and removed entirely from legal protection (see Figure 6.20).

The ESA has become increasingly controversial, as it has been viewed as a major impediment to economic development. The law has been used (and misused in some instances) to stop projects that would be beneficial for society. Violation of the ESA is a criminal offense, and people have been jailed over violations of the act.

The challenge is to build and maintain an adequate list of endangered and threatened species and to provide the enforcement necessary to maintain ecological stability. At the same time, we must make it possible for land use that serves the best interests of the people that inhabit a region. This is no small task. In the future, the debate will continue as both sides analyze the benefits and shortcomings of the ESA.

▼ FIGURE 6.20 Threatened and endangered species. (a) Spineless hedgehog cactus (*Marv Poulson*); (b) loggerhead sea turtle (*Robert L. Pitman*); (c) black-footed ferret (*Dean Biggs/USFWS*).

a

b

c

Probably one of the most important natural resources to preserve is germplasm (Figure 6.21). We are heavily dependent on the many varieties of crop species as our major food source. As a result, we are making significant progress in collecting and preserving germplasm. The International Board for Plant Genetic Resources (IBPGR) was established in 1974 to create and coordinate a worldwide network of germplasm resource conservation centers. The IBPGR receives funds from the World Bank, the Food and Agriculture Organization of the United Nations (FAO), and the United Nations Development Program. Board membership consists of these three sponsors, as well as 14 donor governments; three regional development funds; the European Economic Community; the Ford, Rockefeller, and Kellogg Foundations; the International Development Research Center (Ottawa, Canada); and two representatives from each of five major developing regions.

The most significant result of the board's work has been its stimulation of genetic resource activities in many nations. Many international, regional, and national agricultural research centers have responded. Some 60 research institutions serve as the repositories for the world's base collections of seed of the principal food crops. In addition, the IBPGR has helped establish storage and information management systems. It has also helped to develop training programs to

FIGURE 6.21 Some of the ear and kernel types in the U.S. Department of Agriculture's collection of corn germplasm from Yugoslavia, Guatemala, the former Soviet Union, and Turkey. *(Raymond Clark, North Central Regional Plant Introduction Station, Ames, Iowa)*

provide personnel for genetic resources work. In 1978, the National Plant Genetic Resources Board (NPGRB) was established by the United States Secretary of Agriculture. This group cooperates closely with the IBPGR.

 QUESTIONS & TASKS

Record your responses in your science notebook.

1. Why should we set aside large expanses of land as wilderness? Why is this becoming more difficult to do?

2. How do seed banks preserve seeds for future generations?

3. What is the economic justification for maintaining a network of seed banks (see Figure 6.22)?

FIGURE 6.22 Two varieties of cabbage show a difference in susceptibility to bacterial black rot. The variety in the row on the left, typical of commercially available cabbages, is susceptible. The leaf tips die, turn brown, and roll downward. Eventually, the heads rot off. The variety in the row on the right is highly resistant. It is derived from an old Japanese variety known as Early Fuji. Early Fuji is no longer available commercially; it exists only as stored inventory in one or two seed banks in Japan. This variety remains the most valuable source of black rot resistance known today. *(Paul H. Williams, University of Wisconsin)*

6.9 Plant Biotechnology and Agriculture

For centuries, farmers have used a variety of techniques to improve the quality of their crops and livestock. The process they used is called biotechnology. **Biotechnology** uses living organisms to make products such as medicines and improved crops. At first, this was done by selective breeding. Two parents are purposefully chosen to crossbreed to hopefully produce offspring with specific characteristics. This particular process is called **hybridization**, a form of selective breeding. The farmer or scientist controls which plant will be used to pollinate the crop that will produce the seeds. The seeds are then collected to be planted the next growing season.

Biotechnology uses living organisms to make useful living products.

Genetic engineering

Scientists have been able to refine the process by which information from parents is transferred to offspring. This technique is called genetic engineering. Genetic engineering allows for the transfer of very specific information so that only a few, beneficial traits are added to the new plant. Less specific methods, such as hybridization, often transfer undesired traits along with the desired, beneficial traits.

Genetic engineering involves changing characteristics one gene at a time.

Genetic engineering is possible because of what scientists understand about DNA (deoxyribonucleic acid). DNA is found in the nucleus of the cell. It contains the information that directs the cell to make the proteins that are the basis of life. DNA is a very long, submicroscopic substance. Scientists refer to sections of this long chain of DNA as **genes**. On one strand of DNA, there are many, many genes. Each gene provides the code for the cell to make a particular protein. This code may help a plant resist a certain disease or withstand times of low water.

Helpful Hint!

Refer back to Special Focus: A Primer on Cells, DNA, Chromosomes, and Genes to clarify terms.

Figure 6.23 shows a comparison of traditional plant biotechnology to genetic engineering. Notice how specific the gene transfer is in genetic engineering.

How is new genetic information transferred? The first step is to isolate the gene for the desired trait. After the gene (piece of DNA) is isolated, it is spliced into the DNA of bacteria, such as *Agrobacterium*. *Agrobacterium* is a bacterium that normally lives in the soil and causes the plant disease called crown gall. After scientists splice in the new DNA, they take

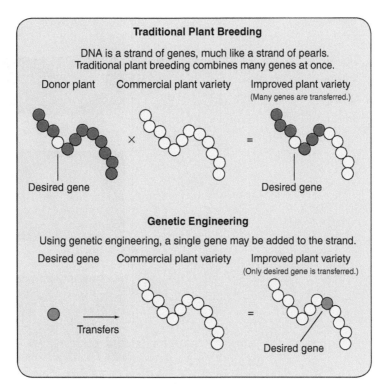

◀ FIGURE 6.23 A comparison of traditional plant breeding and genetic engineering.

out the genes for forming galls. *Agrobacterium* can then be helpful, rather than harmful, to the plant.

To be helpful, the new DNA has to be put inside a plant cell. This plant cell must then be grown into a whole new plant that has the DNA for the desired characteristic. For plants such as beans and cotton, scientists remove a piece of the plant and grow it in a petri dish with special nutrients. When the piece of plant has grown a "bunch" of new cells, called a *callus*, the callus is wounded and *Agrobacterium* is introduced to the wound. This combination of plant tissue and *Agrobacterium* are grown together for a few days. Scientists then apply antibiotics to the plant tissue that kills the *Agrobacterium*. Even though the *Agrobacterium* is dead, the new DNA is now inside some of the plant cells of the callus. By applying special chemicals, scientists can induce just these cells to grow. Before long, they have grown new plants with the DNA that codes for the desired traits. Scientists use these plants to produce seeds that have the engineered DNA inside. From these, they can grow a new population of plants with the new trait. Figure 6.24 shows a diagram of this process.

For plants such as wheat or corn, the new DNA must be introduced in a slightly different way. Scientists still start by growing a callus. This time the callus must be grown with immature plant embryos. Then, instead of introducing *Agrobacterium* to the callus, scientists

▶FIGURE 6.24 The basic steps scientists use to engineer plants such as cotton or beans with new DNA for specific, desired traits. This is a form of genetic engineering. *(Courtesy of Monsanto.)*

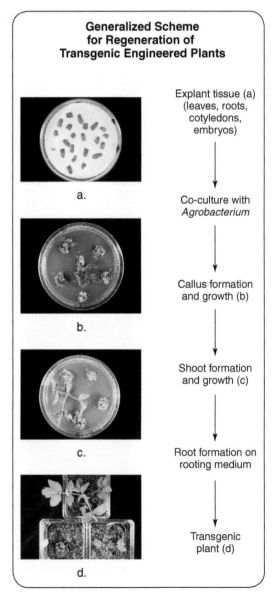

Generalized Scheme for Regeneration of Transgenic Engineered Plants

a.

Explant tissue (a) (leaves, roots, cotyledons, embryos)

Co-culture with *Agrobacterium*

b.

Callus formation and growth (b)

c.

Shoot formation and growth (c)

Root formation on rooting medium

d.

Transgenic plant (d)

must bombard the callus with very small (0.4–1.0 micron) particles of gold or tungsten that are coated with the new DNA. They do this by placing the callus tissue into a special container. They then use a particle gun to move the microscopic particles at high speed, forcing them into the plant cells. After this process, the cells are left to develop. During this time, they are treated with chemicals that encourage the growth of the cells with the new DNA.

Examples of plants improved through biotechnology are shown in Figures 6.25 and 6.26.

Future Needs

The future will require plants and animals that can survive a variety of climatic changes, diseases, and insects. A storehouse of genetic material is our best hope for developing plants and animals that can survive. However, the process of natural selection will enable harmful organisms to evolve and make the new and old varieties ineffective if we are not constantly alert. Hence, our commitment to the future must be sufficient and ongoing. We must enable researchers to draw on the numerous plant and animal varieties that are now quickly diminishing.

Plant A   Plant B

◀ FIGURE 6.25 Cotton that has in-plant protection against attacking insects can be produced. An insect-toxic protein inhibits the working of the insect's digestive system. Plant A is the traditional plant showing complete devastation of the leaves. Plant B is the insect-protected plant showing little insect damage. (*Courtesy of Monsanto.*)

Row A   Row B

◀ FIGURE 6.26 Soybeans that are tolerant to the herbicide glyphosate (Roundup™) were developed through biotechnology. Row A is the traditional soybean plant showing plant death after application of glyphosate. Row B is the glyphosate-tolerant plant showing complete tolerance to the glyphosate herbicide. (*Courtesy of Monsanto.*)

Record your responses in your science notebook.

1. How does genetic engineering differ from traditional biotechnology?

2. How does genetic engineering add to the diversity of our supply of seeds?

ACTIVITY 6.8

Why Preserve Biological Diversity?

In this activity, you will think about human values with regard to biological diversity.

Background

There are various reasons for preserving biological diversity. These include the following:

1. All life has a right to exist. Ethics should extend beyond *Homo sapiens*. Most of us have no knowledge or appreciation of the millions of organisms and species in nature that help us in countless ways. The least we can do is allow them to exist.

2. The variety of nature adds to the enjoyment and meaning of life.

3. Variety adds to the diversity of ecosystems. Diversity provides stability to the biosphere—our life-support system. For example, a mountain meadow is more stable than a field of corn.

4. Every different organism is a genetic marvel that may someday be valuable to us or to other species. For example, many of our pharmaceutical drugs originate from tropical rain forest plants.

These four reasons stem from human values. A value is a principle or belief that is regarded as being desirable by an individual or a group of individuals.

Procedure

1. Figure 6.27 lists 8 types of human values. The middle column briefly defines each value. Reproduce this table in your science notebook.

2. Answer the questions that follow.

QUESTIONS & TASKS

Record your responses in your science notebook.

1. Which of the four reasons in the background information are scientific statements? That is, which are based on repeatable observations, can be tested, and are supported by evidence?

2. In the right column of Figure 6.27, place the number of a reason (1, 2, 3, or 4) that matches that type of value. Some values may have more than one reason.

[Adapted from Botkin and Keller, *Environmental Science: Earth as a Living Planet*, 3rd ed. © 2000 John Wiley & Sons, Inc.]

Types of Value	Definition	Reason Number
a. Ethical	Ties to correct conduct	
b. Aesthetic	Ties to a sense of beauty	
c. Economic	Has potential for income and wealth	
d. Ecological	Contributes to the health of ecosystems	
e. Intellectual	Has potential to contribute to knowledge	
f. Emotive	Has potential to inspire (awe and wonder)	
g. Religious	Ties to creation, purpose	
h. Recreational	Is a diversion that offers enjoyment	

◀ **FIGURE 6.27** Sample table for matching human values to reasons for preserving biological diversity.

Summary

An ecosystem is a region in nature that functions for the purpose of maintaining life on Earth. All living things grow and repair themselves, reproduce, change, move, respond, and die. The basic unit of life is the cell. A cell functions like a small factory to perform its task and stay alive. Seeds are the connection between soil and the food we eat. Most animal species depend on seeds as a food source. Seeds also have practical uses in industry. Significant amounts of food are lost to nonhuman organisms. Food spoilage can be reduced in a variety of ways. Some ways involve combating insects. This is difficult because insects adapt so readily (natural selection).

The natural environment is a very diverse environment. This diversity is important because diversity adds to the stability of an ecosystem. Human activity is causing the variety in nature to diminish. Various ethical, scientific, economic, and religious reasons argue for the preservation of this diversity. The primary methods for preserving diversity are setting aside large expanses of land, establishing preservation in seed banks and zoos, using genetic engineering, and providing legal protection to some species. Our commitment to the future must include the preservation of biodiversity.

REFERENCES

Christensen, Teri L. *Germination of 91 Native California Species After 50 Years in Vacuum Storage* (Greeley, CO: Graduate School, University of Northern Colorado), 2000.

Committee on Genetically Modified Pest-Protected Plants. *Genetically Modified Pest-Protected Plants: Science and Regulation* (Washington, DC: National Research Council), 2000.

Hayden, Thomas. All in the Family. *U.S. News & World Report* (June 3, 2002): 58–60.

Margulis, L. and D. Sagan. *What Is Life?* (New York: Simon & Schuster), 1995.

Monsanto. *Sustainability—Seeds for Thought*, Issue 2, undated.

Reid, W. V. and K. R. Miller. *Keeping Options Alive: The Scientific Basis for Conserving Biodiversity* (Washington, DC: World Resources Institute), 1989.

U.S. Department of Agriculture (USDA). *Seeds for Our Future: The U.S. National Plant Germplasm System* (Washington, DC: USDA), April 1996.

WEBSITES

Biodiversity: http://www.mnh.si.edu/biodiversity

Convention on International Trade in Endangered Species http://www.cites.org

Information on threatened and endangered species: http://www.fws.gov

Information on toxicology and pesticides: http://ace.orst.edu/info/extoxnet

National Center for Genetic Resources Preservation:
   http://www.ars.usda.gov/npa/ftcollins/ncgrp

James Shaffer Photography

CHAPTER 7

Agriculture and Nutrition

GOAL

- To understand agriculture by examining the relationships among soil makeup, soil conservation, plant and human nutrition, and carrying capacity.

Give a person a fish, and you feed him for a day. Teach that person to fish, and you can feed him for a lifetime.

—*Ancient Chinese proverb*

The Essence of Agriculture

What does it take to put food on the table at your house (see Figure 7.1)? Consider this question in terms of economics, energy, and ecology. What does it cost to feed a family? What kinds of nutrients and how much energy are used to produce food? What relationships among living and nonliving things result in plant and animal products that we eat? What is a good diet? Most people do not know how to answer these questions. In this chapter, we will begin to consider the issues involved in agriculture.

What is agriculture all about?

7.1 The Strategy of Agriculture

The challenge of agriculture is to feed the world and preserve our biosphere. How can that be done? The first step is to determine the most efficient way to grow food. To do this, we must revisit the topic of ecological succession. Examine Figure 7.2, which shows the change in biomass with succession (see Figure 2.38 in Chapter 2).

From Figure 7.2, we see that at the beginning of ecological succession, biomass increases the fastest. This happens because photosynthesis mainly goes to plant growth. Hence, the most efficient way to grow plants and, thus, crops, is in good sunlight on well-fertilized and watered open land. First, the seed bed is prepared (see Figure 7.3). Then the crop is planted. Fertilizer and water (either by rain or irrigation) are added. When the crop is ready, it is harvested (see Figure 7.4). Unused parts of the plant are returned to the soil, and the process is repeated. The time from beginning to end is most often 1 year. The whole process is then repeated year after year. This does not include crops such as tree (for example, apple) and shrub (for example, blueberries) crops or crops that use natural succession.

▶ FIGURE 7.1 Sometimes, it seems as though food just appears on the table ready for us to eat. In reality, that food came from somewhere. (*James Shaffer Photography*)

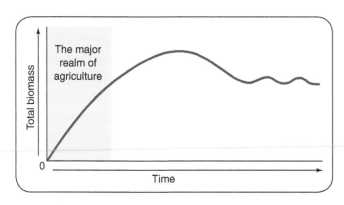

◀ FIGURE 7.2 The realm of agriculture.

◀ FIGURE 7.3 Four-wheel drive tractor plows a hillside with a semimounted, three-furrow reversible plow. *(© Pegasus/Visuals Unlimited)*

This method of farming has been highly successful in the developed world. It is why most people on Earth eat well. The success, however, has produced some problems, including the following:

1. Traditional plowing of large areas of land (Figure 7.3) increases the potential for soil erosion and can affect the soil profile.

2. Planting large areas with a single crop (monoculture) makes it easy for pests (diseases and insects) to find food sources and habitat (see Figure 7.4).

3. Significant energy is required to produce food and fertilizer using high-tech farming.

◀ FIGURE 7.4 Combining wheat; harvesting a monoculture. *(Science VU/ Visuals Unlimited)*

Agriculture and Nutrition   257

Because the human population is so large, we cannot go back to simpler methods of farming. Instead, we must find ways to combat these problems. In this chapter, we will examine ways to prevent soil erosion, use our knowledge of diversity preservation and genetic engineering, and improve the energy efficiency of crop production.

Soil: Linking the Nonliving to the Living

Though we use many minerals directly, some come to us indirectly. Minerals are mixed with organic matter to become soil, or they dissolve in water. Minerals from soil and water are taken up by plants during the process of photosynthesis. In this way, the nonliving world is linked to the living.

The abundant good soil and climate in the United States have made it possible for U.S. farmers to feed our own population and export many foods as well. Many other countries also are successful in agriculture. New varieties of wheat and rice bring record harvests in some regions of the world, yet thousands die of starvation. Deserts expand, arable land and forests shrink, and people argue. When considering sustainable agriculture, we have to think about the growth, production, and distribution of food from a global perspective. Even though many countries have the land to grow their own food, other countries do not.

7.2 Introduction to Soils

Terrestrial life is supported by soil. Without good soil, there isn't enough plant growth to feed many animals and people. Key to healthy living is a healthy ecosystem, and one key to a healthy ecosystem is good soil.

When Earth was formed, there was no soil. But as time passed, the action of wind, rain, ice, water flow, and gravitational forces all served to break down rock into smaller and smaller particles. This weathering process is called erosion. Primitive plants grew in the early products of weathering, and soil formation began. The expanding roots of the growing plants also contributed to the process. They helped weather rocks. When the roots died, they added material to the soil. **Soil** is a mixture of minerals, organic matter, water, and air. It has a definite structure and composition, and forms on the surface of the land.

Think about This!

Some nations of the world have an excess of food, while people in other nations nearly starve. Can these two facts be related to help solve a problem?

Topic: soil
Go to: www.scilinks.org
Code: GloSci7e258

What is soil?

ACTIVITY 7.1

What's in the Soil?

In this activity, you will conduct a series of tests on a soil sample to learn more about soil. As you test your soil, think about how soil links the nonliving world to living organisms.

Materials

- soil samples (collected in advance)
- hand lens
- soil test kit
- safety goggles

Procedure

1. Collect 3 different soil samples as directed by your teacher.

2. Work with a partner to develop a description of what you think soil is. Your description should

BE SAFE

Wear safety goggles when working with chemicals. Wash with water any areas where chemicals spill. Report any spills to your teacher.

Soil Type	Characteristics When Wet	Capacity to Hold Water	Looseness
Sand	Gritty, not plastic	Poor	Very loose
Loam	Smooth, slick, somewhat gritty or sticky	Good to excellent	Very loose
Clay	Smooth, plastic, very sticky	High (holds water too tightly for plants to use)	(Sticks together, not loose)
Silt	Smooth, slick	Good	Somewhat loose

▲ FIGURE 7.5 Soil types and characteristics.

include at least 5 characteristics that help define soil. Record your description in your science notebook.

3. Test your 3 soil samples for pH, nitrogen, phosphorus, and potash according to your teacher's directions. Note the safety cautions.

> **Helpful Hint!**
>
> Nitrogen, phosphorus, and potash are important for the growth of plants. The *acidity* or *alkalinity* of the soil as measured by pH will give you an idea of how well the plants will be able to use the nutrients in your soil sample. You can read more about these nutrients and pH in section 7.3 What Is Soil?, which follows this activity.

4. Determine the texture of your soil samples by rubbing a small, moist sample between your fingers. Use the information in Figures 7.5 and 7.6 to decide if your soil is mostly sand, loam, clay, or silt.

5. Determine the structure of your soil by examining it with a hand lens. Use the information in Figure 7.7 to help you identify the structure of your soil.

> **Helpful Hint!**
>
> Structure refers to how the soil is put together in geometric shapes. You can read more about texture and structure in section 7.3.

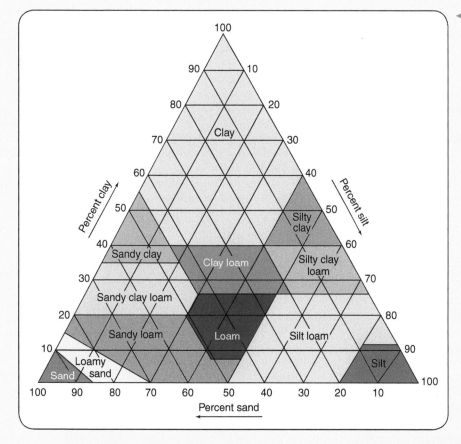

◀ FIGURE 7.6 Classification of soil textures. *(From USDA Soil Survey Manual.)*

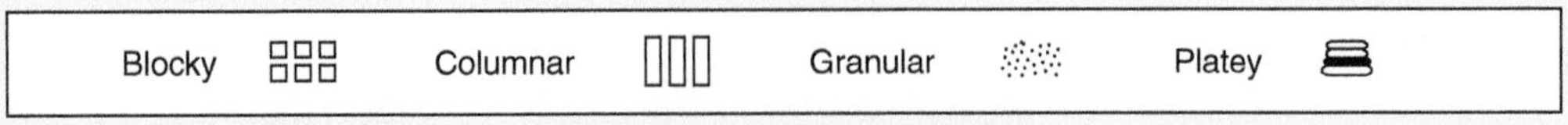

▲ FIGURE 7.7 Four key classifications of soil structure.

6. Reproduce the table in Figure 7.8 in your science notebook. Record the results of your tests in the 3 columns.

7. Combine your results on a class data table.

8. Review the class data and consider these 3 questions:

   a. How are the data similar?

   b. How are the data different?

   c. What patterns do you see in the data?

9. According to your teacher's instructions, join one of 4 expert groups. You will become an expert on one of the nutrients (nitrogen, phosphorus, or potash) or pH. If you are a *nutrient expert*, you should be able to answer these questions:

   Helpful Hint!

   Use the information in section 7.3 What Is Soil?, library books, or the Internet to help you answer the questions in step 9.

   a. What is your nutrient and where does it come from?

   b. Why is your nutrient important for agricultural plants?

   c. What causes your nutrient to be depleted from the soil?

   d. How can the level of your nutrient be changed?

   If you are a *pH expert*, you should be able to answer these questions:

   a. What does pH stand for?

   b. Why do farmers have to pay attention to pH?

   c. What is a "good" pH level for agricultural use of soil?

   d. How can the pH level of the soil be changed?

QUESTIONS & TASKS

Record your responses in your science notebook.

1. Each expert group should give a report to the whole class.

2. After listening to the expert reports, review your soil data. Choose one sample that you think is the best for agriculture. Be sure you can justify your choice.

	Results from Sample 1	Results from Sample 2	Results from Sample 3
pH			
Nitrogen			
Phosphorus			
Potash			
Texture			
Structure			

▲ FIGURE 7.8 Sample table for recording test results.

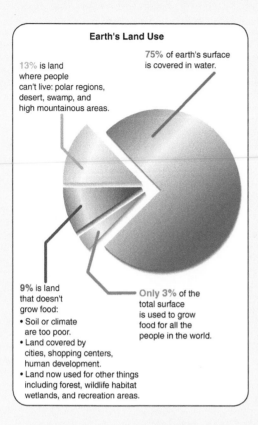

Earth's Land Use

13% is land where people can't live: polar regions, desert, swamp, and high mountainous areas.

75% of earth's surface is covered in water.

9% is land that doesn't grow food:
• Soil or climate are too poor.
• Land covered by cities, shopping centers, human development.
• Land now used for other things including forest, wildlife habitat wetlands, and recreation areas.

Only 3% of the total surface is used to grow food for all the people in the world.

◀ FIGURE 7.9 At present, only 3 percent of Earth's surface is used to grow food. This is only 12 percent of the total land surface. (*Mineral Information Institute*)

3. Based on the class data, choose the soil sample you think is the worst for growing crops.

4. Review what you wrote in step 2 about the characteristics of soil. Add or delete characteristics from the list based on your experience in this activity.

5. Why do you think it is important to conserve soils that are good for growing crops?

6. Look at Figure 7.9. How much of Earth's surface is suitable for growing food? What are the implications of this figure?

7. How can we conserve soil?

7.3 What Is Soil?

Soil is generally found in layers called **horizons**. Many soils have three major layers: top soil, subsoil, and parent material. Because soil formation has many variables, you may find more or fewer layers. If you take a close look at a road cut through a hill covered with vegetation, you may see soil layers that have different colors and compositions. These layers make up the soil profile (see Figure 7.10). A **soil profile** is the succession of distinctive soil layers from the surface down to the unchanged parent material beneath it.

Soil Horizons

The top layer of soil is referred to as the O-horizon. It consists of organic matter such as fallen leaves, dead grasses, and partially decomposed organisms.

The topsoil is the A-horizon. High-quality topsoil is usually dark brown, dark gray, or black because of the humus it contains. **Humus** is the highly decomposed plant and animal residue that is part of the soil. The mixture of organic and inorganic nutrients makes this layer valuable economically because it supports agricultural crops. The living and nonliving link

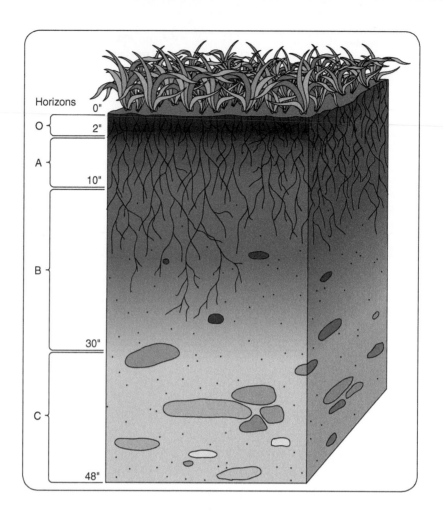

FIGURE 7.10 A soil profile. *(From USDA, SCS.)*

together in this layer to produce the food that supports all life on Earth. The thickness of this layer of topsoil may be anywhere between 1 inch (in) to 2 feet (ft) or 2 centimeters (cm) to 0.7 meters (m). Eight inches (20 cm) is about average. Because of its texture, a good topsoil will hold adequate moisture and will allow air to circulate. The A-horizon is also known as the "zone of leaching." Some nutrients can be leached out (carried away) as water percolates through the layer from the surface.

The B-horizon is made up of subsoil. This is a zone of accumulation, and it is poor in organic content. It contains part of what has been leached from the A-horizon.

The C-horizon is part of the profile, but it is not part of the soil itself. It is part of the parent material from which the soil in the region originated. The C-horizon has no distinct lower limit.

Color, Composition, and Texture

Soils come in a variety of colors. Color can serve as an indicator of soil condition (see Figure 7.11).

Soil is a mixture of minerals, organic matter, water, and air. It has a definite structure and composition, and it forms on the surface of the land. Figure 7.12 shows the average composition of a typical soil. There is a relationship between the composition of soil and the nutritional needs of plants. The elements plants need for healthy growth originate in the mineral particles. Decomposers break down the organic matter and free the nitrates (NO_3^{-1}), phosphates (PO_4^{-3}), and sulfates (SO_4^{+2}) that plants require.

Topsoil (A Horizon)

Condition	Color		
	Dark Gray, Brown, or Black	Moderately Dark Brown or Yellow Brown	Light Brown or Yellow
High organic material	X		
Medium organic material		X	
Low organic material			X
High erosion			X
Medium erosion		X	
Low erosion	X		
High aeration	X		
Medium aeration		X	
Low aeration			X
High available nitrogen	X		
Medium available nitrogen		X	
Low available nitrogen			X
High fertility	X		
Medium fertility		X	
Low fertility			X

Subsurface Soil (B Horizon)

Condition	Color		
	Dull Gray	Yellow, Red Brown, Black (forest)	Mottled Gray
Water-logged	X		
Well-drained		X	
Poorly drained			X

▲ **FIGURE 7.11** This table shows the relationship between soil condition and color. *(Source: Forest Service: USDA.)*

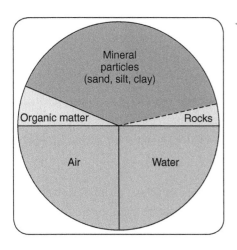

◄ **FIGURE 7.12** Composition (by volume) of a typical loam soil. The proportions vary somewhat with soil type and environmental conditions.

► FIGURE 7.13 This soil ecosystem shows some of the organisms that live in the soil and decompose organic matter. *(From U.S. Department of Agriculture, Nature Resource Conservation Service [NRCS].)*

How rapidly soil forms depends on the "parent" material in the region and on the climate and surface features. If the parent material is hard rock, formation may take hundreds of years. If the parent material is shale, sandstone, volcanic ash, or some other softer material, formation may require only 20 to 30 years under warm, moist conditions.

The upper layer of a typical fertile soil is teeming with life. Bacteria, fungi, molds, ants, earthworms, centipedes, spiders, and a host of other creatures live here. They burrow, dig, and act as decomposers of organic matter (see Figure 7.13). As they go through their life processes, they free up soil nutrients, maintain soil **porosity** (space for air and water), and hold solid particles together.

The mineral particles in soil are classified in three main categories based on particle size. The larger, coarse particles are **sand**. Somewhat finer particles are **silt**. The extremely fine particles are **clay**. The relative amounts of sand, silt, and clay in a given soil sample make up its texture. Figure 7.6 shows how soil texture is classified.

A soil's **texture** determines how much water the soil can hold and how rapidly water will percolate through it. A sandy soil can absorb a lot of water. However, these soils also drain very quickly, so they retain almost no water. At the other extreme are clay soils. Clay particles are so small and packed so close together that water can hardly penetrate. These soils are poorly aerated and do not drain well. Plant roots have trouble penetrating them.

From Figure 7.6, we see that a **loam** soil has about equal amounts of sand and silt, but very little clay. Loam is the best soil for growing crops. Porosity is sufficient to allow air circulation and good water drainage; still, enough water is retained for good plant growth.

The suitability of a soil for agricultural production depends on both its texture and its structure. The most productive soils have a crumbly structure of small particles held together by organic materials. Such soils are well aerated and have a large capacity for retaining water.

Nutrients

A fertile soil is one that contains and is able to supply the complete set of **nutrients** required by growing plants. This means a wide variety of ions must be available to the plant's root system. These ions must be available in the correct proportions. A chemical analysis of a soil provides information that can be used to determine whether or not essential nutrients are needed and how much fertilizer should be applied.

Helpful Hint!

A *nutrient* is an element or compound that is needed for the survival, growth, and reproduction of a plant or animal.

The *major* essential nutrient elements supplied through the soil are nitrogen (N), phosphorus (P), potash (any number of compounds containing potassium [K]), calcium (Ca), magnesium (Mg), and sulfur (S). Other major nutrients, carbon (C), hydrogen (H), and oxygen (O), come from water and atmospheric carbon dioxide. The nutrients absorbed from the soil by plants are supplied by several means. Minerals are released through the erosion of native rocks. They also come from the decomposition of organic matter and deposition with the soil from floodwaters. Nutrients are also supplied by the application of limestone, commercial fertilizer materials, animal manure, and plant materials.

Nitrogen, phosphorus, and potassium are of particular interest to farmers and other plant growers. Plants require relatively large quantities of these elements. So when plant materials are harvested and removed from the area, the soils are quickly depleted of these elements. Measures do exist, however, to replace these nutrients.

Nitrogen produces the rich green color that is characteristic of a healthy plant. It also influences the quality of a plant's fruit, and increases the fruit's protein content. A plant's use of other major elements is stimulated by the presence of nitrogen in the plant. Nitrogen can be added to the soil by growing legumes, adding organic matter, or applying commercial nitrogen fertilizers.

Phosphorus is abundant in the fruits of plants and seeds. It is also in parts of the root such as the root hairs, which are involved in the rapid uptake of water and nutrients. Phosphorus plays a major role in those processes requiring a transfer of energy. Phosphorus compounds are added to the soil in the form of farm manure and commercial fertilizers.

Potassium or *potash* has much to do with the vigor and vitality of a plant. It encourages the development of a healthy root system, and offsets the harmful effect of excessive nitrogen. Potassium appears to play a role in the synthesis of starch and the movement of carbohydrates within a plant. Potassium deficiencies are usually corrected with the application of a commercial fertilizer.

A calcium deficiency is rarely a problem because of the widely accepted practice of applying lime to soil to raise the pH to the proper range for optimum plant growth. Also, soils have many sources of magnesium. Any deficiency can usually be corrected with the application of lime (pulverized dolomite or limestone). Almost all of the sulfur found in soils is located in the organic matter.

In addition to all these elements, fertile soils must contain very small quantities of manganese, iron, boron, copper, zinc, molybdenum, and chlorine. Plants also need small quantities of cobalt, iodine, and fluorine. The micronutrients taken up by plants are essential to animal health, including the health of humans. Carefully monitored, agricultural soils can provide a well-balanced ration of nutrients necessary for the proper maintenance of health.

The pH Level of Soil

The term **pH** refers to the degree of acidity or alkalinity (basicity) of a substance. The pH scale ranges from 0 to 14. A pH value of 7.0 is neutral (that is, neither acidic nor alkaline). Values below 7.0 are acidic; values above 7.0 are alkaline (see Figure 7.14).

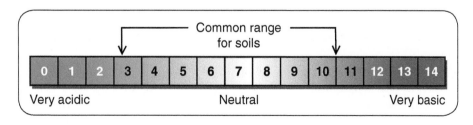

◀ FIGURE 7.14 The pH scale showing the common range for soils.

A soil's pH level is important. It affects the availability of soil nutrients that a plant needs for efficient growth. Soils that are too acidic or too alkaline do not favor the solution of compounds. Therefore, they restrict the presence of ions of essential plant nutrients. As a result, most plants prefer a soil that is neutral or near the neutral point (pH range of 6.0 to 8.0). Farmers and gardeners can change the pH of the soil by adding chemicals to it. To increase the pH, lime is usually added. To decrease the pH, commercial alum or sulfur is added.

Soil Conservation

Soil erosion is the process by which soil particles are carried away by wind and water. Human activities such as wood gathering, overgrazing, poor farming practices, and clearing for construction may increase erosion (see Figure 7.15). When plants are removed or damaged, their roots no longer hold the soil in place, and wind and rain can more easily reach the surface. Erosion often results.

Because soil formation is such a slow process, we should regard topsoil as a nonrenewable resource. **Soil conservation** programs are designed to help people learn how to manage soil in ways that help prevent erosion.

Major progress is being made in soil conservation efforts in the United States and in other countries. The Natural Resources Conservation Service (an agency of the U.S. Department of Agriculture) was formed after the Dust Bowl drought of the 1930s. This federal agency provides technical assistance and cost-sharing to landowners who apply conservation practices. Local conservation districts also help farmers and ranchers apply soil and water conservation measures on a voluntary basis. A variety of conservation practices have proven effective in combating soil erosion. They are explained as follows.

Conservation Tillage

There are several methods of crop production that minimize cultivation and leave crop residues on the surface throughout the year. Holding cultivation to a minimum helps maintain soil structure, reduce compaction, and prevent plowpans (plow-caused paths followed by water). Leaving crop residue on the surface reduces erosion, conserves moisture, and improves root development and soil aeration. It also increases water infiltration and improves ease of cultivation.

Of all methods of conservation tillage, **no-till** is the most effective in reducing erosion and providing food or cover for wildlife. All crop residue is left on the surface. In many areas, farmers using no-till plant the crop and apply fertilizer, herbicides, and other chemicals in one trip across the field (see Figure 7.16). This method also saves energy.

Cover and Green-Manure Crops

With this strategy, grasses or legumes are planted in a cropping system to reduce erosion, add organic matter to the soil, fix nitrogen, and

▲ FIGURE 7.15 Soil erosion. *(From USDA, NRCS, Ron Nichols.)*

▲ FIGURE 7.16 An example of no-till corn in Iowa. *(From USDA, NRCS, Gene Alexander.)*

▲ FIGURE 7.17 An example of strip cropping. *(From USDA, NRCS.)*

produce forage (food for horses and cattle) or hay. These crops hold soil and moisture as they grow. Green plants that are plowed under for the purpose of soil building are called *green manure.*

Strip Cropping

In strip cropping, strips of a row crop are alternated with soil-conserving strips of small grain or a cover crop, such as grass or a grass-legume mixture. The soil-conserving strips trap soil that erodes from the row crop strips (see Figure 7.17).

As storm water runoff flows downhill, it tends to form streams and gullies. To prevent gullying, a grass waterway can be planted to carry storm runoff slowly off the field. The waterway's depth and width are based on the size of the drainage area, topography, amount and distribution of rainfall, and other factors (see Figure 7.18).

Terraces

A **terrace**, or step, reduces erosion on sloping cropland by intercepting runoff and shortening the slope. With narrow-base terraces, the slopes are not cropped. Instead, they are planted with permanent vegetation (Figure 7.19).

Field Windbreaks and/or Borders

A field **windbreak** is a strip of large plants planted in or next to a field (Figure 7.20). This reduces wind erosion, traps blowing snow, conserves moisture, and protects crops, orchards, and livestock from wind. Nearly all field windbreaks consist of trees or shrubs, or both. However, there are exceptions. For example, giant reed is planted to control erosion in southwest citrus orchards; it also provides nesting cover for birds.

A field border is a strip of perennial vegetation. Usually, it is established to control erosion, protect field edges used as turn areas or travel

▲ FIGURE 7.18 This is what grass waterways look like. *(From USDA, NILES, Erwin Cole.)*

▲ FIGURE 7.19 A farmer uses terraces to reduce erosion on this farm. *(From USDA, NRCS, Tim McCabe.)*

Agriculture and Nutrition 267

▲ FIGURE 7.20 This windbreak of small plants, shrubs, and trees helps slow soil erosion due to wind and adds diversity to the local habitat. *(From USDA, NRCS, Gene Alexander.)*

lanes for farm machinery, or reduce competition from adjacent woodland.

Focus Questions & Tasks

1. List five strategies used to conserve soil. Briefly describe each strategy.

Topic: soil conservation
Go to: www.scilinks.org
Code: GloSci7e268

2. Land developers and highway departments often use erosion control blankets to minimize soil erosion. Obtain information on these products and write a short description of how they work.

Nutrition: Nurturing Life

The word *nutrition* comes from the word *nurture*. To nurture means to feed or support growth. Hence, **nutrition** refers to nourishing by taking in food. All living things must be nourished to stay alive (see Figure 7.21).

7.4 Plant Nutrition

A food chain has three main levels: producers, consumers, and decomposers. Producers make their own food. Consumers rely on what the producers make. Decomposers are special types of consumers that break down plant and animal refuse into simpler chemicals that plants and animals can use. Hence, decomposers are necessary for the recycling of nutrients. They also help maintain soil structure and aeration.

A plant's nutritional needs are the following:

- sunlight
- carbon dioxide (CO_2)
- water (H_2O)
- minerals (soil nutrients)
- oxygen (O_2)

Plants also need an adequate growing season to reach maturity.

During photosynthesis (an energy-trapping process), plants combine carbon dioxide and water to form organic compounds. From these, they make their body parts (stems, leaves, and so on) and obtain their energy. Oxygen is a product of photosynthesis. Both plants and animals use oxygen during respiration. During respiration (an energy-releasing process), organic materials are broken down as oxygen is consumed. Carbon dioxide and heat are given off. Heat is necessary to maintain an acceptable body temperature in which chemical (metabolic) reactions can occur.

Minerals are essential for the growth of healthy plants. The necessary minerals must contain 13 different elements. Nitrogen, potassium, and phosphorus are required in relatively

Apply Your Understanding

What is nutrition?

Name the nutritional needs of plants. Know why each is important.

large quantities. The remaining ten nutrients—calcium, magnesium, sulfur, manganese, boron, iron, zinc, copper, molybdenum, and chlorine—are needed in lesser amounts. For some, only a trace is needed.

The minerals a plant needs must be absorbed from the soil. Thus, the nutrition of plants is dependent on the ability of the soil to store essential elements. The elements must be made available in a form that can be used by plants. If a soil is poor in some minerals, farmers can apply manure and synthetic fertilizers. Farmers can use modern technology to help them plan fertilizer application (see Figures 7.22 and 7.23). In nature, this replacement occurs more slowly as rock weathers and organic matter decomposes.

7.5 Animal Nutrition

The nutritional needs of animals are the following:

- water (H_2O)
- oxygen (O_2)
- minerals
- vitamins
- proteins
- carbohydrates
- fats

Apply Your Understanding

List the nutritional needs of animals. Explain why each is important.

▶ **FIGURE 7.22** Farmers can use technology to help document grain moisture and yield to make production more efficient. When clean grain passes along this combine's elevator in route to the grain tank, grain samples are taken randomly to probe for moisture and measure yield. These data, combined with data from a Global Positioning System (GPS) telling exactly where in the field the samples were taken, allow the farmer to adjust seed levels during planting, as well as fertilizer and chemical levels in the areas identified by the GPS. *(Courtesy: New Holland North America, Inc.)*

▶ **FIGURE 7.23** As the wheat combine moves back and forth across a field, its position on Earth is accurately determined by the GPS in the cab. The position of the combine and the data from the yield and moisture monitoring system are color-coded and plotted on a graph. This color-coded graph (shown here) becomes a map of the field. The farmer then uses this map to plan fertilizer and moisture application for the next crop. *(Courtesy: New Holland North America, Inc.)*

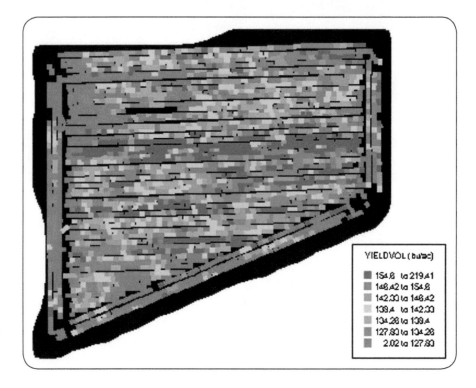

Animals obtain their food either directly or indirectly from green plants. They get their energy by first breaking down the energy-rich products of photosynthesis into simpler molecules. Many of these less energetic molecules become the nutrients that the animal absorbs for the building of its own body parts. The chemical reactions that take place in an organism as food is used are referred to as **metabolism**. Nutrition is the uptake of materials necessary for metabolism.

Water regulates the body temperature, transports nutrients, carries waste, participates in metabolic reactions, and carries water soluble vitamins. An adult human body is 65 percent water by weight.

◀ FIGURE 7
must moni...
nutritional n...
cattle. (Kansas
Sustainable Agri...
John S. Bradley.)

Oxygen is required for respiration. Respiration is the breakdown of food by organisms to release nutrients, energy, carbon dioxide, and water. Both animals and plants carry on respiration.

Essential *minerals* are involved in the functions of nerves and muscles, the formation of bones and teeth, the activation of *enzymes* (organic catalysts) and, in the case of iron, the transport of oxygen. Minerals are widely distributed in nature. Mixing foods from around the globe makes dietary deficiencies rare. However, changes in the balance among foods may have important consequences for health. Excess intake of certain minerals can cause problems.

Vitamins are organic molecules that are needed in small quantities in the diet of higher animals to perform specific biological functions. For example, vitamin K is important in blood clotting. Vitamins and enzymes often work in combination.

Proteins in food are broken down by the body into amino acids. The amino acids are then reassembled into body proteins. Some proteins serve to give structure to the organs of the cell. Others act as enzymes, antibodies, hormones, and metabolically active compounds.

The breakdown of **carbohydrates** provides our body's main source of energy. Adequate carbohydrate intake prevents the breakdown of fat and protein for energy needs. This "protein sparing" is important because protein is best used for body-building functions.

Fats and *oils* (or **lipids**) help maintain cell membrane structure and function. They also serve as building blocks for some hormones, provide a concentrated source of energy, carry fat-soluble vitamins, and provide insulation and protection for important organs and body structures.

Proper nutrition is essential for the growing of healthy plants and animals. Humans need sufficient amounts of fats, proteins, and carbohydrates. If humans eat excessive amounts, however, they are converted to body fat.

Topic: nutrition
Go to: www.scilinks.org
Code: GloSci7e271

Molecules of Life: Macromolecules

Life is tied to the unique properties of the carbon atom. One of these properties is that carbon can bond to other carbon atoms and form long carbon chains. For example,

H H H H
H—C—C—C—C—H
H H H H

Helpful Hint!

Each line represents one shared electron pair.

Butane

Another property is that carbon bonds strongly to other elements such as hydrogen, oxygen, and nitrogen.

In addition to forming long carbon chains, carbon can also bond to other carbons to form rings in a variety of ways. For example,

Cyclopropane   and   Benzene

or

Macromolecule	Building Blocks
Carbohydrates	Monosaccharides (for example, glucose)
Lipids (fats and oils)	Fatty acids, glycerol
Protein	Amino acids
Nucleic acid	Nucleotides

▲ FIGURE 7.25 The four main types of macromolecules and the building blocks that form them.

▲ FIGURE 7.26 The carbohydrate cellulose in plant cell walls can be broken down into sugars by microbial proteins. (*USDOE Genomics: GTL Program, http://doegenomestolife.org*)

Many of the molecules in living cells are so large, they are called macromolecules. These macromolecules are all carbon based. They are made of repeating units of smaller molecules that are referred to as building blocks. The four main types of macromolecules are carbohydrates, lipids

Helpful Hint!

Macro- is a prefix that means large.

(fats and oils), proteins, and nucleic acids. Figure 7.25 summarizes the building blocks of their structures. Figures 7.26–7.29 show ways of representing the structure or function of the four types of macromolecules. Figure 7.30 summarizes the composition, function, and production of the four types of macromolecules found in all living organisms.

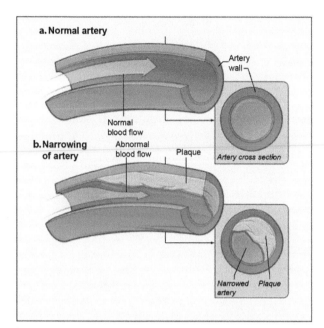

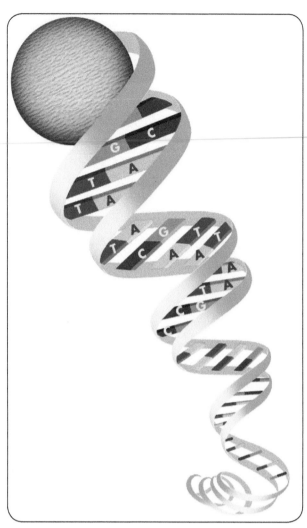

▲FIGURE 7.27 (a) An artery with normal blood flow. (b) An artery containing plaque buildup. Plaque is made up of fat, cholesterol, calcium, and other substances from the blood. *(U.S. Department of Health & Human Services, National Institute of Health.)*

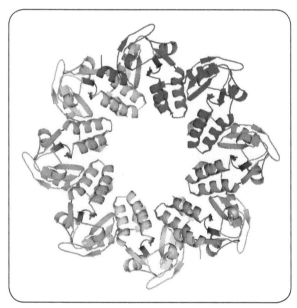

▲FIGURE 7.29 A representation of DNA strands and a cell. Nucleic acids are chains assembled from nucleotides. Both DNA and RNA are nucleic acids. *(USDOE Human Genome Program, www.ornl.gov/hgmis)*

▲FIGURE 7.28 Protein molecules are huge and have three-dimensional structures. Understanding structures is a focus of cancer research. *(USDOE Human Genome Program, www.ornl.gov/hgmis)*

The composition, function, and production of the four main types of macromolecules.

Composition	Function	Production (how made)
Carbohydrates Carbohydrates are compounds made from carbon, hydrogen, and oxygen usually in a ratio of 1:2:1. Carbohydrates include sugars, starches, and cellulose. The smallest carbohydrates are simple sugars such as glucose. Glucose may be represented as or $C_6H_{12}O_6$ Starch and cellulose (fiber) are polymers (chains) of glucose and are called polysaccharides, which means "many sugars."	When eaten, complex carbohydrates such as starch are broken down into glucose. This simple sugar is absorbed through the intestinal walls and taken into the bloodstream. The body then uses the glucose as a source of energy as it breaks the glucose down through a complex set of chemical reactions. This produces CO_2 and H_2O, and releases energy (cellular respiration). These reactions are the reverse of photosynthesis. The steps in this process to break down glucose are catalyzed by enzymes (special protein molecules). Humans and many other animals cannot break down cellulose (plant fiber). Grazing animals and termites can because of the action of bacteria in their digestive tract.	Carbohydrates are made (synthesized) as plants photosynthesize CO_2 and H_2O into sugars, starches, and cellulose.
Lipids (fats and oils) Lipids are compounds of carbon, hydrogen, and oxygen. Lipids, however, differ structurally from carbohydrates. Instead of containing a "ring" like glucose, lipids contain long carbon chains that are hooked together. For example, Triglyceride	Lipids play a dual role in the diet. Some are "burned" as fuel. Others are used to build important parts of a cell's body. Some lipids are stored as a future source of energy. Lipids also serve to insulate the body against loss of heat and to protect vital organs from injury. They also can carry vitamins to desired locations.	Fats are synthesized by both plants and animals. They are supplied to us when we eat butter, cream, margarine, vegetable oils, shortenings, meats, and some seeds and nuts.

Composition	Function	Production (how made)

Proteins

Proteins are a vital part of all life. No living part of an organism is without protein. All proteins contain the elements carbon, hydrogen, oxygen, and nitrogen. Most proteins also contain sulfur.

The general formula of a protein is

$$R - \underset{\underset{NH_2}{|}}{\overset{\overset{H}{|}}{C}} - \underset{OH}{\overset{O}{C}}$$

where R is shorthand meaning a continuous carbon side chain. It is the side chain that distinguishes one protein from another.

Proteins serve as the structural material of animals much as cellulose does for plants. Muscle tissue is largely protein. So are the skin and hair. Proteins are used by organisms for growth and for the repair of body tissues. If eaten in excess, proteins can serve as a source of energy.

Both the composition and shape of protein molecules determine how they function.

Plants can synthesize proteins from carbon dioxide, water, and minerals such as nitrates (NO_3^-) and sulfates (SO_4^{-2}). Animals break down proteins in their digestive tracts from plants or other animals into the component amino acids. From these, the animal then synthesizes proteins for growth and repair of body tissues. Twenty amino acids occur in the protein of organisms.

Nucleic acids

Nucleic acids are macromolecules that contain carbon, hydrogen, oxygen, nitrogen, and phosphorus. Nucleic acids are polymers (chains) assembled from nucleotides. The nucleotides consist of three parts: a 5-carbon sugar, a phosphate group, and a nitrogenous base as shown in Figure 7.31.

Nucleic acids function in living organisms to store and express genetic memory. There are two types of nucleic acids: *deoxyribonucleic acid* (DNA) and *ribonucleic acid* (RNA). The nuclei of living plant and animal cells contain the genetic memory bank of DNA molecules. DNA, with assistance from RNA, determine the presence and structure of protein molecules. Proteins are the end product of genetic expression.

Nucleotides join together to make a single helical (helix) strand. A sequence of nucleotides of a single strand of DNA is a given amount of genetic information. A DNA molecule is constructed from two single-stranded nucleic acid molecules that are joined together by hydrogen bonds between nitrogen rings (see Figure 7.32).

- Phosphate Molecule
- Deoxyribose Sugar Molecule
- Nitrogenous Bases
- A — T
- C — G
- G — C
- T — A
- Weak Bonds Between Bases
- Sugar-Phosphate Backbone

▲ FIGURE 7.31 A representation of a segment of a DNA molecule. (*USDOE Human Genome Program, www.ornl.gov/hgmis*)

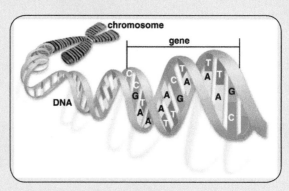

▲ FIGURE 7.32 A representation of a DNA molecule. (*USDOE Human Genome Program, www.ornl.gov/hgmis*)

Composition	Function	Production (how made)
Nucleic acids *(continued)* There are five nitrogenous bases that code into nucleic acid molecules (see Figure 7.33). The DNA double helix molecule consists of a sugar-phosphate backbone or ribbon. Arranged along the backbone in a particular order (the DNA sequence) are the nitrogenous bases represented by their initial letters (A, T, C, G). Normally, we simply use the capital letter to identify the nitrogenous base in drawings (see Figures 7.31 and 7.32). The sequence encodes all genetic instructions for an organism. The two DNA strands are held together by weak bonds between the bases (see Figure 7.31).		The self-replicating property built into the DNA molecule is the basis of life. The master molecule, DNA, also controls the production of RNA. RNA controls the production of proteins—the "building blocks" of living cells.

▼ FIGURE 7.33 The five nitrogenous bases that code into nucleic acid molecules.

Adenine A

Thymine T (from DNA)

Uracil U (from DNA)

Guanine G

Cytosine C

QUESTIONS & TASKS

Record your responses in your science notebook.

1. Summarize the composition and function of the four types of macromolecules.

2. In Activity 7.4, you will test for the presence of sugars, starch, lipids, and protein.

How Much Food Energy Do I Need?

In this activity, you will estimate the number of Calories you need per day and compare that figure to your average daily diet. You will then determine what that number means in terms of agriculture.

Background

A calorie is usually thought of as a unit of heat. One calorie is the amount of heat required to raise the temperature of 1 gram of water 1 degree Celsius. One thousand calories is known collectively as a kilocalorie (kcal) and as a Calorie. Food value is measured in Calories.

Food Calories are a measure of the energy content of a specified portion of a given food.

> **Content Clue**
>
> One kilocalorie = 1 Calorie = 1,000 calories.

Each day you must take in a definite number of Calories if you are to maintain a constant physical condition. People vary in their Calorie requirements primarily because of age, gender, size, and daily physical activities. This activity will help you compute your Caloric need.

Materials

- Calorie Counter (Appendix 10)
- scale
- meterstick or measuring tape

Procedure

Part A: How much food energy do you need to stay alive?

1. Convert your height (ht) from feet and inches into centimeters. (1.0 in = 2.54 cm, so ht. in cm = ht. in inches × 2.54)

> **Helpful Hint!**
>
> Make all your calculations in your science notebook. DO NOT WRITE IN THIS BOOK.

2. Convert your weight into kilograms (1 kg = 2.2 lbs) (mass in kilograms = weight in pounds/2.2)

3. Use Figure 7.34 to determine your surface area in m².

4. Use Figure 7.35 and your age and gender to determine your normal basal metabolic rate (BMR) in Cal/m²/hr.

> **Helpful Hint!**
>
> Your *basal metabolic rate (BMR)* is the approximate amount of energy required/ m²/hr just to stay alive.

5. Multiply your BMR by your surface area to determine your basal energy requirement (BER) in Cal/hr.

6. Add 10% of your BER to the BER total from step 5 to get your "dynamic BER" in Cal/hr.

> **Helpful Hint!**
>
> Your *basal energy requirement (BER)* is the number of Calories/hr a person of your age, gender, and size needs just to stay alive.

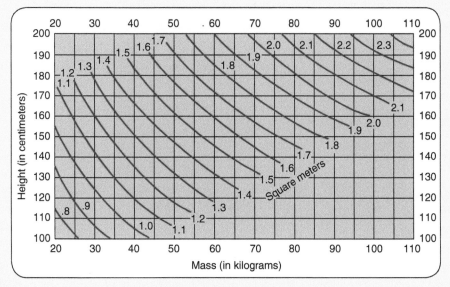

◄ **FIGURE 7.34** Use this table to determine your body surface area by finding the intersection of your height and mass. (*From Dubois, E.F.: Basal Metabolism in Health and Disease, 3rd ed., Lea A. Febiger.*)

► FIGURE 7.35 This graph shows the average or typical basal metabolic rates (BMR) of males and females at different ages. (*Figure from* Physiology of the Human Body, *Fifth Edition by Arthur C. Guyton, copyright © 1979 by Saunders College Publishing.*)

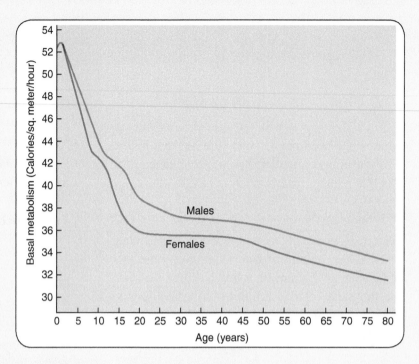

7. Multiply your dynamic BER by 24 hr/day to get your dynamic daily basal energy requirement in Cal/day.

For any daily activity beyond sleeping, you need additional Calories. Also, the greater your dynamic BER, the greater number of Calories you will need to perform the same activity. Figure 7.36 lists the number of additional Calories/hr that would be needed for each activity by a male 17 years old who is 172 cm tall (5 ft 8 in) and weights 68 kg (152 lb). His daily BER is 1,728 Calories/day, and his dynamic daily BER (10% more) is 1,900 Cal/day.

8. Reproduce the table in Figure 7.37 in your science notebook. List your daily activities with the additional Calories needed. Use Figure 7.36. Complete the table for your average day. Then find your total additional Calories used/day. Work in decimals, not fractions.

> **Content Clue**
>
> In addition (depending on the food combination you eat), you need an average of 10% more to stimulate the body to use your food and maintain body temperature (step 6).

> **Helpful Hint!**
>
> Use an average day and be realistic about the kind of things you do and the amount of time you spend doing them.

9. You now must adjust the figures in the table to yourself. Since the table was designed for a person who has a dynamic BER of 1,900 Cal/day,

find your adjustment by dividing your dynamic daily BER (step 7) by 1,900.

For example, for a person who has a dynamic daily BER of 1,500,

$$\text{adjustment factor} = \frac{1,500}{1,900} = 0.79$$

$$\text{Your adjustment factor} = \frac{\text{your dynamic daily BER}}{1,900}$$

$$= \frac{}{1,900} = \underline{}.$$

10. Multiply your total additional Calories used/day (step 8) by your adjustment factor (step 9) to find your total additional Calories needed.

11. Add the results of steps 7 and 10. This is the number of Calories you need to carry out your daily activities and maintain constant physical condition.

Part B: How much food energy do you consume?

1. Reproduce the table in Figure 7.38 in your science notebook. Use a Calorie counter (see Appendix 8) to determine the Caloric value of each item consumed. Then total up your daily intake. You may also obtain Caloric information from food packaging.

2. Make a statement summarizing how your total daily intake and total daily requirement (step 11, Part A) pertain to you. See note, Figure 7.38.

Activity	Cal/hr	Activity	Cal/hr
Sleeping	0	Mopping floors	300
Awake lying down	10	Gardening	280
Sitting (watching TV or reading)	30	Digging, lifting	330
Sitting—riding in a car	40	Aerobics	420
Sitting—eating	45	Badminton	130
Sitting—studying	50	Playing pool	140
Sitting—sewing	55	Horseback riding (slow)	145
Sitting—playing cards	55	Dancing (slow)	400
Sitting—typing rapidly	70	Dancing (fast)	600
Kneeling	30	Ping-pong	270
Standing (relaxed)	50	Golf	300
Standing (light activity)	65	Swimming—relaxed	420
Bicycling (moderate)	200–400	Swimming—competitive	700
Driving a car	75	Tennis	430
Squatting	85	Rowing	400
Walking—indoors	100	Bowling	200
Walking—outdoors (2.5 mph)	130	Running (5.3 mph)	530
Walking—outdoors (3.0 mph)	150	Basketball	540
Jogging—outdoors (5.6 mph)	580	Football	680
Walking downstairs	470	Sprinting (100 yds)	860
Climbing stairs	1,030	Wrestling	900
Showering, dressing	35	Ice skating	300
Dishwashing, ironing	60	Volleyball	150
Washing clothes	135	Skiing	500
Making beds	300		

▲ FIGURE 7.36 This table lists the Calories required to do each of the activities listed for 1 hour beyond the basal requirement. If one of your activities is not listed in this table, use the table to help you estimate the Cal/hr for that activity.

Part C: How much land does it take to grow the food you eat?

1. Examine Figure 7.39. This table provides information for estimating the amount of land required to raise the food eaten by a 17-year-old American male. The food column is for a daily diet. This diet was not selected because it is healthy. It was selected because it is made up of foods most teenagers are familiar with. Note that the hamburger bun and cookies are divided into the flour, sugar, and fat that those foods are made from.

Form of Activity	Additional Cal/hr	Hours per Day	Total Additional Calories Used
	Totals:	Counting sleep, this column should total 24.	____ Cal/day

Your total additional Calories used per day.

▲FIGURE 7.37 Sample table for recording daily activities.

2. Total the column titled "Calories" to determine how many Calories per day this diet provides. Record your answer in your science notebook.

3. The land area calculation is made much easier if you assume this diet is eaten every day for 1 year. Multiply each of the numbers in column 2 by 365 and record the answers in column 4.

4. To determine the land used to provide a year's supply of each food item, multiply the number you recorded in column 4 by the related conversion factor. (See the hint box for information on conversion factors.) Record the number of acres in column 6 in your science notebook. It is best to record that number as a decimal. (This calculation requires the use of scientific notation. If you need to improve your ability to use scientific notation, see Appendix 3.)

5. Total the numbers in column 6 and record your answers in your science notebook.

Helpful Hint!

Reproduce columns 4 and 6 from Figure 7.39 in your science notebook. DO NOT WRITE IN THIS BOOK.

Helpful Hint!

Column 5 contains the conversion factors needed to determine how much land is required to produce a year's supply of a related food item. The conversion factors were determined using agricultural production data provided by the U.S. Department of Agriculture (USDA), various state agriculture statistics agencies, growers' associations, and industry.

QUESTIONS & TASKS

Record your responses in your science notebook.

1. What does your answer from step 5 mean? If the average size of a residential lot in suburban America is 0.25 acres, how many lots does your answer represent?

Items Eaten	Calories
Breakfast	
_____	_____
_____	_____
_____	_____
_____	_____
Mid-morning snacks	
_____	_____
_____	_____
Lunch	
_____	_____
_____	_____
_____	_____
Afternoon snacks	
_____	_____
_____	_____
Dinner	
_____	_____
_____	_____
_____	_____
_____	_____
_____	_____
TV snacks	
_____	_____

Your total *intake* for an average day   = _____

Your total *requirement* for the day   = _____ (step 11)

Note: For every 3,500 Calories you consume more than you use, you gain a pound of body weight. You lose a pound of weight by using 3,500 more Calories than you eat.

▲ **FIGURE 7.38** Sample table for recording daily Calorie intake.

2. Determine the amount of arable land there is per person on Earth using the following information. Compare this number to the number you calculated in question 1.

   a. Average radius of Earth = 3,963 mi.
   b. Area of a sphere = $4\pi r^2$.
   c. One square mile = 640 acres.

d. Three percent of Earth's surface is arable land.

e. Present population of the world.

3. Determine some of the conversion factors in Figure 7.39 using information provided by your teacher. (Your teacher will tell you whether to try this task.) Place your work on Handout 7.2.

▼FIGURE 7.39 Food analysis of a daily diet for a 17-year-old male.

Food	Amount Eaten	Calories	Amount if Eaten Every Day for 1 Year	Conversion Factor	Land Used to Provide (acres)
Corn flakes	1 oz	110		1.63×10^{-5} acre/oz	
Milk (1%)	8 fl oz	100		3.5×10^{-6} acre/oz	
Orange juice	8 fl oz	106		3.13×10^{-6} acre/oz	
Apple, raw (unpeeled)	1	73		2.35×10^{-5} acre/apple	
Hamburger	4 oz	350		5.2×10^{-5} acre/oz	
Bun	49 g*	130	—	—	
fat	1.5 g	—		2.7×10^{-8} acre/g	
flour	29 g	—		1.41×10^{-6} acre/g	
sugar	3 g	—		2.29×10^{-7} acre/g	
Cheese	1 oz	110		5.5×10^{-6} acre/oz	
Large fries	147 g	450		6.5×10^{-8} acre/g	
Ketchup	1 oz	30		4.2×10^{-6} acre/oz	
Small shake	414 mL	360		3.0×10^{-8} acre/mL	
Large Coke	32 fl oz (86 g sugar)	310	—	— 2.29×10^{-7} acre/g	
Chicken	9 nuggets	430		3.5×10^{-5} acre/nugget	
Sugar cookies	42 g	180	—	—	
fat	5 g	—		2.7×10^{-8} acre/g	
flour	22 g	—		1.41×10^{-6} acre/g	
sugar	15 g	—		2.29×10^{-7} acre/g	
Large Hi-C Orange	32 fl oz (94 g sugar)	350	—	— 2.29×10^{-7} acre/g	
	Total Calories _____			Total acres _____	

*32% of the weight (mass) of the bun is moisture. This diet consumes more than twice the per capita sugar consumption in the United States.

Nutrition

In this activity, you will use the Food Guide Pyramid to analyze your diet.

Background

What is good nutrition for humans? There is no simple answer to that question. Nutrition is a complex subject, and there are many points of view about what people should eat.

The U.S. Department of Agriculture developed the Food Guide Pyramid to help people make daily food choices for better health (see Figure 7.40). Eating as the pyramid suggests will enable you to fulfill your nutritional requirements. The Food Guide Pyramid helps you choose what and how much to eat from the five food groups shown in the three lower sections of the pyramid. The number of servings that are right for you depends on how many Calories you need. This is determined partially by your age, gender, size, and daily activities.

From the pyramid, you can see that a person should

- go easy on fats, oils, and sweets;
- eat a variety of foods;
- choose a diet with plenty of vegetables, fruits, and whole grain products;
- use table salt and other sodium products in moderation (they are not even on the chart); and
- eat meat, poultry, fish, and eggs in moderation.

Each of the food groups provides some, but not all, of the nutrients you need. Foods in one group can't replace those in another. No one group is more important than another. For good health, you need them all.

Procedure

1. Keep a record in your science notebook of the foods you eat for 1 week (include quantities).

2. Organize your data.

3. Analyze your data in terms of the Food Guide Pyramid.

4. Write a conclusion that summarizes your findings.

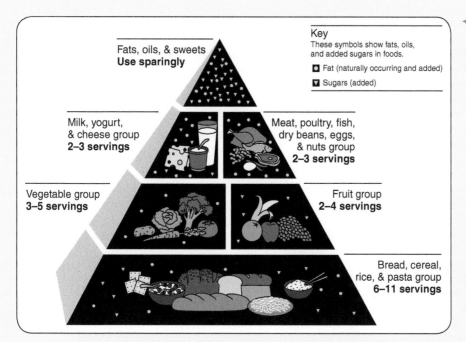

Key
These symbols show fats, oils, and added sugars in foods.

■ Fat (naturally occurring and added)
▼ Sugars (added)

Fats, oils, & sweets
Use sparingly

Milk, yogurt, & cheese group
2–3 servings

Meat, poultry, fish, dry beans, eggs, & nuts group
2–3 servings

Vegetable group
3–5 servings

Fruit group
2–4 servings

Bread, cereal, rice, & pasta group
6–11 servings

◄ **FIGURE 7.40** The Food Guide Pyramid. *(USDA)* Another version of the Food Guide Pyramid can be viewed at www.mypyramid.gov.

ACTIVITY 7.4

Connecting Seeds and Human Nutrition

In this activity, you will test a variety of seeds for the presence of four different nutrients.

Materials

- assorted seeds (soaked 24 hours) or edible seeds
- starch-detecting solution (iodine-iodide)
- sugar-detecting solution (Benedict's)
- protein-detecting solution (Biuret)
- lipid (fat)–detecting solution (Sudan III)
- boiling apparatus
- sliced turkey, butter patty, honey
- slice of potato
- grease pencil to label petri dishes
- distilled water
- 6 petri dishes
- paper towels
- scalpel or single-edge razor blade
- 2 beakers, 250-mL
- stirring rod with flat end
- dropping pipette
- 4 small test tubes
- safety goggles

Procedure

Part A: Preparing standards for comparison

1. Reproduce the table in Figure 7.41 in your science notebook.

2. To test for *starch*, place a small slice of potato in a petri dish. Note the color of the iodine-iodide solution. Place a drop of iodine-iodide solution on the potato slice. Wait 2 minutes (min). Observe any color change and record it on your data chart. Starch is a granular, solid carbohydrate.

3. To test for *protein*, start with a clean test tube. (Contamination from dirt will make your results inaccurate.) Add 4 milliliters (mL) of

   BE SAFE

   Read the warnings on the four chemical solutions before you proceed. Wear your safety goggles throughout this entire activity.

   Biuret solution (*corrosive!*) to the test tube. Note the color of the solution. Add a small piece (size of a nickel) of sliced turkey to the test tube. *Do not heat.* Use a clean stirring rod to thoroughly crush the turkey. Wait 2 min. Record any color change in your data chart. Rinse and clean the test tube.

4. Place about 100 mL of water into a 250-mL beaker. Bring the water to a boil as instructed by your teacher (*safety goggles!*). This is your water bath for step 5 in Part A and step 7 in Part B.

5. To test for *sugars*, start with a clean test tube. Add 1 mL of distilled water. Then add 1 mL of clover honey. Heat the honey/water mixture in

Material or Seed	Starch (iodine-iodide)	Protein (Biuret)	Sugar (Benedict's)	Lipid (fat) (Sudan III)
Potato (rich in starch)				
Turkey (protein source)				
Honey (sugar source)				
Butter (rich in fat)				
Lima bean				
Sweet corn				
Fresh soybean				
Mammoth sunflower				

▲ FIGURE 7.41 Sample table for recording test results.

a hot-water bath for 2 min. Note the color of the Benedict's solution. Add 2 mL of Benedict's solution to the test tube. Tap the test tube with your fingers to mix the solutions. Heat the mixture in a water bath for 4 min. Remove and let cool for 2 min. Observe and record any color change in your data chart. Clean the test tube. Sugars are sweet, high-energy carbohydrates.

6. To test for *lipids* (fats), place ¼ of a butter patty in a petri dish. Make a small indentation in the butter so it will hold liquid. Note the color of the Sudan III solution. Place a drop of Sudan III solution in the indentation. Let stand for 4 min. Note and record any color change in your chart.

Part B: How nutritious are the seeds we eat?

1. Obtain 4 petri dishes. Label the first dish *starch*, the second *protein*, the third *sugar*, and the fourth *lipid* (fat).

2. Obtain 2 each of the 4 different soaked seeds you will be testing.

3. Place the seeds on a paper towel and *carefully* cut each seed in half lengthwise.

4. Place half of each seed that you cut into each of the 4 petri dishes.

BE SAFE

Use caution when using a sharp blade. Wear safety goggles when using chemicals. Wash any spills liberally with water. Report any spills. Do not place any of these seeds in your mouth.

5. Place 1 drop of iodine-iodide solution on each half seed in the petri dish labeled *starch*. Iodine-iodide solution changes color from brown to royal blue or purple in the presence of starch. Record your findings on your data chart using both words and pictures.

Helpful Hint!

Note that seeds have three major parts: seed coat (protection), embryo (undeveloped plant), and food storage tissue.

6. Remove each half seed from the petri dish labeled *protein*. Place each one in its own clean test tube. Add 3 mL of Biuret solution (*corrosive!*) to each test tube. Use a clean stirring rod to crush each seed in the solution. Wait 2 min. Record any color change in your data chart. Biuret solution changes from blue to pink-to-violet in the presence of protein. Rinse and clean the test tubes.

7. Remove each half seed from the petri dish labeled *sugar*. Place each one in its own clean test tube. Add 2 mL distilled water to each. Use a clean stirring rod to thoroughly crush each half seed. Then add 2 mL of Benedict's solution to each mashed-up seed/water mixture. Heat each mixture in a hot-water bath for 5 min. Benedict's solution changes from light blue/turquoise to a cloudy brownish red in the presence of sugar. Various colors of a cloudy green or cloudy yellowish green also indicate smaller amounts of sugar are present. Record any color changes in your data chart.

8. Place 1 drop of Sudan III solution on each half seed in the petri dish labeled *lipid*. Wait 4 min. When Sudan III dye is added to a mixture of

lipids and water, the dye will move into the lipid layer and stain it red. Sudan III dye is red when dissolved in lipids. Record your findings in your data chart in both words and pictures.

QUESTIONS & TASKS

Record your responses in your science notebook.

1. Which of the seeds you tested were the most nutritious?

2. What evidence supports your answer to question 1?

3. Sugar is used as a sweetener in many countries. Since seeds are not a major source of sugar, where does most of our sugar come from?

4. We grow plants from seeds, but humans also eat a variety of seeds. List at least five different seeds you have eaten recently.

5. Give two or three reasons why humans eat such a variety of seeds.

6. How do people in developing countries stay healthy even though they don't have the food choices people in developed regions have?

7. Examine Figure 7.40 in Activity 7.3. What does the Food Guide Pyramid represent?

8. Why do seeds and seed-related foods have such an important role in the Food Guide Pyramid?

9. How does the way you eat compare to the recommendations in the Food Guide Pyramid? Explain.

10. Soybeans are one of the largest cash crops in the United States, yet most people don't know what they are or how they are used. What are soybeans used for?

The Challenge of Agriculture: Feeding the World and Saving Diversity

To live the good life, we must maintain a healthy biosphere and provide a healthy diet for all the world's people. Science can help achieve that goal. Also important, however, is skill at conflict resolution. We will examine the scientific issues next; conflict resolution will be examined in Chapter 17.

ACTIVITY 7.5

Seeds for the Future

Seeds are powerful packets of information. In this activity, you will examine three issues about seeds and the future. As you respond to these issues, consider the information you have read and the data you have collected prior to this activity.

Procedure

1. Divide into 3 groups: genetic engineers, experimental agronomists, or visiting agronomists.

2. Work with your group to develop a response to your question. The question for each group is in one of the following boxes. Record your response in your science notebook.

3. Present your response to the class.

4. After you listen to the group presentations, answer the following questions.

Apply Your Understanding

What is a genetic engineer? What is an agronomist?

QUESTIONS & TASKS

Record your responses in your science notebook.

1. What is the value of seed banks?

2. What is the value of genetic engineering?

3. What other strategies can you think of to use seeds as one of the keys to feeding a growing human population?

Genetic Engineer

Question: If you could design the perfect seed, what would that seed be like?

As you consider your response, address these issues:

a. What properties would you design into your seed? List the properties you desire and why you desire them.

b. What seed species would you be most likely to work with?

c. What might your seed look like? Include a drawing (see Figure 7.42).

d. What problems might arise during your work?

Review the material in Chapter 6 on genetic engineering.

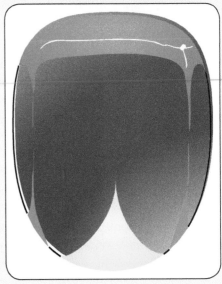

▲ FIGURE 7.42 Make a drawing of your "perfect" seed and list its properties.

Experimental Agronomist

Question: If you had the only known seeds of an endangered plant, what would you do with them?

As you consider your response, address these issues:

a. Who should know that the seeds exist?

b. Where should the seeds be kept?

c. What experiments or activities are acceptable to do with the seeds?

d. What experiments or activities are unacceptable to do with the seeds?

e. What are the trade-offs of your decisions related to your responses to questions a–d?

Review the material in Chapter 6 on seed storage.

Visiting Agronomist

Question: If you needed to feed a village of 100 people and you had only 10 seeds, what would you do?

As you consider your response, address these issues:

a. What kind(s) of seed do you think are most valuable in this situation?

b. What will you do with your seeds?

c. What is your goal when you leave the village?

d. How does this scenario reflect the Chinese proverb at the opening of this chapter?

The Politics of Hunger

If you want to live in Camelot, you've got to build Camelot; and you have to build it using the hand you've been dealt.

—J. W. Christensen

In this activity, you will examine possible reasons why some people eat well and others do not.

Background

Figure 7.43 shows a map of the world where countries are sized by population. Each country is numbered. Country numbers, names, and populations (in millions) are listed below the figure. Figure 7.44 is the same illustration as in Figure 7.43. However, for each country, the average daily Calorie supply per person has been added. Figure 7.44 shows the daily Calorie supply per person. Categories can be renamed as follows:

- Nearly starving: Less than 2,000 Calories/day
- Poorly fed: 2,001–2,400 Calories/day
- Well fed: 2,401–3,000 Calories/day
- Very well fed: Over 3,000 Calories/day

Materials

- poster board
- markers or colored pencils

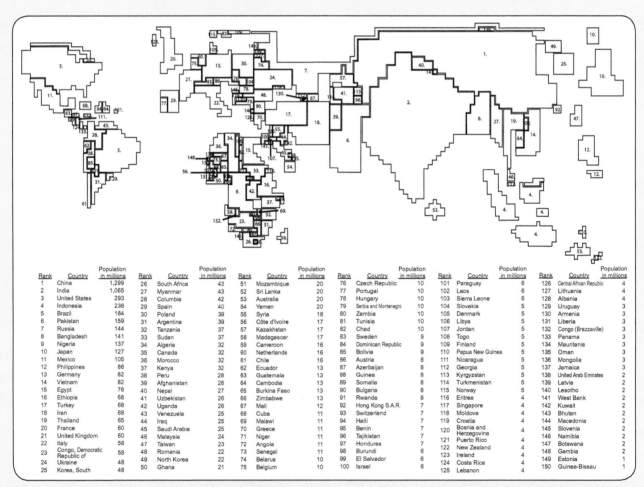

Rank	Country	Population in millions	Rank	Country	Population in millions	Rank	Country	Population in millions	Rank	Country	Population in millions	Rank	Country	Population in millions	Rank	Country	Population in millions
1	China	1,299	26	South Africa	43	51	Mozambique	20	76	Czech Republic	10	101	Paraguay	6	126	Central African Republic	4
2	India	1,065	27	Myanmar	43	52	Sri Lanka	20	77	Portugal	10	102	Laos	6	127	Lithuania	4
3	United States	293	28	Columbia	42	53	Australia	20	78	Hungary	10	103	Sierra Leone	6	128	Albania	4
4	Indonesia	238	29	Spain	40	54	Yemen	20	79	Serbia and Montenegro	10	104	Slovakia	5	129	Uruguay	3
5	Brazil	184	30	Poland	39	55	Syria	18	80	Zambia	10	105	Denmark	5	130	Armenia	3
6	Pakistan	159	31	Argentina	39	56	Côte d'Ivoire	17	81	Tunisia	10	106	Libya	5	131	Liberia	3
7	Russia	144	32	Tanzania	37	57	Kazakhstan	17	82	Chad	10	107	Jordan	5	132	Congo (Brazzaville)	3
8	Bangladesh	141	33	Sudan	37	58	Madagascar	17	83	Sweden	9	108	Togo	5	133	Panama	3
9	Nigeria	137	34	Algeria	32	59	Cameroon	16	84	Dominican Republic	9	109	Finland	5	134	Mauritania	3
10	Japan	127	35	Canada	32	60	Netherlands	16	85	Bolivia	9	110	Papua New Guinea	5	135	Oman	3
11	Mexico	105	36	Morocco	32	61	Chile	16	86	Austria	8	111	Nicaragua	5	136	Mongolia	3
12	Philippines	86	37	Kenya	32	62	Ecuador	13	87	Azerbaijan	8	112	Georgia	5	137	Jamaica	3
13	Germany	82	38	Peru	28	63	Guatemala	13	88	Guinea	8	113	Kyrgyzstan	5	138	United Arab Emirates	2
14	Vietnam	82	39	Afghanistan	28	64	Cambodia	13	89	Somalia	8	114	Turkmenistan	5	139	Latvia	2
15	Egypt	78	40	Nepal	27	65	Burkina Faso	13	90	Bulgaria	8	115	Norway	5	140	Lesotho	2
16	Ethiopia	68	41	Uzbekistan	26	66	Zimbabwe	13	91	Rwanda	8	116	Eritrea	4	141	West Bank	2
17	Turkey	68	42	Uganda	26	67	Mali	12	92	Hong Kong S.A.R.	7	117	Singapore	4	142	Kuwait	2
18	Iran	68	43	Venezuela	25	68	Cuba	11	93	Switzerland	7	118	Moldova	4	143	Bhutan	2
19	Thailand	65	44	Iraq	25	69	Malawi	11	94	Haiti	7	119	Croatia	4	144	Macedonia	2
20	France	60	45	Saudi Arabia	25	70	Greece	11	95	Benin	7	120	Bosnia and Herzegovina	4	145	Slovenia	2
21	United Kingdom	60	46	Malaysia	24	71	Niger	11	96	Tajikistan	7	121	Puerto Rico	4	146	Namibia	2
22	Italy	58	47	Taiwan	23	72	Angola	11	97	Honduras	7	122	New Zealand	4	147	Botswana	2
23	Congo, Democratic Republic of	58	48	Romania	22	73	Senegal	11	98	Burundi	6	123	Ireland	4	148	Gambia	2
24	Ukraine	48	49	North Korea	22	74	Belarus	10	99	El Salvador	6	124	Costa Rica	4	149	Estonia	1
25	Korea, South	48	50	Ghana	21	75	Belgium	10	100	Israel	6	125	Lebanon	4	150	Guinea-Bissau	1

▲ **FIGURE 7.43** This world map shows the size of each country according to its population as estimated for the year 2005.

(From Population, An Introduction to Concepts and Issues, 9th edition by WEEKS. © 2005. Reprinted with permission of Wadsworth, a division of Thomson Learning: www.thomsonrights.com.)

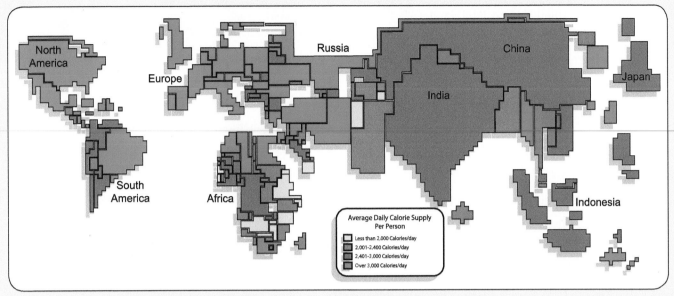

FIGURE 7.44 In this map of the world, each country's size is proportional to its population. Thus, China and India dominate the map, each having more than 1 billion people. Trinidad and Tobago are just dots in the Caribbean Sea. *(From* Population, An Introduction to Concepts and Issues, *9th edition by WEEKS. © 2005. Reprinted with permission of Wadsworth, a division of Thomson Learning: www.thomsonrights.com.)*

- reference materials such as atlases, almanacs, encyclopedias, and online resources
- Handout: *Map of the World* (optional)
- Handout: *Politics of Hunger Poster* (optional)

Procedure

1. You will be assigned a country from one of the 4 categories.

2. Make a 12 × 18-inch poster for your country and organize it as shown in Figure 7.45.

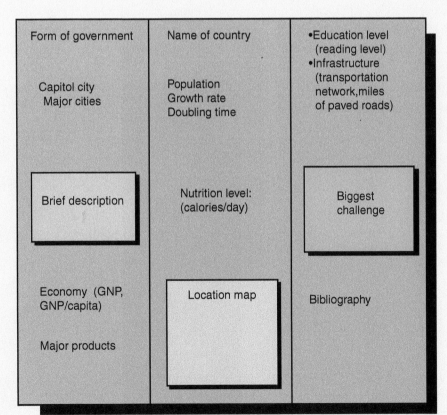

◀**FIGURE 7.45** Model for the poster of your assigned country.

3. Gather information from libraries, atlases, almanacs, references, and the Internet.

4. Give a short (2 min) report on your country to your class.

5. Reproduce the table in Figure 7.46 in your science notebook. As the reports are given, fill in the table. Add as many rows as needed to include all countries. Group the countries into the 4 categories.

Record your responses in your science notebook.

1. After all reports are given, analyze your data. Look for similarities, trends, and patterns.

2. Make a statement that relates your findings to the problem of hunger.

Country	Category Cal/Day	Population	G.R. / D.T.	Form of Government	Distribution System	Education Level	GNP/Capita

▲ FIGURE 7.46 Sample chart for recording information from reports about assigned countries.

7.6 The Concept of Carrying Capacity

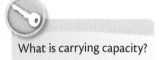

What is carrying capacity?

As you learned in Chapter 5, carrying capacity is the maximum number of a given organism that a given ecosystem can support. When we refer to Earth's carrying capacity, we are generally referring to the capacity for people (Figure 7.47). Of course, no single number

▶ FIGURE 7.47 There is some point beyond which we cannot adequately support everyone. (*Courtesy Bill Garner.*)

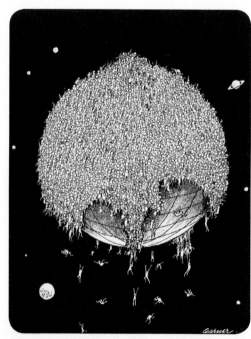

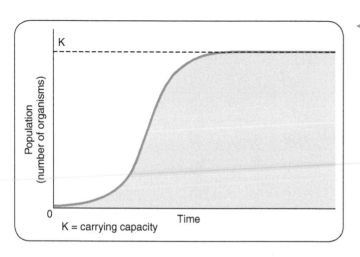

◄FIGURE 7.48 An idealized approach to carrying capacity. This type of graph is often referred to as a sigmoid curve.

can be given as the carrying capacity. The number of people Earth can support is tied to the standard of living and to our ability to preserve genetic diversity. The idealized approach to carrying capacity is shown in Figure 7.48. The matter of determining Earth's carrying capacity is quite controversial from both a scientific and a political point of view. Can you think of reasons why this is so?

ACTIVITY 7.7

How Many Squirrels Can an Oak Forest Support?

In this activity, you will model a small ecosystem and examine the concept of carrying capacity.

Background

Oak forests are quite common in the eastern United States. Sometimes, they occur naturally. Other times, they have been planted in parks, on school campuses, or in cemeteries. Gray squirrels living in oak forests often use acorns as their major, or even sole, source of food.

In this activity, you will create a model of an oak forest. You will determine the size and species of the oak trees. You will also calculate the energy present in their average annual production of acorns. From this, you will be able to determine the theoretical carrying capacity of the area for squirrels. In other words, you can discover how many squirrels your model oak forest can support.

Materials (for each team of 2–3 students)

- cardboard, poster board, or other stiff material approximately 0.5 m square

- colored construction paper circles of varying diameters (25, 30, 35, 40, 45, 50, 55, 60, and 65 mm)

- metric ruler

Procedure

1. Your piece of cardboard represents an oak forest that comprises a few acres of land. Your first task is to decide on the topography of your piece of land. Think about these questions as you make your decisions:

   a. Will you have hills and valleys?

   b. Should there be a stream?

   c. Is your area a natural forest or a human-made area like a park or school campus?

Diameter of Tree at Breast Height (cm)	Black	Chestnut	Northern Red	Scarlet	White
25.0	0.50	0.40	0.18	1.10	0.85
30.0	0.77	1.40	0.99	1.80	1.60
35.0	1.00	2.30	2.60	2.50	2.30
40.0	1.30	2.70	4.50	4.60	3.10
45.0	1.50	3.60	6.50	5.40	3.90
50.0	1.80	4.00	7.10	6.60	4.60
55.0	2.10	4.40	7.70	7.90	5.40
60.0	2.30	4.50	6.90	8.00	6.10
65.0	2.60	4.70	6.20	8.20	6.80

▲FIGURE 7.49 Table of annual average acorn production in kilograms for various oaks. (*Based on U.S. Department of Agriculture, Forest Service, Managing Woodland for Wildlife, 1970.*)

2. Once you have decided on the physical features of the land, choose a species of oak tree. The colored circles represent oak trees of particular species and of varying diameters. The scale for diameter is 1 millimeter (mm) = 1 cm. In other words, a circle of 25 mm in diameter represents an oak tree of 25 cm in diameter. The circles are color-coded to represent different species. The color key is as follows:

Black   Black oak (*Quercus velutina*)
Brown   Chestnut oak (*Quercus pinus*)
Red   Northern red oak (*Quercus rubra*)
Orange   Scarlet oak (*Quercus coccinea*)
White   White oak (*Quercus alba*)

3. Place your oak trees on your land. Think about these questions:

a. Will the trees be scattered or clustered in one place?

b. Will there be both large and small trees? If so, where will they grow?

c. Have you left enough room for the oaks to grow and get water and nutrients from the soil?

4. To determine how many squirrels can live in your forest, follow these steps:

a. Make a data table in your science notebook with the following column headings: Tree Diameter, Number of Trees, Kilograms of Acorns/Tree, Total Kilograms. Make sure your table title includes your name and the species name of your tree.

b. Measure the diameter of each tree. Record the number of trees of each diameter in your data table.

c. Determine the average annual acorn production of each tree on your land. Record this information in your data table. (See Figure 7.49 for information about acorn production.)

d. Use the information in your data table to calculate the total annual acorn production in kilograms for all your trees.

e. Convert the calculated total acorn yield in kilograms to kilocalories. One kilogram of acorns produces approximately 4,500 kcal.

f. Calculate the number of squirrels that can live in your forest for a year by relating the number of kilocalories to the population of gray squirrels. Researchers have determined that a 0.5-kg squirrel requires 137 kcal *each day* for maintenance in the laboratory.

5. Create a class data table by combining your results with those of other teams.

6. Review the class data table and respond to the following questions.

Record your responses in your science notebook.

1. Which team achieved the greatest carrying capacity? What factors affected the outcome?

2. Why was it necessary to convert kilograms to kilocalories before making the calculations?

3. Do you think the actual carrying capacity of an oak forest is more or less than the calculations you made in this activity. Why?

4. Is the carrying capacity greater with many small trees or a few larger ones?

5. As much as 25 percent to 50 percent of the diet of the black bear, raccoon, white-tailed deer, and wild turkey is made up of acorns. What would happen to the carrying capacity of your plot if any of these animals were present?

6. Does the carrying capacity for squirrels depend on acorn production alone?

7.7 How Many People Can Earth Support?

How many people can Earth feed (Figure 7.50)? At first glance, one might think that a question like this can be answered by simply putting data into this equation:

$$\text{number of people (P)} = \frac{\text{quantity of food the world can produce/day}}{\text{average food requirement/day/person}}$$

Topic: carrying capacity
Go to: www.scilinks.org
Code: GloSci7e293

A closer evaluation of this equation reveals the task is much more difficult than this.

People have been attempting to calculate Earth's carrying capacity for humans since the late 1600s. An analysis of these attempts is contained in the book *How Many People Can the Earth Support?* by Joel E. Cohen. Cohen is one of the foremost theoretical biologists in the world. Of particular interest are his analyses of the seven carrying capacity estimates, which are summarized in Figure 7.51. These estimates range from less than 1 billion people to 1,000 billion people! How can there be such a range? The answer is that each estimate is based on a set of assumptions. Since the assumptions are all different, the answers are all different. However, the answers are not nearly as important as understanding the assumptions. If we understand the assumptions, we can then make sense of the differences.

◀FIGURE 7.50 The unquenchable appetite. *(Cartoon by Gene Bassett. Winner of Editorial Category Award in the 1974 Population Cartoon Contest. Credit: Scripps-Howard newspapers.)*

Primary Thinker/ Publication Date	Estimate of Maximum Population	Key Ideas behind Calculations
E. G. Ravenstein England, 1891	**5.994 billion** people (almost 6 billion)	The potential of different types of land (zones) to support a population of a given size. The populations of the various zones were then added together.
Albrecht Penck Germany, 1924	**15.9 billion** people possible, but 7.689 billion is more probable (the 11 climatic zones of Earth added together to give total)	The carrying capacity of a region = (the production area × production per unit of area)/average nutritional requirements of one person.
C. T. De Wit Netherlands, 1967	**1,000 billion** people (if space not considered) or 146 billion (providing 750 sq. meters/person for *all* space needs)	The rate of photosynthetic production is the *only* limiting factor in determining how many people Earth can support. Assumes adequate water and minerals. All people are vegetarians.
H. R. Hulett United States, 1970	**Less than 1 billion** people (The world's population was already 3.7 billion when Hulett calculated this number.)	The average U.S. citizen's rate of consumption of food and other raw materials determines an *optimal* size for the world's population.
Roger Ravelle United States, 1976	**40 billion** people. (Assumes a vegetarian diet.)	Food limits population size. Determining the amount of arable land in the world and *potential* crop yields enables you to calculate Earth's carrying capacity.
Food and Agricultural Organization (FAO) United Nations, 1983	**33 billion** people in Africa, Southeast Asia, Southwest Asia, South America, and Central America	The physical potential of lands in the *developing* world to grow enough food (assuming high resource inputs) to support minimal nutritional requirements.
Robert Kates United States, 1991	**5.9 billion** people on a basic vegetarian diet **3.9 billion** people on a diet of 85% vegetarian and 15% animal products **2.9 billion** people on a diet of 75% vegetarian and 25% animal products	How many people can live on the known primary food supplies in the world (similar to Penck's equation).

▲ FIGURE 7.51 A summary of seven estimates of carrying capacity. (*Summarized from Cohen, Joel E. How Many People Can the Earth Support? W.W. Norton & Co. 1995.*)

Think about This!

Why is Dewit's estimate so high and Hulett's estimate so low?

When we make these calculations, should we assume that photosynthesis is the only factor that limits how fast Earth can grow plants? What role do water and minerals (soil nutrients) play in plant production? We all know that plants don't grow rapidly in the desert. Should we assume that everyone will be a **vegetarian**? Some people believe Earth could support more vegetarians than meat eaters (Figure 7.52). But is that what people want? Half of the land available for food production is only sustainable as pastureland or rangeland and cannot or should not grow crops. It is also true that animals in agriculture can transform food that humans don't eat into nutritious human food. We can show that from the standpoint of nutritional requirements, a world population of 50 billion or more could

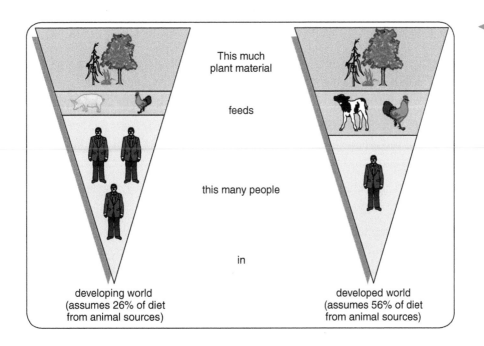

◀FIGURE 7.52 This figure shows the relative proportion of people and livestock fed by the same amount of plant material in the developing world compared to the developed world. *(Adapted from United Nations: Food and Agriculture Organization.)*

easily be fed from the products of algae farms and yeast factories. But people don't choose to eat such material.

QUESTIONS & TASKS

Record your responses in your science notebook.

1. What do you think the pros and cons of a vegetarian diet are?

2. Make an argument for or against this type of diet based on economics, personal values, nutrition, and/or personal health.

How many people can Earth *support*? This is a different question than how many people can Earth *feed*? Support implies more that biological survival. What do *you* want out of life? How much space do you require? Do you want enjoyment as well as a job? Do you want to view and experience nature? Can we learn to get along with one another? What roles should culture, religion, politics, economics, and government play in our lives?

Your answers to these questions, as well as the answers given by society as a whole, will determine what the carrying capacity of the Earth probably is. It all hinges on what people want.

In the chapters that follow, we will examine the roles that energy, water, air quality, and land use play in our efforts to build a sustainable world.

Apply Your Understanding

What do *you* think Earth's carrying capacity is? Defend your point of view.

Apply Your Understanding

Part C of Activity 7.2 enables you to make a carrying capacity calculation. What assumptions is this calculation based on?

QUESTION & TASK

1. At the beginning of this chapter, we implied that agriculture can be more efficient if (a) soil erosion is reduced, (b) diversity is increased, (c) energy efficiency is improved, and (d) more land-efficient transportation systems are developed. State at least one way each of these can be done.

Agriculture and Nutrition 295

Summary

Most agriculture is a deliberate attempt to keep land in the early stage of ecological succession. This is done because, in the early stage, photosynthesis mainly goes to plant growth. Thus, with sufficient sunlight, water, and soil nutrients, crops can be grown most efficiently.

Soil is the link between the living and the nonliving. Several factors determine the quality of a soil, including its texture, structure, and the availability of key nutrients. There are many ways to conserve the soil we use for farming.

Both plants and animals have specific nutritional needs. Knowledge of the needs and the use of technology can help us satisfy those needs.

The quality and quantity of food available to people has a direct impact on their nutrition. The number of Calories we need depends on our age, gender, size, and daily activities. The number of Calories we receive depends on the type and quantity of food we eat. People need a certain balance of food products to stay healthy. A diet high in carbohydrates, medium in protein, and low in fats is currently thought to be optimal for maintaining human health.

Most people on Earth receive the bulk of their nutrition by eating seeds and seed products. They can be very healthy and eat less meat because seeds contain rich stores of essential nutrients.

To maintain an adequate food supply for all people, we need to store seeds for future use, improve our ability to genetically engineer desirable properties into seeds and other foods, and learn how to better distribute the food that is available.

How many people the world can feed is difficult to determine. This is because so many variables are involved. What average standard of living shall we assume? What kind of food will the people eat? How will conflicts be resolved, and what will the people want? It is impossible to accurately answer all of these questions about the future. However, it is important to plan ahead and attempt to offer the greatest number of opportunities to the greatest number of people.

 REFERENCES

Avery, Dennis T. High-yield Agriculture a Boon to Humanity and Environment. *Wheat Life* (July-August 1997).

Avery, Dennis T. and Alex Avery. Farming to Sustain the Environment. *Hudson Briefing Paper* 190 (May 1996).

Brown, Lester B. *Outgrowing the Earth: The Food Security Challenge in an Age of Falling Water Tables and Rising Temperatures* (New York: W.W. Norton & Co.), 2004.

Cohen, Joel E. *How Many People Can the Earth Support?* (New York: Norton & Company), 1995.

International Food Policy Research Institute. *A 2020 Vision for Food, Agriculture, and the Environment* (Washington, D.C.: IFPRI), 1995.

United Nations Food and Agriculture Organization. *The State of Food and Agriculture* (Rome: United Nations), annual.

United Nations World Food Council. *The Global State of Hunger and Malnutrition* (Rome: United Nations), annual.

United States Department of Agriculture (USDA). *Agricultural Research—whole issue.* (Washington, D.C.: USDA), September 1997.

Soil Information-USDA/NRCS site: http://soils.usda.gov

Kansas Sustainable Agriculture Series, Kansas State University: http://www. kansassustainableag.org/

Sustainable Agriculture Network: www.sare.org/

University of Minnesota Extension Service: www.extension.umn.edu

Sustainable Agriculture Research and Education Program, University of California:www.sarep.ucdavis.edu/concept.htm

World Sustainable Agriculture Association: Do a web search.

Food Guide Pyramid: www.mypyramid.gov

CHAPTER 8

Energy Today

GOAL

- To understand the energy sources
  currently relied on by modern societies.

To chart a course through the cross currents of varying points of
view and opinion, one must understand the fundamental facts
about where our energy comes from, how we use it, and how
efficient these uses are.

—Energy: The Critical Choices Ahead
(U.S. Department of Commerce)

Energy for the Global Economy

Modern societies require huge amounts of energy. If we are to continue to live in a world where energy fuels our industry, transportation, and communications, we have the responsibility to understand where this energy comes from and how we use it. If we desire to change our energy-use patterns in an intelligent way, we must understand this as well. An orderly future won't just happen. It must be planned carefully.

Although the United States is currently the world's largest consumer of energy, energy use is increasing rapidly in other countries. Their uses of energy, like ours, affect world resources and pollution. As a result, patterns of energy production and consumption have become global in scope.

Think about This!

Why is energy so important to modern societies?

ACTIVITY 8.1

Where Do We Get Our Energy?

In this activity, you will examine the sources of the energy we use in the United States and in the world.

Materials

- protractor
- calculator

Procedure

1. In your science notebook, plot the energy/percentages shown in Figure 8.1 on 2 pie graphs—one for the United States and the other for the world. Label your graphs.

   Helpful Hint!

   Conversion factor: 100% = 360° or 1% = 3.6°

2. Study the 2 graphs you have drawn and answer the questions that follow.

▼ FIGURE 8.1 Percentage of commercial energy consumed in the United States and the world by energy source. *(World data from International Energy Agency World Energy Outlook; U.S. data from EIA Annual Energy Review.)*

2005 Commercial* Consumption—United States			2008 Commercial† Consumption—World		
Oil	40.4 quads	40.4%	Oil	154.4 quads	34.1%
Natural gas	22.6	22.6	Natural gas	109.4	24.1
Coal	22.8	22.8	Coal	109.2	24.1
Nuclear	8.1	8.1	Nuclear	10.1	2.2
Biomass	2.8	2.8	Biomass	48.4	10.7
Renewables**	3.3	3.3	Renewables**	21.8	4.8
Total	100.0 quads	100%	Total	453.3 quads	100%

*Commercial energy does not include energy from wood, waste, geothermal, wind, photovoltaic, and solar thermal energy unless it is used by electric utilities to generate electricity for distribution.

**Renewables includes wind, hydro, solar PV (photovoltaics), and solar thermal.

†Commercial energy means commercially traded sources only. Not included are sources such as wood, peat, and animal waste, which, though important in many countries, are unreliably documented in terms of consumption data.

QUESTIONS & TASKS

Record your responses in your science notebook.

1. What three energy sources are most widely used in both the United States and in the world?

2. What do these three energy sources have in common?

3. What percentage of the world's oil consumption is consumed in the United States? What does this tell you about the pattern of energy use in the United States?

Helpful Hint!

Compare the number of quads of oil consumed by the United States and the world. Remember, a *quad* is a large quantity of energy equal to 1 quadrillion Btu.

8.1 How We Use Energy

Figure 8.2 shows how Americans use energy. Note that the uses are divided into three main use sectors or areas.

1. The *residential and commercial sector* includes houses, apartments, office buildings, stores, and shopping malls. Well over half the energy used in residential and commercial buildings goes for space heating. The second highest use is for space cooling, followed closely by lighting and water heating.

2. The *industrial sector* includes manufacturing plants, paper mills, oil refineries, chemical and fertilizer plants, steel mills, and auto assembly plants, as well as agriculture, mining, and construction. The largest industrial energy consumers are the manufacturers of chemicals, rubber, and plastics, as well as oil refineries.

3. The *transportation sector* includes all light-duty vehicles, freight trucks, air transport, boats/ships, and trains. It is important to note that U.S. transportation is almost entirely oil-dependent. U.S. transportation obtains more than 97 percent of its energy from petroleum. This is because liquid fuels, such as gasoline, are easy to transport, store, and use in our vehicles. As one might expect, light-duty vehicles consume more than 60 percent of all fuels that are used for transportation.

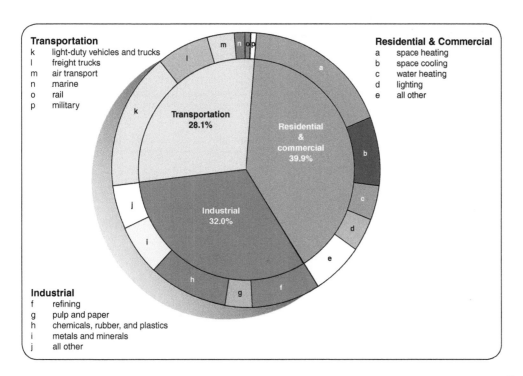

Transportation
- k light-duty vehicles and trucks
- l freight trucks
- m air transport
- n marine
- o rail
- p military

Residential & Commercial
- a space heating
- b space cooling
- c water heating
- d lighting
- e all other

Industrial
- f refining
- g pulp and paper
- h chemicals, rubber, and plastics
- i metals and minerals
- j all other

Transportation 28.1%

Residential & commercial 39.9%

Industrial 32.0%

◄ FIGURE 8.2 U.S. end-use consumption by sector in 2005. Total consumption = 99.89 quads. (*Source: U.S. Department of Energy, Energy Information Administration.*)

ACTIVITY 8.2

An Energy History of the United States

In this activity, you will look for patterns of historical energy use in the United States.

Procedure

Study the line graph shown in Figure 8.3. Each curve represents a dominant form of energy over the past 160 years of U.S. history.

QUESTIONS & TASKS

Record your responses in your science notebook.

1. The United States has already gone through two major energy transitions. It appears we are now going through a third. List the three transitions and the approximate time they occurred.

2. Speculate as to why each transition happened. Evaluate the impact of each transition.

3. Predict what will happen to these curves over the next 50 years. Defend your prediction.

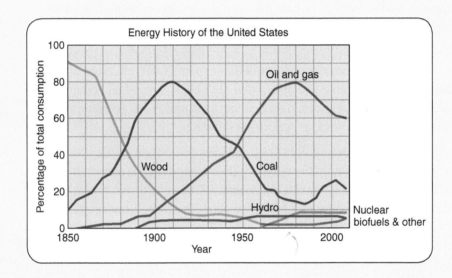

Industrial Revolution begins in Europe	1760
Revolutionary War	1775–1783
Railroads *begin* in eastern U.S.	1830–1850
Civil War	1861–1865
Ford *begins* mass production of automobiles	1908
World War I	1914–1918
World War II	1939–1945
Most American families have a car; modern air travel begins	1950–1965
Strong economy fueled by inexpensive energy	1960–2000

▲ FIGURE 8.3 The energy history of the United States in graphical form. The abbreviated U.S. history timeline gives clues to what the curves actually mean. (*Source: U.S. Department of Energy.*)

8.2 Historical Energy Use

At the dawn of human history, our ancestors relied on renewable sources of energy. The first humans used solar energy. Photosynthesis stores the sun's energy in the form of carbohydrates—the food derived from the living tissues of plants. Like us, early humans ate fruits, vegetables, and animals (which ate plants and/or other animals). Early humans also used solar energy stored in other plant parts. For example, they burned wood from fallen trees. Eventually, people learned to broaden their energy base, using wind to move ships and flowing water to drive their machines. But even this was solar powered.

By the mid 1700s, people turned to other fuels to meet their growing needs for heating, for cooking, and for the new technology of making steel. In Europe, where much of this technology began, the forests were largely depleted. As a result, another fuel had to replace wood. The answer was **coal**, a carbon-rich mineral-like substance that gave energy users a convenient and abundant supply of stored energy. Where the burning of fuel wood represented the combustion of recently stored solar energy, burning coal (which is formed from plant matter) represented the unlocking of solar energy stored long ago. Thus, the age of fossil fuels had begun.

Energy use in the New World, however, followed a different schedule. In colonial North America, pioneers gazed out across a largely untouched continent. The virgin forests of America represented a treasure trove of fuel for early settlers. Wood accounted for about 90 percent of U.S. energy consumption in 1850 (review Figure 8.3). The average wood consumption in the frontier American home was 17.4 cords per year. (A cord of wood is a stack of wood measuring 4 ft by 4 ft by 8 ft.) Most of the wood (140 million cords in 1850) was used for heating homes; it was the only readily available source of heat. Its total energy was two to four times the average amount of energy used to heat a home today.

Wood also was an important source of energy for the country's young industry and transportation system. Nearly 2 million cords of wood were turned into charcoal for smelting iron. In addition, trains and steamboats burned 7 to 8 million cords of wood annually.

What caused U.S. energy patterns to shift so dramatically at the turn of the 20th century? The explosion of technology coupled with the growing demand for energy required that a new fuel be plentiful and have a high energy content. This new fuel had to produce more energy per volume than the fuel it was replacing. The energy content of a fuel is a concept that has played, and will continue to play, a vital role in all energy-use decisions.

ACTIVITY 8.3

Counting Calories . . . the Energy Content of a Fuel

In this activity, you will determine the energy content of a fuel and relate its importance to energy-use decisions.

Background

The **energy content** of a substance is the amount of heat produced or given off by the combustion of 1 gram (g) of that substance. For example, burning 1 g of wood yields approximately 2,760 calories (cal) of heat. Knowledge of the energy content of various fuels (as well as foods) is a valuable tool for scientists, business executives, economists, and government planners.

This lab shows you how to determine the energy content of paraffin wax, an easily combustible fuel. Paraffin wax is produced when crude oil is processed at an oil refinery.

Data Collected		
Mass of empty cardboard juice can (step 2)	_____	g
Mass of cardboard juice can + water (step 3)	_____	g
Initial temperature of the water (step 5)	_____	°C
Final temperature of the water (step 7)	_____	°C
Initial mass of candle and base (step 2)	_____	g
Final mass of candle and base (step 8)	_____	g

Materials

- graduated cylinder
- large tin can chimney
- Celsius thermometer (°C)
- matches
- set of standard masses
- ring stand and ring
- cardboard frozen juice can
- candle on cardboard base
- glass stirring rod
- double pan balance
- cold water
- safety goggles

WARNING

Working around open flames and combustible fuels can be dangerous. Wear safety goggles. Work carefully. Know where the fire extinguisher and other safety equipment are located and how to use them.

Procedure

1. Reproduce the data sheet in Figure 8.4 in your science notebook. Record your measurements in your notebook.

2. Determine the mass of the empty cardboard juice can. Also determine the initial mass of the candle and cardboard base (see Figure 8.5). Make all mass determinations to the nearest 0.1 g.

3. Add about 300 mL of cold water to the cardboard juice can. Determine the mass of the juice can plus water.

4. Set up a tin can calorimeter as shown in Figure 8.6. Make adjustments so that the flame from the candle (do not light it yet) will almost, but not quite, touch the bottom of the juice can.

▲ FIGURE 8.5 Determining the mass of objects is an important science skill. *(Photo © Paul Hartmann.)*

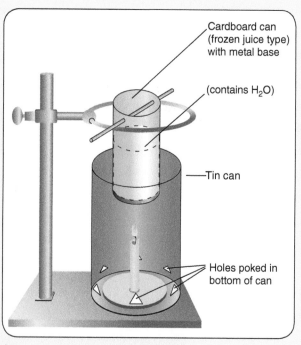

▲ FIGURE 8.6 Tin can calorimeter.

Mass of water heated ____________ g
Temperature change of the water ____________ C°
Number of calories = mass of water in grams × temperature rise in C°:
____________ cal = ____________ g × ____________ C°
Mass of paraffin burned = ____________ g
What is the value for the energy content of paraffin that you determined in this experiment?
Energy content of paraffin = ____________ cal/g

▲FIGURE 8.7 Calculations for determining the energy content of paraffin wax.

Helpful Hint!

One calorie = the amount of heat required to raise the temperature of 1 g of water 1C°.

Remember, *energy content* is the amount of heat produced by the combustion of 1 g of a substance.

5. Record the initial temperature of the water to the nearest 0.2C°.
6. Light the candle and heat the water until the temperature has risen about 15C°–20C°. Then blow out the candle flame.
7. Stir the water until the temperature stabilizes at its maximum value. Record this maximum (final) temperature on your data sheet.
8. Finally, determine the final mass of the candle and cardboard base.
9. Clean up your lab station as instructed.
10. Use your data to determine the energy content of paraffin wax. Do this by reproducing Figure 8.7 in your science notebook. Then make the calculations.

QUESTIONS & TASKS

Refer to Figure 8.8, which shows the average energy content for some selected fuels and foods, and complete the following. Record your responses in your science notebook.

1. How does your value for the energy content of paraffin compare with the value given in Figure 8.8? Give your answer in terms of a percentage.

$$\% \text{ accuracy} = \frac{\text{your answer}}{\text{accepted answer}} \times 100\%$$

2. Account for the difference.
3. Refer back to Figure 8.3 in Activity 8.2. Did energy content have anything to do with the transition from wood to coal? Is this the major reason, or is it one of several reasons? Explain.
4. Give one or two reasons why it is useful to know the energy content of various foods and fuels.

Item	Energy Content (cal/g)
Wood	2,760
Coal (stove coal)	7,200
Fuel oil	10,800
Natural gas	11,000
Gasoline	11,530
Alcohol (denatured)	6,400
Alcohol (scotch, 80 proof)	2,580
Paraffin wax	11,250
Bread	2,660
Butter	7,950
Sugar	4,100
Beef steak	1,840

▲FIGURE 8.8 The energy content of selected fuels and foods.

8.3 America's Energy Transitions

Apply Your Understanding

Give two reasons for the wood to coal transition.

As shown in Figure 8.3, the U.S. conversion away from wood to fossil fuels began at the end of the 1800s. Forests near cities had been cut down, and it became necessary to transport logs from far away. The transition was also based on energy content. Wood, when burned, produces about 2,760 calories per gram. Coal has more than twice that energy content. If you have to transport energy, you want to carry as much per gram as you can. Thus, coal replaced wood. By 1910, coal accounted for more than three-quarters of the total energy used. Railroad transport made coal a good source of energy.

Apply Your Understanding

Give two reasons for the coal to oil and gas transition.

The use of petroleum products (oil and natural gas) began to grow during the 1920s. Petroleum is easier to use and cleaner than coal. Because it occurs either in liquid or gaseous form (unlike solid coal), it was also easier and cheaper to transport by pipeline. At the end of World War II, the petroleum age arrived.

It now appears that the dominance of petroleum products may also be drawing to a close. In 2006, petroleum products dropped to less than 60 percent of the total. Is a transition to a new dominant source beginning? The current data are unclear. We see two small surges. Nuclear energy's contribution has grown from less than 1 percent in 1970 to about 8 percent. Some see in this growth the beginning of a nuclear age. Also, coal is showing a revival. Coal contributed 17 percent of the total in 1975, but almost 23 percent in 2001.

Think about This!

Why is it difficult to predict our energy future?

It would be foolish to predict the future of either coal or nuclear energy right now. What happens will depend on the outcome of a complicated and interrelated set of environmental, economic, and political considerations. We will pursue questions about energy for the future in Chapters 11 and 12 (see Figure 8.9).

▶FIGURE 8.9 This mosaic of satellite images shows Earth at night. Major cities, transportation routes, controlled fires, and natural gas burn offs are clearly visible. What does this pattern reveal about the worldwide use of energy? How might this pattern have looked 100 years ago? How might it change in the future? (NASA *Visible Earth image catalog*, Earth's City Lights.)

ACTIVITY 8.4

Unquenchable Energy Thirst

In this activity, you will examine historical energy-use figures to learn more about past and future energy use in the United States.

Materials

- Handout: *U.S. Energy Consumption from 1875–1980*

Procedure

1. Figure 8.10 summarizes U.S. energy consumption from 1875 to 1980. Your teacher will provide you with a full-size copy.

2. Use this graph to analyze energy consumption and to guess what the future of energy consumption might be.

QUESTIONS & TASKS

Record your responses in your science notebook.

1. What was our principal energy source in 1875? in 1910? in 1960?

2. What new factor became significant about 1960 that enabled U.S. energy consumption to continue to grow?

3. What is the general shape of the energy demand curve? (Choose one.)
   a. exponential growth curve (J-shaped)
   b. bell-shaped curve
   c. simple linear relation
   d. sigmoid curve (S-shaped)

4. What caused the big drop in energy consumption in the 1930s?

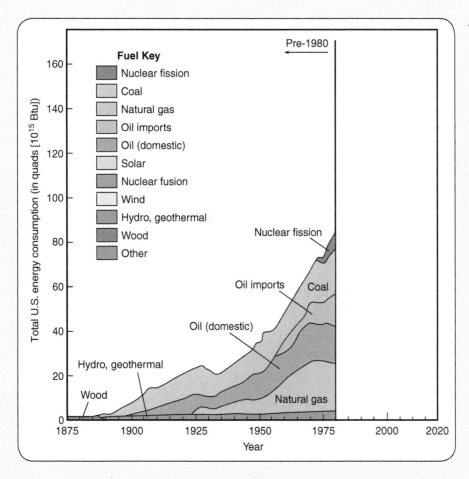

◀ FIGURE 8.10 U.S. energy consumption from 1875 to 1980.

5. Energy consumption in the United States totaled approximately 10 quads in 1900. How many years did it take to double that consumption?

6. How many years did it take to double that figure (that is, to grow from a 20- to a 40-quad economy)?

7. How many years did it take to double that figure (that is, to become an 80-quad economy)?

8. What is the average doubling time you discovered in the previous three questions?

9. The equation that relates doubling time to percentage annual growth is

$$\text{doubling time (years)} = \frac{70}{\text{\% annual growth rate}}$$

Use your answer to question 8 to determine the approximate percentage annual increase in American energy consumption for the time period you examined.

10. If we continue to grow (from 1975) at the rate you calculated in question 9, what will our energy consumption be (in quads) in the year 2050? Mark this on your extended energy consumption graph.

11. Do you think this type of growth can continue to 2050? Can it continue forever? Explain your answer.

Helpful Hint!

Dramatic annual increases in U.S. energy consumption ceased starting about 1980. This change lasted for about 15 years. Consumption again began to rise in the late 1990s. This was caused mostly by global economics and extremely low world energy prices.

Fossil Fuels

Topic: fossil fuels
Go to: www.scilinks.org
Code: GloSci7e308

Why is oil useful as an energy source?

Content Clue

Petroleum consists chiefly of flammable carbon and hydrogen compounds that occur naturally in liquid, gaseous, and solid form.

Current sources of energy are dominated by **fossil fuels**. These fuels—oil, gas, and coal—were formed eons ago by the compression, decay, and heating of plant and animal matter buried in mud and sand.

8.4 Oil

Crude oil is consumed in great quantities because of the widespread use of the automobile. Since oil is a liquid, it is more usable than the other forms of primary energy. Oil is fairly easily stored, transported, and consumed. For these reasons, oil is the leading source of energy in the United States.

Crude oil is a product of the decay of **organic** (carbon-containing) matter, both plant and animal. The hydrogen and carbon atoms (**hydrocarbons**) in today's petroleum are derived from the remains of ancient plants and animals. In a similar way, tiny amounts of petroleum are being formed today. Most **petroleum** exists in the earth in one of two forms—liquid or vapor. The liquid is called **crude oil**. The vapor is known as **natural gas**. Petroleum also exists as a solid in deposits like the Athabasca tar sands of Alberta, Canada, and in the oil shale beds of Colorado, Wyoming, Utah, and elsewhere in the world. Figure 8.11 shows a chemical representation of some of the hundreds of petroleum molecules.

Although scientists report finding traces of hydrocarbons in rocks that are more than a billion years old, they think that most petroleum was formed less than 500 million years ago. Some formed as recently as 10 million years ago.

Most scientists believe that oil was formed from the remains of countless tiny creatures and plants that lived in the sea, or washed into the sea with mud and silt from streams. This material settled to the bottom of the ancient seas and piled up, layer atop layer. Compressed by the tremendous weight gathering above them, these deeply buried layers of mud, silt, and sand were gradually formed into layers of sedimentary rock. The rocks included sandstones,

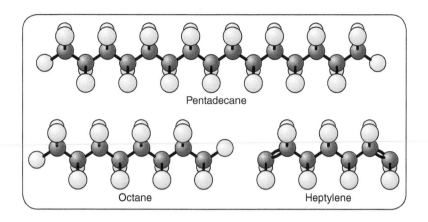

◀ FIGURE 8.11 Chemical models of three petroleum molecules: pentadecane, octane, and heptylene. The yellow spheres represent hydrogen, the purple spheres represent carbon, and the black connectors represent chemical bonds. *(Enterprise for Education)*

shales, limestones, dolomites, and other rock types. Rock formation was further aided by heat, which came both from pressure and from interior parts of Earth.

Over millions of years, the organic matter was transformed. Billions of bits of decayed plant and animal matter, held captive by the mud and silt, were changed to petroleum by heat and compression. The action of bacteria, chemicals, and radioactive materials also contributed. As ages passed, the sea withdrew and Earth's crust heaved and buckled, creating structures that trapped the oil and gas.

Layers of sediment in which petroleum was formed are referred to as **source beds**. After its formation, petroleum migrated from these source beds into layers of **porous** and **permeable** rock. These are the **reservoirs** sought by today's petroleum geologists (Figure 8.12). Just how petroleum moved from these source beds to reservoirs is not fully understood. One line of thinking is that because oil and gas are less dense than water, they tended to rise to the top of the ancient seawater that filled the porous spaces when the sedimentary formations were laid down. The oil and gas seeped upward and outward through porous and permeable layers until stopped by dense **impermeable** rocks. When further movement was halted, oil and gas collected or were "trapped" between impermeable layers. The lighter gas rose to the upper parts of the traps. Oil remained beneath the gas. Seawater, the most dense, sank to the lowest parts.

Most scientists agree that many of the trapped oil and gas concentrations resulted from uplifts and movements of rock strata layers. Originally, the seafloors were nearly horizontal. Over millions of years, the continental plates moved, and horizontal layers were shifted, bent, and broken. Ancient sea bottoms often became dry land area. These movements sometimes rearranged permeable and impermeable rock layers so that either the movement of oil was stopped or the oil vanished.

Apply Your Understanding

How did oil and gas become trapped underground?

◀ FIGURE 8.12 The geologist. *(Courtesy of Exxon Corporation.)*

SCIENCE at work

Energy Today 309

►FIGURE 8.13 Offshore rig.
(© 1992 ARCO Photography Collection, Los Angeles, CA.)

Topic: oil and gas traps
Go to: www.scilinks.org
Code: GloSci7e310

Only rarely are concentrations of oil found near Earth's surface. Most are thousands of feet deep. Today, these traps are the object of a search for oil throughout the world (see Figure 8.13). Exploratory techniques to locate rock formations in which oil or gas might have formed or might have been trapped are very complex and expensive. Only drilling can prove the presence of oil or gas, outline the field, and determine potential amounts.

In deciding where to begin exploratory drilling, geologists and geophysicists usually look for three things. First, they look for source beds of shales or limestones that originally contained an abundance of organic remains. Next, they seek the porous and permeable sandstones or limestones that later became reservoir beds. Finally, they look for a trap that sealed off the reservoir beds and held the oil and gas in place.

Two basic types of trap are most important to petroleum geologists: structural and stratigraphic. The **attitude** of rocks—folded, fractured, or displaced—is called their geologic structure. Therefore, the **structural trap** for oil or gas is the result of folding, faulting, or other deformation.

As a result of folding, oil may be trapped in the crest of an **anticline** or upward bulge of rock layers. The oil lies in tiny spaces between grains in porous rock, but is trapped by impermeable rock layers (see Figure 8.14a).

Faulting can create structural traps. A **fault** is a break in Earth's crust along which movement has occurred. This movement may result in a permeable rock layer being offset by a nonporous and impermeable layer. The oil moving along a permeable layer is "dammed" or blocked by the impermeable rock (see Figure 8.14b).

Another type of structural trap is called a **salt dome** trap. Salt dome traps are found along the gulf coasts of Texas and Louisiana and in the western Colorado/eastern Utah area. This type of structure results from the upward surge of a great mass of salt far below

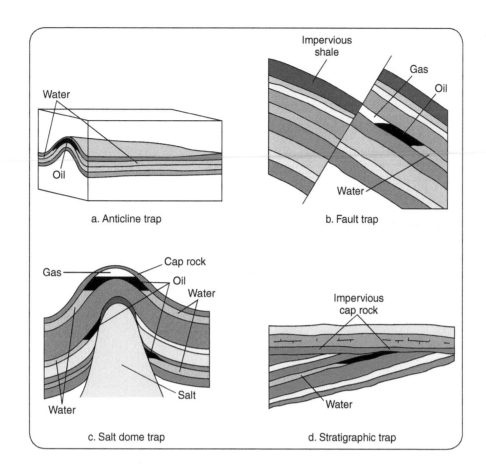

◀ **FIGURE 8.14** Four traps where oil and gas may be found. (*Adapted from Primer of Oil and Gas Production, 3rd ed., American Petroleum Institute, 1971.*)

a. Anticline trap

b. Fault trap

c. Salt dome trap

d. Stratigraphic trap

Earth's surface. When a salt dome rises through an oil-bearing layer, oil may be trapped (see Figure 8.14c).

One of the hardest places to find oil is in a **stratigraphic trap**. Here, the porous layers bearing oil taper off under nonporous layers (**strata**) of rock. The stratigraphic trap is formed by the thinning out (sometimes called pinch-out) of porous and permeable sandstone between two layers of impermeable shale. This creates an "envelope" where oil and gas may accumulate. This type of trap may have formed from buried beaches and sandbars. The famous East Texas field is a "strat" trap (see Figure 8.14d).

It takes a combination of the latest in earth science and technology and sound economic evaluation to explore for hydrocarbons profitably. By searching for source beds, reservoirs, and traps, geologists can greatly increase the likelihood of finding oil. Earth scientists develop hypotheses about where oil may occur; however, only the drill holes can prove the existence of oil (see Figure 8.15). Many discoveries are geologic successes, but economic failures.

As already stated, oil consists of a mixture of liquid hydrocarbons of varying composition. During burning, the hydrogen and carbon in a hydrocarbon each combine with oxygen, forming water and carbon dioxide. The burning of oil to obtain energy may be represented by this equation:

$$\text{oil} + \text{oxygen}(O_2) \rightarrow CO_2 + H_2O + \text{heat energy} + \text{wastes}$$

The wastes usually consist of unburned hydrocarbons, carbon monoxide, nitrogen oxides, and some sulfur gases.

Refined petroleum is used for more than just gasoline for automobiles. Refining crude oil yields a host of products. Figure 8.16 shows what an "average" barrel of oil is used

Apply Your Understanding

Name some useful products that are produced when oil is refined.

Energy Today 311

▶FIGURE 8.16 Average annual yields from a barrel of crude oil. (One barrel of oil contains 42 gallons.) (*Source of percentage yield, USDOE. Gallons per barrel computed by American Petroleum Institute. Percentage yield totals more than 100 because of "processing gains."*)

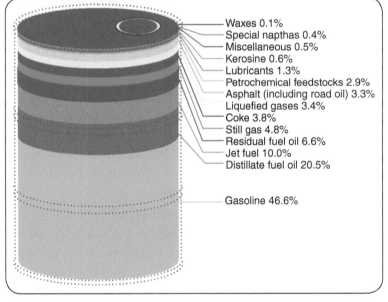

Waxes 0.1%
Special napthas 0.4%
Miscellaneous 0.5%
Kerosine 0.6%
Lubricants 1.3%
Petrochemical feedstocks 2.9%
Asphalt (including road oil) 3.3%
Liquefied gases 3.4%
Coke 3.8%
Still gas 4.8%
Residual fuel oil 6.6%
Jet fuel 10.0%
Distillate fuel oil 20.5%

Gasoline 46.6%

for. Many of our lubricants, plastics, and pharmaceuticals have their origin in crude oil. Figure 8.17 illustrates how the petroleum industry fuels much of the U.S. economy.

8.5 Natural Gas

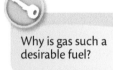

Why is gas such a desirable fuel?

Oil and gas originated together and are searched for together. At first, natural gas was an unwanted by-product of the search for oil. It was considered of little value. For a long time, only the gas associated with oil was produced. Part of the production was used locally; the rest was simply flared to the atmosphere. After World War II, the true value of natural gas as a primary source of energy was recognized. There were strong efforts to develop widespread markets. Because of its excellent fuel qualities and the low price charged for

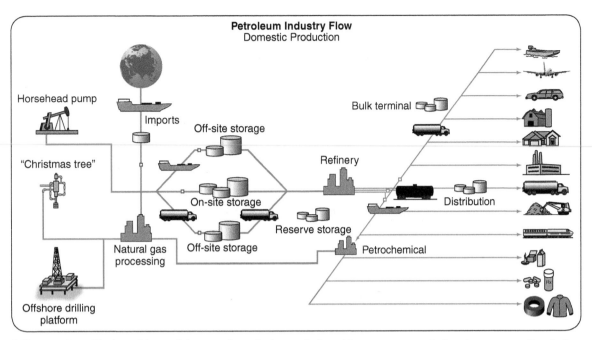

▲ **FIGURE 8.17** The broad base of the petroleum industry. *(Adapted from U.S. Bureau of Mines, Department of Interior.)*

it, gas began to be used at a rapidly increasing rate. By 1958, gas had displaced coal as the nation's second most important source of energy. Gas is a much cleaner fuel than coal or oil. It burns almost completely, and produces practically no harmful by-products.

The basic equation for the burning of natural gas is the same as that for oil:

$$\text{natural gas} + \text{oxygen} \rightarrow CO_2 + H_2O + \text{heat}$$

The only difference is that the hydrocarbon molecules that make up natural gas are smaller. Almost no wastes are formed, although some nitrogen oxides and some SO_2 are produced.

Natural gas is primarily a fuel resource. The industrial sector is the largest consumer of natural gas. In addition, more U.S. homes are heated with natural gas than with any other fuel. Among other uses, natural gas is used for raw material processing, food preparation, petrochemical feedstocks, refinery fuel, and power generation.

Apply Your Understanding

What products result when gas is burned?

 # ACTIVITY 8.5

Simulating Oil Refining—the Distillation Process

In this activity, you will learn more about the process of distillation by distilling *simulated* crude oil. We will use a mixture other than oil because toxic fumes are released during oil distillation.

Background

We do not use crude oil as it comes directly out of the ground. Instead, the oil is taken to a refinery where it is processed and divided into components. Crude oil is a mixture of many different substances.

The oil is separated on the basis of different boiling points for different substances. This separation is done by heating, evaporating, cooling, and condensing in a process known as **distillation**. Crude oil can be distilled into a variety of gasolines, alcohols, additives, and oils.

Materials

- simulated crude oil, 50 mL
- clear plastic tubing
- beaker, 400-mL

- ring stand
- wire gauze
- Erlenmeyer flask, 250-mL
- test tube (25 × 150 mm)
- matches
- crushed ice
- utility clamp
- Bunsen burner
- rubber stopper (No. 6) with glass connector
- metal ring
- graduated cylinder, 50-mL
- colored pens or pencils
- safety goggles

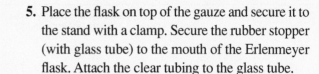

BE SAFE

Working around open flames can be dangerous. Wear safety goggles. Work carefully and know where the fire extinguisher, safety blanket, and other safety equipment are located. Know how they are to be used.

Procedure

1. Draw Figure 8.18 in your science notebook. Correctly label all the main parts of your lab setup. Use a colored pen or pencil to indicate where *heating*, *vapors*, *cooling*, and *condensation* occur.

2. Place the Bunsen burner on the base of the ring stand.

3. Position the ring that supports the wire gauze over the Bunsen burner.

4. Pour 50 milliliters (mL) of simulated crude oil ("simcrude") into the Erlenmeyer flask.

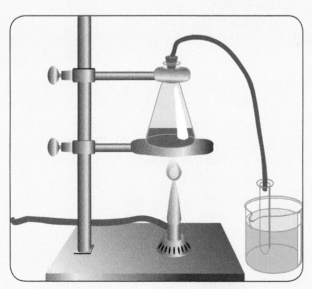

▲ FIGURE 8.18 The setup for distilling simulated crude oil.

5. Place the flask on top of the gauze and secure it to the stand with a clamp. Secure the rubber stopper (with glass tube) to the mouth of the Erlenmeyer flask. Attach the clear tubing to the glass tube.

6. Write down your *hypothesis* (guess) to state what you think will happen once the Bunsen burner is lit and the simulated crude oil is heated.

7. Light the Bunsen burner and begin heating the simcrude with a small, blue flame.

8. Have your partner fill a beaker with ice. Insert the other end of the clear tubing into the test tube and place the test tube in the beaker of ice.

9. Bring the liquid to a slow boil, and watch it evaporate.

10. Collect about 5 mL of liquid in the test tube. Compare it to the simcrude.

QUESTIONS & TASKS

Record your responses in your science notebook.

1. Record the following observations:
   a. colors
   b. odors
   c. quantities collected and remaining
   d. time for events to occur
   e. appearance of vapors
   f. anything else that seems important

2. Was your hypothesis correct? Explain. What happened and why?

EXTENSIONS

1. Figure 8.19 shows the apparatus usually used for laboratory distillation in more advanced classes and labs. How is this apparatus like the setup you used? How is it different?

2. Crude oil is a mixture of many different liquids, each with a different boiling point. Distillation is the beginning of the complex process of oil refining. The initial separation of all the liquids and gases occurs in the fractionating tower (see Figure 8.20). Notice that all these liquids are separated by boiling point. From this point forward, a variety of processes with such names as cracking, reforming, isomeriza-

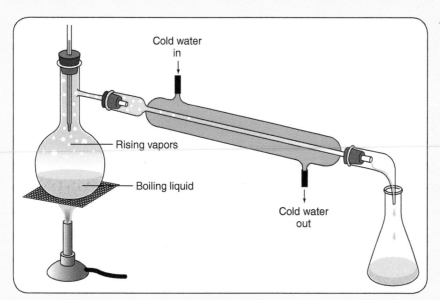

◄FIGURE 8.19 Advanced laboratory distillation apparatus.

Cold water in

Rising vapors

Boiling liquid

Cold water out

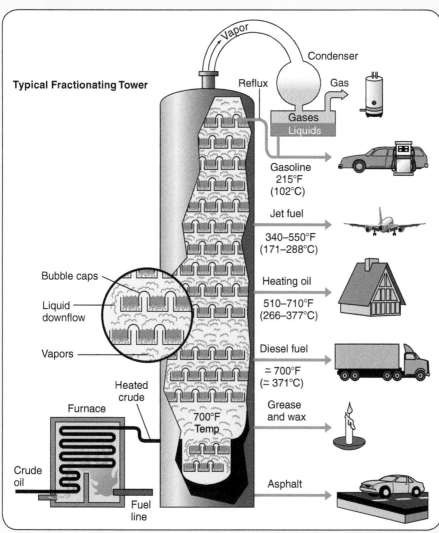

Vapor

Condenser

Typical Fractionating Tower

Reflux

Gas

Gases

Liquids

Gasoline
215°F
(102°C)

Jet fuel

340–550°F
(171–288°C)

Bubble caps

Heating oil

Liquid downflow

510–710°F
(266–377°C)

Vapors

Diesel fuel

≃ 700°F
(≃ 371°C)

Heated crude

Furnace

Grease and wax

700°F
Temp

Crude oil

Asphalt

Fuel line

◄FIGURE 8.20 A typical fractionating tower for separating crude oil. (*Adapted from and reprinted courtesy of the American Petroleum Institute.*)

tion, alkylation, polymerization, and hydrogenation occurs. These processes are the subject of more advanced science classes. The result is the different products listed in Figure 8.16 that come from crude oil. To learn more about oil refining, visit http://www.api.org and select education materials.

ACTIVITY 8.6

Coal

In this activity, you will examine samples of the main types of coal and list their distinguishing characteristics. You will then read more about coal and use maps, charts, and diagrams to complete a matching exercise.

Materials

- 4 coal samples

Procedure

1. Reproduce the table in Figure 8.21 in your science notebook. Enter a short (2–5 word) description of each type of coal. Your descriptions should make it possible for a person to distinguish between these 4 grades of coal even if the samples were not labeled.

2. To learn more about the different types of coal and why they are of interest to us, read section 8.6 Coal. Carefully examine Figures 8.23, 8.25, and 8.26. As you work, complete the following 2 sets of matching items. Match each numbered statement about coal to the type of coal or region listed in the 2 answer keys. Record your answers in your science notebook.

Set 1: Types of Coal

1. The major U.S. deposits are located in eastern Montana and western North Dakota.

2. The major U.S. deposits are located in eastern Pennsylvania.

3. The major U.S. deposits are in the Rocky Mountain West.

4. The most common type of coal in terms of its occurrence around the United States.

5. A brownish black organic material that is used to build up garden soil.

6. This high-grade coal is hard to ignite, but once lit, it burns with almost no smoke.

7. A very low-grade coal that is rich in volatiles and is good feedstock for coal gasification.

8. Because of its wide availability around the country, this type of coal is most often burned at electric power generation plants.

9. This type of low-grade coal is only 70 percent carbon.

10. The energy density (calories/kilogram) of this type of coal ranks highest.

Set 1: Answer Key
A. Peat
B. Lignite
C. Subbituminous
D. Bituminous
E. Anthracite

Set 2: Geographic Regions

1. Coal from this region has a higher sulfur content.

2. Coal from this region is generally closer to the surface and is commonly strip-mined.

3. Because of higher labor intensity, coal from this region is more expensive.

4. Because of low annual rainfall, reclamation of mined land in this region is more difficult.

Set 2: Answer Key
F. Eastern
G. Western

▼ FIGURE 8.21 Sample table for recording descriptions of coal samples.

Coal Type	Description
Peat	
Lignite	
Bituminous	
Anthracite	

8.6 Coal

Coal ranks second or third as a source of energy in world use of commercial energy. In the United States, coal is of interest because reserves are large and it is the main source of energy for producing electricity. U.S. coal production has doubled since the mid-1960s. Today, production is more than 1 billion tons annually. Eight out of every 10 tons of coal used in the United States goes toward generating electricity. More electricity than ever before is being used to power appliances, computers, and a host of other high-tech devices.

The chemical equation for the burning of coal is

$$\text{coal (C)} + \text{oxygen (O}_2) \rightarrow CO_2 + \text{heat} + \text{waste}$$

The wastes consist of sulfur dioxide, nitrogen oxides, carbon monoxide, soot, fly ash, and bottom ash. Sulfur is found in varying amounts in all coal deposits. Nitrogen oxides are formed in all engines and furnaces that burn very hot. Carbon monoxide is produced when the amount of air supplied to a furnace is not adequate. Soot is unburned coal. Fly ash and bottom ash come from impurities in coal. As technology improves, problems related to these wastes are diminished. Because carbon dioxide is a greenhouse gas, ways to capture it at coal-fired power plants and sequester (store) it in the ground are being perfected (see Chapter 15).

The Origin of Coal

Coal occurs in strata (miners call them "seams") along with other sedimentary rocks—mostly shale and sandstone. A look through a magnifying glass at a piece of coal (Figure 8.22) reveals bits of fossilized wood, bark, leaves, roots, and other parts of land plants. This shows that coal is fossilized plant matter. Thus, coal is an organic substance. It is made up primarily of carbon. It also contains varying amounts of hydrogen, oxygen, nitrogen, and sulfur.

The places where coal accumulated were ancient swamps and marshes in equatorial regions. Only under these conditions is plant matter likely to become coal. On dry land, dead

Apply Your Understanding

Why is there a renewed interest in coal?

Helpful Hints!

Fly ash is the nonflammable impurities in burning coal that are carried away by the draft.

Bottom ash is the inorganic residue that remains after incineration.

Apply Your Understanding

How was coal formed?

◄ FIGURE 8.22 A close-up view of coal. *(From AMAX Coal Industries, Inc.)*

plant matter (composed chiefly of carbon, hydrogen, and oxygen) rots away. This happens because bacteria use atmospheric oxygen to form carbon dioxide and water from dead material. Under stagnant or nearly stagnant water, little oxygen is present. The plant matter is attacked by **anaerobic** (without air) bacteria. The bacteria partly decompose the matter by splitting off oxygen and hydrogen. These two elements escape, combined in various gases. Carbon gradually becomes concentrated in the remains. The bacteria themselves are destroyed before they can finish the decay. Acids liberated from the dead plants kill the bacteria. This could not happen in a stream because flowing water would bring in new oxygen and dilute the acids.

With the destruction of bacteria, the plant matter is converted to peat. **Peat** is brownish black organic material that looks very much like decayed wood. Dried peat will burn and produce heat. Because peat still contains some water, it is very smoky when burned. This chemical equation represents the formation of peat from plant material:

$$6\ C_6H_{10}O_5 \xrightarrow{\text{anaerobic bacteria}} 7\ CO_2 + 3\ CH_4 + 14\ H_2O + C_{26}H_{20}O_2$$

plant cellulose · · · carbon dioxide · marsh gas · water · peat

Apply Your Understanding

What are the four types of coal and what are their uses? (Do not include peat because it is not sold as an energy source.)

As peat is buried beneath more plant matter and beneath accumulating sand, silt, or clay, both temperature and pressure increase. This brings about a series of continuing changes. As peat is compressed, water is squeezed out. Gases such as methane (CH_4) escape, leaving an ever-increasing proportion of carbon. The peat is converted first into **lignite**, then into **subbituminous coal**, and finally into **bituminous coal**. These coals are sedimentary rocks. A still later phase, **anthracite**, is a metamorphic rock. The stages of coal formation are summarized in Figure 8.23.

As anthracite generally occurs in folded strata, we infer that it has undergone a further loss of volatiles. This is the result of the pressure and heat that accompany folding. Because of

▼ FIGURE 8.23 Accumulating plant matter is converted into coal by decomposition, pressure, and heat. By the time a layer has been changed from peat to bituminous coal, it has decreased to one-tenth of its original thickness. During the same time, the energy content has risen continually. (*From Physical Geology, 2nd ed., by R. F. Flint and B. J. Skinner, copyright © 1977, John Wiley & Sons, Inc. Reprinted by permission of John Wiley & Sons, Inc.*)

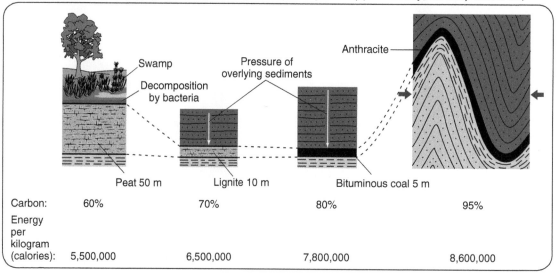

	Peat 50 m	Lignite 10 m	Bituminous coal 5 m	Anthracite
Carbon:	60%	70%	80%	95%
Energy per kilogram (calories):	5,500,000	6,500,000	7,800,000	8,600,000

◄FIGURE 8.24 Advances in technology have enabled the electric arc furnace to replace the less efficient blast furnace and basic oxygen furnace in making steel. In most cases, the electricity for operating these furnaces is generated at coal-fired power plants. *(Barry McGee/Ispat Sidbeck Inc.—Canada)*

its low content of volatiles, anthracite is hard to ignite. Once alight, however, it burns with almost no smoke. This quality makes it the most desirable of all coals for space heating. In contrast, lignite ignites so easily that it is dangerously subject to spontaneous combustion. It burns with a great deal of smoke.

The energy content of coal helps to determine its quality and usefulness as a fuel. The higher the proportion of carbon to moisture, the higher the coal's energy content. Lignite ranks lowest among coals. Anthracite ranks highest. (The use of lignite in coal gasification processes may generate a new demand for this type of coal. This is discussed in Chapter 11.)

Subbituminous coal is used primarily for producing steam. The principal uses of bituminous coal are for electric power generation and steel production (see Figure 8.24).

The Location of Coal Deposits

Proven coal deposits exist on every continent, even on Antarctica. This can be explained by continental drift. Coal formed in swampy equatorial regions, but it was "rafted" by the moving lithosphere to other areas.

As the map in Figure 8.25 shows, coal has been found in most of the United States. In fact, nearly one-eighth of the country lies over coal beds. For discussion, it is convenient to divide the coal fields of the United States into eastern and western regions.

Eastern coals occur generally in continuous seams up to 12 feet (ft) or 3.6 meters (m) thick. They run throughout 2,000 to 3,000 ft (600–900 m) of stratified clay, sandstone, or limestone. The eastern coal fields are mostly high-grade deposits.

Western deposits are usually isolated from one another and are less predictable. They are usually smaller in area than eastern deposits. Most are also thicker, closer to the surface, and of lower rank.

Coal seams vary considerably in thickness, from a few inches to more than 100 ft (30 m). The average thickness of bituminous coal seams in the United States is 5.4 ft (1.6 m). Most of the coal mined in this country is from beds varying in thickness from 3 to 10 ft (1–3 m). Many of the seams strip-mined in the West are more than 80 ft (24 m) thick and very close to the surface.

Helpful Hint!

Volatiles are easily evaporated and are passed off as vapors.

Content Clue

U.S. coal deposits are divided into eastern and western coal.

U.S. Coal Deposits

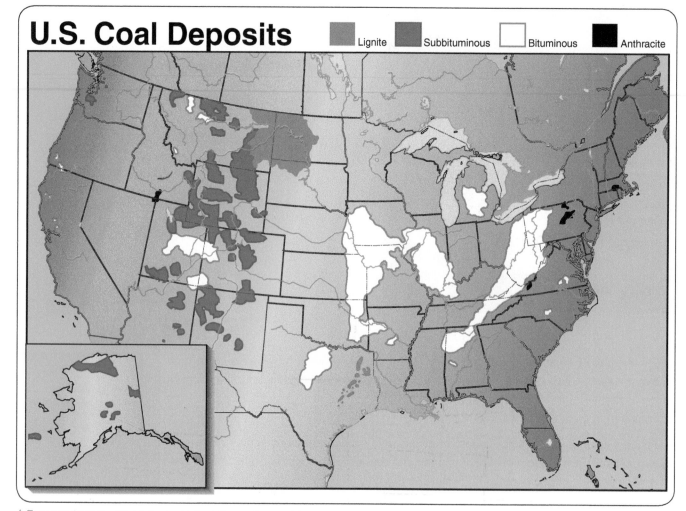

Lignite Subbituminous Bituminous Anthracite

▲ FIGURE 8.25 Coal fields in the United States. *(Adapted from National Coal Association.)*

Figure 8.26 highlights important differences between eastern and western coal. We will return to some of this information in later chapters.

Mining Methods

In the beginning, most coal was obtained by mining underground. (Underground mining methods are shown in Figure 8.27.) Generally, a series of large underground rooms are cut into the coal seam. **Pillars** (columns) of coal are left standing to help support the roof. Once a particular area is mined out, the pillars are systematically removed and the roof is allowed to fall.

In the past, underground miners recovered no more than about 50 percent of the coal present. The work was hard, unpleasant, and dangerous. Today, underground mining has been modernized by huge automatic coal-cutting and loading machines (see Figure 8.27). This modernization has improved mine safety. It has also increased coal production (by 10 to 20 times) and coal seam recovery (to about 80 percent). Figure 8.27 shows a **continuous mining** machine at work. This machine can cut the coal loose and load it in one operation. Two men operating it can mine coal at the rate of about 12 tons a minute. That's a lot of coal compared to the days of "Big John," the pick-and-shovel miner. The continuous mining machine is like a gigantic coal-eating monster. It chews coal from the mine face, gathers it in its claws, feeds it onto a moving belt, and dumps the coal at its rear end.

Topic: coal mining
Go to: www.scilinks.org
Code: GloSci7e320

Apply Your Understanding

What is continuous mining?

Apply Your Understanding

What is a "continuous miner"?

Item	Eastern	Western
% of U.S. production	53%	47%
% of U.S. demonstrated reserves	46%	54%
Primary types	Bituminous, anthracite	Subbituminous, bituminous, lignite
Average sulfur content	High to low	Low to medium
Seam depth	200 ft (60 m) (average)	Shallow
Mining methods*	Underground/surface	Primarily surface
Average $ value (2005)	38.47/ton	$11.01/ton
Recovery**	81%	90%
Water supply	Adequate for both human needs and coal processing	Low for both human needs and coal processing
Reclamation challenges	Wet; acid mine drainage, spoil banks, sinking of the surface	Dry; lack of water for slurries, gasification, and reclamation
Labor	Mostly union	Mostly nonunion
Safety	Some problems remain, but improved overall	Few problems
Socioeconomic impact	Low; many long-established mining communities to absorb additional population and provide infrastructure needs	Medium; lack of large communities near mining sites can result in strain on infrastructure

*Some eastern coal is surface-mined; some western coal is mined underground.
**Represents the average rate of recovery for accessible coal resources.

▲ FIGURE 8.26 A comparison of eastern and western coal.

Apply Your Understanding

How is longwall mining done?

Another underground mining method gaining popularity in the United States is **longwall mining** (illustrated in Figure 8.27). In this system, coal is mined by a cutter (shears) that is pulled back and forth across a mine face 300 to 800 ft (90–240 m) long. The loosened coal drops onto a conveyor belt that lies along the bottom of the face. As the mining machine cuts its way into the seam, hydraulic jacks automatically push steel roof supports forward toward the receding face. This creates a space in which workers and machines can operate without being endangered by falling roof material. When the coal is removed from a section, its roof is allowed to fall.

Using longwall techniques, miners can recover up to 90 percent of a coal seam. There is no need to leave pillars supporting the roof. Another benefit is that roof subsidence (sinking) occurs more uniformly with longwall operations than over room-and-pillar systems. Short-wall mining, a modification of longwall mining, is used to mine odd, irregular sections of a coal seam.

About 60 percent of the coal produced annually in the United States is recovered by **surface mining**. If coal lies less than 200 ft (60 m) beneath the surface and the seam is thick enough, it may be mined by removing the overlying surface rock (called **overburden**) with

Types of Underground-Mining Equipment

The type of equipment that an underground mine requires depends on the method of mining it uses. Mechanized mines use three main methods: (1) the conventional method, (2) continuous mining, and (3) longwall mining. Each of the three methods calls for a different type of equipment.

WORLD BOOK illustrations by Robert Addison

Conventional-Mining Equipment. The conventional method of mining involves a series of steps, three of which require special machinery. First, a cutting machine, *left*, cuts a deep slit along the base of the coal face (coal exposed on the surface of a mine wall). Another machine, *center*, drills holes into the face. Miners load the holes with explosives and then set the explosives off. The undercutting along the bottom of the face causes the shattered coal to fall to the floor. A loading machine, *right*, gathers the coal onto a conveyor belt.

Continuous-Mining Equipment eliminates the need for separate steps in mining a face. A continuous-mining machine, *right*, gouges out the coal and loads it onto a shuttle car in one operation.

Longwall-Mining Equipment. Longwall mining differs from the other methods of underground mining in its system of roof support. The other methods are used only in room-and-pillar mines, where pillars of coal are left to support the mine roof. In the longwall method, movable steel props support the roof over one long coal face. The miners move a cutting machine back and forth across the face, shearing off coal. The coal falls onto a conveyor. As the miners advance the cutter into the bed, the roof supports are moved forward. The roof behind the miners is allowed to fall.

▲FIGURE 8.27 Types of mining equipment and methods. *(From* The World Book Encyclopedia. *© 1999,* World Book, Inc. *By permission of the publisher.)*

◄ FIGURE 8.28 The surface mining of coal.

◄ FIGURE 8.29 This huge truck is typical of those used in modern surface mines. (*Courtesy Caterpillar, Inc.*)

draglines, shovels, or bucket wheels (see Figure 8.28). Power shovels then dig the coal and load it onto huge trucks (see Figure 8.29). The trucks carry the coal to a nearby processing plant where it is separated from impurities, crushed, sorted into various sizes, and washed. Then it may be trucked or loaded onto railroad cars for shipping.

Surface mining, or *open pit mining*, greatly reduces the danger to miners, and permits recovery of 90 percent or more of the coal in the ground. Less than 10 percent of all coal in the United States is shallow enough to be surface-mined. Because much of this shallow, strippable coal occurs in rich farming areas, farming and farmland may be disturbed. However, the land is restored after mining is completed. Both mining and reclamation can go on at the same time. With good planning, the cost is moderate. Reclaimed land may even look better than before the surface was disturbed (see Figure 8.30).

Apply Your Understanding

How is surface mining done?

 QUESTIONS & TASKS

Record your responses in your science notebook.

1. Why is there a renewed interest in coal?

2. Coal is mostly (by mass) what element?

3. What waste products are produced when coal is burned?

4. Since coal combustion produces some undesirable wastes, why is the United States returning to coal as a significant source of energy?

5. Why can coal be used so readily in our economy?

6. List and distinguish among the four different kinds of coal (don't include peat).

7. Describe a major use for each kind of coal you listed in question 6.

8. What determines the usefulness of coal as a fuel? Which kind of coal ranks highest as a fuel?

9. List the ways in which modern underground mining has improved.

10. How is longwall mining superior to room-and-pillar mining?

⟹ Electrical Energy

Coal is the largest and most important source of energy for generating electricity. Because of environmental and regional choices, other energy sources are also used. The three major alternative sources are nuclear energy, hydropower (energy from water), and natural gas. Scientists are continuously trying to perfect new and more desirable methods for producing electric power.

8.7 Hydropower

Apply Your Understanding

What is hydropower?

The potential energy of dammed water is used as an energy source in certain regions of our country where there are rivers and hills or mountains (see Figure 8.31). **Hydropower** is

◄ FIGURE 8.31 Aerial view of Shasta Dam. (*U.S. Bureau of Reclamation*)

used almost entirely for generating electricity. Of the total amount of primary (beginning) energy used in the United States in 2005, hydropower represented about 2.7 percent.

The basic equation for the use of hydropower can be represented as follows:

potential energy → kinetic energy → electrical energy (as wires
(of dammed   (of rotating   spin in a magnetic field
up water)   turbine)   in a generator)

Trace the parts of this equation through the cutaway view of a hydroelectric power plant (see Figure 8.32).

In spite of the relative low cost and cleanliness of hydropower, its role is not expected to increase in the years ahead. Few large hydroelectric sites remain that can be developed and effectively used. The Southwest has the elevation changes necessary for good sites, but lacks the water. The eastern portion of the United States has the water, but not the elevation changes. In the Northwest, hydropower has been developed to its capacity.

Apply Your Understanding

Why is the use of hydropower not expected to greatly increase the amount of energy available?

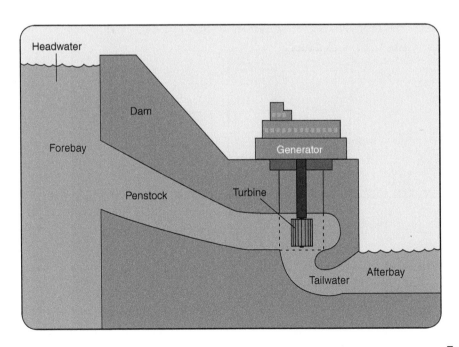

◄ FIGURE 8.32 Cutaway view of a hydroelectric power plant. (*U.S. Bureau of Reclamation*)

Energy Today 325

How Is Electricity Generated?

In this activity, you will gain a basic knowledge of what happens in the generator unit of a large power plant. No matter how electrical energy is produced at large electric power plants (hydroelectric, nuclear, coal, solar thermal), the electricity ultimately originates in the generator unit. You will examine what happens in the generator and determine why motion is necessary.

Topic: electricity
Go to: www.scilinks.org
Code: GloSci7e326

Background

Examine the drawings of the hydroelectric, nuclear, coal-fired, and solar thermal electric power plants (see Figures 8.33–8.36). Notice that they all have a turbine and a generating unit. In the solar thermal drawing (Figure 8.36), the generator is part of the electrical power generation subsystem. The purpose of the water and the dam in the hydroelectric system is to rotate the turbine. This is also the purpose of the steam produced in the nuclear, solar, and coal-fired power plants. The turbine then causes rotational movement in the generator. Finally, after

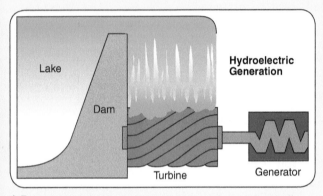

▲ **FIGURE 8.33** Hydroelectric generation. The water actually flows through the dam. (*Public Service Company of Colorado*)

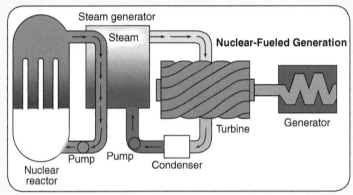

▲ **FIGURE 8.34** Nuclear-fueled generation. (*Public Service Company of Colorado*)

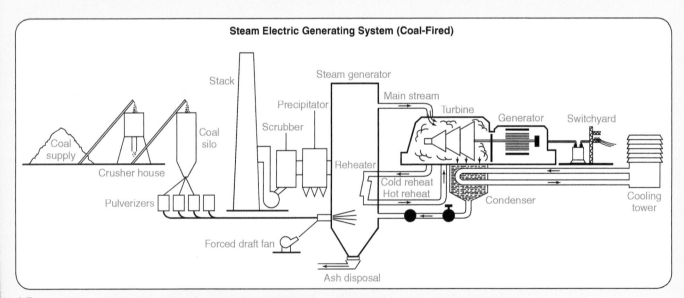

▲ **FIGURE 8.35** Schematic drawing of a steam electric generating station. (*Public Service Company of Colorado*)

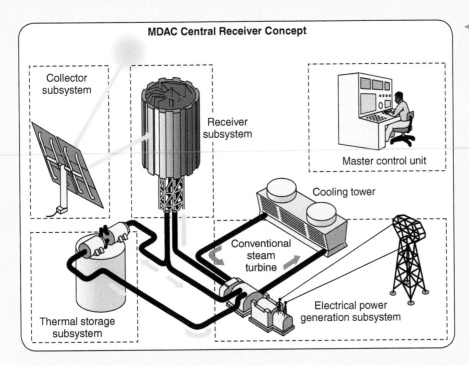

MDAC Central Receiver Concept

Collector subsystem

Receiver subsystem

Master control unit

Cooling tower

Conventional steam turbine

Electrical power generation subsystem

Thermal storage subsystem

◀ **FIGURE 8.36** How a solar thermal electric power plant works. *(Adapted from McDonnell Douglas Corporation.)*

the electricity is produced in the generator, it goes to a transformer. There the voltage is increased. The electricity is then sent on transmission lines to where it is to be used.

Procedure

Part A: How do you make a complete circuit?

Materials

- size D battery, 1.5 V
- flashlight bulb
- jumbo paper clip
- safety goggles

BE SAFE

Be sure to wear safety goggles throughout this entire activity.

1. Find a way to light the bulb using only the battery, bulb, and paper clip. Have your teacher initial your lab notes when you can do this.

Helpful Hint!

Scientists use symbols to represent electrical equipment. The symbols for the equipment you are using are shown in Figure 8.37.

2. In your science notebook, draw a diagram to show the circuit that lights the bulb. First, draw the symbols exactly as shown in Figure 8.37. Then use lines to connect the symbols to show how connections were made.

Part B: What can we learn from using a compass galvanometer?

Materials

- compass
- air core solenoid
- 2 connecting wires (12–18 inches long)
- insulated #18 copper wire, coil of 40 turns
- bar magnet
- metal paper clips (optional)
- safety goggles

1. Examine the coil of insulated wire. The insulation on the wire is a resin (like clear fingernail polish). Note that the insulation has been scraped off at the ends where electrical connections are made.

◀ **FIGURE 8.37** Electrical symbols.

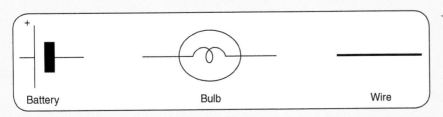

+

Battery

Bulb

Wire

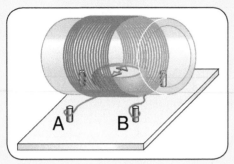

▲FIGURE 8.38 Coil of insulated wire with compass inside.

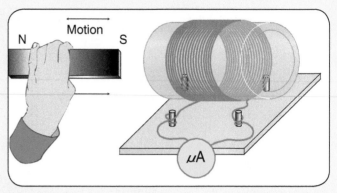

▲FIGURE 8.39 The movement of a magnet relative to a coil.

2. Place the small magnetic compass inside the coil as shown in Figure 8.38. This is our compass galvanometer. A galvanometer is a device that detects both the presence and direction of electric current.

3. Align (position) the compass galvanometer so the compass points in a direction parallel to the wires of the coil (as shown in Figure 8.38).

4. Touch wires A and B to the battery in the same way you made contact with the battery to light the bulb in Part A. You may need to use metal paper clips to complete these connections.

5. Respond to the following in your science notebook:

   a. When electric current flows in the coil of wires, what does the compass needle do?

   b. Reverse connections A and B on the battery. When the flow of electric current in the coil is reversed, what does the compass needle do?

6. Replace the battery with the air core solenoid. A solenoid is simply a coil of wire with a hollow core. Connect wire A to the left binding post on the solenoid and wire B to the right binding post. Position the solenoid so it is as far from the galvanometer as your wire will allow (12 to 18 inches).

7. Place the bar magnet inside the hollow center of the solenoid. Grab the solenoid in your hand and move it back and forth parallel to the bar magnet. Keep the bar magnet *stationary* and inside the solenoid. Observe the compass needle.

8. Respond to the following in your science notebook:

   a. When the solenoid is moved back and forth with respect to the stationary magnet in its core, what does the compass needle do?

   b. What is produced in the circuit when the coil (solenoid) is moved by the magnet?

Part C: What's happening between the magnet and the coil?

Materials

- air core solenoid
- micrometer or galvanometer
- bar magnet
- safety goggles

1. Disconnect the compass galvanometer in Part B from the solenoid. In its place, connect the micrometer. The micrometer is a device for detecting and measuring small amounts of current.

2. Move the bar magnet in and out of the solenoid core (see Figure 8.39). Observe the micrometer needle.

3. Respond to the following in your science notebook:

   a. What is produced in the circuit when the bar magnet is moved in and out of the solenoid?

   b. How do the results of question 3a change when rapid movement is compared to slow movement of the magnet?

Part D: What can we learn from a hand-crank generator?

Materials

- hand-crank generator

1. Examine the apparatus in Figure 8.40. Compare this apparatus to those used in Parts B and C. Note the magnet, the coil of wire, and the bulb. Trace the wires from the bulb back to the coil.

2. Using your hand-crank generator, turn the crank slowly and observe the bulb. Then turn the crank rapidly and observe the bulb again.

BE SAFE

Use the hand-crank generator only as instructed in this activity. Careless use could be dangerous. Wear your

3. As you turn the crank, have someone unscrew the bulb. What does it take to generate electricity?

QUESTIONS & TASKS

Record your responses in your science notebook. DO NOT WRITE IN THIS BOOK.

1. To produce electric current without a battery, we need both a _____ and a _____.

2. To produce electric current, the circuit has to be _____ and there has to be _____ between the two items you listed in question 1.

3. The method we use for producing electric current without a battery is called electromagnetic induction. Based on what you have done and seen, complete the following definition: *Electromagnetic induction* is the production of electric current in a closed circuit caused by _____.

8.8 Electric Power Generation

Electrical energy is popular because it is easily transformed into motion, heat, or light. It also easily activates electronic switches in high-tech circuits. All we have to do is flip a switch. With that, a motor starts, heat is available, a light goes on, or a computer works. At our command, a radio plays or a TV brings us news and pictures from around the globe. What is electricity? How is it produced? You just looked at the major ideas in Activity 8.7.

Electric **current** consists of electrons moving in an organized way in a wire. Electrons are already in the wires. However, they will not move in an organized way without a source of power. One source of power is a battery; another is an electric power plant. Most of the electricity we use is generated at electric power plants. From there, power lines bring the electricity to our homes. Figure 8.41 shows the basic parts of a typical electric power plant: a boiler, a **turbine**, and a **generator**. Let's take a closer look at how each of these units functions.

Topic: electric power generation
Go to: www.scilinks.org
Code: GloSci7e329

How is electric energy produced?

► FIGURE 8.41 The
basics of electric power
generation. (*Adapted from
Public Service Company of
Colorado.*)

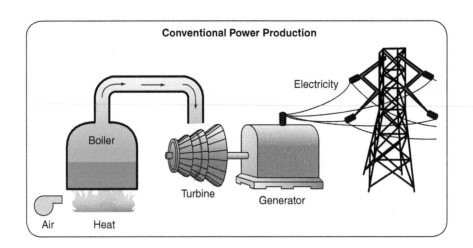

Conventional Power Production

► FIGURE 8.42 The
rotation of the coil
between the poles of
the magnet induces
alternating current.
(*From Modern Science 3,
by Blanc, Fischler and
Gardner. Copyright © 1963
by Holt, Rinehart & Winston,
Publishers.*)

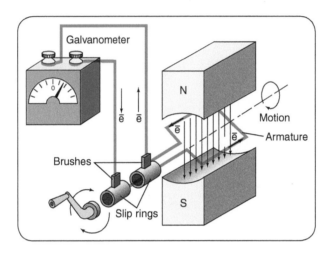

Helpful Hint!

Remember that a
galvanometer is a meter
that detects both the
presence of electric
current and the direction
of current flow.

Electric power generation is built around an event called electromagnetic induction. In 1831, Michael Faraday, an English physicist, found that if a copper wire was moved in a magnetic field, electrons in the wire would move. He used a galvanometer to detect the movement. If the wire was made part of a complete **circuit**, electricity would flow through the circuit. To produce electricity, it is necessary to change the magnetic field continuously. The easiest way to do that is to rotate a coil of wire between the poles of a strong magnet. The basic principles involved in this procedure are illustrated in Figure 8.42.

The rotating coil is called an **armature**. As the armature spins around, current flows back and forth in the coil; this is called alternating current (AC). One coil moving through a magnetic field produces very little current. However, thousands of coils spinning rapidly in a powerful magnetic field can produce enough electricity to satisfy the needs of a small town. In a power plant, it is the electric generator that contains the coils of wire and the powerful magnet.

Apply Your Understanding

What does the turbine do?

The coils do not spin easily. It takes energy to drive electrons through the electric circuit. The conservation of energy law says we cannot get something for nothing. Therefore, to power an electric circuit, the coils must be forced to rotate. To do that, the generator is connected to a turbine. The turbine consists of a series of thousands of blades that are carefully shaped and directed to transfer the force of moving steam or water to a central shaft. As the shaft spins, the armature coils spin and electric current flows. Figure 8.43 shows the blades of a typical turbine. Figure 8.44 shows the structures that enclose the turbine blades.

Electric power plants differ primarily in how they are designed to turn the turbine. Most direct high-pressure steam onto turbine blades. The steam is produced in a steam generator.

◀ FIGURE 8.43 Turbine blades. *(USDOE)*

This is usually heated by burning coal, but some power plants burn oil or natural gas. Others obtain their heat from nuclear reactors. Hydroelectric plants use the pressure of water behind a dam to turn turbines.

Electric power plants are large-scale operations (see Figure 8.45). A 1,000-megawatt, coal-fired plant may burn 10,000 tons of coal a day to provide for the needs of a million people. Some power plants are located at the coal mines. In other cases, the coal is often brought to these plants by a unit train. A **unit train** may consist of one hundred 100-ton cars. One megawatt serves the needs of about 1,000 homes.

At the plant, the coal is carried by conveyor to a crusher and a storage silo. The coal is fed by gravity into a pulverizer, where it is continuously hammered into particles as fine as flour. The pulverized coal is then blown into the boiler where steam is produced (see Figure 8.35).

For steam to rush through the turbine, the pressure must be high at the incoming end and low at the exit. Steam leaves the boiler at very high pressure and is blown onto the

▲ FIGURE 8.44 Giant turbine generators at a large nuclear power plant. *(U.S. Council for Energy Awareness)*

▲ FIGURE 8.45 A typical coal-fired electric power generating plant. This plant is located on the Mississippi River in Minnesota. *(Northern States Power Company)*

Energy Today   331

►FIGURE 8.46 Cooling tower operation.

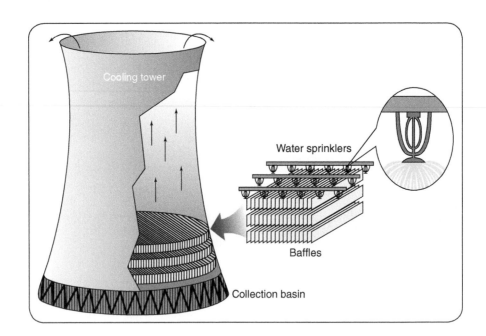

Apply Your Understanding

What tasks do cooling towers perform?

Helpful Hint!

Voltage is a measure of the electrical force for driving an electric current. It is often compared to the concept of pressure.

turbine blades. At the exit end of the turbine, the steam comes in contact with cool pipes from the **cooling towers** (see Figure 8.35). The steam quickly condenses back to water, and the pressure drops sharply. The water in the cool pipes absorbs the released heat and is warmed. This warmed water goes to the radiator unit of the cooling tower. Here sprinklers spray the water onto tile baffles. The baffles provide a huge surface area for the warm water to flow over. As heat and steam rise in the tower, cooler air flows into the bottom of the tower and past the spray of water. This causes some of the water to evaporate, cooling the lower region. Water is cooled, collects at the bottom of the cooling tower, and is returned to the low-pressure end of the turbine. The cycle then repeats (see Figure 8.46).

Electricity is typically generated at approximately 20,000 **volts** (V). Before being transmitted to consumers, it flows to the power **transformer**. Here the voltage is increased, or stepped up. A transformer is a highly efficient electrical device used to either increase (step up) or decrease (step down) voltages (see Figure 8.47).

All wires offer some **resistance** to the flow of electric current. This resistance results in the heating of the wire. The more current in the wire, the greater the heating. Unfortunately, if these wires are the power transmission wires, energy is being lost to space in the form of heat. To cut down on this energy loss, electrical energy must be transmitted at the lowest current possible. To step down the current, the transformer steps up the voltage. Transmission voltages may be as high as 760,000 V (see Figure 8.48).

►FIGURE 8.47 Generation, transmission, and distribution of electricity. (*National Energy Foundation*)

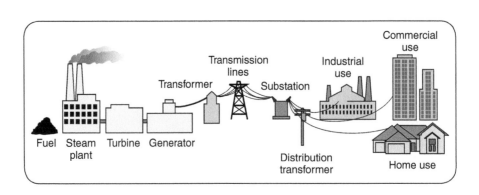

▲FIGURE 8.48 A high-voltage (500 kv) transmission tower under construction. (*Northern States Power Company*)

▲FIGURE 8.49 Utility pole transformer. (*Public Service Company of Colorado*)

High-voltage transmission lines carry electric power over many miles. The electric power eventually ends up at a local substation. The transformer at the substation then steps down the voltage again (12,000 V is common). As the voltage is stepped down, the electric current increases to the current that the consumer wants. Current flows from the local substation through a network of lines attached to power poles. However, before the lines go to homes and buildings, they first pass through the smaller step-down transformer that is fastened high up on the power pole (see Figure 8.49).

From these transformers, 240- and 120-V lines extend to homes and smaller commercial buildings. Electrical devices that heat, such as electric stoves and clothes dryers, require more current and a higher voltage (220–240 V). Most other appliances are built to operate at 110–220 V.

Before passing into a building, the lines pass through the **watt-hour meter** (see Figure 8.50). This meter monitors and records electrical energy usage. The lines then enter the circuit breaker box, where all the circuits in a building originate.

Content Clue

Resistance to current flow depends on the kind of wire (copper, aluminum) and the diameter of the wire. The larger the diameter, the lower the resistance.

Apply Your Understanding

What does a transformer do?

◀FIGURE 8.50 A home watt-hour meter. (*Public Service Company of Colorado*)

Energy Today 333

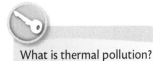

What is thermal pollution?

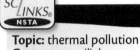

Topic: thermal pollution
Go to: www.scilinks.org
Code: GloSci7e334

Electricity is a unique form of energy in that it cannot be stored, except for the relatively small amounts stored in batteries (or pump-filled reservoirs). Electricity must be used immediately on generation; thus, it must be produced on demand. The demand is signaled by someone turning on an additional air conditioner or TV, for instance. The signal is sent at nearly the speed of light, and it must be met just as swiftly.

8.9 Thermal Pollution

As you learned in section 8.8, for the turbine at an electric power generating plant to spin, the low-pressure end of the turbine must be kept relatively cool. This is accomplished by cooling the water in the cooling loop. The process for keeping this water cool can lead to thermal pollution. **Thermal pollution** is the addition to air or water of abnormal amounts of heat, resulting in environmental changes. In the past, electric power plants often dumped the heated water from the cooling loop into a nearby body of water. Figure 8.51 shows an infrared photo of such an operation.

Because this heat dumping usually has an adverse effect on the aquatic environment, most states have laws that prohibit power plants from returning hot water directly to nearby bodies of water. In fact, most states have laws that prohibit increasing water temperature by more than 5.04°F (2.8°C) at the point where water is discharged into a river, lake, or bay. These laws were enacted to prevent a variety of problems. The water taken into the plant contains small fish and smaller organisms. These are killed by heat as the water is pumped through the pipe that cools the condenser. The result is a reduced food supply for larger organisms. The warm discharged water also holds less dissolved oxygen than cold water does. Lack of adequate oxygen may cause organisms to die. At the same time, the increased temperature increases the metabolic rate, and hence the need

▶ FIGURE 8.51 An infrared photo of the thermal plume from a power plant located on Lake Michigan. The plume extends approximately 4,900 ft (1,470 m) offshore. The photo was taken during relatively calm waters. Discharges to this extent are no longer allowed. *(From Professor T. Green, Marine Studies Center, University of Wisconsin-Madison.)*

for oxygen, for both microorganisms and fish. The result can be a large fish kill due to suffocation.

Thermal pollution often leads to changes in species composition. Desirable algae may be replaced by undesirable blue-green algae. Desirable fish populations, such as trout, may diminish. On occasion, some desirable fish populations, such as bass and catfish, have benefited.

To prevent negative impacts, many utilities have special artificial lakes called **cooling ponds**. Warm water from the condenser is pumped into these ponds. Evaporation of the water and transfer of heat to the outside air result in cooling. Cool water is drawn from the deepest point of the pond and returned to the cooling loop. To be effective, cooling ponds must be large.

Modern electric power plants use cooling towers to remove heat from the condenser and dump it into the air (see Figure 8.52). Cooling towers are typically giant hollow cylinders about 500 ft (150 m) high. These cylinders are pinched in near the top. They are supported on legs that allow air to flow under the tower.

Inside the top of the cooling tower are several layers of special tiles called baffles. The baffles provide a huge surface area for the cooling water to trickle over. Water that was warmed in the condenser is returned to the cooling tower and sprayed onto the baffles. As the water trickles down the baffles, it loses heat. The large surface area of the baffles causes the heat to be quickly transferred into the air.

Since hot air rises, the warmed air moves up through the cooling tower. Cooler air flows under the tower, replacing the heated air. As this process continues, a natural breeze begins to blow up through the baffles and out of the cooling water. On a cool day, a huge cloud of steam can be seen rising from a cooling tower.

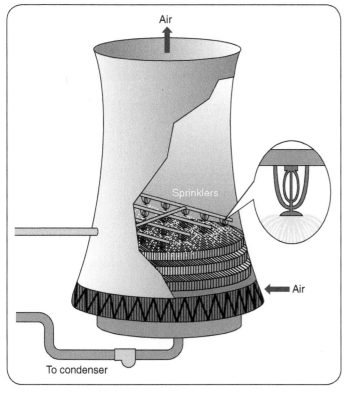

◄ FIGURE 8.52 Cooling towers are designed to dump waste heat into the air.

Most of the cooling water does not evaporate. It is cooled to about 75°F (24°C) and collected at the bottom of the cooling tower. Some of this water may be returned to a nearby river, but most is used again in the cooling loop. (In a nuclear power plant, however, none of this water ever comes in contact with the reactor core, so the water carries no radioactive materials.)

Dry cooling towers have been designed for use in arid regions where water is scarce and expensive. These towers cool the water from the condenser, but do not evaporate large quantities of water. Unfortunately, they are more expensive to build and to operate.

Think about This!

Why are dry cooling towers of interest?

Despite their high cost, cooling towers are being constructed at most new power plants. The waste heat dumped into the atmosphere doesn't seem to have a noticeable negative impact on the local environment. In the future, we hope to capture and use the waste heat from power plants. This heat could be used for heating homes, for growing green-houses crops, or for fish farming near the power plants. These uses only cool the water slightly. Unfortunately, the water must still be cooled further for efficient use at the power plant.

Summary

Americans use primarily the energy stored in oil and gas molecules to operate their society. These fuels are easily adapted to a variety of tasks—moving vehicles, heating homes, and running machines. Unfortunately, domestic reserves of oil and gas are running low. As a result, there is continuing interest in coal, especially for electric power generation.

Coal is mined underground using a variety of mining techniques. Where it is located near the surface, coal is strip-mined. The heat from burning coal can be used to boil water and make steam. The steam then forces a turbine to rotate. If the rotating turbine is attached to a generator, electric power is produced. This is because a coil of wire in the generator is forced to move across a magnetic field. Electricity can also be generated using the energy stored in water held behind a dam.

 REFERENCES

American Petroleum Institute. *All about Petroleum* (Washington, D.C.: American Petroleum Institute), 1998.

BP p.l.c. *BP Statistical Review of World Energy* (London: BP p.l.c.), annual.

United Nations. *Yearbook of World Energy Statistics* (New York: United Nations), annual.

U.S. Bureau of Reclamation. *Hydropower: Water at Work* (Washington, D.C.: GPO), 1991.

U.S. Department of Energy. *Annual Energy Outlook 1999: With Projections to 2020* (Washington, D.C.: GPO), 1998.

U.S. Department of Energy. *Annual Energy Review* (Washington, D.C.: GPO), annual.

U.S. Geological Survey: http://www.usgs.gov/

U.S. Dept. of Energy—Office of Fossil Energy: http://www.fe.doe.gov/

American Petroleum Institute: http://www.api.org—select educational materials

BP p.l.c. http://www.bp.com

CHAPTER (9)

Nonrenewable Resource Depletion

GOALS

- To examine the depletion pattern for non-renewable resources.

- To examine how resource lifetimes are determined.

Civilization as we know it will come to an end sometime in this century unless we can find a way to live without fossil fuels.

—David Goodstein, vice provost and Frank J. Gilloon, Distinguished Teaching and Service Professor, California Institute of Technology, 2004

The prospect of running out of energy is purely a bogeyman. The availability of energy has been increasing, and the meaningful cost has been decreasing, over the entire span of humankind's history.

—*The Resourceful Earth*, by Simon and Kahn

Diminishing Resources of Energy

The central focus in discussions of energy resources has always been the eventual exhaustion of fossil fuel resources, especially oil. As the two quotations at the beginning of this chapter illustrate, it is difficult to find agreement on the seriousness of the possible oil shortage, or when it will occur. This chapter will help you to understand why experts disagree. It will also help you to distinguish between *reserves* and *resources*. We will provide current "best guesses" about how much of our nonrenewable (depletable) fuel resources remain. We will then consider some projected rates of fuel usage and discuss what these numbers might tell us about resource lifetimes.

9.1 Depletion of Nonrenewable Resources

How are **nonrenewable resources** obtained? Let's begin by examining this in Activity 9.1.

Nonrenewable resources are resources that are not replaced within a reasonable period of time.

Topic: nonrenewable resources
Go to: www.scilinks.org
Code: GloSci7e340

➤ FIGURE 9.1 Heavy freeway traffic. *(National Renewable Energy Laboratory)*

ACTIVITY 9.1

Resource Depletion

Think about products you use or consume—food, clothes, bicycles, and tools. What resources are these products made of? Are the resources grown or mined?

In this activity, you will model the mining of a nonrenewable resource. Your goal is to discover the patterns of resource

Content Clue

Do not jump to conclusions about resource depletion until you have finished this chapter.

removal from the earth. Before you begin, you need to understand how this simulation will work. Read the following background information carefully. *Make sure you understand this model.*

Background
Parts of the Model

- Beads = valuable resource such as oil, coal, or a mineral that can be removed from the earth.

- Dried corn = other parts of Earth's crust that are not valuable; these are called gangue.

- Plastic box with beads and corn = Earth.

- You = a developer who removes and makes use of the valuable resource.

- Plastic cup = mining car.

Assumptions

Helpful Hint!

The assumptions determine what happens.

1. Earth and its resources are finite.

2. Demand for and consumption of the nonrenewable resources grows exponentially until it encounters barriers.

Rules

1. When you are mining, you can only use a pinching action with your index finger and thumb. Improper mining practices are illegal.

2. Try to remove one bead at a time; try not to remove corn with the beads.

3. Two people (executive + miner) represent a large mining company. One person represents a small independent operator.

4. Beads are placed in a cup that your partner holds. Hold the cup yourself if you don't have a partner.

5. Fifteen seconds (sec) of mining represent 1 year of production.

6. The number of beads you extract in 15 sec equals your annual production.

7. You need to extract a minimum number of beads to stay in business. This number depends on economic conditions and is determined by your teacher.

8. Process your ore at the company mill by separating the minerals (beads) from the gangue (corn).

Helpful Hint!

Extract means to remove.

Production is separated at the mill site.

9. Keep the beads at the mill. They will be enriched and sold at some future time.

10. Return the tailings (milled gangue) to the earth.

11. Report your annual production to the designated government official each year.

12. New developers enter the mining business when existing companies make profits. Companies are added in a roughly exponential manner (see Figure 9.2).

13. Companies are not added when profits become marginal.

14. You will be charged an environmental fine if you are careless in your mining practices. The fine equals 40 percent of your total production that year.

Helpful Hint!

Since four miners are about all you can crowd around the box, eight miners are equivalent to four miners mining for 2 years (30 sec). The number of miners seldom exceeds eight because few new companies go into mining as profit margins narrow.

Content Clue

When profits cease, companies fail.

15. Mining will continue until total production drops to near what it was the first year or when class ends.

Procedure

1. Form mining companies according to your teacher's directions.

2. Go to the table that contains the Earth (plastic box) in which you will mine.

3. Choose 1 or 2 EPA (Environmental Protection Agency) officials. They will inspect the mining sites and assess fines for environmental damage, if necessary.

4. Choose 1 or 2 Department of the Interior officials. They will obtain, process, tabulate, and display the data for each round (year) of production.

5. Reproduce the table in Figure 9.2 in your science notebook.

6. Decide who will mine in the first round. In the first year, only 1 company will extract nuggets (beads) from the Earth box.

7. Your teacher will announce when mining begins and stops.

Time (years)	Number of Developers	Production Rate (nuggets/year)	Total Resources Withdrawn (nuggets)
1	1		
2	2		
3	4		
4	8		
5			
6			
7			
8			
9			
10			
11			
12			

8. When the first year is over (15 sec), determine your production and report it to the Department of the Interior. The Department of the Interior then reports to the class.

Helpful Hint!

In an *accumulative summation*, the production of the present year is added to the total resources withdrawn previously.

9. Record the results in your data table. Note that the total resource withdrawn is an accumulative summation of all the nuggets withdrawn. Your final number will be very close to the total number of nuggets in the box.

10. Have your mine site inspected by the EPA. Determine your net production, which equals gross production less damage fine. Then determine how many companies will mine in the next round.

11. Repeat steps 7–10 until the production rate returns to year 1 levels or the class period is about to end.

QUESTIONS & TASKS

Record your responses in your science notebook.

1. Divide a sheet of graph paper in half by drawing a line down the center. (Turn the sheet of paper so the longest side is at the bottom.)

2. On the left side of the sheet, plot a graph of production rate vs. time.

3. On the right side of the sheet, plot a graph of total resource withdrawn vs. time.

4. What pattern do you see in the graph of production rate vs. time?

5. What pattern do you see in the graph of total resource withdrawn vs. time?

Apply Your Understanding

Look up the word *sigmoid* in a dictionary. Why is this graph called a sigmoid graph?

6. Write a conclusion about resource depletion based on your experience in this activity and the related graphs. Start your conclusion as follows: *Production of the nonrenewable resource started slowly because . . .*

Applying a Model to a Real Situation

M. King Hubbert was a petroleum engineer who projected crude oil production rates for the United States (not including Alaska). He did most of his work in the 1960s and 1970s.

In this activity, you will use Hubbert's projection (Figure 9.4 in the Questions & Tasks section) as another model for resource depletion. You will compare his projection (prediction) to what is actually happening.

> **Think about This!**
>
> Are models useful tools for predicting the future and planning for it?

Materials

- graph paper

Procedure

1. Plot a graph of U.S. petroleum production vs. time. Use the data provided in Figure 9.3. Begin the time axis at 1910 and extend it to 2030. This will allow you to extrapolate back to 1910 and forward into the future.

> **Helpful Hint!**
>
> Remember, *extrapolate* means to estimate an unknown quantity by using the data and trends you know.

2. Compare your graph of production rate vs. time from Activity 9.1 to the one you just plotted. State 3 similarities and 3 differences.

3. Look at Hubbert's graph (Figure 9.4). Because the graph was made in the late 1960s, everything after that date is an extrapolation (educated guess).

QUESTIONS & TASKS

Record your responses in your science notebook.

1. How does Hubbert's projection in Figure 9.4 compare to actual U.S. petroleum production (shown on the graph you just plotted)?

2. When did Hubbert predict U.S. petroleum production would peak? When did it actually peak?

▼ FIGURE 9.3 U.S. petroleum production exclusive of Alaska. (*Source: American Petroleum Institute.*)

In Billions of 42-Gallon Barrels	
1925	.77
1930	.90
1935	1.00
1940	1.35
1945	1.71
1950	1.97
1955	2.48
1960	2.57
1965	2.84
1970	3.43
1975	2.99
1980	2.56
1985	2.61
1990	2.04
1995	1.85
2000	1.77
2004	1.65

3. When did Hubbert predict the United States would have used up 90 percent of its petroleum reserves? Assume the depletion curve is symmetrical.

> **Think about This!**
>
> *Symmetrical* means that if a line is drawn down through the center, the left side will be a mirror image of the right side.

4. Why are we still driving our vehicles and powering them with gasoline when our domestic supplies appear to be so low?

▼FIGURE 9.4 Complete cycle of crude oil production in the United States and adjacent continental shelves, exclusive of Alaska. *(From Hubbert, M. King: "Energy Resources." Reproduced from Resources and Man, 1969, Fig. 8.17, p. 183, by permission of the National Academy of Sciences, Washington, D.C., and M. King Hubbert.)*

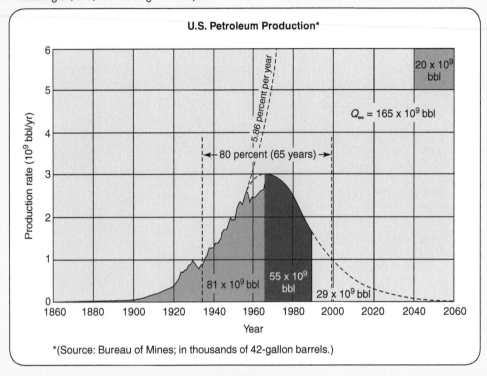

U.S. Petroleum Production*

*(Source: Bureau of Mines; in thousands of 42-gallon barrels.)

Helpful Hint!

The abbreviation bbl/yr stands for barrels per year.

Content Clue

Since the beginning and end of a resource depletion curve are so uncertain, many experts talk about the 80 percent life span (see Figure 9.4). This is the period of time during which 80 percent of a resource is expected to be withdrawn. Generally, when 90 percent of a resource is withdrawn, the resource is considered exhausted. The remaining 10 percent is just too expensive to extract.

5. Why hasn't the price of gasoline shot up? In normal economics, as the supply goes down, the price should go up.

6. If Hubbert is right and the domestic supply is very low, how should the United States respond to this situation?

7. Running out of a resource is not the only reason a depletion curve may plunge. What are some other reasons why a depletion curve may peak and then fall?

9.2 Resource Depletion Curves

The history of crude oil is a typical production cycle. A typical production cycle, called a **resource depletion curve**, is illustrated in Figure 9.5. When crude oil was first discovered, its rate of consumption was very low. It had some uses as a lubricant and as a fuel for lamps. Eventually, people learned to separate crude oil into products such as gasoline and kerosene. Its use expanded. Automobiles were invented that used gasoline as their source of power.

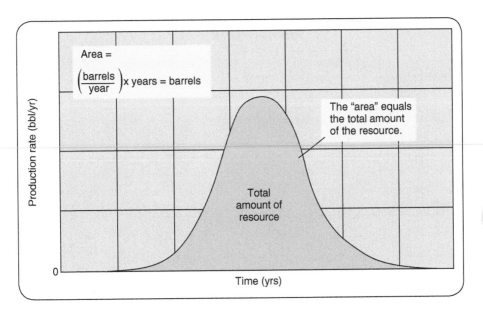

A resource depletion curve represents the complete production cycle of a resource in a given region.

Soon, mass production made cars available for millions of people. The demand for gasoline rose; this caused similar growth of oil production. Then came the diesel locomotive, the airplane, trucks, asphalt, the motorcycle, heating oil, and oil-fired electric power generating plants. Demand and production continued to grow at an exponential rate.

Earth's resources are finite; they are limited. Oil is one of these nonrenewable resources. Thus, the production rate will eventually peak and then decrease. As crude oil gets harder to find, more dry holes will be drilled. Wells that do produce will be deeper and located in more remote regions. Because this is expensive, it is more difficult to make a profit. As a result, some companies will drop out of the oil business. Economical substitutes for the oil-based products will be developed. The demand for crude oil will drop.

A resource depletion curve represents the complete production cycle of a resource in a given region. A curve like this is a useful tool. For example, look at Figure 9.7 in section 9.5 Hubbert Theory of Resource Estimation. Imagine a vertical line running through any given time on the horizontal axis. The area under the curve to the left of the vertical line represents the quantity of the resource that has been extracted from that region. This has implications for the economics of oil in the region the curve represents.

SCLINKS.
NSTA

Topic: resource depletion curve
Go to: www.scilinks.org
Code: GloSci7e345

What does the area under a resource depletion curve represent?

9.3 Resources and Reserves

We use the terms *resources* and *reserves* to discuss how much of some material exists. The terms are often misused as synonyms; however, they do not mean the same thing.

Resources are amounts of materials that are known or assumed to exist, and for which extraction is economically possible now or in the future with potential technology. **Reserves** are known amounts of a material that can be extracted profitably with existing technology under present economic conditions. So, reserves are part of resources. The general relationship between resources and reserves is shown in Figure 9.6.

We see from Figure 9.6 that resources are much larger than reserves. But they are also less certain. Some resources can be assumed to exist, but have not been discovered. Extracting them may or may not be profitable. It is important to understand that total resource estimates are always highly unsure. There is no way to know when, or even if, resources will be discovered or whether they actually exist.

Reserves represent deposits that have been studied long enough for the amount and grade of the material to be estimated. They can be mined under present economic conditions

What is the difference between resources and reserves?

Think about This!

Reserves may be thought of as a working inventory.

Content Clue

Resources are larger than reserves.

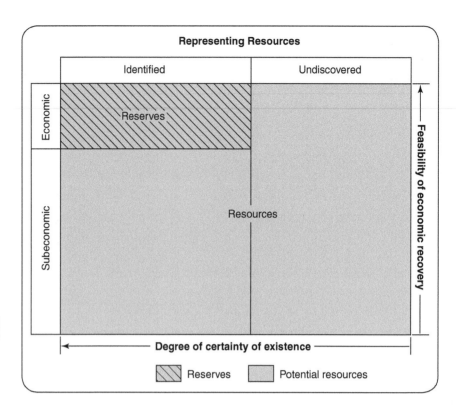

Think about This!

As technology changes and improves, so do our estimates of both reserves and resources.

Resource estimates are useful for future planning.

using the technology available. However, even in a well-known deposit, reserve estimates change from year to year. Material is extracted, thereby reducing the reserves. At the same time, further exploration of the deposit may *add* measurable quantities of reserves. Moreover, new technologies or possible changes in economic conditions may shift known deposits from the resource to the reserve category. A decline in economic conditions may result in a shift from the reserve to the resource category.

Although reserve estimates are essential to short-range planning, they rarely give a good long-term picture. When used with caution, resource estimates are a better tool for probing the future.

❓ QUESTIONS & TASKS

1. Why are reserves usually much smaller than resources?

2. Why do reserves of resources usually last much longer than most early estimates predict?

9.4 Estimating the Size of Resources

Content Clue

Estimating resources is difficult.

Estimating the size of our energy and mineral resources is a complex task. It involves gathering and processing data, and making educated guesses based on scientific hypotheses and historical trends.

Once estimates are made, we must interpret their meaning. This can be problematic. Opinions vary about the amount of any given resource that can be extracted profitably. Thus, we find a wide variety of figures stating what our reserves are. To interpret the meaning of an estimation of resources, we must ask several questions: Who is making and paying for the estimates? For what purpose are their estimates being made? What techniques are being used? How are terms being defined? How reliable have their estimates been in the past?

The Problem of Estimating the Size of a Resource

In this activity, you will look at the problem of estimating reserves and some possible solutions to that problem. You will do this by answering a series of questions about the model you worked with in Activity 9.1.

Procedure

1. In Activity 9.1, you modeled the depletion of a nonrenewable resource and plotted a resource depletion curve. Refer to the depletion curve you plotted to answer the questions that follow. You will also need to recall how you obtained the data that are plotted on that curve.

2. This activity will help you analyze the Hubbert theory of resource estimation discussed in section 9.5, which follows this activity.

QUESTIONS & TASKS

Record your responses in your science notebook.

1. Before you began your mining activities, did you have any idea of how many nuggets (beads) were in the Earth box? Explain.

   Helpful Hint!

   Recall both the appearance of the Earth box and your thoughts.

2. After three rounds of mining, what ideas did you have about the number of nuggets in the box? Explain.

3. How many years (rounds) did it take for production to peak?

4. At the time production peaked (round), were you aware that about half of the nuggets were removed from the box? Explain.

5. When did you become aware that the supply of nuggets was running out?

6. What evidence made you aware of that fact?

7. If you know when production peaks, and you know the number of nuggets extracted by that time, you can make a pretty good estimate of how many nuggets remain. Explain how this can be done.

8. Develop a way to estimate how many nuggets are in the box before you know production has peaked. Be creative.

9. How reliable do you think the estimate is that you suggested in question 8?

9.5 Hubbert Theory of Resource Estimation

You can predict the overall shape of a resource depletion curve if you know two things: (1) the actual shape of the beginning of the curve, and (2) an estimate of the total quantity of the resource. The area under the curve is equal to the total quantity of the resource. This technique was used by M. King Hubbert in 1956. At that time, he predicted that if the accepted figure of 150–200 billion barrels was the amount of crude oil that could be pumped out of the ground in the 48 contiguous states, then U.S. production should have peaked between 1966 and 1971. Production actually peaked in 1970. Figure 9.7 shows his prediction.

In 1971, Hubbert made a similar projection for world crude oil production (see Figure 9.8). In this projection, he used two different estimates of the total amount of the resource. Note that the larger estimate led to a curve that both rose and fell more steeply. Because of this,

Content Clue

If you know the beginning of the curve and can estimate the amount of a resource, you can sketch the rest of the curve.

Helpful Hint!

Contiguous means to touch or join at a border.

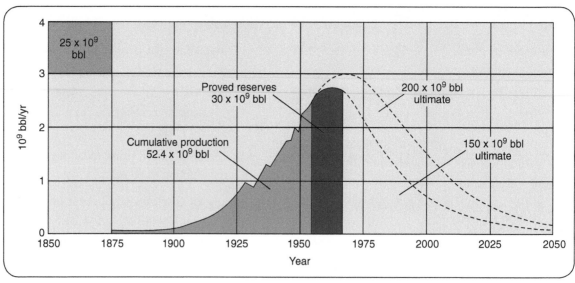

▲FIGURE 9.7 Hubbert's 1956 prediction of the future production of crude oil in U.S. contiguous states and adjacent continental shelves. *(From M. King Hubbert, 1956, Fig. 21, p. 17, with permission of the author and the American Petroleum Institute.)*

▶FIGURE 9.8 The cycle of world oil production. This cycle is plotted on the basis of two estimates of the amount of oil that will ultimately be produced. The high curve assumes $2,100 \times 10^9$ barrels, and the low curve $1,350 \times 10^9$ bbl. *(From "The Energy Resources of the Earth" by M. King Hubbert. Scientific American, September 1971, p. 69. Reprinted by permission of the author.)*

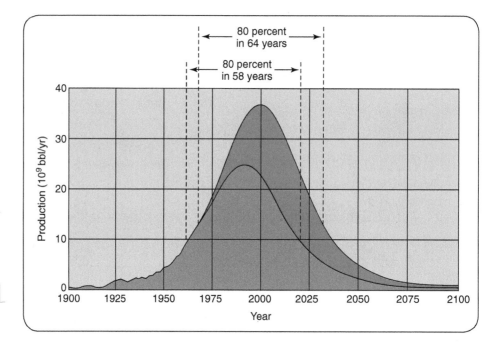

Think about This!

How would the exhaustion of the world's crude oil supply affect your lifestyle, world politics, and the future?

Content Clue

A variety of methods are used to estimate the size of a resource before production peaks.

Apply Your Understanding

Identify the strengths and weaknesses of the Hubbert theory.

Hubbert's projection about when 90 percent of the world's crude oil will be gone is nearly the same in both cases. The prediction for the exhaustion of the world's crude oil supply in 2025 is one you will want to watch.

Dr. Hubbert was one of the early thinkers about resource depletion. His 1956 warning to U.S. oil producers of the oncoming decline in production in the early 1970s was dismissed by many. The reliability of his projections has earned him great respect and recognition.

There are a number of ways to estimate the size of a resource before its production peaks. Dr. Hubbert both developed and used some of these methods. Some involve analyzing the geology of a region. Some involve analyzing the results of exploratory drilling. Others involve the analysis of production data and reserve estimates. The greater the quantity, quality, and variety of data available, the more reliable the estimate.

How Much Do We Have?

The amount of energy available to us from nonrenewables depends on the remaining resources of different fuels. This quantity is hard to analyze because oil is sold by the barrel, coal by the ton, and natural gas by the cubic foot. This makes it hard to compare amounts of energy. To make comparisons, we need to compare "apples to apples," as the expression goes. We need to know the amount of energy *available* from a barrel of oil or a ton of coal.

The amount of energy released when one unit of mass of that fuel is consumed is its *energy content*. A bomb calorimeter is used to determine the energy content of flammable fuels (see Figure 9.9). The table in Figure 9.10 shows how the average energy content varies from fuel to fuel. Oil and natural gas provide more energy per pound than coal does. Nuclear fuels have a huge energy content. We can use this table, along with estimates of how much oil, gas, coal, and uranium remain, to gain some idea of the amount of energy available to the United States and the world from these fuels.

What do we mean by the energy content of a fuel?

Helpful Hint!

In Activity 8.3, you determined the energy content of a fuel.

◀ FIGURE 9.9 A scientist uses a bomb calorimeter to determine the energy content of a sample of coal. Electric power utilities do this on a routine basis to make certain the coal they purchase contains the energy they are paying for. (*Public Service Company of Colorado*)

◀ FIGURE 9.10 Energy content of various fuels.

Fuel	Common Units	Energy per Pound	Energy per Kilogram
Coal	25×10^6 Btu*/ton	3,150 Calories** (13×10^6 joules)	6,930 Calories (2.9×10^7 joules)
Crude oil	5.8×10^6 Btu/bbl†	4,900 Calories (20.5×10^6 joules)	10,780 Calories (4.5×10^7 joules)
Natural gas	1,031 Btu/cf†	5,000 Calories (20.9×10^6 joules)	11,000 Calories (4.6×10^7 joules)
Uranium	—	8.86×10^9 Calories (3.71×10^{13} joules)	1.95×10^{10} Calories (8.17×10^{13} joules)

*Btu = British thermal unit
**1,000 calories = 1 kilocalorie = 1 Calorie
†bbl = barrel, cf = cubic foot

Nonrenewable Resource Depletion 349

9.6 Nonrenewable Resources

As discussed in Chapter 8, the United States relies primarily on fossil fuels—coal, oil, and natural gas—for its energy. In 2005, the burning of these fuels accounted for about 86 percent of U.S. energy use. The United States obtained an additional 8 percent from uranium used in nuclear reactors that year. Another 6 percent came from **renewable** sources. The world-use pattern is similar.

The deposits of fossil fuels and uranium are finite. Therefore, it is useful to know how much we have of these fuels. Remember, however, experts strongly disagree on estimates of these resources.

Coal

Apply Your Understanding

Why is it difficult to accurately estimate coal reserves?

To estimate coal reserves, you need a variety of information. You need to know the thickness, extent, and quality of individual **coal seams**. If a seam isn't thick enough, mining is not practical. It is also important to know how deeply these coal seams are buried and how easily they can be mined. Some coal seams lie close to the surface and can be mined there. Others dip deeply into Earth, even thousands of feet below the surface. Most of this coal is available only through underground mining methods. The structural condition of the rocks enclosing the seam must also be considered. All of this information is necessary for estimating the quantity of recoverable coal (see Figure 9.11).

Total identified coal resources in the United States are about 1.7 trillion tons. An equal amount may be in coal deposits that have not yet been discovered. Reserves of coal are estimated to be 494 billion tons (see Figure 9.12). World reserves are estimated to be 1.0 trillion tons.

Crude Oil

Apply Your Understanding

Why is it difficult to accurately estimate crude oil reserves?

Estimating resources and reserves of crude oil is a very difficult task. Before the full extent of an oil field can be known, many wells must be drilled. This process may extend over several years. Furthermore, the oil in a field is never fully recovered.

▶ FIGURE 9.11 Multiple coal seams outcrop on this pristine bluff in the Hoseanna (also known as Lignite) Creek Basin, near Healy, Alaska. The most prominent coal seam is approximately 40 feet (12 meters) thick. This area is known as the Popovitch Bad-lands, named after an early prospector. *(From Usibelli Coal Mine, Inc.)*

Energy Type	Region	Recoverable Proven Reserves	Estimated Total Resource Remaining*
Crude oil (billion bbl)	World	1,180	1,600
	U.S.	23	175
Natural gas (trillion cf)	World	6,500	7,000
	U.S.	193	1,430
Coal (billions of short tons**)	World	998	5,220
	U.S.	494	1,670
Uranium (U_3O_8) (thousands of short tons)	World	6,140	14,000
	U.S.	445	2,100
Oil shale/tar sands (billion bbl)	World	471	2,400
	U.S.	25	1,050

*Average of the estimates for 2001 reported in various recent studies.
**1 short ton = 2,000 pounds; 1 metric ton = 2,204.62 pounds

◄FIGURE 9.12
Nonrenewable energy reserves and resources.

With our current technology, there is always a portion that cannot be recovered economically. Some reservoirs may yield 90 percent of their oil. However, the current average recovery of oil from all the oil fields in the United States is estimated at between 30 percent and 40 percent.

World crude oil resources are estimated to be about 1.6 trillion barrels. World reserves are about 1,180 billion barrels—over half of that located in the Middle East (see Figure 9.13).

◄FIGURE 9.13 The development of crude oil reserves in the Middle East. (*Science VU-API/Visuals Unlimited*)

▶FIGURE 9.14 The flaring and storage of natural gas. *(William Ober/Visuals Unlimited)*

The U.S. resources are estimated to be around 175 billion barrels; U.S. reserves are about 23 billion barrels (see Figure 9.12).

Natural Gas

Natural gas is even more elusive than oil. It can be found with oil or alone. We are much more efficient at extracting natural gas than we are in extracting coal or oil (see Figure 9.14). Because it is free-flowing and often under pressure, natural gas can be extracted at a national average of 80 percent of identified reserves. U.S. resources are estimated to be 1,430 trillion cubic feet, with reserves of 193 trillion cubic feet (see Figure 9.12). World resources are estimated to be about 7,000 trillion cubic feet; world reserves are placed at 6,500 trillion cubic feet.

Uranium

Apply Your Understanding

How long might it take the nuclear power plants in the United States to use up all U.S. uranium reserves? Why will the reserves probably last longer than this estimate?

The United States has about 455,000 tons of uranium oxide (U_3O_8) in proven reserves. A 1,000-megawatt (mW) nuclear-fueled electric power generating plant uses about 5,500 tons of uranium oxide in its 30-year lifetime. Hence, there is enough uranium oxide in U.S. reserves to fuel 83 1,000-mW nuclear power plants through their full 30-year lifetime. At the present time, there are about 100 nuclear power plants operating in the United States (see Figure 9.15). Most of these are smaller than 1,000 mW.

Uranium Resources in a Breeder Economy

The energy content of uranium is based on the current, inefficient methods of using nuclear fuel. A nuclear program based on the more efficient breeder reactor could enable a nation to obtain 60 to 100 times more energy from its nuclear reserves (see Figure 9.16). How this is done is one of the topics in the next chapter.

◀ FIGURE 9.15 Nuclear fuel rods. The rods are underwater. The glow is called Cerenkov radiation. *(Science VU-API/Visuals Unlimited)*

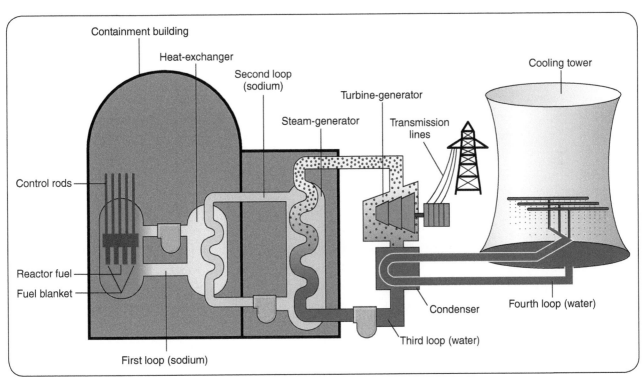

▲ FIGURE 9.16 Diagram of a fast breeder reactor. *(From USDOE.)*

Oil Shale and Tar Sands

Oil shale is sedimentary rock containing **kerogen**, a solid organic substance (see Figure 9.17). When heated, kerogen breaks apart. This breakup can produce large quantities of synthetic crude oil (**syncrude**) and flammable gas.

Apply Your Understanding

Why is oil shale important?

Helpful Hint!

Synthetic means not fully of natural origin. Human intervention is required for the production.

► FIGURE 9.17 Oil shale cliffs in Colorado's Grand Valley region. (*Courtesy Atlantic Richfield Company [ARCO].*)

Syncrude means synthetic crude oil.

Apply Your Understanding

Why are tar sands of interest?

Tar sands are very old deposits of rock or sediment from which the light fuels have escaped. The asphaltic residue left behind is a heavy oil or tarlike fuel (bitumen). That fuel, however, is too thick to be pumped to the surface. The technology for treating tar sands to make synthetic crude oil is relatively simple.

Tar sands and oil shale are of economic interest. The synthetic crude oil they provide can become a substitute for our shrinking supply of crude oil. Oil shale and tar sands will be discussed in greater detail in Chapter 11.

ACTIVITY 9.4

Comparing Nonrenewable Reserves

In this activity, you will compare nonrenewable energy sources and the reserve estimates for each.

To compare the nonrenewable sources, we will use a common unit of measure. Since we are dealing with national and world energy reserves and demands, we will use a very large unit, the quad. One quad can provide the energy required to run the entire United States for approximately 4 days.

Apply Your Understanding

How large is a quad?

Materials

- graph paper
- calculator

Procedure

1. Reproduce the table in Figure 9.18 in your science notebook. Note the following about each of the columns:

   a. The first column is a list of the nonrenewable energy sources that can be extracted from deposits within the United States.

   b. The second column gives a reserve estimate for each source. (Note that the units used are the customary units.)

Source	Reserve Estimate	Conversion Factor	Quads
Crude oil	23×10^9 bbl	181×10^6 bbl/quad	127
Natural gas	193×10^{12} cf	0.797×10^{12} cf/quad	
Coal	494×10^9 tons	44.3×10^6 tons/quad	
Uranium (U_3O_8)	445×10^3 tons	7.67×10^3 tons/quad	
Syncrude (oil shale, tar sands)	25×10^9 bbl	181×10^6 bbl/quad	

c. The third column lists the conversion factor. This allows you to change the customary units to a common energy unit, the quad (Q).

d. The last column shows how much energy, in quads, can be obtained from the reserve. The number of quads is obtained by dividing the reserve by the conversion factor.

Helpful Hint!

Eggs/eggs per day = days.

2. Complete the last column. The quads for crude oil are listed so you can check the process. The answer was rounded off to the nearest whole number.

Content Clue

Convert all data to a common unit.

Helpful Hint!

For help working with numbers written in scientific notation, refer to Appendix 4.

3. To understand the meaning of these numbers, you must estimate how much energy the United States will use between 2010 and 2030. Estimating a number like this is very risky. The crystal ball is foggy at best, and much can change in 20 years. However, projections are necessary for planning ahead. Make your estimates as follows:

a. Assume energy consumption in the United States will average approximately 100 Q/yr for the 20-yr span. Hence: U.S. requirement (2010–2030) = _____ Q.

b. In summary, list all the assumptions your estimate was based on.

4. Graph your various reserve and requirement estimates on a single bar graph, as follows:

a. Reproduce the bar graph in Figure 9.19 in your science notebook.

b. Extend the horizontal axis, in quads, out a little past your largest reserve number.

c. Assume that nuclear with breeder could provide 60 times more energy than conventional nuclear. (You will examine the details of the breeder option in the next chapter.)

QUESTIONS & TASKS

Record your responses in your science notebook.

1. Use your bar graph to explain why the United States imports so much crude oil.

2. Do you think conventional nuclear will become a big part of the U.S. energy future? Explain.

3. Why is there interest in the nuclear breeder option?

4. Why don't we have breeder reactors in the United States today? (Use your imagination. You will learn more about this later.)

5. Your graph should show that U.S. reserves of coal could provide huge amounts of energy. Give at least two reasons why we don't use more coal.

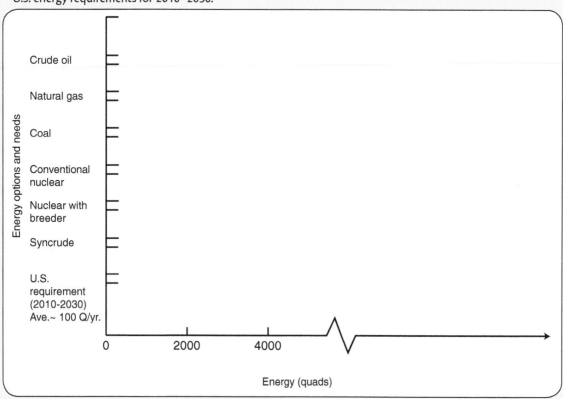

'Hydrocarbons! . . . Hydrocarbons! . . .

6. At present, the United States has not made any real commitment to synthetic fuels. Why might this be the case?

7. The cartoon in Figure 9.20 shows Uncle Sam (a symbol of the United States) crawling on a desert desperately crying out "Hydrocarbons! Hydrocarbons!" What is the cartoonist attempting to show?

How Long Will Our Reserves Last?

The lifetime of reserves is one of the most controversial issues in any debate over energy policy. This controversy is fueled by the wide range of answers that are given. The primary reason for the wide range of answers is the hidden assumptions behind them. We will examine these assumptions next.

9.7 The Static Lifetime

The lifetime of a resource depends on (1) how much we have and (2) how fast we use it. If we assume that the use rate doesn't change (that is, it remains static) and that no discoveries of the resource are made as we use it, it is easy to calculate its lifetime. We simply use this equation:

What variables determine the lifetime of a nonrenewable resource?

$$\text{reserve lifetime } (T_s) = \frac{\text{reserve}}{\text{constant use rate}}$$

Unfortunately, this method gives only a rough projection; no resource is consumed at a constant rate. A constant (static) use rate does not occur—especially over long periods of time. More important, the quantity of a resource classified as a reserve also changes over time because of new discoveries, economic conditions, and new technologies.

The static method for calculating the lifetime of a reserve can be shown on a graph (see Figure 9.21).

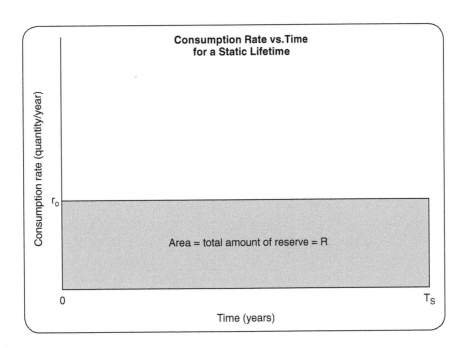

◀ FIGURE 9.21 Use rate vs. time for a nonrenewable resource that is consumed at a constant rate. Notice that the area of R (a rectangle) equals its length (time) times its width (use rate).

ACTIVITY 9.5

Calculating Resource Lifetimes

In this activity, you will solve a number of problems that will help you understand how to calculate resource lifetimes.

Problems

Record your responses in your science notebook.

1. A local grocery store has 300 16-oz (454 grams) cans of baked beans on the shelf. It has 300 more

Nonrenewable Resource Depletion 357

cans in a back storage area. On average, 75 cans of baked beans are sold each day.

a. At this consumption rate, how long will the store's supply of baked beans last?

b. After the lifetime you just calculated, will the store be out of baked beans, never to sell them again? If not, why not?

c. How is the baked bean problem *somewhat* like the U.S. situation for crude oil?

2. In 2006, proven reserves of crude oil in the United States were estimated to be 23 billion barrels. The United States produced 1,869 million barrels of crude oil that year. At this production rate, how long will the proven reserves last? (Both figures in this problem include Alaska.)

3. At the present time, the United States has a recoverable reserve of about 494 billion tons of coal. Current production of coal is about 1,133 million tons per year. Use these two facts to calculate how long U.S. reserves will last under current conditions.

4. World-known reserves of crude oil are estimated to be about 1,200 billion barrels. World oil production is about 29 billion barrels per year.

At this rate, how long should it take to use up the known reserves?

5. In addition to the 1,000 billion barrels of estimated known reserves, Earth probably contains 200–600 billion barrels of undiscovered crude oil. This range of numbers averages 400 billion barrels. If these barrels are discovered, how many years do they add to the lifetime supply of world oil? Assume the production rate remains at 29 billion barrels per year.

6. What are the major problems with the information you just calculated in problems 2–5? Which answer do you think is the most accurate? Why? Which answer do you think is the least accurate? Why?

> **Think about This!**
>
> Give serious thought to your answers. They are critical to your understanding of why we haven't "run out" of mineral and energy resources.

7. What is the value in doing these kinds of calculations? Explain.

> **Helpful Hint!**
>
> Remember, these calculations are based on reserves, not resources.

9.8 The Exponential Lifetime

Demand for energy can often increase rapidly. The energy problem is partially a problem of growth. Demand grows, but reserves are finite. In other words, the numerator in our static lifetime equation is in some ways fixed, but the denominator increases. To really understand the problem and to make realistic assessments of reserves lifetimes, we have to apply our knowledge of the mathematics of growth. We have to be able to deal with the exponential function. Think about the important properties of exponential growth that you examined in Chapter 5.

In real life, the rate of consumption may increase as time passes. This is the case with exponential growth. In these cases, the lifetime equation becomes

$$\text{lifetime } (T_e) = \frac{\text{reserve}}{\text{exponentially increasing consumption}}$$

You can use calculus to solve this equation, or you can use a graph to analyze the situation.

From Figure 9.22, we see that the consumption rate is growing exponentially. The area under the graph represents the total amount of the resource (R), and T_e is the exponential lifetime. However, this graph does not represent reality because no resource is consumed exponentially until the day it may run out.

> **Think about This!**
>
> Why doesn't this graph represent reality?

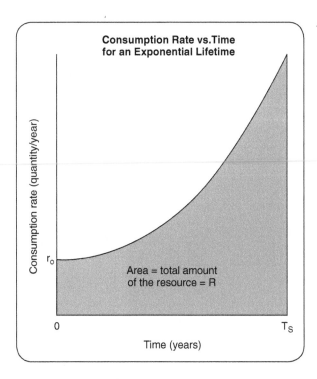

 QUESTIONS & TASKS

Record your responses in your science notebook.

1. In the real world, we don't consume resources at an ever-increasing rate until the day they may run out. Explain why.

2. Explain why resource lifetime estimates are useful but must be used with caution.

9.9 The Way Things Are

No resource is consumed at an ever-increasing rate until the day it is exhausted. Increasing rates of demand become harder and harder to fill as the resource becomes harder to find. This results in higher prices. Higher prices then lower demand.

Also, both the static and the exponential **lifetime calculations** assume that no resources will be discovered and become new reserves. In reality, both the known reserves and the use rates change depending on economics, technology, and world politics. There is some upper limit to the reserves since Earth (and each country) is finite. However, some reserves (like coal) are so enormous that calculating a lifetime is not a useful activity. In a practical sense, we will probably never completely use them up (see Figure 9.23).

Content Clue

Lifetimes in terms of the way things really are in the real world.

QUESTIONS & TASKS

Record your responses in your science notebook.

1. In terms of this chapter, what might the buffalo of Figure 9.23 represent?

2. Is this a proper analogy for our mineral resources? Explain why this cartoon may not relate to Earth's mineral situation.

▲FIGURE 9.23 "Buffalo shortage? What buffalo shortage? Just give me more money for scouts and guns, and I'll get you all the buffalo you need!" (*Stein '77—* Rocky Mountain News)

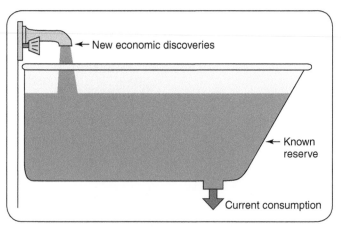

▲FIGURE 9.24 The real-world situation regarding reserves. New reserves are being discovered as known reserves are being depleted.

Why do resource lifetime calculations often give very different answers?

In addition, lifetime calculations are made more difficult by these uncertainties: Should we assume an increasing or a decreasing preference for a certain resource with time? Should you include only reserves in your calculation? Or, should you try to guess at the quantity of undiscovered resources and assume you will be able to afford to extract them? It is important to understand that the assumptions one starts with determine the lifetime one calculates.

The real-world situation regarding reserves is much like a bathtub that is being filled while the drain is left open (see Figure 9.24). The quantity of water in the tub at any given time represents the known reserve. The water coming in represents new economic discoveries. The water that is leaving represents our consumption.

In the early use of a resource, new discoveries are more significant than consumption. The reserve builds up. Eventually, the resource becomes harder to find and reserves are drawn down. The historical depletion pattern (Activity 9.2) examined at the beginning of this chapter holds true.

Content Clue

Environmental restrictions affect lifetimes.

Another factor that makes estimating lifetimes more difficult is government-imposed environmental restrictions. We are placing many areas off limits to resource extraction. Depending on your point of view, some of these rules are justified; others seem unjustified. Whatever the reason, the resources are not available.

The graphs in Figure 9.25 summarize the relationship between static lifetime (T_s), exponential lifetime (T_e), and real-world lifetime (T_{rw}) for a given reserve (R) of a resource.

Apply Your Understanding

Give three possible reasons why a resource depletion curve may peak and then drop.

From the information in this section and the data contained in Figures 9.12, 9.18, and 9.19, we can agree on one conclusion: No matter how lifetime is determined, both the United States and the world are using up crude oil reserves. However, the drop after the peak on a depletion curve can also occur because of improved efficiency of vehicles and/or a shift to substitute fuels. Both of these are becoming significant factors. Also, lack of supply of crude oil isn't the only reason we may choose to move to other fuels.

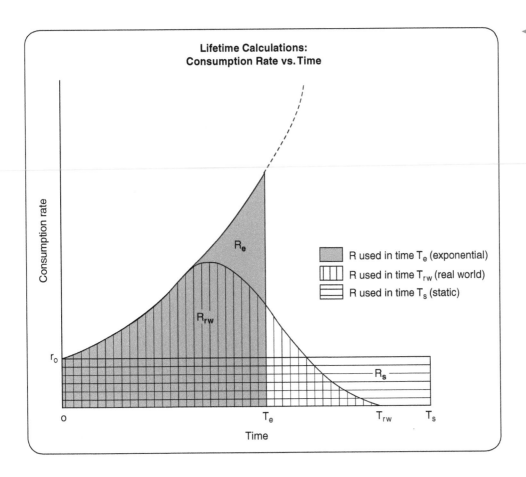

Lifetime Calculations:
Consumption Rate vs. Time

Consumption rate

R used in time T_e (exponential)
R used in time T_{rw} (real world)
R used in time T_s (static)

R_e

R_{rw}

r_0

R_s

0   T_e T_{rw} T_s

Time

We also have *renewable* energy resources. These we will call "continuous" resources. Greatest among these are the solar energy sources. In Chapter 11, we will look at continuous resources and assess the contributions they can make to our energy needs. We will then examine strategies for providing energy for the future.

Crude oil isn't our only energy option!

Reducing Problems Related to Resource Depletion

Problems related to the depletion of nonrenewable resources can be reduced by doing the following:

- Expand known resource reserves through continued exploration and improved ability to extract all the fuel.

- Improve the efficiency of machines (automobiles, power plants, and furnaces) that consume these resources.

- Improve the quality of technical devices (catalytic converters, scrubbers, and so on) that reduce the pollution related to the combustion of these fuels.

- Expand the use of renewable energy sources.

- Examine use patterns to eliminate wasteful consumption.

- Plant trees and conserve forests to tie up excess CO_2 emissions.

Think about This!

If the oil age is ending, what's next?

Summary

The data in this chapter indicate the oil age may be drawing to a close. It has been a unique age in the history of humans—an age of inexpensive, abundant energy and rapid growth in both technology and technology-related problems. As we move into the post-oil world, we are challenged to develop and use the sources, technologies, and attitudes that will carry us into the next phase of our journey.

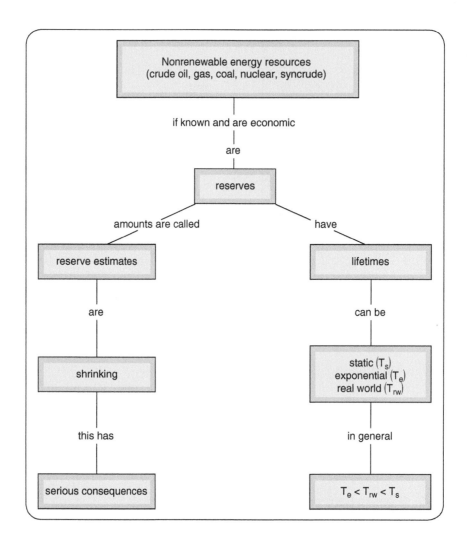

REFERENCES

American Petroleum Institute. *Basic Petroleum Data Book* (Washington, D.C.: American Petroleum Institute), biannual.

BP p.l.c. *B P Statistical Review of World Energy* (London: BP p.l.c.), annual.

Campbell, Colin J. and Jean H. Laherrere. The End of Cheap Oil. *Scientific American* 278, no. 3 (March, 1998): 78–83.

Deffeyes, Kenneth S. *Hubbert's Peak: The Impending World Oil Shortage* (Princeton, NJ: Princeton University Press), 2001.

Gerling, Peter, et al. *Brief Study: Reserves, Resources and Availability of Energy Resources 2004* (Hannover: Federal Institute for Geosciences and Natural Resources), 2004.

Goodstein, David. *Out of Gas: The End of the Age of Oil* (New York: W.W. Norton & Company), 2004.

Ivanhoe, L. F. Updated Hubbert Curves Analyze World Oil Supply. *World Oil* 217, no. 11 (November, 1996): 91–94.

McCabe, Peter J. Energy Resources: Cornucopia or Empty Barrel? *AAPG Bulletin* 82, no. 11 (November, 1998): 2110–2134.

Roberts, Paul. *The End of Oil: On the Edge of a Perilous New World* (Boston: Houghton Mifflin Co.), 2005.

U.S. Department of Energy. *Annual Energy Review* (Washington, D.C.: GPO), annual.

WEBSITES

U.S. Department of Energy: http://www.eia.doe.gov

BP Statistical Review of World Energy: www.bp.com/centres/energy

Compliments of Georgia Power Company

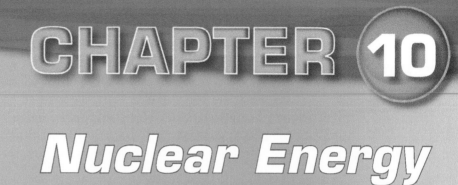

CHAPTER 10

Nuclear Energy

GOAL

• To examine the basic principles of nuclear energy and consider its potential as an energy option.

We nuclear people have made a Faustian bargain* with society. On the one hand, we offer an inexhaustible source of energy. But the price that we demand of society for this magical energy source is both a vigilance and a longevity of our social institutions that we are quite unaccustomed to.

—A. Weinberg, former director, Oak Ridge National Nuclear Laboratory, 1972

*According to legend, Faust was an old philosopher who sold his soul to the devil in exchange for knowledge and power.

The Concept of the Atom

To understand the basics of nuclear energy, it is best to start with the concept of the atom. Why do scientists believe atoms exist? How are atoms put together?

The belief that atoms exist developed over a long period of time—mostly during the last 200 years. No one has ever seen an atom. They are much too small. And because no one can see an atom, the evidence for them is indirect. No one experiment can prove there are atoms; our belief in their existence is based on many experiments. By doing Activity 10.1 carefully, however, you should understand why the concept that matter is made up of small building blocks is so useful.

ACTIVITY 10.1

Atoms and Molecules

In this activity, you will conduct an experiment to begin your investigation into the unseen world of atoms.

Materials

- demineralized water
- 2 iron nails
- small beaker containing a few copper sulfate crystals
- pennies (old and new)
- copper sulfate solution
- 2 beakers, 50-mL
- steel wool
- safety goggles
- disposable lab gloves

> ⚠ **WARNING**
>
> All the soluble compounds of copper are poisonous. Wash off any copper sulfate that comes in contact with your skin. Wear safety goggles.

Procedure

Day 1

1. Read steps 2–13 *before* you begin your experiment.

2. Form a lab group and obtain a group symbol to label your beakers.

3. Gather the materials, including 2 nails and 2 beakers. Label your beakers.

4. Place 35–40 milliliters (mL) of H_2O in one beaker.

5. Place 35–40 mL of copper sulfate ($CuSO_4$) solution in another beaker. The copper sulfate solution is made by dissolving copper sulfate crystals in water. Compare your beakers to those shown in Figure 10.1.

6. Examine the following items and record your observations in your science notebook. Then explain why it is important to record these beginning observations.

▶ FIGURE 10.1 Three beakers and their contents.

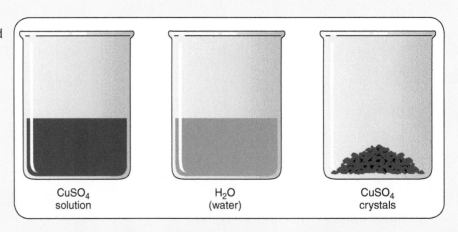

| $CuSO_4$ solution | H_2O (water) | $CuSO_4$ crystals |

a. Demineralized water

b. Copper sulfate (CuSO4) crystals

c. Copper sulfate solution

d. Iron (Fe) nail

7. In step 9, you will place a nail into the copper sulfate solution. *Before* you do this, complete steps a and b:

> **Helpful Hint!**
>
> An *atom* is a small piece of matter that is made of protons, neutrons, and electrons. It is a fundamental building block of nature. A *molecule* is a group of atoms bonded together in a particular way.

a. Review the definitions of *atom* and *molecule* in the hint box.

b. Guess (hypothesize) what will happen when you put the nail in $CuSO_4$.

8. Observe the differences between a new penny and an old penny. Record your descriptions in your science notebook.

9. *Read this step completely before you do it. Timing is critical.* Clean the nails by rubbing them with steel wool. Place 1 iron nail in the copper sulfate solution. Place the other in the demineralized water. Let the nails stand in the liquids for *2 seconds* (sec) and then remove and examine them. Do *not* clean the nails again. Repeat the process of immersing the nails and examining them two or more times. Then record your observations.

> **BE SAFE**
>
> Remember, be very careful not to get the copper sulfate on your hands. If you do, wash them off and dry.

10. Place the nails back into the solutions and let them stand overnight.

11. Now look at the periodic table in Figure 10.4. What does a periodic table show? Check the glossary and/or a reference in the library.

12. Record the names of the following substances:

> **Helpful Hint!**
>
> For help with step 12, see question 1 under Questions and Tasks and Figure 10.5.

a. Cu

b. S

c. O

d. Fe

13. Answer question 1 under Questions & Tasks.

14. Find out what happened in the beakers of the other lab groups. Are the results of this lab predictable and repeatable?

Day 2

1. Observe the 2 beakers that stood overnight. Note the color of the solutions as well as the color and quantity of new solids formed. Record your findings. You may assume the nail in the water rusted.

2. Remove the 2 nails; clean and dry them. Then feel them. Has iron left any of the nails? Now answer questions 2–4.

QUESTIONS & TASKS

Record your responses in your science notebook.

Before it is placed in the water, $CuSO_4$ = copper sulfate. The equation for the copper-iron reactions is

> **Helpful Hint!**
>
> The "+" sign separates different small particles. If a particle is charged (+ or −), it is called an *ion*. The (s) means a solid.

$$Cu^{+2}_{(blue)} + SO_4^{-2} + Fe_{(s)} \rightarrow Cu_{(s)} + Fe^{+2} + SO_4^{-2}$$

1. What elements make up copper sulfate? Use the periodic table (Figure 10.4) and the chart of element names (Figure 10.5) to identify the symbols.

2. Why is the copper sulfate solution blue? (See the equation for help.)

3. Why does the blue color leave the solution as time passes? (Again, study the equation.)

4. What happened to the nail in this experiment? Use the equation to help you with your explanation.

5. Was your hypothesis correct? Explain.

6. Can you use the equation to explain what happened? Record an explanation based on the equation.

7. How does copper change in this reaction?

8. Figure 10.2a represents an atomic explanation of what happened in this experiment. Figure 10.2b represents a nonscientific explanation that gives matter the qualities of life. Examine both drawings and the related explanations.

a. Which explanation do you prefer?

b. Why?

c. Why do scientists believe in small particles called atoms? (Use your lab results to help you answer this question.)

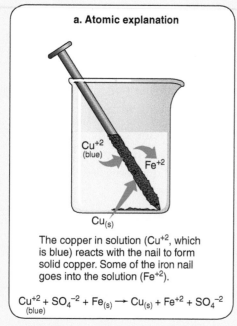

a. Atomic explanation

Cu^{+2}
(blue)

Fe^{+2}

$Cu_{(s)}$

The copper in solution (Cu^{+2}, which is blue) reacts with the nail to form solid copper. Some of the iron nail goes into the solution (Fe^{+2}).

$$Cu^{+2} + SO_4^{-2} + Fe_{(s)} \rightarrow Cu_{(s)} + Fe^{+2} + SO_4^{-2}$$
(blue)

b. Nonscientific explanation

When the nail is placed in the blue solution, the solution becomes angry and deposits brown material on the nail.

and

When a nail is placed in water, the nail breaks out with an orange rash.

▲ FIGURE 10.2 Two explanations of your lab results. (a) Atomic explanation—matter is made of small particles. (b) Nonscientific explanation—matter has living qualities.

 # Energy from Atoms

Since the beginnings of civilization, humans have made use of most forms of energy. Only nuclear energy is new to us. Science and technology had to develop to the point where nuclear events could be detected, understood, and controlled. Our understanding began in the early 1900s. The potential and danger of nuclear energy were brought to the world's attention with the atomic bomb explosion at Hiroshima in World War II. It wasn't until the 1960s, however, that nuclear energy began to make a real contribution to the energy mix.

Nuclear energy is potentially a huge source of energy that can help satisfy our increasing desire for electricity. Several features of nuclear energy make it attractive. It can lessen our dependence on fossil fuels. It does not cause easily seen pollution. It does not add to the "greenhouse" effect.

In this chapter, we will discuss how nuclear reactors work. We will also explain how breeder reactors make fuel as they operate. But first, we must understand some basic ideas about atoms and how they are put together.

Fundamental Particle	Symbol	Electric Charge	Relative Mass
Proton	p	Positive = (+ 1)	1
Neutron	n	Neutral = (0)	1
Electron	e	Negative = (−1)	1 / 1837 ≈ 0

◄ FIGURE 10.3 Basic properties of protons, neutrons, and electrons.

10.1 The Atomic Model

Today, scientists think that all matter is built of basic units called atoms. There are more than 100 kinds of atoms. The atoms of any particular kind make up an *element*. For example, one kind of atom makes up the element we call gold; another is silver. All of the known elements are listed on a chart called the **periodic table** (Figure 10.4).

Atoms themselves are believed to be made up of smaller units called protons, neutrons, and electrons. Scientists think that an atom is mostly empty space, and that almost all of its mass is concentrated at the center in a small, very dense, positively charged **nucleus**. Nuclear particles called **nucleons** are found in the nucleus. Nucleons are of two types: **protons** and **neutrons**. Protons are positively charged; neutrons are neutral. All nucleons have about the same mass. Moving around the nucleus are the **electrons**. Electrons, on a relative scale, have practically no mass. They have a negative charge. Under ordinary conditions, atoms are neutral because they have equal numbers of electrons and protons. Figure 10.3 summarizes the basic properties of protons, neutrons, and electrons.

The number of protons in a nucleus determines which element an atom is. The number is referred to as that atom's **atomic number**. The elements are listed on the periodic table by atomic number. The table starts with the simplest and lightest atoms first, and works up to the heavier, more complicated ones.

Scientists use symbols to summarize what we have just covered. Study the diagrams in Figure 10.6 and the periodic table carefully. Also, study the three definitions that follow. Relate them to the symbols in Figure 10.6. It is important that you understand what the number and letter symbols mean. They are the keys to understanding much of what we will learn as we survey the nuclear energy option.

Atomic number: The number of protons in an atom's nucleus.

Mass number: The number of nucleons (protons and neutrons) in an atom's nucleus.

Isotopes: Atoms of the same element that differ in the number of neutrons they contain. Isotopes are named by their mass numbers. For example, U-235 is an isotope of uranium that has a mass number of 235. Another uranium isotope, U-238, has a mass number of 238.

What is an atom and how are atoms put together?

Helpful Hint!

Be sure you know these definitions.

Content Clue

Remember, atoms normally have the same number of protons and electrons, and are electrically neutral.

Periodic Table of the Elements

22
Ti
Titanium
47.87

— Atomic number
— Element symbol
— Element name
— Average atomic mass

Gases

Nonmetal solids and liquids

Metals

Transuranium elements

1																	2
H Hydrogen 1.0079																	**He** Helium 4.0026
3 **Li** Lithium 6.941	4 **Be** Beryllium 9.0122											5 **B** Boron 10.811	6 **C** Carbon 12.011	7 **N** Nitrogen 14.007	8 **O** Oxygen 15.999	9 **F** Flourine 18.998	10 **Ne** Neon 20.179
11 **Na** Sodium 22.990	12 **Mg** Magnesium 24.305											13 **Al** Aluminum 26.982	14 **Si** Silicon 28.086	15 **P** Phosphorus 30.974	16 **S** Sulfur 32.066	17 **Cl** Chlorine 35.453	18 **Ar** Argon 39.948
19 **K** Potassium 39.098	20 **Ca** Calcium 40.08	21 **Sc** Scandium 44.956	22 **Ti** Titanium 47.87	23 **V** Vanadium 50.941	24 **Cr** Chromium 51.996	25 **Mn** Manganese 54.938	26 **Fe** Iron 55.847	27 **Co** Cobalt 58.933	28 **Ni** Nickel 58.71	29 **Cu** Copper 63.546	30 **Zn** Zinc 65.38	31 **Ga** Gallium 69.72	32 **Ge** Germanium 72.59	33 **As** Arsenic 74.922	34 **Se** Selenium 78.96	35 **Br** Bromine 79.904	36 **Kr** Krypton 83.80
37 **Rb** Rubidium 85.468	38 **Sr** Strontium 87.62	39 **Y** Yttrium 88.906	40 **Zr** Zirconium 91.224	41 **Nb** Niobium 92.906	42 **Mo** Molybdenum 95.94	43 **Tc** Technetium (97)	44 **Ru** Ruthenium 101.07	45 **Rh** Rhodium 102.91	46 **Pd** Palladium 106.4	47 **Ag** Silver 107.87	48 **Cd** Cadmium 112.41	49 **In** Indium 114.82	50 **Sn** Tin 118.69	51 **Sb** Antimony 121.76	52 **Te** Tellurium 127.60	53 **I** Iodine 126.90	54 **Xe** Xenon 131.30
55 **Cs** Cesium 132.91	56 **Ba** Barium 137.33	57-71 **La•** Series	72 **Hf** Hafnium 178.49	73 **Ta** Tantalum 180.95	74 **W** Tungsten 183.85	75 **Re** Rhenium 186.21	76 **Os** Osmium 190.2	77 **Ir** Iridium 192.22	78 **Pt** Platinum 195.09	79 **Au** Gold 196.97	80 **Hg** Mercury 200.59	81 **Tl** Thallium 204.37	82 **Pb** Lead 207.2	83 **Bi** Bismuth 208.98	84 **Po** Polonium (209)	85 **At** Astatine (210)	86 **Rn** Radon (222)
87 **Fr** Francium (223)	88 **Ra** Radium (226)	89-103 **Ac*** Series	104 **Rf** Rutherfordium (261)	105 **Db** Dubnium (262)	106 **Sg** Seaborgium (263)	107 **Bh** Bohrium (264)	108 **Hs** Hassium (265)	109 **Mt** Meitnerium (266)	110 **Ds** Darmstadtium (281)	111 **Rg** Roentgenium (280)	112						

•**Lanthanide** Series

57 **La** Lanthanum 138.91	58 **Ce** Cerium 140.12	59 **Pr** Praseodymium 140.12	60 **Nd** Neodymium 144.24	61 **Pm** Promethium (145)	62 **Sm** Samarium 150.4	63 **Eu** Europium 151.96	64 **Gd** Gadolinium 157.25	65 **Tb** Terbium 158.93	66 **Dy** Dysprosium 162.50	67 **Ho** Holmium 164.93	68 **Er** Erbium 167.26	69 **Tm** Thulium 168.93	70 **Yb** Ytterbium 173.04	71 **Lu** Lutetium 174.97
89 **Ac** Actinium (227)	90 **Th** Thorium 232.04	91 **Pa** Protactinium 231.04	92 **U** Uranium 238.03	93 **Np** Neptunium (237)	94 **Pu** Plutonium (244)	95 **Am** Americium (243)	96 **Cm** Curium (247)	97 **Bk** Berkelium (247)	98 **Cf** Californium (251)	99 **Es** Einsteinium (254)	100 **Fm** Fermium (257)	101 **Md** Mendelevium (258)	102 **No** Nobelium (259)	103 **Lr** Lawrencium (260)

***Actinide** Series

▲ **FIGURE 10.4** Periodic table of the elements.

Element	Symbol	Element	Symbol	Element	Symbol	Element	Symbol
Actinium	Ac	Erbium	Er	Mercury	Hg	Samarium	Sm
Aluminum	Al	Europium	Eu	Molybdenum	Mo	Scandium	Sc
Americium	Am	Fermium	Fm	Neodymium	Nd	Seaborgium	Sg
Antimony	Sb	Fluorine	F	Neon	Ne	Selenium	Se
Argon	Ar	Francium	Fr	Neptunium	Np	Silicon	Si
Arsenic	As	Gadolinium	Gd	Nickel	Ni	Silver	Ag
Astatine	At	Gallium	Ga	Niobium	Nb	Sodium	Na
Barium	Ba	Germanium	Ge	(Columbium)		Strontium	Sr
Berkelium	Bk	Gold	Au	Nitrogen	N	Sulfur	S
Beryllium	Be	Hafnium	Hf	Nobelium	No	Tantalum	Ta
Bismuth	Bi	Hassium	Hs	Osmium	Os	Technetium	Tc
Bohrium	Bh	Helium	He	Oxygen	O	Tellurium	Te
Boron	B	Holmium	Ho	Palladium	Pd	Terbium	Tb
Bromine	Br	Hydrogen	H	Phosphorus	P	Thallium	Tl
Cadmium	Cd	Indium	In	Platinum	Pt	Thorium	Th
Calcium	Ca	Iodine	I	Plutonium	Pu	Thulium	Tm
Californium	Cf	Iridium	Ir	Polonium	Po	Tin	Sn
Carbon	C	Iron	Fe	Potassium	K	Titanium	Ti
Cerium	Ce	Krypton	Kr	Praseodymium	Pr	Tungsten	W
Cesium	Cs	Lanthanum	La	Promethium	Pm	(Wolfrum)	
Chlorine	Cl	Lawrencium	Lr	Protactinium	Pa	Uranium	U
Chromium	Cr	Lead	Pb	Radium	Ra	Vanadium	V
Cobalt	Co	Lithium	Li	Radon	Rn	Xenon	Xe
Copper	Cu	Lutetium	Lu	Rhenium	Re	Ytterbium	Y
Curium	Cm	Magnesium	Mg	Rhodium	Rh	Yttrium	Y
Darmstadium	Ds	Manganese	Mn	Roentgenium	Rg	Zinc	Zn
Dubnium	Db	Meitnerium	Mt	Rubidium	Rb	Zirconium	Zr
Dysprosium	Dy	Mendelevium	Md	Ruthenium	Ru		
Einsteinium	Es			Rutherfordium	Rf		

▲ FIGURE 10.5 Alphabetical list of elements and symbols.

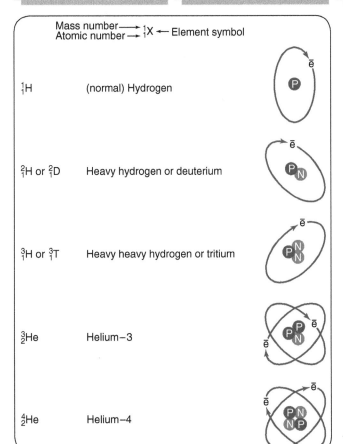

Mass number ⟶ ^1_1X ⟵ Element symbol
Atomic number ⟶

^1_1H — (normal) Hydrogen

^2_1H or ^2_1D — Heavy hydrogen or deuterium

^3_1H or ^3_1T — Heavy heavy hydrogen or tritium

^3_2He — Helium–3

^4_2He — Helium–4

◄ FIGURE 10.6 Element symbols.

ACTIVITY 10.2

Working with Atomic Symbols

In this activity, you will fill in missing information in a chart about elements. This will help you become more familiar with atomic symbols.

Materials

- *Working with Atomic Symbols* handout

Procedure

1. Shown below is a chart of atomic symbols. The first row of the chart is complete. The boxes in the remaining rows have blanks.

2. Fill in the blanks with names, numbers, or symbols using the definitions provided in section 10.1: The Atomic Model, and the information in Figures 10.4 and 10.5. DO NOT WRITE IN YOUR BOOK. Your teacher will provide a handout of this chart.

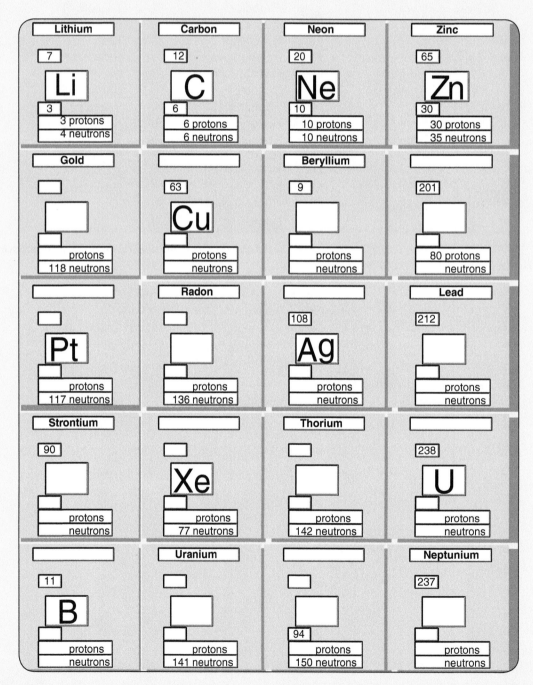

10.2 Radioactivity

Radioactivity is both a sign and a measure of the instability of certain atoms.

—E. Rutherford, physicist

Helpful Hint!

Radiation is energy in the form of moving particles or waves.

The nuclei of most atoms are very stable. They are put together in such a way that they never change. However, some nuclei are unstable and emit **radiation** to gain stability. These nuclei are said to be *radioactive*. The reasons for instability vary. Some nuclei have a neutron-to-proton ratio that is too high or too low. Some nuclei are in an excited state, while others are just too heavy for stability. To remedy instability, nuclei decay. Since the conditions of instability differ, the ways nuclei decay also differ. The three most common ways are as follows:

1. α–particle emission

2. β–particle emission

3. γ–ray emission

Helpful Hint!

The symbols α, β, and γ stand for *alpha, beta,* and *gamma,* the first three letters of the Greek alphabet.

Alpha particles ($^4_2$He) are the nuclei of fast-moving helium atoms. They are easily absorbed by thin sheets of paper or a few centimeters of air.

Beta particles ($^{\ 0}_{-1}\beta$) are fast-moving electrons. They can penetrate a few millimeters of aluminum or about 100 centimeters (cm) of air. The mass of an electron is so small that compared to other nucleons, it is 0. With no proton to balance the electron, it has a charge of -1.

Know what α, β, and γ radiations are.

Gamma rays (γ) are electromagnetic radiations of very high frequencies. They have an indeterminate range in matter. On average, they can penetrate long distances through air or several centimeters through lead. Figure 10.7 summarizes some of the properties of radiation.

Content Clue

You can observe the effects of alpha and beta radiation if you do Activity 10.3, Observations in a Cloud Chamber.

When an alpha or a beta particle is emitted by a nucleus, the atom becomes a new element. What it becomes can be determined by the rules in Activity 10.4, Writing Nuclear Equations. You must understand this information. It is crucial to an understanding of nuclear science.

In a sample of radioactive material, the unstable nuclei do not all decay at the same time. Instead, decay is a random event. However, since most radioactive samples contain literally billions of radioactive nuclei, the average rate of decay is "smooth." The amount of time it takes half of the unstable nuclei of a sample to decay into more stable nuclei is called the **half-life**. Each kind of radioactive element has a unique half-life. The half-life can serve as a "fingerprint" for identifying a radioactive material.

What do we mean by half-life?

	Charge	Rest Mass	Description	Speed (% speed of light)	Range in Air	Method of Interacting with Matter	Effective Shielding Materials
α	+2	4	Nucleus of helium atom $^4_2$He or $^4_2\alpha$	3–8	Few inches	Ionizing collisions	Paper, dead skin
β	-1	$\frac{1}{1837}$	High-speed electron, $^{\ 0}_{-1}\beta$	20–99	Several feet	Ionizing collisions	Plastic, glass, aluminum
γ	0	0	High-energy radiation	100	Indefinite	Discrete interactions; only direct hits or nearly direct hits	Lead, concrete, water

▲ FIGURE 10.7 Some properties of α, β, and γ radiation.

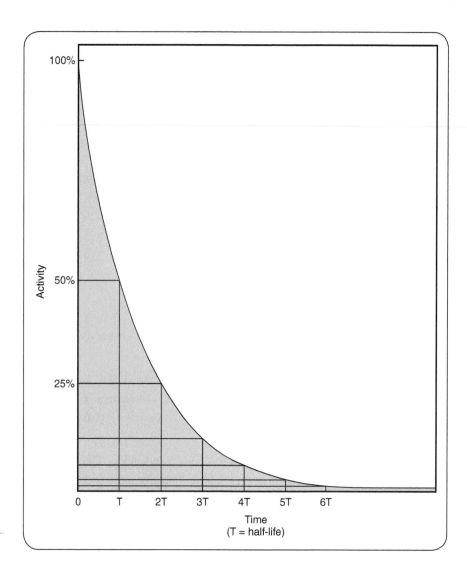

Think about This!

Spent fuel rods from
nuclear power plants
lose about half their
radioactivity in 3 months
and about 80 percent after
1 year of storage. However,
the spent fuel is still
radioactive for thousands
of years.

A typical radiation intensity vs. time curve is shown in Figure 10.8. From this, you can see
that although the half-life for a given radioactive material is a specific amount of time, a
radioactive sample theoretically never completely decays. "Half" is always left. Some half-
lives are only small fractions of a second; others are hundreds to billions of years.

ACTIVITY 10.3

Observations in a Cloud Chamber

In this activity, you will observe evidence of nuclear radiation. You will also observe evidence of
probable background (cosmic) radiation.

Background

A **cloud chamber** is a device for observing evidence of nuclear radiation. The cloud chamber you
will be using is called a diffusion cloud chamber. It
consists of a container with clear sides, a clear lid,

and a dark base. The container rests on dry ice. The
cover at the top remains at room temperature. The
temperature difference between the top and bottom
of the chamber is about 150F° (65C°) or more (dry
ice = −109°F or −78.5°C).

Under these conditions, the alcohol vapor in the
chamber forms a very dense (supersaturated) layer.
Alpha and beta particles and certain cosmic rays
strongly ionize (charge) the materials through which
they pass. This means that when they enter the

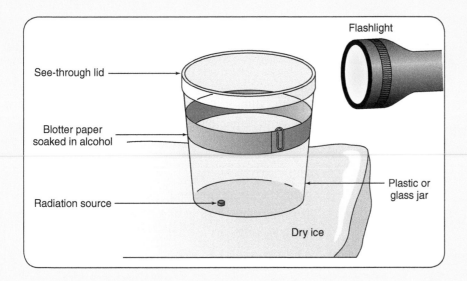

Flashlight

See-through lid

Blotter paper soaked in alcohol

Radiation source

Plastic or glass jar

Dry ice

dense alcohol layer, they create hundreds of ion pairs (electron + alcohol or air molecule with electron removed). These charged particles serve as condensation nuclei. Neutral alcohol molecules are attracted to them, forming small droplets that are visible. The result is a thin trail much like the "vapor trail" that forms behind a high-flying jet plane. When an intense light beam (a good flashlight works fine) is projected into the chamber, the tracks become easy to observe.

Materials

- cloud chamber (with radioactive source)
- methyl alcohol
- dry ice slab
- flashlight
- several rags
- thick gloves or tongs
- tweezers (optional)

Procedure

1. Examine your cloud chamber and note the blotter ring. Soak (saturate) the blotter ring liberally in alcohol (methyl or ethyl alcohol).

2. Place the chamber on top of a surface of dry ice, and level it using some of the rags provided. Also, cover exposed portions of the dry ice with rags. This will speed up the cooling of your chamber and slow the subliming (changing directly from a solid to a gas) of the dry ice.

3. Place the radioactive source into the chamber. Replace the lid.

4. Using a swirling motion, rub the top of the chamber for a few seconds with a dry rag. This creates a static charge on the top of the chamber and drives unwanted charged particles from the chamber volume.

5. Darken the classroom, and shine a bright light (such as a good flashlight) into the chamber volume. Tracks should appear in less than 5 minutes (min). If the tracks become fuzzy and indistinct, rub the top of the chamber with the dry cloth again. This should sharpen their appearance.

6. Carefully view the inside of the chamber. List as many different observations as you can in 20 minutes (see steps 6a–e). You are not required to interpret what you see at this time.

   a. intervals (regular or random)

   b. appearance

   c. direction

   d. length

   e. anything else you observe

7. Remove the radioactive sample with gloves or tweezers. See if you can observe any tracks in its absence. If you do, why might these be there?

8. Draw a circle about 3 inches (in) in diameter (about 8 cm) in your science notebook. In it, sketch some of the things you saw in the cloud chamber.

Writing Nuclear Equations

In this activity, you will learn and apply the rules for writing nuclear equations.

Background

Model: $\begin{array}{c}\text{Mass number}\\ \quad\quad X \longleftarrow \textit{Chemical symbol}\\ \text{Atomic number}\end{array}$

The rules for writing the nuclear equations you will be studying are as follows:

1. When a nucleus emits an α particle, the mass number decreases by 4 and the atomic number decreases by 2.

   ex. $^{232}_{90}\text{Th} \longrightarrow {}^{228}_{88}\text{Ra} + {}^{4}_{2}\alpha$

2. When a nucleus emits a β particle, the mass number doesn't change; however, the atomic number increases by 1.

   ex. $^{228}_{88}\text{Ra} \longrightarrow {}^{228}_{89}\text{Ac} + {}^{0}_{-1}\beta$

3. When a nucleus emits a gamma ray, both the atomic number and the mass number remain unchanged.

   ex. $^{113m}_{49}\text{In} \longrightarrow {}^{113}_{49}\text{In} + {}^{0}_{0}\gamma$, m = metastable

4. When a nucleus absorbs a neutron, the mass number increases by 1 and the atomic number remains unchanged.

   ex. $^{238}_{92}\text{U} + {}^{1}_{0}\text{n} \longrightarrow {}^{239}_{92}\text{U}$

5. In all nuclear reactions, the sum of the mass numbers on the left side of the equation equals the sum of the mass numbers on the right side of the equation. The same is true for the atomic numbers.

Procedure

With these rules in mind, and with the help of your periodic table (Figure 10.4), complete the following nuclear equations in your science notebook.

1. $^{222}_{86}\text{Rn} \longrightarrow \underline{} + {}^{4}_{2}\alpha$

2. $^{214}_{82}\text{Pb} \longrightarrow \underline{} + {}^{0}_{-1}\beta$

3. $^{9}_{4}\text{Be} + {}^{4}_{2}\alpha \longrightarrow \underline{} + {}^{1}_{0}\text{n}$

4. $^{235}_{92}\text{U} + {}^{1}_{0}\text{n} \longrightarrow {}^{138}_{56}\text{Ba} + \underline{} + 3{}^{1}_{0}\text{n}$

5. $^{14}_{7}\text{N} + {}^{4}_{2}\alpha \longrightarrow {}^{18}_{9}\text{F} \longrightarrow \underline{} + {}^{1}_{1}\text{H}$

6. $^{241}_{95}\text{Am} \longrightarrow \underline{} + {}^{4}_{2}\alpha$

7. $^{27}\text{Al} \longrightarrow \underline{} + {}^{4}_{2}\alpha$

8. $^{144}_{58}\text{Ce} \longrightarrow \underline{} + {}^{0}_{-1}\beta$

9. $^{209}\text{Pb} \longrightarrow \underline{} + {}^{0}_{-1}\beta$

10. $^{27}\text{Al} + {}^{1}_{1}\text{H} \longrightarrow {}^{28}_{14}\text{Si} + \underline{}$

11. $^{239}_{94}\text{Pu} + {}^{1}_{0}\text{n} \longrightarrow \underline{} + {}^{144}_{58}\text{Ce} + 2{}^{1}_{0}\text{n}$

12. $^{235}_{92}\text{U} + {}^{1}_{0}\text{n} \longrightarrow {}^{99}_{42}\text{Mo} + \underline{} + 2{}^{1}_{0}\text{n}$

13. $^{23}\text{Na} + {}^{1}_{1}\text{H} \longrightarrow {}^{23}_{12}\text{Mg} + \underline{}$

14. $^{55}_{26}\text{Fr} + {}^{0}_{-1}\beta \longrightarrow \underline{}$

15. $^{68}_{30}\text{Zn} + {}^{1}_{0}\text{n} \longrightarrow \underline{} + {}^{4}_{2}\alpha$

Investigating Half-Life

In this activity, you will determine the half-life of a simulated radioactive sample and relate this information to the problem of radioactive waste disposal.

Background

Radioactive nuclei are unstable. To become more stable, they spontaneously emit radiation. The emission of radiation is a random event.

As time goes by, a given radioactive sample emits less and less radiation. This is because radioactive material decays into more stable material. The amount of time required for a radioactive sample to decay to half its present activity is called the half-life. During the second half-life, the sample decays to one-fourth the starting activity, and so on. The lifetime of the sample is theoretically infinite. But as time elapses, the activity becomes less and less. The half-life is also the amount of time it takes for half of the radioactive atoms (of a particular type) to become more stable atoms.

Each kind of radioactive nuclei has a unique half-life. Some half-lives are only small fractions of a second; others are for hundreds or thousands of years. Because nuclear radiations can cause physical and structural damage, and because some radioactive materials last so long, the storage of long-lived **radioactive wastes** is both a difficult and serious problem.

Materials

- "radioactive sample" (plastic box)
- dice
- graph paper
- semi-log paper

Procedure

1. The plastic box you have been given represents a radioactive sample. The dice inside represent radioactive atoms. Each atom can gain stability in 1 step by becoming a six when rolled.

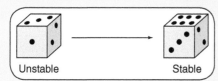

Unstable → Stable

2. Reproduce the table in Figure 10.9 in your science notebook. Number the first column, Elapsed Time, from 0 to 20.

3. Count the number of radioactive atoms in your sample. Record that number at time T = 0 on the data table.

4. Place all the atoms (dice) into the plastic box, and attach the lid. Then briefly shake and dump the atoms onto a tabletop. Each throw of the dice represents 1 unit of time.

5. Count the number of 6s that occur. Record this as the number of decays for T = 1.

6. Subtract the number of decays from the number of radioactive atoms in the container before you shook it. Record this number as the number of radioactive atoms remaining.

7. Remove the 6s from the rest of the dice and place them off to the side. They are now stable and won't change. Place the others back into the container.

8. Shake the remaining radioactive atoms and dump them out again. Repeat steps 5–8. Continue this procedure until the table is filled in.

QUESTIONS & TASKS

Record your responses in your science notebook.

1. Plot the following graphs. Draw the best line or smooth curve through the points you plot. (You are averaging the values plotted, not connecting all the plotted points.)

   a. number of radioactive atoms vs. elapsed time (on ordinary graph paper)

   b. number of radioactive atoms vs. elapsed time (on semi-log paper)

2. What is the half-life of your radioactive sample (number of throws)?

3. Why is the lifetime of a radioactive sample not a meaningful concept?

> **Helpful Hint!**
>
> See the background information for help in answering question 3.

4. Before the spent (used) fuel rods are removed from a nuclear reactor site, they are placed in a deep pool of water and kept underwater for a minimum of several months. Why is this done?

▶ FIGURE 10.9 Sample table for half-life simulation.

Data		
Elapsed Time	Number of Radioactive Atoms	Number of Decays
0		—
1		
2		
3		
20		

10.3 Sources of Nuclear Energy

Nuclear energy is the energy released by a nuclear reaction (fission or fusion), or by radioactive decay.

Nuclear energy is the energy released by a nuclear reaction or by radioactive decay. This energy depends on changes in the nuclear particles.

Any nucleus consists of a certain number of protons and neutrons. Therefore, you would expect that the total weight of the nucleus could be predicted by adding together the individual weights of the particles in it. In the case of nuclear weights, however, the whole is not equal to the sum of the parts! All nuclei (except hydrogen) weigh less than would be expected from the number of particles in them (see Figure 10.10). In fact, the weight per particle depends on the number of particles, as shown in Figure 10.11.

The weight of the protons and neutrons in a nucleus depends on which nucleus they are in. The curve in Figure 10.11 shows that if light nuclei (atoms near the beginning of the periodic table) could be combined to make a somewhat heavier nucleus (that is, nearer the middle of the periodic table), the nucleus would weigh less than the sum of the original nuclei. It is also clear that if a very heavy nucleus could be separated into parts that fell near the middle of the table, the sum of the product weights would be less than the original (Figure 10.11).

In both types of nuclear reactions just described, a small amount of matter would actually vanish. Einstein's special theory of relativity accounts for the vanished matter by saying that it would reappear as an incredibly large amount of energy.

The energy released is shown by the equation $E = mc^2$. E represents energy, m represents the "vanished" mass, and c is the speed of light. The amount of energy released in the splitting (fission) of one uranium nucleus is not large; however, there are billions and billions of nuclei in a pound of uranium. One pound of uranium-235 has the energy equivalence of 1,500 tons of coal. Figure 10.12 shows the equivalence for plutonium.

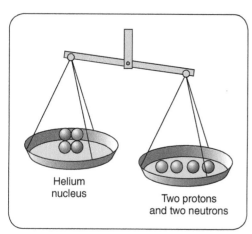

▲ FIGURE 10.10 A helium nucleus weighs less than the sum of the individual weights of the particles that make it up. *(USDOE)*

Helium nucleus

Two protons and two neutrons

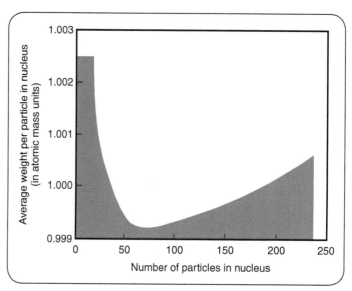

▲ FIGURE 10.11 Number of particles in a nucleus. The weight per nucleon varies with the number of particles in the nucleus in a significant way. *(USDOE)*

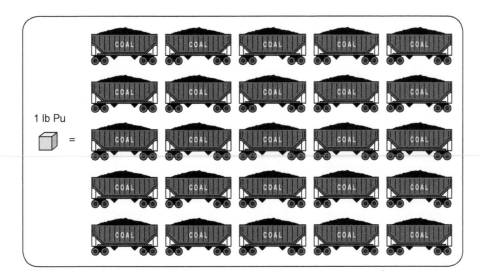

The two types of nuclear reactions are called fission and fusion. *Fission* is the splitting of a heavy nucleus into two approximately equal **fission fragments** (which are nuclei of lighter elements). This is always accompanied by the release of a relatively large amount of energy. It is also generally accompanied by the loss of one or more neutrons. Fission can occur spontaneously. However, it usually is caused by nuclear absorption of gamma rays, neutrons, or other particles (see Figure 10.13). *Fusion* is the combining of two lighter nuclei (such as hydrogen isotopes) to form a heavier nucleus. This action releases energy (as in a hydrogen bomb).

What is the difference between fission and fusion?

10.4 Fissionable Isotopes

The only naturally occurring **fissionable isotope** is U-235. There are two humanmade fissionable isotopes of interest: Pu-239 and U-233. Pu-239 can be made from U-238; U-233 can be made from Th-232. These two reactions are diagrammed here:

$$^{238}_{92}U + {}^{1}_{0}n \longrightarrow {}^{239}_{92}U \xrightarrow[2.35m]{\beta^-} {}^{239}_{93}Np \xrightarrow[2.35d]{\beta^-} {}^{239}_{94}Pu \ (\text{h.1.} = 24,360 \text{ yrs})$$

$$^{232}_{90}Th + {}^{1}_{0}n \longrightarrow {}^{233}_{90}Th \xrightarrow[23m]{\beta^-} {}^{233}_{91}Pa \xrightarrow[27d]{\beta^-} {}^{233}_{92}U \ (\text{h.1.} = 163,000 \text{ yrs})$$

Some typical fission reactions are

$$^{235}_{92}U + {}^{1}_{0}n \longrightarrow {}^{138}_{56}Ba + {}^{95}_{36}Kr + 3{}^{1}_{0}n + \text{energy}!$$

$$^{239}_{94}Pu + {}^{1}_{0}n \longrightarrow {}^{90}_{38}Sr + {}^{147}_{56}Ba + 3{}^{1}_{0}n + \text{energy}!$$

Helpful Hint!

Pu is the symbol for **plutonium**.

Helpful Hint!

In these two reactions, m = minutes and d = days.

Apply Your Understanding

What are the three fissionable fuels and how are they obtained?

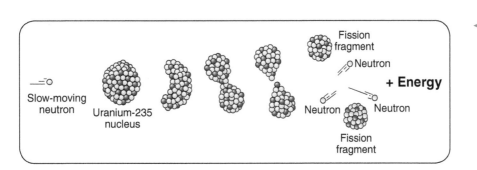

◀ FIGURE 10.13 A typical fission reaction.

Slow-moving neutron — Uranium-235 nucleus — Fission fragment — Neutron — **+ Energy** — Neutron — Neutron — Fission fragment

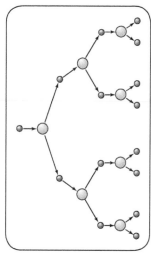

▲FIGURE 10.14 Nuclear fission of uranium. A neutron hits the nucleus of an atom of uranium. The neutron splits the nucleus in two parts and creates energy. At the same time, other neutrons are released from the splitting nucleus. These continue the fission process in a chain reaction. (USGS)

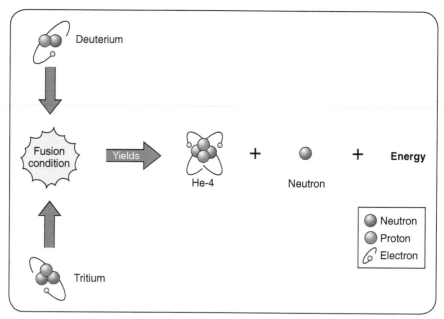

▲FIGURE 10.15 Nuclear fusion.

Uranium and **thorium** are the sources of our fission-energy fuels. The uranium atoms in natural uranium (as it is taken from the ground) are approximately 99.3 percent U-238 and 0.7 percent U-235. The thorium atoms in natural thorium are all Th-232. It is important to note that in its initial stages, the fission process is solely dependent on the isotope U-235.

There are two reasons that U-233, U-235, and Pu-239 are fissionable fuels. First, when bombarded with neutrons, they split into lighter elements, releasing huge amounts of energy. Second, when they split, they release more than one neutron, making possible a **chain reaction**. Use Figures 10.13 and 10.14 to help you describe what happens in a chain reaction.

10.5 Fusion Fuels

Fusion involves the combination of light nuclei to produce heavier nuclei and large amounts of energy. The light nuclei used for fusion are two isotopes of hydrogen (**deuterium** and **tritium**) and lithium 6. Figure 10.15 shows nuclear fusion.

Deuterium is found in all water. Therefore, the enormous amount of water available on Earth represents a huge potential source of energy. Tritium, however, is a different story. Tritium is made from lithium, and lithium ore is scarce. Lithium 6, required for fusion, is only 7.4 percent of natural lithium. The scarcity of lithium could mean that the total amount of energy that might be realized from fusion on Earth might be no more than what could be obtained from the combustion of the world's fossil fuels.

 Using Nuclear Fuels

Wood and coal require little preparation for use as fuels. Even petroleum products are much like the crude oil from which they were refined. Uranium ore, however, must pass through several steps before becoming nuclear fuel. Also, the disposal of nuclear waste is much more difficult than the disposal of waste from fossil fuels.

Simulating a Radioactive Decay Chain

In this activity, you will simulate a three-member radioactive decay chain. The knowledge you gain will help you understand some of the current problems related to the use of nuclear power.

Background

Uranium-235, uranium-238, and thorium-232 all decay in a series of steps to stable isotopes of lead. This series of steps is called a decay chain. The beginning member of a decay chain is called the parent atom. U-235, U-238, and Th-232 are all parent atoms. The parents decay into a series of daughter products until a stable end product is formed. A lack of understanding the decay process and the health effects of not properly managing radioactive wastes caused problems resulting from the mining and milling of our uranium reserves.

Materials (for each lab group)

- 100 dice (six-sided)
- 75 dice (20-sided)
- 100 marbles
- 3 to 6 plastic containers
- graph paper

Procedure

1. Reproduce the table in Figure 10.16 in your science notebook. Number the first column, Throw Number, from 0 to 30.

2. Place 100 ordinary dice into a container. The dice represent parent atoms.

3. Shake the container and dump the dice out onto a large table. Remove and record all the 1s that occur. They represent parent atoms that have decayed.

4. The parent atom decays into a daughter product. In this simulation, the daughter product is a 20-sided geometric figure called a bead. Replace each 1 with a bead.

5. Place all the "surviving" ordinary dice back into the container along with the beads. Shake the container and pour the contents out onto the table.

6. Remove all the beads that have a 10 or 20 on the top side. For each bead removed, add a marble. The marble represents the stable end product.

7. Remove all ordinary dice that have the 1 side up. For each 1 that is removed, add a new bead.

8. Keep a record of what happens on each throw by filling in the table as you proceed.

▼FIGURE 10.16 Sample table for radioactive decay chain simulation.

Data					
Throw Number	Number of Decayed Parents (N_1)	Number of Surviving Parents (N_2)	Number of Decayed Beads	Number of Beads Present after the Throw (growth − decays) (N_3)	Number of Marbles Present (N_4)
0	0	100*	—	—	—
1					
2					
3					
30					

*Because the number of major particles is conserved, $N_2 + N_3 + N_4 = 100$ after each throw.

9. Keep repeating this procedure until the number of beads has peaked and less than 20 beads remain.

QUESTIONS & TASKS

Record your responses in your science notebook.

Helpful Hint!

Be sure to label the different lines you plot on your graph.

1. Plot a graph of the number of surviving dice vs. number of throws for the ordinary dice. On the same graph, plot both the total number of beads present and the number of marbles present vs. number of throws.

2. Summarize what happened in this simulation.
  a. What does your graph show?
  b. How does this relate to radioactivity?

EXTENSIONS

Look up the U-235 and/or the U-238 decay series in a nuclear physics textbook. Record that information in your science notebook and use it to answer these questions:

1. Radon gas is an α-emitter. In the past, underground uranium miners had a higher incidence of lung cancer than the national average. (This conclusion comes from statistical evidence similar to the evidence that links smoking to lung cancer.) Why did these miners have a higher cancer rate?

2. At a uranium mill, the uranium in the ore is separated from the gangue, the worthless material. The first step in the milling operation involves crushing the ore. After crushing, several steps may be involved. The net result is that the uranium is concentrated, and the remaining material disposed of. This discarded material is called the tailings. If the uranium is efficiently removed, why are the tailings still radioactive?

3. In the 1950s, some uranium tailings were used as fill dirt for housing developments. Why wasn't this a good idea? What do you suppose the residents of those communities are doing about the problem?

ACTIVITY 10.7

Nuclear Fuel Cycle

The **nuclear fuel cycle** comprises all the steps involved in the use of nuclear material. The cycle starts with the removal of ore from the ground; it ends with the eventual disposal of related waste materials. In this activity, you will put the nine steps of the nuclear fuel cycle in sequential order.

Materials

- 11 × 17-inch paper
- scissors
- tape or glue
- colored pencils (optional)
- *Nuclear Fuel Cycle* handout

Procedure

1. Figure 10.17 contains boxes that illustrate the 9 steps of the cycle. Your teacher will provide a handout of this figure.

2. Using scissors, cut out these 9 steps, as well as the 9 descriptions below the drawings. Pair each drawing with its description, as explained in step 3.

3. Place the 9 drawing/description pairs on an 11 × 17-inch sheet of paper in a meaningful arrangement. Draw arrows to show how the 9 pairs relate. Use solid arrows to show connections that actually exist in the real world. Use dashed arrow lines to show connections that could exist, but don't at the present time in the United States. The descriptions give you clues.

Helpful Hint!

➤ Fuel cycle as it operates currently.

■ ■ ■➤ Fuel cycle as it would operate with spent fuel reprocessing and federal waste storage.

4. Tape or glue your cutout items to the paper. Put your name(s) in the upper left corner. Turn in your diagram.

Conversion	Federal final disposition	Milling
Interim storage	Enriching	Reactor
Fuel fabrication	Exploration Mining	Spent fuel reprocessing
Used fuel rods are temporarily stored underwater in an above-ground storage unit. This allows the short half-life radioactive wastes to decay. After several months, the rods become safer to handle. When removed, the used fuel rods can go to two possible places. At the present time, neither of these places exists in the United States.	Enriched U-235 is made into pellets and the pellets placed in fuel rods.	UF_6 molecules are forced through a porous barrier. U-235 is a little lighter than U-238. Therefore, the concentration of U-235 increases after several hundred barriers have been penetrated.
Used fuel rods are dissolved in acid. Uranium is removed and sent to enriching. Plutonium is removed and sent to fuel fabrication. The remaining wastes are placed in federal final disposition. At present, the United States has no operating final disposition.	Radioactive wastes remain dangerous for hundreds of years. They must not be allowed to enter the environment. They are to be placed in carefully designed and monitored permanent storage deep beneath the surface of Earth.	Exploration geologists search for and locate rich uranium deposits. Mining companies remove the uranium ore from the ground.
Uranium ore is crushed and concentrated as a product called yellowcake. What is left over after the uranium is removed is called the mill tailings.	Fuel rods are placed into the reactor core. Fission reactions in the core produce heat that boils water to make steam. The steam turns a turbine that turns a generator. Electricity is produced.	Yellowcake is changed into a gaseous uranium compound — uranium hexafluoride (UF_6).

10.6 The Nuclear Fuel Cycle—A Closer Look

In Activity 10.7, you examined the flow of the nuclear fuel cycle. You discovered that the cycle has a front end where fuel enters the cycle and a back end where wastes are parceled and stored. The nuclear power plant is located near the middle of the cycle. Since waste reprocessing and long-term storage don't exist at present in the United States, nothing is fed back to the front end. Thus, we have no cycle at all. The following paragraphs describe each step of the cycle.

Exploration and Mining

Most rocks contain small amounts of uranium. To be mined profitably, the uranium must be sufficiently concentrated. Uranium fuel production begins with a search for a deposit that is rich enough to mine. Even then, a lot of rock and dirt must be moved in the process (see Figure 10.18). Uranium is mined by open pit and various underground methods.

Milling

The crude uranium ore (U_3O_8) is crushed, sampled, and concentrated as a product called *yellowcake* (see Figure 10.19). When the uranium is removed, *mill tailing* is left over. Mill tailings contain some radioactive material. In the past, these leftovers piled up at the mine/mill site. Today, the wastes are recognized as a potential hazard. A government-sponsored program is underway to place them in designated sites for burial.

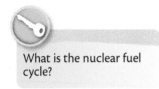

What is the nuclear fuel cycle?

SCIENCE at work

Apply Your Understanding

Why is uranium ore milled?

▶ FIGURE 10.18 An open-pit uranium mine in New Mexico. *(U.S. Bureau of Mines)*

SCiLINKS®
NSTA

Topic: nuclear fuel cycle
Go to: www.scilinks.org
Code: GloSci7e384

▶ FIGURE 10.19 Yellowcake. *(USDOE)*

Conversion and Enrichment

Most American nuclear reactors use *enriched* U-235 for fuel. In its natural state, only 0.7 percent of uranium is U-235. For nuclear fuel rods, this must be increased to 3 or 4 percent. (The concentration of bomb-grade material is at least 85 percent.)

Enrichment is a difficult, energy-consuming step. Since U-235 and U-238 are chemically identical, they must be separated by physical means. They differ in mass by only three parts in 235 (1.3 percent). Thus, there is little margin in which to work.

Gaseous diffusion is the most common enrichment technique. In a conversion plant, the yellowcake is converted to a gaseous uranium compound—uranium hexafluoride (UF_6). This gas is then passed through a porous barrier. The UF_6 molecule containing U-235 is slightly lighter than the one with U-238. Therefore, it moves a little faster and passes through the barrier more easily. Many such passages (there are hundred of barriers) build up the concentration of U-235.

Apply Your Understanding

Since U-235 and U-238 are chemically the same, how are they separated?

Gaseous diffusion is a complicated, expensive process. For less-developed countries, it is the most difficult step to carry out in using nuclear fuel.

Enrichment is also possible by newer techniques. One technique uses the ultracentrifuge. Centripetal force is used to separate the differing masses. Another technique is laser enrichment. Laser light selectively activates (excites) U-235 so that chemical separation can be performed. The perfection of one of these techniques could radically change today's "balance" of nuclear power among various nations.

Fuel Fabrication

The enriched gas is converted to the ceramic powder UO_2 (uranium oxide) or UC (uranium carbide). The powder is formed into pellets that are installed in fuel rods (see Figure 10.20).

Fuel Burning

Fuel rods are transported to the reactor and inserted into the reactor core. The present practice is to replace one-third of a reactor's fuel each year. Unlike fossil fuels, uranium fuel is

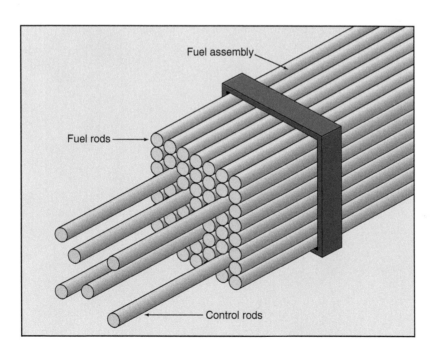

◄FIGURE 10.20 Fuel rods in the reactor core. *(USDOE)*

not totally consumed in ordinary reactors. Only about 1 percent of the total energy content of all the uranium in the original fuel is converted. The fuel rods need to be removed before all the U-235 is fissioned. This is because the buildup of fission products begins to interfere with the overall operation.

Spent Fuel Reprocessing

At this stage in the process, highly radioactive "fission products" have built up in the fuel rods. (These are radioactive wastes.) The fuel rods also contain unused U-235 and some Pu-239. The Pu-239 was produced as a result of neutron absorption by some of the U-238 in the fueled rods.

If the fuel were to be reprocessed, the first step would be to store the fuel rods underwater for several months to let the short-lived fission products decay (see Figure 10.21). Currently, this is the only step taken in reprocessing.

Apply Your Understanding

At the present time (in the United States), where are used fuel rods stored?

At present, the interim storage facilities at U.S. reactor sites are filling up. We are rapidly approaching the point where it will be necessary to either provide some away-from-reactor storage or begin reprocessing. The federal government is required by law to provide a permanent site for spent fuel storage.

In reprocessing, fuel rods are dissolved in acid. Radioactive wastes are separated out and prepared for long-term storage. Plutonium is removed and sent to fuel fabrication. Unused uranium is removed and prepared for enrichment.

The political problems involved in waste disposal and reprocessing are growing. State after state is now saying "not in my backyard." No one wants to live near a nuclear processing plant or by radioactive waste storage. As the debate goes on, however, the spent fuel rods continue to fill up reactor site interim storage facilities. Tests are progressing at potential sites for the final disposal of **nuclear wastes**.

Waste Storage

Fission products (nuclear wastes) are radioactive and can remain so for thousands of years. In assessing the danger to people, you have to consider the type of radiation and

▶ FIGURE 10.21 Spent fuel rod storage at a reactor pool.
(*U.S. Council for Energy Awareness*)

the half-life. You also must consider the biological effects of the radioactive material. (We will learn more about this in a later section of this chapter.)

Because of the dangers, radioactive wastes must be kept isolated for thousands of years. This need for isolation is the real challenge of radioactive waste disposal. The debate is intense and often bitter. Questions raised are both moral and scientific. We are, in effect, leaving these materials to our children. After disposal, the wastes will have to be monitored for generations.

Nuclear waste can be divided into five different categories.

1. **Spent fuel**—waste resulting from the production of electricity in commercial nuclear power plants.

2. **High-level waste**—waste resulting mainly from the production of nuclear materials for U.S. defense activities. They are highly radioactive and will not decay to background (safe) levels for thousands of years.

3. **Transuranic waste**—waste left mainly from the production of nuclear weapons, such as contaminated clothing, tools, rags, and other such items. These items contain trace amounts of radioactive elements—mostly plutonium. Since they have an atomic number greater than uranium (92), they are called transuranic (beyond uranium). The contamination contains alpha particle emitters with half-lives greater than 20 years.

4. **Low-level waste**—radioactive waste that does not fall into any other category. Low-level waste is usually rags, papers, filters, tools, equipment, and discarded protective clothing. This type of waste is generated at nuclear power plants, hospitals, research facilities, industries, and universities. These wastes will decay to background levels in reasonable amounts of time.

5. **Uranium mine/mill tailings**—naturally occurring radioactive rock and soil that are the waste product of uranium mining/milling operations.

Nuclear waste must be disposed in ways that permanently isolate it from people and the environment. This is usually done by burial. The type of waste determines the type of burial. For instance, uranium mill tailings are usually contained and buried near the mill where they were produced.

In the United States, each state is responsible for the management and disposal of its own low-level radioactive waste in disposal facilities. A state has the option of forming a compact with one or more other states to accomplish disposal.

The Waste Isolation Pilot Plant (WIPP) located in southeastern New Mexico is the designated site for the safe and permanent disposal of transuranic waste left from the production of nuclear weapons and the cleanup of nuclear weapon production facilities. WIPP is not allowed to accept any commercial (spent fuel) or high-level waste.

The selected disposal site for spent fuel and high-level waste is located at Yucca Mountain, Nevada (see Figure 10.22). Extensive studies are in progress to determine the ability of this site to completely contain this waste for the next 10,000 years (see Figure 10.23). For a rock, 10,000 years is not long. For humans, that span of time is hard to grasp. The United States has existed as a nation for only 235 years. The whole history of nuclear power spans about 100 years. At present, legal battles over the use of this site are being fought. In the meantime, spent fuel accumulates at reactor sites.

Apply Your Understanding

Why must radioactive wastes be totally isolated?

What are the five categories of nuclear waste?

How are nuclear wastes to be disposed of in the United States?

Think about This!

Your teacher can provide information on how other countries deal with radioactive waste.

►FIGURE 10.23 The
proposed Yucca
Mountain nuclear
waste repository in
Nevada. The cross
section shows the
potential repository
area. (U.S. Department of
Energy/Rocky Mountain
News)

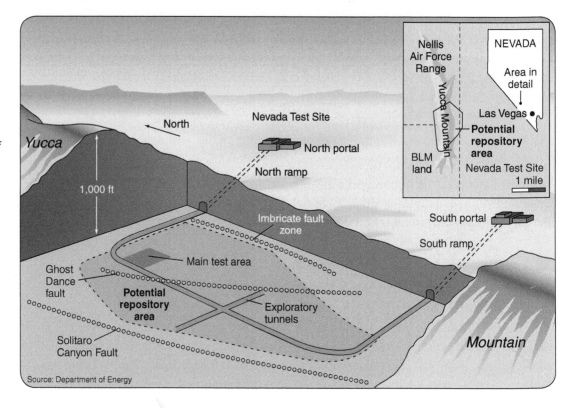

ACTIVITY 10.8

Transporting Nuclear Waste: An Engineering Design Project

In this activity, you will act as an engineer with the U.S. Department of Energy to create and test a package (a cask) designed to contain waste (an egg) and withstand accidents. The outer layer of the cask will be made from 2-liter (L) soda bottles. The interior packaging can be made from your choice of materials and design.

▲ FIGURE 10.24 What would happen if a truck carrying simulated radioactive waste in an approved cask stopped on a railroad track and was struck by a train going 80 mph? See for yourself! Though the truck was destroyed, the cask was only slightly dented. (USDOE)

Background

One of the functions of the U.S. Department of Energy (DOE) is to oversee the research and production of nuclear materials used in weapons. Today, with the decreased need for such weapons, the primary role of the DOE is environmental restoration and waste management. This means the DOE must clean up waste and contamination produced in the past. Many cleanup activities require the moving of waste to a processing or disposal site. For this purpose, the DOE has designed packages (casks) that must retain their contents and withstand severe accidents, whether being moved by truck, train, or ship (see Figure 10.24).

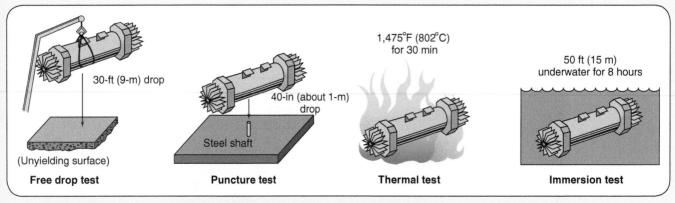

▲ FIGURE 10.25 The testing of casks designed for transporting nuclear waste. *(USDOE)*

Casks of radioactive waste must survive extensive testing. Tests include being dropped from 30 feet (ft) or 9 meters (m) onto an unyielding surface, then being dropped 40 inches (in) (about 1 m) onto a steel shaft. Casks are exposed to 1,475°F (802°C) flames for 30 min, then submerged 50 ft (15 m) underwater for 8 hours (see Figure 10.25).

Cask Requirements

1. All of your packing and materials must fit in no more than two 2-L plastic soda bottles that have a combined length of 2 ft (about 0.5 m) or less.

2. The maximum allowable weight of the entire cask with egg must be equal to or less than 1 pound (lb) or 454 grams (g).

3. The cask must withstand a drop of 20–30 ft (6–9 m) without the egg breaking.

4. The cask must withstand the force of a swinging 1-lb (454-g) weight striking the side of the cask without the egg breaking.

5. When dropped from a height of 3 ft (1 m) onto a post 2 in (5 cm) tall and 0.5 in (1.27 cm) in diameter, the egg in the cask must not break.

Scoring

If more than one cask survives all the tests, the cask that weighs the least wins. (Less weight means greater fuel efficiency during transportation.)

10.7 Nuclear Power Plants

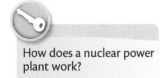

How does a nuclear power plant work?

Topic: nuclear power plants
Go to: www.scilinks.org
Code: GloSci7e390

Aside from its environmental impact, a nuclear power plant differs from ordinary power plants only in how energy is made available for turning the turbine that connects to the generator. In a nuclear power plant, a **nuclear reaction** produces heat, which is used to produce steam to drive the turbine. The main parts of a **nuclear reactor** are

- fuel
- moderator
- control system
- heat removal system
- radiation shield

Each of these parts is described briefly in the following paragraphs. They are also shown in Figures 10.26 and 10.27. Refer to these figures as you read about each part.

The Fuel

Ceramic pellets made of enriched uranium oxide (UO_2) or uranium carbide (UC) are the fuel for the reactor. The pellets are stacked end-to-end in long metal tubes called fuel rods.

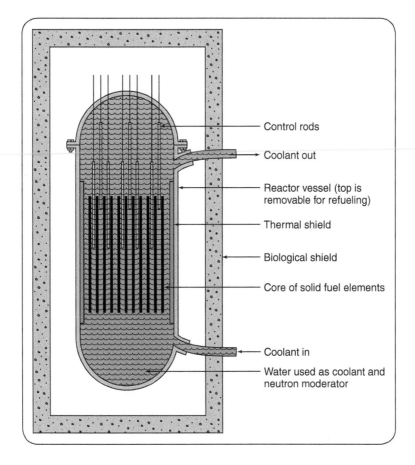

Control rods

Coolant out

Reactor vessel (top is removable for refueling)

Thermal shield

Biological shield

Core of solid fuel elements

Coolant in

Water used as coolant and neutron moderator

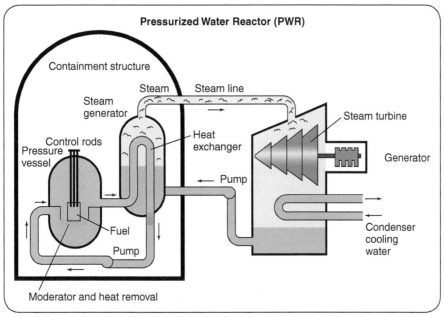

Pressurized Water Reactor (PWR)

Containment structure

Steam

Steam line

Steam generator

Steam turbine

Control rods

Heat exchanger

Pressure vessel

Generator

Pump

Fuel

Pump

Condenser cooling water

Moderator and heat removal

◀FIGURE 10.27 A complete nuclear power plant. In the pressurized water reactor, the primary cooling system is closed and under pressure. It exchanges heat energy with a secondary system that provides the steam. *(U.S. Council for Energy Awareness)*

The fuel rods are then precisely arranged as bundles within the reactor with spaces between them for control rods. Water flowing through the bundles removes the heat and puts it to work. The fuel assembly bundles make up the reactor core (see Figure 10.20).

The Moderator

Neutrons are the bullets that penetrate the nucleus and cause it to split or fission. They make excellent bullets because they have no electric charge. This lack of charge enables them to move toward a nucleus without any electric forces to deflect them.

Nuclear Energy 391

When most nuclei are bombarded with neutrons, they absorb them. The nuclei then emit alpha or beta particles or gamma rays and are changed themselves (see Activity 10.4). However, when uranium-235 absorbs a neutron, its nucleus fissions into two parts whose weights place them somewhere near the middle of the periodic table (see Figure 10.13). The movement of these fission fragments produces a huge amount of heat energy. The fission process also causes the release of several fast neutrons.

Each new neutron can cause another neutron to split, if properly slowed down by a **moderator**. Slow neutrons have a greater probability of causing U-235 nuclei to fission. The moderator must be made of light atoms. Fast neutrons lose more energy upon colliding with light atoms than with heavy atoms. Good moderators include graphite, H_2O, or D_2O (heavy water). Most U.S. reactors use water.

The Control System

A minimum amount of fuel is required for a reactor to work. This is called the **critical mass**. In a bomb, an uncontrolled fission chain reaction takes place. In a reactor, the fission chain reaction is controlled.

On the average, 2.5 neutrons are emitted per fission. If the reactor is just critical, then there must be one neutron, which, after slowing down, is left to produce another fission. If more than one is available, the number of neutrons increases rapidly as a chain reaction begins. If less than one is available, the reactor will shut down.

All reactors have some adjustable neutron-absorbing rods, containing boron or cadmium, called **control rods**. The control rods may be thought of as neutron sponges. When they are pushed into the fuel assembly, they soak up neutrons and the reactor starts to cool down.

The Heat Removal System

As the fission products (and neutrons) collide with surrounding matter, their kinetic energy is quickly converted to heat.

Power plant reactors operate at extremely high power levels (measured in kilowatts or megawatts of heat output). Therefore, they must be cooled to prevent overheating and melting of the core. In these reactors, the heat that is carried away is the primary product of the reactor. This heat is used for steam production. A forced circulation system carries the heat from the reactor to the steam generator. Various coolants are used, including gases, water, and liquid metals (see Figures 10.27, 10.28, and 10.29).

The Radiation Shield

The part of the released fission energy that does not instantly appear as heat appears as penetrating radiation. Nuclear reactors must, therefore, be heavily shielded.

Reactors have an internal, or "thermal," shield to protect the walls of the reactor vessel from radiation damage. This internal shield usually consists of a steel lining. Reactors also have an external, or "biological," shield to protect workers from radiation exposure. The external shield is also called the containment structure (see Figure 10.26). It is typically made of several feet of high-density concrete surrounding the reactor installation.

Fission reactions occur continually as the reactor runs. Fission equations have this general form:

$$\text{fissionable nuclei} + {}_0^1n \rightarrow \text{fission products (nuclear wastes)} + \text{neutrons} + \text{energy}$$

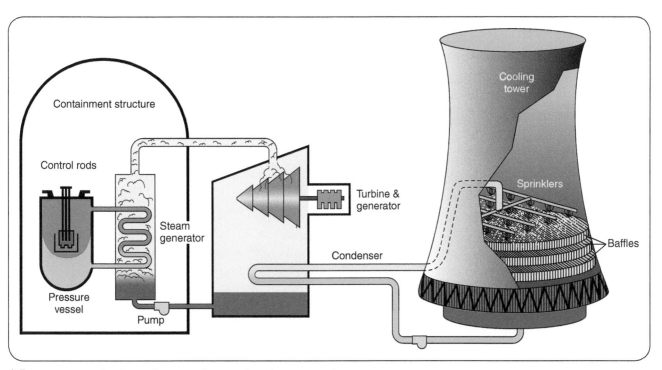

▲ FIGURE 10.29 The design features of a typical nuclear power plant.

The fission products are by far the largest source of radioactive waste in terms of radioactivity. They go through one or more steps of radioactive decay before reaching a stable, harmless end product. Most of the fissionable products decay rapidly and represent no real hazard to humans. A few of them, however, are a problem for one or more of these reasons: amount produced, long half-life, efficiency of transfer to humans, and metabolism in the human body.

Nuclear Energy   393

►FIGURE 10.30 Tanks for the storage of high-level radioactive waste. *(USDOE)*

What are some of the advantages and disadvantages of using nuclear power?

Our biggest problem with these wastes today is storing them effectively (see Figure 10.30). Much research is being directed toward solving the waste storage challenge.

10.8 The Pros and Cons of Nuclear Power

Nuclear energy is the most controversial of all our energy sources. Figure 10.31 summarizes the major advantages and disadvantages of nuclear energy.

►FIGURE 10.31 Summary of the advantages and disadvantages of nuclear power.

	Advantages	Disadvantages
Energy source	A significant amount of energy is available to us in the form of nuclear energy.	The fission process consumes uranium- and thorium-based nuclear fuels. A significant shift to nuclear power could result in the depletion of our readily available nuclear reserves.
Operation	We know how to build and operate fission reactors. We have been doing so for many years.	The fission process produces long-lived, hazardous radioactive wastes. Methods of storing them safely are being developed; however, as yet there is no general agreement on where to do this.
Dependency	A significant shift to nuclear energy will reduce our country's dependence on foreign sources of petroleum-based products.	A shift to nuclear energy could result in a partial dependence on foreign sources of uranium and thorium.
Pollution	No obvious pollutants, such as smoke or ashes, are formed by consuming nuclear fuels. Nuclear power does not contribute to the "greenhouse" effect.	Expensive cooling towers and cooling ponds that dissipate heat out into the atmosphere must be constructed to minimize the environmental impact of large-scale heat disposal. In addition, we must safely dispose of radioactive waste.

Radiation: Benefits and Problems

10.9 Biological Effects of Radiation

Radiation is any event that spreads out in all directions from some source. Hence, the emissions from radioactive nuclei (mostly α, β, and γ) are radiations. Radiation also includes X-rays and the **cosmic rays** that enter our atmosphere from outer space.

Topic: radiation
Go to: www.scilinks.org
Code: GloSci7e395

For radiations to act in helpful or harmful ways, they must interact with the medium they pass through. For example, the interaction of α and β particles with alcohol molecules produces the tracks in a cloud chamber (see Figure 10.32).

An atom consists of a tiny, centrally located nucleus that has a positive charge. Negatively charged electrons circle the nucleus. Ordinarily, the negative charges of the electrons equal the positive charge on the nucleus.

Atoms and molecules tend to be electrically neutral. However, an alpha or beta particle or a cosmic ray entering an atom can knock electrons loose. This leaves the atom with a positive electric charge. An atom carrying an electric charge is called an *ion*. Radiation that produces ions is called **ionizing radiation**. Ions have chemical properties that are different from the properties of the atoms from which they came (see Figure 10.33).

Alphas and betas interact continuously as they enter matter. In contrast, X-rays and g-rays have discrete interactions with the atoms of the materials they enter. (They must hit the particles they interact with directly.) These interactions result in the creation of ions. Hence, α, β, and γ emissions, X-rays, and cosmic rays are all ionizing radiation.

Like all matter, plants and animals are made of atoms and can be affected by radiation. The basic unit of any living thing is the cell. Each cell is a tiny chemical factory made up of millions of atoms. In it, several thousand different kinds of chemical changes are constantly taking place. The average human adult consists of about 50 trillion cells.

Growth occurs when cells divide. The instructions for division and growth are contained in the cell's **chromosomes**. On the chromosomes are the instructions that determine growth, eye color, number of fingers, gender, and so on. Each species has a characteristic number of chromosomes in each cell. As a cell divides, its chromosomes also divide, and they line up in pairs. Because one chromosome of each pair goes to each new cell, the new cells are replicas of the old cell. (In the formation of sex cells, however, a sperm or egg cell gets only half as many chromosomes as a body cell would.)

Ionizing radiation can alter chromosomes. This results in **mutations**, or changes, in cells. Mutations may be invisible, like a change in one enzyme, or they may lead to missing fingers, toes, or other visible changes. Mutations caused by ionizing radiation are random.

Helpful Hint!

A *species* is one kind of animal or plant, such as humans, flies, or oak trees.

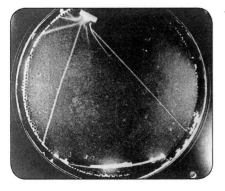

◀ FIGURE 10.32 Cloud chamber tracks produced by alpha emissions from a plutonium source. (*Argonne National Laboratory*)

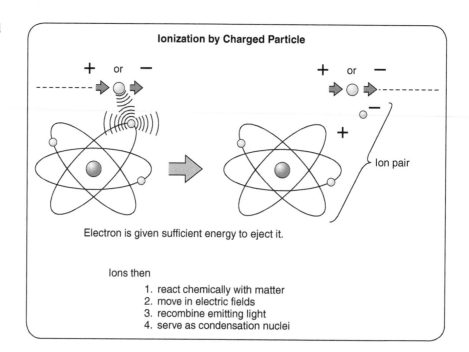

Since living organisms are such complex, nearly perfect functioning chemical factories, very few mutations are believed to be beneficial (Figure 10.34).

Humans have always lived in an environment that includes a great deal of natural radiation. It comes from within Earth and from outer space. For example, radioactive materials such as uranium and thorium, and the decay products associated with them, exist everywhere in Earth. The places where they are mined are simply the locations of concentrations of these minerals. Likewise, small amounts of the radioactive gas radon is present in the soil. It is even present in the air we breathe.

Cosmic radiation is made up of particles of very high energy that strike Earth's atmosphere from outer space. They contribute both directly and indirectly to the amount of radiation to which we are exposed. Cosmic rays contribute directly by striking our bodies. They contribute indirectly by creating radioactive carbon 14 when cosmic neutrons strike atmospheric nitrogen. Carbon 14 is then quickly converted into $^{14}CO_2$. The $^{14}CO_2$ is used by plants in photosynthesis; the plants are eaten by animals. The radioactive carbon eventually finds its way into our bodies through our food.

The disintegration of ^{14}C results in the liberation of about 200,000 beta particles per minute in the average adult. Potassium 40 is also in our bodies. It liberates approximately 240,000 beta particles per minute in the average adult. Other radioactive materials occur naturally

Helpful Hint!

Strontium 90 is a radioactive isotope of strontium that easily deposits in bone.

► FIGURE 10.34 "Strontium 90." *(Reprinted from* The Saturday Evening Post. © 1966. The Curtis Publishing Company.)

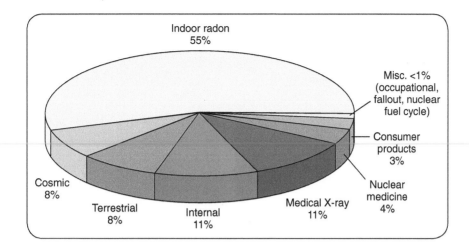

◀FIGURE 10.35 Sources of ionizing radviation: natural and humanmade. National average per person. (*Adapted from Science, Society, and America's Nuclear Waste, USDOE.*)

in our bodies. These include radium 226, strontium 90, cesium 137, and iodine 131 (see Figure 10.35). We seem to suffer no ill effects from this natural dosage of radiation.

Humans have explored nature and hunted for ways to improve our control and use of nature. In doing so, we have created new sources of radiation. One source of human-produced radiation that contributes to our total exposure to radiation is medical X-rays. Other sources include radioactive fallout, television tubes, radioactive wastes from nuclear reactors, and so on.

Depending on the type, radiation can be either an external or an internal hazard. X-rays and gamma rays must undergo discrete interactions (direct hits) with matter before they create ions. Hence, they can penetrate deep into wood, water, and the human body. They are thus considered *external hazards*. People who were a mile or so away from the bomb dropped on Hiroshima suffered radiation effects, even though they were not injured by flying debris, intense heat, or the shock wave created by the explosion.

Alpha and beta radiations are not very penetrating, so they are not classified as external hazards. Their range in air, paper, and skin is very short. However, they intensely ionize the material through which they do pass (as seen in the cloud chamber). This makes them a serious *internal hazard*. That is why plutonium is so dangerous. Plutonium is a strong alpha emitter. Cancer may result if even a minute amount of it is breathed in and deposited in the lungs.

Large doses of radiation can cause severe injury—even death. But what about smaller doses? All exposures to ionizing radiation present some risk. However, humans are continuously exposed to radiation at low intensity without any apparent or readily identifiable harmful effects. To a certain extent, the body can adjust to and counteract the harmful effects of small doses of radiation.

In a couple of ways, however, we cannot adjust even to low levels of ionizing radiation. For example, rates of genetic mutations and all forms of cancer increase with increased exposure.

Genetic damage and cancer production have been the subjects of much public concern. Some scientists believe that low levels of radiation have been producing genetic effects since the beginning of life. Cumulative changes in heredity have apparently helped to accomplish the evolution of plant and animal species. Although this may be the case, most scientists feel we should not speed up the process of evolution by increasing our radiation exposure.

Cancer is believed to result from a mutation in which certain cells lose the capacity to regulate their growth properly. In every cell in the body, there is a regulatory gene that controls the rate at which the cell divides. A cell normally divides about 50 times. A cancerous cell, however, produces millions and millions of cells. These mutations do not involve the sex cells. Thus, they are confined to the individual and are not passed on to the offspring.

Nuclear Energy 397

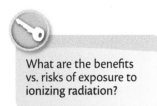

What are the benefits vs. risks of exposure to ionizing radiation?

These facts pose a real dilemma. Surely it makes sense to have one's leg X-rayed if one suspects it has been broken. If the information gained from the X-ray results in the proper treatment of the break, the benefit incurred most likely is greater than the increased risk of cancer or genetic damage.

However, the dangers of increased exposure to ionizing radiation must not be taken lightly. For example, the handling and disposal of our radioactive wastes are serious problems. How we decide to handle them is important.

10.10 Measuring Radiation: The Units

Several units have been developed for measuring radioactivity and radiation. A common set of units was developed first. This set of units is being replaced by the International System (SI) units. Figure 10.36 summarizes the units, what they measure, and the related conversion factors.

▶FIGURE 10.36 Unit names, descriptions, and conversion factors for radioactivity and radiation.

SI Unit	Description	Common Unit
Becquerel (Bq) 1 Bq = 1 disintegration/sec	Measures the number of nuclear transformations (disintegrations) that occur in a certain time period.	Curie (Ci) 1 Ci = 3.7×10^{10} disintegrations/sec
Roentgen (R)	Measures the exposure (ionization) of air by X-rays and γ-rays.	Roentgen (R)
Gray (Gy)	Measures the energy deposited in any material by any type of ionizing radiation.	Rad—means radiation absorbed dose.
Sievert (Sr)	An estimate of the biological damage or health risk to humans due to the absorption of ionizing radiation.	Rem—means radiation effect on man.

Conversion Factors

1 becquerel (Be) = 2.7×10^{-11} curie (Ci)

1 gray (Gy) = 100 rad

1 sievert (Sv) = 100 rem

1 curie (Ci) = 3.7 3 10^{10} becquerel (Bq)

1 rad = 0.01 gray (Gy)

1 rem = 0.01 sievert (Sv)

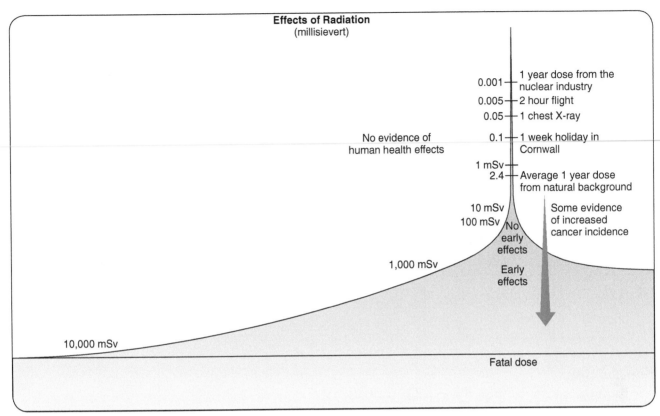

Effects of Radiation
(millisievert)

0.001	1 year dose from the nuclear industry
0.005	2 hour flight
0.05	1 chest X-ray
0.1	1 week holiday in Cornwall
1 mSv	
2.4	Average 1 year dose from natural background

No evidence of human health effects

10 mSv
100 mSv — No early effects

Some evidence of increased cancer incidence

1,000 mSv

Early effects

10,000 mSv

Fatal dose

▲ FIGURE 10.37 The effect of various doses of ionizing radiation on people. (*Source:* Radiation: Doses, Effects, Risks. *United Nations Environment Program.*)

10.11 Dosage and Effect

The effect various doses of ionizing radiation has on humans is our main concern. Figure 10.37 shows one way to illustrate this. Note that an annual radiation dose of less than 5 mSv appears to provide no evidence of human health effects.

ACTIVITY 10.9

Calculate Your Personal Radiation Dose

In this activity, you will estimate your personal radiation dose based on your own lifestyle and living conditions.

Background

Radiation is all around us and in us. It is part of our natural environment. In the United States, radiation is usually measured in millirems (mrem). The annual dose per person from all sources is about 360 mrem. However, it is not uncommon for a person to receive far more than this amount in a given year (usually as the result of medical procedures).

For those who work with nuclear materials, the international standards allow up to 5,000 mrem per year exposure.

Materials

* *Personal Radiation Dose* handout

Procedure

1. Fill in the blanks on the handout your teacher provides (Figure 10.38). Base your responses on your activities during the past year.

2. Total your annual exposure and answer the questions that follow.

Nuclear Energy 399

Where You Live

Cosmic radiation (from outer space) at sea level 26

For your **elevation** in feet above sea level, add one of these numbers:

1,000–2	4,000–13	7,000–40
2,000–5	5,000–21	8,000–48
3,000–9	6,000–26	9,000–70

House construction: If stone, concrete, or masonry, add 7. _____

Ground radiation: Add one of the numbers below: _____

    a. Atlantic and Gulf Coast Plains 16

    b. Colorado Plateau (Four Corners area) 81

    c. Rest of the United States 32

What You Eat, Drink, and Breathe

From food and water: U.S. average 40

From radon in the air (mostly indoor air) 200

How You Live

Jet plane travel: For each 2,500 miles, add 1 mrem. _____

TV viewing: For each hour per day _____ × 0.15 mrem. _____

If natural gas heating or cooking, add 2. _____

X-rays and radiopharmaceutical diagnosis:

    Number of chest X-rays _____ × 10. _____

    Number of lower gastrointestinal tract X-rays _____ × 500. _____

    Number of radiopharmaceutical exams _____ × 300. _____

How Close You Live to a Nuclear Plant

At site boundary: Average number of hours per day _____ × 0.2. _____

One mile away: Average number of hours per day _____ × 0.02. _____

Five miles away: Average number of hours per day _____ × 0.002. _____

Over 5 miles away: None. _____

Note: These are maximum allowable doses established by the U.S. Nuclear Regulatory Commission. Experience has shown that most people receive far less than these limits.

Add the right-hand column to get your total.   **Total mrem:** _____

▲ FIGURE 10.38 Determine your personal radiation dose.

QUESTIONS & TASKS

Record your responses in your science notebook.

1. The U.S. annual average dose is 360 mrem. How does your total dose compare to that figure?

2. Convert your annual dose to mSv: 1 mrem = 0.01 mSievert (mSv).

3. Find your annual dose in mSv on Figure 10.37. Does your annual exposure seem to put you in any apparent danger? Explain.

Medicine	Industry	Agriculture	Research	Home
• Myocardial imaging • Bone/lung scans • "Hooking" radioisotopes to antibodies • Surgery "gamma knife" • Pacemakers • Pulmonary embolism • Surgical gloves	• Imaging flaws • Measure thickness • Test quality (metals) • Test strength • Shrink wrap • Smoke detectors • Nuclear power plants • Nuclear-powered spacecraft • Remote weather-monitoring stations	• Insect control • Cultivate seeds • Test hydrology • Irradiation of food • Astronauts' food • Study germination • Fertilizer studies	• Carbon-14 dating • Artifacts • Analyzing moles • 95% all new drugs tested by radiation • Treatment of AIDS • Cancer treatment	• Microwave cooking • Remote control device • Smoke detectors • TV and radio broadcast waves • Irradiated foods

▲ FIGURE 10.39 Some beneficial ways nuclear materials and radiation applications are used.

10.12 Beneficial Uses of Radiation

The proper application of nuclear science and the properties of radiation have brought countless benefits to humans. Figure 10.39 summarizes some of these benefits.

Learn more about one or more of these by doing a library or Internet search. See the website section at the end of this chapter.

Looking to the Future

10.13 The Breeder Option

Most of the uranium found in nature (99.3 percent) is made of atoms containing 238 protons and neutrons, U-238. This uranium is quite stable, but is not a practical source of energy. The uranium used to fuel today's nuclear reactors is uranium-235 (the remaining 0.7 percent of natural uranium). When hit with a high-speed (thermal) neutron, it will split and produce heat energy, fission products (nuclear wastes), and more neutrons. These neutrons can be used to split more U-235 atoms and produce more energy. Uncontrolled, we have a bomb; controlled, we have a source of energy. This sequence is summarized as follows:

Topic: breeder reactor
Go to: www.scilinks.org
Code: GloSci7e401

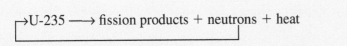

$$\rightarrow \text{U-235} \longrightarrow \text{fission products + neutrons + heat}$$

As pointed out earlier, this reaction uses up the U-235. That is why our present nuclear reactors are called burner reactors. They use up the U-235. Today, reserves of uranium-235 are such that if this were the complete story on nuclear energy, there would be little interest in it.

In a **breeder reactor**, the U-235 fissions. In the process, some of the spare neutrons produced are captured by the rather useless U-238. When that happens, the U-238 changes (in a series of steps) to plutonium-239. This isotope can be split by neutrons, as in the fission of uranium-235, and used to produce heat in a reactor. The same thing can be done to thorium-232, the natural form of thorium. The equations are as follows:

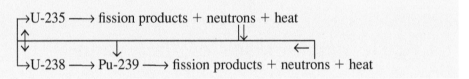

$$^{238}_{92}\text{U} + {}^{1}_{0}\text{n} \longrightarrow {}^{239}_{92}\text{U} \xrightarrow{{}^{0}_{-1}\beta} {}^{239}_{93}\text{Np} \xrightarrow{{}^{0}_{-1}\beta} {}^{239}_{94}\text{Pu}$$

$$^{232}_{90}\text{Th} + {}^{1}_{0}\text{n} \longrightarrow {}^{233}_{90}\text{Th} \xrightarrow{{}^{0}_{-1}\beta} {}^{233}_{91}\text{Pa} \xrightarrow{{}^{0}_{-1}\beta} {}^{233}_{92}\text{U}$$

Thus, if U-238 and Th-232, which are natural and mined from the ground, are placed in a breeder reactor and bombarded with neutrons, they can be changed into Pu-239 and U-233, respectively. Both P-239 and U-233 are fissionable. This means they can be used to fuel other reactors. Therefore, a breeder reactor makes fuel as it operates.

Theoretically, our uranium fuel supply could be increased by a factor of $99.3/0.7 = 142$. (In reality, we cannot build reactors that bombard every uranium-238 atom placed in them.) Engineers have determined that a breeder program is capable of increasing the energy available to us from uranium by a factor of about 60. We also gain access to the nuclear energy available in our thorium reserves. We are just beginning to determine the extent of those reserves. This diagram illustrates the breeder reaction:

$$\begin{array}{l}
\rightarrow \text{U-235} \longrightarrow \text{fission products + neutrons + heat} \\
\uparrow\ \downarrow \qquad\qquad\qquad\qquad\qquad\qquad \Downarrow \qquad\qquad \leftarrow \\
\rightarrow \text{U-238} \longrightarrow \text{Pu-239} \longrightarrow \text{fission products + neutrons + heat}
\end{array}$$

Once a supply of Pu-239 (or U-233) is built, U-235 is no longer necessary for the breeder program. However, it is absolutely necessary to have uranium-235 in the beginning.

By careful selection and arrangement of materials in a reactor, the neutrons not needed in the fission chain reaction can be used to convert U-238 and Th-232 into Pu-239 and U-233. Thus, scientists and engineers may be able to make use of most of the uranium and thorium in nature for the release of nuclear energy and the production of electric power (see Figure 10.40).

▼FIGURE 10.40 A breeder reactor. *(USDOE)*

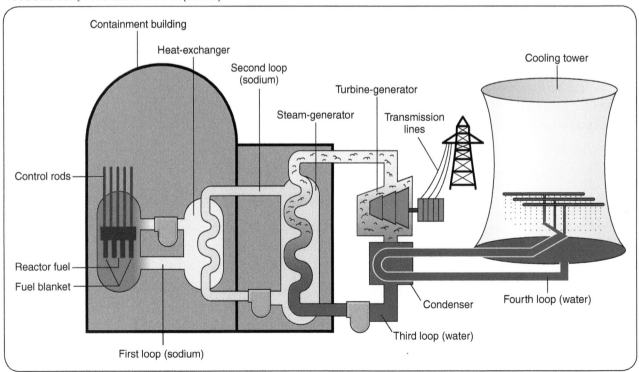

There are several advantages to a breeder-based nuclear program.

- A significant amount of energy is available to us in the form of nuclear energy.

- A significant shift to nuclear energy could reduce a country's dependence on fossil fuels and foreign sources of petroleum-based products.

- Because breeders make nuclear fuel as they run, they will greatly extend the lifetime of nuclear fuel reserves.

But this is only half the story. There are also disadvantages of breeder-based technology.

- Like ordinary fission reactors, breeder reactors produce long-lived radioactive wastes. If we increase the energy available to us from nuclear fission by a factor of 60 or more, we also increase the quantity of radioactive wastes by the same factor. Should we venture into a new program that produces additional wastes without proven storage and disposal techniques?

- Like ordinary fission reactors, breeders produce large quantities of "waste" heat. This is released into the air and bodies of water. How should this potential thermal-pollution problem be handled?

- The fissionable materials produced in a breeder should be used to power new breeder reactors. However, they could also be used by terrorists to make nuclear weapons. Any country that has the capability of producing plutonium-239 and uranium-233 also has the capability of becoming a nuclear power (Figure 10.41).

  A reactor producing 300 kilograms (kg) of plutonium per year is theoretically producing the equivalent of some 30 or more nuclear bombs. What are the implications of this kind of information?

- Dr. John Goffman has spent the major portion of his career studying the biological effects of nuclear materials. He states, "One pound of plutonium represents the potential of producing nine billion human lung cancers. As a toxic substance, it will be in our environment, if released, for the next half million years." Should we go ahead and produce this kind of material by the ton?

Breeder-based technology does present a magnitude of problems. However, because it is a promising source of energy, scientists and engineers are looking at alternative breeder reactor designs. One such alternative is the gas core reactor power plant. This reactor has a low inventory of fissionable material. If as little as 4 kg of fissionable material is removed from the reactor (less than a critical mass), the reactor will shut down. Fuel is processed on-site. A high fuel burn up is featured. Waste production is drastically reduced.

Other scientists are working on transmuting long-lived nuclear wastes to isotopes that are short-lived. These possibilities, if successful, could make the breeder option an acceptable

◀ FIGURE 10.41 All God's chillun got N-power. (*Copyright © 1975 by the* Washington Star. *Reprinted with permission of Universal Press Syndicate. All rights reserved.*)

one to the American public. However, the investigation of these possibilities will take money and time.

 QUESTIONS & TASKS

1. How does a breeder reactor make fuel as it operates?

2. What kinds of pollution would increase with the widespread use of breeder reactors? What kinds of pollution would decrease?

3. A breeder reactor produces Pu-239. For what purpose other than fueling nuclear reactors can the Pu-239 be used?

4. By how much might the nuclear resources of a nation be extended if it committed itself to using the breeder option?

10.14 The Fusion Future

Topic: nuclear fusion
Go to: www.scilinks.org
Code: GloSci7e404

The sun and other stars generate energy by nuclear fusion. Fusion involves joining together the nuclei of two atoms, which results in the release of energy. Normally, nuclei repel each other. This happens because all nuclei are positively charged, and like charges repel each other. However, if the nuclei can be brought very close to each other, the force of nuclear attraction becomes stronger than the repelling electrical force, and fusion takes place. To get the nuclei close enough, the fuel for the fusion process (isotopes of hydrogen) must be heated to about 100 million degrees (Celsius, Fahrenheit, or Kelvin). At this temperature, the nuclei are moving fast enough so that fusing conditions are met as the nuclei move together. A heavier element is formed, neutrons are produced, and a huge amount of energy is released (see Figure 10.15).

It has been difficult to accomplish controlled fusion on Earth. This is because of the problem of heating something to 100 million degrees and containing it. Normally, we contain gases in bottles and cans. However, any container would vaporize long before the 100 million-degree temperature was reached. No known material substance exists as a solid or liquid at such high temperatures. Two attempts to sidestep this problem are being tried. One is **magnetic confinement fusion**; the other is **laser fusion**.

The idea in magnetic confinement fusion is to contain the hot nuclei, called a **plasma**, in a strong magnetic field often referred to as a magnetic bottle. One of these bottles is shaped like a doughnut. It is produced by bending a circular coil of wire into the shape of a doughnut. This is called a torus. When electric current is passed through the coil, a magnetic field is produced both in and around the torus. When charged particles are placed inside the torus (where the dough of a doughnut would be), they cannot get out. They are trapped in a magnetic bottle. An electric current is then driven through the plasma and heats it (as in a microwave oven) to fusing temperatures. The heat produced is drawn off and exchanged to water for steam production (see Figure 10.42). That is how it *should* work. Technical difficulties with this process have kept teams of scientists and engineers busy since the late 1940s. The goal is to have the plasma produce more energy than the apparatus consumes.

Another method of accomplishing fusion is to embed some heavy hydrogen (deuterium) inside a small glass pellet. If the pellet is zapped with a series of powerful laser beams, the outside layer evaporates almost instantly. The counterforce generated by the rapid expansion of the outer material drives the remaining portion inward. As the material is driven inward, it is forced into a smaller volume and is heated by compression. At the high densities and temperatures generated, the fuel will fuse (see Figures 10.43 and 10.44). The fusion chamber in this case is spherical, like a basketball. Lasers are mounted like spokes on a wheel to give

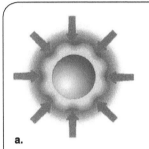 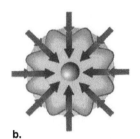 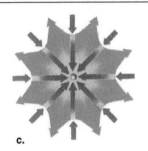 

a.

Laser or ion beams rapidly heat the surface of the fuel pellet.

b.

The fuel is compressed by the rocketlike blow off of the hot surface material.

c.

When the fuel core reaches 20 times the density of lead, it ignites at 100,000,000°C.

d.

Thermonuclear burn quickly spreads through the compressed fuel, yielding many times the input energy.

▲FIGURE 10.43 How inertia fusion works. (*Source: The American Physical Society.*)

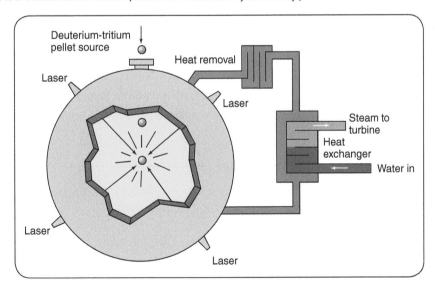

◀FIGURE 10.44 The laser fusion chamber.

perfect geometry. So far, no laser fusion device has transferred energy to a pellet rapidly enough to ignite plasma. Teams of scientists continue working on that goal as well.

Fusion power has a number of advantages over most future energy sources.

1. Because deuterium is found in water, abundant fuel in the form of deuterium is available to all countries.

2. Fusion involves no chemical combustion that contributes to air pollution.

3. There is no threat of diversion for making weapons.

4. Perhaps most important, there is no possibility of nuclear explosion, nuclear runaway (meltdown), or reactor-core cooling problems.

There is a major problem in assessing the contribution of fusion. No one knows for sure whether it can be accomplished regularly under controlled conditions in laboratories and power plants. Even if a breakthrough occurs, it will take years to move from the demonstration of feasibility to the reality of large-scale power generation.

Apply Your Understanding

Which of the fusion reactions is the easiest to make work?

The Equation of Fusions

The reactions of interest are

$$\frac{2}{1}D + \frac{2}{1}D \longrightarrow \frac{3}{2}He + \frac{1}{0}n + energy$$

$$\frac{2}{1}D + \frac{2}{1}D \longrightarrow \frac{3}{1}T + \frac{1}{1}H + energy$$

$$and \frac{2}{1}D + \frac{3}{1}T \longrightarrow \frac{4}{2}He + \frac{1}{0}n + energy$$

It is difficult to make tritium (T) from deuterium (D). However, there is another way to produce tritium atoms.

$$\frac{6}{3}Li + \frac{1}{0}n \longrightarrow \frac{4}{2}He + \frac{3}{1}T + energy$$

The deuterium-deuterium reactions are much more difficult to accomplish than the deuterium-tritium reactions. Unfortunately, the world's supply of lithium (Li), from which we can make tritium, is small. Hence, until we increase our ability to run the deuterium-deuterium reactions, the fusion option is limited.

What is the future outlook for nuclear power?

10.15 The Future of Nuclear Power

Nuclear power worldwide is increasing slowly, with about 30 reactors under construction in 12 countries. U.S. electric utilities are hesitant to build new nuclear power plants. This is because a number of social, political, and economic concerns must be addressed. These concerns center around the following questions:

Apply Your Understanding

What are some of the social, economic, and political issues that relate to the use of nuclear energy?

1. What are the long-term effects of exposure to low levels of radiation?

2. Where will a repository for high-level waste be built?

3. Can nuclear waste be disposed of and kept out of the environment for thousands of years?

4. Can nuclear waste be transported safely?

5. Are further security measures needed to protect against terrorism?

6. Does nuclear power compete economically with other energy options?

U.S. nuclear power will not move forward until the public believes it has satisfactory answers to these questions. It is important to know all sides of the nuclear power issue before intelligent decisions are made. Ask questions, get information from all sides, and then make up your mind. The references for this chapter can help you begin that search.

Summary

Nuclear energy is the only new source of energy available to us. It is used as a source of heat to make steam for electric power generation.

In nuclear fission, heavy nuclei are bombarded with neutrons, made unstable, and caused to split. This splitting results in the production of lighter, but unstable, nuclei. Heat is produced in the process. Unfortunately, the lighter nuclei are radioactive waste. Since portions of this waste have undesirable biological effects on all living things, they cannot be allowed to enter our ecosystem.

Extra neutrons from the fission process can be used to produce more nuclear fuel. This is done in a breeder reactor. Unfortunately, this new nuclear fuel can also be used to make nuclear bombs.

Nuclear fusion has the potential for providing huge amounts of energy for the future. However, very difficult technical problems must be overcome.

Before nuclear power expands as an energy option, serious social, political, technical, and economic issues must be addressed. To solve the nuclear dilemma, we must do one of two things:

1. Give up on the nuclear option and safely store the nuclear waste that currently exists.

2. Carefully research nuclear waste disposal options, alternative breeder reactor designs, fusion, and reactor technologies. At the same time, a meaningful public debate must bring public acceptance of a safe, reliable way to use nuclear power and handle all related waste.

 ## REFERENCES

Deutch, John M. and Ernest J. Moniz. The Nuclear Option. *Scientific American* (September, 2006): 76–83.

Garwin, Richard L. and Georges Charpak. *Megawatts and Megatons: A Turning Point in the Nuclear Age?* (New York: Knopt), 2001.

U.S. Department of Energy. *Closing the Circle on the Splitting of the Atom* (DOE/Office of Environmental Management), 1995.

U.S. Department of Energy. *International Nuclear Fuel Cycle Fact Book* (DOE/RW-0371P), 1992.

U.S. Department of Energy. *Site Characterization Plan Overview, Yucca Mountain Site* (DOE/RW-0198), 1991.

U.S. Department of the Interior. *Uranium, Its Impact on the National and Global Energy Mix* (USGS Circular 1141), 1997.

 ## WEBSITES

Uranium Information Ctr.; Melbourne, Australia: http://www.uic.com.au

Penn State Nuclear Engineering Program: http://www.mne.psu.edu

American Nuclear Society: http://www.ans.org

Canadian Nuclear Society: http://www.cns-snc.ca/society.html

General nuclear science: http://www.nuc.berkeley.edu

Basic information on radioactivity: http://www.epa.gov/radiation/students/

Nuclear medicine: http://www.uca.edu—choose academics & research, then colleges & departments, then nuclear medicine technology

World Nuclear Association: http://www.world-nuclear.org/

CHAPTER 11

Energy Alternatives

GOAL

- To examine the energy sources that can be alternatives to the use of oil, natural gas, coal, and nuclear power.

Our choices for the future rest in how we perceive and use our resources.

—Glenn T. Seaborg

Our Energy Future

An examination of the data in Figure 8.3, an energy history of the United States, shows that our reliance on oil and gas is diminishing. At the same time, coal is showing a small revival. It also indicates that the nuclear option has, as yet, not been accepted by the public. Can any alternative sources of energy do for us what oil, gas, coal, and nuclear have? In this chapter, we will examine alternative sources.

Synthetic Fuels

What are synfuels? Why is there interest in them?

By processing naturally occurring materials, humans can produce new substances called **synthetic fuels** (synfuels). Synthetic fuels originate in the processes of coal gasification and liquefaction, heating of oil shale, and refining of fuels from tar sands (also called oil sands).

11.1 New Fuels from Coal

About 90 percent of our nation's fossil fuels are coal, which is easily converted to electricity at electric power generating plants. However, most of the nation's energy consumption (about 63 percent) is of oil and gas. Coal represents only 23 percent of the total energy consumption. To reverse this trend, while maintaining high environmental standards, the United States could convert some of its vast reserves of coal into clean gaseous and liquid fuels. These could be used for transportation since most cars and trucks are built to run on liquid fuels. They could be used in residences since most of the homes in the United States are heated with natural gas and many people cook with gas. They could also be used by industry. Changing coal to gas and a liquid makes sense if it can be done economically.

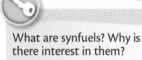

Topic: synthetic fuel
Go to: www.scilinks.org
Code: GloSci7e410

Both coal **gasification** (conversion to gas) and **liquefaction** (conversion to liquid and solid fuels) require high temperature and pressure. Coal is mostly carbon, with only a small amount of hydrogen. Hydrogen must be added to make synthetic hydrocarbons. Water is the cheapest source of hydrogen.

Coal can be converted to three types of gases:

1. High-Btu (or high-energy) gas, which can be directly substituted for natural gas.

2. Medium-Btu gas, which can be used for utility boilers, industrial fuel, electric power, and chemical feedstocks.

3. Low-Btu gas, which can be used for electrical power generation.

The major steps in coal gasification are shown in Figure 11.1. Hard coal is ground into a fine powder, then sprayed into a gasifier where it reacts with hot steam under high pressure. The resulting gases are cleaned up. Some gas is drawn off and used as a power plant fuel. The rest is made into a more valuable gas in the methanation process. This gas can be used for home heating purposes. Liquefaction can produce as much as three barrels of synthetic liquids from each ton of coal.

For both gasification and liquefaction, environmental problems must be overcome. For example, large quantities of water are consumed in both of these processes. As a rule of thumb, processing a pound of coal uses about 1.5 to 3 pounds, or 0.7 to 1.4 quarts, of water. This is about twice the water requirement of an electric power plant of the same energy output. Since much of the coal to be gasified is located in the semiarid West, this is a major concern. In addition, some water must be treated before it is discharged.

C	H₂O	CO	CO₂	H₂	CH₄
Carbon	Water	Carbon monoxide	Carbon dioxide	Hydrogen gas	Methane

Recovery and treatment systems will also be needed to minimize air pollution. Solid wastes, such as ash, require disposal.

Then there is the question of net energy. It takes energy to process coal and change it to oil or gas. Does the final product provide enough energy to justify the whole process?

Finally, at the high temperatures used in these coal conversion processes, molecules known as polycyclin aromatic hydrocarbons (PAHs) are formed. There is evidence that many of the PAHs are carcinogenic—that is, they cause cancer. This problem must be solved before synthetic fuels can be safely made or used.

11.2 Oil Shale

Oil shale is sedimentary rock (marlstone) that contains a high-molecular-weight organic solid called kerogen. When heated (**retorted**), the kerogen breaks down into synthetic crude oil and hydrocarbon gas. The world's largest reserves of oil shale are found in the Rocky Mountain region of the western United States (see Figure 11.2). One ton of oil shale may yield as much as 140 gallons of oil. To be of potential commercial interest, the yield must average at least 25 gallons per ton, and the oil must sell for at least $80 per barrel.

Apply Your Understanding

Why is oil shale important?

◄FIGURE 11.2 Oil shale country in Colorado's Grand Valley region. (*Atlantic Richfield Company [ARCO]*)

Energy Alternatives   411

► FIGURE 11.3 Oil shale, crushed shale, and the synthetic crude that can be extracted from it.

The primary advantage of shale oil is that it is a fossil fuel. The synthetic crude (Figure 11.3) that results from the heating of the shale can be refined. In fact, the products we now obtain from the refining of ordinary crude oil can be obtained from shale oil. Thus, we do not need to make major changes to use the products of oil shale development. Our present automobiles, trucks, furnaces, and motors do not need modification. Another advantage of oil shale is that some of the by-products are raw materials for the petrochemical industry.

The most common method for developing oil shale consists of mining the shale, then crushing the rocks into fist-size chunks. These chunks are further crushed to grain-size rock particles. These are then fed into the top of a tall (20 stories) retort tower (see Figure 11.4). Here the shale is heated in the absence of air (retorted). The high temperature breaks the solid kerogen molecule into liquid and gaseous vapors. The vapors are fed into a condenser where synthetic crude oil collects. Some of the flammable gas is fed back into the retort to provide the heat necessary for the breakup of more kerogen. Retorted (spent) shale must then be disposed of (see Figure 11.5).

There are some disadvantages to oil shale. Its development causes environmental damage. The land is disrupted, and air may be polluted at the retort and refinery. Large amounts of water are consumed in the waste disposal process, and new towns are built in remote areas.

Net energy is another concern related to oil shale development. Does the synfuel provide enough energy to justify the large expenditure of energy that went into producing it?

► FIGURE 11.4 A surface retort used to extract the synthetic crude from oil shale. Raw shale is introduced at the top of the retort vessel. Retorted shale is removed at the bottom. Oil and gas are taken off as a vapor at the top of the retort. (ARCO)

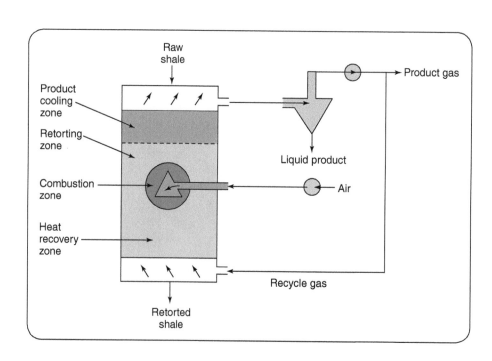

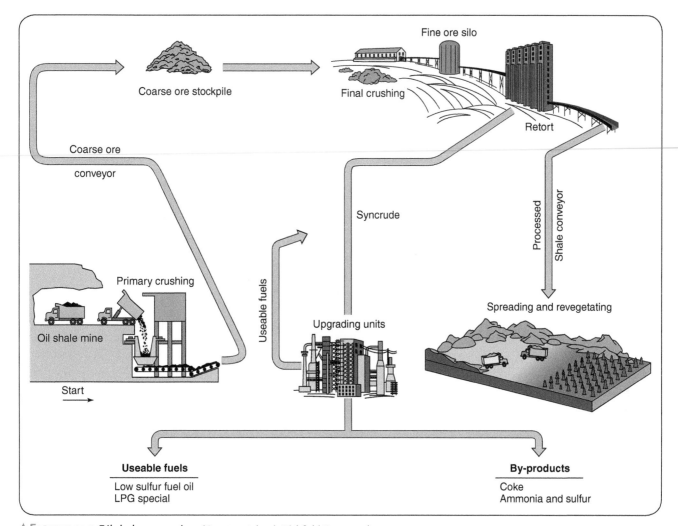

▲ FIGURE 11.5 Oil shale processing. *(Courtesy Atlantic Richfield Company.)*

Oil shale resources in the United States total more than 4 trillion barrels of potential oil. At present, however, very little is being done to develop oil shale. The world price of oil is too low for a profit to be made.

11.3 Tar Sands (Oil Sands)

Tar sands are deposits of rock or sediment that contain a heavy oil- or tar-like fossil fuel substance called **bitumen**. They are very old hydrocarbon deposits from which the light hydrocarbons have escaped, leaving the heavy, asphaltic residue behind. In the summer, tar sands look like a fine-grain asphalt road mix.

The raw material of the tar sands deposits can be changed to a whole range of fuels—from gases to heavy furnace oils and solids. These are the fuels on which our present economy depends. Many tar sands can be surface-mined. Currently, however, deep-lying deposits are difficult to extract. Bitumen is too thick to be pumped to the surface by drilling. It does not flow at room temperature; however, it flows freely when heated to about 180°F (82°C).

The Canadian tar sands are a mixture of 84–88 percent sand and clay, 8–12 percent bitumen, and 4 percent water. There, the overburden is removed from a drained muskeg (swamplike) area by huge draglines. The tar sand is then scooped up and loaded onto huge trucks that carry it to the extraction plant.

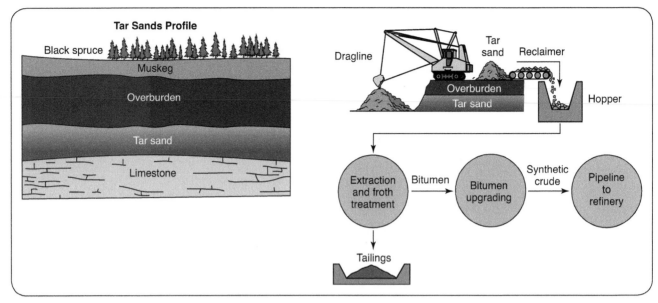

▲ Figure 11.6 Tar sands development. *(Courtesy Syncrude Canada Ltd.)*

In the extraction plant, the tar sands are mixed with chemically treated water at 180°F (82°C) in huge, horizontal rotating drums. This mixture is then pumped into separation cylinders where the sand and clay settle to the bottom and the bitumen floats to the surface. The sand and clay (the tailings) are disposed of near the plant. The bitumen is then upgraded and piped to a refinery. This whole operation is summarized in Figure 11.6.

Why is there such interest in a material that is so difficult to extract? The tar sands in the United States are small compared with those in Venezuela, Canada, and Russia. The tar sands in Alberta alone may contain the equivalent of 1 trillion barrels of petroleum. This is more than the petroleum resources of Saudi Arabia's oil fields. A similar deposit in Venezuela holds as much as 2 trillion barrels. And a deposit in Russia is estimated to be somewhat less than 1 trillion barrels.

Because of the increasing demand for crude oil, tar sand development in Canada is booming. Engineers and scientists continue to address environmental issues and study the question of net energy.

 Local Options

As our fossil fuels run low, the heat energy stored in Earth's interior (geothermal) and the mechanical energy of waves and tides begin to look more attractive. None of these can contribute more than a fraction of the total energy that will be needed in the future. In certain locations, however, they can be important.

11.4 Geothermal Energy

Geothermal energy, the natural heat of Earth, is an important supplemental power source in certain areas of the world. Currently about 6,000 megawatts (mW) of geothermal electricity serve millions of people in 20 countries. The 500 mW of electrical generating capacity at The Geysers geothermal installation near San Francisco is the largest in the world (see Figure 11.7).

Geothermal energy uses the heat produced by natural processes under Earth's surface to provide energy. These processes occur at great depths everywhere on Earth, but the heat

Apply Your Understanding

How do the sizes of tar sands deposits around the world compare?

Content Clue

Oil shale and tar sands are called nonconventional petroleum sources.

What are some nonsolar energy options that are of local interest?

414 Chapter 11

◀ FIGURE 11.7 Geothermal power plant at The Geysers near the city of Santa Rosa in northern California. The Geysers area is the largest geothermal development in the world. *(Photograph by Julie Donnelly-Nolan, USGS.)*

must be concentrated close enough to the surface to be useful. Geothermal reservoirs provide hot water or steam that can be used for heating and cooling buildings, processing foods, producing other consumer goods, and generating electricity (see Figure 11.8). Geothermal energy is the major energy source in Iceland.

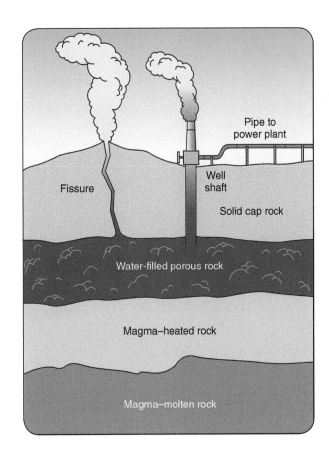

◀ FIGURE 11.8 A vapor-dominated geothermal system. *(Adapted from PEEC Packet: Energy for the Future, National Science Teachers Association.)*

ACTIVITY 11.1

Geothermal Convection Currents

In this activity, you will produce a convection current and relate convection currents to geothermal activity inside Earth.

Background

Heat energy inside Earth is transferred mostly by conduction and convection to groundwater. **Conduction** is the transfer of heat from one part of an object or region to another. For example, if you place a metal spoon in hot tea, the handle of the spoon soon becomes hot. Conduction occurs when heat is transferred from molecule to molecule. Another way to transfer heat is by convection. **Convection** is the transfer of thermal energy by moving currents of molecules.

▲ FIGURE 11.9 Convection setup.

Materials (for each lab group)

- large, open-mouth, straight-sided jar or beaker

BE SAFE

Use care when working with hot objects. Wear gloves or mitts when moving hot objects. Use tongs to move very hot items.

- small, clear glass bottle (or vial) that fits easily inside the jar (or beaker)

- dark food coloring or ink with dropper

- cold water and a way to boil water

BE SAFE

Wear safety goggles when working around open flames and boiling water. Know where the fire extinguisher and safety blankets are located, and how to use them.

- mitts or gloves and tongs

- colored pencils

- safety goggles (for each student)

Procedure

1. Add cold water to the large jar or beaker until it is about 80 percent full.

2. Fill the small glass bottle with boiling water to just below the rim.

3. Add a few drops of dark food coloring or ink to the small bottle of hot water.

BE SAFE

Be sure to wear your safety goggles throughout the lab steps.

4. Using tongs or gloves, carefully lower the small bottle of hot, colored water into the jar of cold water. Make sure the cold water completely covers the small bottle (see Figure 11.9).

5. Carefully observe what happens to the hot, colored water.

6. Reproduce Figure 11.9 in your science notebook. Label all items. Use arrows and colors or shading to show what happened.

QUESTIONS & TASKS

Record your responses in your science notebook.

1. Why didn't you get a nice convection loop like those you often see in textbook drawings (see Figure 11.10.)?

2. How might you modify this activity to get a full convection cell or loop?

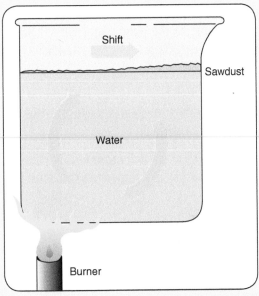

FIGURE 11.10 A convection cell in a beaker. The sawdust models a plate being rifted.

3. Use concepts you have learned about energy, thermodynamics, molecules, matter, and density to explain a convection loop. Explain clearly in a paragraph or two.

4. Imagine that the small glass bottle of hot water models a thermal hot spot inside Earth and the cold water represents groundwater. Explain how heat might be transferred inside Earth.

[Adapted from materials provided by the Geothermal Education Office, 664 Hilary Drive, Tiburon, CA 94920; http://geothermal.marin.org.]

To learn more about convection currents and geothermal activity, visit the Geothermal Education Office website at http://geothermal.marin.org.

11.5 Tidal Energy

Tidal energy has its source in the gravitational interaction between Earth and the moon. The relative contribution of tidal energy is small. It may be important, however, at some sites where energy is expensive and the rise and fall of the tides is large. A difference of about 16 feet (ft) or about 5 meters (m) between low and high tides is needed for a site to be considered. With the method commonly used, water is dammed in a reservoir at high tide, then allowed to run out through a turbine. The turbine has reversible blades, so it can spin when the tide comes in and when it goes out (see Figure 11.11).

Apply Your Understanding

What causes the tides?

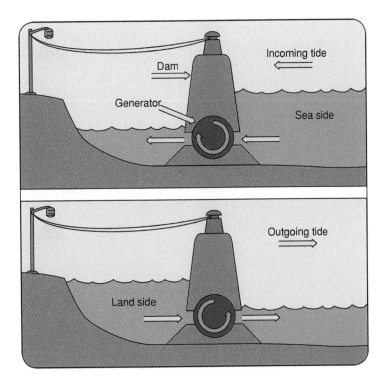

◄ FIGURE 11.11 At a tidal power station, both the incoming tide and the outgoing tide are held back by a dam. The reversible blades on the turbogenerator allow electricity to be produced both as water flows into the reservoir and as it leaves. Tidal power sites usually are large bays with small openings that can be dammed.

There are few suitable sites for tidal energy generation around the world. Those in the Bay of Fundy (Maine) are the only sites available to the continental United States, although there is impressive tidal power potential at the Cook Inlet site in Alaska.

11.6 Ocean Waves

Energy is also available from ocean waves. The kinetic energy carried by these ocean oscillations comes from wind and ocean current interactions.

Waves have considerable energy. Ask any surfer! An active region may have as much as 10,000 watts/m^2 of wave front. Several clever devices designed to extract this kinetic energy are undergoing small-scale testing.

Living in Harmony with Nature

To live in a sustainable world, we must live in harmony with nature. *Global Science* provides many strategies for such living.

ACTIVITY 11.2

Design an Environmental Home

In this activity, you will use information from upcoming readings and activities to design an environmentally responsible home.

Background

Of all the energy consumed in the United States, 40 percent is consumed in homes and buildings. About half of that energy is for space heating. With this kind of consumption, the home is something that should be examined in terms of its design, use, and potential modification.

Many of our homes are energy inefficient. In the winter, the furnace consumes fuel to keep the home warm as heat leaks out through the windows, walls, cracks, roof, and foundation. In the summer, the process is reversed. The air conditioner labors on as heat seeps in through walls, cracks, roof, and foundation (see Figure 11.12).

Procedure

1. Examine some of the methods that can be used to keep us comfortable in our homes and yet not waste energy. To do this, read sections 11.7–11.9, 11.11, and 11.12. Also complete

▶ FIGURE 11.12 Heat-loss areas in a typical home. (*Adapted from Crowther, R. L.: Sun Earth, A. B. Hirschfeld Press, Inc.*)

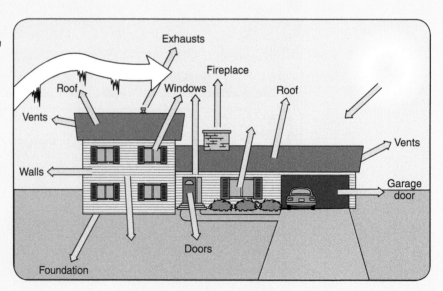

Activities 11.3, 11.6, and 11.7. For information on insulation and lighting, read sections 12.1 and 12.3 in the next chapter. You will then have the background and quantitative information to design your home and justify your decisions.

2. Your assignment is to design a home that exists in harmony with its surroundings, uses the forces of nature to perform its functions, and uses the natural forms of energy that are continuously available to us. With this kind of planning, you will be able to live in your home and cause minimal disruption to the natural cycles of Earth.

3. As you design your home, you will want to consider the following factors. Read more about these factors in the paragraphs that follow step 4 (Location of the Home and The House Itself).

   a. The location:
      - site
      - climate
      - seasons
      - daily and seasonal movement of the sun

   b. The house itself:
      - function the house is to perform
      - energy conservation principles
      - available materials
      - likes/dislikes of the occupants

   - lighting requirements
   - windows and other openings
   - entrances
   - ventilation
   - mechanical systems

4. Use the illustrations and information in this chapter, information you gather, and your own ingenuity to design and build a model of an environmental home. Write a short paper that describes its features, and present your model home to your class.

Location of the Home

In designing to the site and for the climate, one first determines the placement, orientation, and dimensions of the building. Where do the coldest and hottest winds come from? Does the site provide any natural protection from these winds? What are the daily and seasonal changes in the movement of the sun? Figure 11.13 summarizes site considerations, and section 11.7 Passive Solar describes this strategy.

The House Itself

A house can be designed to use energy wisely, and use both passive and active solar collection. An entire building can function as a solar collector in the winter and prevent solar gains in the summer. (Strategies are described in sections 11.7–11.9.)

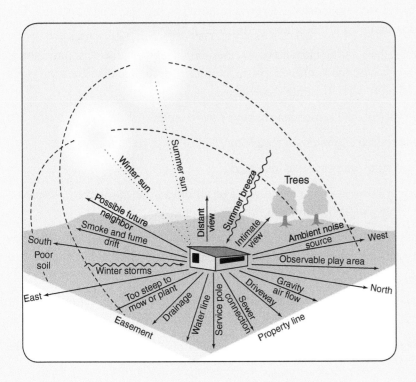

◀ FIGURE 11.13 Site analysis. (*Source: The Owner-Built Home by Ken Kern, Box 817, North Fork, CA 93643. Adapted by the author.*)

With proper planning, one can design an environmentally responsive building that has minimal negative impact on its site and efficient use of all energy. The house can also maximize human comfort, effort, and talents by providing a pleasant atmosphere in which to live and work. Figure 11.14 shows one such home.

▶FIGURE 11.14 Farmland residence. *(From Crowther, R. L.: Sun Earth, A. B. Hirschfeld Press, Inc.)*

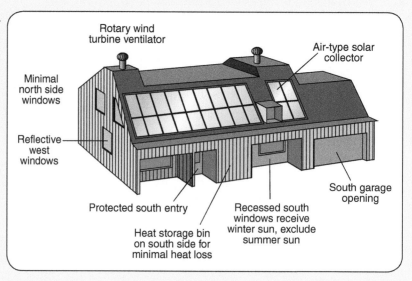

Solar Heating and Cooling of Buildings

11.7 Passive Solar

What is meant by passive solar?

Topic: passive solar energy
Go to: www.scilinks.org
Code: GloSci7e420

Passive solar is the simplest way to make use of the sun's energy to heat a home. The strategy is called passive because no outside energy is required to operate fans or pumps. The key elements of the system just sit there and perform their tasks.

In passive solar homes, the familiar elements of the building itself—walls, floors, windows, and other features, along with the landscaping—help collect, store, and distribute the sun's energy. Figures 11.15 and 11.16 illustrate these ideas.

The following list highlights the basic ideas behind passive solar:

- The home faces south to capture the greatest amount of solar radiation.

- Outside walls and attics must be well insulated.

- The south-facing window area is maximized and all others are minimized. Windows have double or triple panels or high-tech (low-E) design.

- Roof overhangs or shades block out the high summer sun to cut cooling costs. Recessing the windows accomplishes the same thing. In the winter, the low-angle sun rays are allowed to enter.

- **Thermal mass** in the interior absorbs and stores energy in the daytime and radiates it at night. The thermal mass can be a dark brick or stone wall, or dark tiles on a concrete floor.

- Insulated drapes or shutters can be opened in the daytime and drawn to provide insulation at night.

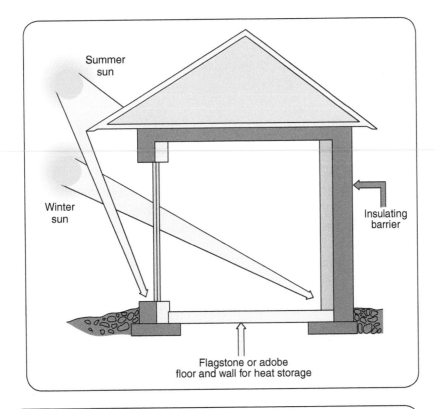

◀ FIGURE 11.15 A passive solar home.

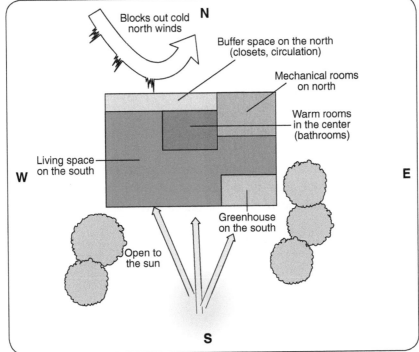

◀ FIGURE 11.16 A generalized floor plan. *(From Crowther, R. L.: Sun Earth, A. B. Hirschfeld Press, Inc.)*

- Deciduous trees on the south side shade and cool the house in the summer. The sun is allowed to enter in the winter when the leaves have fallen. Coniferous trees make a good windbreak when they are planted on the north side of the home.

- Well-placed vents help with summer cooling.

- Small openings and cracks in outside walls are caulked to prevent undesired energy losses. Door and window frames have weather stripping.

- Dirt banking, especially on the north side of a building, can be very effective in deflecting winds. Small hills or burms also deflect wind.

Energy Alternatives 421

- Energy loss can be minimized at entrances by the use of wing walls (solid barriers attached to and perpendicular to the walls of a building), landscaped barriers, storm doors, weather stripping, insulated doors, and airlocks.

- Natural lighting should be used as much as possible, and it should be indirect and diffuse. Windows, skylights, and skyshafts must be placed carefully so they provide proper lighting, yet don't cause excessive summer heat gain.

- Air is normally circulated using motors and fans. However, it can be circulated naturally using the fact that warm air is less dense than cold air. In the summer, dampered vents located at the high points in a building can be opened. As the hot air exits, cool air can be drawn in through openings near ground level on the shady side of a building. Solar plenums (ducts that, when heated, act to initiate the movement of air) can also be designed to initiate passive ventilation. In the winter, the warm air, which collects at the high points in a building, can be redirected to the cooler locations with fans. The air can be humidified by houseplants or in an attached greenhouse. (You may want to research Trombe walls at your local library or online.)

11.8 Earth-Sheltered Homes

Combining passive strategies with the underground placement of a home is slowly gaining some popularity. Moderate soil temperatures dramatically reduce the total heating and cooling energy requirements of a residence. Proper placement of a dwelling in the ground and the correct location of insulation are necessary for good performance. Usually three walls are in the ground. The south wall is exposed and designed to let the sun's rays penetrate the interior only during the winter months. Some **earth-sheltered homes** have earthen roofs.

In addition to their significant energy savings, earth-sheltered homes have the potential to withstand tornadoes. They have long-term design life and negligible exterior maintenance. Acceptance, however, has been low. This is probably because they do not look like most other homes, and people may have visions of feeling trapped in a cave. The latter is primarily a cost and architectural problem. When the principles of handling the earth-sheltered environment are understood, a subterranean architecture may evolve. The homes will be limited in their beauty, quality, and individuality only by the abilities of architects and engineers and the costs involved (see Figure 11.17).

▶FIGURE 11.17 An earth-sheltered home that is both functional and attractive. *(Designers: Tom Ellison and John Carmody. Underground Space Center, University of Minnesota.)*

Passive Solar Home

In this activity, you will examine some passive solar strategies. The activity is built around the equipment shown in Figure 11.18.

You can do this activity outside in direct sunlight or inside using sunlight through a window or a sun simulator. Regardless of your light source, conditions must be standardized so that the only quantity that varies is the one you are testing. If you use the sun simulator, it should be placed *exactly* 10 inches (in) or 25 centimeters (cm) directly out from the south window in all situations studied. If sunlight is used, all houses must directly face the sun.

Materials

- passive solar home (Sunpower House)
- thermometer (°C/°F)
- water storage container (thermal mass)
- dark- and light-colored floor panels
- reflective insulation panel
- sun simulator (clamp with 8-inch diameter reflector and 150W lightbulb)
- graph paper
- clock or watch

Procedure

1. Reproduce the table in Figure 11.19 in your science notebook.

2. Cover the front window with the reflective insulation panel. Decide which variable you will test and set up to test that variable.

3. When you are ready to begin, plug in the lamp and/or remove the reflective cover from the window.

4. If you are testing reflector and black floor, place the reflector on the floor (ground) directly in front of the window.

5. Take your initial temperature reading (at time = 0).

6. Record temperatures every 2 minutes (min) for 16 min.

7. Unplug the sun simulator and cover the window with the reflective insulation panel. You are now ready to do the "in shade" portion of the activity.

8. Take temperature readings every 2 min for another 16–18 min.

> **Helpful Hint!**
>
> If you do this activity as a class, groups can test different variables. You must, however, make sure conditions are standardized. Only then can data be compared.

> **Helpful Hint!**
>
> You may take temperatures in degrees Fahrenheit if that is the temperature scale you are familiar with.

QUESTIONS & TASKS

Record your responses in your science notebook.

1. Use graph paper to plot temperature vs. time for this lab. Plot all four situations on the same graph. Use some system to distinguish one line from the other. Label each of the four graphs.

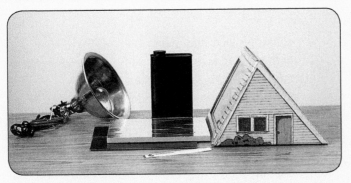

◀ **FIGURE 11.18** This model of a passive solar home can be used for experiments and demonstrations involving passive principles.

Home with →	White Floor	Black Floor	Reflector and Black Floor	Thermal Mass and Black Floor
Time (min)	Temp. (°F)	Temp. (°F)	Temp. (°F)	Temp. (°F)
0				
2				
4				
6				
8				
10				
12				
14				
16				
18				
20				
22				
24				
26				
28				
30				
32				
34				

In sun ↕ In shade

▲ FIGURE 11.19 Sample table for collecting data on passive solar homes.

2. Write a conclusion that summarizes the results of this lab.

   a. What is the best strategy for designing a passive solar home?

   b. How can indoor temperatures be kept most comfortable for living?

   c. Are there any strategies we didn't investigate?

   d. How might more heat be kept in at night?

   e. Are the best strategies economical?

ACTIVITY 11.4

Build and Use a Solar Oven

In this activity, you will design and build a solar oven and use it to cook food.

Background

While the solar oven will probably never replace the conventional gas or electric stove, for some it could replace the backyard barbecue. It is true that solar ovens only work when the sun is shining—but then, who barbecues outside in the rain? With some preplanning and an eye to the weather, a

BE SAFE

Use your solar oven to heat only precooked food until you gain the skills to determine when the food is "done."

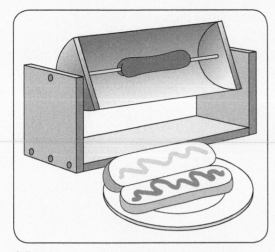

▲ FIGURE 11.20 Sun-powered hot dog cooker.
(*Courtesy Thomas Alva Edison Foundation.*)

▲ FIGURE 11.21 The Sunspot™ Solar Oven.

good deal of enjoyment and some tasty meals can be had with a solar oven.

Solar ovens come in a variety of shapes and sizes (see Figures 11.20 and 11.21). Although their appearance differs greatly, solar ovens operate on the same principles. The oven gathers solar radiation from a large area, and then concentrates it by reflecting it to a small central location. By taking a large amount of sunlight and concentrating it in a small area, very high temperatures can be achieved quickly. Food can be cooked efficiently by placing it in the area of concentrated sunlight.

Except in the case of the hot dog cooker, food is placed inside an oven (cavity) that has a black interior and a glass or special clear plastic top window. Using the "greenhouse effect," the window allows the passage of sunlight, but serves as a barrier to the transfer of heat. The black surfaces absorb the radiation and change it into long-wavelength heat rays. With the combination of window and blackened surfaces, excessive heat loss is prevented and cooking temperatures are maintained. A dark-colored, teflon-coated aluminum pan makes an excellent cooking container. Roasting bags (by Reynolds Aluminum and Glad Bags) are also convenient to use. A well-designed solar oven can cook, bake, or brown food the same as a conventional oven and in about the same amount of time.

The highest oven temperatures are reached when the solar cooker is faced directly toward the sun. Temperature is controlled simply by positioning the oven off-focus to the sun by the desired amount.

With proper design, you have an ecological, safe, nonpolluting way to quickly cook tasty meals year-round. Your oven is reusable and comes with a lifetime supply of free fuel on sunny days.

The following suggestions will increase your enjoyment and knowledgeable use of your oven:

- Preheat your oven for about 10 min before placing the food in it.

- Cooking containers and canned foods *must* be vented for steam. Closed cans will explode when heated!

- Use sunglasses when looking at your oven in bright sunlight at close range.

- Keep reflective surfaces clean with window cleaner.

- Clean spilled juices and food as soon as you are through cooking.

- Use an inexpensive oven thermometer to check the temperature inside your oven. This information will help improve your skill as a solar chef.

- Because the solar hot dog cooker does not have an oven designed to retain heat, you should only use precooked meats when using it. Use hot dogs, Spam™, or any delicious shishkebob you invent.

Procedure

You can build or purchase a solar oven from the following sources. Discuss these options with your teacher.

- To obtain directions for building a solar-powered hot dog cooker, send $1 to Charles Edison Fund, 101 S. Harrison St., East Orange, NJ 07018. Request the publication *Energy Conservation Experiments You Can Do.* A website is planned, so do a web search. This experiment may be available online for free!

- To learn about the Sunspot™ Solar Oven, contact Scott Resources, P. O. Box 2121F, Ft. Collins, CO 80522. This educational device is designed to stimulate interest in solar energy and recreational or emergency solar cooking. This inexpensive oven can be used to cook foods such as hamburgers and hot dogs in 20 min. It comes with simple instructions and cooking hints.

11.9 Active Solar

What is meant by active solar?

Active solar heating systems work like this: **Flat-plate collectors** are usually installed on the sunny side (on the roof or ground near the building) and covered with transparent glass or plastic. Between the cover and a black plate is an air space. (Black is used because it is an efficient absorber of sunlight.) The transparent cover traps heat in the collector much like glass does in a greenhouse (see Figure 11.22).

Water or air is circulated (in pipes) through the collectors to absorb captured heat and carry it to a storage tank (usually in the basement). If air is circulated, the heat is absorbed in hot rocks. If water is circulated, the storage tank is usually a large tank of water. Fans or pumps, powered by electricity, deliver the heat to the various rooms of the house (see Figure 11.23). If solar cooling is also desired, the flat-plate collectors must be replaced by parabolic reflectors. This kind of system is much more expensive.

Think about This!

Would you be willing to pay more to install a solar-heating system in your house?

Hopefully in the future, the cost (when spread out over 20 years) will be competitive with other types of heating. Currently, however, the initial costs for installing solar heating systems are still quite high. Because sunshine is unpredictable, storage must be provided. To keep costs down, the storage is usually enough for only two sunless days. After that, a backup heating system must be used. This additional heating system adds to the expense.

►FIGURE 11.22 Flat-plate collector.

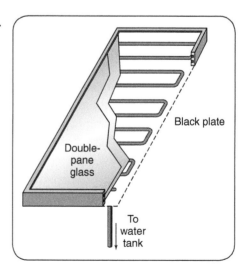

Black plate

Double-pane glass

To water tank

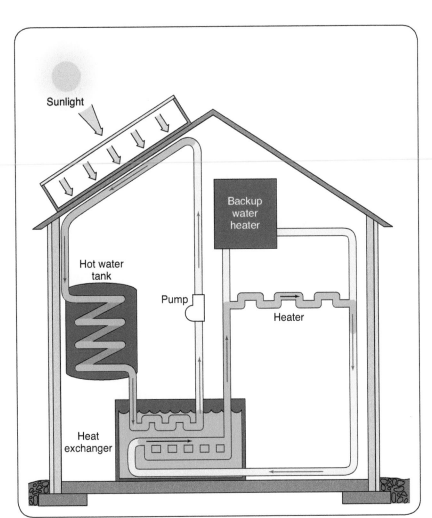

SCLINKS®
NSTA

Topic: active solar energy
Go to: www.scilinks.org
Code: GloSci7e427

ACTIVITY 11.5

Analysis of a Solar Collector

In this activity, you will determine the maximum output of a simple solar collector.

On average, enough solar energy strikes the roof of most American homes to provide for all, or a very significant portion of, their heating needs. This is true throughout the year.

In this activity, you will circulate a measured amount of water through a solar collector, and measure the temperature change and the time for circulation. You will then determine the amount of heat energy gained by the water. Finally, after determining the area of the window of the collector, you will determine the energy output of the collector. This information can be used to give you some insights into the promise and problem of using flat-plate solar collectors as home energy providers.

Materials

- flat-plate collector
- 2,000-mL container with spout (located near bottom), or 2,000-mL beaker and siphon bulb
- styrofoam cooler
- stopwatch or wristwatch
- meterstick or yardstick
- 2 Fahrenheit thermometers
- screw-type tubing clamp (optional)
- 1,000-mL graduated cylinder

Energy Alternatives 427

- chair (or prop)
- cold water
- calculators

Procedure

1. Reproduce the data sheet in Figure 11.25 in your science notebook. Record your measurements in your notebook.

2. Determine and record the outside (ambient) air temperature, the pollution level, and the percentage of cloud cover.

3. Examine the solar collector. Note the transparent window, the air space, the black plate, and the circulating coils. Measure and record (in feet) the length and width of the window.

4. Set the collector in the sun so that it *directly* faces the sun. Minimize the shadow inside the collector to help you get the best angle. Keep the collector in this orientation by positioning it on a chair or some other support.

WARNING

Do not suck on the hose (from the solar collector) in step 7 to pull water through it. The water could be very hot and scald your mouth!

Helpful Hint!

This activity must be done on a sunny day.

5. Go to a cold water tap and run water until it is as cold as that system delivers. This is the temperature of unheated water for that system. Fill a 2,000-milliliter (mL) beaker with this cold water.

6. Make adjustments to your system so your setup looks like the one in Figure 11.24.

7. *Use the siphoning bulb* to start pulling water from the 2,000-mL container through the collector and into the styrofoam cooler.

8. Adjust the flow rate by raising or lowering the large beaker (or with a screw-type tubing clamp) so that 2,000 mL will pass through the system in about 4 min. (This assumes the collector window is approximately 2 to 4 ft².)

9. After almost 1,000 mL of cold water has flushed out the system, pinch the lower hose to stop the flow.

10. Place 2,000 mL of cold water into the upper container. Place the upper hose of the collector in the container. Also, place a thermometer

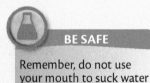

BE SAFE

Remember, do not use your mouth to suck water through the system!

▶FIGURE 11.24 Lab setup for analyzing a solar collector.

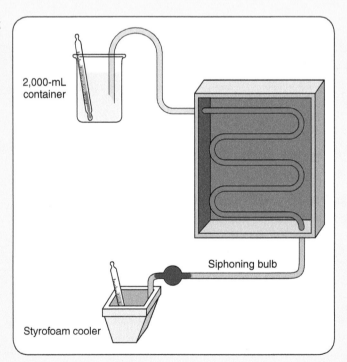

Data Collected

Make sure your collector is aimed directly at the sun.

1. Outside air temperature: _____ °F

2. Pollution level: _____ (estimate high, medium, low)

3. Cloud cover blocking the sun: _____% (ideally 0%)

4. Area of collector window = _____ ft × _____ ft = _____ ft²

5. Volume of water = _____ mL

6. Water temperature   Time of reading
   Incoming water: _____ °F   Start: 0.0 min
   Exiting water: _____ °F   End: _____ min

7. Mass of water = _____ grams (g) = _____ kilograms (kg).
   (Use 1 mL of water = 1 g and 1,000 g = 1 kg.)

8. Weight of water = _____ pounds (lb). (Use 1 kg = 2.2 lb.)

in the water, and record the temperature. Position the container arrangement so that it is *above* the collector. You will run 2,000 mL of water through the collector 1 time.

11. Get ready to determine the following:

    a. amount of time it takes the 2,000 mL of water to pass through the collector,

    b. the incoming water temperature, and

    c. exiting water temperature.

12. Start timing as soon as the water begins to flow. Stop timing when 2,000 mL has passed through the system.

13. As the system runs, record the incoming water temperature and the exiting water temperature.

14. Record the time it took the water to flow through the system.

15. Determine the mass and weight of the water.

QUESTIONS & TASKS

Record your responses in your science notebook.

1. Calculate the amount of heat gained by the water as follows:

   a. Number of Btu = weight of water in pounds × temperature rise in F°.

      = _____ lb × _____ F° × 1 Btu/lb F°

      = _____ Btu

   b. Now determine the maximum output of your collector in Btu/ft²/min.

      Max. output = _____ Btu/ _____ ft²/ _____ min

      = _____ Btu/ft²/min

2. Imagine you tracked the sun so that your collector faced the sun continuously. What is the potential maximum output of your collector in *Btu/ft²/hr*?

Helpful Hint!

The unit of heat most commonly used in the American solar heating industry is the Btu. One Btu = the amount of heat required to raise the temperature of 1 lb of water 1F°.

Helpful Hint!

This is called the *maximum output* of the collector because the collector is directly facing the sun and there is no cloud cover.

Solar Water Heating

In Activity 11.5, you determined the maximum output of a flat-plate collector. Is this a good way to provide hot water to a home? Let's find out.

In this activity, you will calculate the approximate collector area required for heating the hot water required by a family of four. You will then analyze the economics of providing hot water to a home using flat-plate collectors.

Background

At midday in cloudless weather, at central latitudes in the United States, about 300 Btu/hour of solar radiation strike a square foot of surface that is facing the sun. However, flat-plate collectors are almost always fixed in place on a roof facing south. They are mounted at a given angle that is determined by the latitude of the home. In addition to this, the weather is not always cooperative (cloudy part of the time). Also, the sun's angle changes during the day and during the different seasons. Thus, during winter months most flat-plate solar collectors provide about 120 Btu/ft^2/hour during a 6-hour period (9:00 AM–3:00 PM). Before and after that period, the sun provides little additional heat.

Materials

- calculators

Procedure

Work through the calculations and answer the questions in the Question & Task section. Be sure to show your work, not just your answers.

QUESTIONS & TASKS

Record your responses in your science notebook.

1. Determine the average output of a flat-plate collector/day (assume winter months).

   Average output/day = (Btu/ft^2/hour) × (collecting hours/day) = _____ Btu/ft^2.

2. The average family of four uses about 60 gallons of hot water/day. Hot water is used for showers, baths, sinks, dishwasher, and washing clothes. Assume that the water is provided to the home at 45°F and water is heated to 120°F for home use. How many Btu/day are required to provide hot water to a family of four?

   Helpful Hint!

   One gallon of water weighs 8.33 lb.

3. How many square feet of flat-plate collector are required to provide for the hot water needs of a family of four?

4. Assume that the average flat-plate collector panel measures 4 ft × 8 ft or 4 ft × 10 ft. How many collector panels must be placed on a roof?

5. Now assume that the average suburban home in America has a roof area of 1,000 ft^2. If the roof slopes both north and south, how many square feet of south-facing roof are available for installing the hot water system?

6. What percentage of the south-facing roof will be covered by flat-plate collectors? Sketch the house outlined in Figure 11.26 in your science notebook. Shade the roof on your sketch.

7. Let's now assume that the average cost of installing a complete flat-plate solar water heating system is $100/ft^2. How much does a flat-plate water heating system cost? Is this cost reasonable?

   Helpful Hint!

   A complete solar water heating system includes collectors, heat exchange, storage, pumps, controls, and installation costs (see Figure 11.26).

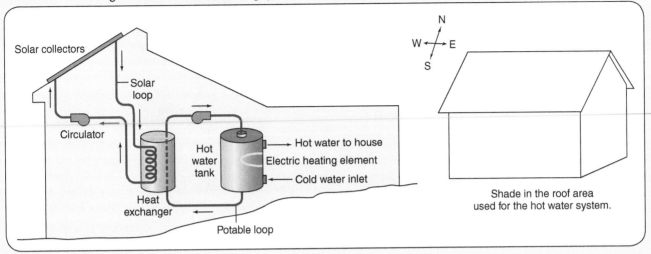

Solar Electricity

Solar energy can be harnessed in several ways to produce electricity.

11.10 Concentrating Solar Power (CSP)

Concentrating solar power (CSP) is a collection system that concentrates enough sunlight onto a boiler or a fluid (water or heat-conducting oil) to make large quantities of steam. The steam, in turn, is used to spin a turbine that rotates the coil of a generator that produces electricity.

Two methods of CSP are being studied. The first method is called the *distributed collector concept*. In its most common form, a long reflecting trough with a parabolic cross section concentrates solar energy onto a collector tube. A heat-conducting oil flows through the tube and into a heat exchanger. Here the oil transfers its heat to water and produces steam. Excess heat is stored for use at night and on cloudy days (see Figure 11.27).

The second method is called *solar thermal power*. This method produces higher temperature. A field of computer-guided mirrors (heliostats) tracks the sun and focuses the sun's

How can the sun be used to produce electricity?

Apply Your Understanding

What is the purpose of CSP?

◀ FIGURE 11.27 The distributed collector concept. (*From USDOE, Sandia Laboratories.*)

rays onto a boiler. The boiler is mounted on top of a central receiving tower. Here the radiant solar energy is absorbed and used for producing steam (see Figure 11.28).

The main advantage of both CSP methods is that sunshine is free. In addition, the environmental impact of these systems is relatively minor.

Only direct sunlight is usable by CSP. This restricts solar thermal power plants primarily to the sunny areas of the country. There are no basic technical limitations in this method. The main questions are overall efficiency and economics. One key consideration is space, as sunlight is diffuse and must be collected over a wide area. It is estimated that in the southwestern United States, approximately 10 square miles (mi^2) or 26 square kilometers (km^2) would be needed to operate a 1,000-mW plant working at an average capacity of 60 percent. This is enough power to supply a city of a million people. At present, there is no economically feasible method for storing heat for use at night and on overcast days.

Scientists and engineers are working to develop concentrating solar power plants that are both economical and of low technical risk to investors.

11.11 Solar Photovoltaic Energy (Solar Cells)

A **solar cell** is an electronic device that converts sunlight directly into electricity. Basically, solar cells work this way. If a particle of light (a **photon**) of appropriate wavelength (and energy) enters a solar cell, it will free an electron from its chemical bond within the cell. The electron is now free to wander forward within the cell, leaving behind a "hole." The hole essentially moves backward when an electron from a neighboring bond exchanges places with it. Such movement of electrons and holes is the essence of electricity. Because this movement builds up an electrical potential (voltage), a solar cell is essentially a small, light-activated battery.

If circuitry is provided, as shown in Figure 11.29, current will flow with electrons moving toward the negative terminal and holes in the opposite direction. Thus, electric power is produced.

Solar cells have been used for years to power highway call boxes, offshore buoys, and other remote devices. Once installed, they essentially require no maintenance. They are now economical for use in homes in remote areas. (Remote means one-quarter mile or more from the nearest utility pole.)

The chief barrier to the widespread use of solar cells is cost. Much current research is being done, however, particularly in "thin-film" technology. Research breakthroughs and mass production should lower the cost. This could make photovoltaics commercially competitive.

It is possible to construct solar cell arrangements that have enough capacity for electric power production (see Figure 11.30). Figure 11.31 shows a photovoltaic system that produces alternating current (AC) for use in a home or cabin.

Helpful Hint!

A **photovoltaic cell** is another name for a solar cell.

Apply Your Understanding

What are some other uses of solar cells?

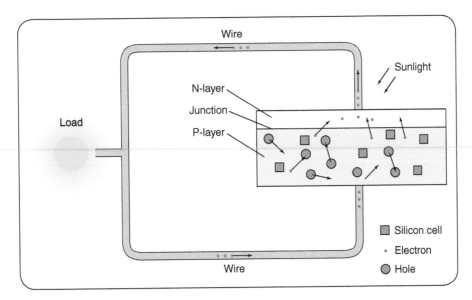

Wire

N-layer

Junction

P-layer

Load

Sunlight

Silicon cell

Electron

Hole

Wire

◀ FIGURE 11.29 Diagram of a solar cell. The **load** is the electrical device (appliance, lightbulb) in the circuit that the current operates. The load offers resistance to the flow of current. *(From Solar Energy Research Institute.)*

◀ FIGURE 11.30 One-axis tracking photovoltaic panels at the 8.2 megawatt SunEdition photovoltaic power plaut near Alamosa, Colorado.

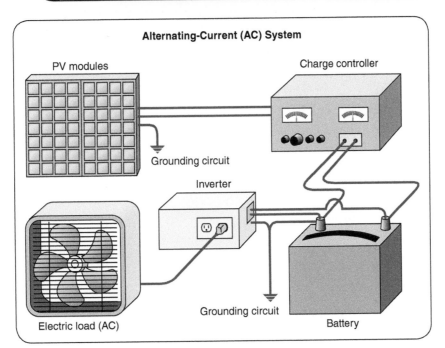

Alternating-Current (AC) System

PV modules

Charge controller

Grounding circuit

Inverter

Electric load (AC)

Grounding circuit

Battery

◀ FIGURE 11.31 Most household appliances operate on alternating current (AC). This diagram illustrates a basic configuration of the PV modules and equipment in an AC system. (Circuit breakers and safety fuses are not shown.) *(NREL)*

Energy Alternatives 433

Solar Cells

In this activity, you will calculate the power output of a solar cell and determine its efficiency as an energy converter. You will also analyze some of the factors that must be considered in appraising the potential of solar cells for providing electrical and heating/cooling requirements in the home.

Materials

- solar cell

- resistor (matched to the cell)

- 4 lead wires (connecting wires) with alligator clip

- voltmeter (high resistance), 0–2 V or 0–5 V

- milliammeter (0–100 mA)

- metric ruler

- calculators

Procedure

1. Reproduce the data sheet in Figure 11.32 in your science notebook. Record all data and do all calculations in your notebook.

▼FIGURE 11.32 Data sheet for recording measurements and calculations.

Data Collected/Calculations

1. Current = _____ milliamps = _____ amps

2. Electrical potential = _____ volts

3. Length of cell = _____ cm; width of cell = _____ cm

> **Helpful Hint!**
>
> 1,000 mA = 1 amp

4. Use the following information to estimate the solar input where you live.

   The strength of the sun as a power provider is called the **solar input**. The value of the solar input depends on several factors. The main factor is usually the amount of atmosphere that lies between the sun and the absorber. Here is the approximate value of the solar input for three locations.

Location	Solar Input (on a clear day)
Sea level	0.100 watts/cm^2
2,000 ft	0.103 watts/cm^2
5,000 ft	0.108 watts/cm^2

   Solar input = _____ watts/cm^2

5. Power output of our solar cell:

   Power (watts) = _____ volts × _____ amps = _____ watts

6. Area of our solar cell:

   Area = length × width = _____ cm × _____ cm = _____ cm^2

7. Power density of our solar cell:

   Power density = power output/area = watts/cm^2 = _____ watts/cm^2

8. Efficiency of our solar cell as an energy converter:

   Efficiency = power density/solar input × 100% = _____ %

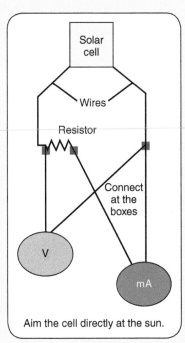

▲FIGURE 11.33 A diagram of
what your circuit looks like.

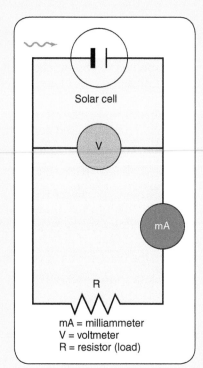

▲FIGURE 11.34 Schematic
drawing of the solar cell circuit.

2. Set up the circuit shown in Figure 11.33. Figure 11.34 shows how an electrician would draw the circuit.

3. Aim the solar cell directly at the sun so that both meters give maximum readings.

4. Note and record the current flow (I) in milliamps and amps.

5. Note and record the electrical potential (V) in volts.

6. Measure and record the length and width of the solar cell in centimeters (cm).

Helpful Hint!

In this circuit, the solar cell acts as a battery and produces current that passes through the load. The load (resistor or R) represents the portion of the circuit that uses the power produced by the cell. The **milliammeter** measures the current that flows through the circuit (mA), and the **voltmeter** measures the electrical potential (voltage or V) across the solar cell.

Helpful Hint!

The solar cell is inside a plastic case. Be sure to measure the dimension of the cell and not the case.

7. Estimate and record the approximate solar input where you live using the information provided in Figure 11.32.

8. Make the following calculations:

   a. Determine the power output of your solar cell. (Power in watts is equal to volts times amps.)

   b. Determine the area of your solar cell. (Area = length × width.)

   c. Determine the power density of your solar cells by dividing the power output by the area.

   d. Determine the percentage efficiency of your solar cell by dividing the power density by the solar input and multiplying by 100 percent.

Record your responses in your science notebook.

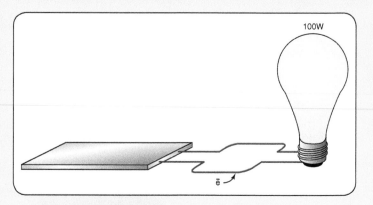

1. How many solar cells of the type you worked with would it take to light a 100W bulb? (Assume that the bulb is used during the sunny part of the day, or that you have a way to store the energy the solar cell produces during the day for use at night or when it is cloudy.)

2. How much does it cost a homeowner to use electricity for 30 years if the electricity is purchased from the electric power company?

Helpful Hint!

- An average house uses 15 kilowatt hour (kWh)/day.
- Electricity costs $0.10/kWh.

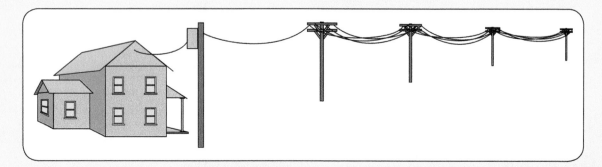

3. Suppose a homeowner wants to use solar cells to provide the electricity for a home. How much power does the solar cell system need to produce?

Helpful Hint!

- An average house uses 15 kWh/day.
- An average day has 6 hr of collecting time.
- Power $= \dfrac{\text{energy}}{\text{time}}$, so

$$P_{(KW)} = \dfrac{e(kWh)}{t(h)}$$

4. If solar cell systems cost $8,000 per kilowatt (installed), what is the cost of putting a solar cell system on a house?

5. How much electrical energy can be obtained from a square meter of solar cells each day? Solar cells are approximately 12 percent efficient.

Helpful Hint!

Earth's surface receives approximately 4 kWh/m² of sunlight each day. This is a 24-hr average figure for the United States (the lower 48 states).

6. The average American home uses approximately 15 kWh of electrical energy each day. How many square meters of solar cells are required to produce 15 kWh of electrical energy?

7. The area of the average American roof is 1,000 ft².

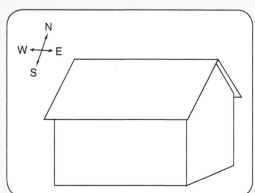

a. How many square meters is this?

Helpful Hint!

1 ft = 0.3045 m
Hint: Square both sides.

1 ft² = _____ m²

1,000 ft² = _____ m²

b. What percentage of the roof will need solar cells?

c. What percentage of the south-facing roof must be solar cells?

d. Make a sketch of the house shown. Shade in the solar cells on the roof.

8. How do you plan to heat your solar home? (See table for information.) Show this on your drawing.

9. How will you provide hot water? Show this on your drawing.

10. Do you have any other ideas for providing for the energy needs of your environmental home?

Heating Region	Daily Heating Requirement (Btu/day)	Daily Heating Requirement (kWh/day)
Cold northern	1,000,000	300
Mid-climate	700,000	200
Sun Belt	50,000	100

11.12 Wind Power

The wind's energy originates in the uneven heating of Earth. The sun's rays strike the equatorial regions almost directly, but they approach the poles at an angle (see Figure 11.35). This causes large-scale currents in the atmosphere. Hot air rises from the tropical regions, flows toward the poles, and sinks to Earth. A flow of cooler air goes back across the surface toward the equator. Wind patterns would be simple if Earth were a smooth, solid sphere, and if it were not rotating. The planet's axial spin breaks this simple flow into the major wind belts—the prevailing westerly and trade winds. Differences in local surface conditions (mountains, oceans, forests, and so forth.) provide the almost infinite variety that makes wind and weather so hard to predict.

Using the wind's energy is not a new idea. Wind has been used for centuries for grinding grain, moving sailing ships, and pumping water. In the early 20th century, 6 million small windmills of about one horsepower each dotted the Midwest. They were used mainly for pumping water. In the 1930s, inexpensive electricity provided through the REA (Rural

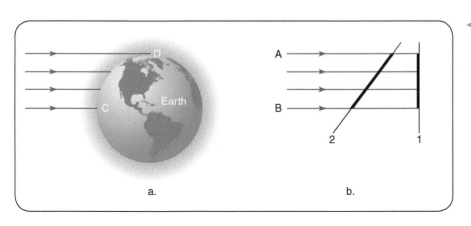

◀ FIGURE 11.35 (a) Radiant energy hitting Earth's surface at an angle, as at point D, is less intense because it must pass through a greater thickness of the atmosphere than that coming straight down, as at C. (b) The energy carried by rays A–B is spread over a greater area on the inclined surface (2) than on the perpendicular surface (1) and so produces less heating per unit area. (*From Physics of the Earth, by Robert B. Gordon. New York: Holt Rinehart and Winston, Inc., 1972.*)

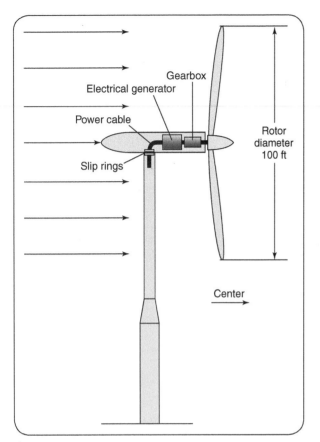

▲ FIGURE 11.36 Horizontal-axis wind turbine. (*From* Energy Alternatives: A Comparative Analysis. *Science and Public Policy Program, University of Oklahoma. Photo by Sandia Laboratories.*)

Electrification Administration) put most of the windmills out of business. However, uncertain fuel prices, coupled with environmental and political concerns, have revived interest in wind machines as a source of electricity.

Wind power is economic and nonpolluting. It has features that are well-adapted to farm and remote site use. This eliminates the need for long and expensive transmission lines. Before the wind can provide meaningful amounts of power for us, several major problems must be solved.

There are different **wind generator** designs. The most important distinction is between the horizontal-axis machines (Figure 11.36) and the vertical-axis machines such as the Darrieus rotor (Figure 11.37).

In general, the horizontal-axis machines have higher power factors (as shown in Figure 11.38). The vertical-axis machines have the advantage of not having to be steered into the wind. They also allow placement of the generator at the base of the machine. Such placement, however, has the disadvantage of putting all the wind machine's weight on the pivot. At present, the vertical-axis machines are considered most suitable for smaller machines, while the very large machines are all horizontal-axis devices.

Other considerations enter into designing wind machines. How is the machine to be used? If water is to be pumped, then a high torque (or turning force) is required to enable the wind machine to start with a heavy load on it. The multibladed Jacobson windmill of the old Midwest and the Dutch windmill gave away efficiency for torque. If the machine is designed to generate electricity, a high starting torque is not required and a higher power coefficient can be obtained.

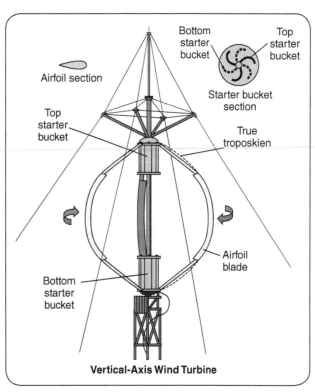

▲ **FIGURE 11.37** Vertical-axis wind turbine (showing modified troposkien configuration). *(USDOE, Sandia Laboratories)*

Wind as a source of energy is erratic, like solar energy. On average, wind machines have capacity factors of 25 to 30 percent. This means that wind machines either need significant storage capacity or they need backup.

Wind-generated electricity can be stored in batteries. This is done in many small-scale operations. However, battery storage is expensive. Other storage options are available. Some of them, like hydrogen production, still require much research. The most practical systems at present are those that would take advantage of a large grid of interconnected wind machines. Interconnection averages power over a large area, increasing the odds that some machines are generating power. It is likely that an interconnected grid system like this would include some nuclear or fossil fuel backup–generating capacity (see Figure 11.39.)

Solar energy and wind energy can be used to complement each other. The wind is likely to be blowing when the sun doesn't shine, and vice versa. Connecting a solar generator to a wind generator would be more reliable than using either alone.

Helpful Hint!

A *capacity factor* is the rate of energy delivered to the total energy that could be delivered if the machine ran its rated capacity all the time.

Think about This!

What are other possibilities involving wind?

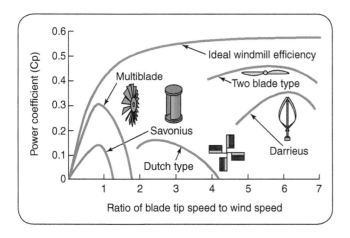

◀ **FIGURE 11.38** Typical performances of wind machines. *(USDOE)*

► FIGURE 11.39 This
California windmill
complex is part of a
growing independent
power industry. *(Pacific
Gas & Electric Company)*

At present, wind power is the fastest growing energy alternative. It is cost competitive with coal-fired, gas-fired, and nuclear electric power. However, wind farms do require the construction of new expensive transmission lines.

Wind power is not a single answer to the energy problem, even though it has significant potential. Used imaginatively, and in connection with other sources, it can be an important component of the energy mix of the future. Wind could satisfy up to 5 percent of our energy needs in a couple of decades.

ACTIVITY 11.8

Build a Model Wind Generator

In this activity, you will build one or more model wind generators and test some of the variables involved.

Background

In our nation's effort to obtain power from the wind, a variety of devices are being tested. In some devices, the rotors look like bicycle wheels; in other devices, the rotors look like eggbeaters and airplane propellers. Each design has its features and drawbacks. Here are some of the factors that you should consider when designing your wind generator.

1. *Self-starting.* Will your generator start by itself, or do you need an external power source to get it going?

2. *Directional properties.* Will your generator accept wind from any direction, or do you need to add directional equipment?

3. *Vertical or horizontal axis.* Where is the electric generator to be mounted (near the ground or high on a tower)? Is efficiency-reducing, right-angle drive involved in transferring power from the rotor to the generator?

4. *Stress and strain.* How are stress and strain on the rotors and the tower to be handled? The size of your rotor, the speed at which it rotates, the speed of the wind, and its gustiness all are factors that produce stress and strain. They all must be considered.

5. *Constancy of electric output.* Normally, you want to generate constant voltage power that

has a constant frequency and is in phase. However, wind is unpredictable and its speed will vary. How do you allow for this and still generate proper current?

6. *Vibrations.* As the wind blows and your rotor spins, vibrations will be produced. The generator, the rotor, and the tower all have natural vibration frequencies. You must keep the frequencies of vibration set up by the rotor different from those of the tower. If they aren't, the tower could tear itself apart with vibration.

7. *Airfoil design.* Is the foil thickest where it moves slowest and thin where it moves fast? At what angle does it attack the wind? Should this angle vary along the foil? Do you want the pitch angle to change with wind speed (feathering), or do you want to keep it constant? How many blades work best?

8. *Energy storage.* What happens when the wind doesn't blow? Do you plan to store energy in batteries or to generate hydrogen? Is it practical to do this on a large scale, or are you limiting yourself to remote homes and farms?

9. *Cost effectiveness.* How much energy do you get per dollar spent? When your wind generator is scaled up in size, what happens to the amount and cost of materials per dollar ratio?

Procedure

1. Look at the series of vertical-axis and horizontal-axis wind generator models shown in Figures 11.40 and 11.41. For indoor testing, the fan type shown in Figure 11.41 works well.

2. Since you will only be able to generate at about 1.5 V, you can use a 1.5-V motor as your generator. Because the rate of rotation of the shaft will probably be relatively slow, it may be better to use a 12-V motor. If the shaft of a 12-V motor is rotated at 1/10 normal operating speed, you will generate current at a potential of approximately 1.2 V. Since the amount of current is so little, connect a 1.5-V @ 25 mA mini-lamp (bulb) to the wires of your generator.

3. Design one or more model generators, test some of the variables, and consult various library references as necessary.

4. Write a short report on your findings.

> **Helpful Hint!**
>
> The small motors used in toys and sold in hobby shops make excellent generators for model wind generators. Because they have a coil and permanent magnets inside, they will generate electricity when their shaft is forced to rotate.

> **Helpful Hint!**
>
> These bulbs can be purchased at radio and electronic parts stores.

▼ FIGURE 11.40 A variety of vertical-axis wind generator models.

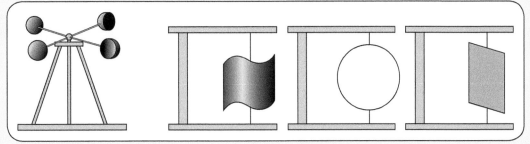

▼ FIGURE 11.41 A variety of horizontal-axis wind generator models.

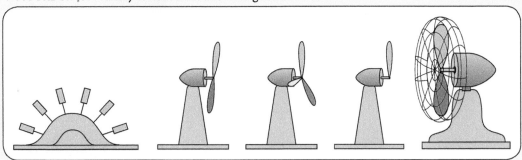

11.13 Ocean Thermal Energy Conversion (OTEC)

The largest collectors of energy on Earth are the oceans. This fact makes possible the concept of **ocean thermal energy conversion (OTEC)**. OTEC uses temperature differences between surface waters and ocean depths to generate electricity. Basically, this is how it works.

1. In the tropics, the ocean's top layer, heated by sunlight and mixed by wind and waves, is relatively warm (80°F/27°C). The lower, dark layers (1,500–4,000 ft down 450–1,200 m) are cold (40°F/4.5°C). A power plant in the ocean would draw warm water from the surface to heat a working fluid such as ammonia, propane, or Freon™ in a closed container until the fluid evaporates.

2. Confining the fluid to a small container would produce pressure that rotates a turbine, which would power a generator. Cold water drawn from the depths would cool the working fluid until it condenses back into a liquid. The entire cycle would then be repeated.

All this takes place at a power plant on a large, floating platform (see Figure 11.42). Electricity can either travel to land through cables for conventional uses, or be used to extract hydrogen from seawater. Hydrogen can replace fossil fuels in many ways. Electricity could also be used to combine nitrogen from the air and hydrogen from the water to make ammonia. This is the primary ingredient for fertilizer.

The temperature difference between deep and shallow ocean waters represents a continuous and considerable source of energy. However, this process is still highly speculative. The potential for capturing this power is largely unproved because little experimentation has been done. Many questions remain. Can a design and materials be found that will resist the corrosive power of seawater? What impact will mixing warm and cold water have on aquatic life and ocean cycles? Is a net energy yield possible? What are the legal and political considerations? Finally, cold water contains large amounts of dissolved carbon dioxide, which would be released upon warming. What long-term environmental effects would this have?

▶ FIGURE 11.42 An ocean thermal power plant. For size comparison, note the helicopter in the upper left corner. (*Lockheed Missiles & Space Co., Inc.*)

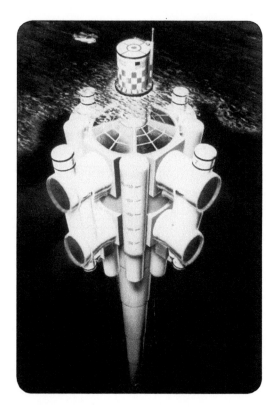

11.14 Orbiting Solar Satellite Energy

Putting solar collectors in outer space and relaying energy back to Earth may be possible. The solar radiation reaching Earth could supply more useful power than the world needs. The idea is to put solar collectors in orbit and beam the captured energy back to Earth in the form of microwaves. Advantages of such an undertaking are that solar radiation is more intense in outer space and the sun shines continuously. The clouds that interfere with collecting solar energy near Earth's surface would have no effect on orbiting collectors.

Think about This!

How can solar satellites provide energy to people on Earth?

The orbiting satellites would have solar panels more than 40 square miles in area. A single power station might provide as much as 5,000 mW of power. This is about half the present capacity of New York City's generating plants. The microwaves, transmitted by the satellite, would be received by a ground-based antenna some 5 mi (8 km) in diameter. Here the microwave energy would be converted into alternating current electricity and distributed for use (see Figure 11.43). Princeton physics professor Gerard K. O'Neill calculates that a 5,000-mW satellite station and its ground receiver could possibly produce electricity for less than the 8 to 12 cents per kilowatt-hour consumers now pay for electricity from coal-fired power plants.

The economics of collecting and using this energy presents a major obstacle to scientists and engineers. It has been suggested, for example, that we mine the moon for raw materials for building the space stations and collectors. However, a closer examination of this idea puts it in the realm of pure fantasy. Not all the needed raw materials are found on the moon. Also, the production of steel and special alloys is a complex operation even on Earth. It is difficult to explore for and develop mineral deposits in isolated regions on Earth. Attempting similar operations on the moon seems questionable at best.

Another problem is that we know little about the short- or long-term effects of exposing living organisms (including humans) to microwaves. Scientists generally believe that exposure is probably not healthy. A more specific answer to this problem will require more study.

How would a nation defend its solar satellites? Clearly, if a significant portion of a nation's energy supply were orbiting the globe, it would have to be defended. Would this prompt the development of a space-oriented military? Would "Star Wars" become a reality? What would the price tag be?

Think about This!

Why would a solar satellite need to be defended?

◄ FIGURE 11.43 An artist's conception of solar satellites beaming microwave energy back to Earth. (*NASA*)

In a project of this nature, energy is being captured, relayed to Earth, and retained for a time. This is energy that otherwise would not have reached Earth. If this is done on a large enough scale, Earth will become warmer. What are the long-term implications? Will our climate change? Will polar ice begin to melt?

Finally, can we justify spending billions on solar space stations when human problems on Earth are so great? Calculations may indicate that space-produced energy is economical, but do these calculations include all the hidden costs? One thing is sure: A society powered by an energy system located in space would be much more dependent on technology than our society is today.

11.15 Water Power

Apply Your Understanding

How is water power used?

Water power is another use of solar energy that has a long history. Water is evaporated by solar heat, lifted, and carried by the winds. It has energy stored in many forms. It has gravitational energy that is converted by hydroelectric power plants (see Figure 11.44). Flowing water has kinetic energy, which can be used to turn a waterwheel or a modern turbine.

We are already using a large percentage of our available hydropower (see Figure 11.45). Many of the undeveloped sites are in areas of great scenic beauty, however, and are protected by legislation such as the Scenic Rivers Act.

Future development of hydropower in the United States may proceed in two directions. There is growing interest in using the energy available from small dams and from

▶ FIGURE 11.44 Cross section of a hydroelectric dam. (*Adapted from Hydroelectric Handbook, 2nd ed., by Creager and Justin. New York: John Wiley & Sons, Inc.*)

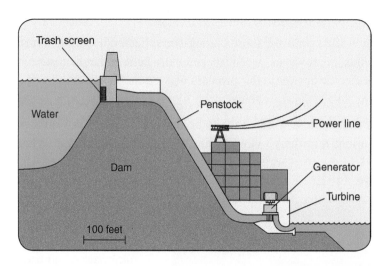

▶ FIGURE 11.45 Aerial view of Hoover Dam on the Colorado River. (*U.S. Bureau of Reclamation*)

undammed flowing water ("nondam" hydropower). These installations would use totally immersible turbogenerators placed in rivers or in artificially constructed diversions. They could also be used in aqueducts, irrigation ditches, and so on. Such systems would be small and of local interest. They could be important components of the "appropriate technology" approach to energy, which we will consider in the next chapter.

Fuels from the Sun

In photosynthesis, solar energy causes CO_2 and H_2O to combine to form carbohydrates. The energy stored in the carbohydrates is released when they are digested, burned, or decomposed.

11.16 Wood

Wood (a form of biomass) was the first solar energy option to be used widely. After accounting for as much as 90 percent of our total energy consumption in the mid-19th century, the use of wood as an energy source has dropped to under 0.5 percent.

Areas where many woodstoves and fireplaces are in constant use are experiencing a good deal of pollution related to wood burning. Some areas have banned, and others are considering banning, their use—at least on high-pollution days.

Wood will make only a small contribution to our nation's energy future. This contribution will be in areas of low population density and where wood is abundant and inexpensive.

11.17 Energy from Trash

Various cities throughout the world burn trash to produce electric power. Municipal trash is mostly paper, cardboard, plastic, and food scraps. Mixed in with that flammable trash, however, are bottles, cans, and a variety of other materials. If these items are not removed ahead of time, they melt in the boiler and then condense as a hard scale on the inside walls of the boiler. This scale must be removed periodically at great expense.

Various methods are being sought to separate municipal trash into its various components before it is burned. Figure 11.46 diagrams one such proposal. It would be much easier if trash were separated before being picked up. It is a challenge to get people to do this in an effective way. Even if trash is separated, burning paper and other biological materials add

How can the sun be used to provide solid, liquid, and gaseous fuels?

Content Clue

Municipal trash has an average energy content of about 4,500 Btu/lb.

Think about This!

What are some ways of getting people to separate their trash? How might these strategies be made more effective?

▼ FIGURE 11.46 A proposed resource recovery plant. (*From* Energy Alternatives: A Comparative Analysis, *Science and Public Policy Program, University of Oklahoma.*)

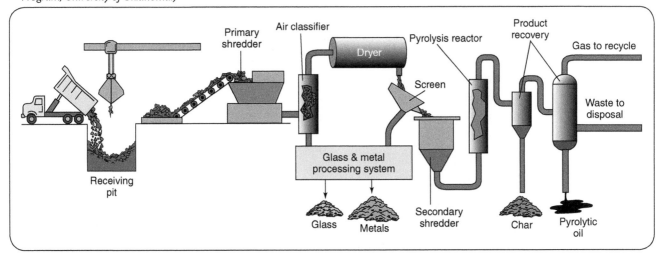

to air pollution. Thus, scrubbers must be added to the incinerators. New technologies may improve our ability to turn trash into fuel.

11.18 Bioconversion

Topic: bioconversion
Go to: www.scilinks.org
Code: GloSci7e446

Living materials that can be used as fuels are called **biofuels**. (Biofuels may also be referred to as **biomass**.) Biofuels are living organic material such as trees, grass, crops, and seaweed or other algae. Municipal solid waste (trash) can also be included as it consists mainly of biofuel products (paper, cardboard, food residues). The energy stored in biofuels is derived from photosynthesis. The energy may be released by direct combustion (burning), or by converting biofuels into solid, liquid, or gaseous fuels. The by-products (leftovers) of biofuels can be used for food, fertilizer, and chemicals. Biofuels can be used to produce electricity, heat, steam, and transportation fuels to reduce the use of nonrenewable sources.

Sources of Biofuels

Many of the biofuels now available for energy are waste materials left over from other processes. Here are some typical sources and examples.

- Forest products: for example, sawdust, bark, paper pulp, wood shavings, scrap lumber, wood dust, and paper

- Agricultural and food-processing waste: for example, fruit pits, walnut shells, rice hulls, corn cobs, manures, and sugarcane residue

- Municipal sewage and solid waste

Converting residues and other wastes to energy also solves waste-disposal problems.

Residues are another source of biofuels for conversion to energy. Examples of forest residues are wood material or "slash" left in the forest after cutting and harvesting timber, noncommercial timber, and diseased trees. Agricultural residues include corn stalks as well as straw from rice, wheat, barley, and oats.

High-yield, high-energy crops such as sugarcane, sugar beets, and sweet sorghum, or rapidly growing trees such as eucalyptus, willow, and sweet gum, can be grown specifically for use as biofuels. Existing technology for short-rotation forestry can be adapted to biofuel tree plantations. The annual yield of usable material from managed short-rotation tree farms could be as much as 10 short tons per acre (22,000 kg/hectare). Organic materials for biofuels could be grown in nearly every region of the United States.

Conversion Processes

Biofuels can be converted into gaseous, liquid, or solid fuels, as illustrated in Figure 11.47. The type of fuel you end up with depends on the conversion process. The processes can produce liquid fuels similar to crude oil and alcohols, including methanol and ethanol. The gas methane is a common product.

Sewage treatment plants have used anaerobic digestion for many years to treat waste and generate methane gas. It is also possible to capture and burn the methane gas formed by natural anaerobic breakdown of municipal solid waste in old landfills. The methane gas produced in these processes can be used as a direct substitute for the natural gas used to heat most American homes.

Biofuels in Our Future

Interest in biofuels is growing because of the following reasons: competition for crude oil is increasing, crude oil is mainly supplied by countries that the developed world considers to be unstable, air pollution from burning fossil fuels is affecting our health, and the

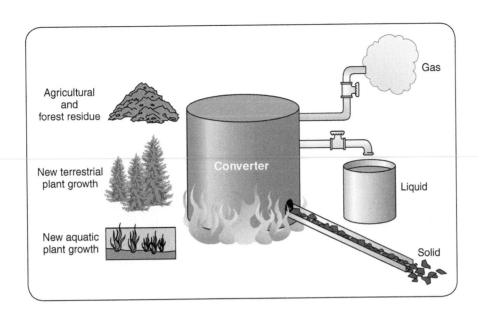

◀ FIGURE 11.47 Fuels from biomass. *(USDOE)*

demand to reduce carbon dioxide emissions is increasing. Figure 11.48 reveals that carbon atoms move around the biofuels cycle in a year or so. Thus, under the right conditions, biofuels can have little to no impact on global warming.

At the present time, most biofuels are made from sugarcane and corn. Brazil currently meets more than 40 percent of its gasoline demand with ethanol made from sugarcane. American ethanol is almost exclusively made from the kernels of corn, accounting for about 20 percent of the corn crop.

▼ FIGURE 11.48 The biofuel cycle. It takes a carbon atom about 1–2 years to go around the cycle. This can mean no net contribution to global warming.

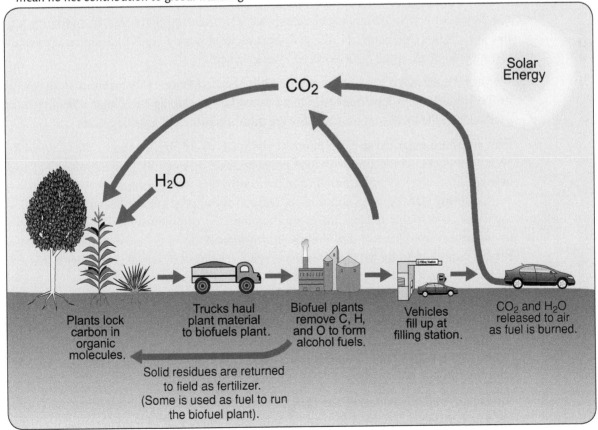

The sugar to ethanol equation is shown below. Fermentation is the catalytic action of yeast enzymes that act on biomass.

$$C_6H_{12}O_6 \xrightarrow[\text{heat}]{\text{yeast}} 2C_2H_5OH + 2CO_2$$
$$\text{sugars} \qquad\qquad \text{ethanol}$$

As we look to the future, it is unlikely that corn will be the major source of ethanol in the United States. This is because corn competes with food crops for land, and the net energy yield for corn-based ethanol is not as high as what is possible from cellulose-based ethanol.

Cellulose is a polymer of glucose (sugar) that makes up the fiber (structure) of plant material. Sources of cellulose include biomass wastes from forests and fields, fast-growing hays like switchgrass (see Figure 11.49), and short-rotation woody crops like poplar. Freshwater farms could grow algae, duckweed, and water hyacinth.

Marine (ocean) farms can also have high biomass production. This means that all regions of the United States have fuel-producing potential. Producing fuels near where they are used adds to the local economy and lowers transportation and handling costs.

Fuel crops are expected to have biomass yields of 10–15 dry tons/acre. These crops can be grown without competing with food crops because they can be grown in marginal areas unsuited for food crop production. In addition, crops like switchgrass are deep-rooted perennials; growing them prevents soil erosion. The soil doesn't have to be plowed and maintained each year, which also reduces the energy requirement of production. The greatest energy saving results from the fact that biotech enzymes break down cellulose to fuel. Corn-based ethanol requires heat for the fermentation process. The most recent studies indicate that only 0.2 units of energy are required to produce 1.0 units of cellulosic ethanol.

To produce ethanol, cellulosic materials are converted into a synthesis gas composed of carbon oxides and hydrogen. The gas is then converted into ethanol via either a biological process using microorganisms or a catalytic reactor. In another process, enzymes and bacteria are used to break down plant cell walls such as in corn residues (leaves, stalks, and cobs) into sugars that can be converted into ethanol.

An intense search is on to find the most cost-effective and efficient microorganisms, catalysts, and enzymes necessary for making biofuels a major part of our energy mix.

Apply Your Understanding

Why is cellulose-based ethanol of interest?

Think about This!

Roses are red,
violets are blue.
Cows eat grass,
and cars can too!
—Sign along an Iowa road

Summary

Global reserves of oil and natural gas are shrinking. Coal is a solid fuel and its direct use presents special environmental challenges. The public has not, as yet, accepted the nuclear option. For those reasons, we can develop synfuels; develop local energy options such as geothermal power; and use the sun's energy to heat and cool buildings, provide electricity, and produce solid, liquid, and gaseous fuels.

Topic: renewable energy resources
Go to: www.scilinks.org
Code: GloSci7e449

In this chapter, we have examined our energy alternatives. Synthetic fuels enable us to obtain fuels like the oil and gas we rely on so heavily at the present time. We have examined renewable (sustainable) energy options. These options are always with us. They include the secondary solar sources (wind, waves, hydroelectric power, and biomass) and direct solar options (active and passive solar, CSP, photovoltaic cells, OTEC, and solar satellites).

Some of these options produce minimal amounts of energy. However, they are of interest because they can help satisfy local needs. Others offer significant amounts of energy on a national scale. They all have environmental impacts that must be considered.

Solar applications are many and varied. Some are simple, such as passive solar and flat-plate collectors. Some, such as photovoltaic cells, CSP, and OTEC, require major engineering efforts. Solar satellites require a space program and military capability.

REFERENCES

Anderson, Bruce, ed. *Solar Building Architecture* (Cambridge, MA: MIT Press), 1990.

Deffeyes, Kenneth S. *Beyond Oil: The View from Hubbert's Peak* (New York: Hill and Wang), 2005.

Flavin, Christopher. Power Shock: The Next Energy Revolution. *World Watch* (January/February, 1996): 10–19.

Kammen, Daniel M. The Rise of Renewable Energy. *Scientific American* (September, 2006): 84–93.

Lemley, Brad. Anything into oil. *Discover* (May, 2003): 51–57.

Wells, Malcomb. *Underground Buildings* (Brewster, MA: Malcomb Wells), 1990.

U.S. Department of Energy. *Solar Water Heating* (Washington, D.C.: GPO), May, 1996.

WEBSITES

Alternative Fuels Data Center: http://www.eere.energy.gov/afdc/

American Wind Energy Association: http://www.awea.org

Bioenergy Information Network: http://bioenergy.ornl.gov/

Energy Efficiency and Renewable Energy (USDOE): http://www.eere.energy.gov/

Energy Information Administration (USDOE): http://www.eia.doe.gov/

Geothermal Energy http://geothermal.marin.org

National Renewable Energy Laboratory (NREL): http://www.nrel.gov/

Courtesy Owens Corning

CHAPTER (12)

Strategies for Using Energy

GOALS

- To examine strategies for using energy.

- To begin to sort out our options as a basis for future planning.

The energy problem should be not how to expand supplies to meet the postulated extrapolated needs of a dynamic economy, but rather how to accomplish social goals elegantly with a minimum of energy and effort.

—Amory B. Lovins

The First Priority: Conservation

Our energy situation is a matter of how we use energy and a challenge of supply. Strategies for making the best use of our available energy can be as significant as large discoveries of new supplies.

The U.S. economy was built on human enterprise and abundant cheap energy sources. As we have seen, abundant supplies of clean, cheap energy cannot be guaranteed. For this reason, we must begin to carefully plan our energy future. The easiest and sometimes most cost-effective way to save energy is to use energy wisely and to eliminate waste. This is called energy conservation. Conservation does not create new supplies of energy. It can, however, reduce the amount of energy we all use. This is where we will start looking at how to use energy wisely.

SPECIAL FOCUS

Heat Transfer

If we want to focus on saving energy, it is important to know how heat moves from one place to another. There are three ways heat can transfer from one place to another (see Figure 12.1).

Heat is infrared electromagnetic *radiation* (radiant energy). It can travel in waves away from hot objects to cooler regions (Figure 12.1a). As radiation, heat can move through space and the air. As it is absorbed by matter, heat changes the kinetic or potential energy of the molecules of that matter. If the molecules are free to move, they move faster. If they are locked in place, they will vibrate faster.

Conduction is the type of heat transfer in which the kinetic energy of molecules is given by contact to other molecules (Figure 12.1b). For example, the heat from a frying pan is conducted to an egg as it is fried, and the egg becomes more solid. If you touch a hot stove, your hand is heated by conduction.

When a liquid or gas is heated, its molecules move faster and farther apart. This makes the density of the heated portion less than that of the surrounding unheated portion. The heated portion, being less dense, rises and begins a convection current. More-dense material moves in to replace the rising less-dense volume, which

▼FIGURE 12.1 The three methods of heat transfer.

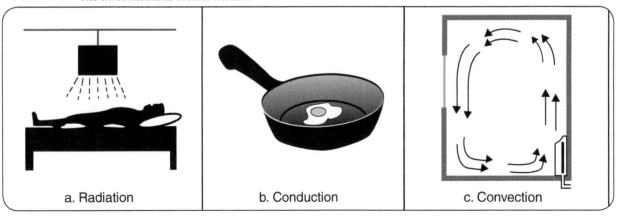

| a. Radiation | b. Conduction | c. Convection |

results in a convection cell. Heat transfer by fluid movement is called *convection*. Analyze the convection cell shown in Figure 12.1c.

Radiant energy is the only method of heat transfer that can travel through the vacuum of space. Your face feels warmer when the sun reappears from behind a cloud because your skin absorbs radiation arriving from the sun. Conduction and convection require contact between molecules of matter.

Heat transfer (energy flow) can be slowed using poor conductors of heat. Insulation is an example. Sealing off air spaces can prevent convection currents from forming. Reflecting materials can return radiation to where it came from. In Section 12.1, you will read about some of these strategies and relate them to energy conservation in the home.

Focus Questions & Tasks

1. Give an example of heat transfer by conduction.

2. Give an example of heat transfer by convection.

3. How does energy get from the sun to Earth?

4. How can heat transfer be slowed?

5. Does a "warm" blanket heat your body?

ACTIVITY 12.1

Home Energy Plan

In this activity, you will analyze the energy status of your home and determine how you can use energy more wisely. To help you with your analysis, you will first read about well-insulated buildings and more efficient vehicles and appliances.

Background

From the pie chart you studied in Figure 8.2, we saw that as consumers of energy, most of our use is for the cars we drive, heating and cooling our homes, home lighting, and heating water. Since most of this consumption is centered at home, it makes sense to start with a home energy plan. Figure 12.2 can help with that plan. This pie chart shows how most Americans use energy in their homes (based on national averages).

Figure 12.3 shows an outline of a generic home. Various parts of the home are labeled and numbered. If Figure 12.3 is not at all like your home, you may redraw the figure to represent your living environment. Figure 12.4 is an outline of the areas of your home you are to examine.

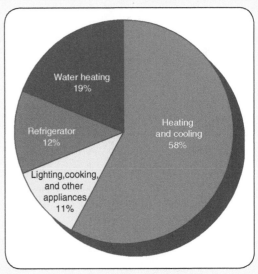

▲ FIGURE 12.2 Home energy use by task for the energy supplied by a utility company. *(U.S. Department of Energy)*

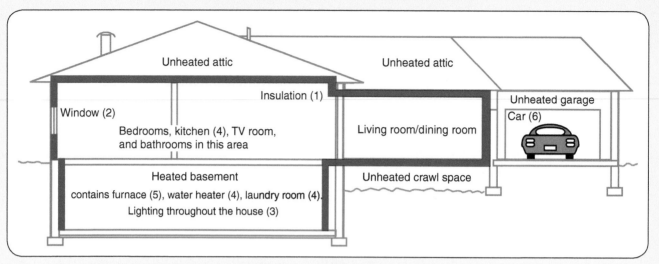

▲FIGURE 12.3 A generic home with attached garage. Recommended areas for insulation are shown in dark blue. The numbers correspond to items in Figure 12.4.

Materials

- *Home Energy Analysis* handout

Procedure

1. Examine Figures 12.3 and 12.4.

2. Read sections 12.1–12.3. Use this information to help you analyze the energy status of your home.

3. Fill out your energy plan as outlined in Figure 12.4. Record your fundings and recommendations on your *Home Energy Analysis* handout.

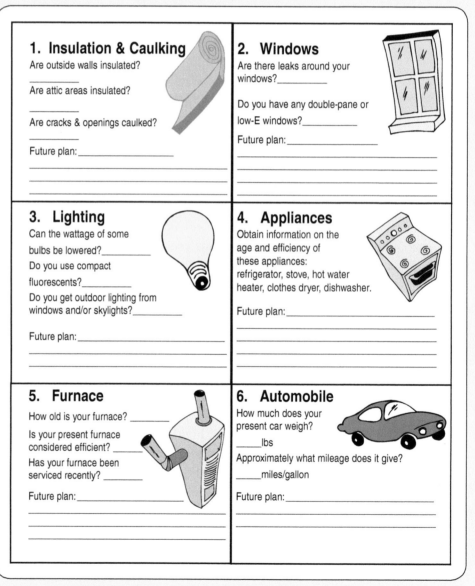

1. Insulation & Caulking
Are outside walls insulated?
_____
Are attic areas insulated?
_____
Are cracks & openings caulked?
_____
Future plan: _____
_____
_____

2. Windows
Are there leaks around your windows?_____

Do you have any double-pane or low-E windows?_____

Future plan: _____
_____
_____

3. Lighting
Can the wattage of some bulbs be lowered?_____
Do you use compact fluorescents?_____
Do you get outdoor lighting from windows and/or skylights?_____

Future plan: _____
_____
_____

4. Appliances
Obtain information on the age and efficiency of these appliances: refrigerator, stove, hot water heater, clothes dryer, dishwasher.

Future plan: _____
_____
_____

5. Furnace
How old is your furnace? _____
Is your present furnace considered efficient? _____
Has your furnace been serviced recently? _____

Future plan: _____
_____
_____

6. Automobile
How much does your present car weigh?

_____lbs
Approximately what mileage does it give?
_____miles/gallon

Future plan: _____
_____
_____

▲FIGURE 12.4 This chart will help you determine the present situation at your home in each of six categories. Make suggestions about what you can do to use energy more wisely; assume you can afford to make a change. If no change is possible, tell why.

◄ FIGURE 12.5 This thermograph (infrared photo) shows heat flow from a home during cold weather. Red and yellow indicate the areas of greatest heat loss. Well-placed insulation and low-E windows can greatly reduce such losses. *(Photo courtesy of Inframetrics, Inc., N. Billerica, MA.)*

12.1 Well-Insulated Buildings

As the Second Law of Thermodynamics states, heat naturally flows from hot to cold. This is why poorly insulated buildings are cold in the winter and hot in the summer. Heat simply moves through the walls and windows to the cooler location (see Figure 12.5).

Five features can greatly reduce heat transfer, lower energy bills, make indoor temperatures more comfortable year-round, and provide cleaner indoor air. These features are a well-insulated building shell, a vapor barrier, well-designed windows, a controllable ventilation system, and a carefully selected heating system.

A Well-Insulated Building Shell

Insulation is material that greatly slows the transfer of heat both in winter and summer. The ability of a material to stop heat from passing through it is indicated by its **R-value**. The higher the R-value, the greater the *resistance* to heat loss. An uninsulated wall typically has an R-value of R-1. Figure 12.6 shows the poorly insulated design of a typical home built in the 1960s when energy was cheap. Compare this to that of the home built in the 1980s and to that of the superinsulated home. Note the difference in the amount of insulation. Foundations and floors, which can be large sources of heat loss, also require much more attention (see Figure 12.7). In the past, they were often left uninsulated.

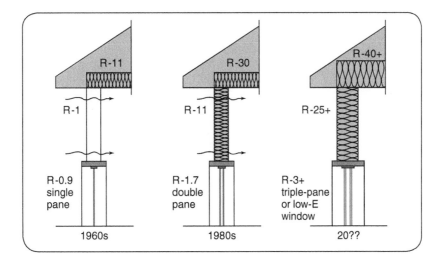

◄ FIGURE 12.6 Past and future insulation levels for residential buildings in cold climates. *(Courtesy Denver Energy Resource Center. Adapted by the author.)*

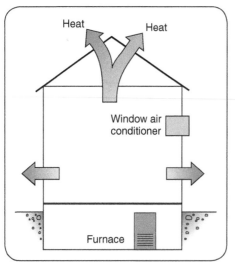

▲ FIGURE 12.7 Poorly insulated homes built in the 1960s and 1970s leaked heat through walls and ceilings. The structures also had many cracks and openings. It was common for these homes to have a large furnace and air conditioner. Heat flow through foundations was ignored.

▲ FIGURE 12.8 Rigid insulation panels made of fiberboard and coated with a reflecting surface are nailed to the outside walls. (*Owens Corning*)

Today, insulating is done in a variety of ways. In new homes, rigid insulation in the form of thick fiberboard panels is nailed to the outside walls. This is done before the siding is attached (see Figure 12.8). Blanket insulation fills the space between the fiberboard panels and the drywall (see Figure 12.9). Loose-fill insulation is blown into unfinished floors, walls, and unheated attics, or through temporary holes drilled into finished walls (see Figure 12.10).

A Vapor Barrier

A sealed vapor barrier stops cold air drafts, keeps valuable heat inside, and prevents moisture damage in exterior walls (see Figure 12.11). The vapor barrier can be either a continuous polyethylene (plastic-type) sheet in walls and ceilings or a foam skin on the outside of the structural frame.

▲ FIGURE 12.9 Blanket insulation, sold in thick rolls, can be installed on the inside surface of outside-facing walls or in an attic to retard the flow of heat and thus reduce heating and cooling bills. (*Owens Corning*)

▲ FIGURE 12.10 Loose-fill insulation consists of small pieces of fiberglass or other insulating material. It can be blown into unfinished floors, walls, or through small, temporary holes drilled into finished walls. (*Owens Corning*)

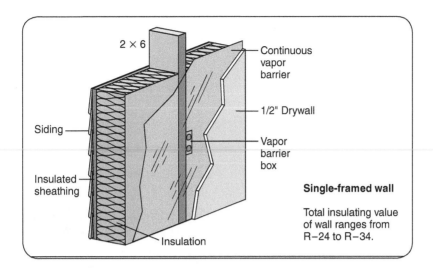

2 × 6

Continuous vapor barrier

Siding

1/2" Drywall

Vapor barrier box

Insulated sheathing

Insulation

Single-framed wall

Total insulating value of wall ranges from R−24 to R−34.

Putting in the vapor barrier requires attention to detail. For example, when a polyethylene vapor barrier is used, any holes put in it for electrical wiring, pipes, and fixtures must be sealed. A pressure-door test of a well-insulated home can assure that the desired airtightness has been achieved.

Well-Designed Windows

Windows are thermal "soft spots" in a tight, well-insulated home, and so they need special attention. Double- or triple-paned windows should be used. Also available are special high-tech windows called low-emissivity (low-E) windows. These provide an insulating value between R-3 and R-7. Another consideration is proper window size and placement. This can provide a well-insulated home with a large percentage of heat from solar energy. An ideal area of south-facing windows—expressed as a percentage of the home's floor area—would be roughly 5 to 6 percent (see Figure 12.12).

Apply Your Understanding

How can a well-insulated home get much of its energy from the sun?

▼ FIGURE 12.12 A cold-climate, superinsulated home in Montrose, Colorado. *(Courtesy of Dick Busing.)*

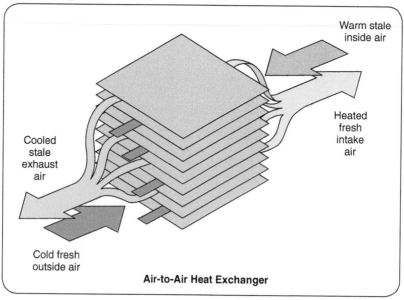

Air-to-Air Heat Exchanger

A Controllable Ventilation System

An automated ventilation system provides a controllable supply of fresh air. There are two kinds of ventilation systems. One is a combination of several fans that exhaust odors and pollutants at the locations where they are generated, such as in the kitchen or bathroom. The other is a general ventilation system that recovers heat from the exhausted warm air. This is called a heat exchanger (see Figure 12.13). The result is a home that has fresher and more healthful air than most homes. Added humidistats can provide a controlled and more desirable humidity level. The ventilation system is a must. Without it, well-sealed homes become traps for indoor pollutants.

A Carefully Selected Heating System

A well-insulated home loses heat so slowly that most furnaces on the market today are larger than needed. Thus, the size of the system, type of fuel, and provision of outside air for combustion heating systems all must be considered. Some well-insulated homes can be heated economically with electricity. If gas is used for heating, through-the-wall sealed combustion minifurnaces are a good choice (see Figure 12.14). Since the combustion process is isolated from the home, these furnaces are quite safe.

In an airtight home, it is not safe to draw air from the living space for the combustion gases, as that can deplete oxygen in the house. Woodstoves and fireplaces are not recommended for well-insulated homes. Stoves tend to overheat easily. Also, because it is difficult to make them airtight and limit their combustion air to an outside source, they lower indoor air quality. Figure 12.15 summarizes the insulation strategy.

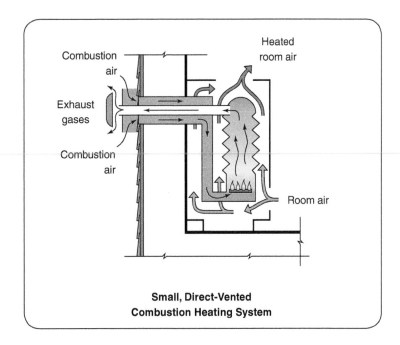

Combustion air

Exhaust gases

Combustion air

Heated room air

Room air

Small, Direct-Vented Combustion Heating System

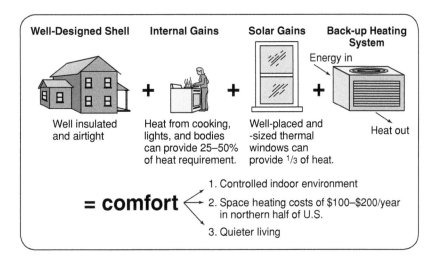

Well-Designed Shell

Well insulated and airtight

Internal Gains

Heat from cooking, lights, and bodies can provide 25–50% of heat requirement.

Solar Gains

Well-placed and -sized thermal windows can provide 1/3 of heat.

Back-up Heating System

Energy in

Heat out

= comfort ← 1. Controlled indoor environment
2. Space heating costs of $100–$200/year in northern half of U.S.
3. Quieter living

◀FIGURE 12.15 The strategy for designing a well-insulated home.

Think about This!

Building "green" and near-zero energy homes are strategies builders are now using. Are they being used where you live?

12.2 More Efficient Vehicles

As world supplies of crude oil shrink and laws tied to air pollution force change, the demand for more fuel-efficient vehicles should increase. A revolution in the design of automobiles is underway. Figure 12.16 summarizes the changes. At the present time, several vehicles are being mass-produced that average 35 miles or more per gallon. These are purchased mainly by people interested in economy, the environment, or both. A series of limited-production vehicles is also available to consumers in selected regions. In addition, auto manufacturers are working on a series of prototype (built and tested) vehicles that are a stage beyond the limited-production vehicles. Most interesting is the concept vehicle.

Although not yet built, the concept vehicle is being tested and refined on the computer by engineers. The Special Focus: The Car of the Future, provides more information on its features. If this is the direction we are headed, we can look forward to cleaner, sleeker, lighter, safer, more fuel-efficient cars. These cars would be about the same size of today's cars. They would also have approximately the same passenger capacity and acceleration ability. However, they would result in lower oil consumption and reduced hydrocarbon and greenhouse gas emissions.

Apply Your Understanding

Describe the revolution in automobile design that is happening.

Topic: hybrid vehicle
Go to: www.scilinks.org
Code: GloSci7e459

Apply Your Understanding

What is the difference between a concept car and a prototype car?

Strategies for Using Energy 459

▼ FIGURE 12.16 A summary of the current revolution in vehicle choices available both now and in the future.

Vehicle	Fuel	Fuel Economy (hwy)		Curb Weight		Power		Passengers (persons)
		(liters/ 100 km)	(miles/ gal)	(kg)	(lb)	(kW)	(horse-power)	
Mass Production (2007)								
Kia Rio (automatic, 4-speed)	Gasoline	6.1	38	1,092	2,403	82	110	5
Chevrolet Monte Carlo (automatic, 4-speed)	FFV	8.6	27	1,525	3,354	158	211	5
Honda Civic Hybrid*	Gasoline	4.6	51	1,724	3,792	82	110	5
Toyota Prius Hybrid*	Gasoline	4.6	51	1,333	2,932	57	76	5
Limited Production								
Honda Civic GX	Natural gas	6.0	39**	1,449	3,188	85	113	5
Volkswagen Polo Blue Motion***	Diesel	3.2	73	1,085	2,389	59	80	5
Prototype								
Ford Advanced Focus FCV	Compressed hydrogen	4.7	50**	1,602	3,525	85	113	5
Chevrolet Equinox FCV	Compressed hydrogen	3.9–2.9	60–80**	2,010	4,431	93	124	4
Concept								
RMI Ultralight Hybrid Hypercar™	Gasoline/ alcohol/gas	2.6	90	585	1,289	30 (50 max)	40 (67 max)	4

*Continuously variable transmissions.
**Based on the conversion to gasoline "equivalent" energy.
***Not sold in the United States in 2007.

Terms: Mass production: available to consumers for purchase.
            Limited production: limited availability to consumers at some locations.
            Prototype: built and being tested, but not sold.
            Concept: designed on paper, but not yet built.
            Hybrid: a vehicle that uses electric motors to power the wheels, but gets its power from a small internal-combustion engine and energy conversion rather than from heavy, costly batteries.
            FCV: fuel cell vehicle.
            FFV: Flex-fuel vehicles operate on gasoline, E85, or any mixture of the two fuels.
            E85: a mixture of 85% ethanol and 15% gasoline.

Note: Diesel-powered vehicles typically get 30%–35% more miles per gallon than comparable vehicles powered by gasoline.
      FFVs operating on E85 usually experience a 20%–30% drop in miles per gallon because of ethanol's lower energy content.

The Car of the Future? The Ultralight Hybrid (or RMI Hypercar™ Concept)

Because today's cars are made of steel, they are heavy. And as we know, it takes energy to speed up and slow down mass. Hence, most of the energy that moves a car and its passenger(s) goes into changing the speed of the mass. For that reason, Hypercars are designed more like airplanes than tanks. They are made of synthetic composites such as carbon fibers, which are lighter and stronger than steel (as demonstrated by crashes at the Indy 500 each year). Polymer composites are a combination of high-strength nonmetallic fibers embedded in a polymer matrix. These cars are shaped to cut through the air with little resistance. They are light and slippery, fuel efficient, attractive, and safe to drive (see Figure 12.17).

The Hypercar is called a hybrid because it is powered by both an electric motor and a fuel-burning engine. It is an electric car, but it doesn't carry heavy batteries around. Instead, it has a small tank of fuel (such as gasoline). This fuel is burned in a modest, onboard engine to produce electricity to power the wheels. Since an electric motor running backwards becomes a generator, as the car is braked, it can generate electric power that can be stored in a small pack of batteries and used later for acceleration. With its power so distributed, the engine needs to provide only the maximum continuous load, not the peak load as present engines must do. This means it only needs to be about one-third as powerful.

In the relatively near future, the small engine used to produce the electricity to run the wheels could be replaced by fuel cells that have no moving parts and are even more efficient (see Activity 12.3 on fuel cells).

Near-term Hypercars are estimated to average about 70–110 miles per gallon. Advanced-design Hypercars are projected to give up to 200 miles or more per gallon.

To learn more about the development of the Hypercar Concept, write to Rocky Mountain Institute, 1739 Snowmass Creek Road, Snowmass, CO 81654-9199, or view online at http://www.rmi.org/. See also www.hypercar.com and www.fiberforge.com.

Reduced heating, cooling, and accessory loads

Reduced aerodynamic drag

Small, clean, and efficient hybrid power unit

Efficient electric drive

Reduced rolling resistance

Long range from small fuel tank

Ultralight advanced materials throughout

Electronically managed energy flow and traction

Small, high-power load-leveling device

▲FIGURE 12.17 The RMI HypercarTM concept showing the main features and components. (*Illustration by Timothy Moore. Courtesy Rocky Mountain Institute, Hypercar Center^SM.*)

ACTIVITY 12.2

Fuel Efficiency vs. Weight

In this activity, you will graph and compare the fuel efficiency and curb weight of five commercially available vehicles. All five vehicles have primarily steel construction and are powered by gasoline-driven internal-combustion engines. All have four-speed automatic transmissions and are gasoline powered.

Materials

- graph paper

Procedure

1. Familiarize yourself with the data provided in Figure 12.18.

2. Plot a graph of fuel economy (mpg) vs. curb weight (lb). Draw a smooth curve that passes near all the points. Record the name of each vehicle by its point. Then write a conclusion that summarizes your graph.

3. Repeat step 2, but plot fuel economy (km/L) vs. mass (kg).

4. Plot a graph of fuel economy vs. 1/weight. If you get a straight line that extrapolates through the origin, it means the variables plotted are *inversely proportional*. For example, when one is doubled, the other is cut in half. What do you conclude?

5. Using data from Figure 12.16, plot a point for either the Toyota Prius or the Honda Civic Hybrid on your fuel economy vs. curb weight graph. Write a statement about the location of this point on the graph.

> **Helpful Hint!**
>
> You may need to replot your graph to get the point to fit on the graph.

▼ **FIGURE 12.18** Fuel efficiency and curb weight statistics for five commercially available vehicles.

Vehicle—2007 (all internal-combustion, all automatic transmission)	Fuel Economy (hwy)*		Curb Mass or Weight	
	(km/liter)	(miles/gal)	(kg)	(lb)
Toyota Yaris	16.7	39	1,055	2,321
Ford Focus (front-wheel drive)	14.5	34	1,224	2,692
Pontiac Grand Prix	12.0	28	1,584	3,484
Ford Escape 4WD SUV	10.3	24	1,586	3,490
Hummer 3, 4WD SUV (3.7 liter/5 cylinder)	8.1	19	2,136	4,700

* Fuel economy is EPA highway.

12.3 More Efficient Appliances

Apply Your Understanding

What are some of the major benefits of an effective energy conservation program?

Refrigerators in the United States consume about 6 percent of the nation's electricity. This is the energy output of about 25 large electric power plants. A 1972 refrigerator with a top-mounted freezer and automatic defrost typically used about 2,000 kilowatt-hours (kWh) of energy per year. A similar model sold in 2006 runs on about 600 kWh a year. If every household in the United States had the most efficient refrigerator currently available, the electricity savings would eliminate the need for about 12 large power plants (see Figure 12.19).

◀FIGURE 12.19 Energy-efficient refrigerators.

But this is only the beginning! Similar savings are possible with other appliances—lightbulbs, stoves, freezers, washers, dryers, furnaces, and so on. For example, compact fluorescent lamps (CFLs) are more efficient than incandescent lightbulbs (see Figure 12.20). Incandescent lightbulbs produce light by passing an electric current through the filament in the bulb, heating it hot enough to glow. Unfortunately, only about 10 percent of the electricity is changed to light. The other 90 percent is lost as heat. CFLs produce light directly without heat. This makes them more efficient. CFLs are the most significant lighting advance developed for homes since the lightbulb was invented. They are best used in places where they will be on for several hours at a time. They cost ten times as much as incandescent lightbulbs, but they last ten times as long. Since they are three to four times as efficient, they reduce energy costs greatly.

A newer type of light is the light-emitting diode or LED. LEDs are tiny chips made of semiconductor materials. When an electric current is applied to the LED, electrons move in the chip and photons of light are emitted. Because very little heat is released, LEDs are very efficient and they last much longer than both incandescent and fluorescent lights. With the development of white light LEDs, the technology has moved into the home lighting market. This technology is developing rapidly and costs are dropping significantly.

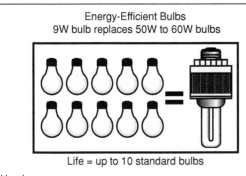

Energy-Efficient Bulbs
9W bulb replaces 50W to 60W bulbs

Life = up to 10 standard bulbs

Energy Used
Compact fluorescent: 9 watts X 10,000 hour life = 90 kWh
Standard incandescent: 50 watts X 1,000 hour life X 10 bulbs = 500 kWh
Savings: 410 kWh X 10¢/kWh = $41.00

◀FIGURE 12.20 A comparison of compact fluorescent lamps (CFLs) to incandescent lightbulbs.

Although energy conservation may be less exciting than controlled nuclear fusion experiments or space-based solar collection systems, the potential benefits of conservation are enormous. These include a cleaner environment, reduced world tensions, and an increased opportunity for more people to enjoy some of those benefits we refer to as the good life. And energy conservation is something you can contribute to every day.

Energy Conversion and Storage

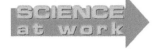

Describe some energy conversion methods.

Although they are not energy sources, several methods for converting and storing energy are important to understand as we examine our energy future. These strategies can help us improve the efficiency of processes and thus conserve energy, reduce pollution, and improve economics. Four of these strategies are described in the next section.

12.4 Energy Conversion Technologies

Cogeneration

SCIENCE at work

Cogeneration is the production of two useful forms of energy (for example, hot gases and electricity) from the same fuel source. As discussed in Chapter 8, waste heat from most electric power plants is dumped into space. That is the purpose of cooling towers. At a cogeneration power plant, called a combined-cycle power plant, some of the "waste" heat is captured and used before it is released at a lower temperature. Other examples of cogeneration are forest product mills that use waste heat to generate electricity, and sugar companies that burn shredded, processed sugarcane to produce steam for their electric generators and other uses.

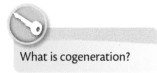

What is cogeneration?

In Figure 12.21, natural gas fires a gas turbine to drive an electric generator. Heat from the exhaust of the gas turbine is used to provide steam to drive a steam turbine that drives a second electric generator. Waste heat is exhausted, but at a lower temperature. This combined use increases the efficiency of producing electricity.

SCI LINKS NSTA
Topic: cogeneration
Go to: www.scilinks.org
Code: GloSci7e464

FIGURE 12.21 A combined-cycle power plant. *(Calpine)*

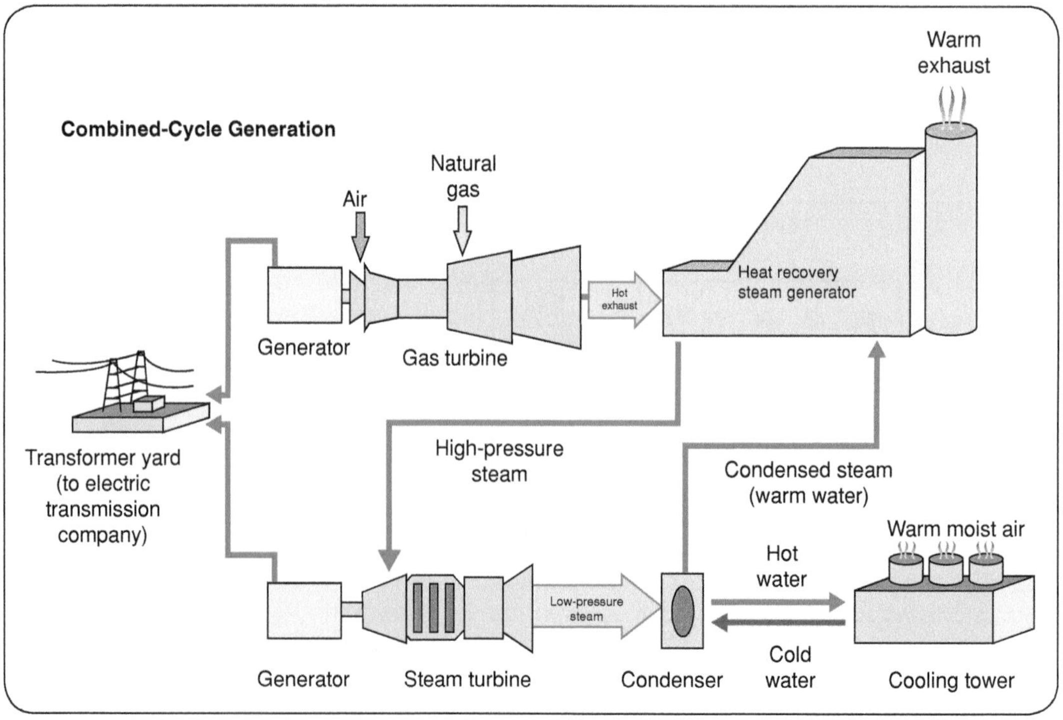

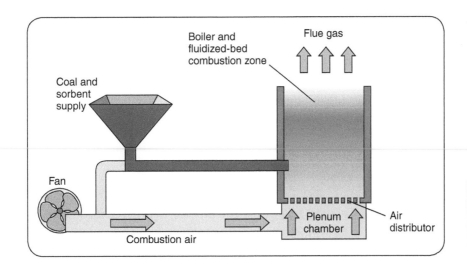

◀ FIGURE 12.22 The fluidized-bed combustion process. (*Reproduced from Annual Review of Energy and the Environment. Vol. 16,* © *1991 Annual Reviews, Inc.*)

Content Clue

The plenum chamber contains air under high pressure.

Fluidized-Bed Combustion

Fluidized beds are simple devices that add the fuel (usually pulverized coal) to a much larger mass of small, red-hot particles called the sorbent. The efficiency of combustion and of heat transfer is high because of the turbulent mixing and large surface area of the particles. Current research is attempting to perfect the process and adapt it to large power generation plants.

Figure 12.22 illustrates the **fluidized-bed combustion** process. Coal and particles (sorbent) are injected into the boiler, while air is blown upward through the air distributor in the bottom of the boiler. In the boiler, coal is burned efficiently, and sulfur dioxide (produced from sulfur impurities in the coal) reacts with a sorbent-related chemical to form calcium sulfate. The calcium sulfate can be removed as a dry, harmless solid.

Fluidized-bed combustion is of interest because it improves efficiency and because it reduces sulfur oxide and nitrogen oxide emissions at electric power plants. This means that less fuel is burned and air quality is improved.

Heat Pumps

Heat pumps are devices such as air conditioners or refrigerators that move heat around, rather than producing it. They are similar to air conditioners, with a reverse cycle for heating. In the winter, the refrigerant (colder than the outside air) picks up heat from the outdoors and releases it inside the house (see Figure 12.23).

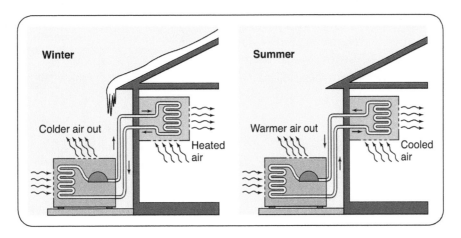

◀ FIGURE 12.23 The operation of a heat pump. (*Reprinted from Popular Science with permission* © *1973 Times Mirror Magazines, Inc., Frank R. Buonocare (artist). Adapted by the author.*)

Heat pumps are more efficient than electrical resistance heating and somewhat more efficient than gas furnaces. They are clean and don't need a chimney. Their only chimney is at the electric power company. However, a major drawback of heat pumps is the initial high cost. Also, they do not work well in very cold climates. Not surprisingly, it is difficult to draw heat from outside air that is below 0°F (-17.8°C).

Fuel Cells

A **fuel cell** is a device that produces electrical energy directly from chemical energy. It is somewhat like a battery. However, it differs from a battery in that the chemicals are not stored in the cell. Rather, they are fed into the cell as power is needed. In most fuel cells, hydrogen is combined with oxygen from the air to produce electricity plus water. Because the chemicals are not stored, fuel cells are much lighter than battery packs. This is one of the reasons they are being designed as possible power sources for electric vehicles.

Fuel cells have many uses besides powering vehicles. They are used as stand-alone power generators for office buildings, hospitals, and schools. In the future, refrigerator-size fuel cell units in the attic, garage, or outside will provide the electricity for individual homes.

Fuel cells can be stacked together to deliver a wide range of power. That means fuel cells can power something as small as a laptop computer or as large as an automobile. Stack enough fuel cells together and they can power homes, office buildings, or small towns.

How does a fuel cell work? The following is a brief summary; refer to Figure 12.24 as you read the summary.

Every fuel cell has two *electrodes*. They are the anode and the cathode. The chemical reactions that produce electricity occur at the electrodes. Fuel cells also contain an *electrolyte*. An electrolyte carries electrically charged particles from one electrode to the other. A *catalyst* is also needed. A catalyst speeds up the reactions that take place at the electrodes. Hydrogen is the basic *fuel*, but fuel cells also need oxygen. As the cell operates, the hydrogen and oxygen combine to form water. The process is as follows:

Helpful Hint!

Remember, an ion is a particle that carries an electric charge.

1. Hydrogen enters the fuel cell at the anode. There, a chemical reaction takes away electrons, which carry a negative charge. The hydrogen atoms are now ionized and carry a positive charge. This enables them to pass through the electrolyte.

$$2H_2 \rightarrow 4H^+ + 4e^-$$

2. The negatively charged electrons cannot move through the electrolyte. They must travel a different route to reconnect with the hydrogen ions. Their movement through wires (see top of Figure 12.24) provides an electric current. We can use this current to do many useful tasks.

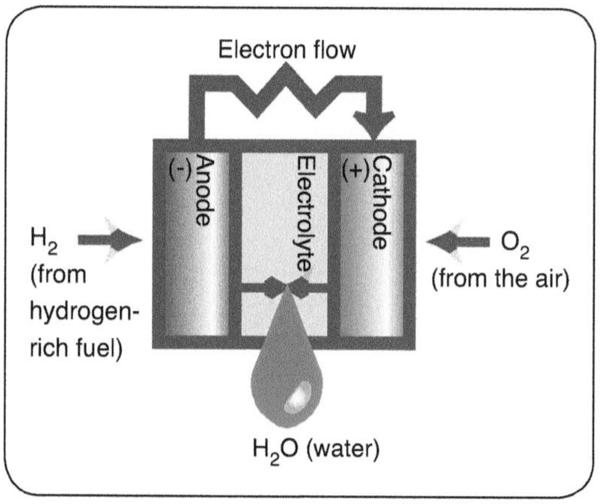

Content Clue

The electrolyte controls charge flow.

▶ FIGURE 12.24 A simplified fuel cell using hydrogen and oxygen. The electron flow that results can be used to power an electric vehicle, a home, or a space station. (USDOE)

3. Oxygen now enters the fuel cell at the cathode. It combines with the electrons returning from the electric circuit as follows:

$$O_2 + 4e^- \rightarrow 2O^{-2}$$

4. The hydrogen ions, which passed through the electrolyte membrane, now combine with the oxygen ions to form water, which drains from the cell. Some heat is also given off.

$$4H^+ + 2O^{-2} \rightarrow 2H_2O$$

5. As long as a fuel cell is supplied with hydrogen and oxygen, it will produce electricity and clean water.

Fuel cell systems have many advantages over most power sources. They are more efficient (50–60 percent). In addition, the only moving parts are fans and pumps. The cells themselves have no moving parts, so fuel cells are very quiet. Third, because they only produce electricity and water, they last for years. And finally, they greatly reduce pollution.

One of the problems related to fuel cell development is to find the best source of hydrogen. In the future, it will most likely come from electrolyzing or splitting water into hydrogen and oxygen. To begin with, the hydrogen will probably come from natural gas, ethanol, methanol, or gasoline. One method extracts hydrogen from gasoline within the vehicle through a device called a *reformer*. A reformer can do the same with methanol, ethanol, or natural gas. This means that vehicles will be able to use the existing system of gas stations, and they won't be limited in range like battery-powered vehicles are. And even though carbon dioxide is produced in this process, it is less than that produced by internal-combustion engines because fuel cells are more efficient.

Topic: fuel cell
Go to: www.scilinks.org
Code: GloSci7e467

ACTIVITY 12.3

Operate and Analyze a Fuel Cell

In this activity, you will operate and analyze a fuel cell and relate what you learn to the operation of a hydrogen economy.

Background (Equipment)

This activity is designed around the hydro-Genius™ Solar Hydrogen Technology Science Kit shown in Figure 12.25. This kit is an experimentation and demonstration model that provides hands-on experiences with hydrogen technology and its components.

The hydro-Genius science kit allows you to assemble, operate, and analyze a miniature solar-hydrogen plant. The four main parts of your solar-hydrogen plant (Figure 12.25) are as follows:

a. *solar module:* directly converts light into electricity.

b. *electrolyser:* uses electric current to split water into hydrogen and oxygen. These gases may be stored for later use.

c. *fuel cell:* produces electric current when hydrogen and oxygen are fed into it.

d. *load measurement box:* designed as an electrically wired box containing a small motor and lamp that can accept current from the fuel cell. (It contains other features that can be used in various experiments tied to the kit.)

BE SAFE

Before using the kit, you *must* read the operating manual for both safety reasons and to prevent damage to the equipment. The steps in the Procedure assume that the operator has read the operating instructions. Wear safety goggles when operating this unit.

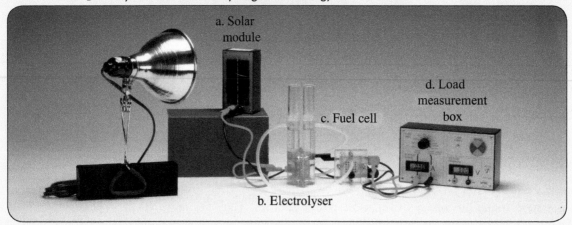

Materials

- hydro-Genius Solar Hydrogen Technology Science Kit

⚠ **WARNING**

Use no flames near the electrolyser or the fuel cell.

- light source (lamp)
- clear, 100W lightbulb
- distilled water
- squeeze-type wash bottle
- metric ruler
- safety goggles

Procedure

1. Set up the solar module (solar cells) as follows:

   a. Place the solar module on the workplace surface so it stands upright with the red and black connecting jacks at the bottom.

   Helpful Hint!

   This procedure assumes you are setting up the miniature solar-hydrogen plant. If it is already set up, read the Procedure and examine the components/connections so you understand how the plant runs.

   b. Place the *unplugged* light source in front of the module. Position the light source so it will illuminate the solar module perpendicularly.

2. Set up the electrolyser as follows:

   a. Moisten the ends of the 2 overflow pipes with distilled water.

   b. Insert the 2 overflow pipes into the stoppers at the top of the storage cylinders, and press them in tightly. (See page 12 of the operating instructions in the kit.)

   c. Before the solar-hydrogen plant can be started up, the electrolyser must be filled with *distilled* water. *Do not use any other liquid!* Use a clean squeeze-type wash bottle to fill each storage cylinder to the 0 milliliter (mL) mark. (See the drawing in the operating instructions.)

   d. Push the two 40 centimeter (cm) long silicone tubes onto the gas outlets of the storage cylinders.

3. Use 2 power cables (one red, one black) to connect the solar module to the electrolyser. Connect red to red and black to black.

4. Position the fuel cell so the H_2 and O_2 labels are at the top (right side up). Connect the hydrogen gas (H_2) outlet of the electrolyser to the top hydrogen gas (H_2) inlet of the fuel cell using the silicone tube. Repeat for the oxygen (O_2) side. Plug the lower 2 inlets on the fuel cell using the tubing stoppers provided.

5. Illuminate the solar module sufficiently to observe a distinct development of gas in the electrolyser. Oxygen forms in one of the half-cells, hydrogen

    ⚠ **WARNING**

   The light source and reflector become *hot!* Do not touch them directly when the light is on.

   in the other. You should get good results using a clear, 100W filament lightbulb placed in a socket with reflector positioned a minimum of 25–30 cm from the solar module.

6. Use 2 power cables (one red, one black) to make the following connections:

   a. positive (red) terminal of the fuel cell to the left positive terminal (red) of the load measurement box

b. negative (black) terminal of the fuel cell to the left negative terminal (black) of the load measurement box

7. Turn the ON/OFF switch of the load measurement box to the ON position. Adjust the rotary switch to the MOTOR position.

8. After a maximum of 10–20 minutes (min), the fuel cell should be sufficiently supplied with gas to be able to drive the electric motor. If the electric motor does not turn, pull the tubing stopper from the lower outlet on the hydrogen side of the fuel cell. It should start. If the motor stops turning, replug the outlet and let gas generate for 5 min. Then pull the plug. The motor should start again. Then replug the outlet.

9. If you want to keep the plant running for several hours, pull the tubing stoppers from the outlets on both the hydrogen and oxygen sides of the fuel cell when the overflow pipes fill up. They will both drain. Then replug the outlets. Repeat every hour.

10. You are now ready to make the following observations:

a. Observe how the light illuminates the solar module (solar cells).

b. Observe the production of gas at both the oxygen and hydrogen half-cells.

c. Observe that there are no moving parts in the fuel cell.

d. Watch the motor turn.

QUESTIONS & TASKS

Record your responses in your science notebook.

1. Compare the volume of hydrogen gas produced to the volume of oxygen gas produced.

2. How does this miniature solar-hydrogen plant illustrate how a hydrogen economy centered on fuel cells might function?

3. In regions where there is not a lot of sunlight (northern United States, Canada), how might hydrogen be obtained? Assume hydrogen is expensive to transport.

> **Helpful Hint!**
>
> See the reading titled Hydrogen Storage and Infrastructure in Section 12.5 if you need help getting started.

[Adapted from instructions provided by heliocentris Energiesysteme GmbH, Rudower Chaussee 29, D-12489 Berlin, Germany.]

12.5 Energy Storage Techniques

Hydrogen Storage and Infrastructure

Hydrogen can be used as a medium for storing energy. There are, however, some major issues that must be addressed before fuel cells become widely used in vehicles and as power-generating units.

What are some energy storage techniques?

Hydrogen can come from three possible sources:

1. Electrolyze water using available electricity from the power grid (where the primary source may have been coal, natural gas, nuclear, wind, or geothermal), or solar cells located in sunny climates. The equation is

$$2H_2O(l) + electricity \rightarrow 2H_2(g) + O_2(g)$$
where l = liquid and g = gas

2. Use reformers to extract hydrogen from natural gas, ethanol, methanol, or gasoline. The reformer can be placed in a vehicle, or it can operate at a hydrogen refueling station near a road.

3. Use a variety of chemical and biological processes that can produce hydrogen. Research scientists are working on developing this source.

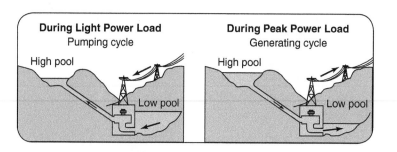

During Light Power Load
Pumping cycle
High pool
Low pool

During Peak Power Load
Generating cycle
High pool
Low pool

As we move into the hydrogen economy, a hydrogen refueling infrastructure will be built. Once that happens, vehicles powered by fuel cells will be able to refuel at stations just as we refuel our vehicles with gasoline today.

Pumped Storage

Because electricity cannot be stored in large quantities, and the demand for electricity fluctuates greatly, electric power companies must maintain a large reserve generating capacity. However, this sits idle much of the time. One way of leveling the demand is to pump water uphill and store it behind a dam during off-peak hours. During high-demand periods, the water can then be used to turn the pumps in a hydroelectric plant (see Figure 12.26).

Of course, electricity must be used to run the pumps. However, even though the reversible turbines (pumps) are only 66 percent efficient (34 percent of energy is lost in the storage step), the difference between the cost of peak and off-peak power often makes the pumps practical.

Heat Storage

One problem with the use of solar energy is that the sun goes down every night. This is when the heat is needed most. To solve this problem, heat must be stored for nighttime use. Storage is often in dark-colored bricks and tiles or in large tanks of water. These are called *thermal masses*. During the day, these thermal masses are heated by the sun; they then radiate the heat back at night.

The tanks of water are used for heat storage only, not as a source of drinking water. Thus, a useful substance called a *eutectic salt* can be added to the tanks. A eutectic salt is a solid at room temperature and a liquid at 120°F–150°F (50°C–65°C), the typical operating temperature of solar-heated water. The solar-heated water melts the eutectic salt in the daytime. At night, the salt solidifies as it cools, releasing the stored heat. The amount of stored heat given off when the salt solution cools and solidifies is many times what would be emitted if the solution remained a liquid as it cooled. This makes it possible to store much more heat in a smaller amount of water, saving space. The heat released at night could be used for heating water tanks and for space heating.

 # Comparing Sources—How Much Is Available?

When planning for the energy needs of a large region or nation, it is useful to know the quantity of energy the various sources can supply. These facts, combined with environmental goals, conservation strategies, and the use of efficient technologies, are key elements in wise energy planning. The next two sections summarize data on energy availability in the United States.

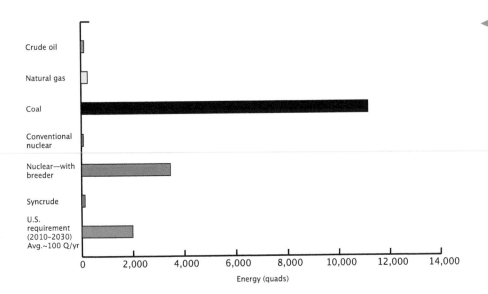

12.6 Energy Available from Nonrenewable Reserves

Figure 12.27 illustrates how nonrenewable reserves may be compared in terms of the amount of energy potentially available from each of them. Remember, however, that as reserves are used, some resources become new reserves. So the situation for oil and natural gas is not as bad as Figure 12.27 implies.

Some people conclude that our crude oil and natural gas reserves are small compared to our demands. Therefore, they believe we should reduce our reliance on them. Instead, we should emphasize sources that can more easily meet our demands in environmentally acceptable ways.

Apply Your Understanding

What is the status of nonrenewable energy reserves in the United States?

12.7 Renewable Resources—A Projection

Projecting future use of energy resources is difficult because of the many variables and unknowns. However, current trends all indicate that the role played by renewable sources will continue to increase. This is because new deposits of crude oil and natural gas are getting harder to find. The costs for exploration and drilling are going up. Ninety percent of the world's oil reserves are held by governments that do not know or will not reveal the size of their holdings. Much of that oil is located in regions that are politically unstable. Competition for available oil and natural gas is increasing. Concern about global warming and efforts to slow carbon emissions are also on the increase.

Topic: renewable energy resources
Go to: www.scilinks.org
Code: GloSci7e471

Figure 12.28 summarizes U.S. current use of renewables and shows a projection to 2030. Note that in 2005, renewables made up only 6 percent of the energy supply. The largest portion came from hydroelectric power. By 2030, the contribution made by renewables could double to 12 percent of the total.

Twelve percent may not seem that much, but it does imply that the U.S. economy is moving quite rapidly toward the goals of reducing dependence on foreign sources of oil and lowering emissions of carbon dioxide from fossil fuel combustion. Note that the greatest changes are in the expanded use of biofuels and in the use of wind power.

▼ FIGURE 12.28 The contribution of renewable energy sources to the U.S. economy now and projected to 2030.

Renewable Source	Current Use (2005)	Potential in 2030
Biofuels (corn-based, cellulosic, biodiesel)	4+ billion gallons/year 0.3	30 billion gallons/year 2.5Q
Wind	30 billion kWh 0.1	300 billion kWh 1.0
Solar (photovoltaics and concentrated solar)	24 billion kWh 0.1	100 billion kWh 0.4
Wood	Mainly industrial heating 1.9	Growth due to availability 3.8
Geothermal	Electric generation + heating 0.4	Electric generation + heating 0.6
Hydroelectric	800 billion kWh 2.7	800 billion kWh 2.7
Waste (MSW + LFG)*	Municipal solid waste, landfill gas 0.5	Expanded use 1.0
Total renewable use in quads	6% of total U.S. use 6.0	12% of total U.S. use 12.0
U.S. economy	100.0 quads	100.0 quads**

(*Sources: Current (2005)*: Annual Energy Review *(USDOE)*. *Potential in 2030*: Annual Energy Outlook Projections *(USDOE)*, Power Technologies Energy Data Book *(NREL)*, and author's assumptions.)

*Municipal Solid Waste (MSW) and Landfill Gas (LFG)

**Assumes no growth in U.S. annual energy use because of cost increases, efficiency improvements, and national conservation efforts.

 # Appropriate Technology

12.8 Appropriate Technology: A Strategy for Using Energy

What is appropriate technology?

Appropriate technology is neither a source of energy nor a way of converting or storing energy. Instead, it is a strategy for using energy wisely. **Appropriate technology** attempts to lower demand and promote the use of renewable resources in a social and political climate based on the following two beliefs: smaller is often better, and, whenever possible, people should be able to understand and control the devices and systems on which they depend. This strategy is summarized in the following six topics.

Apply Your Understanding

What is the advantage of primarily relying on renewable resources?

Renewable Resources

Our major energy sources should be renewable (continuous) sources such as the sun, wind, and vegetation. These sources are always with us whether we use them or not. We must spend "energy income," not deplete our capital (like fossil fuels) (see Figure 12.29).

Apply Your Understanding

Why might it be better to rely on many energy sources rather than just a few?

Diverse Sources

Our energy supply should come from several sources, with each source making only a modest contribution to the whole. No single source is best for all needs. Our future risks should be distributed among many technologies.

FIGURE 12.29 Many cattle roam on land in remote areas where power lines are nonexistent or are very expensive to maintain. In these cases, it is appropriate to use photovoltaic systems to pump and maintain water supplies for cattle. (Photo by Carrol E. Hamon, Western Area Power/DOE.)

Minimizing our reliance on fossil fuels would make us less vulnerable in times of war or natural disaster. Also, the environmental impact is lessened, manageable, and reversible.

Simplicity

Appropriate technology implies that the energy collection and distribution system should be relatively simple. Large numbers of people should be able to understand and use it without having to obtain advanced skills. People who support this concept believe that hard technologies and power complexes are remote and uncontrollable. They would like the decisions about the sources we use and the prices we pay to be more local.

Apply Your Understanding

What are some of the advantages of simple technology?

Matching Size and Quality to End Use

Energy systems should be matched in size to end-use needs. Large power plants and grids increase the size of malfunctions, mistakes, and deliberate disruptions.

Similarly, energy quality should be matched to end-use needs. So-called "waste" heat from power plants and some industries could be used to perform the low-quality tasks of heating water, buildings, and residences near them. Where we want only to create temperature differences of tens of degrees, we should meet the need with sources whose potential is tens or hundreds of degrees, not with flame and nuclear temperatures of hundreds and thousands of degrees. For some applications (electronics, smelting, subways, most lighting, some kinds of mechanical work, and a few others), electricity is appropriate and indispensable.

Apply Your Understanding

Why might smaller be better? When is bigger better?

Apply Your Understanding

Why should we match quality to end use?

Efficiency

Energy should be used more efficiently. We should strive to do more with less energy through strategies like conservation. If the problem is to move yourself from point A to point B, maybe you could take a bus or train instead of a car. If you must go by car, one weighing 1,800 lb may do just as well as one weighing 3,600 lb. For shorter trips, you might consider walking, bicycling, car-pooling, or using mass transit. Instead of using an elaborate "climate control" system, you can insulate your home and dress to suit the weather. An attic fan might make you as comfortable as an air conditioner. Recycling may accomplish much of what expanded resource extraction provides. Almost all of these strategies require significant evaluation and would require a substantial change in personal habits (see Figure 12.30).

Think about This!

List three ways you could use energy more efficiently in your day-to-day living.

Strategies for Using Energy   473

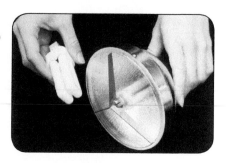

►FIGURE 12.30 A compact fluorescent lightbulb at the left and a patented small heat sink at the right. *(USDOE)*

Apply Your Understanding

Why might appropriate technologies be best for developing countries?

Energy Opportunity

Appropriate technology can provide developing nations with the chance to build strong economies based on small scale, variety, and simplicity.

ACTIVITY 12.4

Appropriate Technology

In this activity, you will look at a number of situations that involve making choices about using resources and technology. You will select one or more of these situations and analyze and defend your choice.

Background

We make decisions on a daily basis about the use of resources and technology. Some of these decisions are ours alone; others involve us as members of society. Because these decisions have an impact on natural resources, economics, our freedoms, and the environment, we want to make good decisions. Unfortunately, not all of our options are clear. We must think clearly and gather good information if we are to choose wisely.

The word *appropriate* means fitting the situation or use. *Technology* is the methods, tools, or machines people use to meet their needs. Hence, *appropriate technology* is the use of methods and/or tools to best do a job or task. That is, the task is done correctly, economically, and cleanly.

Procedure

1. Figure 12.31 describes 15 situations that you (or society) might face. Each situation requires you to make a choice. Select 1 or more of these situations and do the following:

   a. Analyze the energy, resource, and economic implications of both choices.

   b. Decide between the 2 choices and defend your decision.

   c. Record your choices and your thinking in your science notebook.

2. Think about the following as you evaluate your choices:

   a. Most choices depend on the situation. Thus, most of these items have no single answer. Tie your choice to your situation.

   b. Appropriate technology does not necessarily require you to give up comfort or convenience.

   c. Laws can force new behaviors, but methods that allow people to choose are accepted more readily.

   d. In some cases, you may not be able to gather enough information in the time you have to make a good decision. In these cases, state this and explain why.

1. Personal correspondence to a friend Choice: letter vs. e-mail	2. Drive to and from work Choice: SUV vs. fuel-efficient car	3. Eliminate insect pests in the home Choice: fly swatter vs. chemical spray
4. Trim trees Choice: hand saw vs. chain saw	5. Heat/cool a home Choice: passive strategies vs. furnace/air conditioner	6. Bring electricity to a home 1/2 mile from nearest utility pole Choice: photovoltaic system vs. bring in lines to connect to utility company
7. Forecasts imply an increased demand for electricity in your region Choice: build a new 500-mW natural gas–fired electric power plant vs. encourage conservation, provide rebates for use of compact fluorescents, and charge higher rates for excess electrical usage	8. Cool a home in the summer Choice: air conditioner vs. attic fan	9. Transportation Choice: vehicle with internal-combustion engine vs. similar hybrid vehicle
10. Fueling automobiles Choice: gasoline vs. biomass fuels	11. Provide lighting in a home Choice: incandescent lightbulbs vs. compact fluorescents	12. Make a home warmer in the winter Choice: add insulation, improve windows, and caulk cracks vs. buy a larger furnace
13. Provide electricity to a large region Choice: large utility vs. distributed generation*	14. Meeting the demand for metals in a modern society Choice: recycling vs. mining virgin resources	15. Purchasing beverages Choice: aluminum cans vs. plastic bottles vs. glass bottles vs. disposable cardboard containers

*Consumers can either generate their own power, or choose their own power provider from a list of options.

12.9 Can Appropriate Technologies Power the World?

The International Energy Agency (IEA) is a self-governing body that carries out an extensive program of energy cooperation among 26 countries. Its members include most of the countries of Europe, the United States and Canada, plus Japan, the Republic of Korea, Australia, and New Zealand. It was formed to deal with oil supply disruptions, promote rational energy policies, improve the world's energy supply by developing alternative energy sources and increasing the efficiency of use, and assist in the merging of environmental and energy policies. The IEA recently developed a series of scenarios to assist its members in energy planning.

One of the scenarios developed by the IEA is called the Sustainable Development (SD) Vision scenario for member countries of the Organization for Economic Cooperation and Development (OECD). These are the IEA members plus a few other countries. The energy requirement and sources for this projection are shown in Figure 12.32.

The scenario shown in Figure 12.32 was built with the goal or vision of providing energy security for member nations, reducing climate change emissions, and maintaining strong

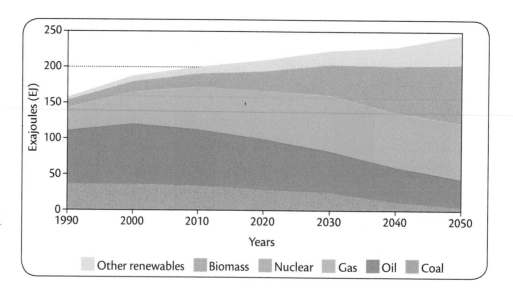

Helpful Hint!

1 quad (Q) = 1.06 exajoules (EJ)

➤ FIGURE 12.33 Solar energy is projected to increase in significance (*USDOE*)

Apply Your Understanding

What might happen in the future based on past and present experience and on speculation about how there trends may further evolve.

economies. The OECD countries make up about one-eighth of the world's population and use about one-fourth of the world's energy supply each year. An examination of Figure 12.32 shows that by 2050, the use of coal is almost phased out, oil consumption is greatly reduced, and the use of gas grows slowly for a time and then stabilizes. Conservation receives heavy emphasis, resulting in only gradual increases in energy use. Three sources grow to major status: nuclear, biomass, and other renewables. Nuclear grows because it does not produce greenhouse gases. It is important to note, however, that none of the OECD countries have solved the nuclear waste disposal problem. It may be that wind will replace coal as the source for electric power generation. The use of biofuels, hydrogen, and wind power receive major emphasis.

The IEA prepared a similar scenario for the world based on the assumptions proposed in Figure 12.32. It showed similar trends, with nuclear, biofuels, and other renewables growing in importance (Figure 12.33). In summary, according to the IEA, appropriate technologies will not completely power member nations or the world by 2050, but the world seems headed in that direction.

QUESTIONS & TASKS

1. What is the IEA?

2. Why does the IEA make energy-use projections?

3. Can IEA members power their countries using appropriate technologies by the year 2050?

4. Can appropriate technologies power the world by 2050?

Energy Policy

An **energy policy** is a plan that is put together by a government. To be effective, it must have broad support from both the business community and the public. If you want to influence that policy, you must be informed and speak out.

What energy strategies do you think are best for the present and the future—both for yourself and for your country?

 ACTIVITY 12.5

World Oil: Supply, Demand, Use

In this activity, you will take a closer look at the distribution of oil reserves around the world.

Procedure

1. This activity centers around an analysis of the three maps in Figures 12.34, 12.35, and 12.36. Examine them carefully.

2. Answer the questions that follow.

QUESTIONS & TASKS

Record your responses in your science notebook.

1. What region of the world has, by far, the largest proven crude oil reserves?

2. Identify two large world regions that have relatively small proven crude oil reserves.

3. Where does western Europe get most of its oil from? Name the top three suppliers.

4. Where does the United States get most of its oil from? Name the top three suppliers.

5. Where does Japan get most of its oil from? Name the top two suppliers.

6. Determine the gross domestic product (GDP) or gross national income (GNI) of the following countries: United States, United Kingdom, France, Germany, Japan, China, and India. Place this information in a chart with

Helpful Hint!

Use a world almanac or an Internet source such as www.studentsoftheworld.info.

▼ **FIGURE 12.34** Proven oil reserves at end of 2006 in thousand million barrels. (BP Statistical Review of World Energy, *June 2006*.)

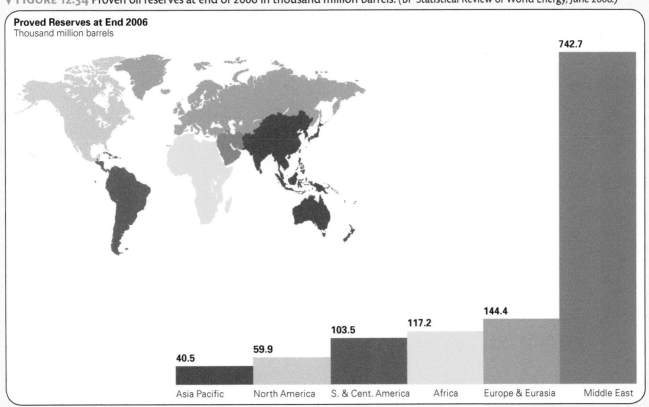

Proved Reserves at End 2006
Thousand million barrels

40.5	59.9	103.5	117.2	144.4	742.7
Asia Pacific	North America	S. & Cent. America	Africa	Europe & Eurasia	Middle East

▼ **FIGURE 12.35** Major oil trade movements in million tonnes. A *tonne* is a metric ton equal to 2204.6 pounds. (BP Statistical Review of World Energy, *June 2006.*)

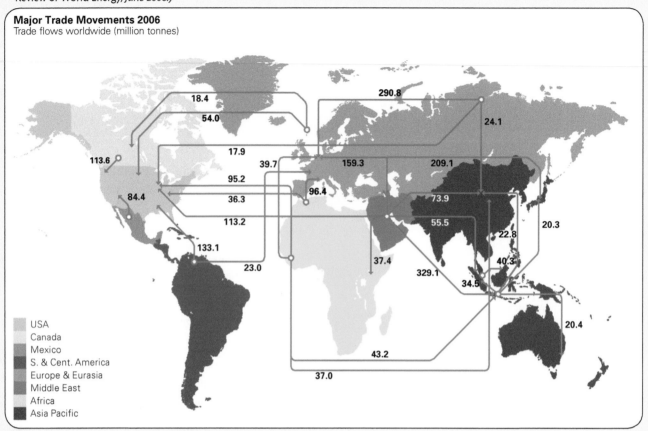

Major Trade Movements 2006
Trade flows worldwide (million tonnes)

USA
Canada
Mexico
S. & Cent. America
Europe & Eurasia
Middle East
Africa
Asia Pacific

▼ **FIGURE 12.36** Consumption of oil per capita in tonnes per person. (BP Statistical Review of World Energy, *June 2006.*)

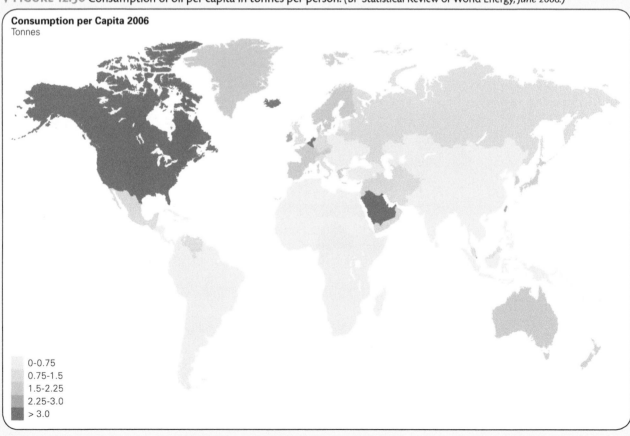

Consumption per Capita 2006
Tonnes

0-0.75
0.75-1.5
1.5-2.25
2.25-3.0
> 3.0

3 columns labeled "Country," "GDP (or GNI)," and "Relative Size of Economy."

a. What does your chart show?

b. What does your chart have to do with the use of world crude oil?

Helpful Hint!

To determine the relative size of the economy, divide the smallest GDP into all of the GDP values. Hence, the smallest economy is assigned a value of 1.00.

7. Identify four countries that have very high per capita (per person) oil consumption.

8. Identify four large countries that have very low per capita oil consumption.

9. If Americans do not want to give up larger cars or SUVs, how can they cut down on crude oil consumption? List several ways.

12.10 Energy Policy

There is little disagreement about the overall value of having an energy policy. Our economy requires an adequate and affordable supply of energy, but the use of energy affects the environment in many ways. Potential energy supply disruptions from unreliable sources make energy a national security issue. Free-market forces do not guarantee clean air or reliable supplies.

The problems of putting together an energy policy are large. Governmental interference with market forces often creates more problems than it solves. Many Americans waited in long lines in their cars to buy gasoline after the government used price controls and supply rationing in response to the Arab oil embargo in 1973 (see Figure 12.37). Also, our economic system is geared primarily to rewarding short-term gains. This makes it difficult to target long-term issues and research projects.

If we can overcome these problems, an energy policy should build mechanisms that encourage business and government to work together to do the following:

1. Provide the research and development (R&D) for those technologies that can advance energy efficiency. Federally initiated R&D programs on energy-conserving technologies have already saved taxpayers billions of dollars. These programs have targeted fluorescent lighting, low-emissivity (low-E) coatings for windows, and high-efficiency refrigeration. Well-conceived federal R&D can continue to reinforce private industry initiatives.

Think about This!

Why is an energy policy important?

Think about This!

Why is it hard to agree on an energy policy?

◀ FIGURE 12.37 Americans waited in long lines to fuel their cars in the 1970s when major oil-producing countries increased the price of oil and reduced supply. *(USDOE)*

▲ FIGURE 12.38 Alternative fuel vehicle. *(USDOE)*

▲ FIGURE 12.39 Domestic natural gas production. *(USDOE)*

2. Encourage a mixed energy supply, including renewables and alternatives to oil and gas (see Figure 12.38). Because of environmental concerns and the geographic locations of known global oil and gas reserves, it is wise to develop energy alternatives.

3. Lessen the conflict between environmental interests and energy industries so that natural resources can be used in an environmentally acceptable manner. It is true that ecological diversity must be preserved. But it is also true that some plots of land are much more diverse and more valuable ecologically than others. The careful selection of sites for energy exploration and extraction, coupled with the application of appropriate technology and environmental knowledge, enables us to use natural resources without destroying the surrounding environment (see Figure 12.39).

4. Determine the role that goals, taxes, and regulations should play in reducing energy consumption and related environmental problems.

The goal of any energy policy should be to accomplish these four tasks, and at the same time minimize government interference in people's lives. Activities 12.7 and 12.8 will help you propose your own national energy policy.

ACTIVITY 12.6

Summarize Your Options

In this activity, you will prepare a summary outline of alternative energy sources and strategies for using energy. This outline will help you write your national energy policy in Activity 12.7.

Procedure

1. In the last 5 chapters, you have examined alternatives to oil and natural gas fuels. Figure 12.40 outlines the various sources and strategies available to us. In your science notebook, list each alternative or strategy.

2. For each alternative or strategy you listed in step 1, *briefly* tell what it is and how it works. Then state both an advantage and a problem with expanding its use. Make a chart that looks something like this:

Source or Strategy	Brief Description	Advantage	Related Problem

Nonrenewable	Sustainable

1. *Fossil fuels*
   a. Coal
   b. Oil shale
   c. Tar sands
   d. Coal gasification
   e. Coal liquefaction
 	
2. *Nuclear*
   a. Ordinary fission reactors
   b. Breeder reactors
   c. Fusion — — — — — — — → ?
	1. *Direct solar*
	   a. Passive solar
	   b. Active solar (solar panels)
	   c. Concentrating solar power (CSP)
	   d. Photovoltaic (solar) cells
	   e. Solar satellites
	
	2. *Secondary solar*
	   a. Wind power
	   b. Hydroelectric power
	   c. Bioconversion
	   d. Energy from trash
	   e. Ocean thermal energy conversion (OTEC)
	   f. Ocean waves and ocean currents
	
	3. *Geothermal*
	
	4. *Tidal*

Energy Conversion and Storage	**Conservation**

1. *Energy conversion technologies*
   a. Cogeneration
   b. Fluidized-bed combustion
   c. Heat pumps
   d. Fuel cells
 	
2. *Energy storage techniques*
   a. Hydrogen storage
   b. Pumped storage
   c. Heat storage
	1. *Reduce*
	2. *Reuse*
	3. *Recycle*
	4. *Improved efficiency*

	Energy Policy (government)
	1. *Provide direction and goals* 2. *Fund research and development* 3. *Tax to influence behavior* 4. *Regulate use*

ACTIVITY 12.7

Sorting Out Your Options

In Activity 12.6, you summarized alternative energy sources and strategies for using energy. Now that you are familiar with our energy options, the next step is to begin sorting them out (see Figure 12.41). In this activity, you will sort out your options and develop your own national energy policy. Record your answers and your thinking in your science notebook.

Procedure

1. List 3 alternatives to oil and gas that result in the production of a fuel that is like oil and/or natural gas. Why is this an important consideration?

2. Give 1 advantage and 1 disadvantage of developing nuclear power.

3. Name 3 energy options that have serious environmental problems related to their development.

Strategies for Using Energy 481

▲ FIGURE 12.41 Making decisions. (*Wright*—The Providence Journal-Bulletin)

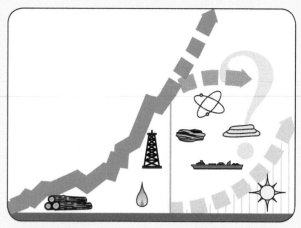

▲ FIGURE 12.42 Sort out the options. What should our energy future be? (*Adapted from USDOE*)

Does this mean we should stop development/use of these options? Why or why not?

4. Name 2 or 3 energy alternatives that have absolutely no negative environmental impacts related to their large-scale development.

5. Name 6 energy options that are directly or very closely related to the sun.

> **Helpful Hint!**
>
> Coal, oil shale, and tar sands were all formed from living matter. But since the organic materials from which they were formed lived so long ago, they are not considered solar options.

6. List 2 or 3 energy options that are smaller in size and considered to be only of local interest.

7. The main problem with this energy alternative is that it is too spread out (not concentrated enough) for many applications. Also, the use of this alternative requires many acres (hectares) of land. What is this option?

8. Name an energy option that could provide huge amounts of energy, but that will require a major research breakthrough before it becomes used widely.

9. What energy option, or combination of options, do you think is the best strategy for providing energy for the United States (or your country) for the next 30 years? Explain why. This is *your* national energy policy. Before writing out your policy, review Sections 12.6–12.10. Plan carefully before you write!

Summary

The wise use of energy includes a variety of strategies.

1. Conservation through superinsulated buildings, high-mileage vehicles, and more efficient appliances.

2. Energy conversion and storage techniques.

3. Knowledge of a variety of energy sources. This includes the quantity of energy the sources can provide and the environmental impacts related to their development and use.

4. A plan or policy for using energy that

   a. supports increased-efficiency R&D,

   b. encourages a balanced and mixed energy supply,

c. lessens the conflict between environmental issues and national resource use, and

d. determines the role taxes should play in reducing energy consumption and related environmental problems.

REFERENCES

American Council for an Energy-Efficient Economy. *The Most Energy-Efficient Appliances* (Washington, D.C.: ACEEE), annual.

DeCicco, John and James Kliesch. *Green Guide to Cars and Trucks* (Washington, D.C.: American Council for an Energy-Efficient Economy), annual.

Enterprise for Education. *Climate & Comfort* (Santa Monica, CA: Enterprise for Education), 1998. This is a more detailed version of the activity Home Energy Plan. Written for classroom use, it is recommended for students who wish to do this activity in more depth. It can be obtained from Enterprise for Education, 1316 Third Street, Suite 103, Santa Monica, CA 90401.

International Energy Agency. *Energy to 2050: Scenarios for a Sustainable Future* (Paris: IEA), 2003.

International Energy Agency. *Renewables in Global Energy Supply* (Paris: IEA), 2007.

Lovins, Amory B. and L. Hunter Lovins. Reinventing the Wheels. *The Atlantic Monthly*, Volume 275, January, 1995.

Siblerud, Robert. *Our Future is Hydrogen!* (Wollington, Co: New Science Publication), 2001.

Socolow, Robert H. and Stephen W. Pacala. A Plan to Keep Carbon in Check. *Scientific American* (September, 2006): 50–57.

U.S. Environmental Protection Agency. *Fuel Economy Guide* (Washington, D.C.: GPO), annual.

Vaitheeswaran, Vijay V. *Power to the People* (New York: Farrar, Straus and Girouy), 2003.

Wilson, Alex, Jennifer Thorne and John Morrill. *Consumer Guide to Home Energy Savings* (Washington, D.C.: American Council for an Energy-Efficient Economy), 2002.

WEBSITES

American Council for an Energy-Efficient Economy: www.aceee.org

EPA Fuel Economy Guide: www.fueleconomy.gov

Fuel Cell Information Center: www.fuelcells.org

International Energy Agency: www.iea.org

National Renewable Energy Laboratory: www.nrel.gov

U.S. Department of Energy: www.energy.gov

U.S. EPA Energy Star Program: www.energystar.gov

CHAPTER 13

Water Quantity

GOAL

- To understand the importance of adequate quantities of quality water for meeting the needs of modern societies.

It seems that the relatively balmy climates of eastern North America and northern Europe—and more generally the movement of the sun's heat around the Earth—are highly sensitive to the balance of fresh and salty water in the North Atlantic Ocean.

—Thomas Homer-Dixon, Centre for the Study of Peace and Conflict, University of Toronto

Earth's Water

How does almost every human activity involve the use of water?

Water is a necessary substance for all organisms; every life process demands water. Land without water is land without life. Water controls the political geography and economic life of nations. Ancient civilizations fought over water and collapsed for lack of it. Too much water brings floods; too little brings drought and famine.

Water is also important as a carrier of other substances. On its long journey from the clouds to the faucet, water picks up or dissolves a little bit of almost everything it touches. Rain washes the air, removing dust, fumes, and microscopic living organisms. Water flowing over Earth's surface becomes turbid or cloudy as it gathers impurities such as silt, sand, mud, and clay. As it flows through swampy areas, water picks up different colors, tastes, and odors from decaying plant and animal life. As water seeps into the ground, it dissolves minerals from rocks and soils.

No matter how much water is used and reused, it is never really consumed. Instead, water cycles. When this cycling process becomes overburdened, water pollution occurs. As citizens, we must become aware of water as an important resource to care for and use wisely (Figure 13.1).

▶FIGURE 13.1 The beauty of a freshwater lake is a wonder of nature. What can we do to keep it pristine? (© Minnesota Office of Tourism)

ACTIVITY 13.1

Water, Water Everywhere

There is water all over Earth, but very little of it is suitable for human consumption (Figure 13.3). In this activity, you will watch a demonstration that shows how the water on Earth is distributed. Consider the implications for your life of both where the water is and how safe it is for you to drink. After the demonstration, respond to the questions that follow.

QUESTIONS & TASKS

Record your responses in your science notebook.

1. Where is most of the water in the world?

2. Where is the least water in the world?

3. What surprised you the most during the demonstration?

◀ **FIGURE 13.2** This aerial view of the Antarctic shows the kind of place where more than 2 percent of Earth's water supply (and 86 percent of the world's frozen water) is stored. *(Ann Bancroft)*

▼ **FIGURE 13.3** An estimate of the world's water supply. *(U.S. Geological Survey)*

Location	Surface Area (square miles)	Water Volume (cubic miles)	Total Water (%)
Surface Water			
Freshwater lakes (Figure 13.1)	330,000	30,000	.009
Saline lakes and inland seas	270,000	25,000	.008
Stream channels (average)	—	300	.0001
Water Below Surface			
Water in soils	—	16,000	.005
Groundwater within half a mile of surface	50,000,000	1,000,000	.31
Deep-lying groundwater	—	1,000,000	.31
Other Water			
Ice caps and glaciers (Figure 13.2)	6,900,000	7,000,000	2.15
Atmosphere (at sea level)	197,000,000	3,100	.001
World oceans	139,500,000	317,000,000	97.20
Total (rounded)	394,000,000	326,000,000	100.00%

Helpful Hint!

Study the information in Figure 13.3. Based on that information, respond to questions 4–7.

4. Describe three ways that the amounts of surface water, water below the surface, and other water differ from one another.

5. According to the data in Figure 13.3, where is the most water found?

6. What sources of water in the figure are easiest to access?

7. Which sources of water are most difficult to access?

13.1 Water Distribution in the World

What portion of the world's water supply is available for human use?

Water seems abundant on Earth. It covers nearly three-quarters of Earth's surface. Of that water, however, less than 1 percent is readily available for human use. The other 99 percent is found mainly in the oceans (too salty for most human uses), or locked in remote ice caps and glaciers as freshwater. The Antarctic ice cap alone covers 6 million square miles (15.5 million square kilometers), and it contains 86 percent of the world's frozen water (see Figure 13.2).

The Oceans and Their Role

The oceans contain more than 97 percent of all the water on Earth, and they cover about 70 percent of Earth's surface. They are part of all the geochemical cycles—especially the water and carbon cycles.

Because water has a high heat capacity, the oceans moderate global climate. They reduce the extremes in temperature that Earth would otherwise experience.

The oceans support a variety of aquatic plants. As a result, the oceans generate oxygen. Because of their size, varying depth, and water circulation, the oceans generate more oxygen and biomass than any other ecosystem (see Figure 13.4).

►FIGURE 13.4 World net primary productivity by ecosystem type. *Net primary production* refers to the portion of matter that plants produce that remains after the respiration of those plants. Data are in billion metric tonnes dry biomass/year. *(From Lieth, Helmut, and Whittaker, editors.* Primary Productivity of the Biosphere, *New York: Springer-Verlag, 1975.)*

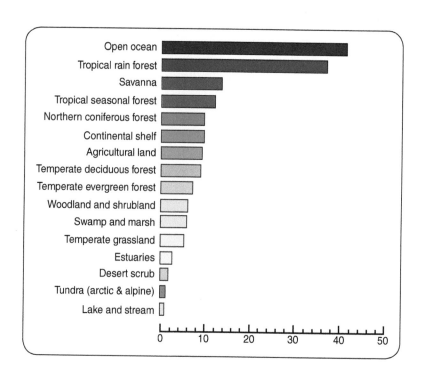

The oceans contain many food webs that tie to humans. Aquatic plants grow only where they receive light, oxygen, and an ample supply of the nutrients they require. Hence, most of the world's fish catch occurs on continental shelves.

Fish are an important part of the human diet. They provide about 16 percent of the world's protein and are especially important to those who live in the developing world. Since the global harvest of fish is declining, we must do a better job of managing ocean fisheries. Cooperation among the major countries that harvest fish is key.

Topic: ocean fisheries
Go to: www.scilinks.org
Code: GloSci7e489a

Surface Waters

Rivers are an important source of freshwater. In addition, since rivers carry surface run-off back to the sea, they help maintain the world's water balance. Figure 13.5 shows the world's major river basins.

Earth's land areas are dotted with hundreds of thousands of lakes. Lakes are important in supplying domestic water to many communities. The volume of all large freshwater lakes in the world totals nearly 30,000 cubic miles (125,000 cubic kilometers). The Great Lakes and other large North American lakes contain about 26 percent of all freshwater in the world. Large freshwater lakes in Africa contain 29 percent of the world's supply. And Asia's large lakes (primarily Lake Baykal in the Soviet Union) contain about 21 percent of the total.

Saline lakes throughout the world contain almost as much water as freshwater lakes. However, their distribution and usefulness to people are very different. The Caspian Sea contains about 75 percent of the total water content of saline lakes. Most of the remainder is in Asia. North America's shallow Great Salt Lake is relatively insignificant in terms of its water content.

Apply Your Understanding

Why are freshwater lakes so important to humans?

Groundwater

Groundwater is water found in porous rock layers and in soils below Earth's surface. While people obtain most of their water from rivers, lakes, and reservoirs, water under the ground is also important. In Germany, more than 70 percent of the water supply comes

Topic: groundwater
Go to: www.scilinks.org
Code: GloSci7e489b

▼ FIGURE 13.5 The world's major river basins. (*From* World Resources 1992–93: A Guide to the Global Environment *by World Resources Institute. Copyright © 1992 by World Resources Institute. Used by permission of Oxford University Press, Inc.*)

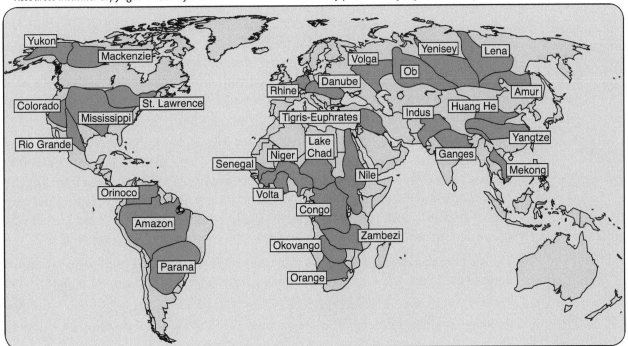

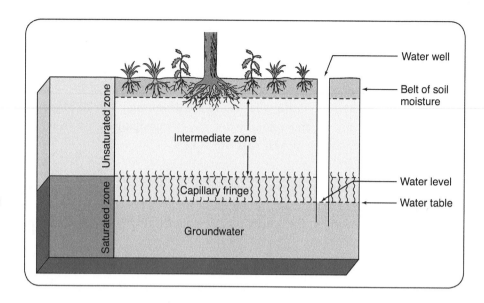

Underground water lies in both an unsaturated zone and a saturated zone. At the top of the saturated zone, water is held in a capillary fringe by surface tension. At any one spot, the water table is the point in the saturated zone where the water is under a pressure equal to atmospheric pressure. Its position is indicated by the water level in shallow wells.

from groundwater. In Israel, this figure is about 54 percent. In Britain and the United States, it is about 20 percent.

Groundwater may be near the surface, only 8–10 feet (ft) or 2.5–3 meters (m) underground, or as deep as 0.5 mile (mi) or about 1 kilometer (km) below the surface. Tremendous amounts of water—more than 30 times the water in all the world's rivers and lakes—exist as groundwater.

Above the saturated zone of groundwater, a small amount of water is held within the soil (see Figure 13.6). This is a very small percentage of Earth's total water, but it is vital to life. Practically all Earth's vegetation depends on natural soil moisture, which, in turn, depends on the proper functioning of the water cycle.

Two serious threats to groundwater are pollution and overuse. Because the **recharge** (replacement) rate of groundwater is slow, pollution affects these water supplies for centuries. In addition, pumping water out of an aquifer faster than it can be recharged depletes this important source of water.

The Problem of Freshwater

The available amount of usable freshwater may become critical because people have become so numerous and because modern economies use and process so much water. If current trends of population growth and increased water use continue, lack of freshwater may threaten the vitality of many regions.

Our personal use of water accounts for one-tenth of the total renewable supply and about one-fourth of the stable supply. Agriculture claims the "lion's share," about 70 percent of the world's water use (see Figure 13.7). Roughly a third of the present-day harvest comes from irrigated croplands. Industry is second, using one-quarter of all water. Production of energy from nuclear and fossil-fueled power plants is the greatest single industrial water user. Water provides the source of steam that drives the turbine generators and cools power plant condensers.

The seeming abundance of water has made us complacent about the need to manage it and adapt to the limits of a fixed supply. Warning signs appear in the form of polluted water supplies, depletion of groundwater, and falling water tables.

As water shortages develop and competition for limited supplies increases, we must develop new strategies to conserve this valuable resource.

◀FIGURE 13.7 Irrigated cropland in an arid region. (*U.S. Soil Conservation Service*)

13.2 The Ocean System

The ocean is part of a giant global heat transfer system that links the atmosphere to the large-scale flow of water—the ocean **currents**. In the process of moving, the currents help distribute the sun's energy throughout Earth's climate system. So also do atmospheric currents, winds, the jet stream, and hurricanes. These interactions are all part of the complex forces that work to balance out Earth's solar influx. Climate modeling is a scientific effort to describe, quantify, and calculate the links between these interactions on land, in the atmosphere, and in the oceans.

Some of the ocean currents are *surface currents*. A comparison of the global wind patterns (see Figure 13.8) and the pattern of surface currents (see Figure 13.9) shows a connection between the two. This is because wind is the driving force of surface currents. Note that the surface currents form circular paths called **gyres**. These gyres result from winds, the continental boundaries, and the influence of Earth's rotation. Their influence on climate is significant.

The ocean is part of the global climate system.

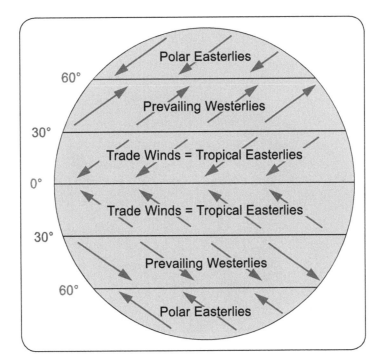

◀FIGURE 13.8 The global wind circulation pattern. The winds that come from the east are drier than the winds that come from the west.

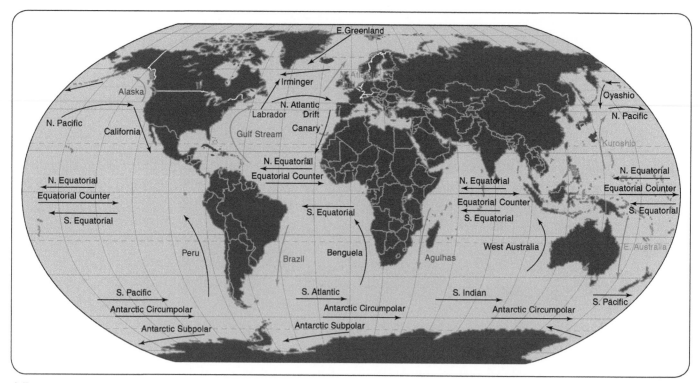

The Gulf Stream, for example, carries 500 times the flow of the Amazon, Earth's largest river, toward Labrador, Greenland, and the Norwegian seas! The climate of eastern North America and northwestern Europe is warmer and wetter as a result. The dry trade winds create arid regions such as the deserts of the American Southwest. The polar regions are also giant deserts. Knowledge of these currents was important to early sailors as they planned their journeys.

Differences in water temperature, salt content, and density drive a huge current called the Great Ocean Conveyor. The conveyor snakes around the globe as it seeks equilibrium. The whole process is driven by the sun. Follow the arrows in Figure 13.10 as we take a trip around the conveyor.

Think about This!

As you read about the Great Ocean Conveyor, think about its importance to global climate and where people live.

▶FIGURE 13.10 The Great Ocean Conveyor of global thermohaline circulation. (Blue represents cold currents; red represents warmer currents.) (*National Oceanic and Atmospheric Administration*)

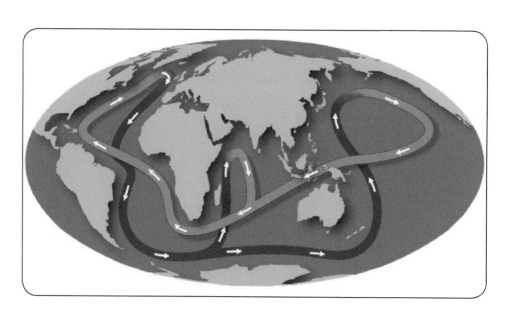

Let's start in the Atlantic's tropical regions in the Caribbean. Here heat from direct sun rays rapidly evaporates the ocean's water. Because evaporated water is fresh, the seawater left behind is saltier. Some of this relatively salty water flows north. This huge current is 75 times larger than the Amazon River. Coming from the equator, the current contains an immense quantity of heat. In the North Atlantic region, it releases some of that heat to the atmosphere, warming the North American coast and northern Europe. The cooled water is salty, and thus relatively dense. As a result, it sinks deep into the ocean and flows back toward the tropics and on toward and along the Antarctic. Here the conveyor splits. One portion flows north into the Indian Ocean. The remainder flows toward New Zealand where it turns north and heads toward Japan and Alaska. As it moves north from Antarctica, the current is soon forced upward where it reaches the surface near India and Japan. A full trip around the conveyor takes about 1,000 years!

One of the great debates of our time centers on the impact global warming *could* have on the Great Ocean Conveyor. As the climate warms, polar ice melts faster. Snow and ice reflect the sun's rays; dark ocean water absorbs them. If the polar ice regions shrink, the dark ocean areas will expand and absorb more solar energy. The polar regions will warm at an increasing rate. Ice and snow are made of freshwater. Freshwater is less dense than salty water. As all this freshwater arrives in the North Atlantic, it is less likely to sink. If it cannot sink, the conveyor will stop moving. If that happens, northeastern America and northern Europe will become much colder. Droughts could increase across the planet. A recent report from the Pentagon claims this could trigger mass migrations of people, and interstate and civil wars in many regions of the world.

It should concern us that scientists have recently recorded that water near the equator is becoming saltier and warmer than normal, while water near Greenland is becoming colder and fresher. We must remember, however, that the uncertainties of these scenarios are great. The projections may be wrong. We have much to learn. However, because the stakes are high, we must proceed into the unknown with caution and, in ignorance, refrain from foolish behavior.

Helpful Hint!

Thermohaline circulation refers to vertical movement of ocean water caused by differences in water temperature and salinity.

Apply Your Understanding

Why does the conveyor water sink in the North Atlantic?

Apply Your Understanding

What could cause the conveyor to stop?

ACTIVITY 13.2

Currents and Continents

In this activity, you will observe a model of liquid currents. You will also observe the effect of land-masses on current flow.

Materials (for each team)

- pie plate
- 3/4 cup whole milk (about 1/2 inch deep on pie plate)
- food coloring, 2 contrasting colors (for example, red and blue)
- dish soap (preferably clear or light colored)
- several small stones (1–2 inches in diameter)
- safety goggles

Procedure

Part A: What do you observe about currents?

1. Pour the milk into the pie plate.

2. Place 5 or 6 drops of 1 food coloring near the edge of the plate.

3. Place 5 or 6 drops of the other food coloring on the *opposite* side of the pie plate (near the edge as well).

4. Put a couple of squirts of dish soap on *opposite* sides of the pie plate, near the 2 groupings of food coloring.

Helpful Hint!

Make sure your drops of food coloring are each closely grouped.

5. Observe any movement of the food coloring.

Part B: How do landmasses influence currents?

1. Empty the pie plate and start again.

2. After adding the milk, place a couple small stones on the plate to represent continents.

3. Add the food coloring and dish soap.

4. Observe the influence of the landmasses on current flow.

QUESTIONS & TASKS

Record your responses in your science notebook.

1. What did the addition of dish soap cause the food coloring to do?

2. What influence did the landmasses have on the movement of food coloring?

3. Compare your observations to surface current flow in the oceans.

[Adapted from "Swirled World," Barbara Z. Tharp, Baylor College of Medicine, Division of School-Based Programs.]

13.3 El Niño

Think about This!

Have you ever heard of El Niño? In what context was it discussed?

El Niño is an interaction between the ocean and the atmosphere in the tropical waters of the Indian and Pacific oceans that occurs about every 2 to 7 years. El Niño events usually last about a year. The events are linked to unusual weather patterns throughout the world. In fact, El Niño events are second only to the normal march of the seasons in their impact on world climate.

Under normal conditions, the trade winds blow over the Pacific from the east and create gyres that flow westward in higher latitudes (see Figures 13.8 and 13.9). The winds and currents keep warm water in the *western* Pacific. The warm water warms the air above it, creating lower atmospheric pressure and frequent heavy rain (see Figure 13.11).

Apply Your Understanding

Why is rainfall normally high in the western Pacific?

A layer of water called a **thermocline** separates warm surface waters from the coldest depths. The thermocline is deep in the western Pacific and Indian Ocean. It slopes upward toward the surface as one moves east toward South America where cold water rises upward. This upwelling carries nutrients to the surface, which results in a greater fish catch off the coast of Peru.

During an El Niño event, the trade winds weaken for reasons that are not fully understood. This allows the warm water in the western Pacific to move eastward. The thermocline in the eastern Pacific deepens and prevents colder deep water in the ocean from rising to the surface. This lowers the fish catch off the coast of Peru (see Figure 13.12). Weather systems with lower atmospheric pressures move eastward and bring heavy rain and flooding to the Pacific coast of South America and drought conditions and fires to Southeast Asia. Thus, El Niño events temporarily disrupt the weather patterns that plants, animals, and people have grown accustomed to.

During El Niño, weather patterns in other parts of the world are also changed. In the United States, there are milder winters in the Midwest, heavy rains and flooding in the South and Southwest, and dry conditions in the Pacific Northwest. El Niño events are not tied directly to global warming. However, global warming probably enhances their impact.

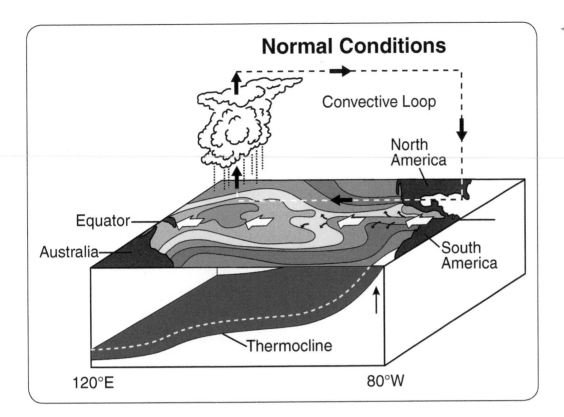

▲FIGURE 13.11 Normal conditions in the Pacific Ocean near the equator. *(National Oceanic and Atmospheric Administration)*

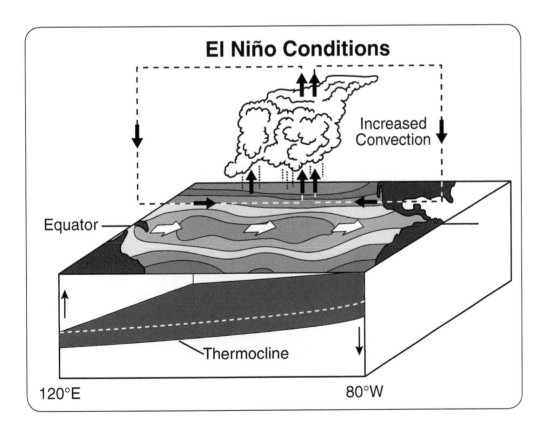

▲FIGURE 13.12 El Niño conditions in the Pacific Ocean near the equator. *(National Oceanic and Atmospheric Administration)*

Think about This!

Have you ever heard of La Niña? In what context was it discussed?

Why will the prediction of an El Niño be beneficial?

A La Niña event often develops after an El Niño. La Niña is the climatic opposite of El Niño and occurs when strong trade winds push warm surface water westward. This causes cold water to be pulled up along the coast of Peru. This situation can result in severe storms in Southeast Asia and drought in South America.

Because of the economic impact, scientists are working to more fully understand the El Niño/Southern Oscillation (ENSO) cycle and improve their ability to predict when these events will occur.

13.4 Hurricanes

A hurricane is a type of tropical cyclone—an organized, rotating weather system that develops in the tropics. Hurricanes rotate counterclockwise in the Northern Hemisphere (see Figure 13.13). They are the most destructive storms that occur on Earth. The greatest number of hurricanes—an average of 20 per year—occur in the western Pacific, where they are called typhoons. Those in the Indian Ocean are called cyclones.

Tropical cyclones are classified as follows:

Tropical depression. An organized system of persistent clouds and thunderstorms with a closed, low-level circulation and maximum sustained winds of 38 mph (33 knots) or less.

Tropical storm. An organized system of strong thunderstorms with a well-defined circulation and maximum sustained winds of 39–73 mph (34–63 knots).

Hurricane. An intense tropical weather system with a well-defined circulation and sustained winds of 74 mph (64 knots) or higher.

The potential of hurricanes to cause loss of life and property is enormous. Those in hurricane-prone areas need to be prepared for hurricanes and tropical storms. Even inland areas, well away from the coastline, can experience destructive winds, tornadoes, and floods from tropical

▶FIGURE 13.13 Hurricane Katrina is about to slam into shore on August 28, 2005. New Orleans was hit with 145 mph winds and the possibility of a 20-ft storm surge. (*NASA/Jeff Schmultz, MODIS Land Response Team*)

storms and hurricanes. In the United States, one in six Americans lives along the East and Gulf coasts. This is the most hurricane-prone region.

Hurricanes form over warm, tropical oceans. Their winds spiral rapidly in toward an intense low-pressure storm center. They begin when very warm, moist air over the evaporating ocean rises rapidly. When moisture in the rising warm air condenses, a large amount of energy in the form of stored heat is released. This heat increases the force of the rising air. Moist tropical air continues to be pulled into the column of rising air. More heat is released, which drives the powerful heat engine. A rising global temperature should enhance this process.

The most dangerous effect of a hurricane is rising sea level and large waves that can submerge vast areas of low-lying coastline. On average, 10 tropical storms, six of which become hurricanes, develop in the Atlantic Ocean, Caribbean Sea, or Gulf of Mexico each year. In a typical 3-year span, the U.S. coastline is struck on average five times by hurricanes.

Of particular concern is the **storm surge**. This is the large dome of water, often 50 to 100 mi wide (about 80–160 km), that sweeps across the coastline near where a hurricane makes landfall. The surge of water topped by waves is devastating. The stronger the hurricane and the shallower the offshore water, the higher the surge will be. Along the immediate coast, storm surge is the greatest threat to life and property. However, more people die from freshwater flooding tied to landfalling tropical cyclones than from any other weather hazard related to them.

Hurricane warnings are issued by the National Hurricane Center. They use a combination of numerical models, observations over the open ocean, and a knowledge of the physics of hurricane movement. These warnings plus a plan of action has and will continue to save thousands of lives.

A family disaster action plan looks something like this:

- **Gather information about hazards.** Contact your local National Weather Service office, emergency management office, and American Red Cross chapter.

- **Meet with your family and make a disaster plan.** Pick two places to meet: a spot outside your home for an emergency and a place away from your neighborhood in case you can't return home. Choose an out-of-state friend as a contact to call if the family gets separated.

- **Implement your plan.** Post emergency telephone numbers. Install safety features in your home. Prepare an emergency kit. Keep enough supplies in your home to last 3 days.

- **Practice and maintain your plan.**

  Government planning for future hurricanes should include the following:

- **Reinforce levees and floodgates.** Floodgates in the Netherlands keep the 10 million Dutch citizens who live below sea level safe.

- **Replenish wetlands.** Wetlands dampen the height of an approaching storm surge, thus protecting people and property farther in from the coast. Every 4 mi (about 6.5 km) of wetlands can reduce the height of Gulf storm surges by a foot.

- **Establish evacuation plans.** Protect the poor, the elderly, and the disabled.

- **Coordinate the plan.**

 To learn more about hurricanes, contact the National Oceanic and Atmospheric Administration (NOAA) at http://www.climate.noaa.gov/education/hurricanes or the National Hurricane Center at www.nhc.noaa.gov.

Waves, Currents, and Coastal Erosion

Waves and currents are a form of energy transfer. Since energy is the ability to move matter around, waves and currents have the ability to both build and rearrange coasts. (Refresh your understanding of wave terms by rereading section 3.7 on Radiant Energy in Chapter 3.)

Most people think of land as a stable platform on which we can safely and easily build and enjoy. This thinking is reasonable in most cases, because most land changes very slowly. Coasts, however, are not static. They change shape and location quickly in response to natural forces and human activity. This poses a dilemma to many because more than 60 percent of the U.S. population lives within an hour's drive of a coast. Coastal areas across the United States have population densities five times the national average. Hence, changes to coasts can have an impact on property, vacation plans, investments, and ecosystems.

Sand and other materials are moved onto and off of beaches by currents and waves. The seasonal movement of coastal materials creates broad summer beaches followed by narrow winter beaches in an annual cycle. During major storms, huge waves and storm surges can move large amounts of coastal sediments and can flood vast areas in a matter of hours.

On a larger scale, the coast itself moves as it tries to achieve equilibrium with the forces acting on it. Barrier islands and offshore sandbars (see Figure 13.14) move landward and along the coast, driven by longshore currents. Headlands are eroded back, moving the

▼ FIGURE 13.14 Ocean City, Maryland, is a popular beach resort. It is also an urbanized barrier island. These two facts combine to create a unique set of conditions the community must struggle with. (*Town of Ocean City Tourism Office*)

coast inland. Sediment is deposited on river deltas, extending the coast out into the water. Coastlines also move in response to changes in sea level. Even if the land remains stationary, a rise in sea level will move the coastline inland.

Sources of coastline-related problems include the following:

- Building on floodplains and in low-lying coastal areas.

- Damming rivers for flood control and water management that affects the stability of coastlines by restricting the supply of new sediments being carried to the coasts.

- Increased production of greenhouse gases, causing worldwide sea level rise as glaciers melt.

The key to understanding and solving coastal problems is to collect information and build a solid foundation of earth science data on these problems. We must then use this foundation as a basis for sound coastal management policies. Think about the following seven points that apply to coastal issues:

1. Coasts are the dynamic junction of water, air, and land. Some coasts are more stable than others. Rocky shores are more stable than sandy beaches. Barrier islands and beaches are constantly migrating, eroding, and building in response to natural processes and human activity (see Figure 13.15).

2. Coastal wetlands are complex and diverse ecosystems. They are valuable habitats for commercial and recreational fish. They also support an abundance of wildlife, moderate the impact of tropical storms, and clean up significant quantities of human pollution. Draining wetlands has had disastrous environmental impacts.

3. Human actions can modify coastlines. Knowledge of coastal dynamics can quantify those changes and improve our ability to predict coastal responses to human actions.

4. Breaking waves move sand along the coast. Rivers carry sediment to the coast and build deltas into the open water. Storms cause

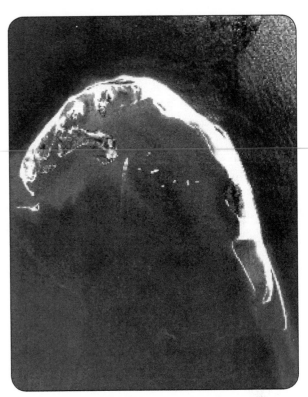

▲ **FIGURE 13.15** Aerial view of a barrier island off the south coast of Louisiana. The Gulf of Mexico is at the bottom of the photo. Rapid erosion of the protecting barrier islands has exposed Louisiana's valuable wetlands and estuaries to increased storm waves and currents. (*Barataria-Terrebonne National Estuary Program*)

major erosion. Plants retain sediment in wetlands and slow the movement of coastal dunes.

5. As the result of climate change, the sea level is slowly rising. This shifts coastlines dramatically on gently sloping coasts such as the U.S. East Coast and the Gulf of Mexico. This problem is increasing.

6. Disasters such as Hurricane Katrina in 2005 are making it harder for insurance companies to insure property in coastal storm–prone areas. Some insurance companies are leaving these areas. Should some communities be abandoned or relocated?

7. Groins, jetties, breakwaters, seawalls, revetments, levees, and other engineered structures affect coastal processes. Some of these impacts are positive; others cause new problems.

Choose one of the seven coast-related facts listed above. Do a library/Internet search. You might want to focus on the work of one or more of the following agencies or on those that conduct research in your area. Write a paper that describes the nature of the concern and some of the possible solutions. Emphasize the scientific aspects.

Federal agencies with regulatory or research responsibilities for our coasts:

FEMA

NOAA (Dept. of Commerce)

NPS (Dept. of Interior)

EPA

NSF

Mineral Management Service (Dept. of Interior)

Army Corps of Engineers (Dept. of Defense)

U.S. Coast Guard (Dept. of Transportation)

FWS (Dept. of Interior)

USGS (Dept. of Interior)

NRCS (Dept. of Agriculture)

In addition, many state agencies have similar responsibilities.

SPECIAL FOCUS

Tsunamis

On December 26, 2004, an earthquake with a *moment magnitude* of 9.3 shook the bottom of the Indian Ocean just below the northwest tip of the Indonesian island of Sumatra. The tremors jolted the seabed upward, producing a series of towering waves called tsunami waves. The waves spread outward in expanding circles and moved at speeds of up to 500 mi (800 km) per hour! They raced across the Indian Ocean and onto the shores of Asian and African nations. Somalia, on the horn of Africa, 3,500 mi (about 5,600 km) away, was reached in just over 7 hours.

About 15 minutes after the earthquake, waves at least 66 ft (20 m) high hit the north and west coasts of Sumatra (see Figure 13.16). When the tsunami was over, at least 175,000 people were dead. In addition, hundreds of thousands were injured, millions were left homeless, and buildings, roads, farms, and property were destroyed.

As the above description implies, a **tsunami** (pronounced tsoo-NAH-me) is a series of powerful ocean waves produced by an earthquake, landslide, volcanic eruption, or asteroid impact. Tsunami waves are much longer (farther apart) than common wind-caused ocean waves. On the open ocean, tsunami waves are long and low. They are not easily seen from airplanes or boats. As the waves enter shallow water, they slow, causing their height to grow dramatically. The waves then surge onto land. In shallow water, the waves can be over 100 ft (30 m) tall (see Figure 13.17).

How can such devastation be reduced? A number of things can be done, including the following:

1. **Improve the warning system.** Seismic waves travel through the ground much faster than tsunami waves travel over the water. For that reason, scientists can often warn people several hours before tsunami waves strike. Another forecasting method uses pressure

◄ FIGURE 13.16 A village near the coast of Sumatra lays in ruin after the tsunami that struck southeast Asia in December 2004. *(U.S. Navy photo by Photographer's Mate 2nd Class Philip A. McDaniel)*

sensors placed on the ocean floor. When the sensor detects a large tsunami wave overhead, it relays the information to a buoy above on the surface. The buoy then transmits the data to a warning center. This information can be matched to seismic information as a means of confirmation. This method of detection is being expanded. At the time of the 2004 tsunami, the Indian Ocean lacked tsunami detection devices.

2. **Educate people about warning signs and safety measures.** When a tsunami warning is issued, sirens should go off and radio and television announcements made. Best evacuation routes must be clearly marked. People need to know that they must move quickly to higher ground and/or inland. Since there can be only a few minutes' warning of a local tsunami, as soon as the ground begins to tremble, one must move quickly upward and inland. It is also important to know that a second and third wave may strike. These waves can be 10–60 minutes apart. One should not return to low-lying areas until an "all clear" is announced by local authorities. A tsunami can easily wrap around an island and be just as dangerous on coasts not facing the source of the tsunami.

When on a beach, sometimes the first sign of a tsunami is a withdrawal of water from the shore, exposing the ocean floor including shells, seaweed, and fish. Tilly Smith, a 10-year-old from England, learned this in a geography lesson. After watching the ocean recede while on a beach in Thailand with her family, she warned her family and others on the beach. About 100 people quickly fled. No one on that beach was killed.

3. **Scientifically assess the conditions that lead to the development of tsunamis.** This is the work of international tsunami research groups. The work is ongoing. For more information, go to http://www.prh.noaa.gov/itic/.

QUESTIONS & TASKS

Record your responses in your science notebook.

1. What is a tsunami?

2. Why can a tsunami be so deadly?

3. How can tsunami warning systems be improved and death tolls reduced?

4. When on or near a beach, what should *you* do to protect yourself from a tsunami?

▼ FIGURE 13.17 A tsunami may begin with a below ocean earthquake. Upward (or downward) movement of the seabed displaces a huge quantity of water. Circular surface waves travel rapidly out from the source. As the waves move over shallow water, they grow in height. (*Adapted from International Tsunami Information Center*)

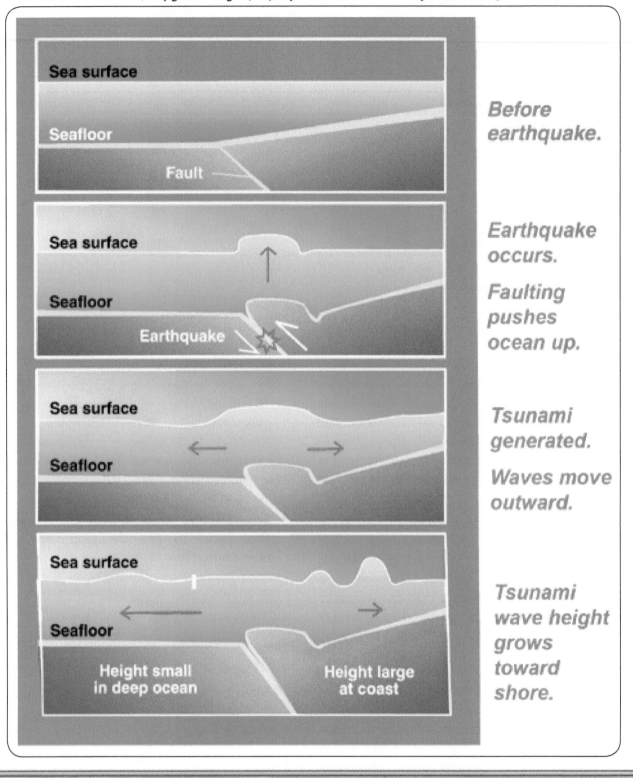

13.5 Water in the United States

The Water Budget

One way to study the water supply in an area is to set up a water budget. A water budget is a type of balance sheet that shows the water available in different parts of the water cycle. Figure 13.18 presents a water budget for the United States. Data are given as millions of gallons per day (Mgal/d). From this illustration, we see that 4,200,000 Mgal/d of moisture enter the United States in the form of precipitation—mainly rain and snow. Water leaves the United States landmass in a variety of ways. It evaporates from moist surfaces and transpires from plants. (These losses are grouped under the term **evapotranspiration**.) The total evapotranspiration over the United States averages 2,800,000 Mgal/d. Both surface water and groundwater leave the United States, flowing into the oceans, Canada, and Mexico. This total outflow amounts to 1,300,000 Mgal/d.

Finally, some water is bound into products (like concrete), crops, and animals, or otherwise removed from the water environment of a region. This is referred to as *consumptive use*. For the United States, consumptive use totals 92,000 Mgal/d.

The water budget is based on averages for the 48 contiguous states. Actually, two-thirds of the precipitation falls in the East and one-third in the West. Western states show considerable variation. The annual precipitation of the Mojave Desert of California is a low 0.8 inches (in) or 5 centimeters (cm). In the Olympic Mountains of Washington, it is 98 in (250 cm). Each region has its own water budget.

Since water does not disappear, the input should equal the output. Thus, P ~ ET + TO + CU. (The slight difference of 8,000 Mgal/d is due to estimates and rounding off numbers and is not significant.)

Human Water Use

Think about the ways we use water. Water for drinking is a necessity for life. In addition, we use water for cooking, washing dishes, bathing, washing clothes, and flushing the toilet.

Apply Your Understanding

What is the difference between TO and SWO?

▼ **FIGURE 13.18** Estimated water budget for the contiguous United States. Data are given in millions of gallons per day (Mgal/d). P = precipitation; ET = evapotranspiration; CU = consumptive use; SWO = surface-water outflow to the oceans, Canada, and Mexico; TO = total surface and groundwater outflow to the oceans, Canada, and Mexico. (*Source: USGS.*)

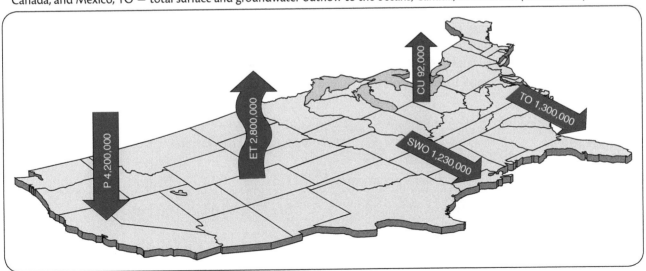

►FIGURE 13.19 Average U.S. indoor home water use. (*U.S. Environmental Protection Agency*)

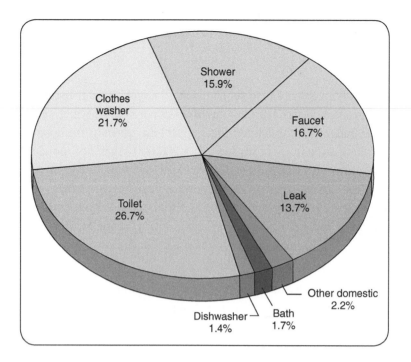

Helpful Hint!

Conversion factor:
3.785 liters = 1 gallon

We use water for our gardens and for recreation. Almost every human activity involves water either directly or indirectly.

In the average American home, each person uses about 80 gallons (gal) or 300 liters (L) of water per day. This use is summarized in Figure 13.19. From this figure, we see that close to 75 percent of the water used in the home is used in the bathroom. Can you think of ways to use less water at home?

The table in Figure 13.20 summarizes U.S. water use. From this table, we see that home and commercial use is only about 12 percent of the total picture. The remainder is used by industry, for electric power generation, and for agriculture.

Think about This!

In terms of U.S. water use, where are the largest opportunities for saving water?

Agricultural water use is primarily for irrigation. Much can and is being done to reduce irrigation losses. Irrigation ditches can be lined with clays, concrete, or plastics to reduce seepage into the ground. Spray irrigation on hot afternoons can be reduced. Trickle irrigation techniques release water closer to the plant roots.

Availability

Because of its dry climate, increasing population, and agricultural demands, much of the western half of the United States is faced with water-supply problems (see Figure 13.21). In the midwestern and western regions of the United States, low precipitation, population, and industrial growth have led to increased use of groundwater. Huge underground

►FIGURE 13.20 This is how the average person in the United States uses water every day. Compare home/commercial, agriculture, and industrial use per person based on this information. (*USGS*)

Sector	Percent	Use/Person/Day
Domestic (home)/commercial	11.5	587 L = 155 gal
Industrial/mining	8.2	416 L = 110 gal
Thermoelectric power	38.6	1,960 L = 518 gal
Agriculture	41.7	2,112 L = 558 gal

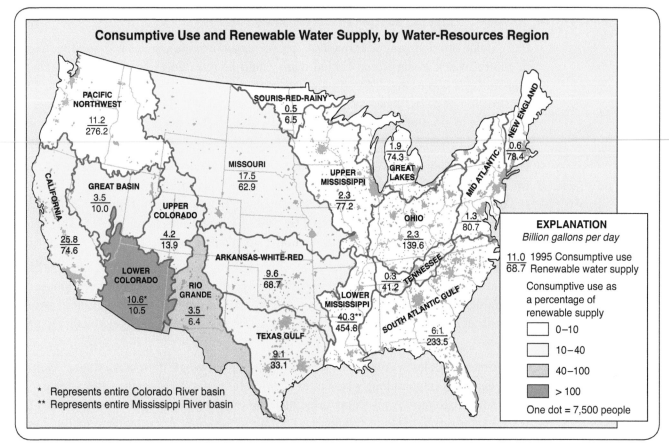

▲ FIGURE 13.21 Comparisons of average consumptive use (see section 13.5, The Water Budget) and renewable water supply for the 18 water-resource regions of the contiguous United States. Superimposed is the U.S. population distribution where one dot = 7,500 people. *(From USGS Water Use in the United States. http://water.usgs.gov/watuse/misc/consuse-renewable.html Population distribution: U.S. Department of Commerce, U.S. Census Bureau.)*

reservoirs that have been filled through the centuries are now being used at a rate greater than their recharge rate. "Mining" of water, accompanied by a drop in the water table, has occurred in the central and San Joaquin valleys of California, south-central Arizona, and throughout the Ogallala **aquifer** underlying the midwestern United States. The Ogallala aquifer may have less than 30 years of useful life left, and in some localities depletion of underground water will occur even sooner.

With adequate precipitation and numerous rivers, the eastern part of the United States seems well endowed with water. The problems there are related more to the quality of the water than the quantity of the water. The eastern section of the United States has many large population centers and a history of pollution of lakes, rivers, and groundwater (see Figure 13.21).

Think about This!

What is meant by "mining" water?

Water Management

Although we cannot easily increase the overall supply of freshwater, we can manage it more effectively. One approach involves increasing water supplies through building dams and diverting water to areas of greatest need. A second approach emphasizes using water more efficiently and conserving water supplies. Both approaches are being used to solve our growing water problems.

13.6 Dams and Reservoirs

Early in the development of agriculture, people began irrigating crops and building dams to control water. Water stored behind dams could be released as needed so crops could flourish. This was essential for growing crops in arid areas such as Israel and Egypt. The construction of dams, aqueducts, canals, and pipes to store and carry water from areas of abundance to areas of need has grown with the growth of human population and with the growth and needs of water by industry.

Dams store or impound water that can be used for irrigation, for drinking and home use, for generating electricity, and for industry. A dam regulates the rate of water flow downstream, thus reducing flooding. Electricity generated by water flowing through turbines can be transmitted long distances to population centers where electricity is needed. The water used in generating electricity is returned to the stream after use.

Figure 13.22 shows the recreational value of impounding water. In this particular case, the lake that was created improved the scenery. The people it displaced built new homes on the lakeshores. The lake and stream that flow in and out provide excellent fishing, swimming, water skiing, and sailing. Ice fishing is popular in the winter, along with other winter activities.

Apply Your Understanding

Debate the pros and cons of damming water.

Sometimes, problems created in damming rivers outweigh their advantages. Building a dam and impounding water alter scenic areas, displace people, and alter natural wildlife habitats. A reservoir prevents low-impact recreational activities such as white-water rafting, stream fishing, and wilderness hiking. A dam interrupts the natural stream flow, disrupts natural fish migrations, and alters the water's temperature and oxygen content.

Water losses from a reservoir are tremendous. Large amounts of water evaporate from the surface of a reservoir, and even more water seeps into the ground. For example, 270,000 cubic meters of water evaporate from Lake Powell each year. This is enough water to serve the needs of a city of 500,000 people. Because the evaporation of water leaves dissolved particles of salt behind, the water remaining in the reservoir becomes saltier. When water with too much salt is used for irrigation, soils become increasingly salty, and eventually become too saline for agriculture.

▶ **Figure 13.22** Lake Dillon was formed by damming Colorado's Blue River (a tributary of the Colorado River). Some of the impounded water is used by the Denver metropolitan area. It is diverted through a tunnel (23 miles long) under the Continental Divide (see Figure 13.23). *(Denver Water Department)*

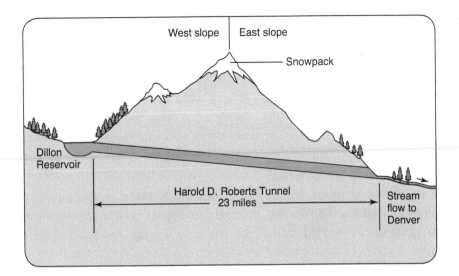

◄ FIGURE 13.23 The Roberts Tunnel is located in the Rocky Mountains of Colorado. It carries water from the west side of the Continental Divide, through a 23-mile-long tunnel, to the east side. The purpose is to provide more water to the large population in the Denver metropolitan area.

Water in a reservoir moves slower and is calmer than the river or stream entering it. In the faster-moving stream, sand and soil particles are carried in the water. In the reservoir, these particles, called silt, settle to the bottom. Each year during the spring runoff, as water from the stream slows down upon entering the reservoir, more silt is deposited. Eventually, the reservoir fills up in this process of siltation.

Think about This!

Why is siltation a problem?

13.7 Water Diversion Projects

Channeling or diverting water from a water-rich to a water-poor area also has mixed blessings. Extensive systems of channels and human made aqueducts carry water to dry, thirsty Southern California. In 1913, the Los Angeles aqueduct first brought water from the Owens River in central California to Los Angeles. Later, a canal was built to carry water from the Colorado River to the Imperial Valley east of San Diego. Both projects brought prosperity to these regions.

Think about This!

What is meant by "water diversion"?

Recently, other, very costly, water projects have been proposed to carry water from northern California to the southern part of the state. Proponents of these projects claim the water is essential for economic growth in Southern California. Opponents think the projects are too costly, encourage waste of a precious resource, and cause increased salinity of soils and other ecological disruption.

SPECIAL FOCUS

The Colorado River Basin and Water Law

The Colorado River, one of the major rivers in the United States, drains much of the American Southwest. It extends more than 1,400 mi (about 2,300 km) from its headwaters in north-central Colorado to its mouth in the Gulf of California. With hundreds of tributaries, the Colorado River basin drains a vast area— 242,000 square miles in the United States and 2,000 square miles in northern Mexico. The Colorado River basin includes some of the driest lands in the United States. So water in the Colorado River is precious. The water resources of the river have been the subject of major legal battles; many landmark cases of water law involve the use of Colorado River water.

The history of the development of the Colorado River is highlighted by brilliant engineering achievements, the production of large supplies of electrical power, agricultural successes, and legal power struggles. The original flow of this mighty river is now almost completely tamed and altered.

The first use of water in the Colorado River basin was for irrigation. The Ancestral Puebloans built ditches, diverting water to their fields. Modern irrigation practices date from the 1850s. At first, only stream bottom lands were irrigated, and the facilities were simple. By the 1890s, it was recognized that storage reservoirs were needed in order to provide a reliable source of water for crops during the latter part of the growing season. It was also necessary to store water from one year to the next to guard against particularly dry years. One of the first laws regarding Colorado River water was the Reclamation Act passed by Congress in 1902. Various diversion projects and dams were planned and built, each to address a particular local problem of water need.

When Rocky Mountain National Park was created in 1915, the Colorado River flowed southwesterly from its origin in the park across the high Colorado Plateau into southeastern Utah, and down through northwestern Arizona. It slashed through a wilderness of mountains, plateaus, and deserts. The Colorado River traveled 1,000 mi (about 1,600 km) through deep gorges, including the spectacular Grand Canyon (see Figure 13.24). The river then bent south, forming the boundaries between Nevada and Arizona, Arizona and California, and Sonora and Baja California in Mexico. Finally, the Colorado River flowed into the Gulf of California.

For purposes of water distribution and control, the Colorado River basin was divided. Lees Ferry in northern Arizona was chosen as the division point (see Figure 13.25). The Colorado and its tributaries above Lees Ferry were "upper basin"; those below, "lower basin." In 1922, use of river water was portioned out by an agreement (the Colorado River Compact) among the upper and lower basin states and the federal government. The compact allocated 7,500,000 **acre-feet** of water use to each of the two basins. Later, in a 1944 agreement, the United States guaranteed Mexico the delivery of 1,500,000 acre-feet of water per year. In years of low water, both upper and lower basins were to share equally in supplying water to Mexico. Thus, the 1922 compact was essential in appropriating water equally to both parts of the river basin. The states (see Figure 13.26) had become bitter rivals for water.

In spite of these agreements, the mighty Colorado River no longer flows to the sea. Its water is being used up. South of Yuma, Arizona, the remnant of the once mighty river now sinks out of sight into the sands. Where has the Colorado River gone? Who used it up?

It became apparent that the natural flow of the Colorado River could not supply all the uses contemplated by the seven Colorado River basin states. In addition, it was obvious that the lower basin states, particularly California and Arizona, were growing much more rapidly in population and water use than were the upper basin states. The upper basin states were concerned that the lower states would legally appropriate all of the water. People in Colorado even charged that the U.S. Congress deprived them of water that was their birthright, while giving California and Arizona all the development funds they could spend.

Solving the conflict required a federal policy directed at helping all seven states develop their compact share. The Bureau of Reclamation's

▲FIGURE 13.24 The Grand Canyon with the Colorado River below. (Ivo Lindauer)

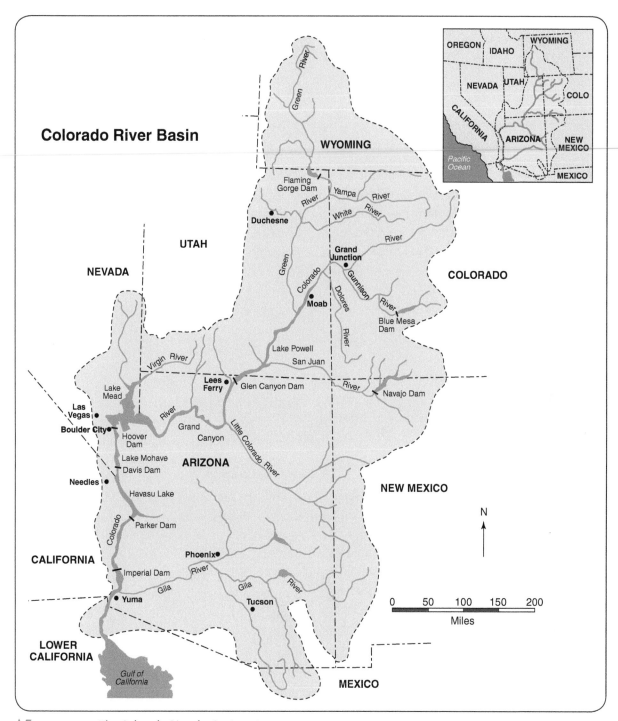

Colorado River Basin

▲ FIGURE 13.25 The Colorado River basin. *(USGS)*

inventory of possibilities for river regulation, irrigation, and power generation stimulated action. The technical and political leaders in the upper Colorado River basin accepted and aggressively promoted the comprehensive development of the upper basin. The Upper Colorado River Basin Compact, signed in 1948, led to the Colorado River Storage Project Act. This allowed authorization for the construction of four large storage reservoirs capable of holding 33,583,000 acre-feet of water for river regulation, power generation, and consumptive use. These storage reservoirs are Glen Canyon Dam and Lake Powell (see Figure 13.27) on the Colorado River in Arizona and Utah; Navajo Dam and Reservoir on the San Juan River in New Mexico and Colorado; Flaming Gorge Dam and Reservoir on the Green River in Wyoming; and Blue Mesa Dam and Reservoir on the Gunnison River in Colorado.

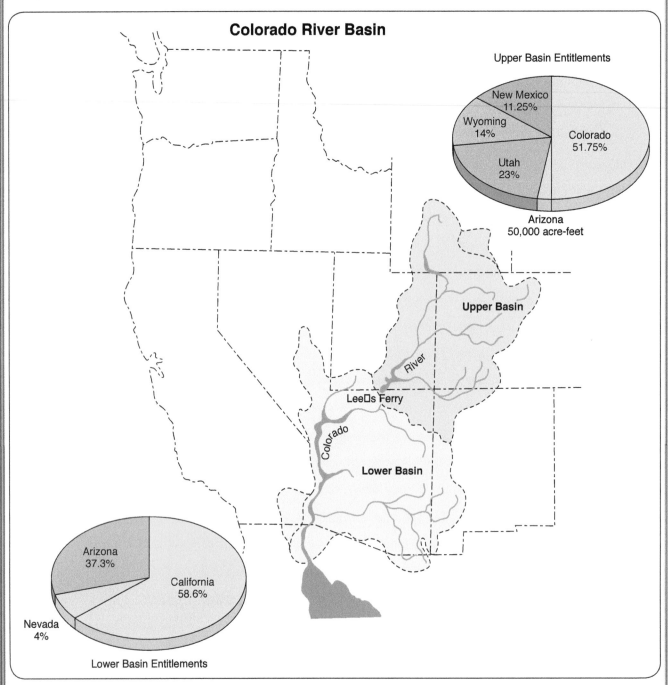

Colorado River Basin

Upper Basin Entitlements

New Mexico 11.25%

Wyoming 14%

Colorado 51.75%

Utah 23%

Arizona 50,000 acre-feet

Upper Basin

River

Lee's Ferry

Colorado

Lower Basin

Arizona 37.3%

California 58.6%

Nevada 4%

Lower Basin Entitlements

▲ FIGURE 13.26 The upper and lower Colorado River basin watershed. A **watershed** is a physiographic (geologic) division. The Colorado River Compact divided states in the Colorado River basin (watershed) into upper and lower basin states. The upper basin states are Colorado, Wyoming, New Mexico, and Utah. The lower basin states are Arizona, Nevada, and California. This division is a legal/political division. Entitlements to water were granted as shown. (*From Water Education Foundation, 717 K Street, Sacramento, California 95814.*)

The upper division states were opposed and harassed by both Arizona and California during the initial filling of the storage units of the Colorado River Storage Project, especially during the filling of Lake Powell behind Glen Canyon Dam. It was also during this period that the upper states recognized that the average stream flow of the Colorado River was only 14.8 million acre-feet annually. This was far less than the 26 million acre-feet estimate that had been used as the basis for the Colorado River Compact in 1922. Tree ring studies confirmed this finding. Thus, upper basin states were fearful that future allocation laws would require upper basin states to give up some of their water rights.

Topic: watershed
Go to: www.scilinks.org
Code: GloSci7e510

▲FIGURE 13.27 Lake Powell was created by Glen Canyon Dam. (*John S. Flannery/Visuals Unlimited*)

After several years of negotiations between upper and lower basin states, the Colorado River Basin Project Act became law in 1968. This was the last of the reclamation laws. It is now a basin-wide comprehensive law aimed at balancing resources and needs throughout the entire basin.

Through all of these projects, the Colorado River has become totally utilized. In the words of critics of these projects, "the river was plumbed to put water on arid lands and to generate electricity." The relationship among all these projects is represented in Figure 13.28.

With the Federal Water Pollution Control Act of 1972, people have become more and more

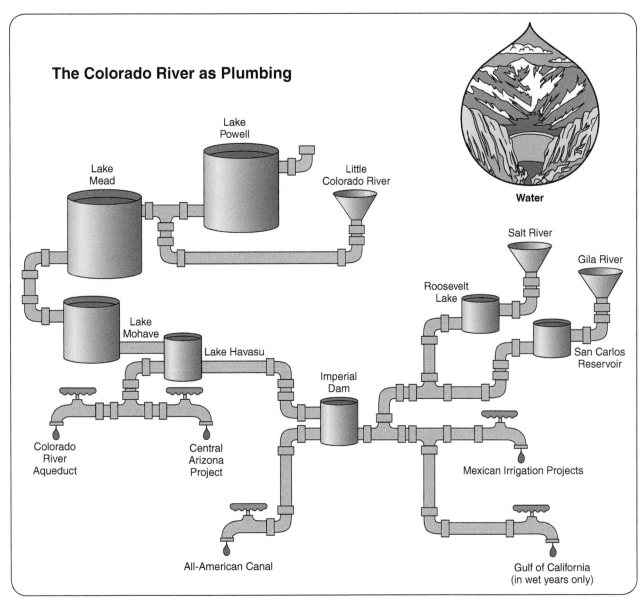

▲FIGURE 13.28 The Colorado River as plumbing. (*Reprinted with permission from* Western Water Made Simple, *Island Press, 1987,* © *High Country News.*)

Water Quantity 511

concerned with the increased salinity (salt) in the Colorado River. About half the salt may be from natural sources and half from human influence. At its headwaters, the average salinity is less than 100 milligrams per liter (mg/L). However, it progressively increases downstream. At Imperial Dam, below Lake Mead, salinity averages approximately 800 mg/L. Projections indicate that the salinity may rise to nearly 1,100 mg/L by the year 2010. Should that occur, the agricultural, municipal, and industrial use of water in Southern California would be affected severely.

Engineers are trying to reduce or eliminate the problems of scale buildup in boilers and pipes, damage to agricultural land, and the high cost of desalination. The various procedures under trial mainly involve modifying irrigation practices above Lake Powell. These include lining irrigation ditches to prevent water loss and salt buildup in soil, and using techniques to increase irrigation efficiency once water reaches the crop (see Figure 13.29). Diversion of water away from natural sources of salt is also being tested. Finally, scientists are genetically engi-

▲ FIGURE 13.29 Trickle irrigation is a strategy for delivering water to the root zone of plants.

neering crop plants so the plants can thrive in salty soils.

Recreational activities in the Colorado River basin are beginning to influence the direction of development and legal actions concerning water policy. More people are beginning to appreciate as never before that the natural landscapes of the Colorado River are unique in the country and probably in the world.

ACTIVITY 13.3

Topographic Maps

In this activity, you will make a topographic map and interpret its meaning.

Background

Like most maps, a **topographic map** shows a portion of Earth's surface by reducing it to a practical size. Various symbols represent features in the mapped area. Unlike common two-dimensional maps, topographic maps add a representation of the vertical dimension through the use of contour lines. Each contour line represents a particular elevation above sea level. To a person with a bit of training, these squiggly lines provide an accurate view of the countryside.

Materials (for each team)

- potato
- clear plastic deli tub with clear plastic lid
- dry erase marker
- permanent marker
- metric ruler
- kitchen knife

BE SAFE

Use the kitchen knife with care. Report any injuries to your teacher.

- blue water (blue food coloring)
- colored pencils
- 8½ × 11-inch white paper
- *Topographic Map Symbols* booklet (USGS)

Procedure

1. Use a dry erase marker and the metric ruler to make a scale on the side of the deli tub. Mark increments of 1 cm. Start with zero at the bottom.

2. Cut the potato in half to make one side of the potato flat.

3. Place the potato in the plastic deli tub with the freshly cut flat side facing down.

4. With the permanent marker, draw an arrow on the top of the potato indicating true north.

5. Place the sheet of white paper on the table in front of you. Position the 8½-in side to your left. Place the deli tub on the paper, slightly to the right of center.

6. Adjust the tub so true north is straight up. Then use a pencil to lightly trace the base of the tub onto the paper. Mark true north on the paper near the top.

7. Place the clear lid on the deli tub. Use the dry erase marker to label north on the lid. Looking *straight down*, use the dry erase marker to trace the bottom edge of the potato (all the way around) onto the plastic lid.

8. Remove the lid and carefully add blue water until the level reaches the 1-cm mark on the side of the tub. Be careful not to pour the water directly onto the potato. Instead, pour it toward the side of the tub.

9. Replace the lid and orient it with the north arrow on the potato. Looking *straight down*, trace on the lid the boundary of the potato with the water.

10. Repeat steps 8 and 9 until there are several contours drawn as the water level moves up 1 cm at a time and the potato is finally submerged.

11. Remove the lid and, as carefully as you can, transfer the contour lines on the lid to the marked area on the sheet of white paper. Use a brown pencil to draw your contour lines.

12. Then record the following information on your paper:

    a. Place your name in the upper-left corner of the paper. Write Potato Mountain National Monument in the upper-right side.

    b. At the lower left, indicate true north with a labeled arrow.

    c. At the lower center, write SCALE 1:24,000. This means 1 measurement on this map represents 24,000 of the same measurements in the real world.

    d. Below the scale, write LINEAR SCALE: 1 inch = 2,000 feet.

    e. Below the linear scale, write CONTOUR INTERVAL = 80 feet. This means the *vertical distance* between each contour line is 80 ft.

13. Develop Potato Mountain National Monument by putting in a road, a trail to the summit of the mountain, a trailhead, a picnic area, a water well, and a ranger station. Color in any woodland areas, a small intermittent stream, and an intermittent pond. (The contour lines should be brown.)

> **Helpful Hint!**
>
> The USGS booklet *Topographic Map Symbols* will show you the correct symbols to use on your topographic map.

QUESTIONS & TASKS

Record your responses in your science notebook.

1. How tall is Potato Mountain?

2. When are the contour lines closest together?

3. How long is the trail up Potato Mountain?

4. How does your topographic map of Potato Mountain National Monument compare to the topographic map of Capulin Mountain National Monument shown in Figure 13.30?

5. How does the photo of Capulin Mountain in Figure 13.31 compare to the topographic map shown in Figure 13.30?

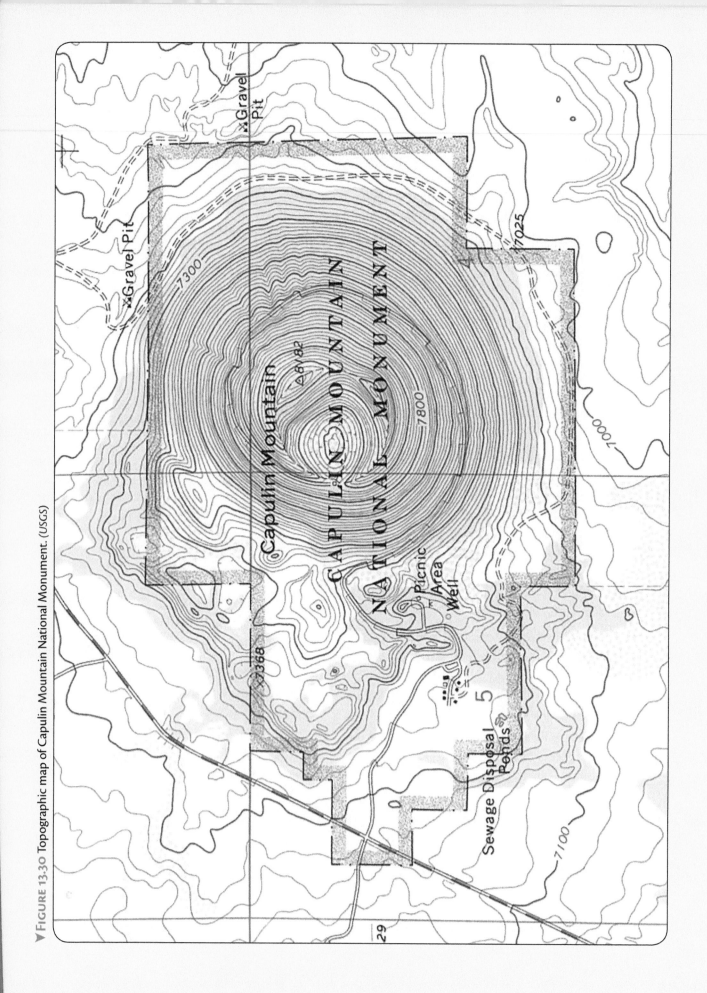

▼ Figure 13.30 Topographic map of Capulin Mountain National Monument. (*USGS*)

◄ FIGURE 13.31 Photo of Capulin Mountain located in northeast New Mexico near the town of Raton. *(Courtesy of National Park Service.)*

 ACTIVITY 13.4

Map and Analyze Your Watershed

In this activity, you will study the watershed in your area. In particular, you will concentrate on the following three purposes:

1. Determine the boundaries of the watershed in your area and develop a plan for monitoring the human impact on the watershed. You will take measurements of relevant variables.

2. Make suggestions on how to minimize the human impact and maximize the benefits of the watershed to those who live within its boundaries.

3. Develop a strategy to use the scientific information you gain to bring about the social action necessary to maximize the benefits.

Background

We all live in a watershed. As you recall, a watershed is an area of land that delivers (drains) the water, sediment, and dissolved substances via a main stream and its tributaries to a major stream or river. A **basin** is a giant watershed. For example, in Colorado, the Piney Creek watershed delivers water to the Cherry Creek watershed, which delivers water to the South Platte watershed, which delivers water to the Missouri River basin. See Figures 13.5, 13.21, and 13.25–13.26.

Materials (for each team)

- blue pens
- local topographic maps
- *Topographic Map Symbols* booklet (USGS)

Procedure

1. Study the USGS topographic maps that contain the watershed in your area, find the creek or stream that drains your watershed, and trace it back to its origin.

> **Helpful Hint!**
>
> The USGS booklet *Topographic Map Symbols* will help you interpret the map symbols.

(You may need to join maps together to do this, or you may choose to map only a portion of your local watershed.)

2. Use a blue pen to draw in your local creek or stream from its beginning to where it ends.

3. Locate all of the tributaries that feed into the creek or stream. Use a blue pen to trace each of the tributaries from its origin to the creek or stream.

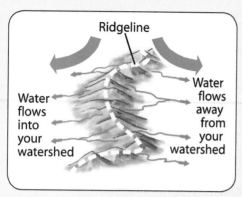

▲ FIGURE 13.32 A high ridgeline separates water flow into two different watersheds.

4. Starting near your creek's origin, locate a high point. Using contour lines as a guide, locate the high ridge where water would flow on one side into your watershed. On the other side, water would flow into another watershed. Draw a line along that ridge and extend it in both directions. Indicate occasionally (with arrows) how water would flow (see Figure 13.32).

> **Helpful Hint!**
>
> On the topo map, a closed oval represents the upper portion of a hill or mound.

5. Extend the ridgeline in both directions until it encloses the entire watershed. The area inside this boundary is your watershed.

QUESTIONS & TASKS

Record your responses in your science notebook.

1. Use the scale on the map to determine the approximate area of your watershed in square miles.

2. Use area road maps to help sketch in roads of interest not shown on your topographic map. Roughly outline the boundaries of any golf courses, parks, or other areas of interest.

3. List some of the native plants, animals, birds, and insects that live in your watershed. Are any of them threatened or endangered? In what biome is the watershed located?

4. Develop a key, and label the various types of land use within the watershed. Is any portion of your watershed a floodplain? (see glossary.) Color and label this area. Is there a plan if flooding should occur?

5. How and where do pollutants enter your watershed? List some of the pollutants that might be found in the waters of your watershed.

Select a site (near your school) for monitoring the creek. Use a GPS receiver to determine the exact longitude and latitude of your site. Record this information and write a short description of your site. Then complete items 6–8.

6. Determine which variables you will test for and how often you will test.

7. Develop a strategy to take measurements that are accurate enough to share with others who may be interested in your data.

8. Find other interested groups to share your data with. You may also want to contact interested groups and join in the dialogue and actions that can make your watershed a positive part of your community.

Topic: aquifer
Go to: www.scilinks.org
Code: GloSci7e516

13.8 Managing Groundwater

Air travelers often notice great circles of green on the brown landscapes as they fly over the Great Plains. These circular fields of corn, alfalfa, and other crops are irrigated by automatic, center-pivot irrigation systems. Each circle usually has a shallow well in its center and a rotating sprinkler system that delivers water to the field (see Figure 13.33).

◄FIGURE 13.33 Center-pivot irrigation. Each circle in the photo has a diameter of one-half mi (about 1 km) and an area of 126 acres (about 51 hectares). *(U.S. Soil Conservation Service)*

Water for this irrigation comes from the Ogallala Formation, a vast aquifer extending from Texas to the Dakotas. This use of water seems beneficial. However, when an aquifer is pumped faster than the water can be replaced, the area is left without sufficient ground-water. Overpumping of the Ogallala aquifer has lowered the water table and is increasing the cost of pumping to a prohibitive level. Some farmers in the area are returning to dry-land farming.

Another problem related to groundwater depletion is subsidence. As water is removed from water-holding rock layers, empty spaces are created. Pressure from overlying material compresses some earth materials, resulting in a lowering of the land surface (**subsidence**). Subsidence rates of 2–4 in (5–10 cm) per year have been observed in the San Joaquin Valley of California, in Texas, and in Florida. Subsidence cannot be reversed. And once an area has collapsed, the water-holding capacity of the underground aquifer is diminished. Figure 13.34 shows how much damage can be caused when subsidence occurs.

◄FIGURE 13.34 The great Winter Park Sinkhole of 1981. Some 360 ft (110 m) across and over 125 ft (38 m) deep, this sinkhole caused more than $4 million in damages. It consumed parts of two streets, a house, two Porsches, and one end of an Olympic-size swimming pool. It also disrupted utilities and tied up traffic for weeks. *(Florida Sinkhole Research Institute)*

Water Quantity 517

Apply Your Understanding

Why does saltwater intrusion ruin an underground water supply?

Along a seacoast, subsidence can lower the land below sea level. The land then either becomes flooded, or dikes must be built to keep out the seawater. If seawater does get in, the aquifer becomes salty and useless for drinking and irrigation.

Hydrologists are currently working on methods to increase groundwater through artificial recharge, that is, pumping water back into the ground. One method channels natural stream water into wells, increasing the natural infiltration of the water through the soil. Water soaks down to the aquifer and fills it. Another recharge method feeds in water from industrial cooling and wastewater. Water is pumped into recharge wells rather than being withdrawn. However, we must be careful not to pollute groundwater during recharging.

13.9 Desalination

As odd as it sounds, people die of dehydration if they drink seawater. The high concentration of salt in seawater draws water out of body cells. In trying to find ways of making seawater usable by humans, scientists have studied seagulls. Seagulls can obtain usable water from seawater because they have a membrane system that allows them to separate the salt from seawater and cough out the excess salt (see Figure 13.35).

Apply Your Understanding

Why do you think desalination is of interest?

Copying the seabirds' technique, engineers have designed a membrane for desalinating seawater. Salt water under pressure is forced through a selective membrane that permits only the passage of water molecules. The salt is left behind. This process is costly and uses a great deal of energy, but new technologies may make it more affordable in the future.

SCi LINKS®
NSTA

Topic: desalination
Go to: www.scilinks.org
Code: GloSci7e518

Another method for removing salt from seawater is evaporative desalination (see Figure 13.36). This may be used in seaside communities where solar energy can be used efficiently to evaporate the water.

13.10 Water from Icebergs

Content Clue

As seawater freezes, the salt remains in the liquid.

In October 1987, a huge iceberg broke away from Antarctica (see Figure 13.37). The iceberg, twice the size of Rhode Island and hundreds of meters thick, is made up of great quantities of freshwater.

What if this iceberg could be towed and its water used? An iceberg of that size would contain enough water to supply Los Angeles for 600 years! The idea of towing icebergs

▶FIGURE 13.35 This seagull can use seawater by excreting the extra salt. (© S. Maslowski/Visuals Unlimited)

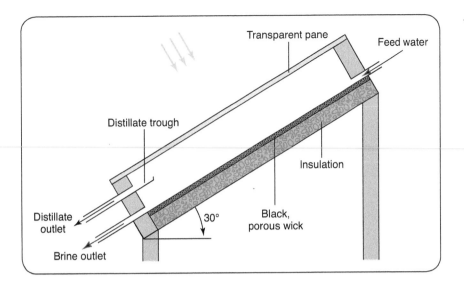

◀ FIGURE 13.36 The principle of evaporative desalination.

◀ FIGURE 13.37 This Landsat satellite image shows a large iceberg that broke away from the Ross Ice Shelf of Antarctica in October 1987. The iceberg measured over 153 km long and 36 km wide (approximately 96 × 23 mi). This is twice the size of Rhode Island. (*Reproduced with permission of Earth Observation Satellite Company, Lanham, Maryland, U.S.A.*)

sounds wild, and no one knows whether it is even feasible. Saudi Arabia's former King Khalid was so intrigued with the idea of towing icebergs to the Middle East that he funded research into the possibility. A French engineering firm concluded that it could be done. However, towing a typical iceberg would cost $80 million and take 6 to 12 months. What the ecological consequences would be, and whether enough water would be available by the time the iceberg reached its destination, are questions that still need to be answered.

Think about This!

Why is there interest in towing icebergs?

13.11 Cloud Seeding

Some scientists and engineers have tried to modify the weather by seeding clouds. Flying over certain types of clouds and sprinkling them with silver iodide crystals causes the formation of ice crystals and water droplets. These precipitate as snow or rain.

Weather can be modified in certain areas in this way, but how cloud seeding affects overall weather patterns is not clear. It may increase rainfall in one locality at the expense of another. In addition, because cloud seeding requires rain clouds, it is not effective in very dry areas that rarely have rain clouds. There is also some concern about using silver iodide

Apply Your Understanding

What are the legal implications of cloud seeding?

Water Quantity 519

to induce a cloud to give up its moisture. Silver iodide is a poison that may, in sufficient quantities, harm plants, animals, or people. Finally, legal questions remain unanswered. Do the people in one state have the right to remove water that might otherwise have fallen in another state?

ACTIVITY 13.5

How Much Water Do You Use?

In this activity, you will keep a diary of your water use. From the information you collect, you will try to figure out how much water you use each day.

Materials

- table of water-use numbers

Procedure

1. With your class, create a list of the possible ways you might use water.

2. Based on the class list, create a data table (diary) in which you record your personal water use. Your table should have a list of water-consuming activities down the left side and the hours of the day across the top. Make a table that will let you record your water use for 24 hours.

3. Collect data about your water use. Record how many times you conduct each water-using activity such as washing clothes, flushing the toilet, or drinking a glass of water. Make sure it is a day you consider "typical." If your days vary a lot, you could record your water use for several days, and then calculate an average for each water-consuming activity.

4. Use the water-use table to convert your activities to gallons of water used (Figure 13.38). For example, if you flushed the toilet 5 times in 24 hours, you would multiply 5×1.6 gal/flush for new toilets (purchased after 1992) or 5×3.5 gal/flush for old toilets (purchased before 1992).

5. After converting each activity to a number of gallons of water, add all the numbers to get your total amount of water used in 1 day.

6. Create a class data table according to your teacher's instructions.

▲ FIGURE 13.38 Your teacher may be able to help you find data that are hard to obtain. (Photo © Paul Hartmann.)

QUESTIONS & TASKS

Record your responses in your science notebook.

1. How much variance is there in the amount of water people use in one day?

2. Why do you think the amount varies?

3. Do you think the numbers each person calculated for the total represent an accurate number for the total amount of water used? Why or why not?

4. Do you think you could lower the amount of water you use? How? Why? Make a list of ten to twelve ways water use can be reduced at home.

13.12 Water Conservation

A variety of factors place limits on our ability to expand water supplies to a region. Some factors are higher energy prices, water laws, increased competition for water, and higher water prices. So, if the supply cannot be increased, the resource must be used wisely. Wise water use includes both using new technologies that require less water and having a water conservation ethic. A water conservation ethic is a way of thinking about water use so that every action that uses water is thought about in terms of conserving this valuable resource. Here are some ideas for developing a water conservation ethic.

A variety of technical solutions are available for the home. These include ultra-low-flush toilets, low-flow faucets and showerheads, space-filling bottles added to toilet tanks, and short cycles on dishwashers and washing machines. The volume of water used for watering lawns during summer months can be huge. Carefully planned landscaping, featuring less grass and more native plants that require little water, result in large savings (see Figure 13.39). Automatic car washes can wash a car with a small amount of water or with recycled water. Plumbing supply stores, lawn and garden shops, and your local water supplier can provide other ideas for reducing water use.

Figure 13.20 shows that on a national basis, the greatest water savings can be made in electric power generation and in agriculture. Dry cooling towers can cut the use of water at electric power plants by one-fourth. These towers circulate water in pipes instead of evaporating it in open air. Unfortunately, dry cooling towers require more energy to operate and cost more to build than conventional towers.

◀ FIGURE 13.39 Low-water landscaping strategies make use of native grasses, trees, and plants.

In agriculture, irrigation ditches should all be lined with cement or plastic, or replaced with closed pipes. Unlined ditches can lose 40–50 percent of the water flowing through them before the water reaches the crops. Crop sprinklers, which often waste up to half the water used, can be replaced by **drip irrigation** systems. These deliver water directly to the root area and, thus, lose only 5–10 percent of the water to the atmosphere.

ACTIVITY 13.6

Can You Improve Your Water Use?

Most people in the United States can find a way to use less water. Sometimes, this requires doing things that are not as easy, fast, or comfortable as we are used to doing. Each person has to decide what his or her water conservation ethic will be. In this activity, you will make some decisions about your own water use and check the results of your decisions.

Materials

• data table on water use (from Activity 13.5)

Procedure

1. Think about the ideas for conserving water that you read about in section 13.12 Water Conservation.

2. Discuss ways that individuals can conserve water.

3. Choose 1 or 2 ideas to try out.

4. Record your own water-use data as you did in Activity 13.5.

5. Calculate your total water use in gallons.

6. Make a class data table.

QUESTIONS & TASKS

Record your responses in your science notebook.

1. How did your water use change?

2. How difficult was the change?

3. Do you think you could keep up the change?

4. How much did the total class use of water change?

5. What do you think is the significance of each person's actions with regard to water use?

What can you do to reduce water problems?

 Solving Water Problems

Up until now, water management in the United States has mainly focused on arranging the nation's abundant supplies of freshwater to meet the needs of users. This "supply management" approach has resulted in the building of large reservoirs and delivery systems, especially in the West. Several concerns, however, are forcing water managers and planners to rethink their strategies. Development costs are increasing, and there is a shortage of funds. Water supplies are shrinking, while the amount of polluted water is increasing. Also, government restraint and a growing concern for the environment are contributing to the rethinking of strategies. We are moving into a time for water-demand management and conservation (see Figure 13.40). Figure 13.41 summarizes some of these strategies.

◄FIGURE 13.40 The goal is to provide adequate quantities of high-quality water. *(Copyright: Press Publishing, Ltd., Provo, Utah. Used by permission.)*

- **Technical solutions.** A variety of technical devices are available to conserve water and to avoid polluting it. These include ultra-low-flush toilets, low-flow sink faucets, and low-flow showerheads. Other solutions include low-water landscaping, lined irrigation ditches, and trickle irrigation systems. Automatic car washes also help to conserve water, as do dry cooling towers. Nontoxic chemicals can substitute for toxic chemicals.

- **Water conservation ethic.** Clean water is such a valuable resource that wasting it is extremely harmful. The value of using resources wisely must be taught and practiced at home, at school, and in the workplace. We can save a lot of water if citizens are responsible.

- **Economic solutions.** The price of a resource should fully reflect its true value. If water costs more, waste will shrink.

- **Water policy and water law.** The laws and policies of our nation determine who gets to use water and how it is used. Wise laws and policies can help resolve conflicts and promote the best use of resources.

◄FIGURE 13.41 Water quantity and quality problems can be solved using a variety of strategies.

Summary

Water is the most abundant compound in all living organisms. The resources of water on this planet are vast; yet, the amount of freshwater available for human use is limited. Therefore, it is important to use this valuable resource wisely and conservatively. We must be careful not to waste or pollute our water resources. Economic growth and the quality of our life depend on having enough water for our needs.

The global water supply—mainly the ocean—is an important part of the global climate system. Currents in the ocean help distribute the sun's energy and moderate climates worldwide. Disruptions to this system such as El Niño produce abnormalities to local climates that can cause hardship. Powerful hurricanes spawned over the ocean can devastate the lives of thousands. Tsunamis can devastate hundreds of thousands. Understanding these events and having action plans in place can save lives and greatly reduce damage.

Some of our supply of usable freshwater has been set aside behind dams in reservoirs. While this has made it possible for people to live and farm in arid areas, it has not increased the total water supply. As the population grows, the demand for available water also grows.

Scientists and engineers have developed the technology to use less water in many home and industrial applications. We should all develop a personal water-use ethic.

 REFERENCES

Academy of Natural Sciences. *Ground Water Contamination: Sources, Effect, and Options to Deal with the Problem* (Philadelphia: Academy of Natural Sciences), 1987.

Clarke, Robin. *Water: The International Crisis* (Cambridge, MA: The MIT Press), 1993.

Gottlieb, Robert. *A Life of Its Own: The Politics and Power of Water* (San Diego: Harcourt Brace Jovanovich), 1988.

Newcom, S. Joshua. *Layperson's Guide to the Colorado River* (Sacramento, CA: Water Education. Foundation), 2001.

Postel, Sandra. *Pillar of Sand: Can the Irrigation Miracle Last?* (Washington D.C.: Worldwatch Institute), 1999.

Rocky Mountain Institute. *Catalog of Water-Efficient Technologies for the Urban/Residential Sector* (Old Snowmass, CO: Rocky Mountain Institute), 1990.

U.S. Geological Survey. *Estimated Use of Water in the United States in 1990,* USGS Circular 1081 (Washington, D.C.: USGPO), 1993.

 WEBSITES

Water Quantity

USGS-Water Resources of the United States:

http://water.usgs.gov/

National Water and Climate Center:

http://www.wcc.nrcs.usda.gov/

World Water Council:

http://worldwatercouncil.org/

Ocean System

National Oceanic and Atmospheric Administration

http://www.noaa.gov

National Hurricane Center

www.nhc.noaa.gov

International Tsunami Information Center

http://www.tsunamiwave.info/

El Niño Information

http://elnino.wr.usgs.gov/

Remy Williams Mill Creek Restoration Project, Ohio
© La Motte (www.lamotte.com)

CHAPTER 14

Water Quality

GOAL

- To understand the role of quality water in modern societies.

The care of rivers is not a question of rivers but of the human heart.

—Tanaka Shozo, Japan's conservationist pioneer

Access to Clean Water

Nonpolluted water is essential for quality human life. It is a vital component of all life-support systems. Sadly, the United Nations Development Report* on the global water crisis documents that one-sixth of the world's population (1.1 billion people) lacks access to clean water to drink and wash. Forty percent of the human population (2.6 billion people) do not have access to adequate sanitation. This means that people are forced to defecate in ditches, plastic bags, or on roadsides. In rural sub-Saharan Africa, millions of people share their domestic water sources with animals, or they rely on unprotected wells that are breeding grounds for pathogens. They are aware of the dangers, but they have no other choice.

Apart from the health risks, inadequate access to water means that women and young girls spend hours each day collecting and carrying household water supplies (see Figure 14.1). One-sixth of humanity lives in regions that suffer from water scarcity. And this figure is increasing rapidly.

Think about This!

In most of Africa and Asia, women are responsible for collecting water for their families.

In the previous chapter, you examined issues of water supply. In this chapter, we will examine water pollutants and their impacts on aquatic environments, human health, and groundwater. We will explore water delivery systems. You will test the quality of local bodies of water and examine wastewater treatment strategies.

*United Nations Development Program. *Human Development Report—Beyond Scarcity: Power, Poverty and the Global Water Crisis* (New York: UNDP), 2006.

▼ FIGURE 14.1 Three girls carry water by the Sudanese refugee camp near the town of Guereda in eastern Chad. Temperatures in the region often exceed 109°F (43°C). (© UNICEF/HQ04-0408/Christine Nesbitt)

Pollution of Water

The causes of water **pollution** fall into two broad categories. The first category is untreated or inadequately treated wastes from easily identified points, such as sewage treatment plants. The second category is waste from nonpoint or diffuse sources, such as silt or fertilizers washed into a stream from many farms during heavy rainstorms.

14.1 Point and Nonpoint Sources

Point sources include pipes from cities and industries that dump untreated wastes into waterways and oceans; sewage treatment plants that remove some, but not all, pollutants; feedlots in which animals are confined in a small space; and oil spills. The materials that flow out of a pipe or tank are called the **effluent**.

Nonpoint sources spread pollution over a wide area. These sources include runoff that carries sediments from erosion that results from activities such as logging, fire, construction, or farming; runoff of chemical fertilizers or pesticides from agricultural land and lawns; drainage of acids, minerals, sediments, and metals from abandoned mines; acid precipitation; and untraceable oil spills or dumping of hazardous wastes. Nonpoint pollution is more difficult to control than pollution from point sources.

Distinguish between point and nonpoint sources of water pollution.

14.2 Major Water Pollutants

A water **pollutant** is any substance picked up by water that makes the water impure. Chemically pure water is not found in nature because water dissolves so many substances. Some substances, not actually dissolved by water, are suspended in or dispersed by water.

Drinking water is not pure water. To make water suitable for drinking, many suspended solids are removed and harmful bacteria destroyed. However, many substances still remain in solution. The taste of drinking water varies because different dissolved minerals give water distinctly different tastes. Thus, the term "pure," when used in the sense of water pollution, means water in which no substance is present in sufficient concentration to prevent the water from being used for normal purposes.

Different standards are set for water depending on its use. Water clean enough for agricultural use or clean enough to support a healthy aquatic ecosystem may not be clean enough to drink. More than 2,000 substances can be found in drinking water. For each substance, there is an acceptable level above which harmful effects can result. The processes used for removing these substances are diagramed in Figure 14.2.

Water quality standards change from time to time as new information becomes available. We may need to change the acceptable levels of a particular substance as we learn more about the effects of a particular pollutant. Until the 1960s, for example, the acceptable level of selenium in drinking water was 0.05 milligrams per liter (mg/L). The level was then dropped to 0.01 mg/L. It has now returned to 0.05 mg/L. Selenium is found as a trace element in soils and is a metabolic requirement in trace amounts. However, selenium is toxic when ingested at high levels. Levels of 2.0 mg/L (40 times today's acceptable levels) kill goldfish. Selenium itself does not dissolve in water, but compounds containing selenium are soluble.

Apply Your Understanding

Why do water quality standards change from time to time? How does this reflect the nature of science?

Water pollutants can be divided into eight categories. Each of these categories is discussed in the paragraphs that follow this list.

- **disease-causing agents:** bacteria, parasites, and viruses
- **inorganic chemicals:** salts, acids, and toxic metals

Briefly describe eight categories of water pollutants.

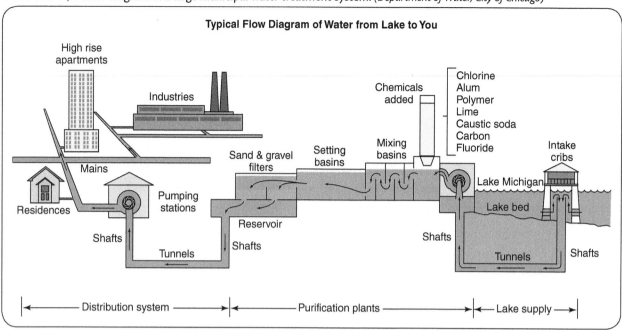

Typical Flow Diagram of Water from Lake to You

- **synthetic organic compounds:** detergents, oil, industrial wastes, pesticides, and solvents
- **fertilizers:** plant nutrients from agricultural runoff (mostly nitrates and phosphates)
- **sediments:** soil, silt, and clay from land erosion
- **oxygen-using wastes:** sewage, animal manure, and some industrial wastes
- **radioactive materials**
- **thermal pollution:** heat from industrial and electric power plants

Disease-Causing Agents

Parasites and microbes are particularly common in water in countries where drinking water standards are not as strict as those in the United States and the developed world. Bacteria, viruses, protozoa, and roundworms are found in water contaminated by human and/or animal feces. The obvious solutions are to prevent untreated sewage from entering drinking water supplies and to treat all drinking water to kill harmful organisms.

In a complete water treatment plant, water is disinfected with chlorine. Chlorine kills bacteria and microorganisms. Various chemicals are then added to coagulate (clot) minerals, to remove suspended particles, and to neutralize unpleasant tastes and smells. Then more chemicals are added to remove the corrective ones. The water is filtered through sand or charcoal, and chlorinated again to prevent contamination as the water is distributed through the community's system (see Figure 14.2).

Although chlorine kills bacteria, it is not capable of destroying all of the hundreds of viruses that can be waterborne. Other processes remove some, but not all, viruses. So far, the only known way to eliminate all viruses is to boil the water.

Inorganic Chemicals

Many chemicals that dissolve in water are very toxic. Heavy metals such as lead, mercury, copper, arsenic, and chromium inhibit or destroy enzymes essential to life. Metals affect decomposers as well as higher forms of life. Adding them to an aquatic system can be quite destructive. These pollutants may be absorbed by the bottom mud and released whenever bottom deposits are disturbed.

Because mercury is used for many purposes, contamination of water by mercury is common. Mercury compounds are found in dental fillings, furniture polishes, floor waxes, antibacterial and antimildew powders, medicines, fungicides for seeds, fluorescent lights, air conditioners, and paints. They are used in making plastics, paper, clothing, and film. Mercury dumped into rivers as an industrial waste was once thought to be safe because liquid mercury is relatively inert. It was believed that the mercury would settle into the river sediment. However, two Swedish scientists discovered that anaerobic bacteria (bacteria that do not require oxygen for their life cycles) found in murky stream sediments could change relatively inert mercury into highly toxic methyl mercury. This transformation occurs more readily in slightly acidic waters.

Methyl mercury poisoning has been reported in Japan, Mexico, Sweden, Iraq, and the United States. In Japan, 52 people died and 150 suffered serious brain and nerve damage from methyl mercury discharged into Minamata Bay by a chemical plant. The methyl mercury in the water was absorbed by fish, and then people became contaminated by eating the fish.

Think about This!

Why are we concerned about inorganic chemicals that dissolve in water?

Synthetic Organic Compounds

Compounds such as detergents, oil, industrial wastes, pesticides, and solvents can cause a multitude of problems. Oil and grease get into water from industries, automobiles, offshore oil drilling operations, pipeline leaks, and tanker spills. Damage to aquatic ecosystems can be drastic, but not always long lasting (see Figure 14.3).

A second source of considerable concern is sudsy, synthetic detergents. Many detergents contain plant nutrients that enhance the growth of algae and aquatic weeds. When these small plants die, they use up oxygen as they decompose. This causes fish to die, which causes foul odors.

Another source of concern is the pesticides used to kill mosquitoes or flies. These also kill many other organisms. Pesticides can build up in aquatic food chains, contaminating foods used by humans. You may recall that this is called biomagnification.

▼FIGURE 14.3 (a) Prince William Sound after the Exxon tanker *Valdez* ran aground in 1989 creating a 1,000-square-mile oil slick. (b) Prince William Sound 3 years later after cleanup. (*Exxon Mobil Corporation*)

a.   b.

Water Quality 531

► FIGURE 14.4

Biomagnification of toxic DDT/DDE as it moves up a food chain in samples from an estuary on Long Island, New York.

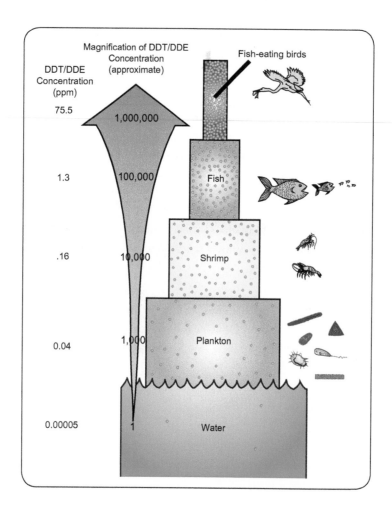

A historical example that traces the accumulation of DDT and related chemicals is shown in Figure 14.4.

Fertilizers

Plant nutrients from agricultural runoff can also cause algal blooms (population explosions). This depletes fish populations as the water becomes clogged with vegetation. The balance of the ecosystem is upset, water becomes stagnant and foul, and dissolved oxygen declines.

Excessive use of nitrogen-rich fertilizers results in nitrate residues that dissolve and seep into groundwater (see Figure 14.5). Water that contains nitrates can be especially dangerous to the health of infants. Soil organisms convert the nitrates to nitrites. The nitrites enter infants' red blood cells and interfere with the cells' ability to carry oxygen. Careful use of fertilizers can prevent such effects.

Sediments

Soil, silt, and clay eroded from land are deposited in bodies of water. As reservoirs become filled, aquatic life is affected, fish populations decline, and dissolved oxygen is reduced.

Oxygen-Demanding Wastes

Sewage, manure, and industrial wastes enter water ecosystems as natural runoff from land. Untreated human or animal wastes may be dumped into rivers. Some of these wastes also come from decaying vegetation and from industries such as food processing plants, paper mills, and oil refineries. Decomposition of these products by aerobic bacteria depletes the

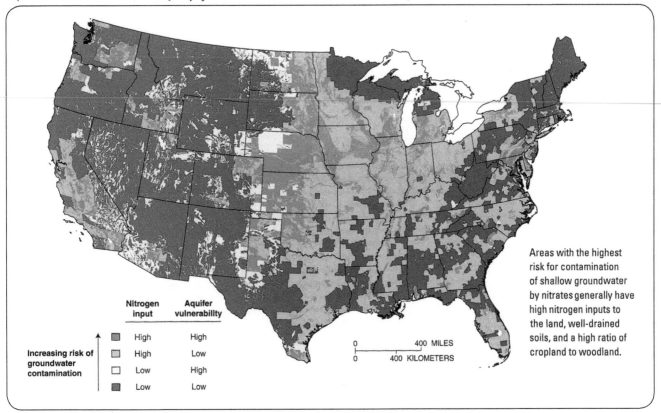

amount of dissolved oxygen, causing fish populations to decline. The aquatic ecosystem changes considerably and the water may give off foul odors.

Radioactive Wastes

Erosion of naturally occurring radioactive rock, mining and processing of radioactive materials, nuclear power plants, and nuclear weapons testing may result in pollution by radioactive wastes. When radioactive wastes become part of drinking water, they are extremely toxic. Radiation damages the cells within a person's body, which can adversely affect the individual. This damage can also lead to genetic defects passed on to offspring. This includes radioactive burns, miscarriages, cataracts, leukemia, and various cancers.

Thermal Pollution

When the steam used to drive turbines is condensed, the excess heat may be released into waterways. Increasing the temperature of a body of water affects the entire ecosystem. The composition of the ecosystem changes as a result. For example, cold-water fish cannot survive and are thus replaced by warm-water species. The amount of dissolved oxygen in water also decreases. Since increased temperatures affect plants as well as animals, species of both plants and animals in the thermally altered ecosystem change. Lakes that normally freeze in winter may not freeze because of the heat discharged into them. Figure 14.6 shows Canada geese overwintering far north of their normal winter range at a pond thermally heated by a power plant.

▶ FIGURE 14.6 Canada geese overwintering on a cooling pond next to an electric power plant in Baldwin, Illinois. *(Photo courtesy of Illinois Power Company.)*

ACTIVITY 14.1

How Clean Is Your Water?

Anyone can be a scientist and test the quality of a local stream, pond, or other water source. In this activity, you will collect a water sample and test it for five key indicators of water quality: dissolved oxygen, pH, nitrates, phosphates, and coliform bacteria.

Materials

- 2 water samples
- water test kit (DO, pH, N, P, and coliform bacteria)
- thermometer

BE SAFE

Obtaining water from lakes, swamps, streams, and rivers can be dangerous. Make sure an adult knows what you are doing and where you are going before you collect your sample. Never work alone.

Procedure

1. Read the background information to help you understand what you are testing for and how to analyze your results. This information follows the Questions & Tasks.

2. Collect a water sample in your community. Remember, be safe!

3. Create a data table like the one in Figure 14.7 in your science notebook.

4. Complete each test as directed by your teacher.

5. Record the results of your tests in your data table.

▶ FIGURE 14.7 Sample table for recording test results from a team working with four water samples.

	Sample 1	Sample 2	Sample 3	Sample 4
Temperature				
DO				
pH				
Nitrates				
Phosphates				
Coliform bacteria				

QUESTIONS & TASKS

Record your responses in your science notebook.

1. Describe what each of your test results means.

Helpful Hint!

Use the background information to help you with your interpretation.

2. Describe the overall quality of your water sample.

3. Would you drink your water sample? Why or why not?

4. Would you swim in the place where you collected your water sample? Why or why not?

5. How is the body of water you tested used right now? Do you think the current use is the best use of the water? Why or why not?

6. How much do you trust the results of your work? Explain your response.

7. What sources of error do you think exist in your testing?

Background

Unless it has been distilled to remove the minerals and pollutants, all water contains impurities. How clean water needs to be is determined by its use. The water you drink needs to be cleaner than the water used for irrigation. Different kinds of industries require different levels of purity in their water based on how the water is being used.

Water can be tested for many characteristics. In this lab, you will complete five tests. The following sections include information about each characteristic you are testing.

Dissolved Oxygen

Dissolved oxygen (DO) is the amount of oxygen dissolved in the water. This characteristic is a rough indicator of the quality of your water supply. Generally, the more oxygen in the water, the better the quality of the water. The amount of oxygen that can dissolve in water is limited by the temperature of the water, as illustrated in Figure 14.8. At a temperature of 68°F (20°C) and normal atmospheric pressure, the maximum DO is 9 parts of oxygen per million parts of water (9 ppm). Figure 14.9 shows the temperature and DO requirements for some freshwater fish and the organisms they eat.

pH

The term *pH* stands for "parts of hydrogen." The hydrogen ion concentration in a water sample indicates how acidic or basic the water is. A pH of 7 is considered neutral. An acidic sample has a pH below 7; a basic sample has a pH above 7. Figure 14.10 shows the pH tolerance of different aquatic organisms.

Topic: pH
Go to: www.scilinks.org
Code: GloSci7e535

Nitrates

Nitrates also come from chemical fertilizers. In small amounts, nitrogen compounds are essential for healthy plant growth. In large amounts, nitrates are harmful to aquatic ecosystems and, therefore, the quality of our drinking water. The Environmental

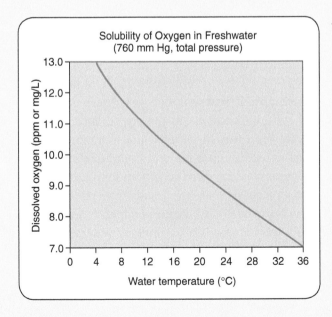

◄ FIGURE 14.8 This graph shows the relationship between water temperature and dissolved oxygen. What happens to the DO level as the temperature of the water increases? (Note that ppm and mg/L are equivalent.)

▼FIGURE 14.9 What does this table tell you about the relationships among temperature, DO, and the aquatic life?

Freshwater Organisms	Temperature Requirements	DO Requirements
Lots of plant life Bass, crappie, bluegill, catfish Caddisfly	Greater than 68°F (20°C)	5 ppm
Some plant life Salmon, trout Stonefly, mayfly, caddisfly Water beetles	55°F–68°F (12.8°C–20°C)	6 ppm or greater
Little plant life Trout Caddisfly, stonefly, mayfly	Less than 55°F (12.8°C)	8 ppm or greater

►FIGURE 14.10

Most organisms can survive in a range of pH. Some organisms are more tolerant than others. Based on this chart, which organisms could survive in your water sample? (Source: Forest Sevice, USDSA.)

pH Ranges That Support Aquatic Life

Most acidic   Neutral   Most alkaline

1   2   3   4   5   6   7   8   9   10   11   12   13   14

Bacteria   1.0 ———————————————————————— 13.0

Plants (algae, rooted, etc.)   6.5 ————————————— 12.0

Carp, suckers, catfish, some insects   6.0 ————— 9.0

Bass, crappie   6.5 ——— 8.5

Snails, clams, mussels   7.0 ——— 9.0

Largest variety of animals (trout, mayfly, stonefly, caddisfly)   6.5   7.5

Protection Agency (EPA) sets the standard for drinking water at 10 ppm or less of nitrates.

Phosphates

Phosphates are an important part of chemical fertilizers. As a result, high levels of phosphates are most often associated with residential and agricultural runoff. Phosphates are also part of some laundry detergents. Some municipal sewer plants release phosphates in their effluent because it is very expensive to remove them, and the community chooses not to include this treatment. Water that is not polluted usually has 0.1 ppm phosphates or less.

Coliform Bacteria

Coliform bacteria live in the intestines of many mammals. They are excreted with feces. In general, these types of bacteria do not cause disease in humans. If coliform bacteria are present in large amounts, however, it may be an indication that other bacteria and viruses are also present. Both harmful and safe bacteria need the same conditions to live. If coliform bacteria are present, it is usually from pasture runoff and occasionally from untreated human sewage. The EPA sets the standard for drinking water at no more than one coliform bacteria colony per 100 milliliters (mL) of water. Swimming water should contain no more than 200 colonies per 100 mL.

14.3 Pollution of Aquatic Ecosystems

Flowing aquatic ecosystems such as streams and rivers have different water pollution problems than standing ecosystems such as lakes and ponds. However, there are three indicators of water quality that are important in both lakes and rivers: the concentrations of dissolved oxygen (DO); the biological oxygen demand (BOD); and the coliform bacteria count.

Dissolved Oxygen (DO)

The dissolved oxygen, or DO, content is the amount of oxygen gas dissolved in water. At a temperature of 68°F (20°C) and normal atmospheric pressure, the maximum DO level is 9 ppm. DO level is an important indication of the ecological health of a waterway. If the DO level drops below 4 ppm, fish populations decline.

Describe three indicators of water quality.

Biological Oxygen Demand (BOD)

In breaking down organic wastes dumped into aquatic ecosystems, decomposing bacteria use dissolved oxygen. The amount of this depletion is called the **biological oxygen demand (BOD)**. Bacterial decomposition may reduce the DO content so much that some aquatic organisms die. Water is considered seriously polluted when the BOD of the decomposers causes the DO to fall below 5 ppm. Compare the typical BOD values shown in Figure 14.11.

Coliform Bacteria

Another measure of water quality is based on the number of coliform bacteria in the water. Coliform bacteria are intestinal microorganisms that are found in soils and in the feces of humans and other animals. Although most of these bacteria are harmless, their presence indicates that harmful microorganisms, which can cause such diseases as viral hepatitis, cholera, dysentery, or encephalitis, may be there also. Bacteria can be grown in the laboratory, producing visible colonies that can be counted.

At a site where untreated sewage is added to a stream, bacteria start feasting on the sewage. The BOD increases enormously. In areas immediately downstream, the DO levels drop drastically and fish die. Fish do not die from the sewage directly, but from a lack of oxygen.

Flowing rivers have a remarkable ability to dilute many wastes and renew their DO content if not overloaded with pollutants. Farther downstream, the amount of sewage

Type of Water	BOD (mg/L)
Pure water	0
Typical fresh, natural water	2 to 5
Domestic sewage	Hundreds
Sewage after treatment	10 to 20

◀ FIGURE 14.11 Sample values of biological oxygen demand.

► **FIGURE 14.12** Typical changes in water chemistry and biology in a river below a source of organic pollution. (*Adapted from* The Biology of Polluted Waters, *H. B. N. Hynes, Liverpool University Press, 1978.*)

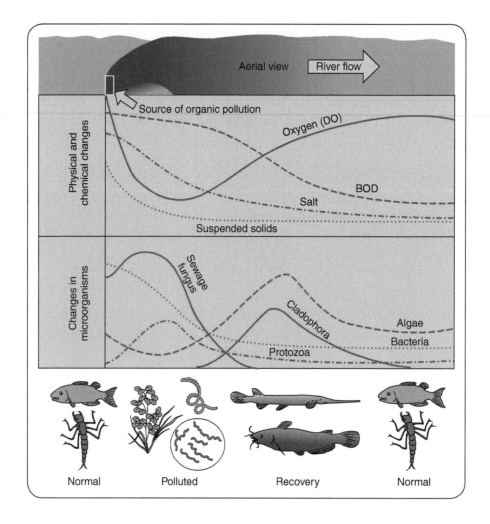

decreases because bacteria have decomposed most of the organic material. BOD levels decrease and DO increases. Some oxygen comes from air mixing with water in the stream, and some is replenished by the photosynthesis of aquatic plants. The stream begins to purify itself again (see Figure 14.12). Because of their ability to purify themselves, most rivers can recover fairly rapidly from a discharge of biodegradable pollutants.

If additional untreated sewage is added before recovery is complete, the river becomes polluted again. Such polluted rivers (which, unfortunately, are found in many densely populated areas all over the world) have no fish, have a high bacterial count, appear muddy to blue green in color, and smell from the odors of decay.

Additional problems occur when nonbiodegradable wastes and toxic substances are dumped into streams and rivers. Bacteria have no effect on those pollutants. Through the tightening and enforcing of treatment standards, many rivers in the eastern United States are cleaner now than they were in the 1960s. Rivers such as the Hudson and the Potomac, once "flowing sewers," have regained fish and other wildlife.

In lakes and ponds, water flows more slowly. They have less ability to purify themselves than streams and rivers. Thus, pollution problems become magnified when water movement is slow.

Apply Your Understanding

Describe the changes in a flowing river as it moves downstream from a source of organic pollution.

The Effects of Pollutants on Pond Water

As we continue to develop land in the United States and in other countries, we increase the quantity of nutrients in natural waterways. Runoff from farms and feedlots, increased population densities, and sprawling suburban areas contribute to the reduced quality of water. In this activity, you will determine the effects and changes that occur when nutrients are added to pond water.

Background

Fertilizers and animal waste products contain nitrogen in the form of nitrates. They also contain phosphorous in the form of phosphate. These chemicals are nutrients for plants. If large amounts of these chemicals get into aquatic ecosystems, algae (microscopic plants) begin to grow rapidly. This rapid growth is often referred to as an algal bloom. When the algae die and begin to decompose, dissolved oxygen in the water is depleted. Some organisms cannot survive in the lower amount of oxygen. Thus, the ecosystem changes.

Nitrogen and phosphorus are naturally occurring elements on Earth. Nitrogen is the major gas in the atmosphere. Both of these elements exist in the bodies of all living things. In small amounts, they are helpful compounds. In large amounts, these compounds are not helpful in aquatic ecosystems. Human activity contributes to increased amounts of both nitrogen and phosphorus compounds being released into natural waterways.

Some sources of nitrogen compounds include the following:

- the ammonia in sewage effluent
- runoff from farmland treated with nitrate fertilizers
- seepage from cattle feedlots
- industrial effluent

Some sources of phosphorus compounds include the following:

- detergents
- runoff from land treated with phosphorus fertilizers
- sewage effluent
- industrial effluent

Materials

- phosphate solution
- nitrate solution
- testing container
- pond water
- water test kit
- graduated cylinder
- safety goggles

Procedure

1. After reading the background information about nitrates and phosphates, discuss their effects on pond water.

2. Develop a hypothesis about the effects of nitrates and phosphates on pond water.

BE SAFE

Obtaining water from lakes, swamps, streams, and rivers can be dangerous. Make sure an adult knows what you are doing and where you are going before you collect your sample. Take a partner with you.

3. Based on your understanding of the effects of nitrates and phosphates, design a simple experiment to test your hypothesis. Ask your teacher to review your experimental design.

BE SAFE

Wear safety goggles when using chemicals. Use chemicals as directed.

4. Collect pond water in your community as directed by your teacher.

5. Conduct your experiment. Record your test results in a data chart in your science notebook.

6. Make a class data table.

Record your responses in your science notebook.

1. How did your pond water change during your experiment?

2. What is your explanation for the changes?

3. How did your pond water sample compare to those of the other teams in your class?

4. Why were the samples the same or different?

5. Based on your experiment, what are your recommendations for controlling the input of phosphate- and nitrate-containing effluents into natural waterways?

14.4 Eutrophication of Lakes

Topic: eutrophication
Go to: www.scilinks.org
Code: GloSci7e540

What is eutrophication?
How can it be slowed?
How can it be speeded up?

All freshwater lakes have various stages of development. When an area drained by a lake (called a drainage basin) has few nutrients, the lake is nutrient poor, or **oligotrophic**. These lakes support little plant life; they are crystal clear with low algae populations. They also have high DO levels and support populations of fish such as lake trout and small mouth bass (see Figure 14.13a).

On the other hand, when a lake is located in an area in which nutrients are released into the lake, the lake is nutrient rich, or **eutrophic.** These lakes support a great deal of plant life, which often chokes out other organisms. Such lakes have large algae populations, low DO content, and fish species such as carp and bullhead (see Figure, 14.13b).

Nutrients tend to stay in a lake and accumulate. Over time, most lakes tend to become more eutrophic. Sediments are added by streams that feed the lake. Lake sediments become thicker, and more recycling of nutrients takes place. Over hundreds to thousands of years, even an oligotrophic lake eventually becomes eutrophic. This natural successional process is called **eutrophication** (see Figure 14.14). Pollution accelerates this natural process by increasing the nutrients in lakes. The nutrients come from the leaching of soil fertilizers or the dumping of nitrates and phosphates from treated sewage into waterways. Because this

▼FIGURE 14.13 (a) A typical oligotrophic lake. This kind of lake is characterized by clear blue water and a lack of algae. In Oregon's Crater Lake, a small, white disc can often be seen as deep as 100 feet (30 meters), compared to only about 5 feet (1.5 meters) in eutrophic lakes. (b) A typical eutrophic lake. A major characteristic of these lakes is the abundance of blue-green algae, also called cyanobacteria, which give the lake a yellow green color. Algae are a nuisance, particularly when they die and decay. In this photo, a thick scum of dead algae is shown as a light-colored band just offshore. (*Both photos by Alex J. Horne.*)

a.

b.

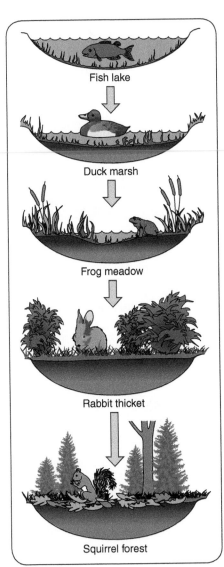

Fish lake

Duck marsh

Frog meadow

Rabbit thicket

Squirrel forest

acceleration of eutrophication is caused by human activities, it is called **cultural eutrophication**. In a few decades, people can produce the same effect that would normally take nature thousands of years.

When a lake becomes overloaded with nutrients, plant growth accelerates. Algal blooms cover the lake's surface. These large plant populations produce oxygen in the upper layers of the water. But when the plants die, they fall to the bottom and are decomposed by bacteria that use a great deal of the dissolved oxygen in the lower layers. As the DO levels of the bottom waters decline, trout, whitefish, and other deep-water species die from oxygen starvation. Fish that live in the upper layers (such as perch) thrive and may increase. But, overall, the number of fish species decreases.

Of all the overfertilized lakes in the world, Lake Erie is one of the largest and best known. The lake is 240 miles (mi) or 386 kilometers (km) long, 50 mi (80 km) wide, and has a volume of 109 cubic miles (450 cubic kilometers). One might think that such a large body of water is capable of handling and purifying an enormous amount of pollutants. However, Lake Erie, with an average depth of 58 feet (ft) or 17.4 meters (m), is the shallowest of all the Great Lakes. Its shallowness is the root of Lake Erie's problems (see Figure 14.15).

► FIGURE 14.15 Lake Erie in the 1960s. Note the algae in the water and on the rocks. *(Kenneth Mantai/Visuals Unlimited)*

At one time, Lake Erie was clear and filled with valuable fish. As large population centers developed around its shore, its pristine beauty was changed. Many factories poured wastes into its waters, including Detroit's steel mills, paper factories, and automobile plants; Toledo's glass and steel industries; Cleveland's petrochemical and steel plants; Erie's paper mills; and Buffalo's flour mills and chemical factories. Large cities poured sewage, both treated and raw, into Lake Erie. Agricultural land between the cities added pesticides, herbicides, and fertilizers.

The first symptom of a lake-wide problem was seen in the 1920s when the fish crop started to decline. By 1950, the catch—which once had been as high as 50 million pounds (23 million kilograms) annually—dropped to less than 1,000 pounds (450 kilograms). The valuable species of whitefish, pike, and sturgeon had been replaced by catfish, carp, and smelt.

With the Water Pollution Control Act of 1972, the EPA spent billions of dollars on the construction of municipal sewage treatment plants. Industries spent billions cleaning up their wastes. Nonpoint pollution from agricultural lands, however, is difficult to curb. Though much still remains to be done, the trend has been reversed, and Lake Erie continues to recover.

SPECIAL FOCUS

The Florida Everglades

The history of the Everglades region shows how people can impact a fragile ecosystem. Until recently, the importance of swampy wetlands were not appreciated. Swamps, bogs, and mud were viewed as problems to be dredged, ditched, and drained. Now, people realize that the nation's most exotic swamp must be preserved.

The Everglades is a broad, swampy region of southern Florida that extends 100 mi (about 160 km) from the shores of Lake Okeechobee to the ocean. Figure 14.16 is a satellite photograph of southern Florida, showing the nature of the Everglades. The water from Lake Okeechobee does not flow to the ocean in a well-defined river. Instead, a wide sheet of water flows slowly through the swamp on its way to the ocean or Gulf of Mexico.

The water in the Everglades never runs deep. It ranges from only a few centimeters to no more than about 6.5 feet (ft) or 2 m. Water depth determines the plant communities. Sprouting

▼ FIGURE 14.16 A satellite photograph of southern Florida. Locate Lake Okeechobee and track the south and then west flow of water through the Everglades marsh. Note the population concentration along the eastern coast. The red color below Lake Okeechobee is the sugarcane fields. (USGS)

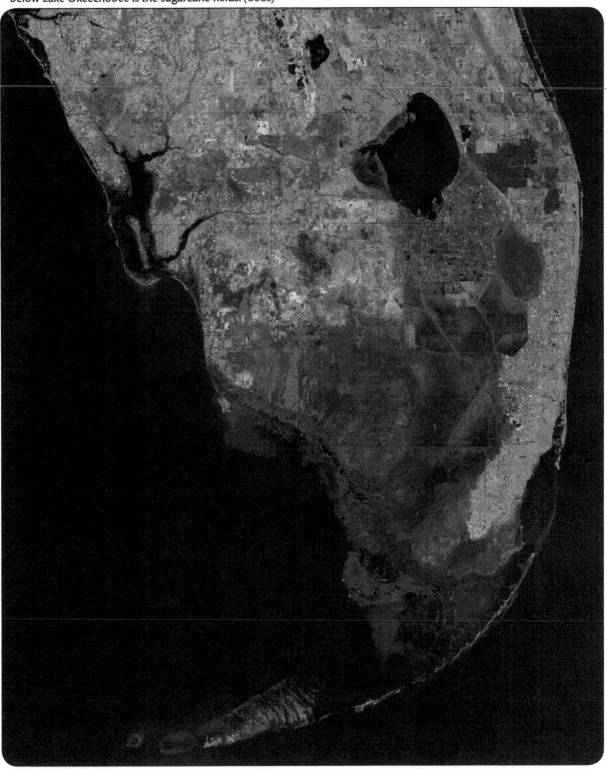

from the shallow water are vast areas of saw-grass—a tall, grasslike plant with slender saw-toothed leaves. The sawgrass grows out of a bed of muck. **Muck** is a rich soil produced by the slow, centuries-long buildup of decaying plants. On scattered outcrops of bedrock, tree islands dot the "river of grass" all along its length (see Figure 14.17). Here, hardwood

▲FIGURE 14.17 Tree islands in the Everglades. (*Photo by Harold Hungerford. Reprinted with permission.*)

▲FIGURE 14.18 Alligator in a 'gator hole. (*Bruce S. Cushing/Visuals Unlimited*)

trees, including live oaks and mahogany, teem with wildlife. These islands provide nesting grounds and shelter for many species of birds, mammals, and reptiles. **Sloughs**—areas with slightly deeper water—are largely free of sawgrass and are dominated by free-floating plants, such as the white waterlily.

The Everglades are always changing. In a typical year, rains drench lower Florida from May through October, and the wetlands flow with an abundance of water. The rainy season is followed by a 6-month dry season. Before the rains return, much of the Everglades turns to mud and then to dry, cracked earth. The balance of wet and dry seasons is important to plants and animals adapted to these conditions. During the wet season, the sawgrass swamp is covered with a meter of water (about 3 ft), and the plants grow rapidly. If this wet growing season continued all year long, plants would choke out the swamp, and forests would invade the area.

During the dry season, the water table drops. The sawgrass dries up and turns yellow. Lightning-caused fires are part of the natural system during the fall and winter, but only the tops of the sawgrass are burned. The roots, still covered by a few centimeters of water, are undisturbed. Tree islands, too, are generally safe from the fast-moving fires.

As the drought continues and the mud dries, most of the aquatic life would be threatened if it were not for the most famous Everglades reptile, the American alligator. The alligator is often referred to as the "keeper of the Glades" because biologists have found that the alligator's behavior helps maintain the marsh ecosystem. Alligators scoop out large depressions with their tails, creating 'gator holes that collect water. During the dry winter season, 'gator holes provide refuge for fish, turtles, snails, and other water-dwelling animals (see Figure 14.18).

The plants and animals of the Everglades have adapted to this complex cycle of seasonal growth, fire, and drought. The wide spectrum of habitats supports a very diverse set of plants and animals that are all interconnected.

Everglades National Park was established in 1947 to preserve this unique ecosystem and the migratory birds that go there to breed and nest. Now it is in danger of environmental collapse. The number of wading birds has declined 90 percent since 1936. Between 1962 and 1981, park biologist Bill Robertson found that the breeding populations of all bird species declined at least 50 percent. Alligator populations have declined because water control projects flooded the mounds on which they lay their eggs. Deer populations have also suffered from floods. Deer feed on vegetation

▲FIGURE 14.19 A canal southwest of Miami is part of a flood-control network that starves the Everglades of water. (*Gerald Davis*)

in the marshes, and tree islands provide dry land where deer can rest and breed. When flooding occurs, deer become stranded on the islands and starve.

What caused these problems for the Everglades? What is being done to turn around this tide of destruction?

In an effort to build Florida as an agricultural state, water from the wetlands and excess water from Lake Okeechobee were channeled and wetlands were drained. Farms replaced many former swamplands. Water development projects grew until there was a maze of 1,400 mi (about 2,250 km) of canals, dikes, levees, and pumping stations throughout the lower third of Florida (see Figures 14.19 and 14.20).

To accommodate both agriculture and the concerns of citizens wanting to preserve the Everglades, the U.S. Army Corps of Engineers designed several water conservation districts. These guaranteed that the park would receive at least a minimum annual water delivery. In 1967, an extension to a canal was dug to serve as a new water route to the park. Designed to get water to the park quickly and in large quantities, the new canal eliminated any remaining trace of the wetlands' historic sheet-flow pattern. Flooding then became a problem. The park was getting too much water, too often, and in too

concentrated a stream. Water released during the dry season flooded the areas around 'gator holes, so that fish were farther apart. To nesting birds, this meant loss of easily accessible prey during critical periods. Release of water during wet periods increased the water level, flooding alligator nests.

One more problem plagued the Everglades: runoff of water from the new agricultural lands led to eutrophication of water in Lake Okeechobee, the main water source for the Everglades. The runoff from fertilized fields added nutrients to the water and increased algae growth, which choked out fish populations.

It was once thought that areas of land could be preserved forever by making them into national parks. But national parks are not isolated islands. They are affected greatly by what happens outside their boundaries. Since water quantity, quality, and timing are at the root of the Everglades's problems, they must be the focus of the solution.

The South Florida Water Management District, the Corps of Engineers, the National Park Service, and private agricultural interests are the principal players when it comes to saving the Everglades. These groups must move quickly to accomplish three tasks. First, they must clearly define what "restore" means. It is hard to accomplish any task without a clear goal. Second, they must develop a plan to reach their goal. Must some lands be removed from agricultural production? Should price supports for the sugar growers be removed? How are nutrients best removed from agricultural runoff, and how can that be paid for? And third, they must develop the leadership to ensure that the principal players work together to accomplish the task. The U.S. Secretary of the Interior, the governor of Florida, and the directors of the principal agencies and associations are all charged with the mandate to save the Everglades. The public must be responsible for holding them to that task. An agreement between the sugar growers and various governmental agencies may prove to be a significant step forward.

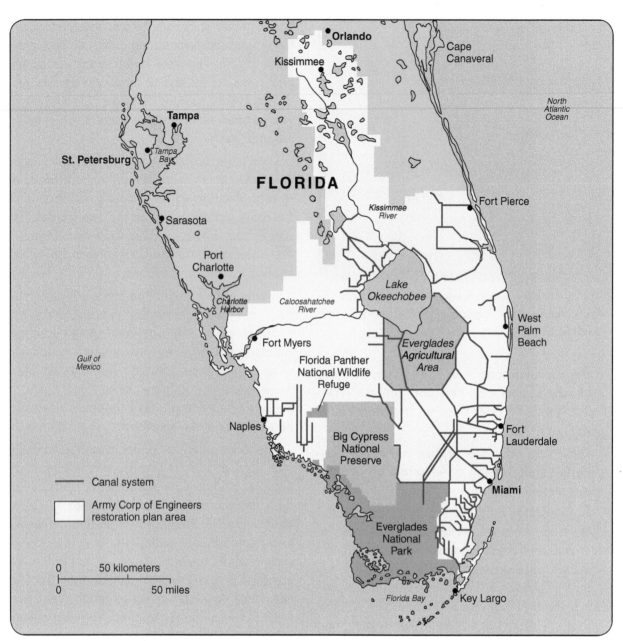

▲FIGURE 14.20 Plan to restore the Florida Everglades. In October 1998, the U.S. Army Corps of Engineers unveiled a plan to restore the ecological health of the Everglades, a large area of wetlands in southern Florida. Over the previous several decades, the corps had built an extensive system of canals to prevent flooding and provide water to urban centers in southern Florida. However, this water-control system severely reduced the Everglades's natural flow of water, drastically altering its plant and animal communities. The 30-year, $8 billion plan calls for removing many canals and levees and capturing much of the water flow (presently channeled to the sea) in underground reservoirs for later release back into the Everglades. In 1999, the corps worked on details of the plan, which it began implementing in 2002. (*From Science Year 2000. The World Book Annual Science Supplement © 1999 World Book, Inc. By permission of the publisher.*)

14.5 Pollution of Groundwater

Of growing concern to many people is the contamination of groundwater. Since groundwater flows slowly, the flow does not purify the water. Soil particles are not effective in filtering out most pollutants found in water. Once these pollutants reach the groundwater, it is almost impossible to clean up the water. Some engineers are investigating the possibility of pumping out an aquifer, cleaning the water, and pumping clean water back in. If this is possible, it will be very costly. Preventing contamination in the first place appears to be the most and currently the only effective solution.

Why can't groundwater purify itself?

Wastewater Treatment

Each American produces about 53 gallons (200 liters) of wastewater each day. This includes suspended solids, dissolved organic and inorganic materials, and microorganisms such as viruses and bacteria. What happens to all those wastes we flush down toilets, sinks, garbage disposals, and drains? To most of us, when wastes disappear down the drain, they are gone. Out of sight, out of mind!

A look at polluted rivers and lakes, however, reminds us that we cannot ignore the problem of what happens after we flush the toilet. There is a need for more wastewater treatment plants that treat and purify our wastewater, so that towns and cities downstream can safely reuse water from upstream users (see Figure 14.21).

The path of wastes from our sewers through a modern treatment plant will explain the problems and the advances in recently developed wastewater treatment technology. After the toilet is flushed, wastes travel through a network of sewer pipes until they arrive at a wastewater treatment plant. The plant consists of a series of tanks, screens, and filters that use both physical and chemical processes to remove wastes from the water.

Topic: wastewater treatment
Go to: www.scilinks.org
Code: GloSci7e547

14.6 Primary Treatment

Sewage contains human wastes, paper, soap, detergent, cloth, food residues, microorganisms, and a variety of other substances. The first stage in wastewater treatment, called

◄ FIGURE 14.21 Aerial photograph of a large metropolitan wastewater treatment plant. *(Metro Wastewater Reclamation District)*

► **FIGURE 14.22** Primary clarifier. *(Metro Wastewater Reclamation District)*

► **FIGURE 14.23** Primary treatment. *(U.S. Environmental Protection Agency)*

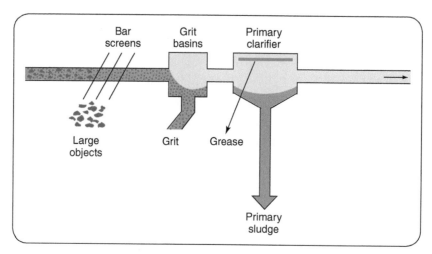

primary treatment, removes large solid objects and materials that settle out. Large objects such as rags and disposable diapers are screened out first. Then things like sand, grit, and coffee grounds settle to the bottom of a grit-removal basin. In a large settling tank, called the primary clarifier, suspended particles settle to the bottom, and grease floats to the top. The grease is skimmed off, and the raw sludge, the bottom sediment, is removed. Primary treatment is shown in Figure 14.22 and diagramed in Figure 14.23.

For many years, this was where sewage treatment ended. The liquid was simply discharged into lakes or streams. The discharge contains millions of microorganisms, some that cause disease, and large quantities of organic nutrients. These can destroy aquatic ecosystems.

14.7 Secondary Treatment

In modern wastewater treatment plants, the sewage goes through **secondary treatment** to remove the dissolved or suspended organic matter and to kill microorganisms. The liquid from primary treatment is pumped into large aeration tanks (see Figure 14.24). There, oxygen can work with microorganisms to decompose the organic materials. In the aeration tank, air (or in some facilities, pure oxygen) is bubbled through wastewater to

◀FIGURE 14.24 An aeration basin.

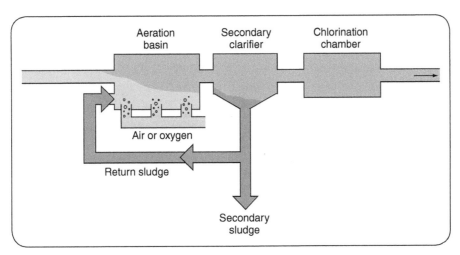

Aeration
basin

Secondary
clarifier

Chlorination
chamber

Air or oxygen

Return sludge

Secondary
sludge

◀FIGURE 14.25 Secondary treatment. (*U.S. Environmental Protection Agency*)

create a swirling action that increases the biological activity. That is, the interaction of oxygen, microorganisms, and the organic nutrients occurs more rapidly. Microorganisms grow and break down the organic matter. When the microorganisms complete their job of digesting the available food in the organic materials, they die and settle to the bottom of the tank.

The liquid from the aeration tanks then flows into the secondary clarifier (settling tank). Sludge settles to the bottom. The liquid, still containing microorganisms, is treated with chlorine, which kills 99 percent of the viruses, bacteria, and protozoa. This completes the secondary stage of treatment. In most cities, the liquid (effluent) is discharged into a nearby river or stream at this point. Figure 14.25 illustrates secondary treatment.

Another method of secondary treatment is called the **trickling filter** process. In this process, effluent from the primary clarifier is sprayed onto a bed of stones. The bed of stones, about 3–6.5 ft (1–2 m) deep, is covered with a slimy coating of bacteria and other microorganisms. Sewage is sprayed over the stones, and a food chain of various organisms is started. Bacteria eat the various nutrients in the sewage, breaking it down into smaller components. The bacteria are then eaten by protozoans that, in turn, are eaten by worms, snails, flies, and spiders. After the trickling filter process, effluent flows into the secondary clarifier.

Water Quality 549

Apply Your Understanding

How do primary, secondary, and tertiary treatments differ from one another?

14.8 Tertiary Treatment

Primary and secondary treatments remove more than 90 percent of all the solids and organic wastes. Chlorination eliminates most of the disease potential. However, most of the phosphates, nitrates, salts, radioactive materials, and pesticides that were in the original sewage still remain. Since high concentrations of these materials can cause severe ecological damage, many cities are now adding a third stage of treatment to remove some (usually not all) of these materials.

Tertiary treatments consist of a series of chemical or physical processes such as absorption, oxidation, or reverse osmosis for removing specific pollutants. The type and amount of tertiary treatment depend on local conditions and community goals.

14.9 Solids Processing

Sludge that results from sewage treatment must be further treated and digested. Figures 14.26, 14.27, and 14.28 illustrate possible approaches to solids processing. First, the sludge is decomposed in anaerobic conditions. The anaerobes break down the organic compounds into harmless solids, organic acids, carbon dioxide, hydrogen sulfide, and methane. Since methane gas (CH_4) is flammable, it may be captured and used to operate generators or to heat buildings.

The final disposal of the sludge may be by incineration (burning), landfill, or composting. **Composting** is the breakdown (rotting) of moist organic matter in solid wastes by aerobic bacteria to form compost. **Compost** is a humuslike material that can be used as a fertilizer or a soil conditioner for lawns and gardens. Because the heat given off as composting occurs kills disease-causing organisms, compost can be used by gardeners and farmers as a fertilizer.

▶ FIGURE 14.26 Solids processing. (*Metro Wastewater Reclamation District*)

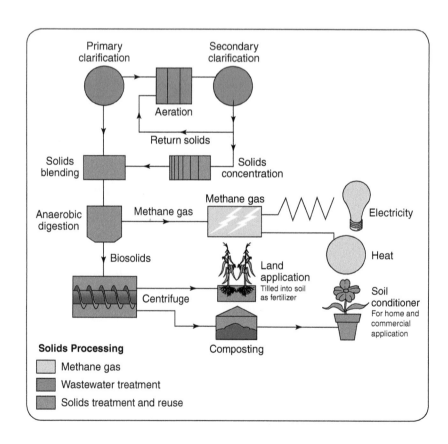

◀ FIGURE 14.27 Compost-mixing machine turning compost. *(Metro Wastewater Reclamation District)*

◀ FIGURE 14.28 Land application of biosolids. *(Metro Wastewater Reclamation District)*

Properly done, the agricultural application of sludge reduces the need for chemical fertilizers. When wastewater is thoroughly treated with aerobic bacteria, the sludge can be used as a fertilizer without being composted. New technologies offer the prospect of producing sludge with fewer disease-causing microorganisms at a lower cost.

14.10 On-Site Sewage Treatment Systems

One-third of all American families use on-site sewage treatment systems. Eighty-five percent of U.S. on-site systems use **septic tanks**. Most of the rest use aerobic tanks (with an air agitator). The purpose of the on-site system is to remove wastewater from its source, separate contaminants from the wastewater, and return an effluent to the soil for further filtration. This is all done on the property where the sewage originated. On-site disposal systems may offer economic advantages over municipal sewage systems. The soil and water conditions must be suitable and a home should not be close to a city sewer line.

An on-site system has two parts: a sewage tank and a soil filter (leach field) (see Figure 14.29). The sewage tank separates out the large solids. Bacteria digest organic materials and cause scum and sludge to separate from the wastewater. Liquid

Topic: septic tank
Go to: www.scilinks.org
Code: GloSci7e551

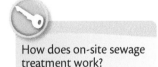

How does on-site sewage treatment work?

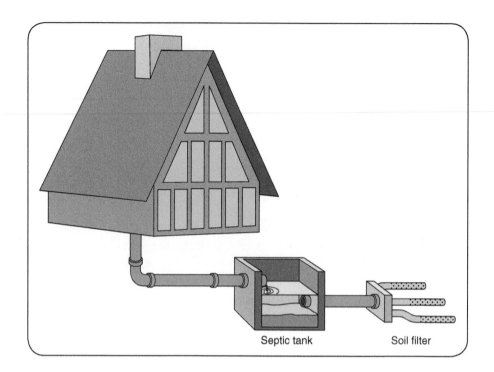

Septic tank   Soil filter

effluent from the sewage tank flows into the soil filter. A soil filter is a network of porous pipes located in trenches covered with soil and turf. Gravel surrounding the pipes promotes even distribution of the effluent. This effluent contains high levels of bacteria and phosphorus, which must be removed or inactivated before reaching the water table.

The improper siting or construction of many on-site sewage treatment systems has caused groundwater pollution around the country. Homeowners must use care in selecting a contractor, or know what they are doing if they do the work themselves.

The only maintenance required for a properly operating system may be the occasional removal of accumulated solids from the sewage tank. Most septic system problems can be reduced if homeowners are careful with their use of water. For example, garbage disposals should be used only sparingly, if at all. It is better to compost the garbage.

14.11 Natural Wastewater Treatment Strategies

Small and moderate-size towns (up to about 50,000 people) can use the nutrient-absorbing capacity of wetlands to treat their wastewater. The task is either to find suitable wetlands or to construct them, creating a chain of shallow lakes and ponds. Some communities discharge nutrient-rich effluent into their wetland system following secondary treatment. Others go from primary treatment to such a system. The key is not to overload the system beyond what the natural processes can handle. Various inorganic chemicals and other pollutants may also have to be removed before effluents are discharged. In the United States, more than 500 restored or artificially constructed wetlands are being used for this purpose. These areas are often used as wildlife preserves or community nature trails.

Summary

Nonpolluted water is essential for quality human life and for the survival of healthy ecosystems. Scientists have identified a host of water pollutants and placed them in categories to study. Students and scientists can test the quality of water samples. An analysis of those data can aid in making decisions about the proper and best use of that water.

By analyzing the condition of aquatic ecosystems, scientists and citizens can make informed decisions about their treatment and use. Such studies help in the restoration of Lake Erie, the Florida Everglades, and large and small areas of ecological concern around the globe.

Wastewater can be treated so that water becomes clean and can be reused. Large cities maintain complex municipal water treatment systems and wastewater treatment plants. On-site sewage treatment can be used where population density is low and soil conditions are right. The wastes that accumulate at large wastewater treatment plants can be processed for recycling. In future years, as populations and waste products increase, improved treatment and reuse of water will be combined.

REFERENCES

Water Quality in the United States

Adler, Robert W., et al. *The Clean Water Act: 20 Years Later* (Washington, D.C.: Island Press), 1993.

Natural Resources Defense Council. *Clean Water: Citizen's Handbook on Water Quality Standards* (Washington, D.C.: NRDC), 1987.

U.S. Geological Survey. *The Quality of Our Nation's Waters: Nutrients and Pesticides*, USGS Circular 1225 (Washington, D.C.: USGPO), 1999.

Global Water Quality

Gleick, Peter H. and H. Cooley. *The World's Water, 2006–2007: The Biennial Report on Freshwater Resources* (Washington, D.C.: Island Press), 2006.

United Nations Environment Programme. *GEMS Water Quality Report* (Burlington, Ontario: UNEP GEMS/Water Programme), 2005.

United Nations Development Programme. *Human Development Report—Beyond Scarcity: Power, Poverty and the Global Water Crisis* (New York: UNDP), 2006.

United Nations Environment Programme. *Water Quality Outlook* (Burlington, Ontario: UN GEMS/Water Programme), 2007.

World Health Organization. *Guidelines for Drinking-water Quality* (Geneva: WHO), 2003.

The Everglades

Grunwald, Michael. *The Swamp: The Everglades, Florida, and the Politics of Paradise* (New York: Simon & Schuster), 2006.

Water Quality

USDA Water Quality Database:
http://www.nal.usda.gov/wqic/dbases.shtml

Environmental Protection Agency (EPA):
http://www.epa.gov/safewater

USGS–National Water Quality Assessment Program:
http://water.usgs.gov/nawqa/

UNICEF/WHO:
http://www.who.int/

United Nations Development Program:
http://www.undp.org/

United Nations GEMS/Water Program:
http://www.gemswater.org

Water Aid:
http://www.wateraid.org

Water Quality Association:
http://www.wqa.org/

Water Quality Information Center:
http://www.nal.usda.gov/wqic/

Everglades Information

The Everglades Ecosystem:
http://www.nps.gov/ever/

A Guide to the Everglades and 10,000 Islands:
http://www.florida-everglades.com/rt.htm

Everglades Pictures:
http://photo.net/photo/everglades/

Everglades Nutrient Removal:
http://www.floridaplants.com/horticulture/enr.htm

Friends of the Everglades:
http://everglades.org/

Great Lakes Information

Great Lakes National Program Office:
http://www.epa.gov/glnpo

Great Lakes Atlas:
http://www.epa.gov/glnpo/atlas/index.html

Great Lakes Environmental Reasearch Laboratory:
http://www.glerl.noaa.gov/

Great Lakes Information Network:
http://www.great-lakes.net/

CHAPTER 15

Resource Management: Air

GOAL

- To understand how human activities affect our atmosphere and global climate.

Given the current level of uncertainty and the complexity of the climate system, the future will likely bring surprises, which could be of either the pleasant or the unpleasant variety.

—*"Reports to the Nation: Our Changing Climate,"* NOAA

Caretakers of the Global Environment

15.1 Human Actions and Our Environment

How can our environment be restored naturally?

When there were fewer people in the world, they had little impact on the environment. Natural processes eventually repaired damage that arose from the stresses of human pollution, land use, and resource extraction. Winds and rains removed pollutants from the air. Flowing streams and decomposers acted together to purify dirty water. Those areas changed by fire, flood, or human actions were slowly restored by natural movements of minerals and soil. The diversity of available vegetation and seeds also helped the land to recover.

A main factor in this recovery process was time. Over time, winds dispersed airborne particles to less toxic concentrations. Over time, decomposers broke down solid and liquid pollutants. Over time, the surrounding ecosystem advanced into and restored disrupted lands. But, as the human population has become larger and more consumption-oriented, we have lost time as our ally.

How can ecosystems be damaged?

The human impact on the global environment comes from many sources. Some of our actions have environmental connections. There are three major causes of severe change in ecosystems. Humans are damaging ecosystems in all three ways (see Figure 15.1) First, essential chemical cycling systems can be disrupted. The widespread use of artificial fertilizers, herbicides, and pesticides is an example of how we disrupt natural chemical cycles. Second, the flow of energy through ecosystems can be disrupted. This can be caused by the introduction of waste heat, carbon dioxide (CO_2), and air pollutants into the atmosphere. Third, the diversity of ecosystems can be reduced. Single-crop farming on great expanses of land is reducing plant diversity. As living organisms totally dependent on what the ecosphere provides, we must look carefully at what we are doing.

Good resource management demands that environmental impacts be examined scientifically. We must understand these impacts before action is taken. Today, we are doing just that. This chapter takes a close look at some of the environmental impacts of our attempts to achieve the good life. We will look at some of the corrective measures we have taken, and can take. We will focus on the atmosphere and on our current knowledge of how human activities may be changing our community, our region, and ultimately, our global climate.

▶ FIGURE 15.1 Ecosystems can be changed in three principal ways.

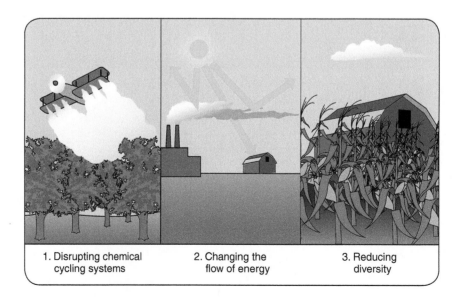

1. Disrupting chemical cycling systems
2. Changing the flow of energy
3. Reducing diversity

The Atmosphere

The first step in managing our atmosphere is to know its structure and how it functions. Activity 15.1 will help you make that analysis.

What's Up There?

Any discussion about the atmosphere must begin with some basic concepts. In this activity, you will learn about the most important layers of the atmosphere (see Figure 15.2).

Think about This!

Our atmosphere is often referred to as a "protective blanket of gas." What does it protect us from?

You will discover what those layers are composed of, and what they do for life on our planet. This will be especially important as we continue to examine how human activities affect different parts of our atmosphere.

Materials

- colored markers or pencils
- research materials such as textbooks, encyclopedias, online resources, or CD-ROMs

Procedure

1. Leave plenty of room in your science notebook for this exercise. Begin by brainstorming a list of all the possible functions of our atmosphere.

2. Using this list, develop a concept map that shows visually how these functions relate to other Earth systems you have learned about.

3. Study Figure 15.3. Create a pie graph that includes all the major gases in the atmosphere. This is the atmosphere's **composition**. Complete the last column labeled "Property or Fact about This Gas" in your science notebook.

4. Using the information from step 3, add facts from your graph and chart to your concept map.

Topic: atmospheric layers
Go to: www.scilinks.org
Code: GloSci7e559

◀FIGURE 15.2 Earth and its atmosphere as seen from space. What atmospheric features are obvious from this vantage point? What features are not obvious? (*NASA photo*)

► FIGURE 15.3 The composition of our atmosphere measured in terms of relative percentage. Complete the last column by researching facts about each atmospheric gas.

Gas	Chemical Formula	Percentage in Atmosphere	Property or Fact about This Gas
Nitrogen	N_2	78.00%	
Oxgen	O_2	21.00%	
Argon	Ar	0.90%	
Carbon dioxide	CO_2	0.030%	
Water vapor	H_2O	<.001%	
Nitrous oxide	N_2O	<.001%	
Ozone	O_3	<.001%	
Methane	CH_4	<.001%	
Neon	Ne	<.001%	
Helium	He	<.001%	

Content Clue

Ninety percent of Earth's atmosphere lies within 10 miles (16 km) of the surface. If Earth were shrunk to the size of an apple, our atmosphere would be the thickness of its skin.

5. Study Figure 15.4. Note that this figure is incomplete. Turn to encyclopedias, atlases, CD-ROMs, or online resources such as the Internet and SciLinks for help in filling in the blanks. Record the missing information in your science notebook.

6. Add facts from Figure 15.4 to your concept map.

7. On a separate page in your notebook, draw a scale model of the atmosphere. Add facts from Figure 15.4. (Your teacher will tell you whether to complete this step.)

▼ FIGURE 15.4 The major layers of the atmosphere. Complete the table by researching facts about each atmospheric layer.

Layer	Location	Temperature	Facts
Troposphere	Over North/South Pole: 0–6 miles (0–10 km) thick; over equator: 0–10 miles (16 km) thick		• Layer in which we live. • 90% of atmosphere's mass is concentrated here. • Most weather occurs here.
Stratosphere	Above the troposphere: 7–30 miles (11–48 km) thick		
Thermosphere		Temperature of some molecules can exceed 1,100°F (about 600°C) at 120 miles (193 km) above Earth.	

Air Quality

15.2 Air Quality

Although there have been minor changes in the atmosphere, the basic composition of Earth's air has remained much the same for millions of years. Most living things developed in that atmosphere and depend on it for survival. Today, when human activities change the air's composition, we may threaten the health (or even the existence) of some species—including our own.

It was one of the worst cases of air pollution in history. Poisonous gas, smoke, and fumes polluted the once-sweet air of the Italian coastal city. The sky grew dark. Many died simply from breathing the air.

In this case, air pollution had come from a natural source—the eruption of Mt. Vesuvius (see Figure 15.5) that buried the city of Pompeii in the year AD 79. Since then, volcanoes and fires have periodically poured natural pollutants into the atmosphere. Wind adds dust, and plants add pollen and vapors to the air. Wind and natural circulation, together with rain and gravity, removed much of the natural pollutants.

Starting around 1800 with the Industrial Revolution, the air's composition was altered by the widescale combustion (burning) of fossil fuels. Today, more than 85 percent of the energy used each year in the United States involves the combustion of fossil fuels. Figure 15.6 summarizes the carbon cycle for fossil fuels.

The five emissions (air pollutants) listed in Figure 15.6 cause the most concern. To emphasize the origin of these pollutants, the combustion equations from Chapter 8 are summarized in Figure 15.7.

An **air pollutant** is any substance in the air that is concentrated enough to harm living things or damage humanmade objects. Some familiar pollutants are smoke, carbon monoxide, and sulfur dioxide.

Content Clue

Other ways gases enter the atmosphere naturally: Plants release oxygen, animals release CO_2, and forest fires release solid carbon (soot), gaseous carbon (CO_2), and most of the compounds listed in this section.

Think about This!

Several volcanoes have erupted recently in populated areas. What is the impact of these eruptions on the local populations?

◀Figure 15.5 Mt. Vesuvius overlooking scenic Naples Bay, Italy. This volcano has been dormant since 1944, but its condition is cause for concern for the more than 2 million people who live in its shadow. (© Jeff Greenberg/Visuals Unlimited)

► **FIGURE 15.6** The carbon cycle, involving the combustion of fossil fuels, begins with solar energy/photosynthesis millions of years ago. When plant material is buried where oxidation is not possible, chemical changes can result in the formation of fossil fuels. These fuels are extracted and burned to do useful tasks. In the process, heat is released into the atmosphere along with such products of combustion as carbon dioxide and water vapor. Other related emissions are shown at the right.

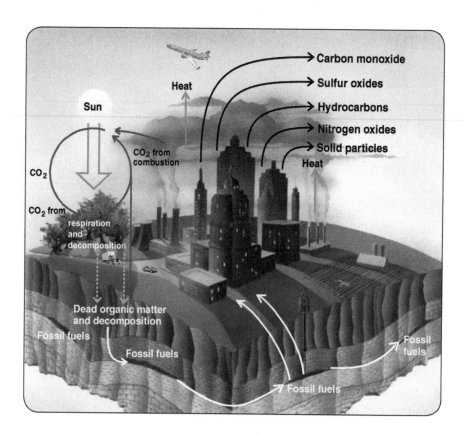

► **FIGURE 15.7** The origins of air pollutants.

Think about This!

Some scientists are concerned about the possible future eruption of Mt. Vesuvius in Italy or Mt. Rainier near Seattle, Washington. Why are they concerned? Predict the possible impact of these eruptions.

Combustion (Burning) Equations

Oil

oil + oxygen → CO_2 + H_2O + heat + wastes*

*wastes = unburned hydrocarbons, carbon monoxide (CO), NO_x, and SO_x

Natural gas

natural gas + oxygen → CO_2 + H_2O + heat

Coal

coal + oxygen → CO_2 + heat + wastes

More specifically,

coal (C) + oxygen (O_2) → CO_2 + heat + soot (unburned coal) + sulfur gases + nitrogen oxides + fly ash + CO

The ebb and flow of pollutants in our atmosphere is carefully watched (in the United States) by the federal government's **Environmental Protection Agency (EPA)**, the National Center for Atmospheric Research (NCAR), and the National Oceanic and Atmospheric Administration (NOAA). The EPA regulates pollution while it and the other organizations study the air's composition and processes.

Driving Our Atmosphere Crazy

In this activity, you will learn about the local and global implications of burning fossil fuels. You will quantitatively analyze and evaluate the link between the automobile and air pollution.

We will talk about air pollution in terms of *pollution units*. Pollution units are representative of those measured in the downtown areas of many major cities in developed countries (that are not near major industrial operations). Pollution units (PUs) can be CO, NO_x, SO_x, VOC, or particulates. You will read more about PUs in section 15.3 Air Pollution: The Big Five.

Materials

- calculator
- measuring cup
- teaspoon
- sugar
- scale
- graph paper (optional)

Procedure

1. List the 3 worst sources of pollution for cities in your science notebook.

2. Graph the data provided in Figure 15.8. Connect all points with a smooth curve. How can you explain the shape of your graph?

Helpful Hint!

There are 1,000 grams in a kilogram and 1,000 kilograms in a metric ton. The average auto in the United States is driven 16,000 kilometers per year. In the United States, there is one car for every 2.5 individuals.

QUESTIONS & TASKS

Record your responses in your science notebook.

1. Nitrogen oxide (NO_x) is one of the ingredients of smog. The average car produces 2.5 grams (g) of nitrous oxides for every kilometer driven. To give you a feel for what 2.5 g is, determine which of the following contains about 2.5 g of sugar:

- 1 grain of sugar
- 1 teaspoon of sugar
- 1 cup of sugar

▼ FIGURE 15.8 Data table showing units of pollution during a 24-hour period. (*Adapted from* Investigations in Science *by Eric D. Miller,* © 1998, Hubbard Scientific, Inc., Fort Collins, Colorado 80522.)

Time	Pollution Units	Time	Pollution Units	Time	Pollution Units
12:00 M	6	9:00 AM	33	6:00 PM	42
1:00 AM	5	10:00 AM	30	7:00 PM	38
2:00 AM	5	11:00 AM	28	8:00 PM	36
3:00 AM	7	12:00 N	26	9:00 PM	20
4:00 AM	9	1:00 PM	29	10:00 PM	12
5:00 AM	19	2:00 PM	31	11:00 PM	9
6:00 AM	28	3:00 PM	35	12:00 M	6
7:00 AM	31	4:00 PM	38		
8:00 AM	35	5:00 PM	40		

2. Estimate the total number of kilometers that your family's autos are driven each year.

3. Multiply the answer for question 2 by 2.5 to see how many grams of nitrogen oxides your family's autos produce each year.

4. Estimate how many autos are in your community. How many kilograms of nitrogen oxides are produced by your community in a year?

5. A large dump truck can haul about 15 metric tons of gravel. Based on the information you calculated in question 4, determine how many trucks full of gravel would equal the nitrogen oxides produced each year by your community.

6. How many dump trucks full of gravel would equal the weight of the nitrogen oxides produced by your state in a year?

7. Make a list of the things that you and your friends can do right now to help reduce automobile pollution.

[Adapted from *Investigations in Science* by Eric D. Miller, © 1998, Hubbard Scientific, Inc., Fort Collins, Colorado 80522.]

15.3 Air Pollution: The "Big Five"

What is an air pollutant? What are the five major air pollutants in the United States?

Topic: air pollutants
Go to: www.scilinks.org
Code: GloSci7e564

What causes carbon monoxide to form?

Many substances pollute the air, but five pollutants cause most of the problems. Most of these occur within the **troposphere**—the lowest layer of the atmosphere. However, some are carried by currents into the **stratosphere**. These five are carbon monoxide (CO); unburned hydrocarbons (also called volatile organics), which are related to ozone (O_3); nitrogen oxides (NO_x); sulfur oxides (SO_x); and particulates (suspended particles, such as soot, ash, dust, and so forth). Carbon dioxide (CO_2) is not usually considered a pollutant, but you will read about possible problems associated with this gas later in this chapter. Again, examine the combustion equations in Figure 15.7.

Carbon Monoxide (CO)

Ninety percent of our atmosphere's *naturally occurring* carbon monoxide is formed and dispersed in the upper troposphere where it poses little risk to people. Near Earth's surface, *human-caused* carbon monoxide is formed when carbon is not completely burned. It is a major problem in cities at higher altitudes. This is because the lower oxygen content of the air causes more carbon monoxide (and less carbon dioxide) to be formed.

High levels of carbon monoxide pose health risks for humans because carbon monoxide binds to the hemoglobin in our blood. Ordinarily, hemoglobin carries oxygen to our cells. By reacting with hemoglobin, carbon monoxide causes oxygen deprivation (loss) in the body. Exposure to moderate concentrations of carbon monoxide causes headache and fatigue. Continued exposure to large concentrations can be fatal.

By improving emission-control systems on automobiles (through the use of **catalytic converters**) and increasing the oxygen content of fuels, carbon monoxide levels in large cities are reduced.

Carbon monoxide can cause problems indoors as well (see Figure 15.9). In homes where woodstoves, kerosene heaters, faulty furnaces, or other combustion devices are not properly installed, incomplete burning can produce excess CO. This form of indoor pollution is rare, but it can be prevented through periodic inspection of home furnaces, fireplaces, or any indoor device that burns fuel. Running automobiles that are parked in unventilated garages can also cause an unwanted buildup of toxic CO gas.

◀ FIGURE 15.9 Indoor carbon monoxide detectors warn homeowners about dangerous levels of indoor CO. Because carbon monoxide is colorless and odorless, it is difficult for people to detect on their own. CO detectors are rapidly joining smoke detectors as a relatively inexpensive (less than $50) safety investment for the home.

Unburned Hydrocarbons

Another related source of atmospheric pollution comes from unburned hydrocarbons (also called volatile organic compounds, or VOCs). VOCs arise from incomplete combustion of gasoline and from evaporation of petroleum fuels, industrial solvents, paints, and dry cleaning fluids. They are most closely related to transportation, industrial processes, and home heating. The primary problem with hydrocarbons is their role in forming **photochemical smog**. VOCs react with nitrogen oxides in sunlight to form ozone and other reactive compounds.

Ozone (O_3) is a highly reactive gas that is a pollutant when found in the troposphere. It comes from a reaction involving sunlight and unburned hydrocarbons. It is also created by lightning. As a pollutant, ozone causes eye, throat, and lung irritation. It may cause unwanted chemical reactions in various materials, such as rubber.

Ozone in the stratosphere, on the other hand, is necessary for screening out ultraviolet radiation. It is sometimes called "good" ozone. We'll revisit ozone later in this chapter.

Catalytic converters are designed to break apart unburned hydrocarbons and change them into carbon dioxide and water. Federal emission standards, regulations, and technology have led to reduced emissions of unburned hydrocarbons from automobiles.

Nitrogen Oxides (NO$_x$)

Air is 78 percent nitrogen. At normal temperatures, nitrogen is relatively inert (that is, it does not combine with other elements). However, at the high temperatures associated with combustion, furnaces, and engines, some nitrogen gas (N_2) combines with oxygen to form nitric oxide (NO).

In the air, nitric oxide reacts quickly with additional oxygen to form nitrogen dioxide (NO_2) and/or nitrogen tetroxide (N_2O_4). These compounds are referred to as nitrogen oxides, symbolized as NO_x. Nitrogen dioxide absorbs light. It is largely responsible for the brownish color of photochemical smog (see Figure 15.10).

Smog is a term that was first used to talk about the combination of smoke and fog in major cities. Smog was primarily industrial in origin. Today, the term is also applied to the brownish photochemical haze produced by the reaction between sunlight, atmospheric gases, automobile exhausts, and industrial emissions. Most sunlight-driven chemical reactions

> **Content Clue**
>
> Ozone is called a *secondary pollutant* because it is formed when a primary pollutant (one of the big five) comes into contact with other primary pollutants or with naturally occurring substances.

> Distinguish between tropospheric ozone and stratospheric ozone. Which is harmful? Which is helpful?

►FIGURE 15.10 Denver's infamous "brown cloud" as it looked in the 1980s. The cloud is not as distinct today, nor is it as harmful. However, because of the population growth, it is more diffuse and covers a much larger area. *(Courtesy of Colorado Department of Health and Environment.)*

Which of the big five air pollutants occur naturally? Check your science notebook from Activity 15.1.

involve nitrogen oxides and unburned hydrocarbons. The reactive chemicals produced harm living organisms. They also damage paint, rubber, and other materials.

Catalytic converters are now designed to greatly reduce nitrogen oxides from automobiles. The converters include the elements platinum and rhodium, which, when heated by the exhaust, aid in stripping oxygen atoms from NO_x to release harmless N_2 and O_2 gas.

Sulfur Oxides (SO_x)

Among the largest contributors to *naturally occurring* sulfur dioxide (SO_2) and other sulfur oxides in the troposphere are volcanoes. Sulfur oxides are also generated by humans (see Figure 15.11). They are formed when sulfur-containing fuels are burned. When electric power plants burn coal, oil, or gas (all of which contain small amounts of sulfur) to generate electricity, a by-product is sulfur oxide. Automobiles also emit sulfur oxides. And, since metal ores can contain various amounts of sulfur, some metal smelters emit sulfur oxide gases as well.

Sulfur oxides do their damage as corrosive and lung-damaging sulfuric acid in smog. They irritate respiratory passages and worsen conditions such as asthma, bronchitis, and emphysema.

Emissions of sulfur oxides have decreased as the result of improved control technology. For example, the sulfur oxides from fossil fuels are reduced most effectively by removing sulfur from them before they are burned. Sulfur oxides can also be removed from smoke-stack emissions by using powdered limestone or trona. This process is called **scrubbing**.

Particulates

Particulates are very small solid particles or liquid droplets suspended in air currents. Most particulates are natural. But they are also found in automobile and truck emissions, and in some industrial and combustion (power plants, heating) emissions. Particulates damage the respiratory tract directly. They stain buildings and other materials, and reduce visibility. In addition, particulates may contribute to long-term climatic changes.

Efforts to reduce air pollution have been most successful in the case of particulates. The installation of pollution control equipment on industrial and power plant furnaces is a

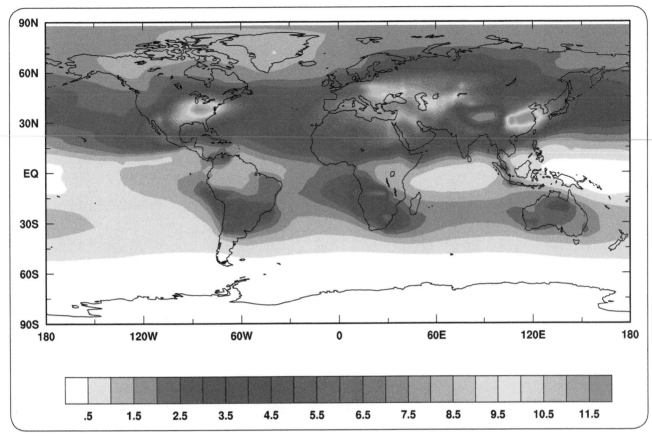

▲ FIGURE 15.11 Map of the world showing plumes of sulfate particles. Red depicts greater concentrations; white, less concentrations. Why are the greatest concentrations of sulfate particles located in eastern North America and eastern Asia? *(Copyright University Corporation for Atmospheric Research.)*

major reason for this reduction. Another is the stricter regulation of the burning of solid wastes. Emission controls on automobiles have been important as well.

Monitoring Our Air Quality

The EPA developed the **Air Quality Index (AQI)** to make information about outdoor air quality understandable and accessible to the public. The AQI is an index for reporting daily air quality. It tells you how clean or polluted the local air is and what associated health effects might be of concern to you. The EPA calculates the AQI for five major air pollutants regulated by the Clean Air Act: ground level ozone, particulates, carbon monoxide, sulfur dioxide, and nitrogen dioxide. The AQI scale runs from 0 to 500. The higher the AQI value, the greater the level of air pollution and the greater the health concern. In large cities (more than 350,000 people), state and local agencies are required to report the AQI to the public daily. The reporting is done in local newspapers, on TV and radio, and on the Internet.

Heath-related effects caused by air pollution are serious (see Figure 15.12). Fortunately, the air in the cities of most developed countries is cleaner now than it was 25 years ago. There is still room for improvement, but the strategies being used to attack the problem are working. We will examine these strategies in section 15.7 Strategies for Reducing Air Pollution. The rapid industrial development in Asia, however, is an air quality challenge.

 To learn more about the AQI, go to www.epa.gov/airnow.

QUESTIONS & TASKS

Record your responses in your science notebook.

1. Go to www.epa.gov/airnow and obtain information to explain the different levels of the AQI 0–500 scale.

2. Make a chart of the five major air pollutants. List the causes, health effects, and ways to reduce the pollutant.

SPECIAL FOCUS

Thermal Inversions

The air pollution problem in many areas is magnified by what is called a **thermal inversion** (see Figure 15.13). Thermal inversions occur when a layer of cool air near Earth's surface is trapped below a layer of warm air. This can happen if a warm air mass moves to-ward a city that sits in a valley. The less-dense warm air will move over the more-dense cooler air in the valley.

Polluted air given off by chimneys and smokestacks is generally much warmer than the surrounding air. Under normal conditions, this

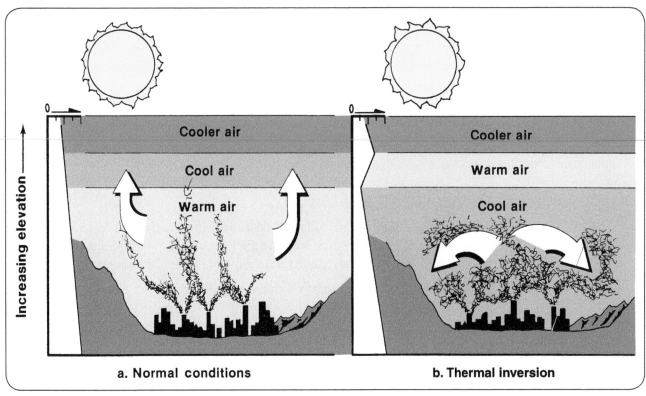

▲ FIGURE 15.13 In a thermal inversion, pollutants are trapped in a layer of cool air that cannot rise into the warm air above it.

air is less dense than the air into which it escapes. Hence, the polluted air rises, spreads out, and becomes diluted. This is shown in Figure 15.13a.

When polluted air is free to rise, its effects are short-lived. But when there is a thermal inversion, the area may be polluted for a long time. Pollutants released at ground level rise until they reach the warm air layer. Here they collect and form the brown cloud that many of our cities try to prevent. This is shown in Figure 15.13b.

If a cold air mass moves into the region, the warm layer may be pushed away. Or, if intense sunlight can warm the cooler air at Earth's surface, the inversion condition can be broken. During lengthy cold-calm periods,

however, the pollutants may stay for several days. Since the pollutants are building up in a fixed volume of air, their concentrations can increase to harmful levels. To prevent this, traffic volumes, industrial activity, and wood burning are watched carefully and possibly restricted.

Focus Questions

1. How does air temperature normally change as distance above the ground increases?

2. What is a thermal inversion? What causes thermal inversions?

3. Why do thermal inversions often create health hazards?

15.4 Indoor Air Pollution

Topic: indoor air
pollutants
Go to: www.scilinks.org
Code: GloSci7e570

Most people today spend much more time indoors or in enclosed spaces than they do outside. Because indoor air is confined, it can pose problems different from the air outside. Indoor air pollution ties to such factors as the material a building is made of, where the building is placed, and the furnishings inside the building. The heating and cooling systems are also factors. As a result, the sources of indoor air pollution are varied.

Figure 15.14 is a drawing of a typical American home. Refer to it as you read about the following seven sources of indoor air pollution.

Bacteria and Mold

Bacteria, mites, and mold breed in air-conditioning units, air ducts, and humidifiers. They are often spread throughout the building via the air duct system. So air filters should be changed regularly. Molds also breed under rugs and wherever moisture accumulates.

Molds and bacteria are most easily reduced by making sure the ground slopes away from a building's foundation to prevent the buildup of moisture. Regularly clean roof gutters and repair any leaks. Make sure rooms have adequate ventilation, especially areas where moisture accumulates quickly (such as bathrooms). Clean bathrooms often with detergent and water or with mold-killing products to prevent the growth of mold spores. Fix leaking pipes and other water problems inside a home as soon as they are discovered. Keep humidity levels indoors below 60 percent (ideally between 30 and 50 percent). Use a dehumidifier during humid months to keep rooms dry. Dust the floors, and open windows on clean air days.

▼ FIGURE 15.14 Sources of indoor air pollution are varied. (*Adapted from American Lung Association.*)

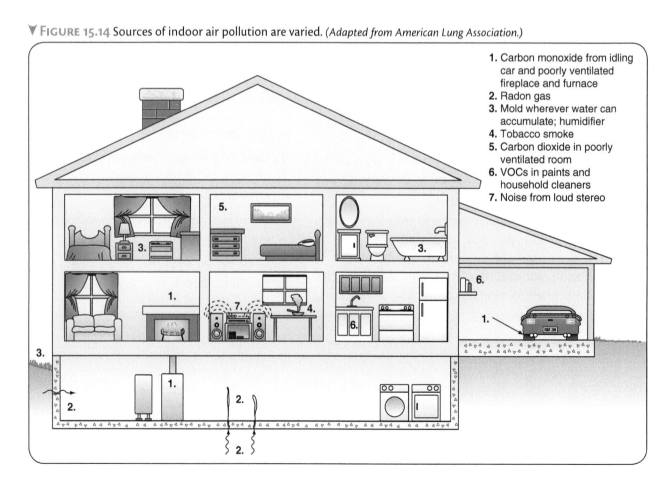

1. Carbon monoxide from idling car and poorly ventilated fireplace and furnace
2. Radon gas
3. Mold wherever water can accumulate; humidifier
4. Tobacco smoke
5. Carbon dioxide in poorly ventilated room
6. VOCs in paints and household cleaners
7. Noise from loud stereo

Tobacco Smoke

Tobacco smoke causes health problems including lung cancer and heart disease. Many restaurants and office buildings do not allow people to smoke inside.

Carbon Monoxide (CO)

Poorly maintained furnaces, a car left idling in the garage, cigarettes, and improperly operated fireplaces all produce carbon monoxide. CO detectors can warn of high levels of this toxic gas. The best defense is to know the causes, keep furnaces serviced, and never leave a car idling in the garage.

Carbon Dioxide (CO_2)

Carbon dioxide can build up to abnormal levels in buildings with poor circulation. Most local utilities can assist you with a building circulation appraisal.

Radon Gas

This deadly gas primarily originates in the rocks and soil a building sits on. Most locations produce very little radon because there is very little uranium or thorium in the soil. Some regions, however, contain high concentrations of uranium or thorium. In these locations, radon can enter the home by migrating up from soil and rock into basements and lower floors—especially through cracks. Radon dissolves in groundwater and can enter a home through the water system. Finally, bricks and cement may contain higher than normal concentrations of uranium. The best way to solve this problem is to have your home/building checked for radon if you suspect it is present.

Volatile Organic Compounds (VOCs)

VOCs can be present in paints, household cleaners, cooking oils, dry-cleaned clothing, and carpets. Some VOCs are carcinogenic. Closing containers after use and not storing excess materials reduces this problem.

Noise

Appliances and stereos can create noise levels that are unhealthy. Knowledge of this problem can easily lead to a solution.

 To learn more about indoor air quality, visit www.epa.gov/iaq.

QUESTIONS & TASKS

Record your responses in your science notebook.

1. Why should the quality of indoor air concern you? Give two reasons.

2. List seven indoor air pollutants and tell how each can be reduced.

15.5 Acid Precipitation

In recent years, much attention has been given to a form of regional air pollution known as acid rain. Natural rainfall is always slightly acidic. Strongly acidic rain, snow, or even fog can result from natural processes. They may also be the result of human-generated

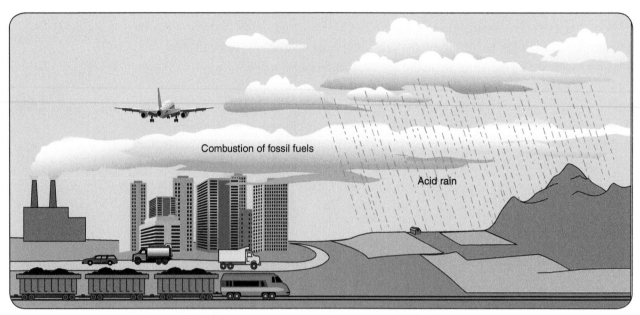

▲ FIGURE 15.15 Human-caused production of acid rain. (*Adapted from NCAR/NSF.*)

acid-forming chemicals combining with natural moisture in the troposphere. The term **acid deposition** is preferred because it refers to all forms of this kind of atmospheric pollution.

One of the unique aspects of acid deposition is that the effects can occur far from the sources of emission. Ironically, this kind of air pollution may have been made worse by efforts during the 1960s and 1970s to ease local air pollution by constructing tall smokestacks. Adding height to the outflow of these chemicals could have enhanced acid rainfall in distant places. Pollutants simply hitched a ride with local air masses that drifted downwind of the tall smokestacks. Thus, air pollution can occur in areas where there is no heavy industry (see Figure 15.15). Hundreds of kilometers downwind of industrial areas, some lakes in the eastern United States, Canada, and Sweden are so acidic that fish populations are very low or nonexistent. The next activity will introduce you to the concept of acidity and the pH scale.

Natural rainfall is slightly acidic because of the mixing of CO_2 and water droplets to form weak carbonic acid. Where does natural CO_2 come from?

ACTIVITY 15.3

Home Sweet Lab—Testing pH

In this activity, you will learn about the pH scale and relate it to **acid precipitation**.

Background

Acid precipitation is not new. It has been around since Earth had an atmosphere capable of forming weather. The carbon dioxide in our atmosphere combines with all forms of precipitation to produce a weak solution of carbonic acid according to this chemical equation:

$$H_2O + CO_2 \rightarrow H_2CO_3$$

Normally, rain tends to be acidic with a pH of 5.6 to 5.7. Any precipitation that has a pH less than 5.6 is considered abnormal, and is called *acidic precipitation*.

In 1978, for example, rain in Wheeling, West Virginia, had a measured pH of less than 2.0. Its acid content was approximately 5,000 times greater than normal rain! It was more acidic than household

Content Clue

pH is a measure of hydrogen ion (H^+) content in aqueous solutions. The greater the H^+ concentration, the more acidic the solution. The pH scale ranges from 1 (extremely acidic) to 14 (extremely basic). A pH of 7 is neutral (neither acidic nor basic).

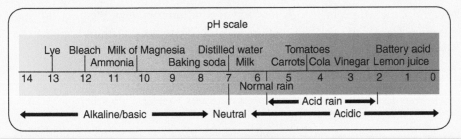

vinegar. Besides carbon dioxide, what can make the various forms of precipitation acidic? Other atmospheric substances such as the chemicals in the smoke and dust from volcanic eruptions and forest fires combine with moisture to produce acids. So do emissions from automobiles and industry.

> **Helpful Hint!**
>
> What are the chemicals that contribute to acid precipitation?

Oxides of nitrogen and sulfur (NO_x and SO_x) combine with water vapor and fall to Earth as acidic precipitation. We will examine these processes in Activity 15.4.

The pH scale is used to measure the degree of acidity (see Figure 15.16). This scale is based on the relative concentration of hydrogen ions in a solution. Hydrogen ions are hydrogen atoms that have lost their electrons (that is, bare protons). They are responsible for the acidic properties of acid solutions. On the pH scale, the highest level of acidity has a value of zero. The highest degree of alkalinity is 14. Distilled water, which is neutral, is neither acidic nor basic (alkaline). It has a pH of 7. The pH scale is logarithmic. Therefore, a solution that has a pH of 6 is 10 times more acidic than distilled water. A solution that has a pH of 8 is 10 times more basic (alkaline) than distilled water. Likewise, a solution that has a pH of 4 is 100 times more acidic than one with a pH of 6.

> **Helpful Hint!**
>
> The "p" in pH represents logarithmic; the "H" is the symbol for hydrogen.

Materials

- pH paper and color comparison charts
- baby food jars or 100-mL beakers (washed, and rinsed with distilled water)
- forceps or tweezers
- metric ruler
- common household solutions of the following:
  - orange juice
  - apple juice
  - baking soda (sodium bicarbonate) solution (5 mg/100 mL distilled water)
  - vinegar
  - tap water
  - distilled water
  - liquid detergent
  - bleach
  - lemon juice
  - ammonia
  - milk of magnesia
  - cranberry juice
  - river (pond) water
  - carbonated soft drink
- acid rain/snow melt
- safety goggles

Procedure

1. Your team will determine the pH of each of the solutions listed above, as well as the acid rain/snow melt. You will then use these data to make a pH chart with the solutions arranged from lowest pH to highest pH. Record your data in your science notebook.

2. Review these key points:
   - The pH scale ranges from 0 to 14 and is logarithmic.
   - Pure water is neutral at pH = 7.
   - Solutions with pH less than 7 are acidic; those with pH greater than 7 are basic (alkaline).

3. Using forceps, dip a small piece (2 cm) of pH paper into a solution. Remove it.

4. Immediately compare the color of the pH paper with the color chart. Determine the pH of the solution, and record the pH in a data table.

5. Repeat the test in steps 3 and 4 for each of the remaining solutions. Use a fresh piece of pH paper for each test.

6. Make a chart with the pH of the various solutions arranged from the lowest to the highest.

QUESTIONS & TASKS

Record your responses in your science notebook.

1. How do your team's pH values compare with those of two other teams?

2. Which of the household solutions had a pH closest to the pH of the acid rain/snow melt?

3. For which solution was there the greatest variation in pH? What do you think caused this variation?

EXTENSIONS

1. Compare the pH of rainwater collected early in a storm or shower with that of a sample collected at the end of the storm. What do you conclude?

2. Compare the pH measurements of storm water from various areas in your community. What do you conclude?

[Adapted from "Teacher's Resource Guide on Acidic Precipitation with Laboratory Activities," Lloyd H. Barrow, Land and Water Resources Center, University of Maine at Orono, 1983.]

ACTIVITY 15.4

Acid Rain—Just the Facts

In this activity, you will investigate how acid rain is produced. You will also speculate on how acid rain production and/or its effects might be reduced.

Background

Acid rain, which is more correctly called acid precipitation, is any precipitation with a high concentration of sulfuric and/or nitric acid. The acidity results when oxides of various nonmetallic elements combine with water vapor. This process may be understood as follows.

1. When many materials are burned or heated intensely in air, oxides are formed. Here are some typical reactions:

   a. The burning of gasoline:

   $$C_8H_{18} + 12.5O_2 \rightarrow 8CO_2 + 9H_2O$$

   gasoline   oxygen   carbon   water
   (octane)   dioxide

   b. The oxidation of sulfur when coal is burned:

   $$S + O_2 \rightarrow SO_2$$

   sulfur oxygen   sulfur
                  dioxide

   c. Nitrogen fixation in hot engines and furnaces:

   $$N_2 + O_2 \rightleftarrows 2NO$$

   nitrogen oxygen   nitric oxide

   d. The burning of phosphorus in an ample oxygen supply:

   $$P_4 + 5O_2 \rightarrow P_4O_{10}$$

   phosphorus oxygen   phosphoral
                       pentoxide

2. Nonmetallic oxides combine with water to form acids. Here are some typical reactions:

   $$H_2O + CO_2 \rightleftarrows H_2CO_3$$

   water   carbon   carbonic acid
          dioxide

   $$H_2O + SO_3{}^* \rightleftarrows H_2SO_4$$

   water   sulfur   sulfuric acid
          dioxide

   $$H_2O + 3NO_2{}^* \rightleftarrows 2HNO_3 + NO$$

   water nitrogen   nitric   nitric
         dioxide   acid   oxide

   $$6H_2O + P_4O_{10} \rightleftarrows 4H_3PO_4$$

   water phosphorus   phosphoric
       pentoxide   acid

3. An *indicator* is a substance that shows the presence of a chemical by changing color. Bromthymol blue (BTB) is an indicator that is green or yellow in the presence of an acid. It is blue in the presence of a base. BTB will be the indicator used in this lab.

Helpful Hint!

*See Figure 15.20 at the end of this activity to see how SO_2 becomes SO_3 and how NO becomes NO_2 in the atmosphere.

Content Clue

A base may be considered the opposite of an acid. That is, bases neutralize acids. They can nullify their effect.

4. Buffers are naturally occurring chemicals that can neutralize the effects of acid precipitation. This is especially true where soils or bedrock contain abundant calcium carbonate in the form of limestone. In areas that lack buffering capacity, lakes can be "limed." This increases their ability to neutralize the effects of acid precipitation.

Helpful Hint!

green or yellow (acid) $\underset{}{\overset{\textbf{BTB}}{\rightleftarrows}}$ blue (base)

Materials

- 100 mL distilled or tap water
- dropper bottle, 1.0M acetic acid
- dropper bottle, limewater
- dropper bottle, 1.0M NH_4OH
- dropper bottle, BTB

- "strike-anywhere" kitchen match
- 4 baby food jars
- 2 lids
- graduated cylinder, 50-mL
- straw
- masking tape and ballpoint pen (to make labels)
- safety goggles

Procedure

1. Use masking tape to label 4 baby food jars as shown in Figure 15.17 (A, B, C, D).

2. Reproduce the table in Figure 15.18 in your science notebook.

3. Place 25 milliliters (mL) distilled or tap water in each jar.

4. Add 4 drops of BTB to the water in each jar.

5. Record the color of the solution in each jar in your data table.

6. Add 2 drops of 1.0M acetic acid to jar A. Swirl, and note and record the color of the resulting solution.

7. Add 2 drops of 1.0M NH_4OH (ammonium hydroxide) to jar B. NH_4OH is a weak base that is commonly used as a cleaning solution. Swirl, and note and record the color of the resulting solution.

BE SAFE

Wear safety goggles when working with chemicals. Use care when striking matches.

▼ FIGURE 15.17 Label jars for testing.

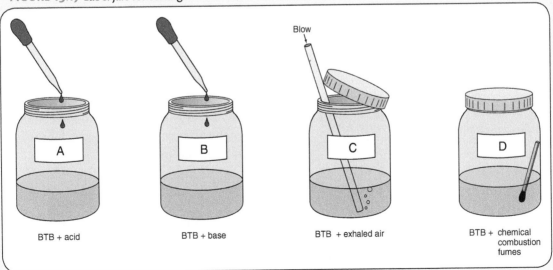

BTB + acid

BTB + base

Blow

BTB + exhaled air

BTB + chemical combustion fumes

▼ FIGURE 15.18 Sample data table for recording test results.

Jar	Color of Water + BTB	Component Added	Color after Requested Change	Color after Limewater Added
A		Acetic acid		✕
B		Ammonium hydroxide (base)		✕
C		Human breath		
D		Match head combustion fumes		

8. Carefully blow exhaled air through a straw into the solution in jar C. Place the lid partially over the jar opening to prevent splashing (see Figure 15.17). After about 1 minute (min) of bubbling, record the color of the resulting solution in the table.

BE SAFE

Be careful not to suck up any solution through the straw.

9. Light a match and *immediately* thrust it into jar D. The goal here is to have almost all the original combustion of the chemicals occur in the air above the water in the jar. Quickly place the lid on the jar, and then swirl the water around so it can interact with the combustion fumes. Record the color of the resulting solution in the table. The major chemical compounds in the match head are shown in Figure 15.19.

Content Clue

The combustion fumes in a match contain chemicals similar to the chemicals in the fumes released by some industrial processes.

► FIGURE 15.19 "Strike-anywhere" match showing the location of chemicals involved in combustion.

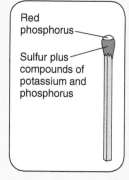

Red phosphorus

Sulfur plus compounds of potassium and phosphorus

10. Add limewater to jars C and D, drop by drop, until there is a color change. Record the resulting color in the table.

11. Clean up your lab station as instructed.

Content Clue

Lime (CaO) is a common chemical. It reacts with water to form slaked lime [CaO + H_2O → $Ca(OH)_2$]. Thus, limewater is a base.

QUESTIONS & TASKS

Record your responses in your science notebook.

1. What color is BTB in the presence of an acid? What color is BTB in the presence of a base?

2. What forms when the oxides of various nonmetallic elements are dissolved in water?

3. Why is an acid produced when exhaled air is bubbled in water?

4. Use your answer to question 3 to explain why natural rainwater is slightly acidic.

5. Why did the fumes from the burning match head cause the water to become acidic?

6. Why is lime sometimes added to lakes that are threatened with acid rain?

7. Acid rain is associated with the combustion of high sulfur coal. List three or four ways of attacking this problem.

8. Nitrogen oxides are formed in engines and furnaces that burn very hot. List three or four ways that nitrogen oxides might be reduced.

Formation of Sulfuric Acid

Step 1.   The oxidation of sulfur when coal is burned:
$$S + O_2 \rightleftarrows SO_2$$

Step 2.   Further oxidation in the atmosphere:
$$SO_2 + 1/2O_2 \rightleftarrows SO_3 \text{ (oxgyen donated by ozone)}$$

Step 3.   Combination with water vapor to form acid:
$$SO_3 + H_2O \rightleftarrows H_2SO_4 \text{ (sulfuric acid)}$$

Formation of Nitric Acid

Step 1.   Nitrogen fixation in hot engines and furnaces:
$$N_2 + O_2 \rightleftarrows 2NO$$

Step 2.   Further oxidation in the atmosphere:
$$NO + 1/2O_2 \rightleftarrows NO_2 \text{ (oxgyen donated by ozone)}$$

Step 3.   Combination with water vapor to form nitric acid and more NO:
$$3NO_2 + H_2O \rightleftarrows 2HNO_3 \text{ (nitric acid)} + NO$$

▲ FIGURE 15.20 Explain how SO_2 becomes SO_3 and how NO becomes NO_2 in the atmosphere.

15.6 The Effects of Acid Precipitation

Until now, we have looked mostly at the details of what causes acid precipitation. Most scientists agree that acid precipitation is initiated when sulfur and nitrogen oxides (SO_x and NO_x) are released as pollution by-products from the combustion of fossil fuels for industry, electricity generation, and transportation. Once airborne, these acid-forming chemicals combine with water to form sulfuric (H_2SO_4) and nitric (HNO_3) acids. These chemicals may be carried thousands of miles away by large air masses before being deposited in freshwater ecosystems or into the soil. At this point, the chemistry of ecosystems can be altered depending on the concentration of the acid precipitation, the nature of the soil or surface waters, or the kinds of vegetation present in the affected areas.

What happens once these chemicals are deposited? The effects of acid rain are not as clear-cut as you might think. There have been instances of lakes so acidic that the lowered pH has caused increases in dissolved aluminum. This has rendered the lakes devoid of life (see Figure 15.21). Some mountaintop clouds are so polluted that they bathe entire forests in acid fog, changing green forests to stands of dying trees.

Apply Your Understanding

Often, we learn that environmental damage is a simple matter of cause and effect. What factors or variables complicate the causal connection between acid rain and damaged ecosystems?

► FIGURE 15.21 Lake Colden is located high in the Adirondack Mountains of northern New York. It is part of the headwaters of the Hudson River. Its water has an average pH value of 5. No fish live in the lake. It is generally believed that acid rain is a contributing factor. The acidic soil and rock, along with other natural occurrences, also contribute to the lake's unique biology. As a result, fish may not have existed in the lake as far back as 1918 (or further). The cause is a complex issue. *(Photo courtesy of Robert Marrone.)*

It is important to remember that not all problems are caused by humans. Unpolluted rain is already slightly acidic. It is made even more so by the periodic addition of acid-forming chemicals from natural forest fires, dust storms, and volcanic eruptions. What's more, many *natural* diseases suffered by fish or other organisms simply resemble (and are not caused by) the effects of acid poisoning.

In recent years, much research has been conducted on the effects of acid precipitation on biologic systems—notably the Appalachian forests of New England and Mid-Atlantic states. A 10-year study called the National Acid Precipitation Assessment Program (NAPAP) found that while acid rain may be harming some lakes and trees, the problem is *much smaller* than is generally believed.

Continued research is important because the effects of acidic precipitation on plant life are not understood as well as the effects on aquatic ecosystems. Some studies have found that acidic precipitation destroys the waxy surfaces on leaves and interferes with transpiration and gas exchange. It poisons the plants via their transport systems, which results in a lower capacity for photosynthesis. It destroys root hairs, and it decreases the percentage of seeds that germinate. The next activity will give you an opportunity to replicate a study used to evaluate the effects of acid precipitation on terrestrial ecosystems.

Effects of Acid Precipitation on Plants

In this activity, you will investigate the effects of acid precipitation on plants.

Background

The pH range for optimum growing conditions for plants varies. Examples for some common plants are shown below.

Plant	Optimum pH
Alfalfa	6.0–7.0
Bean	6.0–7.0
Carrot	5.5–6.5
Dandelion	6.0–8.0
Lettuce	6.0–7.0
Oak	6.0–7.0
Pine	5.0–6.0
Radish	6.0–8.0

Acid precipitation can influence the growth of plants. It can also cause certain minerals (sodium, phosphorus, potassium, magnesium, and calcium) to be leached or carried away from the soil. These minerals can be transported into the aquatic environment, influencing organisms there. Acids can also dissolve metals such as aluminum, manganese, iron, mercury, cadmium, and lead. This makes these metals more soluble and more easily absorbed by plant roots. Experiments have also shown that acidic precipitation kills the microorganisms that decompose plant litter. Nitrogen-fixing bacteria are also destroyed by lower pH.

Surprisingly, growth rates for some plants are improved by acidic precipitation. Dilute nitric acid, for example, can "fertilize" some varieties of plants by adding nitrogen to the soil. Dilute sulfuric acid can also promote plant growth if the soil is deficient in the trace element sulfur. However, too much nitrogen and/or sulfur can cause negative results.

Materials (for each team)

- vermiculite or potting soil
- leaves of coleus, begonia, or African violet
- tap water
- graduated cylinder
- pH paper
- 3 jars with lids
- 3 jars or cups
- distilled water
- acid rain/snow melt
- 30-cm ruler

Procedure

1. Read through the procedure steps quickly. Use your understanding of the activity to design a data table in your science notebook to record all the information you will collect.

2. Determine the pH of the distilled water, tap water, and acid rain/snow melt. Record these pH numbers in your data table. Keep these containers covered and labeled.

3. Obtain 3 jars or cups for your team. Label them as follows:
   Jar 1-distilled water
   Jar 2-tap water
   Jar 3-acid rain/snow melt

4. "Pot" 3 leaves of the plant provided, 1 in each jar. Make sure that you use the same type and amount of soil (or vermiculite).

5. Place all 3 containers so that the leaves will be at the same temperature and receive equal amounts of sunlight.

6. Keep a daily record of the amount of water you add to each plant.

7. Check for the growth of roots on each leaf. Write a description or draw a picture of the roots at various stages of growth. Measure the root length in millimeters (mm). Record all measurements in your data table.

Record your responses in your science notebook.

1. Which of the three jars was the experimental control?

2. In which jar did the roots appear to grow fastest? What was the corresponding pH of this potting?

3. In which jar did the roots appear to grow the slowest? What was the corresponding pH of this potting?

4. Based on the results of your experiment, what pH range would you recommend for starting plant cuttings of the type your team used? Why?

5. How do you think the "acid precipitation" that your team used influenced the growth of your plants?

Extensions

1. Hypothesize which pH—3, 4, 5, 6, 8, 9, or 10—will cause roots of your plant to grow the fastest. Design an experiment to test your hypothesis. Share your design with your teacher.

2. Repeat the laboratory experiment with leaves of a different plant.

[Adapted from "Teacher's Resource Guide on Acidic Precipitation with Laboratory Activities," Lloyd H. Barrow, Land and Water Resources Center, University of Maine at Orono, 1983.]

15.7 Strategies for Reducing Air Pollution
A. Our Love Affair with Vehicles

Think about This!

Who is responsible for creating the "acid rain problem"?

Topic: air pollution reduction
Go to: www.scilinks.org
Code: GloSci7e580

Who is to blame for acid precipitation? Coal-fired electric power plants and industrial sites upwind of sensitive ecosystems may be part of the problem. What about other source areas that are not centers of industry and power production? Everyone who drives an automobile contributes to the acid rain problem. Yet many of us will rally to fight pollution coming only from power plants and industrial sources. Why?

We see the pollution problem in a whole new light when it comes to automobiles. We Americans love our vehicles. Freedom, independence, power, prestige, and individual worth are often tied to a person's vehicle. Moreover, the price of fuel has remained so low (relative to other commodities) that the incentive to conserve fuel is low. These are among the many reasons it has been so difficult to expand mass transit, ride-sharing, or any other alternative mode of transportation in most areas. Only in cities where cars have led to great problems are people willing to use other ways of getting around. Times are changing!

This dependence on the automobile must be seriously considered if any attempt to reduce emissions from automobiles is to be successful. Two general approaches are promising. They revolve around (1) improving automobiles and fuels and (2) making driving less convenient and more expensive. Strategies include the eight ideas discussed below.

Apply Your Understanding

What did you discover and conclude in Activity 12.2, Fuel Efficiency vs. Weight?

1. Improved Automobile Efficiency

Decreasing the total mass of the car is one of the most effective ways to improve fuel efficiency. Composite bodies (plastic and fibers), coupled with hybrid engines, may soon result in many automobiles that give from 40–60 miles per gallon or more. A few cars with mileage ratings in this range exist today. Fuel efficiency standards can also be raised.

2. Improved Fuels

We can develop cleaner-burning fuels for the internal combustion engine. Oxygenated fuels, which have oxygen built into them, reduce carbon monoxide emissions. When burned, they give off more CO_2 and less CO. Likewise, plant-based alcohol fuels add little CO_2 to the atmosphere in the long run. Photosynthesis by new plants can use the CO_2 produced by burning alcohol. Also, hydrogen may become an automotive fuel.

Think about This!

Do alcohol-based fuels contain oxygen in their molecules?

3. Lowered Emissions

Afterburners and the catalytic converter help control emissions from today's internal combustion engines. The catalytic converter oxidizes carbon monoxide to carbon dioxide, and unburned hydrocarbons to carbon dioxide and water. Catalytic converters can also break down NO_X into N_2 and O_2 gas (see Figure 15.22).

4. Smaller Vehicles

Small, quiet, and efficient electric cars and trucks for urban use would allow freedom of movement and greatly reduce transportation pollutants. Excellent batteries are available now. But light, small, and tough bodies need to be designed and built with well-known composites that will not contribute new pollutants.

Think about This!

What is a ceramic engine? Why do you think this would be an improvement?

5. Improved Engines

The internal combustion engine can be modified to lower emissions and improve gasoline mileage. A variety of new engine designs are being tested. This includes ceramic engines.

6. Special Traffic Lanes and Mass Transit

Designate fast lanes for buses and high-occupancy vehicles (HOVs) for use during rush hours. This would make driving alone less appealing.

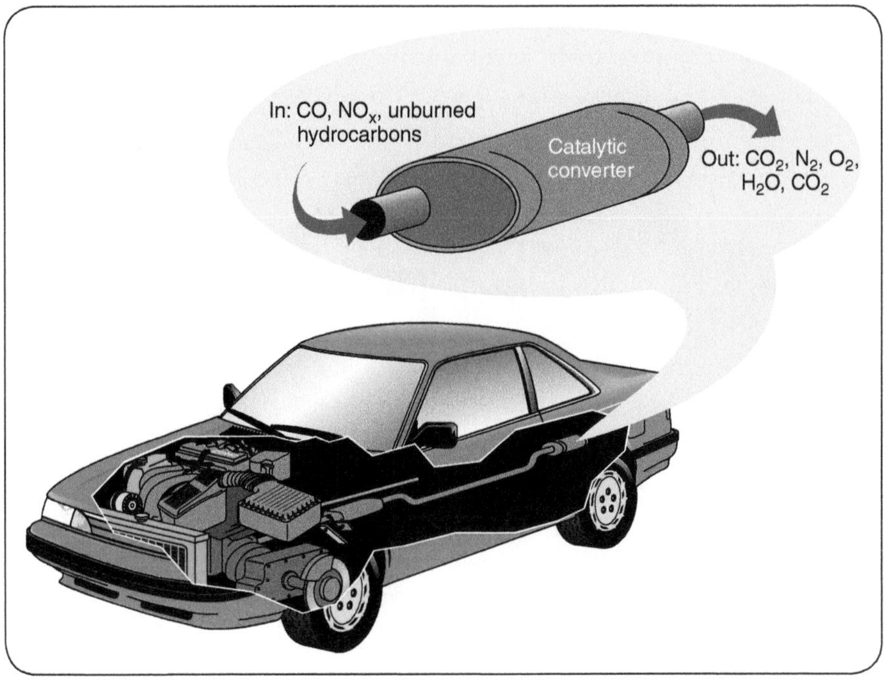

Think about This!

Are there special traffic lanes and/or mass transit options where you live? How could you find out if they are well used?

In: CO, NO_X, unburned hydrocarbons

Catalytic converter

Out: CO_2, N_2, O_2, H_2O, CO_2

◀ FIGURE 15.22 A catalytic converter changes engine exhausts into harmless carbon dioxide, nitrogen, oxygen, and water.

7. Increased Automobile Costs

The cost of operating an automobile can be increased by raising the tax on gasoline. Also, motorists could be charged a fee for entering certain areas during rush hour. The cost of parking downtown might be increased as well. As demand for gasoline rises, so does cost.

8. Transit-Oriented Design (TOD)

In response to traffic gridlock, urban sprawl, and disconnected land use, many cities are implementing transit-oriented design. This means their mass transit systems include sustainable communities where rail lines are or will be placed. These communities have civic plazas near train entrances, pleasant walking areas, diverse (including affordable) housing, and compactness (high density). To build a commitment to the transit system, parking is limited.

B. Reducing Smokestack Emissions

The most striking success in controlling pollution from autos and industry has been in the reduction of particulate emissions. This visible residue—unburned carbon (soot), mineral ash, and particles of tar—is what gives the blackness to smoke.

Because coal is the preferred fuel for electric power plants, emissions from the plants have been a problem. Today, several processes are available for attacking the problem. For example, a baghouse filter can remove up to 99.9 percent of the particles, including the fine ones. A **baghouse** might be likened to a building-size vacuum cleaner. Exhaust gases are forced through fiber bag filters before the gases escape into the environment (see Figure 15.23).

Sulfur dioxide cannot be removed by the baghouse or by other filtration devices. For that reason, the **wet scrubber** is used (see Figure 15.24). The scrubber forces stack gases through a chemical spray that absorbs SO_2. Scrubbers remove up to 99.5 percent of the particles and 80–90 percent of the SO_2. However, they are extremely expensive to build and maintain.

Think about This!

Are the costs of using a vehicle increasing where you live? If so, how?

Think about This!

What are some of the attractions of the TOD? Are there any drawbacks?

Apply Your Understanding

Name four strategies that reduce stack emissions at power plants.

▶ FIGURE 15.23 In a baghouse, the dirty air is carried by pipe to the sides of the hoppers. From there, the air passes up, into, and through the filter bags, and exits, clean, through vents in the walls and roof. (The cleaned air might also be vented through a stack.) The dirt trapped by the bags is periodically shaken into the hoppers, where it can be removed. (*American Lung Association*)

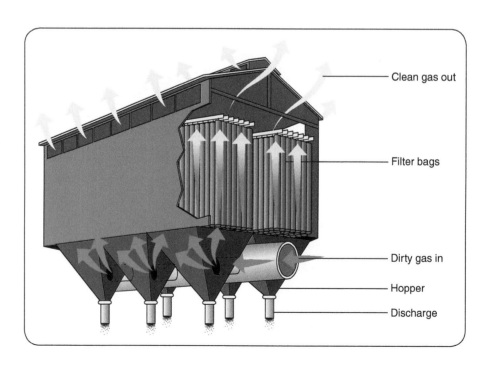

- Clean gas out
- Filter bags
- Dirty gas in
- Hopper
- Discharge

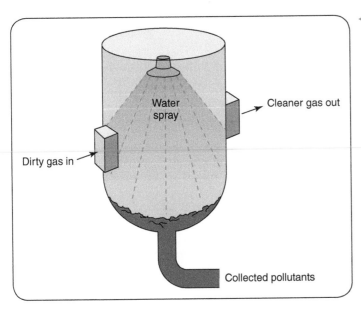

Low-sulfur coals, like those found primarily in the western United States, can be readily dry scrubbed. This process is well advanced and is economically feasible. Dry scrubbing is always combined with baghouse filtering.

A major source of sulfur pollution is the sulfur impurity in coal. The most logical thing to do is to remove the sulfur from the coal before the coal is burned. Although some sulfur compounds can be removed by routine washing, most resist such simple removal. One of the advantages of coal gasification and liquefaction is the removal of sulfur before the gaseous or liquid fuels are formed.

Burning coal in the newer fluidized-bed furnaces also has advantages for similar reasons. Crushed calcium carbonate or limestone ($CaCO_3$) is added to the coal in the furnace, and the sulfur is removed as calcium sulfate ($CaSO_4$).

The next activity introduces you to yet another device that helps remove particulates from coal emissions.

 ## ACTIVITY 15.6

Charge It! For Cleaner Air

In this activity, you will examine the **electrostatic precipitator**—a technology used by coal-fired power plants to clean stack emissions. You will do this by first discovering some of the fundamental properties of electric charges by experimenting with some easily charged objects.

Materials (for each team)

- 2 ringstands with crossbar
- wool cloth (the softer cloth)
- cotton cloth (the coarser cloth)
- 2 strips of cellulose acetate (a clear plastic)
- 2 strips of vinylite (a milky white plastic)
- collection of easily charged objects, including a plastic ruler, balloons, and comb (also, a hard rubber rod and cat's fur, if available)
- masking tape
- *Electrostatic precipitator* handout

Procedure

Part A: What are some of the fundamental properties of electric charges?

1. Using short lengths of masking tape, hang a strip of cellulose acetate from the cross-bar of a ringstand so the plastic strip can swing freely without twisting (see Figure 15.25). Do the same with a second ringstand and a strip of vinylite.

Helpful Hint!

Work through this activity by following instructions from your teacher. Record all answers to questions in your science notebook.

▼ **FIGURE 15.25** Ringstand apparatus with vinylite or cellulose acetate strip.

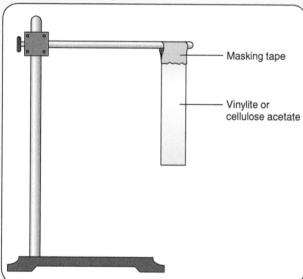

— Masking tape

— Vinylite or cellulose acetate

2. Briskly rub the vinylite strip with a dry woolen cloth.

3. Briskly rub the acetate strip with a dry cotton cloth. Do not touch the rubbed surfaces.

4. Rub another vinylite strip with wool, and bring it near each of the suspended strips. What do you conclude from the results?

5. Now rub another strip of acetate with cotton, and bring it near the hanging strips. What do you infer?

6. Recharge the hanging acetate strip by rubbing it with cotton. Stretch the cotton by grasping it at both ends, and hold it near the acetate. What do you conclude?

7. Have you found 1, 2, or 3 kinds of charge?

8. Do charges have to touch to influence each other?

9. Rub a comb, plastic ruler, balloon, or other objects that charge easily on your clothes. Observe the effect of these objects on the 2 suspended pieces of plastic.

10. What charges did you detect? Record your findings in your science notebook.

Content Clue

Ben Franklin established the names of all electric charges by stating that a hard rubber rod rubbed with cat's fur takes on a negative charge. Thus, anything attracted to the rod is positive; anything repelled by it is negative.

QUESTIONS & TASKS

Record your responses in your science notebook. Some items require you to add the missing word or words. DO NOT WRITE IN THIS BOOK.

1. What charges does cellulose acetate gain when rubbed with cotton?

2. What charge does vinylite gain when rubbed with wool?

3. Like charges _____.

4. Unlike charges _____.

5. When dissimilar materials are rubbed together, they become _____ charged.

6. There appear to be only _____ kinds of charge.

7. Electric charges (do, do not) have to touch to influence each other. Hence, an/a _____ exists around an _____ _____ electric charge. (See box for hint.)

8. List the objects rubbed and the charge detected on each object. It appears that many objects show _____ when rubbed against dissimilar materials.

Content Clue

Scientists have never proven in some cosmic sense that there are only two kinds of electric charge. They simply have never found evidence that there are more than two kinds. An electric field is a region in space in which an electric charge experiences a force on itself if placed there.

Part B: How does an electrostatic precipitator work?

The numbered paragraphs that follow describe how an electrostatic precipitator works. Write the paragraph numbers in the empty circles on the *Electrostatic Precipitator* handout. DO NOT WRITE IN THIS BOOK. In each case, select the circle that is located

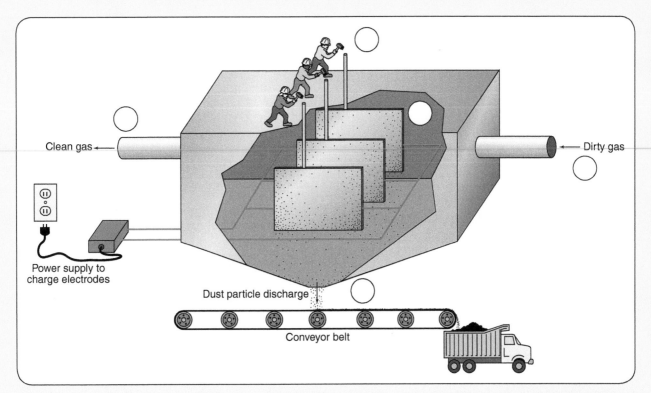

Clean gas

Dirty gas

Power supply to
charge electrodes

Dust particle discharge

Conveyor belt

▲FIGURE 15.26 Electrostatic precipitator.

by the portion of the precipitator that is being described.

1. The basic properties of electric charges examined in Part A are used to make an electrostatic precipitator function. The main component of an electrostatic precipitator is a series of charged metal plates. These, in turn, have a series of highly charged wire electrodes in the space between the plates. The plates (because they are grounded) are charged opposite from the charge on the electrodes. This arrangement produces a strong electric field in the space between the plates.

2. Dirty stack gases are blown into the precipitator. The particulates enter the strong electric field in the space between the plates and become charged with the charge on the electrodes. This means the particulates are charged opposite to the charge that is on the plates. As a result, the particulates are attracted to and cling to the plates.

3. The metal plates are periodically rapped with small hammer-type mechanisms. This causes the plates to vibrate, and solid ash slides off the plates and into a collection hopper.

4. The collection hopper is opened periodically to allow the ash to fall onto a conveyor belt. The conveyor belt carries the ash to trucks, which haul it away for disposal or for recycling into some useful product. Fly ash is a component of certain types of concrete.

5. When functioning properly, electrostatic precipitators can remove up to 99 percent of the particulates, thereby changing a dirty effluent into a visibly clean one.

Despite all the problems in burning coal, the last 30 years has brought new cleanup technologies that are reducing sulfur dioxide emissions. These improvements, however, have not affected a more troublesome emission: waste carbon dioxide gas. The implications of this will be discussed in the next section.

Thunderstorms and Tornadoes

Thunderstorms are small-area storms formed by the upward movement of warm, moist air. They always produce lightning and thunder, and they usually produce rain. A severe thunderstorm is one that produces hail ¾ inch in diameter or larger, and/or wind gusts of 58 mph or more.

All thunderstorms, whether or not they become severe, proceed through a three-stage life cycle (see Figure 15.27). Stage 1 is the cumulus stage where development begins. The storm consists only of upward-moving air currents. Towering cumulus (heap-type) clouds develop as water vapor condenses and droplets form. Heat energy is released in the process. Stage 2 is the mature stage. This is the strongest and most dangerous stage. The storm contains both updraft and downdraft areas. Precipitation occurs in the downdraft areas. When the cool downdraft hits the ground, it spreads out and forms a gust front that may include damaging winds. At the top of the storm, the updraft decelerates and clouds spread out and form an anvil. Stage 3, the final stage, is the dissipation stage. Eventually,

excessive precipitation and downdraft weaken the updraft. This weakens the inflow of energy into the storm, causing it to die out.

Tornadoes are the most violent of all storms. They are much more frequent in the United States than anywhere else on Earth. They are most frequent in the Mississippi River valley and on the Great Plains. The conditions that produce strong thunderstorms can also produce tornadoes. A tornado is a violently rotating column of air attached to a thunderstorm and in contact with the ground (see Figure 15.28). Tornadoes are also associated with hurricanes that make landfall.

The strength of tornadoes varies greatly. The winds can exceed 300 miles per hour or about 480 kilometers (km) per hour. These winds can lift cattle, automobiles, and sheds into the air, and destroy almost everything in their path. Fortunately, most tornadoes are not this powerful. The damage path is usually less than 1,600 feet (ft) or 480 meters (m) wide. The storm and related tornado usually move along the ground at speeds less than 35 miles (about 55 km) per hour.

▼ FIGURE 15.27 Three stages of a thunderstorm. *(Diagram by Cameron Douglas Craig.)*

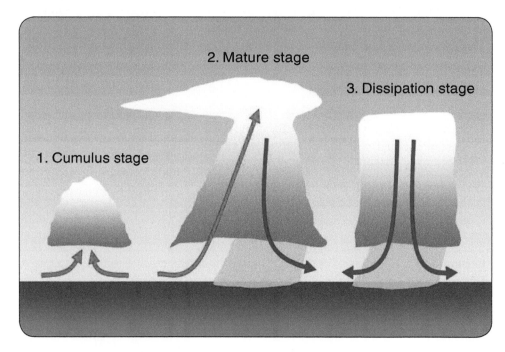

1. Cumulus stage

2. Mature stage

3. Dissipation stage

◀ FIGURE 15.28 This tornado struck south of Dimmitt, Texas, on June 2, 1995. (NOAA Photo Library, NOAA Central Library; OAR/ERL/National Severe Storms Laboratory [NSSL])

Tornado paths are usually less than 18 miles (about 30 km) long. They pass in a few seconds with a roar like that of a passing train. They are accompanied by heavy rain, lightning, and hail.

Because both lightning and tornadoes can be deadly, it is important to take precautions. Examine and memorize the safety cautions in Figure 15.29.

 To learn more about tornadoes, go to www.noaa.gov/tornadoes.html.

▼ FIGURE 15.29 Remember these safety cautions! They will help you to stay safe during a tornado or lightning.

CAUTIONS: Lightning

1. Go indoors if possible.

2. If traveling, stay in your car.

3. If outdoors, do not stand near high objects or be the highest object. Crouch down.

4. If swimming, get out of the water. If in a boat, go to shore.

5. If indoors, stay away from open doors, windows, and metal objects.

6. Do not use the phone or plug-in appliances.

CAUTIONS: Tornadoes

1. Keep an eye on the sky during a thunderstorm. Know where the best tornado shelter area is in your home. Keep a battery-powered radio in this area. This area will be in the basement or an interior room on the lowest level.

2. Stay away from outside walls, windows, and doors. If possible, get under a heavy table or mattress.

3. In a public place, go to the designated shelter area or sit close to an interior wall on the lowest level.

4. Get away from mobile homes and vehicles.

5. If outside, look for a ravine or ditch. Lie flat and protect your head with your arms.

Climate Change

15.8 The Greenhouse Effect

Climate refers to the average weather (including seasonal variations), either locally, regionally, or globally. Over time, Earth's climate has changed dramatically. Eighteen thousand years ago, our planet was still gripped in a global ice age climate. Mile-thick ice covered New England. Occasional snow dusted even the most tropical islands. Today, we are slowly warming as Earth recovers from this deep freeze. The thick glaciers that still cling to parts of Northern Europe, Asia, and North America are mere remnants of Earth's most recent climate shift (see Figure 15.30). The long-term balance of energy of Earth and its atmosphere control this complex ebb and flow of change. The question is not whether we are experiencing climate change; the question is, are humans influencing this change?

Carbon dioxide (along with clouds, water vapor, and other trace gases) keep Earth's climate warm and temperate. This **greenhouse effect** is vital for our survival. Without

▶ FIGURE 15.30 The Qori Kalis glacier in the Peruvian Andes in 1978 and in 2002. The lake began to form in 1991. It is now more than 200 ft deep (60 m) and covers more than 84 acres (34 hectares). (Photos: Lonnie G. Thompson, The Ohio State University, 1978 and 2002.)

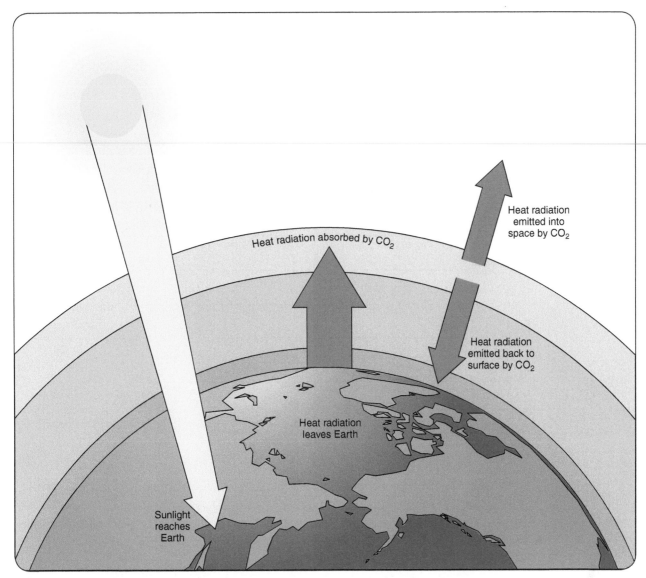

▲ FIGURE 15.31 The greenhouse effect. (*Copyright University Corporation for Atmospheric Research.*)

heat trapping gases, our planet would be frigid and lifeless. How does the greenhouse effect work?

Greenhouse gas molecules allow the passage of visible and ultraviolet radiation from incoming sunlight. But they absorb the longer wavelength infrared (heat) radiated from the warm Earth. This traps heat in the atmosphere. This effect is similar to the heat buildup in a greenhouse or in a car with the windows closed (see Figure 15.31).

When fossil fuels are burned, carbon dioxide (CO_2) is released into the air. Unmined coal, crude oil, natural gas, oil shale, and tar sand deposits represent potential energy for powering future machines. They also represent billions and billions of future carbon dioxide molecules that are not in the atmosphere at the present time. Since burning is oxidation of carbon, burning carbon-containing fuel produces carbon dioxide. At present, fossil fuels are our primary source of energy. Burning them is the major energy conversion process. What are the implications of releasing all that carbon dioxide?

The carbon dioxide content of the atmosphere has increased since the Industrial Revolution. We know this because analysis of air bubbles trapped in glaciers preceding the late 1700s and early 1800s reveal lower concentrations of atmospheric carbon dioxide than later years.

Content Clue

Use Figure 15.31 to explain the greenhouse effect.

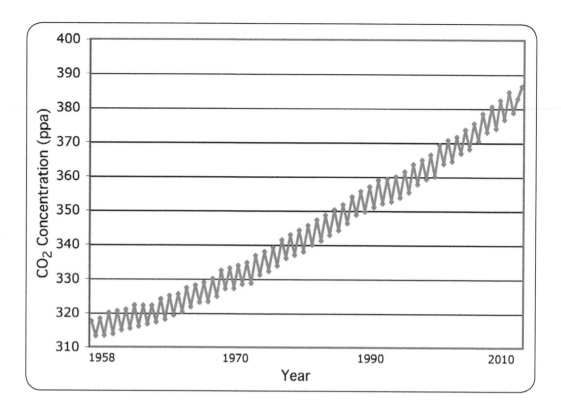

▶FIGURE 15.32 CO_2 concentration at Mauna Loa, Hawaii, 1958–2010. The spiky nature of the curve reflects uptake of CO_2 during spring and summertime in the Northern Hemisphere. What might cause global CO_2 to drop during the growing season? *(Dave Keeling and Tim Whorf—Scripps Institution of Oceanography.)*

Apply Your Understanding

Why do the points on the graph in Figure 15.32 move up and down each year?

More recent measurements from the Mauna Loa Observatory in Hawaii provide a continuous record of the changing CO_2 content of Earth's atmosphere. That record is illustrated in Figure 15.32.

Plants help control the amount of CO_2 in the atmosphere by using it for photosynthesis. Animals and humans breathe in oxygen and exhale CO_2. Plants use the CO_2 and give off oxygen. It is essential to maintain plant growth to balance the effects of animal and human populations. This rhythm of gas exchange is clearly shown in Figure 15.32. More CO_2 is produced in the winter and less in the summer.

 ## ACTIVITY 15.7

The Greenhouse Effect Model

In this activity, you will build a model to simulate the greenhouse effect. You will use the model to generate data, and then analyze and interpret the data. The data will help you judge the validity of the model. You will wrap up the activity by applying knowledge of the greenhouse effect to possible behavior modification on both a societal and an individual level.

Materials (for each team)

- 1 shoebox

- dark-colored soil (enough to fill the shoebox to a depth of 2–3 cm)

- clamp lamp with reflector— attached to a large ringstand

- 100W or 150W incandescent bulb (clear)

Helpful Hint!

Half of the class will complete the lab with boxes that have a plastic wrap that covers the top. The other half will set up boxes that are open at the top. Gather the materials appropriate to your group.

- 1 thermometer, 15 cm (−10°C to 110°C)
- graph paper (1 sheet per student)
- colored pencils
- watch or clock with second hand
- clear plastic wrap and masking tape (for covered-box group)
- metric ruler
- cardboard stand (see Figure 15.33)

Procedure

1. Set up a lab station as shown in Figure 15.33.

   a. Fill a shoebox with dark soil to a depth of 2–3 centimeters (cm).

   b. Place a thermometer in each box. Prop up the thermometer on a cardboard stand so that the bulb is facing upward. Make sure you can read the thermometer from above.

   c. Cover the box with clear plastic wrap. Secure the wrap with masking tape.

2. Put the box in the sun or under a light. If the box is placed under a light, the light source

   Helpful Hint!

   Only half the class will cover their boxes.

   must be exactly 25 cm above the exact center of the top of the box. In all cases, the light should shine on the thermometer bulb.

3. Reproduce the data tables like those shown in Figure 15.34 in your science notebook.

Helpful Hint!

You will exchange information with another group so you get a full set of data for both uncovered and covered boxes.

4. Turn on the lamp and take temperature readings every minute for 15 min. Record your temperatures on the data table. At the end of 15 min, turn off the light. Now take temperature readings every minute for 15 min as the surroundings cool.

5. Exchange data with another group to obtain data for the table you did not complete.

6. Plot a graph of temperature vs. time for each of these 2 situations. Plot both lines on the same graph to make comparison easier. Use a different color for each line.

QUESTIONS & TASKS

Record your responses in your science notebook.

1. In which trial did the greatest temperature change occur? Explain why this happened.

2. What does the plastic covering represent (or model) in this experiment?

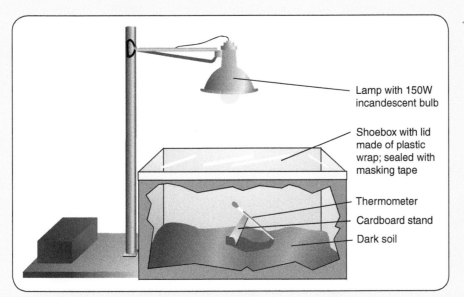

◀FIGURE 15.33 Lab station to simulate greenhouse effect.

Lamp with 150W incandescent bulb

Shoebox with lid made of plastic wrap; sealed with masking tape

Thermometer

Cardboard stand

Dark soil

With Clear Plastic Cover				Without Cover			
Light on		Light off		Light on		Light off	
Time (min)	Temp. (°C)	Time (min)	Temp. (°C)	Time (min)	Temp. (°C)	Time (min)	Temp. (°C)
0		16		0		16	
1		17		1		17	
2		18		2		18	
3		19		3		19	
4		20		4		20	
5		21		5		21	
6		22		6		22	
7		23		7		23	
8		24		8		24	
9		25		9		25	
10		26		10		26	
11		27		11		27	
12		28		12		28	
13		29		13		29	
14		30		14		30	
15		—	—	15		—	—

3. Compare your model to the global greenhouse effect by filling in this chart:

Model	(represents)	Earth
Light	→	Sun
Dark soil at bottom of box	→	
Air in the box	→	
Plastic covering	→	

4. This activity is based on a model. All models are imperfect. List two or three ways this model does not accurately simulate the global greenhouse effect.

5. Why are models used to simulate global heating or cooling?

6. What are the implications of relying solely on models to obtain hard scientific facts?

7. Some argue that more CO_2 in the air "fertilizes" trees and plants. Is this a valid argument? How can you tell?

8. List at least three things that can be done to slow the rate at which greenhouse gases are being added to Earth's atmosphere.

9. List at least three things *you* can do to reduce the increase in greenhouse gases.

10. Can any experiments be conducted safely on Earth's atmosphere directly? Why or why not?

[Adapted from *Understanding the Greenhouse Effect* © 1989 by Ward's Natural Science, P.O. Box 92912, Rochester, New York 14692. The adaptation was made primarily by Alan Sinnwell, science teacher, Weld Central Jr.-Sr. High School, Keenesburg, Colorado.]

15.9 The Climate Question

In recent years, earth scientists, policy makers, and industry experts have become entangled in a heated debate about Earth's climate. Is our planet's recent warming trend simply part of our long-term climate, or does it reflect human pollution in the form of excess greenhouse gases?

Let's look at some evidence. The globally averaged temperature of air at Earth's surface has warmed over the past century and a half (see Figure 15.35). Of the 12 warmest years on record, 11 occurred between 1995 and 2006. Other evidence of warming includes the rise in sea level of between 4 and 10 inches (10 and 25 cm), as well as the retreat of mountain glaciers in many areas. Beyond this recorded data, scientists now have measurements from tree rings, shallow ice cores, and corals. All point to the fact that today's global temperatures are now as warm or warmer than they were at any time in the past 600 years.

Satellite measurements, a relatively new source of data, have given climatologists other information about global temperature change. Initial observations begun in 1979 indicate that the upper troposphere has cooled slightly by about 0.1°C. This apparent cooling is something we need to continue to study.

Topic: global warming
Go to: www.scilinks.org
Code: GloSci7e593

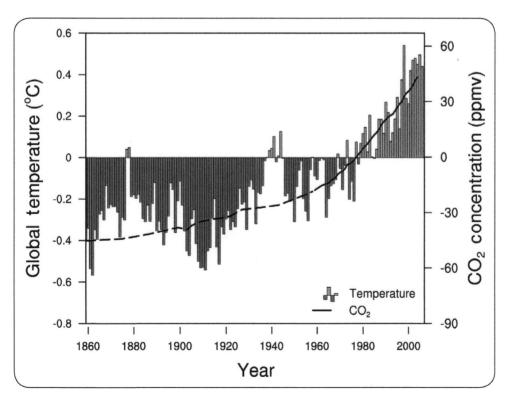

◄ FIGURE 15.35 Globally averaged temperature of the air at Earth's surface from 1860 to 2006. Temperatures are shown relative to the average for the 30-year period 1961 to 1990 (the horizontal line). The average temperature for that period was 14°C. Thus, 0.2 on the graph is 14.2°C. Also shown are CO_2 concentrations in ppmv. (Note: Sunspot cycles influence this graph.) *(Source: Climate Research Unit, School of Environmental Sciences, University of East Anglia, Norwich, UK)*

Greenhouse gases (GHGs) such as CO_2 are known to absorb Earth's re-radiated heat energy. Thus, we must look to see if recent trends in human-generated CO_2 emissions have any relationship with temperature changes over the same period. Recall that natural CO_2 is mainly the by-product of the burning and decay of organic material in nature. In contrast, the source of *added* CO_2 comes entirely from human activity. The burning of fossil fuels alone currently accounts for 80–85 percent of the CO_2 being added to the atmosphere. Land use changes account for about 15–20 percent of the excess CO_2.

Chlorofluorocarbons (CFCs) have also been shown to behave as greenhouse gases. CFCs have been used as refrigerants and for styrofoam. Until recently, they were also used as spray-can propellants. CFCs occupy a unique role as a greenhouse gas. They are entirely humanmade, so any attempts to curb their emissions will eventually bring their levels down.

Methane is another greenhouse gas. It occurs naturally as a by-product of decaying vegetation or from the activity of termites as they digest dead wood. Methane from agriculture is produced from livestock manure. Solid waste landfills are capable of producing large amounts of methane gas.

Water vapor is the most significant greenhouse gas. The amount of water vapor in the atmosphere, however, has not been significantly influenced by human activity.

Content Clue

CFCs, like CO_2, are greenhouse gases because they absorb infrared or heat energy that is radiated from Earth's surface.

ACTIVITY 15.8

CO_2 and Climate Trends: You Decide

In this activity, you will speculate on possible causes of climate change. You will also investigate possible relationships between global carbon dioxide measurements and global temperature readings.

Materials

- graph paper

Procedure

1. On graph paper, plot the CO_2 emissions data from Figure 15.36.

2. Then answer the questions that follow.

Year	CO_2 Emissions	Year	CO_2 Emissions
1860	0.3	1940	4.8
1870	0.5	1950	6.0
1880	0.9	1960	9.4
1890	1.3	1970	14.9
1900	2.0	1980	19.5
1910	3.0	1990	22.5
1920	3.4	2000	24.5
1930	3.9	2003	26.8

◄FIGURE 15.36 Table of CO_2 emissions (in billions of metric tons) from 1860 to 2003. (*Source: Carbon Dioxide Information Analysis Center. Oak Ridge National Laboratory. Oak Ridge, TN.*)

Content Clue

Global emissions of CO_2 reflected here come from the burning of fossil fuels, cement manufacture, and gas flaring.

Record your responses in your science notebook.

1. What are the main sources of CO_2 for this time period?

2. What accounts for the dramatic change in CO_2 emissions shown in your graph?

3. What is the total rise in CO_2 emissions over the past 60 years? What is the percentage rise?

4. What is the total rise in temperature over the past 100 years? Now calculate the rate of temperature change per year.

> **Helpful Hint!**
>
> Refer to Figure 15.35 to answer question 4.

5. Some scientists predict a temperature rise of 2°F–7°F (1°C–3.9°C) is enough to raise the sea level an additional 6–37 in (15–95 cm). Using the rate you calculated in question 4, how long would it take the sea to rise this distance?

> **Helpful Hint!**
>
> Time = distance ÷ rate.

6. What additional information would you want to have to understand these trends more fully?

7. List other greenhouse gases that could contribute to the increasing of global temperatures.

8. What additional data or proof would you need to establish human-generated CO_2 as the principal reason behind greenhouse warming?

> **Think about This!**
>
> Scientists, political leaders, and business executives will be debating these predictions for the next decade and beyond.

15.10 Carbon Sequestration—A Technical Fix

Most of the electricity used in the world today is generated at coal-fired power plants. If the CO_2 produced at these plants could be prevented from entering the atmosphere, there would be a large reduction in greenhouse gas emissions. **Carbon sequestration** is the capture and storage of CO_2 and other greenhouse gases that would otherwise be emitted to the atmosphere. Greenhouse gases can be captured at the point of emission, or they can be removed from the air. Captured gases can be used, or they can be stored in underground reservoirs, or possibly the deep oceans; absorbed by trees, grasses, soils, and algae; or converted to rocklike mineral carbonates or other products (see Figure 15.37).

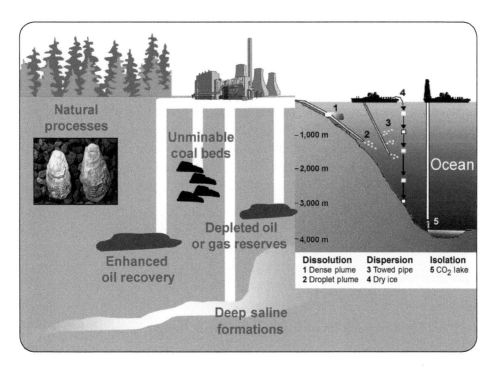

◀ FIGURE 15.37 Summary of carbon sequestration strategies. (*USDOE: National Energy Technology Laboratory*)

There are two types of sequestration: direct and indirect. Direct, or geologic, sequestration involves capturing CO_2 at a source before the CO_2 is emitted to the atmosphere. The most efficient concept uses specialized equipment to capture CO_2 at sources like factories or power plants. The CO_2 is then injected into storage zones deep underground or into the deep ocean. CO_2 that is injected into aging oil and gas wells helps push the remaining fuel out of hidden pockets for recovery. This could greatly reduce the cost of sequestration. Indirect, or terrestrial, sequestration involves removing CO_2 from the atmosphere. This type of sequestration uses land management practices that boost the ability of nature to remove CO_2 from the air. Opportunities for indirect sequestration can be found in forests, grasslands, wetlands, and croplands.

Helpful Hint!

A *carbon footprint* is a measure of one's impact on the environment.

Much research is being directed toward finding affordable and environmentally safe approaches to sequestration. New strategies could help countries reduce their carbon footprint without making more costly changes to their energy infrastructure. Questions to be answered include, Will the CO_2 migrate to the surface and leak out over time? Will the CO_2 contaminate local groundwater, deep freshwater aquifers, or the ocean's depths? Norway has become a leader in this field. Electric utilities are now building new power plants that gasify coal (Chapter 11), use cogeneration (Chapter 12), and sequester carbon dioxide.

15.11 The Debate about Our Future Climate

Think about This!

How should society deal with uncertainty in science?

Is CO_2 buildup the only possible explanation for global warming? Examining the references cited at the end of this chapter can help you learn more about this issue. Whatever conclusion you reach, we are still left with these critical questions: How much of this warming is natural and how much is human-induced? What, if any, action should we be taking to deal with potential changes to our future climate?

One of the most useful tools climatologists have for separating the causes of global change is the supercomputer. Since we can't perform experiments directly on our atmosphere, we use "cyber-earths" to model long-term changes such as temperature, vegetation, and trends in greenhouse gases. Other factors involved include variations in solar radiation received, effects of volcanic eruptions, and the concentration of aerosol particles that tend to block sunlight. But keep in mind, models are imperfect.

Powerful computers allow scientists to ask questions such as, Will our climate warm? And if so, how much? What areas are likely to be most affected? Which areas are likely to be least affected? If warming occurs, how will the climate change affect patterns of rainfall, temperature, or plant growth?

Some experts on the subject estimate that Earth's mean temperature could rise 2°F–7°F (1°C–3.9°C) by the year 2100 if greenhouse gases continue to increase at the current rate. These estimates involve many variables, and the connections between the variables are incomplete and extremely complex. As a result, the predictions cannot be tested easily in the lab. They do, however, imply that we should carefully watch and plan for changes.

Increased warming of Earth by the greenhouse effect is a hypothesis. Remember, there were other "greenhouse warmings" before modern times due entirely to natural variations (see Figure 15.38.) For example, would Earth experience a postglacial warm-up even without the added CO_2 from human activities? What does seem certain is that about half of the CO_2 produced by industrial processes since the beginning of the industrial age is still in the atmosphere. The turnover rate of carbon dioxide seems low. We must, therefore, look ahead carefully. If we get too much CO_2 in the atmosphere, it will be a long time before it can be removed by natural processes.

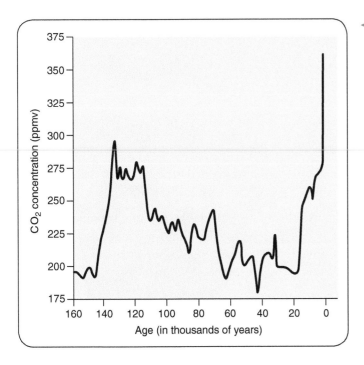

◀ FIGURE 15.38 Record of CO_2 concentration during the past 160,000 years. Glacial and interglacial periods coincide with CO_2 change. *(Reports to the Nation: Our Changing Climate. NOAA.)*

How much CO_2 is too much? This is another question that is difficult to answer with certainty. One computer model predicts that a doubling of the CO_2 content would increase the atmospheric temperature at Earth's surface 2 or 3 degrees Celsius. A temperature change of this size would cause significant changes in climate. Changes in climate could greatly influence Earth's ecosystems and their food-growing capabilities. The very fact that we do not know the consequences is the strongest reason for proceeding with care. Analyzing and understanding what we are doing to our ecosystem should be one of our higher priorities.

15.12 Responding to Climate Change

A majority of the world's atmospheric scientists now agree that both Earth is warming and humans are part of the reason. How should we respond? Our response will include two strategies: adaptation and mitigation.

Adaptation refers to our ability to adjust and safeguard our societies to the warming. How do we live with the problem? By anticipating harm to both natural and human systems, we can lessen the impact on those who will suffer the most. In particular, we can do the following:

- Build and/or improve storm-surge defenses in populated areas; manage coastal zones, including the restoration of wetlands; not allow building in flood-prone areas; and move people out of those areas where possible.

- Perfect storm warnings and response strategies, as the intensity and frequency of storms will increase.

- Enhance fire protection as drought-prone areas expand, and set aside space as natural burn areas.

- Accelerate water conservation strategies in water scarce regions.

- Stop the loss of tropical forests, and encourage the planting of trees and other vegetation that effectively lock up carbon.

- Fund biotech research to genetically engineer food plants that use less water and fewer chemicals, and that thrive in hotter climates. Develop microbes and synthetic

Resource Management: Air 597

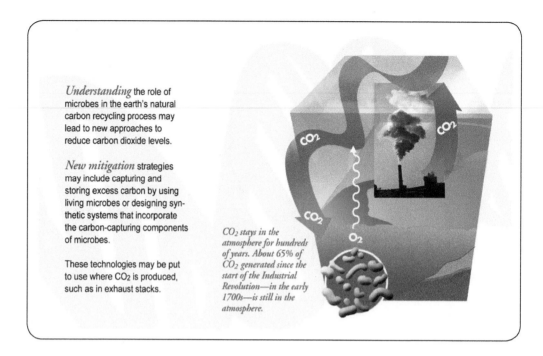

Understanding the role of microbes in the earth's natural carbon recycling process may lead to new approaches to reduce carbon dioxide levels.

New mitigation strategies may include capturing and storing excess carbon by using living microbes or designing synthetic systems that incorporate the carbon-capturing components of microbes.

These technologies may be put to use where CO_2 is produced, such as in exhaust stacks.

CO_2 stays in the atmosphere for hundreds of years. About 65% of CO_2 generated since the start of the Industrial Revolution—in the early 1700s—is still in the atmosphere.

systems that more efficiently capture and store the carbon from carbon dioxide (see Figure 15.39). Expand the capacity of the world's seed banks.

Mitigation refers to the actions and measures we can take to reduce greenhouse gas (GHG) emissions. In particular, we can do the following:

- Place a worldwide cap on GHG emissions. Allocate rights to emit GHGs to different countries and trade those rights in a market-based system. The Kyoto Protocol attempts to do this. Although the United States is not part of the agreement, several states (14), cities (431 mayors), and industries (GE, Alcoa, DuPont, BP America, Wal-Mart, and others) are voluntarily taking action to reduce their GHG emissions.

- Expand the use of renewable energy sources and/or nuclear power.

- Reduce the amount of fuel used in transportation by raising fuel-efficiency standards, promoting car pooling and mass transit, and possibly increasing gas taxes.

- Reduce electrical consumption by increasing the use of CFLs, LEDs, and more efficient appliances.

- Promote a resource conservation ethic in our classrooms, churches, and society as a whole.

- Expand opportunities for all people on a global scale so the demographic transition takes hold in all regions of the world.

15.13 The Effect of Particles on Global Temperature

Think about This!

Jet contrails make regions cooler in the day and warmer at night. How this affects global climate change is still a mystery.

Human activity results in the release of huge quantities of particles—soot, dust, salt, and smoke—into the atmosphere. Scientists refer to these as **aerosols**. Agricultural plowing plus wind creates dust. Clearing of land, in general, does the same. The constant movement of traffic, together with vehicle and airplane emissions, results in particle generation. Airplane emissions create new cloud layers that reflect sunlight that would have reached Earth if the plane had not been there (see Figure 15.40). There also are

◄ FIGURE 15.40 These two photos show jet contrails in the sky over the Juan De Fuca Straight near Victoria, British Columbia. The second photo was taken about 30 min after the first. The contrails have grown to become high cirrus clouds. (*John W. Christensen*)

particulate emissions from industrial smokestacks, power plants, and home chimneys. Some speculate that an all-out nuclear war would create a giant particle effect. To these, we must add all the natural sources such as volcanic eruptions, dust storms, forest fires, and pollens.

Particles can reflect sunlight back into space, and thereby reduce the amount of solar radiation that reaches Earth's surface. The net result is cooling of the ground and atmosphere. Figure 15.41 illustrates this effect. Some small particles in the upper atmosphere absorb sunlight and cause a warming of that region. Once clouds form, they hold in heat energy.

Carbon dioxide may warm Earth; particles may cool it. Might these two cancel each other? We don't know whether the particle effect will rival other events, such as the greenhouse effect. We do know that Earth's weather machine is huge and complex, and that humans affect it in a variety of ways. We are just beginning to understand the extent of this possible "weather modification."

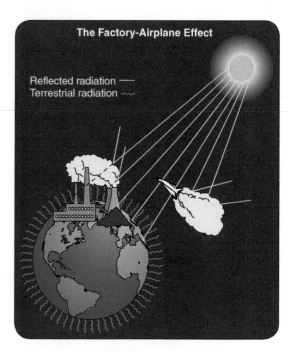

►FIGURE 15.41 The effect of aerosols on incoming sunlight. *(Adapted from a drawing by Jennifer Cole.)*

15.14 Depletion of the Ozone Layer ("Good" Ozone)

Content Clue

Greenhouse gases are important within Earth's lower atmosphere (troposphere) where heat energy is absorbed from Earth's surface. The ozone that protects us from the sun's UV radiation is much higher in the atmosphere (stratosphere).

Topic: ozone shield
Go to: www.scilinks.org
Code: GloSci7e600

While CO_2 and particles have been building up in Earth's troposphere, Earth's protective ozone layer has been thinning out in the stratosphere.

Recall earlier that ozone in the troposphere is regarded as a pollutant. In contrast, the ozone layer that surrounds Earth at an altitude of 12–35 mi (about 20–55 km) is our first line of defense against the sun's ultraviolet rays. This "good" ozone can efficiently absorb ultraviolet light and, as a result, prevent it from reaching life-forms on Earth. Ultraviolet rays cause sunburn and skin cancer, and have been linked to cataracts and other disorders.

Ozone (O_3) is an oxygen gas that exists only rarely at Earth's surface. It is produced during lightning storms and when sparks fly around powerful electrical equipment. It also is produced when sunlight acts on the ingredients that result in photochemical smog. Ozone is produced in the stratosphere when ordinary oxygen molecules (O_2) are bombarded with ultraviolet rays from the sun. Ultraviolet radiation breaks apart O_2 molecules into free oxygen atoms (O). Some of the free oxygen atoms recombine with O_2 to form O_3.

Though ultraviolet radiation continuously creates an abundance of ozone molecules, a variety of natural processes also destroy them. Until recently, these processes remained in balance.

In the 1960s, the group of gaseous chemicals called chlorofluorocarbons (CFCs) became very popular. Because they were nontoxic and inert, they could be used for refrigeration and for propellants in aerosol spray cans. They did what gases should do, and they didn't become involved in unwanted chemical reactions or make people sick. Unfortunately, when released, the gases rise into the stratosphere, where ultraviolet light can break them apart. The resulting free chlorine atoms catalyze the destruction of ozone. Each chlorine atom produced is capable of destroying 100,000 ozone molecules (see Figure 15.42). This may be causing the reduction in the size of the ozone layer, especially over Antarctica. The

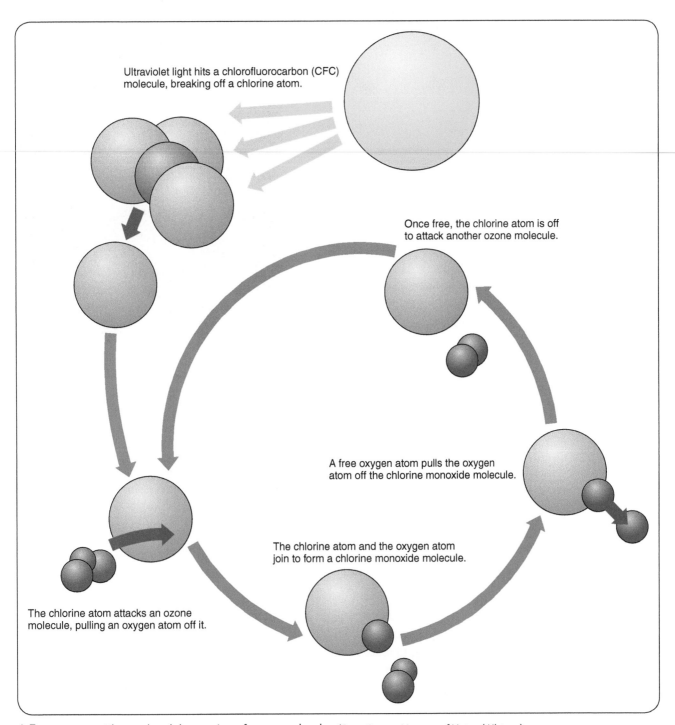

Ultraviolet light hits a chlorofluorocarbon (CFC) molecule, breaking off a chlorine atom.

Once free, the chlorine atom is off to attack another ozone molecule.

A free oxygen atom pulls the oxygen atom off the chlorine monoxide molecule.

The chlorine atom and the oxygen atom join to form a chlorine monoxide molecule.

The chlorine atom attacks an ozone molecule, pulling an oxygen atom off it.

▲ FIGURE 15.42 The catalyzed destruction of ozone molecules. (*From Denver Museum of Natural History.*)

change is shown in the satellite images reproduced in Figure 15.43. Many nations have agreed to sharply curtail the production of CFCs.

Summary

Natural events and human actions can damage ecosystems by disrupting their chemical cycles, changing the flow of energy through them, or reducing their diversity. If the damage is not too great and enough time is available, natural processes can mend the damage. People and technology can help reduce this damage. Today, unfortunately, change can occur rapidly, and time is lost as our ally.

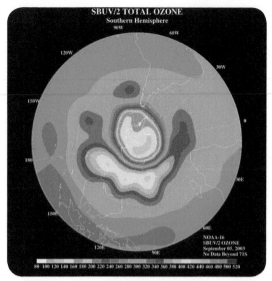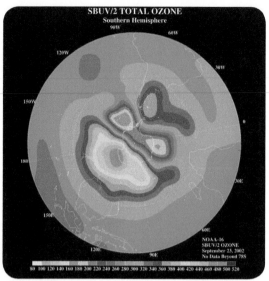

▲ Figure 15.43 Satellite images of the ozone hole over Antarctica. The ozone hole grew to near record size on September 5, 2003. The size of the hole was 27.6 million square km (left image). The record size was set on September 9, 2000, with a size of 28.7 million square km. The right image is of the ozone hole splitting into two separate holes on September 23, 2002. This phenomena was never observed before. A rapid warming of the stratosphere, usually observed only in the Northern Hemisphere during its winter period, caused the ozone hole to divide into two parts. Ozone concentration is measured in Dobson Units (DU). Concentration is indicated using a color scale. Low concentration of ozone corresponds to lower numbers on the Dobson Scale. *(Climate Prediction Center, NOAA)*

The human impact on the global environment comes almost entirely from our need for and use of resources to feed ourselves and provide for our other needs. Cleanup and correction involve the use of new technologies, laws that regulate our behavior, and new attitudes about our relationship to others and to our environment.

Acid rain may cause ecological damage to forests and lakes throughout the world. Progress is being made in combating the formation of acid rain.

Carbon dioxide is normally not considered an air pollutant. However, the increase in the CO_2 content of the atmosphere (related to burning fossil fuels) increases what we call the greenhouse effect. This results in a gradual warming of Earth. Large numbers of particles in our atmosphere could reflect enough sunlight to cause some global cooling. Humans are deciding how to best respond to global warming.

The thinning of the ozone layer is another potential threat to our well-being. Steps have been taken to reduce the production of chemicals that are connected to this thinning.

 REFERENCES

Bernick, Michael and Robert Cervero. *Transit Villages in the 21st Century* (New York: McGraw-Hill), 1997.

Committee on the Science of Climate Change, National Research Council. *Climate Change Science: An Analysis of Some Key Questions* (Washington, D.C.: National Academy Press), 2001.

Flavin, Christopher and Seth Dunn. Responding to the Threat of Climate Change. *State of the World, 1998* (Worldwatch Institute): 113.

Intergovernmental Panel on Climate Change (IPCC). *Climate Change 2007: Impacts, Adaptation, and Vulnerability* (UK: Cambridge University Press), 2007.

Intergovernmental Panel on Climate Change (IPCC). Climate Change 2007: The Physical Science Basis (UK: Cambridge University Press), 2007.

National Academy of Sciences. *Acid Deposition: Long-Term Trends* (Washington, D.C.: National Academy Press), 1986.

Rye, James Andrew. Understanding the Role of Chlorofluorocarbons in Global Atmospheric Change. *Journal of Geoscience Education* 46 (1998): 488.

Trenberth, Kevin E. (editor). Climate System Modeling (New York, Cambridge University Press), 1992.

United Nations Environment Programme & World Meteorological Organization. *Common Questions about Climate Change 1997*. Also on the web at http://www.gcrio.org/ipcc/qa/cover.html.

U.S. Environmental Protection Agency. *Air Quality Index: A Guide to Air Quality and Your Health* (Washington, D.C.: EPA 454/K-03-002), 2003.

U.S. Environmental Protection Agency. *The Inside Story: A Guide to Indoor Air Quality* (Washington, D.C.: EPA), 1995.

U.S. National Acid Precipitation Assessment Program. *1990 Integrated Assessment Report* (Washington, D.C.: The NAPAP Office of the Director), November, 1991.

WEBSITES

Air Quality Index (AQI):

http://www.epa.gov/airnow

Environmental Protection Agency:

http://www.epa.gov

EPA Indoor Air:

http://www.epa.gov/iaq/

University of Illinois at Urbana-Champaign: Meteorology:

http://www.atmos.uiuc.edu—choose Weather Information, then WW2010 Online Guides

Global Change Research Program:

http://geochange.er.usgs.gov

National Center for Atmospheric Research:

http://www.ncar.ucar.edu

National Oceanic & Atmospheric Administration:

http://www.noaa.gov/

Ozone Hole:

http://www.theozonehole.com

CHAPTER 16

Resource Management: Land

GOAL

- To examine ways of improving our ability to use our land.

What is the use of having a house if you don't have a decent planet to put it on?

— *Henry David Thoreau*

Land Use and Land Use Decisions

16.1 Land Use/Cover Categories

Helpful Hint!

Land use is the way people use the land and its resources—for example, farming, forest uses, and housing.

The United States is the third or fourth largest country in the world, depending on how you measure it. It is third largest (behind Russia and Canada) if you include the area covered by water. It is fourth largest (behind China) if you count only the land area. Figure 16.1 shows different ways of representing how U.S. land can be divided up.

Few things are as controversial as land use. To many, the freedom to forge their own destinies is tied to the land.

Helpful Hint!

Land cover describes the physical surface of the land, as in forests, range- and cropland, and urban areas.

Just as there are different ways for determining the size of the United States, there are different groupings used to represent U.S. **land use** and **land cover**. The three pie charts in Figure 16.2 are all developed from reports by the U.S. Department of Agriculture. Each provides accurate information about land use/cover in the United States, yet each provides somewhat different information. It is important to understand the definitions and categories that are used when discussing land use and land cover.

Helpful Hint!

1 acre = 43,560 square feet
football field = 48,000 square feet (300 feet by 160 feet)

Land Area in Acres	
United States	2,263 million
Alaska	365 million
California	100 million
Kansas	52.5 million
Massachusetts	5 million
Mississippi	30.2 million
Rhode Island	677 thousand
Federal land ownership	643 million

Land Areas of the United States

2,263 million acres   50.3 million acres in water

Ownership	Private property, including Native & Indian Trust lands—1,415 million acres, 63%	State govt.— 198 million acres, 9%	Federal govt.— 643 million acres, 28%

Nonfederal Land—Rural or Developed

Rural—1,516 million acres   Developed—107 million acres

Land Use/Cover

Forest use—28% 642 million acres	Range, grassland—26% 580 million acres	Cropland—20% 455 million acres	Misc.—13% 301 million acres	Special uses—13% 286 million acres

▲ FIGURE 16.1 Land area of the United States. *(Primary source: Adapted from U.S. Department of Agriculture, www.ers.usda.gov/publications/sb973/.)*

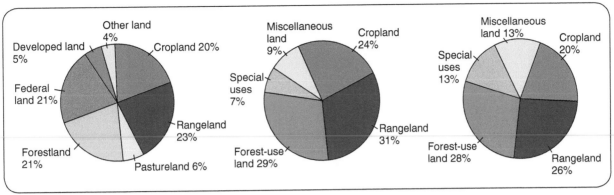

▲ FIGURE 16.2 Land use/cover in the United States. (*Sources: USDA, Natural Resources Conservation Service and Economic Research Service.*)

❓ QUESTIONS & TASKS

1. Name some land cover categories.

2. Name some land use categories.

16.2 Land Ownership and Past Land Use

One of the most important reasons for the rapid growth of America into a great world power was its land. Natural resources of rich soil, forests, mineral deposits, and abundant water were all present on the continent.

When Europeans settled in North America, they were attracted by the concept of privately owned property. People could claim the right to own their own piece of land and develop it as they saw fit. Life, liberty, and private property all became linked to the American way of life. Citizens also had the freedom to move and settle virtually anywhere in the United States in pursuit of a better life.

The Fifth Amendment to the U.S. Constitution states:

> . . . nor (shall any person) be deprived of life, liberty, or property, without due process of law, nor shall private property be taken for public use without just compensation.

This means that property owners can use their land as they desire in a reasonable manner. However, numerous devices have evolved to control the use of property. These include the following:

1. **Zoning regulations** (local government controls) to allow some uses and prohibit others.

2. **Covenants** (private property agreements) between groups of home owners.

3. **Contracts** among private parties and/or with government organizations or agencies.

4. **Traditional controls** based on who owns the land. (For example, there are controls on how the government can use the land it owns.)

5. **Environmental regulations/restrictions** requiring special studies and mitigation to minimize negative impacts.

Content Clue

Changes in land use (for example, grassland to farmland) should not imply a degradation of the land.

Think about This!

Private land ownership is important in the United States.

Think about This!

Why is it important to have restrictions on the use of private property?

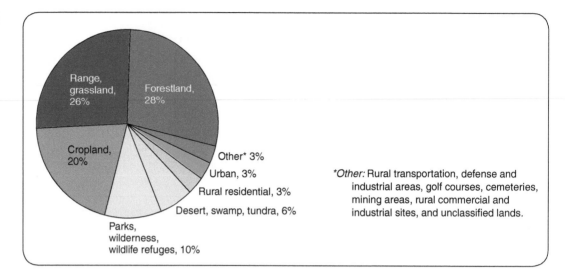

Land use is the use of land by people. Until the 20th century, the goal of the U.S. government was to create private land ownership to encourage settlement and to support the national economy. The Homestead Act of 1862 allowed nearly 290 million acres (15 percent of the area of the United States at the time) to become owned by private citizens. More than 300 million acres were granted to the states to support schools, transportation, and local economies. Another 94 million acres were granted to railroads as an incentive to build transportation systems as a further attempt to settle the vast country.

Major cities and urban areas sprang up where transportation routes came together. Originally, this meant access to harbors and rivers. Then, locations served by major roads and railroads became trade centers for the distribution of the food and raw materials that were produced elsewhere, and for shipping the finished products from factories to other markets.

16.3 Present Land Use

Figure 16.3 shows how land in the United States can be grouped. From this, we see that almost 30 percent of the land is classified as forest-use land. More than 25 percent is range, grassland, or pasture. Cropland covers 20 percent, while parks, wilderness, and wildlife areas cover 10 percent. Deserts, swamps, and tundra cover 6 percent of the total land area. Urban areas cover about 3 percent. Note what the "Other" category includes.

Land often has more than one use. For example, farmlands can also be forested. Likewise, a single forest can have recreational, grazing, timbering, and other uses all at the same time. Urban areas have highways, railroads, and airports. They also include recreational and park areas along with the residential and manufacturing areas. Deserts can have residential and wildlife areas. Mining lands can also provide wildlife and watershed areas, rangeland, and recreational uses.

16.4 Present Land Use Decision-Making Structures

Land use is affected primarily by the resources it offers (forests, crops, minerals, water, location) and by government regulations. More than one-third of all land in the United States is managed by the government, principally the federal government. The highest concentration of federal land is in the far West (see Figure 16.4).

Land Ownership by Federal Government (selected states)		
Rank	State	Percentage
1	Nevada	87.6
2	Utah	67.9
3	Alaska	67
4	Idaho	65.2
5	Oregon	55.5
6	California	49.9
7	Wyoming	49.7
8	Arizona	44.3
43	Iowa	2.1
44	Maryland	2.1
45	Massachusetts	1.7
46	Maine	1.2
47	Kansas	1.1
48	Connecticut	0.6
49	Rhode Island	0.6
50	New York	0.4

◄ FIGURE 16.4 Concentration of federally owned land ranked by state. (*Source: National Wilderness Institute.*)

More than half of the land in the United States is privately owned by individuals and corporations. The owners have considerable freedom to develop and use that land as they desire. This freedom, however, is not total. As pointed out in section 16.2, land use is restricted by environmental regulations, zoning laws, subdivision standards, covenants, and taxes.

Historically, for the most part, regulations for privately owned lands have been the responsibility of local governments. This seemed the best way to develop consistent, desirable use patterns. Agreements could be worked out among people who knew one another or had common interests, and zoning maps could reflect an overall plan. It was thought that responsible individuals would comply with the rules and that local governments would have the power to implement the goals.

Over time, federal regulation of private lands and land use has increased. Floodplains, wetlands, and water quality are examples of local land use issues that, although perhaps administered locally, are now governed by federal regulation.

The standard land use decision-making model used throughout much of the United States is illustrated in Figure 16.5. If an individual or group wishes to use a parcel of land in a different way than stated in the current zoning regulations, a request for a variance or a zoning change must be made and a public hearing held. After hearing discussions about the land use change (both pro and con), local government officials vote on the request. Majority rules.

Originally, the concept of *highest* and *best use* of the land was the dominant factor for deciding land use. That use was often based on improving the value and financial gain the property would bring to the landowner and the community.

Question This!

Is the standard land use decision-making model described here the decision-making model used in your region?

Think about This!

Why is the concept of *highest* and *best use* of the land changing?

► **FIGURE 16.5** The standard land use decision-making model.

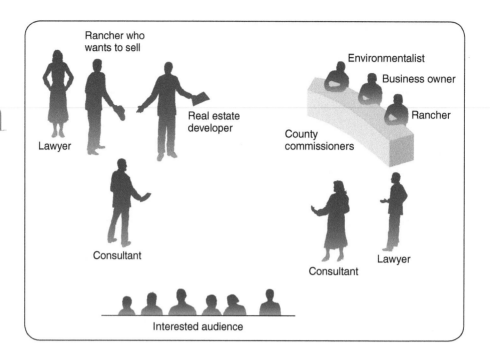

Rancher who wants to sell

Lawyer

Real estate developer

Consultant

Environmentalist

Business owner

Rancher

County commissioners

Consultant

Lawyer

Interested audience

Think about This!

All the commissioners have hidden agendas (not necessarily bad) on why they ran for the position they hold.

The public hearing is usually held during the day. This is a poor time for receiving citizen input.

After hearing arguments from both sides, the county commissioners vote on the request. Majority rules.

Think about This!

What uses of land would *you* not want in your "backyard"?

This attitude is changing as citizen groups are organizing and empowering themselves with requests for priority over landowners' desires. "Environmental impact mitigation" and "environmental sustainability" have become the slogans for this new appeal. Citizen action opposing landowners' development proposals has become so common that planners nationwide have identified it as the "NIMBY" (Not In My Backyard!) syndrome.

ACTIVITY 16.1

Land Use Decision: You Make the Call

In this activity, you will consider a land use issue and think about the consequences of different uses for the land.

Procedure

1. Read the 3 sections of the background information about the land being studied by a county land use commission. Examine the related map (see Figure 16.6).

2. Answer the questions that follow.

Background

Description of Area

- One square mile of farmland (shown by red box in Figure 16.6), 4 miles northeast of the city of Wheatland.

- The population of Wheatland is 220,000 and increasing rapidly.

- The city's boundaries are being extended, but the suburban fringe is expanding even more rapidly.

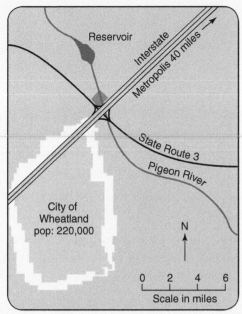

▲ FIGURE 16.6 Map of Wheatland and the surrounding area.

- The rapid population growth is accompanied by demands for more housing, more jobs, additional city services, and recreational areas.

- Power for industrial uses, adequate public transportation, and a skilled labor force are available.

- The Wheatland area is located in productive agricultural land.

- The Pigeon River is relatively clean and is the source of irrigation water and the municipal water supply.

- The river is too small for freight transportation.

- The gravel bed of the river is appropriate raw material for concrete manufacture.

- The present sewage treatment plant and garbage disposal area are at capacity. The citizens of Wheatland are concerned about the maintenance of a scenic regional environment.

- The Pike County commissioners are the authority for land zoning; many citizens' groups are forming to influence zoning decisions.

Issue

Pike County is revising its land use plan. Several proposals are being debated about how to use the farmland located at the intersection of the Interstate and State Route 3.

Land Use Proposals

Six proposals for the use of the present farmland:

A. Keep the present agricultural zoning and continue to farm.

B. Change to a county park and recreation area.

C. Develop into a privately owned regional trucking center.

D. Develop into the campus for a proposed state technical college.

E. Develop into a proposed shopping mall.

F. Mixed use—part residential houses, apartments, and light commercial.

QUESTIONS & TASKS

Record your responses in your science notebook.

1. List the advantages and disadvantages of each of the six proposals given in the background information.

2. List pieces of information about this decision that are not available to you.

3. Some classes take this activity and develop it into a simulation (see Figure 16.5). Students play the different roles.

   a. What is useful about this kind of exercise?

   b. What can be misleading about this kind of activity?

4. What is necessary for the decision to be the best decision? Is the "Not In My Backyard" (NIMBY) syndrome a problem that must be faced?

ACTIVITY 16.2

Environmental Landscaping

In this activity, you will develop a home landscape plan that is both attractive and resource (water/energy/mineral) efficient.

Background

Probably the most important land use decision most people make in a lifetime is the landscaping of their yard. Unfortunately, most people don't think much about it. They imitate what their neighbors do. They accept what is already there. They ask a few friends or wander through a garden shop and buy what looks pretty or seems to be the least expensive.

Well-thought-out site analysis and landscaping can provide an attractive yard and may save you money. They can add to the comfort and enjoyment of life. Planning is essential for the best landscape design. This activity will help you put together a plan.

Materials (for each student)

- graph paper
- ruler
- colored pencils or pens
- design template (to help draw shapes) (optional)

Procedure

1. Design the landscape of a home in the area where you live. Think about the following resource issues in your community:
   a. Is energy expensive?
   b. Is water plentiful or scarce?
   c. How important is the wise use of water?
   d. How are home and yard wastes handled?
   e. What is the local climate?
   f. What native plant species are available?

2. Draw and analyze your site plan. Then sketch your landscape plan on graph paper.

3. Wrap up the activity by summarizing your process and results.

Draw a Site Plan

1. Draw the boundaries of the site on graph paper. How large are most yards in your area? Use the scale of 1 division = 1 foot (ft). This means that each small box on the graph paper is 1 ft × 1 ft.

2. With an arrow, show where NORTH is on your site plan.

3. Block out your house floor plan. Typical outside dimensions of a home are 25 ft by 40 ft. This does not include a garage.

4. Indicate windows and doors and the main entrance of your home. Possible symbols to use include: outside walls (▬▬▬), windows (———), doors (⟋), and sliding doors (▬■▬—▬).

Analyze the Site

Think about and plan around these items. Do not limit yourself to only these items.

1. How will your site be used? Do you want a children's play area, vegetable garden, flowers, trees and shrubs, a circular drive, a patio or deck, room for a boat, extra parking, and privacy? Will your garden have trickle irrigation?

2. How do you approach the house by car and by foot?

3. What views do you want to emphasize and/or block out?

4. Which way does the wind blow? Show this on your plan.

5. Where are the hot and cool spots in your yard? South and west areas will get a lot of hot afternoon sun. East areas get cooler morning sun; north areas get very little sun.

6. Which side of the lot faces the street or road?

7. Is there existing landscape, or are you starting with bare ground?

8. Can you compost organic wastes to reduce the quantity of trash you put out and possibly reduce your garden's fertilizer bill? What will you do with your lawn and yard wastes?

9. Is there a recycling area in your garage or yard?

10. How much can you afford? What is your budget?

11. What benefits do you hope to achieve? Think about water costs and needs. Think about energy bills and passive solar strategies. Think about recycling and trash removal. Is water available?

12. Can emergency services get to the home easily? Are construction materials fire resistant? Is it important to have defensible space around the home in case of grass or forest fires?

Sketch the Landscape Plan

Based on the analysis of your site, sketch your landscape plan on the graph paper. Use symbols and labels to indicate what is located on your plan. Possible symbols to use include the following:

<blockquote>**Helpful Hint!**

The size of the area taken by the symbol indicates the area taken up by the plant when it is fully grown.</blockquote>

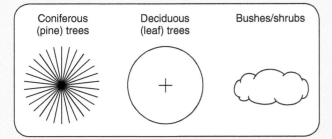

Coniferous (pine) trees   Deciduous (leaf) trees   Bushes/shrubs

1. Place trees for shade on the south and west sides of the house. Plant windbreaks on the north side.

2. Select low-maintenance, low-water shrubs and ground cover around the edge of your house. Do not place turf next to the foundation of your home.

3. Use a low-water-requiring grass in turf areas.

4. Group your plants and gardens according to the amount of water they consume.

5. Consider the use of rock, gravel, bark, and mulch as a way to cut down on grass areas that demand water.

6. Consider an outdoor patio or deck as a way to reduce grass needs.

7. Are there wildfire breaks on the property? What is the slope of the property?

<blockquote>**Helpful Hint!**

Native plants are recommended no matter where you live because they are best suited to your particular climate.</blockquote>

Consider Other Ideas

1. Color your plan to suggest variety of plants and materials.

2. Talk to a landscape architect.

3. Call or visit local garden centers and ask about native plants, costs, and their best ideas.

4. Call your local electric power company and water provider; find out if they provide landscape suggestions. Also check your library.

5. You may want to build a 3-D model of your home and yard.

QUESTIONS & TASKS

Summarize your project as follows:

1. Review your illustrated and labeled landscape plan. The site plan could be color-coded. Make sure your plan is understandable to anyone who examines it.

2. Write a one-page summary that explains the following:

   a. What you did.

   b. Why you chose the vegetation you did.

   c. The estimated cost of the landscape project and how this was determined.

   d. The benefits you hope to get from your plan.

   e. A short list of native plants you could use.

   f. Trees: Shrubs: Grasses:

   g. Where you found your information on native plants.

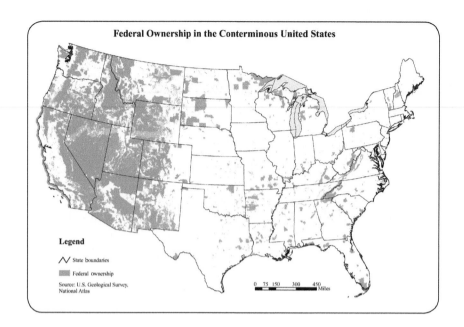

Federal Ownership in the Conterminous United States

Legend

/\\/ State boundaries

▨ Federal ownership

Source: U.S. Geological Survey, National Atlas

0 75 150   300   450 Miles

16.5 Public Lands

Public lands are owned by the people as a whole. They include city and state parks, greenbelts and open space in communities, national parks and monuments, national forests, seashores, wildlife refuges, and military bases. Presidents and Congress and state and local governments set aside public lands. Figure 16.7 shows some of the public lands in the contiguous United States. Most of our public lands are in the western part of our country and Alaska.

The largest area of public lands is on federal land. The federal government owns and manages about one-fourth of the total landmass of the United States. Federal land management agencies include these five groups:

Bureau of Land Management (BLM)

The BLM manages about one-eighth of the land area of the United States. This land provides opportunities for outdoor recreation, and preserves natural, cultural, and historic resources. It also contains valuable energy and mineral resources that are vital to our country.

Forest Service (USFS)

The USFS manages and protects federal forests and grasslands.

National Park Service (NPS)

The NPS manages our national parks, monuments, and important historic sites.

Fish and Wildlife Service (FWS)

The FWS manages our national wildlife refuges, fish hatcheries, and thousands of small wetlands and other special management areas.

Army Corps of Engineers (USACE)

The USACE serves the armed forces and the nation by providing engineering services and capabilities in five areas: water resources, environment, infrastructure, homeland security, and warfare. These involve coastal protection, flood protection, hydropower, water supply, environmental cleanup, and wetland restoration.

Record your responses in your science notebook.

1. Go online and find the mission statement for each of the five agencies listed above. Summarize each statement.

2. Compare and contrast the objectives and activities of these five agencies.

16.6 Land Management Issues

Public lands belong to all of us, and recreational use and economic use often come into conflict. Hence, a series of laws was passed by Congress (after World War II) to guide how these lands are to be managed. These laws include the Wilderness Act, the Endangered Species Act, the National Environmental Protection Act (NEPA), and other laws that regulate the protection of cultural, historic, and archaeological resources. These laws mandate public review in land management decision processes. Our public land management agencies carry out the rules and regulations mandated by Congress and the American public. If the process leads to a decision that a group of individuals does not feel is just, that group can sue in federal court.

How our public land management agencies decide to use and manage land leads to conflict when one group advocates a use that excludes others. Over time, our land management agencies became "multiple use" land managers. This means they seek a balance among competing land uses. This is often difficult because most natural resources, such as minerals, are located where they were formed, not always where we would like them to be. Here are three examples of when conflict can occur:

* Urbanization covers sand, gravel, and stone deposits required for the building of roads, buildings, and homes in a region.

* Zoning restrictions and local interests limit or eliminate a particular land use, forcing an advocacy group to go elsewhere—sometimes to an area (or country) where the impacts might be greater or where there will be fewer (or no) environmental regulations.

* Recreational and aesthetic values ban uses that might be visible—uses that might be vital to our economy.

In the 1970s, a series of laws was passed to address a variety of resource/environmental concerns. The major laws and their original date of passage are summarized in Figure 16.8.

National Environmental Policy Act

The National Environmental Policy Act (NEPA) of 1969 is the foundation of environmental policy making in the United States. It created a review process prior to the federal government undertaking any major action that significantly affects the environment. The Council on Environmental Quality (CEQ) is the agency responsible for overseeing NEPA implementation.

NEPA is considered the basic national charter for protection of the environment. It was enacted for a simple reason: to assure that all branches of government give proper consideration to the environment before taking any major action. An **environmental assessment (EA)** and **environmental impact statement (EIS)** are required. These help determine the likelihood of impacts from alternative courses of action. They are required from all federal agencies and are the most visible NEPA requirements.

Apply Your Understanding

What major contribution did NEPA make to the future protection of the environment?

National Environmental Policy Act (late 1969)

Clean Air Act (1970)

Mining and Mineral Policy Act (1970)

Occupational Safety and Health Act (OSHA) (1970)

Resource Recovery Act (1970)

Clean Water Act (1972)

Coastal Zone Management Act (1972)

Federal Environmental Pesticides Control Act (1972)

Marine Mammal Protection Act (1972)

Marine Protection, Research, and Sanctuaries Act (1972)

National Coastal Zone Management Act (1972)

Endangered Species Act (1973)

Forest and Rangeland Renewable Resources Planning Act (1974)

Renewable Resources Planning Act (RPA) (1974)

Safe Drinking Water Act (1974)

Hazardous Materials Transportation Act (Hazmat) (1975)

Federal Land Policy and Management Act (FLPMA) (1976)

Fishery Conservation and Management Act (1976)

Forest and Rangeland Renewable Resources Planning Act (FRRRPA) (1976)

National Forest Management Act (1976)

Resource Conservation and Recovery Act (1976)

Toxic Substance Control Act (1976)

Soil and Water Conservation Act (1977)

Surface Mining Control and Reclamation Act (1977)

Antarctic Conservation Act (1978)

Endangered American Wilderness Act (1978)

Fish and Wildlife Improvement Act (1978)

Public Rangelands Improvement Act (1978)

Comprehensive Environmental Resource, Compensation, and Liability Act (CERCLA or "Superfund") (1980)

▲ FIGURE 16.8 Major federal environmental laws passed during the 1970's. These laws are routinely amended and updated. Similar laws have been passed at the state level as well.

At a minimum, an environmental impact statement must include these four points:

1. An analysis of the need for the project

2. A rigorous comparison of reasonable alternative projects

3. A description of the environment affected by the project

4. A discussion of the environmental impacts of the proposed project and those of the possible alternatives

In short, an EIS is a scientific analysis of the proposed project in terms of its impact on the surrounding environment.

 To learn more about the EIS process, including how to receive an EIS, go online at www.epa.gov/compliance/nepa/obtaineis/index.html.

Environmental impact statements must be thorough and based in science. They are often lengthy and expensive to produce (see Figure 16.9). Similar statements are also required by local and state laws. Many students who graduate from college with a major in environmental science are employed by energy and mineral companies or by companies hired to do environmental impact studies.

Environmental regulation and compliance place modern societies in a quandary. If we ignore environmental concerns, we risk permanent damage to surrounding ecosystems and to ourselves. If we raise the cost of resource production too high, we risk the loss of

◄FIGURE 16.9 An example of an application for a state permit in 1996. The proposed project (a gold mine in Montana) has been a major controversy for 10 years. *(Photo provided by Canyon Resources.)*

our resource–based industries and the jobs and opportunities they provide. Further, poor environmental practices in foreign countries that do not require careful mining benefit neither their own people and land, nor our planet. We must strive for solutions that lead to quality lives for everyone.

? QUESTIONS & TASKS

Record your responses in your science notebook.

1. Describe the concept of multiple use.

2. An environmental impact statement contains four main parts. List them.

For the 25th anniversary of NEPA, the CEQ set out to examine the law's effectiveness and to identify the factors critical to ensuring success of the NEPA process. Overall, the study reports "that NEPA is a success—it has made agencies take a hard look at the potential environmental consequences of their actions, and it has brought the public into the agency decision-making process like no other statute."

 To learn more about the findings of the CEQ study, you can download the 60-page report at ceq.eh.doe.gov/nepa/nepa25fn.pdf.

The CEQ study also cited several areas where the NEPA process has fallen short of its goals. For example, the study reported:

NEPA is supposed to be about good decision-making—not endless documen-tation. Some federal agencies act as if the detailed statement called for in the statute is an end in itself, rather than a tool to enhance and improve decision-making. As a consequence, the exercise can be one of producing a document to no specific end. (See Figure 16.9.)

Agencies sometimes engage in consultation only after a decision has—for all practical purposes—been made. In such instances, other agencies and the public at large believe that their concerns have not been heard. As a result, they may find themselves opposing even worthy proposed actions.

Other matters of concern to participants in the study included the

- length of NEPA processes,
- extensive detail of NEPA analyses, and
- sometimes confusing overlay of other laws and regulations.

Land Trusts and Conservation Easements

In addition to governments, private nonprofit groups also manage and preserve land. **Land trusts** are local and regional organizations that preserve lands valued by their members. These organizations are funded with a mix of private donations and public monies. They have preserved more than 37 million acres of land in the United States alone. (This is the size of the state of Georgia.) Land trusts accomplish their goals by either owning land outright or by holding conservation easements.

A **conservation easement** is a legal agreement that contains permanent restrictions on the use or development of land. It is recorded in the county real estate records. Typically, it prohibits subdivision and commercial development but can permit agricultural and residential use. Once signed, the easement cannot be changed, even by a new owner. Conservation easements are attractive to many owners because they don't have to wholly give up their land. The public benefits because valuable open space, wildlife habitat, river corridors, wetlands, biodiversity, and scenic overlooks are preserved (see Figure 16.10). The landowner loses potential profit but gains a feeling of having done something good. The landowner also receives a significant tax break.

The size of the tax break to some landowners has come under criticism. The criteria for selecting land for easements is also being examined. Some golf courses have been granted easements even though they offer no real benefit to the tax-paying public (except when they pay to play). It would also be helpful if land trusts could, on occasion, sell easements so that other easements could be obtained to provide corridors for wildlife and longer hiking trails for people. (See the upcoming Special Focus titled Land Fragmentation.)

▶ FIGURE 16.10 A conservation easement in Colorado. This easement protects wildlife and preserves nature trails in an area that is experiencing significant population growth. *(Douglas County Open Space Division.)*

Record your responses in your science notebook.

1. List three ways land trusts could improve their ability to manage land for public benefit.

2. Research land trusts and conservation easements in your area. What are the benefits to your community?

16.7 Mined Land Reclamation

Surface mining can affect land quality more than any other use. In surface mining, the soil and rock covering the mineral deposit are removed. The removed materials are called "overburden." Huge equipment can remove as much as 200 ft or 60 meters (m) of overburden to get to the coal or ore, which can then be mined. Huge trucks haul the mineral away (see Figure 16.11). When mining is complete, the overburden can often be put back into the empty cavity in preparation for reclamation. Although it is evident that surface mining disrupts the land, the land can and is being reclaimed. The record of reclamation in this country was not good until the 1970s.

After years of controversy, a federal surface mining law was passed in 1977. This, along with upgraded state laws, now assures that poor mining practices will not be repeated in new mining regions. Today, many mining companies, through hard work and the expenditure of many dollars, are reclaiming lands that can be used for other purposes.

Many examples of successful reclamation exist in this country and abroad. Overburden (top soil and rock) that was put aside during the mining period is being replaced in the excavation area. Seed mixtures of good starter grass and native vegetation are being planted, fertilized, and watered. The steps in surface mining followed by reclamation are shown in Figure 16.12. Knowledge of the process of ecological succession guides the reclamation project.

Careful land reclamation adds to the cost of mining coal or other material. If the land is bulldozed to resemble its original contours and revegetated, the total cost may run as high as $20,000 per acre. In the arid West, where irrigation is required, the costs can be even higher.

That is a lot of money. To put it into perspective, the cost of reclamation adds only a small percentage to the total value of the coal.

Reclamation can and is being accomplished. We used coal as an example in the previous paragraphs, but the mining sites of other resources, such as sand and gravel, can also be reclaimed. Sand and gravel excavations often make excellent fishing ponds or lakes and water storage reservoirs.

◀ **FIGURE 16.11** Coal loading at a western U.S. mine. (*AMAX Coal Industries, Inc.*)

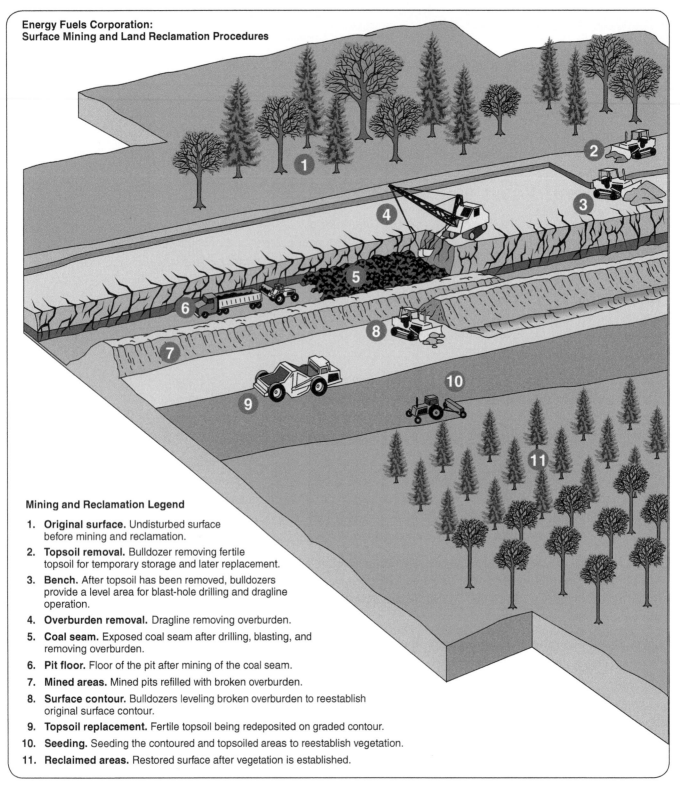

Energy Fuels Corporation:
Surface Mining and Land Reclamation Procedures

Mining and Reclamation Legend

1. **Original surface.** Undisturbed surface
   before mining and reclamation.
2. **Topsoil removal.** Bulldozer removing fertile
   topsoil for temporary storage and later replacement.
3. **Bench.** After topsoil has been removed, bulldozers
   provide a level area for blast-hole drilling and dragline
   operation.
4. **Overburden removal.** Dragline removing overburden.
5. **Coal seam.** Exposed coal seam after drilling, blasting, and
   removing overburden.
6. **Pit floor.** Floor of the pit after mining of the coal seam.
7. **Mined areas.** Mined pits refilled with broken overburden.
8. **Surface contour.** Bulldozers leveling broken overburden to reestablish
   original surface contour.
9. **Topsoil replacement.** Fertile topsoil being redeposited on graded contour.
10. **Seeding.** Seeding the contoured and topsoiled areas to reestablish vegetation.
11. **Reclaimed areas.** Restored surface after vegetation is established.

▲FIGURE 16.12 A modern surface mining and land reclamation procedure. (*Courtesy Energy Fuels Corporation.*)

? QUESTIONS & TASKS

Record your responses in your science notebook.

1. Can mined land be reclaimed? Defend your answer.

2. Briefly summarize the steps of the reclamation process.

ACTIVITY 16.3

Mined Land Reclamation

Land reclamation is becoming an established practice as the human population grows, cities expand, and people become more knowledgeable about the human tie to the environment. Today, much of that reclamation is done by industry, land developers, and governments.

In this activity, you will focus on mined land reclamation. This is because mining companies reclaim significant tracts of land. The Mineral Information Institute (MII) provides ready access to a wealth of information on such projects via the Internet.

Materials (for each student)

- 11 × 17-inch sheet of paper
- reclamation photos (from website)

Procedure

1. You will be assigned one of the mined land reclamation projects listed in Figure 16.13. Record the name of the reclamation project you are to examine in your science notebook. Projects are listed by category.

2. Either in class or outside of class, research your project as follows:

   a. Go online to www.mii.org and click on "Mining and the Environment."

   b. Click on your category; then scroll to your project and click on it.

   c. Print a *color* copy of the description of your reclamation project.

   d. Read the project description, and look up any terms you do not understand.

   e. Have a copy of the description of your project available for your next class.

▼ FIGURE 16.13 Current mined land reclamation projects.

Coal	Sand & Gravel	Gold & Silver
Coal Mining Reclamation	Cherry Valley	Homestake Mining Co.
Pennsylvania D.E.P.	Glaster Sand & Gravel	Jerritt Canyon
Arkadelphia	Lake County	Manhattan Mine
Catenary Coal Co.	Martin Marietta	Ruby Hill
Cravert Coal Co.	Oklahoma Partnership	Santa Fe/Calvada
G&S Coal Co., Inc.	Porters Concrete Service	
Larson Enterprises	Watson Gravel	**Other Metals**
Oakey Creek Coal Mine	Hanson Aggregates-Fossil Park	Bridge Hill
Paramont Coal Corp.		Cabacal Copper & Gold
Sandlick Coal Co.	**Industrial Minerals**	Flambeau Copper
Seneca Coal Co.	Butchart Gardens	Kennecott Utah Copper
Texas Utilities	Columbia Quarry	Steep Rock Iron
Trapper Mine	Fossil Trace Golf Club	Climax Molybdenum-Urad Mine
Twisted Gun Golf Course	Walker Co.	
Vigo Coal Co.		
Wylo Coal Mine		

3. Obtain an 11 × 17-inch sheet of paper on which to make a poster. Your poster will describe the reclamation project you are examining. Figure 16.14 shows a model of how to organize the information on your poster.

4. Review section 16.7 Mined Land Reclamation.

5. Review what you learned about ecological succession in Chapter 2, section 2.5 Ecosystems Change over Time.

6. Use Figure 2.24 in Chapter 2 to determine the biome your project is most likely in.

7. Use Figure 16.15 to estimate mean annual precipitation (inches) and mean annual temperature (°F) for your biome. Also, give the ranges in metric.

Helpful Hint!
1 inch = 2.54 centimeters
°C = 5/9 (°F − 32)

8. Assemble your poster.

9. Answer the questions that follow.

➤ FIGURE 16.14 A model of the land reclamation poster.

Your name   Date   Period

NAME OF THE LAND RECLAMATION PROJECT
LOCATION OF THE PROJECT

Biome in which the project is located

- Approximate mean annual temperature range
- Approximate mean annual precipitation range
- Short description of the restoration project (2–3 paragraphs)
- What has been planted at the site

Some photos
of the reclamation
(Use before and after photos if available.)

Q1   State the question and then answer it.
Q2   State the question and then answer it.

➤ FIGURE 16.15 The influence of temperature and precipitation on biome types.

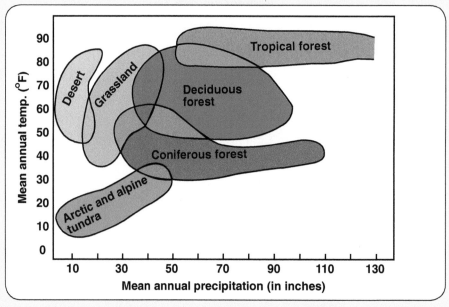

1. What additional information do you need to determine whether or not this reclamation project will be (or is) successful?

2. If left undisturbed by humans for the next 50 years, what would you expect your reclamation site to look like? Justify your answer.

SPECIAL FOCUS

Island Biogeography

The study of island ecosystems reveals some principles that have application to many of the land use issues we face. These include the following:

1. Islands have fewer species than continents.

2. The smaller the island, the fewer the species.

3. The farther an island is from the mainland, the fewer the species that exist on the island. (The island is less likely to be found by migrants from the mainland.)

4. The smaller the island, the smaller the population of a species that can be supported. The smaller the population, the greater the risk of extinction (recall the dice lab).

5. The smaller the island, the greater the risk from predators, disease, competition, or habitat alteration. Figure 16.16 summarizes some of these principles.

These principles have application today as we build parks in cities, designate greenbelts in communities, and set aside open space and wildlife preserves. They also apply to the "islands" of forest that were left as farms, ranches, and towns were established as America grew. This is called *fragmentation*. Fragmentation is the subject of the next Special Focus.

▼ FIGURE 16.16 Some of the main principles of island biogeography. The principles tie to migration from the mainland, odds of being found, and the ability to maintain a diverse ecosystem. *(Source: Summarized from R. H. MacArthur and E. O. Wilson, The Theory of Island Biogeography. Princeton University Press, Princeton, NJ. © 1967 and 2001.)*

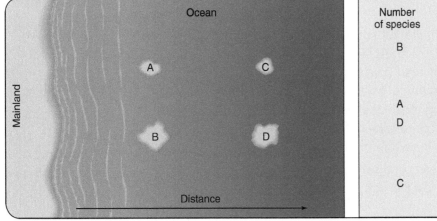

1. Assume your community or county (parish) is considering obtaining land for open space. Use the principles of island biogeography to draw up a set of guidelines for the selection of an open space site. Assume the goal is to create the most stable biotic community.

2. What effect might topography of the islands have on the principles of island biogeography?

SPECIAL FOCUS

Land Fragmentation

As land is developed for human use, it is usually divided up into smaller, often random, isolated pieces. This creates the patchy landscape that is often associated with urban sprawl or that one sees when flying over midwestern farm country. This is called **fragmentation** (see Figure 16.17).

To an ecologist, the boundary between a forest and a farm field or between a suburban lot and an open space is interesting. Often the boundary zone or edge promotes species diversity, as birds might feed in fields or grasslands but nest in the forest. In the process, energy and materials move from one to the other. However, the principles of island biogeography tell us that habitat fragmentation generally reduces habitat stability. The best approach is to preserve larger habitat blocks and link smaller blocks with migration corridors.

Focus Problems

At the top of the next page at the left is a tract of forestland, 1,000 m by 1,000 m. At the right is the same tract of forestland after it was fragmented by a service road running north and south and a railroad running east and west. Assume a domestic cat can penetrate 100 m into the forest from any edge in search of prey.

1. Calculate the area, perimeter, and safe area (the area not penetrated by the cat) of the

▲ FIGURE 16.17 Aerial view of the Texas Hill Country showing the boundary between suburban lots and forestland. (*U.S. Fish and Wildlife Service—Wyman Meinzer*)

original forest. Area = L × W; perimeter = L1 + L2 + L3 + L4.

2. Calculate the area, perimeter, and safe area of each quadrant after the road and railroad were built. Assume quadrants are the same size.

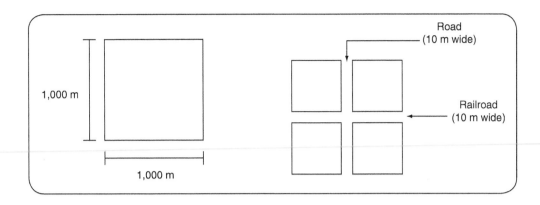

3. How much *total* safe area remains after the road and railroad were built? What percentage is this area of the original safe area?

4. How might the effects of fragmentation on wildlife be minimized? Suggest at least two approaches.

ACTIVITY 16.4

Land Use Analysis

At times, suburban and farmland area developments have been poorly planned and are sprawling. Before wetland laws, valuable wetlands were drained to expand farms or to build more homes or office buildings. Homeowners organize and fight the opening of gravel pits, power plants, and landfills, yet they all need and use their services. Jails, wastewater treatment plants, and trash transfer facilities all serve people's needs, as do business parks and industries.

Most communities run open, well-publicized land use hearings. They seek out the best advice, and use the most advanced tools to enable them to make the best land use decisions possible.

In this activity, you will apply what you have learned about land use management and issues to the questions and tasks that follow.

QUESTIONS & TASKS

Record your responses in your science notebook.

1. Explain what good land use planning should accomplish.

2. Summarize the ways land is managed in your state and/or in your local community (Figure 16.18).

3. Analyze how population change has affected the environment in your area.

4. Ecosystem restoration projects have been attempted in the United States and in other countries. Find a completed project and describe the restoration process. Is fragmentation a problem?

5. Geographic information systems (GIS) provide computer technology that assists land use planners. GIS allow scientists and planners to overlay many layers of data (such as soil types, groundwater layers, topography, zoning laws, and so forth) to produce land use maps for a variety of uses. Use SciLinks and other resources to find out more about GIS. Does your local planning office use this technology? Prepare a report and share the information with your class.

Topic: Geographic Information System
Go to: www.scilinks.org
Code: GloSci7e625

►FIGURE 16.18 Land use decisions are made by people. Make sure you are informed when you become involved with such issues. (*Photo © Paul Hartmann.*)

6. Describe the long-term effect of a local industry on the environment of your community. How can the benefits of having this industry be maximized using good land use planning?

7. Make a land use map to scale of your county. Show major geologic features, towns, parks, and preserves. Show landfills, reservoirs, water treatment plants, wastewater treatment, electric power plants, and other projects. Develop a key. Indicate any future plans. Credit your information sources.

 Land Management Challenges

16.8 Agricultural Land

What challenges do humans face as they attempt to manage land under a variety of conditions?

Topic: range management
Go to: www.scilinks.org
Code: GloSci7e626

Agricultural land includes all of the land used to produce food, fiber, flavorings, flowers, renewable fuel, and crops grown for industrial and pharmaceutical uses. In the United States, this includes 388 million acres of cropland; 788 million acres of range, pasture, and forested land used for grazing; and 7 million acres identified as miscellaneous farmland that makes up the 2.16 million U.S. farms and ranches (see Figures 16.19 and 16.20).

Less than 20 percent of the landmass of the United States is considered cropland. But a good deal of that 20 percent is very good cropland. The United States possesses a quarter of the world's Class 1 soils—the best soil in the world.

On this land, each American farmer produces 2 trillion pounds of food, which is enough food to feed 129 people for a year. Of the world's leading food commodities, the United States produces 43 percent of the soybeans, 43 percent of the corn, 24 percent of the beef, 20 percent of the milk and dairy products and cotton, and more than 10 percent of the wheat and eggs.

One of the challenges facing America's farmers and ranchers is the rapid urban development of farmland. Almost a million acres of farmland are developed each year. Most of this land is on the urban fringes where 74 percent of the nation's fruits, vegetables, and dairy products are produced. This is a challenge faced across the globe as the world's population

▲FIGURE 16.19 Range refers to a large area of open land, whether or not it is actually used for livestock or wildlife forage. (*USDA Natural Resources Conservation Service*)

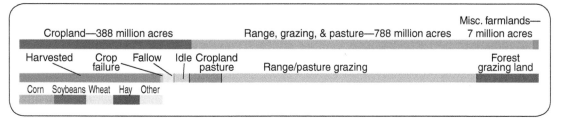

▲FIGURE 16.20 All agricultural lands in the United States: 1,183 million acres. (*Sources: USDA, Economic Research Service and National Resources Inventory, adapted.*)

becomes increasingly urbanized. Farmland also provides habitat and food for wildlife, open space, beauty that enhances tourism, and other environmental enhancements.

QUESTIONS & TASKS

Record your responses in your science notebook.

1. Calculate the total amount of the U.S. landmass that is used to grow crops.

2. Calculate the percentage of the total U.S. landmass that is used to produce food by grazing livestock on pastures, ranges, or on forestland.

3. Why is agricultural land important? What are the benefits of preserving agricultural land and keeping it in production?

16.9 Forestlands

About 33 percent of the U.S. land area, or 747 million acres, is covered by forests. This amounts to about 71 percent of the area that was forested in 1630 (1.05 billion acres) (see Figure 16.21).

When European Americans arrived, they used the forest to meet their basic needs for food and energy, much as Native Americans had done. However, the abundant wealth of the forests was later harvested to build the homes, cities, and industrial infrastructure of a growing nation. The land was also converted to agricultural use to feed a rapidly growing population.

►FIGURE 16.21 Forest resources of the United States, 2002. Percentage of land area in forest, by state. *(Forest Service—U.S. Department of Agriculture)*

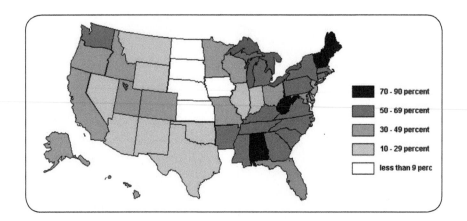

■	70 - 90 percent
■	50 - 69 percent
■	30 - 49 percent
■	10 - 29 percent
□	less than 9 perc

Public/Government-owned	Private property (71%)			
Reserved from timbering	67% is classified timberland, capable of being logged			
Primarily federal and state parks, wilderness and wildlife areas, watershed protection, grazing, and other special uses.	Location of timberlands in U.S.			
	Northeast	Southeast	Rocky Mtns.	Pacific Coast
	72% of all timberlands are in the eastern U.S.			

▲FIGURE 16.22 Forested land, 747 million acres. *(Source: U.S. Forest Service, Forest Resources of the United States, www.ncrs.fs.fed.us)*

By the 1920s, the area of U.S. forests had stopped declining for the first time in 400 years. This was due largely to the stabilization in cropland acreage, which resulted from these two major factors:

1. Draft animals were replaced by internal combustion engines. (In 1900, feeding draft animals took about one-third of the U.S. farmland base.)

2. After 1930, farm productivity increased. This was due to the development of hybrid crops, fertilization, and other practices resulting from agricultural research.

Currently, about 504 million acres of forestland (67 percent of all forestland) are classed as timberland (see Figure 16.22). Timberland is forestland that is capable of producing in excess of 20 cubic feet of wood per acre per year. It is legal to use this land for commercial timber production. (Wilderness areas are legally withdrawn from commercial timber production.) In the East, 94 percent of the forests are classed as timberland. The Pacific Northwest subregion includes 80 percent timberland; the Rocky Mountain region about 50 percent; and Alaska forests include about 10 percent timberland.

Seventy-one percent of timberland is privately owned. In 1996, these lands accounted for 89 percent of growing-stock removals.

Helpful Hint!

Growing stock is a classification of timber inventory that includes trees that meet specified standards of quality or vigor. When associated with volume, it includes only trees that are 5.0 inches and larger dbh (diameter at breast height).

Topic: tree cutting methods
Go to: www.sclinks.org
Code: GloSci7e628

? QUESTIONS & TASKS

Record your responses in your science notebook.

1. Give two reasons why America's forestlands stopped shrinking.

2. Who owns most of America's forested land?

3. Where are most of America's forests located? (See Figure 16.21.)

Western Forest Management

Recent summers in the western United States have been hot and dry. This has resulted in water shortages and rationing, increased demand for air-conditioning, and a significant increase in wildfires. These fires have ignited a public debate about how our public forests have been and should be managed.

In this activity, you will read articles that relate to the topic of forest management. You will be assigned one of the articles to summarize for the class.

Procedure

1. Record the title of the article your teacher assigns in your science notebook.

2. Read the article, and summarize it in about 3 sentences.

3. Meet with the others assigned your article and agree on a short summary.

4. Report your summary to the class.

5. Record the summaries reported by the other groups.

QUESTIONS & TASKS

Record your responses in your science notebook.

1. Assume you were recently elected to the U.S. House of Representatives. You will be voting on the eight bills listed below. After the initial vote, you will prioritize all bills that passed. This must be done because money is limited and allocations must be made.

Pass (Y/N)	Priority	Bill	Short Title (Description)
_____	_____	1	Fight *all* forest fires. Fires are never good.
_____	_____	2	Let some fires burn as long as private property and lives are not threatened.
_____	_____	3	Clear-cut to reduce fire danger and increase water runoff.
_____	_____	4	Institute a moratorium on land development (for homes and cabins) in "red zones."
_____	_____	5	Provide funding for selective thinning in "red zone" areas. (Funding must be provided because Rocky Mountain trees are too "small-bore" to be profitable for logging.)
_____	_____	6	Execute controlled burns to reduce the overgrowth of high-density timber on federal lands.
_____	_____	7	Institute an "Adopt-a-Forest" program to get interested groups and individuals to thin and clear out problem areas.
_____	_____	8	Require insurance companies to assign fire-risk ratings to homes and other buildings they insure that are located in forested areas.

> **Helpful Hint!**
>
> You may not feel fully qualified to vote intelligently on each of these bills. Neither is your actual representative. This is because no single person can be an authority on every bill Congress votes on. You are now more qualified than most people on this topic because you have gathered and processed more material on this subject than most people will ever do.

2. Examine the priorities. This is your class forest management plan.

3. Are there any other possibilities for which a forest management bill could have been proposed?

16.10 Wilderness and Preserves

When you think of wilderness, you may picture deep canyons or fast-running rivers, tall mountains and forests, the howl of a wolf, encountering a bear, or simply a walk through a park on the weekend (see Figure 16.23). The concept of wilderness has evolved to reflect changing attitudes, new information, and the constantly adapting natural world. While most people agree that wilderness is something wild and untamed, how do we know what wilderness is? The practice of designating wilderness areas is unique to North America.

Biologists agree that a wilderness ecosystem is an environment in which both biotic and abiotic components are minimally disturbed by humans. The Wilderness Preservation Act of 1964 defines it this way: Wilderness is a place where "the earth and community of life are untrammeled by man, where man himself is a visitor who does not remain." This act established the country's National Wilderness Preservation System.

Four federal agencies of the U.S. government administer the National Wilderness Preservation System.

- The Park Service manages 51 national parks and more than 300 national monuments, historic sites, memorials, seashores, and battlefields. It oversees 43,616,250 acres of wilderness.

- The USDA Forest Service oversees nearly 200 million acres of national forest and other lands, 34,863,476 of which are wilderness.

- The U.S. Fish and Wildlife Service conserves the nation's wild animals and their habitats by managing a system of more than 500 national wildlife refuges and other areas. These total about 91 million acres of land and water, 20,699,313 of which are wilderness.

- The Bureau of Land Management manages 270 million acres, 6,512,227 of which are wilderness.

Many agree that these different wilderness areas need to be protected. However, wilderness areas throughout the country are managed, or maintained, differently. The communities, government agencies, and resource users who help manage or who use wilderness areas are *stakeholders*. In the United States, the involvement of different stakeholders in planning a wilderness area may affect the way lands are used. In reality, the ability to influence different plans is very small. In the United States, 138 million acres have been set aside as parks and wilderness. Another 99 million acres are wildlife areas.

▼**FIGURE 16.23** Two popular wilderness areas: Elk grazing in a wilderness area near Yellowstone National Park *(Noah Jackson)*. The Boundary Waters Canoe Area Wilderness of northern Minnesota. *(Forest Service, USDA)*

Importance and Use of Preserves

Wilderness preserves attempt to maintain biodiversity. These areas are often created to preserve rare, threatened, or endangered plants and animals.

Interesting Wilderness Facts and Figures

There are 106 million acres of land in 662 designated wilderness areas (as of 2004) in the United States. The largest wilderness area is the Wrangell-St. Elias National Park in Alaska (9.7 million acres). The smallest (and first) wilderness area is the Pelican Island National Wildlife Refuge in Florida (5 acres). Six states (Connecticut, Delaware, Kansas, Maryland, Nebraska, and Rhode Island) have no designated wilderness areas.

The Future of Wilderness

The United States has the largest wilderness preservation system in the world. Still, many valuable areas are not protected. For example, there are nearly 400,000 miles of roads adjacent to or in wilderness areas. These roads may increase logging, grazing, recreational vehicle use, pollution, and fragmentation of habitats. Often, the designation of a wilderness area must be balanced with human use and needs. These areas face increasing pressures as communities and resource needs grow. Here are a few ways we can meet these challenges.

- Link fragmented habitats together with corridors. Corridors are patches that connect separate wilderness enclaves. The corridors allow wildlife greater freedom to move safely.

- Encourage tourism based on outdoor recreation. This can generate income for communities and allow people to realize the economic value of undisturbed wilderness.

- Urge foresters to experiment with new, lower-impact methods for extracting lumber.

- Prompt environmental scientists to look for ways in which stakeholders can resolve conflict over resource use. There are many opportunities of this nature for the future environmental scientist.

> **Apply Your Understanding**
>
> When preserves become too small to maintain their diversity, what strategy can minimize the problem?

 QUESTIONS & TASKS

Record your responses in your science notebook.

1. In what ways might you be a stakeholder in wilderness areas?

2. What are some ways in which wilderness might be managed or used by humans?

3. What are some ways in which humans can minimize their effect on wilderness areas when traveling through them?

4. If you were a park ranger, forester, or wilderness manager, what policies or rules would you make to ensure the preservation of wilderness areas? Who would you include on your advisory board?

16.11 Deserts and Desertification

The impressions that many people have of deserts include sand dunes and parched landscapes, like those in the Namib Desert in southern Africa (see Figure 16.24). These are not necessarily accurate images. For example, the hottest desert in North America is the Sonoran Desert (see Figure 16.25). It has the most complex, and perhaps most varied, desert vegetation on Earth.

► FIGURE 16.24 The Namib Desert is along the west coast of southern Africa. In some places, it borders the Atlantic coastline directly. (*Tom Claytor, www.claytor.com*)

► FIGURE 16.25 The Sonoran Desert is an arid region covering 120,000 square miles in southwestern Arizona and southeastern California, as well as most of Baja California and the western half of the state of Sonora, Mexico. (*DesertUSA.com*)

Arid and extremely arid lands provide the areas we call *deserts*. Deserts cover nearly one-third of Earth's surface. They exist on every continent except Europe, which does have several semiarid (desertlike) regions.

Sand covers only about 20 percent of the world's deserts. Nearly half of desert surfaces are plains where the sands have been removed by wind and erosion.

One characteristic is common to all deserts—they are dry. Deserts and arid areas receive less than 10 inches (in) or 250 millimeters (mm) of annual rainfall. Some deserts have gone more than a year without *any* rainfall. When it does rain in the desert, the storms are often violent, catching some people unprepared. More people drown in deserts than die of thirst! Interestingly, some of the world's driest deserts are located right on an ocean coastline.

Water resources, which are critical to desert life, can occur by natural springs and oases; however, they are rare. Most available water is provided by the rare rain and snowstorms. It is stored inside plants or below the ground's surface where it helps sustain life during dry periods.

Deserts can provide amazingly active ecosystems, teeming with plants and animals. Each desert organism has uniquely adapted to arid conditions. For example, kangaroo rats absorb all of the water out of their urine; they urinate by emitting hard crystals of uric acid.

Desertification

The world's deserts were formed by natural processes over long periods of time. During ice ages of the past, major amounts of water were tied up in glaciers, so less water was available on Earth to fall as rain. This made existing deserts even more arid, and they covered larger areas than they do today.

◀ FIGURE 16.26 A boy carries firewood to his home. *(Kenyan photographer Carol Kaminju.)*

Topic: desertification
Go to: www.scilinks.org
Code: GloSci7e633

People live in many of the arid regions of the world and along the edges of the extremely arid desert areas. This has caused concern about the impact humans can have on the surrounding environment. This impact can facilitate erosion and may lead to a gradual spread of the desert, a process known as **desertification.**

Of special concern are the edges of deserts in poorer nations where local people gather firewood for both cooking and construction (see Figure 16.26). In richer nations, the uncontrolled driving of off-road vehicles (ORVs) on desert lands can do damage that lasts for centuries.

Desertification has received much publicity in the news. However, there is still much that we don't know about the degradation of land and the expansion of the deserts.

> *Contrary to popular belief, the extent of desertification is not at all well known . . . There is extremely little scientific evidence based on field research or remote sensing for the many statements on the global extent of the problem.*
>
> —Ridley Nelson, World Bank, and senior staff to the United Nations Environment Department and its desertification studies

Despite the challenges of living in these arid regions, numerous nomadic communities throughout the world have thrived for centuries near the desert areas. They have provided important trade routes and cultural diversity.

 To learn more about deserts, go to http://pubs.usgs.gov/gip/deserts/.

Throughout the world, innovative solutions are helping preserve these beautiful desert landscapes. In the western United States, for example, the concept of *xeriscaping*—landscaping with native, desert-tolerant plants—has gained popularity. This saves valuable water and

Resource Management: Land 633

encourages habitat and wildlife diversity. Also, *drip irrigation* technology, rather than traditional irrigation systems, is often used for growing crops in deserts. By studying deserts, we are discovering additional ways to further adapt our lifestyles to the desert environment.

? QUESTIONS & TASKS

Record your responses in your science notebook.

1. What should you bring on a day hike into a desert landscape?

2. How can you minimize your impact when exploring desert environments?

3. What are some solutions you might suggest to minimize desertification?

16.12 Wetlands and Floodplains

Swamps, bogs, creeks, shallow lakes, marshes, mudflats, and even shallow rivers are all **wetlands**. Areas that have saturated soils or are water logged for part of the year may also be wetlands. Wetlands may appear as forests or fields. They are found all over our planet, and they are important for the survival of both humans and wildlife (see Figure 16.27).

Wetlands are often located on floodplains. **Floodplains** are the wide level areas that border a stream or river and are covered by water when the streams or rivers flood. As a result, homes should not be built on floodplains.

Wetlands usually have areas of shallow water where sunlight can penetrate to the bottom. These areas provide an important habitat for microscopic plants and animals, grasses, worms, snails, clams, frogs, and a host of other organisms. Shrimp and crabs are protected from predators in shallow water. Migratory birds, waterfowl, and other wading birds feed in shallow waters as well. Together, all these interactions form a wetland ecosystem.

Wetlands are productive. They can produce more biomass per square meter per year than any other ecosystem. Coastal wetlands, also called estuaries, salt marshes, and tidal wetlands, annually produce millions of tons of detritus (broken down organic nutrients) that support sport and commercial fish and shellfish industries (see Figure 16.28).

Preserved wetlands help minimize erosion during flooding. Wetlands hold a stockpile of nutrients. Nearby farms can benefit from both richer soils and a greater diversity of

► FIGURE 16.27 The Upper Klamath National Wildlife Refuge in Oregon. *(U.S. Fish and Wildlife Service)*

Topic: wetlands
Go to: www.scilinks.org
Code: GloSci7e634

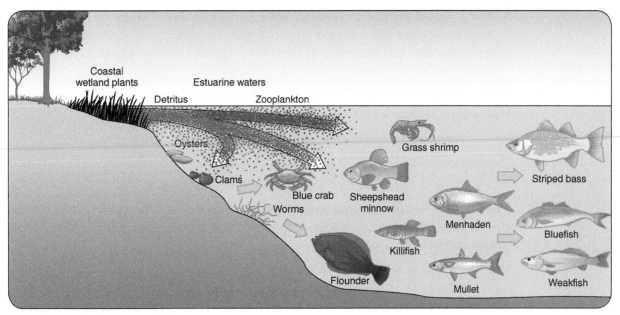

▲**FIGURE 16.28** Coastal wetlands produce millions of tons of detritus annually that support fish and shellfish. (*Adapted from USEPA.*)

wildlife. Wetlands also contribute to groundwater recharge by allowing precipitation to be stored where it can slowly percolate into the ground. Recreation benefits are provided for hunting, fishing, canoeing, and wildlife viewing. Wetlands are also the first line of defense against pollution from surface water runoff. Chemicals from factories, pesticides from agriculture, and sediment can be absorbed by wetlands instead of ending up in rivers, lakes, or reservoirs downstream.

People like to live near water. One in seven Americans lives along the east and gulf coasts. Nearly half of the original wetland habitats in the United States have been converted into agricultural lands and urban areas. As a result, wildlife habitat and water quality have decreased. In response, farmers' environmental organizations, government agencies, and concerned citizens are working to restore and expand wetlands.

Farmers around the world are working to create wetlands to absorb excess nutrients and runoff. When new roads are built, the Department of Transportation (DOT) uses the practice of *mitigation banking*. For each wetland area that is damaged due to road construction, new wetland area is created elsewhere. When road construction must go through a wetland, heavy equipment can be placed on platforms above the delicate land. This may involve the Army Corps of Engineers. The Environmental Protection Agency (EPA) has a special wetland hotline to help planners, developers, and scientists stay informed of new policy and information. The EPA also sponsors community and school "Adopt a Watershed" programs so students and their communities can monitor water quality and be informed.

As wetlands face increasing pressure, the resources that wetlands protect are more threatened. It is important for us to preserve wetlands and find ways to live in harmony with them.

Apply Your Understanding

How can wetlands be preserved?

 QUESTIONS & TASKS

Record your responses in your science notebook.

1. What specific benefits do you think tidal wetlands provide?

2. Does your community restrict or regulate building on floodplains? If so, how?

3. A large wetland near your neighborhood is to be developed for housing. You have been hired to plan the new community. What strategies would you recommend for planners? How should construction be carried out? Would you recommend many individual houses or a single, large housing unit?

16.13 Urban Environments

The future success of humankind is linked to how successful urban living will be as part of the planet's ecosystem.

—Peter Head, Arup (an international engineering firm)

Apply Your Understanding

Where do cities develop? Give several examples.

Since the shift from hunting and gathering to agriculture, people have been creating population centers. These urban environments develop in areas of geographic, political, and resource importance.

Urban environments are places where music, literature, and art can flourish. Cities help support institutions such as libraries, universities, and foundations, which provide the means for nations and economies to grow. Cities need creative environmental scientists to address their special needs and improve the environmental health. When managed well, urban areas can be enjoyable places to live, work, and play.

Urban environments deserve our special attention because 75 percent of Americans live in an urban setting. About 50 percent of all people on Earth live in cities (Figure 16.29). Demographers project that more than 62 percent of the world's population will live in cities by the year 2025.

Cities have needs similar to living organisms and ecosystems. They require (1) a flow of energy (sunlight, food, fuel); (2) material resources (vitamins, minerals, water, air); and (3) ways to remove wastes. Unlike a self-contained ecosystem, however, cities require a large outside region for support. As we examined in Chapter 13, large quantities of water must be brought to cities. That water is cleaned, used, and then cleaned again before it is released downstream. Likewise, major efforts must be made to keep the air clean. In addition, food, raw materials, and fuel must be brought in from remote regions to make the city work. Finally, the challenge of waste disposal must be addressed. We will examine that in the next section.

▶ FIGURE 16.29 More than half of all the people on Earth live in cities.

Despite obstructions created by homes, office buildings, and streets, parks and other open spaces can create corridors or connections between habitats for wildlife. These include paths and forested areas along the side of creeks and rivers. With proper planning, an urban area can support a healthy wildlife community.

A variety of innovative strategies aim to increase the quality of life in urban settings. But good land use planning is critical. Rapid and inexpensive public transportation systems are vital. They both reduce congestion on streets and pollution from vehicles. Transit-oriented design is becoming a popular strategy. New office buildings are being built that decrease energy requirements and use more natural light and fresh air to improve worker health and limit pollution. Waste reduction, compaction, and recycling are strategies receiving more and more emphasis. These are challenges most of us must face as we move into the future.

The challenge of urban planning is to provide the natural resources a city needs as efficiently as possible. This means wastes will be minimized as well as their impact on surrounding regions. Healthy urban environments increase positive values toward nature (for example, a greater environmental connection and respect) and a higher quality of life (community optimism, neighborhood quality, and social civility). As humans, we can shape our environment. In the end, our environment shapes us. We must plan with care.

Think about This!

What can we do to meet the challenge of maintaining great cities?

QUESTIONS & TASKS

Record your responses in your science notebook.

1. Like a living ecosystem, a city must maintain three things. List them.

2. Why is it so important to focus on the needs and functioning of cities?

3. How would you plan for increased population in your city or neighborhood and maintain the current level of environmental health? How would you improve the level of environmental health?

The Problem of Waste

On March 22, 1987, a gigantic load of garbage—3,168 tons—from a New York City suburb was refused as landfill in Islip, New York. It was then acquired by National Waste Contractors, Inc., who hoped to sell it for methane extraction. The trash was loaded onto the barge *Mobro 4,000* and headed for Jones County, North Carolina. However, North Carolina officials ordered the barge away. By this time, it had become a symbol of our nation's mounting waste disposal problems.

For years, we believed the saying "out of sight, out of mind" applied to all our waste products. We learned that matter can't be destroyed, but we acted as if it could. Bury it and it's gone. When it goes down the drain, it disappears. When the trash truck leaves the neighborhood, the trash is gone. Everything that we learned about the conservation of mass and reality didn't seem to connect.

The journey of the *Mobro 4,000* (see Figure 16.30) finally made the connection between science and reality. It traveled 6,000 miles in search of a dump. It was spurned by at least five states and three countries—Mexico, Belize, and the Bahamas. It returned in failure to Gravesend Bay, off Brooklyn, on May 16, 1987. New York state and city officials huddled and negotiated until July 10, 1987, when a solution was announced: **incineration**. The

Think about This!

What does the story about the garbage barge symbolize?

► FIGURE 16.30 The *Mobro 4,000* and its spurned cargo. *(Jeffrey Cardenas)*

3,168 tons of trash would be burned in a Brooklyn incinerator. Here it would be reduced to 400 tons of ash. The ash would then be trucked to the Islip municipal landfill.

In the rest of this chapter, we will take a close look at the problem of waste. How did it begin? How is it being solved?

ACTIVITY 16.6

Not in My Backyard!

What should we do about disposing of our waste? In this activity, you will start to grapple with this problem and the solutions.

Background

Municipal solid waste (MSW) is the term we use for the (mostly) nonhazardous waste generated in households, commercial establishments, and institutions, and light industrial wastes. MSW does not include industrial process wastes, agricultural wastes, mining wastes, and sewage sludge. In its most common form, MSW is the trash we place by the curb in front of our homes.

Americans throw away more than 240 million tons of MSW each year. That averages about 4.5 pounds per person per day. This waste would fill a convoy of 10-ton garbage trucks reaching over halfway to the moon!

The pie chart in Figure 16.31 shows what is in our trash. The percentages are by weight. (Volume percentages are slightly different.) Not shown in the pie graph is the fact that some of these wastes are toxic.

Each year the average household generates 8 to 10 pounds of hazardous waste. These wastes are contained in everyday products such as cleaners (floor, drain, and oven cleaners; furniture polishes; and bleach), paints, pesticides, and auto products (antifreeze, batteries, motor oil, and gasoline). The EPA estimates that approximately 0.4 percent of all MSW is hazardous. Because they are used in the home and can be combined with or hidden among the usual MSW, these materials are very

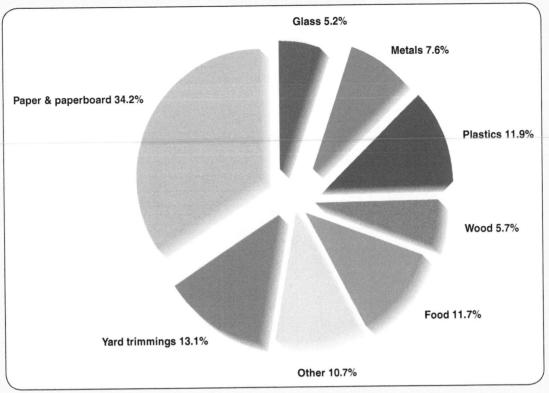

▲ FIGURE 16.31 Gross discards of municipal solid waste materials, 2005; 100% = 245 million tons. (*From EPA–Municipal Solid Waste, Basic Facts.*)

difficult to regulate. As a result, they end up in landfills.

New federal landfill regulations make disposal very expensive as old landfills close and new ones become more difficult to open. Landfills now must have liners and groundwater monitoring.

Many American cities are having difficulty finding new locations for landfills. It is not that there is no more space. Instead, the problem is mainly economic and political. We are running out of acceptable locations close to where the trash is generated. People simply don't want to live by or near landfills and incinerators. Because of problems and disasters related to careless attitudes and practices from earlier times, we fear that new laws and technologies will somehow be ignored or fail to function. Put it somewhere else, but not in my backyard!

As the costs of waste disposal skyrocket, many eastern cities and states are casting their eyes on the great open spaces of the West. The economics of dumping is partly to blame. Tipping fees (what trash haulers must pay to unload their trucks) in the more densely populated eastern states average from $80 to $100 per ton of trash. In the western states, dumping costs range from $4 to $50 per ton.

What should we do?

Materials (for each team)

- *Arriving at a Decision* handout

Procedure

1. Read the background information carefully. Then discuss it with your lab group.

2. As you discuss, fill in the handout *Arriving at a Decision* (Figure 16.32). If the flowchart is too small, recopy it on larger paper.

3. Next, review your plan of action.

4. Near the end of the class session, your group will make a short presentation of your plan.

5. Turn in your written work for evaluation. You will use your plan as a framework for the remainder of this chapter.

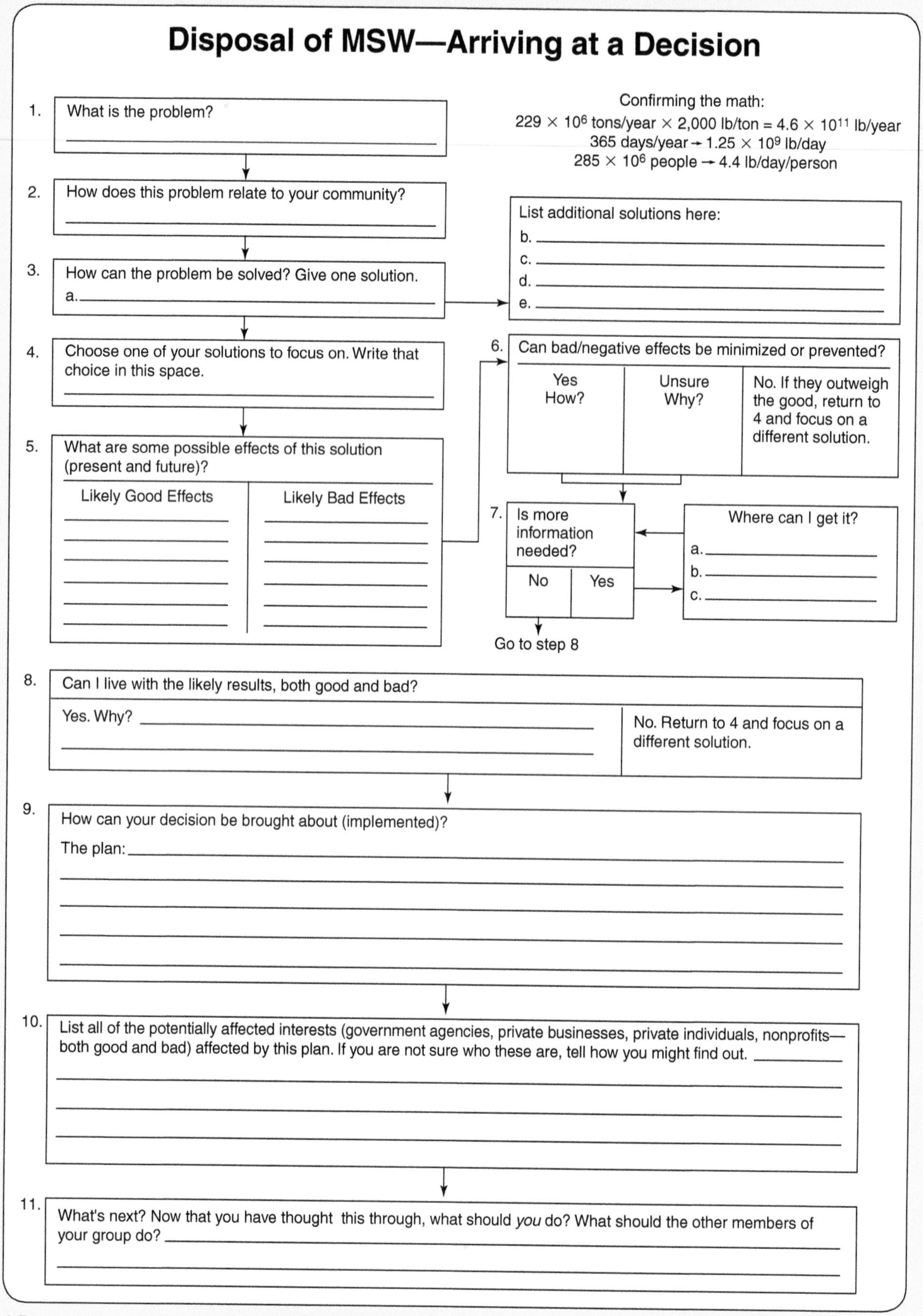

Disposal of MSW—Arriving at a Decision

Confirming the math:

229×10^6 tons/year $\times$ 2,000 lb/ton $= 4.6 \times 10^{11}$ lb/year

365 days/year $\rightarrow 1.25 \times 10^9$ lb/day

285×10^6 people $\rightarrow$ 4.4 lb/day/person

1. What is the problem?

2. How does this problem relate to your community?

3. How can the problem be solved? Give one solution.
   a.

List additional solutions here:
   b.
   c.
   d.
   e.

4. Choose one of your solutions to focus on. Write that choice in this space.

5. What are some possible effects of this solution (present and future)?

Likely Good Effects	Likely Bad Effects

6. Can bad/negative effects be minimized or prevented?

Yes How?	Unsure Why?	No. If they outweigh the good, return to 4 and focus on a different solution.

7. Is more information needed?

No	Yes

   Go to step 8

   Where can I get it?
   a.
   b.
   c.

8. Can I live with the likely results, both good and bad?

   Yes. Why?

   No. Return to 4 and focus on a different solution.

9. How can your decision be brought about (implemented)?
   The plan:

10. List all of the potentially affected interests (government agencies, private businesses, private individuals, nonprofits—both good and bad) affected by this plan. If you are not sure who these are, tell how you might find out.

11. What's next? Now that you have thought this through, what should *you* do? What should the other members of your group do?

▲ **FIGURE 16.32** A flowchart to help you arrive at a decision.

16.14 Disposing of Our Solid Wastes

All living things make wastes. In nature, however, wastes are recycled. Natural wastes are **biodegradable,** meaning that microorganisms break them down and change them into materials that can be used by the living.

Modern societies interrupt natural chemical cycles. We produce metal alloys, glass products, plastics, and a whole host of chemicals that are not biodegradable. Further, our wastes are discarded as a random mixture of organic products (paper, cardboard, food scraps) and inorganic materials (bottles, cans, plastics, chemicals, metals). This makes dealing with the wastes difficult.

The barge incident showed that the problem is now one we must solve. Using natural processes can be a solution.

Much of our problem stems from the fact that, in the past, people got used to hauling wastes out of town to the public dump. Since hauling wastes was expensive (and time consuming), we didn't want to haul them too far. But as the town grew, it surrounded the dump. Often the dump was converted to a park or other recreational area. A new dump was opened a few miles out of town. As the city grew, the story was repeated.

The old dumps often smelled bad and were breeding grounds for flies and rats. They sometimes caught on fire and burned for days. Newer *sanitary landfills* cover newly dumped wastes with soil or some other materials at least once each day. This has solved the rat, odor, and fire problems. However, the chemical makeup of the wastes has changed (see Figure 16.33). New problems have arisen. The sanitary landfill approach is no longer an adequate solution to waste disposal.

An examination of Figure 16.34 explains why the chemical makeup of modern wastes is different now than it was in the early 1900s.

Most of the vast quantity of municipal solid waste is biodegradable. Much of it is paper, metal, and glass that could be recycled. Figure 16.31 summarizes municipal solid waste by type.

This information indicates that waste minimization and a good **recycling** program have great possibilities. Some argue that Americans are too set in their ways and cannot be made to separate their trash. Separating trash means putting paper products in one container, food

Apply Your Understanding

Distinguish between waste minimization and recycling.

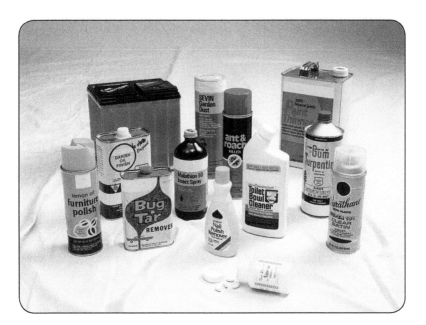

◀ FIGURE 16.33 Some modern products that contribute to the solid waste problem. In Figure 16.31, these are classified as "Other."

Item	Early 1900s	Today
Transportation	Horse and buggy waste = manure and urine.	Automobile wastes = exhausts, old batteries, used motor oil, chemical engine coolants, etc.
Sanitation	Outhouse and wash basin wastes = abandoned toilet pits and dirty water.	Flush toilets and running water wastes = detergents, shampoos, toilet bowl cleaners.
Medication	No cure for serious infections. Peppermint and other natural remedies.	Powerful drugs and antibiotics. All kinds of chemicals to cure minor illnesses.
Pest control	Flyswatter, sticky flypaper, cleanliness, soapy dishwater dumped on garden vegetables and plants, mousetraps.	Insecticides and repellents.
Housecleaning	Mops and water, brooms, dust rags, a few waxes, homemade soap.	Chemical floor cleaners, oven cleaners, scouring powders, rug shampoos, furniture polish, spot removers, room fresheners.
Clothing	Most clothing made from organic fibers—wool, linen, cotton. Leather—animal skins and fur.	Most clothing made of synthetic fibers, which are washed in automatic washing machines with detergents and fabric softeners.
Packaging	Market basket, gunny sack, saddlebag.	Paper, cardboard, plastics, styrofoam.

▲FIGURE 16.34 Modern technology has changed the composition of what we consume.

scraps in a second, metal in a third, glass in a fourth, and so on. (Other separation schemes are possible.) We all seem to respond to financial incentives. Perhaps if the pickup charge for sorted trash was significantly less than that for unsorted trash, a meaningful behavioral change would result. (It costs more to do this, and someone must pay.) Or, the return deposit on containers could be increased. Although plastics make up a small percentage of municipal trash by weight, they take up a great deal of space. In addition, most plastics are not degradable. Some plastics can be recycled. The "Other" category in Figure 16.31 may be a small percentage, but in today's society, it is a very significant one. Included in this category is hazardous waste (see Figure 16.35).

▼FIGURE 16.35 Hazardous wastes.

Classification	Characteristics
Highly flammable or explosive	React chemically to produce fires, explosions, or other violent reactions that may harm humans.
Corrosive or reactive	React chemically to eat away other substances including human flesh. Reactive materials combine with other things to become dangerous.
Toxic	Act as a poison or cause cancer, birth defects, or other health problems.
Infectious*	Cause living organisms to become diseased.
Radioactive*	Can cause illness and increase a person's chance of developing cancer.

*Infectious and radioactive wastes are not legally defined as hazardous wastes in all cases. However, they fit the definition.

16.15 Classifying Wastes

We have a variety of wastes, some of which are dangerous. As a result, it has become necessary to classify them. Once classified, mandated (legal) disposal procedures must be followed. Wastes are classified as nonhazardous and hazardous.

Nonhazardous Wastes

1. **Biodegradable:** Substances that have their origin in living materials and are broken down by the action of microorganisms. These substances include paper products, food wastes, wood, some fibers, and leather.

2. **Nonbiodegradable:** Discarded substances that are not biodegradable and are not potentially dangerous to humans. These include glass, most metal products, and plastics. With time, chemical action corrodes many metal products.

Hazardous Wastes

Hazardous wastes are discarded chemical or biological substances that are potentially dangerous to humans. Figure 16.35 summarizes the types of hazardous waste. Hazardous wastes must be handled so they do not escape into the environment in concentrations that could be dangerous. We especially want to prevent them from getting into groundwater and municipal water systems (see Figure 16.36).

16.16 Industrial Processes

Modern societies rely on products such as automobiles, airplanes, computers, televisions, home appliances, and communications systems. To produce these, a host of items is required. These include, but are not limited to, fuels, lubricants, machine tools, paints, solvents, alloys, and glues. Consider, for example, what is involved in the building of an integrated circuit for use in a computer:

1. Growing, slicing, and polishing pure crystals.

2. Creating the circuitry on each crystal chip. This involves chemical coating and heating.

Distinguish between nonhazardous and hazardous wastes.

Topic: hazardous waste
Go to: www.scilinks.org
Code: GloSci7e643

What are the different types of hazardous waste?

Helpful Hint!

An *integrated circuit* is a miniaturized electrical circuit designed to perform a specific function.

► **FIGURE 16.37** Printed circuits are the foundation on which "high-tech" industry is built. *(Courtesy: Merix Corporation.)*

3. Diffusing impurities into the chip to alter its electrical characteristics.

4. Etching the surface into the desired pattern, including the electrical connection points.

5. Mounting the circuit in a frame, wiring it, and testing it.

Helpful Hint!

Soldering is the process of uniting the surfaces of metals using a metallic cement called solder.

One of the processes used in producing **printed circuits** (see Figure 16.37) is **electroplating**. The surfaces that are to be wired must be prepared for soldering. Such surfaces can be produced by electroplating with tin, tin-lead alloys, or gold. The next two activities focus on the electroplating process.

ACTIVITY 16.7

Conducting Solutions

In this activity, you will investigate the electrical conductivity of water, salt solution, and sugar solution.

Materials (for each team of 4 students)

- 9-volt battery
- graduated container (medicine cup)
- small packet of sugar
- water
- battery harness with lightbulb
- small packet of table salt
- plastic spoon or stirring rod

- paper towel
- 4 safety goggles

BE SAFE

Wear safety googles.

Procedure

1. Attach the battery clips with the bulb to your 9-volt battery. Touch the 2 clips at the end together; notice how brightly the bulb shines.

Helpful Hint!

To avoid wearing out the battery, do not allow the clips to touch each other except when performing the experiment.

2. Fill the graduated container to the 30 milliliter (mL) mark with tap water.

3. Attach the clip from the black wire (negative) to the lip of the container so that the end of the clip is in the water (see Figure 16.38).

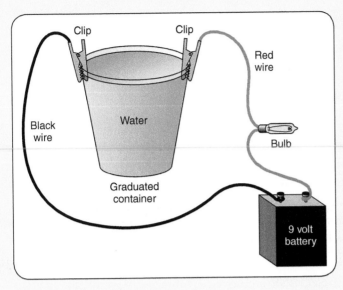

◀ FIGURE 16.38 The setup for testing electrical conductivity.

4. Attach the clip from the red wire (positive) to the opposite side of the container as you did in step 3. Record your observations in your science notebook. Is water a good conductor of electricity? What did you observe that proves this?

5. Add a very small amount of table salt from the packet to the water in the cup. Slowly stir and note what happens to the bulb. What do you observe?

6. Now add the rest of the packet and stir. What do you observe?

7. Why did the bulb glow more brightly?

8. Take off the clips and rinse; dry them with a paper towel. Dispose of the solution as directed. Rinse out the container. Add 30 mL of water to the container.

9. Attach the clips again to the container, and slowly add the small packet of sugar and stir. What do you observe?

10. Does sugar form ions when it dissolves? What is your evidence?

11. Take off the clips, and rinse and dry them. Rinse out the container. Clean up as instructed.

QUESTIONS & TASKS

Record your responses in your science notebook.

1. Define *toxic*.

2. Define *waste*.

3. Give examples of some toxic wastes that could be found in your home or in homes in your neighborhood.

4. How do you dispose of household toxic wastes?

5. Complete the following definitions:

   a. **Conductor:** a material that is capable of transferring . . .

   b. **Conducting solution:** a solution that can carry . . .

   c. **Ion:**

   d. **Electrolyte:** a substance that breaks up into ions when it . . .

   e. **Nonelectrolyte:** a substance that . . .

16.17 Why Some Substances Dissolve and Some Solutions Conduct

Water molecules have a positive and a negative side (see Figure 2.7). Salt and sugar molecules have positive and negative sides.

Scientists think that water molecules are free to move around in water solutions. What happens when salt and sugar crystals are dropped into water? Since like charges repel and unlike charges attract, water molecules can orient themselves to attack and pull on the opposite-charged portions of both salt and sugar crystals. This pulls them apart, and we say they dissolve. In the case of salt (NaCl), the sodium part (Na^+) can be pulled away from the chloride part (Cl^-). We thus end up with a conducting solution with charged particles (ions) floating around (see Figure 16.39.)

Once a salt crystal dissolves, the sodium ions (Na^+) and chloride ions (Cl^-) are free to move around in solution. If electrodes are inserted into a salt solution, the ions drift and current flows (see Figure 16.40).

Unlike salt, sugar molecules are not pulled apart into ions, so the sugar solution does not conduct.

► FIGURE 16.39 Water molecules attack sodium and chlorine sites at the surface of a salt crystal and pull it apart. (See also Figure 2.7.)

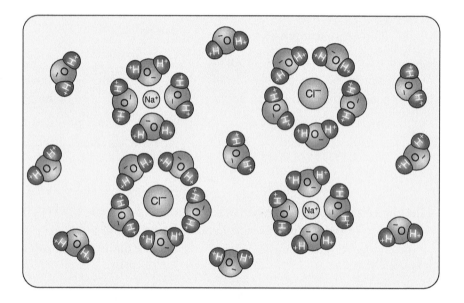

► FIGURE 16.40 As sodium and chloride ions move toward electrodes, current flows in the electric circuit. What happens at each electrode depends on the chemistry of both the ion and the electrode. (We'll talk more about that later. See also Figure 2.7.)

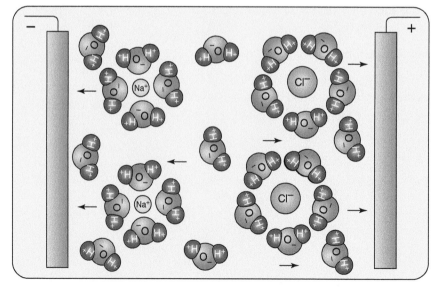

ACTIVITY 16.8

Copper Plating

In this activity, you will investigate the process of electroplating and learn about the potential disposal problems of a toxic substance.

Materials

WARNING

For the class:

- labeled container to collect plating solution

DO NOT TASTE the copper plating solution. Copper chloride is toxic if taken internally. Wash your hands thoroughly before leaving class. Wear safety goggles.

For each team of 4 students:

- 9-volt battery
- graduated container
- paper clip (steel)
- paper towel
- battery harness with lightbulb
- 250 mL bottle of a 50,000 ppm copper chloride solution
- copper strip
- 4 safety goggles

Procedure

1. Add 30 mL of a 50,000 ppm copper chloride solution to the container.

   Content Clue

   Copper chloride is an electrolyte. It was dissolved in water to make the solution.

2. Bend a strip of copper metal in the shape of a "J." Hook the end of the strip over the side of the container, as shown in Figure 16.41.

Clip the red wire to the strip (see Figure 16.41).

3. Bend one end of the paper clip slightly, as shown in the diagram. Attach the black wire to the bent end of the paper clip.

BE SAFE

Be careful not to touch the wire clips directly to the copper solution or to spill the copper solution from the container.

4. Carefully lower the paper clip into the solution. Allow the current to flow for 2 minutes. In your science notebook, reproduce the table shown in Figure 16.42 and record your observations.

5. Remove the paper clip and allow it to dry on a paper towel.

6. Disconnect the battery clip.

7. Carefully pour the plating solution from your graduated container into the class container labeled USED COPPER CHLORIDE SOLUTION.

8. Rinse and dry your container, the clips, and the strip of copper.

QUESTIONS & TASKS

Record your responses in your science notebook.

1. What happened to the paper clip? What seems to be coating it?

   Helpful Hint!

   Copper ions are blue in color, $Cu^{+2}_{(blue)}$. They are toxic.

2. Copper ions are positively charged. Which clip of the

◄ FIGURE 16.41 The setup for investigating the process of electroplating.

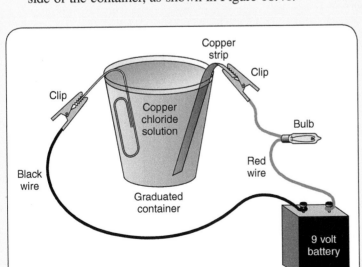

Copper strip

Clip

Clip

Copper chloride solution

Bulb

Black wire

Red wire

Graduated container

9 volt battery

Appearance	Paper Clip	Plating Solution	Copper Strip
Before the reaction			
After the reaction			

battery are they attracted to? From your observations, how would you prove that?

3. As a group, discuss what should be done with the toxic copper chloride solution you used.

Give at least two points of view. Summarize your discussion in three short paragraphs.

[Used with permission of the Science Education for Public Understanding Program, Lawrence Hall of Science, University of California at Berkeley.]

ACTIVITY 16.9

Disposing of Toxic Waste: The Decision

In this activity, you will examine and rank alternative methods for disposing of toxic waste.

Materials

* *Disposing of Toxic Waste* handout

Procedure

1. Review your suggestions for disposing of the toxic copper ions in Activity 16.8. Compare your ideas to the alternative disposal methods summarized in Figure 16.43.

2. Read the information about waste management in section 16.18.

3. Then rank the 6 strategies on the *Disposing of Toxic Waste* handout from 1 = best to 6 = worst. Finally, justify your ranking.

▼ FIGURE 16.43 Analysis of alternative methods for disposing of toxic waste.

Method	Description and/or Examples	Ranking (1 = best to 6 = worst)	Justification
Dilution	Add H_2O until down to legal level and dispose.		
Out of sight	• Shoot into space. • Bury it. • Burn it. • Dump in ocean.		
Waste reclamation	• Change waste to valuable product. Recover and sell. • Recycle.		
Chemical alteration	• Change waste to nontoxic substance and dispose.		
Containment dump	• Tie up in concrete, a barrel, or special landfill.		
Waste minimization	• Buy only what you need. • Substitute nontoxic for toxic.		

16.18 Waste Management

Wastes in general, and hazardous wastes in particular, are dealt with in all of the following ways.

Reduction (Waste Minimization)

The quantity of wastes produced can be reduced in a variety of ways. Substitution reduces the demand for a hazardous substance. Recycling enables us to continually enjoy the benefits of a substance without having to dispose of it. Substances like DDT may be banned. People should learn to purchase no more than they need, or they could buy clothes at a thrift store, for example. This would automatically reduce the quantity of waste.

What are some ways of reducing solid-waste problems?

Substitution

In some cases, substitutes can be found. Many toxic insecticides have been replaced by synthetic substitutes that can be broken down into nontoxic materials. Nontoxic pigments, such as titanium oxide, have replaced the lead compound used in house paint. Lead was phased out of gasoline as an octane booster; certain organic compounds can accomplish the same thing.

Apply Your Understanding

Give an example of how a waste material was reduced by substitution.

Recycling and Waste Reclamation

Lead is a toxic metal, but it is also a useful metal. The lead in automobile storage batteries can be recovered and reused (65 percent of all lead is recycled). This way, the concentration of lead in our environment is partially controlled and does not increase. We also get much more use of the lead. Many industries can reclaim valuable materials before the waste stream leaves their plant.

Chemical Alteration

Some toxic substances can be chemically altered (changed) to make them nontoxic. Nerve gases can be detoxified, for example.

Think about This!

Why should we chemically alter wastes?

Labeling Instructions

Special and clear instructions, through proper labeling of hazardous materials, are essential to prevent improper use. We must learn how to read and follow these instructions. The first step in proper disposal is knowing what *proper disposal* means.

Think about This!

How should potential waste products be labeled?

Sanitary Landfills and Secure Landfills

It is necessary to place certain wastes in specially designed, sealed landfills. Hazardous wastes cannot simply be buried because they may eventually seep into aquifers and end up in someone's drinking water. They also must not be dumped down the drain. Dilution is not acceptable because the toxins do not disappear. Instead, they are just spread out. Some could become biologically concentrated and cause new problems. Sewage-treatment plants were not designed to handle toxic wastes. Many will kill the microorganisms that make a sewer plant work. For these reasons, new municipal (sanitary) landfills are required by law to be constructed in such a manner that they prevent the escape of hazardous materials. Hazardous wastes must go to secure landfills.

Topic: landfills
Go to: www.scilinks.org
Code: GloSc7e649

Incineration

Incineration is the burning of wastes under carefully controlled procedures. It is described in more detail in section 16.19 Disposal of Municipal Solid Waste.

Regulation/Enforcement

It is essential to our well-being that the proper disposal of hazardous wastes be regulated and enforced. The Environmental Protection Agency (EPA) has been charged with this responsibility. Proper disposal is expensive, and there are always some who will try to avoid regulations. Unlicensed waste haulers are known as "gypsy haulers" and "midnight dumpers." Enforcement of our laws against them must be swift and effective.

Public Education

Think about This!

Who is responsible for the proper disposal of a product?

Whenever you buy a product, *you* take the responsibility to use and dispose of the product properly. If this attitude can be etched in people's minds and reflected in their behavior, we will have come a long way in dealing with our solid waste problems.

Our waste disposal problem has increased greatly since World War II. Our nation's rapid industrial growth just after the war was matched by a surge in consumer demand for new products. The country seized upon new "miracle" products, such as plastics, nylon stockings, and coated paper goods, as soon as industry introduced them. Our appetite for material goods also created a problem: how to manage the increasing amounts of waste produced by industry and consumers alike.

Apply Your Understanding

Summarize waste management legislation at the federal level.

As part of a general response to pollution, Congress passed the **Solid Waste Disposal Act** in 1965. It was the first federal law to require safeguards. It also encouraged environmentally sound methods for the disposal of household, municipal, commercial, and industrial refuse.

In 1970, Congress amended this law by passing the Resource Recovery Act. A third amendment, passed in 1976, gave us the **Resource Conservation and Recovery Act (RCRA)**. The primary goals of RCRA are as follows:

- Protect human health and the environment from the potential hazards of waste disposal.

- Conserve energy and natural resources.

- Reduce the amount of waste generated, including hazardous waste.

- Ensure that wastes are managed in an environmentally sound manner.

As our knowledge about the health and **environmental impacts** of waste increased, Congress revised RCRA, first in 1980 and again in 1984. The 1984 amendments—referred to as the Hazardous and Solid Waste Amendments (HSWA)—significantly expanded the scope of RCRA. HSWA was created in response to strongly voiced citizen concerns that existing methods of hazardous waste disposal, particularly land disposal, were not safe.

Problems associated with past mismanagement of hazardous wastes are covered by RCRA's companion law—the **Comprehensive Environmental Response, Compensation, and Liability Act of 1980 (CERCLA)**—more commonly known as Superfund. It addresses the cleanup of inactive and abandoned hazardous waste sites.

The term "RCRA" (pronounced rick-ruh) is often used interchangeably to mean (1) the law, (2) the regulations, and (3) EPA policy and guidance. The law describes the waste management program mandated by Congress and gives EPA the authority to develop means to carry it out. The regulations carry out the Congressional intent by providing explicit requirements for waste management that are legally enforceable. The EPA policy statements clarify issues related to the implementation of the regulations. Together, these three elements are essential parts of the RCRA program.

Record your responses in your science notebook.

1. How should you properly dispose of used paint thinner?

2. How should insect sprays, garden pest powders, and ant poison be disposed of in your community?

3. Does your school have a recycling program?

16.19 Disposal of Municipal Solid Waste

What is municipal solid waste?

As you learned earlier, solid waste from homes, office buildings, and restaurants is called municipal solid waste or MSW. Modern disposal techniques consist of five main strategies.

1. Recycling

The benefits of recycling have already been discussed. Recycling must be part of any modern municipal solid waste program.

2. Biological Breakdown

The largest portion of municipal solid waste is biodegradable. As we described in Chapter 11, these materials can be broken down into liquid and gaseous fuels. To obtain full value from them, they should be separated from the other categories of waste.

Topic: municipal solid waste (MSW)
Go to: www.scilinks.org
Code: GloSci7e651

3. Sanitary Landfills

Modern sanitary landfills cause little damage to the environment (see Figure 16.44). The site is carefully selected, and liners are used to prevent leaching of the soluble portions of

▼FIGURE 16.44 A modern sanitary landfill.

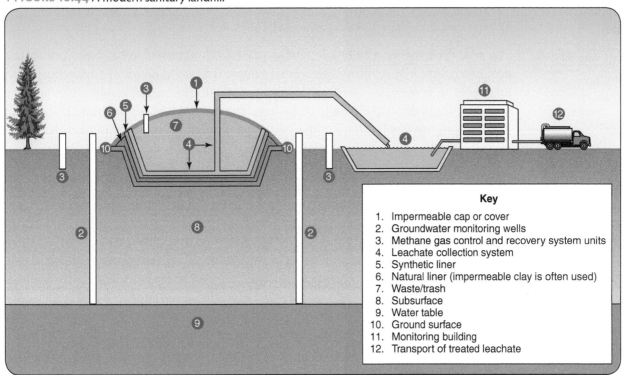

Key
1. Impermeable cap or cover
2. Groundwater monitoring wells
3. Methane gas control and recovery system units
4. Leachate collection system
5. Synthetic liner
6. Natural liner (impermeable clay is often used)
7. Waste/trash
8. Subsurface
9. Water table
10. Ground surface
11. Monitoring building
12. Transport of treated leachate

the wastes into groundwater. At these landfills, wastes are packed firmly together by heavy tractors and covered with soil each day. The soil cover prevents insects and rodents from getting into the refuse. It also greatly reduces fire danger and foul odors. Some landfills are designed to become a source of useful methane gas as the organic materials decompose. However, many communities have run out of nearby potential landfill sites. Future landfill sites can become controversial issues. Hauling solid wastes (see Figure 16.45) great distances is expensive; it also is a waste of energy.

4. Special Handling Procedures for Hazardous Wastes—Secure Landfills

Question This!

Does your community have a program for handling household hazardous waste?

The need for properly handling hazardous wastes has already been discussed. Industries are already carefully regulated. However, many cities and states do not have regulations that apply to households. Find out if your community has a hazardous waste program. If it does, try to develop a plan to make more people aware of the program. If it doesn't, find out how one can be started. Many successful programs began with the concern of a single person.

5. Incineration

Incineration is the process of burning wastes (see Figure 16.46). To prevent the release of hazardous substances into the atmosphere, the products of incineration must be treated. Solid particles are removed, and the gases are mixed with chemicals. The remaining solids and ashes from the incinerator are taken to a hazardous waste landfill called a secure landfill. There are several advantages to incineration.

- Some valuable substances can be reclaimed from the ashes.

- Incineration results in a huge reduction in volume.

- In some communities, the heat from municipal incinerators is used to produce steam. The steam is used to drive the turbines that generate electrical power.

The problem of waste disposal is monumental. However, if we want to continue to enjoy the products of modern technology, we must manage the wastes we generate. In the near future, it is projected that more than half of all MSW in the United States will be either incinerated, recycled, or composted.

Technology: Friend or Foe?

Technology is the application of science to produce useful goods and services. In this chapter, we have seen (again) that the process of producing those goods and services can also produce new problems. The building of desired products can add to our waste disposal problem when unwanted by-products are not degradable by natural systems (see Figure 16.47).

What is technology?

◄Figure 16.47 "Someday, my boy, this will all be yours." (Copyright 1966 by Bill Mauldin. Reprinted courtesy of the Mauldin Estate.)

The analysis of processes and new technologies can help solve waste disposal problems. So, which is it? Is technology causing more and more problems? Or, is technology part of the solution? Can any problem caused by science be solved by science? Let's take a closer look.

The marvels of science and technology are impressive.

- With a handheld calculator, one can do in seconds and minutes math problems that used to take hours.
- With the Internet, a home computer can become a powerful reference library.
- With a properly installed sound system, one's living room can become a seat at a world-class symphony.
- With an automobile, a person can travel in comfort and safety through the most difficult terrain.

And the list goes on and on. But there is also a not-so-pleasant side of technology.

- With modern weaponry, a single person can now become a killing machine.
- With the Internet, trash and filth can be brought into one's home just as easily as useful information.
- Video games and simulations can be made so lifelike that some users have difficulty separating reality from fantasy. It is argued that these experiences can make a person insensitive to real pain, suffering, and death. Uncontrolled technology seems to be attacking our moral fiber.

The ethical neutrality dilemma discussed in Chapter 1 has returned. Science and technology come with no instructions on how to use them. Science brings us knowledge, but it does not bring us wisdom. Wisdom is knowledge tempered with judgment. Good science proceeds into the unknown with caution, and in ignorance, refrains. So how do we refrain?

It seems there are two approaches. One is to form groups or committees that assess the impact of new technologies before they have widespread application. These groups or committees can be funded by taxes and/or with private contributions. This "Office of Technological Assessment" would be charged with the development of better systems to identify and monitor the impacts of new technologies. The costs and benefits of new technologies would be weighed before they could be funded or licensed.

It has been argued that scientists should not be given a blank check to perform thousands of uncontrolled, unmonitored, and unrestrained experiments with the whole world as the subject and our survival as a civilized society at stake.

The second approach is to examine your own ethical commitments. Who are you? What do you want to become? What kind of world do you want to live in? Once you have answered these questions, you have established your identity. Your identity determines your behavior, and your behavior determines your purchases. Technologies are not developed if no one wants them.

In the final analysis, technology does not make us better people. It simply expands what people can do. We, as individuals and society, must decide what we want to do.

Think about This!

List some technological marvels that affect you.

Think about This!

List some not-so-pleasant sides of technology.

Think about This!

What is the difference between knowledge and wisdom?

Apply Your Understanding

How might the direction of technology be influenced?

Helpful Hint!

A *fact* is a piece of information. *Knowledge* is organized information. *Wisdom* is knowledge tempered with judgment.

Record your responses in your science notebook.

1. It is one thing to understand life. It is another thing to alter life. How does this statement relate to biotechnology and the dilemma focused on in this section?

2. Are social and scientific controls defensible in a nation that is founded on the premise of liberty for all? How much control is too much? Is it ethical *not* to control for the benefit of society?

Summary

> How can we solve the problems related to the wise use of land?
> - Education—understand the problems and the full range of solutions available.
> - Technology—line and monitor landfills, substitute products, design products for recycling, incinerate.
> - Lifestyle changes—carefully select products purchased, buy only what is needed, reuse products, recycle, buy recycled products.
> - Laws and agreements—RCRA, HSWA, CERCLA, require design for recycling, zoning laws, land use planning.

Land is a resource that needs to be properly managed for the benefit of the owner and society as a whole. Various mechanisms have been developed to accomplish this goal.

We are to be stewards of the land. Wise land use management can begin with good management of your own yard. In addition, business, industry, and governments can manage their impacts on the environment and reclaim damaged land.

Waste management is important in societies that produce products and by-products that natural systems cannot degrade. For management purposes, it is useful to classify waste and manage it according to its properties.

Technology is part of the environmental problem and part of the solution. It is also confronting us with some ethical dilemmas. With technology, we can now do things that some think ought not to be done. Can we restrain ourselves? If we do, how much restraint should we impose? The decisions we make concerning our use of science and technology are important. They will have a definite impact on the quality of life both now and in the future.

Beatley, Timothy. *Ethical Land Use: Principles of Policy and Planning* (Baltimore: John Hopkins University Press), 1994.

Devito, Steven C., and Roger L. Garrett, eds. *Designing Safe Chemicals: Green Chemistry for Pollution Prevention* (Washington, D.C.: American Chemical Society), 1996.

Fielder, Peggy L., and Subodh K. Jain, eds. *Conservation Biology: The Theory and Practice of Nature Conservation, Preservation and Management* (New York: Chapman & Hall), 1992.

Kane, Hal. "Shifting to Sustainable Industries." In Lester R. Brown, et al. *State of the World* (Washington, D.C.: Worldwatch Institute), 1996.

League of Women Voters. *The Garbage Primer. A Handbook for Citizens* (New York: Lyons & Burford), 1993.

Millennium Ecosystem Assessment. *Ecosystems and Human Well-Being: Synthesis* (Washington, DC: World Resources Institute), 2005.

Nilon, C. H. et al. Understanding Urban Ecosystems: A New Frontier for Science and Education. *Urban Ecosystems* 3-1 (1999), 3–4.

Parker, Dominic P. *Conservation Easements: A Closer Look at Federal Tax Policy* (Bozeman, MT: PERC), 2005.

Portney, Kent E. *Siting Hazardous Waste Treatment Facilities: The NIMBY Syndrome* (New York: Auburn House), 1992.

Pyne, Stephen J. *Fire in America: A Cultural History of Wildland and Rural Fire* (Seattle: University of Washington Press), 1997.

Centers for Disease Control:
http://www.cdc.gov/page.do
(Select Environmental Health, click Hazardous Substances, Hazardous
Waste Sites, or Toxic Substances.)

Global Recycling Network:
http://grn.com/index.html

Intl. Registry of Potentially Toxic Chemicals:
http://www.chem.unep.ch/irptc

National Center for Environmental Health:
http://www.cdc.gov/nceh/

National Interagency Fire Center:
http://www.nifc.gov

Recycling Resources:
http://grn.com/library/hot_list.htm
(Try Earth's 911.)

Waste Management:
http://www.epa.gov/epahome/slate.htm
(Try Environmental Topics, click Wastes.)

U.S. Bureau of Reclamation:
http://www.usbr.gov/

U.S. Bureau of Land Management:
http://www.blm.gov/

CORBIS

CHAPTER 17

Options for the Future

GOALS

- To examine some predictions about our planet's future.

- To make some decisions about the best route into the future.

Some people see the world as it is now and ask why. I see the world as it never has been and ask why not?

—Cervantes (paraphrased)

Pioneers and Their Island

In this activity, you will theorize about the growth and development of a population on an imaginary island.

Background

About 350 years ago, 125 people left their homeland for political, economic, and religious reasons. They were in search of new opportunities and a better life. Their ship was at sea for many months, and their voyage was hazardous at times. All that hardship was quickly forgotten on the morning that land was sighted. The captain located a potential harbor, and soon they docked and unloaded.

Since the pioneers were not planning to return to their homeland, they brought along seeds for crops, crude tools, and some domesticated animals. These proved to be very valuable as they established a foothold on their island.

A few years after the first settlement was established, explorers were sent out to try to determine the size of their homeland and the natural resources available to them. Figure 17.1 summarizes the extent of their discoveries after living on the island for about 100 years.

Growing societies generally have a mix of ages (see any population histogram). The male/female ratio is typically close to 1 to 1. The United States is a **pluralistic** society. It has a mix of races, religions, and viewpoints. In nature, such diversity implies stability. For humans, this is not always the case in terms of race and religion. But it can be. *E pluribus unum*, the motto of the United States, means "out of many, one."

Over the 350-year time span, the population had an annual growth rate of 2.8 percent. This growth rate is high for most countries today. However, this rate was not unusual for small populations in agricultural regions where space and resources seemed limitless. In the early years, the mortality

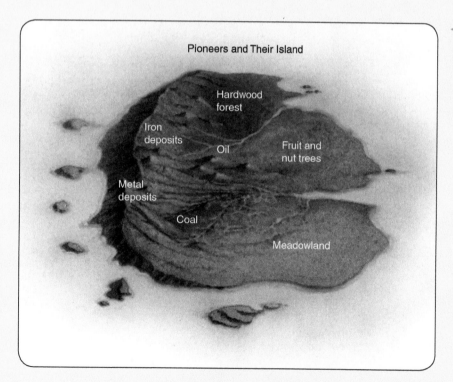

Pioneers and Their Island

Hardwood forest

Iron deposits

Oil

Fruit and nut trees

Metal deposits

Coal

Meadowland

◄ FIGURE 17.1 The island as known to the pioneers approximately 100 years after settlement.

rate was high, and the average life expectancy was not much over 40 years.

Materials (for each team of 4 students)

- large sheet of white paper
- colored markers (red, black, blue, green, yellow, brown)

Procedure

1. On a large piece of paper, make a drawing to show what the island looks like today (350 years after settlement). Use symbols to represent various types of activity, and add a key.

2. Then answer the questions that follow.

Record your responses in your science notebook.

1. Describe how you (or your group) decided to develop the island. Imports? Exports?

2. What is the present population? How did you determine that number?

3. Throughout history, people have moved or been forced to move for political, economic, ethnic, or religious reasons. Give some examples. Does this apply to your family or to anyone you know? Explain.

4. Explain what the people on the island do for work and fulfillment.

5. Be ready to explain the growth and development of your island to the class.

[Adapted from Man and Nature/Biological Sciences Curriculum Study.]

ACTIVITY 17.2

Graphing the Status of the Island

Sometimes, it is useful to graph change over time, and to represent more than one quantity on the same graph. One way to do that is shown in Figure 17.2. In this activity, you will graph some of the growth and development of your island from Activity 17.1.

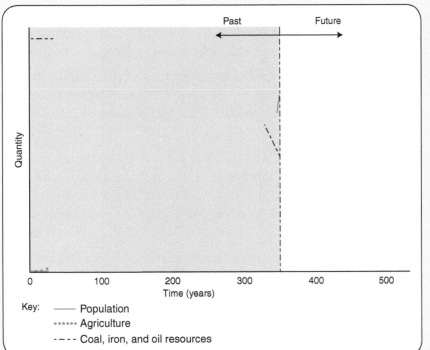

◄ FIGURE 17.2 Graphic representation of the island.

Materials (for each team of 4 students)

- graph paper
- *Graphic Representation of the Island* handout
- colored pencils

Procedure

1. Interpolate the graph (Figure 17.2) for the first 350 years of life on your island from Activity 17.1. Time (t) = 0 is the day the pioneers landed. On that day, you may assume the agricultural production was zero and the population was 125 people. At t = 350, the population is what you calculated in Activity 17.1.

2. At time = 0, the quantities of coal, iron, and oil resources were unknown. Assume that the total quantity humans can develop on the island is represented by the dashed line segment on the upper left portion of the graph. Assume also that the people on the island need these resources. After 350 years, the resources of natural coal, iron, and oil have been drawn down to the dashed lines shown on the graph. Interpolate the resource graph between t = 0 and t = 350 years. Explain and justify the line you drew.

3. Sketch in the agricultural production line that joins t = 0 to t = 350 years. Explain why you drew the line the way you did.

4. Extrapolate your 3 graph lines for the next 150 years.

5. Explain why you extended each line the way you did.

6. What assumptions did you make about each extended line? List your assumptions.

The Growth Issue

17.1 Growth in a Finite System

What three factors caused major growth in early America?

Throughout most of U.S. history, Americans have believed that growth is good and essential to the maintenance of a vibrant nation and a healthy economy. Growth was important in the evolution of America into a major world power for three reasons. First, the human population in early America was small. Second, the space available seemed unlimited. Third, natural resources appeared almost limitless. As frontiers moved westward, the country grew, dreamed, and prospered. Opportunities abounded for those with an adventurous spirit. The frontiers called for development. Growth was the key.

Apply Your Understanding

How did growth help America to become a major world power?

As the expansion continued, so did the dream (see Figure 17.3). The midwestern farmlands were developed, oil wells were drilled, and gold was discovered farther west. As environmental problems appeared and new opportunities arose, pioneers migrated west—all the way to the Pacific Ocean.

Around 1900, some people became worried about the growing immigrant population that crowded the cities. Progressive reformers encouraged birth control and sanitation. At the same time, others were concerned about the loss of forests that provided lumber and held soil in place. National forests were set aside. These steps seemed to help ease growth-related problems.

By the 1960s, we could no longer ignore environmental issues. Parts of the country seemed filled with people. Smog was overpowering in many cities, and some rivers and lakes literally stank. For some, the dream had failed. Increasingly, Americans had to import several strategic metals and even petroleum. Something had gone wrong. Many wondered if the system had failed. Scholars began reexamining our assumptions. Even the doctrine of growth was attacked.

▲ Figure 17.3 The westward movement. (*From Denver Regional Transportation District.*)

In the atmosphere of the 1960s, it was only natural that the idea of "growth as the key to success" should be questioned. And it was, as you will read about in the following pages. Keep in mind, however, that the assumptions upon which the following "no growth" philosophy are based are *only* assumptions; many were shown to be false. Other assumptions must be given equal consideration. There is no instant solution. The following suggestions are yours to consider, critique, and then use to form your own ideas.

17.2 The *Limits to Growth* Report

The Club of Rome is a loosely knit, multinational group of scientists, scholars, and other assorted professionals. The club's stated purpose is to develop ways of dealing with a more complicated world. Because of the worldwide scope and complexity of the growth issue, the club hired an international team of scientists to head a study. This team was led by computer experts from the Massachusetts Institute of Technology (MIT). The study group identified five basic factors that determine and, in their interactions, ultimately limit growth on our planet.

Apply Your Understanding

What is the Club of Rome?

- Population
- Agricultural production
- Consumption of nonrenewable resources
- Industrial output
- Pollution

What are the five factors that determine growth on Earth?

The study group further identified three features that these five factors have in common.

1. The factors are all **interrelated** and cannot be studied separately.
2. At the time of their study, the factors were all growing exponentially.
3. Since Earth is finite, the factors all appear to have upper limits.

What characteristics do the five factors have in common?

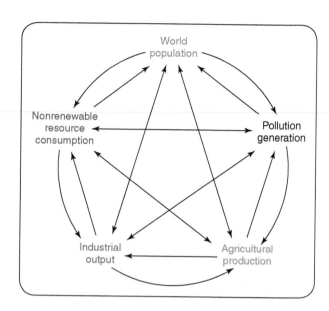

► **FIGURE 17.4** A simplified diagram of the Club of Rome's world model. Each arrow indicates that one factor influences another. For example, an increase in population size leads to increased industrial output.

What is *The Limits to Growth* report?

What was the major conclusion of *The Limits to Growth* report?

A simplified diagram of the interrelationships of the five factors is shown in Figure 17.4.

Using data about the five factors and their growth rates, the scientists built a computer model to **simulate** the major ecological forces at work in the world. The model related the important **variables**. For example, a rise in population is ordinarily accompanied by a rise in agricultural production because more food is needed.

A nontechnical report of the findings called *The Limits to Growth* came out in 1972. The results of the simulation were startling. The basic finding was this: *If there are no major changes in the physical, economic, or social relationships that have historically governed the development of the world system, the system will continue to grow exponentially until the rapidly diminishing resource base forces a collapse* ($\approx$ AD 2020) This conclusion, shown in Figure 17.5, illustrates the change in the five basic factors over time. The message was loud and clear: If we don't change our ways of doing things, we've had it.

► **FIGURE 17.5** The standard computer run. (*From* The Limits to Growth: A Report for The Club of Rome's Project on the Predicament of Mankind, *by Donella H. Meadows, Dennis L. Meadows, Jorgen Randers, and William W. Behrens III. A Potomac Associates book published by Universe Books, New York, 1972. Graphics by Potomac Associates. Used with permission.*)

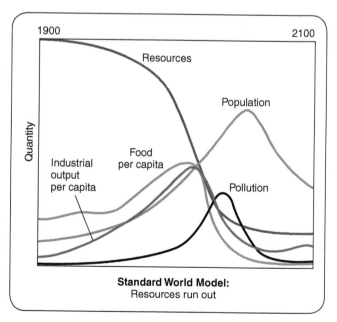

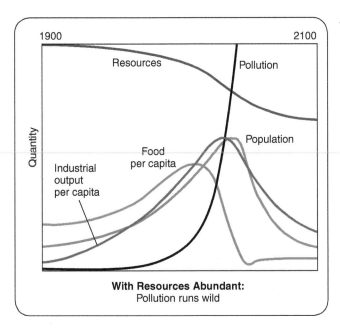

With Resources Abundant:
Pollution runs wild

◀ FIGURE 17.6 With resources abundant, pollution runs wild. (*From* The Limits to Growth. *Used with permission.*)

17.3 Responding to the Prediction of Doom

The logical next question was, What should we do? The computer was asked a series of "what if" questions as different scenarios were modeled:

Q. Since the main cause of global collapse was nonrenewable resource depletion (Figure 17.5), what if nonrenewable resources are searched for and developed in great abundance?

A. With traditional resources in great abundance, pollution would reach such high levels collapse would follow (Figure 17.6).

Q. What if nonrenewable resources are found in great abundance and the effectiveness of pollution control is increased by a factor of four?

A. This strategy would buy time, but the demand on land, water, and fuel supplies, plus population growth, strains the food supply to the point of collapse (see Figure 17.7).

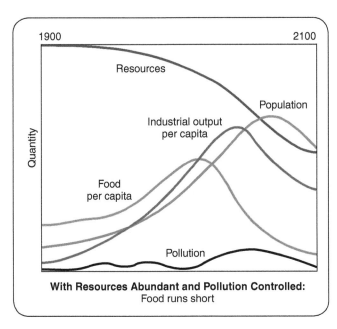

With Resources Abundant and Pollution Controlled:
Food runs short

◀ FIGURE 17.7 With resources abundant and pollution controlled, food runs short. (*From* The Limits to Growth. *Used with permission.*)

► FIGURE 17.8 *The Limits to Growth* report.

What two global factors must be controlled if growth is to stop?

Many other strategies were modeled. The overall conclusion was that without constraints, exponential growth would continue. Two factors dominated the situation: exponentially increasing *population* and *nonrenewable resource consumption*. In any program designed to produce a future world that is stable, the exponential growth of both of these factors would have to cease. Any combination of the variables that influence growth that did not stabilize both population and nonrenewable resource consumption would eventually lead to collapse.

The Limits to Growth study (Figure 17.8) hit the world's thinkers like a bomb. It attacked some fundamental beliefs of modern-day society. It predicted a doomsday that was soon to be. There was hardly time to debate the study or make plans for a change. Either we were to accept the conclusions and change our values, or the world would collapse around us. It was repent or perish.

17.4 Criticism of *The Limits to Growth* Report

What are the flaws in *The Limits to Growth* report?

Many criticized the study, and flaws were found. The most serious charges were these five shortcomings.

1. *The study sponsors (The Club of Rome) had hidden agendas.* Should an elitist group of wealthy people be telling the rest of us what direction we ought to be taking? The club members had already reaped the benefits of the growth they now abhorred.

2. *The assumptions determined the conclusion.* The assumption was made that Earth and its resources are finite. The authors of the study also assumed that nonrenewable resource consumption and population would grow exponentially. In any simulation, the results depend on the assumptions. In this case, nothing could happen but collapse.

3. *Skimpy and insufficient evidence was extrapolated years into the future.* The human inventive genius was ignored. We were assumed to be utterly incapable of adjusting

◀ FIGURE 17.9 Free at last! (Copyright 1975 by Bill Mauldin. Reprinted courtesy of the Mauldin Estate.)

to problems of scarcity. Would humans really sit by idly as technology stagnated, pollution built, and millions choked to death? (See Figure 17.9.) Couldn't we learn to invent and adapt?

4. *Some important variables were not included.* As you know, pricing and behavior are linked. Pricing, however, was not a variable in the Club of Rome model. In the real world, rising prices would act as an economic signal to conserve scarce resources. They would stimulate research efforts to develop ways to substitute or save on resources and make exploration attempts more profitable. Rising prices would provide incentives to use cheaper materials and/or substitutes. Some of these goals could be accomplished with less impact on the poor through rationing. Currently, some minerals have no substitutes; their prices could reflect their true value (see Figure 17.10).

◀ FIGURE 17.10 Automobile bumpers used to be made of steel and chrome. Now, they contain aluminum, plastic, and synthetic rubber. (*James Shaffer Photography*)

The demographic transition shows that as the standard of living goes up, the population growth rate goes down. As modern ways and knowledge expand, global population growth should slow.

5. *The book told us what the world of the future should be like, but it didn't tell us how to get there.* The recipe for recovery was too generalized to be useful for policy-making. It is easy to say that population should be stabilized by equating birthrates to death rates. It is harder to deal with how this can be done. The strategies for reducing population growth, redefining the good life, changing value systems, and reordering priorities are what the problem is all about.

The above shortcomings in *The Limits to Growth* study deserve serious examination. We will examine these issues as you move through this chapter (see Figure 17.11).

▲ FIGURE 17.11 How do we get there from here? (*Mineral Information Institute*)

17.5 Accomplishments of *The Limits to Growth* Report

The Limits to Growth study can be praised for accomplishing the following:

1. It forced us to look at the direction in which we seem headed. It nailed down the fact that exponential growth is abnormal in a finite system. It put that fact in a time reference that hits us all—now. Every living thing reaches a limit beyond which it cannot grow. Trees reach a certain height. Animals and humans do the same. When growth continues beyond maturity, we call it obesity or cancer. Abnormal growth is dangerous.

2. It pointed to historical evidence that there are limits to the five basic factors. The study organized and documented much of this evidence.

3. It provided a glimpse of what the future might be like—if we chose their proposed road to survival. Figure 17.12 depicts that future.

What were the beneficial results of *The Limits to Growth* report?

Think about This!

Growth in knowledge is good. However, growth for the sake of growth is the mission of the cancer cell.

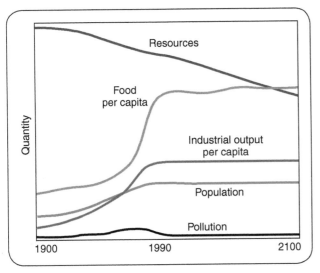

◀ FIGURE 17.12 The sustainable society. (*From* The Limits to Growth. *Used with permission.*)

The "Limits" sketch of what a no-growth world would be like was vague. And the route to get there was not clearly defined in the study. However, the idea of a **sustainable** future is of value in itself. Certainly, changes are required if life as we know it is to survive on this planet. Though not the last word on predicting the future, *The Limits to Growth* was of value because it served to make us more aware of important issues.

Content Clue

Population and traditional consumption cannot grow forever on a finite planet. *The Limits to Growth* study provided a glimpse into the future.

17.6 New Efforts to Project the Future

Since the release of *The Limits to Growth*, a whole series of future projections have been published. The reference section at the end of this chapter lists some of them. (See, for example, Bloom, 2003; Brown, 2001, 2006; Hughes, 2006; Meadows, 1992; and Raskin, 2002.)

Figure 17.13 summarizes the projected future proposed in the study *Beyond the Limits*. Most of these studies have optimistic scenarios, all of which center on punishing waste and rewarding modernization. Fossil fuels are replaced with the efficient use of renewable resources. Ecological limits are addressed seriously. Issues of **equity** and quality of life are faced boldly. People learn to distinguish between growth and development. Growth means to get larger; development means to make adjustments and changes. There are limits to growth, but there need not be limits to development.

Content Clue

Renewable means to live off nature's flow while maintaining its capital stock.

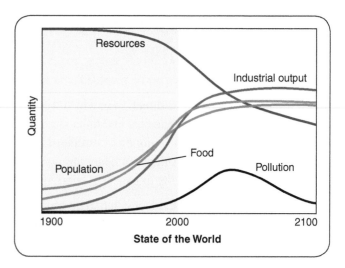

►FIGURE 17.13 In this projected future, population and resources used per person are moderated starting in 1995. The desired family size is two children, and the standard of living is fixed to near European levels. Technologies increase the efficiency of resource use, decrease pollution emission, protect agricultural land, and increase land yields. The resulting society sustains 7.7 billion people at a comfortable standard of living with high life expectancy and declining pollution until at least the year 2100. (*Reprinted from Beyond the Limits copyright © 1992 by Meadows, Meadows, and Randers. With permission from Chelsea Green Publishing Co, White River Junction, Vermont.*)

Topic: global forecasting
Go to: www.scilinks.org
Code: GloSci7e670

17.7 Other Views of the Future

The 1972 release of *The Limits to Growth* triggered a heated debate concerning the issue of growth. However, it also prompted a series of other studies about the future of human life on Earth. These studies present different images of what the future holds.

The Limits to Growth warned that population size is shooting out of control. It concluded that population must be stabilized—and soon. Two of the many who disagreed include Herman Kahn (the director of a "think tank" called the Hudson Institute) and Julian Simon. Simon was an economist associated with the Heritage Foundation. Simon argued that the world would be better off with more people (see Figure 17.14). The more people, the greater the knowledge base. The greater the knowledge base, the more likely we are to

►FIGURE 17.14 The future as some humorists view it. This illustrates part of the philosophy of Kahn and Simon.

solve our resource/environmental problems. Kahn and Simon maintained that our lack of nonrenewable resources is only temporary. Improvement in our abilities to locate, extract, and use nonrenewable resources continues. Invention, substitution, and human ingenuity have no limits. Many of their predictions, made over 25 years ago, have been correct.

Some studies argue that pollution is not out of control and, in fact, our environment is now cleaner than it was in the 1960s. The overall quality of the air in many of the world's major cities is better than it was during that time period.

Some of the greatest differences of opinion are about how best to respond to the problems we face. Some advocate swift action coupled with strong governmental control. Some even call for a revolution. Others argue that problems are best solved by letting individuals respond to situations locally. They think that individual action coupled with free market choice produces the best solution in most cases. Some studies advocate a complete redistribution of world economic and political power. This would lead to the resolution of the problem of inequities. Only then can the problems of population and resource depletion be addressed adequately.

What is a worldview?

Think about This!

Which worldview in Figure 17.15 reflects your ideology?

Why such different conclusions? Barry Hughes, in his book *World Futures: A Critical Analysis of Alternatives*, maintains that these differences are natural outcomes of differing worldviews. A *worldview* is a comprehensive set of beliefs and basic assumptions about the way the world works, coupled with the resulting "understandings" of complex events and processes. The worldview you have leads to the solutions you propose to various problems. It dictates what you recommend as appropriate individual, social, and political behavior. Figure 17.15 summarizes various worldviews with regard to global problems addressed in this course. It is a simplified version of the analysis done by Hughes.

Why can futurists look at the same data and come to very different conclusions?

These views of the world and how it works differ greatly. Because of this, forecasts of the future differ greatly, and so do recommended solutions to problems.

But, you ask, can't a look at the "facts" lead to movement toward a common viewpoint. The answer is—probably not. Facts are a nebulous thing. There are so many facts and bits of data to deal with that each of us has to decide which are important and which to toss out. Our worldview helps us with that selection. The net result is that we cling to those facts that support our viewpoint, and we ignore those that don't.

A second dilemma is that facts can be interpreted differently. Think about the old story of the pessimist who looks at the glass of water and says it's half empty and the optimist who looks at the same glass and says it's half full (see Figure 17.16). That behavior applies here. We color our interpretations of data with our own perspective. Each of us is born with our own individual mental and physical abilities and characteristics. As we journey through life, we each have a variety of unique experiences. As a consequence, no one views the world in the exact same way as another. Thus, reasonable compromise is vitally important throughout our lives.

Think about This!

Why is the need to compromise at times so critical?

Finally, our data may be incomplete. Do we have enough data to predict, with certainty, a worldwide warming trend? How much data do we need? Have we been collecting data long enough to detect a cycle or a trend of significance? A reliable scientific data base may only go back a hundred years. Is that long enough? Many of the environmental changes we are now monitoring are relatively recent concerns. Hence, accurate record-keeping in many areas has been all too brief. In some cases, we have almost no data

Think about This!

What can happen when we base decisions on incomplete data?

Title	Assumption/Beliefs	Typical Forecasts	Recommendations
Technologists	• The global environment can be understood and controlled by humans. Humans are increasingly in control of the natural environment. • Technology is the key to a better future.	• Technological progress will steadily increase. • Environmental problems will be solved. • Resource limitations will be overcome.	• A governmental hands-off policy is best for most technological projects. • Research and development programs should be supported by governments.
Naturalists	• The universe is orderly and law-abiding. Humans are tied into the global environment. • The environment is more complex and delicate than most people realize. • Lifestyles consistent with natural laws are the key to a better future.	• Material wealth and technological progress will prove unsatisfying. • Environmental problems will appear faster than we can solve them, unless . . . • Resource scarcities will intensify unless . . .	• Selectively use and control new technologies. • Minimize rate at which resources pass through societies to conserve resources and limit environmental impact. • Stabilize global populations.
Free market advocates	• Free markets benefit both producers and consumers. • Economic growth (betterment) occurs in stages.	• The gap between the rich and the poor will narrow over the next few decades. • The population problem will solve itself as a result of this. • Price mechanisms will solve energy and food problems.	• Globally, minimize government intervention in domestic and international economics. Intervention only hinders the natural solution.
Internationalists	• Free markets are unequally beneficial. • Economic benefits can be accelerated with help.	• The rich-poor gap will close only slowly. • Population might overwhelm resources in some countries and create a poverty cycle. • Agricultural and energy problems are long term and might worsen.	• Wealthy nations should assist poorer nations with foreign aid and trade concessions.
Revolutionists	• Free markets are controlled by the rich. • Wealthy nations hold poorer nations in perpetual poverty.	• The rich-poor gap will not close; therefore, the population issue cannot be resolved, and agriculture and energy will remain problems for the poor.	• Poorer nations must either break away from the international system, and deny the rich the benefit of their natural resources; or, change via revolution must occur in the wealthy countries.

◄ FIGURE 17.16 Different worldviews can lead to very different conclusions—even when the same data are used.

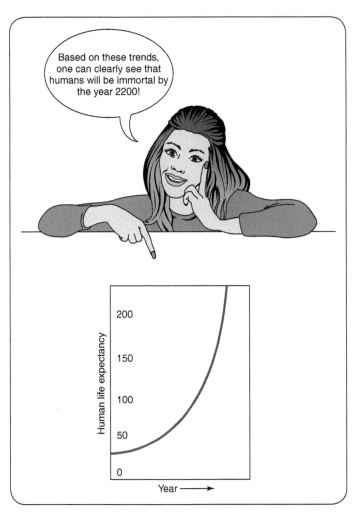

◄ FIGURE 17.17 The dangers of blind extrapolation.

base at all. Blind extrapolation of insufficient data can lead to bizarre conclusions (see Figure 17.17).

At this point, how should we proceed? The problem posed by conflicting worldviews makes it difficult. All of these views cannot be correct. Only time will make that determination.

What assumptions does your author make about the world and how it works?

What we will do is move forward with the assumption that Earth and its resources are finite. We will assume that natural laws govern how the world works, and that humans are tied into the natural system. We will also assume that humans are clever, resourceful, and capable of acting in their own best interest. We will assume that the vast majority want to live meaningful and productive lives. The story of human history seems to bear this out. With this in mind, we will return to our consideration of the sustainable world.

ACTIVITY 17.3

Trade-Offs

In this activity, you will interpret a graph that compares pollution damages and the costs of cleanup.

Procedure

1. Carefully analyze Figure 17.18. Discuss the meaning of the graph in groups or as a class.

2. Then complete the items below.

QUESTIONS & TASKS

Record your responses in your science notebook.

1. Complete these statements:

   a. Figure 17.18 shows that as pollution levels are reduced, the cost of pollution control . . .

   b. As pollution gets worse, the cost of pollution-related damage . . .

   c. If we increase the amount we are willing to pay for pollution control, the acceptable pollution level . . .

2. The minimum cost to the consumer is labeled as the acceptable cost. What is meant by acceptable cost?

3. Why are we willing to accept some pollution?

4. Can nature accept "small amounts" of pollution? Justify your answer.

5. How can the acceptance of only small amounts of pollution from various technological devices (such as the automobile) lead to serious problems?

6. Write a paragraph that ties this activity to the issue of growth.

► FIGURE 17.18 An idealized graph showing costs paid by the public vs. the percentage of pollution remaining in the environment. The line labeled "Total cost to the consumer" (at any point) is the sum of the cost of pollution control plus the cost of pollution damage.

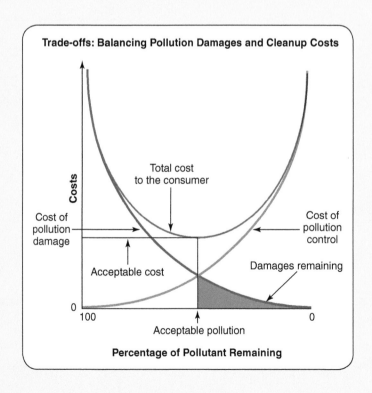

The Challenge of Sustainability

A sustainable world is a worthwhile goal. However, obtaining it will involve overcoming some major obstacles. We will examine some of them in this section.

ACTIVITY 17.4

Do We Live in Two Different Worlds?

In this activity, you will explore your own world-view by ranking a series of assumptions about Earth and how we live on it.

Background

As we go through life, we interact with our environment. Many of our actions reflect two different world-views. The assumptions for each view are listed in Figure 17.19. These two sets of assumptions seem to be in conflict. On the left are eight assumptions of the "Plentiful Earth" point of view (see Figure 17.20). On the right are the matched assumptions of the "Finite Earth" point of view (see Figure 17.21).

Materials

- *Assumptions of Two Different Worldviews* handout

▼ FIGURE 17.19 Assumptions of two different worldviews.

Assumptions: Plentiful Earth	2L	L	0	R	2R	Assumptions: Finite Earth
1. Developed nations have unlimited growth potential.						1. All living entities (organisms, cities) have a carrying capacity (biological/social).
2. Nations and regions can be totally self-sufficient.						2. Nations are interdependent.
3. For every problem, there is a definite and best solution.						3. New solutions breed new problems (ad infinitum).
4. Private freedoms are more important than public responsibilities.						4. Public responsibilities are more important than private freedoms.
5. Material wealth accumulation is good and is an indication of one's own worth.						5. Happiness is more than just owning things
6. Gross inequities in wealth distribution are both acceptable and inevitable.						6. Gross inequities in wealth are intolerable because stability is not possible.
7. The concept of finite resources holds us back. We can invent new resources.						7. Earth is finite. Resources can be depleted. There are environmental limits.
8. Free markets regulate themselves. Governments need not interfere.						8. Governments need to regulate markets to accomplish accepted social goals.

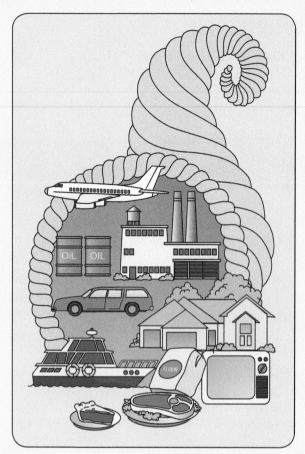

▲ FIGURE 17.20 The Plentiful Earth (horn of plenty) worldview.

▲ FIGURE 17.21 The Finite Earth worldview.

Procedure

1. Read each pair of assumptions in Figure 17.19. Place a dot on the number line of the handout that indicates your degree of agreement with the assumption.

> **Helpful Hint!**
>
> A "2L" means you are in *strong agreement* with the assumption on the left. A "0" means you are *very unsure*. A "2R" means you *strongly agree* with the assumption on the right. "L" or "R" means you *agree* with the assumption on the left or right, but your belief in that assumption is not well established.

2. After ranking the 8 assumptions, write a short statement in your science notebook that summarizes your view of the world. Your statement should consist of 8 sentences. Write a sentence on why you ranked each item as you did.

EXTENSIONS

In his commencement address to the graduates of Yale University on June 11, 1962, President John F. Kennedy said, "The great enemy of the truth is very often not the lie—deliberate, contrived, and dishonest—but the myth—persistent, persuasive, and unrealistic. Too often we hold fast to the clichés of our forebears. We subject all facts to a prefabricated set of interpretations. We enjoy the comfort of opinion without the discomfort of thought."

1. Relate this quote to the idea that our worldview helps determine what "facts" we keep and what "facts" we ignore.

2. How can this process hinder the acceptance of new ideas?

17.8 Life in a Sustainable World

No one likes the thought of world collapse and chaos. No matter what our worldview, most people seem to desire stability, a clean environment, and reasonable comfort. A sustainable world is a worthwhile goal. However, the route to it is not agreed upon by all.

What would the sustainable world be like? Would life be boring? According to many futurists, a sustainable world would have the following characteristics:

1. It would be sustainable without sudden and uncontrolled collapse.

2. It would be capable of satisfying the basic material requirements of *all* of its people.

3. The average life expectancy could be about 80 years.

4. Material inequalities between groups of people would be fewer. (Most people would be neither very rich nor very poor.)

5. There would be more leisure time to devote to less-polluting and less-consuming activities.

6. Education, art, music, religion, basic scientific research, athletics, and social interactions would flourish.

7. Technical advances would continue, because the desire to improve the quality of life would still exist. Scientific research would focus on controlling pollution, finding alternative energy sources (see Figure 17.22), developing improved contraceptives, developing better recycling techniques, improving conservation practices for energy and resources, enhancing human relations, and improving mental, physical, and spiritual health.

8. Incentive would be there. Instead of wealth, the incentive would be a better quality of life.

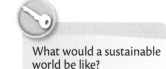

What would a sustainable world be like?

Think about This!

Are *you* willing to settle for "basic material requirements"?

Topic: sustainability
Go to: www.scilinks.org
Code: GloSci7e677

▼ FIGURE 17.22 Photovoltaic panels at SunEdison's 8.22 mW power plant near Alamosa, Colorado. *(Photo courtesy of SunEdison and Zinn Photography.)*

ACTIVITY 17.5

Resource Allocation

In this activity, you will play a game to learn more about resource allocation.

Materials (for each team of 6–10 students)

- tokens
- hard candies

Procedure

1. You will be assigned to a group of 6–10 people. Your group should sit around a table or in a circle on the floor.

2. In the center of your table or circle is a small pile (pool) of tokens. The tokens represent valuable resources that can be traded in for desired goods—in this case, candy.

3. When your teacher says "Go," you may take resources (tokens) for yourself.

4. When you have accumulated 10 tokens, trade them in for a piece of candy (or other reward).

5. When your teacher says "Stop," he or she will double the number of tokens remaining in the center. The activity will then continue.

6. Do not talk to anyone during the activity.

7. Your teacher will provide instructions on how this activity will continue.

> **Helpful Hint!**
>
> There will never be more tokens in the pool than there were at the start of this activity. This is the maximum number of tokens the pool can hold.

QUESTIONS & TASKS

After you have finished this activity, record your responses to the following questions in your science notebook.

1. What do the tokens represent?

2. Why was there a limit to the number of available tokens in each round?

3. How is the way groups competed for tokens similar to the way you (as an individual) compete for things you need (want)?

4. How does this activity illustrate how some families and/or family members compete for resources?

5. How does this activity illustrate how nations or groups of nations compete for resources?

6. How were tokens taken out of the pool in different rounds of the game? How many candies were gained using each strategy? How did you feel about other members of your group based on each outcome?

7. Which strategy produced the most candy for the group and the best feeling among group members?

8. What had to be realized before the greatest gain was available to the greatest number?

9. If groups or nations are competing for land, water, energy, or minerals, for example, how might you maximize benefits and minimize conflicts?

10. What is meant by a "win-win" situation? Relate this to the concept of conflict resolution.

[Adapted from *People and the Planet*, an activity guide produced by Population Connection. Washington, D.C., copyright 1996, 2004.]

17.9 Conflict Resolution

This is a time when violence is not strength and compassion is not weakness. We are civilized.

—King Arthur (in *Camelot*)

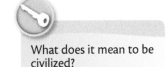

What does it mean to be civilized?

The first human who hurled an insult instead of a stone was the founder of civilization. A test of how civilized we have become is to measure the number of violent disputes that occur at a given point in time. This number can be compared to the number of disputes that are settled peacefully during the same time period.

A look at events around the world clearly indicates that humans need to improve their ability to *resolve* conflicts (see Figure 17.23). Conflicts occur between individuals, between groups of people (governments, industries, and communities), and between regions or nations.

We know that global collapse can be avoided. We also know that to avoid collapse, major conflicts must be resolved. Activity 17.5 should have provided you with some insights into how the process might work. First, there must be some desire to resolve the conflict. Then there must be some discussion between the parties involved. Finally, a solution must be available where all parties believe they can gain something they want. This is called a win-win solution.

Think about This!

Why is world cooperation important?

Is it reasonable to expect that the rich nations of the world will make short-term sacrifices to achieve long-term gains? Will people act in their own best interests if they must forego some immediate pleasure? Can we build a new global economic order? A new economic order might feature regional specialization tied to local strengths and the most effective use of labor, technology, and available resources. Each region would maximize the economic and human resources it has. Growth would stop in some regions and continue in others. Some regions would need to develop in order to meet the material needs of their people. Growth would be carefully controlled.

Our current crises are not temporary. They are tied to historical events. Cooperation among nations has been the exception rather than the rule. For stability to happen, our ability to **foresee** and **forestall** will be taxed to the limit.

◀ FIGURE 17.23 We must learn to reduce violence in all aspects of our lives—in our personal interactions, in athletics, and in the ways our governing bodies settle disputes. (*David Klutho/Sports Illustrated*)

►FIGURE 17.24 The United Nations was formed in 1945 under a permanent charter that was ratified by 51 countries. Is it an effective organization for promoting stability and peace? Can it be? (UN Photo #10395 by Y. Nagata.)

The role international organizations, such as the **United Nations** (UN), can play is not clear (see Figure 17.24). The UN is more a debating society than anything else. It is not a world government nor a major military power. It is a meeting place for countries large and small. It is a forum for dialogue, debate, and occasionally, reconciliation. At present, it is the major system we have for resolving international conflict. When people speak in a civilized forum, the likelihood that they will fight is reduced. Who knows? Sometimes, they may even listen to each other.

Economics and Growth

17.10 Major Economic Systems

Think about This!

Why should we study economics in a global science class?

Economic decisions have a major impact on resource use and the environment. Manipulation of economic factors can create problems as well as play a major role in solving problems. To be ignorant of the basic principles of economics is to be ill-prepared to study problems of energy, resources, and the environment.

Economics is the study of the ways individuals and societies distribute their goods in an attempt to satisfy their wants (see Figure 17.25). Economics is a very broad field and is difficult to define. We will not consider all aspects of economics. Instead, we will define and develop those areas of economics that meet our needs for this course.

What is economics?

The most fundamental question any economic system must answer is this: How should goods be distributed? In other words, how much of the total production does each person get to have or to use? Throughout history, a variety of answers to this question have been tried.

In the world today, two major economic systems exist: government-dominated economy and market economy (or free enterprise). In their purest form, they may be summarized as follows.

Government Dominated

Helpful Hint!

Allocative mechanism is a technique for distributing a portion of the production of a society among its members.

The government often decides who gets what. How this is best done is not obvious. The two common approaches involve "equal shares" and "need."

In the equal shares approach, everyone gets the same amount. At first glance, this simple system seems fair and efficient. However, individual needs are not identical. Babies need more milk than adults. Farmers need more tractors than musicians do. Not everyone likes yogurt.

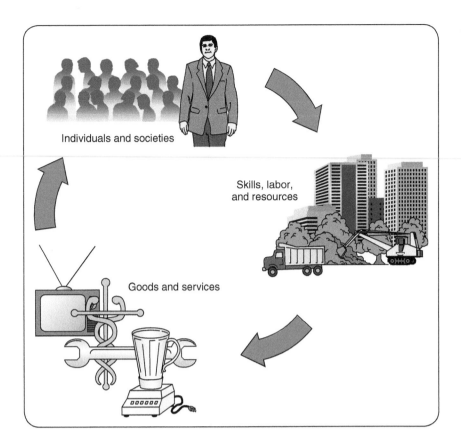

◄ FIGURE 17.25 Economics is the study of the ways individuals and societies distribute their goods in an attempt to satisfy their wants.

Individuals and societies

Skills, labor, and resources

Goods and services

The need approach is based on the philosophy "from each according to his or her ability, to each according to his or her need." However, it is difficult for governments to determine other people's needs accurately and fairly. Why not exaggerate your needs to get more for yourself? Why not send a lobbyist to Washington to make decision makers aware of your special interest's situation? Why work hard if you're not included with the "needy"?

Think about This!

What do we mean by "need"?

Market Economy

A **market economy (free enterprise)** is the system in which anyone is allowed to produce any product and attempt to sell it to others (see Figure 17.26). The producer is allowed to keep the profit (or a portion of it) and use that profit to maximize his or her own happiness.

◄ FIGURE 17.26 Free enterprise in action.

How much product is produced is the decision of the producer and is determined by free market decisions.

Even though each of these systems is used to some degree in the United States, most economic decisions are made in the marketplace. Expected demand and price determine what is produced and who gets what.

Although much of a market economy operates on its own, government does play a role. Government is involved when it regulates the safety, health, and well-being of workers and the products they produce. It also plays other roles, as we shall see.

Content Clue

Governments can manipulate the market system.

17.11 Free Market Economics

The natural forces that drive a market economy are the law of demand and the law of supply.

Law of demand: The demand for a product or service depends on its price. Low prices lead to high demand; high prices lead to low demand.

Law of supply: The quantity of goods and services offered for sale will vary with price. The higher the price, the greater the quantity offered, and vice versa.

These two laws interact with each other, as is shown on the graph in Figure 17.27. The interaction produces market equilibrium prices. At **market equilibrium**, producers can supply an amount of a good or service equal to demand at a price low enough to be acceptable to consumers but high enough so that producers can make an acceptable profit. Without profit, an enterprise cannot provide for its future.

17.12 Evaluating the Market (Free Enterprise) System

As you have seen, the principles of supply and demand are quite simple. However, the actual functioning of the system is complex. Further, the whole system operates primarily on enlightened self-interest. Consumers purposely act to maximize their personal satisfaction through the goods they obtain. While suppliers attempt to maximize their profits, competition keeps suppliers from exploiting their customers. In addition, suppliers must constantly be on the lookout for new and better ways to produce their goods. If they don't, their competitors will undersell them and still make a profit. In this way, competition guarantees that the market price is very close to the cost of producing an item.

Once goods are produced, how are they distributed? The answer is simple. Those who want the goods and can afford the price get the goods. Those who can't afford the goods or are unwilling to pay the market price don't get them.

▶ FIGURE 17.27 Graphic representation of the free market economy.

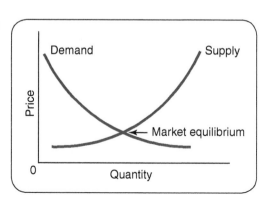

The market system may seem unfair, cold, or impersonal. Cold as it may seem, however, there are some major arguments in favor of the market (free enterprise) system.

1. The major argument for the market system is that it is *efficient*. Resources are distributed among the people as efficiently and, hence, as cheaply as possible. Competition forces suppliers to adopt the most efficient methods of production and to sell goods as attractively and cheaply as possible.

2. The market system *emphasizes personal freedom*. No one tells you what you must buy or what you can or cannot have. Those decisions are made by the individual consumer (see Figure 17.28).

What are the major features of the market system?

In spite of its efficiency and its emphasis on personal freedom, the market system also has some flaws.

1. Markets can be manipulated and made noncompetitive. When a few large firms dominate a portion of the market, they can work together to limit competition and keep the price of their goods high.

2. Since it takes money to make money, the free market can allow the rich to hold on to economic power. In some cases, tradition instead of free market forces determines who gets what.

3. Free market forces by themselves do not provide for social needs (such as schools and police protection), nor do they automatically absorb all the costs of goods. For example, the costs of pollution damages are not naturally included in the initial cost of a car, unless it has an emissions control system. Automobile producers did not voluntarily choose to include such systems. Another example would be a rapid shift to using solar energy. If solar options cannot, by themselves, compete economically with traditional energy sources, solar energy will not grow quickly in popularity.

4. Free markets tend to be unstable. Cycles of boom and depression or recession are common. Large numbers of people are hurt in these swings, which affects all classes from rich to poor. Competition breeds efficiency of production, but it also breeds stress.

5. The coldness of the market can cause alienation between the labor force and management (see Figure 17.29). Each seems to be motivated by opposing interests, although

What problems are associated with the market system?

this need not be the case. Many firms seem to have bridged this gap by promoting teamwork by workers and managers. The result is that both benefit.

6. Free markets fluctuate according to short-term factors. These factors include such things as crop failures, international conflicts, and labor disputes. Long-term study and planning can often soften the blows of some of these short-term factors.

7. Free market forces by themselves do not provide for long-term planning. It is often difficult to fund needed research and development when the required funding cuts into short-term profits.

17.13 The Role of Government in a Market Economy

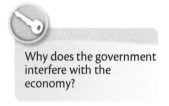

Why does the government interfere with the economy?

Every human system has some inherent flaws. The free market system is no exception. Any system run by individuals, some of whom may be very selfish, can create problems. Thus, some citizens have encouraged their governments to become involved in the economy and to interfere with and/or manipulate the free market. The government's role in our economy is the subject of great political and philosophical debate. Like any other program of human creation, government intervention in our economic system has had varying degrees of success.

Our government has been charged with five main economic functions. The goals are to lessen the injustices and to improve the benefits of the free market system.

1. *To ensure economic trust.* For businesses to function, contracts must be firm. Through their legislative powers, governments can establish rules for property ownership, standards for weights and measures, money standards and policy, and rules for legal agreements between parties.

2. *To promote and maintain competitive markets.* Competition is necessary for the free market to function efficiently. New production techniques and new products drive outmoded practices out of existence. Price increases conserve scarce goods. They also promote the wise use of goods.

Unfortunately, it is possible to stifle competition and prevent free market forces from functioning. Firms can band together and control supply and demand. Supply can be restricted and then higher prices obtained. To prevent this, governments can pass and enforce antitrust laws.

3. *To meet social goals by providing for public needs and wants.* As we mentioned earlier, the costs of both preventing pollution and pollution cleanup are not automatically included in the price of goods. To prevent innocent parties from having to pay for the pollution caused by others, governments have intervened. They may either force a supplier to eliminate or reduce a problem, or they may force someone to pay for the cleanup. The net result is that the cost of the good in question rises to reflect its true cost.

In other cases, the entire public may be taxed to provide goods and services that the market system would not provide equally to the entire population. For example, people want police protection, roads, schools, immunizations, emergency response, disaster relief, and other goods and services. If a majority believes that everyone is entitled to these things, governments supply them (see Figure 17.30).

4. *To promote fairness (equity).* So often we hear, "The rich get richer and the poor get poorer." It is true that to make money you generally must have money to invest. Because of this, those who are wealthy have a distinct advantage over those who are not. The poor find it difficult to work up the ladder of success. They have trouble saving for their old age, paying for emergencies, and providing opportunities for their children. To remedy some of this, our government provides such things as Social Security, Medicare, disaster relief, and educational assistance. Further, the majority of our federal government's expenditures are financed with a progressive income tax. This means that those with higher incomes pay proportionately more in taxes.

5. *To stabilize national income, employment, and the price level.* Free markets have a tendency to go through cycles. Alternating periods of strong economic activity and recession are particularly hard on the poor. They have nothing saved to "tide them over." It would be helpful to control the economic cycle so that employment would constantly be high and prices relatively stable.

Our government has a variety of mechanisms for stabilizing the economy. It can increase or decrease the money supply. Interest rates are manipulated for a variety of reasons. We will not explain these mechanisms further. It is sufficient for now to recognize that these stabilization activities exist and are a major effort of the federal government.

◀ FIGURE 17.30 How is police protection paid for in your community? (*James Shaffer Photography*)

The Economic Role of the Government

In this activity, you will take a closer look at the role of government in the economy.

Background

Americans have given some economic power to the federal government so our society can meet certain goals. The five major economic functions of the U.S. government are to promote the following:

1. Economic trust

2. Competitive markets

3. Social goals by providing certain public wants and needs

4. Fairness in taxation on businesses and individuals

5. Economic stability of national income, employment, and price level

Procedure

Listed below are 15 actions that the government could take to fulfill its economic functions. In your science notebook, record the following for each action:

a. Identify which function (1–5 above) is accomplished by the specific action below.

> **Helpful Hint!**
>
> There may be more than one function that pertains to an action. Choose the *best* answer for each item. Other possibilities will be brought out in class discussion.

b. Explain why the action promotes that function.

1. A lawsuit by the Department of Justice breaks up the American Telephone and Telegraph monopoly. Why?

2. The environmental impacts of mining and milling projects are researched before permission is given to mine on federal lands. Why?

3. Regulation of the money kept in circulation is entrusted to the Federal Reserve Board. Why?

4. A 100 percent tax on inheritance of money and property is instituted. Why?

5. A 40 percent tax on imported automobiles is passed in Congress.

6. Free public education for all under the age of 18 years is provided.

7. Work programs are created for the unemployed.

8. Federal scholarships and college loan programs are offered.

9. An increase in the defense budget is made possible by increasing the national debt and taxes on the citizens.

10. Women and minorities, by law, receive the same pay as Caucasian men holding similar jobs.

11. National standards for weights and measures are set by the Department of Commerce (National Bureau of Standards is established).

12. A wage and price freeze is instituted nationally.

13. Microcomputer software is left unregulated.

14. Emission standards for coal-fired electric power plants are set.

15. Small business loans are made available by the federal government.

Note: These actions and possible actions are for purposes of discussion only. Listing does not imply acceptance by the authors nor anyone else associated with this course.

◀ FIGURE 17.31 Solar electric power generation. (*National Renewable Energy Laboratory*)

17.14 Sustainable Economics

A sustainable nation or world must operate under an economic system that has somewhat different goals than the economic systems that are prevalent today. A sustainable world must have a sustainable economy. A **sustainable economy** is one in which both the number of people and the flow of resources are maintained at some desired, *sufficient* level. This economy recognizes the fact that the world is a complex, but finite system that has evolved with reference to a fixed rate of solar input. It views humans as dependent on what a finite ecosystem can provide.

In a sustainable economy, the free market is allowed to control the transfer of goods and services. However, a sustainable economy must provide **mechanisms** for accomplishing the following three tasks:

1. Maintaining a stable population

2. Preventing rapid depletion of critical resources

3. Providing maximum opportunity to all people

These three mechanisms could come about by government policy and laws. They could also be the result of education, which brings about changes in personal preferences, beliefs, and values (see Figure 17.31).

The three mechanisms that might make sustainable economics work.

Helpful Hint!

A *mechanism* is a way of doing something.

Topic: sustainable economics
Go to: www.scilinks.org
Code: GloSci7e687

The Sustainable Planet

We will now focus on building the sustainable planet.

In the sections that follow Activity 17.7, you will obtain ideas for planning the world of your future. In Activity 17.10, you will design such a future.

Strategies for Building a Sustainable World

A sustainable world requires the establishment of three mechanisms:

1. Maintaining a stable population.

2. Preventing the depletion of critical resources.

3. Maximizing opportunities for all people.

In this activity, you will brainstorm strategies for accomplishing each mechanism.

Materials

- *Strategies for Building a Sustainable World* handout (optional)

Procedure

1. Reproduce the table in Figure 17.32 in your science notebook or use the handout *Strategies for Building a Sustainable World*.

2. List any strategies you can think of in the second column of your chart.

3. During the class discussion, record any new ideas in the third column of your chart.

> **Helpful Hint!**
>
> At this point, you are not to determine which ideas are good and which are not. At this point, they are all simply ideas. The goal is to generate long lists of ideas to analyze, debate, and sort out.

▼ **FIGURE 17.32** Strategies for building a sustainable world.

Mechanism	Strategies to Make It Function	Other Ideas
Maintaining a stable population	1 2 3 4 5	6 7 8 9 10
Preventing the depletion of critical resources	1 2 3 4 5	6 7 8 9 10
Maximizing opportunities* for all people	1 2 3 4 5	6 7 8 9 10

*By maximizing opportunities, the largest number of people are committed to the system. This minimizes social unrest and leads to a stable society.

17.15 Maintaining a Stable Population

Some social forces in the United States and in other developed nations may bring about a stabilization of population. These include (1) the demand for new roles by women, (2) the promotion of the benefits of smaller families and/or the choice to begin a family at a later age, (3) the demand by many women for control over their reproductive functions, (4) the widespread availability of birth control devices and information, (5) available retirement plans, and (6) the removal of **tax incentives** for having large families.

The population situation in the less-developed countries (LDC) is difficult for those of us in the more-developed countries (MDC) to comprehend. Many people hope that the demographic transition will work for LDC as it has for us. The demographic transition is a phenomenon seen in populations of modern nations. As modernization proceeds and wealth accumulates, population growth slows. However, a decline in the death rate usually precedes the decline in the birthrate, producing a period of rapid growth before stabilization. The demographic transition is thought to occur because children are more important to family budgets in the agricultural economies of LDC than in the MDC. Also, in most LDC, parents look to their children to care for them in their old age. Because many infants and children die, large families ensure that some will survive long enough to care for their parents. The better medical care in developed countries leads to the survival of more children, making large numbers of children unnecessary.

It is not known if the demographic transition will occur without significant industrialization. Some believe that population will always stabilize when living standards reach a level when basic human needs are met and life becomes enjoyable and meaningful to both men and women (see Figure 17.33).

Although a topic of debate, it may be that wealthy nations (MDC) will have to help poorer nations (LDC) while their populations stabilize. They may need help with population control, with industrial development, and with financial assistance.

◀ FIGURE 17.33 Will the demographic transition occur in less-developed countries as they begin to modernize? (*Adobe EyeWire*)

Changes in Attitudes

A **value** is a principle or belief that is regarded as being desirable by an individual or a group of individuals. Often, there is an emotional and traditional attachment to values. People and societies have certain values because those values serve various desires and/or needs.

People's lives change with time and so, often, do their values. The values of our forefathers don't always meet our present needs.

> **Think about This!**
>
> Some values, such as The Ten Commandments, are believed to be absolute. They don't change over time.

In this activity, you will think about how values reflect the needs of society.

Procedure

Listed under Questions & Tasks are 9 statements that reflect some of the values and beliefs of early Americans. Figure 17.34 is a list of some values related to a sustainable society.

1. Match the old value (1–9) with the one in Figure 17.34 that could replace it.

2. For each value pair, do the following:

   a. Give a reason the old value was held.

   b. Give evidence, if any, why the old value is being replaced.

> A. We're all in it together.
> B. Happiness is more than just things.
> C. Good science proceeds into the unknown with caution and in ignorance, refrains.
> D. Humans are partners with nature.
> E. To every task, there is an optimum completion time.
> F. Earth and its resources are finite.
> G. The tool must match the task.
> H. There is no "away."
> I. Replenish means to replace oneself (and that's all).
>
> **Helpful Hint!**
>
> Each item has only one answer. Don't use a letter more than once.

▲ **FIGURE 17.34** Some values related to a sustainable society.

Record your responses in your science notebook.

1. Man is master of nature. ☐

   a.

   b.

2. The bigger the better. ☐

   a.

   b.

3. Material wealth is a measure of your worth as an individual. ☐

   a.

   b.

4. The faster the better. ☐

   a.

   b.

5. Americans were given a special land to occupy. ☐

   a.

   b.

6. People ought to have large families. ☐

   a.

   b.

7. We'll never run out of resources. ☐

   a.

   b.

8. There is no problem that science and technology can't solve. ☐

   a.

   b.

9. Out of sight, out of mind. ☐

   a.

   b.

17.16 Values Regarding Resource Use

People have beliefs and attitudes about everything. This includes our natural resources and how we should use them. The pioneers who settled America had basic beliefs (values) about how natural resources should be used. These values served their needs well. The nation they established grew, became great, and provided a comfortable and meaningful life to most of its people. But the situation of most Americans today is vastly different than that faced by the early pioneers. In many cases, this requires a change in some of our values. The values of our ancestors do not always meet our present needs. This is especially true in the case of natural resources.

Early pioneers believed that man was *master* of nature. To them, the natural environment was hostile and needed to be tamed. They had to cut down forests to grow food and build roads. Today, we realize that we are *partners* with nature. Nature provides us with the food, air, soil, water, and minerals we need to stay alive and live a quality life. We can work with nature to make sure that these benefits will always be with us.

We used to think that bigger was better. The tasks of the early pioneers were large, and they required large tools. However, this is not always the case. A large, heavy car can waste valuable resources. Often, a more efficient car can be faster and more comfortable than a larger, more massive one (see Figure 17.35).

When America was being developed, it appeared that our resources would never run out. However, the settlement of the nation has shown that there are limits. Earth is only so big.

We once thought that the wastes of society could simply be buried. But, there is no "away." We now realize that the conservation of mass applies to everything.

Large families were the norm in early America. Life on the farm was hard, and many hands were necessary to get the job done. Today, children are usually not an economic gain. They add to our lives in other ways. American couples now have two children on the average.

It was once believed that material wealth was a measure of one's success as an individual. Rich people and families were highly regarded simply because they were rich. The gathering of land and belongings became a goal in itself. This helped fuel the economy.

> **Content Clue**
>
> Some values change over time.

◀ FIGURE 17.35 This 1958 Buick Riviera Special is representative of American cars of the late 1950s and 1960s—heavy, large, much chrome, and low mileage. It averages 12 to 15 miles per gallon.

However, evidence supports the observation that wealth, in and of itself, does not guarantee happiness.

A look at Earth from space forces us to realize, once again, that we are all on this planet together. To survive into the future, we must use our natural resources with care. With a resource-use ethic, our resources can sustain generation after generation on our planet.

17.17 Promoting the Wise Use of Natural Resources

It is important that we understand the interactions and limits of the ecosphere. These limits will determine future economic activity. How much waste can a given lake, river, or ocean absorb without undergoing irreversible ecological damage? How much pollution can a given volume of air absorb and still be able to cleanse itself? Our present environment demonstrates that limits exist, but we need to know what those limits are. More research is needed on environmental impact and pollution control.

Even with limited knowledge, we can see that producing and using goods produces pollutants. Probably the most effective way to limit pollution is to carefully examine the flow of resources through the economy. How can the flow of resources through an economy be changed? There are many ways.

First, nonrenewable resource flow could be limited through government control. Governmental action might include the required use of biomass fuels or the placement of high taxes on materials we want to conserve. Also, the advertising of products that contain scarce resources could be banned.

Second, we may simply choose to allow the free market to function. Increased scarcity causes prices to rise. Higher prices encourage conservation. They also enable mining companies to develop lower grade ore deposits because the potential for profit would be there. Higher prices also stimulate the search for new ore bodies and substitute materials.

Third, individuals can make conscious efforts to conserve, eliminate waste, choose products in which materials are used wisely, and recycle and reuse when possible.

▶ FIGURE 17.36 The wide use of fiber optic cables is causing the partial replacement of a traditional resource (copper) with a new (invented) resource (sand). (CORBIS/D. Boone)

Fourth, technology can also play a significant role. In many ways, the technological solutions are the preferred solutions. They enable us to continue doing many things we have grown to enjoy and yet reduce resource consumption. Technology can bring us the energy-efficient automobile (lighter in mass due to its composite body) that can be powered with hydrogen using a fuel cell. Technology also enables us to extract more completely the resources we mine, and to find or develop substitutes for many of the materials that may become scarce.

With technology, we can also "invent" resources. For example, fiber optic cable now replaces communication cable that uses strands of copper wire. Fiber optic strands are made from sand (see Figure 17.36). In the past, synthetic rubber replaced natural rubber. Rubber and aluminum have replaced chrome on bumpers. Synthetic diamonds replaced natural diamonds in industry. The list is long and will continue to grow.

In the attempt to achieve a more stable world, one of the great debates will center on what role government should play in dealing with our natural resource issues. The government, in cooperation with the business community and an informed public, can help formulate and carry out a national natural resource strategy. It is equipped to reconcile conflicting interests and balance various national needs (see Figure 17.37 and 17.38). It is capable of formulating policies, setting objectives, and establishing appropriate incentives for the private sector to achieve those objectives. It can also monitor progress and provide leadership. How well our government performs these functions will, in large measure, determine our future (see Figure 17.39).

As you can see, the matter of a resource policy is complex. There is no *one* best road to follow, no *one* best solution that is fair to all. That is what makes policy development so difficult. Solutions come from ideas. Dialogue, debate, and compromise bring results.

◀ FIGURE 17.37 Arctic energy development. (*From Atlantic Richfield Corporation.*)

◀ FIGURE 17.38 The panic of irrational thought. (*Gene Bassett. Scripps-Howard Newspapers.*)

Options for the Future   693

Wise resource use offers exciting possibilities for the future. Figure 17.40 illustrates this. Curve 1 is a familiar resource depletion curve. Curve 2 shows how some commitment to conservation, recycling, and research and development can buy us time and new possibilities. Curve 3 illustrates the dream. A nonrenewable resource-use ethic assures prudent use. Proper application of economic forces stifles waste. Invention and substitution could enable us to change materials that are not economic today into valuable raw materials in the future. In that way, our total supply of useful resources could even increase.

Which curve we follow is yet to be determined. You will help to determine its course.

In Figure 17.41, we list ten of the most important natural resource options that we have. We then briefly outline the political issues that center on those options. Filling in the rest of the table is up to you. The opinions you express constitute your own natural resource policy. The soundness of your opinions is an indication of how well-thought-out and workable your plan may be. The collective decisions of our people and our leaders on these issues will be our national resource plan. It should evolve from sound national debate and introspection, not just happen at random. You can be part of formulating a positive attitude toward national natural resource issues, if you choose to.

Helpful Hint!

Remember, do not write in your textbook. Use your science notebook or a separate piece of paper for your answers. Did you complete the table?

Apply Your Understanding

What should our resource policy be?

► FIGURE 17.40 The shape of a resource depletion curve for a nonrenewable resource depends on human attitudes. Which curve is most likely to represent our future?

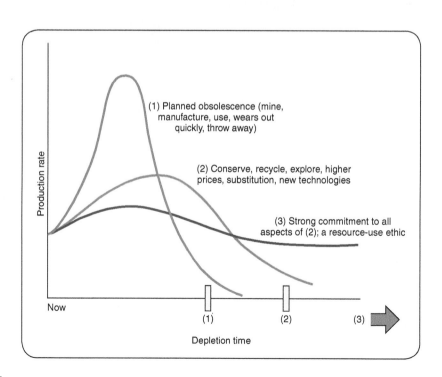

Resource Options	Political Issues	Effectiveness Rating (1 to 10)*	What the United States Should Do (and how)
1. Slow the flow of natural resources through the world economy (use less, greater efficiency).	Economic disruption. Unemployment. Design for recycling. Retraining. Use of leisure time. Price and/or tax incentives. Government regulation. Education of the public. Free market interactions.		
2. Invest in more public transportation.	Effect on auto industry and auto-related businesses. Access for elderly and disabled. Are there better ways to transport people? Taxes to build. Toll roads.		
3. Recycle materials.	Economic incentives. Creating new behavioral patterns.		
4. Reduce population growth.	Reproductive freedom. Religious issues. Reversing some present economic incentives.		
5. Live more simply (lifestyle change).	Redefining the "good life." Economic readjustment. Preference for nonconsuming activities.		
6. Increase exploration and development of natural resources.	Terms of access to resources. Producers' economics. Environmental impact.		
7. Resolution of coal development uncertainties.	Carbon sequestration. Air pollution. Land reclamation. Mine safety.		
8. Resolution of nuclear program uncertainties.	Siting and licensing of plants. The breeder program. Safeguarding plutonium. Spent fuel handling and storage.		
9. Research and development of alternative energy sources.	Choice of priorities. Role of the government.		
10. International cooperation.	Energy trade controls. Economic impact of rising energy prices. Technology and emergency supply sharing.		

*1 = most effective option; 10 = least effective option

Recycling Aluminum

In this activity, you will examine the energy issues related to the recycling of aluminum.

Materials

- grocery sack filled with crushed aluminum cans
- balance
- calculator (optional)

Procedure

1. Examine the table in Figure 17.42. Note that the life-cycle energy cost of using aluminum cans is similar to that of other containers that perform similar functions. This is because the recycling rate for aluminum cans is quite high. Why is the recycling rate high?

2. Reproduce Figure 17.43 in your science notebook.

3. Collect aluminum cans, crush them, and place them in a standard size grocery sack until the sack is full.

4. Dump the sack out and count the cans. Record your answer in Figure 17.43.

5. Determine the weight of the sack in pounds (1 lb = 454 grams). Record your answer.

6. It requires 0.40 kilowatt-hours (kWh) to produce 1 aluminum can from bauxite ore, which is mined. Record this in your data table.

7. Make the calculations and answer the questions that follow. Show all your work.

QUESTIONS & TASKS

Record your responses in your science notebook.

1. What is the weight of one aluminum can (in pounds)?

2. How long, in hours, can a 100W (.1 kW) bulb be lit with the energy required to produce one aluminum can?

Helpful Hint!

Electrical energy in kilowatt-hours equals kilowatts multiplied by hours.

Energy (kWh) = kilowatts × hours

Thus, a 100W lightbulb consumes 100 watt-hours (.1 kWh) of energy in 1 hour, 200 watt-hours (.2 kWh) of energy in two hours, and so forth.

▼ FIGURE 17.42 The life-cycle* energy cost of various packaging materials.

Type of Container	Energy Requirements per Container (thousand Btu/container)
Aluminum can** (12 oz, pop-top)	2.22
Steel vegetable can** (two piece, drawn, 15 oz)	6.93
Glass bottle (nonreturnable, 12 oz)	2.69
Plastic bottle (16 oz)	2.10
Plastic milk jug (1 gal = 128 oz)	10.0
Paperboard (coated) milk carton (1 gal = 128 oz)	no longer in use
Paper grocery sack (1/6 barrel, 0% recycling)	2.180
Plastic grocery sack (1/6 barrel, 0% recycling)	0.700

*Life-cycle means from manufacturing through use and recycling.

**58% of steel cans are recycled (2001); 49% of aluminum cans are recycled (2001). Note: The decrease in the recycling rate for the aluminum can (from 1990 to 2001) is due to a change in the EPA methodology.

(Sources: Franklin Associates [2004], Aluminum Association [2004], CIWMB website [2004], AISI website [2004], NAPCOR.)

1. Number of crushed cans per grocery sack: _____
2. Weight of sack in pounds: _____
3. Energy required to produce an aluminum can from ore: _____

3. If your local recycling center pays $ .40 per pound for aluminum, how much money would you receive by bringing in the sack of aluminum cans?

4. If a family of four consumes four six-packs of beverages in aluminum cans per week, how long will it take them to fill the sack with crushed Cans? Weeks? Months?

5. How many kilowatt-hours of energy went into the production of the aluminum cans in the sack?

6. If 95 percent of the energy required to produce new aluminum from bauxite is saved by recycling, how much energy is saved by recycling the aluminum in the sack of cans?

7. Let's assume the average American home consumes 15 kWh of electrical energy per day. How many days of home electrical energy are represented by the energy saved as the result of recycling the sack of cans?

8. There were 53.8 billion aluminum cans recycled in 2002. If this represents 53.4 percent of the cans produced in 2002, how many aluminum cans are produced in a year in the United States?

9. How much do the 53,800,000,000 aluminum cans weigh? If aluminum is valued at $1,200/ton,

Grocery sack

what is the dollar amount of this recycled aluminum?

10. Suppose one aluminum can requires the consumption of 0.40 kWh of electrical energy to produce, and 95 percent of this energy can be saved by recycling. How much energy goes into the production of a recycled aluminum can?

11. True or false: In terms of the use of beverage containers, the best thing one can do is to recycle an aluminum can.

17.18 Expanding Opportunities for All People

To build a sustainable world, people must be committed to that goal. Stable societies offer many opportunities to their citizens. Stable societies also do not reward people who do not work. (There are, of course, exceptions based on physical/mental disabilities.) It is difficult to produce the wealth necessary to expand opportunities if creativity and work are not rewarded.

The most effective ways to expand opportunities seem to revolve around education. Education, however, isn't free. The funds to improve education come from tuition, taxes, gifts, and loans—usually, a mix of all of these. The available monies support all of the following:

1. Education programs that focus on the disadvantaged.

2. Scholarships and low-interest loans that target fields that need trained individuals or groups that are underrepresented.

3. Reading and basic skill improvement for individuals and groups that lack the skills to be productive in society.

4. Job training in fields where there are not enough workers.

5. Scholarships and grants to reward high achievement.

6. Higher minimum wages so those who do manual labor can raise a family.

In summary, successful societies create ways to enable the maximum number of people to develop to the fullest (see Figure 17.44).

17.19 Maximizing Stability and Freedom

Think about This!

The challenge is to maximize both stability and freedom.

The building of the sustainable planet will take cooperation among private citizens, corporations, and governments. Cooperation will be required if we are to maintain a stable world that recognizes both finiteness and the full potential of all humans.

Suggestions and hints of a new way of living that can lead toward stability are beginning to appear. For example, the Japanese have voluntarily made a two-child family the norm; the Chinese are trying to make a one-child family the norm. Environmental pollution is now unacceptable in the United States, Canada, and western Europe. Automobile engines may shortly be made from ceramics to conserve metals. Automobiles can be made to use much less gasoline than thought possible not that many years ago. We may even be able to use solar cells to produce hydrogen from water. That hydrogen may then power the fuel cell that powers our cars (see Figure 17.45).

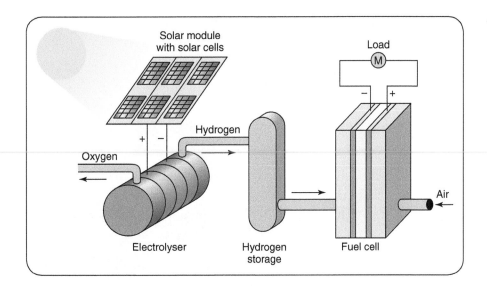

◀ FIGURE 17.45 A solar hydrogen system for powering a fuel cell. The load (M) could be an automobile. *(Heliocentris Energie-systeme GmbH, Berlin, Germany)*

As new technologies, political frameworks, and ideas spread, there is a good chance that growth will be materially slowed. This should give the ingenuity of humans a chance to reorder our world. At the same time, we should be able to preserve the opportunity to strive for true freedom for all people.

ACTIVITY 17.10

The Island Revisited

Humans are travelers, not lemmings. We can ask the traveler's question—Where do we want to go?

—Stockholm Environmental Institute

You and your classmates have been stranded on an island in the South Pacific. You have the same resources as specified in Activity 17.1, Pioneers and Their Island (see Figure 17.1). In this activity, you will examine the conditions necessary for long-term survival on Spaceship Earth.

Procedure

You have already decided how the resources of this island could potentially be used. In Activity 17.1, those decisions led to collapse (in most cases). Your task is to rethink the priorities and plan an island that survives. Work individually or as a group. If you work as a group, each member must have a specific task.

1. Make a graph that projects the ideal future for your population, your resource situation, and your agricultural production (see Figure 17.2 to get started). Draw in what happened during the first 350 years to show what you must deal with as you plan the future. Everyone in your group must agree on this graph.

> **Helpful Hint!**
>
> Your lists from Activity 17.7 will be helpful.

2. Write a scenario (possible future) explaining the social processes your island people will go through to attain your goals. Do this by working through the 4 steps under Questions & Tasks. Write 1 or 2 paragraphs per step. Your decisions must agree with the information illustrated on your graph. Work carefully and thoughtfully. This is the blueprint for your future (see Figure 17.46).

> **Helpful Hint!**
>
> Review sections 17.8–17.19 and use other references for ideas.

QUESTIONS & TASKS

Record your responses in your science notebook.

1. *Social structure and decision making.* Every society has a way to interact and make decisions. Historically, dictatorships and anarchy have not been mechanisms for producing positive social change. Do not model after those types of government.

   a. How are decisions made?

   b. What is your social structure? (Family units, community, government? Will you promote two-parent families? Will both parents work?)

   c. How did you select the governing structure (elections, town meetings, electronic voting)?

   d. How do you promote and reward responsible behavior? Will people still enjoy freedom?

2. *Economic structure and values.* Your economic structure is how you make and distribute goods (objects and services) in order to satisfy the needs and wants of your people.

   a. What objects and services will your island produce?

   b. Who will get the benefits of that production (labor, management, both)?

   c. Will you attempt to limit greed? How?

   d. Will you attempt to limit inequities between people? How?

   e. How will you provide incentives to work hard and to be inventive?

   f. How will people find fulfillment in life?

   g. What values do your people have that promote the achievement of stability, quality of life, and environmental sustainability?

   > **Think about This!**
   >
   > Read "An Essay on Values." Your teacher can provide this.

   h. Will most of your people be committed to your system? How do you know?

3. *Population growth.* To achieve stability, the population must eventually level off. To have a high-tech society, however, you must have several million people. Assume you start with the original 125 people and grow to about 4 million.

   a. Will your population grow exponentially?

   b. Will it stabilize and when?

   c. How will you accomplish changes in growth? Be specific.

4. *Resource use.* All material objects come from natural resources (agriculture and mining). High-tech objects require a variety of minerals, some of which have to be imported.

  a. Will you attempt to stabilize resource consumption? If so, how?

  b. Will you promote the wise use of resources and minimize waste? If so, how?

  c. How will you accomplish your resource goals? Be specific.

  d. Does your plan rely mostly on the government, or on the inventive nature of people?

  e. Identify any renewable resources that must come (be imported) from outside your (island) ecosystem.

  f. Identify any nonrenewable resources that must come (be imported) from outside your (island) ecosystem.

17.20 Possible Futures for Humankind

It is up to us to determine whether the years ahead will be for humankind a curse or a blessing. We always must remember that it is given to men and women to choose life and living, not death and destruction.

—Elie Wiesel, Nobel Laureate

The future will happen. What kind of future we have depends a good deal on how we face the important issues we have been discussing (see Figure 17.47).

Can the good life be redefined? Must happiness be tied to consumption? Can technology help make our choices easier?

If we assume the laws of science will continue to hold true—that mass and energy are conserved and that disorder steadily increases—then it is safe to say that the vast majority of us are bound to this planet. With nearly all of us bound to Earth, the laws and principles of human ecology take on new meaning. The interplay of human actions and natural forces

> **Think about This!**
>
> What is the good life?

> **Think about This!**
>
> Most of us will spend our entire lives on planet Earth.

◄ FIGURE 17.47 *"I'm not asking you to actually read my future. Just tell me that I've got a future." (© Tribune Company Syndicate, Inc. All rights reserved.)*

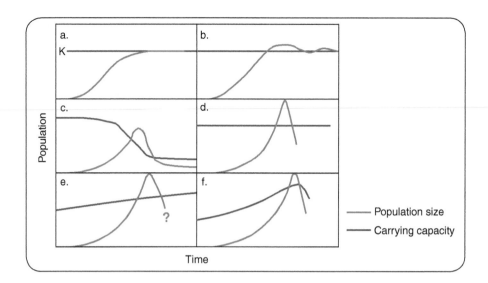

seems to imply that humankind can follow a course that will lead to any one of six possible outcomes. These outcomes are illustrated in the graphs in Figure 17.48.

Note that each graph has a solid red line that depicts a pattern for stable or unstable growth in relation to resource limit or carrying capacity (K). In this case, as before, we are referring to the *world's carrying capacity for humans*. This is the size of the human population that can be supported on a long-term, sustainable basis by the world's resources. As you learned, carrying capacity cannot be defined unless a standard of living and a role for technology are specified. Although you cannot accurately calculate a global world carrying capacity for humans, you can compute some rough estimates based on a variety of assumptions (as in *Beyond the Limits*) and draw some conclusions. With these ideas in mind, let's take a closer look at the graphs.

Figure 17.48a is the optimistic view. It assumes that humans plan well and follow through on those measures that allow us to slowly ease into a sustainable world (Figure 17.49).

►FIGURE 17.49 Wind surfing is relatively nonconsuming. The wind provides the energy; you provide the challenge. The surfboard, sail, and swimwear, however, are all high-tech. It took energy and resources to make them. *(Mark Müller)*

Figure 17.48b assumes that humans react to uncontrolled growth, but not quite soon enough. Hence, for a time, we overshoot our limits. Readjustment, however, allows stabilization to take place. Fortunately, the overshoot isn't too severe, and the ecosystem experiences no permanent damage.

Figure 17.48c assumes that humans react to uncontrolled growth, but not until our limits have been exceeded and some ecological damage has been done. Earth's carrying capacity is permanently lowered. An equilibrium is eventually established, but at a lower level than before.

Figure 17.48d shows humans continuing their consumptive patterns of exponential growth until Earth can no longer satisfy them. Civilization then experiences a sudden and irreversible collapse.

In Figure 17.48e, technological advances and planet management result in a steadily increasing carrying capacity. However, growth in both population and human demand is more rapid than the growth in carrying capacity. The limits are overshot, and a collapse occurs. We may or may not survive.

Figure 17.48f is a slight modification of Figure 17.48e. Again, technological advances and planet management result in an increased carrying capacity. However, growth in population and material well-being overshoot and damage the limiting factors. As a result, both collapse.

Which of these patterns most closely reflects our future? We do not know. Perhaps there will be some unexpected turn of events that will dramatically alter our future and cause us to move rapidly in a completely new direction. Who knows!

By taking this course, you may have caught a glimpse of a world that has never been. You may have caught a vision of a world that could be—a world where people might live in harmony with one another and their environment.

ACTIVITY 17.11

It's Time to Take Action!

In this activity, you will write a letter, make a phone call, send an e-mail, or pay a visit to a person, business, or organization that is involved with resource/environmental matters. You will match consumer choices with environmental commitments.

Background

Do you know the names of your local, state, and national governmental officials? Do you belong to or help a political party? Do you send donations to or attend the meetings of the League of Women Voters, the Environmental Defense Fund, or the Mineral Information Institute? Have you ever written a manufacturer about the packaging of a product or to an industry complimenting or criticizing their mode of operation?

Knowing about resource/environmental issues is not enough. The decisions that are to be made by industry, by government, by ordinary people, and by you in these areas in the next several years will have a tremendous effect on your future, your lifestyle, and your economic situation. Science is a powerful tool that can serve both our selfish and our nobler instincts. How it is used can be influenced by ordinary people—by people who care. Today, the direction in which science moves is probably determined more by the decisions of industry and government and by the buying habits of people than by the desires of scientists. Industry and government are very sensitive to what people want. *You* can make a difference.

Even though you can make a difference, surprisingly few people ever write their congressperson.

Perhaps 90 percent of our citizens live and die without ever taking pen in hand and expressing a single opinion to the person who represents them in Congress. A vote or two could greatly influence the direction of our national energy policy, the location of a power plant, or a water quality standard.

Because congressional sessions are long, and because each member of Congress represents so many people and votes on so many issues, the mailbag is probably a legislator's best link to the people back home. This activity is your chance to get involved and make a difference—or to increase your involvement if you already have taken action on one or more of these issues.

Finally, industries and agriculture produce what people want. Our buying habits determine what kind of cars they build, the efficiency of the appliances they build, and the kind of food they raise. The purchases we make are, in a way, votes for a certain type of future.

Procedure

1. This activity is divided into 4 parts: writing government officials; contacting the business community; investigating organizations; and analyzing your consumption habits. Do any or all 4 parts and then report your results to your teacher.

2. In addition to summarizing what you did, turn in copies of the letters you wrote, replies received, and information gathered. If you can document a well-though-out consumption pattern, also turn that in.

Part A: What is the best way to write government officials?

You may choose to write to your congressperson, your senator, a governmental agency, a state legislator, your governor, or the President. You may write to request information, ask for an opinion, give a compliment for taking a particular stand on an issue, support a position, or recommend action. When writing the President or members of Congress, the proper way to address your letter or e-mail is as follows:

President _____
The White House
1600 Pennsylvania Ave.
Washington, DC 20500

Senator _____
Senate Office Building
Washington, DC 20510

(Your Representative)
The Honorable _____
House Office Building
Washington, DC 20515

The following suggestions will help your letter be more effective.

1. Identify the bill or issue. About 20,000 bills are introduced in each Congress. Be specific. Try to give the bill number or describe it by popular title ("truth in lending," "minimum wage," etc.).

2. Be timely. Sometimes a bill is out of committee, or has passed the House, before a helpful letter arrives. Inform your congressperson while there is still time to take effective action.

3. Concentrate on your own delegation.

4. Be reasonably brief.

5. Identify yourself as a student.

6. Express your own views.

7. Give your reasons for taking a stand.

8. Be constructive.

9. If you have expert knowledge, share it with your congressperson.

10. Say "well done" when it's deserved.

11. Don't make threats or promises.

12. Don't berate your congressperson.

13. Don't pretend to wield vast political influence.

14. Don't become a constant "pen pal." Quality, rather than quantity, is what counts.

15. Don't demand a commitment before the facts are in.

Part B: Why should you contact the business community?

Our country is committed to the free enterprise system. Private industry will mine the coal and uranium that will power our nation; attempt to restore the land; design, build, and run the coal-fired and solar power plants; and handle industrial waste. Their actions will be regulated by our government, but they will do the work. Because they are private, and because of governmental regulation, industries are very concerned about how the public feels about what they do and how they do it. In the United States, all industries must perform their work in an environmentally sound manner.

What industries concern you? Do you know what they are doing about your concerns? Do you know why they are doing what they are doing? If they are located in your area, call them and arrange for a visit to address your questions. If your concerns are not of a local nature, write for information. Your librarian can help you choose the proper place to write and determine the address. Be informed.

Part C: What will you learn by investigating organizations?

Many organizations concern themselves with resource/environmental issues. Investigate some of these organizations. Find out what they stand for and how reasonable their actions are. Your parents, teachers, the library, and the Internet can help you get started.

Part D: Why is it important to analyze, and perhaps change, your consumption habits?

Every purchase you make is a vote that helps direct the economy. What you do with that purchase has an environmental impact. Recycling is a loop. If people don't purchase recycled products, the loop is broken. Document your consumption pattern; make changes when appropriate. Give your analysis to your teacher.

ACTIVITY 17.12

Introspection

Introspection is the process of observing and analyzing oneself. This is a good way to end a course that deals with so many aspects of life. In this activity, you will reflect on what you have studied, and tie it all together (Figure 17.50).

Take a quiet walk early in the morning, preferably by yourself. Watch the sunrise. Walk through a meadow, by a lake, in the woods, or follow a trail in the mountains. Look at the sky, listen to the birds, smell the flowers, and touch the leaves, the rocks, and the grass. Take your time. Think about where you are, how you relate to what's around you, and about the relationship between humans and nature. Then think about the way you live, what's important to you, and what you and your friends plan to do in the future. Finally, either while you rest or after your walk, write down some of your thoughts and share them with your teacher.

Helpful Hint!

Find a quiet place where you can really think.

Hope is not a prognostication, it is an orientation of the spirit, an orientation of the heart. It transcends the world as immediately experienced. Hope is an ability to work for something because it is good, not because it stands a chance to succeed. It is not the same thing as optimism. It is not the conviction that something will turn out well, but the certainty that something makes sense regardless of how it comes out.

—Vaclav Havel

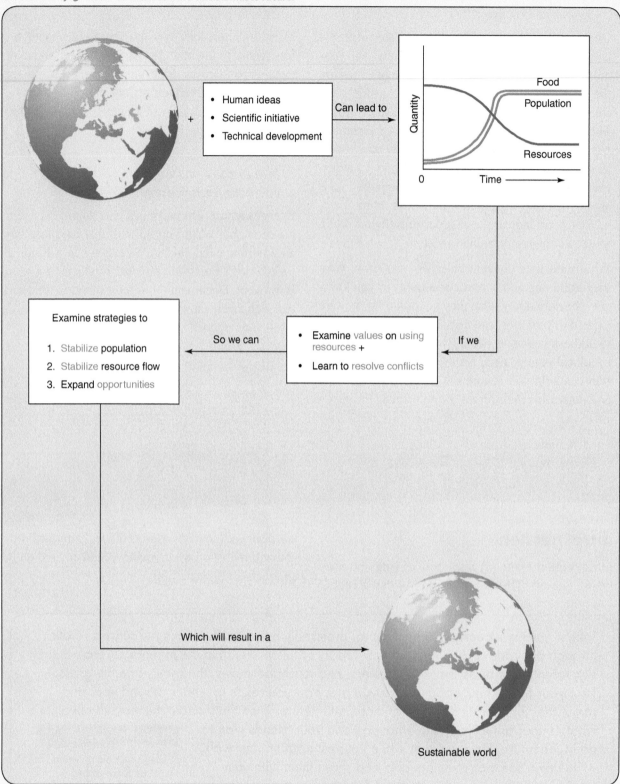

Summary

Growth was important as America evolved into a major world power. The population had to increase so that every region of the nation could become productive and use its resources. For a time, all the results of this expansion seemed positive.

Eventually, however, some problems appeared. Smog appeared in many of our major cities, many rivers and lakes literally died, and large sections of land became eroded and useless. Waste accumulation became overpowering. For many people, their hopes and dreams ended in despair. The westward migration was over.

In the early 1970s, the doctrine of growth came under serious attack. The attack was based largely on the study *The Limits to Growth*. This study identified five factors that determine and, in their interactions, ultimately limit growth on our planet. These factors are population, agricultural production, consumption of resources, industrial output, and pollution generation. These five factors have three things in common: (1) they are all interrelated; (2) at the time of the study, they were all growing exponentially; and (3) they all appear to have upper limits.

The Limits to Growth study predicted that if human behavior doesn't change, we are headed toward a global collapse. And there is only one way to prevent it—population and resource consumption must be stabilized.

There's no place like home. —Dorothy (Photo by NASA.)

The study was interesting, but it was attacked for several reasons. The rich were telling the poor how their behavior must change; economics was not considered as a tool for modifying human behavior; and the result was fixed, because growth in a finite system has to fail. The study also was vague in spelling out how a sustainable world could be achieved.

The study was praised, however, for forcing us to look at the direction in which we seem to be headed. It also documented evidence of environmental stress and provided a glimpse of what a sustainable future may be like.

A sustainable system must have a sustainable economy. This economy must have a way to control the flow of the physical resources that pass through it, a way to achieve a stable population, and a way to maximize opportunities for all people. Human ingenuity must be brought into play to preserve freedom and the opportunity for individual fulfillment.

The world we are being asked to shape is like no other. It involves a general realization that we are all passengers on a wonderful, but fragile, spaceship. We are part of everything, and everything is a part of us. Why not make a personal commitment to help build a better tomorrow?

> Vision without action is a waste of time. Action without vision is pointless and often dangerous. Vision with action can change the world.

Ashworth, William. *The Economy of Nature: Rethinking the Connections between Ecology and Economics* (Boston: Houghton Mifflin), 1995.

Baily, Martin N., et al. *Growth with Equity* (Washington, D.C.: Brookings Insititution), 1993.

Bloom, David E., et al. *The Demographic Dividend* (Santa Monica, CA: RAND), 2003.

Brown, Lester R. *Eco-Economy: Building an Economy for the Earth* (New York: W.W. Norton), 2001.

——— *Plan B 2.0: Rescuing a Planet Under Stress and a Civilization in Trouble* (New York: W.W. Norton), 2006.

Club of Rome. (See Meadows, *The Limits to Growth*).

Cole, H. S. D., et al., eds. *Models of Doom: A Critique of The Limits to Growth* (New York: Universe Books), 1973.

Daly, Herman. *Steady-State Economics*, 2nd ed. (Washington, D.C.: Island Press), 1991.

Diamond, Jared. *Collapse: How Societies Choose to Fail or Succeed* (New York: Viking), 2005.

Hammond, Allen. *Which World? Scenarios for the 21st Century: Global Destinies, Regional Choices* (Washington, D.C.: Island Press), 1998.

Hawken, Paul and Amory & L. Hunter Lovins. *Natural Capitalism: Creating the Next Industrial Revolution* (New York: Little, Brown and Company), 1999.

Hughes, Barry B. and Evan E. Hillebrand. *Exploring and Shaping International Futures* (Boulder, CO: Paradigm), 2006.

Hughes, Barry B. *World Futures: A Critical Analysis of Alternatives* (Baltimore: The Johns Hopkins University Press), 1985.

Johnson, Warren. *The Future Is Not What It Used to Be: Returning to Traditional Values in an Age of Scarcity* (New York: Dodd, Mead), 1985.

Meadows, Donella H., et al. *The Limits to Growth* (New York: Universe Books), 1972.

——— *Limits to Growth: The 30-Year Update* (Post Mills, VT: Chelsea Green), 2004.

Miles, Ina. World Views and Scenarios. *World Futures: The Great Debate*, edited by Christopher Freeman and Marie Johoda (New York: Universe Books), 1978.

Pirages, Dennis and Ken Cousins, eds. *From Resource Scarcity to Ecological Security: Exploring New Limits to Growth* (Cambridge, MA: MIT Press), 2005.

Raskin, Paul, et al. *Great Transition: The Promise and Lure of the Times Ahead* (Boston: Stockholm Environment Institute), 2002.

Rees, William, and Mathis Wackernagel. *Our Ecological Footprint* (Philadelphia: New Society), 1995.

Rolston, Holmes, III. *Conserving Natural Values* (New York: Columbia University Press), 1994.

Scientific American Magazine. *Crossroads for Planet Earth* Entire issue – September, 2005.

Simon, Julian L. *The Ultimate Resource 2* (Princeton, NJ: Princeton University Press), 1996.

United Nations Department of Economic and Social Affairs. *Global Challenge, Global Opportunity: Trends in Sustainable Development* (New York: United Nations), 2002.

WEBSITES

Club of Rome:
http://www.clubofrome.org/

International Institute for Sustainable Development:
http://www.iisd.org/

Institute for Global Communications
Issues Search Feature: click EcoNet:
http://www.igc.org/

UN Division for Sustainable Development:
http://www.un.org/esa/sustdev/csd.htm

APPENDICES

SCIENCE at work

Chapter 2: Traveling the Grand Oasis

You can't get away from Spaceship Earth, but you can vacation in areas that are remote or unfamiliar. Jim Sano helps people who really want to get away from it all—at least for 3 weeks or so. As President of InnerAsia Expeditions in San Francisco, California, Jim focuses on special-interest travel. Would you like to follow Marco Polo's route through China? Do you want to research rare butterflies in Micronesia? Jim knows how to help you take advantage of our widely diverse global ecosystems.

Courtesy of Jim Sano

Most of InnerAsia's clients have unusual interests and a higher-than-average sense of adventure. They may want to explore an especially remote place such as Patagonia, or sample the cuisines of various provinces in China. Jim often assists filmmakers in finding inaccessible locations for movie sets. He also helps scientists and students travel to areas where they can observe the unique characteristics of those areas.

It's interesting and challenging to arrange travel in these unusual lands and circumstance; however, Jim's efforts aren't always completely successful. One trip to the Himalayas, for example, was designed for people who wanted to look for the rare snow leopard. Reservations fell off when folks realized they'd spend most of their vacation hanging out in parkas and snowshoes at 15,000 feet with little chance of a hot meal and a lesser chance of seeing the beautiful leopard.

In arranging tours, Jim has help from a variety of experts. Usually a tour guide in San Francisco is responsible for the overall planning and logistics of the trip. An accompanying tour leader, naturalist, scientist, professor, or other knowledgeable person handles the daily educational needs of the travelers in the destination locale. Local tour guides who live in the area may have little formal education, but know their country, its climate, and its culture. Translators, too, are often on hand.

Travelers signing up for one of InnerAsia's expeditions receive an extensive itinerary with detailed instructions for preparing for their excursion. Annotated reading lists help them study the geography, etiquette, environment, and local culture of the country they will visit. On returning, travelers may continue studying about the country, using the lists as references.

Jim Sano's graduate work in biochemistry was a long way from the travel industry, but as he used computers in his education, he appreciated more and more their usefulness in data analysis and problem solving. Today, computers help him with everything from airline reservations to market analysis. In planning his ad mailing lists, for instance, he uses a customized statistical database to identify potential customers, their geographical interests, and spending limits. An online medical information service provides the latest information for travelers on subjects such as immunization requirements and current disease outbreaks.

Most travel industry training consists of standard travel-agent instruction in handling packaged tours, airline reservations, and hotel arrangements. Jim says, however, that there is little formal training available for a career in his type of travel. Still, if you're interested in learning and teaching about Earth's people, ecosystems, and geography, the travel industry may have a place for you. You might start as a guide in a museum, theme park, or state park. Look for experience handling groups of people, and develop your confidence and leadership abilities. When he was in college, Jim worked as a naturalist at Yosemite National Park in California, in charge of the naturalist programs at Tuolumne Meadows. Now, aided by his computer skills, he continues his role in education in other ways.

Task

Research the potential for employment as an "eco-travel" agent. Summarize your findings.

SCIENCE at work

Chapter 3: Here Today, Still Here Tomorrow

England, 1709. Imagine an old, shabbily dressed junk man, carrying a worn and stained bag of cast-off shoes, looking up at Queen Anne's palace. Today. The junk man's great-great-great-grandson kneels before Queen Elizabeth II, who taps him on each shoulder with her ceremonial sword and says solemnly, "I dub thee Sir Recycler."

Bill Cohen has watched the salvage business acquire new dignity; yesterday's "rags-and-bones" junk dealers are today's superstars. Bill knows about the importance of recycling because he owns and runs ABC Recycling Industries, Inc., in Santa Clara, California. His company is one of many in the United States working to conserve the world's resources and to decrease pollution from manufacturing. He's making a living at it, too.

Businesses such as Bill Cohen's collect or purchase various discarded materials, separate and package them, and forward them to companies for reuse. Take aluminum, for example. ABC repackages discarded aluminum cans, pots and pans, automobile and aircraft parts, screen doors, and so on, according to the specifications of companies such as Alcoa.

Courtesy of Bill Cohen

They melt down and recast these materials—sometimes as pure aluminum, sometimes combined with other metals to make alloys. ABC sends other materials, too, on this journey to recovery: copper wire, sheeting, and solar panels; brass doorknobs and valves; stainless steel sinks and pipes; zinc and lead. All can be reclaimed and reformed. Glass bottles, plastic jugs, newspapers, cardboard, and paper can also be recycled. These and many other materials are removed from the waste stream at Bill's company and used in new products or as fuel.

Up early most days, Bill enjoys the hands-on involvement with his business. After reviewing the weights of yesterday's collections and current prices offered for these items, he's outside with his workers, supervising packaging operations and shipments. Ten percent of ABC's suppliers are businesses recycling industrial waste; 90 percent are "just folks"—scout troops, community organizations, families that collect their own recyclables, and scavengers who wheel in shopping carts full of stuff found in alleys and vacant lots. Bill usually pays cash for the "junk" he collects.

Bill got started in recycling in Canada. His father was an early recycler; he and one truck provided "curb service" for folks wanting to get rid of things they weren't using any more. Bill worked in a neighbor's recycling business, learning it from the ground up. Later, he started his own company with one truck, just like his father.

Bill thinks his industriousness, perseverance, and natural curiosity about science have helped him in studying recycling methods and economics. To keep up on modern advances in industry and their uses for recycled material, he attends seminars and trade shows. One kind of information he needs for meeting his customers' needs is the physical properties of metals and other minerals. For example, one company might want materials that are very ductile (capable of being drawn out) for making wire. Another might need metals that conduct electricity easily. Still another might

be combining different materials to create a new alloy with certain properties. The more Bill knows about the properties of the materials he recycles, the better service he can provide to these companies. It also helps him decide whether materials must be separated from each other.

Recycling is a real equal-opportunity field, Bill says. And it needs the participation of more people who want to decrease pollution, conserve Earth's resources, help produce useful and efficient products, and provide jobs. As one way to begin, he suggests starting out in government recycling programs.

Task

List some of the kinds of information a successful recycler needs to know. Place a check (√) by those items requiring knowledge of science.

SCIENCE at work

Chapter 5: Information, Please . . .

In her job at the Los Angeles regional office of the U.S. Census Bureau, Nenet (pronounced "Nanette") Magpayo knows how valuable *information* is in our country's efforts to understand population. This information does not include only numbers of people; it also includes housing distribution, utility and transportation usage, education, and so forth. Each person or family Nenet interviews has been carefully selected to represent thousands of others throughout the country. She and other field representatives in 13 regional offices throughout the United States collect the data. Statisticians in a central office interpret the data and predict future patterns.

Courtesy of Nenet Magpayo

For instance, the bureau's recent estimate of population by the year 2020 is that 50 to 53 million people will live in California. That is 15 percent of the estimated U.S. population. (This depends on what happens to the state and elsewhere economically.) Because of the information obtained by Nenet and other field representatives, we know much more about the ebb and flow of our nation's population. We have facts such as what proportion are immigrants and what proportion arrive by birth. We also have an idea about the number of folks who look for greener pastures in other states. Through these data, the experts can estimate the resources we'll need.

After participating in the 1990 census, Nenet stayed on as a part-time employee of the Los Angeles office. Now, in addition to her survey work, she supervises other field representatives. She also recruits interviewers for the surveys. In the last few years, in addition to working for the Census Bureau, Nenet has gathered many different kinds of data for other government agencies and some private organizations. She has delved into people's spending habits for use in preparing the Consumer Price Index. For the U.S. Bureau of Labor, she has asked questions about employment. She has talked to people about AIDS and other issues for the National Institute of Health's Center for Health Statistics. She also has interviewed crime victims for monthly Department of Justice studies. By law, the identity of everyone interviewed is kept confidential.

Nenet gathers data both in person and over the phone. At times, a survey of one household or individual may take as long as 5 hours, depending on the questions. So, even though she deals with cold, hard facts, Nenet's approach to interviewing is more personable. She must be persistent, but friendly and polite; she must put folks at ease. Therefore, she has learned to be an excellent communicator.

Nenet follows up on about 40 cases a week; some of this occurs on weekends, when working people have more time to talk to her. In addition, Nenet attends many meetings and sends thousands of letters to potential respondents. She also helps other representatives prepare for interviews.

Special skills help Nenet with her job. She has been trained to use a laptop computer with customized programs. This helps her with recording, organizing, and summarizing interview data, which she then transmits over a modem. Also, Nenet speaks several languages, which has been helpful in her Census Bureau work. She worked as an electronics engineer in the Philippines before coming to the United States. Thus, she speaks her native Tagalog in addition to English and Spanish.

The latest population and housing census was in the year 2000; Nenet worked on that one, too. Those who joined her in this work were U.S. citizens who were at least 18 years old and who had a high-school diploma or GED certificate. Nenet says it was a great job for college students, parents of young children, and others who needed a part-time job to provide some insurance and other benefits.

Question

Is census taking only part-time work? Can analysis of census-type data lead to full-time employment?

SCIENCE at work

Chapter 7: Eating Wisely, Not Too Well

Diners in modern restaurants tend to be sophisticated and health-conscious, whether they can afford to spend a lot or only a little. They expect to eat foods from Mediterranean countries in particular. While some want to end a meal with elaborate Viennese-style desserts, others insist on beginning

Courtesy of Nathan Peterson

with wine from little-known California wineries. Nathan Peterson tries to satisfy them all.

Nathan once planned to be a florist. In creating and delivering floral arrangements for special occasions, he met the caterers who were providing the food. As Nathan himself loved to cook, he started working with the caterers, and today he is the chef at the Bay Wolf, one of the most popular restaurants on the east side of San Francisco Bay.

Nathan didn't become a chef overnight. When he became serious about entering that field, an older relative helped him by paying his tuition at a renowned culinary academy. For 16 intense months, Nathan studied cooking, pastry baking, and other aspects of being a chef and managing a restaurant. At the end of that time, he took a low-paying job at a Bay Area restaurant where he got practical experience to complement his formal training. Not long after, he began working at the Bay Wolf.

The dinner menu at the Bay Wolf changes monthly to feature a cuisine that is appropriate for the season. For instance, a summer dinner might begin with a cold tomato soup—gazpacho—from Spain; in winter, a hot stew from the Provence region of France might appear on the table.

All year-round, lunches reflect the foods and seasons of California. On the cold November day when Nathan was interviewed, one entree was crab cakes—it was the beginning of the local crab season—in a sauce made from Meyer lemons (a local citrus fruit), cole slaw (from California's winter crop of red and green cabbage) with a light vinaigrette dressing, and a few thin slices of roasted potato. Other entrees were similarly seasonal and from local sources. One, goat cheese and butternut squash cannelloni, also would make vegetarians happy.

While having seasonal foods is good for attracting customers, it also has the advantage of using local sources. Vegetables and fruit that have been transported for long distances, then stored in warehouses, have little flavor and may lose some of their nutritional value. The effect on the environment also is bad, as much energy must be used in carrying foods from other parts of the country or world.

Nathan is concerned about the environment, as are his customers, and he tries to buy organic foods when possible. As a practical person, though, he must control costs for the restaurant and for customers by using nonorganic

foods in some cases. For the same reason, he orders free-range chickens, but cannot insist on beef that is free of antibiotics and added hormones. By making some compromises, he can provide delicious, gourmet meals that are as healthful and affordable as possible.

Fad diets come and go, but basic nutrition remains much the same. Nathan's meals include moderate amounts of proteins and carbohydrates plus a little oil or fat. Fish is often available, and most meals include herbs and vegetables that add to their nutritional value as well as their flavor. When customers have special dietary needs, Nathan makes an effort to please them.

The desserts tend to be more "sinful," but the dessert list usually includes a fruit-based item that adds few calories. Again, fresh fruits in season are featured.

Nathan was drawn to his work because of its creative aspect, and that is still what he enjoys most. The meals served at the Bay Wolf are as appealing to the eyes as to the taste buds. When asked what he dislikes about being a chef, Nathan said that it is extremely demanding and sometimes painful physically because the continual repetitive motions—lifting, stirring, and chopping—are stressful to the arm and shoulder joints. In fact, he thinks upper-body strength may be one of the main prerequisites for being a chef.

Nathan's workday varies greatly, from 4 to 16 hours, depending on the season and the restaurant's monthly schedule. Once each month, he must plan the menus for that month, test recipes, and train cooks to prepare everything to his standards. New menus must be printed, and food suppliers must be alerted about what they will need to provide. During the winter holidays, the restaurant is especially busy with people having parties, but the cuisine must be as good as at slower times.

While Nathan was very fortunate in having formal culinary schooling (which can be extremely expensive), he emphasizes that anyone wanting to be a chef can get the necessary experience more gradually and at little cost by taking an entry-level job in a good restaurant.

In fact, Nathan feels his own education really began when he had the chance to work for Michael Wild (a famous chef and owner of the Bay Wolf) and other excellent chefs.

Task

Make a career plan for becoming a chef. Include a timeline, cost analysis, and the science of nutrition. Summarize your findings.

SCIENCE at work

Chapter 8: Finding Tomorrow's Energy

Famous petroleum geologist Wallace Pratt said in 1952, "Where oil is first found, in the final analysis, is in the minds of men." Pratt's opinion was that people exploring for oil will continue to find it as long as they believe more oil is left to be found. Jason Cansler, an earth scientist specializing in petroleum geology, knows that "before you can find the oil, you need the data proving that it exists."

Courtesy of Jason Cansler

Jason works for Chevron-Texaco's San Joaquin Valley Business Unit (SJVBU) headquartered in Bakersfield, California. The SJVBU is one of ChevronTexaco's largest development operations—it includes four major oil fields producing about 250,000 barrels of oil per day. Jason's team of scientists and engineers is working on one series of sandstone reservoirs in an oil field between 7,500 and 11,000 feet deep, containing about 20 wells across an area of 3 square miles. Oil and gas have been obtained here for almost 100 years already.

From a geologic standpoint, this reservoir in central California presents real challenges for Jason and his team. First, they must locate the remaining oil and gas, and then find ways to improve its *permeability* (the ease with which fluid flows through rock). This particular reservoir contains rocks with very low porosity (the percent of oil-bearing pores) and thus has less "connectivity" between the pores. That

means the rocks contain less oil and that the oil is harder to get. Engineers must find ways to improve permeability by perforating the wellbore and hydraulically fracturing the reservoir, which connects the oil-bearing pores. This is called "completing and stimulating" the well. Another challenge is the many faults that alter this reservoir's elevation and change its physical character down through the layers of earth. The geometry of these faults has considerable impact on how the reservoir is managed.

Jason provides earth science support for his team. He collects, analyzes, and interprets an array of geologic data about the reservoir, such as rock samples and existing well logs. He then maps the area's underground features and constructs three-dimensional geologic models. A key aspect of his job is calculating the amount of oil and gas trapped in the reservoir and determining how much remains to be extracted, to identify areas where existing wells can be reworked or new wells drilled. When these targets are identified, the team designs wells that will penetrate the earth safely and efficiently. Jason uses a wide range of databases, software, and operating systems in his work, ranging from basic office programs such as Excel and PowerPoint to complex geologic mapping and modeling software. The data he uses come from seismic imaging and many kinds of lab techniques for rock measurement and analysis (electron microscopes, X-ray diffraction, fossil identification, and more).

About 20 percent of Jason's time is spent out in the field, where he selects surface well sites, works with drillers and other technicians to identify geologic hazards, and evaluates rock samples and data from well logs as the drilling proceeds. In the office, study of the rocks and rock outcrops continues after wells are drilled, and the wells are evaluated with electric and nuclear tools. Most of Jason's days are spent in collaboration with other team members (reservoir, drilling, production, and facilities engineers; project managers; oil-field operators; and various engineering and geologic technicians). Together, they interpret and evaluate all the information that is the basis for their team's success: getting more oil out of a mature site. In 2003, Jason's team at SJVBU drilled and completed what was one of the highest producing wells in California at that time.

After earning a B.S. in geology from Kansas State University, Jason's graduate study at the University of Kansas included an internship at Chevron Texaco's Bakersfield office. His geologic computer model of one heavy oil reservoir in the San Joaquin Valley is still in use today. Jason says students preparing for work in his field will do course work in subjects such as geophysics, structural geology, geomechanics, stratigraphy, sedimentology, geochemistry, and geostatistics. His continued training has included subjects such as petroleum economics, reservoir engineering, and decision analysis. He travels several times a year within the United States and occasionally to other countries for training, seminars, recruiting, and other meetings.

In the past, petroleum explorers faced huge challenges as they looked for oil. Without today's advanced technology, they relied heavily on their observations of Earth's surface to figure out the best sites to drill for oil. But they learned as they worked, and gradually developed the science, equipment, and tools that made them more skillful at finding additional resources. Jason Cansler considers it a personal challenge to continue in a creative and innovative spirit, improving technology in the search for tomorrow's energy.

Task

Select a field of employment mentioned in this vignette. Determine the nature of the job and the type of training required.

SCIENCE at work

Chapter 9: Energy Efficiency: A Bridge to Tomorrow

High on a hillside in Berkeley, California, sits the Lawrence Berkeley National Laboratory (LBNL). As Lynn Price drives up the winding road to get to her job there every day, she enjoys breathtaking views of the San Francisco Bay Area. Sometimes, fog makes it hard to see out over the treetops, but on a fine day the air is usually clear and crisp. Fresh air all over the world is threatened every day by industrial emissions, and Lynn works on projects

Courtesy of Lynn Price

designed to lessen the harmful effects of a primary source of those emissions: the inefficient consumption of energy.

Lawrence Berkeley is managed by the University of California for the U.S. Department of Energy. In the Energy Analysis Department, Lynn is deputy group leader of the International Energy Studies Group.

She is one of many scientists at LBNL studying climate changes related to the consumption of nonrenewable energy. Lynn's department is part of a larger unit called the Environmental Energy Technologies Division (EETD). She and her colleagues look for ways to reduce energy use and emissions for industries ranging from iron and steel mills to cement factories, paper and pulp processing plants, chemical producers, automobile assembly plants, and even wineries and breweries. These industries, located in the United States and abroad, are the users of the technologies and processes analyzed by Lynn and her colleagues.

Some industries are more damaging to Earth's environment because they use chiefly nonrenewable fuel sources and release more emissions and by-products as a result. These energy-intensive industries are most costly in terms of environmental damage because they are transforming raw materials into products such as chemicals, steel, paper, and cement, and the many stages of production consume large quantities of fuel along the way. The analyses done by Lynn's team help these industries to convert, store, and use energy more efficiently and with less environmental impact.

Making things more efficient for these industries is high on the list of priorities at EETD. Lynn and her colleagues create reports that analyze energy consumption and trends and the associated environmental emissions. They study industrial technologies that can reduce energy use. They contribute to the work of policymakers trying to address the problems of industrial energy consumption. And they devise tools and models that help industries measure their energy usage and its effects on the surrounding air and land. For example, one spreadsheet tool they have developed helps create benchmarks for a steel plant's energy consumption and provides options for making the plant more efficient. With some customization, this tool can also be used in other industries—for example, a winery or an auto-mobile assembly plant. Other tools devised by Lynn and her colleagues help industries measure and reduce their greenhouse gas emissions. These models are being used in several developing countries.

The international aspects of Lynn's job make it very exciting. She often works with industry representatives, policymakers, climate change experts, and researchers from countries in Europe and Asia. China, for example, which produces more cement and steel than any other country, has many outdated and inefficient facilities, but has great opportunity to improve them because of the country's rapid economic growth.

A typical day for Lynn starts very early. At home, she monitors e-mail from clients and associates in the eastern United States and Europe. Then she spends the main part of her workday in her LBNL office, where there are meetings to attend and reports to write. She does a lot of research, works with spreadsheets on her computer, and uses various resources at the nearby University of California campus. Frequently she talks, often through an interpreter, with international visitors about their work in climate change and energy. Then it's back to her computer at home, where in the evening she looks at yet more e-mail—this time from Asia and other parts of the Eastern Hemisphere. Her work takes her on the road a lot, too, traveling within the United States and to countries around the globe.

Lynn studied at the University of Wisconsin in Madison and has a bachelor's degree in geography. Her master's degree is in environmental science. After college, she gained additional training in her field by working as a consultant; then she joined LBNL. She says her on-the-job training has never stopped, and she is continually setting new goals for herself.

Lynn sees the work in energy efficiency as a major link in the bridge to renewable, cleaner energy. She says, "We're getting closer all the time. Wind energy is already cost effective. More and more businesses are using green energy such as photovoltaic cells." She thinks the arguments about the Hubbert prediction for exhaustion of the world's crude oil supply are less important than acknowledging that these resources are finite and environmentally damaging, and then using them more efficiently. "Energy efficiency is an essential step in reducing our dependence on fossil fuels."

Questions

1. What are some advantages of energy efficiency in terms of reducing air pollution?

2. Why might a developing country tend to use inefficient methods of using energy?

Chapter 10: Using Nuclear Energy for Medicine

Have you ever had an X-ray? Probably—or you know someone who has. X-rays are used to show images of bones and other hard tissues. Newer methods show the soft tissues, too. MRI (magnetic resonance imaging), for example, is used for scanning the brain and other soft tissues. MRI is not a nuclear process and exposes the patient to no ionizing radiation.

Today, nuclear medicine provides still another way to examine organs. Nuclear medicine uses radioisotopes (radioactive materials) to show the functions of organs—blood flow or metabolic rate, for example—rather than their structures.

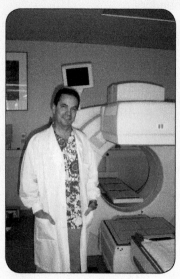

Courtesy of Emil Germanov

Emil Germanov is a nuclear medicine technologist at Alameda Hospital, a community hospital in Northern California. His field is one of the benefits of nuclear energy. Today, nearly 100 nuclear procedures are used in medical specialties from cardiology to psychiatry to pediatrics. Cardiac examinations account for 40 to 50 percent of the procedures, and cancer-related examinations for another 35 to 40 percent.

The results of nuclear medicine techniques can be combined with traditional X-rays and MRI scans to give physicians a complete picture of any organ's anatomy and physiology, while subjecting the patient to a minimum dose of radiation, and without requiring surgery, anesthesia, or expensive laboratory tests. Often nuclear medicine provides an early warning of a disease, when medical intervention can make a greater difference than if the disease is discovered later.

Emil does most of his work with a gamma camera. The camera is suspended above a large bed where the patient lies quietly during the procedure. In some cases, such as when the thyroid gland or other small area is being studied, Emil uses a small probe linked to a computer, rather than the large gamma camera.

The first step in creating an image is to inject a radiopharmaceutical (a radioisotope that is attracted to a particular organ) into the patient. Technetium (Tc-99) and other radioisotopes that emit gamma rays are used. Emil waits for the radiopharmaceutical to reach the organ and then switches on the camera. Gamma rays emitted from the organ are recorded by the camera, which transmits electrical signals to a nearby computer. In the computer, the signals are translated into numerical code and then converted into the digital images Emil and physicians read on the monitor.

These remarkable images are in full color, and they move. An image may show blood passing through a pumping heart, electrical signals passing through a brain, or urine collecting in kidneys—with data about those functions. Images can even be viewed as three-dimensional objects that can be turned in any direction for examination. Usually, to confirm a diagnosis, a physician needs to examine a particular part of an organ. The images and data coming from a gamma camera are of great usefulness for that purpose.

Emil likes the fact that there is no such thing as a "typical day" in his work. Most of the patients he sees are not hospitalized; their physicians send them in for diagnoses at early stages of illness. A child having bone pain may be referred for evaluation. The Emergency Room may suddenly call Emil because an elderly woman has been rushed in by paramedics who think she may have had a stroke. Or, a man recovering from an amputation may need to be examined so that his physician can see if normal blood circulation has returned to the area. Another patient's kidneys may appear to have shut down.

In every case, the gamma camera provides useful information. Just as important, Emil feels he has been able to help every one of these patients and their physicians.

Some universities now offer undergraduate degrees with majors in nuclear medical technology. Because this is a fairly new field, people may enter it from various backgrounds, such as medical technology or nursing. Whatever their past education, they must undergo special training and be certified, usually by a state board. (The website, http://www.snm.org/nuclear contains links to related education sites.)

Emil himself was educated in the physical sciences and became a mechanical engineer. He enjoyed the problem-solving aspects of engineering but wanted to work with people. With the additional training in nuclear technology, he can do both.

Questions

1. Technetium-99 is produced for medical use by bombarding molybdenum-98 with neutrons. Write a balanced equation showing that reaction.

2. Why might an engineer's education be a good background for this field of medicine?

3. Are there hospitals near your home that use nuclear medicine techniques? List them.

SCIENCE at work

Chapter 11: Harnessing the Wind

In 1997, David Blecker was in Alaska, working on energy-related concerns for Alaska's native Indians and Eskimos. He was struck by the irony of their having to purchase fuel derived from oil drawn from under their own land and piped hundreds of miles away for processing. He became interested in seeking a more creative, less destructive approach to energy production and use. For David, the answer was to found Seventh Generation Energy Systems (SGES) in Belleville, Wisconsin.

Courtesy of David Blecker

Since then, SGES has worked with governments, communities, schools, and tribes to plan, design, and install wind and solar energy systems (about 10 per year) in several states. His customers include a family-owned wood mill and a poultry farm in Wisconsin, and the Omaha Tribe of Nebraska. In western South Dakota, a large radio station serving the Sioux nation is powered by energy from one of SGES's systems.

Working with Native Americans has profoundly affected David's approach to his work. Indeed, the name of his organization comes from a Native American belief that we should consider the effect of our actions today on the world "seven generations into the future." He is committed to honoring the rights of indigenous peoples, and he believes every project should include community outreach and education. "I want to take a systemic approach to building energy systems, rather than just sell the systems themselves."

SGES is a nonprofit group, so its projects are funded by federal agencies such as the U.S. Department of Energy and Environmental Protection Agency, state agencies and energy programs, foundations, and occasionally by private donations. The Administration for Native Americans, a branch of the U.S. Department of Health and Human Services, has subsidized projects, as well.

David does all the front-end work—research and analysis, planning, managing customer education and participation, site assessment, permits, and more—until construction begins. Then he hires skilled construction workers. In some situations, he uses labor provided by the customer. For example, on the Omaha Nation project, he worked with local Native Americans who had been trained in an SGES workshop at the Nebraska Indian Community College.

Every wind system, whether a small (less than 20 kilowatts) residential system or a large commercial system (as much as 1.5 megawatts), begins with research. For a home-size system, David looks at published wind-resource maps and the site topography. He considers the users' power needs and their own observations about local wind patterns. For a larger system, he studies spreadsheets of detailed data from a meteorological tower that records wind speed and direction at various heights.

A licensed professional engineer, David uses math and statistical analysis to interpret the collected data. He uses project planning and communication skills to set the project's milestones and to work with the system's users and the local utility companies. Site assessment, infrastructure planning, and economic analysis are next. He considers factors such as the size and elevation of the land parcel, vegetation that affects the wind, distance to power lines, sensitive wildlife and environmental resources, and zoning laws. Finally, actual work on the site begins. This includes excavation, assembly of the towers and turbines, laying power cables, wiring and electronics tasks, and thorough testing. SGES uses only horizontal wind turbines.

Wind systems need maintenance twice a year. David or a hired worker has to climb the tower and check the structure, its connections and moving parts, and various safety and control components. Most systems last about 20 years.

Seventh Generation wind systems don't need costly (and toxic) batteries for storing the generated power. In a home-size system, the generator produces "wild" AC power; the frequency and voltage continously change with wind speed. This power is then converted to utility-grade 120V or 240V AC power that ties into the local power grid on the customer's side of the meter. When the system produces more power than what is needed, the power company maintains a credit for when the user's needs are higher. In a larger commercial system, transmission and control electronics allow the generated power to flow directly into the power grid for sale to the local utility or to distant markets.

Because he may have several projects in different stages, David's daily tasks vary widely. About half his time is spent on development of what he calls "sane" energy policy. For example, he works with utilities and regulators to promote increased use of renewable energy. He has developed new energy-delivery planning models, with the support of the U.S. DOE, that have been used to identify lower-cost, lower-impact alternatives to high-voltage power lines.

David began by working on nuclear submarines for the U.S. Navy and on submarine power systems for the General Electric Company. Then he studied electrical engineering and received a bachelor's degree from Rensselaer Polytechnic Institute in New York. Today, he continues his graduate work at the University of Wisconsin, Madison. His message to students is to "hang in there" when the going gets tough—math and science are important. His knowledge in these areas has given him the chance to work in beautiful places, in exciting new technologies, and with dedicated people.

David has a deep commitment to teaching people about sustainable energy. "Let's not say 'alternative' energy—we have clean, economic, and reliable choices *now*, so let's have the will to make them. Each and every wind turbine we put up says yes, this works, and we can do it now."

Questions

1. Why might a wind turbine be a good choice for providing energy at various points on a large farm or ranch?

2. If there is fossil-fuel energy available, is there any need for alternative wind- or solar-powered systems? Why or why not?

Chapter 12: Designing for the Future

Courtesy of Nicki Kwee

Nicki Kwee drives through the streets of Paris in his silver Ford Ka, an attractive car that also has the small size and fuel economy demanded in Europe. More than most drivers, though, Nicki can appreciate the design of his car because he is a car designer.

Born in the Netherlands, Nicki remains a Dutch citizen. As a child, he lived in California; later he enrolled in the Center for Creative Studies in Detroit to learn about industrial design. Following college, he joined Ford in Germany. Now he works for Renault in France.

A car designer is only one member of the team that develops a new car. The process takes about 3 years, beginning with a rough plan that incorporates customers' wishes, the availability of suitable materials, and the manufacturer's emphasis on fuel economy. In the beginning stages, Nicki may spend many hours meeting with other designers and engineers to plan the new car. Engineers specify the parts of the motor, other under-hood parts, the suspension, and the chassis. Designers are responsible for proposing an overall design for the exterior and interior that looks good and incorporates the engineers' technical specifications. That can sometimes lead to disagreements about how to accomplish the company's goals for the car. Often, for example, a design proposal is deemed too expensive, and a less costly alternative must be chosen. The team's project leader makes the final decisions after weighing the options.

At the beginning of a project, designers work on the creative phase of research and making drawings. They make several presentations to management until a few design themes are chosen for development as a CAD (computer-assisted design) or physical model. The next weeks are spent working with CAD or with a team of two to five clay modelers. Clay models, made in a large workshop, may be on a scale of anywhere from one-fifth to full size. As the models evolve, more presentations are made to company managers and, eventually, one design is chosen for production. During the whole process, designers and engineers work together to ensure that the designs are viable and will meet the objectives set by the product planners. Toward the end of a project, there is a series of meetings with engineers and suppliers—for Nicki, the least favorite aspect of his job.

Nicki works with about 10 other designers in an open office that also contains a support staff of CAD operators, technical assistants, a secretary, and managers. He has no typical work day; it all depends on the number and status of the team's projects.

Nicki's training in art and sculpture makes it possible for him to draw rough sketches in the beginning, and to work with the modelers in later stages of the project. While CAD software is used increasingly to simplify some parts of the job, designers must still be trained in the principles of art and design.

Strict demands for fuel economy affect the design. Because the shape affects the car's aerodynamics, which in turn determine the amount of energy needed for movement, overall shape is extremely important. While a long, fishlike shape might seem preferable, there are conflicting demands from engineers to design cars that can accommodate fuel-efficient diesel engines; these are generally larger, heavier, and require more cooling. Another important aspect involves the "packaging" of the car, which determines its size and the placement of components, the driver and passengers, and their luggage. In Europe, designers try to keep the cars compact on the outside, yet very roomy on the inside. This keeps the weight down, as does using aluminum or composite materials rather than steel for some parts.

The future of car design will depend on the types of cars people ask for. At this time, people tend to buy cars that project their self-image. In the United States, especially, a car buyer may choose a large car with low economy for psychological reasons. That attitude may become a luxury if the world's oil supply diminishes, and the kind of cars in demand may change dramatically.

Manufacturers are trying to plan for an uncertain future. Some companies are developing car models that run on alternative fuels, including compressed natural gas, propane, and ethanol. In November of 2003, U.S. DOE Secretary Abraham released a "road-map" for putting hydrogen fuel cells in U.S. vehicles, which committed the United States to a hydrogen-based system of transportation. Meanwhile, some all-electric and gasoline-electric hybrid cars and trucks are being produced. No one really knows what cars of the future may be like. Whatever happens, Nicki and other designers will need to come up with the right combinations of attractiveness and necessary features.

Questions

1. How might a tall, boxy shape affect a vehicle's fuel efficiency?

2. Why do Europeans demand more fuel economy in their cars than Americans do?

SCIENCE at work

Chapter 15: Forecasting Future Climates

Will farms in Iowa turn into deserts? Will oceans cover Florida and other low-lying areas? Will ski resorts have to close down for lack of snow? Caspar Ammann tries to find the answers to climate-related questions like these. He is a climatologist at the National Center for Atmospheric Research (NCAR) in Boulder, Colorado, who creates computer models of climates and interprets their results.

Courtesy of Caspar Ammann

Caspar focuses on natural climate variability. The time span he studies may cover recent centuries and millennia, or may go back a few million years (during which all humans and human civilizations have existed and large continental glaciations have occurred). His primary goal is to understand what climate did during these times, how it changed, and what might have been responsible for these fluctuations. Climatic variations often depend on the amount of solar radiation reaching Earth, resulting either from changes in the sun itself or from variations in Earth's orbit. Caspar and his co-workers look at changes in average solar energy as well as how it is distributed over the annual cycle and in different regions of Earth. They also study the impact of volcanic eruptions on climate. Some eruptions were very large explosive events, after which humans recorded strange hazes high up in the sky. Such observations can often be found together with historical records of harvest failures, pestilence, and other effects.

The computer models represent the climate system as completely as possible: Having an atmosphere, an ocean, sea ice, and a land surface component, they are driven by solar radiation that hits the planet on the day side. Every 15 or 20 minutes, the system solves equations that describe how solar radiation is transmitted through the atmosphere, how it gets absorbed in the air or ground, and how it is reflected by clouds or on the surface. The model then shows how the heat drives the steps in the hydrologic cycle—evaporation, convection, cloud formation, rain, snow, and so on. The new models can even "grow" vegetation, simulate rivers with their seasonal runoff, and represent complex biogeochemical systems like the carbon cycle.

The models, by definition, can be run to represent any time in the past or the future. For showing the past, Caspar has to make sure that he gives the model realistic boundary conditions, such as distribution of the continents, atmospheric composition, and vegetation. In interpreting the results and validating his conclusions, he may collaborate with people who study climate's effects on tree rings, ocean sediments, or ice cores, or with other modeling groups.

As the exact future atmospheric composition is unknown, generally the models are run 100 to 300 years into the future under different scenarios. While climatologists look at the absolute changes to determine how different climate will be, the different responses to the scenarios are also of great practical interest to politicians and others. The model can provide hints about how useful emission reductions or cleaner fuels are for keeping climate from completely getting out of control.

While the climate models are not perfect, they are the only means to capture the effects of the processes within as well as between the different subsystems. In recent years, these climate models have proven to be remarkably good in explaining the variability in the climate system. They can begin to explain features like El Niño and changes in the storm track. The models are now increasingly used for long-range (about 6 months) climate forecasts, for which farmers in particular are grateful.

The models have also reproduced the natural climates of the past remarkably well. However, for the 20th century, the models' picture of natural climate matches actual records only through about 1950. Only when models include observed greenhouse gases and human-made aerosols do they reproduce the rapid warming of the last 30 years. That seems to be strong support for the hypothesis that greenhouse gases have already contributed to the warming that is inarguably going on.

The Paleoclimatology Group in which Caspar works consists of four scientists and a few associate scientists. They generally work on different experiments and time periods, but get together on a regular basis to compare notes. Sometimes, the group meets for more formal talks or seminars, or hosts visiting scientists from other research centers. Caspar travels about once per month. He needs to collaborate with many people.

Caspar grew up in Switzerland, getting a Master's Degree in geography and geology. His education was very broad, with lots of emphasis on interdisciplinary and integrative thinking. He earned a Ph.D. at the University of Massachusetts in the Department of Geosciences. His course work included all sorts of climate-related courses, some statistics, and other courses of interest.

Questions

1. Why are insurance companies interested in climate change?

2. Make a list of careers that tie to climate change studies. What skills are needed for each career?

SCIENCE at work

Chapter 16: The Challenge of Compromise

No matter what your worldview, saving the future of Earth and its people will require compromise—and that's the vocation of Diane Henderson, founder of DMH Land Use Planning in San Rafael, California. Working with city planners, land developers, and other professionals, as well as landowners, Diane's goal is to foster cooperation when development is planned in a community. Whether a project is large or small, Diane helps to plan growth that will have as few negative effects on the community's citizens and environment as possible. This work has a personal side for her, too—in addition to making a living at it, she often gets to watch over development projects in her own area of residence.

Diane especially enjoys the variety of her work. Building methods and techniques are always changing, and she is pleased with the strong movement toward sustainability. In her home county of Marin, there is more and more emphasis on "green" development, recycling, and energy efficiency.

Courtesy of Diane Henderson

One interesting new trend is for building using "straw" bales—the agricultural waste left behind after wheat, rye, barley, rice, or other cereal grain has been harvested. No trees are cut down; less energy goes into constructing the house; and the straw has two to four times the insulating quality of traditional wall materials. Diane has also seen much new interest in the recovery and remilling of materials such as wood and slate from demolished structures for reuse in new ones.

Working freelance means Diane's role in every project is different. Planning takes many forms—for example, she was part of a special staff guiding a large retail development project so that its changes would fit the requirements of everyone involved: business owners, city government, and environmentalists. In Salinas, California, she joined a planning team that was temporarily expanded to handle a high-priority development project. She has filled in as a city planning director until a new, permanent director was hired. The locales of her work cover a broad range, too, from planning department counters to specific building sites, and even a boat in the San Francisco Bay, from which she can inspect developments along the coastline.

Varied projects mean varied tasks. As a planner, she has to understand the review process in a given city or county. Often she writes or collaborates on reports to planning boards. In addition to local government officials, she works with many other professionals, such as transportation planners, architects, engineers, and attorneys—and, of course, with the area's citizens. To make development easier on the environment, she may suggest changes in bus service, installation of bike racks, and so forth.

Sometimes her task is to answer questions for people who visit a planning department, seeking information. A big part of her work is communication and negotiation.

Variety is also reflected in the needs of the people Diane serves, and that's where the concept of compromise comes in. She wants to achieve the best possible outcome for everyone involved. Choosing her clients carefully, she will turn down a job if the people in charge don't want to consider environmental issues and the needs of the community. "Developers often need to be guided toward doing things right," she says. Always, however, her focus is to encourage cooperation. On all land use projects, it's important for changes to be reviewed for their impact on the neighbors. This applies to an individual home owner making changes to a house and its grounds just as much as the developer of a large shopping mall that is near other businesses, homes, and parks.

Diane has a B.S. in Environmental Planning and Management. This area of specialization and others like it involve studies in architecture, design, engineering, mapping, various sciences, sociology, and psychology—all tools that contribute to Diane's skill in planning and communication. She has taken additional classes from University of California Extension and the American Planning Association. Related paraprofessional careers in this field—planning technicians, for instance—are also available to people with 2-year degrees.

Diane says it's crucial that we "strike a balance between growth and protecting the natural environment." Growth and its problems are inevitable on our planet, so we must "provide for the future as well as preserve the past" as we search for global solutions to save Planet Earth.

Question

For whom might a land use consultant work? List several possibilities.

Chapter 17: Self-Contained and Self-Sustained

On 4,500 acres in southwest Kansas, Reeve Agri Energy is nothing like the old-fashioned family farm it once was. Employing 30 to 35 people as well as several members of the Reeve family, the company is a complex, profitable ecosystem that conserves more than one of Earth's nonrenewable resources.

Oxygenated fuels are important to U.S. energy needs now that oil is less plentiful, more expensive, and contributing too much to pollution. Ethanol—the same form of alcohol found in beer and whiskey—is mixed with gasoline to provide the cleaner-burning, higher-octane automobile fuel you know as "unleaded plus" or "super-unleaded." Every year, the Reeve facility produces 9.2 million gallons of ethanol. The process starts with corn, molasses, and other material high in sugars and starches, and water from the Ogallala aquifer that underlies much of the Midwest. The plant uses many energy-efficient tools such as heat exchange systems and electricity from natural gas generators.

But ethanol is only part of the story. A by-product of the ethanol production is used to feed the Reeve cattle. After cooling, sifting, and removal of water, the stillage that remains is heavy in protein. The starch used for the ethanol production is replaced in the form of corn, alfalfa, and milo, and some vitamins and minerals are added. This enhanced mash is then given to the 21,000 head of cattle raised on the ranch. It's important to keep it wet, because drying the product would take as much energy as producing the ethanol in the first place.

Further down the ecosystem line, cattle manure is used to fertilize the surrounding cropland. The leftover hot water from the ethanol plant is cooled and used to raise white tilapia, a mild-flavored, warmwater fish. This same water, nutrient-rich after housing the fish, is then returned to the land in irrigation.

Courtesy of Lee Reeve

Many branches of science contribute to the Reeve effort. A remarkable assortment of people contribute their talent and knowledge—farmers, veterinarians, microbiologists, nutritionists, attorneys, accountants, and those who run the ethanol facility—and Lee Reeve has to communicate with all of them. He sees every day the value of understanding scientific ideas. When the family added the fish breeding operation to its business, he learned a lot about biology and ecology, and was glad for the good scientific beginnings his high school textbooks gave him. Lee has a B.S. in Agricultural Economics from Kansas State. He also knows the value of community college instruction, and emphasizes the importance of on-the-job training such as apprenticeship programs.

Critics of ethanol say it's too expensive to produce and that our tax dollars should not be spent to make it. But there's no doubt ethanol is a cleaner fuel than oil, and supplies of oil are decreasing. According to Lee, the critics should remember the First and Second Laws of Thermodynamics. We can't make new energy, but we can take advantage of its transformation from one form to another.

Reeve Agri Energy is an excellent example of economic development that contributes both jobs and products in a setting that does not harm the environment or waste energy. Lee wants to see other industries evolve from and support one another, just as his family's business has. "The first requirement of success is to find out what happens in nature, and then try to duplicate that, not fight it."

Task

List potential jobs in the field of sustainable farm operation.

Graphing Data

Making Tables of Data

In the lab, collected data is often put in a table. A table may be a simple table of rows and columns (like Table 1), or a more complex one.

Distance (m)	Time (s)
0.0	0
2.5	1
5.0	2
7.5	3
10.0	4

Table 1: A table of distance (meters) and time (seconds) for a battery-driven toy car.

Note that Table 1 clearly indicates both the quantities that were measured and the units. Also note that data are recorded in decimal form and not in fractions.

It is often difficult to simply look at numbers in a table and see how the data are related. For this reason, scientists use graphs to visually show how data are related to each other.

Choosing the Axes of a Graph and Naming Them

Many of the experiments you will do will involve two or more variables that change together. Scientists often try to control an experiment so that only two variables change at the same time. This allows them to record data, plot graphs, and look for relationships.

When there are two variables, the graph maker names one the *independent* variable and the other the *dependent* variable. In Table 1, for example, time is the independent variable, and distance is the dependent variable. This is because the distance traveled from a starting point depends on the amount of time.

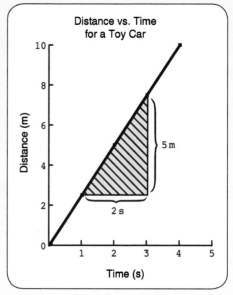

▲ FIGURE 1 The graph for the data given in Table 1.

By agreement, the independent variable is plotted along the horizontal axis, or x-axis, while the dependent variable is plotted along the vertical axis, or y-axis. The title of the graph, which should be written near the top of the graph, should state the dependent variable vs. the independent variable. See Figure 1 for an example.

Choosing the Scale

After determining which variable is to be plotted on which axis, the next step is to choose a scale that will easily fill most of the graph area. Easily means that divisions on the scale should be multiples of 1, 2, 4, 5, 10, and so forth. In Figure 1, the distance divisions are multiples of 2. The time divisions are multiples of 1.

Labeling the Axes

After the axes are named and scales chosen, the scale numbers should be written along the axes (see Figure 1). Use only as many numbers as are needed. Too many numbers adds confusion. Then state, in words, what is being plotted. Finally, place the symbol for the unit used in parentheses next to the word (see Figure 1).

Plotting the Points

The points to be plotted are contained in the table. Locate each data pair (from the table) on the graph and plot a dot. Do this until all points are plotted.

Drawing the Curve

The type of curve to be drawn depends on what is being plotted. If the plotted points line up pretty well, a ruler can be used to draw a straight line—even if every point does not fall exactly on it. This is because experimental errors (errors made in making measurements) may cause the points to slightly miss the line. If things change smoothly during an experiment, a smooth curve can often be drawn that connects or lies close to each plotted point. You will get better at making these decisions and drawing graph lines and curves as you gain lab experience.

Finding the Slope of a Line Graph

If a graph is a straight line, the slope of the line can be determined. This is done by marking two points on the line. These points do not have to be plotted points. They should be points that are easy for you to work with. From the upper point, draw a vertical line straight down. From the lower point, draw a horizontal line to the right until it touches the vertical line. You should have formed a triangle (see Figure 1). Use the scale of the graph to determine the length of the vertical side of the triangle. Also, use the scale of your graph to determine the length of the horizontal side of your triangle (see Figure 1 for an example). By definition, the slope is the ratio of the vertical length divided by the horizontal length. The slope is given the symbol m.

Thus, $m = \dfrac{\Delta y}{\Delta x} = \dfrac{\text{vertical distance}}{\text{horizontal distance}}$

where Δ is a symbol that means *change in*.

For Table 1,

$$m = \frac{\Delta \text{ distance}}{\Delta \text{time}} = \frac{5 \text{ m}}{2 \text{ s}} = 2.5 \text{m/s}$$

Sometimes, the slope has a physical meaning. In the case of Table 1, 2.5 m/s is the speed of the toy car.

APPENDIX 3

Scientific Notation

In the study of science, very large and very small numbers are encountered regularly. For example, the total power incident from the sun at the top of Earth's atmosphere is 173,000,000,000,000,000 watts. It would be difficult to deal with such numbers if we didn't have a special method for handling them. Scientific notation is the method for doing just that. Learn it well. With scientific notation, problems that look almost impossible to solve become relatively simple.

Most of what you need to know about scientific notation involves four ideas.

1. *A system for writing multiples of 10.* The following is a partial list of powers of 10:

$10^0 = 1$

$10^1 = 10$

$10^2 = 10 \times 10 = 100$

$10^3 = 10^2 \times 10 = 1,000$

$10^4 = 10 \times 10 \times 10 \times 10 = 10,000$

$10^{-1} = \dfrac{1}{10} = 0.1$

$10^{-2} = \dfrac{1}{10^2} = \dfrac{1}{100} = 0.01$

$10^{-3} = \dfrac{1}{10^3} = \dfrac{1}{1,000} = 0.001$

2. *A way of writing any number involving powers of 10.* Any number can be written as the product of a number between 1 and 10 and a number that is a power of 10.

ex. $769 = 7.69 \times 10^2$

$$5,200,000 = 5.2 \times 10^6$$

$$0.124 = 1.24 \times 10^{-1}$$

$$0.0000003 = 3 \times 10^{-7}$$

3. *A system for multiplying numbers.* In multiplication, exponents of like bases are added.

$$10^2 \times 10^3 = 10^{2+3} = 10^5$$

$$10 \times 10 = 10^{1+1} = 10^2$$

$$(4 \times 10^4)(2 \times 10^{-6})$$

$$= 8 \times 10^{4-6} = 8 \times 10^{-2}$$

4. *A system for dividing numbers.* In division, exponents of like bases are subtracted.

$$\frac{10^2}{10^5} = 10^{2-5} = 10^{-3}$$

$$\frac{8 \times 10^2}{2 \times 10^{-6}} = \frac{8}{2} \times 10^{2+6} = 4 \times 10^8$$

After studying the four ideas, practice using scientific notation by doing these problems.

Problems

1. Express the following in scientific notation:

   a. 720

   b. 32,600

   c. 1,006

   d. 59,000,000

   e. 0.831

   f. 0.02

2. Evaluate the following and express the results in scientific notation:

   a. $1,700 \times 340$

   b. $220 \times 35,000$

   c. $40/20,000$

   d. $61,900/0.48$

   e. $\dfrac{3.17 \times 7,230}{0.000289} =$

   f. $\dfrac{(16,000)(0.0003)(2.4)}{(2,000)(0.007)(0.00051)} =$

Answers

Note that the answers to all calculations in this text are never given to more than three figures.

1. 7.2×10^2, 3.26×10^4, 1.006×10^3, 5.9×10^7, 8.31×10^{-1}, 2×10^{-2}.

2. 5.78×10^5, 7.7×10^6, 2×10^{-3}, 1.29×10^5, 7.93×10^7, 1.61×10^3.

APPENDIX 4

SI Units Prefixes

Prefix	Abbreviation	Factor by Which Unit Is Multiplied
exa	E	10^{18}
peta	P	10^{15}
tera	T	10^{12}
giga	G	10^9
mega	M	10^6
kilo	k	10^3

(continued)

Prefix	Abbreviation	Factor by Which Unit Is Multiplied
hecto	h	10^2
centi	c	10^{-2}
milli	m	10^{-3}
micro	μ	10^{-6}
nano	n	10^{-9}
pico	p	10^{-12}
femto	f	10^{-15}
atto	a	10^{-18}

1 thousand = 10^3 1 billion = 10^9 1 quadrillion = 10^{15}

1 million = 10^6 1 trillion = 10^{12} 1 quintillion 10^{18}

APPENDIX 5

International System (SI) Units

Names, symbols, and conversion factors of SI units used in this text:

Quantity	Name of Unit	Symbol	Conversion Factor
Distance	meter	m	1 km = 0.621 mile
			1 m = 3.28 ft
			1 cm = 0.394 in
			1 mm = 0.039 in
			1 μm = 3.9×10^{-5} in = 10^4 Å (see below)
			1 nm = 10 Å
Mass	kilogram	kg	1 tonne = 1.102 tons (tonne = metric ton)
			1 kg = 2.20 lb
			1 gm = 0.0022 lb = 0.035 oz
			1 mg = 2.20×10^{-6} lb = 3.5×10^{-5} oz
Time	second	sec	1 yr = 3.156×10^7 sec
			1 day = 8.64×10^4 sec
			1 hr = 3,600 sec

(continued)

Quantity	Name of Unit	Symbol	Conversion Factor
Temperature	kelvin	K	$273°K = 0°C = 32°F$ $373°K = 100°C = 212°F$
Area	square meter	m^2	$1\ m^2 = 10^4\ cm^2 = 10.8\ ft^2$
Volume	cubic meter	m^3	$1\ m^3 = 10^6\ cm^3 = 35\ ft^3$
Frequency	hertz	Hz	$1\ Hz = 1\ cycle/sec$ $1\ kHz = 1,000\ cycles/sec$ $1\ MHz = 10^6\ cycles/sec$
Density	kilogram per cubic meter	kg/m^3	$1\ kg/m^3 = 0.001\ gm/cm^3$ $1\ gm/cm^3 = $ density of water
Speed, velocity	meter per second	m/sec	$1\ m/sec = 3.28\ ft/sec$ $1\ km/sec = 2240\ mi/hr$
Force	newton	N	$1\ N = 10^5\ dynes = 0.224\ lbf$
Pressure	newton per square meter	N/m^2	$1\ N/m^2 = 1.45 \times 10^{-4}\ lb/in^2$
Energy	joule	J	$1\ J = 0.239\ calorie$
Photon energy	electronvolt	eV	$1\ eV = 1.60 \times 10^{-19}\ J;\ 1\ J = 10^7\ erg$
Power	watt	W	$1\ W = 1\ J/sec$
Atomic mass	atomic mass unit	amu	$1\ amu = 1.66 \times 10^{-27}\ kg$

Customary units used with the SI units:

Quantity	Name of Unit	Symbol	Conversion Factor
Wavelength of light	angstrom	Å	$1\ Å = 0.1\ nm = 10^{-10}\ m$
Acceleration of gravity	g	g	$1\ g = 9.8\ m/sec^2$

APPENDIX 6

Common Conversion Factors
(Related to Energy and Resources)

Weight

1 short ton	contains	2,000 pounds
1 metric ton	contains	1.102 short tons
1 long ton	contains	1.120 short tons

Conversion Factors for Crude Oil (Average Gravity)

1 barrel	contains	42 gallons
1 barrel	weighs	0.136 metric tons (0.150 short tons)
1 metric ton	contains	7.33 barrels
1 short ton	contains	6.65 barrels

Conversion Factors for Uranium

1 short ton (U_3O_8)	contains	0.769 metric tons
1 short ton (UF_6)	contains	0.613 metric tons
1 metric ton (UF_6)	contains	0.676 metric tons

Conversion Factors for Energy

1 calorie = 3.968×10^{-3} Btu = 4.184 joules

1 kilocalorie = 1,000 calories = 1 dietic Calorie

1 Btu = 252.0 calories = 772 ft·lbs. = 1,055 joules

1 foot·pound = 1.285×10^{-3} Btu = 0.3239 cal

1 joule = 0.2389 cal = 0.7376 ft·lb

1 ton of TNT = 1.04×10^9 cal = 4.14×10^6 Btu

1 barrel of oil = 5.8×10^6 Btu

1 kilowatt·hour = 3,413 Btu = 860,000 cal
              = 1,000 watt·hours

1 therm = 100,000 Btu

Very Large Energy Units

1 exajoule (EJ) = 10^{18} joules

1 quad = 10^{15} Btu

1 quad (Q) = 1.06 exajoules (EJ)

Fuel-Related Conversion Factors

1 kilowatt-hour	3,413 Btu
1 short ton of coal	25,000,000 Btu
1 bbl crude oil	5,800,000 Btu
1 gallon of gasoline	125,000 Btu
1 gallon of No. 2 fuel oil	140,000 Btu
1 cubic foot of natural gas	1,031 Btu
1 therm of gas (or other fuel)	100,000 Btu
1 cord of wood	20,000,000 Btu

1 gram fissionable U-235 = 74,000,000 Btu

1,000 kWh = 0.123 metric tons of coal (heating value)

1 metric ton of peat = 0.3 to 0.45 metric tons of anthracite or bituminous coal

Coal (per 2,000 lb ton)

Anthracite	= 25.4×10^6 Btu
Bituminous	= 26.2×10^6 Btu
Subbituminous	= 19.0×10^6 Btu
Lignite	= 13.4×10^6 Btu

Required to Generate 1 kWh of Electricity

1 kilowatt·hour = 0.88 lb of coal
              = 0.076 gallons of oil
              = 10.4 cu ft of natural gas

Temperature

$°F = \frac{9}{5}°C + 32$

$°C = \frac{5}{9}(°F - 32)$

APPENDIX 7

Table of Energy Conversion Factors

This table summarizes the relation among several common energy units. Use this table to help solve those problems that require the conversion from one unit to another.

Unit	Btu	Ft·lb	Joule	Cal	kWh
1 British thermal unit =	1	778	1,055	252	2.93×10^{-4}
1 foot · pound =	1.29×10^{-3}	1	1.356	0.324	3.77×10^{-7}
1 joule =	9.48×10^{-4}	0.738	1	0.239	2.78×10^{-7}
1 calorie =	3.97×10^{-3}	3.09	4.19	1	1.16×10^{-6}
1 kilowatt·hour =	3,413	2.66×10^6	3.6×10^6	8.6×10^5	1

APPENDIX 8

Useful Data About Energy Production Facilities *

Comparative Sizes

Large coal mine	10–20,000 tons/day
Large electric generating plant	500–1,000 megawatts
Large coal gasification plant	500×10^6 ft³/day
Large oil shale plant	100,000 bbl/day
Typical oil refinery	50,000 bbl/day

*All of these operations have approximately the same energy output/day, and all cost about the same to build, that is, approximately $1–2 billion.

APPENDIX 9

Plate Tectonic Maps

A. Plate Boundary Map

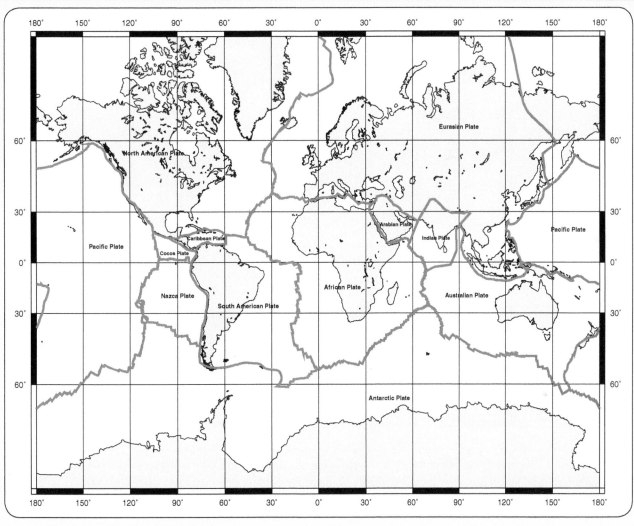

Source: Dietmar Mueller, University of Sydney.

This map is part of "Discovering Plate Boundaries," a classroom exercise developed by Dale S. Sawyer at Rice University (dale@rice.edu). Additional information about this exercise can be found at http://terra.rice.edu/plateboundary.

B. Seismology (Earthquakes)

Earthquake locations 1990–1996 (magnitudes 4 and greater).

Color indicates depth: red 0–20 mi (0–33 km); orange 20–43 mi (33–70 km); green 43–186 mi (70–300 km); blue 186–434 mi (300–700 km).

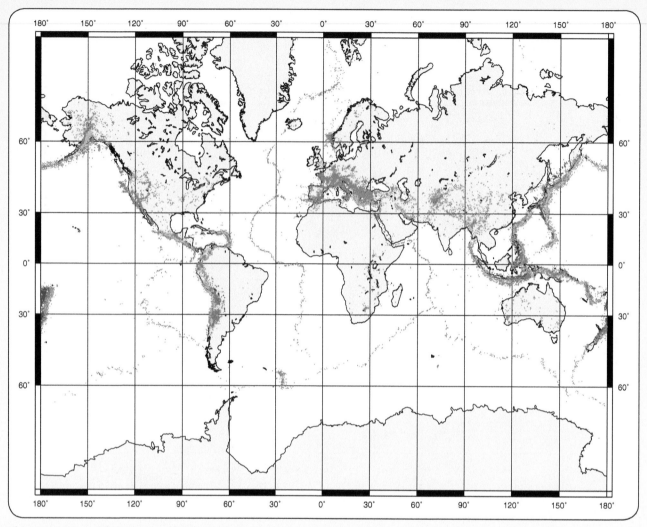

This map is part of "Discovering Plate Boundaries," a classroom exercise developed by Dale S. Sawyer at Rice University (dale@rice.edu). Additional information about this exercise can be found at http://terra.rice.edu/plateboundary.

C. Volcanology (Volcanoes)

Red dots indicate currently or historically active volcanic features.

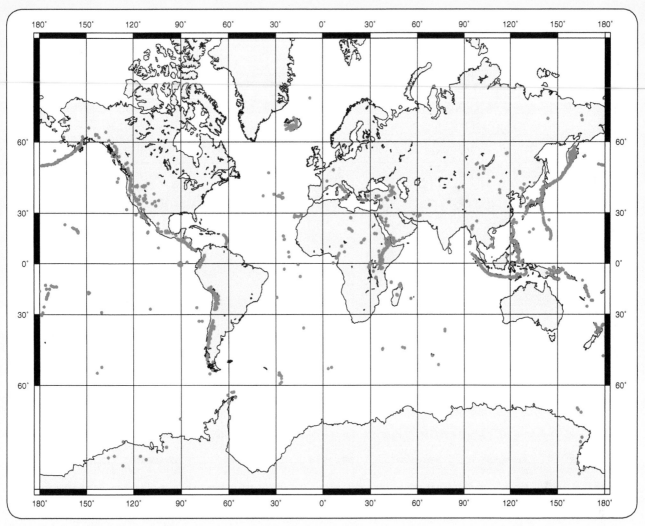

Source: The Smithsonian Institution.

This map is part of "Discovering Plate Boundaries," a classroom exercise developed by Dale S. Sawyer at Rice University (dale@rice.edu). Additional information about this exercise can be found at http://terra.rice.edu/plateboundary.

D. Geochronology (Seafloor Age)

Seafloor age in millions of years.

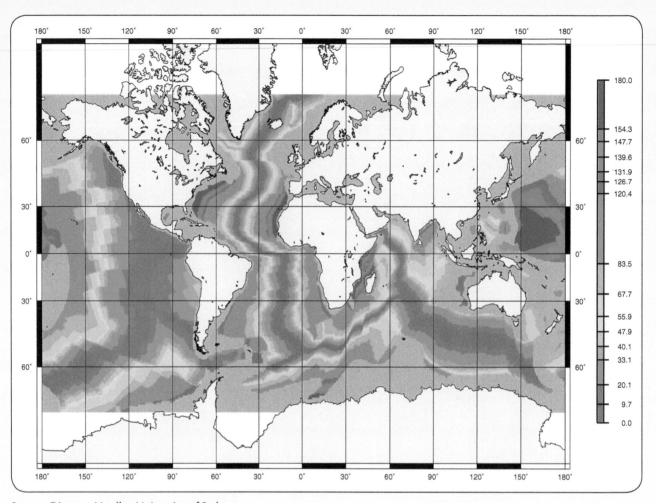

Source: Dietmar Mueller, University of Sydney.

This map is part of "Discovering Plate Boundaries," a classroom exercise developed by Dale S. Sawyer at Rice University (dale@rice.edu). Additional information about this exercise can be found at http://terra.rice.edu/plateboundary.

E. Geodesy (Pull of Gravity at the Sea Surface)

Anomalies in acceleration of gravity (in milligals) at the sea surface.

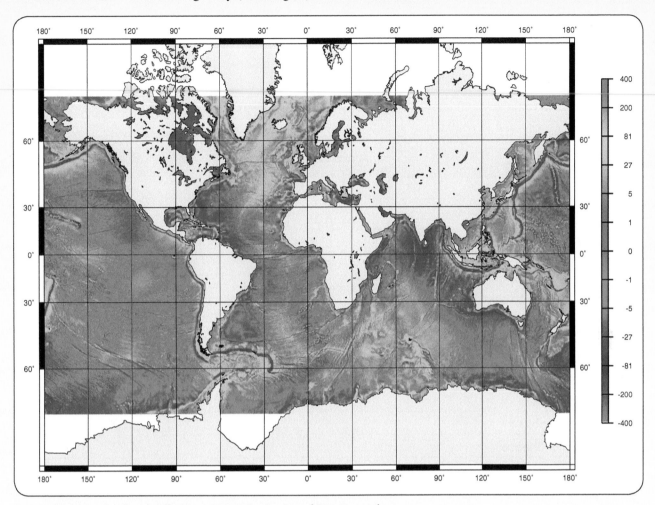

Source: David Sandwell and colleagues, Scripps Institution of Oceanography.

This map is part of "Discovering Plate Boundaries," a classroom exercise developed by Dale S. Sawyer at Rice University (dale@rice.edu). Additional information about this exercise can be found at http://terra.rice.edu/plateboundary.

Calorie Counter

Conversion Factors

1 cup = 8 ounces (oz)   3 teaspoons (tsp) = 1 tablespoon (tbsp)   2 tablespoons = 1 ounce

Food	Amount	Calories
Bread-Cereal Group		
Bagel (Einstein)	1 each	330
Bagel with cream cheese	1 each	420
Bran flakes	3/4 cup	100
Bread, rye	1 slice	60
Bread, white	1 slice	60
Bun, hamburger or hot dog	each	140
Cornflakes	1 cup	110
Cornflakes, sugar coated	1 cup	165
Cream of Wheat	1 cup, cooked	135
Macaroni, cooked	3/4 cup	115
Macaroni & cheese	1 cup	470
Oatmeal, cooked	2/3 cup	100
Pancake	1 average	60
Pancake, 1/2 pat butter & 1 tbsp syrup	1 average	145
Rice, cooked	3/4 cup	150
Rice, puffed	1 cup	55
Rice, puffed, sugar coated	1 cup	80
Roll, Danish	4.5 in diam.	200
Spaghetti	1 cup, cooked	220
Spaghetti & meatballs	1 serving	220
Toast, French	1 average	180
Waffle	7 in. waffle	210
Wheat flakes	1 cup	125
Fats, Oils, Butter		
Butter or margarine	1 pat	40
Butter or margarine	1 tbsp	100
Corn oil	1 tbsp	125
Corn oil	1 cup	1,950
Mayonnaise	1 tbsp	100

(continued)

Food	Amount	Calories
Salad dressing:		
Blue cheese	1 tbsp	75
French	1 tbsp	65
Italian	1 tbsp	85
Thousand Island	1 tbsp	80
Salad oil	1 tbsp	125
Salad oil	1/4 cup	500
Fruits & Fruit Juices		
Apple, raw	1 medium	70
Apple sauce, canned	1/2 cup	115
Apricots, canned in syrup	4 halves, 2 tbsp syrup	110
Apricots, dried	5 small halves	50
Avocado	1/2	190
Banana	1 small	85
Cantaloupe	1/4 medium melon	40
Cherries	20	60
Cranberry sauce	1 tbsp	30
Dates	3–4 pited	85
Fruit cocktail, canned, heavy syrup	1/2 cup	100
Grapefruit, raw	1/2 medium	50
Grapefruit, canned with liquid	1 cup	175
Grapes, seedless	30 grapes	35
Orange, whole	1 medium	70
Peaches, raw	1 medium	40
Peaches, canned	2 halves with syrup	90
Peaches, frozen	1/2 cup	105
Pears, raw	1 medium	100
Pears, canned	2 halves with syrup	90
Pineapple, raw	1/2 cup diced	40
Pineapple, canned	1/2 cup with syrup	90
Plums, raw	1 plum	25
Prunes, cooked with sugar	4–5 with liquid	105
Raisins, dried	1 tbsp	25
Raspberries, red, raw	3/4 cup	55
Raspberries, red, frozen	1/2 cup	120
Strawberries, raw	10 large	35
Strawberries, frozen	1/2 cup	120
Watermelon	1 slice, 1.5 in. thick	170

(continued)

Food	Amount	Calories
Fruit Juices		
Apple juice, canned	1 cup	120
Grape, frozen diluted	1 cup	170
Grapefruit, canned or frozen (ready-to-serve) unsweetened	1 cup	100
sweetened	1 cup	130
Lemonade	1 cup	110
Orange, fresh	1 cup	110
Orange, canned, unsweetened	1 cup	120
Orange, frozen, ready-to-serve	1 cup	110
Meat, Poultry, Fish		
Bacon	1 strip	50
Beef brisket	3 slices	340
Beef stew with vegetables	1 cup	185
Bologna	1 slice	65
Chicken, fried	½ breast	230
Chicken, fried	med. leg	140
Chicken pot pie	1 pot pie	460
Egg	1 medium	80
Eggs & bacon	2 eggs, 2 medium strips of bacon	320
Fish sticks, breaded	5 sticks	200
Haddock	1 fillet	140
Ham	average slice	140
Hamburger	1 medium patty	250
Hamburger	on bun	400
Hot dog	1	140
Hot dog	on bun	280
Lamb chop	1 chop	110
Liver	2 oz, fried	120
Meat loaf	1 slice	260
Pork chop	1 chop	260
Pork roast	3 oz	310
Pot roast	3 oz	300
Salami	1 slice	135
Salmon, baked	1 steak	175
Shrimp, fried	1 serving	180

(continued)

Food	Amount	Calories
Steak	3 oz	250
Tuna, canned	3 oz, drained	170
Turkey, roasted	3 slices	200
TV Dinners		
Beef	complete dinner	350
Chicken	complete dinner	540
Chopped sirloin	complete dinner	480
Ham	complete dinner	310
Meat loaf	complete dinner	370
Turkey	complete dinner	320
Veal cutlet	¼ cutlet	235
Sweets Group		
Beverages, cola type	12 oz	160
Chocolate syrup	1 tbsp	50
Dream Whip	1 tbsp	15
Honey	1 tbsp	65
Jams, commercial	1 tbsp	55
Jellies, commercial	1 tbsp	50
Miracle Whip	1 tbsp	50
Molasses	1 tbsp	50
Reddi-whip	1 average serving	30
Sugar, white	1 tbsp	30
Table syrup	1 tbsp	55
Whipped cream	1 tbsp	50
Dairy Products		
Cheese, American	1 oz	115
Cheese, cheddar	1 in cube	115
Cheese, cottage	¼ cup	60
Cheese, swiss	1 slice	105
Cheese, Velveeta	1 slice	90
Cream	1 tbsp	35
Ice cream	1 scoop	270
Milk, skim	1 cup	90
Milk, whole	1 cup	165
Sherbet	1 scoop	120
Yogurt	1 cup	120

(continued)

Food	Amount	Calories
Vegetables		
Asparagus, canned	6 medium spears	20
Beans, pork & tomato sauce	½ cup	140
Bean, green, cooked	½ cup	30
Bean, kidney, cooked	½ cup	110
Bean sprouts, raw	½ cup	15
Beets, diced, cooked	½ cup	35
Broccoli, cooked	3 med. stalks	30
Cabbage, cole slaw	½ cup	60
Carrots, raw	2 small	40
Carrots, cooked	½ cup, diced	25
Celery, raw	3 stalks	10
Corn, sweet, cooked	1 ear	100
Corn, sweet, canned	½ cup	70
Cucumber, raw	6 slices	5
Lettuce, raw	6 small leaves	10
Onion, raw	1 tbsp, chopped	5
Peas, green	½ cup	65
Pickle, dill	*1 large*	10
Potato, baked	1 medium	110
Potato, baked with 1 pat butter	1 medium	125
Potato chips	10	115
Potato, french fried	10	200
Potato, hash browns	½ cup	210
Potato, mashed with butter & milk	½ cup	110
Spinach, cooked	½ cup	25
Sweet potatoes, baked	1 medium	170
Sweet potatoes, candied	1 half	180
Tomato juice	1 cup	40
Tomatoes, raw	1 small	20
Tomatoes, canned	½ cup	20
V-8	1 cup	50
Alcoholic Drinks		
Beer	12 oz can	150
Hard liquor, 90 proof	1.5 oz jigger	110
Wine	3.5 oz glass	90

(continued)

Food	Amount	Calories
Beverages		
Carbonated drinks	12 oz can or bottle	160
Chocolate, hot	¾ cup	210
Chocolate malt	1 large glass	500
Diet Pepsi	12 oz can	6
Ice cream soda	1 serving	320
Milk shake	1 large glass	420
Tea or coffee, black	1 cup	0
Tea or coffee, with 2 tbsp cream or 2 tsp sugar		45
Candies		
Caramels, plain	2 medium	90
Chocolate bars: plain,		
sweet milk	1 bar (1 oz)	160
with almonds	1 bar (1 oz)	140
Chocolate-covered bar	1 bar	270
Cough drops	1 piece	10
Gum	1 stick	10
Lifesavers	1 roll	95
M&M's, plain	small bag	140
Peanut brittle	1 square	110
Popcorn	1 cup, no butter	55
Desserts		
Banana split	large	1,170
Cake & frosting	3 in. section	300
Coffee cake	3 in. wedge	260
Cupcake, icing	1 medium	230
Dixie cup	1 regular	280
Doughnuts:		
cake	1 average	135
cake, sugared	1 average	150
jelly	1 average	225
Ice cream	1 scoop	270
Pop, ice	1 regular pop	120
Sandwich, ice cream	1 regular	250
Sherbet	1 scoop	120

(continued)

Food	Amount	Calories
Sundaes, chocolate with nuts & whipped cream	average	350
Turnover, apple	medium	275
Fruits		
Apple	1 medium	80
Banana	1 small	95
Grapes	30 medium	70
Orange	1 medium	70
Peach	1 medium	40
Pear	1 medium	80
Sandwiches		
Cheese sandwich	1	280
Ham sandwich	1	320
Ham and swiss sandwich	1	570
Hamburger on bun	1	400
Hero sandwich	1	800
Hot dog and bun	1	280
Peanut butter sandwich	1 tbsp	330
Pizza, cheese	1/4 pie	360
Fast Foods/Franchises		
Big Mac		560
Quarter Pounder with cheese		530
McDonald hamburger		260
Small french fries		210
Large french fries		450
Chicken McNuggets (6 pc.)		290
KFC Original breast		400
KFC Original drumstick		140
KFC Original thigh		250
Pizza Hut (Personal Pan-cheese)		813
Pizza Hut (Personal Pan-pepperoni)		810
Coke, small	16 oz	150
Coke, medium	21 oz	210
Coke, large	32 oz	310
Coke, diet		0
Subway club	6 in.	312

(continued)

Food	Amount			Calories
Subway turkey	6 in.			289
Whopper				640
Starbucks:	Tall (12 oz)	Grande (16 oz)	Venti (20 oz)	
Latte (whole milk)	210	270	350	
Mocha (whole milk)	340	420	510	
Frappuccino-coffee	180	240	300	
Frappuccino-mocha	210	280	350	

Munchies

Food	Amount	Calories
Animal crackers	1	10
Cashews	6–8	90
Chocolate chip cookie	1	100
Fritos corn chips	small bag	120
Ginger snap	1	30
Graham cracker	1	30
Onion rings, fried	10 rings	75
Oreo	1	40
Peanuts	15–17	85
Potato chips	8–10	110
Pretzel	1 large	140
Pretzels, 3 ring	1 small	10
Ritz cracker	1	15
Ry-Krisp	1	20
Saltines	1	15
Vanilla wafer	1	15

Soups

Food	Amount	Calories
Bean with pork	1 cup	170
Chicken noodle	1 cup	60
Clam chowder, Manhattan	1 cup	80
Cream of chicken with milk	1 cup	180
Pea, split	1 cup	145
Tomato with milk	1 cup	170
Vegetable with beef broth	1 cup	80

Puddings, Jello

Food	Amount	Calories
Butterscotch pudding	½ cup	210
Chocolate pudding	½ cup	220

(continued)

Food	Amount	Calories
Gelatin, fruit, D-Zerta	1/2 cup	10
Jello, plain	1 serving	65
Jello, with fruit	1 serving	75
Tapioca pudding	1/2 cup	135
Vanilla pudding	1/2 cup	150
Salads		
Lettuce with french dressing	1 wedge	130
Mixed green, plain	1 cup	35
Mixed green with blue cheese	1 cup	160
Tossed salad	1 cup	120

Source: Adapted from U.S. Department of Agriculture materials and information provided on packages.

Note: Products vary greatly. Check package labels and information posted in stores and restaurants to improve accuracy in counting calories.

Geologic Time

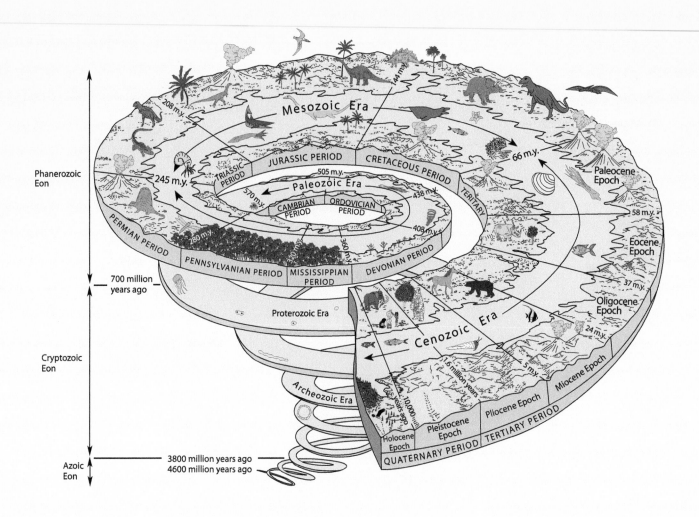

GLOSSARY

— A —

abiotic nonliving.

abrasives substances that can be used to rub or wear away, especially by friction.

acid deposition the falling of acids and acid-forming compounds from the atmosphere to Earth's surface. Acid deposition includes acid rain. It also includes acid snow, acid smog, and other acidic material.

acid (rain) precipitation any precipitation having a high concentration of sulfuric and/or nitric acid. Any precipitation that has a pH value of less than 5.6. Acidic precipitation includes acid rain, acid snow, acid sleet, acid hail, acid fog, and dry pollutants that form acid when they encounter moisture. All of these forms of precipitation are naturally acidic due to the carbon dioxide in the atmosphere. Generally, rain has a pH of 5.6 or 5.7. The average pH of a rainstorm in the Northeast (USA) is 4.0.

acre-foot the quantity of water used (indoor and outdoor) by a family of four for about a year in the United States. One acre-foot will cover an acre of land with a foot of water. One acre-foot = 325,851 gallons.

active solar those techniques for collecting, storing, and releasing solar energy that require some outside source of energy for fans and/or pumps.

adaptation an inherited characteristic of an organism in a population that improves the organism's chances of survival and reproduction in its environment compared with other organisms in the population.

aerobic able to live and grow only if free oxygen is present.

aerosols suspended tiny particles in a gas.

air pollutant any substance in sufficient concentration in the air to produce a "harmful" effect on humans or other animals, vegetation, or materials.

Air Quality Index (AQI) an index for reporting daily air quality that tells how clean or polluted the air is and what associated health effects might be of concern. The EPA calculates the AQI for five major air pollutants regulated by the Clean Air Act.

alcohol a colorless, volatile, flammable, organic liquid that is formed by the fermentation of biomass.

allocative mechanism a technique for distributing part of the production of a society among its members.

alloy a metal that is a mixture of a metal(s) with a non-metal or another metal.

alpha particle the nucleus of a fast-moving helium atom ($^4_2$He).

alpine growing on mountain heights above the timberline; as in alpine plants.

alternative breeder a breeder reactor that contains a much lower inventory of fissionable material than breeders at present.

ambient surrounding; outside; as in the ambient air.

ammeter the instrument used for measuring the rate of flow of electricity.

anaerobic able to live and grow in the absence of air or free oxygen.

anaerobic digestion the biochemical decomposition of organic matter by anaerobic bacteria.

annual plants terrestrial plants that die off each year during periods of temperature and moisture stress but leave behind seeds to germinate during the next favorable climatic season.

anthracite the most highly metamorphosed form of coal. Anthracite has a high energy content. It is black, hard, and glassy.

anticline an upward fold of sedimentary rocks. The layers slope down, from the top on all sides.

appliance a device or machine, especially for household use.

appropriate technology a strategy for approaching the energy future based on the general belief that "simpler is better" and that sources should be matched to end-use tasks.

aquatic pertaining to water; growing or living in or upon water.

aquifer a porous and permeable formation that stores and transmits enough groundwater to supply wells.

armature the part of an electric generator that revolves; consists of a series of coils of insulated wire surrounding a laminated iron core.

asthenosphere the zone of Earth that geologists believe flows like thick tar.

atmosphere the layer of air surrounding Earth.

atom a small piece of matter that is composed of protons, neutrons, and electrons.

atomic number the number of protons in an atom's nucleus.

attitude   in geology, the position or angle of a rock layer in relation to a point of reference.

— B —

background radiation   normal radiation in the lower atmosphere from cosmic rays and from Earth sources.

bacteria   single-celled microorganisms that lack chlorophyll. Some bacteria are capable of causing human, animal, or plant diseases; others are essential in pollution control because they break down organic matter in air and water.

baghouse   an installation containing thousands of heat-resistant fiberglass bags to control particulate emissions. A baghouse works as a room-size vacuum cleaner.

basal metabolic rate (BMR)   the rate at which heat is given off by a healthy human body when it is completely relaxed in comfortable surroundings and has not eaten food for 10 hours. It is expressed in Calories/hour/square meter of skin surface.

beta particle   a fast-moving electron ($_{-1}^{0}\beta$) that can penetrate a few millimeters of aluminum or about 100 centimeters of air.

bioconversion   a general term that refers to the transformation of solar energy to chemical energy during photosynthesis.

biodegradable   decomposing quickly as a result of the action of microorganisms.

biofuels   fuels produced from recently living material.

biological control   use of naturally occurring predators, parasites, bacteria, and viruses to control pests.

biological oxygen demand (BOD)   amount of dissolved oxygen gas required for bacterial decomposition of organic wastes in water.

biomagnification   the increased concentration of toxic chemicals, heavy metals, and certain pesticides in the tissues of organisms as these materials move up the food chain; also called *biological amplification.*

biomass   the total weight or mass of all living matter in a particular habitat or area.

biome   a large ecosystem characterized by a distinctive type of vegetation and maintained under the climatic condition of the region. Biomes cover large areas.

biosphere   (see ecosphere)

biotechnology   the use and manipulation of organisms to produce useful products.

biotic   living.

birth control   all methods for controlling conception or impregnation.

bitumen   hard or semisolid material occurring as natural asphalt.

bituminous coal   a soft intermediate grade of coal. The most common grade of coal.

breeder reactor   a reactor that both produces and consumes fissionable fuel, especially one that produces more than it consumes.

Btu (British thermal unit)   the amount of heat required to raise the temperature of 1 pound of water 1 degree Fahrenheit.

— C —

calorie   the amount of heat necessary to raise the temperature of 1 gram of water 1 Celsius degree. One thousand calories is a kilocalorie (Calorie): 1 kilocalorie = 1 Calorie = 1,000 calories. Food value is measured in Calories. Food Calories are a measure of the energy content of various foods.

capillary action   the movement of liquids in narrow tubes that is the result of adhesion, cohesion, and surface tension. The movement is referred to as capillarity.

carbohydrate   any of various compounds of carbon, hydrogen, and oxygen (as sugars, starches, cellulose), most of which are formed by green plants and which constitute a major class of animal foods.

carbon cycle   a chemical cycle in which the element carbon is circulated in various forms through the ecosphere.

carbon dioxide (CO_2)   a gaseous molecule containing one atom of carbon and two atoms of oxygen, formed by respiration in organisms or the complete combustion of fossil fuels.

carbon monoxide (CO)   a gaseous molecule containing one atom of carbon and one atom of oxygen, formed by the incomplete combustion of fossil fuels.

carbon sequestration   the capture and storage of CO_2 and other greenhouse gases that would otherwise be emitted to the atmosphere and potentially contribute to global climate change.

carnivore   an animal that uses other animals as a food source.

carrying capacity   the maximum number (population size) of a given organism that a given ecosystem can support.

catalyst   a substance that speeds a chemical reaction without being permanently changed itself.

catalytic converter   a device added to the exhaust pipe of an automobile that converts the air pollutants carbon monoxide (CO) and unburned hydrocarbons to carbon dioxide (CO_2) and water. The newer converters also break down nitrogen oxides.

cell a group of atoms and molecules interacting in an organized way to exhibit life.

cementation a uniting or joining together, as with cement.

ceramics one of the most important classes of materials on which modern societies rely. Ceramics are a class of inorganic, nonmetallic products that are subjected to high temperatures during manufacture. They are of interest because of their resistance to the action of chemicals and their ability to withstand high temperatures.

chain reaction a series of reactions in which each reaction causes one or more new reactions to occur. A reaction that stimulates its own repetition.

chaparral a biome characterized by a dry climate with little or no summer rain. Vegetation is dominated by shrubs that have adapted to regrow rapidly after the fires that occur frequently during the dry season.

chemical alteration the process of chemically rearranging a substance for the purpose of changing its properties. To change from toxic to nontoxic.

chemical energy the energy that is stored in the chemical bonds that hold molecules together.

chemical sedimentary rock rock that was formed by chemical precipitation, usually from seawater.

chemical weathering the chemical alteration of rock material during exposure to air, moisture, and organic material.

chlorofluorocarbons (CFCs) organic molecules consisting of chlorine and fluorine bonded to carbon. Used as spray-can propellants and coolants. Previously thought to be inert but now known to destroy the stratospheric ozone layer.

chromosome a centrally located, threadlike cell structure that contains hereditary material (genes).

circuit the path an electric current follows as it moves through wires and electrical devices.

clarifier a tank in which partially treated wastewater is allowed to separate into settleable solid, liquid, and floatable components.

clastic rock a sedimentary rock formed from particles (clasts) that were mechanically transported.

clay a very fine-grained sediment consisting of particles less than 1/256 millimeter in diameter. Clay is plastic when wet, cracks on drying out, and hardens on heating.

cleavage the tendency of some minerals to break along smooth, flat, parallel surfaces.

climate the average weather conditions of a place or area over a period of years.

closed system a system where nothing enters or leaves; hence, a system that must use and reuse everything in it.

cloud chamber a device in which the tracks of charged atomic particles, such as cosmic rays or radioactive emissions, are displayed. It consists of a glass-walled chamber filled with a supersaturated vapor, such as alcohol. When charged particles pass through the chamber, they trigger a process of condensation, thus producing a track of tiny liquid droplets, much like the vapor trail of a jet plane.

cloud seeding dispersion of small particles (condensation nuclei) into the atmosphere to stimulate cloud formation and precipitation.

coal a black or brownish-black organic solid primarily carbon but containing varying proportions of hydrogen, oxygen, nitrogen, and sulfur. Coal releases energy when burned and is a widely used natural fuel.

coal gasification a process for converting coal into a synthetic fuel similar to natural gas. The process involves applying heat, pressure, and steam to pulverized coal.

coal liquefaction a process for producing a synthetic crude oil by adding hydrogen to coal.

coal seam a layer or stratum of coal.

coarse-grained large visible crystals or particles.

cogeneration the production of two forms of energy (ex. hot gases and electricity) from the same fuel source; also called *combined-cycle generation*.

coliform bacteria a normally harmless type of bacteria that resides in the intestinal tract of humans and other animals and whose presence in water indicates that the water may be contaminated with disease-causing organisms found in untreated human and animal waste.

combustion the production of heat and light energy through a chemical process—usually oxidation. Burning is combustion.

commercial involved in the interchange of goods, wares, productions, or property of any kind.

community a group of populations living in a given area.

composite plastics plastics combined with fiberglass for added strength.

compost relatively stable decomposed organic material.

composting the controlled biological decomposition of organic solid waste under aerobic (in the presence of oxygen) conditions. Organic wastes are broken down into soil components such as humus or mulch.

Comprehensive Environmental Response, Compensation and Liability Act (CERCLA) the federal law that addresses the cleanup of inactive and abandoned hazardous waste sites. It is sometimes referred to as Superfund.

concentrating solar power (CSP) the name given to those strategies for concentrating and collecting enough solar energy to make large quantities of steam.

conduction the transfer of thermal energy from molecule to molecule.

conflict resolution the process(es) of softening and eventually ending struggles, clashes, sharp disagreements, and other forms of contention between people or groups of people.

coniferous trees cone-bearing trees, mostly evergreens that have needle-shaped or scalelike leaves.

conservation a careful preservation and protection of something; especially the planned management of a natural resource to prevent waste.

conservation easement a legal agreement between a land trust or a government entity that permanently restricts the use or development of land.

conservation law a law stating that in a closed system some quantity of mass or energy remains conserved (unchanged) forever.

conservation of energy (law of) energy can neither be created nor destroyed. It can, however, be transformed from one form to another.

conservation of matter (law of) matter can neither be created nor destroyed. It can, however, be rearranged.

consumers individuals or groups that buy/use resources, goods, and services.

consumptive use a use that consumes or uses up a resource.

containment strategies for locking up or enclosing and holding in toxic material.

continuous mining a method of mining in which the continuous mining machine cuts or rips coal from the face and loads it onto conveyors or into shuttle cars in one continuous operation.

continuous resources those resources that renew themselves and hence are always available if used sensibly. Also called renewable resources.

control the norm (unchanged part) in an experiment. It is selected to be like the examined part except for the one variable being tested.

controlled experiment a planned investigation in which all the variables are held constant except the one under study. That variable is then compared to the control in which the investigated variable does not change. The purpose is to control external influences so that every change produces its effect under known conditions so that the cause of an effect can be identified.

control rod a rod, plate, or tube containing a material that readily absorbs neutrons; used to control the power of a nuclear reactor. By absorbing neutrons, a control rod prevents the neutrons from causing further fission.

convection the transfer of heat by the mass movement of the heated particles, as in air or liquid currents.

conversion factor a number that enables you to change from one measurement unit to another.

cooling pond a lake or pond used to cool heated water from an electric power plant or factory.

cooling system the system for removing heat from the core of a nuclear reactor and transferring it to the steam generator.

cooling tower a device used to remove excess heat from water used in industrial operations, notably in electric power generation.

core the center of Earth.

cosmic rays radiation of many sorts; mainly atomic nuclei (protons) with very high energies, originating outside Earth's atmosphere. **Cosmic radiation** is part of natural background radiation.

critical mass the smallest mass of fissionable material that will support a self-sustaining chain reaction under stated conditions.

crude oil unrefined petroleum. Petroleum as it is taken from the ground.

crust the upper part of the lithosphere.

crustal abundance pertaining to the average concentration of a particular element or isotope in Earth's crust.

crystal a form of matter in which the atoms, ions, or molecules are arranged regularly in all directions to form a regular, repeating network.

cultural eutrophication (see eutrophication)

current the flow of charged particles through a conductive material.

— D —

deciduous trees trees, such as oak and maple, that lose all their leaves during part of the year.

decomposers the tiny organisms (such as bacteria, fungi, and some protozoa) that break down the complex compounds in dead animals and plants.

decomposition reduction of the net energy level and change in chemical composition of organic matter because of the actions of aerobic or anaerobic microorganisms.

dehydrate to remove water from; to dry.

demand the quantity of a good or service that people are willing and able to buy at various prices. Demand is influenced by advertising and prices of other goods, for example.

demographer a person who studies the vital statistics of populations—births, deaths, or marriages, for example.

demographic transition a phenomenon witnessed in the populations of many industrialized nations. As the standard of living increases, both birth and death rates decline. Gradually zero or low population growth is achieved. The decline in death rate usually precedes the decline in birthrate, producing a period of rapid growth before stabilization occurs.

demography the study of human populations.

desalination the removal of salt, especially from seawater, to make it drinkable.

desert a biome that receives less than 25 centimeters (10 inches) of precipitation per year.

desertification the process by which arid lands become transformed by loss of vegetation and soil into barren desert.

design vehicle a vehicle that is designed on paper (and on computer programs) but not yet built.

deuterium an isotope of hydrogen whose nucleus contains one neutron and one proton and is therefore about twice as heavy as the nucleus of normal hydrogen, which is only a single proton. Deuterium is often referred to as heavy hydrogen.

developed regions regions characterized by high standard of living, low population growth rate, low infant mortality, high material consumption, high per capita energy consumption, high per capita income, urban population, and high literacy. Also called MDRs.

developing regions regions characterized by low standard of living, high population growth rates, high infant mortality, low material consumption, low per capita energy consumption, low per capita income, rural populations, and low literacy. Also called LDRs.

diffuse to spread out; to mix by diffusion as in gases and liquids.

digestion biochemical decomposition of organic matter. Digestion of sewage sludge takes place in tanks where the sludge decomposes, resulting in partial gasification, liquefaction, and mineralization of pollutants.

dilution the process of lowering the concentration of a solution by adding water (or other solvent).

dipolar having two equal but oppositely charged ends.

dissolved oxygen (DO) amount of oxygen gas (O_2) dissolved in a given quantity of water at a given temperature and atmospheric pressure.

distillation the process of evaporating a liquid and condensing its vapors.

distribution mechanism (see allocative mechanism)

diversity the physical or biological complexity of a system. In many cases, it leads to ecosystem stability.

DNA deoxyribonucleic acid; the heredity material of most organisms. DNA has a helical structure made of two linked strands. DNA makes up the genes. It contains deoxyribose, a phosphate group, and one of four bases.

doubling time the amount of time it takes a growing quantity of something to double in number or volume.

drip irrigation (see trickle irrigation)

— E —

Earth a grand oasis in space.

earthquake the shaking of Earth's crust caused by a sudden release of energy.

earth-sheltered home a home that combines passive strategies with underground placement. These homes are usually open to light on the south side, with the other walls and floor placed in the ground. Some earth-sheltered homes have earthen roofs.

ecological succession The process by which the organisms that occupy a given area gradually change that area so that different and usually more complex communities replace them.

ecology the study of organisms in their homes. The study of the relationships of living organisms with one another and with their environment.

economics the study of ways that individuals and societies distribute their goods in an attempt to satisfy their unlimited wants.

ecosphere the global ecosystem; the biosphere. The sum total of all the various ecosystems on Earth.

ecosystem any area of nature that includes living organisms and nonliving substances interacting to produce an exchange of materials between the living (biotic) and nonliving (abiotic) parts.

effervesce to give off gas bubbles, as carbonated beverages.

efficiency   the efficiency of a machine or, more generally, of any process in which some energy or work is put in and some combination of useful work or energy comes out. Efficiency is the ratio of the desired output (work or energy) to the input.

efficient   to accomplish with the minimum use of time, energy, money, or effort.

effluent   a discharge of pollutants into the environment, partially or completely treated or in their natural state. Generally used in regard to discharges into water.

electric power transmission   the method by which electric power is transferred from the power generating plant to where the power is to be used.

electrical energy   a special kind of kinetic energy. Electrical energy is the energy of electrical charges, usually electrons in motion.

electrolyte   a substance whose aqueous solution conducts electricity.

electromagnetic induction   the production of electric current in a closed circuit caused by a change in the magnetic field that passes through that circuit.

electromagnetic wave   a wave of energy radiated into space by the sun, a light, or an antenna.

electrons   the tiny, negatively charged particles that orbit or migrate about the nucleus of an atom.

electroplating   the deposition of a coating on an object by use of an electric current.

electrostatic precipitator   a device used for removing particulates from smokestack emissions. The charged particles are attracted to an oppositely charged metal plate, where they are precipitated out of the air.

element   one of the approximately 108 known chemical substances that cannot be divided into simpler substances by chemical means. A substance whose atoms all have the same atomic number.

El Niño   the interaction between the ocean and the atmosphere in the tropical waters of the Indian and Pacific oceans that occurs about every 2–7 years. It is linked to disrupted weather patterns throughout the world.

emigration   movement out of an area that was once one's place of residence.

endangered species   a species in immediate danger of extinction.

end-use   the final and intended use of a resource. The major end-uses of energy resources include transportation, space heating, refrigeration, lighting, and cooking.

energy   the ability to move matter around. Something that is necessary to maintain life and a vibrant society.

energy content   the amount of heat energy released by the combustion (or reaction) of one unit mass of that fuel.

energy conversion   (see energy transformation)

energy policy   a plan of action for using energy resources usually drawn up by a government.

energy pyramid   a diagram representing the flow of energy through a food chain or web. The base of the pyramid represents the usable energy stored in the producers.

energy quality   the ability of an energy source to do useful work as measured by the ease with which it can be transformed to mechanical energy or electrical energy. Energy quality is also referred to as *energy usefulness.*

energy transformation   the process of changing energy from one form to another. For example, a match transforms chemical energy to heat energy.

entropy   a measure of the degree of disorder of a situation. A measure of energy's gradual degeneration to a useless condition.

environment   the sum of all external conditions and influences affecting the life, development, and ultimately the survival of an individual organism or population.

environmental assessment (EA)   a brief document for which a federal agency is responsible that serves to provide sufficient evidence and analysis for determining whether to prepare an environmental impact statement or a finding of no significant impact.

environmental impact   the total effect of an environmental change, either natural or humanmade, on the ecology of an area.

environmental impact statement (EIS)   a written report that examines and analyzes the possible impacts of a particular project (and possible alternative projects) on the surrounding environment. In the United States, such a statement is required by the National Environmental Policy Act.

Environmental Protection Agency (EPA)   the federal agency empowered to determine environmental standards and enforce federal environmental laws.

enzyme   organic catalysts produced in plant and animal cells that regulate chemical reaction rates in those cells.

equilibrium   a stable state of a system. A state of balance or equality between opposing forces.

equity   that which relates to fairness. The general principles of fairness and justice.

estuary   coastal regions such as inlets or mouths of rivers, where saltwater and freshwater mix.

eutrophic lake a lake characterized by nutrient-rich water supporting an abundant growth of algae or other aquatic plants at the surface. Deep eutrophic water has little or no dissolved oxygen (DO).

eutrophication accumulation of nutrients in a lake or pod due to human intervention (cultural eutrophication) or natural causes (natural eutrophication). Contributes to the process of succession.

evaporation the process of changing from a solid or liquid state to a vapor or gas.

evaporites chemical sedimentary rocks consisting of minerals precipitated by evaporation waters, especially salt and gypsum.

evapotranspiration the combination of water evaporation from Earth's surface and transpiration from plants.

evolution a process of continual change in organisms caused by changes in successive generations.

exponential growth growth that starts slowly but has the potential to shoot out of control rapidly. Growth that is characterized by doubling in a fixed amount of time.

exponential lifetime (T_e) an estimate of the amount of time the reserves of a resource will last, assuming they are consumed at an exponentially increasing rate.

externalities costs (or benefits) that are external to the actual act of production, or uses that are passed on involuntarily to someone else.

extinction the total loss of a species worldwide.

extrapolate to estimate a quantity beyond the known base of data by assuming the present trends will continue.

extrusive rock rock formed from lava or from other volcanic material spewed out onto the surface of Earth.

— F —

family planning process by which couples determine the number and spacing of children.

famine the situation in which people in a given area suffer from lack of access to food sufficient for good health. This may be due to drought, flood, earthquake, or political/economic conditions.

fault a crack in the crust of Earth along which rocks have moved.

fermentation the breakdown of complex molecules in organic compounds caused by bacteria. The souring of milk is an example.

fertile material a material, not itself fissionable, that can be converted into a fissionable material by irradiation in a reactor. There are two basic fertile materials, uranium-238 and thorium-232.

fertilization (conception) the fusion (uniting) of egg and sperm that begins embryonic development.

fertilizer a substance that makes the land or soil capable of producing more and healthier vegetation or crops.

fine-grained barely visible crystals or particles.

finite having bounds or limits. Not infinite, subject to limitations.

First Law of Thermodynamics energy cannot be created or destroyed. It can, however, be transformed from one form to another. This is also known as the law of conservation of energy.

fission the splitting of a heavy nucleus into two nearly equal parts (which are nuclei of lighter elements) accompanied by the release of a large amount of energy and generally one or more neutrons.

fission fragments the two nuclei that are formed by the fission of a nucleus. Also referred to as *radioactive waste*.

fissionable isotopes isotopes that can be fissioned (split) by neutrons to release nuclear energy. Nuclear fuel.

flat-plate collector a device for collecting solar energy and converting it into heat.

floodplain the wide, level area that borders a stream or river that is covered by its water in time of flood.

flotation separation of ore constituents by binding in a froth, then skimming the froth from the liquid.

fluidized-bed combustion a method of producing heat from low-grade coal. Air is blown into a bed of sand, or of powdered coal and limestone, causing the bed to churn almost like a boiling fluid. The bed is heated red-hot by the injection and ignition of a start-up gas, and more ground or powdered coal is slowly fed in. Steam is generated in boiler tubes laid in the bed, and the exhaust gases are captured under pressure and used to drive a gas turbine.

foliation a parallel or nearly parallel structure caused by a parallel arrangement of platy minerals.

food chain the sequence transferring energy in the form of food from one organism to another.

food web a complex, interlocking series of food chains.

foot-pound the amount of work done or energy used when a force of 1 pound acts through a distance of 1 foot.

foresee to see beforehand; to see into the future.

forestall to hinder or prevent by doing something beforehand.

fossil fuels the remains of once-living plants and animals that can be burned to release energy. Examples are coal, oil, natural gas, oil shale, and tar sands.

fracture zone a crack in Earth's crust where plates slide past each other horizontally.

fragmentation the dividing up of land into smaller, often random, isolated pieces. This creates a patchy landscape.

free enterprise (market) an economic system in which individuals are free to start and operate their own businesses in a competitive environment.

freshwater water that contains little salt.

fuel cell a device for converting chemical energy directly into electrical energy without combustion. Chemicals are fed into the cell.

fuel fabrication the step in the nuclear fuel cycle in which the enriched UF_6 gas is converted into a solid (UO_2 or UC) and formed into a usable fuel.

fusion the formation of a heavier nucleus from two lighter ones (such as hydrogen isotopes), resulting in the release of energy.

— G —

galvanometer an instrument that indicates both presence and direction of electric current.

gamma rays high-frequency electromagnetic radiations that have an indeterminate range in matter. They are very penetrating.

gangue the fraction of ore rejected as tailing in a separation process. It is usually of no value but may have some secondary commercial use.

gas the phase of matter that easily moves and has neither a definite shape nor a definite volume.

gaseous diffusion a method of isotopic separation based on the fact that gas atoms or molecules with different masses will diffuse through a porous barrier (or membrane) at different rates.

gasohol a mixture of gasoline and alcohol. The alcohol is generally formed from the fermentation of grains and plant residue.

generator a device for converting mechanical energy into electrical energy.

genetic engineering any technique used to identify or change genes at the molecular level.

genome an organism's complete set of DNA.

geologist one who studies the makeup, structure, and history of Earth's crust, including rock layers, fossils, and mineral content.

geothermal energy energy originating in Earth's crust, especially in volcanic regions.

germplasm the substance in seeds by which hereditary characteristics are transmitted.

global science the study of how individuals and societies use their living and nonliving resources and influence the environment in their attempts to satisfy human needs and wants.

glucose a variety of sugar less sweet than cane sugar, occurring naturally in fruits and honey.

gradient the rate of change of temperature, pressure, and so on. A diagram or curve representing this.

grasslands found in both temperate and tropical regions and characterized by periodic drought, flat or slightly rolling terrain, and large grazers that feed off the lush grasses.

greenhouse effect the trapping of heat in the atmosphere. Incoming solar radiation penetrates the atmosphere, but outgoing radiation (heat) is absorbed by water vapor, carbon dioxide, and ozone. Some of this is reradiated toward Earth, causing a rise in temperature.

greenhouse gases (GHG) gases in the atmosphere that absorb infrared energy and raise the temperature of the air. These gases include CO_2, water vapor, methane, nitrous oxide, CFCs, and other halocarbons.

groundwater water below the water table.

growth rate in simplest form, the growth rate of a population equals the birthrate minus the death rate.

— H —

habitat the specific region in which an organism lives.

half-life the time it takes half the atoms of a particular radioactive substance to disintegrate to another nuclear form.

hazardous wastes potentially harmful solid, liquid, or gaseous waste products of manufacturing or other human activities.

HCl hydrochloric acid.

heat capacity the quantity of heat required to raise the temperature of a body (object) 1 degree.

heat energy a form of kinetic energy that flows from one body to another because of a temperature difference between them. The effects of heat energy result from the motion of molecules.

heat engine any device that converts heat energy into mechanical energy.

heat exchanger any device that transfers heat from one fluid (liquid or gas) to another or to the environment.

heat pump a device that transfers heat from a cooler region to a warmer one using mechanical or electrical energy.

hemoglobin the red coloring matter of the red blood corpuscles. Hemoglobin carries oxygen from the lungs to the cells and some carbon dioxide from cells to the lungs.

herbivore a plant-eating animal.

high-level waste material generated by chemical reprocessing of spent fuel and irradiated targets. High-level waste contains highly radioactive, short-lived fission products, hazardous chemicals, and toxic heavy metals.

horizons layers found in most soils.

human ecology the study of the growth, distribution, and organization of human communities and how they interact with other humans, with other species, and with their environment.

humus decaying organic matter that increases soil fertility, aeration, and water retention.

hurricane a strong tropical storm. Hurricanes are the most destructive storms on Earth.

hybrid the offspring of two animals or plants of different races, varieties, or species, for example.

hybridization a breeding process that involves crossing (mating) different individuals for the purpose of developing the most ideal heredity traits.

hydrocarbon any of a vast family of compounds containing carbon and hydrogen in various combinations; found especially in fossil fuels.

hydrogen storage any technique for producing and storing hydrogen as a fuel source. The production usually involves electrolyzing water because water is plentiful, and electricity is difficult to store.

hydrologic cycle the water cycle.

hydropower techniques for converting the gravitational energy of water stored behind a dam to electrical energy.

hydrosphere the surface water on Earth.

hypothesis a possible explanation of an event that is assumed for the purpose of testing it.

— I —

igneous rock rock that solidified from a molten state.

immigration migration of people into a country or area to take up permanent residence.

immiscible liquids liquids that cannot mix.

impermeable not permitting the passage of fluids such as water.

incineration the burning of household or industrial waste.

industry the practice of making goods as distinguished from agriculture (growers) and exchanges of goods and services (commerce).

inequity lack of justice or fairness; an instance of injustice or unfairness.

inertia the property of matter that opposes any change in its state of motion.

infiltration the movement of groundwater or hydrothermal water into rock or soil through joints and pores.

insectary a place where insects are raised, especially for study or for the purpose of breeding natural predators to control pests.

in situ in the natural or original position or location.

insulation a nonconducting material used to retard the flow of heat.

integrated circuit the circuit on a computer chip that is made up of electronic components built into the chip.

integrated pest management (IPM) a pest-control strategy based on natural forces, such as the use of natural insect enemies, weather, crop rotation, use of pest-resistant plants, and carefully applied doses of pesticides.

interdependent mutually dependent. Depending on each other.

interpolate to supply or infer information between known data or points, assuming the same trends hold.

interrelated the idea that in an ecosystem everything is mutually related to everything else.

intrusive rock igneous rock that forced its way in a molten state into surrounding (country) rock before it cooled.

invasive species a nonnative species that is introduced to an ecosystem and whose introduction causes or is likely to cause economic or environmental harm or harm to human health.

ion an atom or molecule that has lost or gained one or more electrons and has become electrically charged.

ionizing radiation radiation with enough energy to dislodge one or more electrons from an atom, forming ions. These ions can react with and damage living tissue.

isotope one of two or more atoms with the same atomic number (the same chemical element) but with different mass numbers. The nuclei of isotopes have the same number of protons but different numbers of neutrons.

— J —

Joule   the amount of work done or energy used when a force of 1 newton acts through a distance of 1 meter.

— K —

kerogen   the solid organic matter of high molecular weight contained in oil shale. When heated (retorted), kerogen breaks down, yielding synthetic crude oil and hydrocarbon gas.

kilowatt-hour   a common unit of electrical energy. The energy expended when 1,000 watts of electrical power are used for 1 hour.

kinetic energy   the energy possessed by a moving object. Energy of motion.

— L —

land trust   a non-profit organization that preserves land for the purpose of protecting the natural environment and the biota that inhabit it. The Nature Conservancy is the world's largest land trust.

land use   the use of land by humans.

laser fusion   an approach to nuclear fusion in which a small solid sphere crammed with deuterium and tritium is bombarded with powerful laser beams in an attempt to drive the fuel inward to the point where the nuclei fuse.

lava   magma that pours out onto Earth's surface.

law of demand   a law of economics that says that the demand for a product or service depends on its price. Low prices lead to high demand; high prices lead to low demand.

law of supply   a law of economics that says that the quantity of goods and services offered for sale will vary with price. The higher the price, the greater the quantity offered for sale; the lower the price, the less offered for sale.

leaching   the process of extracting or removing a soluble substance from a material or rock layer by causing water to filter through the material or layer.

lead time   the time span from when a project is first proposed to when it is completed.

lifetime calculation   a calculation done for the purpose of determining how long a resource will last.

lignite   a very soft grade coal formed by the burial of peat.

limiting factor   a factor such as temperature, light, or water that limits the ability of an organism to grow and be productive.

Limits to Growth, The   a nontechnical report of the findings of the Club of Rome's study of growth on our planet. The report came out in 1972.

lipids   energy-rich organic compounds containing carbon, hydrogen, and small amounts of oxygen. Lipids help make up the cell membrane. Fats, oils, and waxes are examples.

liquefaction   to change into a liquid.

lithosphere   the solid portion of Earth's crust.

load   the electrical devices (appliances, lightbulbs) in an electric circuit that the current operates. The load offers resistance to the flow of current.

loam   a soil that is a sandy and clay mixture.

longwall mining   a method of subsurface mining in which a narrow tunnel is cut and then supported by movable metal pillars. After the ore is removed, the roof supports are moved forward, allowing the earth behind them to collapse.

low-level waste   a catchall term for any radioactive waste that is not spent fuel, high-level, or transuranic waste.

— M —

macro   of or involving larger quantities or objects.

magma   molten rock beneath Earth's surface. Magma is a supersaturated solution containing nonvolatile minerals and volatile constituents.

magnetic confinement fusion   a fusion process in which tritium and deuterium are heated to a plasma that is confined in a chamber by means of electromagnetic forces.

magnetic field   a region in space in which a magnet or compass needle will experience a force.

magnetometer   an instrument for measuring the force and variations in the force of magnetism.

malnutrition   the state of poor health in which an individual's diet lacks one or more of the essential vitamins and nutrients, especially protein.

mantle   a thick shell of Earth below the asthenosphere that behaves like a solid.

marine   of the sea or ocean; inhabiting, found in, or formed by the sea.

market   a situation in which buyers and sellers communicate with one another concerning the exchange of goods and/or services.

market economy   an economic system in which most of the businesses are owned and operated by private citizens. Most economic decisions are made by individual producers and consumers through buying and selling in the market. Also called a free market.

market equilibrium   the point where the consumer is able to purchase the largest amount of a product or service at the cheapest price, and the producer is able to produce the most at the highest price.

mass   a number that measures the quantity of matter. It is obtained on Earth's surface by dividing the weight of a body by the acceleration due to gravity.

mass number   the number of protons plus neutrons in an atomic nucleus.

matter   anything that occupies space and has mass.

mechanical concentration   any concentration of a mineral caused by the movement of a fluid.

mechanical energy   the energy of an object as represented by its movement, its position, or both.

mechanism   any system, means, or strategy for doing something.

meltdown   an event at a nuclear reactor if a pipe ruptures or there is some other major interference with the normal cooling system. This would allow the reactor's hot fissionable fuel to quickly overheat. The fuel could quickly form itself into a heavy, white-hot blob of molten metal that could penetrate through the reactor and melt its way down through the basement of the plant and into the ground. Large quantities of contaminated steam and other vapors would be released into the environment.

metabolism   the chemical reactions that take place in an organism as food is used.

metamorphic rock   sedimentary or igneous rock in which the minerals or texture or both have been changed by high temperature and pressure without melting.

methane   a gaseous hydrocarbon, CH_4, that is flammable and formed by the decomposition of organic matter. It is the main constituent of natural gas.

methodology   the application of the principles of reasoning to scientific and philosophical inquiry. The science of method or orderly arrangement.

metric system   a system of measurement that is based on decimal multiples and subdivision of the basic units. The official name of the modern metric system is Systeme International or simply SI.

micro   of or involving smaller quantities or objects.

microorganisms   any living things of microscopic size; examples include bacteria, yeasts, simple fungi, some algae, slime molds, and protozoans.

mill   a building or collection of buildings containing machinery for separating the valuable portion of an ore from the waste rock.

milling   the process of separating valuable minerals from waste rock. The mill is the building in which milling takes place.

mine   an excavation made in the earth for the purpose of extracting ore.

mineral   any naturally occurring crystalline inorganic material. A naturally occurring substance or phase with a characteristic internal structure determined by a regular arrangement of the atoms or ions within it, and with a chemical composition and physical properties that are either fixed or that vary within a definite range.

mineral/nutrient cycle   the generic chemical cycle in which the minerals/nutrients necessary for life are circulated in various forms through the ecosphere. Does not usually contain a gas phase.

model   something that imitates the behavior of something else.

moderator   a material, such as ordinary water, heavy water or graphite, used in a reactor to slow down high-velocity neutrons, thus increasing the likelihood of further fission.

molecule   a group of atoms held together in a particular way.

monoculture   cultivation of one plant species (such as wheat or corn) over a large area. Highly susceptible to disease and insects.

municipal solid wastes   combined residential and commercial solid waste materials generated in a given municipal area.

mutation   a sudden fundamental change in heredity producing a new individual unlike its parents in some way.

— N —

natural gas   a gas mixture that is trapped in many places in the upper strata of Earth. Natural gas is mostly methane and ethane. It can be found alone but is often found with petroleum.

natural resources   the materials that nature provides that can be used in production. Natural resources are often called gifts of nature.

natural selection   the process by which the individuals in a population that are best suited to their environment survive and pass their characteristics on to their offspring.

need   a lack of something essential, desirable, or useful. A condition requiring supply or relief.

net energy   the difference between total energy produced and total energy used.

neutron   an uncharged elementary particle with a mass slightly greater than that of the proton and found in the nucleus of every atom heavier than ordinary hydrogen.

niche   all the physical, chemical, and biological factors a species needs to survive, stay healthy, and reproduce in an ecosystem.

nitrogen cycle a chemical cycle in which the element nitrogen is circulated in various forms through the ecosphere.

nitrogen oxides (NO$_x$) gases formed in great part from atmospheric nitrogen and oxygen when combustion takes place under conditions of high temperature and high pressure; for example, in internal combustion engines; considered major air pollutants.

no-till a method of cultivation in which the soil is left undisturbed to reduce soil erosion, lower labor costs, and save energy.

nonpoint source a source of pollution in which wastes are not released at one specific, identifiable point, but from a number of points that are spread out and difficult to identify and control.

nonrenewable resources resources that are not replaced or regenerated naturally within a reasonable period of time. For example, fossil fuels and minerals.

nuclear energy the energy liberated by a nuclear reaction (fission or fusion) or by radioactive decay.

nuclear fuel cycle all of the steps involving the use of a nuclear material, starting with the removal of ore from the ground and ending with the eventual disposal of related waste materials.

nuclear proliferation (see proliferation)

nuclear reaction a reaction involving a change in an atomic nucleus, such as fission, fusion, neutron capture, or radioactive decay.

nuclear reactor a device in which a fission chain reaction can be initiated, maintained, and controlled.

nuclear waste equipment and materials (from nuclear reactions and operations) that are radioactive and thus not usable.

nucleon a nuclear particle; a proton or neutron in the nucleus of an atom.

nucleus the small, positively charged core of an atom. The nucleus contains nearly all the atom's mass. Both protons and neutrons are found in all nuclei, except that of ordinary hydrogen, which consists of a single proton.

nutrient an element or compound that is needed for the survival, growth, and reproduction of a plant or animal.

nutrition nourishing or being nourished by taking in and assimilating food.

— **O** —

ocean thermal energy conversion (OTEC) an energy option that uses temperature differences between surface waters and ocean depths to vaporize a working fluid and generate electricity.

oil (see crude oil)

oil shale a sedimentary rock containing kerogen. Heated kerogen yields synthetic crude oil, which can be processed into gasoline and other petroleum products. Flammable gas is also produced.

oligotrophic lake a lake with low dissolved plant nutrient (nitrate and phosphate) content.

omnivore an animal, such as a human, that can use both plants and other animals as food sources.

open pit mining surface mining of materials that creates a large hole or pit.

open system a system, such as a living organism, in which both matter and energy are exchanged between the system and the environment.

ore a mineral or mineral aggregate containing precious or useful material and that occurs in such quantity, grade, and chemical combination as to make extraction commercially profitable.

ore body a more or less solid mass of ore that may consist of low-grade as well as high-grade ore and is of different character than the adjoining rock.

organ a group of tissues that perform a similar function. For example, the heart and the lungs.

organ system a group of organs that perform a similar function. For example, the digestive system.

organic derived from living organisms; the branch of chemistry dealing with carbon compounds.

organic farming a method of producing crops and livestock naturally by using organic fertilizer (manure, legumes, compost, crop residues); crop rotation; natural (biological) pest control (good bugs that eat bad bugs, plants that repel bugs); and environmental controls (such as crop rotation) instead of using commecial, synthetic fertilizers and pesticides and herbicides.

organism any living thing.

overburden material of any nature that covers a deposit of useful materials or ores that are to be mined.

oxygen (O) an element that is found free as a colorless, tasteless, odorless gas in the atmosphere; or combined in water, in most rocks and minerals, and in numerous organic compounds. It can combine with all elements except the inert gases, is active in life processes, and is involved especially in combustion processes.

ozone (O$_3$) a highly reactive molecule made up of three atoms of oxygen. High in the atmosphere ozone forms a layer that filters out harmful ultraviolet radiation, thus protecting life on Earth. Ozone is also formed at Earth's surface as a damaging component of photochemical smog.

— P —

particulates solid particles and liquid droplets suspended or carried in the air. Particulates include soot, ashes, and dust.

passive solar those techniques for using solar energy to heat an enclosure that require no nonsolar energy for fans or pumps.

peat a mixture of plant fragments formed from partly decayed vegetation that is slowly built up in swamps.

periodic table a pictorial arrangement of the elements based on their electron arrangements and hence their properties.

permafrost a permanently frozen aggregate of ice and soil occurring in very cold regions.

permeable open to passage or penetration by fluids, especially by water or crude oil.

pesticide a generic term used to refer to anything used to kill or control pests.

petroleum an oily, flammable liquid that may vary from almost colorless to black and occurs in many places in the upper strata of Earth. It is a complex mixture of hydrocarbons and is the raw material for many products.

pH a numeric value that indicates the relative acidity or alkalinity of a substance on a scale of 0 to 14, with the neutral point at 7. Acid solutions have pH values lower than 7, and basic or alkaline solutions have pH values greater than 7.

photochemical smog a complex mixture of air pollutants (oxidants) produced in the atmosphere by the reaction of hydrocarbons and nitrogen oxides under the influence of sunlight. Photochemical smog produces localized dead spots, yellowing, and growth alterations in plants. It is an eye and respiratory irritant in humans.

photon a small bundle of radiant energy. A photon carries a quantum of electromagnetic energy.

photosynthesis the process by which plants use sunlight to combine carbon dioxide, water, and various minerals into carbohydrates (such as glucose).

photovoltaic cell an electronic device that converts sunlight directly into electrical energy.

photovoltaic effect the ejection of electrons from the surface of a material that is exposed to visible light.

physical weathering breaking down of rock into bits and pieces by exposure to temperature changes and the physical action of moving ice and water, growing roots, and human activities such as construction and farming.

pillar the mass of coal or ore left to support the ceiling of a mine.

placer a deposit of gold or other metal-bearing alluvial gravel.

plasma an electrically neutral gaseous mixture of positive and negative ions. Sometimes called the "fourth state of matter" since it behaves differently from solids, liquids, and gases.

plate tectonics theory the theory that there are six large crustal plates, and many smaller ones, that move around on the surface of Earth.

platy made of flat, broad, thin sheets.

pluralistic containing many parts, views, or features. A pluralistic society contains many nationalities, religions, and customs.

plutonium (Pu) a heavy, radioactive, humanmade metallic element with atomic number 94. Its most important isotope is fissionable plutonium-239, produced by neutron irradiation of uranium-238. It is used for reactor fuel and in weapons.

point source (of pollution) easily discernible source of pollution, such as a factory.

pollutant something that pollutes; especially a harmful chemical or other waste material discharged into the water or atmosphere.

pollution the presence of matter or energy whose nature, location, and/or quantity produces undesired environmental effects.

population all the organisms of the same type living in a certain area.

population histogram graphical representation of population by age and sex.

population pyramid a more general term that refers to a population histogram.

porosity the percentage of space between soil or rock particles.

porous full of pores or tiny holes that can be occupied by fluids such as water or crude oil.

potential energy stored energy. Energy that is due to the position or configuration of a mass.

precipitation the process by which water vapor molecules condense to form drops or ice crystals that are heavy enough to fall to Earth's surface.

predator an organism that lives by preying on other organisms.

prey an animal taken by a predator as food.

price the value, in monetary terms, placed on a good or service.

primary consumer first consumer organism in a given food chain.

primary succession ecological succession in an area where no soil is present and the area is devoid of organisms.

primary treatment the first stage in waste water treatment in which the floating or settleable solids are mechanically removed by screening and sedimentation.

printed circuit a conductive pattern formed in a predetermined design on the surface of an insulating base in an accurately repeatable manner.

priorities a preferential ranking of goals, projects, or actions.

producers organisms (such as plants) that synthesize organic substances from inorganic substances.

production vehicle a new vehicle that has limited availability to consumers at some locations.

profit the amount of revenue left for a producer after all costs of production are paid.

proliferation the process of growing or increasing rapidly in number or amount.

proteins the principal organic substances within cells. Proteins contain carbon, hydrogen, nitrogen, oxygen, and usually sulfur. Proteins are synthesized from raw materials by plants but assimilated as separate amino acids by animals.

proton an elementary particle with a single positive electrical charge and a mass approximately 1,837 times that of the electron. Protons are found in all nuclei.

protoplasm the living part of a cell.

prototype vehicle a vehicle that has been built and is being tested but not sold.

pumped storage reversible pump turbines that use surplus electric power to lift water into a reservoir when demand is low and then use it to generate power when it is needed.

pyrolysis to heat, for the purpose of breaking up, in the absence of air. Chemical decomposition by heat.

— Q —

quad (Q) a large quantity of energy equal to 1 quadrillion Btu. $1Q = 10^{15}$ Btu.

quality energy (see energy quality)

— R —

R-value a measure of a material's ability to stop heat from passing through it. The higher the R-value, the greater the resistance to heat flow.

radiant energy the energy of electromagnetic waves, including light.

radiation that which is sent out from an object such as the sun, a planet, a lightbulb, a heater, or an atom. Radiation can either be in the form of particles or waves.

radioactive waste materials that are radioactive and for which there is no further use.

radioactivity the spontaneous transformation of an atomic nucleus during which it changes from one nuclear species to another, with the emission of particles and energy.

randomness a measure of the disorder or chaos of a situation. Also an indication of the degree of degradation of an energy supply.

rationing the process of distributing or dividing up a commodity in short supply in an equitable manner, or so as to achieve a particular objective.

real world lifetime (T_{rw}) the amount of time the reserves of a resource actually last under real-world conditions.

recharge in hydrology, the replacement of ground water by infiltration of water from the atmosphere.

reclamation the process of restoring to cultivation, useful purpose, or original state.

recycling the process by which waste materials are transformed into new useful products in such a manner that the original products may lose their identity.

refining the process by which a mineral concentrate is brought to a fine or a pure state.

remote sensing a technique used to gather information about an object without actually touching it.

renewable resource a resource that can be used continuously without being used up.

renewal time the time it takes a depleted resource to be restored to its original condition.

replacement deposit a deposit of ore minerals by hydrothermal solutions. The minerals were first dissolved in the hot solution and then substituted for some other mineral in the surrounding rock.

reserves the amount of an identified resource that can be extracted profitably with existing technology under present economic conditions. Reserves are a subclass of resources.

reservoir a source or place of residence of some valuable material.

residual enrichment a mineral concentration process in which a material of no value is dissolved away, leaving behind a valuable substance.

resistance opposition to the passage of electric current, causing electric energy to be transformed into heat.

resistor   an electrical device used in a circuit primarily to resist the flow of electric current.

resolve   to work out; to come to a decision.

Resource Conservation and Recovery Act (RCRA)   the federal law that regulates hazardous waste generation, storage, transportation, treatment, and disposal. The emphasis is on resource conservation.

resource depletion curve   a plot of production rate versus time that represents the complete production cycle of a resource in a given region.

resources   identified and unidentified deposits of a mineral that can be economically recovered with existing technology or that may become economically recoverable when prices rise or mining technology improves.

respiration   the oxidation of food by organisms that releases usable energy, carbon dioxide, and water.

retort   a vessel in which substances are distilled or decomposed by being heated in the absence of air.

rift   an opening made by splitting.

rift zone   the region where tectonic plates separate and move away from each other. Rift zones are located mostly on the ocean floor. The process of plate separation and formation of new crust is called *seafloor spreading*.

rock   the basic solid material of Earth's crust. Rock is a collection of minerals.

rock-forming minerals   the minerals that make up the most common rocks in Earth's crust.

room-and-pillar mining   a method of underground mining in which a series of rooms are cut and pillars (columns) left standing to support the roof. Once a particular area is mined out, the pillars are systematically removed and the roof allowed to fall.

run off   water that flows on the surface into streams, lakes, and oceans.

— S —

salt dome   a solid mass of salt that was once fluid and flowed into fractures and other weaknesses in surrounding geologic structures. Oil and gas traps formed against the side of this salt, in faults caused by the movement of salt, and in arched formations above the salt.

sanitary landfill   an engineered method of solid waste disposal on land in a manner that protects the environment. Waste is spread in thin layers, compacted to the smallest practical volume and covered with soil at the end of each working day.

scenario   a possible future or outcome that is based on a series of assumptions or criteria.

science   the study of measured facts about the natural world and the relationships among those facts. Science is based on measurements of the natural world and interpretations of those measurements.

scientific explanation   a statement that says that an event is a logical consequence of a theory or model, which serves to unify a host of related facts or occurrences.

scrubber/scrubbing   a device used in controlling particulate and/or gaseous emissions. The process involves washing impurities out of the stream of flue gas and carrying them off in a slurry of ash and water.

seafloor spreading   the process by which material rising at the ocean ridges moves toward the ocean trenches, carrying the seafloor with it.

Second Law of Thermodynamics (Form 1)   in any conversion of energy from one form to another, there is always a decrease in the amount of useful energy.

Second Law of Thermodynamics (Form 2)   heat cannot by itself flow from cold to hot. It spontaneously flows from hot to cold.

Second Law of Thermodynamics (Form 3)   in any closed system, randomness always tends toward a maximum.

secondary consumer   animals that obtain their food by feeding only on plant-eating animals.

secondary enrichment   a mineral concentration process in which a valuable substance is dissolved and carried to a new location where it is redeposited in a concentrated state.

secondary succession   ecological succession in an area where a community has been cleared by a disturbance (fire, flood, plow, tornado) that has not destroyed the soil.

secondary treatment   wastewater treatment, beyond the primary stage, in which bacteria consume the organic parts of the wastes. The biochemical action is accomplished by the use of trickling filters or the activated sludge process. Customarily, disinfection by chlorination is the final stage of the secondary treatment process.

sediment   any matter or mass deposited by water or wind.

sedimentary rock   rock made up of fragments of other rocks and minerals, usually deposited in water.

seed   the part of a flowering plant that contains the embryo and will develop into a new plant if sown.

seed bank   a facility in which a variety of seeds are kept under ideal conditions for the purpose of preserving genetic diversity.

seismic   of or having to do with an earthquake.

seismograph an instrument that detects and records earthquake (seismic) waves.

selective advantage a biological trait that enables an organism to survive in a particular environment better than other similar organisms.

semiconductor a material, such as silicon, whose electrical conductivity can be greatly increased by exposing it to heat, light, or voltage.

septic tank a tank in which waste matter is putrefied and decomposed through bacterial action.

severance tax a tax on the taking and use of natural resources, imposed at the time the mineral or other product is extracted or severed from the earth.

sewage the total of organic waste and wastewater generated by residential and commercial establishments.

shortage the market condition that occurs when people cannot buy the full quantity of an economic good or service they desire at the going price.

shrublands lands covered with bushy, woody plants that have several permanent stems instead of single trunks.

silt a fine-grained sediment of particle size between the clay and sand grades.

simulate to imitate; to look or act like.

slough a place of deep mud or mire. A swamp, bog, or marsh.

sludge solid organic material produced during sewage treatment.

smelting the fusing or melting of an ore in order to separate out the metal it contains.

smog a combination of fog and smoke. The term is now also applied to the photochemical haze produced by the action of sun and atmosphere on automobile and industrial exhausts.

soft technology (see appropriate technology)

soil loose weathered material at the surface of Earth, in which plants can grow.

soil conservation strategies to reduce soil erosion and to prevent depletion of soil nutrients.

soil erosion movement of topsoil and other soil components from one place to another, usually by wind and flowing water.

soil nutrients food and minerals found in soil that organisms must take in to live, grow, or reproduce. Fertilizer contains soil nutrients.

soil profile the layers in a particular sample of soil.

solar cell (see photovoltaic cell)

solar collector a device for collecting solar energy and converting it into heat.

solar energy energy from the sun that is received by Earth.

solar input the amount of solar power received by a square meter of land on a clear day when the sun is directly overhead.

solenoid a coil of wire that can carry an electric current. When current flows, a solenoid is surrounded by a magnetic field.

Solid Waste Disposal Act (1965) the first federal law to require safeguards and encourage environmentally sound methods for disposal of household, municipal, commercial, and industrial refuse.

solution mining a method of removing soluble materials from underground deposits by pumping hot water down a drill hole and recovering the salt by evaporation of the resulting brine.

solvent a medium, usually liquid, in which other substances can be dissolved.

source bed the layer of rock that was the origin of a valuable material.

species all individuals and populations of a particular kind of organism, maintained by biological mechanisms that result in their breeding only with their kind.

spillover costs the costs (or benefits) external to the actual act of production or use of a product that are passed on involuntarily to someone else.

starch a white food substance found in potatoes, cereals, and many other foods; it is a granular, solid carbohydrate.

static lifetime (T_s) an estimate of the amount of time the reserves of a resource will last, assuming both the quantity of the reserve and the use rate don't change.

steady state a balanced condition in a system because a substance (or energy) is entering and leaving at the same rate.

steel a hard, tough metal composed of iron alloyed with various small percentages of carbon; steel may be alloyed with other metals to produce specific properties.

sterilization any procedure by which an individual is made incapable of reproduction.

stockpile a reserve supply of a raw material.

storm surge a current formed when a hurricane piles up water along the shore and blows it inland.

strata layers of rock, especially layers of sedimentary rock.

strategic minerals minerals that are essential to the economic and military strength of a nation.

stratigraphic trap a trap for underground fluids that results from the orientation of the layers or strata. Stratigraphic traps occur when an upward-sloping porous layer is pinched between two nonporous layers.

stratosphere the part of Earth's atmosphere beginning at an altitude of about 7 miles (12 kilometers) and continuing to the ionosphere; it is characterized by an almost constant temperature at all altitudes.

structural trap a trap for underground fluids that is the result of the geologic structure. Anticlines, salt domes, and fault traps are all examples.

subbituminous coal a form of coal produced at pressures and temperatures greater than those that produce lignite but less than those required for bituminous coal.

subduction the process where converging lithospheric plates collide and the more dense plate moves downward and enters the mantle.

subduction zone the shear zone between a sinking oceanic plate and an overriding plate.

subsidence the act or process of sinking or settling to form a depression.

substitution to replace one resource with another. The replaced resource is usually more expensive or more scarce.

succession the gradual (and sometimes rapid) changing sequence of species that occupy a given area. This change is somewhat predictable, starting with initial colonization by pioneer organisms and ending with a climax community.

sugar a sweet, usually crystalline substance, $C_{12}H_{22}O_{11}$, extracted chiefly from sugar cane and sugar beets and used as a food and sweetening agent; also called *sucrose*.

sulfur oxides (SO$_x$) pungent, colorless gases formed primarily by the combustion of fossil fuels; considered major air pollutants. Sulfur oxides may damage the respiratory tract, as well as vegetation.

supply the amount or quantity of goods or services available for purchase at a given price.

surface mining a mining technique used when the deposits of a resource lie relatively near the surface. Overburden is stripped away, the resource removed, and overburden from an adjoining area (as it is mined) placed in the void that was formed.

surface tension a property of liquids in which the exposed surface tends to contract to the smallest possible area.

surface water water falling on the surface of Earth that runs off into lakes and streams. It stays on the surface.

sustainable able to continue indefinitely.

sustainable agriculture agriculture that maintains the quality of soil and water resources so that it can continue indefinitely. Organic farming strategies are maximized.

sustainable economics an economic system that can operate in a nongrowing environment. In a sustainable economy, both the number of people and the stock of available resources are maintained at some desired, sufficient level.

syncrude crude oil that requires some human intervention in its production rather than crude that is pumped from the ground.

synthetic fuels fuels that involve some type of human intervention (technology) to produce. Examples are oil shale, coal gasification, and tar (oil) sands.

system an orderly working totality that can be isolated within a real or imaginary boundary and studied.

system efficiency the overall efficiency of a process that occurs in a series of steps. The efficiency of a system is equal to the product of the efficiencies of the various steps in the process.

— T —

tailing the inferior or refuse material separated as residue in the milling process.

tar sands a sandy geologic deposit containing a heavy oil or tarlike fuel too thick to be pumped to the surface, but which can be mined and treated to obtain synthetic fuels. Tar sands are also called *oil sands*.

tax incentive tax cuts that either encourage people to work and spend or accomplish some action advantageous to the public.

technology applications of science that provide objects used for human sustenance and comfort. The application of scientific knowledge for practical purposes.

terrace small earthen embankments on hilly or mountainous terrain constructed to reduce the velocity of water flowing across the soil and reduce soil erosion.

terrestrial pertaining to or consisting of land, as distinguished from water.

tertiary consumer an animal that eats a secondary consumer.

tertiary treatment wastewater treatment beyond the secondary, or biological, stage that includes removal of nutrients such as phosphorus and nitrogen and a high percentage of suspended solids. Tertiary treatment, also known as *advanced waste treatment*, produces a high-quality effluent.

texture (rock) the size and arrangement of mineral grains.

texture (soil) the relative proportions of sand, silt, and clay in a soil sample. Texture can be estimated by rubbing a small, moist sample of soil between your fingers and using the information in Figures 7.5 and 7.6.

thermal inversion the situation that results when a layer of dense cool air is trapped under a layer of thinner warm air. The warm gaseous pollutants cannot rise through the warm air, so they accumulate at the boundary between these layers.

thermal mass a mass of material, such as rock or water, that can absorb solar radiation in the daytime and then radiate away heat at night. Inside a building, thermal mass tends to moderate indoor temperatures.

thermal pollution an increase in water or air temperature that disturbs the ecology of the area. Most often, thermal pollution is associated with electric generating plants, which require large amounts of cooling water to remove waste heat.

thermocline the transitional layer between warm surface waters and cold bottom waters in oceans or lakes.

thermosphere the uppermost region of Earth's atmosphere. It begins at an altitude of about 53 miles (85 kilometers) and continues about 300 miles (480 kilometers) into space. The thermosphere contains only a tiny fraction of the gases that are in the atmosphere.

thorium (Th) a naturally radioactive element with atomic number 90 and, as found in nature, an atomic weight of approximately 232. The fertile thorium-232 isotope is abundant and can be transmuted (changed) to fissionable uranium-233 by neutron irradiation.

threatened species species that are likely to become endangered within the foreseeable future.

tidal energy the kinetic energy of the ocean's tides that can be converted to electric energy.

tilth tilled land; land that has been cultivated and prepared for raising crops.

tissue a group of similar cells that perform a similar function. Examples include muscle tissue and blood tissue.

topographic map a map that represents the surface forms of an area.

total abstinence the complete (total) avoidance of sexual relations before marriage.

toxic waste waste that acts as a poison or causes cancer, birth defects, or other health problems.

transform fault a plate boundary along which two plates slide past each other.

transformer an electrical device that is used to step up or step down voltage. When voltage goes up, current goes down. When voltage goes down, current increases.

transition a passing from one condition, form, or stage, for example, to another.

transpiration the process by which moisture is carried through plants from the roots to the leaves, where it changes to vapor and escapes to the atmosphere through leaf openings.

transuranic waste waste contaminated with uranium-233 or transuranic elements (atomic numbers greater than 92) having half-lives over 20 years in concentrations of more than 1 ten-millionth of a curie per gram of waste.

trickle irrigation supplying irrigation water through tubes that drip or trickle water onto the soil at the base of each plant; also called *drip irrigation.*

trickling filter a form of secondary sewage treatment in which aerobic bacteria degrade organic materials in wastewater as it seeps through a large vat filled with crushed stones.

tritium a radioactive isotope of hydrogen with two neutrons and one proton in the nucleus. It is humanmade and is heavier than deuterium (heavy hydrogen).

tropical forest a biome with warm, relatively constant temperature where there is no frost. They receive more than 200 centimeters (80 inches) of rain per year in rains that fall almost every day.

troposphere the innermost layer of the atmosphere. It contains about 75 percent of the mass of Earth's air and extends about 11 miles (17 kilometers) above sea level.

tsunami a series of powerful ocean waves produced by an earthquake, landslide, volcanic eruption, or asteroid impact.

tundra treeless, boggy regions of both low average temperature and low average annual precipitation. There is both alpine tundra and arctic tundra.

turbine a bladed, wheel-like device that converts the kinetic energy of a gas or liquid into the mechanical energy of a rotating shaft.

— U —

unburned hydrocarbons air pollutants that come from the incomplete combustion of gasoline and from the evaporation of petroleum fuels, industrial solvents, and painting and dry cleaning activities.

underground mining the mining method used when the mineral deposit lies beneath the surface of Earth and which cannot economically be removed using surface mining methods.

undernourishment a state of poor health in which an individual is obtaining too little food.

unit train a long train of approximately 100 cars, all of which carry the same product (usually coal).

United Nations an international organization established immediately after World War II for the purpose of working for world peace, security, and the betterment of humanity.

uranium (U) a radioactive element with the atomic number 92 and, as found in ores, an average atomic weight of approximately 238. The two principal natural isotopes are uranium-235 (0.7% of natural uranium), which is fissionable, and uranium-238 (99.3% of natural uranium), which is fertile. Natural uranium also includes a minute amount of uranium-234. Uranium is the basic raw material of nuclear energy.

uranium enrichment any process in which the relative abundance of uranium-235 in a sample is increased from 0.7 percent to some higher value.

U.S. Customary System the system of measurement in common use in the United States. It is sometimes called the inch-pound system.

useful energy energy that can easily be transformed to do mechanical or electrical tasks.

— V —

value the worth of a thing in money or goods at a certain time; market price.

variable anything changeable; a thing or quantity that changes or can change.

vegetarian a person who eats no meat, and sometimes no animal products.

vein deposit a mineralized zone or belt lying within boundaries clearly separating it from neighboring rock.

vitamins organic molecules that are needed in small quantities in the diet of higher animals to perform specific biological functions.

volatile evaporating rapidly; diffusing freely into the atmosphere.

voltage a measure of the electrical force for driving an electric current.

voltmeter the instrument used for measuring difference of potential (voltage).

— W —

wastewater the collective discharges from toilets, sinks, showers, washing machines, storm sewers, and so on.

water budget a water balance. It accounts for the income, storage, and loss of water over an area.

water cycle the total process by which water is circulated through the ecosphere.

water diversion a method for increasing the supply of freshwater in a water-poor area by bringing in water from a water-rich area.

water table the top of a saturated soil zone.

watershed the area of land that delivers (drains) the water, sediment, and dissolved substances via a main stream and its tributaries to a major stream or river.

watt-hour If the potential difference across a portion of an electrical circuit is 1 volt, a current of 1 ampere flowing continuously through that portion for 1 hour will furnish 1 watt-hour of electrical energy.

weathering the natural process of breaking down rocks.

wet scrubber an antipollution device that uses a liquid spray to remove pollutants from a stream of air.

wetlands mostly semiaquatic lands that are either inundated or saturated by water for varying periods of time during the growing season.

wilderness an area where the biological community is nearly undisturbed by humans.

windbreaks rows of trees or hedges planted to partially block wind flow and hence reduce soil erosion and water loss on cultivated lands located in high-wind areas.

wind generator a generator operated by the wind's rotation of turbine blades that radiate from a shaft. Wind generators can be a cheap source of electricity if used properly.

work the transfer of energy that involves a force acting through a distance.

INDEX

Boldface page references refer to the primary discussion of the term.

— A —

Abiotic, **45**
Abstinence, 212
AC generators, 92
Acid deposition, **572**
Acidity, of soil, 259
Acid precipitation (rain), 571–574
 effects of, 577–578
 human causes of, 572
 pH testing of, 572–574
 plants and, 579
Acre-feet, of water, **508**
AC systems, 433
Active solar energy, **426–427**
Adaptation, 597–598
Aeration basis, 549
Aerosols, **598**
 sunlight reflection and, 600
Africa
 population rates in, 199
 vegetation density, 98
Ag, 135
Age, population growth by, 209
Agricultural land, 626–627
Agriculture and nutrition, 256–296.
  See also Nutrition; Soil
 ecological succession in, 256–257
 feeding the world, 286–296
 genetic engineering, 249–251
 land surface used for, 261
 machinery for, 257, 270
 major realm of, 257
 nutrition, 268–286
 plant biotechnology, 249
 soil and, 258–268
 strategy of, 256–258
Agrobacterium, 249–250
Air, 44
Air pollutants, **561**
 origins of, 562
 secondary, 565
Air pollution, 564–567
 AQI for, 567
 carbon monoxide, 564
 health-related effects of, 568
 indoor, 570–571
 nitrogen oxides, 565–566
 particulates, 566–567
 reduction strategies, 580–583
 sulfur dioxides, 566
 thermal inversion and, 568–569
 unburned hydrocarbons, 565
Air pollution reduction, 580–583
 with automobile efficiency, 580
 fuel efficiency, 581
 of smokestack emissions, 582–583

Air quality, 561–562
Air Quality Index (AQI), **567**
Air resource management, 558–602
 for air quality, 561–562
 climate change, 588–590
Air-to-heat exchangers, 458
Alkalinity, of soil, 259
Alloys, **167–168**
Alpha particles, **373**
 interactions with matter, 396
Alpine tundra, 54
Alternate current (AC) generators, 92
Alternate current (AC) systems, 433
Aluminum recycling, 696
Ambient temperature heat, 115
Anaerobic bacteria, **318**
Angiosperms, 230
Animal nutrition, 269–271. *See also*
  Human nutrition
 carbohydrates, 271
 lipids, 271
 metabolism and, 270
 minerals in, 271
 proteins, 271
 vitamins, 271
Antarctic, 487
Anthracite, **318**
Anticline traps, **310**
Appropriate technology, for energy use,
 472–476
 efficiency in, 473
 for renewable resources, 472
 worldwide applications of, 475–476
AQI, **567**
Aquatic ecosystems, **58–60**
 estuaries, 60–61
 freshwater, 58–59
 marine, 60
 pollution of, 537–538
 ponds, 539
Arab oil embargo, 479
Arachnicides, 236
Arctic tundra, 53
Arid lands, 632
Armature, **330**
Asthenosphere, 145
Astronomical units (AUs), 38
Atmosphere, **30,** 559–560
 composition of, 560
 layers of, 560
Atomic model, 369–372
 periodic table, 369–370
Atomic number, **369**
Atoms, **47,** 366–372
 atomic model, 369–372
 energy from, 368
 molecules and, 366–368
 structure of, 369
Attitude of rocks, in oil traps, **310**
Au, 135–136
 in seawater, 153

AUs, 38
Automobiles
 air pollution reduction, 580
 bumpers, 667
 ceramic engines, 581
 concept, 459
 crude oil production and, 345
 energy efficiency of, 112, 459–461
 hypercars, 461
 mineral uses in, 172–173
 prototype, 459

— B —

Bacteria, 570
Baffles, 335
Baghouse, **582**
Barrel of oil (bbl), **99**
Bartlett, Albert A., 191
Basal energy requirement (BER), 277
Basal metabolic rate (BMR), 277–278
Base metals, 169
Bbl, **99**
Benedict's solution, 284
BER, 277
Beta particles, **373**
 interactions with matter, 396
"Big Muskie," 90
Bingham Canyon Mine, Utah, 156, 164
Bioconversion, 446–448
Biodegradable waste, **641, 643**
Biodiversity, 239–248
 among Finches, 241
 importance of, 241–243
 invasive species and, 243–244
 preservation of, 245–248
 symbiosis in, 240
Biofuel cycle, 447
Biofuels, **446–448**
 biomass, 256, 446–447
 conversion processes, 446
 cycle, 447
 future applications of, 446–447
 sources of, 446
Biogeochemical cycles, 76–81
 carbon, 79–80
 mineral/nutrient, 78–79
 nitrogen, 80–81
 water, 77–78
Biogeography, of islands, 623
Biological control, **236**
Biological oxygen demand (BOD), 537
Biomagnification, **237**
 with synthetic organic compounds, 531
Biomass, 256, **446–447**
Biomes, 51–58. *See also* Terrestrial
  ecosystems
Biosolids, 551
Biospheres, **30–31,** 49
Biotechnology, for plants, 249
Biotic, **45**

APÉNDICES

La ciencia en acción (viñetas profesionales)

La ciencia en acción

Capítulo 2: Un viaje por el gran oasis

No puedes escapar de la nave espacial Tierra, pero puedes pasar tus vacaciones en áreas remotas o desconocidas. Jim Sano ayuda a aquellas personas que quieren alejarse del mundanal ruido, al menos durante unas tres semanas. Como presidente de Inner-

Cortesía de Jim Sano

Asia Expeditions, una empresa de San Francisco, California, Jim se dedica a viajes de intereses especiales. ¿Te gustaría seguir la ruta de Marco Polo a través de China? ¿Quieres investigar mariposas exóticas en Micronesia? Jim sabe cómo ayudarte a aprovechar la gran diversidad de ecosistemas mundiales.

La mayoría de los clientes de InnerAsia tiene intereses insólitos y un sentido de aventura superior al promedio de las personas. Quizá quieran explorar un lugar muy alejado, como la Patagonia, o probar los estilos culinarios de las diferentes provincias de China. Jim con frecuencia ayuda a los productores de cine a encontrar sitios inaccesibles para la filmación de las películas. También ayuda a científicos y estudiantes a viajar a lugares donde puedan observar las características únicas de estas regiones.

Planificar un viaje por estas regiones y en estas circunstancias atípicas es interesante y constituye un gran desafío. Sin embargo, los esfuerzos de Jim no siempre resultan exitosos. Por ejemplo, se planificó un viaje al Himalaya para personas que querían observar el exótico leopardo de las nieves. Las reservaciones decayeron cuando los posibles viajeros se dieron cuenta de que pasarían la mayor parte de sus vacaciones vistiendo parkas y usando

raquetas para nieve a 15,000 pies de altura, con pocas expectativas de conseguir una comida caliente y muchas menos oportunidades de ver al hermoso leopardo.

Para organizar las excursiones, Jim recibe ayuda de varios expertos. Generalmente, un operador turístico en San Francisco es responsable de toda la planificación y logística del viaje. Un acompañante, ya sea un guía turístico, naturalista, científico, profesor o cualquier otra persona con conocimiento del tema, se encarga de las necesidades educativas diarias de los viajeros en el lugar de destino. Los guías turísticos locales que viven en la zona quizá tengan poca educación formal, pero conocen el país, el clima y la cultura. También, a menudo, hay traductores disponibles.

Los viajeros que contratan las excursiones de InnerAsia reciben un extenso itinerario con instrucciones detalladas de cómo prepararse para el viaje. Una lista de lecturas con comentarios les ayuda a estudiar la geografía, las reglas de cortesía, el medio ambiente y la cultura del país que visitarán. Cuando regresan, los viajeros pueden seguir estudiando sobre el país, usando las listas como referencia.

Los estudios de posgrado de Jim Sano en el área de bioquímica no tenían mucha relación con la industria turística, pero al usar las computadoras para su educación comenzó a valorar cada vez más su utilidad para el análisis de la información y la resolución de problemas. Hoy en día, las computadoras le ayudan en todo, desde reservaciones en las líneas áreas hasta análisis de mercado. Por ejemplo, para planificar la lista de correo de anuncios comerciales, utiliza una base de datos estadística personalizada para identificar a los posibles clientes, sus intereses geográficos y sus límites de gasto. Un servicio de información médica en Internet brinda a los viajeros la información más reciente sobre temas de salud, como los requisitos de vacunación o los brotes de enfermedades actuales.

La mayor parte de la capacitación en la industria turística consiste en instrucciones convencionales para el agente de viajes, de modo que pueda manejar paquetes turísticos y reservaciones en líneas aéreas y hoteles. Sin embargo, Jim opina que hay poca capacitación formal disponible para una carrera profesional con su estilo de viajes. De todas formas, si estás interesado en aprender y enseñar sobre los habitantes, ecosistemas y geografía de la Tierra, la industria turística puede ser una opción para ti. Podrías comenzar como guía en un museo, parque temático o parque estatal. Trata de obtener experiencia manejando grupos de personas y desarrolla tu confianza y capacidades de liderazgo. Mientras Jim estaba en la universidad, trabajó como naturalista en el parque nacional Yosemite, en California, donde estaba a cargo de los programas naturalistas en Tuolumne Meadows. Ahora, con la ayuda de sus habilidades con la computadora, continúa desempeñando su papel en la educación de otras maneras.

Tarea

Investiga el potencial que existe para trabajar como agente de "ecoturismo". Resume lo que has aprendido.

La ciencia en acción

Capítulo 3: Hoy aquí, mañana también

Inglaterra, 1709. Imagina un viejo y andrajoso trapero cargando una bolsa usada y manchada llena de zapatos viejos, admirando el palacio de la reina Ana de Inglaterra. Hoy. El nieto del tataranieto del trapero se arrodilla ante la reina Isabel II, quien lo toca en cada hombro con su espada ceremonial y solemnemente le dice: "Te nombro Sir Reciclador".

Bill Cohen ha visto como el negocio de recuperación de objetos adquiere nueva

Cortesía de Bill Cohen

dignidad. Los comerciantes "ropavejeros" de ayer son las superestrellas de hoy. Bill conoce la importancia del reciclaje, ya que es dueño y gerente de ABC Recycling Industries, Inc., en Santa Clara, California. Su compañía es una de tantas en los Estados Unidos que trabajan para conservar los recursos del mundo y reducir la contaminación producida por la industria manufacturera. Además, con esto se gana la vida.

Las empresas como las de Bill Cohen colectan o compran diversos materiales desechados, los separan y embalan y los envían a empresas para que vuelvan a ser utilizados. Por ejemplo, veamos el caso del aluminio. ABC vuelve a embalar latas, ollas y utensilios de cocina, piezas de automóviles y aeronaves, puertas mosquiteras y otros objetos de aluminio que han sido desechados, de acuerdo con las especificaciones de empresas, tales como Alcoa. Funden y vuelven a moldear estos materiales, a veces como aluminio puro y otras veces combinados con otros metales para obtener aleaciones. En este viaje de recuperación, ABC también envía otros materiales: cables de cobre, planchas de metal, paneles solares, perillas y llaves de bronce, lavabos y tuberías de acero inoxidable, cinc y plomo. Todo se puede recuperar y reformar. También se pueden reciclar botellas de vidrio, jarras de plástico, periódicos, cartones y papel. Éstos y muchos materiales más son retirados de la corriente de desperdicios en la empresa de Bill y utilizados para nuevos productos o como combustible.

Bill madruga la mayoría de los días y disfruta de su participación activa en el negocio. Luego de revisar el peso de la recolección del día anterior y los precios actuales que se ofrecen para esos artículos, sale a supervisar los trabajos de embalaje y embarque. El diez por ciento de los proveedores de ABC son empresas que reciclan desperdicios industriales. El 90 por ciento son "personas comunes", como grupos de niños exploradores, organizaciones comunitarias, familias que recolectan sus propios materiales reciclables y vagabundos con carritos de compra llenos de objetos que han encontrado en callejones y lotes baldíos. Generalmente Bill paga en efectivo por la "basura" que recibe.

Bill comenzó con el negocio del reciclaje en Canadá. Su padre fue un pionero del reciclaje. Con un camión, ofrecía "servicio a domicilio" para las personas que querían librarse de las cosas que ya no usaban. Bill trabajó en el negocio de reciclaje de un vecino donde aprendió el oficio desde cero. Luego, inició su propia empresa con un camión, al igual que lo hizo su padre.

Bill cree que su esmero, perseverancia y curiosidad innata por la ciencia le han ayudado a estudiar los métodos y el aspecto económico del reciclaje. Asiste a seminarios y exposiciones comerciales para mantenerse actualizado sobre los avances en la industria y los usos de materiales reciclados. Un tipo de información que necesita conocer para satisfacer las necesidades de sus clientes es las propiedades físicas de los metales y demás minerales. Por ejemplo, una empresa puede solicitar materiales que sean muy dúctiles (capaces de ser estirados) para hacer cables. Otra puede necesitar materiales que conduzcan la electricidad con facilidad. Otra más puede combinar diferentes materiales para crear una nueva aleación con propiedades específicas. Cuánto más conozca Bill sobre las propiedades de los materiales que recicla, mejor es el servicio que puede ofrecer a estas empresas. También le ayuda a decidir si los materiales deben ser separados.

Bill dice que el reciclaje es un campo con igualdad de oportunidades, y que necesita la participación de más personas que deseen disminuir la contaminación, conservar los recursos de la Tierra, ayudar a producir productos útiles y eficientes y generar empleos. Sugiere comenzar con programas gubernamentales de reciclaje como una manera de iniciar esta tarea.

Tarea

Haz una lista del tipo de información que un reciclador exitoso necesita conocer. Marca (3) aquella información para la cual se necesita conocimiento de ciencias.

Capítulo 5: Información, por favor. . .

Cortesía de Nenet Magpayo

En su trabajo en la oficina regional de la Oficina del Censo de EE.UU. ubicada en Los Ángeles, Nenet Magpayo sabe cuán valiosa es la información para el esfuerzo que realiza nuestro país con el objetivo de comprender a la población. Esta información no sólo consiste en el número de personas, sino que también incluye información sobre la distribución de viviendas, el uso de servicios públicos y transporte, la educación y mucho más. Cada persona o familia que Nenet entrevista ha sido cuidadosamente seleccionada para representar a miles de personas más de todo el país. Ella y otros agentes de campo de las 13 oficinas regionales en los Estados Unidos recopilan la información. Los especialistas en estadística de la oficina central interpretan los datos y prevén los patrones futuros.

Por ejemplo, el cálculo más reciente de la oficina sobre la población para el año 2020 es que California tendrá entre 50 y 53 millones de habitantes. Esto representa el 15 por ciento de la población estadounidense prevista. (Esto depende de lo que suceda económicamente en el estado y en otros lugares.) Gracias a la información que obtienen Nenet y otros agentes de campo, sabemos mucho más sobre el flujo de la población de nuestra nación. Contamos con datos concretos, como por ejemplo, qué proporción de la población es inmigrante y que proporción nació en el país. También tenemos una idea sobre la cantidad de personas que buscan nuevos horizontes en otros estados. Con estos datos, los expertos pueden calcular los recursos que necesitaremos.

Nenet se quedó en la oficina de Los Ángeles como empleada de tiempo parcial después de haber participado del censo de 1990. Ahora, además de su trabajo de encuestas, supervisa a otros agentes de campo. También recluta entrevistadores para las encuestas. En los últimos años, además de trabajar para la Oficina del Censo, Nenet ha recopilado distintos tipos de datos para otras agencias gubernamentales y para algunas organizaciones privadas. Ha investigado los hábitos de consumo de las personas para la preparación del Índice de Precios al Consumidor. Ha realizado encuestas sobre empleo para la Oficina de Trabajo de EE.UU. Ha hablado con las personas sobre el SIDA y otros temas para el Centro de Estadísticas sobre la Salud del Instituto Nacional de Salud. También ha entrevistado a victimas de delitos para los estudios mensuales que realiza el Departamento de Justicia. Por ley, la identidad de las personas entrevistadas es confidencial.

Nenet recopila la información tanto personalmente como por teléfono. A veces, una encuesta a una familia o a una persona puede durar hasta cinco horas, dependiendo de las preguntas. Por lo tanto, aunque trabaja con datos fríos y precisos, Nenet utiliza una estrategia mucho más personal para realizar las entrevistas. Debe ser persistente pero amigable y amable; necesita que las personas estén tranquilas. Por ende, ha aprendido a ser una excelente comunicadora.

Nenet realiza el seguimiento de aproximadamente 40 casos semanales, algunos durante los fines de semana, cuando las personas que trabajan tienen más tiempo para hablar con ella. Además, Nenet asiste a muchas reuniones y envía miles de cartas a posibles encuestados. También ayuda a otros agentes a prepararse para las entrevistas.

Nenet cuenta con habilidades especiales que le ayudan con su trabajo. Se capacitó en el uso de una computadora portátil con programas personalizados. Esto le ayuda a registrar, organizar y resumir los datos de las entrevistas, que luego envía por medio de un módem. Nenet también habla varios idiomas, lo que le ha sido de mucha utilidad para su trabajo en la Oficina del Censo. Antes de viajar a los Estados Unidos, trabajó como ingeniera electrónica en Filipinas. Por lo tanto, además de su idioma nativo, tagalo, también habla inglés y español.

El último censo sobre población y vivienda se realizó en el año 2000 y Nenet también trabajó en él. Quienes trabajaron con ella eran ciudadanos estadounidenses de 18 años de edad como mínimo y con diploma de la escuela secundaria o el diploma equivalente de educación general (GED, por sus siglas en inglés). Nenet comenta que fue un gran trabajo para los estudiantes universitarios, padres de niños pequeños y otras personas que necesitaban un trabajo de tiempo parcial que les brindara algún tipo de seguro y otros beneficios.

Preguntas

¿Es la realización de censos sólo un trabajo de tiempo parcial? ¿Puede el análisis de los datos de censos convertirse en un trabajo de tiempo completo?

La ciencia en acción

Capítulo 7: Comer bien y con sabiduría

Los comensales de los restaurantes modernos suelen ser sofisticados y conscientes de la importancia de la salud, ya sea que puedan gastar mucho o no tanto. En particular, esperan comer alimentos de países del Mediterráneo. Mientras que algunos quieren finalizar una comida con elaborados postres de estilo vienés, otros insisten en comenzar con vinos de bodegas californianas poco conocidas. Nathan Peterson trata de satisfacer a todos ellos.

Cortesía de Nathan Peterson

Alguna vez, Nathan quiso ser florista. Mientras creaba y entregaba los arreglos florales para ocasiones especiales, conoció a las personas encargadas del servicio de comidas. Como a Nathan le encantaba cocinar, comenzó a trabajar con ellos y hoy es el chef de Bay Wolf, uno de los restaurantes más concurridos del área este de la bahía de San Francisco.

Nathan no se convirtió en chef de la noche a la mañana. Cuando decidió dedicarse a esa profesión, un pariente mayor lo ayudó y le pagó su matrícula en una afamada academia culinaria. Durante unos 16 meses de intensa actividad, Nathan estudió cocina, repostería y los demás aspectos necesarios para ser un chef y administrar un restaurante. Cuando finalizó sus estudios, consiguió un empleo de bajo salario en un restaurante de la zona de la bahía, donde adquirió la experiencia práctica para complementar su capacitación formal. Al poco tiempo, comenzó a trabajar en el Bay Wolf.

En el Bay Wolf, la carta para la cena cambia todos los meses para ofrecer platillos apropiados para la época del año. Por ejemplo, una cena de verano puede comenzar con una sopa fría de tomate, llamada gazpacho, de España. En invierno, puede encontrarse en las mesas un guiso caliente de la región de Provenza, Francia.

Durante todo el año, los almuerzos representan los alimentos y estaciones de California. En los días fríos de noviembre, cuando entrevistamos a Nathan, uno de los platos principales eran las croquetas de cangrejo, ya que era el comienzo de la temporada local de pesca de cangrejo, con una salsa hecha de limones Meyer (un cítrico local), ensalada de col (de la cosecha invernal de col morada y verde de California) con un ligero aderezo a la vinagreta, y unas rodajas finas de papas asadas. Otros platos principales también representaban de forma similar las distintas temporadas y los alimentos disponibles en la zona. Los canelones rellenos de queso de cabra y calabaza también habrían deleitado a los vegetarianos.

El uso de alimentos de temporada no sólo es bueno para atraer a los clientes, sino que también ofrece la ventaja de utilizar los recursos locales. Las verduras y frutas que se transportan grandes distancias y luego se almacenan en depósitos tienen poco sabor y pueden perder parte de su valor nutritivo. También es nocivo el efecto que esto tiene en el medio ambiente, ya que se debe utilizar mucha energía para transportar estos alimentos desde otras partes del país o del mundo.

Tanto Nathan como sus clientes se preocupan por el medio ambiente y por eso él trata de comprar alimentos orgánicos cuando es posible. Sin embargo, como persona práctica, debe controlar los costos para el restaurante y los clientes, y a veces utiliza alimentos no orgánicos convencionales. Por ejemplo, compra pollos de granja, pero sabe que no puede asegurar que la carne de res esté libre de antibióticos y hormonas. Al hacer ciertas concesiones, puede brindar deliciosas comidas *gourmet* que son las más saludables y accesibles posibles.

Las dietas de moda van y vienen, pero la nutrición básica casi no cambia. Las comidas de Nathan incluyen cantidades moderadas de proteínas y carbohidratos, más una pequeña cantidad de aceite o grasa. El pescado está siempre disponible y la mayoría de las comidas incluyen hierbas y verduras que les dan más valor nutritivo y sabor. Nathan se esfuerza por complacer a los clientes que tienen dietas especiales.

Los postres suelen ser más "pecaminosos", pero el menú de postres generalmente incluye uno de frutas que aporta pocas calorías. Por supuesto, se destacan las frutas frescas de estación.

El aspecto creativo es lo que llevó a Nathan a este trabajo y es lo que aún más disfruta. Las comidas que se sirven en el Bay Wolf son apetecibles tanto a la vista como al paladar. Cuando le preguntaron qué le disgustaba de ser un chef, Nathan dijo que era una profesión muy exigente y en ocasiones dolorosa, ya que los continuos movimientos repetitivos (levantar, batir y picar) son actividades que tensan las articulaciones del hombro y el brazo. De hecho, piensa que la fuerza de las extremidades superiores puede ser uno de los principales requisitos para ser un chef.

El trabajo diario de Nathan varía bastante, de cuatro a 16 horas, según la temporada y el calendario mensual del restaurante. Una vez al mes, debe planificar el menú del mes, probar las recetas y capacitar a los cocineros para que preparen todo como él lo desea. Se deben imprimir los menús y avisar a los proveedores de alimentos qué deberán proveer. En las vacaciones de invierno, el restaurante tiene mucha actividad por las personas que ofrecen fiestas, pero los platillos deben ser tan buenos como en la época de baja temporada.

Aunque Nathan tuvo la fortuna de recibir una educación culinaria formal (lo que puede resultar muy costoso), hace hincapié en que cualquiera que desee ser un chef puede obtener la experiencia necesaria de manera más gradual y a menor costo, si comienza a trabajar en un puesto de principiante en un buen restaurante. De hecho, Nathan siente que su propia educación realmente comenzó cuando tuvo la oportunidad de trabajar para Michael Wild, famoso chef y dueño del Bay Wolf, y para otros excelentes chefs.

Tarea

Realiza un plan profesional para convertirte en chef. Incluye un cronograma, un análisis de costos y la ciencia de la nutrición. Resume lo que has aprendido.

Capítulo 8: En la búsqueda de la energía del mañana

En 1952, el famoso geólogo petrolero, Wallace Pratt, dijo: "A final de cuentas, es en la mente de los hombres donde primero se encuentra el petróleo". Pratt pensaba que la gente que realiza exploraciones en busca de petróleo lo seguirá encontrando mientras crea que queda petróleo por encontrar. Jason Cansler, un científico especializado en la geología petrolera sabe que "antes de encontrar petróleo, se necesitan datos que demuestren que existe".

Cortesía de Jason Cansler

Jason trabaja en la Unidad Comercial del Valle de San Joaquín (SJVBU, por sus siglas en inglés) de ChevronTexaco, con sede central en Bakersfield, California. La SJVBU constituye una de las operaciones de explotación más importantes de Chevron-Texaco, con cuatro yacimientos petrolíferos principales que producen cerca de 250,000 barriles de petróleo por día. El equipo de científicos e ingenieros de Jason trabaja en un conjunto de depósitos de arenisca de un yacimiento petrolífero a una profundidad de entre 7,500 y 11,000 pies, que contiene alrededor de 20 pozos en un área de 3 millas cuadradas. Aquí se ha obtenido petróleo y gas durante casi 100 años.

Desde un punto de vista geológico, este yacimiento ubicado en la región central de California presenta grandes desafíos para Jason y su equipo. En primer lugar, deben localizar el petróleo y gas que queda y luego encontrar la manera de mejorar su *permeabilidad* (la facilidad con la que fluyen los líquidos a través de las rocas). Este yacimiento en particular contiene rocas de muy baja *porosidad* (el porcentaje de poros petrolíferos) y, por lo tanto, tiene menos "conectividad" entre poros. Ello significa que contiene menos petróleo y que

éste es más difícil de extraer. La tarea de los ingenieros es encontrar la manera de mejorar la permeabilidad mediante perforaciones y la fractura hidráulica del yacimiento para conectar los poros petrolíferos. Esto se denomina "completar y estimular" el pozo. Las numerosas fallas que alteran la elevación del yacimiento y modifican su característica física a través de las distintas capas de la tierra constituyen otro desafío. La geometría de estas fallas tiene un impacto considerable en la manera como se maneja el pozo.

Jason apoya a su equipo con sus conocimientos de geología. Recopila, analiza e interpreta una serie de datos geológicos sobre el yacimiento, como muestras de roca y registros del pozo. Luego, elabora un mapa de las características subterráneas del área y construye modelos geológicos tridimensionales. Un aspecto clave de su trabajo es calcular la cantidad de petróleo y gas atrapados en el yacimiento y determinar cuánto queda por extraer, identificar las áreas en las que los pozos existentes pueden volver a producir o dónde pueden perforarse nuevos pozos. Una vez que los objetivos son identificados, el equipo diseña pozos que penetran la tierra de manera segura y eficiente. Jason utiliza en su trabajo una amplia variedad de bases de datos, software y sistemas operativos, desde programas básicos de oficina, como Excel y PowerPoint, hasta software complejo de mapas y modelado geológico. Los datos que utiliza se obtienen de imágenes sísmicas y con diversas técnicas de laboratorio para la medición y análisis de rocas (microscopios electrónicos, difracción de rayos X, identificación de fósiles y otras).

Jason pasa alrededor del 20 por ciento de su tiempo en el campo, donde selecciona los emplazamientos de los pozos, trabaja con perforadores y demás técnicos en la identificación de riesgos geológicos y evalúa las muestras de roca y datos de los registros del pozo mientras que se realiza la perforación. En la oficina, después de que se han perforado los pozos, se continúa con el estudio de las rocas y el afloramiento rocoso y se evalúan los pozos con herramientas eléctricas y nucleares. La mayoría de los días, Jason trabaja conjuntamente con otros miembros del equipo (ingenieros especialistas en yacimientos, perforación, producción e instalaciones; gerentes de proyecto; operadores de yacimientos petrolíferos y diversos técnicos en ingeniería y geología). En conjunto, interpretan y evalúan toda la información que constituye la base del éxito del equipo: la extracción de más petróleo de un emplazamiento desarrollado. En 2003, el equipo de Jason en la SJVBU perforó y completó lo que resultó ser uno de los pozos de mayor producción en California en la época.

Después de obtener una licenciatura en Geología en la Universidad Estatal de Kansas, los estudios de posgrado de Jason en esa universidad incluyeron una pasantía en las oficinas de Chevron Texaco en Bakersfield. Su modelo geológico por computadora de un yacimiento de petróleo denso en el Valle de San Joaquín sigue utilizándose en la actualidad. Jason dice que los estudiantes que se preparan para trabajar en su campo profesional estudian geofísica, geología estructural, geomecánica, estratigrafía, sedimentología, geoquímica y geoestadística. Su capacitación continua ha incluido temas como la economía del petróleo, ingeniería de yacimientos y análisis de decisiones. Viaja varias veces al año dentro de los Estados Unidos y a otros países para capacitación, seminarios, selección de personal y otras reuniones.

En el pasado, los exploradores de petróleo enfrentaban enormes desafíos en su búsqueda del oro negro. Sin contar con la avanzada tecnología actual, dependían en gran medida en sus observaciones de la superficie terrestre para calcular los mejores emplazamientos en los que realizarían perforaciones para extraer petróleo. Pero aprendieron de su trabajo y desarrollaron gradualmente la ciencia, los equipos y las herramientas que les facilitaran el descubrimiento de recursos adicionales. Para Jason Cansler, es un desafío personal seguir trabajando con espíritu creativo e innovador a fin de mejorar la tecnología para la búsqueda de la energía del mañana.

Tarea

Selecciona un campo de empleo mencionado en esta viñeta. Determina la naturaleza del trabajo y el tipo de capacitación necesaria.

La ciencia en acción

Capítulo 9: Eficiencia energética: un puente al futuro

En lo alto de una colina en Berkeley, California, se encuentra el Laboratorio Nacional Lawrence Berkeley (LBNL, por sus siglas en inglés). Mientras conduce por el sinuoso camino hacia su trabajo cotidiano, Lynn Price disfruta de los paisajes imponentes

Cortesía de Lynn Price

de la región de la bahía de San Francisco. A veces, la niebla dificulta la visibilidad por encima de las copas de los árboles, pero en un buen día el aire por lo general está despejado y claro. En todo el mundo, el aire limpio se ve amenazado todos los días por las emisiones industriales, y Lynn trabaja en proyectos diseñados para mitigar los efectos perjudiciales de una de las principales fuentes de dichas emisiones: el consumo ineficiente de energía.

El laboratorio Lawrence Berkeley es administrado por la Universidad de California para el Departamento de Energía de los EE.UU. En el Departamento de Análisis de Energía, Lynn es subdirectora del Grupo de Estudios Internacionales sobre Energía. Es una de los numerosos científicos del LBNL que estudia los cambios climáticos relacionados con el consumo de recursos de energía no renovables. El departamento de Lynn forma parte de una unidad más amplia, denominada División de Tecnologías Energéticas Ambientales (EETD, por sus siglas en inglés). Ella y sus colegas tratan de buscar maneras de disminuir las emisiones y el consumo de energía en diversas industrias, como siderúrgicas, fábricas de cemento, plantas de procesamiento de papel y pulpa de papel, productores de sustancias químicas, plantas de montaje de automóviles e incluso vinicultores y cervecerías. Estas industrias, ubicadas en los Estados Unidos y en el extranjero, son los usuarios de las tecnologías y procesos analizados por Lynn y sus colegas.

Algunas industrias causan más daños al medio ambiente terrestre, debido a que utilizan principalmente combustibles de fuentes no renovables y liberan, en consecuencia, más emisiones y productos derivados. Estas industrias de gran consumo de energía son más costosas en cuanto al daño que ocasionan al medio ambiente, ya que transforman materias primas en productos tales como sustancias químicas, acero, papel y cemento, y las numerosas etapas de producción consumen grandes cantidades de combustible. Los análisis realizados por el equipo de Lynn contribuyen a que estas industrias conviertan, almacenen y utilicen la energía de manera más eficiente y con menor impacto en el medio ambiente.

Una de las prioridades principales del EETD es la mayor eficiencia energética de estas industrias. Lynn y sus colegas elaboran informes que analizan las tendencias y el consumo de energía y las emisiones ambientales asociadas. Estudian las tecnologías industriales que puedan disminuir el consumo de energía. Contribuyen al trabajo de las autoridades responsables de la formulación de políticas

que tratan de buscar una solución a los problemas del consumo de energía de las industrias. También diseñan herramientas y modelos que ayudan a las industrias a medir la utilización de energía y sus efectos en el aire y suelo. Por ejemplo, una hoja de cálculo que han desarrollado facilita la creación de puntos de referencia para evaluar el consumo energético de una planta siderúrgica y ofrece opciones para aumentar la eficiencia de la planta. Esta herramienta también puede adaptarse y utilizarse en otras industrias, por ejemplo, en una empresa vinicultora o en una planta de montaje de automóviles. Otras herramientas diseñadas por Lynn y sus colegas ayudan a las industrias a medir y reducir las emisiones de gases que producen el efecto invernadero. Estos modelos se emplean en muchos países en vías de desarrollo.

Los aspectos internacionales del trabajo de Lynn lo hacen muy apasionante. A menudo colabora con representantes de industrias, autoridades responsables de la formulación de políticas, expertos en cambios climáticos e investigadores de países europeos y asiáticos. China, por ejemplo, que es el mayor productor de cemento y acero del mundo, cuenta con instalaciones ineficientes y anticuadas, pero tiene una gran oportunidad de mejorarlas gracias al rápido crecimiento económico del país.

Un día típico de Lynn comienza muy temprano. En su casa, revisa el correo electrónico de clientes y socios de Europa y de la región este de los Estados Unidos. Luego, pasa la mayor parte de su día de trabajo en su oficina de LBNL, donde asiste a reuniones y elabora informes. Realiza muchas tareas de investigación, trabaja con hojas de cálculo en su computadora y utiliza varios recursos del campus cercano de la Universidad de California. Con frecuencia habla, a menudo a través de un intérprete, con visitantes internacionales acerca de su trabajo sobre cambio climático y energía. A la noche, sigue trabajando en la computadora de su casa, donde lee más correo electrónico, esta vez los mensajes recibidos de Asia y otras partes del hemisferio oriental. Su trabajo también implica viajar mucho por los Estados Unidos y a países de todo el mundo.

Lynn estudió en la Universidad de Wisconsin en Madison y obtuvo una licenciatura en Geografía. Realizó su maestría en ciencias del medio ambiente. Después de la universidad, obtuvo capacitación adicional en su especialidad al trabajar como consultora y luego se unió al LBNL. Lynn afirma que su capacitación en el trabajo es permanente y que siempre se fija nuevas metas.

Considera al trabajo en eficiencia energética como un componente de gran importancia en el puente a una energía renovable y más limpia. Afirma que "cada día nos acercamos más a la meta. La energía eólica ya es rentable. Cada vez más negocios utilizan energía ecológica, como las células fotovoltaicas". Cree que los argumentos de la predicción de Hubbert sobre el agotamiento de las reservas de crudo del mundo son menos importantes que el reconocimiento de que estos recursos son finitos y perjudiciales para el medio ambiente, y que en consecuencia se deben usar de forma más eficiente. "La eficiencia energética es un paso esencial para reducir nuestra dependencia de los combustibles fósiles".

Preguntas

1. ¿Cuáles son algunas de las ventajas de la eficiencia energética en cuanto a la disminución de la contaminación del aire?

2. ¿Por qué es posible que un país en vías de desarrollo tienda a utilizar métodos ineficientes de uso de la energía?

La ciencia en acción

Capítulo 10: El uso de energía nuclear en la medicina

¿Alguna vez te sacaron una radiografía? Tal vez sí, o quizás conozcas a alguien a quien se la hicieron. Las radiografías se utilizan para mostrar imágenes de los huesos y de otros tejidos duros. Hay nuevos métodos que también muestran los tejidos blandos. Por ejemplo, las imágenes por resonancia magnética (IRM) se utilizan para explorar el cerebro y otros tejidos blandos. La IRM no es un proceso nuclear y no expone a los pacientes a la radiación ionizante.

En la actualidad, la medicina nuclear es otra forma de examinar los órganos. Utiliza radioisótopos (materiales radiactivos) para mostrar las funciones de los órganos, por ejemplo, el flujo sanguíneo o el índice metabólico, más que las estructuras.

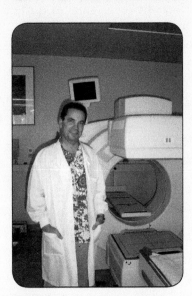

Cortesía de Emil Germanov

Emil Germanov es tecnólogo en medicina nuclear en el hospital Alameda, un hospital comunitario en el norte de California. Su especialidad es uno de los beneficios de la energía nuclear. En la actualidad, se utilizan aproximadamente 100 procedimientos nucleares en distintas especialidades médicas, que abarcan la cardiología, psiquiatría y pediatría, entre otras. Los exámenes cardíacos representan entre un 40 y un 50 por ciento de los procedimientos, y los exámenes relacionados con el cáncer, otro 35 a 40 por ciento.

Los resultados de las técnicas de la medicina nuclear pueden combinarse con las radiografías tradicionales y los exámenes de diagnóstico por IRM para brindar a los médicos un panorama completo de la anatomía y fisiología de cualquier órgano, a la vez que el paciente está expuesto a una dosis mínima de radiación sin necesidad de cirugía, anestesia ni costosas pruebas de laboratorio. A menudo, la medicina nuclear permite identificar una enfermedad en las primeras etapas, cuando una intervención médica puede lograr mejores resultados que si la enfermedad fuera descubierta con posterioridad.

Emil realiza la mayor parte de su trabajo con una cámara gamma. La cámara se encuentra suspendida sobre una gran cama donde el paciente se acuesta tranquilamente durante el procedimiento. En algunas situaciones, por ejemplo, cuando se examina la glándula tiroides u otra área pequeña, Emil utiliza una pequeña sonda conectada a una computadora, en vez de una cámara gamma de grandes dimensiones.

El primer paso para obtener una imagen es inyectar al paciente un radiofármaco, es decir, un radioisótopo que es atraído por un órgano en particular. Se utilizan tecnecio (Tc99) y otros radioisótopos que emiten rayos gamma. Emil espera a que el radiofármaco llegue al órgano y luego enciende la cámara. La cámara registra los rayos gamma que el órgano emite y luego transmite señales eléctricas a una computadora cercana. Una vez en la computadora, las señales son traducidas a un código numérico y luego convertidas en imágenes digitales que Emil y los médicos observan en la pantalla.

Estas excepcionales imágenes aparecen a todo color y se mueven. Una imagen puede mostrar la sangre que pasa por un corazón que está latiendo, las señales eléctricas que viajan por el cerebro o la orina que acumula en los riñones, junto con datos sobre esas funciones. Incluso, las imágenes se pueden ver como objetos tridimensionales que pueden moverse en cualquier dirección para estudiarlas. Generalmente, a fin de confirmar un diagnóstico, un médico necesita examinar una parte específica de un órgano. Las imágenes y los datos que se obtienen de una cámara gamma son de gran utilidad para dicho fin.

A Emil le gusta saber que en su trabajo no hay "días típicos". La mayoría de los pacientes que él atiende no están internados. Sus médicos los envían para realizarse estudios de diagnóstico en las primeras etapas de la enfermedad. Un niño con un dolor óseo puede ser remitido para un estudio. La sala de urgencias puede llamar a Emil de inmediato porque una señora mayor ingresa de emergencia y los paramédicos que la traen creen que puede haber sufrido una apoplejía. O bien, un hombre que se recupera de una amputación necesita un estudio para que su médico pueda ver si se recuperó la circulación sanguínea normal en esa área. Los riñones de otro paciente parecen haber dejado de funcionar.

En todos estos casos, la cámara gamma brinda información útil. Lo importante para Emil es que siente que ha podido ayudar a cada uno de estos pacientes y a sus médicos.

Algunas universidades ofrecen grados de licenciatura con especialización en tecnología médica nuclear. Debido a que es un campo relativamente nuevo, las personas pueden ingresar con diferente formación, por ejemplo, en tecnología médica o enfermería. Cualquiera sea su educación previa, deben recibir capacitación especial y una certificación, por lo general de una junta estatal. En http://www.snm.org/nuclear encontrarás enlaces a sitios educativos relacionados.

Emil estudió ciencias físicas y se convirtió en ingeniero mecánico. A él le gustaba el aspecto de resolución de problemas de la ingeniería pero deseaba trabajar con personas. Gracias a la capacitación adicional en tecnología nuclear, puede hacer ambas cosas.

Preguntas

1. El tecnecio 99 se produce para uso médico mediante el bombardeo del molibdeno 98 con neutrones. Escribe una ecuación equilibrada que muestre esa reacción.

2. ¿Por qué una educación formal en ingeniería puede ser una buena formación para este campo de la medicina?

3. ¿Existen hospitales cerca de tu casa que utilicen técnicas de medicina nuclear? Haz una lista de ellos.

Capítulo 11: El aprovechamiento del viento

En el año 1997, David Blecker se encontraba en Alaska trabajando en asuntos relacionados con la energía y los indígenas y esquimales de Alaska. Le asombró la ironía de que ellos tuvieran que comprar el combustible que se obtenía del petróleo que se extraía de su propia tierra y se transportaba por un oleoducto a un centro de procesamiento a cientos de millas de distancia. Le interesó buscar un método más creativo y menos destructivo para la producción y uso de la energía. Para David, la respuesta fue fundar Seventh Generation Energy Systems (SGES) en Belleville, Wisconsin.

Cortesía de David Blecker

Desde entonces, SGES ha trabajado con gobiernos, comunidades, escuelas y tribus en la planificación, diseño e instalación de sistemas de energía solares y eólicos (unos 10 por año) en diferentes estados. Entre sus clientes está una familia propietaria de un aserradero y una granja avícola en Wisconsin, así como la tribu Omaha de Nebraska. En el oeste de Dakota del Sur, una gran estación de radio de la nación Sioux se alimenta con energía de uno de los sistemas de SGES.

El trabajo con los nativos americanos ha cambiado la forma de trabajo de David. Tal ha sido el efecto, que el nombre de su organización proviene de una creencia de los nativos americanos que dice que debemos tener en cuenta el efecto que nuestras acciones tendrán en el mundo "dentro de siete generaciones". Está decidido a honrar los derechos de los indígenas y cree que cada proyecto debería incluir un programa de servicios a la comunidad y educación. "Quiero emplear un enfoque sistémico en la construcción de los sistemas de energía, más que simplemente vender los sistemas."

SGES es un grupo sin fines de lucro, por lo que sus proyectos son financiados por agencias federales, como el Departamento de Energía de los Estados Unidos y la Agencia para la Protección del Medio Ambiente, agencias estatales, programas energéticos, fundaciones y en ocasiones por donativos privados. La Administración para los Nativos Americanos, una rama del Departamento de Salud y Servicios Humanos de los Estados Unidos, también ha subsidiado proyectos.

David realiza todo el trabajo inicial, es decir, investigación, análisis, planificación, gestión de la participación y educación del cliente, evaluación del lugar, tramitación de permisos y muchas otras tareas, hasta que comienza la construcción. Luego, contrata obreros calificados para la construcción. A veces, utiliza la mano de obra provista por el cliente. Por ejemplo, en el proyecto de la nación Omaha, trabajó con los nativos americanos del lugar que habían sido capacitados en un taller de SGES en el Colegio Comunitario Indígena de Nebraska.

Todo sistema eólico, ya sea un pequeño sistema residencial (menos de 20 kilovatios) o un gran sistema comercial (de 1.5 megavatios), comienza con la investigación. Para un sistema doméstico, David estudia los mapas que existen sobre los recursos eólicos y la topografía del lugar. Tiene en cuenta las necesidades de energía de los usuarios y sus propias observaciones sobre los patrones del viento en el lugar. Para un sistema de mayores dimensiones, estudia hojas de cálculo con información detallada de una torre meteorológica que registra la velocidad y la dirección del viento a distintas alturas.

Como todo ingeniero profesional matriculado, David utiliza las matemáticas y el análisis estadístico para interpretar la información recopilada. Utiliza las habilidades de planificación de proyectos y de comunicación para establecer las metas del proyecto y trabajar con los usuarios del sistema y las empresas locales de servicios públicos. Luego sigue la evaluación del lugar, la planificación de la infraestructura y el análisis económico. Tiene en cuenta factores como el tamaño y elevación de la parcela del terreno, la vegetación que afecta el viento, la distancia a las líneas de alta tensión, los recursos silvestres y ambientales sensibles y las leyes de zonificación. Por último, comienza el trabajo en el lugar. Esto comprende la excavación, el montaje de las torres y las turbinas, el tendido de los cables de alta tensión, las tareas de cableado y de sistemas electrónicos y la meticulosa prueba del sistema. SGES sólo utiliza turbinas eólicas horizontales.

Los sistemas eólicos necesitan mantenimiento dos veces por año. David o un obrero contratado deben subir a la torre y verificar la estructura, conexiones, piezas móviles y distintos componentes de seguridad y control. La mayoría de los sistemas duran aproximadamente 20 años.

Los sistemas eólicos de Seventh Generation no requieren baterías costosas (ni tóxicas) para almacenar la energía generada. En un sistema doméstico, el generador produce una corriente alterna "descontrolada" ya que la frecuencia y el voltaje cambian continuamente con la velocidad del viento. Esta energía luego se convierte en una corriente alterna de 120 V o 240 V que se acopla a la red de energía local después del medidor del cliente. Cuando el sistema produce más energía que la necesaria, la empresa de energía eléctrica acumula un crédito para cuando la demanda del usuario sea mayor. En un sistema comercial más grande, el sistema electrónico de control y transmisión permite que la energía generada fluya directamente hacia la red de energía para la venta a las empresas de energía locales o para mercados más alejados.

Debido a que puede tener varios proyectos en diferentes etapas, las tareas diarias de David varían mucho. Aproximadamente la mitad del tiempo lo dedica al desarrollo de lo

que él llama política energética "sana". Por ejemplo, trabaja con las empresas de energía y organismos reguladores para promover el incremento en el uso de energía renovable. Ha desarrollado nuevos modelos de planificación de suministro de energía con el respaldo del Departamento de Energía de los Estados Unidos (DOE, por sus siglas en inglés), que han sido utilizados para identificar alternativas de menor costo e impacto que las líneas de alta tensión.

David comenzó trabajando en submarinos nucleares para la Armada de los Estados Unidos y en sistemas de energía para submarinos para la empresa General Electric. Luego, estudió ingeniería eléctrica y obtuvo una licenciatura en el Instituto Politécnico Rensselaer de Nueva York. En la actualidad, continúa su trabajo de posgrado en la Universidad de Wisconsin en Madison. Su mensaje para los estudiantes es "perseverar" cuando las cosas se ponen difíciles: las matemáticas y la ciencia son importantes. Sus conocimientos en esas áreas le han dado la oportunidad de trabajar en hermosos lugares, con nuevas y apasionantes tecnologías y con personas de gran dedicación.

David tiene el firme compromiso de enseñar a las personas sobre la energía sostenible. "No digamos energía 'alternativa'. Ya tenemos opciones limpias, económicas y confiables; entonces, tengamos la voluntad de hacerlo. Cada una de las turbinas eólicas que colocamos es prueba de que sí funciona y que podemos hacerlo ahora."

Preguntas

1. ¿Por qué una turbina eólica podría ser una buena opción para suministrar energía en distintos lugares de una gran granja o rancho?

2. Si existe energía de combustibles fósiles disponible a bajo costo, ¿hay alguna necesidad de sistemas de energía alternativos solares o eólicos? ¿Por qué? ¿Por qué no?

Capítulo 12: Diseño para el futuro

Nicki Kwee recorre las calles de París en su Ford Ka plateado, un vehículo atractivo que también posee el tamaño pequeño y el ahorro de combustible exigidos en Europa. Nicki, sin embargo, aprecia el diseño de su automóvil más que la mayoría de los conductores porque es diseñador de automóviles.

Cortesía de Nicki Kwee

Nicki nació en los Países Bajos y sigue siendo ciudadano holandés. Durante su niñez vivió en California y luego se inscribió en el Centro de Estudios Creativos en Detroit para aprender diseño industrial. Después de la universidad, comenzó a trabajar para Ford en Alemania. Ahora lo hace para Renault en Francia.

Un diseñador de automóviles es sólo uno de los integrantes del equipo que desarrolla un nuevo automóvil. El proceso lleva alrededor de tres años. Comienza con un plan general que incorpora los deseos de los clientes, la disponibilidad de materiales adecuados y el énfasis del fabricante en el ahorro de combustible. En las primeras etapas, Nicki puede pasar muchas horas en reuniones con otros diseñadores e ingenieros para planificar el nuevo automóvil. Los ingenieros especifican los componentes del motor, otras piezas debajo del capó, la suspensión y el chasis. Los diseñadores son los responsables de proponer un diseño del exterior e interior que luzca bien e incorpore las especificaciones técnicas de los ingenieros, lo cual puede llevar a desacuerdos sobre cómo lograr las metas de la compañía para el automóvil. A menudo, por ejemplo, una propuesta de diseño se considera demasiado costosa y se elige una alternativa más barata. El líder de proyecto toma las decisiones finales después de analizar las opciones.

Al comienzo de un proyecto, los diseñadores se ocupan de la fase creativa de la investigación y la elaboración de planos. Llevan a cabo varias presentaciones a la dirección hasta que se eligen unos cuantos temas de diseño para ser desarrollados en forma de modelo CAD (diseño asistido por computadora) o modelo físico. Durante las siguientes semanas, se trabaja con CAD o con un equipo de dos a cinco modeladores de arcilla. Los modelos de arcilla, realizados en un amplio taller, pueden ser a una escala de un quinto a tamaño completo.

A medida que los modelos evolucionan, se llevan a cabo más presentaciones a los directores de la compañía y, finalmente, se elige un diseño para la producción. Durante todo el proceso, los diseñadores e ingenieros trabajan juntos para garantizar que los diseños sean viables y cumplan con los objetivos establecidos por los planificadores del producto. Cerca de la finalización de un proyecto, hay una serie de reuniones con ingenieros y proveedores, que para Nicki resulta ser el aspecto menos agradable de su trabajo.

Nicki colabora con alrededor de 10 diseñadores más en una oficina abierta, en la que también trabaja un equipo de apoyo de operadores de CAD, asistentes técnicos, una secretaria y directores. No existe un día típico en el trabajo de Nicki. Todo depende de la cantidad y estado de los proyectos del equipo.

La capacitación de Nicki en arte y escultura le permite dibujar esbozos al comienzo y trabajar con los modeladores en etapas posteriores del proyecto. Si bien se utiliza cada vez más el software de diseño asistido por computadora (CAD) para simplificar algunas tareas, los diseñadores aún deben tener capacitación en los principios del arte y del diseño.

Las exigencias estrictas de ahorro de combustible afectan el diseño. Debido a que la forma afecta la aerodinámica del automóvil, lo que a su vez determinará la cantidad de energía necesaria para moverlo, la forma general es extremadamente importante. Si bien una forma alargada como un pez sería la preferida, los ingenieros exigen diseños de automóviles que puedan utilizar motores diesel de buen rendimiento. Estos automóviles son, por lo general, más grandes, pesados y requieren más refrigeración. Otro aspecto importante involucra la "organización" del automóvil, que determina su tamaño y la ubicación de las piezas, el conductor, los pasajeros y el equipaje. En Europa, los diseñadores buscan que los automóviles sean compactos en el exterior pero muy amplios en el interior. Esto reduce el peso, lo que también se logra con el uso de aluminio o materiales compuestos en vez de acero para algunas piezas.

El futuro del diseño de automóviles dependerá de los tipos de automóviles que la gente busque. En la actualidad, la gente tiende a comprar automóviles que reflejen su propia imagen. Sobre todo en los Estados Unidos, es posible que un comprador elija un automóvil grande con bajo rendimiento del combustible por razones psicológicas. Esta actitud se puede convertir en un lujo si el suministro de petróleo del mundo disminuye, y es posible que el tipo de automóvil solicitado cambie de manera drástica.

Los fabricantes intentan elaborar planes para un futuro incierto. Algunas empresas están desarrollando modelos de automóviles que funcionan con combustibles alternativos, como gas natural comprimido, propano y etanol. En noviembre de 2003, Spencer Abraham, Secretario del Departamento de Energía (DOE, por sus siglas en inglés) de los EE.UU. dio a conocer una guía para introducir células de combustible de hidrógeno en los vehículos estadounidenses, lo que comprometía a los Estados Unidos a utilizar un sistema de transporte basado en el hidrógeno. Al mismo tiempo, se están produciendo algunos automóviles y camiones eléctricos y otros híbridos, que utilizan gasolina y electricidad. Nadie sabe realmente cómo serán los automóviles del futuro. No importa lo que suceda, Nicki y otros diseñadores deberán idear combinaciones correctas de atractivo y funcionalidad.

Preguntas

1. ¿Cómo afectaría una forma alta y cuadrada al rendimiento de combustible de un vehículo?

2. ¿Por qué los europeos exigen mayor ahorro de combustible en sus automóviles que los estadounidenses?

La ciencia en acción

Capítulo 15: Predicción de climas futuros

¿Se convertirán las granjas de Iowa en desiertos? ¿Cubrirán los océanos la Florida y otras áreas bajas? ¿Deberán cerrar los centros de esquí por falta de nieve? Caspar Ammann intenta encontrar las respuestas a preguntas como éstas, relacionadas con el clima. Como climatólogo del Centro Nacional de Investigación Atmosférica (NCAR, por sus siglas en inglés) de Boulder, Colorado, genera modelos por

Cortesía de Caspar Ammann

computadora de climas e interpreta los resultados.

Caspar se centra en la variabilidad natural del clima. El período que estudia puede abarcar siglos o milenios recientes, o bien puede ir millones de años atrás, durante los cuales han existido la humanidad, todas las civilizaciones humanas y las grandes glaciaciones continentales. Su meta principal es comprender cómo era el clima en esas épocas, cómo cambió y qué factores pudieron haber generado esas fluctuaciones. Las variaciones climáticas a menudo dependen de la cantidad de radiación solar que llega a la Tierra, ya sea por cambios en el Sol o las variaciones en la órbita del planeta. Caspar y sus colegas observan estos cambios en la energía solar media y su distribución durante el ciclo anual y en las diferentes regiones de la Tierra. También estudian el impacto de las erupciones volcánicas sobre el clima. Algunas erupciones fueron eventos explosivos muy grandes, después de los cuales los seres humanos registraron brumas extrañas en el cielo. Tales observaciones a menudo pueden encontrarse en los registros históricos de pérdidas de cosechas, pestilencia y otros efectos.

Los modelos por computadora representan el sistema climático de la forma más completa posible. Estos modelos, que contienen como componentes una atmósfera, un océano, hielo marino y la superficie terrestre, son impulsados por la radiación solar que llega al planeta durante las horas correspondientes al día. Cada 15 ó 20 minutos, el sistema resuelve ecuaciones que describen cómo se transmite la radiación solar a través de la atmósfera, cómo se absorbe en el aire o la tierra y cómo es reflejada por las nubes o la superficie. Luego, el modelo muestra cómo el calor actúa en los pasos del ciclo del agua (evaporación, convección, formación de nubes, lluvia, nieve, etc.). Los nuevos modelos incluso pueden "hacer crecer" vegetación, simular ríos con su escorrentía estacional y representar sistemas biogeoquímicos complejos, como el ciclo del carbono.

Los modelos, por definición, se pueden ejecutar de manera que representen cualquier período en el pasado o futuro. Para mostrar el pasado, Caspar tiene que asegurarse de que proporciona al modelo condiciones límite realistas, tales como la distribución de los continentes, composición atmosférica y vegetación. Para interpretar los resultados y validar sus conclusiones, puede colaborar con la gente que estudia los efectos climáticos en los anillos de los árboles, los sedimentos oceánicos o los núcleos del hielo, o con otros grupos de modelado.

Como no se sabe con exactitud cuál será la futura composición atmosférica, por lo general los modelos se realizan para 100 a 300 años en el futuro en diferentes situaciones. Mientras que los climatólogos observan los cambios absolutos para determinar cuán diferente será el clima, las diferentes respuestas a las situaciones también despiertan un gran interés práctico entre los políticos y otras personas. El modelo puede ofrecer pistas sobre cuán útiles son las reducciones de emisiones o los combustibles más limpios para evitar que el clima salga de control.

A pesar de que los modelos climáticos no son perfectos, son el único medio para reproducir los efectos de los procesos entre los subsistemas y dentro de ellos. En fechas recientes, estos modelos climáticos han demostrado ser sorprendentemente buenos para explicar la variabilidad en el sistema climático. Pueden comenzar a explicar fenómenos como El Niño y los cambios en el trayecto de las tormentas. En la actualidad, los modelos se usan cada vez más para las predicciones climáticas de largo alcance (alrededor de seis meses), de gran utilidad sobre todo para los agricultores.

Además, los modelos reproducen los climas naturales del pasado de manera extraordinaria. Sin embargo, para el siglo XX, la imagen de los climas naturales creada por los modelos sólo coincide con los registros reales hasta alrededor de 1950. Solamente cuando los modelos incluyen los gases del efecto invernadero y los aerosoles hechos por el hombre, reproducen el calentamiento rápido de los últimos 30 años. Esto parece apoyar la hipótesis de que los gases del efecto invernadero ya han contribuido al calentamiento que sin lugar a dudas está ocurriendo.

El Grupo de Paleoclimatología en el que trabaja Caspar consta de cuatro científicos y un puñado de científicos asociados. Por lo general trabajan en experimentos y períodos diferentes, pero se reúnen con regularidad para comparar observaciones. A veces, el grupo concurre a charlas formales o seminarios, o recibe a científicos visitantes de otros centros de investigación. Caspar viaja alrededor de una vez por mes. Debe colaborar con mucha gente.

Caspar creció en Suiza y obtuvo una maestría en Geografía y Geología. Su educación fue muy amplia, con mucho énfasis en el pensamiento interdisciplinario e integrador. Realizó un doctorado en el Departamento de Geociencias de la Universidad de Massachusetts. Los cursos que estudió incluyeron todo tipo de cursos relacionados con el clima, algo de estadística y otros cursos de interés.

Preguntas

1. ¿Por qué las aseguradoras se interesan por el cambio climático?

2. Haz una lista de profesiones que se relacionan con los estudios del cambio climático. ¿Qué aptitudes se necesitan para cada profesión?

La ciencia en acción

Capítulo 16: El desafío del compromiso

Independientemente de cuál sea tu opinión del mundo, salvar el futuro de la Tierra y a su gente requerirá de un compromiso, y ésa es la vocación de Diane Henderson, fundadora de DMH Land Use Planning, en San Rafael, California. La meta de Diane, quien trabaja con urbanistas, promotores inmobiliarios y otros profesionales, al igual que con propietarios de tierras, es fomentar la cooperación al planificar la urbanización de una comunidad. Ya sea un proyecto grande o pequeño, Diane ayuda a planificar un crecimiento que tenga el menor efecto negativo en los ciudadanos y el medio ambiente de una comunidad. Este trabajo también tiene un aspecto personal para ella. Además de ser su fuente de ingresos, a menudo tiene la oportunidad de supervisar proyectos de urbanización en la zona donde vive.

Cortesía de Diane Henderson

Diane disfruta especialmente de la variedad de su trabajo. Los métodos y técnicas de construcción cambian en forma constante y ella se complace con el fuerte movimiento hacia lo sustentable. En su condado natal de Marin existe cada vez más énfasis en el desarrollo ecológico, el reciclaje y la eficiencia en el uso de la energía. Una nueva tendencia interesante es la construcción con pacas de "paja",

los residuos agrícolas después de cosechar trigo, centeno, cebada, arroz y otros granos. No se cortan árboles, se consume menos energía para construir la casa y la paja es de dos a cuatro veces más aislante que los materiales tradicionales para las paredes. Diane también ha notado mucho interés por la recuperación y el reprocesamiento de materiales, tales como madera y pizarra de estructuras demolidas, que son reutilizados en nuevas estructuras.

El trabajo independiente significa que el papel de Diane es diferente en cada proyecto. La planificación asume muchas formas. Por ejemplo, formó parte de un equipo especial que guiaba un gran proyecto de desarrollo de negocios minoristas, de manera que los cambios estuvieran de acuerdo con los requisitos de todas las personas involucradas: propietarios de negocios, gobierno municipal y ecologistas. En la ciudad de Salinas, California, se incorporó a un equipo de planificación que se amplió en forma temporal para administrar un proyecto de urbanización de alta prioridad. Ocupó el cargo de directora de planificación de la ciudad hasta que se contrató a un nuevo director permanente. Los escenarios de su trabajo comprenden una amplia gama, desde la atención en mostradores del departamento de planificación hasta emplazamientos de construcción específicos, e incluso un barco en la bahía de San Francisco, desde el cual puede inspeccionar los desarrollos urbanos a lo largo de la costa.

Proyectos diversos implican tareas diversas. Como planificadora, debe comprender el proceso de revisión en una ciudad o condado determinado. A menudo, escribe o colabora en la redacción de informes para los consejos de planificación. Además de los funcionarios del gobierno local, trabaja con muchos otros profesionales, como planificadores de transporte, arquitectos, ingenieros, abogados y, por supuesto, los ciudadanos de la región. Para evitar que el desarrollo urbano perjudique el medio ambiente, sugiere cambios en el servicio de autobuses, la instalación de soportes para bicicletas, etc. A veces, su tarea es responder preguntas de la gente que visita un departamento de planificación en búsqueda de información. Una gran parte de su trabajo es la comunicación y la negociación.

La variedad también se ve reflejada en las necesidades de la gente que Diane atiende y es justo allí donde aflora el concepto del compromiso. Ella desea lograr el mejor resultado posible para todas las personas involucradas. Elige a sus clientes con mucho muy cuidado y rechazaría un trabajo si las personas a cargo no desean tener en cuenta cuestiones ambientales o las necesidades de la comunidad. "Los urbanizadores a menudo necesitan ser guiados hacia lo correcto", afirma Diane. Sin embargo, su énfasis siempre es el fomento de la coop-

eración. En todos los proyectos de utilización de la tierra, es importante que se revisen los cambios para considerar su impacto sobre los vecinos. Esto se aplica tanto a un propietario individual que realiza cambios en una casa y sus tierras, como al promotor del desarrollo de un centro comercial grande que se encuentra cerca de otros negocios, casas y parques.

Diane tiene una licenciatura en Planificación y Administración Ambiental. Esta área de especialización y otras parecidas requieren estudios de arquitectura, diseño, ingeniería, cartografía, diversas ciencias, sociología y psicología, herramientas que contribuyen a la habilidad de Diane para la planificación y la comunicación. Tomó cursos adicionales de educación continua de la Universidad de California y de la Asociación Estadounidense de Planificación. También hay carreras paraprofesionales relacionadas con este campo, como técnicos en planificación, con diplomas de dos años.

Diane afirma que es crucial que "mantengamos un equilibrio entre el crecimiento y la protección del medio ambiente natural". El crecimiento y sus problemas resultan inevitables para nuestro planeta, de manera que debemos "asegurar el futuro a la vez que se preserva el pasado" a medida que buscamos las soluciones para salvar al planeta Tierra.

Pregunta

¿Para quién puede trabajar un consultor de planificación del uso de la tierra? Haz una lista de varias posibilidades.

La ciencia en acción

Capítulo 17: Autosuficiente y sostenible

En los 4,500 acres del suroeste de Kansas, Reeve Agri Energy no se parece en nada a la tradicional granja familiar que alguna vez fue. La empresa es un complejo y redituable ecosistema que conserva más de un recurso no

renovable de la Tierra y emplea a alrededor de 30 a 35 personas y a varios miembros de la familia Reeve.

Los combustibles oxigenados son importantes para las necesidades energéticas de los

Estados Unidos en este momento en el que el petróleo es más escaso, más caro y contribuye demasiado a la contaminación. El etanol, la misma forma de alcohol presente en la cerveza y el whisky, se mezcla con la gasolina para obtener el combustible para automotores con una combustión más limpia y de mayor octanaje conocido como "extra sin plomo" o "súper sin plomo". Cada año, la familia Reeve produce 9.2 millones de galones de etanol. El proceso comienza con maíz, melaza y otros materiales con alto contenido de azúcares y almidón, y con agua que se obtiene del acuífero Ogallala, que subyace gran parte de la región central de los Estados Unidos. La planta utiliza muchas herramientas de ahorro de energía, como sistemas de intercambio térmico y electricidad de generadores de gas natural.

Cortesía de Lee Reeve

Pero el etanol sólo es una parte de la historia. Un derivado de la producción de etanol se utiliza para alimentar al ganado de los Reeve. La vinaza que se obtiene luego de enfriar, tamizar y extraer el agua posee una gran concentración de proteínas. El almidón que se utiliza para la producción del etanol se reemplaza con maíz, alfalfa y sorgo milo, y se agregan algunos minerales y vitaminas. Con esta masa mejorada se alimentan las 21,000 cabezas de ganado que se crían en el rancho. Es importante mantenerla húmeda, ya que secar el producto consumiría tanta energía como la necesaria para producir el etanol.

En una etapa posterior del ecosistema se encuentra el estiércol del ganado, que se utiliza para fertilizar la tierra de cultivo de los alrededores. El agua caliente que queda de la planta de etanol se enfría y se utiliza para criar la tilapia blanca, un pez de aguas calientes de sabor suave. Esta misma agua, rica en nutrientes luego de albergar los peces, es devuelta a la tierra en forma de riego.

Muchas de las ramas de la ciencia ayudan en las tareas de los Reeve. Un destacado grupo de personas aportan su talento y conocimiento, entre ellas granjeros, veterinarios, microbiólogos, nutricionistas, abogados, contadores y quienes administran la planta de etanol, y Lee Reeve debe comunicarse con todos ellos. Comprende a diario el valor de lo que significa entender las ideas científicas. Cuando la familia incorporó la cría de peces a su negocio, aprendió mucho sobre biología y ecología, y se alegró de los buenos conocimientos científicos iniciales que le brindaron los libros de texto de la escuela secundaria. Lee tiene una licenciatura en Economía Agrícola de la Universidad Estatal de Kansas. También valora la enseñanza de las universidades técnicas y remarca la importancia de la capacitación en el lugar de trabajo como, por ejemplo, los programas de aprendizaje.

Los críticos del etanol dicen que cuesta demasiado producirlo y que el dinero de nuestros impuestos no debería gastarse en su producción. Pero no hay duda de que el etanol es un combustible más limpio que el petróleo y que los suministros de éste están disminuyendo. Según Lee, los críticos deberían recordar la primera y segunda leyes de la termodinámica. No podemos crear energía nueva, pero podemos aprovechar su transformación de un estado a otro.

Reeve Agri Energy es un excelente ejemplo de desarrollo económico que aporta tanto empleos como productos en un entorno que no daña el medio ambiente ni derrocha energía. Lee desea ver que otras industrias evolucionen y se respalden entre sí, tal como lo ha hecho su negocio familiar. "El primer requisito para lograr el éxito es descubrir qué sucede en la naturaleza y tratar de copiarlo, no combatirlo."

Tarea

Haz una lista de posibles trabajos en el área de las operaciones de una granja sostenible.

Representación gráfica de datos

Cómo realizar tablas de datos

Muchas veces los datos que se obtienen en el laboratorio se recopilan en una tabla. Una tabla puede ser una tabla simple de dos columnas y varias filas, como el ejemplo de la Tabla 1, o una más compleja.

Distancia (m)	Tiempo (s)
0.0	0
2.5	1
5.0	2
7.5	3
10.0	4

Tabla 1: Una tabla de distancia (en metros) contra tiempo (en segundos) para un automóvil de juguete con pilas.

Observa que la Tabla 1 indica claramente tanto las cantidades medidas como las unidades. También observa que los datos se registran en forma de decimales y no de fracciones.

A menudo, es difícil saber cómo se relacionan los datos con sólo mirar los datos en una tabla. Por esta razón, los científicos utilizan gráficas para mostrar visualmente cómo se relacionan los datos.

Cómo elegir los ejes de una gráfica y nombrarlos

Muchos de los experimentos que realizarás constarán de dos o más variables que cambian al mismo tiempo. Muchas veces los científicos tratan de controlar un experimento de manera que sólo dos variables cambien al mismo tiempo. Esto les permite registrar los datos, trazar gráficas y buscar las relaciones.

Cuando existen dos variables, la persona que realiza la representación gráfica denomina una de ellas variable *independiente*, y la otra, variable

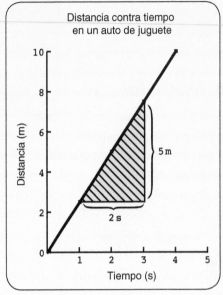

▲ Figura 1 Gráfica de la información suministrada en la Tabla 1.

dependiente. Por ejemplo, en la Tabla 1, el tiempo es la variable independiente y la distancia, la variable dependiente, ya que la distancia que se recorre desde un punto de inicio depende de la cantidad de tiempo.

Por acuerdo la variable independiente se traza a lo largo del eje horizontal, o eje x, y la variable dependiente se traza a lo largo del eje vertical, o eje y. El título de la gráfica, que debe escribirse cerca de la parte superior de la misma, debe enunciar la variable dependiente contra la variable independiente. Observa el ejemplo que se presenta en la Figura 1.

Cómo elegir la escala

Luego de determinar qué variable se representará en cada eje, el siguiente paso es elegir una escala que ocupe *de manera fácil* la mayor parte de la gráfica. De manera fácil significa que las divisiones de la escala deben ser múltiplos de 1, 2, 4, 5, 10, etc. En la Figura 1, las divisiones de la distancia son múltiplos de 2. Las divisiones del tiempo son múltiplos de 1.

Cómo rotular los ejes

Después de que se nombran los ejes y se eligen las escalas, los números de la escala se deben anotar a lo largo de los ejes (ver Figura 1). Utiliza sólo la cantidad de números necesarios. Demasiados números crean confusión. Luego, redacta con palabras lo que se está representando en forma gráfica. Por último, coloca junto a la palabra, entre paréntesis, el símbolo de la unidad que se utiliza (ver Figura 1).

Cómo marcar los puntos

Los puntos que deben marcarse se encuentran en la tabla. Localiza cada par de datos (de la tabla) en la gráfica y marca un punto. Haz esto hasta que todos los puntos estén marcados.

Cómo dibujar la curva

El tipo de curva que se dibujará depende de lo que se esté representando. Si los puntos están bastante alineados, se puede utilizar una regla para unirlos mediante una línea recta, aun cuando no todos los puntos se ubiquen exactamente sobre la línea. Esto sucede porque los errores experimentales, es decir, los errores que se cometen cuando se realizan mediciones, pueden hacer que los puntos queden un poco fuera de la línea. Si durante un experimento las cosas cambian con uniformidad, a veces se puede dibujar una curva suave que una o se ubique cerca de los puntos marcados. Irás mejorando estas decisiones y el trazado de las líneas y curvas de una gráfica a medida que adquieras experiencia en el laboratorio.

Cómo encontrar la pendiente de una gráfica lineal

Se puede determinar la pendiente de la línea si la gráfica es una línea recta. Esto se hace marcando dos puntos de la línea. Estos puntos no necesitan ser los puntos marcados a partir de los datos. Deben ser puntos fáciles de utilizar. Desde el punto superior, traza una línea vertical recta hacia abajo. Desde el punto inferior, traza una línea horizontal hacia la derecha hasta que toque la línea vertical. Debes haber formado un triángulo (ver Figura 1). Utiliza la escala de la gráfica para determinar la longitud del lado vertical del triángulo. Utiliza también la escala de la gráfica para determinar la longitud del lado horizontal del triángulo (ver la Figura 1 como ejemplo). Por definición, la pendiente es la longitud vertical dividida entre la longitud horizontal. A la pendiente se le asigna el símbolo m.

Por lo tanto, $m = \dfrac{\Delta y}{\Delta x} = \dfrac{\text{distancia vertical}}{\text{distancia horizontal}}$

dónde Δ es un símbolo que significa *el cambio en*. Para la tabla 1,

$$m = \frac{\Delta \text{ distancia}}{\Delta \text{ tiempo}} = \frac{5 \text{ m}}{2 \text{ s}} = 2.5 \text{ m/s}$$

Algunas veces, la pendiente tiene un significado físico. En el caso de la Tabla 1, 2.5 m/s es la velocidad del automóvil de juguete.

APÉNDICE 3

Notación científica

Al estudiar ciencias, con frecuencia se encuentran números muy grandes y números muy pequeños. Por ejemplo, la incidencia total de energía del Sol en la parte superior de la atmósfera de la Tierra es de 173,000,000,000,000,000 vatios. Sería difícil manejar estos números si no tuviéramos un método especial. La notación científica es este método. Recuérdalo bien. Los problemas que parecen casi imposibles de resolver se tornan relativamente simples con la notación científica.

Lo que necesitas saber sobre la notación científica se resume en cuatro conceptos:

1. *Un sistema para escribir múltiplos de 10.* A continuación se presenta una lista parcial de las potencias de 10:

$$10^0 = 1$$

$$10^1 = 10$$

$$10^2 = 10 \times 10 = 100$$

$$10^3 = 10^2 \times 10 = 1,000$$

$$10^4 = 10 \times 10 \times 10 \times 10 = 10,000$$

$$10^{-1} = \frac{1}{10} = 0.1$$

$$10^{-2} = \frac{1}{10^2} = \frac{1}{100} = 0.01$$

$$10^{-3} = \frac{1}{10^3} = \frac{1}{1,000} = 0.001$$

2. *Una forma de escribir cualquier número que comprenda potencias de 10.* Cualquier número puede escribirse como el producto de un número entre 1 y 10 y un número que sea una potencia de 10.

Ej.

$$769 = 7.69 \times 10^2$$

$$5,200,000 = 5.2 \times 10^6$$

$$0.124 = 1.24 \times 10^{-1}$$

$$0.0000003 = 3 \times 10^{-7}$$

3. *Un sistema para multiplicar números.* En la multiplicación, los exponentes de igual base se suman.

$$10^2 \times 10^3 = 10^{2+3} = 10^5$$

$$10 \times 10 = 10^{1+1} = 10^2$$

$$(4 \times 10^4)(2 \times 10^{-6})$$

$$= 8 \times 10^{4-6} = 8 \times 10^{-2}$$

4. *Un sistema para dividir números.* En la división, los exponentes de igual base se restan.

$$\frac{10^2}{10^5} = 10^{2-5} = 10^{-3}$$

$$\frac{8 \times 10^2}{2 \times 10^{-6}} = \frac{8}{2} \times 10^{2+6} = 4 \times 10^8$$

Luego de aprender estos cuatro conceptos, practica la notación científica resolviendo estos problemas.

Problemas

1. Expresa los siguientes números en notación científica:

   a. 720

   b. 32,600

   c. 1,006

   d. 59,000,000

   e. 0.831

   f. 0.02

2. Resuelve las siguientes operaciones y expresa los resultados en notación científica:

   a. $1,700 \times 340$

   b. $220 \times 35,000$

   c. $40/20,000$

   d. $61,900/0.48$

   e. $\dfrac{3.17 \times 7,230}{0.000289} =$

   f. $\dfrac{(16,000)(0.0003)(2.4)}{(2,000)(0.007)(0.00051)} =$

Respuestas

Ten en cuenta que las respuestas a todos los cálculos de este texto nunca tienen más de tres dígitos.

1. 7.2×10^2, 3.26×10^4, 1.006×10^3, 5.9×10^7, 8.31×10^{-1}, 2×10^{-2}.

2. 5.78×10^5, 7.7×10^6, 2×10^{-3}, 1.29×10^5, 7.93×10^7, 1.61×10^3.

APÉNDICE 4

Prefijos de las unidades del Sistema Internacional (SI)

Prefijo	Abreviatura	Factor por el cual se multiplica la unidad
exa	E	10^{18}
peta	P	10^{15}
tera	T	10^{12}
giga	G	10^{9}
mega	M	10^{6}
kilo	k	10^{3}
hecto	h	10^{2}
centi	c	10^{-2}
milli	m	10^{-3}
micro	μ	10^{-6}
nano	n	10^{-9}
pico	p	10^{-12}
femto	f	10^{-15}
atto	a	10^{-18}

1 mil $= 10^3$ 1 mil millones $= 10^9$ 1 mil billones $= 10^{15}$

1 millón $= 10^6$ 1 billón $= 10^{12}$ 1 trillón $= 10^{18}$

APÉNDICE 5

Unidades del Sistema Internacional (SI)

Los nombres, símbolos y factores de conversión de las unidades del Sistema Internacional que se utilizan en este texto son los siguientes:

Cantidad	Nombre de la unidad	Símbolo	Factor de conversión
Distancia	metro	m	1 km = 0.621 millas 1 m = 3.28 ft 1 cm = 0.394 in 1 mm = 0.039 in $1 \mu m = 3.9 \times 10^{-5}$ in $= 10^4$ Å (ver abajo) 1 nm = 10 Å
Masa	kilogramo	kg	1 tonelada métrica = 1.102 toneladas (EE.UU.) 1 kg = 2.20 lb 1 gm = 0.0022 lb = 0.035 oz 1 mg $= 2.20 \times 10^{-6}$ lb $= 3.5 \times 10^{-5}$ oz
Tiempo	segundo	s	1 año $= 3.156 \times 10^7$ s 1 día $= 8.64 \times 10^4$ s 1 h = 3,600 s
Temperatura	kelvin	K	273°K = 0°C = 32°F 373°K = 100°C = 212°F
Superficie	metro cuadrado	m²	1 m² $= 10^4$ cm² $= 10.8$ ft²
Volumen	metro cúbico	m³	1 m³ $= 10^6$ cm³ $= 35$ ft³
Frecuencia	hertz	Hz	1 Hz = 1 ciclo/s 1 kHz = 1,000 ciclos/s 1 MHz $= 10^6$ ciclos/s
Densidad	kilogramo por metro cúbico	kg/m³	1 kg/m³ = 0.001 gm/cm³ 1 gm/cm³ = densidad del agua
Velocidad	metro por segundo	m/s	1 m/s = 3.28 ft/s 1 km/s = 2240 mi/h
Fuerza	newton	N	1 N $= 10^5$ dinas $= 0.224$ lbf
Presión	newton por metro cuadrado	N/m²	1 N/m² $= 1.45 \times 10^{-4}$ lb/in²
Energía	julio	J	1 J = 0.239 calorías
Energía fotónica	electronvoltio	eV	1 eV $= 1.60 \times 10^{-19}$ J; 1 J $= 10^7$ erg
Potencia	vatio	W	1 W = 1 J/s
Masa atómica	unidad de masa atómica	uma	1 uma $= 1.66 \times 10^{-27}$ kg

Unidades habituales utilizadas con las unidades del Sistema Internacional:

Cantidad	Nombre de la unidad	Símbolo	Factor de conversión
Longitud de onda de la luz	ångström	Å	$1\ \text{Å} = 0.1\ \text{nm} = 10^{-10}\ \text{m}$
Aceleración de la gravedad	g	g	$1\ g = 9.8\ \text{m/s}^2$

APÉNDICE 6

Factores de conversión de uso frecuente (relacionados con la energía y los recursos)

Peso

1 tonelada corta	contiene	2,000 libras
1 tonelada métrica	contiene	1.102 toneladas cortas
1 tonelada larga	contiene	1.120 toneladas cortas

Factores de conversión para el petróleo crudo (a gravedad media)

1 barril	contiene	42 galones
1 barril	pesa	0.136 toneladas métricas (0.150 toneladas cortas)
1 tonelada métrica	contiene	7.33 barriles
1 tonelada corta	contiene	6.65 barriles

Factores de conversión para el uranio

1 tonelada corta (U_3O_8)	contiene	0.769 toneladas métricas
1 tonelada corta (UF_6)	contiene	0.613 toneladas métricas
1 tonelada métrica (UF_6)	contiene	0.676 toneladas métricas

Factores de conversión para la energía

1 caloría $= 3.968 \times 10^{-3}$ BTU $= 4.184$ julios

1 kilocaloría $= 1,000$ calorías $= 1$ Caloría alimenticia

1 BTU $= 252.0$ calorías $= 772$ ft · lb $= 1,055$ julios

1 pie · libra $= 1.285 \times 10^{-3}$ BTU $= 0.3239$ cal

1 julio $= 0.2389$ cal $= 0.7376$ ft · lb

1 tonelada de TNT $= 1.04 \times 10^9$ cal $= 4.14 \times 10^6$ BTU

1 barril de petróleo $= 5.8 \times 10^6$ BTU

1 kilovatio · hora $= 3,413$ BTU $= 860,000$ cal $= 1,000$ vatio · hora

1 termia $= 100,000$ BTU

Unidades de energía muy grandes

1 exajulio (EJ) $= 10^{18}$ julios

1 quad $= 10^{15}$ BTU

1 quad (Q) $= 1.06$ exajulios (EJ)

Factores de conversión relacionados con el combustible

1 kilovatio-hora	3,413 BTU
1 tonelada corta de carbón	25,000,000 BTU
1 barril de petróleo crudo	5,800,000 BTU
1 galón de gasolina	125,000 BTU
1 galón de fuel-oil núm. 2	140,000 BTU
1 pie cúbico de gas natural	1,031 BTU
1 termia de gas (u otro combustible)	100,000 BTU
1 cuerda de leña	20,000,000 BTU

1 gramo fisionable de U-235 = 74,000,000 BTU

1,000 kWh = 0.123 toneladas métricas de carbón (valor de calefacción).

1 tonelada métrica de turba = 0.3 a 0.45 toneladas métricas de antracita o carbón bituminoso

Carbón (por tonelada de 2,000 libras)

Antracita	$= 25.4 \times 10^6$ BTU
Bituminoso	$= 26.2 \times 10^6$ BTU
Subbituminoso	$= 19.0 \times 10^6$ BTU
Lignito	$= 13.4 \times 10^6$ BTU

Requerido para generar 1 kWh de electricidad

1 kilovatio · hora = 0.88 lbs de carbón
$= 0.076$ galones de petróleo
$= 10.4$ pies cuadrados de gas natural

Temperatura

$°F = \frac{9}{5}°C + 32$

$°C = \frac{5}{9} (°F - 32)$

APÉNDICE 7

Tabla de factores de conversión de energía

En la siguiente tabla se resume la relación entre varias unidades de energía comunes. El uso de esta tabla puede ayudar a resolver problemas que requieren la conversión de una unidad a otra.

Unidad	BTU	Ft·lb	julio	cal	kWh
1 unidad térmica británica (BTU, por sus siglas en inglés) =	1	778	1,055	252	2.93×10^{-4}
1 pie·libra =	1.29×10^{-3}	1	1.356	0.324	3.77×10^{-7}
1 julio =	9.48×10^{-4}	0.738	1	0.239	2.78×10^{-7}
1 caloría =	3.97×10^{-3}	3.09	4.19	1	1.16×10^{-6}
1 kilovatio·hora =	3,413	2.66×10^6	3.6×10^6	8.6×10^5	1

APÉNDICE 8

Información útil relacionada con instalaciones de producción de energía*

Dimensiones comparativas

Mina grande de carbón	10–20,000 toneladas/día
Planta grande de generación eléctrica	500–1,000 megavatios
Planta grande de gasificación de carbón	500×10^6 ft^3/día
Planta grande de esquisto petróleo	100,000 barriles/día
Refinería típica de petróleo	50,000 barriles/día

*Todas estas operaciones tienen aproximadamente la misma producción de energía por día, y tienen casi el mismo costo de construcción, es decir, de 1 a 2 mil millones de dólares.

APÉNDICE 9

Mapas de placas tectónicas

A. Mapa de los límites de placas

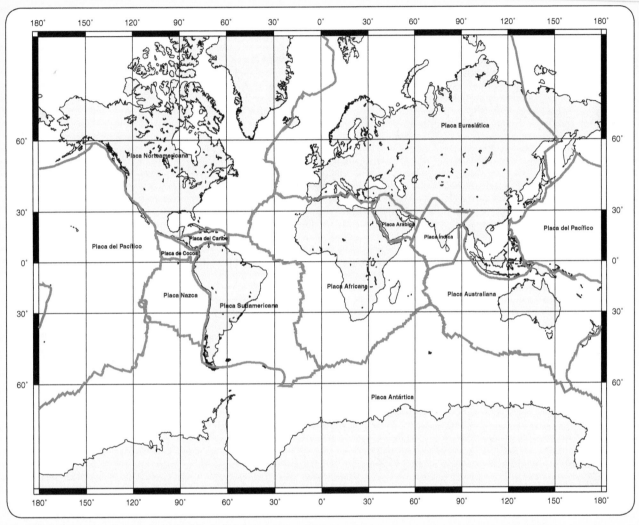

Fuente: Dietmar Mueller, Universidad de Sydney.

Este mapa forma parte de "Descubra los límites de placas", un ejercicio para el salón de clases desarrollado por Dale S. Sawyer en la Universidad Rice (dale@rice.edu). Se puede obtener información adicional sobre este ejercicio en http://terra.rice.edu/plateboundary.

B. Sismología (terremotos)

Ubicación de terremotos de 1990 a 1996 (magnitud de 4 o mayor)

El color indica la profundidad: rojo de 0 a 20 millas (0 a 33 kilométros); anaranjado de 20 a 43 millas (33 a 70 kilométros); verde de 43 a 186 millas (70 a 300 kilométros); azul de 186 a 434 millas (300 a 700 kilométros).

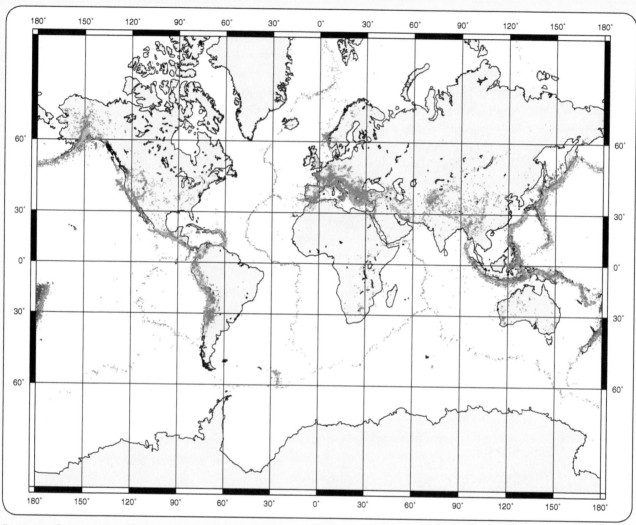

Este mapa forma parte de "Descubra los límites de placas", un ejercicio para el salón de clases desarrollado por Dale S. Sawyer en la Universidad Rice (dale@rice.edu). Se puede obtener información adicional sobre este ejercicio en http://terra.rice.edu/plateboundary.

C. Vulcanología (volcanes)

Los puntos rojos indican rasgos volcánicos activos en la actualidad o en el pasado.

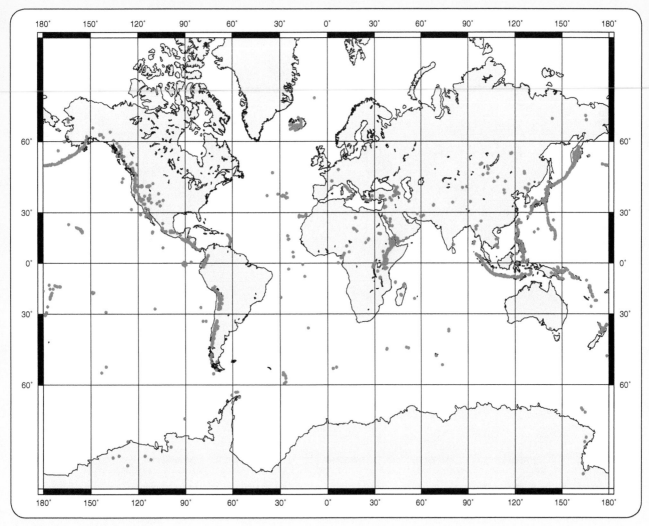

Fuente: Instituto Smithsoniano.

Este mapa forma parte de "Descubra los límites de placas", un ejercicio para el salón de clases desarrollado por Dale S. Sawyer en la Universidad Rice (dale@rice.edu). Se puede obtener información adicional sobre este ejercicio en http://terra.rice.edu/plateboundary.

D. Geocronología (edad del lecho marino)

Edad del lecho marino en millones de años.

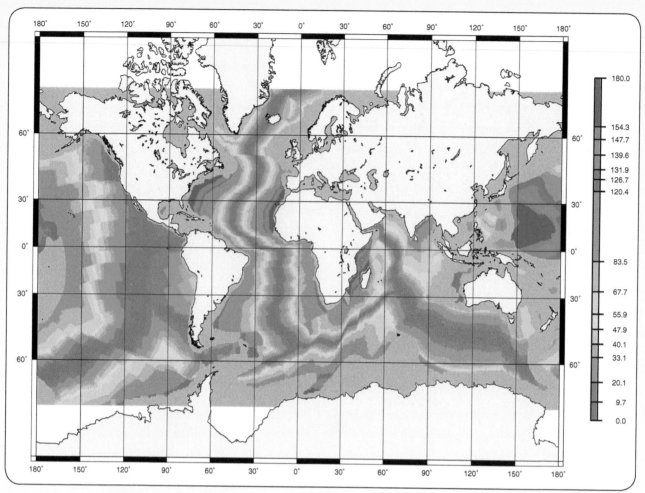

Fuente: Dietmar Mueller, Universidad de Sydney.

Este mapa forma parte de "Descubra los límites de placas", un ejercicio para el salón de clases desarrollado por Dale S. Sawyer en la Universidad Rice (dale@rice.edu). Se puede obtener información adicional sobre este ejercicio en http://terra.rice.edu/plateboundary.

E. Geodesia (atracción gravitacional en la superficie del mar)

Anomalías en la aceleración de la gravedad (en miligales) en la superficie del mar.

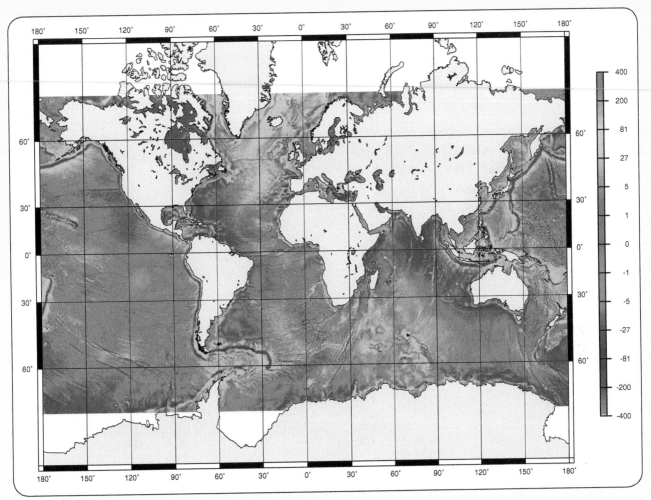

Fuente: David Sandwell y colegas, del Instituto Scripps de Oceanografía.

Este mapa forma parte de "Descubra los límites de placas", un ejercicio para el salón de clases desarrollado por Dale S. Sawyer en la Universidad Rice (dale@rice.edu). Se puede obtener información adicional sobre este ejercicio en http://terra.rice.edu/plateboundary.

Contador de Calorías

Factores de conversión

1 taza = 8 onzas (oz)   3 cucharaditas = 1 cucharada   2 cucharadas = 1 onza

Alimento	Cantidad	Calorías
Grupo de panes y cereales		
Bagel (Einstein)	1	330
Bagel con queso crema	1	420
Hojuelas de salvado	3/4 taza	100
Pan de centeno	1 rebanada	60
Pan blanco	1 rebanada	60
Pan de hamburguesa o perro caliente	cada uno	140
Hojuelas de maíz	1 taza	110
Hojuelas de maíz azucaradas	1 taza	165
Crema de trigo	1 taza, cocido	135
Macarrones, cocidos	3/4 taza	115
Macarrones con queso	1 taza	470
Avena, cocida	2/3 taza	100
Panqueque	1 promedio	60
Panqueque con 1/2 porción de mantequilla y 1 cucharada de jarabe	1 promedio	145
Arroz, cocido	3/4 taza	150
Arroz, inflado	1 taza	55
Arroz, inflado azucarado	1 taza	80
Bollo danés	4.5 in de diámetro	200
Espagueti	1 taza, cocido	220
Espagueti con albóndigas	1 porción	220
Tostada francesa	1 promedio	180
Waffle	7 pulgadas	210
Hojuelas de trigo	1 taza	125
Grasas, aceites, mantequilla		
Mantequilla o margarina	1 porción	40
Mantequilla o margarina	1 cucharada	100
Aceite de maíz	1 cucharada	125
Aceite de maíz	1 taza	1,950

(continuación)

Alimento	Cantidad	Calorías
Mayonesa	1 cucharada	100
Aderezo para ensaladas:		
de queso Roquefort	1 cucharada	75
francés	1 cucharada	65
italiano	1 cucharada	85
mil islas	1 cucharada	80
Aceite para ensaladas	1 cucharada	125
Aceite para ensaladas	¼ taza	500
Frutas y jugos de frutas		
Manzana, fresca	1 mediana	70
Puré de manzana, en lata	½ taza	115
Albaricoques (chabacanos), en lata en almíbar	4 mitades, 2 cucharadas de almíbar	110
Albaricoques (chabacanos), secos	5 mitades pequeñas	50
Aguacate	½	190
Plátano	1 pequeño	85
Melón	¼ de melón mediano	40
Cerezas	20	60
Salsa de arándano	1 cucharada	30
Dátiles	3–4 deshuesados	85
Ensalada de frutas, en lata almíbar espeso	½ taza	100
Toronja, fresca	½ mediana	50
Toronja, en lata con líquido	1 taza	175
Uvas sin semillas	30 uvas	35
Naranja, entera	1 mediana	70
Duraznos, frescos	1 mediano	40
Duraznos (melocotones), en lata	2 mitades en almíbar	90
Duraznos (melocotones), congelados	½ taza	105
Peras, frescas	1 mediana	100
Peras, en lata	2 mitades en almíbar	90
Piña, fresca	½ taza, en dados	40
Piña, en lata	½ taza, con almíbar	90
Ciruelas, frescas	1 ciruela	25
Ciruelas pasa, cocidas con azúcar	4–5 con líquido	105
Uvas pasas, secas	1 cucharada	25
Frambuesas, frescas	¾ taza	55

(continuación)

Alimento	Cantidad	Calorías
Frambuesas, congeladas	½ taza	120
Fresas, frescas	10 grandes	35
Fresas, congeladas	½ taza	120
Sandía	1 rebanada, 1.5 pulgadas de espesor	170

Jugos de frutas

Alimento	Cantidad	Calorías
Jugo de manzana, en lata	1 taza	120
Uva, congelado diluido	1 taza	170
Toronja, en lata o congelado (listo para servir) sin azúcar	1 taza	100
con azúcar	1 taza	130
Limonada	1 taza	110
Naranja, fresca	1 taza	110
Naranja, en lata, sin azúcar	1 taza	120
Naranja, congelado, listo para servir	1 taza	110

Carnes, aves, pescado

Alimento	Cantidad	Calorías
Tocino	1 lonja	50
Falda de res	3 rebanadas	340
Estofado de carne con verduras	1 taza	185
Mortadela	1 rebanada	65
Pollo, frito	½ pechuga	230
Pollo, frito	pierna mediana	140
Pastel de pollo	1 porción de pastel	460
Huevo	1 mediana	80
Huevos con tocino	2 huevos, 2 lonjas medianas de tocino	320
Palitos de pescado, empanados	5 bastones	200
Abadejo	1 filete	140
Jamón	rebanada promedio	140
Hamburguesa	1 porción de carne mediana	250
Hamburguesa	con pan	400
Salchicha	1	140
Salchicha	con pan	280
Chuleta de cordero	1 chuleta	110
Hígado	2 oz, frito	120
Pan o pastel de carne	1 rebanada	260
Chuleta de cerdo	1 chuleta	260

(continuación)

Alimento	Cantidad	Calorías
Cerdo asado	3 oz	310
Carne a la cacerola	3 oz	300
Salami	1 rebanada	135
Salmón, al horno	1 filete	175
Camarón, frito	1 porción	180
Bistec	3 oz	250
Atún, en lata	3 oz, escurrido	170
Pavo, asado	3 rebanadas	200
Comidas rápidas		
Carne de res	comida completa	350
Pollo	comida completa	540
Lomo molido	comida completa	480
Jamón	comida completa	310
Pan o pastel de carne	comida completa	370
Pavo	comida completa	320
Chuleta de ternera	1/4 chuleta	235
Grupo de dulces		
Bebidas, tipo cola	12 oz	160
Salsa de chocolate	1 cucharada	50
Dream Whip	1 cucharada	15
Miel	1 cucharada	65
Mermeladas, comerciales	1 cucharada	55
Jaleas, comerciales	1 cucharada	50
Miracle Whip	1 cucharada	50
Melaza	1 cucharada	50
Reddi-whip	1 porción promedio	30
Azúcar, blanca	1 cucharada	30
Jarabe de mesa	1 cucharada	55
Crema batida	1 cucharada	50
Productos lácteos		
Queso, tipo americano	1 oz	115
Queso, cheddar	cubo de 1 in	115
Requesón	1/4 taza	60
Queso, suizo	1 rebanada	105
Queso, Velveeta	1 rebanada	90
Crema	1 cucharada	35
Helado	1 bola	270

(continuación)

Alimento	Cantidad	Calorías
Leche, descremada	1 taza	90
Leche, entera	1 taza	165
Sorbete	1 bola	120
Yogur	1 taza	120
Verduras		
Espárragos, en lata	6 espárragos medianos	20
Frijoles, con cerdo y salsa tomate	1/2 taza	140
Habichuelas, cocidas	1/2 taza	30
Frijoles, cocidos	1/2 taza	110
Brotes de frijol, crudos	1/2 taza	15
Remolacha, en cubos, cocida	1/2 taza	35
Brócoli, cocido	3 troncos medianos	30
Col (repollo), ensalada de col	1/2 taza	60
Zanahorias, crudas	2 pequeñas	40
Zanahorias, cocidas	1/2 taza, en cubos	25
Apio, crudo	3 troncos	10
Maíz, cocido	1 mazorca	100
Maíz, en lata	1/2 taza	70
Pepino, crudo	6 rodajas	5
Lechuga, cruda	6 hojas pequeñas	10
Cebolla, cruda	1 cucharada, picada	5
Arvejas (chícharos)	1/2 taza	65
Pepinillos curtidos	1 grande	10
Papa, al horno	1 mediana	110
Papa, al horno con 1 porción de mantequilla	1 mediana	125
Papas fritas	10	115
Papas a la francesa	10	200
Papas, picadas y doradas	1/2 taza	210
Puré de papas con mantequilla y leche	1/2 taza	110
Espinacas, cocidas	1/2 taza	25
Batata (camote), al horno	1 mediana	170
Batata (camote), acaramelada	1 mitad	180
Jugo de tomate	1 taza	40
Tomates, crudos	1 pequeño	20
Tomates, en lata	1/2 taza	20
V-8	1 taza	50

(continuación)

Alimento	Cantidad	Calorías
Bebidas alcohólicas		
Cerveza	lata de 12 oz	150
Licor fuerte, 90 grados	vaso de 1.5 oz	110
Vino	vaso de 3.5 oz	90
Bebidas		
Gaseosas	lata o botella de 12 oz	160
Chocolate, caliente	¾ taza	210
Batido de chocolate	1 vaso grande	500
Pepsi dietética	lata de 12 oz	6
Refresco con helado (Ice cream soda)	1 porción	320
Malteada	1 vaso grande	420
Té o café, negro	1 taza	0
Té o café, con 2 cucharadas de crema o 2 cucharaditas de azúcar		45
Golosinas		
Caramelos, comunes	2 medianos	90
Tabletas de chocolate:		
con leche	1 tableta (1 oz)	160
con almendras	1 tableta (1 oz)	140
Barra con cobertura de chocolate	1 barra	270
Caramelos para la tos	1 unidad	10
Goma de mascar	1 unidad	10
Salvavidas (Lifesavers)	1 paquete	95
M&M, comunes	paquete pequeño	140
Crocante de cacahuete	1 unidad	110
Palomitas de maíz	1 taza, sin mantequilla	55
Postres		
Banana split	grande	1,170
Pastel glaseado	porción de 3 pulgadas	300
Bizcocho con fruta seca	porción de 3 pulgadas	260
Magdalena, glaseada	1 mediana	230
Dixie cup	1 mediano	280
Rosquillas (donas):		
bizcocho	1 promedio	135
bizcocho, con azúcar	1 promedio	150
con jalea	1 promedio	225

(continuación)

Alimento	Cantidad	Calorías
Helado	1 bola	270
Refresco	1 refresco mediano	120
Sándwich de helado	1 mediano	250
Sorbete	1 bola	120
Sundaes, de chocolate con nueces y crema batida	mediano	350
Empanada, de manzana	mediana	275
Frutas		
Manzana	1 mediana	80
Plátano	1 pequeño	95
Uvas	30 medianas	70
Naranja	1 mediana	70
Durazno (melocotón)	1 mediano	40
Pera	1 mediana	80
Emparedados		
Emparedado de queso	1	280
Emparedado de jamón	1	320
Emparedado de jamón y queso suizo	1	570
Hamburguesa con pan	1	400
Emparedado Hero	1	800
Perro caliente con pan	1	280
Emparedado de mantequilla de cacahuete	1 cucharada	330
Pizza, de queso	¼	360
Comida rápida de franquicias		
Big Mac		560
Cuarto de libra con queso		530
Hamburguesa de McDonald's		260
Porción pequeña de papas a la francesa		210
Porción grande de papas a la francesa		450
McNuggets de pollo (6 unidades)		290
Pechuga de pollo KFC Original		400
Pierna de pollo KFC Original		140
Muslo de pollo KFC Original		250
Pizza Hut (Pizza individual de queso)		813
Pizza Hut (Pizza individual con pepperoni)		810

(continuación)

Alimento	Cantidad		Calorías
Coca Cola, pequeña	16 oz		150
Coca Cola, mediana	21 oz		210
Coca Cola, grande	32 oz		310
Coca Cola, dietética			0
Club sándwich Subway	6 pulgadas		312
Sándwich de pavo Subway	6 pulgadas		289
Whopper			640

Starbucks:	Tall (12 oz)	Grande (16 oz)	Venti (20 oz)
Latte (leche entera)	210	270	350
Mocha (leche entera)	340	420	510
Café Frappuccino	180	240	300
Mocha Frappuccino	210	280	350

Bocadillos

Alimento	Cantidad	Calorías
Galletas de animales	1	10
Castaña de cayú	6–8	90
Galletas con chispas de chocolate	1	100
Tostadas de maíz Fritos	paquete pequeño	120
Galleta de jengibre	1	30
Galletas integrales	1	30
Aros de cebolla, fritos	10 anillos	75
Galletas Oreo	1	40
Cacahuetes	15–17	85
Papas fritas	8–10	110
Pretzel	1 grande	140
Pretzels, de 3 anillos	1 pequeño	10
Galletas Ritz	1	15
Ry-Krisp	1	20
Galletas Saltines	1	15
Oblea de vainilla	1	15

Sopas

Alimento	Cantidad	Calorías
Frijoles con carne de cerdo	1 taza	170
Fideos con pollo	1 taza	60
Crema de almejas, Manhattan	1 taza	80
Crema de pollo con leche	1 taza	180
Arvejas, secas	1 taza	145

(continuación)

Alimento	Cantidad	Calorías
Tomate con leche	1 taza	170
Verduras con caldo de res	1 taza	80
Pudines, gelatina		
Pudín de caramelo y mantequilla	½ taza	210
Pudín de chocolate	½ taza	220
Gelatina, de fruta, D-Zerta	½ taza	10
Gelatina, común	1 porción	65
Gelatina, con fruta	1 porción	75
Pudín de tapioca	½ taza	135
Pudín de vainilla	½ taza	150
Ensaladas		
Lechuga con aderezo francés	1 porción	130
Verde mixta, común	1 taza	35
Verde mixta con aderezo de queso Roquefort	1 taza	160
Ensalada mixta	1 taza	120

Fuente: Adaptación de material e información provista por el Departamento de Agricultura de los EE.UU. en los envases.

Observación: Los productos pueden variar mucho. Verifique las etiquetas de los envases y la información publicada en las tiendas y restaurantes para mejorar la exactitud al contar las calorías.

Eras Geologicas

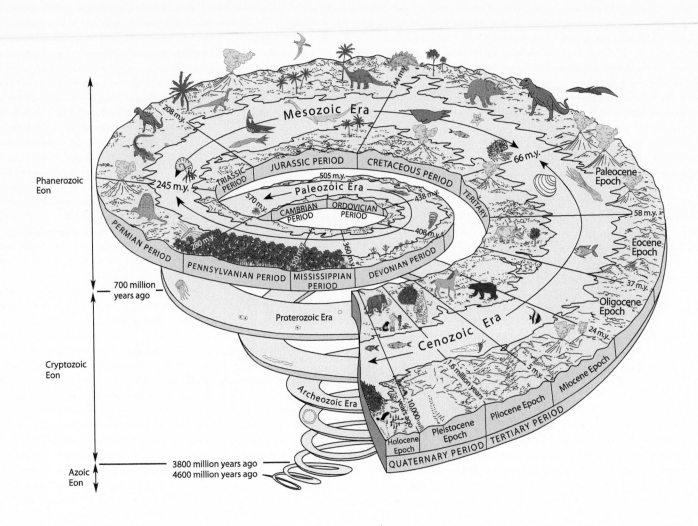

— A —

abiótico sin vida.

abono es la descomposición biológica controlada de desperdicios sólidos bajo condiciones aeróbicas (en la presencia de oxígeno). Los desperdicios orgánicos se descomponen en abonos tales como la mantilla, (tierra vegetal), el estiércol.

abono orgánico material orgánico descompuesto, relativamente estable.

abrasivos sustancias que se pueden usar para desgastar o pulir, especialmente por fricción.

abstinencia total la completa privación de las relaciones sexuales antes del matrimonio.

abundancia cortical relativo a la concentración media de un elemento o isótopo específico en la corteza de la Tierra.

acción capilar el movimiento de líquidos dentro de tubos angostos como resultado de la adhesión, cohesión y tensión superficial. El movimiento se denomina capilaridad.

acero metal duro y resistente, compuesto aleaciones de hierro con porcentajes pequeños de carbono; el acero se puede alear con otros metales para obtener propiedades específicas.

acre-pie la cantidad de agua utilizada (en el interior y exterior) por una familia de cuatro miembros durante aproximadamente un año en los Estados Unidos. Un acre-pie cubre un acre de terreno por un pie de agua. Un acre-pie = 325,851 galones.

acuático perteneciente al agua; que crece o vive en, o sobre el agua.

acuerdo de conservación acuerdo legal entre una entidad gubernamental y una entidad no lucrativa que se encarga del cuidado de terrenos para restringir de forma permanente el uso o desarrollo de las tierras

acuífero formación porosa y permeable que almacena y transmite suficiente agua subterránea para abastecer pozos.

acumulación de reservas suministro de reserva de una materia prima.

adaptación característica heredada de un organismo de una población que mejora sus probabilidades de supervivencia y reproducción en su medio ambiente, en comparación con otros organismos de la misma población.

ADN ácido dioxirribonucleico; material hereditario de muchos organismos. El ADN que forma los genes, tiene una estructura en espiral compuesta de dos hileras unidas y contiene dioxirribo, que es un compuesto que pertenece al grupo de los fosfatos y una de cuatro bases.

aeróbico que requiere oxígeno para vivir y crecer.

aerosoles partículas diminutas suspendidas en un gas.

agencia para la Protección Ambiental (EPA, Environmental Protection Agency) agencia federal con poder para fijar normas ambientales y ejercer las leyes federales sobre el medio ambiente.

agricultura sostenible agricultura que mantiene la calidad de las fuentes del suelo y el agua para continuar indefinidamente. Se maximizan las estrategias de cultivo orgánico.

agua dulce agua que contiene poca sal.

agua residual descargas colectivas de inodoros, lavabos, duchas, lavadoras, alcantarillas pluviales, etc.

agua subterránea agua debajo del nivel freático.

agua superficial agua que cae sobre la superficie de la Tierra y corre hacia lagos y riachuelos. Permanece en la superficie.

aguas residuales el total de residuos orgánicos y aguas negras que generan los establecimientos residenciales y comerciales.

aislante material no conductor que se usa para frenar el flujo del calor.

alcohol líquido incoloro, volátil, combustible y orgánico, producto de la fermentación de biomasa.

aleación metal que resulta de la mezcla de uno o más metales con otro metal o con un elemento no metálico.

aleatoriedad medida del desorden o caos de una situación. Indicación del grado de degradación de una fuente de energía.

almacenamiento bombeado turbinas con bombas reversibles que usan electricidad excedente para elevar agua a un depósito cuando la demanda es baja y luego la usan para generar energía cuando se necesita.

almacenamiento de hidrógeno cualquier técnica para la producción y almacenamiento de hidrógeno como fuente de combustible. La producción por lo general comprende la electrolización de agua, ya que ésta es abundante y la electricidad es difícil de almacenar.

almidón sustancia alimenticia blanca que se encuentra en papas, cereales y muchos otros alimentos; es un carbohidrato granular sólido.

alpino que crece en elevaciones montañosas superiores al límite de la vegetación arbórea; como las plantas alpinas.

alteración química proceso de reorganizar químicamente una sustancia con el propósito de alterar sus propiedades. Cambiar de tóxico a no tóxico.

ambiental circundante, exterior; como el aire ambiental.

amperímetro instrumento que se usa para medir la corriente eléctrica.

anaerobio que puede vivir y crecer sin aire u oxígeno.

anticlinal plegamiento ascendente de rocas sedimentarias. Las capas descienden desde la cima por todos los costados.

antracita la forma de carbón más metamorfoseada. La antracita tiene un elevado contenido de energía. Es negra, dura y vidriosa.

aparato electrodoméstico dispositivo o máquina, especialmente para uso doméstico.

aprovechamiento solar activo técnicas para la recolección, almacenamiento y liberación de energía solar que requieren una fuente de energía externa para sus ventiladores o bombas.

aprovechamiento solar pasivo técnicas para usar la energía solar para la calefacción de un recinto que no requieren energía convencional para ventiladores y bombas.

árboles coníferos árboles de fruto coniforme, principalmente los de hojas perennes en forma de aguja o escama.

árboles de hoja caduca árboles, como el roble y el arce, que pierden todas sus hojas durante parte del año.

arcilla sedimento de grano muy fino, compuesto por partículas de menos de 0.004 de diámetro. La arcilla es plástica cuando está mojada, se agrieta al secarse y se endurece al calentarse.

arenas alquitranosas depósito geológico arenoso que contiene un combustible similar al alquitrán o petróleo espeso, demasiado denso para bombearlo a la superficie, pero que puede ser extraído y tratado para obtener combustibles sintéticos. Las arenas alquitranosas son llamadas también *arenas aceitosas*.

armadura parte de un generador eléctrico que gira; consiste en una serie de espirales de alambre aislado que rodea un núcleo de hierro laminado.

astenosfera zona de la Tierra que los geólogos creen fluye como alquitrán espeso.

atmósfera la capa de aire que rodea la Tierra.

átomo partícula pequeña de materia compuesta por protones, neutrones y electrones.

azúcar sustancia dulce, usualmente cristalina, $C_{12}H_{22}O_{11}$, extraída principalmente de la caña de azúcar y la remolacha azucarera, y que se usa como alimento y agente edulcorante; también se le llama *sacarosa*.

— **B** —

bacteria coliforme tipo de bacteria normalmente benigna que reside en el tracto intestinal de los seres humanos y otros animales, y cuya presencia en el agua indica que ésta puede estar contaminada con organismos causantes de enfermedades presentes en desperdicios humanos y animales que no han sido tratados.

bacterias microorganismos unicelulares que carecen de clorofila. Algunas bacterias son capaces de causar enfermedades en seres humanos, animales o plantas; otras son esenciales para el control de la contaminación, ya que descomponen materia orgánica presente en el aire y el agua.

banco de semillas local en el cual se almacena una variedad de semillas en condiciones ideales con la finalidad de preservar la diversidad genética.

barra de control una barra, placa o tubo que contiene material que absorbe neutrones con facilidad; usada para controlar el poder de un reactor nuclear. Al absorber neutrones, la barra de control evita que los neutrones causen fisión adicional.

biocombustibles combustibles producidos por materiales recientemente vivos.

bioconversión término general que se refiere a la transformación de energía solar en energía química durante la fotosíntesis.

biodegradable que se descompone rápidamente como resultado de la acción de microorganismos.

bioma ecosistema de gran tamaño, caracterizado por su vegetación distintiva y mantenido por las condiciones climáticas locales.

biomagnificación el aumento en la concentración de sustancias químicas tóxicas, metales pesados y ciertos pesticidas en los tejidos de los organismos a medida que estos materiales ascienden por la cadena alimenticia. También se conoce como *amplificación biológica*.

biomasa el peso o masa total de toda la materia viva en un hábitat o área en particular.

biosfera (ver ecosfera)

biotecnología el uso y la manipulación de organismos para producir productos útiles.

biótico vivo.

bitumen material sólido o semisólido que se presenta en forma de asfalto natural.

bomba de calor dispositivo que transfiere calor de una región más fría a una más caliente, usando energía mecánica o eléctrica.

bosques tropicales un bioma caliente con temperatura relativamente constante en la que no hay congelación. Los bosques tropicales (selvas) llueve a diario y reciben más de 80 pulgadas (200 centímetros) de lluvia por año.

— C —

cadena alimenticia secuencia que transfiere energía en forma de alimentos de un organismo a otro.

cálculo de vida cálculo para determinar cuánto tiempo durará una fuente de recursos.

calidad de la energía capacidad de una fuente de energía para producir trabajo útil, medida como la facilidad con que se puede transformar en energía mecánica o eléctrica. También se conoce como *utilidad de la energía*.

caloría cantidad de calor necesaria para elevar la temperatura de un gramo de agua un grado centígrado. A mil calorías se les da el nombre de kilocaloría (Caloría): 1 kilocaloría = 1 Caloría = 1,000 calorías. El valor de los alimentos se mide en Calorías. Las Calorías alimenticias son una medida del contenido energético de varios alimentos.

cámara de filtros instalación que contiene miles de bolsas de fibra de vidrio resistentes al calor para el control de emisiones. Funciona como si fuera una aspiradora del tamaño de una habitación.

cámara de niebla dispositivo en el cual se registran las trayectorias de partículas atómicas cargadas, tales como rayos cósmicos o emisiones radiactivas. Consiste en una cámara con paredes de vidrio llena de un vapor supersaturado, como alcohol. Cuando las partículas cargadas pasan por la cámara, inician un proceso de condensación, formando así un rastro de gotas minúsculas muy similar al rastro de vapor de un avión a chorro.

campo magnético región del espacio donde un imán o aguja de brújula experimentarán el efecto de una fuerza.

capacidad calorífica cantidad de calor necesaria para elevar la temperatura de un cuerpo (objeto) un grado centígrado.

capacidad de carga número máximo (tamaño de la población) de un organismo dado que un ecosistema determinado puede mantener.

carbohidrato cualquiera de varios compuestos de carbono, hidrógeno y oxígeno (como azúcares, almidones o celulosa), la mayoría de los cuales están formados por plantas verdes y constituyen una clase importante de alimentos animales.

carbón materia orgánica sólida, de color negro o negro pardusco, principalmente formada por carbono pero que contiene diversas proporciones de hidrógeno, oxígeno, nitrógeno y azufre. El carbón libera energía al quemarse y es un combustible natural de uso muy difundido.

carbón bituminoso grado de carbón intermedio blando. El grado más común de carbón.

carbón subbituminoso forma de carbón producido a presiones y temperaturas mayores que las que producen lignito, pero menores que las requeridas para el carbón bituminoso.

carga dispositivos eléctricos (aparatos electrodomésticos, bombillas) de un circuito eléctrico operado por la corriente. La carga presenta resistencia al flujo de la corriente.

carnívoro un animal que usa otros animales como fuente de alimento.

casa subterránea casa que combina estrategias pasivas con ubicación subterránea. Estas casas generalmente están abiertas a la luz en el lado sur, y sus otras paredes y el piso están en la tierra. Algunas de estas casas tienen techos de tierra.

catalizador sustancia que acelera una reacción química sin tener una alteración permanente.

celda de combustible dispositivo para convertir energía química directamente en energía eléctrica sin combustión. Esta celda es alimentada con químicos.

celda fotovoltaica dispositivo electrónico que convierte luz solar directamente en energía eléctrica.

celda solar (ver celda fotovoltaica)

célula grupo de átomos y moléculas que actúa en conjunto de manera organizada exhibiendo vida propia.

cementación acción de unir o juntar, como con cemento.

cenagal un lugar de lodo o fango profundo. Un pantano, ciénaga o marisma.

cerámicas una de las clases de materiales más importantes de la que dependen las sociedades modernas. La cerámica es un tipo de producto inorgánico no metálico que se expone a altas temperaturas durante su fabricación. Es de interés por su resistencia a la acción de sustancias químicas y por su capacidad para resistir altas temperaturas.

chaparral bioma caracterizado por un clima seco con poca o ninguna lluvia estival. La vegetación predominante consiste en arbustos que se han adaptado para crecer de nuevo con rapidez después de los incendios que ocurren con frecuencia en la temporada de sequía.

ciclo de minerales y nutrientes ciclo químico genérico en el cual los minerales y nutrientes necesarios para la vida circulan en varias formas por la ecosfera. Por lo general no comprende una fase gaseosa.

ciclo del agua proceso por el cual el agua circula por la ecosfera.

ciclo del carbono ciclo químico en el cual el elemento carbono circula en varias formas por la ecosfera.

ciclo del combustible nuclear todos los pasos que tienen que ver con el uso de un material nuclear, comenzando por la remoción de mineral de la tierra y terminando con la eliminación de materiales de desecho relacionados.

ciclo del nitrógeno ciclo químico en el cual el elemento nitrógeno circula en varias formas por la ecosfera.

ciclo hidrológico el ciclo del agua.

ciencia el estudio de datos medidos sobre el mundo natural y la relación entre estos datos. La ciencia se basa en mediciones del mundo natural e interpretaciones de esas mediciones.

ciencia global el estudio de cómo los individuos y las sociedades usan sus fuentes de recursos vivos y no vivientes e influyen en el medio ambiente en su afán por satisfacer sus deseos humanos.

circuito trayectoria que sigue una corriente eléctrica al avanzar por cables y dispositivos eléctricos.

circuito impreso disposición de conductores en la superficie de una base aislante siguiendo un diseño predeterminado en una forma correctamente repetible.

circuito integrado circuito de un chip de computadora, formado por componentes electrónicos incorporados en el chip.

clarificador tanque en el cual aguas residuales parcialmente tratadas se separan en componentes sólidos, líquidos y flotantes.

clima las condiciones meteorológicas medias de un lugar o región a lo largo de varios años.

clorofluorocarbonos (CFC) moléculas orgánicas compuestas por cloro y flúor unidos a carbono. Se usan como propulsores de latas de aerosol y como refrigerantes. Se creía que eran inertes, pero ahora se sabe que destruyen la capa de ozono estratosférica.

cogeneración producción de dos formas de energía (por ejemplo: la electricidad y los gases calientes) a partir de la misma fuente de energía. También se le conoce como *generación de ciclo combinado*.

colector solar dispositivo para recolectar energía solar y convertirla en calor.

combustibles fósiles restos de plantas y animales que vivieron hace tiempo y que pueden quemarse para liberar energía. Por ejemplo: carbón, petróleo, gas natural, esquisto de petróleo y arenas alquitranosas.

combustibles sintéticos combustibles que requieren intervención humana (tecnología) para su producción. Por ejemplo, esquisto de petróleo, carbón gasificado y arenas alquitranosas.

combustión producción de energía térmica y luminosa mediante un proceso químico, generalmente la oxidación. Quemar es combustión.

combustión en lecho fluidizado método para la producción de calor con carbón de baja calidad. Se sopla aire en un lecho de arena o de carbón y caliza pulverizados, haciendo que se arremoline casi como un líquido en ebullición. El lecho se calienta al rojo vivo mediante la inyección e ignición de un gas inicial y lentamente se añade más carbón molido o pulverizado. Se genera vapor en tubos colocados en el lecho y los gases de emisión se atrapan bajo presión y se utilizan para hacer funcionar una turbina de gas.

comercial involucrado en el intercambio de mercancías, bienes, producciones o propiedades de cualquier tipo.

comunidad grupo de poblaciones que habitan en un área determinada.

concentración de energía solar nombre dado a las estrategias para recolectar y concentrar suficiente energía solar para hacer grandes cantidades de vapor.

concentración mecánica cualquier concentración de un mineral causada por el movimiento de un fluido.

conducción la transmisión de energía térmica de una molécula a otra.

conservación preservación y protección cuidadosa de algo; en particular la gestión planificada de recursos naturales para evitar desperdicios.

conservación de la energía (ley de la) la energía no se puede crear ni destruir. Puede, no obstante, transformarse de una forma a otra.

conservación de la materia (ley de la) la materia no se puede crear ni destruir. Puede, no obstante, reorganizarse.

conservación del suelo estrategias para reducir la erosión del suelo y para evitar el agotamiento de los nutrientes del suelo.

constante solar cantidad de energía solar recibida por metro cuadrado de tierra en un día claro en que el Sol está directamente encima.

consumidor primario el primer organismo consumidor en una cadena alimenticia.

consumidor secundario animales que obtienen sus alimentos consumiendo sólo animales que comen plantas.

consumidor terciario animal que se alimenta de consumidores secundarios.

consumidores individuos o grupos que compran o usan recursos, bienes y servicios.

contaminación presencia de materia o energía cuya naturaleza, localización o cantidad produce efectos ambientales no deseados.

contaminación térmica aumento en la temperatura del agua o el aire que perturba la ecología del área. Frecuentemente, la contaminación térmica está relacionada con plantas generadoras de electricidad, las cuales requieren grandes cantidades de agua refrigerante para eliminar el calor residual.

contaminante algo que contamina; especialmente una sustancia química dañina u otro residuo en el agua o en la atmósfera.

contaminante del aire toda sustancia presente en el aire en concentración suficiente para producir un efecto "dañino" en seres humanos, animales, plantas o materiales.

contención estrategias para encerrar y contener materiales tóxicos.

contenido energético la cantidad de energía térmica liberada por la combustión (o reacción) de una unidad de masa de ese combustible.

control la norma (parte que no cambia) de un experimento. Se selecciona de manera que sea igual a la parte examinada excepto por la variable que se está examinando.

control biológico uso de depredadores naturales, parásitos, bacterias y virus para el control de plagas.

control de la natalidad todos los métodos para el control de la concepción o fecundación.

control integral de plagas estrategia para el control de plagas basado en fuerzas naturales, como el uso de enemigos naturales de los insectos, clima, rotación de cultivos y uso de plantas resistentes a las plagas; y dosis de pesticidas cuidadosamente aplicadas.

convección la transferencia de calor mediante el movimiento en masa de partículas calientes, como en corrientes de aire o líquidas.

conversión de energía (ver transformación de energía)

conversión de la energía térmica oceánica (OTEC) opción de obtención de energía que utiliza diferencias de temperatura entre las aguas superficiales y las profundidades de los océanos para vaporizar un fluido activo y generar electricidad.

convertidor catalítico dispositivo que se añade al tubo de escape de un automóvil para convertir el monóxido de carbono (CO) y los hidrocarburos sin quemar, que contaminan el aire, en dióxido de carbono (CO_2) y agua. Los convertidores más recientes también descomponen óxidos de nitrógeno.

corriente el flujo de partículas cargadas por un material conductor.

corteza la parte superior de la litosfera.

costos de derrame costos (o beneficios) externos de la producción o uso de un producto que se pasan involuntariamente a otra persona.

crecimiento exponencial crecimiento que comienza lentamente pero puede dispararse en forma descontrolada con rapidez. Crecimiento caracterizado por la duplicación en un tiempo fijo.

cristal forma de materia en la cual los átomos, iones o moléculas están ordenados regularmente en todas las direcciones, formando una red regular y repetitiva.

cromosoma estructura celular central, parecida a un hilo, que contiene material hereditario (genes).

crudo sintético petróleo crudo que requiere intervención humana para su producción, a diferencia del crudo que se extrae de la tierra.

cultivo orgánico método para producir cosechas y ganado en forma natural, usando fertilizantes orgánicos (estiércol, legumbres, abono orgánico y residuos de cosechas); rotación de cultivos; control de plagas natural (biológico; insectos buenos que comen insectos malos, plantas que repelen insectos) y controles ambientales (como la rotación de cultivos) en lugar de usar fertilizantes, pesticidas y herbicidas sintéticos.

curva de agotamiento de recursos gráfica de la tasa de producción contra el tiempo, que representa el ciclo completo de producción de una fuente de recursos en una región determinada.

— D —

Declaración de Impacto Ambiental (*Environmental Impact Statement*) informe escrito que examina y analiza el posible impacto de un proyecto (y posibles proyectos alternativos) en el medio ambiente. En los Estados Unidos, la Ley de Política Ambiental Nacional (National Environmental Policy Act) exige dicho informe.

declaración sobre el medio ambiente documento breve por el cual la agencia federal es responsable de proveer la suficiente evidencia y análisis para determinar si debe preparar una declaración que afecte significativamente al medio ambiente.

demanda la cantidad de un bien o servicio que las personas están dispuestas a comprar a distintos precios. La demanda es afectada por la publicidad y por los precios de otros bienes, etc.

demanda bioquímica de oxígeno (DBO) cantidad de oxígeno disuelto requerida para la descomposición bacteriana de desechos orgánicos en el agua.

demografía estudio de las poblaciones humanas.

demógrafo persona que estudia las estadísticas vitales de poblaciones: nacimientos, muertes, matrimonios, etc.

deposición ácida la precipitación de ácidos y compuestos generadores de ácidos desde la atmósfera a la superficie de la Tierra. La deposición ácida incluye la lluvia ácida, nieve ácida, smog ácido y otros tipos de materia ácida.

depósito fuente o lugar donde se encuentra un mineral valioso.

depósito de reemplazo depósito de minerales por soluciones hidrotermales. Los minerales primero se disolvieron en la solución caliente y luego sustituyeron a otros minerales en la roca adyacente.

depredador organismo que mata otros organismos para comérselos.

depurador dispositivo utilizado para controlar las emisiones de partículas o gases. El proceso consiste en lavar las impurezas del flujo de gas del tubo de la chimenea y desecharlas mediante una mezcla de ceniza y agua.

depurador húmedo dispositivo que usa un rocío líquido para eliminar contaminantes de una corriente de aire.

desalinización quitar la sal, especialmente de agua de mar para hacerla potable.

descomponedores pequeños organismos (como bacterias, hongos y algunos protozoos) que descomponen los compuestos complejos de animales y plantas muertos.

descomposición reducción del nivel de energía neta y cambio en la composición química de materia orgánica a causa de la acción de microorganismos aerobios o anaerobios.

desertización proceso mediante el cual tierras áridas se transforman en un desierto estéril por la pérdida de vegetación y suelo fértil.

deshidratar eliminar el agua de algo, secar.

desierto un bioma o región que recibe menos de 10 pulgadas (25 centímetros) de precipitación pluvial al año.

desigualdad falta de justicia o imparcialidad; una instancia de injusticia o parcialidad.

desnutrición estado de mala salud en el cual la dieta de un individuo carece de una o más de las vitaminas y nutrientes esenciales, especialmente proteínas.

destilación proceso de evaporar un líquido y condensar sus vapores.

destrucción por fusión suceso en un reactor nuclear cuando se rompe un conducto u ocurre una interferencia grave en el sistema de enfriamiento normal. Esto haría que el combustible fisionable caliente del reactor se sobrecalentara con rapidez. El combustible podría transformarse en una masa candente y pesada de metal fundido que podría atravesar el reactor y descender derritiendo todo lo que toca, hasta el sótano de la planta y el suelo. En este caso, se liberarían grandes cantidades de vapor contaminado al medio ambiente.

desviación del agua método para aumentar las existencias de agua dulce en un área con escasez de agua, trayendo agua de un área rica en agua dulce.

deterioro ambiental físico es la constante exposición de las rocas a los cambios de temperatura en conjunto con el movimiento físico del hielo y del agua, el crecimiento de las raíces, las actividades humanas, tales como, la agricultura y la construcción ocasionan que se quiebren en pedazos.

deterioro ambiental químico alteración química de material rocoso por la exposición al aire, humedad y materiales orgánicos.

deuterio isótopo de hidrógeno cuyo núcleo contiene un neutrón y un protón y es, por lo tanto, aproximadamente dos veces más pesado que el núcleo del hidrógeno normal, el cual está formado por un solo protón. El deuterio con frecuencia se denomina hidrógeno pesado.

difundir esparcir; mezclar por difusión, como en gases y líquidos.

difusión gaseosa método de separación isotópica basado en el hecho de que átomos o moléculas de gas con diferentes masas se difundirán a través de una barrera porosa (o membrana) en diferentes proporciones.

digestión descomposición bioquímica de materia orgánica. La digestión de sedimentos de las aguas residuales se efectúa en tanques donde el sedimento se descompone, resultando en la gasificación parcial, la licuefacción y la mineralización de agentes contaminantes.

digestión anaerobia descomposición bioquímica de la materia orgánica por bacterias anaerobias.

dilución proceso de reducir la concentración de una solución al agregar agua (u otro solvente).

dióxido de carbono (CO_2) molécula gaseosa que contiene un átomo de carbono y dos átomos de oxígeno, producida por la respiración de organismos o la combustión completa de combustibles fósiles.

dipolar que tiene dos extremos iguales pero con cargas opuestas.

diversidad   complejidad física o biológica de un sistema. En muchos casos lleva a la estabilidad del sistema.

domo de sal   masa sólida de sal que era líquida y fluía por las fracturas y otras fallas de las estructuras geológicas circundantes.   En los lados de esta sal, en fallas causadas por el movimiento de la sal en formaciones arqueadas encima de la sal, se formaron bolsas de petróleo crudo y gas.

duración en la vida real (T_{rw})   tiempo que las reservas de un recurso duran en condiciones del mundo real.

— E —

ecología   el estudio de organismos en sus hogares. El estudio de las relaciones de los organismos vivos con otros organismos y el medio ambiente.

ecología humana   estudio del crecimiento, la distribución y la organización de las comunidades humanas y cómo interactúan con otros seres humanos, otras especies y su medio ambiente.

economía   el estudio de las maneras en que los individuos y las sociedades distribuyen sus bienes con la finalidad de satisfacer sus deseos ilimitados.

economía de mercado   sistema económico en el cual ciudadanos del sector privado son dueños y operarios de la mayoría de los negocios. La mayoría de las decisiones económicas son tomadas por productores y consumidores individuales mediante la compraventa en el mercado.

economía sostenible   sistema económico que puede operar en un ambiente sin crecimiento. En una economía sostenible, tanto el número de personas como las fuentes de recursos disponibles se mantienen en un nivel de suficiencia deseado.

ecosfera   el ecosistema global; la biosfera. La suma de los diversos ecosistemas de la Tierra.

ecosistema   toda área de la naturaleza que incluye organismos vivos y sustancias sin vida, que interactúan para producir un intercambio de materiales entre sus partes vivas (bióticas) y sin vida (abióticas).

efecto de invernadero   calor atrapado en la atmósfera. La radiación solar penetra en la atmósfera, pero la radiación saliente (calor) es absorbida por el vapor de agua, dióxido de carbono y ozono. Parte de esta radiación vuelve a ser emitida hacia la Tierra, causando un aumento en la temperatura.

efecto fotovoltaico   expulsión de electrones de la superficie de un material expuesto a la luz visible.

efervescencia   emitir burbujas de gas, como las bebidas carbonatadas.

eficiencia   la eficiencia de una máquina o, más generalmente, de cualquier proceso en el que se aplica energía o trabajo y el resultado es una combinación de trabajo o energía útil.   Eficiencia es la proporción entre el resultado deseado y el trabajo o energía aplicado.

eficiencia de sistema   eficiencia total de un proceso que ocurre en una serie de pasos. La eficiencia de un sistema es igual al producto de la eficiencia individual de los pasos del proceso.

eficiente   alcanzar un fin con mínimo uso de tiempo, energía, dinero o esfuerzo.

efluente   descarga de agentes contaminantes al medio ambiente, parcial o completamente tratados o en su estado natural. Por lo general se usa para referirse a descargas al agua.

electrolito   sustancia cuya solución acuosa conduce la electricidad.

electrones   partículas minúsculas con carga negativa que orbitan o se mueven alrededor del núcleo de un átomo.

elemento   una de las aproximadamente 108 sustancias químicas conocidas que no pueden ser divididas en sustancias más simples por medios químicos. Sustancia cuyos átomos tienen todos el mismo número atómico.

El Niño   fenómeno climatológico que ocurre cada 2 ó 7 años debido a la interacción del océano y la atmósfera en aguas tropicales de los océanos Índico y Pacífico. Este fenómeno esta conectado a los cambios de temperaturas de todo el mundo.

emigración   salida de un área que fue lugar de residencia.

encierro del carbón   captura y almacenaje del carbón (CO_2) y otros gases que de alguna manera son emitidos a la atmósfera y que potencialmente contribuyen al cambio climatológico global.

energía   la capacidad de mover materia. Aquello que es necesario para mantener la vida y una sociedad vibrante.

energía cinética   energía poseída por un objeto en movimiento. Energía de movimiento.

energía de calidad   (ver calidad de la energía).

energía eléctrica   una clase especial de energía cinética. La energía eléctrica es la energía de las cargas eléctricas, por lo general electrones en movimiento.

energía geotérmica   energía que se origina en la corteza de la Tierra, sobre todo en regiones volcánicas.

energía hidráulica   técnica para convertir en energía eléctrica la energía gravitacional del agua almacenada detrás de una presa.

energía mareomotriz   energía cinética de las mareas oceánicas que puede convertirse en energía eléctrica.

energía mecánica   energía de un objeto representado por su movimiento, posición o ambas.

energía neta diferencia entre la energía total producida y la energía total utilizada.

energía nuclear energía liberada por una reacción nuclear (fisión o fusión) o por desintegración radiactiva.

energía potencial energía almacenada. Energía que se debe a la posición o configuración de una masa.

energía química la energía almacenada en los enlaces químicos que mantienen unidas las moléculas.

energía radiante energía de ondas electromagnéticas, inclusive la luz.

energía solar energía del Sol que recibe la Tierra.

energía térmica forma de energía cinética que fluye de un cuerpo a otro debido a la diferencia de temperatura entre ambos. Los efectos de la energía térmica son el resultado del movimiento de moléculas.

energía útil energía que puede transformarse fácilmente para realizar tareas mecánicas o eléctricas.

enriquecimiento del uranio cualquier proceso en el cual la abundancia relativa de uranio-235 en una muestra es aumentada del 0.7 porciento a un valor más alto.

enriquecimiento residual proceso de concentración mineral en el cual un material sin valor es disuelto, dejando atrás una sustancia valiosa.

enriquecimiento secundario proceso de concentración mineral en el cual una sustancia valiosa es disuelta y transportada a un nuevo lugar, donde es redepositada en un estado concentrado.

entropía medida del grado de desorden de una situación. Medida de la degeneración gradual de la energía a una condición inútil.

enzima catalizadores orgánicos producidos en las células de plantas y animales, que regulan la proporción de reacciones químicas de esas células.

equilibrio condición estable de un sistema. Estado de equilibrio o igualdad entre fuerzas opuestas.

equilibrio de mercado punto en el cual el consumidor puede comprar la mayor cantidad de un producto o servicio al precio más bajo, y el productor puede producir lo máximo al precio más alto.

erosión del suelo movimiento de la capa superior del suelo y otros componentes del suelo de un lugar a otro, generalmente provocado por el viento y el agua.

escasez condición del mercado que ocurre cuando las personas no pueden comprar la cantidad deseada de un bien o servicio al precio vigente.

escenario una posibilidad futura o resultado que se basa en una serie de criterios y suposiciones.

escisión la tendencia de algunos minerales a romperse a lo largo de superficies lisas, planas y paralelas.

especie todos los individuos y poblaciones de una clase particular de organismo, mantenidos por mecanismos biológicos que resultan en su reproducción solamente con organismos del mismo tipo.

especies en peligro especies que podrían estar en peligro de extinción dentro de un futuro anticipado.

especie invasora especie no autóctona que se introduce en un ecosistema y que como resultado causa o puede causar daños económicos, medioambientales o afectar la salud de los seres humanos.

esquisto de petróleo roca sedimentaria que contiene kerógeno. El kerógeno caliente produce petróleo crudo sintético, el cual se puede procesar para producir gasolina y otros productos de petróleo.

estado constante condición equilibrada de un sistema debido a que la tasa de entrada y salida de una sustancia (o energía) es constante.

estanque de enfriamiento un lago o estanque usado para enfriar agua caliente de una planta de energía eléctrica o fábrica.

esterilización cualquier procedimiento mediante el cual un individuo resulta incapaz de reproducirse.

estratos capas de rocas, especialmente capas de rocas sedimentarias.

estratosfera la parte de la atmósfera terrestre que comienza a una altitud de unos 12 kilómetros (7 millas) y continúa hasta la ionosfera; está caracterizada por una temperatura casi constante en todas las altitudes.

estuario regiones costeras, como ensenadas o desembocaduras de ríos, donde se mezclan aguas dulces y saladas.

eutrofización acumulación de nutrientes en un lago o estanque a causa de la intervención humana (eutrofización cultural) o causas naturales (eutrofización natural). Contribuye al proceso de sucesión.

eutrofización cultural (ver eutrofización)

evaporitas rocas sedimentarias químicas que consisten en minerales precipitados por la evaporación de aguas, especialmente sal y yeso.

evapotranspiración la combinación de evaporación de agua de la superficie de la Tierra y la transpiración de las plantas.

evolución proceso de cambio continuo en los organismos, causado por cambios en generaciones sucesivas.

experimento controlado una investigación planeada en la cual todas las variables se mantienen constantes, excepto la que se estudia. La variable se compara con el control, donde la variable investigada no cambia. La finalidad es controlar las influencias externas de manera que cada cambio produce su efecto en condiciones conocidas, para que la causa de un efecto pueda ser identificada.

explicación científica declaración que afirma que un suceso es la consecuencia lógica de una teoría o modelo, que sirve para unificar un grupo de datos o sucesos relacionados.

externalidades costos (o beneficios) externos al acto de producción o usos que se transmiten involuntariamente a otra persona.

extinción pérdida total de una especie en todo el mundo.

extracción por disolución método para extraer materiales solubles de depósitos subterráneos, bombeando agua caliente por una perforación y recuperando la sal por evaporación de la salmuera resultante.

extrapolar calcular una cantidad más allá de la base de datos conocida, suponiendo que las tendencias actuales continuarán.

— F —

fabricación de combustible paso del ciclo de combustible nuclear en que el gas UF_6 enriquecido se convierte en un sólido (UO_2 o UC) y toma la forma de combustible utilizable.

factor de conversión número que permite convertir una unidad de medida en otra.

factor limitante factor, como temperatura, luz o agua, que limita la capacidad de un organismo para crecer y ser productivo.

falla grieta en la corteza de la Tierra a lo largo de la cual se han desplazado las rocas.

falla de transformación límite entre placas a lo largo del cual se desplazan dos placas separadas.

fecundación (concepción) fusión (unión) de huevo y esperma que da comienzo al desarrollo embriónico.

fermentación descomposición de moléculas complejas en compuestos orgánicos, causada por bacteria. Un ejemplo es cuando la leche se vuelve agria.

fertilizante sustancia que hace que el suelo sea capaz de producir mayor cantidad de vegetación o cultivos más saludables.

filtro percolador forma de tratamiento secundario de aguas residuales en la cual bacterias aerobias degradan los materiales orgánicos de las aguas residuales al filtrarse en un tanque grande lleno de piedras trituradas.

finito que tiene cotas o límites. No infinito, sujeto a limitaciones.

fisión la división de un núcleo pesado en dos partes casi iguales (que son núcleos de elementos más ligeros) acompañada por la liberación de una gran cantidad de energía y generalmente uno o más neutrones.

fisura apertura causada por una ruptura.

flotación separación de componentes minerales, realizada mediante su unión en una espuma que luego se quita de la superficie del líquido.

foliación estructura paralela o casi paralela causada por una distribución paralela de minerales en placa.

fosa séptica tanque en el que la materia residual se pudre y descompone por la actividad bacteriana.

fotón pequeño haz de energía radiante. Un fotón tiene un cuanto de energía electromagnética.

fotosíntesis proceso mediante el cual las plantas usan la luz solar para combinar dióxido de carbono, agua y varios minerales y producir carbohidratos (como la glucosa).

fragmentación división de la tierra en partes pequeñas, aisladas y a menudo aleatorias. Esto crea un paisaje irregular.

fragmentos de fisión los dos núcleos que se forman por la fisión de un núcleo. Se conoce también como *residuo radiactivo*.

fuente dispersa fuente de contaminación en la cual los residuos no se liberan en un punto específico e identificable, sino desde varios puntos dispersos y difíciles de identificar y controlar.

fuente fija (de contaminación) fuente de contaminación fácilmente discernible, como una fábrica.

fundición fundir o derretir una mena para separar el metal que contiene.

fusión formación de un núcleo más pesado con dos más livianos (como isótopos de hidrógeno), resultando en la liberación de energía.

fusión láser tipo de fusión nuclear en la cual una pequeña esfera sólida atiborrada de deuterio y tritio es bombardeada con poderosos rayos láser con la finalidad de dirigir el combustible hacia el interior hasta que los núcleos se fusionen.

fusión por confinamiento magnético proceso de fusión en el cual el tritio y el deuterio se calientan hasta convertirse en plasma, que se aísla en una cámara mediante fuerzas electromagnéticas.

— G —

galvanómetro instrumento que indica la presencia y la dirección de la corriente eléctrica.

galvanoplastia descomposición del revestimiento de un objeto mediante el uso de una corriente eléctrica.

ganancias la cantidad de ingresos finales de un productor después de pagar todos los gastos de producción.

ganga fracción de mineral rechazada como desecho en el proceso de separación. Por lo general, no tiene valor pero puede tener usos comerciales secundarios.

gas fase de la materia que se mueve con facilidad y no tiene forma ni volumen definidos.

gases atrapados en la atmósfera que absorben energía infrarroja ocasionando el aumento de temperatura en el aire. Estos gases incluyen al dióxido de carbono (CO_2), al vapor de agua, metano, óxidos nitrosos, clorofluorocarbonos (CFC) y otros carbonos.

gas natural mezcla de gases que se encuentra atrapada en varias partes de los estratos superiores de la Tierra. El gas natural es mayormente metano y etano. Puede encontrarse aislado pero con frecuencia se encuentra con petróleo.

gasificación de carbón proceso para convertir carbón en un combustible sintético similar al gas natural. Durante el proceso se aplica calor, presión y vapor a carbón pulverizado.

gasohol mezcla de gasolina y alcohol. El alcohol generalmente se obtiene de la fermentación de trigo u otros granos echados a perder o de calidad inferior.

generador dispositivo para convertir energía mecánica en energía eléctrica.

generador eólico generador en el cual el viento hace girar las aspas de turbinas que se extienden desde un eje. Los generadores eólicos pueden ser una fuente de electricidad económica si se usan en forma apropiada.

genotipo (genome) organismo completo del ADN.

geólogo persona que estudia la composición, estructura e historia de la corteza terrestre, incluyendo las capas rocosas, fósiles y contenido mineral.

glucosa variedad de azúcar, menos dulce que el azúcar de caña, que se encuentra naturalmente en frutas y miel.

gradiente proporción del cambio de temperatura, presión etc. Diagrama o curva que la representa.

grano fino, de cristales o partículas apenas visibles.

grano grueso, de cristales o partículas grandes y visibles.

greda tierra que es una mezcla arenosa y arcillosa.

— H —

hábitat región específica donde vive un organismo.

hambruna situación en la cual las personas de un área determinada sufren por falta de acceso a alimentos suficientes para la buena salud. Esto se puede deber a sequías, inundaciones, terremotos o condiciones políticas o económicas.

HCl ácido hidroclórico.

hemoglobina materia que da el color rojo a los glóbulos rojos de la sangre. La hemoglobina transporta oxígeno de los pulmones a las células y dióxido de carbono de las células a los pulmones.

herbívoro animal que se alimenta de plantas.

hibridización proceso de unión que incluye diferentes tipos de animales, razas o especies con el fin de desarrollar una descendencia mejor.

híbrido descendencia de dos animales o plantas de diferentes razas, variedades o especies, etc.

hidrocarburo cualquiera de los compuestos de una vasta familia que contienen carbono e hidrógeno en diversas combinaciones, encontrados especialmente en combustibles fósiles.

hidrocarburos no quemados contaminantes del aire que proceden de la combustión incompleta de gasolina y de la evaporación de combustibles de petróleo, solventes industriales y actividades de pintura y limpieza en seco.

hidrosfera superficie de agua de la Tierra.

hipótesis explicación posible de un suceso que se presupone con la finalidad de ponerlo a prueba.

histograma de población representación gráfica de la población por edad y sexo.

horizontes capas que se encuentran en la mayoría de los suelos.

humus materia orgánica en descomposición que aumenta la fertilidad, aireación y retención de agua del suelo.

huracán tormenta tropical muy fuerte. Los huracanes son las tormentas mas destructoras de la Tierra.

— I —

igualdad lo que está relacionado con la imparcialidad. Los principios generales de imparcialidad y justicia.

impacto medioambiental el efecto total de un cambio ambiental, ya sea de origen natural o causado por el ser humano, en la ecología de una región.

impedir obstaculizar o prevenir haciendo algo de antemano.

impermeable que no permite el paso de fluidos como el agua.

impuesto sobre la extracción impuesto sobre uso de fuentes de recursos naturales, que se aplica cuando el mineral u otro producto se extrae o separa de la tierra.

in situ en su posición o lugar natural u original.

incentivos fiscales reducciones en los impuestos que animan a las personas a trabajar y gastar dinero o sirven para realizar algo provechoso para el público.

incineración quema de residuos domésticos o industriales.

índice de la calidad del aire un índice que reporta a diario la calidad del aire diciendo que tan limpio o contaminado se encuentra; además que asocia los efectos que puedan tener con la salud. La agencia protectora del medio ambiente calcula el índice en cinco principales contaminantes del aire, mismas que están reguladas por el Acta de Aire Limpio.

índice de crecimiento en su forma más simple, el índice de crecimiento de una población es igual al índice de natalidad menos el índice de mortalidad.

inducción electromagnética producción de corriente eléctrica en un circuito cerrado como resultado de un cambio en el campo magnético que pasa por ese circuito.

industria la práctica de fabricar bienes, a diferencia de la agricultura (cultivadores) y el intercambio de bienes y servicios (comercio).

inercia propiedad de la materia que se opone a todo cambio en su estado de movimiento.

infiltración movimiento de agua subterránea o hidrotérmica a las rocas o el suelo a través de uniones y poros.

ingeniería genética toda técnica utilizada para identificar o modificar genes en el nivel molecular.

inmigración migración de personas a un país para radicar en él de manera permanente.

insectario lugar donde se crían insectos, especialmente para su estudio o con la finalidad de procrear depredadores naturales para controlar plagas.

intercambiador de calor cualquier dispositivo que transfiere calor de un fluido (líquido o gas) a otro o al medio ambiente.

interdependiente mutuamente dependiente. Que depende uno del otro.

interpolar proveer o inferir información entre datos conocidos presuponiendo que serán válidas las mismas tendencias.

interrelacionado la idea de que en un ecosistema todo está mutuamente relacionado.

inversión de temperatura situación que resulta cuando una capa densa de aire frío queda atrapada bajo una capa más delgada de aire caliente. Los contaminantes gaseosos calientes no pueden elevarse a través del aire caliente y se acumulan en la frontera entre estas capas.

ion átomo o molécula que ha perdido o ganado uno o más electrones y ha adquirido carga eléctrica.

irrigación por goteo suministrar agua de riego mediante tubos que gotean agua al suelo en la base de cada planta; también se le llama *riego por goteo*.

isótopo uno o más átomos con el mismo número atómico (el mismo elemento químico) pero con distintos números de masa. Los núcleos de los isótopos tienen el mismo número de protones pero diferente número de neutrones.

isótopos fisionables isótopos que pueden ser fisionados (divididos) por neutrones para liberar energía nuclear. Combustible nuclear.

— J —

joule cantidad de trabajo realizado o energía utilizada cuando se aplica una fuerza de un newton en una distancia de un metro.

— K —

kerógeno materia orgánica sólida de alto peso molecular contenida en esquisto de petróleo. Al calentarse (en retorta), el kerógeno se descompone, produciendo petróleo crudo sintético y gas de hidrocarburo.

kilovatio-hora unidad de energía eléctrica de uso común. La energía consumida cuando se usan 1,000 voltios de electricidad durante una hora.

— L —

lago eutrófico se caracteriza por ser rico en nutrientes; ya que apoya al crecimiento de algas y de otros tipos de plantas marinas. La profundidad de este tipo de lagos tiene muy poco o casi nada de oxígeno.

lago oligotrófico lago con un contenido bajo de nutrientes de plantas disueltas (nitrato y fosfato).

laminado hecho de láminas delgadas, planas y anchas.

lava magma que se vierte sobre la superficie de la Tierra.

Ley Completa de Responsabilidad, Compensación y Respuesta al Medio Ambiente (CERCLA, *Comprehensive Environmental Response, Compensation and Liability Act*) ley federal que aborda la limpieza de depósitos de residuos peligrosos inactivos o abandonados. A veces se hace referencia a esta ley con el nombre "Superfondo".

ley de conservación ley que establece que en un sistema cerrado cierta cantidad de masa o energía se conserva (sin cambios) para siempre.

Ley de Eliminación de Residuos Sólidos (1965) (*Solid Waste Disposal Act*) la primera ley federal en re-querir medidas preventivas y fomentar métodos que no dañen el medio ambiente para deshacerse de los residuos domésticos, municipales, comerciales e industriales.

ley de la demanda ley de la economía que dice que la demanda de un producto o servicio depende de su precio. Los precios bajos conducen a alta demanda, los precios altos producen baja demanda.

ley de la oferta ley de la economía que dice que la cantidad de bienes y servicios ofrecidos a la venta variará con el precio. Cuanto más alto el precio, mayor la cantidad ofrecida en venta; cuanto más bajo el precio, menor la cantidad a la venta.

Ley para la Conservación y Recuperación de los Recursos Naturales (RCRA, *Resource Conservation and Recovery Act*) ley federal que regula la producción, almacenamiento, transporte, tratamiento y eliminación de residuos peligrosos. Se hace hincapié en la conservación de fuentes de recursos.

libre empresa (mercado) sistema económico en el cual los individuos son libres para emprender y operar sus propios negocios en un ambiente competitivo.

licuefacción convertir en líquido.

licuefacción de carbón proceso para producir petróleo crudo sintético agregando hidrógeno al carbón.

lignito grado muy suave de carbón, formado al enterrar turba.

Límites de crecimiento informe no técnico de los hallazgos del estudio del Club de Roma sobre el crecimiento en nuestro planeta. El informe se publicó en 1972.

limo sedimento de grano fino, con partículas de tamaño intermedio entre la arcilla y la arena.

lípidos compuestos orgánicos ricos en energía que contienen carbono, hidrógeno y pequeñas cantidades de oxígeno. Los lípidos son parte de la membrana de las células. Algunos ejemplos son grasas, aceites y ceras.

líquidos inmiscibles líquidos que no pueden mezclarse.

litosfera parte sólida de la corteza terrestre.

lixiviación proceso de extraer una sustancia soluble de un material o capa rocosa filtrando agua a través del material o capa.

llanos área ancha que colinda con arroyos o ríos y que es cubierta por el agua en época de inundación.

lodo residual material orgánico sólido producido durante el tratamiento de aguas residuales.

— M —

macro compuesto por grandes cantidades u objetos.

magma roca fundida bajo la superficie de la Tierra. El magma es una solución supersaturada que contiene minerales no volátiles y constituyentes volátiles.

magnetómetro instrumento para medir la fuerza y variaciones en la fuerza del magnetismo.

manto corteza gruesa de la Tierra, debajo de la astenosfera, que se comporta como un sólido.

mapa topográfico representa la superficie y forma de un área o región.

maremoto (sunami) serie de ondas marinas muy fuertes, ocasionadas por terremotos, deslaves, erupciones volcánicas o impacto de un asteroide.

marino del mar u océano; que habita o se encuentra en el mar o es formado por él.

masa número que mide la cantidad de materia. En la superficie terrestre, se obtiene dividiendo el peso de un cuerpo entre la aceleración causada por la gravedad.

masa crítica la masa más pequeña de material fisionable capaz de mantener una reacción en cadena independiente en determinadas condiciones.

masa de mena masa más o menos sólida de mena que puede consistir tanto en mena de baja graduación como en mena de alta graduación y tiene características diferentes a las rocas adyacentes.

masa térmica masa de material, como roca o agua, que puede absorber radiación solar durante el día y luego irradiar calor por la noche. Dentro de un edificio, la masa térmica tiende a moderar las temperaturas interiores.

materia cualquier cosa que ocupa espacio y tiene masa.

material de recubrimiento material de cualquier naturaleza que cubre un depósito de materiales útiles o menas que se van a extraer.

material fértil material, de por sí no fisionable, que puede convertirse en material fisionable mediante la irradiación en un reactor. Hay dos materiales fértiles básicos: uranio-238 y torio-232.

matorrales tierras cubiertas con plantas espesas y leñosas que tienen varios tallos permanentes en lugar de troncos únicos.

mecanismo cualquier sistema, medio o estrategia para hacer algo.

mecanismo de adjudicación técnica que distribuye parte de la producción de una sociedad entre sus miembros.

mecanismo de distribución (ver mecanismo de adjudicación)

medio ambiente suma de todas las condiciones e influencias externas que afectan la vida, el desarrollo y en última instancia la supervivencia de un organismo o población.

mena mineral o agregado mineral que contiene metales preciosos o útiles y que se da en cantidades, graduación y combinación química tales que hacen que la extracción comercial sea lucrativa.

mercado situación en la cual los compradores y vendedores se comunican unos con otros para el intercambio de bienes o servicios.

metabolismo reacciones químicas que tienen lugar en un organismo al utilizar los alimentos.

metano hidrocarburo gaseoso, CH4, que es combustible y se forma por la descomposición de materia orgánica. Es el principal constituyente del gas natural.

meteorización proceso natural de descomposición de las rocas.

metodología aplicación de los principios de razonamiento a estudios científicos y filosóficos. La ciencia del método y organización.

micro compuesto por pequeñas cantidades o por objetos pequeños.

microorganismos todas las cosas vivas de tamaño microscópico, como bacterias, levaduras, hongos simples, algunas algas, mohos y protozoos.

mina excavación en la tierra para extraer minerales.

mineral cualquier material cristalino inorgánico natural. Sustancia o fase natural con una estructura interna característica determinada por la distribución regular de sus átomos o iones, y con una composición química y propiedades físicas que son fijas o que varían dentro de una gama definida.

minerales estratégicos minerales esenciales para el poderío económico y militar de una nación.

minerales formadores de rocas minerales que componen las rocas más comunes de la corteza terrestre.

minería a cielo abierto técnica minera usada cuando los depósitos de una fuente de recursos yacen relativamente cerca de la superficie. Se quita el material de recubrimiento, se extrae el recurso y se coloca material de recubrimiento de un área cercana (mientras se explota) en el vacío que se formó.

minería continua método de minería en el cual maquinaria minera de funcionamiento continuo corta o extrae carbón de la superficie y lo carga en transportadores en una operación continua.

minería de cámaras y pilares método de minería subterránea en el cual se abre una serie de cámaras y se alzan pilares (columnas) para sostener el techo. Una vez que finaliza la explotación de un área, se quitan los pilares y se deja que el techo se desplome.

minería de frente largo método de minería subterránea en el cual se abre un túnel angosto que se sostiene con pilares metálicos movibles. Después de extraer los minerales, los soportes del techo se mueven hacia adelante, dejando que la tierra se derrumbe tras ellos.

minería de hoyo abierto técnica minera en que los recursos materiales se encuentran en la superficie y que al ser extraídos crean un hoyo grande y profundo.

minería subterránea método que se usa cuando los depósitos minerales se encuentran debajo de la superficie del suelo y no puede ser extraído usando métodos superficiales.

modelo algo que imita el comportamiento de otra cosa.

moderador material, como agua común, agua pesada o grafito, que se usa en un reactor para frenar neutrones de alta velocidad, incrementando así las probabilidades de fisión adicional.

molécula grupo de átomos unidos de una manera particular.

molino edificio o grupo de edificios que contiene maquinaria para separar la porción valiosa de un mineral de los desperdicios de roca.

monocultivo cultivo de una especie de planta (como trigo o maíz) en un área extensa. Muy susceptible a enfermedades e insectos.

monóxido de carbono (CO) molécula gaseosa que contiene un átomo de carbono y un átomo de oxígeno, producida por la combustión incompleta de combustibles fósiles.

motor térmico cualquier dispositivo que convierte energía térmica en energía mecánica.

mutación cambio fundamental repentino en la herencia que produce un individuo nuevo que difiere de sus progenitores en algún aspecto.

— N —

Naciones Unidas organización internacional establecida inmediatamente después de la Segunda Guerra Mundial con la finalidad de trabajar por la paz mundial, la seguridad y el mejoramiento de la humanidad.

necesidad la falta de algo esencial, deseable o útil. Condición que requiere abastecimiento o alivio.

neutrón partícula elemental sin carga, con una masa ligeramente mayor que la del protón, que se encuentra en el núcleo de todos los átomos más pesados que el hidrógeno común.

nicho todos los factores físicos, químicos y biológicos que una especie necesita para sobrevivir, mantenerse saludable y reproducirse en un ecosistema.

nivel freático parte superior de una zona de suelo saturado.

no labranza método de cultivo en el cual no se trabaja la tierra para reducir la erosión del suelo, reducir los costos de mano de obra y ahorrar energía.

núcleo centro pequeño con carga positiva de un átomo. El núcleo contiene casi toda la masa del átomo. En todos los núcleos hay protones y neutrones, excepto en el de hidrógeno común que consiste en un solo protón. *También*, el centro de la Tierra.

nucleón partícula nuclear, un protón o neutrón en el núcleo de un átomo.

número atómico el número de protones en el núcleo de un átomo.

número de masa número de protones y neutrones en un núcleo atómico.

nutrición nutrirse ingiriendo y asimilando alimentos.

nutriente elemento o compuesto necesario para la supervivencia, el crecimiento y la reproducción de una planta o animal.

nutrientes del suelo alimentos y minerales que se encuentran en el suelo y que los organismos deben consumir para vivir, crecer o reproducirse. Los fertilizantes contienen nutrientes del suelo.

— O —

oferta la cantidad de bienes o servicios disponibles para ser adquiridos a un precio dado.

omnívoro animal, como el ser humano, que puede usar tanto plantas como otros animales como fuente de alimentos.

onda electromagnética onda de energía irradiada hacia el espacio por el Sol, una luz o una antena.

orgánico derivado de organismos vivos, la rama de la química que trata con los compuestos de carbono.

organismo cualquier ser viviente.

Organización territorial no lucrativa (land trust) se encarga de cuidar y proteger el medio ambiente natural y sus seres que lo habitan. La organización *Nature Conservancy* es la más grande del mundo y se encarga del cuidado de la naturaleza.

órgano grupo de tejidos que realizan una función similar. Por ejemplo, el corazón y los pulmones, etc.

óxidos de azufre (SO_x) gases incoloros, acres, formados principalmente por la combustión de combustibles fósiles considerados grandes contaminantes del aire. Los óxidos de azufre pueden dañar las vías respiratorias y la vegetación.

óxidos de nitrógeno (NO_x) gases formados en gran parte por nitrógeno atmosférico y oxígeno cuando se da la combustión en condiciones de alta temperatura y presión; por ejemplo, en motores de combustión interna; considerados grandes contaminantes del aire.

oxígeno (O) elemento que se encuentra libre en forma de gas incoloro, sin sabor y sin olor en la atmósfera, combinado en el agua, en la mayoría de las rocas y minerales y en numerosos compuestos orgánicos. Puede combinarse con todos los elementos excepto gases inertes, es activo en los procesos vitales y es parte de los procesos de combustión.

oxígeno disuelto (OD) cantidad de oxígeno gaseoso (O_2) disuelto en una cantidad de agua dada, a determinada temperatura y presión atmosférica.

ozono (O_3) molécula altamente reactiva compuesta por tres átomos de oxígeno. En la parte alta de la atmósfera, el ozono forma una capa que filtra la radiación ultravioleta dañina, protegiendo así la vida en la Tierra. El ozono también se forma en la superficie de la Tierra como componente dañino del smog fotoquímico.

— P —

partícula alfa el núcleo de un átomo de helio ($_2^4 He$) que se desplaza a gran velocidad.

partícula beta un electrón ($_{-1}^0 \beta$) que se desplaza a alta velocidad y es capaz de penetrar unos cuantos milímetros de aluminio o aproximadamente 100 centímetros de aire.

partículas materia sólida y gotas líquidas suspendidas o transportadas en el aire. Las partículas incluyen hollín, cenizas y polvo.

pastizales se encuentran tanto en regiones templadas como tropicales y se caracterizan por sequías periódicas, terrenos llanos o levemente ondulados, y grandes animales de pastoreo que se alimentan con la exuberante hierba.

perfil del suelo capas de una muestra de suelo.

permafrost capa de hielo y tierra permanentemente congelada, propia de regiones muy frías.

permeable abierto al paso o penetración de fluidos, especialmente agua o petróleo crudo.

pesticida término genérico utilizado para referirse a todo lo que se usa para eliminar o controlar plagas.

petróleo líquido aceitoso inflamable, que varía de casi incoloro a negro y que se presenta en varios lugares de los estratos superiores de la Tierra. Es una mezcla compleja de hidrocarburos y es la materia prima de muchos productos.

petróleo crudo petróleo sin refinar. El petróleo tal cual es extraído de la tierra.

pH valor numérico que indica la acidez o alcalinidad relativa de una sustancia en una escala de 0 a 14, cuyo punto neutro es 7. Las soluciones ácidas tienen valores de pH inferiores a 7 y las soluciones básicas o alcalinas tienen valores de pH superiores a 7.

pie-libra la cantidad de trabajo realizado o energía utilizada cuando se ejerce una fuerza de una libra en una distancia de un pie.

pilar masa de carbón o mena que se deja para sostener el techo de una mina.

pirámide de energía diagrama que representa el flujo de la energía por una cadena o red alimenticia. La base de la pirámide representa la energía aprovechable almacenada en los productores.

pirámide de población término más general que se refiere a un histograma de población.

pirólisis calentar en ausencia de aire, con la finalidad de descomponer. Descomposición química por calentamiento.

placer depósito aluvial de grava rico en oro u otros metales.

planificación familiar proceso mediante el cual las parejas determinan el número de hijos y el lapso entre un hijo y otro.

plantas anuales plantas terrestres que mueren todos los años durante los períodos de temperatura o humedad adversa pero dejan semillas para germinar en la próxima estación climática favorable.

plasma mezcla gaseosa eléctricamente neutra de iones positivos y negativos. A veces se le llama el "cuarto estado de la materia", debido a que se comporta de manera diferente de los sólidos, líquidos y gases.

plasma germinal sustancia de las semillas mediante la cual se transmiten las características hereditarias.

plásticos compuestos plásticos combinados con fibra de vidrio para aumentar su resistencia.

plazo de entrega tiempo que transcurre entre el momento en que se propone inicialmente un proyecto y su culminación.

pluralista que contiene varias partes, vistas o características. Una sociedad pluralista contiene varias nacionalidades, religiones y costumbres.

plutonio (Pu) elemento artificial, altamente radiactivo, con un número atómico de 94. Su isótopo más importante es plutonio fisionable-239, producido por la irradiación neutrónica del uranio-238. Se usa como combustible para reactores y en armamentos.

población todos los organismos del mismo tipo que viven en cierta área.

política de energía plan de acción para el uso de los recursos energéticos, generalmente trazado por un gobierno.

porosidad porcentaje de espacio entre partículas de tierra o roca.

poroso lleno de poros o pequeños orificios que pueden ser ocupados por fluidos como agua o petróleo crudo.

posición en geología, la orientación o ángulo de una capa rocosa en relación a un punto de referencia.

precio valor, en términos monetarios, que se asigna a un bien o servicio.

precipitación proceso mediante el cual las moléculas de vapor de agua se condensan para formar gotas o cristales de hielo con el peso suficiente para caer a la superficie de la Tierra.

precipitación (lluvia) ácida toda precipitación que contiene una alta concentración de ácido sulfúrico o nítrico. Toda precipitación que tiene un valor de pH inferior a 5.6. Entre las precipitaciones ácidas están la lluvia ácida, nieve ácida, aguanieve ácida, granizo ácido, niebla ácida y contaminantes secos que forman ácidos al entrar en contacto con la humedad. Todas estas formas de precipitación son ácidas por naturaleza debido al dióxido de carbono existente en la atmósfera. Generalmente, la lluvia tiene un pH de 5.6 ó 5.7. El pH medio de una tormenta en el noroeste de los Estados Unidos es de 4.0.

precipitador electrostático dispositivo utilizado para quitar partículas de las emisiones de chimeneas. Las partículas cargadas son atraídas hacia una placa de metal con carga opuesta, donde se precipitan del aire.

presa animal atrapado por un depredador como alimento.

presupuesto de agua saldo del agua disponible. Considera el ingreso, almacenamiento y pérdida de agua en un área determinada.

prever ver de antemano; ver hacia el futuro.

primera ley de la termodinámica la energía no puede ser creada o destruida. Puede, no obstante, transformarse. Esto también se conoce como la ley de la conserva-ción de la energía.

prioridades catalogación preferencial de metas, proyectos o acciones.

productores organismos (como las plantas) que sintetizan sustancias orgánicas de sustancias inorgánicas.

proliferación proceso de crecer o aumentar rápidamente en número o en cantidad.

proliferación nuclear (ver proliferación)

proteínas principales sustancias orgánicas dentro de las células. Las proteínas contienen carbono, hidrógeno, nitrógeno, oxígeno y usualmente azufre. Las proteínas son sintetizadas de materias primas por las plantas, pero son asimiladas por los animales como aminoácidos separados.

protón partícula elemental con una sola carga eléctrica positiva y una masa aproximadamente 1,837 veces mayor que la del electrón. Los protones se encuentran en todos los núcleos.

protoplasma parte viva de una célula.

— Q —

quad (Q) gran cantidad de energía igual a mil billones BTU. 1 Q = 10^{15} BTU.

— R —

racionamiento proceso de distribuir o dividir un bien escaso de manera equitativa para alcanzar un objetivo en particular.

radiación aquello que emite un objeto como el Sol, un planeta, una bombilla, un calentador o un átomo. La radiación puede ser en forma de partículas o de ondas.

radiación de fondo radiación normal de rayos cósmicos y fuentes terrestres en la atmósfera inferior.

radiación ionizante radiación con suficiente energía para desprender uno o más electrones de un átomo, formando iones. Estos iones pueden reaccionar con tejidos vivos y dañarlos.

radiactividad transformación espontánea de un núcleo atómico, en la cual cambia de una especie nuclear a otra, con la emisión de partículas y energía.

rayos cósmicos radiación de varios tipos, principalmente núcleos atómicos (protones) con altos niveles de energía, que se originan fuera de la atmósfera de la Tierra. La **radiación cósmica** es parte de la radiación de fondo natural.

rayos gamma radiaciones electromagnéticas de alta frecuencia que tienen una extensión indeterminada en la materia. Son muy penetrantes.

reacción en cadena una serie de reacciones en la cual cada reacción causa una o más reacciones nuevas. Una reacción que estimula su propia repetición.

reacción nuclear involucra un cambio en el núcleo atómico; tales como la fisión, fusión, captura de neutrones o la descomposición radiactiva.

reactor nuclear dispositivo en el cual se puede iniciar, mantener y controlar una reacción de fisión en cadena.

reactor reproductor un reactor que produce y consume combustible fisionable, especialmente el que produce más de lo que consume.

recarga en hidrología, el reemplazo de agua subterránea por infiltración de agua de la atmósfera.

reciclado proceso por el cual se transforman materiales residuales en productos útiles nuevos, de tal manera que los productos originales pueden perder su identidad.

reclamación propósito de restaurar para el cultivo, para uso útil o al estado original.

recolector solar de panel plano dispositivo para recolectar energía solar y convertirla en calor.

recursos depósitos minerales identificados y no identificados que se pueden recuperar económica-mente con la tecnología existente o que pueden llegar a ser económicamente recuperables cuando suben los precios o mejora la tecnología minera.

recursos continuos aquellos recursos que se renuevan y por lo tanto siempre están presentes si se usan con prudencia.

recursos naturales materiales provistos por la naturaleza que pueden usarse para la producción. A los recursos naturales muchas veces se les llama regalos de la naturaleza.

recursos no renovables recursos que no se reemplazan o regeneran en forma natural dentro de un lapso razonable. Por ejemplo, combustibles fósiles y minerales.

recursos renovables recursos que pueden usarse de manera continua sin que se agoten.

red alimenticia compleja serie entrelazada de cadenas alimenticias.

refinación proceso mediante el cual un concentrado mineral alcanza un estado más puro.

regiones desarrollados regiones caracterizados por tener alto nivel de vida, bajo índice de crecimiento de población, bajo nivel de mortalidad infantil, consumo excesivo de materiales, alto nivel de consumo de energía per capita, alto nivel de ingresos per capita, población urbana y alto nivel de alfabetización. También conocidos como regiones más desarrollados.

regiones en vías de desarrollo regiones caracterizados por tener bajo nivel de vida, alto índice de crecimiento de población, alto nivel de mortalidad infantil, bajo consumo de materiales, bajo nivel de consumo de energía per capita, bajos ingresos per capita, poblaciones rurales y bajo nivel de alfabetización. También conocidos como regiones menos desarrollados.

relleno sanitario método para el desecho de residuos sólidos en la tierra, en una forma que protege el medio ambiente. Los residuos se esparcen en capas delgadas, se compactan al menor volumen posible y se cubren con tierra al final de cada día de trabajo.

reproductor alternativo reactor reproductor con un contenido de material fisionable mucho menor que los reproductores actuales.

reservas cantidad de una fuente de recursos identificada que puede ser extraída lucrativamente con tecnología existente en las condiciones económicas actuales. Las reservas son una subclase de fuentes de recursos.

residuo tóxico residuo que actúa como veneno o causa cáncer, defectos de nacimiento u otros problemas de salud.

residuos material inferior o residual resultante del proceso de molienda.

residuos de alto nivel material generado por el reprocesamiento químico de combustible usado y objetivos irradiados. Esos residuos contienen productos de fisión altamente radiactivos y de corta vida, sustancias químicas peligrosas y metales pesados tóxicos.

residuos de bajo nivel término general para todos los residuos radiactivos que no sean combustibles gastados, de alto nivel o residuos transuránicos.

residuos nucleares equipos y materiales (de reacciones y operaciones nucleares) que son radiactivos y por lo tanto no se pueden usar.

residuos peligrosos productos residuales sólidos, líquidos o gaseosos, potencialmente dañinos, de la fabricación u otra actividad humana.

residuos radiactivos materiales que son radiactivos y para los cuales no hay más usos.

residuos sólidos municipales materiales de desechos sólidos, de origen residencial y comercial, generados en una zona municipal.

residuos transuránicos residuos contaminados con uranio-233 o elementos transuránicos (números atómicos superiores a 92) que tienen una vida media superior a 20 años y están presentes en concentra ciones de más de 1 diezmillonésima de curie por gramo de residuos.

resistencia oposición al paso de corriente eléctrica que hace que la energía eléctrica se transforme en calor.

resistor dispositivo eléctrico que se usa en un circuito, principalmente para resistir el flujo de la corriente eléctrica.

resolución de conflictos proceso para apaciguar y eventualmente poner fin a luchas, discordias, desacuerdos intensos y otras formas de contienda entre personas o grupos de personas.

resolver solucionar; llegar a una decisión.

respiración oxidación de alimentos por organismos, que libera energía utilizable, dióxido de carbono y agua.

retorta recipiente en el cual se destilan o descomponen sustancias calentándolas en ausencia de aire.

riego por goteo (ver irrigación por goteo)

roca material sólido básico de la corteza de la Tierra. Una roca es una colección de minerales.

roca clástica roca sedimentaria formada por partículas (clastos) mecánicamente transportadas.

roca extrusiva roca formada por lava u otros materiales volcánicos arrojados a la superficie de la Tierra.

roca ígnea roca solidificada, producto de un estado fundido.

roca intrusiva roca ígnea que en un estado fundido se abrió paso por otra zona rocosa antes de enfriarse.

roca madre capa de roca que originó un material valioso.

roca metamórfica roca sedimentaria o ígnea en la cual los minerales, la textura o ambos han sido transformados por altas temperaturas y presión sin que la roca se funda.

roca sedentaria química roca formada por precipitación química, generalmente de agua de mar.

roca sedimentaria roca compuesta de fragmentos de otras rocas y minerales, generalmente depositados en el agua.

rompevientos hileras de árboles o matorrales plantados para bloquear parte del viento y así reducir la erosión del suelo y la pérdida de agua en tierras cultivadas de áreas muy ventosas.

— S —

sedimento cualquier materia o masa depositada por el agua o el viento.

segunda ley de la termodinámica (forma 1) en toda conversión de energía de una forma a otra, siempre hay una disminución en la cantidad de energía útil.

segunda ley de la termodinámica (forma 2) el calor no puede fluir por sí solo de frío a caliente. Fluye de caliente a frío espontáneamente.

segunda ley de la termodinámica (forma 3) en todo sistema cerrado, la aleatoriedad o grado de desorden tiende a alcanzar su punto máximo.

selección natural proceso mediante el cual los individuos de una población que están mejor equipados para su medio ambiente sobreviven y transmiten sus características a sus descendientes.

semiconductor material, como el silicio, cuya conducti-vidad eléctrica puede aumentarse considerablemente exponiéndolo a calor, luz o voltaje.

semilla parte de una planta que contiene el embrión y que se convertirá en una nueva planta si se siembra.

sensores remotos técnica usada para recopilar información sobre un objeto sin tocarlo.

separación proceso de fundición que separa minerales de gran valor de deshechos de rocas. La fundición es el lugar donde se realiza este proceso de separación.

siembra de nubes dispersión de pequeñas partículas (núcleos de condensación) en la atmósfera para estimular la formación de nubes y la precipitación.

simular imitar; lucir o actuar como otro.

sísmico relativo o perteneciente a un terremoto.

sismógrafo instrumento que detecta y registra los movimientos sísmicos.

sistema forma de trabajo ordenado y total que puede ser aislado y estudiado dentro de los limites reales o imaginarios.

sistema abierto sistema, como un organismo vivo, en el cual se intercambian materia y energía entre el sistema y el medio ambiente.

sistema cerrado sistema en el que nada entra o sale. Por lo tanto, es un sistema que debe usar y reutilizar todo lo que contiene.

sistema de enfriamiento sistema para extraer calor del núcleo de un reactor nuclear y transferirlo al generador de vapor.

sistema de órganos grupo de órganos que realizan una función similar. Por ejemplo: el aparato digestivo.

sistema métrico sistema de medidas basado en múltiplos decimales y subdivisiones de las unidades básicas. El nombre oficial del sistema métrico moderno es *Système International* (Sistema Internacional) o simplemente SI.

sistema Normativo de los Estados Unidos (*U.S. Customary System*) sistema de medidas de uso común en Estados Unidos. A veces se le denomina sistema inglés o de pulgadas y libras.

smog combinación de niebla y humo. El término también se aplica a la bruma fotoquímica producida por la acción del Sol y la atmósfera sobre las emisiones de los automóviles e industrias.

smog fotoquímico mezcla compleja de contaminantes del aire (oxidantes) producida en la atmósfera por la reacción del hidrógeno y los óxidos de nitrógeno bajo la influencia de la luz solar. El smog fotoquímico produce puntos muertos localizados, amarillamiento y alteraciones en el crecimiento de las plantas. Es un irritante ocular y respiratorio en los seres humanos.

solenoide espiral de alambre que puede conducir una corriente eléctrica. Cuando fluye corriente, el solenoide es rodeado por un campo magnético.

solvente medio, generalmente líquido, en el cual se pueden disolver sustancias.

sostenible capaz de continuar indefinidamente.

subalimentación estado de mala salud en el cual un individuo no obtiene suficiente alimento.

subsidencia acto o proceso de hundirse o asentarse formando una depresión.

substracción proceso de convergencia (choque) de placas litosfericas en donde la placa más densa se mueve hacia abajo y entra en la capa.

sucesión ecológica el proceso mediante el cual los organismos que habitan una región gradualmente la modifican, de manera que son reemplazados por comunidades diferentes y usualmente más complejas.

sucesión primaria sucesión ecológica en un área donde no hay suelo ni organismos.

sucesión secundaria sucesión ecológica en una región donde una comunidad ha sido eliminada por una perturbación (incendio, inundación, arado, tornado) que no ha destruido el suelo.

sucesión secuencia de cambio gradual (y a veces rápida) de especies que habitan en una área determinada. Este cambio es relativamente predecible y comienza con la colonización inicial de organismos pioneros y finaliza con un clímax de la comunidad.

suelo material erosionado suelto en la superficie de la Tierra, en el cual crecen las plantas.

sustitución reemplazar una fuente de recursos con otra. La fuente de recursos reemplazada generalmente es más costosa o escasa.

— T —

tabla periódica disposición gráfica de los elementos basada en la disposición de sus electrones y, por ende, sus propiedades.

tasa de metabolismo basal (TMB) el ritmo al que un cuerpo humano sano irradia calor cuando está completamente relajado en un ambiente cómodo y no ha ingerido alimentos en diez horas. Se expresa en Calorías/horas/metros cuadrados de superficie cutánea.

tecnología aplicaciones de la ciencia que proveen objetos que se usan para el sustento y la comodidad de los seres humanos. La aplicación de conocimientos científicos a usos prácticos.

tecnología apropiada una estrategia para encarar el futuro de la energía, basada en la creencia general de que "lo más simple es mejor" y que las fuentes de recursos deben coordinarse con las aplicaciones finales.

tecnología blanda (ver tecnología apropiada)

tejido grupo de células similares que realizan una función similar. Ejemplos: tejido muscular y tejido sanguíneo.

tensión superficial propiedad de los líquidos en la cual la superficie expuesta tiende a contraerse a la menor área posible.

teoría de la tectónica de placas teoría que sugiere que hay seis grandes placas en la corteza terrestre, y muchas más de menor tamaño, que se mueven en la superficie de la Tierra.

térmico zona de transición entre aguas tibias que se encuentran en la superficie y aguas frías que se encuentran en la profundidad de los lagos y océanos.

termosfera la región más alta de la atmósfera de la Tierra. Comienza a una altitud de aproximadamente 53 millas (85 kilómetros) y se extiende aproximadamente 300 millas (480 kilómetros) hacia el espacio. La termosfera sólo contiene una ínfima fracción de los gases que hay en la atmósfera.

terrazas terraplenes pequeños en terreno montañoso construidos para reducir la velocidad del agua que corre por el suelo y reducir la erosión.

terremoto movimiento de la corteza terrestre causada por una inesperada descarga de energía.

terrestre perteneciente a la tierra o formado por ella, a diferencia de agua.

textura del suelo es la proporción relativa de la arena, arcilla, fango, en un ejemplo de la tierra. La textura puede ser calculada de la siguiente manera, frotando una pequeña partícula de tierra entre los dedos de la mano y usando la información que se da en las figuras 7.5 y 7.6.

textura (roca) tamaño y disposición de granos minerales.

tiempo de duplicación el tiempo necesario para que una cantidad creciente de algo duplique su cantidad o volumen.

tiempo de renovación tiempo que tarda una fuente agotada en volver a su condición original.

tiempo de vida estático (T_s) cálculo del tiempo que durarán las reservas de una fuente de recursos, presuponiendo que no cambien ni la cantidad de la reserva ni su ritmo de uso.

tiempo de vida exponencial (T_e) cálculo aproximado del tiempo que durarán las reservas de una fuente de recursos, suponiendo que se consuman a un paso exponencialmente creciente.

tierra un gran oasis en el espacio.

tierra labrada tierra arada, cultivada y preparada para cultivo.

torio (Th) elemento naturalmente radiactivo con número atómico de 90 y, en su estado natural, peso atómico de aproximadamente 232. El fértil isótopo torio-232 es abundante y puede ser trasmutado (convertido) a uranio-233 fisionable mediante bombardeo neutrónico.

tormenta embravecida se forma cuando un huracán junta agua a lo largo de las playas y la arroja a la tierra.

torre de enfriamiento dispositivo usado para extraer el exceso de calor del agua utilizada en operaciones industriales, especialmente en la generación de electricidad.

trabajo transferencia de energía que comprende una fuerza por una distancia.

trampa estratigráfica fluidos subterráneos atrapados por la orientación de las capas o estratos. Las trampas estratigráficas se forman cuando una capa porosa ascendente queda atrapada entre dos capas no porosas.

trampa estructural fluidos subterráneos atrapados como resultado de la estructura geológica. Algunos ejemplos son anticlinales, domos de sal y planos de fallas.

transformación de la energía proceso de cambiar la energía de una forma a otra. Por ejemplo: una cerilla transforma energía química en energía térmica.

transformador dispositivo eléctrico que se usa para aumentar o reducir voltajes. Cuando el voltaje aumenta, la corriente disminuye. Cuando el voltaje disminuye, la corriente aumenta.

transición pasar de una condición, forma, etapa a otra.

transición demográfica fenómeno que se observa en las poblaciones de varias naciones industrializadas. Al aumentar el nivel de vida, disminuyen las tasas de natalidad y de mortalidad. Gradualmente se alcanza un crecimiento de población bajo o nulo. La reducción en la tasa de mortalidad por lo general precede la caída de la tasa de natalidad, causando un período de rápido crecimiento antes de que se produzca la estabilización.

transmisión de electricidad método por el cual la electricidad es transferida de la planta generadora al lugar donde se usará.

transpiración proceso mediante el cual la humedad pasa de las raíces de las plantas a las hojas, donde cambia a vapor y escapa a la atmósfera a través de aberturas en las hojas.

tratamiento primario primer paso en el tratamiento de aguas residuales, en el cual los sólidos suspendidos o asentables son extraídos mecánicamente mediante la sedimentación y depuración.

tratamiento secundario tratamiento de aguas residuales más allá de la etapa primaria, en el cual las partes orgánicas de la materia son consumidas por bacterias. La acción bioquímica se logra mediante el uso de filtros de goteo o el proceso de sedimento activado. Generalmente, la cloración es la etapa final del proceso de tratamiento secundario.

tratamiento terciario tratamiento de aguas residuales más allá de la etapa secundaria o biológica, que incluye la remoción de nutrientes como fósforo y nitrógeno y un alto porcentaje de sólidos en suspensión. El tratamiento terciario, también conocido como *tratamiento de residuos avanzado*, produce efluentes de alta calidad.

tren unitario tren largo, de aproximadamente 100 vagones, todos los cuales transportan el mismo producto (generalmente carbón).

tritio isótopo de hidrógeno radiactivo con dos neutrones y un protón en el núcleo. Es artificial y más denso que el deuterio (hidrógeno pesado).

troposfera la capa interior de la atmósfera. Contiene aproximadamente el 75 porciento de la masa del aire de la Tierra y se extiende aproximadamente 11 millas (17 kilómetros) sobre el nivel del mar.

tundra regiones cenagosas, carentes de vegetación arbórea, con bajo promedio de temperatura y precipitación anual. Hay tundras alpinas y árticas.

turba mezcla de fragmentos de plantas formada por vegetación parcialmente descompuesta que se acumula con lentitud en los pantanos.

turbina dispositivo con aspas, similar a una rueda, que convierte la energía cinética de un gas o líquido en la energía mecánica de un eje rotativo.

— U —

unidad térmica británica (BTU) cantidad de calor requerida para elevar la temperatura de una libra de agua en un grado Fahrenheit.

uranio (U) elemento radiactivo con número atómico 92 y, como se encuentra en mena, con un peso atómico aproximado de 238. Los dos isótopos naturales principales son uranio-235 (0.7% del uranio natural), que es fisionable y uranio-238 (99.3% del uranio natural), que es fértil. El uranio natural incluye además una cantidad diminuta de uranio-234. El uranio es la materia prima para la energía nuclear.

uso consuntivo uso que consume o agota un recurso.

uso de la tierra el uso de la tierra por los humanos.

uso final el uso final deseado de un recurso. Los principales usos finales de las fuentes de energía son transporte, calefacción, refrigeración, iluminación y cocción.

— V —

valor lo que vale algo en dinero o bienes en un momento dado; precio en el mercado.

valor-R medida de la capacidad de un material para impedir el paso del calor. Cuanto más elevado el valor-R, más resistencia al paso del calor.

vaporización cambio de un estado líquido a vapor o gas.

variable todo lo que es cambiable; una cosa o cantidad que cambia o puede cambiar.

vatio-hora si la diferencia de potencial en una parte de un circuito eléctrico es un voltio, una corriente de un amperio que circula continuamente por parte durante una hora generará un vatio-hora de energía eléctrica.

vegetariano persona que no come carne ni, a veces, productos de origen animal.

vehículo de producción vehículo nuevo con disponibilidad limitada para los consumidores de ciertas localidades.

vehículo diseñado vehículo que ha sido diseñado en papel (y en programas de computadora) pero que aún no se ha fabricado.

vehículo prototipo vehículo que ha sido fabricado y está a prueba pero no está a la venta.

ventaja selectiva característica biológica que permite que un organismo sobreviva en un medio ambiente en particular mejor que otros organismos similares.

vertiente región de la tierra que envía agua, sedimento y substancias disueltas a través de arroyos y afluentes hacia una corriente principal o rió.

veta de carbón una capa o estrato de carbón.

vida media tiempo que tarda la mitad de los átomos de una sustancia radiactiva específica en desintegrarse a otra forma nuclear.

vitaminas moléculas orgánicas que son necesarias en pequeñas cantidades en la dieta de los animales mayores para realizar funciones biológicas específicas.

volátil que se evapora con rapidez; se dispersa libremente en la atmósfera.

voltaje medida de fuerza eléctrica para impulsar una corriente eléctrica.

voltímetro aparato que se emplea para medir diferencias de potencial (voltaje).

— Y —

yacimiento en veta zona o franja mineralizada que yace dentro de límites que claramente la separan de roca adyacente.

— Z —

zona de fractura grieta en la corteza de la Tierra donde las placas se desplazan separadas horizontalmente.

zonas agrietadas región donde las placas tectónicas de la corteza terrestre se separan y se alejan la una de la otra. Estas zonas se encuentran comúnmente en el suelo marino. Al proceso de separación de las placas y formación de una nueva capa se le conoce como la *propagación del suelo marino*.

zona de subducción zona marginal entre una placa oceánica en hundimiento y una placa que se sobrepone a ella.

zona virgen área donde la comunidad biológica está prácticamente imperturbada por los seres humanos.

zonas pantanosas tierras principalmente semiacuáticas que están inundadas o saturadas con agua por períodos variables durante la temporada de crecimiento.